WYCLIFFE'S OLD TESTAMENT

Translated by

JOHN WYCLIFFE
and JOHN PURVEY

VOLUME ONE

GENESIS – 2ND CHRONICLES

*A modern-spelling edition
of their 14th century Middle English translation,
the first complete English vernacular version,
with an Introduction by*

TERENCE P. NOBLE

My thanks to
QUYNH M. DANG,
for your patience, support,
and word processing expertise;

the JEWISH PEOPLE,
who, for millennia, preserved
and protected these Holy Scriptures,
their greatest gift to ALL humanity;

my parents, AL and FRIEDA NOBLE,
and everyone else, including pets,
who showed kindness along the way.

Thanks be to
GOD
for this opportunity of a lifetime.

With love for my mother,
Helen Frieda Noble

Library and Archives Canada Cataloguing in Publication

Bible. O.T. English (Middle English). Wycliffe. 2010.
Wycliffe's Old Testament translated by John Wycliffe and John Purvey: a modern-spelling edition of their 14th century Middle English translation, the first complete English vernacular version, with an introduction by Terence P. Noble/Terence P. Noble, editor.

Includes bibliographical references.
ISBN 978-1-4538104-7-7

I. Wycliffe, John, d. 1384. II. Purvey, John, 1353?-1428?
III. Noble, Terry, 1954-. IV. Title.
BS835 2010 225.5'201 C2001-911689-6

For more information, contact:

Terry Noble
702-1955 Haro Street,
Vancouver, B.C.
Canada V6G 1J1
(phone: 604-689-7095; email: terry@smartt.com)

Table of Contents

Introduction

...and I shall give to thee tables of stone, and the law, and commandments, which I have written, that thou teach them.

From within a cloud or a burning bush, from the midst of the Holy of Holies in the Temple in Jerusalem or above the summit of Mount Sinai in the desert, to prophets, priests, and patriarchs alike, YAHWEH, the Great "I AM", "the God of revelation and grace", spoke to His people in words they could all understand.

Moses came down from Mt. Sinai with the ten commandments written in stone by the finger of God in a language the entire nation of Israel could read.

David composed his poems of praise and petition, promises and pleadings, to the Lord God of hosts, in the everyday language of his people.

Solomon penned his proverbs of wise fatherly counsel, and his songs of passionate love, in Hebrew, the language of many of his sons, and at least some of his lovers.

But 2300 years later, in England, the Word of God was written almost exclusively in Latin[1], an unknown language to 99% of that society. Indeed, Latin was only understood by some of the clergy, some of the well-off, and the few who were university educated. This did not disquiet the Church princes, who long before had transformed the "Divine Commission" – to preach the Word and save souls – into the more temporal undertaking of an all-consuming drive to wield authority over every aspect of life, and in doing so, to accumulate ever-greater wealth.

John Wycliffe, an Oxford University professor and theologian, was one of those few who had read the Latin Bible. And although a scholar living a life of privilege, he felt a special empathy for the poor, the uneducated, those multitudes in feudal servitude whose lives were "nasty, brutish, and short". He challenged the princes of the Church to face their hypocrisy and widespread corruption – and repent. He railed that, because of them, the Church was no longer worthy to be The Keeper of the Word of God. And he proposed a truly revolutionary idea:

"The Scriptures," Wycliffe stated, "are the property of the people, and one which no party should be allowed to wrest from them. Christ and his apostles converted much people by uncovering of scripture, and this in the tongue which was most known to them. Why then may not the modern disciples of Christ gather up the fragments of the same bread? The faith of Christ ought therefore to be recounted to the people in both languages, Latin and English."

Indeed, John Wycliffe earnestly believed that all of the Scriptures should be available to all of the people all of the time in their native tongue.

---

[1] Following King Edward I's expulsion edict of 1290, decreeing the banishment of all Jews from England, the Jewish people were absent from its soil until the mid-17TH century. However, Hebrew Old Testaments, commentaries, and other scholarly writings concerning the Hebrew Scriptures, were studied when the Old Testament of the "Wycliffe Bible" was written and revised (as were Greek sources when its New Testament was written and revised). For more on this, see *'A Word Regarding the Primary Source'* below.

He believed that with the Word of God literally in hand, each individual could have a personal relationship with God, with no need for any human or institutional intermediary.

And so John Wycliffe and his followers, most notably John Purvey, his secretary and close friend, translated Jerome's Vulgate, the "Latin Bible", into the first English Bible (for a limited time, Nicholas Hereford[2] also helped). Their literal, respectful translation was hand-printed around 1382. Historians refer to this as the "Early Version" of the "Wycliffe Bible".

The Church princes, long before having anointed themselves as sole arbitrator (indeed "soul" arbitrator!) between God and man, condemned this monumental achievement as heretical – and worse:

> "This pestilent and wretched John Wycliffe, that son of the old serpent... endeavour[ing] by every means to attack the very faith and sacred doctrine of Holy Church, translated from Latin into English the Gospel, [indeed all of the Scriptures,] that Christ gave to the clergy and doctors of the Church. So that by his means it has become vulgar and more open to laymen and women who can read than it usually is to quite learned clergy of good intelligence. And so the pearl of the Gospel, [indeed of the Scriptures *in toto*,] is scattered abroad and trodden underfoot by swine."
>
> (*Church Chronicle,* 1395)

The Church princes decreed that Wycliffe be removed from his professorship at Oxford, and it was done. Two years later, his health broken, he died.

In the decade following John Wycliffe's death, his friend John Purvey revised their Bible. Portions of that revision, in particular the Gospels and other books of the New Testament, were likely circulated as early as 1388. The complete text, including Purvey's "Great Prologue", appeared by 1395.

Historians refer to this as the "Later Version" of the "Wycliffe Bible". This vernacular version retained most of the theological insight and poetry of language found in the earlier, more literal effort. But it was easier to read and understand, and quickly gained a grateful and loyal following. Each copy had to be hand-printed (Gutenberg's printing press would not be invented for more than fifty years), but this did not deter widespread distribution. The book you now hold in your hands is that Bible's Old Testament (*with modern spelling*).

---

[2] Nicholas (de) Hereford, an associate of Wycliffe's and Purvey's, helped write 2/3RDS of the highly literal "Early Version" of the Old Testament (up to "Baruch", an apocryphal book then placed before "Ezekiel"), before he was summoned to Rome to explain his actions. Threatened with death by the Synod of Black Friars, he recanted. Pope Urbanus VI sentenced him to prison, where he possibly spent two years. When a civil insurrection broke out in Rome, the rioters set all the captives free. Hereford fled back to England and resumed his work to educate the ignorant and aid the poor. Arrested again, this time his recantation stuck. Thenceforth, he worked tirelessly against his former colleagues, testifying at their trials, vociferously and vituperatively condemning the writing of the English Bible. For his efforts, the Church princes rewarded him with the position of Chancellor and Treasurer of Hereford Cathedral, as well as a lifelong stipend. Finally, after a long life of shifting alliances, of activities of both grace and perfidy, Hereford retired to a Carthusian monastery, an austere, ascetic order that embraced solitude, silence, and midnight masses. Perhaps, at long last, he felt he had said enough.

For his efforts, the Church princes ordered John Purvey arrested and delivered to the dungeon. He would not see freedom again until he recanted of his "sin" – writing the English Bible. His spirit ultimately broken, he eventually did recant. Upon release, he was watched, hounded at every step, the Church princes determined that he would tow the party line. His life made a living hell, the co-author of the first English Bible eventually disappeared into the mists of history and died unknown.

But the fury of the Church princes was unrelenting. Edicts flew. John Wycliffe's bones were dug up – and burned. Wycliffe's writings were gathered up – and burned. All unauthorized Bibles – that is, all those in the English language – were banned. All confiscated copies were burned. Those who copied out these Bibles were imprisoned. Those who distributed these Bibles were imprisoned. Those who owned an English Bible, or, as has been documented, "traded a cart-load of hay for but a few pages of the Gospel", were imprisoned. And those faithful souls who refused to "repent" the "evil" that they had committed, were burned at the stake, the "noxious" books that they had penned, or even had merely owned, hung about their necks to be consumed by the very same flames. In all, thousands were imprisoned, and many hundreds executed. Merry olde England was engulfed in a reign of terror. All because of an English Bible. This Bible.

But the spark that John Wycliffe, John Purvey, and their followers had ignited could not, would not, be extinguished. The Word of God was copied, again, and again, and again. The Word of God was shared, from hand, to hand, to hand. The Word of God was spoken, and read, and heard by the common people in their own language for the first time in over 1000 years. At long last, the Word of God had been returned to simple folk who were willing to lose everything to gain all.

And so the pearl of the Scriptures was spread abroad and planted in their hearts by the servants of God....

216 years after Purvey's revision appeared, somewhat less than a century after Martin Luther proclaimed his theses (thereby sparking the Protestant Reformation), and Henry VIII proclaimed his divorce (thereby creating the Church of England), what would become the most famous, enduring, beloved, and revered translation of the Bible, the "Authorized" or "King James Version" (KJV), was published in 1611.

In their preface, "The Translators to the Reader", in the 1ST edition of the KJV, the 54 translators detail many sources utilized and arduous efforts undertaken to achieve their supreme accomplishment. Interestingly enough, they make scant mention of even the existence of earlier, unnamed English versions. And they make no specific reference to the work of John Wycliffe and John Purvey. It is not my desire or intention here to speculate on the political-ecclesiastical reasons for this omission, simply to state its fact.

From 1611 until today, historians of the English Bible have uniformly followed the lead of the KJV translators, and have ignored, dismissed, or denigrated John Wycliffe's and John

Purvey's contributions to, and influences upon, that ultimate translation, the KJV. To wit:

> "The Bible which permeated the minds of later generations shows no direct descent from the Wycliffite versions; at most a few phrases from the later version seem to have found their way into the Tudor translations....Tyndale's return to the original languages meant that translations based on the intermediate Latin of the Vulgate would soon be out of date."
>
> (*Cambridge History of the Bible,* Vol. 2, p. 414.)

When you finish reading this book, you may reach a different conclusion.

Regarding *Wycliffe's Old Testament*

Wycliffe's Old Testament comprises the Old Testament found in extant copies of the "Later Version" of the "Wycliffe Bible", with modern spelling. For 99.9% of *Wycliffe's Old Testament,* the word order, verb forms, words in *italics,* and punctuation are as they appear in the "Later Version". In addition, words and phrases found only in the "Early Version" are presented within square brackets, "[ ]", to provide more examples of John Wycliffe's and John Purvey's groundbreaking scholarship, as well as to aid comprehension and improve passage flow. (Literally thousands of "Early Version" verses were transcribed, but limited space meant most could not be printed in this book. See the *Wycliffe's Bible* CD or the online efiles for these significant and interesting textual variations.)

Because their lives were ever at risk, and personal glory was of no consequence to either man, neither Wycliffe nor Purvey signed any extant copy of either version, attesting to authorship. This omission has allowed some historians to debate the matter. *Wycliffe's Old Testament* is unambiguously credited: "Translated by John Wycliffe and John Purvey". While authorship of particular chapter or verse can be argued by those concerned with such matters, there is absolutely no doubt about the essential role that each of these men played in the momentous effort to bring the English Bible to the English people.

Middle English

The "Wycliffe Bible" was written in Middle English in the last three decades of the 14TH century. "Middle English" is the designation of language spoken and written in England between 1150 and 1450. The year 1300 is used to divide the period into "Early Middle English" and "Late Middle English". During the time of "Late Middle English", there were 5 regional dialects in England (with a sixth dialect eventually developing in London). Examples of at least three dialects are found in the "Later Version" of the "Wycliffe Bible".

What does one encounter reading the "Wycliffe Bible"? An alphabet with a widely used 27TH letter, "*ȝ*", and a 28TH letter, "*þ*", that already was frequently being replaced with "*th*" (even within the same sentence). A myriad of words which today are **obsolete** ("anentis": "with"), **archaic** ("culver": "dove"), or at best, strangely-spelled **precursors** to our modern words ("vpsedoun": "upside-down"). Spelling and verb forms that are not standardized, in part because they were phonetic to different dialects. For example, the word "saw" is spelled a dozen different ways (even differently within the same sentence), and differently for singular and plural nouns (similarly, the word "say"); "have take" and "have taken" are found in the same sentence, as are "had know" and "had known"; and so forth. Prepositions and pronouns that often seem misplaced and incorrectly used: "at", "for", "in", "of", "on", "there", "to", "what", and "which" again and again seem wrongly situated; "themself" and "themselves" are found in the same sentence, as are "youself" and "yourselves"; and so forth. Capitalization, punctuation, and other grammatical conventions that are rudimentary by today's standards, and vary greatly from sentence to sentence. For example, the *past tense* of a verb was made by adding nothing to the present tense, or an "e", "en", "ed", "ede", "id", "ide", or still other suffixes. One encounters, in short, formidable obstacles to being able to understand (what will become) a single verse of Scripture.

And so the need for *Wycliffe's Old Testament. Wycliffe's Old Testament* is the "Later Version" of the Old Testament of the "Wycliffe Bible" (henceforth referred to as the WOT or Wycliffe Old Testament), with its irregular spelling deciphered, the verb forms made consistent, and numerous grammatical variations standardized. *Wycliffe's Old Testament* is the key that unlocks the amazing secrets found within the WOT.

Three types of words: obsolete, archaic, and precursors

As stated above, with the spelling modernized, three types of words are found in the Wycliffe Old Testament: **obsolete** ("dead words", unknown and unused for centuries); **archaic** ("old-fashioned words", now chiefly used poetically); and, the vast majority, "**precursors**", which are strangely-spelled forerunners of words that we use today. To understand the text, each group of words must be dealt with in a particular way.

Obsolete Words

Perhaps 2% of the words in the "Later Version" of the WOT are "dead" words that are not presently used, or found in current dictionaries. This percentage is significantly lower than the estimated 5% of obsolete words found in the "Later Version" of the Wycliffe New Testament (WNT). It is amazing how in little more than a decade, the time taken to revise the "Early Version" of the "Wycliffe Bible", the language so quickly evolved, and how much more modern the lexicon of the "Wycliffe Bible" became, particularly its Old Testament. But to understand the text, these obsolete words must be **replaced**.

Fortunately, the "Later Version" of the WOT was created at an exciting time of transition, just as the nascent language was beginning to blossom into the English that we know today. Many modern equivalents for words that we consider "dead" are found in the text itself, already in use alongside their soon-to-be-discarded doublets. Examples of "in-house" replacement words include: again, alley, ascend, ashamed, basket, besides, call, choir, desire, diminish, disturb, follow, hair shirt, harm, hinge, knew, know, mad, pasture, path, praise, reckon, repent, restore, rider, shame/d, snare, strong hold, strong vengeance, stumble, trap, trouble, uncle, weigh (both as a balance or scales and as the verb), weight, with, and still other words (including "that" and "those", which are replacements for "thilke"). So most of the obsolete or "dead" words of the WOT were replaced with words already there in the text.

For the relatively few remaining obsolete words, reference works were consulted, and appropriate replacement words were chosen and utilized. Older words, in use as close as possible to the time of the "Wycliffe Bible", were favored over more recent words. When selecting replacements not already found in the text, words were chosen, as often as possible, that were different from those used in the KJV, so as not to artificially produce similar phraseology. But sometimes the only appropriate replacement word was that which the KJV also used.

When an obsolete word was replaced, an effort was made to use the same replacement word as often as possible to reflect word usage found in the original text. However many words have more than one meaning, and differing contexts at times required multiple renderings for an individual "dead" word. So "departe", usually rendered "part" ("to divide"), also became "separate"; "meyne" usually rendered "family", also became "household"; "wilne" usually rendered "desire", also became "to delight in" and "to take pleasure in"; "out-takun" usually rendered "except", also became "besides". Of these particular nine replacement words, only "separate", "family", and "except" are not found in the original text.

In all, approximately 100 individual replacement words (and their various forms and tenses) were utilized. Some replacement words ("benumbed", "creaketh", "creditor", "mocked", "satisfy", etc.) were used infrequently; other replacement words ("ascend", "call", "except", "pour", etc.) were used repeatedly.

Archaic Words

About 4% of the words used in the "Later Version" of the WOT are today considered "archaic", that is, not widely used, but still found in good, current dictionaries. Words in this category include: "comeling" (stranger or newcomer), "culver" (dove), "forsooth" ("for truth" and "but"), "knitches" (bundles), "livelode"/"lifelode" (livelihood), "quern" (hand-mill), "soothly" (truly), "strand" (stream), "sweven" (dream), "trow" (to trust or to believe), "ween" (to suppose), and "youngling" (young person). Once understood, these words are valid and vital, and evoke the atmosphere and colour of the original text. Most archaic words have been retained. Sometimes the KJV follows the "Later Version" in the use of an archaic word – such as "anon" (at once), "baken" (baked), "holden" (held), "holpen" (helped), "leasing" (lying), "letting" (hindering!), "washen" (washed), "wist" (knew), and "wot" (know) – and *Wycliffe's Old Testament* also follows the WOT.

Significantly, and of great benefit for our purposes, many archaic words in the WOT have their own modern equivalents right there in the original text. So in *Wycliffe's Old Testament,* following the original text, you will find both "alarge" and "enlarge"; "alure" and "lattice" (and "alley"); "anon" and "at once"; "araneid" and "spider"; "barnacle" and "bit" (part of a "bridle", which is also found); "cheer" and "face"; "close" and "enclose"; "darked" and "darkened"; "dure" and "endure"; "err" and "wander"; "flower" and "flourish"; "forgat" and "forgot"; "gat" and "begat"; "gender" and "engender"; "get" and "beget"; "gobbets" and "pieces"; "gotten" and "begotten"; "grave" and "engrave"; "gree" and "degree"; "grene" and "snare" (and "trap"); "half" and "hand" (and "side"); "harded" and "hardened"; "leasing" and "lying"; "lessed" and "lessened"; "liquor" and "liquid"; "manyfold" and "manifold"; "marishes" and "marshes"; "maumet" and "idol"; "nurse" and "nourish"; "owe" and "ought"; "paddocks" and "frogs"; "painture" and "painting"; "plage" and "region"; "says" (and "serges") and "curtains"; "simulacra" and "idols"; "sop up" and "swallow"; "spelunk" and "cave" (and "den"); "strain" and "constrain"; "sweven" and "dream"; "thank" (past tense of "think") and "thought"; "tree" and "beam" (and also "stick", and "timber", and "wood"); "venge" and "avenge"; "vinery" and "vineyard"; "virtue" and "strength" (and "host"); "volatiles" and "birds"; "waiter" (and "waker") and "watcher" (and "watchman"); "waking" and "watching"; "wem" and "spot"; and still more doublets of archaic and modern words. For definitions, see the Glossary, two pages after Malachi.

Precursors

But the vast majority of words in the "Later Version" of the WOT, about 94%, are the direct precursors of words that we use today. Although these words are spelled quite differently from words that we know, once their spelling has been modernized, they can be understood – with the following caveats.

In *Wycliffe's Old Testament,* you will encounter familiar words in unfamiliar settings: "deem" in place of "judge"; "defoul" in place of "defile"; "doom" in place of "judgement"; "dread" in place of "fear"; "either" in place of "or"; "enhance" in place of "exalt"; "health" in place of "salvation" or "deliverance" (and also "victory"); "wed" in place of "pledge"; and so on. Consult a good dictionary. Even as currently defined, these words remain relevant in their particular context. Their retention here breathes new life into familiar passages and brings fresh insight and illumination.

However, some words that we recognize have significantly changed definition in the intervening six centuries (in most cases, their meanings have become more specialized, less inclusive, than they were before). Reading the original text, these words sound jarring to our ears and appear out of place. Confusion would result if they were retained in *Wycliffe's Old Testament.* So different words were **substituted**, words whose definitions have remained constant over the centuries, are conducive to the context, and aid, rather than hinder, passage flow. Of vital importance, almost all of the substitution words used in *Wycliffe's Old Testament* were already present in the original text (some were previously noted above in the list of doublets of archaic and modern words); many are given as alternate renderings by the translators themselves (either in italics or in another verse dealing with the same subject matter).

The "in-house" substitution words used include: arms (for "armours"); at once (for "anon"); basin (for "cup", and for "vial", as corrected in glosses citing the Hebrew text); beam (for "tree"); box tree (for "beech tree", as corrected in glosses citing the Hebrew text); cause to stumble (for "sclaundre"); cave (for "swallow" as a noun); chamber (for "treasury"); chiefs (for "corners"); curtains (for "tents"); denounce (for "defame"); depraved (for "shrewide"); feeble (for "sick"); foreyard (for "hall"); half (for "middle"); hooks (for "heads" of pillars); host (for "strength"); hosts (for "virtues"); joined (for "applied"); knowing (for "cunning"); let go (for "leave" and for "left"); lookers (for "tooters"); loves (for "teats"); lie and lying (for "leasing"); mad (for "wood"); meek (for "debonair"); meekness (for "debonairness"); one (for "to" and for "toon"); only (for "properly"); own (for "proper"); pieces (for "plates"); pit (for "lake" and for "swallow" as a noun); posts (for "fronts" and for "trees"); remember (for "record"); remnant (for "relief"); servant (for "child"); servants (for "children"); species (for "spices"); spoon (for "mortar", as corrected in glosses citing the Hebrew text); stick (for "tree"); stranger or visitor (for "pilgrim"); strength or power (for "virtue"); strengthened (for "comforted"); strong hold (for "strength" and for "strengthening"); stumble (for "offend"); swallow (for "to sop up"); table (for "board"); tent (for "roof"); tents (for "castles"); timber (for "tree"); turn/ed again (for "convert" and "converted"/"return" and "returned"); vessel (for "gallon"); watch (for "wake"); watcher (for "waiter" and for "waker"); a weigh, that is, a balance or scales (for "a peis"); to weigh and weight (for "peise"); well (for "lake" and for "pit"); wild (for "wood"); wood (for "tree"); young (for "birds"); young man (for "child"); and young men (for "children"). **All of these substitution words are frequently found in the original text.** Nine other substitutions were used which are not found in the original text: boy (for "child"); cloak (for "cloth", the singular of "clothes"); consecrate/d (for "make sacred" and "made sacred", though "consecration" is found); drowned (for "drenched"); firm (for "sad"); physician (for "leech"); pledge (for "wed"); and promise (for "behest").

This seems a lengthy list. About 70 individual words. Yet the total number of substitution words in *Wycliffe's Old Testament* is approximately 500, out of more than 550,000 words in all (or about 1/10TH of 1%). Many of these words were used as substitutions five times or less. So when you read any of these words (with the exception of the final nine), almost all of the time they are there in the original text. Substitution words were only used to aid comprehension and were kept to an absolute minimum.

Other Minor Modifications

To aid comprehension and readability, two separate words in the WOT are often joined together in *Wycliffe's Old Testament.* Examples include: "in+to", "to+day", "-+self", "-+selves", "no+thing", and a few others. Conversely, and for the same reasons of comprehension and readability, many unfamiliar compound nouns found in the WOT are hyphenated in *Wycliffe's Old Testament*. For example, "a3enstondynge" became "against-standing" ("opposing"), "a3einseiyng" became "against-saying" ("contradicting"), etc. It can also be helpful to reverse the order of hyphenated words when reading them, so "against-stand" can be read "stand against", "against-said" can be read "said against", and so on.

Occasionally a prefix or suffix was added to a root word to aid comprehension: "ac" to "knowledge"; "al" to "together"; "be" to "gat", "get", and "loved"; "con" to "strained"; "di" to "minished"; "en" to "close", "compass", "dure", "during", "gender", and "grave"; "re" to "quite"; and "ly" to "most". These prefixes and the suffix are found in the original text, as are the words "altogether", "begat", "beget", "constrained", "diminished", "enclose", "endure", "enduring", "engender", and "engrave".

Inconsequential prepositions, conjunctions, and pronouns ("a", "the", "and", "selves", etc.) not found in particular "Later Version" phrases, but present in the same "Early Version" phrases, were occasionally added to the text of *Wycliffe's Old Testament* to aid comprehension and improve passage flow. They appear in square brackets, "[ ]", and are regular type size. Such words were also added even when not found in the comparable "Early Version" verses; these inserts appear in parentheses, "( )", and are regular type size.

Parentheses were also used to contain phrases and even entire verses which were re-ordered, re-punctuated, and, sometimes, re-worded, to aid comprehension and readability. Working with Hebrew and Latin sources, the translators produced a highly literal text that is often convoluted and confusing in English. So an effort was made to make better sense out of these passages by putting the available words (or, at times, different, but more accurate words,) into a more fluent order, with more appropriate punctuation. But this was only done with words that are found within parentheses. Such re-working always appears after the original unaltered text, and can easily be ignored, if so desired.

Punctuation overall follows the original text. Occasionally a comma was inserted to aid readability. For chapters of repetitive lists of names, numbers, places, or temple accoutrements (such as those found in Numbers, Ezra, Nehemiah, and 1ST Chronicles), verses were made consistent with one another. To accomplish this, commas and semi-colons were sometimes interchanged. As well, in various Psalms, it seems that semi-colons were employed to aid in oral presentation (perhaps to indicate a significant pause for breath), for their usage does not follow grammar found elsewhere in the text. So sometimes commas were substituted. The occasional interchange of commas and semi-colons in these books aids comprehension and improves passage flow, but does not alter the meaning of any verse.

To sum up: More than 98% of the words found in *Wycliffe's Old Testament* are modern spellings of the original words found in the 14TH century manuscript. Less than 2% are "replacement words", that is, appropriate words chosen to replace obsolete or "dead" words. Almost all of these replacements – about 100 individual words along with their various forms and tenses – are found in the original text. As well, about 500 times throughout all of *Wycliffe's Old Testament* (about 1 word for every two pages of this book), a word more conducive to the context was substituted for another whose meaning had radically changed over the intervening 600 years. Almost all of the substitution words (about 70 in all) were taken from elsewhere in the original text.

Ultimately, each word in *Wycliffe's Old Testament* was selected for its fidelity to the original text, as well as its ability to aid comprehension and passage flow.

Use of the KJV

When transforming the "Later Version" of the WOT into *Wycliffe's Old Testament*, reference was made to the KJV in regard to verse number, book order, book names, and (most) proper names.

Verses are not found in either version of the "Wycliffe Bible". Each chapter consists of one unbroken block of text. There are not even paragraphs. In creating *Wycliffe's Old Testament*, the "Later Version" of the WOT was defined, word by word. Then the KJV was placed alongside and used to divide each chapter into the traditional verses. (The English Bible was first divided into numbered verses in the middle of the 16TH century, 60 years before the KJV was printed. The King James translators copied what was already established.) As the blocks were broken up, it became readily apparent that Wycliffe and Purvey had often written first what would appear two centuries later in the KJV. (This debt is particularly obvious in the New Testament. See *Wycliffe's New Testament*.)

The sequence of the books of the Old Testament to which we are accustomed long pre-dates the KJV. It appeared in some Latin Bibles at least as early as the 5TH century A.D. (Those Bibles in turn were influenced by the order of the books in the Septuagint, the Old Greek version of the Hebrew Scriptures, from the 3RD century B.C., which is our earliest complete translation of them.) The sequence was formally established in the accepted order at the time that the verse divisions were made (again, about 60 years before the KJV was printed). This is the same order found in the WOT, which was written 150 years earlier. *Wycliffe's Old Testament* simply follows the WOT (but excludes the apocryphal books found intermittently within it).

The names of the books of the Old Testament have minor variations among the copies of the "Wycliffe Bible", but they are basically what is found in the KJV. Most are prefaced by the phrase, "The Book of...". The exceptions: 1ST and 2ND Samuel are called 1ST and 2ND Kings in the WOT (the same alternate names also found in early editions of the KJV); "our" 1ST and 2ND Kings are called 3RD and 4TH Kings in the WOT (again, the same alternate names also found in early editions of the KJV); 1ST and 2ND Chronicles (named by Jerome) are called 1ST and 2ND Paralipomena in the WOT (the name is taken from the Septuagint and means "things left over", referring to Samuel and Kings; however, it is a misnomer, for the Chronicles are distinct from the other historical books, focusing on God's intervention in history, and omitting Northern Kingdom annals); Nehemiah is called 2ND Ezra; the Song of Solomon is usually called the Song of Songs (as it is often named in Jewish and modern English Bibles); and Jeremiah is referred to as "Jeremy" in the titles of the book of his prophecies and the book of his lamentations. On the whole, book names in *Wycliffe's Old Testament* follow those found in the KJV.

To aid comprehension and also comparison with other translations, proper names in *Wycliffe's Old Testament* were generally made to conform to those in the KJV. However, surprisingly, the modern names of such countries as Africa, Greece, Libya, and Ethiopia are found in the WOT, where the KJV often uses their archaic and/or Hebrew names (respectively Put, Javan or Grecia, Lubim, and Cush), and they were not changed. As well, the WOT often shows its debt to the Septuagint by using the Greek names for such cities as Heliopolis, Memphis, Pelusium, Sidon, Tanis, and Thebes, instead of the Hebrew names which the KJV uses (respectively On, Noph, Sin, Zidon, Zoan, and No); these names were also not changed. A list of "Alternate Names of People and Places" appears after Malachi, before the Glossary.

Infrequently, apparently confusing an object name with a proper name, a **Hebrew** word was not translated in the WOT, but simply transliterated (the KJV and other translations do translate these words). These transliterations were left as found in the original text of the WOT, with a translation following in parentheses. They are also defined in the Glossary.

Finally, the few times where a proper name in the WOT is distinctly different from its counterpart in the KJV, it was not changed in *Wycliffe's Old Testament*; however the more familiar name is given immediately following in parentheses.

Names of God are a special circumstance. God has many names and titles in the WOT, including "God", "Lord", "God Almighty", "Almighty God", "the Almighty", "the Lord of hosts" (sometimes written "the Lord of virtues"), "the Lord God of hosts" (sometimes written "the Lord God of virtues"), "the High", "the most High", "the Highest", "the alder-Highest", "the Holy", "my Maker", "the old of days", "creator", "the overcomer", and still others as well (including "king", which is also given as a title for the coming Messiah). In the WOT, the first seven titles in this list are always capitalized, the next six are infrequently capitalized, and the others are never capitalized. In *Wycliffe's Old Testament*, the capitalized titles were left as such, those in the second grouping ("the High", "the most High", "the Highest", "the alder-Highest", "the Holy", and "Maker") were consistently capitalized to aid comprehension, and the other remaining titles were also capitalized for the same reason. The KJV, and other translations, including Jewish Bibles, capitalize some, or even all, of these titles, but not in uniformity with one another.

Surprisingly, the words "christ", "christs", and "Christ" appear in the WOT. The English word "christ" is from the Greek word "christos" ("christus" in Latin), and means "the anointed (one)"; the transliterated Hebrew for the same word is the familiar "messiah". The word "christos" appears in the Septuagint (e.g., in Psalms 2:2 and Daniel 9:25). It was borrowed from there by the writers of the Greek New Testament in the 1st century A.D. to refer specifically and only to Jesus Christ (and so it is capitalized). But in the WOT, "christ" uncapitalized can refer to King Saul, the Persian king Cyrus, David in particular, the patriarchs in general (here the word "christs" is used), and others who were "anointed by God" (but with no messianic overtones). The WOT self-defines the term with the words "the anointed", "the king", or "the anointed king" (sometimes in an alternate rendering, sometimes in italics).

However, reference is made to "Christ" in a prophetic manner, that is, in regard to the coming Messiah, in 1ST Samuel 2:10 and 2:35, 2ND Samuel 23:1, Psalms 2:2 and 45:2, and Lamentations 4:20, all verses where the KJV and other translations say "anointed king" or "anointed prince"; throughout the Song of Songs, where the "Early Version", and one copy of the "Later Version", present the entire book as an allegorical dialogue between Christ and his bride, the Church; in Daniel 9:25 and 9:26, where the KJV says "Messiah", but modern translations simply say "prince"; and in Zechariah 3:8, where the KJV and other translations say "the Branch"/"The Branch", and Jewish Bibles suggest a formal name, rather than a messianic term. (In Isaiah, where one might expect to find the word, if anywhere, it does occur, once, at 45:1, but only as "my christ", and refers to King Cyrus of Persia; in the KJV and other translations, the term used here is "his anointed".)

Other titles in the WOT which also refer to the coming Messiah include "king", "duke", "prince", "saviour", "a just burgeoning", "a burgeoning of rightwiseness", "a seed of rightfulness", and "the sun of rightwiseness". None of these titles is ever capitalized in the WOT. However, in one verse, Zechariah 6:12, the coming Messiah is referred to as "a man, Coming forth, *either Born, is* his name," in the "Later Version", and as "a man, East, *or Springing,* (*is*) his name," in the "Early Version" (both examples capitalized in the original text). The equivalent title used here in the KJV, and in several modern translations as well, is "The Branch". Overall, the KJV and other translations, including Jewish Bibles, capitalize words such as "King", "Prince", "Branch", and "Sun", as titles for the coming Messiah, but not always consistently internally, or in uniformity with one another. To aid comprehension, all are consistently capitalized in *Wycliffe's Old Testament.*

In Habakkuk 3:18, where the KJV has "God my saviour", and other translations have "God my deliverer"/"God my deliverance", *Wycliffe's Old Testament,* following the WOT (both versions), has "God my Jesus". The name "Jesus" is not here in the original Hebrew or Greek texts. Its insertion here in this verse by Christian preachers Wycliffe and Purvey illustrates their belief in the essential unity of the two testaments.

"Spirit" in the WOT can refer to God, His breath, or simply "the wind". So "the Spirit" and "the Spirit of God" are sometimes capitalized, sometimes not. Occasionally, the WOT has "the Spirit of the Lord", where the KJV and other translations have "the spirit of the Lord". But overall, "the Spirit of the Lord" is capitalized more often in the KJV Old Testament and other translations than in the WOT. This term is problematic. *Wycliffe's Old Testament* simply follows the WOT. As always, the goal was to provide an accurate representation of the original text, while remaining true to the context, and enhancing reader comprehension.

Words in *italics* are words added by the translators to aid comprehension. The KJV contains more *italicized* words than the "Later Version" of the WOT, but less than the

"Early Version" of the WOT. *Wycliffe's Old Testament* simply follows the WOT.

Comparing *Wycliffe's Old Testament* and the KJV, sometimes the KJV follows the WOT, other times the KJV helps decipher a passage in the WOT; sometimes the two texts are identical, other times they are as different as two versions of the same verse could be.

A Word Regarding the Primary Source

The primary source for this book was Forshall & Madden's 4-volume magnum opus, *The Holy Bible, Containing the Old and New Testaments, With the Apocryphal Books, In the Earliest English Versions, Made from the Latin Vulgate by John Wycliffe and His Followers*. Today, it is most likely found in a university library or on the Internet.

Written over a period of twenty years in the mid-19TH century, this monumental work of scholarship was the crowning achievement of The Rev. Josiah Forshall and Sir Frederic Madden. From about 160 extant hand-printed copies of the two versions of the "Wycliffe Bible" (about 40 copies of the "Early Version", and about 120 copies of the "Later Version"), they selected one copy from each version to serve as "master" texts, and then, by utilizing over 90,000 footnotes, correlated the other copies with the two "master" texts.

Both versions of the "Wycliffe Bible" contain prologues (introductions to each book, or group of related books, mostly taken from Jerome), and marginal glosses (explanations of the text by the translators, and some alternate renderings of words and phrases). The prologues are not utilized in *Wycliffe's Old Testament*. The glosses are a different story.

Some revisions of the "Later Version" of the WOT, particularly the copies Forshall & Madden labelled "C", "G", "K", "Q", and "X", and to a lesser extent, "B", "I", and "N", contain glosses which prove that Hebrew Bibles, commentaries, and scholars were consulted during the copying/revising process. Over 300 times throughout the WOT, gloss after gloss states: "in Hebrew, it is", "is not in Hebrew", "as Hebrews say", "as Hebrews understand", "this verse is not in Hebrew", "this title is not in Hebrew". As well, at least 7 times, a "Rabbi Solomon" is quoted as commenting on a particular verse: "as Rabbi Solomon saith". This "Rabbi Solomon" was most likely the scholar "Rashi", the leading commentator on the Jewish Bible and the Talmud in the 11TH century, or possibly another commentator from history, or perhaps even a contemporary of the translators (although this is the least likely possibility). Another 5 times, reference is made to (Jerome's) "Book of Hebrew Questions", a book of the master translator's own corrections of the Greek and Latin texts, which he made by referencing the Hebrew Scriptures. Jerome believed that the Hebrew provided a truer text to translate from than either the earlier Latin versions or the Septuagint (a fact agreed to by all modern translators). So, where appropriate, the words and phrases from these glosses have been either incorporated into the main text of *Wycliffe's Old Testament* or are presented as alternate renderings. A few of the alternate renderings from the glosses are printed in this book, but all of them can be found in files on the *Wycliffe's Bible* CD and the online efiles. As well, gleanings from other glosses are placed in footnotes here.

The footnotes in Forshall & Madden's four volumes are another source of invaluable information. As noted, there are over 90,000 footnotes, with about 65,000 pertaining to the Old Testament alone (both versions). These footnotes delineate textual divergence – changes, omissions, insertions, copyist errors – between the "master" texts and the other hand-printed copies of both versions of the "Wycliffe Bible". (A footnote can refer to a single copy or to multiple copies.) Close reading of the footnotes indicates that many times when a copy of either version was written (though less frequently with the "Early Version"), original language texts were also consulted. For time and again, words were added, or changed, to produce a more accurate rendering of the original Hebrew of the Old Testament, and the original Greek of the New Testament. In creating *Wycliffe's Old Testament,* many of these footnotes were utilized to provide the most precise translation, as well as the best phrasing – the most satisfying, balanced, rhythmic read – that is found within all extant copies of the WOT.

In *Wycliffe's Old Testament,* a forward slash, "/", separates different renderings of the same phrase from two different hand-written copies, usually the "master" text and an alternate rendering found in a footnote. Most of these renderings from the footnotes came from the copies labelled "I", "N", and "S". It is interesting to note that numerous textual variations indicated in footnotes for only the "Early Version" also appear in the KJV. This suggests that several copies of the "Wycliffe Bible" were studied during the writing of the KJV. See the files on the *Wycliffe's Bible* CD or the online efiles for most of these alternate renderings taken from the footnotes.

In creating *Wycliffe's Old Testament,* textual errors that were found in the WOT were not changed (they are also part of the original text); none are of major doctrinal significance. Corrections of names, numbers, and places, most often needed in chapters of repetitive lists, were placed in parentheses, immediately following the error, to enable better comparison with other translations.

A handful of printing errors – reversed letters or misread vowels of pronouns, prepositions, and adverbs – were discovered in the "Later Version" of the WOT. These were confirmed by referring to the "Early Version", which in each case agreed with the Hebrew, and not with the "Later Version". These were corrected.

Use of the "Early Version"

The "Later Version" of the WOT is the foundation upon which *Wycliffe's Old Testament* was built. Strictly speaking, *Wycliffe's Old Testament* is not a composite of the "Later" and "Early" versions. However, the "Early Version" of the WOT was utilized in a number of significant ways in the writing of *Wycliffe's Old Testament.*

First, the "Early Version" was used to define unknown words found in the "Later Version". Irregular spelling can make even the simplest words difficult to decipher. The "Early Version" served as a second source for such words. Often it had a more recognizable spelling, and so helped to identify them. As well, modern equivalents of "dead" words (to be used as replacement or substitution words) were often found only in the "Early Version". Modern verb forms were also often found only in the "Early Version". Their existence helped achieve verb form consistency in *Wycliffe's Old Testament*.

Second, the "Early Version" served as a source of "missing" words and phrases. About two dozen times, a textually significant word or partial phrase was not found in the "Later Version", but was present in the "Early Version" (following the Hebrew and also found in the KJV). Examples include: Genesis 35:5 and 50:22; Leviticus 4:21; Numbers 32:29 and 35:27; Deuteronomy 3:22; Joshua 16:8; 1ST Samuel 1:9; 2ND Samuel 17:28; 1ST Kings 8:2, 8:34, 21:7, and 21:19; 2ND Kings 1:4; Ezra 4:8; Proverbs 5:4 and 21:21; Isaiah 64:2; Jeremiah 52:22; Ezekiel 15:4; Hosea 2:12; and Zechariah 7:4. (An even greater number of significant phrase fragments are "missing" from the "Early Version".) As well, less consequential "missing" words, mostly "and" and "the", were often found only in "Early Version" verses. These "missing" words, significant and insignificant alike, were inserted into *Wycliffe's Old Testament* to improve its accuracy, reader comprehension, and passage flow. All "missing" words are contained within square brackets, and are regular type size.

Third, like the glosses and footnotes, the "Early Version" itself served as a source of "alternate" words and phrases. When the "Early Version", the "Later Version", and the KJV are compared side-by-side, one discovers numerous instances where the KJV follows the "Early Version" and not the "Later Version". Sometimes it is a single word, sometimes it is a phrase, and sometimes it is the order of several phrases within a verse. This usually occurs where the "Early Version" more closely follows the Hebrew than does the "Later Version". These textually significant "alternate" renderings from the "Early Version" are also contained within square brackets, but have reduced type size, to distinguish them from "missing" words.

Fourth, the "Early Version" served as a source of "interesting" words and phrases, no more accurate than what is found in the "Later Version", and many not utilized by the KJV, but fascinating nevertheless. These renderings are also contained within square brackets, and also have reduced type size.

Fifth, in 1ST Chronicles 8:16-26 (one of the "list" chapters), the text of the "Early Version" was used, rather than that of the "Later Version", because of more accurate punctuation. There are no major differences in wording between the two versions; consistency in punctuation and aid to comprehension were the only reasons for using these "EV" verses. Each verse is marked with a superscript E to denote its origin.

To sum up: All of the words in square brackets, "[ ]", in *Wycliffe's Old Testament* are from the "Early Version" of the WOT. Regular-size words were added to aid textual accuracy, reader comprehension, and passage flow; reduced-size words are either "alternate" words that are textually closer to the original Hebrew and/or what is found in the KJV, or simply "interesting" variations too fascinating to ignore. A limited number of these "EV" words are printed in *Wycliffe's Old Testament*, but all of them can be found in files on the *Wycliffe's Bible* CD and the online efiles.

All of this understood, it needs to be stated that *Wycliffe's Old Testament* can be read, and comprehended, without reference to any of the words or phrases found in the square brackets. The "Later Version" of the WOT – as represented by *Wycliffe's Old Testament* – can stand on its own. These additional words simply provide an another dimension of this seminal work in the English translation of the Old Testament.

A Final Note

With the spelling up-dated and the obsolete words replaced, the document you now hold in your hands is a fair and accurate representation of John Wycliffe's and John Purvey's 14TH century translation of the very first English vernacular Old Testament. This is *their* Old Testament *with modern spelling* – not some 21ST century variation on a medieval theme. The melodies and harmonies are Wycliffe's and Purvey's. Only now they are sung with words that we can all understand. Six centuries later, you can now read what those common folk were themselves at long last able to read (or, more likely, have read to them). Simple, direct words, with their own rhythm and charm, their own humble, cogent beauty. Sophisticated and graceful words, their originality and newness making the well-known and fondly remembered fresh, alive, and interesting once again. All because Wycliffe, Purvey, and their compeers cared so deeply and sacrificed so dearly.

Today there are many modern translations of the Old Testament in English, available at the library, in bookstores, and on the Internet. But once, there was just one. This one. Try to imagine the impact on hearing or reading these words for the very first time:

In the bigynniyng God made
of nouȝt heuene and erthe.
Forsothe the erthe was idel and voide,
and derknessis weren on the face of
depthe; and the Spiryt of the Lord
was borun on the watris[3].
And God seide, Liȝt be maad, and
the liȝt was maad.
And God seiȝ the liȝt,
that it was good, and he
departide the liȝt fro derknessis;
and he clepide the liȝt, dai,
and the derknessis, nyȝt. And
the euentid and the morwetid
was maad, o daie.

"Later Version", *Genesis, Chapter 1,*
The Holy Bible, 1395, unaltered.

In the beginning God made
of nought heaven and earth.
Forsooth the earth was idle and void,
and darknesses were on the face of
(the) depth; and the Spirit of the Lord
was borne on the waters.
And God said, Light be made, and
the light was made.
And God saw the light,
that it was good, and he
parted the light from (the) darknesses;
and he called the light, day,
and the darknesses, night. And
the eventide and the morrowtide
was made, one day (the first day).

Genesis 1:1-5,
Wycliffe's Old Testament, 2010.

[3] The "Early Version" phrase here is: "and the Spiryt of God was born vpon the watrys" ("and the Spirit of God was borne upon the waters").

Wycliffe's Old Testament

Genesis – 2nd Chronicles

GENESIS

CHAPTER 1

1 In the beginning God made of nought heaven and
earth. (In the beginning God made out of nothing the
heavens and the earth.)
2 Forsooth the earth was idle and void, and
darknesses were on the face of (the) depth; and the Spirit
of the Lord was borne on the waters [and the Spirit of God
was borne upon the waters].
3 And God said, Light be made, and the light was made.
4 And God saw the light, that it was good, and he
parted the light from (the) darknesses;
5 and he called the light, day, and the darknesses,
night. And the eventide and the morrowtide was made,
one day (the first day).
6 And God said, The firmament be made in the midst
of (the) waters, and part (the) waters from (the) waters.
7 And God made the firmament, and parted the
waters that were under the firmament, from the waters
that were on the firmament [from these that were above the
firmament]; and it was done so.
8 And God called the firmament, (the) heaven(s). And
the eventide and the morrowtide was made, the second
day.
9 Forsooth God said, The waters, that be under (the)
heaven(s), be gathered into one place, and a dry place
appear; and it was done so.
10 And God called the dry place, earth; and he called
the gatherings together of waters, the seas. And God saw
that it was good;
11 and said, The earth bring forth green herb, and
making seed, and an apple tree making fruit by his kind,
whose seed be in itself, on [the] earth; and it was done
so. (and said, Let the earth bring forth green herbs, which
make seed after their kind, and trees making fruit after
their kind, whose seed be in them, all over the earth; and
it was done so.)
12 And the earth brought forth green herb and making
seed by his kind, and a tree making fruit, and each having
seed by his kind. And God saw that it was good. (And the
earth brought forth green herbs, which make seed after
their kind, and trees making fruit, and each having seed
after its kind. And God saw that it was good.)
13 And the eventide and the morrowtide was made, the
third day.
14 Forsooth God said, Lights be made in the firmament
of (the) heaven(s), and part they the day and (the) night;
and be they into signs, and times, and days, and years;
15 and shine those in the firmament of (the) heaven(s),
and lighten they the earth; and it was done so.
16 And God made two great lights, the greater light that
it should be before to the day, and the less(er) light that it
should be before to the night; and *God made* (the) stars;
17 and setted them in the firmament of (the) heaven(s),
(so) that they should shine on [the] earth,
18 and that they should be before to the day and
(before) [to the] night, and should part (the) light and (the)
darkness. And God saw that it was good.
19 And the eventide and the morrowtide was made, the
fourth day.
20 Also God said (And God said), The waters bring
forth a reptile, *either a creeping beast,* of living soul, and
a volatile, *either a bird flying* above [the] earth, under the
firmament of (the) heaven(s).
21 And God made of nought great whales, and each
living soul and movable, which the waters have brought
forth in their kinds; and God made of nought each
volatile by his kind. And God saw that it was good; (And
God made out of nothing great whales, and each living
soul that moveth, which the waters brought forth after
their kind; and God made out of nothing each bird after
its kind. And God saw that it was good;)
22 and blessed them, and said, Wax ye, and be ye
multiplied, and fill ye the waters of the sea, and [the]
birds be multiplied on [the] earth.
23 And the eventide and the morrowtide was made, the
fifth day.
24 And God said, The earth bring forth a living soul in
his kind, work beasts, and reptiles, *either creeping beasts,*
and unreasonable beasts of [the] earth, by their kinds; and
it was done so. (And God said, Let the earth bring forth
living souls after their kind, yea, work beasts, and
reptiles, *or creeping beasts,* and unreasoning beasts of the
earth, all after their kind; and it was done so.)
25 And God made unreasonable beasts of the earth by
their kinds, and work beasts, and each creeping beast of
the earth in his kind. And God saw that it was good;
(And God made the unreasoning beasts of the earth after
their kind, and the work beasts, and the reptiles of the
earth, each after its kind. And God saw that it was good;)
26 and said, Make we man to our image and likeness,
and be he sovereign to the fishes of the sea, and to the
volatiles of (the) heaven(s), and to [the] unreasonable
beasts of [the] earth, and to each creature, and to each
creeping beast/each reptile, which is moved in [the]
earth. (and said, Let us make man in our image and
likeness, and be he sovereign over the fishes of the sea,
and over the birds of the air, and over the unreasoning
beasts of the earth, yea, over each creature, and over
each reptile which creepeth on the earth.)
27 And God made of nought a man to his image and
likeness; God made of nought a man, to the image of
God; God made of nought them, male and female. (And

so God made out of nothing a man in his image and
likeness; God made out of nothing a man in the image of
God; yea, God made them out of nothing, male and
female.)
28 And God blessed them, and said, Increase ye, and
be ye multiplied, and fill ye the earth, and make ye it
subject; and be ye lords to the fishes of the sea, and to
[the] volatiles of (the) heaven(s), and to all living beasts
that be moved on [the] earth (and be ye lords, *or rule ye*,
over the fishes of the sea, and the birds of the air, and all
the living beasts that move on the earth).
29 And God said, Lo! I have given to you each herb
bearing seed on [the] earth, and all (the) trees that have in
themselves the seed of their kind, that they be into meat
to you (so that they can be food for you);
30 and to all living beasts of [the] earth, and to each
bird of (the) heaven(s), and to all things that be moved in
[the] earth, and in which is a living soul, that they have
(them) to eat; and it was done so. (and also for all the
living beasts of the earth, and for each bird of the air, and
for all the things that creep on the earth, and in which is
a living soul, so that they have them to eat; and it was
done so.)
31 And God saw all (the) things which he (had) made,
and they were full good (and they were very good). And
the eventide and the morrowtide was made, the sixth day.

CHAPTER 2

1 Therefore heavens and earth be made perfect, and
all the ornament of those. (And so the heavens and the
earth, and all their ornaments, were finished.)
2 And God [ful]filled in the seventh day his work
which he made; and he rested in the seventh day from all
his work which he had made; (Yea, God finished his
work by the seventh day; and so he rested on the seventh
day from all the work which he had done;)
3 and he blessed the seventh day, and hallowed it; for
in that day God ceased of all his work which he made of
nought, that he should make. (and he blessed the seventh
day, and made it holy; for on that day God ceased from
all his work which he had made out of nothing, that he
had intended to make.)
4 These be the generations of heaven and of earth, in
the day wherein the Lord God made heaven and earth,
(These be the generations, *or the creation*, of the heavens
and the earth, in the days when the Lord God made the
heavens and the earth,)
5 and each little tree of [the] earth before that it sprang
out in [the] earth; and he made each herb of the field
before that it burgeoned. For the Lord God had not (yet)
rained on the earth, and no man there was that wrought
the earth (and there was no man yet to work the earth);
6 but a well went out of [the] earth, and moisted all
the higher part of the earth. (but a well, *or a mist*, went
up out of the ground, and watered all the earth's surface.)
7 Therefore the Lord God formed man of the slime of
[the] earth, and breathed into his face the breathing of
life; and man was made into a living soul. (And so the
Lord God formed man out of the slime of the earth, and
breathed into his face the breathe of life; and then the
man was made into a living soul.)
8 Forsooth the Lord God planted at the beginning (the)
paradise of liking, wherein he set man whom he had
formed. (And the Lord God planted a garden in Eden, in
the east, and he put the man there whom he had formed.)
9 And the Lord God brought forth (out) of the earth
each tree fair in sight, and sweet to eat; also he brought
forth the tree of life in the midst of paradise, and the tree
of knowing of good and of evil (and he brought forth the
tree of life in the middle of the garden, and the tree of the
knowledge of good and evil).
10 And a river went out from the place of liking to moist
paradise, which river is parted from thence into four heads.
(And a river went out from Eden to water the garden, and
this river was parted from there into four rivers.)
11 The name of the one river is Pishon, that it is that
compasseth all the land of Havilah, where gold cometh
forth, (The name of the first river is Pishon, and it
encircleth all the land of Havilah, where gold cometh
from,)
12 and the gold of that land is the best, and there is
found bdellium, *that is, a tree of spicery*, and the stone
onyx; (and the gold of that land is the best, and bdellium,
that is, a spice tree, is also found there, and the onyx
stone as well;)
13 and the name of the second river is Gihon, that it is
that compasseth all the land of Ethiopia (and it encircleth
all the land of Ethiopia);
14 forsooth the name of the third river is Tigris, that
goeth against Assyrians (which floweth east of Assyria);
soothly the fourth river is that Euphrates.
15 Therefore the Lord God took man, and set him in
(the) paradise of liking, that he should work and keep it.
(And so the Lord God took the man, and put him in the
Garden of Eden, so that he would work it, and care for it.)
16 And God commanded to him and said, Eat thou of
each tree of paradise; (And God commanded to him and
said, Thou can eat of every tree in the garden;)
17 forsooth eat thou not of the tree of knowing of good
and of evil; for in whatever day thou shalt eat thereof,
thou shalt die by death. (but thou shalt not eat of the tree
of the knowledge of good and evil; for on the day that
thou shalt eat of it, thou shalt die.)
18 And the Lord God said, It is not good that a man be
alone; make we to him an helper like to himself (let us
make for him a helper like himself).
19 And therefore when all living beasts of [the] earth,
and all the volatiles of (the) heaven(s,) were formed of

[the] earth, the Lord God brought those to Adam, that he should see what he should call those; for all thing that Adam called of living soul, that is the name thereof. (And so when all the living beasts of the earth, and all the birds of the air, were formed from the earth, the Lord God brought them to Adam, to see what he would call them; for whatever name that Adam called each thing with a living soul, that is its name.)
20 And Adam called by their names all living things, and all volatiles [of (the) heaven(s)], and all unreasonable beasts of [the] earth. Forsooth to Adam was not found an helper like him. (And so Adam named all the living things, yea, all the birds of the air, and all the unreasoning beasts of the earth. But there was not found for Adam a helper like himself.)
21 Therefore the Lord God sent sleep into Adam, and when he slept, God took one of his ribs, and filled flesh for it. (And so the Lord God sent sleep into Adam, and while he slept, God took one of his ribs, and then closed up the flesh over that place.)
22 And the Lord God builded the rib which he had taken from Adam into a woman, and brought her to Adam.
23 And Adam said, This is now a bone of my bones, and flesh of my flesh; this shall be called virago, for she is taken (out) of man (she shall be called Woman, for she was taken from Man).
24 Wherefore a man shall forsake [his] father and mother, and shall cleave to his wife, and they shall be twain in one flesh [and two shall be in one flesh].
25 Forsooth ever either was naked, that is, Adam and his wife, and they were not ashamed. (And both of them were naked, that is, the man and his wife, but they were not ashamed.)

CHAPTER 3

1 But the serpent was feller than all living beasts of [the] earth, which the Lord God had made. The which serpent said to the woman, Why commanded God to you, that ye should not eat of each tree of paradise? (And the serpent was more cunning than all the living beasts of the earth. And the serpent said to the woman, Why hath God commanded you to not eat from any tree in the garden?)
2 To whom the woman answered, We eat of the fruit of trees that be in paradise; (To whom the woman answered, We can eat of the fruit of the trees that be in the garden;)
3 soothly God commanded to us, that we should not eat of the fruit of the tree, which is in the midst of paradise (which is in the middle of the garden), and that we should not touch it, lest peradventure we die.
4 Forsooth the serpent said to the woman, Ye shall not die by death (Ye shall not die);
5 for why God knoweth that in whatever day ye shall eat thereof, your eyes shall be opened, and ye shall be as Gods, knowing good and evil. (for God knoweth that on whatever day ye shall eat of it, your eyes shall be opened, and ye shall be like gods, knowing good and evil.)
6 Therefore the woman saw that the tree was good, and sweet to eat, and fair to the eyes, and delightable in beholding; and she took of the fruit thereof, and ate, and gave to her husband, and he ate.
7 And the eyes of both (of them) were opened; and when they knew that they were naked, they sewed [together] the leaves of a fig tree, and made breeches to themselves (and made breeches for themselves).
8 And when they heard the voice of the Lord God going in paradise at the wind after midday, Adam and his wife hid them(selves) from the face of the Lord God in [the] midst of the trees of paradise. (And when they heard the sound of the Lord God walking in the garden in the evening breeze, the man and his wife hid themselves from the face of the Lord God among the trees of the garden.)
9 And the Lord God called Adam, and said to him, Where art thou?
10 And Adam said, I heard thy voice in paradise, and I dreaded, for I was naked, and I hid me. (And the man said, I heard the sound of you walking in the garden, and I was afraid, for I was naked, and so I hid myself.)
11 To whom the Lord said, Who showed to thee that thou were naked, no but for thou hast eaten of the tree of which I commanded to thee that thou shouldest not eat? (To whom the Lord said, Who told thee that thou were naked? hast thou eaten of the tree which I commanded to thee that thou shouldest not eat?)
12 And Adam said, The woman which thou gavest (for) fellow(ship) to me, gave me of the tree, and I ate. (And Adam said, The woman whom thou gavest to me for fellowship, gave to me of the tree, and so I ate.)
13 And the Lord said to the woman, Why didest thou this thing? The which answered, The serpent deceived me, and (so) I ate.
14 And the Lord God said to the serpent, For thou didest this, thou shalt be cursed among all [the] living things, and unreasonable beasts of [the] earth; thou shalt go on thy breast, and thou shalt eat earth in all the days of thy life. (And the Lord God said to the serpent, For thou didest this, thou shalt be cursed among all the living things, and unreasoning beasts of the earth; thou shalt go upon thy breast, and thou shalt eat dust all the days of thy life.)
15 I shall set enmities betwixt thee and the woman, and betwixt thy seed and her seed; she shall break thine head, and thou shalt set ambushes to her heel. (I shall put enmity between thee and the woman, and between thy seed and her seed; her seed shall break thy head, and thou shalt set ambush to her seed's heel.)
16 Also God said to the woman, I shall multiply thy wretchednesses and thy conceivings; in sorrow thou shalt bear thy children; and thou shalt be under (the) power of

thine husband, and he shall be lord of thee.
17 Soothly God said to Adam, For thou heardest the
voice of thy wife, and hast eaten of the tree, of which I
commanded to thee that thou shouldest not eat, the earth
shall be cursed in thy work, *that is, for thy sin*; in travails
thou shalt eat thereof in all the days of thy life; (And God
said to Adam, For thou heardest thy wife's voice, and
hast eaten of the tree, of which I commanded to thee that
thou shouldest not eat, the ground shall be cursed on
account of thee, *that is, because of thy sin*; only after
much travail, *or much labour*, shalt thou get food from it
all the days of thy life;)
18 it shall bring forth thorns and briars to thee, and
thou shalt eat (the) herbs of the earth;
19 in [the] sweat of thy cheer, [*or (thy) face*,] thou shalt
eat thy bread, till thou turn again into the earth of which
thou art taken; for thou art dust, and thou shalt turn again
into dust. (by the sweat of thy brow, thou shalt earn thy
bread, until thou return to the earth of which thou art
taken; for thou art dust, and thou shalt return to dust.)
20 And Adam called the name of his wife Eve, for she
was the mother of all men living (for she was the mother
of all living people).
21 And the Lord God made coats of skins to Adam and
Eve his wife, and clothed them; (And the Lord God made
coats out of skins for Adam and Eve his wife, and clothed
them;)
22 and said, Lo! Adam is made as one of us, and
knoweth good and evil; now therefore *see ye*, lest
peradventure he put [out] his hand, and take [also] of the
tree of life, and eat, and live without end.
23 And the Lord God sent him out of (the) paradise of
liking, that he should work the earth, of which he was
taken. (And so the Lord God sent him out of the Garden
of Eden, to work the earth, from which he was taken.)
24 And God casted out Adam, and setted before (the)
paradise of liking cherubim, *that is, (he gave it into the)*
keeping of angels, and a sword of flame turning about to
keep (charge of) the way of the tree of life. (And so God
cast out Adam, and to the east of the Garden of Eden he
placed cherubim, and a sword of flame which turned
about, to guard the way to the tree of life.)

CHAPTER 4

1 Forsooth Adam knew Eve his wife, which
conceived, and childed Cain, and said, I have gotten a
man by God. (And Adam knew his wife Eve, who
conceived, and bare Cain, and she said, Now, with the
Lord's help, I have begotten a man.)
2 And again she childed his brother Abel. Forsooth
Abel was a keeper of sheep, and Cain was an earth-tiller.
(And then she bare his brother Abel. And Abel was a
shepherd, and Cain was a farmer, who worked the soil.)
3 Soothly it was done after many days, that Cain
offered gifts to the Lord of the fruits of the earth[1];
4 and Abel offered of the first engendered of his flock,
and of the fatness of those. And the Lord beheld to Abel
and to the gifts of him;
5 soothly he beheld not to Cain and to his gifts. And
Cain was wroth greatly, and his cheer felled down (And
Cain was greatly angered, and his face fell).
6 And the Lord said to him, Why art thou wroth, and
why felled down thy face?
7 Whether not if thou shalt do well, thou shalt receive
well; but if *thou doest* evil, thy sin shall be present anon
in the gates? but the desire thereof, *that is, of sin*, shall be
under thee, and thou shalt be lord thereof. (If thou shalt
do well, then thou shalt be accepted; but if *thou doest*
evil, then at once thy sin shall be present at the gates, and
the desire of sin shall take thee under, and so thou must
be lord of it, *or rule over it*.)
8 And Cain said to Abel, his brother, Go we out (But
then Cain said to his brother Abel, Walk with me). And
when they were in the field, Cain rose (up) against his
brother Abel, and killed him.
9 And the Lord said to Cain, Where is Abel thy
brother? Which answered, I know not; whether I am the
keeper of my brother? (And the Lord said to Cain, Where
is thy brother Abel? And he answered, How do I know;
am I my brother's keeper?)
10 And God said to Cain, What hast thou done? the
voice of the blood of thy brother crieth to me from [the]
earth (the voice of thy brother's blood crieth out to me
from the earth).
11 Now therefore thou shalt be cursed on [the] earth,
that opened his mouth, and received of thine hand the
blood of thy brother. (And so now thou shalt be cursed
on the earth, that hath opened its mouth, and received
thy brother's blood from thy hand.)
12 When thou shalt work the earth, it shall not give his
fruits to thee; thou shalt be unstable of dwelling, and
fleeing about on [the] earth, in all the days of thy life.
(When thou shalt work the earth, it shall not give its fruits
to thee; thou shalt be of unstable dwelling, and fleeing
about on the earth, all the days of thy life.)
13 And Cain said to the Lord, My wickedness is more
than that I deserve forgiveness (for); (And Cain said to the
Lord, My punishment is more than that I can bear;)
14 lo! today thou castest me out from the face of the
earth; and I shall be hid from thy face, and I shall be
unstable of dwelling, and fleeing about in (the) earth;
therefore each man that shall find me shall slay me. (lo!
today thou castest me out from the face of the earth; and I
shall be hid from thy face, and I shall be of unstable
dwelling, and fleeing about on the earth; and any man
who findeth me shall slay me.)

---

[1] Not the *first* fruits, or the best, or it would have been so stated.

15 And the Lord said to him, It shall not be done so,
but each man that shall slay Cain shall be punished
sevenfold. And the Lord set a sign in Cain, that each man
that should find him should not slay him. (And the Lord
said to him, It shall not be done so, but any man who
shall kill Cain shall be punished seven times. And the
Lord put a mark on Cain, so that any man who would
find him would not kill him.)
16 And Cain went out from the face of the Lord, and
dwelled fleeing about in [the] earth, at the east coast of
Eden, *that is, of (the) earthly paradise.* (And so Cain went
out from the face of the Lord, and lived in the land of
Nod, to the east of the Garden of Eden, *that is, to the east
of Paradise on earth.*)
17 Forsooth Cain knew his wife, which conceived, and
childed Enoch; and Cain builded a city, and called the
name thereof of the name of his son, Enoch (and Cain
built a city, and named it after his son Enoch).
18 Forsooth Enoch begat Irad; and Irad begat Mehujael;
and Mehujael begat Methusael; and Methusael begat
Lamech;
19 that took two wives, the name to the one wife was
Adah, and the name to the other was Zillah. (and Lamech
took two wives, and his first wife was named Adah, and
the other was named Zillah.)
20 And Adah begat Jabal, that was the father of (the)
dwellers in tents, and of shepherds;
21 and the name of his brother was Jubal; he was the
father of the singers in harp and organ. (and his brother's
name was Jubal; and he was the father of the players of
harps and of organs.)
22 And Zillah begat Tubalcain, that was an hammer-
beater, and [a] smith on all works of brass and of iron
(who used a hammer, and was a smith of all things made
out of bronze and of iron); forsooth the sister of
Tubalcain was Naamah.
23 And Lamech said to his wives, Adah and Zillah, Ye
wives of Lamech, hear my voice, and harken (to) my
word(s); for I have slain a man by my wound(ing), and a
young waxing man by my violent beating (for I have
killed a man with my wounding, and a young man with
my violent beatings);
24 (if) vengeance shall be given sevenfold of Cain,
forsooth of Lamech seventy times seven times. (if
vengeance shall be given seven times for Cain, then for
Lamech *it shall be* seventy-seven times.)
25 Also yet Adam knew his wife, and she childed a
son, and called his name Seth[2], and said, God hath put to
me another seed for Abel, whom Cain killed. (And Adam
knew his wife, and she bare a son, and named him Seth,
for Eve said, God hath given me another child for Abel,
whom Cain killed.)

[2] The name sounds like the Hebrew for "has given".

26 But also a son was born to Seth, which son he called
Enos; this began to call inwardly the name of the Lord.
(And a son was born to Seth, whom he called Enos; and
his generation began to inwardly call on the Lord's name.)

CHAPTER 5

1 This is the book of the generation(s) of Adam, in the
day wherein God made man of nought. God made man
to the image and likeness of God; (This is the book of the
descendants of Adam. On the day when God made man
out of nothing, God made man in the image and likeness
of God;)
2 God formed them male and female, and blessed
them, and called the name of them Adam, in the day in
which they were formed. (God formed them male and
female, and blessed them, and called their name Man, on
the day when they were formed.)
3 Forsooth Adam lived an hundred years and thirty,
and begat a son to his image and likeness, and called his
name Seth. (And Adam lived a hundred and thirty years,
and then begat a son in his image and likeness, and
called his name Seth.)
4 And the days of Adam after that he begat Seth were
made eight hundred years, and he begat sons and
daughters.
5 And all the time in which Adam lived was made
nine hundred years and thirty, and he was dead. (And all
the time in which Adam lived was nine hundred and
thirty years, and then he died.)
6 And Seth lived an hundred and five years, and (then)
begat Enos.
7 And Seth lived after that he begat Enos eight
hundred and seven years, and begat sons and daughters.
8 And all the days of Seth were made nine hundred
and twelve years, and (then) he was dead.
9 Forsooth Enos lived ninety years, and (then) begat
Cainan;
10 after whose birth Enos lived eight hundred and
fifteen years, and begat sons and daughters.
11 And all the days of Enos were made nine hundred
and five years, and (then) he was dead.
12 Also Cainan lived seventy years, and begat
Mahalaleel. (And Cainan lived seventy years, and then
begat Mahalaleel.)
13 And Cainan lived after that he begat Mahalaleel
eight hundred and forty years, and begat sons and
daughters.
14 And all the days of Cainan were made nine hundred
and ten years, and (then) he was dead.
15 Forsooth Mahalaleel lived sixty years and five, and
begat Jared. (And Mahalaleel lived sixty-five years, and
then begat Jared.)
16 And Mahalaleel lived after that he begat Jared eight
hundred and thirty years, and begat sons and daughters.

17 And all the days of Mahalaleel were made eight
hundred [and] ninety and five years, and (then) he was
dead.
18 And Jared lived an hundred and two and sixty years,
and (then) begat Enoch.
19 And Jared lived after that he begat Enoch eight
hundred years, and begat sons and daughters.
20 And all the days of Jared were made nine hundred
and two and sixty years, and (then) he was dead.
21 Forsooth Enoch lived five and sixty years, and (then)
begat Methuselah.
22 And Enoch went with God (And Enoch walked with
God); and Enoch lived after that he begat Methuselah
three hundred years, and begat sons and daughters.
23 And all the days of Enoch were three hundred and
five and sixty years.
24 And Enoch went with God (And Enoch walked with
God), and appeared not afterward, for God took him away.
25 Also Methuselah lived an hundred and seven and
eighty years, and begat Lamech. (And Methuselah lived a
hundred and eighty-seven years, and then begat Lamech.)
26 And Methuselah lived after that he begat Lamech
seven hundred and two and eighty years, and begat sons
and daughters.
27 And all the days of Methuselah were made nine
hundred and nine and sixty years, and (then) he was dead.
28 Forsooth Lamech lived an hundred and two and
eighty years, and (then) begat a son;
29 and [he] called his name Noe[3], and said, This man
shall comfort us of the works and travails of our hands, in
the land which the Lord cursed. (and he called his name
Noah, and said, This son shall bring us comfort from all
the work and labour of our hands, on the land which the
Lord hath cursed.)
30 And Lamech lived after that he begat Noe five hundred
[and] ninety and five years, and begat sons and daughters.
(And after that he begat Noah, Lamech lived five hundred
and ninety-five years, and begat sons and daughters.)
31 And all the days of Lamech were made seven
hundred [and] seventy and seven years, and he was dead.
(And all the days of Lamech were made seven hundred
and seventy-seven years, and then he died.)
32 Forsooth Noe, when he was of five hundred years,
begat Shem, Ham, and Japheth. (And Noah, when he was
five hundred years old, begat Shem, Ham, and Japheth.)

CHAPTER 6

1 And when men began to be multiplied on [the]
earth, and had begat daughters,
2 the sons of God saw the daughters of men that they
were fair, and took wives to them of all which they had
chosen. (the sons of God saw that the daughters of men
were beautiful, and took wives for themselves of all
whom they had chosen.)
3 And God said, My spirit shall not dwell in man
without end, for he is flesh; and the days of him shall be
an hundred and twenty years.
4 Soothly giants were on the earth in those days,
forsooth after that the sons of God entered [in] to the
daughters of men, and those daughters begat; these were
mighty of the world and famous men (these were the
mighty and famous men of the world).
5 Soothly God saw that much malice of men was in
[the] earth, and that all the thought of *their* heart was
attentive, *either given (over)*, to evil in all time, (And God
saw that there was much malice in people on the earth,
and that all the thoughts of *their* hearts were given over
to evil all the time,)
6 and it repented him that he had made man in (the)
earth; and God was wary before against time to coming,
and was touched with sorrow of heart within; (and he
repented that he had made man on the earth; and God
was wary about the time to come, and was touched with
sorrow of heart within;)
7 and said, I shall do away man, whom I made of
nought, from the face of the earth; from man till to living
things, from creeping beast till to the birds of (the)
heaven(s); for it repenteth me that I made them. (and he
said, I shall do away man, whom I made out of nothing,
from the face of the earth; from man to beast, from the
reptiles to the birds of the air; for I repent that I ever
made them.)
8 Forsooth Noe found grace before the Lord. (But
Noah found grace before the Lord.)
9 These be the generations of Noe. Noe was a just
man and perfect in his generations; Noe went with God,
(This is the story of Noah. Noah was a just, *or a
righteous*, man, and the only good man of his generation;
and Noah walked with God,)
10 and begat three sons, Shem, Ham, and Japheth.
11 Forsooth the earth was corrupt before God, and was
filled with wickedness. (And the earth was corrupt in the
sight of God, and filled with wickedness.)
12 And when God saw, that the earth was corrupt, for
each flesh, *or man*, had corrupted his way on [the] earth
(for all people had corrupted their ways upon the earth),
13 he said to Noe, The end of all flesh is come before
me; the earth is filled with wickedness of the face of
them, and I shall destroy them with the earth. (he said to
Noah, The end of all flesh hath come before me, for they
have filled the earth full of wickedness; and so I shall
destroy them all, and the earth with them.)
14 Make thou to thee a ship[4] of wood hewn and planed

[3] This name sounds like the Hebrew for "rest" or "relief".

[4] Throughout Genesis, whenever the "Later Version" refers to Noah's "ship", the "Early Version" refers to Noah's "ark".

(Make thou a ship for thyself out of hewn and planed
wood); thou shalt make dwelling places in the ship, and
thou shalt anoint it with pitch within and withoutforth.
15 And so thou shalt make it. The length of the ship
shall be of three hundred cubits, the breadth shall be of
fifty cubits, and the highness thereof shall be of thirty
cubits. (And thou shalt make it thus. The length of the
ship shall be three hundred cubits, and the breadth shall
be fifty cubits, and the height of it shall be thirty cubits.)
16 Thou shalt make a window in the ship, and thou
shalt end the highness thereof in a cubit (and the distance
from the top of it to the roof shall be one cubit); soothly
thou shalt set the door of the ship in the side beneath;
thou shalt make solars, and places of three chambers in
the ship.
17 Lo! I shall bring waters of deluge, *or great flood*, on
the earth, and I shall slay each flesh in which is the spirit
of life under heaven, and all things that be in [the] earth,
shall be wasted. (Lo! and then I shall bring in waters of a
deluge, *or of a great flood*, on the earth, and I shall kill all
flesh under heaven in which is the spirit of life, and all
the things that be on the earth shall be destroyed.)
18 And I shall set my covenant of peace with thee (But I
shall make my covenant of peace with thee); and thou
shalt enter into the ship, [thou,] and thy sons, and thy
wife, and the wives of thy sons shall enter with thee.
19 And of all living beasts of all flesh, thou shalt bring
into the ship twain and twain, of male kind and female,
that they live (along) with thee; (And of all living beasts of
all flesh, thou shalt bring into the ship two of each kind,
male and female, so that they can continue to live, along
with thee;)
20 of birds by their kind, and of work beasts in their
kind, and of each creeping beast of [the] earth, by their
kind; twain and twain of all shall enter with thee, that
they may live. (of birds by their kind, and of work beasts
by their kind, and of reptiles by their kind; two of each
kind shall enter with thee, so that they will continue to
live.)
21 Therefore thou shalt take with thee of all meats that
may be eaten, and thou shalt bear together at thee, and
those shall be as well to thee as to the beasts into meat.
(And so thou shalt take with thee all kinds of food that
can be eaten, and thou shalt carry it all with thee, and
this shall be food for thee, and for the beasts.)
22 Therefore Noe did all things which God
commanded to him. (And so Noah did everything which
God commanded him to do.)

CHAPTER 7

1 Also the Lord said to Noe, Enter thou and all thine
house into the ship, for I saw (that) thee (alone were) just
before me in this generation. (And then the Lord said to
Noah, Enter thou and all thy household, *or all thy family*,
into the ship, for I have seen that in this generation, thou
alone be righteous before me.)
2 Of all clean living beasts, thou shalt take (with thee)
by seven and by seven, male and female; forsooth of
unclean living beasts, thou shalt take by twain and by
twain, male and female; (Of all clean beasts, thou shalt
take with thee seven pairs, male and female; but of all
unclean beasts, thou shalt take only one pair, male and
female;)
3 and also of [the] volatiles of (the) heaven(s), thou
shalt take, by seven and by seven, male and female, that
their seed be saved on the face of all (the) earth. (and also
of the birds of the air, thou shalt take seven pairs, male
and female, so that their descendants will continue to live
on the face of the earth.)
4 For yet and after seven days, I shall rain on [the]
earth forty days and forty nights, and I shall do away all
substance which I made, from the face of [the] earth. (For
in seven days, I shall send rain on the earth for forty days
and forty nights, and I shall do away all the substance
which I made, from off the face of the earth.)
5 Therefore Noe did all things which the Lord
commanded to him.
6 And he was six hundred years (old), when the
waters of the great flood flowed on [the] earth.
7 And Noe entered into the ship, and his sons, and his
wife, and the wives of his sons, entered with him, for the
waters of the great flood (because of the waters of the
great flood).
8 And of living beasts clean and unclean, and of [the]
birds of (the) heaven(s), and of each beast which is
moved on [the] earth, (And of the clean and unclean
beasts, and of the birds of the air, and of each beast
which creepeth on the earth,)
9 by twain and by twain, male and female entered to
Noe into the ship, as the Lord commanded to Noe. (by
two and two, male and female, they entered into the ship
with Noah, as the Lord had commanded to Noah.)
10 And when seven days had passed, the waters of the
great flood flowed on [the] earth.
11 In the six hundred(th) year of the life of Noe, in the
second month, in the seventeenth day of the month (on
the seventeenth day of the month), all the wells of the
great sea were broken, and the windows of (the)
heaven(s) were opened,
12 and rain was made on the earth (for) forty days and
forty nights.
13 In the end of that day Noe entered, and Shem, and
Ham, and Japheth, his sons (At the end of that day Noah
entered, and his sons Shem, and Ham, and Japheth), and
his wife, and the [three] wives of his sons, entered with
them into the ship.
14 They entered, and each beast by his kind, and all
work beasts in their kind, and each beast which is moved

on [the] earth in his kind, and each volatile by his kind;
all birds and all volatiles, (They entered, and each beast
after its kind, and all the work beasts after their kind, and
each beast which creepeth on the earth after its kind, and
each bird after its kind, yea, all the kinds of birds,)
15 entered to Noe into the ship, by twain and by twain
of each flesh in which the spirit of life was. (entered into
the ship with Noah, two by two of all flesh in which was
the spirit of life.)
16 And those that entered, entered male and female of
each flesh, as God commanded to him. And the Lord
closed him from withoutforth. (And they that entered,
entered male and female of all flesh, as God had
commanded to him. And the Lord enclosed him from
outside.)
17 And the great flood was made (for) forty days and
forty nights on [the] earth, and the waters were multiplied,
and raised (up) the ship on high from the earth.
18 The waters flowed greatly, and filled all things in the
face of the earth (And the waters greatly flowed, and
filled up all the things that were on the face of the earth).
Forsooth the ship was borne on the waters.
19 And the waters had mastery greatly on [the] earth
(And the waters had great mastery over the earth), and all
[the] high hills under all (of) heaven were covered;
20 (yea,) the water was higher, by fifteen cubits, over
(all) the hills which it covered.
21 And each flesh was wasted that moved on [the]
earth, of birds, of living beasts, of unreasonable beasts,
and of all reptiles/all creeping beasts that creep on [the]
earth. (And all flesh that moved on the earth was
destroyed, yea, birds, and living beasts, and unreasoning
beasts, and all the reptiles that creep on the earth.)
22 All men, and all things in which the breathing of life
was in [the] earth, were dead. (And all men, and all the
things on the earth in which was the breath of life, died.)
23 And God did away all the substance that was on
[the] earth, from man till to beast, as well a creeping
beast, as the birds of (the) heaven(s); and those were
done away from [the] earth. Forsooth Noe dwelled
alone, and they that were with him in the ship. (And so
God did away all the life that was on the earth, from man
unto beasts, and reptiles, and the birds of the air, they
were all done away from the earth. And only Noah, and
those who were with him in the ship, remained alive.)
24 And the waters of the great flood over-went the
earth an hundred and fifty days. (And the waters of the
great flood went over the earth for a hundred and fifty
days.)

CHAPTER 8

1 Forsooth the Lord had mind of Noe, and of all living
beasts, and of all work beasts, that were with him in the
ship; and [he] brought a wind on the earth. And [the]
waters were decreased, *or assuaged*, (And the Lord
remembered Noah, and all the living beasts, and all the
work beasts, that were with him in the ship; and he
brought forth a wind on the earth. And the waters
decreased,)
2 and the wells of the sea were closed, and the
windows of (the) heaven(s) were closed, and (the) rains of
(the) heaven(s) were ceased. (and the wells of the sea
were closed, and the windows of the sky were closed,
and the rains from the sky ceased.)
3 And [the] waters turned again from (off) the earth,
and went again, and began to be decreased, *or assuaged*,
after an hundred and fifty days.
4 And the ship rested in the seventh month, in the
seven and twentieth day of the month, on the hills of
Armenia. (And the ship rested in the seventh month, on
the seventeenth day of the month, on Mount Ararat.)
5 And soothly the waters went and decreased till to
the tenth month, for in the tenth month, in the first day of
the month (on the first day of the month), the tops of [the]
hills appeared.
6 And when forty days had passed, Noe opened the
window of the ship which he had made,
7 and sent out a crow, which went out, and turned not
again till the waters were dried on [the] earth. (and sent
out a crow, which went out, and did not return until the
waters were dried up from off the earth.)
8 Also Noe sent out a culver after him, to see if the
waters had ceased then on the face of the earth; (And
then Noah sent out a dove after him, to see if the waters
had now gone from off the face of the earth;)
9 and when the culver found not where her foot
should rest, she turned again to him into the ship, for the
waters were on all [the] earth; and Noe held forth his
hand, and brought the culver, (once) taken, (back) into
the ship. (but when the dove found nowhere to rest her
feet, she returned to him in the ship, for the waters were
still over all the earth; and Noah held forth his hand, and
caught her, and brought the dove back into the ship.)
10 Soothly when other seven days were abided
afterward, again he sent out a culver from the ship; (And
he waited another seven days, and then again he sent out
the dove from the ship;)
11 and she came (back) to him at eventide, and bare in
her mouth a branch of (an) olive tree with green leaves.
Therefore Noe understood that the waters had ceased
(from flowing) on (the) earth (And so Noah understood
that the waters had now gone from off the face of the
earth);
12 and nevertheless he abode seven other days, and
(then) sent out a culver, which turned not again to him.
(nevertheless he waited another seven days, and then
again sent out the dove, but this time she did not return
to him.)

13 Therefore in the six hundred and one year of the life
of Noe, in the first month, in the first day of the month,
[the] waters were decreased on (the) earth; and Noe
opened the roof of the ship, and beheld, and saw that the
face of the earth was dried. (And so in the six hundred and
first year of Noah's life, in the first month, on the first day
of the month, the waters were gone from off the face of the
earth; and Noah opened the roof of the ship, and looked,
and saw that the face of the earth was becoming dry.)
14 In the second month, in the seven and twentieth day
of the month, the earth was made dry. (And by the
second month, on the twenty-seventh day of the month,
the whole earth was made dry.)
15 Soothly the Lord spake to Noe; and said,
16 Go out of the ship, thou, and thy wife, and thy sons,
and the wives of thy sons with thee;
17 and lead out with thee all living beasts that be with
thee of each flesh, as well in volatiles, as in unreasonable
beasts, and all reptiles/all creeping beasts that creep on
[the] earth; and enter ye on the earth, increase ye, and be
ye multiplied on (the) earth. (and lead out with thee all
the living beasts that be with thee of all flesh, yea, the
birds, and the unreasoning beasts, and all the reptiles that
creep on the earth; and go they over the earth, and
increase they, and be they multiplied on the earth.)
18 Therefore Noe went out, and his sons, and his wife,
and the wives of his sons with him;
19 but also all (the) living beasts, and work beasts, (and
birds,) and reptiles that creep on [the] earth, (all) by their
kind, went out of the ship.
20 Forsooth Noe builded an altar to the Lord, and he
took of all clean beasts and birds, and offered burnt
sacrifices on the altar. (And Noah built an altar to the
Lord, and he took one of each kind of the clean beasts
and birds, and offered burnt sacrifices on the altar.)
21 And the Lord savoured the odour of sweetness, and
said to him(self), I shall no more curse the earth for men,
for (I know that) the wit and thought of man's heart be
ready, *either prone*, into evil from (a) young waxing age;
therefore I shall no more smite each living soul, as I did;
(And the Lord savoured the aroma of sweetness, and said
to himself, I shall no more curse the earth for man's sake,
for I know that the wit and the thought of man's heart be
prone toward evil from a young age; and so I shall no
more strike down each living soul, as I have done;)
22 (and so) in all the days of [the] earth, seed and ripe
corn, cold and heat, summer and winter, night and day,
shall not rest. (and so for all the days that remain for the
earth, seed-time and harvest, cold and heat, summer and
winter, night and day, shall never cease.)

CHAPTER 9

1 And God blessed Noe and his sons, and said to
them, Increase ye, and be ye multiplied, and fill ye the
earth;
2 and your dread and trembling be on all [the]
unreasonable beasts of the earth, and on all [the] birds of
(the) heaven(s), with all things that be moved in (the)
earth; all (the) fishes of the sea be given (in)to your hand.
(let the fear of you, and trembling over you, be on all the
unreasoning beasts of the earth, and on all the birds of
the air, and on all the fishes of the sea; yea, let all the
things that move on the earth, be given into your hands.)
3 And all thing which is moved and liveth shall be to
you into meat; (now) I have given to you all things, as (I
gave the) green worts (before), (And everything which
liveth and moveth shall be food for you; yea, as I did
with the green herbs before, now I give you all these
things to eat,)
4 except that ye shall not eat flesh with the blood,
5 for I shall seek the blood of your lives, of the hand
of all unreasonable beasts, and of the hand of man, of the
hand of man, and of his brother, I shall seek the life of
man. (for I shall seek justice for any spilt blood of your
lives, from any unreasoning beast, and from any man,
yea, from any man, and from any of his brothers, I shall
seek their life if any of them take the life of someone.)
6 Whoever sheddeth out man's blood, his blood shall
be shed; for man is made to the image of God (for man is
made in the image of God).
7 Forsooth increase ye, and be ye multiplied, and
enter ye on [the] earth, and fill ye it.
8 Also the Lord said these things to Noe, and to his
sons with him,
9 Lo! I shall make my covenant with you, and with
your seed after you,
10 and to each living soul which is with you, as well in
birds as in work beasts and small beasts of [the] earth,
and to all things that went out of the ship, and to all
unreasonable beasts of [the] earth. (and with each living
soul which is with you, yea, with the birds, and with the
work beasts and the small beasts of the earth, and with all
the unreasoning beasts of the earth, yea, with all the
things that went out of the ship.)
11 I shall make my covenant with you, and each flesh
shall no more be slain of the waters of the great flood,
neither the great flood destroying all [the] earth shall be
(any) more. (I shall make my covenant with you, and
never again shall all flesh be slain by the waters of a great
flood, and never again shall there be a great flood
destroying all the earth.)
12 And God said, This is the sign of (the) bond of
peace, which I give between me and you, and to each
living soul which is with you, into everlasting
generations. (And God said, This is the sign of the
covenant, which I make between me and you, and each
living soul which is with you, unto endless generations.)
13 I shall set my bow in the clouds, and it shall be a

sign of (the) bond of peace between me and [the] earth; (I
shall set my rainbow in the clouds, and it shall be a sign
of the covenant between me and the earth;)
14 and when I shall cover [the] heaven with clouds, my
bow shall appear in the clouds, (and when I shall cover
the heavens with clouds, my rainbow shall appear in the
clouds,)
15 and I shall have mind of my bond of peace which I
made with you, and with each soul living that nourisheth
flesh; and the waters of the great flood shall no more be
to do away all flesh. (and I shall remember my covenant
which I made with you, and with each living soul that
hath flesh; and never again shall the waters of a great
flood do away all flesh.)
16 And my bow shall be in the clouds, and I shall see
it, and I shall have mind of the everlasting bond of peace,
which is made between God and man, and each soul
living of all flesh which is on [the] earth. (And my
rainbow shall be in the clouds, and I shall see it, and I
shall remember the everlasting covenant, which is made
between God and man, and each living soul of all the
kinds of flesh that be on the earth.)
17 And God said to Noe, This shall be a sign of [the]
bond of peace, which I made between me and each flesh
on earth. (And God said to Noah, This shall be a sign of
the covenant, which I made between me and all flesh on
the earth.)
18 Therefore they that went out of the ship were Noe,
Shem, Ham, and Japheth; forsooth Ham, that is the father
of Canaan.
19 These three were the sons of Noe, and all the kind
of men was sown of them on all [the] earth. (These three
were the sons of Noah, and all the kinds of people on all
the earth came from them.)
20 And Noe, an earth-tiller, began to till the earth, and
he planted a vinery, (And Noah, a farmer, began to work
the soil, and he planted a vineyard;)
21 and (one day) he drank wine, and was drunken; and
he was naked, and lay in his tabernacle (and he lay naked
in his tent).
22 And when Ham, the father of Canaan, had seen this
thing, that is, that the shameful members of his father
were made naked, he told his two brethren withoutforth.
23 And Shem and Japheth putted a mantle on their
shoulders, and they went backward, and covered the
shameful members of their father, and their faces were
turned away, and they saw not the privy members of their
father.
24 And Noe waked of the wine, and when he had
learned what things his less(er), *or younger*[5], son had
done to him, (And when Noah awoke from the wine, and
he had learned what his youngest son had done to him,)
25 he said, Cursed be the child Canaan, he shall be (a)
servant of servants to his brethren. (he said, Cursed be
Ham's child Canaan, let him be a slave of slaves to his
brothers.)
26 And Noe said, Blessed be the Lord God of Shem,
and Canaan be the servant of Shem; (And Noah said,
Blessed be the Lord God of Shem, and let Canaan be
Shem's slave;)
27 God alarge Japheth, and dwell he in the tabernacles
of Shem, and Canaan be the servant of him. (May God
enlarge, *or increase*, Japheth, and live he in Shem's tents,
and let Canaan be his slave too!)
28 Forsooth Noe lived after the great flood three
hundred and fifty years;
29 and all the days of him were filled nine hundred and
fifty years, and he was dead. (and all his days filled nine
hundred and fifty years, and then he died.)

CHAPTER 10

1 These be the generations of the sons of Noe; Shem,
Ham, and Japheth (These be the descendants of Noah's
sons, Shem, Ham, and Japheth). And sons were born to
them after the great flood.
2 The sons of Japheth were Gomer, and Magog, and
Madai, and Javan, and Tubal, and Meshech, and Tiras.
3 Forsooth the sons of Gomer were Ashkenaz, and
Riphath, and Togarmah.
4 Forsooth the sons of Javan were Elishah, and
Tarshish, (and) Kittim, and Dodanim;
5 of these sons the isles of the heathen men were
parted in their countries, each by his language, and
families, in his nations. (from these sons the heathen on
the islands separated into their own countries, with their
own languages, and families, and nations.)
6 Soothly the sons of Ham were Cush, and Mizraim,
and Phut, and Canaan.
7 Forsooth the sons of Cush were Seba, and Havilah,
and Sabtah, and Raamah, and Sabtechah. The sons of
Raamah were Sheba, and Dedan.
8 Forsooth Cush begat Nimrod; (and) he began to be
mighty in [the] earth,
9 and he was a strong hunter, *or oppressor, of men*
before the Lord; of him a proverb went out, (saying,) As
Nimrod, a strong hunter before the Lord. (and he was a
strong hunter before the Lord; and a proverb went out
about him, saying, Be ye like Nimrod, a strong hunter
before the Lord.)
10 Soothly the beginning of his realm was Babylon, and
Erech, and Accad, and Calneh, in the land of Shinar.
11 Asshur went out of that land, and builded Nineveh,
and [the] streets of the city, and Calah, (And he went out
of that land to Assyria, and he built the cities of Nineveh,

[5] Most modern translations and Bible dictionaries refer to Ham as Noah's *youngest* son, though he is second in all the lists. The KJV, like the Wycliffe versions, uses "younger" in this verse.

and Rehoboth Ir, and Calah,)
12 and Resen betwixt Nineveh and Calah; this is a great
city.
13 And soothly Mizraim begat Ludim, and Anamim,
and Lehabim, and Naphtuhim, (And Mizraim begat the
Lydians, and Anamites, and Lehabites, and Naphtuhites,)
14 and Pathrusim, and Casluhim; of which the
Philistines and Caphtorim came forth. (and Pathrusites,
and Casluhites, and the Caphtorites, from whom came
forth the Philistines.)
15 Forsooth Canaan engendered Sidon, his first
engendered son, (and) Heth, (And Canaan begat Sidon,
his first-born son, and the Hittites,)
16 and Jebusites, and Amorites, Girgashites,
17 (and) Hivites, and Arkites, (and) Sinites,
18 and Arvadites, (and) Zemarites, and Hamathites; and
[the] peoples of (the) Canaanites were sown abroad by
these men.
19 And the terms of Canaan were made to men coming
from Sidon to Gerar, till to Gaza (And Canaan's borders
went from Sidon to Gerar, and unto Gaza), (and then) till
thou enter into Sodom, and Gomorrah, and Admah, and
Zeboiim, till to Lasha.
20 These were the sons of Ham, in their kindreds, and
languages, and generations, and lands, and folks (and
nations).
21 Also of Shem were born the fathers of all the sons of
Eber, and Japheth was the more, *or elder*, brother (of
Shem) [and Shem was the elder brother of Japheth]. (And of
Shem were born the fathers of all the sons of Eber, and
Shem was the elder brother of Japheth.)
22 The sons of Shem were Elam, and Asshur, and
Arphaxad, and Lud, and Aram.
23 The sons of Aram were Uz, and Hul, and Gether,
and Mash.
24 And soothly Arphaxad begat Salah, of whom Eber
was born.
25 And two sons were born to Eber, the name to the
one son was Peleg, for the land was parted in his days
(for the peoples of the world were divided in his time);
and the name of his brother was Joktan.
26 And that Joktan begat Almodad, and Sheleph, and
Hazarmaveth, (and) Jerah,
27 and Hadoram, and Uzal, and Diklah,
28 and Obal, and Abimael, (and) Sheba,
29 and Ophir, and Havilah, and Jobab; all these were
the sons of Joktan.
30 And the habitation of them was made from Mesha,
as men goeth till to Sephar, an hill of the east. (And they
lived in the hill country of the east, from Mesha unto
Sephar.)
31 These be the sons of Shem, by kindreds, and
languages, and countries, in their folks (and nations).
32 These be the families of Noe, by their peoples, and
nations; [the] folks in [the] earth were parted of these after
the great flood. (These be the families of Noah, by their
peoples, and their nations; all the nations on the earth
came from these *three men*/came from these *people* after
the great flood.)

CHAPTER 11

1 Forsooth (all) the land was of one language, and of
the same speech. [Forsooth the (whole) earth was of one lip,
and of the same words.]
2 And when they went forth from the east, they found
a field in the land of Shinar, and they dwelled therein.
3 And one said to his neighbour (And they said to one
another), Come ye, and make we tilestones, and bake we
those with fire; and they had tile for stones, and pitch,
either strong glue, for mortar;
4 and they said, Come ye, and make we to us a city
and a tower, whose highness stretch till to (the) heaven(s);
and make we solemn our name, before that we be parted
into all lands. (and they said, Come ye, and let us make a
city, and a tower whose height shall stretch up to the sky;
and make we our name well-known, or else we shall
soon be parted from each other into all the earth.)
5 Forsooth the Lord came down to see the city, and
the tower, which the sons of Adam builded (which the
sons of men were building).
6 And he said, Lo! the people is one, and one
language is to all, and they have begun to make this;
neither they shall cease of their thoughts, till they [ful]fill
those in work (and they shall not cease from their
thoughts, until they have fulfilled them in deed);
7 therefore come ye, go we down, and shame we
there the tongue of them, that each man hear not the
voice of his neighbour. (and so come ye, let us go down
there, and confuse their tongues, so that each person
shall not be able to understand their neighbour's voice.)
8 And so the Lord separated them from that place into
all (the) lands; and they ceased to build the city.
9 And therefore the name thereof was called Babel,
for the language of all [the] earth was confounded there;
and from thence the Lord scattered them on the face of
all countries (and from there the Lord scattered them over
all the face of the earth).
10 These be the generations of Shem (These be the
descendants of Shem). Shem was an hundred years (old)
when he begat Arphaxad, two years after the great flood.
11 And Shem lived after that he begat Arphaxad five
hundred years, and begat sons and daughters.
12 Forsooth Arphaxad lived five and thirty years, and
(then) begat Salah;
13 and Arphaxad lived after that he begat Salah three
hundred and three years, and begat sons and daughters.
(and Arphaxad lived after that he begat Salah four
hundred and three years, and begat sons and daughters.)

14 And Salah lived thirty years, and (then) begat Eber;
15 and Salah lived after that he begat Eber four hundred
and three years, and begat sons and daughters.
16 Soothly Eber lived four and thirty years, and (then)
begat Peleg;
17 and Eber lived after that he begat Peleg four hundred
and thirty years, and begat sons and daughters.
18 Also Peleg lived thirty years, and begat Reu; (And
Peleg lived thirty years, and then begat Reu;)
19 and Peleg lived after that he begat Reu two hundred
and nine years, and begat sons and daughters.
20 And Reu lived two and thirty years, and (then) begat
Serug;
21 and Reu lived after that he begat Serug two hundred
and seven years, and begat sons and daughters.
22 Soothly Serug lived thirty years, and (then) begat
Nahor;
23 and Serug lived after that he begat Nahor two
hundred years, and begat sons and daughters.
24 Forsooth Nahor lived nine and twenty years, and
(then) begat Terah;
25 and Nahor lived after that he begat Terah an hundred
and nineteen years, and begat sons and daughters.
26 And Terah lived seventy years, and (then) begat
Abram[6], Nahor, and Haran.
27 Soothly these be the generations of Terah (These be
the descendants of Terah). Terah begat Abram, Nahor,
and Haran. Forsooth Haran begat Lot;
28 and Haran died before Terah, his father, in the land
of his nativity, in Ur of Chaldees (in Ur of the Chaldeans,
later called Babylon).
29 Forsooth Abram and Nahor wedded wives; the
name of the wife of Abram was Sarai, and the name of
the wife of Nahor was Milcah, the daughter of Haran,
(the) father of Milcah, and (also the) father of Iscah. (And
Abram and Nahor wedded wives; the name of Abram's
wife was Sarai, and the name of Nahor's wife was
Milcah, the daughter of his brother Haran, who was also
the father of Iscah.)
30 Soothly Sarai was barren, and had no children.
31 And so Terah took Abram, his son, and Lot, the son
of Haran, his son, and Sarai, his daughter-in-law, the wife
of Abram, his son, and led them out of Ur of Chaldees,
that they should go into the land of Canaan; and they
came unto Haran, and dwelled there. (And Terah took his
son Abram, and Lot, the son of his son Haran, and Sarai,
his daughter-in-law, the wife of his son Abram, and led
them out from Ur of the Chaldeans, to go to the land of
Canaan; and they came to Haran, and lived there.)
32 And the days of Terah were made two hundred
years and five, and he was dead in Haran. (And all the
days of Terah were two hundred and five years, and then
he died in Haran.)

CHAPTER 12

1 Forsooth the Lord said to Abram, Go thou out of thy
land, and (out) of thy kindred, and (out) of the house of
thy father, and come thou into the land which I shall
show to thee;
2 and I shall make thee into a great folk (and I shall
make thee into a great nation), and I shall bless thee, and
I shall magnify thy name, and thou shalt be blessed;
3 I shall bless them that bless thee, and I shall curse
them that curse thee; and all kindreds of [the] earth shall
be blessed in thee (and all the families on the earth shall
pray to be blessed as thou art blessed/and through thee I
shall bless all the nations of the earth).
4 And so Abram went out, as the Lord commanded
him, and Lot went with him. Abram was five and seventy
years (old) when he went out of Haran.
5 And he took Sarai, his wife, and Lot, the son of his
brother, and all the substance which they had in
possession, and the men which they had begotten in
Haran (and all the men, *or all the slaves*, which they had
gotten, *or had acquired*, in Haran); and they went out (so)
that they should go into the land of Canaan. And when
they came into it,
6 Abram passed through the land till to the place of
Sichem, and till to the noble valley. Forsooth Canaanite
was then in the land. (And Abram passed through the
land to the place of Shechem, and to the terebinth tree of
Moreh. And the Canaanites were then in the land.)
7 Soothly the Lord appeared to Abram, and said to
him, I shall give this land to thy seed. And Abram built
there an altar to the Lord, that appeared to him (And
Abram build an altar there to the Lord, who had
appeared to him).
8 And from thence he passed forth to the hill [of]
Bethel, that was against the east, and setted there his
tabernacle, having Bethel from the west, and Hai from
the east. And he builded also there an altar to the Lord,
and inwardly called his name. (And from there he went
on to the hill country that was east of Bethel, and pitched
his tent there, having Bethel on the west, and Hai on the
east. And there he also built an altar to the Lord, and
inwardly called on his name.)
9 And Abram went going, and going forth over to the
south. (And Abram continued on, and went down to the
south.)
10 Soothly hunger was made in the land; and Abram
went down into Egypt, to be a pilgrim there (to live there
for a while), for hunger had the mastery in the land.
11 And when he was nigh to enter into Egypt, he said
to Sarai, his wife, I know that thou art a fair woman,
12 and that when (the) Egyptians shall see thee, they
shall say, It is his wife, and they shall slay me, and keep

---

[6] God would later change Abram's name to Abraham.

thee (and then they shall kill me, but keep thee alive).
13 Therefore, I beseech thee, say that thou art my sister,
that it be well to me for thee, and that my life live for the
love of thee. (And so I beseech thee, say that thou art my
sister, and then all shall be well with me, because of
thee, and I shall remain alive, because thou hast shown
thy love for me.)
14 And so when Abram had entered into Egypt, (the)
Egyptians saw the woman, (and) that she was full fair;
15 and the princes told (about her) to Pharaoh, and
praised her with him; and (so) the woman was taken up
into the house of Pharaoh.
16 Forsooth they used well Abram for her; and sheep,
and oxen, and asses, and servants, and servantesses, and
she-asses, and camels were (given) to him. (And Pharaoh
treated Abram well because of her; and sheep, and oxen,
and donkeys, and male and female slaves, and female
donkeys, and camels were given to him.)
17 Forsooth the Lord beat Pharaoh and his house with
most vengeances for Sarai, the wife of Abram. (But the
Lord struck Pharaoh and his household with great
plagues, because of Sarai, the wife of Abram.)
18 And Pharaoh called (for) Abram, and said to him,
What is it that thou hast done to me? why showedest
thou not to me that she was thy wife?
19 for what cause saidest thou, that she was thy sister,
(so) that I should take her into wife to me? Now therefore
lo! thy wife; take thou her, and go(!).
20 And Pharaoh commanded to men on Abram, and
they led forth him, and his wife, and all things that he
had. (And Pharaoh commanded to *his* men about Abram,
and they sent him away with his wife, and all the things
that he had been given.)

CHAPTER 13

1 Therefore Abram ascended from Egypt (And so Abram
went up from Egypt), he, and his wife, and all things that
he had; and Lot went with him, to the south coast.
2 Forsooth he was full rich in possession(s) of silver,
and of gold. (And now he was very rich with livestock,
silver, and gold.)
3 And he turned again by the way in which he came
from the south into Bethel, till to the place, in which
before he had set a tabernacle (to the place where he had
pitched his tent before), betwixt Bethel and Hai,
4 in the place of the altar which he made before, and
inwardly called there the name of the Lord. (at the place
where he had made the altar before, and had inwardly
called on the Lord's name.)
5 But also flocks of sheep, and droves of oxen, and
tabernacles were to Lot, that was with Abram; (And Lot,
who was with Abram, also had flocks of sheep, and herds
of oxen, and tents;)
6 and the land might not take them, that they should
dwell together, for the cattle of them was much, and they
might not dwell in common. (and the land could not
support both of them, for each of them had many
livestock, and so they could not live there together.)
7 Wherefore also strife was made betwixt the keepers
of [the] flocks of Abram and of Lot. Forsooth Canaanites
and Perizzites (also) dwelled in that land in that time.
8 Therefore Abram said to Lot, I beseech thee, that no
strife be betwixt me and thee, and betwixt my shepherds
and thy shepherds; for we be brethren (for we be kinsmen).
9 Lo! all the land is before thee, I beseech, depart thou
from me; if thou go to the left side, I shall hold the right
side; if thou choose the right side, I shall go to the left side.
10 And so Lot raised [up] his eyes, and saw about all
the country of Jordan, which was all-moisted, before that
the Lord destroyed Sodom and Gomorrah, as (the)
paradise of the Lord, and as Egypt, as men come into
Zoar. (And so Lot raised up his eyes, and saw the Jordan
Valley all about, and that it was well-watered, and that all
the way to Zoar it was like the Garden of the Lord, *that
is, like the Garden of Eden*, and like Egypt, for this was
before the Lord destroyed Sodom and Gomorrah.)
11 And Lot chose to him the country about Jordan, and
departed from the east; and they were parted each from
his brother. (And Lot chose for himself all the Jordan
Valley, and left for the east; and so they parted from each
other, yea, each from his kinsman.)
12 (And) Abram dwelled in the land of Canaan; soothly
Lot dwelled in [the] towns about Jordan, and abode in
Sodom (and lived near Sodom).
13 Forsooth (the) men of Sodom were full wicked, and
sinners greatly before the Lord (and greatly sinned against
the Lord).
14 And the Lord said to Abram, after that Lot was
parted from him (And after that Lot had left, the Lord said
to Abram), Raise [up] thine eyes forthright, and see from
the place in which thou art now, to the north and south,
(and) to the east and west;
15 I shall give all the land which thou seest to thee, and
to thy seed (and to thy descendants), till into without end.
16 And I shall make thy seed as the dust of the earth; if
any man may number the dust of the earth, also he shall
be able to number thy seed (and only if anyone can
count all the dust on the earth, then shall they be able to
count all thy descendants).
17 Therefore rise thou, and pass through the land in his
length and breadth, for I shall give it to thee. (And so rise
thou up, and go through the land in its length and
breadth, for I shall give it all to thee.)
18 Therefore Abram, moving his tabernacle, came and
dwelled beside the valley of Mamre, which is in Hebron;
and he builded there an altar to the Lord. (And so Abram,
moving his tent, came and lived beside the terebinths of
Mamre, which be at Hebron; and he built there an altar

to the Lord.)

CHAPTER 14

1 Forsooth it was done in that time, that Amraphel,
king of Shinar, and Arioch, king of Ellasar, and
Chedorlaomer, king of Elamites, and Tidal, king of folks,
(And it happened at that time, that Amraphel, king of
Shinar, and Arioch, king of Ellasar, and Chedorlaomer,
king of Elamites, and Tidal, king of Goiim,)
2 began battle against Bera, king of Sodom, and
against Birsha, king of Gomorrah, and against Shinab,
king of Admah, and against Shemeber, king of Zeboiim,
and against the king of Bela, that Bela is Zoar (and against
the king of Bela, which is now called Zoar).
3 All these came together into the valley of wood,
which is now the sea of salt. (And they all came together
into the Siddim Valley, which is now the Salt Sea, *that is,
the Dead Sea*.)
4 For in twelve years they served Chedorlaomer, and
in the thirteenth year they departed from him. (For they
served Chedorlaomer for twelve years, and then in the
thirteenth year they rebelled against him.)
5 Therefore Chedorlaomer came in the fourteenth
year, and [the] kings that were with him, and they smited
Rephaims in Ashteroth Karnaim, and Zuzims with them
(and the Zuzims in Ham), and Emims in Shaveh Kiriathaim,
6 and Horites in the hills of Seir (and the Horites in
the hill country of Seir), till to the field places of Elparan,
which is in (the) wilderness.
7 And they turned again, and came till to the well of
Mishpat; that is Kadesh (And then they returned, and
came unto Enmishpat; that is Kadesh). And they smited
all the country of (the) men of Amalek, and (also the)
Amorites, that dwelled in Hazazontamar.
8 And the king of Sodom, and the king of Gomorrah,
and the king of Admah, and the king of Zeboiim, also
and the king of Bela, which is (now called) Zoar, went
out, and [they] dressed (the) battle array against them in
the valley of wood (and they directed the battle array
against them in the Siddim Valley),
9 that is, against Chedorlaomer, king of Elamites, and
Tidal, king of folks (king of Goiim), and Amraphel, king
of Shinar, and Arioch, king of Ellasar; four kings against
five.
10 Forsooth the valley of wood had many pits of pitch,
either strong glue; and so the king of Sodom and the king
of Gomorrah turned the(ir) backs, and felled down there;
and they that (were) left fled to the hill(s). (But the Siddim
Valley had many pits of pitch, *or of strong glue*; and when
the king of Sodom and the king of Gomorrah turned their
backs to flee, they fell into them; but the other three kings
who were left *alive*, fled to the hill country.)
11 Soothly they took away all the chattel of Sodom and
Gomorrah/all the cattle of Sodom and Gomorrah, and all
things that pertain[ed] to meat, and went away; (And
those four kings took away all of the possessions of
Sodom and Gomorrah/all of the livestock of Sodom and
Gomorrah, and all of their food, and went away;)
12 also and they took away Lot and his chattel/Lot and
his cattle, the son of the brother of Abram, which Lot
dwelled in Sodom. (and they also took away Lot, the son
of Abram's brother, who lived in Sodom, and all of his
possessions/and all of his livestock.)
13 And, lo! one that escaped, told to Abram the
Hebrew, that dwelled in the valley of Mamre of (the)
Amorites, [the] brother of Eshcol, and brother of Aner; for
these [had] made (a) covenant of peace with Abram. (And,
lo! one who escaped, went and told all of this to Abram
the Hebrew, who lived by the terebinths of Mamre the
Amorite, the brother of Eshcol, and the brother of Aner;
for they had made a covenant of peace with Abram.)
14 And when Abram had heard this thing, that is, (that)
Lot, (the son of) his brother, (was) taken, he numbered his
born servants made ready, three hundred and eighteen,
and pursued them till to Dan. (And when Abram had
heard this, that is, that Lot, his kinsman, was taken
captive, he called together the three hundred and
eighteen men who were born in his household, and
pursued after the four kings as far as Dan.)
15 And when his fellows were separated (into groups),
he felled on them in the night, and smote them, and
pursued them till to Hobah, and Phenice, which is at the
left side of Damascus (which is north of Damascus).
16 And he brought again all the chattel, and Lot, (the
son of) his brother, with his chattel, also (the) women,
and the people./And he brought again all the cattle, and
Lot, (the son of) his brother, with his cattle, also (the)
women, and the people. (And he brought back all of the
possessions that had been taken, and Lot, his kinsman,
and all of his possessions, and all of the women, and the
other prisoners./And he brought back all of the livestock
that had been taken, and Lot, his kinsman, and all of his
livestock, and all of the women, and the other prisoners.)
17 Soothly the king of Sodom went out into the
meeting of him, after that he turned again from [the]
slaying of Chedorlaomer, and of the kings that were with
him, in the valley of Shaveh, which is the valley of the
king. (And Sodom's king went out to meet him, after that
he had returned from killing Chedorlaomer, and the other
kings who were with him, in the Shaveh Valley, which is
now called the King's Valley.)
18 And soothly Melchizedek, (the) king of Salem,
brought forth bread and wine, for he was the priest of the
highest God (for he was the priest of the Most High God);
19 and he blessed Abram, and said, Blessed be Abram
of [the] (most) high God, that made heaven and earth of
nought, (and he blessed Abram, and said, Blessed be
Abram of the Most High God, who made heaven and

earth out of nothing,)
20 and blessed be [the] (most) high God, by whom
defending (thee), (thine) enemies be betaken into thine
hands. And Abram gave tithes of all things to him. (and
blessed be the Most High God, who hath delivered thy
enemies into thy hands. And Abram gave him a tithe of
all the things that he had recovered.)
21 Forsooth the king of Sodom said to Abram, Give
thou the men to me; take thou (the) other things to thee.
(And the king of Sodom said to Abram, Give thou to me
the people; and thou take the other things for thyself.)
22 And Abram answered to him, I raise [up] mine hand
to the high Lord God, Lord of heaven and of earth, (But
Abram answered to him, I raise up my hand, *and swear*
to the Lord, the Most High God, the Maker of heaven and
earth,)
23 that from the thread of [the] woof till to the lanyard
of the hose, I shall not take (anything) of all things that be
thine, lest thou say, I [have] made Abram rich;
24 except these things which the young men ate, and
the parts of (the) men that came with me, Aner, Eshcol,
and Mamre; these men shall take their parts. (except for
those things which the young men have eaten, and a
portion for the men who came with me, that is, for Aner,
Eshcol, and Mamre; let these men take their portion, *or
their share*.)

CHAPTER 15

1 And so when these things were done, the word of
the Lord was made to Abram by a vision, and said,
Abram, do not thou dread, I am thy defender, and thy
meed is full great (Abram, do not thou fear, for I am thy
defender, and thy reward shall be very great).
2 And Abram said, Lord God, what shalt thou give to
me? I shall go without free children, and this Damascus,
son of Eliezer, the procurator of mine house, shall be mine
heir. (And Abram said, Lord God, what shalt thou give me?
for I have no children, and this Eliezer of Damascus, the
procurator of my household, shall be my heir.)
3 And Abram added, Soothly thou hast not given seed
to me, and, lo! my born servant shall be mine heir. (And
Abram said again, Yea, thou hast not given me any
children, *or any descendants*, and so this slave, born in
my house, must be my heir.)
4 And anon the word of the Lord was made to him,
and said, This shall not be thine heir, but thou shalt have
him heir, that shall go out of thy womb. (And at once the
word of the Lord came to him, saying, Nay, he shall not
be thy heir, but thou shalt have an heir who shall come
from thy womb.)
5 And the Lord led out Abram, and said to him,
Behold thou (the) heaven(s), and number the stars, if thou
mayest. And the Lord said to Abram, So thy seed shall
be. (And the Lord led Abram outside, and said to him,
Look thou up at the night sky, and count the stars, if thou
mayest. And then the Lord said to Abram, So shall be thy
descendants.)
6 Abram believed to God, and it was reckoned to him
to rightwiseness. (And Abram believed God, and it was
reckoned to him as righteousness.)
7 And God said to him, I am the Lord, that led thee
out of Ur of Chaldees, (so) that I should give this land to
thee, and (that) thou shouldest have it in possession.
8 And Abram said, Lord God, whereby shall I know
that I shall wield it?
9 And the Lord answered, and said, Take thou to me a
cow of three years, and a goat of three years, and a ram
of three years, and a turtle, and a culver. (And the Lord
answered, Bring thou to me a cow of three years, and a
goat of three years, and a ram of three years, and a
turtledove, and a pigeon.)
10 Which took all these things, and parted those by the
midst (And he brought him all these things, and divided
them in half), and setted ever either part each against
(the) other; but he parted not the birds.
11 And fowls came down on the carrions, and Abram
drove them away. (And when birds came down onto the
carcasses, Abram drove them away.)
12 And when the sun was gone down, dread felled on
Abram, and a great hideousness and dark assailed him.
(And as the sun went down, fear fell upon Abram, and a
great dark hideousness assailed him.)
13 And it was said to him, Know thou (a) before-
knowing, that thy seed shall be [a] pilgrim four hundred
years in a land not his own, and they shall make them
subject to servage, and they shall torment them; (And the
Lord said to him, Know thou a fore-knowing, that thy
descendants shall be foreigners in a land not their own,
and they shall make them subject to servitude, *or to
slavery*, and they shall torment them for four hundred
years;)
14 nevertheless I shall deem the folk to whom they
shall serve; and after these things they shall go out with
great chattel. (nevertheless I shall judge the nation for
whom they shall be slaves; and after these things they
shall go out with many possessions.)
15 Forsooth thou shalt go to thy fathers in peace, and
shalt be buried in (a) good [eld] age.
16 Soothly in the fourth generation they shall turn again
hither, for the wickedness of [the] Amorites be not yet
[full-]filled, till to (this) present time (until now).
17 Therefore when the sun was gone down, a dark mist
was made, and a furnace smoking appeared, and a lamp
of fire, and (it) passed through those partings. (And when
the sun had gone down, a dark mist came, and a smoking
furnace appeared, and a lamp of fire which passed
between the pieces of the animals.)
18 In that day the Lord made a covenant of peace with

Abram, and said, I shall give to thy seed this land, from
the river of Egypt till to the great river Euphrates; (And on
that day, the Lord made a covenant of peace with Abram,
and said, I shall give this land to thy descendants, from
the River of Egypt, *that is, the Nile, or the Shihor River*,
unto the great Euphrates River;)
19 (yea, the lands of the) Kenites, and Kenizzites, and
Kadmonites,
20 and Hittites, and Perizzites, and Rephaims,
21 and Amorites, and Canaanites, and Girgashites, and
Jebusites.

CHAPTER 16

1 Therefore Sarai, the wife of Abram, had not
engendered [to him] free children; but she had a
servantess of Egypt, Hagar by name, (And so Sarai,
Abram's wife, had not borne him any children; but she
had an Egyptian slave-girl, named Hagar,)
2 and Sarai said to her husband, Lo! the Lord hath
closed me (up), (so) that I should not bear (a) child; enter
thou [in]to my servantess, if in hap I shall take children,
namely of her (and so enter thou to my slave-girl, and
perhaps I shall have children through her). And when he
assented to her praying,
3 she took Hagar (the) Egyptian, her servantess, after
ten years after that they began to inhabit the land of
Canaan, and she gave Hagar (as) [a] wife to her husband.
(she took her slave-girl, Hagar the Egyptian, and she gave
her as a wife to her husband; this was ten years after that
they had begun to live in the land of Canaan.)
4 And Abram entered [in]to Hagar; and (soon) Hagar
saw that she had conceived, and (then) she despised her
lady.
5 And Sarai said to Abram, Thou doest wickedly
against me; I gave my servantess into thy bosom, which
seeth that she [hath] conceived, and (now she) despiseth
me; the Lord deem betwixt me and thee. (And Sarai said
to Abram, Thou doest wickedly against me; I gave my
slave-girl into thy arms, and she seeth that she hath
conceived, and now she despiseth me; the Lord judge
between me and thee.)
6 And Abram answered and said to her, Lo! thy
servantess is in thine hand; use thou her as thee liketh.
Therefore for Sarai tormented her, she fled away. (And
Abram answered and said to her, Lo! thy slave-girl is in
thy hands; do thou with her as thou pleaseth. And so
when Sarai tormented her, she fled away.)
7 And when the angel of the Lord had found her
beside a well of water in (the) wilderness, which well is
in the way of Shur in (the) desert,
8 he said to her, From whence comest thou Hagar, the
servantess of Sarai (Sarai's slave-girl), and whither goest
thou? Which answered, I flee from the face of Sarai, my
lady.
9 And the angel of the Lord said to her, Turn thou
again to thy lady (Return to thy lady), and be thou
meeked under her hands.
10 And again he said, I multiplying shall multiply thy
seed, and it shall not be numbered for multitude. (And
again he said, I multiplying shall multiply thy
descendants, and they shall not be able to be counted for
all their multitude.)
11 And afterward he said (And then he said), Lo! thou
hast conceived, and thou shalt bear a son, and thou shalt
call his name Ishmael, for the Lord hath heard thy torment;
12 this shall be a wild man; his hand shall be against all
men, and the hands of all men shall be against him; and
he shall set (his) tabernacles even against all his brethren
(and he shall be at odds with all of his kinsmen).
13 Forsooth Hagar called the name of the Lord that
spake to her, Thou God that sawest me; for she said,
Forsooth here I saw the hinder things of him that saw me.
(And Hagar called the name of the Lord who spoke to
her, Thou God who sawest me; for she said, Here I saw
him who saw me, and I still lived.)
14 Therefore she called that well, The well of him that
liveth and seeth me (And that is why people call that well
The Well of Lahairoi, *or Beerlahairoi*); (and) that well is
betwixt Kadesh and Bered.
15 And (so) Hagar childed a son to Abram, which
called his name Ishmael (and he named him Ishmael).
16 Abram was eighty years and six, when Hagar
childed Ishmael to him. (Abram was eighty-six years old,
when Hagar bare Ishmael for him.)

CHAPTER 17

1 Forsooth after that Abram began to be of ninety
years and nine, the Lord appeared to him, and said to
him, I am Almighty God; go thou before me, and be thou
perfect; (Now when Abram was ninety-nine years old,
the Lord appeared to him, and said to him, I am Almighty
God; go thou before me, and do thou what is right;)
2 and I shall set my covenant of peace betwixt me and
thee; and I shall multiply thee full greatly (and I shall
greatly multiply thee).
3 And Abram felled down low on his face. And God
said to him,
4 I am, and my covenant of peace is with thee, and
thou shalt be the father of many folks (and thou shalt be
the father of many nations);
5 and thy name shall no more be called Abram, but
thou shalt be called Abraham, for I have made thee [the]
father of many folks (for I have made thee the father of
many nations);
6 and I shall make thee to wax full greatly, and I shall
set thee in folks (and I shall make nations to come out of
thee), and kings shall go out of thee;
7 and I shall make my covenant between me and thee,

and between thy seed after thee, in their generations, by
everlasting bond of peace, that I be thy God, and of thy
seed after thee; (and I shall make my covenant between
me and thee, and thy descendants after thee, in all their
generations, an everlasting covenant, that I be thy God,
and the God of thy descendants after thee;)
8 and I shall give to thee, and to thy seed after thee,
the land of thy pilgrimage, all the land of Canaan, into
everlasting possession, and I shall be the God of them.
(and I shall give to thee, and to thy descendants after
thee, this land where thou art now living, yea, all the
land of Canaan, for an everlasting possession, and I shall
be their God.)
9 God said again to Abraham, And therefore thou
shalt keep my covenant, and thy seed after thee, in their
generations. (And God said to Abraham, And so thou
shalt keep my covenant, thou, and thy descendants after
thee, in all generations.)
10 This is my covenant, which ye shall keep, betwixt
me and you, and thy seed after thee; each male kind of
you shall be circumcised (every male among you shall be
circumcised),
11 and ye shall circumcise the flesh of your man's rod,
that it be into a sign of bond of peace betwixt me and you
(so that it be a sign of the covenant between me and you).
12 A young child of eight days shall be circumcised in
you, all male kind in your generations, as well a born
servant [of your household], as a servant bought, shall be
circumcised, (A newborn child among you shall be
circumcised on the eighth day, yea, all the males of every
generation, as well as a slave born in your household,
and a slave who is bought, yea, all the males shall be
circumcised,)
13 and whoever is of your kindred, he (also) shall be
circumcised; and my covenant shall be in your flesh into
everlasting bond of peace (and so my covenant shall be
made in your flesh as an everlasting covenant).
14 A(ny) man whose flesh of his rod shall not be
circumcised, that man shall be done away from his
people; for he made void my covenant (for he hath
broken my covenant).
15 Also God said to Abraham (And God said to
Abraham), Thou shalt not call Sarai, thy wife, Sarai, but
Sarah;
16 and I shall bless her, and of her I shall give to thee a
son, whom I shall bless, and he shall be into nations, and
kings of peoples shall be born of him. (and I shall bless
her, and I shall give thee a son by her; yea, I shall bless
her, and she shall be the mother of nations, and kings of
many people shall be born from her.)
17 Abraham felled down on his face, and laughed in
his heart, and said, Guessest thou, whether a child shall
be born to a man of an hundred years, and Sarah of
ninety years shall bear a child? (And Abraham fell down
on his face, and laughed in his heart, and said, Thinkest
thou, that a child shall be born to a man who is a
hundred years old, and that Sarah, who is ninety years
old, shall yet bear a child?)
18 And he said to the Lord, I would that Ishmael *might*
live before thee.
19 And the Lord said to Abraham, Sarah, thy wife, shall
bear a son to thee, and thou shalt call his name Isaac, and
I shall make my covenant with him into everlasting bond
of peace, and to his seed after him; (And the Lord said to
Abraham, No, thy wife Sarah shall bear a son for thee,
and thou shalt call his name Isaac, and I shall make my
covenant with him, and his descendants after him, yea,
an everlasting covenant;)
20 also on Ishmael I have heard thee, lo! I shall bless
him, and I shall increase (him), and I shall multiply him
greatly; he shall engender twelve dukes, and I shall make
him into a great folk. (and regarding Ishmael, I have
heard thee, lo! I shall bless him, and I shall increase him,
and I shall greatly multiply him; he shall beget twelve
princes, and I shall make him into a great nation.)
21 Forsooth I shall make my covenant with Isaac,
whom Sarah shall child to thee in this time in the tother
year. (But I shall make my covenant with Isaac, whom
Sarah shall bear for thee at this same time next year.)
22 And when the word of the speaker with him was
ended (And when he was finished speaking), God
ascended from Abraham.
23 Forsooth Abraham took Ishmael, his son, and all the
born servants of his house, and all which he had bought,
all the males of all men of his house, and circumcised the
flesh of their rod(s), anon in that day, as the Lord
commanded to him. (Then Abraham took his son
Ishmael, and all the slaves born in his household, and all
the slaves he had bought, yea, all the males of his
household, and at once circumcised the flesh of their
rods on that day, as the Lord had commanded him.)
24 Abraham was of ninety years and nine when he
circumcised the flesh of his rod, (Abraham was ninety-nine
years old when he circumcised the flesh of his own rod,)
25 and Ishmael, his son, had filled thirteen years in the
time of his circumcision. (and his son Ishmael was
thirteen years old at the time of his circumcision.)
26 Abraham was circumcised in the same day, and
Ishmael his son, (And Abraham and his son Ishmael were
circumcised on the same day,)
27 and all the men of his house, as well born servants,
as (those) bought and aliens, were circumcised together.
(and all the men of his household, yea, the slaves born in
his household, and those bought from foreigners, were
circumcised with him.)

CHAPTER 18

1 Forsooth in the valley of Mamre the Lord appeared

to Abraham, (as he was) sitting in the door of his
tabernacle, in that heat of the day. (And sometime later,
by the terebinths of Mamre, the Lord appeared to
Abraham, when he was sitting by the door of his tent, in
the heat of the day.)
2 And when Abraham had raised up his eyes, three
men appeared to him, and stood nigh [to] him. And
when he had seen them, he ran from the door of his
tabernacle into the meeting of them, and he worshipped
on [the] earth (And when he had seen them, he ran from
the door of his tent to meet them, and he bowed low to
the ground),
3 and said, Lord (My lords), if I have found grace in
thine eyes, pass thou not (by) thy servant,
4 but I shall bring (thee) a little water, and your feet
(can) be washed, and (so) rest ye (yourselves) under the
tree;
5 and I shall set (before you) a morsel of bread, and
your heart (shall) be comforted; (and) afterward ye shall
pass [forth]; for therefore (be) ye bowed (aside) to your
servant. Which said (And they said to him), Do thou as
thou hast spoken.
6 (And) Abraham hasted into the tabernacle, to Sarah,
and said to her, Haste thou, mix (up) three half bushels of
clean flour; and make thou loaves baken under ashes.
7 Forsooth (then) he ran to the drove of beasts, and
took thereof a calf most tender and best, and gave (it) to a
servant, which hasted, and seethed the calf (and boiled
the calf);
8 and (then) he took butter, and milk, and the calf
which he had sodden, and set (it) before them; forsooth
Abraham stood beside them under the tree. And when
they had eaten,
9 they said to him, Where is Sarah thy wife? He
answered, Lo! she is in the tabernacle (she is in the tent).
10 To whom the Lord said, I shall turn again, and I shall
come to thee in this time, if I live; and Sarah, thy wife,
shall have a son. When this was heard, Sarah laughed
behind the door of the tabernacle. (And the Lord said to
him, I shall return, and I shall come back to thee at this
same time next year, as I live; and Sarah, thy wife, shall
have a son. And when she heard this, Sarah laughed
behind the door of the tent.)
11 Forsooth both were old, and of great age, and
woman's terms ceased to be made to Sarah (and a
woman's terms had ceased to be made with Sarah).
12 And (so) she laughed, saying privily, After that I
(have) waxed eld, and my lord is eld, shall I give
diligence to lust?
13 Forsooth the Lord said to Abraham, Why laughed
Sarah, thy wife, saying, Whether I an eld woman shall
bear a child verily? (And the Lord said to Abraham, Why
did thy wife Sarah laugh, and say, Shall I, an old woman,
truly bear a child?)
14 whether anything is hard to God? By the promise I
shall turn again to thee in this same time, if I live; and
Sarah shall have a son. (is there anything too hard for
God to do? By my word, I shall return to thee at this same
time, as I live; and Sarah shall have a son.)
15 (And) Sarah was afeared for dread, and denied (it),
saying, I laughed not. Forsooth the Lord said, It is not so,
but thou laughedest.
16 Therefore when the men had risen (up) from thence,
they (ad)dressed the eyes against Sodom (they directed
their eyes toward Sodom); and Abraham went together
(with them), leading them forth.
17 And the Lord said, Whether I may cover from
Abraham what things I shall do, (And the Lord said to
himself, Can I hide from Abraham what things I am about
to do?)
18 since he shall be into a great folk and most strong,
and all nations of [the] earth shall be blessed in him? (For
he shall become a great and a most strong nation, and all
the nations of the earth shall pray to be blessed as he is
blessed/and through him I shall bless all the nations of
the earth.)
19 For I know that Abraham shall command his
children, and his house(hold) after him, that they keep
the way of the Lord, and that they do rightfulness and
doom, that the Lord bring for Abraham all things which
he spake to Abraham (and that they do what is right and
just, so that I shall bring to Abraham all the things that I
have promised him).
20 And so the Lord said, The cry of men of Sodom and
of men of Gomorrah is multiplied, and their sin is
egregious greatly; (And so the Lord said to him, There is a
great outcry against the people of Sodom and the people
of Gomorrah, and their sin is highly egregious;)
21 I shall come down, and see whether they have
[ful]filled in work the cry that came to me, that I know
whether it is not so. (and so I shall go down there, and
see whether their deeds have warranted the outcry that
came to me, and so that I know if it is so, or not.)
22 And they turned them[selves] from thence, and went
to Sodom. Abraham soothly stood yet before the Lord,
(And then two of the men went forth from there, and went
down to Sodom. But Abraham stood yet before the Lord,)
23 and nighed, and said, Whether thou shalt lose a just
man with the wicked? (and he came over, and said to him,
Shalt thou destroy the righteous along with the wicked?)
24 if fifty just men be in the city, shall they perish
together, and shalt thou not spare that place for fifty just
men, if they be therein? (what if fifty righteous people be
in the city, shall they perish along with the others, and
shalt thou not spare that place for fifty righteous people, if
they be there?)
25 Far be it from thee that thou do this thing, and slay
the just with the wicked, and that a just man be made as

a wicked man; this is not thine that deemest all [the]
earth; thou shalt not make this doom. (Far be it from thee
that thou do this thing, and kill the righteous along with
the wicked, and that the righteous be made like the
wicked; this is not thee who judgest all the earth; nay,
thou shalt not make such a judgement.)
26 And the Lord said to him, If I shall find in Sodom
fifty just men in the midst of the city, I shall forgive to all
the place for them. (And the Lord said to him, If I shall
find in Sodom fifty righteous people in the midst of the
city, I shall forgive the whole place for their sake.)
27 Abraham answered and said, For I began once (For
once I began), I shall speak to my Lord, since I am (but)
dust and ashes;
28 what if less than fifty just men by five be, shalt thou
do away all the city for five and forty? And the Lord said,
I shall not do away, if I shall find five and forty there.
(what if there be five less than fifty righteous people
there, shalt thou do away all the city for forty-five? And
the Lord said, I shall not do them all away, if I shall find
forty-five righteous people there.)
29 And again Abraham said to him, But if forty be
there, what shalt thou do? The Lord said, I shall not
smite for forty (I shall not strike them all down, for the
sake of forty righteous people).
30 Abraham said, Lord, I beseech, take thou (it) not into
indignation, if I speak (again); what if thirty be found
there? The Lord answered, I shall not do (it), if I shall find
thirty there.
31 Abraham said, For I began once, I shall speak to my
Lord; what if twenty be found there? The Lord said, I
shall not slay for twenty. (Abraham said, For once I
began, I shall speak again to my Lord; what if twenty be
found there? The Lord said, I shall not slay them all, for
the sake of twenty.)
32 Abraham said, Lord, I beseech, be thou not wroth, if
I speak yet once (more); what if ten be found there? The
Lord said, I shall not do away for ten. (And Abraham said,
Lord, I beseech thee, be thou not angry, if I speak yet
once more; what if ten be found there? And the Lord
said, I shall not do them all away, if I shall find ten
righteous people there.)
33 The Lord went forth, after that he [had] ceased to
speak to Abraham, and Abraham turned again into his
place. (And then the Lord went forth, after that he had
ceased to speak with Abraham, and Abraham returned to
his home.)

CHAPTER 19

1 And (the) twain angels came to Sodom in the
eventide, while Lot sat in the gates of the city. And when
he had seen them, he rose, and went to meet them, and
worshipped low to the earth, (And the two angels came
to Sodom in the evening, while Lot sat at the city gates.
And when he had seen them, he arose, and went to meet
them, and bowed low to the ground,)
2 and said, My lords, I beseech, bow ye [down] into
the house of your servant, and dwell ye there; wash ye
your feet, and in the morrowtide ye shall go into your
way (and in the morning ye shall go on your way).
Which said, Nay, but we shall dwell in the street.
3 He constrained them greatly, that they should turn
(in) to him. And when they entered into his house, he
made a feast, and baked therf bread, and they ate. (But he
greatly constrained them, that they should turn in at his
house. And so when they had entered into his house, he
made a feast, and baked unleavened bread, and they ate.)
4 Forsooth before that they went to sleep, men of the
city compassed his house, from a child till to an eld man
(from a youth unto an old man), all the people together;
5 and they called (to) Lot, and said to him, Where be
the men that entered to thee tonight? (Where be the men
who have entered into thy house tonight?) bring them out
hither, (so) that we (may) know them, *that is, by lechery
against kind.*
6 And Lot went out to them behind the back, and
closed the door, (And Lot went out to them, and closed
the door behind him,)
7 and said, I beseech, do not ye, my brethren, do not
ye do this evil.
8 I have two daughters, that knew not yet (a) man; I
shall lead out them to you (I shall lead them out to you),
and mis-use ye them as it pleaseth you, so (long as) that
ye do none evil to these men, for they (have) entered
under the shadow of my roof.
9 And they said, Go thou (away) from hence. And
again they said, Thou enteredest [in] hither as a comeling;
whether that thou shalt deem us? therefore we shall
torment thee more than these. And they did violently to
Lot full greatly (And they did great violence to Lot). Then
it was nigh that they would break (down) the doors;
10 and lo! the (two) men put (forth their) hand(s), and
led in Lot to them (and brought Lot back in with them),
and they closed the door.
11 And they smote with blindness they that were
withoutforth (And then they struck with blindness those
who were outside), from the least till to the most; so that
they might not find the door.
12 Forsooth they said to Lot, Hast thou here any man of
thine, (a) husband of thy daughter, or sons, or daughters(?);
(if so,) lead thou out of this city all men that be thine,
13 for we shall do away this place, for the cry of them
increased before the Lord, which sent us that we (should)
lose them. (for we shall do away this place, for the outcry
against them hath increased before the Lord, who sent us
to destroy them.)
14 And Lot went out, and spake to the husbands (to be)
of his daughters, that should take his daughters, and said,

Rise ye, and go ye out of this place; for the Lord shall do
away this city. And he was seen to them to speak as
playing. (And Lot went out, and spoke to the husbands-
to-be of his daughters, who were betrothed to his
daughters, and said, Rise ye up, and go ye out of this
place; for the Lord shall do away this city. But he was
seen by them as only to be joking.)
15 And when the morrowtide was (made), the angels
constrained Lot, and said, Rise thou (up), and take thy
wife, and thy two daughters, which thou hast, lest also
thou perish (al)together in the sin of the city (lest also
thou altogether perish amidst the sin of this city).
16 While he dissembled, they took his hand, and the
hand of his wife, and of his two daughters; for the Lord
spared him. And they led out him, and set *him* without
the city. (And while he hesitated, they took his hand, and
the hand of his wife, and the hands of his two daughters;
for the Lord had spared him. And they led them away,
and brought *them* outside the city.)
17 There they spake to him, and said, Save thou thy
life; do not thou behold behind thy back, neither stand
thou in all the country(side) about, but make thee safe in
the hill(s); lest also thou perish (al)together. (And they
spoke to him there, and said, Save thou thy life; do not
thou look behind thy back, nor stand thou in all the
countryside about, but make thee safe in the hills; lest
also thou altogether perish.)
18 And Lot said to them, My Lord (My lords), I beseech,
19 for thy servant hath found grace before thee, and
thou hast magnified thy grace and mercy, which thou
hast done to me, (so) that thou shouldest save my life, (*I
am most grateful*); (but) I may not be saved in the hill(s),
lest peradventure evil (over)take me, and I die (but I
cannot be saved in the hills, for before that I can get there,
the destruction shall surely overtake me, and I shall die);
20 a little city is here beside (there is a little city here),
to which I may flee, and I shall be safe therein; whether it
is not (such) a little city? and my soul shall live therein.
21 And he said to Lot, Lo! also in this I have received
thy prayers, that I destroy not the city, for which thou hast
spoken; (And he said to Lot, Lo! also in this I have
received thy prayers, and I shall not destroy the city, of
which thou hast spoken;)
22 haste thee, and be thou saved there, for I may not do
anything till thou enter [in] thither. Therefore the name
of that city was called Zoar. (haste thee, and be thou
made safe there, for I shall not do anything until thou hast
entered in there. And so that is why that city was called
Zoar, *or Small*.)
23 (And so) The sun rose (up) on [the] earth, and Lot
entered into Zoar.
24 Therefore the Lord rained on Sodom and Gomorrah
brimstone and fire, from the Lord of heaven, (And so the
Lord rained down fire and brimstone from the heavens
on Sodom and Gomorrah,)
25 and destroyed these cities, and all the country(side)
about; *he destroyed* all the dwellers of those cities (*he
destroyed* all the inhabitants of those cities), and all (the)
green things of [the] earth.
26 And Lot's wife looked aback, and *she* was turned
into an image of salt. (And Lot's wife looked back, and
she was turned into a pillar of salt.)
27 Forsooth Abraham rising (up) early, (went to) where
he (had) stood before with the Lord,
28 (and) beheld Sodom and Gomorrah, and all the land
of that country(side) (about); and he saw a dead spark
going up from the earth, as the smoke of a furnace.
29 For when God destroyed the cities of that
country(side), he had mind of Abraham, and delivered Lot
from [the] destroying of the cities in which he dwelled.
30 And Lot went up from Zoar, and dwelled in the
hill(s), and his two daughters with him, for he dreaded to
dwell in Zoar; and he dwelled in a den (and he lived in a
cave), he and his two daughters with him.
31 And the more daughter said to the less (And the
elder daughter said to the younger one), Our father is eld,
and no man is left on (the) earth that may enter [in] to us,
by the custom of all (the) earth;
32 come thou, make we him drunken of wine, and
sleep we with him, that we may keep the seed of our
father. (come thou, make we him drunk with wine, and
sleep we with him, so that we can keep our father's seed,
or our father's family, alive.)
33 And so they gave to their father to drink wine in that
night (And so that night they gave their father some wine
to drink), and the more, *or the elder*, daughter entered,
and slept with her father; and he feeled not, neither when
the daughter lay down, neither when she [a]rose.
34 And the tother day the more daughter said to the
less, *or the younger (one)*, Lo! I slept yesterday with my
father; give we to him to drink wine also in this night;
and thou sleep with him, that we save the seed of our
father. (And the next day the elder daughter said to the
younger one, Lo! yesterday I slept with my father; tonight
we shall also give him some wine to drink, and then thou
sleep with him, so that we shall most assuredly save our
father's seed, *or our father's family*.)
35 And they gave to their father also in that night to
drink wine, and the less daughter entered, and slept with
him; and soothly he feeled not then when she lay down,
neither when she [a]rose. (And so also that night they
gave their father some wine to drink, and the younger
daughter entered, and slept with him; and truly he felt
nothing when she lay down, nor when she arose.)
36 Therefore the two daughters of Lot conceived of
their father. (And so Lot's two daughters conceived by
their father.)
37 And the more daughter childed a son, and called his

name Moab; he is the father of (the) men of Moab unto
this present day.
38 And the less daughter childed a son, and called his
name Benammi, *that is, The son of my people*; he is the
father of (the) men of Ammon till to [this] day.

CHAPTER 20

1 Abraham went forth from thence into the land of the
south, and dwelled betwixt Kadesh and Shur, and was a
pilgrim in Gerar; (And Abraham went forth from there to
the land of the south, and lived between Kadesh and
Shur, and was a foreigner in Gerar;)
2 and (again) he said of Sarah, his wife, She is my
sister. Therefore Abimelech, king of Gerar, sent (for her),
and took her (And so Abimelech, king of Gerar, had her
brought to him).
3 Soothly God came to Abimelech by a sweven in the
night (And God came to Abimelech by a dream in the
night), and said to him, Lo! thou shalt die, for the woman
which thou hast taken, for she hath an husband.
4 Forsooth Abimelech [had] touched not her; and he
said, Lord, whether thou shalt slay (a) folk unknowing
and just? (But Abimelech had not yet touched her; and he
said, Lord, shalt thou slay an unknowing and a righteous
nation?)
5 Whether he said not to me, She is my sister, and she
said, He is my brother? In the simpleness of mine heart,
and in the cleanness of mine hands, I did this (I did this
with a pure heart, and with clean hands).
6 And the Lord said to him, And I know that thou
didest by simple heart, and therefore I kept thee, lest thou
didest sin against me, and I suffered not that thou
touchedest her; (And the Lord said to him, Yea, I know
that thou didest this with a pure heart, and so I kept thee,
so that thou didest not sin against me, and I did not allow
thee to touch her;)
7 now therefore yield thou the wife to her husband,
for he is a prophet; and he shall pray for thee, and thou
shalt live; soothly if thou wilt not yield *her*, know thou
that thou shalt die by death, thou, and all things that be
thine (but if thou wilt not give *her* back to him, know
thou that thou shalt die, thou, and all who be thine).
8 And at once Abimelech rose (up) by night, and
called (for) all his servants, and spake all these words in
the ears of them; and all men dreaded greatly (and all the
men had great fear).
9 Soothly Abimelech called also Abraham (And then
Abimelech called for Abraham), and said to him, What
hast thou done to us? what sinned we against thee, that
thou hast brought in on me and on my realm (such) a
great sin? thou hast done to us which things thou
oughtest not to do.
10 And again Abimelech asked, and said, What thing
sawest thou, that thou wouldest do this? (And again
Abimelech asked Abraham, Why did thou do this?)
11 (And) Abraham answered, I thought within me, and
said, In hap the dread of God is not in this place; and
they shall slay me for my wife;
12 in other manner forsooth and she is my sister verily,
(for she is) the daughter of my father, and not the
daughter of my mother; and I wedded her into wife; (and
truly in one way she is my sister, for she is the daughter
of my father, but not the daughter of my mother; and so I
wedded her for a wife;)
13 soothly after that God led me out of the house of my
father, I said to her, Thou shalt do this mercy with me in
each place to which we shall enter; thou shalt say, that I
am thy brother. (and after that God led me out of my
father's house, I said to her, Thou shalt do this mercy for
me in each place to which we shall enter; thou shalt say
that I am thy brother.)
14 Therefore Abimelech took sheep, and oxen, and
servants, and handmaids, and gave to Abraham; and he
yielded to him Sarah, his wife, (And so Abimelech took
sheep, and oxen, and male and female slaves, and gave
them to Abraham; and he gave him back his wife Sarah,)
15 and said, The land is before you; dwell thou,
wherever it pleaseth thee.
16 Forsooth Abimelech said to Sarah, Lo! I gave a
thousand pieces of silver to thy brother; this shall be to
thee into (a) covering of (the) eyes, to all men that be
with thee; and whither ever thou goest, have thou mind
that thou art taken. (And Abimelech said to Sarah, Lo! I
have given a thousand pieces of silver to thy brother; this
shall be proof to all thy own people that thou art
guiltless; but wherever thou goest, remember that thou
art already taken.)
17 Soothly for Abraham prayed, God cured Abimelech,
and his wife, and handmaids, and they childed; (And
because Abraham prayed to God, God cured Abimelech,
and his wife, and his slave-girls, and they gave birth;)
18 for God had closed each womb of the house of
Abimelech, for Sarah, the wife of Abraham. (for God had
closed up each womb in Abimelech's household,
because of Sarah, Abraham's wife.)

CHAPTER 21

1 Forsooth God visited Sarah, as he promised, and
[ful]filled those things, that he spake.
2 And she conceived, and childed a son in her eld
(age), in the time wherein God before-said to her. (And
she conceived, and bare a son in her old age, at the time
which God had spoken of before to her.)
3 And Abraham called the name of his son, whom
Sarah childed to him, Isaac.
4 And Abraham circumcised him in the eighth day, as
God commanded to him, (And Abraham circumcised him
on the eighth day, as God had commanded to him,)

5 when he was of an hundred years; for Isaac was
born in this age of the father. (when he was a hundred
years old; for this was the age of his father when Isaac
was born.)
6 And Sarah said, The Lord hath made laughing to me
(The Lord hath made me to laugh), and whoever shall
hear (about this) shall laugh with me.
7 And again she said, Who should hear, and believe
to Abraham (And she added, For who would have said to
Abraham), that Sarah should give sucking to a son, whom
she childed to him, (when he is) now an eld man?
8 Therefore the child increased, and was weaned; and
Abraham made a great feast in the day of his weaning (and
Abraham made a great feast on the day of his weaning).
9 And when Sarah saw the son of Hagar (the)
Egyptian, playing, *or doing idolatry*, with Isaac her son,
(And when Sarah saw the son of Hagar the Egyptian,
mocking her son Isaac,)
10 she said to Abraham, Cast out this handmaid and
her son; for the son of the handmaid shall not be heir
with my son Isaac. (she said to Abraham, Send away this
slave-girl and her son; for the slave-girl's son shall not be
heir with my son Isaac.)
11 Abraham took this heavily for his son; (And
Abraham took this heavily, *or was deeply troubled*, for
Ishmael was also his son;)
12 and God said to him, Be it not seen sharp to thee on
the child, and on thine handmaid; all things which Sarah
saith to thee, hear thou her voice, for in Isaac (the) seed
shall be called to thee; (but God said to him, Do not thou
fret over the boy and the slave-girl; hear thou all the
things which Sarah saith to thee, for thy promised
descendants shall come through Isaac;)
13 but also I shall make the son of the handmaid into a
great folk, for he is thy seed. (but I shall also make the
son of the slave-girl into a great nation, for he is also thy
descendant.)
14 And so Abraham rose early, and took bread, and a
bottle of water, and put it on Hagar's shoulder, and he
betook (to) *her* the child[7], and let go her; and when she
had gone, she went out of the way in the wilderness of
Beersheba. (And so Abraham rose up early, and took
some bread, and a bottle of water, and gave it to Hagar,
and put it on her shoulder, and he gave the boy to *her*,
and sent her away; and when she had gone out a ways,
she went off the way into the wilderness of Beersheba.)
15 And when the water in the bottle was ended, she
cast away the child under a tree that was there; (And
when there was no more water in the bottle, she pushed
the boy away under a tree that was there;)
16 and she went away, and she sat (down) even against
(him), as far as a bow may cast; for she said, I shall not
see the child dying (I shall not watch my own child die!);
and she sat (over) against (him), and raised [up] her voice,
and wept.
17 Forsooth the Lord heard the voice of the child, and
the angel of the Lord called Hagar from heaven, and said,
What doest thou, Hagar? do not thou dread, for God hath
heard the voice of the child, from the place wherein he
is. (And the Lord heard the boy crying, and the angel of
the Lord called to Hagar from heaven, and said, What
doest thou, Hagar? do not thou fear, for God hath heard
your boy crying from where he is.)
18 Rise thou, and take the child, and hold his hand; for
I shall make him into a great folk. (Rise thou up, and have
the boy stand up, and take his hand; for I shall make him
into a great nation.)
19 And God opened her eyes, and she saw a well of
water, and she went, and filled the bottle, and she gave
drink to the child (and she gave her boy a drink);
20 and (God) was with him, and he increased, and
dwelled in wilderness (and lived in the wilderness), and
he was made a young man (who was) an archer,
21 and dwelled in the desert of Paran; and his mother
took to him a wife of the land of Egypt. (and he lived in
the wilderness of Paran; and his mother found him a wife
from the land of Egypt.)
22 In the same time, Abimelech, and Phicol, prince of
his host (Now at that time, Abimelech, with Phicol, the
ruler of his army), said to Abraham, God is with thee in
all things that thou doest;
23 therefore swear thou by God that thou harm not me,
and mine heirs, and my kindred; but by the mercy which
I did to thee, do thou to me, and to the land in which
thou livedest (as) a comeling. (and so swear thou by God
that thou shalt not harm me, nor my heirs, nor my family;
but that thou shalt do the same mercy to me, and to the
land in which thou livedest as a newcomer, which I have
shown to thee.)
24 And Abraham said, I shall swear (I swear).
25 And he blamed Abimelech for the well of water,
which his servants took away by violence. (But then
Abraham complained to Abimelech about a well of water,
which his servants had taken away from him by force.)
26 And Abimelech answered, I wist not who did this
thing, but also thou showedest not to me, and I heard not
(of it) except today. (And Abimelech answered, I do not
know who did this thing, and thou hast not told me about
it, and I have not heard about it until today.)
27 And so Abraham took sheep and oxen, and gave to
Abimelech, and both smote together a bond of peace.
(And Abraham took some sheep and oxen, and gave
them to Abimelech, and they made a covenant together.)
28 And (then) Abraham set seven ewe lambs of the
flock asides half.
29 And Abimelech said to him, What will these seven

[7] Ishmael would be about 15 years old at this time.

ewe lambs (mean) to themselves, which thou madest
stand asides half? (And Abimelech said to him, What
mean ye with these seven ewe lambs, which thou hast
made to stand aside?)
30 And he said, Thou shalt take of mine hand seven
ewe lambs, that those be into witnessing to me, for I
digged this well. (And he said, Take thou these seven
ewe lambs from me, and by accepting them, thou agreeth
that I have dug this well.)
31 Therefore that place was called Beersheba, (*that is, The Well of the Oath*[8],) for ever either swore there;
32 and they made bond of peace for the well of an
oath. Forsooth Abimelech rose, and Phicol, the prince of
his chivalry, and they turned again into the land of
Palestines. (and so they made a covenant at Beersheba.
Then Abimelech, and Phicol, the ruler of his cavalry,
arose, and they returned to the land of the Philistines.)
33 Soothly Abraham planted a wood in Beersheba, and
inwardly called there (on) the name of [the] everlasting
God;
34 and he was an earth-tiller, *or a comeling*, of the land
of Palestines in many days. (and as a newcomer, he worked
the soil in the land of the Philistines, for many days.)

CHAPTER 22

1 And after that these things were done, God assayed
Abraham, and said to him, Abraham! Abraham! He
answered, I am present (I am here).
2 God said to him, Take thine one begotten son, whom
thou lovest, Isaac; and go into the land of vision, and offer
thou him there into burnt sacrifice on one of the hills
which I shall show to thee. (And God said to him, Take
Isaac, thy only son, whom thou lovest, and go into the
land of Moriah; and there thou shalt offer him as a burnt
sacrifice on one of the hills which I shall show to thee.)
3 Therefore Abraham rose by night, and saddled his
ass, and led with him two young men, and Isaac his son;
and when he had hewn trees into burnt sacrifice, he went
to the place which God had commanded to him. (And so
Abraham rose up early in the morning, and saddled his
donkey, and took with him two of his young men, and
his son Isaac; and when he had cut the wood for the
burnt sacrifice, he went to the place to which God had
commanded him to go.)
4 Forsooth in the third day (And on the third day), he
raised [up] his eyes, and saw a place afar (off);
5 and he said to his young men, Abide ye here with
the ass, I and the child[9] shall go thither; and after that we
have worshipped, we shall turn again to you. (and he
said to his young men, Wait ye here with the donkey,
while I and the boy go over there; and after we have
worshipped, we shall return to you.)
6 And he took the wood of burnt sacrifice, and laid (it)
on Isaac his son; forsooth he bare fire, and a sword in his
hands. And when they twain went together, (And he
took the wood for the burnt sacrifice, and laid it on his
son Isaac; and he carried the fire, and a knife in his
hands. And as the two of them went together,)
7 Isaac said to his father, My father! And he
answered, What wilt thou, (my) son? (And) He said, Lo!
fire and wood, where is the beast of burnt sacrifice? (but
where is the beast for the burnt sacrifice?)
8 Abraham said, My son, God shall purvey to him the
beast of burnt sacrifice. Therefore they went together, (And
Abraham said, My son, God himself shall provide the
beast for the burnt sacrifice. And so they went together,)
9 and came to the place which God had showed to
him; in which place Abraham builded an altar, and
dressed [the] wood above; and when he had bound
(al)together Isaac, his son (and when he had bound up his
son Isaac), he laid Isaac on the altar, upon the heap of
wood.
10 And he held forth his hand, and took the sword to
sacrifice his son. (And he stretched forth his hand, and
took the knife to sacrifice his son.)
11 And lo! the angel of the Lord cried from heaven, and
said, Abraham! Abraham! Which answered, I am present
(I am here).
12 And the angel said to him, Hold thou not forth thine
hand on the child, neither do thou anything (of harm) to
him; now I know that thou dreadest God, and sparedest
not thine one begotten son for me. (And the angel said to
him, Do not thou raise thy hand against the boy, nor do
thou any harm to him; for now I know that thou fearest
God, for thou hast not withheld thy only son from me.)
13 Abraham raised [up] his eyes, and he saw behind
him a ram cleaving by the horns among (the) briars,
which he took, and offered (as a) burnt sacrifice for the
son. (And Abraham raised up his eyes, and he saw
behind him a ram caught by his horns among the briars,
and he took the ram, and offered it as a burnt sacrifice in
place of his son.)
14 And he called the name of that place The Lord
seeth; wherefore it is said, till to *this* day, The Lord shall
see in the hill. (And he called the name of that place
Jehovahjireh; and so it is said, unto *this* day, In the hill of
the Lord it shall be provided/it shall be seen.)
15 Forsooth the angel of the Lord called (to) Abraham
the second time from heaven,
16 and said, The Lord saith, I have sworn by myself, for
thou hast done this thing, and hast not spared thine one
begotten *son* for me, (and said, The Lord saith, I swear by
myself, because thou hast done this thing, and thou hast
not withheld thy only *son* from me,)

[8] "Beersheba" also means "the Well of the Seven".

[9] According to Jewish tradition, Isaac was probably 25 years old at this time (Gehman/Josephus).

17 I shall bless thee, and I shall multiply thy seed as the
stars of heaven, and as the gravel, *either sand*, which is in
the brink of the sea; thy seed shall wield the gates of his
enemies; (I shall bless thee, and I shall multiply thy
descendants like the stars of the heavens, and like the
gravel, *or the sand*, which is at the seashore; and thy
descendants shall control the gates of their enemies;)
18 and all the folks of [the] earth shall be blessed in thy
seed (and all the nations of the earth shall pray to be
blessed as thy descendants be blessed/and through thy
descendants I shall bless all the nations of the earth), for
thou obeyedest to my voice.
19 Abraham turned again to his young men (And
Abraham returned to his young men), and they went to
Beersheba together, and he dwelled there.
20 And so when these things were done, it was told to
Abraham that also Milcah had borne sons to Nahor his
brother; (And after these things were done, it was told to
Abraham that Milcah had borne sons to his brother
Nahor;)
21 Huz the first begotten (Huz the first-born), and Buz
his brother, and Kemuel the father of Aram,
22 and Chesed, and Hazo, and Pildash, and Jidlaph,
and Bethuel,
23 of whom Rebecca was born; Milcah childed these
eight to Nahor, the brother of Abraham.
24 Forsooth his concubine, *or secondary wife*, Reumah
by name, childed Tebah, and Gaham, and Thahash, and
Maachah.

CHAPTER 23

1 Forsooth Sarah lived an hundred and seven and
twenty years,
2 and died in the city of Arba (and then she died in
Kiriatharba), which is Hebron, in the land of Canaan; and
Abraham came to bewail and (to) beweep her.
3 And when he had risen from the office of the dead
body, he spake to the sons of Heth, and said, (And when
he had risen up from before his dead *wife's* body, he said
to the Hittites,)
4 I am a comeling and a pilgrim with you; give ye to
me (the) right of [a] sepulchre with you, that I bury my
dead body. (I am a newcomer and a foreigner among
you; sell ye me some land for a burial place, so that I can
bury my dead *wife's* body on it.)
5 And the sons of Heth answered, and said, (And the
Hittites answered, and said,)
6 Lord, hear thou us; thou art the prince of God with
us; bury thou thy dead body in our chosen sepulchres,
and no man shall be able to forbid thee, that not thou
bury thy dead body in the sepulchre of him. (My lord,
hear thou us; thou art the prince of God with us; bury
thou thy dead *wife's* body in the choicest of our burial
places; none of us shall forbid thee, to bury thy dead
wife's body in his burial place.)
7 And Abraham [a]rose, and worshipped the people of
the land, that is, the sons of Heth. (And Abraham arose,
and bowed before the people of the land, that is, the
Hittites.)
8 And he said to them, If it pleaseth your soul that I
bury my dead body (If it pleaseth your soul that I bury my
dead *wife's* body here), hear ye me, and pray ye for me
to Ephron, the son of Zohar,
9 that he give to me the double cave, which he hath
in the uttermost part of his field; for sufficient money give
he it to me before you into possession of [a] sepulchre.
(that he give me the cave at Machpelah, which he hath in
the uttermost part of his field, for the full price; yea, let
him sell it to me for a possession of a burial place here
among you.)
10 Forsooth Ephron dwelled in the midst of the sons of
Heth (And Ephron happened to be sitting there in the
midst of the other Hittites). And Ephron answered to
Abraham, while all (the) men heard that entered [in] by
the gate of that city, and (he) said,
11 My lord, it shall not be done so, but more harken
thou (to) that that I say; I give to thee the field, and the
cave which is therein, while the sons of my people be
present; bury thou thy dead body. (My lord, it shall not be
done so, but more harken thou to what I say; I give thee
the field, and the cave which is in it, while the sons of my
people be present; bury thou thy *wife's* dead body there.)
12 Abraham worshipped before the Lord, and before
the people of the land, (And Abraham bowed low before
the people of the land,)
13 and he spake to Ephron, while his people stood
about, (and said,) I beseech, that thou hear me; I shall
give money (to thee) for the field, receive thou it, and so I
shall bury my dead body in the field (and then I shall
bury my dead *wife's* body there in the field).
14 And Ephron answered,
15 My lord, hear thou me; the land which thou askest
(for) is worth four hundred shekels of silver, that is the
price betwixt me and thee; but (now) how much is this?
bury thou thy dead body (so bury thou thy dead *wife's*
body there).
16 And when Abraham had heard this, he numbered
(out) the money which Ephron asked (for), while the sons
of Heth heard (And when Abraham had heard this, he
counted out the money which Ephron had named, and
which the other Hittites had also heard him say), (that is,)
four hundred shekels of silver, and of proved common
money.
17 And the field that was sometime of Ephron, in which
field was a double den, beholding to Mamre, as well that
field, as the den, and all the trees thereof, in all the terms
thereof by compass, (And so the field that belonged to
Ephron, which field was at Machpelah, to the east of

Mamre, that field, and the cave, and all the trees, within
its boundaries all around,)
18 was confirmed to Abraham into (a) possession,
while the sons of Heth saw, and all men that entered by
the gate of that city. (was confirmed as Abraham's
possession, before the Hittites, and all the other men who
came in by the city gate.)
19 And so Abraham buried Sarah, his wife, in the
double den of the field, that beheld to Mamre; this is
Hebron in the land of Canaan. (And so Abraham buried
his wife Sarah, in the cave in the field at Machpelah, to
the east of Mamre; this is Hebron in the land of Canaan.)
20 And the field, and the den that was therein, was
confirmed of the sons of Heth to Abraham, into
possession of (a) sepulchre. (And the field, and the cave
that was in it, were confirmed by the Hittites to be
Abraham's possession for a burial place.)

CHAPTER 24

1 Forsooth Abraham was eld, and of many days, and
the Lord had blessed him in all things.
2 And he said to the elder servant of his house, that
was sovereign on all things that he had, Put thou thine
hand under mine hip, (And he said to the oldest servant
of his household, who was the ruler over all the things
that he had, Put thy hand under my hip,)
3 that I conjure thee by the Lord God of heaven and of
earth, that thou take not a wife to my son of the daughters
of Canaan, among which I dwell; (and I want thee to
swear by the Lord God of heaven and earth, that thou
shalt not get a wife for my son from the daughters of
Canaan, among whom I live;)
4 but that thou go to my land and kindred, and thereof
take a wife to my son Isaac. (but that thou shalt go to my
land and family, and get a wife from there for my son
Isaac.)
5 The servant answered, If the woman will not come
with me into this land, whether I ought to lead again thy
son to the place, from which thou wentest out? (And the
servant answered, If the woman will not come back with
me to this land, should I lead thy son back to the place
from which thou wentest out?)
6 Abraham said, Beware, lest any time thou lead again
thither my son; (And Abraham said, Nay! Beware, lest
any time thou lead my son back there;)
7 the Lord God of heaven that took me from the house
of my father, and from the land of my birth, which spake
to me, and swore (to me), and said, I shall give this land
to thy seed, (yea,) he shall send his angel before thee,
and thou shalt take from thence a wife to my son (and
thou shalt get a wife from there for my son);
8 forsooth if the woman will not follow thee, thou
shalt not be holden by the oath; nevertheless lead not
again my son thither (but do not lead my son back there).
9 Therefore the servant putted his hand under the hip
of Abraham, his lord, and swore to him on this word (and
swore to him on this matter).
10 And he took ten camels of the flock of his lord, and
went forth, and bare with him of all the goods of his lord
(And then he took ten camels from his lord's herd, and
went forth, and took with him many good things from his
lord); and he went forth, and came to Mesopotamia, to
the city of Nahor.
11 And when he had made the camels to rest without
the city (And when he had made the camels to rest outside
the city), beside a well of water, in the eventide, in that
time in which women be wont to go out to draw water,
12 he said, Lord God of my lord Abraham, I beseech,
meet with me today, and do mercy with my lord
Abraham (and do mercy to my lord Abraham).
13 Lo! I stand nigh the well of water, and the daughters
of the dwellers of this city shall go out to draw water; (Lo!
I stand near to the water well, and the daughters of the
inhabitants of this city shall go out to draw water;)
14 therefore the damsel to which I shall say, Bow down
thy water pot (so) that I (may) drink, and (she) shall
answer, Drink thou, but also I shall give drink to thy
camels, that it is which thou hast made ready to thy
servant Isaac (she it is whom thou hast prepared for thy
servant Isaac); and by this I shall understand that thou
hast done mercy to my lord Abraham.
15 And he had not yet [ful-]filled the words within
himself, and lo! Rebecca, the daughter of Bethuel, son of
Milcah, wife of Nahor, brother of Abraham, went out,
having a water pot in her shoulder (having a water pot on
her shoulder);
16 a damsel full comely/full shapely, and fairest virgin,
and unknown of man. Soothly she came down to the
well, and filled the water pot, and turned again. (a very
shapely young woman, and the most beautiful virgin,
yea, unknown by man. And she went down to the well,
and filled the water pot, and then came up again.)
17 And the servant met her, and said, Give thou to me
a little of the water of thy pot to drink (Give thou to me a
little water to drink from thy water pot).
18 Which answered, Drink thou, my lord. And anon
she did down the water pot on her shoulder, and gave
drink to him (And at once she did down the water pot
from off her shoulder, and gave him a drink).
19 And when he had drunk, she said, But also I shall
draw water to thy camels, till all have drunk. (And when
he had drunk, she said, I shall also draw some water for
thy camels, until all of them have had something to drink
as well.)
20 And she poured out the water pot in(to) (the)
troughs, and ran (down) again to the well, to draw (some
more) water, and she gave (the) water drawn to all the
camels (and so she gave water to all the camels).

21 Soothly he beheld her privily, and would wit
whether the Lord had sped his way, or nay. (And he
secretly watched her, and wanted to know if the Lord had
sped his way, or not.)
22 Therefore after that the camels had drunk, the man
brought forth golden earrings, weighing two shekels, and
as many bands of the arm (and two arm bands), in the
weight of ten shekels.
23 And he said to her, Whose daughter art thou? show
thou to me (and tell me), is [there] any place in the house
of thy father (for us) to dwell in?
24 Which answered, I am the daughter of Bethuel, (the)
son of Nahor, whom Milcah childed to him.
25 And she added, saying, Also full much of provender
and of hay is at us (And we have much provender and
hay), and a large place to dwell in.
26 (And) The man bowed himself (down), and
worshipped the Lord,
27 and said, Blessed be the Lord God of my lord
Abraham, which took not away his mercy and truth from
my lord, and led me by the right way, into the house of
the brother of my lord. (and said, Blessed be the Lord
God of my lord Abraham, who took not away his mercy
and truth from my lord, but led me by the right way to
the house of my lord's brother.)
28 And so the damsel ran, and told in the house of her
mother all (the) things which she had heard.
29 Soothly Rebecca had a brother, Laban by name,
which went out hastily to the man, where he was
withoutforth.
30 And when he had seen the earrings, and bands of
the arm in the hands of his sister, and had heard all the
words of her, telling, The man spake to me these things,
he came to the man that stood beside the camels, and
nigh the well of water, (For when he had seen the
earrings, and the bands on his sister's wrists, and had
heard all of her words, saying, The man spoke these and
these things to me, he went out hastily to the man who
was standing beside the camels, and near the water well,)
31 and said to him, Enter thou, the blessed of the Lord;
why standest thou withoutforth? I have made ready the
house, and a place to thy camels. (and said to him, Come
in, thou blessed of the Lord; why standest thou outside? I
have prepared the house, and there is a place for thy
camels.)
32 And he brought him into the inn, and unsaddled the
camels, and gave provender, and hay, and water to wash
the feet of the camels, and (the feet) of (the) men that
came with him. (And he brought him into the house, and
unsaddled the camels, and gave provender and hay to
them, and then brought water to the man, and to the men
who came with him, so that they could wash their feet.)
33 And bread was set forth in his sight, the which said,
I shall not eat till I speak my words. He answered to the
man, Speak thou. (And bread was set before the man, but
he said, I shall not eat until I speak my words. And Laban
said to the man, Speak thou.)
34 And the man said, I am the servant of Abraham,
35 and the Lord hath blessed my lord greatly, and he is
made great; and God gave to him sheep, and oxen,
silver, and gold, servants, and handmaids, and camels,
and asses. (and the Lord hath greatly blessed my lord,
and he is a great man; and God hath given him sheep,
and oxen, silver, and gold, male and female slaves, and
camels, and donkeys.)
36 And Sarah, my lord's wife, childed a son to my lord
in his eld (age), and *Abraham, my lord,* hath given all
things that he had to that son. (And Sarah, my lord's wife,
bare a son for my lord in her old age, and *Abraham, my
lord,* hath given all the things that he hath to his son.)
37 And my lord charged me greatly, and said, Thou
shalt not take to my son a wife of the daughters of Canaan,
in whose land I dwell, (And my lord greatly charged me,
and said, Thou shalt not get a wife for my son from
among the daughters of Canaan, in whose land I live,)
38 but thou shalt go to the house of my father, and of
my kindred thou shalt take a wife to my son. (but thou
shalt go to my father's house, and thou shalt get a wife
from my family for my son.)
39 Forsooth I answered to my lord, What if the woman
will not come with me?
40 (And) He said, The Lord, in whose sight I go, shall
send his angel with thee, and shall direct thy way; and
thou shalt take a wife to my son of my kindred, and of
my father's house (and thou shalt get a wife for my son
from my family, yea, from my father's house).
41 Thou shalt be innocent from my curse, when thou
comest to my kinsmen, and they give not her to thee.
(But thou shalt be released from this oath, if, when thou
comest to my family, they will not give her to thee.)
42 Therefore I came today to the well of water, and (I)
said, Lord God of my lord Abraham, if thou hast directed
my way in which I go now,
43 lo! I stand beside the well of water, and the maid[en]
that shall go out to draw water, (who) heareth me (say to
her), Give thou to me a little of water to drink (out) of thy
pot, (lo! now I stand beside the water well, and the young
woman who shall go out to draw water, and when I say
to her, Give thou to me a little water to drink from thy
water pot,)
44 and she say to me, And thou drink, and I shall draw
water to thy camels, that is the woman which the Lord
hath made ready to the son of my lord. (and she say to
me, Drink thou, and I shall also draw some water for thy
camels, that is the woman whom the Lord hath prepared
for my lord's son.)
45 While I turned in thought these things with(in) me,
Rebecca appeared, coming with a pot which she bare in

her shoulder; and she went down to the well, and drew
water. And I said to her, Give thou a little to me to drink;
(And while I turned these things about in thought within
me, Rebecca appeared, coming with a pot which she
carried on her shoulder; and she went down to the well,
and drew some water. And I said to her, Give thou to me
a little water to drink;)
46 and she hasted, and did down the pot (from) off the
shoulder, and said to me, And thou drink, and I shall give
drink to thy camels (and said to me, Drink, and I shall
also give drink to thy camels); (and so) I drank, and *she*
watered the camels.
47 And I asked her, and said, Whose daughter art thou?
Which answered, I am the daughter of Bethuel, the son
of Nahor, whom Milcah childed to him. And so I hanged
earrings to adorn her face, and I put bands of the arm in
her hands (and I put bands on her wrists),
48 and low-like I worshipped the Lord, and I blessed
the Lord God of my lord Abraham, which God led me by
the right way, that I should take the daughter of the
brother of my lord to his son. (and I bowed low before
the Lord, and I blessed the Lord God of my lord Abraham,
which God led me by the right way, so that I should find
the daughter of the brother of my lord for his son.)
49 Wherefore if ye do mercy and truth with my lord (So
if ye shall do mercy and truth to my lord), show ye to me;
else if (an)other thing pleaseth (thee), also say ye this, (so)
that I (know to) go to the right side, or to the left side.
50 Laban and Bethuel answered, The word is gone out
of the Lord; we may not speak any other thing with thee
without his pleasance. (And Laban and Bethuel
answered, This thing is from the Lord; we shall not say
anything to thee other than what pleaseth him.)
51 Lo! Rebecca is before thee; take thou her, and go
forth, and be she [the] wife of the son of thy lord, as the
Lord spake.
52 And when the servant of Abraham had heard this,
he felled down, and worshipped the Lord in (the) earth.
(And when Abraham's servant had heard this, he fell
down, and worshipped the Lord on the ground.)
53 And when vessels of silver, and of gold, and clothes
were brought forth, he gave those to Rebecca for (a) gift,
and he (also) gave gifts to her brethren, and (to her)
mother.
54 And when a feast was made, they ate and drank
together, and dwelled there. Forsooth the servant rose
(up) early, and said, Deliver ye me, (so) that I (may) go
(now) to my lord.
55 Her brethren and mother answered, The damsel
dwell namely ten days at us, and afterward she shall go
forth. (And her brothers and her mother answered, Let the
young woman stay with us ten more days, and then she
shall go with thee.)
56 (But) The servant said, Do not ye hold me, for the
Lord hath directed my way; deliver ye me, (so) that I
(may) go (now) to my lord.
57 And they said, Call we the damsel, and ask we her
will.
58 And when she was called, and came, they asked
her, Wilt thou go with this man? And she said, I shall go.
59 Therefore they delivered her, and her nurse, and the
servant of Abraham, and his fellows, (And so they let her
go, and her nurse, and Abraham's servant, and his fellows,)
60 and wished prosperities to their sister (and wished
their sister well), and said, Thou art our sister, increase
thou into a thousand thousands, and thy seed wield the
gates of his enemies.
61 Therefore Rebecca and her damsels ascended on the
camels, and followed the man, which turned again
hastily to his lord.
62 In that time Isaac walked by the way that leadeth to
the well, whose name is of him that liveth and seeth; for
he dwelled in the south land. (Now at that time Isaac
walked by the way that leadeth to The Well of Lahairoi,
or Beerlahairoi; for he lived then in the south land.)
63 And he went out to think in the field, for the day
was bowed [down] then; and when he had raised [up] his
eyes, he saw camels coming (from) afar.
64 And when Isaac was seen, Rebecca lighted down off
the camel,
65 and said to the servant, Who is that man that cometh
by the field into the meeting of us? And the servant said
to her, It is my lord. And she took soon a mantle, and
covered her (And she quickly took a mantle, and covered
herself).
66 Forsooth the servant told to his lord Isaac all (the)
things which he had done;
67 Isaac led her into the tabernacle of Sarah, his
mother, and took her to wife; and so much he loved her,
that he assuaged the sorrow which befell to him of the
death of his mother. (and Isaac led her into the tent of his
mother Sarah, and took her as his wife; and he loved her
so much, that he assuaged the sorrow which befell to him
upon his mother's death.)

CHAPTER 25

1 Forsooth Abraham wedded another wife, Keturah by
name,
2 which childed to him Zimran, and Jokshan, and
Medan, and Midian, and Ishbak, and Shuah.
3 Also Jokshan begat Sheba, and Dedan. Forsooth the
sons of Dedan were Asshurim, and Letushim, and
Leummim.
4 And soothly of Midian was born Ephah, and Epher,
and Hanoch, and Abidah, and Eldaah; all these were the
sons of Keturah.
5 And Abraham gave all (the) things which he had in
possession to Isaac;

6 soothly he gave gifts to the sons of [the] concubines,
that is, (his) secondary wives; and Abraham, while he
lived yet, separated them from Isaac, his son, to the east
coast (but Abraham, while yet he lived, separated them
from his son Isaac, and sent them away to the east parts).
7 Forsooth the days of the life of Abraham were an
hundred and threescore and fifteen years;
8 and (then) he failed, and died in [a] good eld (age),
and of (a) great age, and full of days, and he was gathered
to his people (and he joined his ancestors).
9 And Isaac and Ishmael, his sons, buried him in the
double den, which is set in the field of Ephron, son of
Zohar (the) Hittite, even against Mamre, (And his sons
Isaac and Ishmael, buried him in the cave at Machpelah,
which is set in the field of Ephron, the son of Zohar the
Hittite, east of Mamre,)
10 which den he bought of the sons of Heth; and he
was buried there, and Sarah his wife. (which cave he
bought from the Hittites; and he was buried there, with
his wife Sarah.)
11 And after the death of Abraham, God blessed Isaac
his son, which dwelled beside the well by name of him
that liveth and seeth. (And after Abraham's death, God
blessed his son Isaac, who lived beside The Well of
Lahairoi, *or Beerlahairoi*.)
12 These be the generations of Ishmael, the son of
Abraham, whom Hagar (the) Egyptian, handmaid of
Sarah, childed to Abraham; (These be the descendants of
Ishmael, Abraham's son, whom Hagar the Egyptian,
Sarah's slave-girl, bare for Abraham;)
13 and these be the names of the sons of Ishmael, in
their names and generations. The first begotten of
Ishmael was Nebajoth, afterward Kedar, and Adbeel, and
Mibsam, (and these be the names of Ishmael's sons, by
their names, and in their birth order. Ishmael's first-born
was Nebajoth, and then Kedar, and Adbeel, and Mibsam,)
14 and Mishma, and Dumah, and Massa,
15 and Hadar, and Tema, and Jetur, and Naphish, and
Kedemah.
16 These were the sons of Ishmael, and these were the
names by castles, and towns of them, (named after) [the]
twelve princes of their lineages. (These were Ishmael's
sons, and they were also the names of their fortresses,
and towns, named after the twelve princes of their tribes.)
17 And the years of [the] life of Ishmael were made an
hundred and seven and thirty (years), and (then) he failed,
and died, and was put to his people (and joined his
ancestors).
18 Forsooth he inhabited from Havilah till to Shur, that
beholdeth Egypt, as men entereth into [the] Assyrians;
(and) he died before all his brethren. (And Ishmael's
people dwelled from Havilah unto Shur, which is east of
Egypt, on the way to Assyria; and he died in the presence
of all his kinsmen.)
19 Also these be the generations of Isaac, the son of
Abraham. Abraham begat Isaac, (And these be the
descendants of Isaac, Abraham's son. Abraham begat
Isaac,)
20 and when Isaac was of forty years, he wedded a
wife, Rebecca, the daughter of Bethuel, of Syria, of
Mesopotamia, the sister of Laban. (and when Isaac was
forty years old, he wedded a wife, Rebecca, the daughter
of Bethuel, the Syrian from Paddan-aram, and the sister of
Laban.)
21 And Isaac besought the Lord for his wife, for she was
barren; and the Lord heard him, and gave conceiving to
Rebecca.
22 But the little children were hurtled together in her
womb; and she said, If it was so to coming to me, what
need was it to conceive? (and she said, If such was to
come to me, what meaneth it?) And she went to ask (the)
counsel of the Lord,
23 which answered, and said, Two folks be in thy
womb, and two peoples shall be separated from thy
womb, and one people shall overturn a people, and the
more shall serve the less. (who answered, and said, Two
nations be in thy womb, and two peoples shall be taken
from thy womb, and one nation shall be stronger than the
other nation, and the older shall serve the younger.)
24 Then the time of child-bearing came, and lo! two
children were found in her womb.
25 He that went out first was red, and all rough in the
manner of a skin; and his name was called Esau.
26 Anon the other went out (And at once the other
went out), and held with his hand the heel of his brother;
and therefore he called him Jacob[10]. (And) Isaac was sixty
years eld, when the little children were born.
27 And when they were waxen, Esau was a man
knowing of hunting, and a man (who was) an earth-tiller;
forsooth Jacob was a simple man, and dwelled in
tabernacles. (And when they were fully grown, Esau was
a man knowledgeable about hunting, and who worked
the soil, *or was a farmer*; and Jacob was a simple man,
who stayed at home in the tents.)
28 Isaac loved Esau, for he ate of the hunting of Esau;
and Rebecca loved Jacob.
29 Soothly Jacob seethed pottage (And one day Jacob
boiled some stew); and when Esau came (in) weary from
the field,
30 he said to Jacob, Give thou to me of this red
seething, for I am full weary; for which cause his name
was called Edom (and for this reason he was called
Edom, *or Red*).
31 And Jacob said to him, Sell to me the right(s) of the
first begotten child. (And Jacob said to him, First sell me

[10] The name sounds like the Hebrew for 'He who takes by the heel, or supplants'.

thy birthright/First sell me the rights of the first-born child.)
32 Esau answered, Lo! I die, what shall the first begotten
things profit to me? (And Esau answered, Lo! I am
starving right now, and what good is my birthright to me!)
33 Jacob said, Therefore swear thou to me. Therefore
Esau swore, and sold the first engendered things. (And
Jacob said, And so swear thou to me. And so Esau swore
to Jacob, and sold him his birthright.)
34 And so when he had taken bread and pottage, Esau
ate and drank, and went forth, and charged little that he
had sold the right(s) of the first begotten child (and cared
little that he had sold his birthright as the first-born son).

CHAPTER 26

1 Forsooth for hunger rose on the land, after that
barrenness that befelled in the days of Abraham, Isaac
went forth to Abimelech, king of Palestines, in Gerar.
(And another famine arose in the land, like the one which
had come in Abraham's days, and Isaac went to
Abimelech, the king of the Philistines, in Gerar.)
2 And the Lord appeared to him, and said, Go not
down into Egypt, but rest thou in the land which I shall
say to thee, (For the Lord had appeared to him, and said,
Do not go down to Egypt, but rest thou in this land,
where I tell thee to stay,)
3 and be thou a pilgrim therein; and I shall be with
thee, and I shall bless thee; for I shall give all these
countries to thee, and to thy seed, and I shall [ful]fill the
oath which I promised to Abraham, thy father. (and live
thou there; and I shall be with thee, and I shall bless thee;
for I shall give all these lands to thee, and to thy
descendants, and I shall fulfill the oath which I promised
to thy father Abraham.)
4 And I shall multiply thy seed as the stars of (the)
heaven(s), and I shall give all these countries to thine
heirs, and all folks of the earth shall be blessed in thy
seed, (And I shall multiply thy descendants like the stars
of the night sky, and I shall give all these lands to thy
heirs, and all the nations of the earth shall pray to be
blessed as thy descendants be blessed/and through thy
descendants I shall bless all the nations of the earth,)
5 for Abraham obeyed to my voice, and kept my
behests, and my commandments, and my ceremonies,
and my laws.
6 And so Isaac dwelled in Gerar.
7 And when he was asked of [the] men of that place of
his wife (And when he was asked by the men of that
place about his wife), he answered, She is my sister; for
he dreaded to acknowledge that she was fellowshipped
to him in matrimony, and he guessed lest peradventure
they would slay him for the fairness of her.
8 And when full many days were passed, and he (had)
dwelled there, Abimelech, king of Palestines, beheld by a
window, and saw him playing with Rebecca, his wife.
(And when they had lived there for many days,
Abimelech, the king of the Philistines, looked out a
window, and saw Isaac kissing his wife Rebecca.)
9 And when Isaac was called (to him), the king said, It
is open, that she is thy wife; why saidest thou, that she
was thy sister? Isaac answered, For I dreaded (For I was
afraid), lest I should die for her.
10 And Abimelech said, Why hast thou deceived us?
Some man of the people might do lechery with thy wife,
and thou haddest brought in grievous sin on us. (And
Abimelech said, Why hast thou deceived us? Some man
of my people might have done lechery with thy wife, and
then thou wouldest have brought in a grievous sin upon
us.)
11 And the king commanded to all the people, and said,
He that toucheth the wife of this man shall die by death.
12 Forsooth Isaac sowed in that land, and he found an
hundredfold *increase* in that year (and he received a
hundredfold *increase* that year); and the Lord blessed him.
13 And the man was made rich, and he went profiting
and increasing, till he was made full great.
14 Also he had possessions of sheep and of great
beasts, and full much of menials. For this thing Palestines
had envy to him, (And he had possessions of sheep and
of great beasts, and many servants and slaves. And
because of this, the Philistines envied him,)
15 and they stopped in that time and filled with earth
all the wells which the servants of Abraham his father had
digged, (and so they stopped up, and filled with earth, all
the wells which the servants of his father Abraham had
dug,)
16 in so much that Abimelech himself said to Isaac (and
finally Abimelech himself said to Isaac), Go thou away
from us, for thou art made greatly mightier than we (be).
17 And he went away, that he should come to the
strand of Gerar, and dwelled there. (And so he went
away from that place, and came to the Gerar Valley, and
lived there.)
18 And he digged again other wells, which the servants
of Abraham his father had digged, and which the
Philistines had stopped sometime, when Abraham was
dead (and which the Philistines had stopped up after
Abraham died); and he called those wells by the same
names, by which his father had called (them) before.
19 They digged in the strand (And they dug in the
valley), and they found quick, *or welling up,* water.
20 But also strife of [the] shepherds of Gerar was there
against the shepherds of Isaac, and they said, The water is
ours; wherefore of that strife that befelled, Isaac called the
name of that well False Challenge. (But the shepherds of
Gerar also quarreled with Isaac's shepherds, and they
said, This water is ours; and so for the strife that befell,
Isaac called the name of that well Esek, *or Quarrel.*)
21 And they digged another (well), and they strived

also for that, and Isaac called that well Enmities. (And
they dug another well, and they also quarreled over that
one, and Isaac called that well Sitnah, *or Enmity*.)
22 And he went forth from thence, and digged another
well, for which they strived not, [and] therefore he called
the name of that well Breadth, *either Largeness*; and said,
Now God hath alarged us, and hath made *us* to increase
on [the] earth. (And he went forth from there, and dug
another well, which they did not quarrel over, and so he
called the name of that well Rehoboth, *or Broad Places*;
and he said, Now God hath enlarged us, and we shall be
fruitful in this land.)
23 Isaac forsooth went up from that place into
Beersheba, (And Isaac went up from that place to
Beersheba,)
24 where the Lord appeared to him in that night; and
said, I am [the] God of Abraham, thy father; do not thou
dread (do not thou fear), for I am with thee, and I shall
bless thee, and I shall multiply thy seed for (the sake of)
my servant Abraham.
25 And so Isaac builded there an altar to the Lord; and
when the name of the Lord was inwardly called, he
stretched forth a tabernacle; and he commanded his
servants that they should dig wells. (And so Isaac built an
altar there to the Lord; and after he had inwardly called
on the Lord's name, he pitched his tent there; and then
he commanded his servants to dig a well.)
26 And when Abimelech, and Ahuzzath, (one of) his
friends, and Phicol, [the] duke of knights (the leader of his
soldiers), had come from Gerar to that place,
27 Isaac spake to them, (and said,) What came ye to
me, a man whom ye have hated, and putted away from
you? (Isaac said to them, Why have ye come to me, a
man whom ye hate, and whom ye sent away from you?)
28 Which answered, We saw that God is with thee,
and therefore we said now, An oath be betwixt us, and
make we a covenant of peace, (And they answered, We
saw that God was with thee, and so we said, Now let
there be an oath between us, and make we a covenant of
peace,)
29 (so) that thou do not any[thing of] evil to us, as we
(have) touched nothing of thine, neither did that that
hurted thee, but with peace we let go thee (but we let
thee go away in peace), (and now thou art) increased by
the blessing(s) of the Lord.
30 Therefore Isaac made them a feast; and after meat
and drink, (And so Isaac made a feast for them; and after
food and drink,)
31 they rose early, and swore each to (the) other; and
Isaac let go them peaceably into their place. (they rose up
early, and swore an oath to each other; and then Isaac let
them go away in peace.)
32 Lo! forsooth in that day the servants of Isaac came,
telling to him of the well which they had digged, and
said, We have found water.
33 Wherefore Isaac called that well Abundance; and
the name of the city was set Beersheba till into *this*
present day. (And so Isaac called that well Shebah; and
the city there is called Beersheba unto *this* present day.)
34 Esau forsooth forty years eld wedded two wives
(And when Esau was forty years old he wedded two
wives), Judith[11], the daughter of Beeri (the) Hittite, and
Bashemath[12], the daughter of Elon, of the same place;
35 which both offended the soul of Isaac and of
Rebecca. (and because both *women* were *heathen*, that
offended, *or greatly distressed*, Isaac and Rebecca.)

CHAPTER 27

1 Forsooth Isaac waxed eld, and his eyes dimmed,
and he might not see. And he called Esau, his more son,
and said to him, My son! Which answered, I am present.
(And Isaac grew old, and his eyes dimmed, and he could
not see. And he called his elder son Esau, and said to
him, My son! And he answered, I am here.)
2 To whom the father said, Thou seest that I have
waxed eld, and I know not the day of my death[13].
3 Take thine arms (Take thy weapons), (an) arrow
case, and a bow, and go out; and when thou hast taken
anything by hunting,
4 make me a stew thereof, as thou knowest that I will,
and bring it to me that I eat, (so) that (afterward) my soul
(can) bless thee before that I die. (make for me a stew out
of it, as thou knowest that I like, and bring it to me so that
I can eat it, and then I shall bless thee before that I die.)
5 And when Rebecca had heard this thing, and he had
gone forth into the field that he fulfill the behest of his
father,
6 she said to her son Jacob, I heard thy father speaking
with Esau, thy brother, and saying to him,
7 Bring thou to me of thine hunting, and make thou
meats, that I eat, and that I bless thee before the Lord
before that I die. (Bring thou to me some of thy hunting,
and make thou for me some stew, so that I can eat it, and
then I shall bless thee before the Lord, before that I die.)
8 Now therefore, my son, assent to my counsels,
9 and go to the flock, and bring to me twain (of) the
best kids, that I make meats of those to thy father, which
he shall eat gladly; (and go to the flock, and bring me two
of the best goat kids, so that I can make thy father's
favourite meal out of them, which I know that he shall
gladly eat;)
10 and (so) that when thou hast brought in those meats,
and he hath eaten, he (shall) bless thee before that he die.
11 To whom Jacob answered, Thou knowest that Esau

[11] She is also known as Oholibamah/Aholibamah.
[12] She is also known as Adah.
[13] Isaac would still be alive more than 20 years after this event(!).

my brother is an hairy man, and I am smooth;
12 (so) if my father shall touch (me), or draw me to him,
and feel me, I dread lest he guess that I would scorn him,
and he bring in cursing on me for blessing (and I bring in
a curse upon myself, and not a blessing).
13 To whom his mother said, My son, this cursing be in
me (My son, any curse shall be upon me); only hear thou
my voice, and go, and bring that that I said.
14 (And so) He went, and brought it, and gave it to his
mother. She made ready meats, as she knew that his
father would *have* (And she prepared the meat, in the
way that she knew that his father would like it),
15 and she clothed Jacob in [the] full good clothes of
Esau, which she had at home with herself (which she had
there at home with her).
16 And she wrapped his hands about with little skins of
(goat) kids, and covered the nakedness of his neck;
17 and she gave to him the stew (and then she gave
him the stew), and betook (to) him [the] loaves, which
she had baked.
18 And when these were brought in, he said, My father!
And he answered, I (am) here; (but) who art thou, my son?
19 And Jacob said, I am Esau, thy first begotten son. I
have done to thee as thou commandedest to me; rise
thou up, and sit, and eat of my venison, that thy soul
bless me. (And Jacob said, I am Esau, thy first-born son. I
have done for thee as thou commandedest me; rise thou
up, and sit, and eat my venison, and then afterward thou
can bless me.)
20 Again Isaac said to his son, My son, how mightest
thou find *(this) venison* so soon? Which answered, It was
God's will, that this thing that I would, should come soon
to me. (And Isaac said to his son, My son, how mightest
thou find *this venison* so soon? And Jacob answered, It
was God's will, that what I desired, should come so soon
to me.)
21 And Isaac said, My son, come thou hither, (so) that I
(can) touch thee, and that I prove whether thou be my
son Esau, or nay.
22 (And) Jacob nighed to his father; and when Isaac had
feeled him, he said, Soothly the voice is the voice of
Jacob, but the hands be the hands of Esau.
23 And Isaac knew not Jacob, for the hairy hands
showed the likeness of the elder son. Therefore Isaac
blessed Jacob (And so that is why Isaac would soon bless
Jacob),
24 and (so he) said (again), Art thou my son Esau?
(And) Jacob answered, I am.
25 And Isaac said, My son, bring thou to me meats of
thine hunting, that my soul bless thee. And when Isaac
had eaten these meats brought (to him), Jacob brought
also wine to Isaac, and when this was drunken, (And
Isaac said, My son, bring thou to me the meats of thy
hunting, and then afterward I shall bless thee. And when
Isaac had eaten the meat brought to him, Jacob also
brought him some wine, and when he had drunk it,)
26 Isaac said to him, My son, come thou hither, and
give to me a kiss.
27 Jacob nighed, and kissed him; and anon as Isaac
feeled the odour of his clothes, he blessed him, and said,
Lo! the odour of my son as the odour of a plenteous field
which the Lord hath blessed. (And Jacob came over, and
kissed him; and when Isaac smelled the aroma of his
clothes, at once he blessed him, saying, Lo! the aroma of
my son is like the aroma of a plentiful field which the
Lord hath blessed.)
28 God give to thee of the dew of heaven, and of the
fatness of [the] earth, (and of the) abundance of wheat,
and of wine, and of oil; (May God give thee the dew
from heaven, and the fatness of the earth, and an
abundance of corn, *or of grain*, and wine, and oil;)
29 and (may) peoples serve thee, and lineages worship
thee; be thou lord of thy brethren, and the sons of thy
mother be bowed (low) before thee; be he cursed that
curseth thee, and he that blesseth thee, be he [full-]filled
with blessings (be they cursed who curse thee, but let
those who bless thee, be filled full with blessings).
30 Scarcely Isaac had filled the word, and when Jacob
was gone out, Esau came, (Scarcely had Isaac finished
speaking, and Jacob had gone out, then Esau came in
from his hunting,)
31 and brought in meats sodden of the hunting to the
father, and said, My father, rise thou, and eat of the
hunting of thy son, that thy soul bless me. (and he
brought in boiled meats for his father, and said, My
father, rise thou up, and eat of thy son's hunting, and
then afterward thou can bless me.)
32 And Isaac said, Who art thou? Which answered, I
am Esau, thy first begotten son. (And Isaac said, Who art
thou? And Esau answered, I am Esau, thy first-born son.)
33 Isaac dreaded with a great astonishing; and he
wondered more than it may be believed, and said, Who
therefore is he which a while ago brought to me venison
taken, and I ate of all things before that thou camest; and
I blessed him? and he shall be blessed. (And Isaac
dreaded with great astonishment; and he wondered more
than it can be imagined, and he said, Then who was it,
who just a short while ago, brought me the newly caught
venison, and I ate all of it before that thou camest in; and
I blessed him? and yea, he shall be blessed.)
34 When the words of the father were heard, Esau
roared with a great cry, and was astonished, and said, My
father, bless thou also me. (And when he heard his
father's words, Esau roared with a great cry, and was
astonished, and said, My father, thou must also bless me!)
35 Which said (And Jacob said), Thy brother came
prudently [Thy brother came (be)guilingly], and took (away)
thy blessing.

36 And Esau added, Justly his name is called Jacob, for
lo! he [hath] supplanted me (yet) another time; before he
took away my first begotten things, and now the second
time, he [hath] ravished privily my blessing. And again
he said to the father, Whether thou hast not reserved a
blessing also to me? (And Esau added, His name is rightly
called Jacob, *that is, the Heel, or the Supplanter,* for lo!
now he hath supplanted me the second time; first he took
away my birthright as the first-born son, and now he hath
cheated me out of my blessing. And again he said to his
father, Hast thou not reserved a blessing for me?)
37 Isaac answered, I have made him thy lord, and I
have made subject all his brethren to his servage; I have
stablished him in wheat, and wine, and oil; and (so), my
son, what shall I do to thee after these things? (Isaac
answered, I have made him thy lord, and I have made all
of his brothers to be in servitude to him, *that is, to be his
slaves*; I have established him with corn, *or with grain,*
and wine, and oil; and so now, my son, after all these
things, what is left that I can do for thee?)
38 To whom Esau said, Father, whether thou hast only
one blessing? I beseech *thee*, that also thou bless me.
And when Esau wept with great yelling, (To whom Esau
said, Father, hast thou only one blessing? I beseech *thee*,
that thou also bless me. And when Esau wept with great
yelling,)
39 Isaac was stirred, and said to him, Thy blessing shall
be (not) in the fatness of [the] earth, and in the dew of
heaven from above; (Isaac was stirred, and said to him,
Thy dwelling shall be far from the fatness of the earth,
and far from the dew of heaven above;)
40 thou shalt live by (the) sword, and thou shalt serve
thy brother, and (then the) time shall come when thou
shalt shake away, and unbind his yoke from [off] thy
nolls.
41 Therefore Esau hated evermore Jacob for the
blessing by which the father had blessed him; and Esau
said in his heart, The days of mourning of my father shall
come, and (then) I shall slay Jacob, my brother. (And so
Esau hated Jacob even more for the blessing with which
his father had blessed him; and Esau said in his heart, The
days of mourning for my father shall come, and then I
shall kill my brother Jacob.)
42 These things were told to Rebecca, and she sent,
and called (for) her son Jacob, and said to him, Lo! Esau,
thy brother, menaceth to slay thee (Lo! Esau, thy brother,
hath threatened to kill thee);
43 now therefore, my son, hear thou my voice, and rise
thou up, and flee to Laban, my brother, into Haran (and
flee to my brother Laban, in Haran);
44 and thou shalt dwell with him (for) a few days, till
the strong vengeance of thy brother rest, and his
indignation cease,
45 and till he forget those things which thou hast done
against him. Afterward I shall send, and I shall bring thee
from thence hither. Why shall I be made sonless of ever
either son in one day? (and until he forget those things
which thou hast done against him. And then afterward I
shall send for thee, and I shall bring thee back here. For
why should I be deprived of both sons in one day?)
46 And Rebecca said to Isaac, It annoyeth me of my life
for the daughters of Heth (I am weary to death of the
daughters of the Hittites); if Jacob take a wife of the
kindred of this land, I will not live.

CHAPTER 28

1 And so Isaac called Jacob, and blessed him, and
commanded to him, and said, Do not thou take a wife of
the kin of Canaan;
2 but go thou, and walk forth into Mesopotamia of
Syria, to the house of Bethuel, [the] father of thy mother,
and take to thee from thence a wife of the daughters of
Laban, thine uncle. (but go thou forth to Paddan-aram, to
the house of Bethuel, the father of thy mother, and get a
wife for thyself from there, of one of the daughters of thy
uncle Laban.)
3 Soothly Almighty God bless thee (And may
Almighty God bless thee), and make thee to increase, and
multiply thee, (so) that thou be into companies of
peoples;
4 and God give to thee the blessing of Abraham, and
to thy seed after thee, that thou wield the land of thy
pilgrimage, which he promised to thy grand-sire. (and
may God give thee the blessing of Abraham, and thy
descendants after thee, so that thou possessest this land
where thou art now living, which he promised to thy
grandfather.)
5 And when Isaac had let go Jacob, Jacob went forth,
and came into Mesopotamia of Syria, to Laban, the son of
Bethuel of Syria, the brother of Rebecca, his mother.
(And so when Isaac had let Jacob go, he went forth, and
came to Paddan-aram, and to Laban, the son of Bethuel
the Syrian, the brother of his mother Rebecca.)
6 Forsooth Esau saw that his father had blessed Jacob,
and had sent him (away) into Mesopotamia of Syria, that
he should wed a wife of thence, and that after the
blessing he commanded to Jacob, and said, Thou shalt
not take a wife of the daughters of Canaan; (And Esau
saw that his father had blessed Jacob, and had sent him
away to Paddan-aram, so that he would wed a wife from
there, and that after his blessing he had commanded to
Jacob, and said, Thou shalt not take a wife from the
daughters of Canaan;)
7 and that Jacob obeyed to his father and mother, and
went into Syria; (and that Jacob had obeyed his father and
mother, and had gone away to Paddan-aram;)
8 also Esau proved *thereby* that his father beheld not
gladly the daughters of Canaan. (and so Esau understood

by this that his father did not approve of the daughters of
Canaan.)
9 And (so) Esau went to Ishmael, and wedded
a(nother) wife, without these which he had before (in
addition to the two whom he had already wed),
Mahalath[14], the daughter of Ishmael, son of Abraham, the
sister of Nebajoth.
10 Therefore Jacob went out of Beersheba, and went to
Haran. (And so Jacob left Beersheba, and went toward
Haran.)
11 And when he had come to some place, and would
rest therein after the going down of the sun, he took
(some) of the stones that lay there, and he put (them)
under his head, and slept in the same place.
12 And he saw in [his] sleep a ladder standing on the
earth, and the top thereof touching heaven; and he saw
God's angels going up and going down thereby,
13 and the Lord nighed to the ladder, saying to him, I
am the Lord God of Abraham, thy father, and (the) God
of Isaac; I shall give to thee and to thy seed the land in
which thou sleepest.
14 And thy seed shall be as the dust of [the] earth, (and)
thou shalt be alarged to the east, and west, and to the
north, and south; and all the lineages of [the] earth shall
be blessed in thee and in thy seed (and all the families of
the earth shall pray to be blessed as thee and thy
descendants be blessed/and through thee and thy
descendants, I shall bless all the families of the earth).
15 And I shall be thy keeper, whither ever thou shalt
go; and I shall lead thee again into this land, and I shall
not leave thee, no but I shall fulfill all [the] things which I
have said (and I shall not leave thee, until I have fulfilled
all the things which I have promised).
16 And when Jacob had waked of [the] sleep, he said,
Verily the Lord is in this place, and I knew not. (And
when Jacob had awakened from his sleep, he said, Truly
the Lord is in this place, and I did not know it.)
17 And he said dreading, How fearedful, *or worshipful*,
is this place! Here is none other thing, no but the house
of God, and the gate of heaven. (And he said with fear, *or
with reverence*, How fearful, *or how worshipful*, is this
place! This is nothing else, but the House of God, *or
Bethel*, yea, the gateway to heaven/yea, heaven's gate!)
18 Therefore Jacob rose early, and took the stone which
he had put under his head, and raised (it) up into a title,
or (a) sign, and poured out oil (from) above. (And so
Jacob rose up early, and took the stone which he had put
under his head, and set it up as a sacred pillar, and
poured oil on top of it.)
19 And he called the name of that city Bethel, which
was called Luz before. (And he called the name of that
place Bethel; but the city that was there before was called
Luz.)
20 Also Jacob avowed a vow, and said, If God is with
me, and keepeth me in the way in which I go (And Jacob
vowed a vow, and said, If God is with me, and keepeth
me safe on the way on which I go), and giveth to me
loaves to eat, and clothes to be clothed with,
21 and I turn again in prosperity to the house of my
father, the Lord shall be into God to me. (and I return
safety to my father's house, then the Lord shall be my
God.)
22 And this stone, which I raised into a title, shall be
called the house of God; and I shall offer tithes to thee of
all things which thou shalt give to me. (And this stone,
which I raised up as a sacred pillar, shall be called the
House of God; and I shall offer a tithe, *or a tenth*, to thee,
of all the things which thou shalt give me.)

CHAPTER 29

1 Therefore Jacob passed forth, and came into the east
land;
2 and he saw a well in the field, and three flocks of
sheep resting beside it, for why (the) sheep were watered
thereof, and the mouth thereof was closed with a great
stone.
3 And the custom was that when all the sheep were
gathered together, they should turn away the stone, and
when the flocks were watered, they should put it (back)
again on the mouth of the well.
4 And Jacob said to the shepherds, Brethren, of
whence be ye? Which answered, Of Haran (And they
answered, We come from Haran).
5 And he asked them and said, Whether ye know
Laban, the son of Nahor? (And) They said, We know *him*.
6 Jacob said, Is he whole? (Jacob asked, Is he well?)
(And) They said, He is in (a) good state; and lo! Rachel,
his daughter, cometh with his flock.
7 And Jacob said, Yet much of the day is to come, and
it is not (the) time that the flocks be led again to the folds;
soothly give ye drink to the sheep, and so lead ye them
again to meat (and so give drink to the sheep, and then
take ye them back to the pasture).
8 Which answered, We may not till all the sheep be
gathered together, and till we remove the stone from the
mouth of the well, to water the flocks (then we shall
water the flocks).
9 Yet (while) they spake, and lo! Rachel came with the
sheep of her father.
10 And when Jacob saw her, and knew (her to be) the
daughter of (Laban,) his mother's brother, and the sheep
(to be) of Laban his uncle, he removed the stone with
which the well was closed; and when the flock was
watered,
11 he kissed her, and he wept with voice raised (and

[14] Mahalath is also called Bashemath, but she is a different person than Esau's 2ND wife, who was also called Bashemath(!).

with his voice raised up, he wept for joy).
12 And Jacob showed to her that he was the brother of
her father, and the son of Rebecca; and she hasted, and
told to her father. (And Jacob told her that he was her
father's kinsman, and Rebecca's son; and she hastened
home, and told her father.)
13 And when he had heard, that Jacob, the son of his
sister, came, he ran to meet him, and he embraced Jacob,
and kissed him, and led him into his house. Forsooth
when the causes of the journey were heard,
14 Laban answered, Thou art my bone and my flesh.
And after that the days of a month were filled,
15 Laban said to Jacob, Whether for thou art my
brother, thou shalt serve me freely? say thou what meed
thou shalt take. (Laban said to Jacob, Though thou art my
kinsman, shalt thou serve me for nothing? Nay! say what
reward thou shalt take.)
16 Forsooth Laban had two daughters, the name of the
elder was Leah, soothly the younger was called Rachel;
17 but Leah was bleary-eyed, and Rachel was of fair
face, and lovely in sight. (and Leah was blurry-eyed, but
Rachel had a beautiful face, and was lovely to look at.)
18 And Jacob loved Rachel, and (so he) said, I shall
serve thee seven years for Rachel thy younger daughter.
19 Laban answered, It is better that I give her to thee
than to another man; dwell thou with me.
20 Therefore Jacob served seven years for Rachel; and
the days seemed few to him for the greatness of (his) love.
21 And (at last) he said to Laban, Give thou my wife to
me, for the time is fulfilled that I enter [in] to her.
22 And (so) when many companies of friends were
called to the feast, he made [the] weddings,
23 and in the eventide Laban brought in to him Leah
his daughter, (but in the evening, Laban brought in his
daughter Leah to Jacob, *but Jacob was too drunk to
know,*)
24 and gave an handmaid (and Laban gave his slave-
girl), Zilpah by name, to his daughter.
25 And when Jacob had entered [in] to her (as) by
custom, when the morrowtide was made, he saw Leah,
and he said to his wife's father, What is it that thou
wouldest do? whether I served not thee for Rachel? why
hast thou deceived me? (And after Jacob had slept with
his wife, as by custom, when the morning was made, he
saw that it was Leah, and he said to his wife's father,
What hast thou done to me? did I not serve thee for
Rachel? why hast thou deceived me?)
26 Laban answered, It is not custom in our place that
we give first the younger daughter to weddings; (And
Laban answered, It is not the custom in our place that we
give the younger daughter first in a wedding;)
27 fulfill thou the week of days of this wedding, and I
shall give to thee also this *Rachel*, for the work in which
thou shalt serve me by other seven years. (so fulfill thou a
week of days, *or seven days*, for this wedding, and then I
shall also give thee *Rachel*, for the work in which thou
shalt serve me for another seven years.)
28 Jacob assented to the covenant, and when the week
was passed, he wedded Rachel,
29 to whom her father had given Bilhah (for) an
handmaid. (to whom her father had given his slave-girl
Bilhah.)
30 And at the last Jacob used the weddings desired, and
set the love of the latter wife before the first; and Jacob
served Laban seven other years. (And so at last Jacob had
the desired wedding, and put the love of the latter wife
ahead of the first wife; and Jacob served Laban for
another seven years.)
31 Forsooth the Lord saw that Jacob despised Leah, *that
is, (that he) loved her less than Rachel*, and (so) he
opened Leah's womb, while her sister dwelled barren.
32 And Leah childed a son conceived (And Leah
conceived, and bare a son), and she called his name
Reuben, and said, The Lord hath seen my meekness; now
mine husband shall love me.
33 And again she conceived, and childed a son, and
said, For the Lord saw that I was despised, he gave also
this son to me (he also gave me this son); and she called
his name Simeon.
34 And she conceived the third time, and childed
another son, and she said also (and then she said), Now
mine husband shall be coupled to me, for I have childed
three sons to him; and therefore she called his name Levi.
35 The fourth time she conceived, and childed a son,
and said, Now I shall acknowledge to the Lord; and
therefore she called his name Judah; and ceased to child.
(And the fourth time she conceived, and bare a son, she
said, Now I shall praise the Lord; and so she called his
name Judah; and ceased to bear any more children.)

CHAPTER 30

1 Forsooth Rachel saw, that she was unfruitful, and
she had envy to her sister, and said to her husband, Give
thou free children to me, (or) else I shall die. (And Rachel
saw, that she was unfruitful, and she envied her sister,
and said to her husband, Give thou some children to me,
or else I shall die.)
2 To whom Jacob was wroth, and answered, Whether
I am for God, which have deprived thee from the fruit of
thy womb? (To whom Jacob was angry, and answered,
Can I take the place of God, who hath deprived thee of
the fruit of thy womb?)
3 And she said, I have an handmaid Bilhah; enter thou
[in] to her that she child on my knees, and that I have
sons of her. (And she said, I have a slave-girl Bilhah; sleep
thou with her, so that she can bear some children, and
lay them on my knees, and so I shall have sons by her.)
4 And she gave to him Bilhah into matrimony; and

when her husband had entered [in] to her,
5 she conceived, and childed a son.
6 And Rachel said, The Lord hath deemed to me (The
Lord hath judged me), and hath heard my prayer, and
gave a son to me; and therefore she called his name Dan.
7 And again Bilhah conceived, and childed another
son,
8 for whom Rachel said, The Lord hath made me like
my sister, and I [have] waxed strong; and she called him
Naphtali.
9 (Then) Leah feeled that she ceased to bear child, and
she gave Zilpah, her handmaid (her slave-girl), to her
husband.
10 And when Zilpah, after conceiving, childed a son,
11 Leah said, Blessedly (I am most fortunate); and
therefore she called his name Gad.
12 Also Zilpah childed another son,
13 and Leah said, This is for my bless(ing), for all
women shall say me blessed (for all women shall say that
I am blessed); therefore she called him Asher.
14 Forsooth Reuben went out into the field in the time
of wheat harvest, and found (some) mandrakes, which he
brought to Leah, his mother. And Rachel said, Give thou
to me a part of the mandrakes of thy son.
15 Leah answered, Whether it seemeth little to thee,
that thou hast ravished my husband from me, no but thou
take also the mandrakes of my son? (but now thou
wouldest also take away my son's mandrakes?) (And)
Rachel said, The husband sleep with thee in this night,
(in exchange) for the mandrakes of thy son.
16 And when Jacob came again from the field at the
eventide, Leah went out into his meeting, and said, Thou
shalt enter [in] to me, for I have hired thee with hire for
the mandrakes of my son. He slept with her in that night;
(And so when Jacob came in from the field that evening,
Leah went out to meet him, and said, Tonight thou shalt
sleep with me, for I have hired thee with some of my
son's mandrakes. And so he slept with her that night;)
17 and God heard her prayers, and she conceived, and
childed the fifth son;
18 and said, God hath given meed to me, for I gave
mine handmaid to mine husband; and she called his
name Issachar. (and she said, God hath rewarded me, for
I gave my slave-girl to my husband; and so she named
him Issachar.)
19 (And) Again Leah conceived, and childed the sixth
son,
20 and said, The Lord hath made me rich with a good
dower; also in this time mine husband shall be with me,
for I have engendered six sons to him; and therefore she
called his name Zebulun. (and she said, The Lord hath
made me rich with a good dowry; and now my husband
shall be glad to be with me, for I have borne him six
sons; and so she named him Zebulun.)
21 After whom she childed a daughter, Dinah by name.
22 Also the Lord had mind on Rachel, and he heard
her, and opened her womb. (And the Lord remembered
Rachel, and he heard her *prayers and pleadings*, and
opened her womb.)
23 And she conceived, and childed a son, and said,
God hath (now) taken away my shame;
24 and she called his name Joseph, and said, The Lord
give to me another son. (and she said, May the Lord give
me another son/The Lord hath given me another son, and
she named him Joseph.)
25 Soothly when Joseph was born, Jacob said to his
wife's father, Deliver thou me, that I turn again to my
country, and to my land. (And when Joseph was born,
Jacob said to his wife's father, Let me go, so that I can
return to my country, and my land.)
26 Give thou to me my wives, and my free children, for
which I have served thee, that I go (Give thou to me my
wives, and my children, for whom I have served thee, so
that I can go); forsooth thou knowest the service by
which I have served thee.
27 Laban said to him, Find I grace in thy sight; I have
learned by experience, that God hath blessed me for
thee; (Laban said to him, Let me find grace before thee; I
have learned by experience, that God hath blessed me
for thy sake;)
28 ordain thou the meed which I shall give to thee. (tell
me the reward, *or the payment*, which I should give thee.)
29 And Jacob answered, Thou knowest how I have
served thee, and how great thy possession was in mine
hands (and how great thy possession hath become in my
hands);
30 thou haddest little before that I came to thee, and
now thou art made rich, and the Lord [hath] blessed thee
at mine entering; therefore it is just that I purvey sometime
also for mine house (and so it is only right that I provide
something for my own household, *or my own family*).
31 And Laban said, What shall I give to thee? And
Jacob said, I will nothing (I desire nothing), *that is, of thy
gift*, but if thou doest that that I ask, again I shall feed and
keep thy sheep.
32 Go about all thy flocks, and separate thou all
diverse(ly)-*coloured* sheep, and of spotted fleeces, and
whatever thing shall be of dun *hue*, and spotted, and
diverse of colour, as well in sheep as in goats; that shall
be my meed. (Go about all thy flocks, and separate out
all the diversely-*coloured* sheep, and those with spotted
fleeces, and whichever shall be dunned, or spotted, or
diverse in colour, with the sheep as well as with the
goats, and those shall be my reward.)
33 And my rightfulness shall answer to me tomorrow,
when the time of covenant shall come before thee; and
all that be not diverse, and spotted, and dunned, as well
in sheep as in goats, (that) be found at me thou shalt

reprove me of theft. (And my righteousness shall answer
for me later on, when the time of payment shall come
before thee; and if any that be not diverse, or spotted, or
dunned, with the sheep as well as with the goats, be
found with me, then thou can rebuke me for theft.)
34 And Laban said, I have (it) acceptable that that thou
askest. (And Laban said, I find it acceptable what thou
hast suggested.)
35 And Laban separated in that day [the] goats, and
sheep, goat bucks, and rams, diverse and spotted.
Soothly he betook all the flock of one colour, that is, of
white, and of black fleece, into the hand(s) of his sons;
(And so Laban separated out that day the goats, and
sheep, and goat bucks, and rams, that were diversely-
coloured, or spotted. And all of the flock that had only
one colour, that is, those of white, or of black fleece, he
gave to his sons;)
36 and he set the space of (the) way of three days
betwixt his sons, and the husband of his daughters, that
fed his other flocks.
37 Therefore Jacob took green rods of poplars, and of
almonds, and of planes, and in part he did away the
rind(s) of them; and when the rinds were drawn away,
either shaved, whiteness appeared in these that were
made bare; soothly those that were whole dwelled green,
and by this manner the colour was made diverse. (And so
Jacob took some branches of green poplars, and of
almonds, and of planes, and he partly did away their
rinds; and where the rinds were drawn away, *or shaved*,
whiteness appeared on the places that were made bare,
but where the branches were not touched, they remained
green; and so by this manner the colour was made
diverse.)
38 And Jacob put those rods in the troughs, where the
water was poured out, that when the flocks should come
to drink, (And Jacob put up those branches in the
troughs, where the water was poured out, so that when
the flocks would come to drink,)
39 they should have the rods before their eyes, and
they should conceive in [the] sight of the rods. And it
was done that in that heat of riding, *or engendering*, the
sheep should behold those rods, and that they should
bring forth spotted beasts, and diverse, and besprinkled
with diverse colour. (they would have the branches
before their eyes, and they would conceive in front of the
branches. And so it was done that in the heat of riding, *or
of begetting*, the sheep saw those branches, and later
they brought forth beasts that were spotted, and diverse,
and besprinkled with diverse colour, *like the branches
were*.)
40 And Jacob separated the flock, and put the rods in
the [water] troughs, before the eyes of the rams (And so
Jacob separated out the flock, and put up the branches in
the water troughs, before the eyes of the rams). Soothly
all the white and [the] black were Laban's; soothly all the
others were Jacob's; for the flocks were separated (out)
betwixt themselves.
41 Therefore when the sheep were ridden in the first
time, Jacob put the rods in the water troughs before the
eyes of rams, and of *ewe* sheep, that they should
conceive in the sight of the rods. (And so when the sheep
were ridden by the stronger rams, Jacob put up the
branches in the water troughs before the eyes of the
rams, and the *ewe* sheep, so that they would conceive in
front of the branches.)
42 Forsooth when the late mixing, *or engendering*, and
the last conceivings were, Jacob put not (up) those rods;
and those that were late *engendered*, were made Laban's,
and those that were of the first time *engendered*, were
Jacob's. (But when the weaker rams mated, Jacob did not
put up the branches; and so the weaker offspring were
made Laban's, and the stronger ones were made Jacob's.)
43 And Jacob was made full rich, and had many flocks,
handmaids, and menservants, camels, and asses. (And
Jacob was made very rich, and had many flocks, and
male and female slaves, and camels, and donkeys.)

CHAPTER 31

1 After that, Jacob heard the words of the sons of
Laban, that said, Jacob hath taken away all things that
were our father's, and of his chattel Jacob is made rich,
and noble (and Jacob was made rich, and noble, out of
our father's possessions).
2 Also Jacob perceived the face of Laban, that it was
not against him as yesterday, and the third day ago, (And
Jacob saw that Laban's face was not favourable toward
him, like it was yesterday, and the third day ago,)
3 mostly for the Lord (had) said to Jacob, Turn again
into the land of thy fathers, and to thy generation (Return
to the land of thy fathers, and to thy kindred), and I shall
be with thee.
4 (And so) Jacob sent (for), and called Rachel and Leah
(out) into the field, where he kept [the] flocks,
5 and he said to them, I see the face of your father,
that it is not against me as yesterday, and the third day
ago; but God of my father was with me. (and he said to
them, I see that your father's face is not favourable
toward me, like it was yesterday, and the third day ago;
but the God of my father is with me.)
6 And ye know that with all my strengths I have
served your father;
7 but and your father hath deceived me, and changed
my meed ten times; and nevertheless God suffered not
him to harm me. (but your father hath deceived me, and
changed my reward ten times; but God hath not allowed
him to harm me.)
8 If he said any time (If any time he said), Diverse(ly)-
coloured sheep shall be thy meed, all the sheep brought

forth diverse(ly)-coloured lambs; forsooth when he said,
on the contrary, Thou shalt take all the white for thy
meed, all the flocks brought forth white beasts;
9 and God took away the substance of your father
(and so God took away your father's property), and gave
it to me.
10 For after that the time of conceiving of sheep came, I
raised [up] mine eyes, and saw in sleep males diverse,
and spotty, and of diverse colours, going up on females.
(For when the time of conceiving for the sheep came, I
raised up my eyes, and saw in my sleep males diverse,
and spotted, and of diverse colours, going up on the
females.)
11 And the angel of the Lord said to me in sleep, Jacob!
and I answered, I am ready (I am here).
12 Which said, Raise [up] thine eyes, and see all [the]
males (that be) diverse, [and] besprinkled, and spotty (and
spotted), going [up] on [the] females; for I have seen all
things which Laban hath done to thee;
13 I am (the) God of Bethel, where thou anointedest a
stone, and madest a vow to me. Now therefore rise thou
(up), and go out of this land, and turn again into the land
of thy birth (and return to the land of thy birth).
14 And Rachel and Leah answered, Whether we have
anything residue, *or left*, in the chattels, and heritage of
our father? (And Rachel and Leah asked, Is there anything
left here for us, among our father's possessions, yea of
our inheritance?)
15 Whether he areckoned not, *or held*, us (as) aliens,
and sold (us), and ate our price? (Did he not treat us like
foreigners, *or like strangers*, and sell us, and then eat up
all the money that was paid for us?)
16 But God took away the riches of our father, and
gave those to us, and to our sons; wherefore do thou all
things which God hath commanded to thee.
17 Forsooth Jacob rose, and put his free children and
wives on camels, and went forth; (So Jacob rose up, and
put his children and his wives on camels, and went forth;)
18 and he took all his cattle, (and his) flocks, and
whatever thing he had gotten in Mesopotamia (and
whatever he had gotten in Paddan-aram), and went (back)
to Isaac, his father, into the land of Canaan.
19 In that time Laban went to shear sheep, and Rachel
stole the idols of her father. (Now at that time Laban went
out to shear sheep, and *while he was away*, Rachel stole
her father's household idols.)
20 And Jacob would not acknowledge to the father of
his wives, that he would flee;
21 and when he had gone, as well he as all things that
were of his right, and when he had passed [over] the
water, and he went against the hill of Gilead, (and so
when he had gone forth, he as well as all of the things
that were rightfully his, and when he had crossed over
the Euphrates River, and had gone toward the hill country
of Gilead,)
22 it was told to Laban, in the third day, that Jacob fled.
(Laban learned, on the third day, that Jacob had fled.)
23 And Laban took his brethren [with him], and
pursued him seven days, and [over]took him in the hill of
Gilead. (And Laban took his kinsmen with him, and
pursued Jacob for seven days, and finally overtook him in
the hill country of Gilead.)
24 And Laban saw in sleep the Lord saying to him,
Beware that thou speak not anything sharply against Jacob.
25 And then Jacob had stretched forth the tabernacle in
the hill; and when Laban had followed Jacob with his
brethren, Laban set a tent in the same hill of Gilead; (And
Jacob had pitched his tent in the hill country of Gilead;
and when Laban and his kinsmen caught up to him,
Laban pitched his tent on the same hill;)
26 and he said to Jacob, Why hast thou done so, that
the while I knew not, thou wouldest drive away my
daughters as captives, *either (as those) taken prisoners*, by
sword? (and then he said to Jacob, Why hast thou done
this, that while I knew not, thou hast driven away my
daughters like captives, *or like prisoners,* taken with the
sword?)
27 Why wouldest thou flee the while I knew not,
neither wouldest show (it) to me, that I should follow
thee with joy, and songs, and tympans, and harps? (Why
didest thou flee while I knew not, nor toldest me first, so
that I could send thee on thy way with joy, and with
songs, and tambourines, and harps?)
28 Thou sufferedest not that I should kiss my sons and
daughters; thou hast wrought follily. (Thou hast not
allowed me to kiss good-bye my grandsons and my
daughters; yea, thou hast done foolishly.)
29 And now soothly mine hand may yield evil to thee
(And now truly my hand should yield evil to thee), but
the God of thy father said to me yesterday, Beware that
thou speak not any hard thing with Jacob.
30 Suppose, if thou covetedest to go to thy kinsmen,
and the house of thy father was in desire to thee, why
hast thou stolen my gods? (And even if thou covetedest to
go to thy kinsmen, and thou desiredest to return to thy
father's house, why hast thou stolen my household gods?)
31 Jacob answered, That I went forth while thou
knewest not, I dreaded lest thou wouldest take away thy
daughters *from me* violently; (And Jacob answered, I
went away while thou knewest not, for I feared that thou
wouldest violently take away thy daughters *from me*;)
32 soothly that thou reprovest me of theft, at whomever
thou findest thy gods, be he slain before our brethren;
seek thou, (for) whatever thing of thine (that) thou findest
at me, and take it away (but for thou hast accused me of
theft, yea, with whomever thou findest thy gods, be he
killed here before all our kinsmen; seek thou, and
whatever thing of thine that thou findest with me, take it

away). Jacob said these things, and knew not that Rachel
had stolen the idols.
33 And so Laban entered into the tabernacle(s) of Jacob,
and of Leah, and of ever either menial, and he found not;
and when Laban had entered into the tent of Rachel,
(And so Laban entered into the tents of Jacob, and of
Leah, and of both slave-girls, but he did not find the
idols; but before Laban entered into Rachel's tent,)
34 she hasted, and hid the idols under the strewings of
the camel, and she sat above. (she hastened, and hid the
idols in the camel-bag, and then she sat upon them.)
35 And she said to Laban, seeking (throughout) all the
tent, and finding nothing, My lord, be (thou) not wroth
that I may not rise (up) before thee, for it befelled now to
me by the custom of women (for it hath befallen now to
me by the custom of women); so the busyness of the
seeker was scorned.
36 And Jacob swelled, and said with strife, For what
cause of me, and for what sin of me, hast thou come so
fiercely after me, (And Jacob swelled with anger, and
said, What have I done, and what have I sinned, that
thou shouldest come after me so fiercely,)
37 and hast sought (through) all the purtenance of mine
house(hold)? What hast thou found of all the chattel of
thine house(hold)? Put thou here before my brethren and
thy brethren, and deem they betwixt me and thee (Put
thou it here before my kinsmen and thy kinsmen, and let
them judge between me and thee).
38 Was I (not) with thee therefore twenty years? (Was I
not with thee for twenty years?) Thy sheep and (thy) goats
were not barren, I ate not the rams of thy flock,
39 neither I showed to thee anything taken of a beast; I
yielded all [the] harm; whatever thing perished by theft,
thou askedest of me; (I never showed thee anything
caught by a beast; I even yielded to thee for any harm
that was done; yea, whatever thing perished by theft,
thou askedest for it from me, *and thou received it*;)
40 I was anguished in day and night with heat and
frost, and sleep fled from mine eyes;
41 so I served thee by twenty years in thine house (but I
served thee for twenty years in thy household), fourteen
years for thy daughters, and six years for thy flocks; and
thou changedest my meed ten times.
42 But if [the] God of my father Abraham, and the
dread of Isaac had not helped me, peradventure now
thou haddest left me naked; the Lord hath beheld my
tormenting and the travail of mine hands, and reproved
thee yesterday (and yesterday rebuked thee).
43 Laban answered to Jacob, The daughters, and the
sons, and the flocks, and all things which thou seest, be
mine; what may I do to my sons, and to the sons of my
sons? (but now, what can I do about my daughters, or the
children to whom they have given birth?)
44 Therefore come thou, and make we bond of peace,
that it be a witnessing betwixt me and thee. (And so
come thou, and let us make a covenant, and let it be a
witness between me and thee.)
45 And so Jacob took a stone, and raised it (up) into a
title, *either a sign*, (And so Jacob took a stone, and set it
up as a sacred pillar,)
46 and said to his brethren, Bring ye stones; which
gathered, and made an heap, and ate on it. (and said to
his kinsmen, Bring ye some stones; and they gathered
some, and made a heap, *or a pile*, out of them, and then
they ate a meal beside it.)
47 And Laban called it The heap of witness, and Jacob
called it The heap of witnessing; ever either called it by
the property of his (own) language. (And Laban called it
Jegarsahadutha, and Jacob called it Galeed; each named
it in his own language.)
48 And Laban said, This heap shall be (a) witness
betwixt me and thee today, and therefore the name
thereof was called Galeed, *that is, The heap of witness.*
49 And Laban added, The Lord behold, and deem
betwixt us, when we shall go away from you;
50 if thou shalt torment my daughters, and if thou shalt
bring in other wives on them, none is witness of our
word, except God, which is present, and beholdeth. (if
thou shalt torment my daughters, or if thou shalt take
other wives besides them, no one is a witness of our
word, except God, who is present here, and beholdeth
all of this.)
51 And again Laban said to Jacob, Lo! this heap, and
the stone, (*or the pillar*,) which I have raised (up) betwixt
me and thee,
52 shall be witness(es); soothly this heap, and the stone
be into witnessing (this heap, and the stone, shall be
witnesses for both of us), forsooth if I shall pass (over) it,
and go to thee, either (if) thou shalt pass (over) it, and
think (to do) evil to me.
53 God of Abraham, and God of Nahor, [the] God of
the father of them, deem betwixt us. Therefore Jacob
swore by the dread of his father Isaac;
54 and when slain sacrifices were offered (there) in the
hill (country), Jacob called his brethren to eat bread
(Jacob called his kinsmen to eat with him), and when
they had eaten, they dwelled there (all night).
55 Forsooth Laban rose by night, and kissed his sons,
and daughters, and blessed them, and turned again into
his place. (And the next day, Laban rose up early, and
kissed his grandsons, and his daughters, and blessed
them, and then returned to his home.)

CHAPTER 32

1 Forsooth Jacob went forth in the way in which he
began (And Jacob went forth on the way in which he
began), and the angels of the Lord met him.
2 And when he had seen them, he said, These be the

castles of God (These be the companies of God/This is
God's camp); and he called the name of that place
Mahanaim.
3 Soothly Jacob sent before him also messengers to
Esau, his brother, into the land of Seir, in the country of
Edom; (And Jacob sent messengers on before him to his
brother Esau, who was in the land of Seir, in the country
of Edom;)
4 and he commanded to them, and said, Thus speak
ye to my lord Esau, (and say,) Thy brother Jacob saith
these things, I have been a pilgrim at Laban (I have been
living with Laban), and I was (there) till into this present
day;
5 I have oxen, and asses, and sheep, and menservants,
and handmaids, and I send now a message to my lord,
that I find grace in thy sight. (I have oxen, and donkeys,
and sheep, and male and female slaves, and I have sent
this message to my lord, so that I may find grace in thy
sight.)
6 And the messengers turned again to Jacob, and said,
We came to Esau, thy brother, and lo! he hasteth him into
thy coming, with four hundred men. (And the messengers
returned to Jacob, and said, We came to thy brother Esau,
and told him your message, and lo! now he hasteneth
himself to come to meet thee, with four hundred men.)
7 Jacob dreaded greatly, and he was afeared, and he
parted the people that was with him, and he parted the
flocks, and sheep, and oxen, and camels, into two
companies; (And Jacob greatly feared, and he was afraid,
and so he divided all the people who were with him, as
well as the flocks, and sheep, and oxen, and camels, into
two groups;)
8 and he said, If Esau shall come to one company, and
shall smite it, the other company which is left *unsmitten*,
shall be saved. (and he said, If Esau shall come to one
group, and shall strike them down, the other group which
is left, shall be able to escape.)
9 And Jacob said, O! God of my father Abraham, and
God of my father Isaac, O! Lord, that saidest to me, Turn
thou again into thy land, and to the place of thy birth,
and I shall do well to thee (O! Lord, who saidest to me,
Return thou to thy land, and to the place of thy birth, and
I shall deal well with thee),
10 I am less than all thy merciful doings, and than (all)
thy truth which thou hast [ful]filled to thy servant; with
(only) my staff I passed (over) this Jordan, and now I go
(back over) again with two companies; (I am not worthy
of all thy merciful doings, and all thy faithfulness which
thou hast shown to thy servant; for I crossed over this
Jordan River with only my staff, and now I go back again
with these two plentiful groups;)
11 deliver thou me from the hand of my brother Esau,
for I dread him greatly (for I greatly fear him), lest he
come and smite (me, and) the mothers with the sons.
12 Thou spakest that thou shouldest do well to me, and
wouldest alarge my seed as [the] gravel of the sea, that
may not be numbered for muchliness. (Thou saidest that
thou wouldest deal well with me, and that thou wouldest
enlarge my descendants like the gravel, *or like the sand*, of
the sea, that cannot be counted for all of its muchliness.)
13 And when Jacob had slept there in that night, he
separated of those things which he had, (as) gifts to Esau,
his brother, (And after Jacob had slept there that night, he
separated out from the things which he had, as gifts for
his brother Esau,)
14 two hundred (she) goats, and twenty bucks of goats,
(and) two hundred sheep, and twenty rams,
15 camels full with their foals thirty, forty kine, and
twenty bulls, twenty she-asses, and [the] ten foals of them.
(thirty milk camels with their foals, forty cows, and twenty
bulls, and twenty female donkeys, and their ten foals.)
16 And he sent by the hands of his servants all the
flocks by themselves; and he said to his servants, Go ye
before me, and (let) a space be betwixt (a) flock and (a)
flock.
17 And he commanded to the former, and said, If thou
shalt meet my brother Esau, and he shall ask thee, whose
man thou art, or whither thou goest, or whose be these
things which thou followest, (And he commanded to the
first servant, and said, When thou shalt meet my brother
Esau, and he shall ask thee, Whose man art thou? and
where goest thou? and whose things be these which thou
followest?)
18 thou shalt answer, (They be) Of thy servant Jacob;
he hath sent (them as) gifts to his lord Esau, and he
cometh after us.
19 In like manner, he gave commandments to the
second, and to the third (he gave the same orders to the
second, and the third servants), and to all that followed
the flocks; and said, Speak ye by the same words to Esau,
when ye find him,
20 and ye shall add, Also Jacob himself thy servant
followeth our way (and ye shall add, And thy servant
Jacob himself followeth on our way). For Jacob said, I
shall please Esau with (the) gifts that go before (me), and
(then) afterward I shall see him; in hap he shall be
merciful to me.
21 And so the gifts went before him; soothly he
dwelled in that night in the tents.
22 And when Jacob had risen hastily, he took his two
wives, and so many handmaids, with (his) eleven sons,
and he passed (over) the ford of Jabbok. (And during the
night Jacob rose up, and hastily he took his two wives,
and the two slave-girls, and his eleven sons, and they all
crossed over the ford of Jabbok, *or the Jabbok Crossing*.)
23 And when all things that pertained to him were led
over, (And then he returned, and saw that everything had
been taken over,)

24 (and) Jacob dwelled (there) alone, and, lo! a man
(came, and) wrestled with him till to the morrowtide.
25 And when the man saw that he might not overcome
Jacob, he touched the sinew of Jacob's hip, and it dried
anon (and it dried up at once).
26 And he said to Jacob, Let go thou me, for the
morrowtide goeth up now. Jacob answered, I shall not
let go thee, no but thou bless me. (And he said to Jacob,
Let me go, for the morning cometh now. And Jacob
answered, I shall not let thee go, unless thou bless me.)
27 Therefore he said, What name is to thee? (And) He
answered, Jacob.
28 And the man said, Thy name shall no more be
called Jacob, but Israel; for if thou were strong against
God, how much more shalt thou have power against men.
29 Jacob asked him, Say thou to me by what name thou
art called? He answered, Why askest thou my name,
which is wonderful? And he blessed Jacob in the same
place. (And Jacob said to him, Tell thou to me by what
name thou art called. And he answered, Why askest
thou my name? And then he blessed Jacob there.)
30 And Jacob called the name of that place Penuel, and
said, I saw the Lord face to face, and my life is made safe.
(And Jacob named that place Peniel, *or The face of God,*
saying, For I saw the Lord face to face, and yet my life
was spared.)
31 And anon the sun rose to him, after that he had
passed (over from) Penuel; forsooth he halted in the foot.
(And the sun rose up as he left Peniel; and he limped
because of his hip.)
32 For which cause the sons of Israel eat not unto this
present day the sinew, (like that) that dried in the hip of
Jacob (For this reason, the Israelites do not eat the sinew,
like that which dried up in Jacob's hip, unto this present
day); for the man touched the sinew of Jacob's hip, and it
dried (up).

CHAPTER 33

1 Forsooth Jacob raised up his eyes, and saw Esau
coming, and four hundred men with him; and he parted
the sons of Leah, and of Rachel, and of both the
servantesses (and he divided the children between Leah,
and Rachel, and the two slave-girls).
2 And he put ever either handmaid, and the free
children of them, in the beginning (And he put the slave-
girls, and their children, at the front); soothly he put Leah,
and her sons, in the second place; forsooth he put Rachel
and Joseph (at) the last.
3 And Jacob went before (them), and worshipped
lowly to the earth seven times (and bowed low to the
ground seven times), till his brother nighed.
4 And so Esau ran against his brother (And Esau ran to
meet his brother), and embraced him, and Esau held his
neck, and kissed him, and (they) wept (together).
5 And when *Esau's* eyes were raised up, he saw the
women, and the little children of them, and said, What
will these (mean) to themselves? and whether they
pertain to thee? (And when *Esau* raised up his eyes, he
saw the women, and their little children, and he said,
Who be these? do they pertain to thee?) Jacob answered,
They be the little children, which God hath given to me,
thy servant.
6 And the handmaids and their sons nighed, and were
bowed. (And the slave-girls and their sons came near,
and they bowed.)
7 Also Leah nighed with her free children; and when
they had worshipped in like manner, Joseph and Rachel
last worshipped. (And Leah came near with her children;
and when they had bowed before him in like manner,
then lastly Joseph and Rachel bowed before him.)
8 And Esau said, What be these companies, which I
met? And Jacob answered, (So) That I should find grace
before my lord.
9 And he said, My brother, I have full many things,
thy things be to thee.
10 And Jacob said, I beseech thee, do not thou (say) so,
but if I have found grace in thine eyes, take thou a little
gift of mine hands; for I saw so thy face as (though) I had
seen the cheer of God; be thou merciful to me, (And
Jacob said, I beseech thee, do not thou say that, but if I
have found grace in thine eyes, take thou a little gift from
my hands; for I see thy face as if I see the face of God; be
thou merciful to me,)
11 and receive the blessing which I have brought to
thee, and which blessing God giving all things gave to
me. Scarcely (desiring it), while the brother compelled
(him), he received (it), (and receive the blessing which I
have brought to thee, which blessing God, who giveth all
things, hath given to me. Scarcely desiring it, but
because his brother compelled him, Esau at last accepted
the gifts,)
12 and said, Go we together, and I shall be (a) fellow of
thy way. (and he said, Now let us go together, and I shall
give thee fellowship on the way.)
13 And Jacob said, My lord, thou knowest that I have
little children tender, and sheep, and kine with calves
with me, and if I shall make them for to travail more in
going, all the flocks shall die in one day; (But Jacob said,
My lord, thou knowest that I have tender little children
with me, and sheep, and cows with their calves, and if I
make them go any further this day, all the flocks shall die;)
14 my lord go (on) before his servant, and I shall follow
little and little his steps (and I shall follow his steps little
and little), as I see that my little children be able (to go),
till I come to my lord, into Seir.
15 Esau answered, I pray thee, that (some) of the people
which is with me, dwell they namely fellows of thy way.
Jacob said, It is no need; I have need to this one thing

only, that I find grace in thy sight, my lord. (Esau
answered, Then I pray thee, let some of the people who
be with me give thee fellowship on the way. But Jacob
said, There is no need; yea, I only have need of this one
thing, that I find grace in thine eyes, my lord.)
16 And so Esau turned again in that day in the way by
which he came, into Seir. (And so Esau returned that day
by the way by which he came, back toward Seir.)
17 And Jacob came into Succoth, where when he had
builded an house, and had set tents, he called the name
of that place Succoth, *that is, tabernacles.* (But Jacob
went to Succoth, where when he had built a house, and
some shelters for his beasts, he called that place Succoth,
or Shelters.)
18 And Jacob passed into Shalem, a city of Shechem,
which is in the land of Canaan, after that he turned again
from Mesopotamia of Syria, and he dwelled beside the
city. (And then Jacob passed safely into the city of
Shechem, which is in the land of Canaan, after that he
had returned from Paddan-aram, and he lived there in a
field beside the city.)
19 And he bought for an hundred lambs a part of the
field, in which he set tabernacles, of the sons of Hamor,
the father of Shechem. (And he bought part of that field
from the sons of Hamor, the father of Shechem, for a
hundred lambs, *or for a hundred pieces of money,* and
he pitched his tents there.)
20 And when he had raised an altar there, he inwardly
called on it the full strong God of Israel. (And when he
had raised up an altar there, he called it Elelohe-Israel.)

CHAPTER 34

1 Forsooth Dinah, the daughter of Leah, went out to
see the women of that country.
2 And when Shechem, the son of Hamor (the) Hivite,
the prince of that land, had seen her, he loved her, and
he ravished her, and (he) slept with her, and oppressed
the virgin by violence (and he oppressed the virgin with
violence).
3 And his soul was bound fast with her, and he pleased
her sorry with flatterings. (But his soul was bound fast to
her, and he tried to appease her sorrow with flattery.)
4 And he went to Hamor, his father, and said, Take to
me this damsel (for) a wife. (And he went to his father
Hamor, and said, Get me this young woman for a wife.)
5 And when Jacob had heard this thing, while his sons
were absent, and occupied in the feeding/in the pasturing
of [the] sheep, he was still, till they came again (until they
returned home).
6 Soothly when Hamor, the father of Shechem, was
gone out to speak to Jacob,
7 lo! his sons came from the field. And when this
thing that befelled was heard, they were wroth greatly;
for he had wrought a foul thing in Israel, and he had
done a thing unleaveful in the defouling of the daughter
of Jacob. (lo! his sons came in from the field. And when
they heard what had befallen, they were enraged; for
Shechem had done a foul, *or a vile,* thing in Israel, and
he had done an unlawful thing in the defiling of Jacob's
daughter.)
8 And so Hamor spake to them (And Hamor said to
them), The soul of my son Shechem hath cleaved to your
daughter; give ye her (for) a wife to him,
9 and (so) join we weddings together; give ye your
daughters to us, and take ye our daughters (for yourselves),
10 and dwell ye with us; (yea,) the land is in your
power; till ye, and make ye merchandise, and wield ye it
(work ye it, and make ye merchandise, and possess ye it).
11 But also Shechem said to the father and brethren of
her, Find I grace before you, and whatever things ye
ordain I shall give; (And Shechem said to her father and
her brothers, I pray that I find grace before you, and
whatever things ye ask for, I shall give you;)
12 increase ye the dower, and ask ye (for) gifts, and I
shall give willfully that that ye ask; only give ye this
damsel (for) a wife to me. (increase ye the dowry, and ask
ye for gifts, and I shall willingly give what ye ask; only
give ye to me this young woman for a wife.)
13 The sons of Jacob answered in guile to Shechem and
(to Hamor,) his father, and *they* were (made) fierce for the
defouling of the maidenhood of their sister, (And Jacob's
sons answered guilefully, *or deceitfully,* to Shechem, and
to his father Hamor, for *they* were enraged by the defiling
of their sister's maidenhood,)
14 We may not do this that ye ask, neither we may give
our sister to a man uncircumcised, which thing is
unleaveful and abominable with us. (and they said, We
cannot do this thing that ye ask, for we cannot give our
sister to an uncircumcised man, for such a thing is
unlawful and abominable with us.)
15 But in this we shall be able to be bound in peace, if
ye will be like us, and each of male kind be circumcised
in you; (But by this we shall make a covenant with thee,
if ye will be made like us, and each of your males be
circumcised;)
16 then we shall give and take together our daughters
and yours (then we shall give our daughters to you, and
we shall take your daughters for ourselves); and we shall
dwell with you, and we shall be one people.
17 Forsooth if ye will not be circumcised, (then) we
shall take our daughter, and we shall go away.
18 The proffering of them pleased Hamor, and
Shechem, his son, (And their proffer pleased Hamor, and
his son Shechem,)
19 and the young waxing man delayed not, that not he
fulfilled anon that that was asked; for he loved the damsel
greatly, and he was (the most) noble in all the house of
his father. (and the young man delayed not, but he

fulfilled at once what was asked for; for he greatly loved
the young woman, and he was the most noble in all of
his father's household.)
20 And they entered into the gate of the city, and spake
to the people, (And so they went to the city gate, and said
to the people,)
21 These men be peaceable, and will dwell with us;
make they merchandise in the land, and till they it, which
is large and broad, and hath need to tillers; we shall take
their daughters to wives, and we shall give our daughters
to them. (These men be peaceful, and will live with us;
so let them make merchandise in the land, and let them
work it, which is large and broad, and hath need of men
to work it; and we shall take their daughters for our
wives, and we shall give our daughters to them.)
22 One thing is, for which so great good is delayed; if
we circumcise our males, and follow the custom of the
folk, (But before that they will live with us, and we
become one people, there is one thing which they
require us to do; we must first circumcise all our males,
and so follow this folk's custom,)
23 both their substance, and sheep, and all things
which they wield, shall be ours; only assent we in this,
that we dwell together, and make one people. (then their
chattel, and sheep, and all the things which they possess,
shall be ours; so let us assent in this matter, so that we
can all live together, and be one people.)
24 And all (the) men assented, and (so) all [the] males
were circumcised.
25 And lo! in the third day, when the sorrow of [the]
wounds was most grievous, two sons of Jacob, Simeon
and Levi, [the] brethren of Dinah, took swords, and
entered into the city boldly; and when all [the] males
were slain, (And lo! on the third day, when the pain from
their wounds was most grievous, two of Jacob's sons,
Simeon and Levi, Dinah's brothers, took swords, and
boldly entered into the city, and killed all the males;)
26 they killed Hamor and Shechem together, and took
Dinah, their sister, from the house of Shechem. And
when they were gone out, (and they killed Hamor and
Shechem, and took away their sister Dinah from
Shechem's house. And when they had left the city,)
27 [the] other sons of Jacob felled in on the slain men,
and rifled the city, for the vengeance of [the] defouling of
the virgin (to take vengeance for their sister's defiling).
28 And they wasted the sheep of those men, and
droves of oxen, and asses, and all things that were in the
houses and fields, (And they destroyed the sheep of those
men, and their herds of oxen, and their donkeys, and all
the things that were in their houses and in their fields,)
29 and (they) led *away* (as) prisoners the little children,
and [the] wives of those men. And when these things
were done hardily (And when these things were fully
done),
30 Jacob said to Simeon and Levi, Ye have troubled
me, and have made me hateful to (the) Canaanites and
Perizzites, [the] dwellers of this land; we be few, [and]
they shall be gathered together (against me), and shall
slay me, and I shall be done away, and mine house.
(Jacob said to Simeon and Levi, Ye have brought in
trouble on me, and have made me *to be* hated by the
Canaanites and the Perizzites, the inhabitants of this land;
yea, we be few, and now they shall be gathered together
against me, and shall slay me, and I and all of my
household, *or all of my family*, shall be done away.)
31 Simeon and Levi answered, Whether they ought to
mis-use our sister as a whore? (And Simeon and Levi
answered, Should they be allowed to mis-use our sister
like a whore?)

CHAPTER 35

1 In the meantime the Lord spake to Jacob, (and said),
Rise thou (up), and go up to Bethel, and dwell there; and
make thou (there) an altar to the Lord, that appeared to
thee when thou fleddest Esau, thy brother (who appeared
to thee when thou fleddest from thy brother Esau).
2 Soothly Jacob said, when all his house was called
together, Cast ye away alien gods, that be in the midst of
you, and be ye cleansed, and change ye your clothes;
(And Jacob said, when all his household, *or all his family*,
was called together, Throw ye away the foreign gods, that
be in the midst of you, and purify yourselves, and change
ye your clothes;)
3 rise ye, and go we up into Bethel, that we make
there an altar to the Lord, which heard me in the day of
my tribulation, and was fellow of my way. (rise ye, and
go we up to Bethel, to make there an altar to the Lord,
who answered me on the day of my trouble, and who
gave me fellowship on the way.)
4 Therefore they gave to Jacob all the alien gods
which they had, and [the] earrings, that were in their ears;
and Jacob delved them under a terebinth tree, which is
behind the city of Shechem. (And so they gave Jacob all
the foreign gods which they had, and the earrings that
they were wearing; and Jacob buried them under the
terebinth tree, which is behind the city of Shechem.)
5 And when they went (forth), dread assailed all men
by compass of the city, and they were not hardy to
pursue them going away. (And when they went forth, the
fear *of God* assailed all the men of the cities about, and
they were not hardy to pursue after them.)
6 Therefore Jacob came to Luz, which is in the land of
Canaan, by the sire-name Bethel, he and all his people
with him. (And so Jacob came to Luz, that is, Bethel, in
the land of Canaan, he and all the people who were with
him.)
7 And he builded there an altar to the Lord, and called
the name of that place The house of God, for God

appeared there to him, when he fled his brother. (And he
built there an altar to the Lord, and called the name of
that place El-bethel, for God appeared to him there, when
he fled from his brother.)
8 Deborah, the nurse of Rebecca, died in the same
time, and she was buried at the root[s] of Bethel, under
an oak, and the name of the place was called The Oak of
Weeping. (And Deborah, Rebecca's nurse, died at that
time, and she was buried south of Bethel, under an oak
tree, and that place was called Allonbachuth.)
9 Forsooth God appeared again to Jacob, after that he
turned again from Mesopotamia of Syria, and came into
Bethel, and blessed him, (And God appeared again to
Jacob, after that he had returned from Paddan-aram, and
he blessed him,)
10 and (he) said, Thou shalt no more be called Jacob,
but Israel shall be thy name. And (so) God called him
Israel,
11 and said to him, I am God Almighty (and he said to
him, I am Almighty God); increase thou, and be thou
multiplied, (yea,) folks and peoples of nations shall be of
thee, (and) kings shall go out of thy loins;
12 and I shall give to thee, and to thy seed after thee,
the land which I gave to Abraham and Isaac.
13 And (then) God departed from him.
14 Forsooth Jacob raised (up) a title, *or a memorial*, of
stones, in the place wherein God spake to him, and he
sacrificed thereon flowing sacrifices, and shedded out oil,
(And Jacob raised up a stone pillar, in the place where
God spoke to him, and he offered a sacrifice of wine on
it, and poured oil on it,)
15 and he called the name of that place Bethel.
16 Soothly Jacob went out from thence, and he came in
the beginning of summer to the land that leadeth to
Ephratah; in which land when Rachel travailed in child
bearing, (And Jacob went out from there, and at the
beginning of summer he came to the way that leadeth to
Ephrath; in which land when Rachel struggled, *or
laboured*, to survive while giving birth,)
17 she began to be in peril for the hardness of (the)
childbearing; and the midwife said to her, Do not thou
dread, for thou shalt have also this son (and the midwife
said to her, Do not thou fear, for thou shalt also have this
son/for this is another son for you).
18 Forsooth while the soul passed *from her* for sorrow,
and death nighed then, she called the name of her son
Benoni, *that is, the son of my sorrow*; forsooth his father
called him Benjamin, *that is, the son of the right side.*
(But as her soul passed away *from her*, and death neared,
she named her son Benoni, *that is, The son of my sorrow*;
but his father called him Benjamin, *that is, The son of my
right hand.*)
19 Therefore Rachel died, and was buried in the way
that leadeth to Ephratah, that is Bethlehem. (And so
Rachel died, and was buried on the way that leadeth to
Ephrath, which is Bethlehem.)
20 And Jacob builded a memorial upon the sepulchre
of her; this is the memorial of the burial of Rachel unto
this present day. (And Jacob put up a sacred pillar on her
sepulchre; this is the same pillar that is on Rachel's grave
unto this present day.)
21 Jacob went from thence, and setted a tabernacle
over the tower of the flock. (And then Jacob went from
there, and pitched his tent beyond the tower of
Eder/beyond Migdaleder.)
22 And while he dwelled in that country, Reuben went,
and slept with Bilhah, the secondary wife of his father,
which thing was not hid from him (which was told to
Jacob). Forsooth the sons of Jacob were twelve;
23 the sons of Leah were, the first begotten Reuben
(Leah's sons were Reuben, the first-born), and Simeon,
and Levi, and Judah, and Issachar, and Zebulun;
24 the sons of Rachel were Joseph, and Benjamin;
25 the sons of Bilhah, the handmaid of Rachel (Rachel's
slave-girl), were Dan, and Naphtali;
26 and the sons of Zilpah, [the] handmaid of Leah,
were Gad, and Asher. These were the sons of Jacob, that
were born to him in Mesopotamia of Syria. (and the sons
of Zilpah, Leah's slave-girl, were Gad, and Asher. These
were Jacob's sons, who were born to him in Paddan-aram.)
27 Also Jacob came to Isaac, his father, into Mamre,
(by) the city of Arbah, this is Hebron, in which *Mamre*
Abraham and Isaac was a pilgrim. (And Jacob came to his
father Isaac at Mamre, which is near to Kiriatharba, which
is now called Hebron, in which *Mamre* Abraham and
Isaac were foreigners.)
28 And the days of Isaac were filled an hundred and
fourscore of years; (And so the days of Isaac filled a
hundred and eighty years;)
29 and he was wasted in age, and died, and he was put
to his people, and was eld, and full of days; and Esau and
Jacob his sons buried him. (and then he was destroyed by
age, and died, and he joined his ancestors, being old,
and full of days; and his sons Esau and Jacob buried him.)

CHAPTER 36

1 Forsooth these be the generations of Esau; he is (also
called) Edom.
2 Esau took wives[15] of the daughters of Canaan; Adah,
the daughter of Elon (the) Hittite, and Oholibamah (and
Aholibamah), the daughter of Anah, the son of Zibeon
(the) Hivite;
3 also Bashemath (and Bashemath), the daughter of
Ishmael, the sister of Nebajoth.

[15] Each of Esau's three wives were known by two names: Adah, also known as Bashemath; Judith, also known as Oholibamah (Aholibamah); and another Bashemath, also known as Mahalath.

4 And Adah childed Eliphaz; Bashemath childed
Reuel;
5 Oholibamah childed Jeush, and Jaalam, and Korah
(and Aholibamah gave birth to Jeush, and Jaalam, and
Korah). These were the sons of Esau, that were born to
him in the land of Canaan.
6 Soothly Esau took his wives, and his sons, and (his)
daughters, and each soul of his house(hold), and his
cattle, and (his) sheep, and all things which he had in the
land of Canaan, and went into another country (and went
to another country), and (so) departed from his brother
Jacob;
7 for they were full rich, and they might not dwell
together, and the land of their pilgrimage sustained not
them, for the multitude of flocks. (for they were both very
rich, and they could not live together, for the land where
they now were could not sustain them both, for the
multitude of their flocks.)
8 And Esau dwelled in the hill of Seir; he is Edom.
(And so Esau lived in the hill country of Seir; he is also
called Edom.)
9 Forsooth these were the generations of Esau, father
of Edom, in the hill of Seir, (And these were the
descendants of Esau, the father of the Edomites, in the hill
country of Seir,)
10 and these were the names of his sons; Eliphaz, the
son of Adah, (the) wife of Esau, also Reuel (and Reuel),
the son of Bashemath, (the) wife of Esau.
11 And the sons of Eliphaz were Teman, Omar, Zepho,
and Gatam, and Kenaz.
12 Forsooth Timna was the secondary wife of Eliphaz,
Esau('s) son, which *Timna* childed to him Amalek (And
Timna was the concubine of Eliphaz, Esau's son, and
Timna bare Amalek for him). These were the sons of
Adah, Esau's wife.
13 Forsooth the sons of Reuel were Nahath, and Zerah,
and Shammah, and Mizzah. These were the sons of
Bashemath, Esau's wife.
14 And these were the sons of Oholibamah, the
daughter of Anah, son of Zibeon, Esau's wife, which she
childed to him; Jeush, and Jaalam, and Korah. (And these
were the sons of Esau's wife Aholibamah, the daughter of
Anah, the daughter of Zibeon, whom she bare for him;
Jeush, and Jaalam, and Korah.)
15 These were (the) dukes of the sons of Esau; the sons
of Eliphaz, the first engendered of Esau (Esau's first-born
son); duke Teman, duke Omar, duke Zepho, duke Kenaz,
16 duke Korah, duke Gatam, and duke Amalek. These
were the sons of Eliphaz, in the land of Edom, and these
were the sons of Adah.
17 Also these were the sons of Reuel, Esau's son; duke
Nahath, duke Zerah, duke Shammah, duke Mizzah;
forsooth these dukes were of Reuel, in the land of Edom.
These were the sons of Bashemath, Esau's wife. (And
these were the sons of Reuel, Esau's son; duke Nahath,
duke Zerah, duke Shammah, and duke Mizzah; these
were the leaders who came from Reuel, in the land of
Edom. These were the sons of Esau's wife Bashemath.)
18 Forsooth these were the sons of Oholibamah, Esau's
wife; duke Jeush, duke Jaalam, duke Korah; these were
[the] dukes of Oholibamah, the daughter of Anah, Esau's
wife. (And these were the sons of Esau's wife
Aholibamah; duke Jeush, duke Jaalam, and duke Korah;
these were the leaders who came from Esau's wife
Aholibamah, the daughter of Anah.)
19 These were the sons of Esau, and these were dukes
of them (and they were their leaders); he is (also called)
Edom.
20 (And) These were the sons of Seir (the) Horite,
inhabiters of the land (the people of the land); Lotan, and
Shobal, and Zibeon, and Anah,
21 and Dishon, and Ezer, and Dishan; these dukes
were of Horites (these were the leaders of the Horites),
the son[s] of Seir, in the land of Edom.
22 Forsooth the sons of Lotan were Hori, and Hemam;
soothly the sister of Lotan was Timna.
23 And these were the sons of Shobal; Alvan, and
Manahath, and Ebal, Shepho, and Onam.
24 And these were the sons of Zibeon; Ajah, and Anah;
this is Ahan that found hot waters in the wilderness,
when he kept the asses of Zibeon, his father (this is that
Ahan who found some mules in the wilderness, when he
kept the donkeys of his father Zibeon);
25 and he had a son, Dishon, and a daughter,
Oholibamah. (and Anah had a son, Dishon, and a
daughter, Aholibamah.)
26 And these were the sons of Dishon; Hemdan, and
Eshban, and Ithran, and Cheran.
27 Also these were the sons of Ezer (And these were
the sons of Ezer); Bilhan, and Zaavan, and Akan.
28 And Dishon had sons; Uz, and Aran.
29 These were the dukes of Horites (These were the
leaders of the Horites); duke Lotan, duke Shobal, duke
Zibeon, duke Anah,
30 duke Dishon, duke Ezer, duke Dishan; these were
the dukes of Horites, that were lords in the land of Seir
(duke Dishon, duke Ezer, and duke Dishan; these were
the leaders of the Horites, who were the rulers in the land
of Seir.)
31 Forsooth [the] kings that reigned in the land of
Edom, before that the sons of Israel had a king, were
these; (And the kings who reigned in the land of Edom,
before the Israelites had their own king, were these;)
32 Bela, the son of Beor, and the name of his city was
Dinhabah.
33 Forsooth Bela died, and (then) Jobab, the son of
Zerah of Bozrah, reigned for him.
34 And when Jobab was dead (And when Jobab died),

Husham of the land of Temani reigned for him.
35 And when he was dead, Hadad, the son of Bedad,
that smote Midian in the land of Moab, and the name of
his city was Avith, reigned for him. (And when Husham
died, Hadad, the son of Bedad, who struck down the
Midianites in the land of Moab, reigned for him, and the
name of his city was Avith.)
36 And when Hadad was dead (And when Hadad
died), Samlah of Masrekah reigned for him.
37 And when he was dead, Saul of the flood [of]
Rehoboth reigned for him. (And when Samlah died, Saul
from Rehoboth-on-the-River reigned for him.)
38 And when he was dead, Baalhanan, the son of
Achbor, was successor into the realm. (And when Saul
died, Baalhanan, the son of Achbor, was his successor in
the kingdom.)
39 And when he was dead (And when Baalhanan died),
Hadar reigned for him, and the name of the city of Hadar
was Pau, and the name of his wife was Mehetabel, the
daughter of Matred, the daughter of Mezahab.
40 Therefore these were the names of the dukes of Esau
(And so these were the names of the leaders of the
people of Esau), in their kindreds, and places, and (by
their) names; duke Timnah, duke Alvah, duke Jetheth,
41 duke Oholibamah (duke Aholibamah), duke Elah,
duke Pinon,
42 duke Kenaz, duke Teman, duke Mibzar,
43 duke Magdiel, duke Iram; these were the dukes of
Edom, dwelling in the land of his lordship; he was Esau,
the father of Idumeans. (duke Magdiel, and duke Iram;
these were the leaders of Edom, living in the land of their
possession; and Esau is the father of the Edomites.)

CHAPTER 37

1 Forsooth Jacob dwelled in the land of Canaan, in
which his father was a pilgrim; (And Jacob lived in the
land of Canaan, where his father was a foreigner;)
2 and these were the generations of him. Joseph
when he was of sixteen years, yet a child, kept a flock
with his brethren, and he was with the sons of Bilhah and
Zilpah, the wives of his father; and he accused his
brethren at the father of the worst sin. (and this is the
story of his descendants. Joseph, when he was seventeen
years old, yet a boy, kept a flock with his brothers, and
he was with the sons of Bilhah and Zilpah, his father's
wives; and he accused his brothers of the worst sins to
their father.)
3 Forsooth Israel loved Joseph above all his sons, for
he had begotten him in his eld (age); and he made to
Joseph a coat of many colours (and he made a coat of
many colours for Joseph).
4 Forsooth his brethren saw that he was loved of the
father more than all *they*, and they hated him, and might
not speak anything peaceably to him. (And his brothers
saw that their father loved Joseph more than he loved *any
of them*, and so they hated him, and would not say a
kind word to him.)
5 And it befelled that he told to his brethren a sweven
that he saw, which cause was the seed of more hatred.
(And it befell that he told his brothers about a dream that
he had, which was the reason, yea, the seed, of even
more hatred.)
6 And Joseph said to his brethren, Hear ye the sweven
which I saw,
7 I guessed that we bound together sheaves, *or
handfuls*, [in the field,] and that as mine handful rose up,
and stood (upright), and that your handfuls stood about,
and worshipped mine handful. (I saw that we all bound
up sheaves in the field, and when my sheaf rose up, and
stood upright, all your sheaves stood around, and bowed
before my sheaf.)
8 His brethren answered, Whether thou shalt be our
king, either we shall be made subject to thy lordship?
Therefore this cause of dreams and words ministered the
nourishing of envy, and of hatred (And so these dreams
and words were the reason that envy and hatred were
nourished among them).
9 Also Joseph saw another sweven, which he told to
his brethren, and said, I saw a dream that as the sun, and
the moon, and the eleven stars worshipped me. (And
Joseph saw another dream, which he also told to his
brothers, saying, I saw in a dream that the sun, and the
moon, and the eleven stars all bowed before me.)
10 And when he had told this dream to his father, and
his brethren, his father blamed him, and said, What will
this dream *mean* to itself that thou hast seen? Whether I,
and thy mother, and thy brethren, shall worship thee on
(the) earth? (And when he told this dream to his father,
and his brothers, his father rebuked him, and said, What
meaneth this dream that thou hast seen? Shall I, and thy
mother, and thy brothers, all bow low to the ground
before thee?)
11 Therefore his brethren had envy to him. Forsooth
the father beheld privily the thing, (And so his brothers
envied him, but his father privately considered it all.)
12 and when his brethren dwelled in Shechem, about
[the] keeping of [the] flocks of their father, (And one day,
when his brothers were tending their father's flocks in
Shechem,)
13 Israel said to Joseph, Thy brethren keep (the) sheep
in Shechem (Thy brothers tend the sheep in Shechem);
come thou, I shall send thee to them. And when Joseph
answered, I am ready,
14 Israel said, Go thou, and see whether all things be
wellsome with thy brethren, and (with) the sheep; and
(then come back, and) tell thou to me what is done. (And
so) He was sent from the valley of Hebron, and came into
Shechem;

15 and a man found him erring in the field (and a man
found him wandering in a field), and the man asked him,
what he sought.
16 And he answered, I seek my brethren; show thou to
me where they keep *their* flocks. (And he answered, I am
looking for my brothers; tell thou to me where they tend
their flocks.)
17 And the man said to him, They went away from this
place; forsooth I heard them saying, Go we into Dothan.
And Joseph went after his brethren, and found them in
Dothan.
18 And when they had seen him afar (off), before he
nighed to them, they thought to slay him (they decided to
kill him),
19 and they spake together, (and said,) Lo! the dreamer
cometh,
20 come ye, slay we him, and put we him into an eld
cistern, and we shall say, A wild beast full wicked hath
devoured him; and then it shall appear what his dreams
profit to him. (come ye, let us kill him, yea, we shall put
him into an old cistern, and we shall say, A wicked wild
beast hath devoured him; and then we shall see what his
dreams shall profit him.)
21 Soothly Reuben heard this, and endeavoured to
deliver him from their hands, and said, Slay we not the
life of him (and he said, Nay, we should not kill him),
22 neither shed we out his blood, but cast ye him into
an eld cistern, which is in the wilderness, and (so) keep
ye your hands guiltless. Forsooth he said this, desiring to
deliver him from their hands, and to yield *him* (again) to
his father.
23 Therefore anon as Joseph came to his brethren, they
despoiled him of his coat, (that went) down to the heel,
and (was) of many colours, (And so when Joseph came to
his brothers, at once they tore off the coat, that went
down to his heels, and had many colours,)
24 and they put him in[to] an eld cistern, that had no
water.
25 And (then) they sat (down) to eat bread; and (soon)
they saw that (some) Ishmaelite waygoers came from
Gilead, and that their camels bare sweet smelling
spiceries, and resin, and stacte, into Egypt (to take to
Egypt).
26 Therefore Judah said to his brethren, What shall it
profit to us, if we shall slay our brother, and shall hide his
blood? (And so Judah said to his brothers, What shall it
profit us, if we kill our brother, and then hide his blood?)
27 It is better that he be sold to (the) Ishmaelites, and
our hands be not defouled, for he is our brother and our
flesh. His brethren assented to these words;
28 and (so) when [the] merchants of Midian passed
thereforth, they drew Joseph out of the cistern, and sold
him to (the) Ishmaelites, for twenty pieces of silver; which
led him into Egypt (and they took him down to Egypt).
29 And Reuben turned again to the cistern, and found
not the child; and he rent his clothes, (And when Reuben
returned to the cistern, he did not find the boy; and he
tore his clothes,)
30 and he went to his brethren, and said, The child
appeareth not, and whither shall I go? (and he went to his
brothers, and said, The boy is gone, now what shall I do?)
31 Forsooth they took his coat, and dipped it in the
blood of a kid, which they had slain;
32 and they sent men that bare it to their father, and
said, We have found this coat; see thou, whether it is the
coat of thy son, or nay. (and they brought it to their
father, and said to him, We have found this coat; see
thou, is it thy son's coat, or not.)
33 And when the(ir) father had known it (to be such),
he said, It is the coat of my son; a wild beast full wicked
hath eaten him (a wicked wild beast must hath eaten
him); a beast hath devoured Joseph.
34 And he rent his clothes, and he was clothed with an
hair shirt, and bewailed his son in much time (and for a
long time he bewailed his son).
35 Soothly when his free children were gathered
together, that they should appease the sorrow of their
father, he would not take comfort; but said, I shall go
down into hell, and shall bewail my son. And while
Jacob continued in weeping, (And his children gathered
together, to try to appease their father's sorrow, but he
would not take comfort from them; and he said, I shall go
down into the grave/I shall go down to Sheol, bewailing
my son. And while Jacob continued weeping,)
36 (the) Midianites sold Joseph in Egypt to Potiphar, (a)
chaste and honest servant of Pharaoh [the gelding of
Pharaoh], master of the chivalry. (the Midianites now in
Egypt, sold Joseph to Potiphar, one of Pharaoh's eunuchs,
and the captain of the guard.)

CHAPTER 38

1 In the same time, Judah went down from his
brethren, and turned to a man of Adullam, Hirah by
name; (At that time, Judah went forth from his brothers,
and came to a man of Adullam, named Hirah;)
2 and he saw there a daughter of a man of Canaan,
Shuah by name. And when he had taken her to wife, he
entered [in] to her (her slept with her),
3 and she conceived, and childed a son, and (he)
called his name Er.
4 And again when an*other* child was conceived, she
named the child (that was) born, Onan.
5 And she childed the third son, whom she called
Shelah, and when he was born, she ceased to bear child
more (she ceased to bear any more children). (And she
bare her third son, whom she called Shelah, when she
was at Chezib.)
6 Soothly Judah gave a wife, that was called Tamar, to

his first begotten son Er.
7 And Er, the first begotten son of Judah, was wayward
in the sight of the Lord, and therefore he was slain of the
Lord (and so the Lord killed him).
8 Therefore Judah said to Onan, his son, Enter thou
[in] to the wife of thy brother, and be thou fellowshipped
to her, that thou raise seed to thy brother. (And so Judah
said to his son Onan, Sleep with thy brother's wife, and
be fellowshipped to her, and so raise thou up seed, *or
some sons*, for thy brother.)
9 And he knew that sons should not be born to him;
and he entered [in] to the wife of his brother, and
shedded his seed into the earth, lest the free children
should be born by the name of the *dead* brother; (But
Onan knew that any sons who would be born would not
be his; so he slept with his brother's wife, but he poured
out his seed onto the ground, so that no children would
be born in the name of his *dead* brother;)
10 and therefore the Lord smote him (and so the Lord
struck him down), for he did (an) abominable thing.
11 Wherefore Judah said to Tamar, his son's wife, Be
thou a widow in the house of thy father, till Shelah my
son waxed (until my son Shelah hath grown up); for he
dreaded lest also he should die as his brethren (did). And
(so) she went, and dwelled in the house of her father.
12 Forsooth when many years were passed, the
daughter of Shuah, Judah's wife, died; and when comfort
was taken after mourning, Judah went up to the shearers
of his sheep (After many years had passed, Judah's wife,
the daughter of Shuah, died; and after mourning her,
when comfort was taken, Judah went up to his sheep-
shearers); (yea,) he and Hirah of Adullam, *that was* [the]
keeper of the flock, *went up* into Timnath.
13 And it was told to Tamar, that her husband's father
went up into Timnath, to shear sheep.
14 And she did away the clothes of (her) widowhood,
and she took a rochet cloth with many wrinkles, and
when the clothing was changed, she sat in the way-lot
that leadeth to Timnath; for Shelah had waxed, and she
had not (yet) taken him into husband (for although Shelah
was now a grown man, she had not been given to him
for a wife).
15 And when Judah had seen her, he supposed her to
be a whore; for she had covered her face, lest she was
known.
16 And Judah entered to her, and said, Suffer me that I
lie with thee (And Judah went over to her, and said, Let
me lie with you); for he knew not that she was the wife of
his son. And when she answered, What shalt thou give
to me, that thou lie with me?
17 he said, I shall send to thee a kid of the flocks. And
again when she said, I shall suffer that that thou wilt, if
thou shalt give to me a wed, till thou send that that thou
promisest. (he said, I shall send thee a goat kid from the
flocks. And she said, I shall give thee what thou desirest,
if thou shalt give me a pledge, until thou send what thou
hast promised.)
18 Judah said, What wilt thou that be given to thee for
a wed? She answered, Thy ring, and thy band of the arm,
and the staff which thou holdest in thine hand. Therefore
the woman conceived at one lying-by, (Judah said, What
desirest thou to be given to thee for a pledge? She
answered, Thy ring, and thy arm band, and the staff
which thou holdest in thy hand. And so he gave them to
her, and lay with her, and the woman conceived in one
lying-by,)
19 and she rose (up), and went [away]; and when the
cloth was put away which she had taken, she was
clothed (once again) in the clothes of widowhood.
20 Forsooth Judah sent a kid by his shepherd of
Adullam, that he should receive the wed which he had
given to the woman; and when he had not found her,
(And Judah sent a goat kid by his shepherd from Adullam,
so that he could receive back the pledge which he had
given to the woman; and when Hirah could not find her,)
21 he asked men of that place, Where is the woman
that sat in the way-lot? And when all (the) men
answered, A whore was not in this place;
22 he turned again to Judah, and said to him, I found
not her, but also the men of that place said to me, that a
whore sat never there. (Hirah returned to Judah, and said
to him, I could not find her, and the men of that place
told me, that a whore never sat there.)
23 Judah said, Have she (those things) to herself, that
we be not despised, certainly she may not reprove us of a
leasing; I sent the kid which I promised, and thou
foundest not her. (And Judah said, Let her have those
things for herself, so that we be not despised, certainly
she cannot rebuke us for lying; I sent the goat kid which I
promised, but thou could not find her.)
24 Lo! soothly after three months they told to Judah,
and said, Tamar, thy son's wife, hath done fornication,
and her womb seemeth to wax great. Judah said, Bring
her forth, (so) that she (can) be burnt(!).
25 And when she was led (out) to *her* pain, she sent to
her husband's father, and said, I have conceived of the
man, whose these things be; know thou whose is the
ring, and the band of the arm, and the staff? (And when
she was led out to *her* punishment, she sent to her
husband's father, and said, I have conceived by the man
whose these things be; know thou whose ring, and arm
band, and staff these be?)
26 And when the gifts were known, Judah said, She is
more just than I, for I gave not her to Shelah, my son;
nevertheless Judah knew her no more fleshly. (And when
the gifts were seen, Judah said, She is more in the right
than I am, for I did not give her to my son Shelah; but
Judah did not know her fleshly any more.)

27 Soothly when the childbearing nighed, two children
appeared in the womb,
28 and in that birth of the children, one put forth the
hand, in which *hand* the midwife bound a red thread, and
said, This shall go out before. (and during the birth of the
children, one put out his hand, and the midwife tied a
red thread on his wrist, and said, This one shall go out
first.)
29 Soothly while he withdrew the hand, the tother
went out, and the woman said, Why, was the skin in
which the child lay in the womb parted for thee? And for
this cause she called his name Pharez. (But then he
withdrew his hand, and the other one came out first, and
the woman said to him, Was the skin in which the
children lay in the womb, broken for thee to come out
first? And for this reason she named him Perez, *that is,
Breaking out.*)
30 Afterward his brother went out, in whose hand was
the red thread, whom she called Zarah. (And afterward
his brother came out, with the red thread tied about his
wrist, and she called him Zarah, *that is, Redness.*)

CHAPTER 39

1 Therefore Joseph was led into Egypt, and Potiphar, a
gelding of Pharaoh, prince of the host, a man of Egypt,
bought him of the hand of Ishmaelites, of which he was
brought *thither.* (And so Joseph was taken down to Egypt,
and Potiphar, one of Pharaoh's eunuchs, the captain of
the guard, an Egyptian, bought him from the Ishmaelites,
who had brought him *there.*)
2 And the Lord was with him, and he was a man
doing with prosperity in all things (and made him
prosperous in all things). And Joseph dwelled in the
house of his lord,
3 which knew full well that the Lord was with Joseph,
and that all things which he did, were (ad)dressed of the
Lord in his hand. (who knew full well that the Lord was
with Joseph, and that all the things which he did were
directed by the hand of the Lord.)
4 And Joseph found grace before his lord, and he
served him, of whom Joseph was made sovereign of all
things (who made Joseph the ruler over all his things),
and he governed the house betaken to him, and all (the)
things that were betaken to him.
5 And the Lord blessed the Egyptian's house for
Joseph, and multiplied all his chattel, as well in houses,
as in fields; (And the Lord blessed the Egyptian's
household for Joseph's sake, and multiplied his
possessions, yea, all that he had in his house, and all that
he had in his fields;)
6 neither he knew any other thing, but [the] bread
which he ate. Forsooth Joseph was fair in face, and
shapely in sight.
7 And so after many days the lady (of his lord) cast her
eyes into Joseph, and said, Sleep thou with me; (And so
after many days the lady of his lord cast her eyes upon
Joseph, and said, Lie thou with me;)
8 which assented not to the unleaveful work, and said
to her, Lo! while all things be betaken to me, my lord wot
not what he hath in his house, (who assented not to the
unlawful deed, and said to her, Lo! while he hath
entrusted all his things to me, my lord knoweth not what
he hath in his own house,)
9 neither anything is, which is not in my power, either
which he hath not betaken to me, except thee, which art
his wife; how therefore may I do this evil, and do sin
against my lord? (and there is nothing, which is not in my
power, or which he hath not entrusted to me, except
thee, who art his wife; and so how can I do this evil
thing, and sin against God?/and sin against the Lord?)
10 They spake such words by all days/by long time,
and the woman was dis-easeful to the young man, and he
forsook the adultery. (They spoke such words for a long
time, and the woman distressed the young man, but he
forsook the adultery.)
11 Forsooth it befelled in a day, that Joseph entered
into the house, and did some work without witnesses.
12 And she took the hem of his cloth, and she said,
Sleep thou with me; and he left the mantle in her hand,
and he fled, and went out. (And she took hold of the hem
of his cloak, and said, Lie thou with me; and he left the
cloak in her hands, and he fled away.)
13 And when the woman had seen the cloak in her
hands, and that she was despised,
14 she called to her the men of her house, and said to
them, Lo! *my lord* hath brought in an Hebrew man, that
he should scorn us; he entered to me to do lechery with
me, and when I cried, (she called the men of the
household to her, and said to them, Lo! *my lord* hath
brought in a Hebrew man, and he hath scorned us; yea,
he entered to do lechery with me, and when I cried out,)
15 and he heard my voice, he left the mantle which I
held, and he fled out. (and he heard my voice, he left his
cloak which I held onto, and he fled away.)
16 Therefore into proving of the truth, she showed the
mantle, that she held, to her husband turning again
home. (And so to prove the truth of it all, she showed his
cloak, which she had held onto, to her husband when he
returned home.)
17 And she said (to him), The Hebrew servant, whom
thou broughtest in, entered to me to scorn me (came to
me, and mocked me);
18 and when he saw me cry, he left the mantle that I
held, and he fled out. (and when I cried out, he left his
cloak which I held onto, and he fled away.)
19 And when these things were heard, the lord
believed over much to the words of the wife (the lord
believed too much in his wife's words), and he was full

wroth;
20 and he betook Joseph into prison, where the bound
men of the king were kept, and he was closed there. (and
he took Joseph, and put him in the prison, where the
king's prisoners were kept, and so he was enclosed there.)
21 Forsooth the Lord was with Joseph, and had mercy
on him, and gave grace to him, in the sight of the prince
of the prison (before the ruler, *that is, the warden*, of the
prison),
22 which betook in the hand of Joseph all the prisoners
that were holden in keeping, and whatever thing was
done, it was *done* under Joseph, (who put all the other
prisoners, who were held in the prison, under Joseph's
hand, *or power*, and whatever thing was done, it was
done under Joseph's direction,)
23 neither the prince knew anything (and the ruler of
the prison had no further concerns), for all things were
betaken to Joseph; for the Lord was with him, and
directed all his works.

CHAPTER 40

1 When these things were done, it befelled that two
geldings, the butler and the baker of the king of Egypt,
sinned to their lord. (After these things were done, it
befell that two eunuchs, Pharaoh's butler and baker,
sinned against their lord.)
2 And Pharaoh was wroth against them, for the one
was (the) master butler, and the tother was (the) master
baker.
3 And he sent them into the prison of the prince of
knights, in which also Joseph was bound. (And he sent
them into the prison of the captain of the guard, where
Joseph was also kept.)
4 And the keeper of the prison betook them to Joseph,
which also served, *or kept*, them. Somewhat of time
passed, and they were holden in keeping, (And the ruler
of the prison delivered them unto Joseph, who served
them. Some time passed, and they were still held in the
prison,)
5 and both saw a dream in one night, by covenable
expounding to them. (when both of them had a dream
one night, and they needed their dreams to be
interpreted.)
6 And when Joseph had entered to them early, and
had seen them sorry, (And when Joseph came to them in
the morning, and saw them looking sorrowful, *or sad*,)
7 he asked them, and said, Why is your cheer heavier
today than it is wont (to be)? (he asked them, Why are
your faces so heavy, *or so unhappy*, today?)
8 Which answered, We (each) saw a dream, and there
is no man that expoundeth it to us. And Joseph said to
them, Whether the expounding is not of God? Tell ye to
me what ye have seen. (And they answered, We have
each had a dream, and there is no one to interpret it for
us. And Joseph said to them, Should not the interpretation
come from God? Tell me what ye have seen.)
9 The master butler told first his dream; I saw before
me that a vine, (So the master butler told his dream first,
and he said, I saw that there was a vine before me,)
10 in which were three scions, waxed little and little
into burgeonings, and that after the flowers (came), the
grapes waxed ripe, (which had three branches, that over
time had more and more buds, and after the flowers
came, the grapes ripened,)
11 and (then) the cup of Pharaoh was in mine hand;
therefore I took the grapes, and pressed them out into the
cup that I held, and I gave (the) drink to Pharaoh (and I
gave it to Pharaoh to drink).
12 Joseph answered, This is the expounding of the
dream; three scions be yet three days, (Joseph answered,
This is the dream's interpretation; the three branches be
three days yet to come,)
13 after which Pharaoh shall have mind of thy service,
and he shall restore thee into the first degree, and thou
shalt give to him the cup, by thine office, as thou were
wont to do before. (and then Pharaoh shall remember thy
service, and he shall restore thee to thy place, and thou
shalt give him the cup, as per thy duties, yea, as thou
were wont to do before.)
14 Only have thou mind of me, when it is well to thee,
and thou shalt do mercy with me, that thou make
suggestion to Pharaoh, that he lead me out of this prison;
(And when it is well with thee, remember me, and do
thou mercy to me, so that thou make a suggestion to
Pharaoh, that he release me from this prison;)
15 for thiefly, (*that is, by thievery*), I am taken away
from the land of Hebrews, and (once) here I am sent
innocent into prison. (for I was stolen away from the land
of the Hebrews, and then once here, I was sent into
prison, though innocent.)
16 The master baker saw that Joseph had declared
prudently the dream, and he said, And I saw a dream,
that I had three baskets of meal on mine head, (The
master baker saw that Joseph had prudently interpreted
the dream, and he said, And I had a dream, where I had
three baskets of meal on my head,)
17 and I guessed that I bare in one basket, that was
highest, all (the) (bake)meats that be made (for Pharaoh)
by the craft of bakers, and that birds ate thereof. (and I
saw that I carried in the first basket, that was on top, all
the baked goods that the baker made for Pharaoh, and
the birds were eating them.)
18 Joseph answered, This is the expounding of the
dream; three baskets be yet three days, (Joseph answered,
This is the dream's interpretation; the three baskets be
three days yet to come,)
19 after which Pharaoh shall take away thine head, and
he shall hang thee in a cross, and birds shall draw thy

flesh. (after which Pharaoh shall take away thy head, and
he shall hang thee on a tree, and then the birds shall
draw off thy flesh.)
20 From thence the third day was the day of the birth of
Pharaoh, which made a great feast to his servants, and he
had mind among the meats, of the master butler, and of
the prince of (the) bakers; (And three days later was
Pharaoh's birthday, and he made a great feast for his
servants, and during the feast he remembered the master
butler, and the master baker;)
21 and he restored the one into his place, (so) that he
should direct the cup, *either (the) drink*, to the king,
22 and he hanged the tother in a gibbet, that the truth
of Joseph('s) *declaring (of) the dreams* should be proved.
(but he hanged the other man on a tree, and so the truth
of Joseph's *interpretations of the dreams* was shown.)
23 And nevertheless when prosperities befelled to the
master butler, he forgat Joseph that declared his dream.
(And yet when good things happened to the master
butler, he forgot about Joseph, who had interpreted his
dream.)

CHAPTER 41

1 After two years Pharaoh saw a dream; he guessed
that he stood on a river, (Two years later, Pharaoh had a
dream; he saw that he stood by a river,)
2 from which seven fair kine and full fat went up (from
which seven cows, sleek and very fat, came out), and
[they] were fed in the places of (the) marshes;
3 and (an)other seven, foul and lean, came out of the
river, and were fed in that brink of the water, in green
places; (and then seven others, foul and lean, came out of
the river, and were fed on the bank of the river, in the
green places;)
4 and those (foul and lean) kine devoured those kine
of which the fairness and comeliness of (their) bodies
were wonderful. (And) Pharaoh waked,
5 and slept again, and he saw another dream; seven
ears of corn, full and fair, came forth in one stalk, (and
then he slept again, and he had another dream; seven
ears of corn, full and ripe, came forth on one stalk,)
6 and (then) others, as many ears of corn, (but) thin
and smitten with (the) corruption of (the) burning wind,
came forth,
7 devouring all the fairness of the first. (And) Pharaoh
waked after *this* rest,
8 and when the morrowtide was made, he was
afeared by inward dread, and he sent to all the
expounders of Egypt, and to all the wise men; and when
they were called, he told the dream, and none was that
expounded *it*. (and when the morning came, he was
greatly afraid, and he sent for all the dream readers of
Egypt, and for all the wise men; and when they came to
him, he told his dreams to them, but no one could
interpret *them*.)
9 Then at the last, the master butler bethought (to)
him(self), and said (to Pharaoh), I acknowledge my sin (at
last);
10 the king was wroth to his servants, and commanded
me and the master baker to be cast down into the prison
of the prince of knights, (for the king was angry with his
servants, and commanded me and the master baker to be
throw into the prison of the captain of the guard,)
11 where we both saw a dream in one night, before-
showing of things to come. (and one night we both had a
dream, a fore-telling of things to come.)
12 An Hebrew child, servant of the same duke of
knights, was there, to whom we told the dreams, and
heard whatever thing the befalling of [the] thing proved
afterward(s); (And a young Hebrew man, a slave of the
same captain of the guard, was there, to whom we told
our dreams, and then we heard from him what the
befalling of the dreams later proved to be;)
13 for I am restored to mine office, and he was hanged
in a cross. (for I was restored to my office, and he was
hanged on a tree.)
14 Anon at the behest of the king, they polled Joseph
(At once at the king's command, they shaved Joseph),
(and) led (him) out of the prison, and when his clothing
was changed, they brought him to the king.
15 To whom the king said, I saw dreams, and none
[there] is that expoundeth those things that I saw; I have
heard that thou expoundest *such things* most prudently.
(To whom the king said, I had *two* dreams, and there is
no one who can interpret what I saw; but I have heard
that thou interpretest *such things* most prudently.)
16 Joseph answered, Without me, God shall answer
prosperities to Pharaoh. (And Joseph answered, Not I, but
God himself shall answer good things to Pharaoh.)
17 Therefore Pharaoh told that that he saw; I guessed
that I stood on the brink of the flood, (And so Pharaoh
told him what he had dreamed, saying, I stood on the
bank of the river,)
18 and seven kine, full fair, with flesh able to eating,
went up from the water, which kine gathered green
sedges in the pasture of the marshes; (and seven cows,
sleek and with flesh good for eating, came out of the
water, and they gathered green sedges in the pasture of
the marshes;)
19 and lo! seven other kine, so foul and lean, followed
these, that I saw never such in the land of Egypt; (and lo!
seven other cows followed them, so foul and lean, that I
never before had seen such as these in all the land of
Egypt;)
20 and when the former kine were devoured and
wasted *of the lean kine*, (and when the first cows, *the fat
ones*, were devoured and destroyed *by the lean cows*,)
21 the *lean kine* gave no step, *or token*, of fullness, but

were slow, *or feeble*, by like leanness and paleness. I
waked, (the *lean cows* gave no sign of fullness, but were
as feeble, and with the same leanness and paleness, as
before. I awakened,)
22 and again I was oppressed by sleep, and I saw a
dream (and then again I was oppressed by sleep, and
again I dreamed); seven ears of corn, full and most fair,
came forth on one stalk,
23 and other seven (and seven others), thin and smitten
with [a] burning wind, came forth (out) of the stubble,
24 which devoured the fairness of the former; I told this
dream to [the] expounders, and no man there is that
expoundeth it (I told these dreams to the interpreters, but
there was no one who could interpret them for me).
25 Joseph answered, The dream of the king is one (The
dreams of the king be one dream); God hath showed to
Pharaoh what things he shall do.
26 Seven fair kine, and seven full ears of corn, be seven
years of plenty, and the same things comprehend the
strength of the dream; (The seven fat and sleek cows, and
the seven full ears of corn, be seven years of plenty, and
they tell the same thing, and so the dreams be one dream;)
27 and [the] seven kine, thin and lean, that went up
after *the fair kine*, and the seven thin ears of corn, and
smitten with [a] burning wind, be seven years of hunger
to coming, (and the seven foul and lean cows, that came
out after *the good cows*, and the seven thin ears of corn,
that be struck by a burning wind, be seven years of
famine to come,)
28 which shall be fulfilled by this order. (which shall be
fulfilled in this order.)
29 Lo! seven years of great plenty in all the land of
Egypt shall come, (Lo! seven years of great plenty shall
come in all the land of Egypt,)
30 and seven other years of so great barrenness shall
follow those, that all the abundance before *shall* be given
to forgetting; for hunger shall waste all the land, (and
then seven more years of such great famine shall follow
them, that all the abundance of before *shall* be forgotten;
for the famine shall destroy all the land,)
31 and the greatness of neediness shall waste the
greatness of plenty.
32 Forsooth this that thou sawest the second time (in) a
dream pertaining to the same thing (For what thou sawest
in a second dream pertaining to the same thing), is (a)
showing of firmness, *that is, (a) confirming of the first*, for
the word of God shall be done, and it shall be [ful]filled
full swiftly.
33 Now therefore purvey the king a wise man and a
ready (one), and make the king him sovereign to the land
of Egypt, (And so now, let the king find a wise and able
man, and make him the ruler over all the land of Egypt,)
34 which man ordain governors by all countries, and
gather he into barns the fifth part of fruits by [the] seven
years of plenty, that shall come now; (and that man
ordain governors over all the countryside, and gather he
into the barns the fifth part of the harvest of the land
during the seven years of plenty that shall now come;)
35 and all the wheat be kept under the power of
Pharaoh (and let all the corn, *or the grain*, be kept under
Pharaoh's power), and be it kept in [the] cities,
36 and be it made ready to the hunger to coming of the
seven years that shall oppress Egypt, and the land be not
wasted by poverty. (and have it made ready for the seven
years of famine to come that shall oppress Egypt, and so
the land shall not be destroyed by neediness.)
37 The counsel *of Joseph* pleased Pharaoh, and all his
servants,
38 and he spake to them, Whether we be able to find
such a man which is full of God's spirit? (and Pharaoh
said to them, Could we find any other man who is so full
of God's spirit as this man is?)
39 Therefore Pharaoh said to Joseph, For God hath
showed to thee all things which thou hast spoken,
whether I may find a wiser man *than thou*, and like to
thee? (And so Pharaoh said to Joseph, For God hath
shown to thee all the things which thou hast spoken, I
know that I cannot find a wiser man *than thou*, or anyone
even like thee!)
40 Therefore thou shalt be over mine house(hold), and
all the people shall obey to the behest of thy mouth; I
shall pass thee only by one throne of the realm (only by
my throne of the kingdom shall I be greater than thee).
41 And again Pharaoh said to Joseph, Lo! I have
ordained thee on all the land of Egypt. (And so Pharaoh
said to Joseph, Lo! I ordain thee on all the land of Egypt.)
42 And Pharaoh took (off) the ring from his hand, and
gave it in the hand of Joseph (and put it on Joseph's
finger), and he clothed Joseph with a stole of bis, *or of
white silk*, and he put a golden wreath about his neck;
43 and Pharaoh made Joseph to go upon his second
chariot (and Pharaoh had Joseph ride upon his second
chariot), while a beadle cried, that all men should kneel
before him, and should know that he was (the) sovereign
of all the land of Egypt.
44 And the king said to Joseph, I am Pharaoh, (and)
without thy behest no man shall stir hand either foot in
all the land of Egypt.
45 And Pharaoh turned the name of Joseph, and called
him by the Egyptian language, The Saviour of the World[16]
(And Pharaoh changed Joseph's name, and called him in
the Egyptian language, Zaphnathpaaneah); and he gave to
Joseph a wife, Asenath, the daughter of Potipherah, a
priest of Heliopolis, *that is, The City of the Sun*. And so

---

[16] *In Hebrew, it is 'showing privates', as Jerome and Lira here say. (In Hebrew, it is 'The one showing secrets', or revealing mysteries, as Jerome and Nicholas of Lira say here.)*

Joseph went out (in)to the land of Egypt.
46 Forsooth Joseph was of thirty years, when he stood
in the sight of king Pharaoh, and compassed all the
countries of Egypt. (And Joseph was thirty years old,
when he stood before Pharaoh, the king of Egypt, and
then went forth through all the countryside.)
47 And the plenty of [the] seven years came, and [the]
ripe corns were bound into handfuls/into sheaves (and
the harvest came forth in abundance),
48 and (they) were gathered into the barns of Egypt,
also all the abundance of ripe corns was kept in all cities
(and all the abundance of the harvest was kept in all the
cities),
49 and so great abundance was of wheat (and there
was such a great abundance of corn, *or of grain*), that it
was made even to the gravel, (*or the sand,*) of the sea,
and the plenty passed (any) measure.
50 Soothly two sons were born to Joseph before that
the hunger came, which Asenath, the daughter of
Potipherah, a priest of Heliopolis, childed to him (bare
for him).
51 And Joseph called the name of the first begotten
son, Manasseh, and said, God hath made me to forget all
my travails, and the house of my father; (And Joseph
named his first-born son Manasseh, and said, For God
hath made me forget all my travails, *or all my troubles,*
and my father's household, *or my family;*)
52 and he called the name of the second son Ephraim,
and said, God hath made me to increase in the land of
my poverty. (and he named his second son Ephraim, and
said, For God hath made me to be fruitful in the land of
my tribulation.)
53 Therefore when (the) seven years of plenty that were
(to come) in Egypt were passed,
54 [the] seven years of poverty began to come, which
Joseph before-said, and hunger had the mastery in all the
world; also hunger was in all the land of Egypt; (the
seven years of famine began, which Joseph had forecast,
and the famine had the mastery in all the rest of the
world; but there was still bread in all the land of Egypt;)
55 and (finally) when that land hungered, the people
cried to Pharaoh, and asked (for) meats (but when the
famine finally reached Egypt, the people cried to
Pharaoh, and asked for food); to whom he answered, Go
ye to Joseph, and do ye whatever thing he saith to you.
56 Forsooth hunger increased each day in all the land,
and Joseph opened all the barns, and sold *corn* to the
Egyptians, for also hunger oppressed them; (And the
famine increased each day in all the land, and Joseph
opened all the barns, and sold *corn, or grain,* to the
Egyptians, for now the famine oppressed them too;)
57 and all [the] provinces came into Egypt to buy corns,
and to abate the evil of neediness. (and so the whole
world came to Egypt to buy corn, *or grain,* for the famine
was so severe.)

CHAPTER 42

1 Forsooth Jacob heard that foods were sold in Egypt,
and he said to his sons, Why be ye negligent?
2 I [have] heard that wheat is sold in Egypt; go ye
down, and buy ye necessaries to us, that we may live,
and be not wasted by neediness. (I have heard that corn,
or grain, is being sold in Egypt; go ye down there, and
buy ye the necessities for us, so that we can live, and not
be destroyed by this famine.)
3 Therefore ten brethren of Joseph went down to buy
wheat in Egypt, (And so ten of Joseph's brothers went
down to buy corn, *or grain,* in Egypt,)
4 and Benjamin was withholden of Jacob at home,
that said to his brethren, Lest peradventure in the way he
suffer any evil. (but Benjamin was kept at home by Jacob,
who said to his sons, Lest he suffer any evil on the way.)
5 Soothly they entered into the land of Egypt, with
other men that went *thither* to buy *corn*; forsooth hunger
was in the land of Canaan. (And they entered into the
land of Egypt, with others who went *there* to buy *corn, or
grain*; for the famine was now in the land of Canaan.)
6 And Joseph was the prince of Egypt, and at his will
wheats were sold to [the] peoples. And when his
brethren had worshipped him, (And Joseph was the
prince, *or the ruler,* of Egypt, and at his will corn, *or
grain,* was sold to people from all the lands. And so
when his brothers had bowed before him,)
7 and he had known them, he spake harder *to them,*
as to aliens, and asked them, From whence came ye?
Which answered, From the land of Canaan, that we buy
necessaries to *our* lifelode. (and he knew them, he spoke
harshly *to them,* as to strangers, and asked them, Where
did you come from? And they answered, From the land
of Canaan, so that we can buy necessities to live.)
8 And nevertheless he knew his brethren, and he was
not known of them, (And though he knew his brothers,
he was not known by them,)
9 and he bethought on the dreams which he saw
sometime. And he said to them, Ye be spyers, ye came to
see the feebler things of the land (And he said to them,
Ye be spies, and ye came here to spy out our
weaknesses).
10 Which said, Lord, it is not so, but thy servants came
to buy meats; (And they said, My lord, it is not so, but thy
servants have come to buy food;)
11 all we be [the] sons of one man, we came *hither*
peaceably, and thy servants imagine not any evil. (we all
be the sons of one man, and we be honest men, and thy
servants do not think any evil against thee.)
12 To which he answered, It is in other manner, ye
came to see the feeble things of the land. (To whom he
answered, It is not so, for ye came here to spy out our

weaknesses.)
13 And they said, We thy servants be twelve brethren,
the sons of one man in the land of Canaan; the youngest
is with our father, another is not *alive*.
14 This it is, he said, that I spake to you, ye be spyers,
(But again Joseph said to them, Nay! It is what I have said
to you; ye be spies;)
15 right now I shall take experience of you/I shall take
very knowing of you; by the health of Pharaoh ye shall
not go from hence, till your least brother come *hither*; (by
this I shall prove you; yea, by the life of Pharaoh, ye shall
not go away from here, until your youngest brother first
come *here* to me;)
16 send ye one of you, that he bring him, forsooth ye
shall be in bonds till those things that ye said be proved,
whether those be false or true (whether they be true or
false); (or) else, by the health of Pharaoh, ye be spies.
17 Therefore he betook them into keeping three days;
(And so he put them in the prison for three days;)
18 soothly in the third day, when they were led out of
prison, Joseph said, Do ye that that I said, and ye shall
live, for I dread God; (and on the third day, when they
were let out of the prison, Joseph said, Do ye what I said,
and ye shall live, for I fear God;)
19 if ye be peaceable, one brother of you be bound in
prison; forsooth (the rest) go ye, and bear the wheat,
which ye have bought, into your houses, (if ye be honest
men, then one of your brothers shall be kept here in the
prison; but the rest of you go, and take the corn, *or the
grain*, which ye have bought, back to your hungry
households, *or your hungry families*,)
20 and bring ye your youngest brother to me, that I
may prove your words, and ye die not. They did as he
said, (and bring ye your youngest brother to me, so that
you can prove your words, and then ye shall not die.
And they concurred,)
21 and they spake together, Worthily we suffer these
things (and they said together, We deserve to suffer these
things), for we sinned against our brother, and we saw
the anguish of his soul, while he prayed us, and we heard
him not; therefore this tribulation cometh on us.
22 Of which one, Reuben, said, Whether I said not to
you, Do not ye sin against the child, and ye heard not
me? lo! his blood is sought. (And Reuben said to them,
Did I not say to you, Do not ye do this sin against the
boy, but ye would not listen to me? lo! now his blood is
sought from us.)
23 Soothly they knew not that Joseph understood *them*,
for he spake to them by (an) interpreter/by an expounder.
24 And he turned away himself a little, and wept; and
he turned again, and spake to them (And he turned
himself away a little, and wept; and then he turned back,
and spoke to them). And he took Simeon, and bound
him, while they were present;
25 and (then privily,) he commanded the servants, that
they should fill their sacks with wheat, and that they
should put all their money in their bags, and over this
give *to them* meats in the way; which did so. (and then
privately, he commanded his servants, to fill all their
sacks with corn, *or with grain*, and to put all their money
back into their bags, and, more than this, to give them
food for the way; and this was done.)
26 And they bare [the] wheats on their asses, and went
forth, (And so the brothers loaded the corn, *or the grain*,
on their donkeys, and went away,)
27 and when the sack of one of them was opened that
he should give meat to the work beast in the inn, he
beheld the money in the mouth of the bag, (and at an
inn, when one of them opened his sack to give some
food to his work beast, he beheld the money in the
mouth of the bag,)
28 and he said to his brethren, My money is yielded
(again) to me, lo! it is had in the bag (lo! it is here in the
bag); and they were astonished, and troubled, and said
together, What thing is this that God hath done to us?
29 And they came to Jacob, their father, in the land of
Canaan, and told to him all things that befelled to them,
and said,
30 The lord of the land spake hard to us, and guessed
that we were spyers of the province; (The lord of the land
spoke harshly to us, and said that we went there to spy
out his land;)
31 to whom we answered, We be peaceable (We be
honest men), neither we purpose any treasons;
32 (for) we be twelve brethren, engendered of one
father (begotten by one father), (though) one (of us) is not
alive, (and) the youngest dwelleth with the father in the
land of Canaan.
33 And he said to us, Thus I shall prove that ye be
peaceable; leave ye one brother of you with me, and take
ye meats needful to your houses, and go ye, (And he said
to us, I shall prove that ye be honest men in this way;
leave ye one of your brothers with me, and take the food
needed for your households, *or for your families*, and go
ye home,)
34 and bring ye to me your youngest brother, that I
know that ye be not spyers, and that ye may receive this
brother which is holden in bonds, and that from
thenceforth ye have license to buy what things ye will.
(and bring ye your youngest brother here to me, so that I
know that ye be not spies, and then ye can have this
brother back who is held in prison, and from then on ye
shall have license to buy whatever ye desire.)
35 While these things were said, when they all poured
out the wheats, they found the money bound in the
mouths of their sacks. And when they all together were
afeared, (And after they had said these things, when they
all poured out their corn, *or their grain*, they all found

their money in the mouths of their sacks. And now they
all were very much afraid,)
36 their father Jacob said, Ye have made me to be
without children; Joseph is not alive, Simeon is holden in
bonds, (and) ye shall take away from me Benjamin; all
these evils have fallen in (on) me. (and their father Jacob
said, Ye have made me to be without my children;
Joseph is not alive, Simeon is held in prison, and *now* ye
shall take Benjamin away from me; all these evils be
against me.)
37 To whom Reuben answered, Slay thou my two sons,
if I shall not bring him again to thee; take thou him in
mine hand (give thou him into my hands), and I shall
restore him to thee.
38 And Jacob said, My son shall not go down with you;
his brother is dead, he alone is left; if any adversity shall
befall to him in the land to which ye shall go, ye shall
lead forth mine hoar hairs with sorrow to hell (if any
adversity shall befall him in the land to which ye shall go,
ye shall bring down my hoar hairs in sorrow to the
grave/unto Sheol).

CHAPTER 43

1 In the meantime hunger oppressed greatly all the
land, (In the meantime the famine greatly oppressed all
the land,)
2 and when the meats were wasted, which they [had]
brought from Egypt, Jacob said to his sons, Turn ye again,
and buy ye a little of meats to us. (and when all the corn,
or all the grain. which they had brought from Egypt, had
been eaten, Jacob said to his sons, Return ye, and buy ye
a little food for us.)
3 (And) Judah answered, That man announced to us,
under witnessing of an oath, and said, Ye shall not see
my face, if ye shall not bring with you your least brother
(if ye do not bring your youngest brother with you);
4 therefore if thou wilt send him with us, we shall go
(down) together, and we shall buy necessaries to thee
(and we shall buy all the necessities for thee);
5 else if thou wilt not, we shall not go (down); for as
we said oft, the man announced to us, and said, Ye shall
not see my face without your least brother (for as we
have often said to you, the man announced to us, Ye
shall not see my face without your youngest brother).
6 Forsooth Israel said to them, Ye did this into my
wretchedness, that ye showed to him, that ye had also
another brother. (And Israel, *that is, Jacob,* said to them,
Ye did this unto my wretchedness, that ye told him that
ye also had another brother.)
7 And they answered, The man asked us by order our
generation, (and) if our father lived, (and) if we had
another brother; and we answered followingly to him, by
that that he asked (and we answered accordingly to him,
by what he asked us); whether we might know that he
would say, Bring ye (down) your brother with you?
8 And Judah said to his father, Send the child[17] with
me, that we go, and may live, lest we die, (and thou,) and
our little children; (And Judah said to his father, *I pray
thee,* send our youngest brother with me, so that we can
go, and we can live, otherwise we, and thou, and our
little children shall die;)
9 I (shall) take the child, require thou him (again) of
mine hand; if I shall not bring him again, and betake him
to thee, I shall be guilty of sin against thee in all time; (I
shall take our youngest brother, and thou shalt require
him again from my hand; and if I shall not bring him back
again, and give him to thee, I shall be guilty of sin against
thee for all time;)
10 if *this* delay, *or tarrying,* had not been, we had come
thence now another time. (yea, if *this* delay had not
happened, we could already have gone *there,* and had
come back by now, another time.)
11 Therefore Israel, their father, said to them, If it is
need so *to be (done),* do ye that that ye will (And so their
father Israel said to them, If it is so needed *to be* done,
then do ye what ye must); (and) take ye (some) of the best
fruits of the land in your vessels, and bear ye gifts to the
man, a little of gum, and of honey, and of storax, *that is,
(a) precious gum,* and of myrrh, *that is, a bitter gum,* and
of terebinth, *that is, (the) best resins,* and of almonds;
12 and bear ye with you double (the) money, and bear
ye again that money which ye found in [the] bags, lest
peradventure it be done by error, *or unwitting(ly)/or (by)
negligence*;
13 but also take ye your brother, and go ye to the man;
(and also take ye your brother, and so go ye now to the
man;)
14 forsooth my God Almighty make him peaceable to
you/make him pleasable, *or quemeful,* to you, and send
he again your brother, whom he holdeth in bonds, and
also this Benjamin; forsooth I shall be *now* as (if) made
bare (and) without sons. (and may my Almighty God
make him kindly disposed toward you, and send he again
your brother, whom he now holdeth in prison, and *also*
this Benjamin; but for *now* I shall be as if made barren,
and without my sons.)
15 Therefore the men took gifts (And so the men took
the gifts), and double (the) money, and Benjamin; and
they went down into Egypt, and stood before Joseph.
16 And when he had seen them and Benjamin
together, he commanded the dispenser of his house, and
said (And when he had seen Benjamin together with
them, he commanded to the steward of his house, and
said), Lead these men into the house, and slay (some)
beasts, and make a feast; for they shall eat with me today.
17 He did as it was commanded/as it was bidden *him*

---

[17] Benjamin would have been over 30 years old at this time.

(He did as he was commanded), and he led the men into
the house;
18 and there they were afeared, and they said together,
We be brought in for the money which we bare again
before in our sacks, that he put challenge against us, and
make subject by violence to servage both us and our
asses. (and they were afraid there, and they said together,
We be brought in here for the money which we found
put back in our sacks, and he shall soon challenge us
about it, and by force make both us and our donkeys
subject to servitude, *or to slavery*.)
19 Wherefore they nighed in the gates, and spake to
the dispenser, (And so they went to the door, and spoke
to the steward,)
20 Lord, we pray, that thou hear us; we came down
now before that we should buy meats; (and said, My
lord, we pray *thee*, that thou hear us; we came down
before so that we could buy some food;)
21 (and) when those were bought, (and we headed
home,) when we came to the inn, we opened our bags,
and we found the money in the mouth(s) of our sacks,
which *money* we have brought again now in the same
weight (which *money* in the same amount we have now
brought back);
22 but also we have brought other silver, (so) that we
(can) buy those things that be needful to us; it is not in
our knowing who put the money in our purses.
23 And he answered, Peace be to you, do not ye dread;
your God, and [the] God of your father, gave to you (the)
treasures in your bags; for I have the money proved,
which ye gave to me (for I have the approved money,
which ye gave to me). And he led out Simeon to them;
24 and when they were brought into the house, he
brought (them) water, and they washed their feet, and he
gave their asses meats (and he gave some food to their
donkeys).
25 Soothly they made ready the(ir) gifts till Joseph
entered at midday, for they had heard that they should
eat bread there.
26 Therefore Joseph entered into his house, and they
offered gifts to him, and held them in their hands, and
worshipped low to the earth. (And so Joseph entered into
his house, and they offered him the gifts that they held in
their hands, and they bowed low to the ground before
him.)
27 And he greeted them again meekly; and he asked
them, and said, Whether your father, the eld man, is safe,
of whom ye said to me? liveth he yet? (And he meekly
greeted them; and he asked them, and said, Is your father
well, the old man of whom ye spoke to me? yet he
liveth?)
28 Which answered, He is whole, thy servant our father
liveth yet; and they were bowed, and worshipped him.
(And they answered, He is well, yea, thy servant, our
father, yet liveth; and they bowed low before him.)
29 Forsooth Joseph raised [up] his eyes, and saw
Benjamin, his brother of the same womb, and he said, Is
this your young(est) brother, of whom ye said to me?
And again Joseph said, My son, God have mercy on thee.
(And Joseph raised up his eyes, and saw Benjamin, his
brother from the same womb, and he asked, Is this your
youngest brother of whom ye spoke to me? And Joseph
said to him, My son, may God have mercy on thee.)
30 And Joseph hasted into (another part of) the house,
for his entrails were moved on his brother (for his feelings
were stirred because of his brother), and tears burst out,
and he entered into a closet, and wept.
31 And again when *his* face was washed (And then
when he had washed *his* face), he went out, and
refrained himself *from weeping*, and said, Set ye forth
(the) loaves.
32 Which were set forth to Joseph by himself, and to
his brethren by themselves, and to the Egyptians that ate
together by themselves; for it is unleaveful to Egyptians to
eat with Hebrews, and they guess such a feast unholy.
(And they were set forth for Joseph by himself, and for his
brothers by themselves, and for the Egyptians who ate
together by themselves; for it is unlawful for Egyptians to
eat with Hebrews, for they believe that such a feast, *or
that such a meal*, would be unholy.)
33 Therefore they sat before him, the first begotten by
right of the first begotten, and (so on down to) the
youngest by his age; and they wondered greatly, (And so
they sat down before him, the first-born by right of the
first-born, and so on down to the youngest by his age;
and they greatly wondered,)
34 when the parts were taken which they had received
of him, and the more part came to Benjamin, so that it
passed (the others) in five parts; and they drank, and were
[ful]filled with him. (when they received their portions
from him, and the greatest portion came to Benjamin,
indeed it was five times more than what any of the others
received; and so they drank, and were fulfilled with him.)

CHAPTER 44

1 Forsooth Joseph commanded the dispenser of his
house, and said, Fill thou their sacks with wheat, as much
as they may take, and put thou the money of each in the
height of the sack; (And Joseph commanded to the
steward of his house, and said, Fill up their sacks with as
much corn, *or as much grain*, as they can take, and put
the money of each in the top of his sack;)
2 forsooth put thou in the sack's mouth of the
youngest my silver cup, and the price of the wheat which
he gave; and it was done so. (and put my silver cup in the
mouth of the sack of the youngest, and also the money
which he gave for his corn, *or his grain*; and it was done
so.)

3 And when the morrowtide (a)rose, they were
delivered with their asses. (And when the morning came,
they were let go with their donkeys.)
4 And now they had gone out of the city, and had
gone forth a little; then Joseph said, when the dispenser
of his house was called, Rise thou, pursue the men, and
say thou when they be taken, Why have ye yielded evil
for good? (And when they had gone out of the city, and
had gone forth a little; then Joseph said, when the
steward of his house was called, Rise thou up, and
pursue the men, and say thou when they be taken, Why
have ye given back evil for good?)
5 The cup, which ye have stolen, is that in which my
lord drinketh, and in which he is wont to divine; ye have
done a full wicked thing.
6 He did as Joseph commanded, and when they were
(over)taken (and when he had overtaken them), he spake
by order *these things*;
7 the which answered, Why speaketh our lord so,
(saying) that thy servants have done so great a trespass?
8 We brought again to thee from the land of Canaan
the money that we found in the height of our sacks, and
how is it following that we have stolen from thy lord's
house gold or silver? (We brought back to thee from the
land of Canaan the money that we found in the top of our
sacks, so how followeth it, that we would steal gold or
silver from thy lord's house?)
9 At whomever of thy servants this that thou seekest is
found, die he, and we shall be servants of my lord. (With
whomever of thy servants that the cup which thou
seekest is found, let him die, and the rest of us shall be
my lord's slaves.)
10 Which said to them, Be it done by your sentence; at
whom it is found, be he my servant; forsooth ye shall be
guiltless. (And the steward said to them, So be it done by
your own sentence; with whomever it is found, he shall
be my slave; but the rest of you shall go free.)
11 And so they did down hastily their sacks on the
earth, and all they opened *them*, (And so they hastily did
down their sacks onto the ground, and they all opened
them,)
12 the which he sought (through); and he began at the
most till to the least, and he found the cup in Benjamin's
sack. (and then the steward searched through all the
sacks; and he began at the eldest, and worked down to
the youngest, and he found the cup in Benjamin's sack.)
13 And when they had rent their clothes, and had
charged again their asses, they turned again into the city.
(And when they had torn their clothes, and had loaded
up their donkeys again, they returned to the city.)
14 And Judah entered with *his* brethren to Joseph; for
Joseph had not gone yet from the place; and all they fell
together on the earth before him. (And Judah came in
with *his* brothers to Joseph; for Joseph was still in his
house; and they all fell down together on the ground
before him.)
15 To whom he said, Why would ye do so? whether ye
wot not, that none is like me in the knowing of divining?
(To whom Joseph said, Why have ye done this? do ye not
know that there is no one like me with such a knowledge
of divination? *Of course I would find you out!*)
16 To whom Judah said, What shall we answer to my
lord, or what shall we speak, either *what* may *we* justly
against-say? God hath found the wickedness of thy
servants; lo! all we be the servants of my lord, both we
and he at whom the cup is found. (To whom Judah said,
What shall we answer to my lord, or what shall we
speak, or *what* can we justly say against thy words? God
hath found out the wickedness of thy servants; lo! we
shall all be my lord's slaves, both we and he with whom
the cup was found.)
17 Joseph answered, Far be it from me, that I do so; he
be my servant that stole the cup; forsooth go ye free to
your father. (Joseph answered, Far be it from me, that I
would do such a thing; nay, only he who stole the cup
shall be my slave; the rest of you be free to go back to
your father.)
18 Soothly Judah nighed near, and said trustily (and
plaintively said), My lord, I pray thee, (let) thy servant
speak a word in thine ears, and be thou not wroth to thy
servant; for after Pharaoh thou art my lord.
19 Thou askedest first thy servants (Thou first askedest
thy servants), Have ye a father, or a brother?
20 And we answered to my lord, An eld father is to us,
and a little child that was born in his eld (age), whose
brother of the same womb is dead, and his mother hath
him alone; forsooth his father loveth him tenderly. (And
we answered to my lord, We have an old father, and he
hath a young son who was born in his old age, whose
brother from the same womb is dead, and he alone is left
of his mother's children; and his father tenderly loveth
him.)
21 And thou saidest to thy servants, Bring ye him
(down) to me, and I shall set mine eyes on him.
22 We made (the) suggestion to thee, my lord, the child
may not forsake his father (that the youngest son cannot
leave his father); for if he shall leave his father, his father
shall die.
23 And thou saidest to thy servants, If your youngest
brother shall not come (down) with you, ye shall no more
see my face (ye shall not see my face again).
24 Therefore when we had gone up to thy servant, our
father, we told to him all things which my lord spake *to
us*;
25 and our father said, Turn ye again, and buy ye to
you a little of wheat; (and later our father said to us,
Return ye there, and buy ye some corn, *or some grain*,
for us;)

26 to whom we said, We may not go; (only) if our least
brother shall go down with us, we shall go forth together;
else, if he is absent, we dare not see the lord's face (to
whom we said, We cannot go down there; only if our
youngest brother shall go down with us, then shall we go
forth together; for if he is absent, we shall not be able to
see our lord's face.)
27 To which things our father answered, Ye know that
my wife childed two sons to me;
28 one went out (from me), and ye said, A beast [hath]
devoured him (and it was said, A beast hath devoured
him), and hitherto he appeareth not;
29 if ye take also this son, and anything befall to him in
the way, ye shall lead forth mine hoar hairs with mourning
to hells. (and now if ye take also this son from me, and if
anything should befall him on the way, ye shall lead forth
my hoar hairs in sorrow to the grave/unto Sheol.)
30 Therefore if I enter *again* to thy servant, our father,
and the child fail (to come back with us), since his life
hangeth of the life of the child, (And so if I return *again* to
thy servant, our father, and his youngest son faileth to
come back with us, since his life hangeth on the life of
his youngest son,)
31 and he see that the child is not with us, he shall die,
and thy servants shall lead forth his hoar hairs with
sorrow to hells. (and he see that his youngest son is not
with us, he shall die, and thy servants shall have led forth
his hoar hairs in sorrow to the grave/unto Sheol.)
32 Be I properly thy servant, which received this child
on my faith, and I promised, and said, If I shall not bring
again him (to thee), I shall be guilty of sin against my
father in all time; (So let me be thy slave, for I received
his youngest son on my pledge, and I promised, and said,
If I shall not bring him back to thee, I shall be guilty of sin
against my father for all time;)
33 and so I shall dwell thy servant for the child into the
service of my lord, and the child go up with his brethren;
(and so let me stay here in my lord's service as thy slave
in place of the youngest son, and let him go back with his
brothers;)
34 for I may not go again to my father, if the child be
absent (if his youngest son be absent), lest I stand a
witness of the wretchedness that shall oppress my father.

CHAPTER 45

1 Joseph might no longer abstain himself, while many
men stood *there* before *him*; wherefore he commanded
that all men should go out, and that none alien were
present in the knowing of Joseph and his brethren.
(Joseph could no longer restrain himself, with so many
men standing *there* before *him*; and so he commanded
that all the men go out, so that no stranger was present
when Joseph made himself known to his brothers.)
2 And Joseph raised up his voice with weeping, which
the Egyptians heard, and all the house(hold) of Pharaoh.
3 And he said to his brethren, I am Joseph; liveth my
father yet? (yet liveth my father?) His brethren might not
answer, and were aghast with full much dread.
4 To whom Joseph said meekly, Cometh nigh to me
(To whom Joseph meekly said, Come near to me). And
when they had nighed nigh, he said, I am Joseph your
brother, whom ye sold into Egypt;
5 do not ye dread, neither seem it to be hard to you,
that ye sold me into these countries; for God hath sent
me before you into Egypt for your health. (do not ye fear,
nor be ye harsh with yourselves, that ye sold me into this
country; for God hath sent me before you into Egypt for
your salvation.)
6 For it is (but) two years that hunger began to be in
the land, (and) yet five (more) years (shall) follow, in
which men shall not be able to ear, neither reap;
7 and God before-sent me, that ye be kept (alive) on
(the) earth, and may have meats to live. (and God sent
me ahead, so that ye would be kept alive on this earth,
and have food to eat/and have descendants into without
end.)
8 I was sent hither not by your counsel, but by God's
will, which hath made me as the father of Pharaoh, and
lord of all his house, and prince in all the land of Egypt. (I
was sent here not by your deeds, but by God's will, who
hath made me like a father to Pharaoh, and the lord of all
his household, and the ruler in all the land of Egypt.)
9 Haste ye, and goeth up to my father, and ye shall
say to him, Thy son Joseph sendeth these things to thee;
God hath made me lord of all the land of Egypt; come
down (here) to me, and tarry not,
10 and (then) dwell in the land of Goshen; and thou
shalt be beside me, thou, and thy sons, and the sons of
thy sons, (and) thy sheep, and thy great beasts, and all
things which thou wieldest (and all the things which thou
possessest),
11 and there I shall feed thee; for yet five years of
hunger be left, lest both thou perish, and thine house,
and all things which thou wieldest. (and I shall feed thee
there; for there be five more years of famine to come, and
lest thou, and thy household, *or thy family*, and all the
things that thou possessest, perish.)
12 Lo! your eyes (see), and the eyes of my brother
Benjamin see, that (it is) my mouth (which) speaketh to
you;
13 tell ye to my father all my glory, and all things
which ye saw in Egypt; haste ye, and bring ye him to me.
(tell ye to my father about all of my glory here in Egypt,
and all of the things which ye have seen; then haste ye,
and bring ye him down here to me.)
14 And when he had embraced, and felled into the
neck of Benjamin, his brother, he wept, the while also
Benjamin wept in like manner on the neck of Joseph.

(And he embraced his brother, and fell on Benjamin's
neck, and he wept, and Benjamin also wept in like
manner upon Joseph's neck.)
15 And Joseph kissed all his brethren, and wept on
them all (and wept over *them* all); after which things they
were hardy to speak to him.
16 And it was heard, and published by famous word in
the king's hall, (saying,) The brethren of Joseph be come.
And Pharaoh joyed, and all his house (And Pharaoh and
all of his household were glad);
17 and Pharaoh said to Joseph, that he should
command his brethren, and say to them, Charge ye your
beasts, and go ye into the land of Canaan, (and Pharaoh
said to Joseph, Say to your brothers, Load ye up your
beasts, and go to the land of Canaan,)
18 and take ye from thence your father, and your
kindred, and come ye (back) to me; and I shall give you
all the goods of Egypt, that ye eat the marrow of the land
(and I shall give to you all the good things of Egypt, and
ye shall eat the marrow of the land).
19 Command thou also, that they take wains (out) of
the land of Egypt to the carriage of their little children,
and wives, and say thou, Take ye your father, and haste
ye (in) coming soon, (Command thou also, that they take
wagons from the land of Egypt for the transport of their
little children, and their wives, and say thou *to them,*
Bring ye your father here, and make ye haste in coming
back soon,)
20 neither leave ye anything of the purtenance of your
house, for all the riches of Egypt shall be yours. (nor take
ye anything of your household possessions, for all the
riches of Egypt shall be yours.)
21 The sons of Israel did as it was commanded to them;
to which Joseph gave wains, by the behest of Pharaoh,
and meats in the way; (And the sons of Israel did as they
were commanded; and Joseph gave them wagons, by the
command of Pharaoh, and food for the way;)
22 and he commanded two stoles to be brought forth to
each (and he commanded that two stoles, *or changes of
clothing,* be brought forth for each brother); forsooth he
gave to Benjamin three hundred pieces of silver, with five
(of) the best stoles;
23 and he sent to his father so much of silver, and of
clothes, and he added to them ten male asses, that should
bear of the riches of Egypt, and so many female asses,
bearing wheat and loaves in the way. (and he sent his
father ten male donkeys, carrying gifts of the best things
of Egypt, and ten female donkeys, carrying corn, *or grain,*
and loaves for the journey to Egypt.)
24 Therefore he let go his brethren, and said to them
going forth, Be ye not wroth in the way. (And so he let
his brothers go, and said to them as they went forth, Do
not ye argue on the way.)
25 Which went up from Egypt, and came into the land
of Canaan, to their father Jacob;
26 and they told to him, and said, Joseph, thy son,
liveth, and he is lord in all the land of Egypt. And when
this was heard, Jacob waked as of a grievous sleep;
nevertheless he believed not to them. (and they told him,
and said, Thy son Joseph liveth, and he is the ruler of all
the land of Egypt. And when he heard this, Jacob
appeared as if awakening from a grievous sleep, and he
could not believe them.)
27 They told on the contrary *to him* all the order of the
thing; and when Jacob had seen the wains, and all things
which Joseph had sent, his spirit lived again, (But then
they told *him* everything that Joseph had said; and when
Jacob had seen the wagons, and all the things which
Joseph had sent, his spirit lived again, *or revived,*)
28 and he said, It sufficeth to me, if Joseph my son
liveth yet (It sufficeth for me, if my son Joseph yet liveth);
I shall go and see him before that I die.

CHAPTER 46

1 And Israel went forth with all things that he had, and
he came to the well of (the) oath (And Jacob went forth
with all that he had, and he came to Beersheba); and when
sacrifices were slain there to [the] God of his father Isaac,
2 he heard God by a vision in that night calling to him
(he heard God in a vision that night calling to him), and
saying to him, Jacob! Jacob! To whom he answered, Lo! I
am present.
3 God said to him, I am the full strong God of thy
father; do not thou dread, go down into Egypt, for I shall
make thee there into a great folk; (And God said to him, I
am the very strong God of thy father; do not thou fear,
but go down to Egypt, for there I shall make thee into a
great nation;)
4 I shall go down thither with thee, and I shall bring
thee turning again from thence (and I shall bring thee
back again from there), and Joseph shall set his hand on
thine eyes.
5 Jacob rose from the well of (the) oath (And then
Jacob set out from Beersheba), and his sons took him,
with their little children, and (their) wives, in the wains
which Pharaoh had sent to bear the eld man,
6 and all things which he wielded in the land of
Canaan; and he came into Egypt with [all] his seed,
7 his sons, and their sons, and (all the) daughters, and
all the generation(s) together.
8 Forsooth these be the names of the sons of Israel,
that entered into Egypt; Jacob with his free children. The
first begotten *is* Reuben; (And these be the names of the
children of Israel who went to Egypt; that is, the names of
Jacob and his sons. The first-born *was* Reuben;)
9 the sons of Reuben; Hanoch, and Phallu, and
Hezron, and Carmi.
10 The sons of Simeon; Jemuel, and Jamin, and Ohad,

and Jachin, and Zohar, and Saul, the son of a woman of
Canaan (and Shaul, the son of a Canaanite woman).
11 The sons of Levi; Gershon, Kohath, and Merari.
12 The sons of Judah; Er, and Onan, and Shelah, and
Pharez, and Zarah. Forsooth Er and Onan died in the
land of Canaan; and the sons of Pharez were born,
Hezron, and Hamul. (The sons of Judah; Er, and Onan,
and Shelah, and Perez, and Zarah. And Er and Onan
died in the land of Canaan; and the sons of Perez were
Hezron and Hamul.)
13 The sons of Issachar; Tola, and Phuvah, and Job, and
Shimron.
14 The sons of Zebulun; Sered, and Elon, and Jahleel.
15 These be the sons of Leah, which she childed (to
Jacob) in Mesopotamia of Syria, with Dinah, her
daughter; all the souls of his sons and (of his) daughters
(by Leah), (were) three and thirty. (These be the sons of
Leah, whom she bare for Jacob in Paddan-aram, besides
their daughter Dinah; all of his sons and his daughter by
Leah, were three and thirty.)
16 The sons of Gad; Ziphion, and Haggi, Shuni, and
Ezbon, Eri, and Arodi, and Areli.
17 The sons of Asher; Jimnah, and Ishuah, and Isui, and
Beriah; and Serah, the sister of them (and their sister
Serah). The sons of Beriah; Heber, and Malchiel.
18 These were the sons of Zilpah, whom Laban gave to
Leah, his daughter (whom Laban gave to his daughter
Leah), and (through whom) Jacob begat these sixteen
persons.
19 The sons of Rachel, Jacob's wife, were Joseph and
Benjamin.
20 And *two* sons were born to Joseph in the land of
Egypt, Manasseh and Ephraim, which Asenath, [the]
daughter of Potipherah, priest of Heliopolis, childed to
him (bare for him).
21 The sons of Benjamin were Belah, and Becher, and
Ashbel, Gera, and Naaman, and Ehi, and Rosh, and
Muppim, and Huppim, and Ard.
22 These were the sons of Rachel, the which Jacob
begat (whom Jacob begat through her); all the persons
were fourteen.
23 The son of Dan; Hushim.
24 The sons of Naphtali; Jahzeel, and Guni, and Jezer,
and Shillem.
25 These were the sons of Bilhah, whom Laban gave to
Rachel his daughter (whom Laban gave to his daughter
Rachel). And Jacob begat these (through Bilhah); all the
souls were seven.
26 And all the men that entered with Jacob into Egypt,
and went out of his thigh, without his sons' wives, were
sixty and six. (And so all those who went with Jacob to
Egypt, and came out of his thigh, not including his sons'
wives, were sixty-six.)
27 Forsooth the sons of Joseph, that were born to him
in the land of Egypt, were two men. (So) All the souls of
the house of Jacob, that entered into Egypt, were seventy.
28 Forsooth Jacob sent Judah before him to Joseph, that
he should tell to him, and he meet with them in Goshen.
And when Jacob had come thither, (And Jacob sent Judah
ahead, to tell Joseph to come and meet them in Goshen.
And so when Jacob arrived there,)
29 Joseph went up in his chariot to meet his father at
the same place (Joseph came up in his chariot, and met
his father there). And he saw Jacob, and felled on his
neck, and wept betwixt embracings.
30 And the father said to Joseph, Now I shall die joyful,
for I have seen thy face, and I (shall) leave thee living.
31 And Joseph spake to his brethren, and to all his
father's house(hold), (and said,) I shall go up, and tell to
Pharaoh, and I shall say to him, My brethren, and the
house(hold) of my father, that were in the land of
Canaan, be come to me,
32 and they be men keepers of sheep, and have
busyness of flocks to be fed (and these men be
shepherds, *and herdsmen*, and be busy to feed their
flocks, *and their herds*); (and) they brought with them
their sheep, and (their) great beasts, and all things which
they might have.
33 And when Pharaoh shall call you, and shall say,
What is your work?
34 ye shall answer, We be thy servants, men shepherds
(We, thy servants, be shepherds, *and herdsmen*), from
our childhood till into this present time, both we and our
fathers. Soothly ye shall say these things, (so) that ye may
dwell in the land of Goshen, for Egyptians loathe all
keepers of sheep.

CHAPTER 47

1 Therefore Joseph entered, and told to Pharaoh, and
said, My father and brethren, the sheep and the great
beasts of them, and all things that they wield (and all the
things that they possess), have come from the land of
Canaan; and lo! they stand in the land of Goshen.
2 And Joseph ordained five, the least, *or meekest*, men
of his brethren, *to come* before the king,
3 whom he asked, What work have ye? They
answered, We thy servants be keepers of sheep, both we
and our fathers; (and Pharaoh asked them, What work do
you do? And they answered, We, thy servants, be
shepherds, *and herdsmen*, both we and our fathers;)
4 we came into thy land to be pilgrims, *that is, to
dwell for a time*, for no grass is to the flocks of thy
servants; for hunger waxeth grievous in the land of
Canaan, and we ask that thou command us thy servants
to be in the land of Goshen. (we have come to live in thy
land, *that is, to live here for a time*, for there is no grass
for the flocks, *and herds*, of thy servants, for the famine
hath spread far and wide in the land of Canaan; and we

ask that thou allow us, thy servants, to live in the land of
Goshen.)
5 And so the king said to Joseph, Thy father and thy
brethren have come to thee;
6 the land of Egypt is in thy sight; make thou them to
dwell in the best place, and give thou to them the land of
Goshen; that if thou knowest that witting men be in
them, ordain them masters of my beasts. (the land of
Egypt is before thee; have them live in the best place, and
so give them the land of Goshen; and if thou knowest
that knowledgeable men be among them, ordain them to
be masters of my beasts.)
7 After these things Joseph brought in his father to the
king, and set him before the king, and he blessed the king;
8 and he was asked of the king (and the king asked
him), How many be the days of the years of thy life?
9 And he answered, The days of [the] pilgrimage of
my life be few and evil, of an hundred and thirty years,
and those have not come to the days of my fathers, in
which they were pilgrims. (And he answered, The days of
my life's wanderings be but few and far between, yea,
only a hundred and thirty years, and they have not even
come close to the number of days that my fathers had.)
10 And when Jacob had blessed the king (again), he
went out.
11 Forsooth Joseph gave to his father and [his] brethren
(a) possession in Egypt, in Rameses, the best soil of [the]
earth (the best soil in the land), as Pharaoh commanded;
12 and he fed them, and all the house(hold) of his
father, and gave meats to them all (and gave food to all of
them).
13 For bread (had) failed in all the world, and hunger
oppressed the land, mostly of Egypt and of Canaan (most
of all now in Egypt and Canaan);
14 of which lands Joseph gathered all the money for the
selling of wheat, and brought it into the king's treasury.
(from which lands Joseph gathered all the money from
the selling of the corn, *or the grain*, and put it into the
king's treasury.)
15 And when price failed to the buyers, all Egypt came
to Joseph, and said, Give thou loaves to us; why shall we
die before thee, while money faileth? (And when money
failed in the lands of Egypt and Canaan, all Egypt came to
Joseph, and said, Give thou us bread; why should we die
before thine eyes, even though all our money is gone!)
16 To whom he answered, Bring ye your beasts (to me),
and I shall give you meats for those, if ye have not price
(and I shall give you food in return, if ye have no more
money).
17 And when they had brought those, he gave them
meats for horses, and sheep, and oxen, and asses; and he
sustained them in that year for the (ex)change of beasts.
(And so when they brought their beasts, Joseph gave
them food in return for their horses, and sheep, and oxen,
and donkeys; and so he sustained them with food that
year in exchange for their beasts.)
18 And they came in the second year, and said to him,
We cover not from our lord, that the while money faileth,
also (our) beasts failed altogether, neither it is hid from
thee, that without bodies and land, we have nothing;
(And they came back to him the following year, and they
said to him, We hide it not from our lord, that now our
money is all gone, and that all our beasts be thine; nor is
it hid from thee, that except for our bodies and our land,
we have nothing left;)
19 why therefore shall we die, while thou seest this?
both we and our land shall be thine; buy thou us into the
king's servage, and give thou us seeds *to sow*, lest while
the tiller perisheth, the land be turned into wilderness.
(and so why should we die, in front of thine eyes? let
both us and our land be thine; yea, buy thou us into
slavery to the king, and give us seeds *to sow*, lest while
the worker perisheth, the land be turned into wilderness.)
20 Therefore Joseph bought all the land of Egypt, while
all men sold (him) their possessions, for the greatness of
hunger (for the greatness of the famine); and (so) he made
it and all the peoples thereof subject to Pharaoh,
21 from the last terms of Egypt till to the last ends
thereof,
22 except the land of priests, that was given of the king
to them, to which priests also meats were given of the
common barns, and therefore they were not compelled
to sell their possessions. (except for the priests' land,
which the king gave them, and to whom food was also
given out of the common barns, and so they were not
compelled to sell their land.)
23 Therefore Joseph said to the peoples, Lo! as ye see,
Pharaoh wieldeth both you and your land; (now) take ye
seeds, and sow ye (the) fields,
24 that ye may have fruits; ye shall give the fifth part to
the king; I suffer to you the four residue parts into seed,
and into meats, to you, and to your free children. (so that
ye shall have increase; ye shall give the fifth part to the
king; but I shall grant you the remaining four parts for
seed, and for food, for you, and for your children.)
25 Which answered, Our health is in thine hand(s);
only our God behold us, and we shall joyfully serve the
king. (And they answered, Our salvation is in thy hands;
only let our lord continue to care about us, and then we
shall gratefully be the king's slaves.)
26 From that time till to this present day, in all the land
of Egypt, the fifth part is paid to the kings, and it is made
as into a law, without the land of priests, that was free
from this condition. (And so from that time unto this
present day, in all the land of Egypt, the fifth part of the
harvest is paid to the king, for this was made a law, from
all except the priests, whose land did not become
Pharaoh's property.)

27 Therefore Israel dwelled in Egypt, that is, in the land
of Goshen, and wielded it; and he was increased, and
multiplied full much. (And so Jacob *and his family* lived
in Egypt, that is, in the land of Goshen, and acquired
land; and they increased, and were greatly multiplied.)
28 And he lived therein sixteen years (And he lived
there seventeen years); and all the days of his life were
made an hundred and seven and forty years.
29 And when he saw the day of his death [to] nigh, he
called his son Joseph (to his bed), and said to him, If I
have found grace in thy sight, put thine hand under mine
hip, and (swear that) thou shalt do mercy and truth to me,
that thou bury not me in Egypt (that thou shalt not bury
me here in Egypt);
30 but I shall sleep with my fathers, and take thou away
me from this land (but when I shall sleep with my fathers,
thou shalt take me away from this land), and bury *me* in
the sepulchre of my greater(s). To whom Joseph
answered, I shall do that that thou commandest.
31 And Israel said, Therefore swear thou to me; and
when Joseph swore, Israel turned to the head of the bed,
and worshipped God. (And Jacob said, And so swear
thou to me; and when Joseph swore, Jacob turned to the
head of the bed, and worshipped God.)

CHAPTER 48

1 And so when these things were done, it was told to
Joseph, that his father was sick. And he took his two sons,
Manasseh and Ephraim, and he disposed him to go. (And
so after that these things were done, it was told to Joseph,
that his father was sick. And he took his two sons,
Manasseh and Ephraim, and he went to him.)
2 And it was said to the eld man, Lo! thy son Joseph
cometh to thee; which was comforted (who was
strengthened), and sat up in the bed.
3 And when Joseph entered to him, he said, Almighty
God appeared to me in Luz (Almighty God appeared to
me at Luz), which is in the land of Canaan, and blessed
me,
4 and (he) said, I shall increase thee, and multiply
thee, and I shall make *thee* into companies of peoples,
and I shall give to thee this land, and to thy seed after
thee, into everlasting possession (and I shall give this land
to thee, and to thy descendants after thee, for an
everlasting possession).
5 Therefore thy two sons, that be born to thee in the
land of Egypt, before that I came hither to thee, shall be
mine; Ephraim and Manasseh, as Reuben and Simeon,
shall be areckoned to me (Ephraim and Manasseh, just
like Reuben and Simeon, shall be reckoned as mine);
6 forsooth the others which thou shalt beget after them
shall be thine; and they shall be called by the name of
their brethren in their possessions (and they shall be called
after the names of their brothers in their inheritance).
7 Forsooth when I came from Mesopotamia, Rachel
was dead to me in the land of Canaan, in that way; and it
was the beginning of summer; and (before that) I entered
into Ephratah, and I buried her beside the way of
Ephratah, which by another name is called Bethlehem.
(And when I came from Paddan-aram, Rachel died, and
left me on the way, in the land of Canaan; and it was the
beginning of summer; and before that I entered into
Ephrath, I buried her beside the way to Ephrath, which by
another name is called Bethlehem.)
8 Forsooth Jacob saw the sons of Joseph, and said to
him, Who be these?
9 He answered, They be my sons, which God gave
me in this place (whom God gave to me in this place).
Jacob said, Bring them to me, (so) that I bless them.
10 For the eyes of Israel dimmed for great eld (age), and
he might not see clearly; and he kissed and embraced
those children joined to him, (And Jacob's eyes had
dimmed because of great old age, and he could not see
clearly; and when the boys were brought close to him, he
kissed them, and embraced them,)
11 and he said to his son, I am not defrauded of thy
sight; furthermore God hath showed to me thy seed. (and
he said to his son, I am no longer deprived of the sight of
you; and even more, God hath showed me thy children.)
12 And when Joseph had taken them from his father's
lap, he worshipped low to the earth (he bowed low to the
ground).
13 And he set Ephraim on his right side, that is, on the
left side of Israel; forsooth he set Manasseh on his left
side, that is, on the right side of his father; and he joined
both to him. (And he put Ephraim on his right side, that
is, on Jacob's left side; and he put Manasseh on his left
side, that is, on his father's right side; and he brought
them both close to him.)
14 Which held forth the right hand, and laid it on
Ephraim's head, the younger brother; soothly he laid his
left hand on Manasseh's head, that was the more through
birth. Jacob changed his hands, (And Jacob put forth his
right hand, and laid it on Ephraim's head, the younger
brother; and he laid his left hand on Manasseh's head,
who was the elder. Jacob had crossed his hands,)
15 and blessed his son Joseph[18], and said, God, in
whose sight my fathers Abraham and Isaac went; God
that feedeth me from my young waxing age till into this
present day; (and then he blessed his son Joseph, and
said, May God, in whose sight my fathers Abraham and
Isaac walked; the God who hath fed me from my young
age unto this present day;)
16 the angel that delivered me from all evils, bless
these children, and my name be called on them, and the

[18] *'In blessing Ephraim and Manasseh, Jacob was in fact blessing Joseph'.* (Good News Bible)

names of my fathers, Abraham and Isaac; and wax they in
multitude on (the) earth. (yea, the Angel who delivered
me from every evil, bless these boys, and may they be
called by my name, and the names of my fathers,
Abraham and Isaac; and may they grow into a multitude
upon the earth.)
17 Forsooth Joseph saw that his father had set his right
hand on the head of Ephraim, and he took *that* heavily,
and he endeavoured him(self) to raise his father's hand,
and take it from the head of Ephraim, and to bear it over
upon the head of Manasseh. (And Joseph saw that his
father had put his right hand on Ephraim's head, and he
was displeased, and he endeavoured to raise up his
father's hand, and take it from Ephraim's head, and to
bear it over onto Manasseh's head.)
18 And Joseph said to his father, Father, it accordeth
not so; for this is the first begotten (for Manasseh is the
first-born); set thy right hand on his head.
19 Which forsook *to do so*, and said, I know, my son, I
know; and soothly this child shall be into peoples (and
truly this child shall become a people), and he shall be
multiplied; but his younger brother shall be more than
he, and his seed shall increase into (a multitude of) folks,
(*or into a multitude of nations*).
20 And he blessed them in that time, and said, Israel
shall be blessed in thee, *Joseph*, and it shall be said, God
do to thee as to Ephraim and as to Manasseh. And he set
Ephraim before Manasseh; (And he blessed them at that
time, and said, When they say a blessing in Israel, they
shall say, God do to thee as to Ephraim and Manasseh.
And so he put Ephraim before Manasseh;)
21 and (Jacob) said to Joseph, his son, Lo! I die, and
God shall be with you, and shall lead you again to the
land of your fathers; (and Jacob said to his son Joseph, Lo!
soon I shall die, but God shall be with you, and he shall
lead you back to the land of your fathers;)
22 (and now) I give to thee one part over thy brethren,
which I took from the hand of Amorite, in my sword and
bow. (and now I give thee one more portion than what
thy brothers have, which I took from the hands of the
Amorites, with my sword and my bow.)

CHAPTER 49

1 Forsooth Jacob called his sons, and said to them, Be
ye gathered together, that I tell what things shall come to
you in the last days; (And Jacob called his sons, and said
to them, Be ye gathered together, so that I can tell what
things shall happen to you in the days to come;)
2 be ye gathered [together], and hear, ye sons of Jacob,
hear ye Israel your father (listen to your father Israel).
3 Reuben, my first begotten son, thou art my strength,
and the beginning of my sorrow; *thou oughtest to be* the
former in gifts, the more in lordship (*thou ought to be* the
first in gifts, and the greatest in power, *or in authority*);
4 (but) thou art shed out as water; wax thou not, for
thou ascendedest on the bed of thy father, and
defouledest his bed.
5 Simeon and Levi, brethren, fighting vessels of
wickedness; (Simeon and Levi truly be brothers, and they
use their bodies for fighting, and for wickedness;)
6 my soul come not into the counsel of them, and my
glory be not in the congregation of them; for in their
strong vengeance, they killed a man, and in their [own]
will, they undermined the wall (for in their anger, they
have killed some men, and to make sport, they have
wounded some oxen);
7 cursed be the strong vengeance of them, for it is
obstinate, and the indignation of them, for it is hard; I
shall part them in Jacob (I shall divide them in Jacob), and
I shall scatter them in Israel.
8 Judah, thy brethren shall praise thee, thine hands
shall be in the nolls of thine enemies; the sons of thy
father shall worship thee. (Judah, thy brothers shall praise
thee, thy hands *shall be* upon the necks of thy enemies;
the sons of thy father shall bow before thee.)
9 Judah, the whelp of a lion; my son, thou hast gone
up to the prey; thou restedest, and hast lain as a lion, and
as a lioness, who shall raise him? (thou hast rested, and
hast lain like a lion, and a lioness, and now who shall
dare rouse thee?)
10 The sceptre shall not be taken away from Judah, and
a duke (out) of his hip (nor a ruler from between his hips,
or out of his loins), till he come that shall be sent, and he
shall be the abiding of heathen men;
11 and he shall tie his colt at the vinery, and his she-ass
at the vine; O! my son, he shall wash his stole in wine,
and his mantle in the blood of the grape;
12 (yea,) his eyes be fairer than wine, and his teeth be
whiter than milk.
13 Zebulun shall dwell in the brink of the sea, and in
the standing of ships; and *he* shall stretch till to Sidon.
(Zebulun shall live at the edge of the sea, and his shore
shall be a haven for ships; and *he* shall reach as far as
Sidon.)
14 Issachar, a strong ass, lying betwixt [the] terms,
(Issachar, like a strong donkey, lying between two
burdens,)
15 saw rest, that it was good, and *saw* the land, that *it
was* best, and he underset his shoulder to bear, and he
was made serving to tributes[19]. (saw that the resting place
was good, and that the land *was* the best, and so he
underset his shoulder to carry the burden, and was made
to serve as a slave.)
16 Dan shall deem his people, as also another lineage
in Israel. (Dan shall judge, *or shall rule*, his people, like
another tribe in Israel.)

---

[19] *either to rent (or to pay rent or taxes),* as it is in Hebrew.

17 Dan be made a serpent in the way, and (a) cerastes,
that is, an horned adder, in the path, and bite *he* the feet
of an horse, that the rider of him fall backward; (Let Dan
be made a serpent on the way, and a cerastes, *or a
horned adder*, on the path, and bite *he* the horse's feet,
so that his rider fall backwards;)
18 Lord, I shall abide thine health. (Lord, I wait for thy
salvation!)
19 Gad shall be girded, and he shall fight (them) before
him, and he shall be girded behind. (Gad shall be girded,
and shall be attacked from the front, but he shall fight
back from behind.)
20 Asher, his bread shall be fat, and he shall give
delights to kings.
21 Naphtali shall be an hart sent out, and giving
speeches of fairness.
22 Joseph, a son increasing, (yea,) a son increasing, and
fair in beholding; [the] daughters run about on the wall
(his branches climb up over the wall),
23 but *his brethren* wrathed (at) him, and chided him,
and they had darts, and had envy to him (and they had
arrows, and they envied him).
24 His bow sat in the strong (One), *the Lord*, and the
bonds of his arms and *his* hands were unbound by the
hand of the mighty (God) of Jacob; of him a shepherd
went out, the stone of Israel. (But his bow stood strong,
and the bonds on his arms, and on *his* hands, were
unbound by the power of the mighty God of Jacob; yea,
by his Shepherd, by the Rock of Israel.)
25 (The) God of thy father shall be thine helper, and
Almighty God shall bless thee, with blessings of (the)
heaven(s) from above (with blessings from heaven
above), and with blessings of the sea lying beneath, with
blessings of teats, and of the womb;
26 the blessings of thy father be strengthened, *that is,
be (made) better than* the blessings of his fathers, till the
desire of (the) everlasting hills came; *blessings* be made
on the head of Joseph, and in the noll of (the) Nazarite,
that is, holy, among his brethren (*blessings* shall rest on
Joseph's head, yea, on the noll of the Nazarite, that is, the
one set apart, *or the holy one*, among his brothers).
27 Benjamin, a ravishing wolf (a ravenous wolf), shall
eat the prey early, and in the eventide he shall part (the)
spoils.
28 All these were in [the] twelve kindreds of Israel; their
father spake these things to them, and he blessed them all
by proper blessings, (All these were the twelve tribes, *or
the twelve families*, of Israel; their father spoke these
things to them, and he blessed each of them with their
own blessings,)
29 and he commanded to them, and said, I am (soon to
be) gathered to my people; bury ye me with my fathers in
the double den, that is in the land of Ephron (the) Hittite,
(and he commanded to them, and said, soon I shall join
my people, *yea, my ancestors*; bury ye me with my
fathers in the cave, that is in the field of Ephron the
Hittite,)
30 (that is, in the den in the field at Machpelah,) against
Mamre, in the land of Canaan, which den Abraham
bought with the field of Ephron (the) Hittite, into (a)
possession of a sepulchre. (that is, in the cave in the field
at Machpelah, east of Mamre, in the land of Canaan,
which cave Abraham bought with the field from Ephron
the Hittite, for a burial place.)
31 There they buried him, and Sarah his wife; also Isaac
was buried there, with Rebecca his wife; there also Leah
lieth buried. (They buried him there, with his wife Sarah;
Isaac was also buried there, with his wife Rebecca; and
Leah also lieth buried there.)
32 (This verse is omitted in the original text.)
33 And when the behests were ended, by which he
taught his sons, he gathered together his feet on the bed,
and died, and he was put to his people. (And when Jacob
had finished giving these prophesies to his sons, he drew
his feet up onto the bed, and died, and he joined his
ancestors.)

CHAPTER 50

1 Which thing Joseph saw, and he fell on his father's
face, and wept, and kissed him;
2 and he commanded his servants, (the) leeches, that
they should anoint his father with sweet smelling
spiceries. (and he commanded the physicians, his
servants, to anoint his father with sweet smelling spices.)
3 While they fulfilled his behests, forty days passed,
for this was the custom of dead bodies (that were)
anointed; and Egypt bewept him (for) seventy days.
4 And when the time of wailing was fulfilled, Joseph
spake to the household of Pharaoh, (and said,) If I have
found grace in your sight, speak ye in the ears of Pharaoh
(If I have found grace before you, speak ye to Pharaoh for
me);
5 for my father charged me [with (an) oath], and said,
Lo! I die; thou shalt bury me in my sepulchre which I
digged to me in the land of Canaan; therefore I shall go
up that I bury my father, and I shall turn again. (for my
father charged me with an oath, and said, Lo! now I die;
and thou shalt bury me in my grave which I dug for
myself in the land of Canaan; and so let me go up now,
that I bury my father, and then I shall return.)
6 And Pharaoh said to him, Go up, and bury thy
father, as thou art charged.
7 And when Joseph went up, all the elder men of the
house of Pharaoh went with him, and all the greater men
in birth of the land of Egypt; (And when Joseph went up,
all the elders of Pharaoh's household, and all the men of
great age, *that is, the elders*, of the land of Egypt, went up
with him;)

8 (and all) the house of Joseph with their brethren,
(but) without (the) little children, and flocks, and great
beasts, which they left in the land of Goshen, *went with
him.* (and all of Joseph's household, and his brothers,
went with him, but not their little children, or their
flocks, or their great beasts, which they left in the land of
Goshen.)
9 And he had chariots, and horsemen, and (his)
fellowship (with him), and the company was made not
little.
10 And they came to the cornfloor of Atad, which is set
over Jordan, where they made the service of the dead
body, with great wailing and strong, and filled seven
days. (And they came to the threshing floor of Atad,
which is on the east side of the Jordan River, where they
held a service for the dead man, with much loud wailing,
and filled seven days there.)
11 And when the dwellers of the land of Canaan had
seen this, they said, This is a (time of) great wailing to the
Egyptians; therefore they called the name of that place
The wailing of Egypt. (And when the people of the land
of Canaan had seen this, they said, This is a time of great
wailing, *or of great mourning,* for the Egyptians; and so
they named that place Abelmizraim.)
12 Therefore the sons of Jacob did, as he had
commanded to them; (And so Jacob's sons did, as he had
commanded them;)
13 and they bare him into the land of Canaan, and they
buried him in the double den, which den with the field
Abraham had bought of Ephron (the) Hittite, against the
face of Mamre, into possession of a sepulchre. (and they
carried his body to the land of Canaan, and they buried
him in the cave in the field at Machpelah, east of Mamre,
which Abraham had bought for a burial place from
Ephron the Hittite.)
14 And Joseph turned again into Egypt with his
brethren and all the fellowship, when his father was
buried. (And after his father was buried, Joseph returned
to Egypt with his brothers, and with all of his fellowship.)
15 And when their father was dead, the brethren of
Joseph dreaded, and spake together, (and said,) Lest
peradventure he be mindful of the wrong which he
suffered, and yield to us all the evil, that we did. (And
now that their father was dead, Joseph's brothers were
afraid, and spoke together, and said, Perhaps he shall
remember all the wrong, *or all the harm,* which he
suffered because of us, and give back to us all the evil
that we did to him, *and so we must ask him for mercy.*)
16 And (so) they sent (a message) to him, and said, Thy
father commanded to us, before that he died,
17 that we should say to thee these things by his words;
I beseech thee, that thou forget the wickedness of thy
brethren, and the sin, and [the] malice that they haunted
against thee; also we pray *thee,* that thou forgive this
wickedness (which we did) to thy father, the servant of
God. When these things were heard, Joseph wept. (that
we should say these words of his to thee; *My son,* I
beseech thee, that thou forget the wickedness of thy
brothers, and the sin, and the malice that they did against
thee; and we also pray *thee,* that thou forgive our
wickedness, for we, *like thee,* be servants of the God of
thy father. And when Joseph heard this message, he wept.)
18 And his brethren came to him, and worshipped low
to the earth (and bowed low to the ground before him),
and said, We be thy servants.
19 To which he answered, Do not ye dread; whether we
may against-stand God's will? (To whom he answered,
Do not ye fear; for can we stand against God's will?)
20 Ye thought evil of me, and God turned it into good,
that he should enhance me, as ye see in this present time,
and that he should make safe many peoples; (Ye thought
to do evil to me, but God turned it into good, and he
used what you did to me to advance me, as ye see at this
present time, and by doing so he hath saved many
people;)
21 do not ye dread (do not ye fear), I shall feed you and
your little children. And he comforted them, and spake
sweetly and lightly *to them;*
22 and Joseph dwelled in Egypt, with all the house of
his father (and Joseph lived in Egypt, with all of his
father's household, *or all of his father's family*). And he
lived an hundred [and ten] years,
23 and he saw the sons of Ephraim till to the third
generation; also the sons of Machir, the son of Manasseh,
were borne in the knees of Joseph (were brought up on
Joseph's knees).
24 When these things were done, Joseph spake to his
brethren, (and said,) After my death God shall visit you,
and he shall make you to go up from this land to the land
which he swore to Abraham, Isaac, and Jacob. (When
these things were done, Joseph said to his brothers, Soon
I shall die, but someday, God shall visit you, and he shall
lead you out of this land to the land which he promised
to Abraham, Isaac, and Jacob.)
25 And when Joseph had charged them (with an oath),
and had said, God shall visit you, bear ye out with you
my bones from this place; (And when Joseph had charged
them with an oath, and had said, When God shall visit
you, take ye my bones away with you from this place;)
26 he died, when an hundred and ten years of his life
were filled (then he died, when he was a hundred and
ten years old); and he was anointed with sweet smelling
spiceries, and he was kept in a bier in Egypt. ✡

EXODUS

CHAPTER 1

1 These be the names of the sons of Israel, that
entered into Egypt with Jacob; all entered with their
house(hold)s;
2 Reuben, Simeon, Levi, Judah,
3 Issachar, Zebulun, and Benjamin,
4 Dan, and Naphtali, Gad, and Asher.
5 Therefore all the souls of them that went out of the
hip of Jacob were seventy and five. Forsooth Joseph was
in Egypt; (And so all the souls of those who went out of
the hip of Jacob were seventy. And Joseph was already
in Egypt;)
6 and when he was dead (and after he died), and all
his brethren, and all his kindred,
7 the sons of Israel[1] increased, and were multiplied as
burgeoning, and they were made strong greatly, and
filled the land. (the Israelites increased, and were
multiplied like burgeonings, and they were made very
strong, and filled the land.)
8 (But) A new king, that knew not Joseph, rose [up] in
the meantime on Egypt,
9 and said to his people, Lo! the people of the sons of
Israel is much, and stronger than we;
10 come ye, wisely oppress we it, lest peradventure it
be multiplied; and lest, if battle riseth against us, it be
added to our enemies, and go out of the land, when we
be overcome. (so come ye, and let us wisely oppress
them, lest they be multiplied; and lest, if battle riseth
against us, they join our enemies, and when we be
overcome, they leave here.)
11 And so he made (the) masters of (the) works (to be
the) sovereigns to them, that they should torment them
with charges. And they made [the] cities of tabernacles,
either of treasures, as it is in Hebrew, to Pharaoh,
Pithom, and Raamses. (And so he set the taskmasters to
be their rulers, and to torment them with burdens. And
they made for Pharaoh the cities of treasures, that is,
Pithom, and Raamses.)
12 And by how much they oppressed them, by so
much they were multiplied, and increased the more. (But
the more that they oppressed them, the more they
multiplied, and increased.)
13 And (so) the Egyptians hated the sons of Israel, and
tormented, and scorned them;
14 and they brought their life to bitterness, by hard
works of clay and of tilestone, and by all servage, by
which they were oppressed in the works of [the] earth.
(and they made their life bitter, by hard work with clay
and bricks, and by all the servitude, *or all the slavery*, by
which they were oppressed with their work in the land.)
15 Forsooth the king of Egypt said to the midwives of
(the) Hebrews, of which one was called Shiphrah, [and]
the tother Puah;
16 and he commanded to them, When ye shall do the
office of midwives to [the] Hebrew women, and the time
of child-bearing shall come, if it is a knave child, slay ye
him; if it is a woman (child), keep ye *it*. (and he
commanded to them, and said, When ye shall do
midwifing for the Hebrew women, and the time of child-
bearing shall come, if it is a male child, kill ye him; but if
it is a female child, keep ye *her*.)
17 But the midwives dreaded God, and did not by the
commandment of the king of Egypt, but kept the knave
children. (But the midwives feared God, and did not
comply with the king of Egypt's command, but let the
male children live.)
18 To the which (when) called to him, the king said,
What is this thing that ye would do, that ye would keep
the *knave* children? (To whom, when called to him, the
king said, What is this thing that ye would do, that ye
have let the *male* children live?)
19 The which answered, Hebrew women be not as the
women of Egypt, for they have knowing of the craft of
midwifing, and childed before that we come to them. (And
they answered, Hebrew women be not like the Egyptian
women, for they have knowledge of the craft of midwifing,
and have given birth before that we come to them.)
20 Therefore God did well to the midwives; and the
people increased, and was comforted greatly (and were
greatly strengthened).
21 And for the midwives dreaded God, God builded
them houses. (And because the midwives feared God,
God gave them their own households, *or their own
families*.)
22 Therefore Pharaoh commanded (to) all his people,
and said, Whatever thing of male kind is born to (the)
Hebrews, cast ye into the flood (cast ye them into the
River, *that is, into the Nile*); (but) whatever thing of
women kind (is born), keep ye (them).

CHAPTER 2

1 After these things a man of the house of Levi went
out, and took a wife of his kin *into fleshly coupling*[2],

[1] The phrase 'sons of Israel' sometimes refers to the twelve sons of Jacob (whose name God changed to 'Israel'), sometimes to only the Israelite men, and other times to all of the people of Israel, the twelve tribes of Israel, 'the Israelites'.

[2] *'into fleshly coupling'*; for she was his wife before, and had (already) childed (to him) Aaron, and Marie (and Miriam), his sister.

(And after these things, a man of the house of Levi went
out, and knew his wife, who was of his own kin, *or of his
own tribe*,)
2 which conceived, and childed a son. And she saw
him well-faring, and hid *him* three months. (who
conceived, and bare a son. And she saw that he was a
fine boy, and hid *him* for three months.)
3 And when she might not cover [him], then she took
a basket of sedge, and balmed it with tar and pitch, and
put the young child within, and put him forth in a place
of spires of the brink of the flood, (And when she could
no longer hide him, then she took a reed basket, and
balmed it with tar and pitch, and put the young child in
it, and put him out in a place of reeds by the bank of the
Nile,)
4 the while his sister stood afar, and beheld the
befalling of the thing.
5 Lo! forsooth the daughter of Pharaoh came down to
be washed in the flood, and her damsels walked by the
brink of the flood. And when she had seen a basket in
the place of spires, she sent one of her servantesses, (Lo!
then Pharaoh's daughter came down to wash in the
River, and her slave-girls walked by the river bank. And
when she had seen a basket among the reeds, she sent
one of her slave-girls,)
6 and she opened the basket (when it was) brought to
her, and she saw a little child weeping therein. And she
had mercy on the child, and said, It is (one) of the young
children of (the) Hebrews.
7 To whom the child's sister said, Wilt thou that I go,
and call to thee an Hebrew woman, that may nourish the
young child? (And the young child's sister came over to
her, and said, Wilt thou that I go, and call a Hebrew
woman, so that she can nurse the young child for thee?)
8 She answered, Go thou. (And so) The damsel went,
and called the child's mother.
9 To whom Pharaoh's daughter spake, and said, Take
thou this child, and nourish it to me; and I shall give to
thee thy meed. The woman took, and nourished the
child, (And Pharaoh's daughter said to her, Take thou this
child, and nurse it for me; and I shall give thee thy
payment, *or thy reward*. And so the woman took, and
nursed the child,)
10 and *she* betook him, (when) waxen, to Pharaoh's
daughter, whom she (had) purchased into the place of a
son; and she called his name Moses[3], and said, For I took
him from the water. (and when he was old enough, *she*
took him to Pharaoh's daughter, who adopted him as her
own son; and she called his name Moses, saying, For I
took him out of the water.)
11 In those days, after that Moses increased, he went
out to his brethren, and saw the torment of them, and a
man Egyptian smiting an Hebrew man, one of his
brethren. (And later, when Moses had grown to be a
man, he went to see his brothers, *that is, his fellow
Israelites*; and he saw their torment, and he saw an
Egyptian man striking a Hebrew man, one of his brothers,
or one of his kinsmen.)
12 And when he had beholden hither and thither, and
had seen, that no man was present, he killed the
Egyptian, and hid *him* in the sand.
13 And he went out in another day, and saw twain
Hebrew men chiding, and he said to him that did [the]
wrong, Why smitest thou thy brother? (And he went back
the next day, and saw two Hebrew men fighting, and he
said to the man who did the wrong, Why strikest thou thy
brother?)
14 Which answered, Who ordained thee prince, or
judge, on us? [Who ordained thee prince and doomsman
upon us?] Whether thou wilt slay me, as thou killedest
yesterday the Egyptian? Moses dreaded, and said, How is
this word made open? (Who answered, Who ordained
thee prince and judge over us? Shalt thou kill me, like
yesterday thou killedest the Egyptian? Then Moses feared,
and said, How is this made open?)
15 And Pharaoh heard this word, and sought to slay
Moses, which fled from his face, and dwelled in the land
of Midian; and he sat beside a well. (And when Pharaoh
heard of this, he sought to kill Moses, and so Moses fled
from him, and lived in the land of Midian.)
16 Forsooth seven daughters were to the priest of
Midian, that came to draw water; and when the troughs
were filled, they coveted to water their father's flocks.
(Now the priest of Midian had seven daughters. One
day, as Moses sat beside a well, they came to draw some
water; and when the troughs were filled, they desired to
water their father's flocks.)
17 (But some) Shepherds came upon them, and drove
them away; and Moses rose (up), and defended the
damsels; and (then) he watered their sheep.
18 And when they had turned again to Jethro, their
father, (the son of Reuel,) he said to them, Why came ye
swifter than ye were wont (to do)?
19 They answered, A man of Egypt delivered us from
the hand of the shepherds; furthermore and he drew
water with us, and gave drink to the sheep. (And they
answered, An Egyptian man saved us from the hands of
the shepherds; and then he drew water for us, and gave it
to the sheep to drink.)
20 And he said, Where is that man? why left ye the
man? call ye him, that he eat bread (call ye him, so that
he can come and eat with us).
21 Therefore Moses swore, that he would dwell with
Jethro (And so later, Moses agreed, that he would live
with Jethro); and he took (for) a wife, Zipporah, Jethro's
daughter.

[3] In Hebrew, 'Moses' sounds like the words for 'pull out'.

22 And she childed a son to him, whom he called
Gershom[4], and said, I was a comeling in an alien land
(And she bare a son for him, whom he called Gershom,
and said, For I am a newcomer in a foreign land).
Forsooth she childed another son, whom he called
Eliezer[5], and said, For [the] God of my father is mine
helper, and he delivered me from the hand of Pharaoh.
23 Forsooth after much time the king of Egypt died, and
the sons of Israel inwardly wailed for [the] works, and
they cried [out], and the cry of them for their works went
up to God. (And after much time the king of Egypt died,
and the Israelites wailed over all the hard work they were
forced to do, yea, they cried loudly, and their cries over
all their hard work went up to God.)
24 And he heard the wailing of them, and he had mind
of the bond of peace, which he had made with Abraham,
Isaac, and Jacob; (And he heard their wailing, and he
remembered the covenant, which he had made with
Abraham, Isaac, and Jacob;)
25 and he beheld the sons of Israel, and knew them,
that is, showed love to them. (and he looked upon the
Israelites, and he had concern for them, *that is, he loved
them.*)

CHAPTER 3

1 Forsooth Moses kept the sheep of Jethro, his wife's
father, priest of Midian; and when he had driven the flock
to the inner parts of the desert, he came to Horeb, the hill
of God. (And Moses kept the sheep of Jethro, his father-
in-law, the priest of Midian; and when he had driven the
flock to the inner parts of the desert, he came to Mount
Sinai, God's mountain.)
2 Forsooth the Lord appeared to him *there* in a flame
of fire from the middle of a bush, and Moses saw that the
bush burnt, and it was not burnt up (and Moses saw that
the bush burned, but that it did not burn up).
3 Therefore Moses said, I shall go and see this great
sight, (and) why the bush is not burnt (up).
4 Soothly the Lord saw that Moses went to see, and he
called (to) him from the midst of the bush, and said,
Moses! Moses! Which answered, I am present (Who
answered, I am here).
5 And the Lord said, Nigh thou not hither, but (first)
unbind thou the shoes of thy feet, for the place in which
thou standest is holy land (for the place where thou
standest is holy ground).
6 And the Lord said, I am (the) God of thy father(s),
(the) God of Abraham, God of Isaac, and God of Jacob.
Moses hid his face, for he durst not look against God (for
he dared not look at God).
7 To whom the Lord said, I saw the affliction of my
people in Egypt, and I heard the cry thereof, for the
hardness of them that be sovereigns of the works (and I
heard their cry, for the hardness of those who be their
taskmasters). And I knew the sorrow of the people,
8 and I came down to deliver them from the hands of
(the) Egyptians, and lead out of that land into a good land
and broad (and to lead them out of that land into a good
and broad land), into a land that floweth with milk and
honey, to the places of Canaanites, and of Hittites, of
Amorites, and of Perizzites, and of Hivites, and of
Jebusites.
9 Therefore the cry of the sons of Israel came to me,
and I saw the torment of them, by which they be
oppressed of the Egyptians (And so the cry of the
Israelites came to me, and I saw their torment, and how
they were oppressed by the Egyptians.)
10 But come thou, I shall send thee to Pharaoh, that
thou lead out my people, the sons of Israel, from Egypt.
(But come thou, I shall send thee to Pharaoh, so that thou
can lead my people, the Israelites, out of Egypt.)
11 And Moses said to him, Who am I, that I go to
Pharaoh, and lead out the sons of Israel from Egypt? (And
Moses said to him, Who am I, that I go to Pharaoh, and
lead out the Israelites from Egypt?)
12 And the Lord said to Moses, I shall be with thee, and
thou shalt have this sign, that I have sent thee; when thou
hast led out my people from Egypt, thou shalt offer to
God on this hill (when thou hast led my people out of
Egypt, thou shalt worship God here on this mountain).
13 Moses said to God, Lo! I shall go to the sons of
Israel, and I shall say to them, [The] God of your fathers
sent me to you; (and) if they shall say to me, What is his
name, what shall I say to them?
14 The Lord said to Moses, I am that I am. (And) The
Lord said, Thus thou shalt say to the sons of Israel, He
that is, sent me to you.
15 And again God said to Moses, Thou shalt say these
things to the sons of Israel, The Lord God of your fathers,
God of Abraham, and God of Isaac, and God of Jacob,
sent me to you; this name is to me without end, and this
is my memorial in generation and into generation. (And
then God said to Moses, Thou shalt say this to the
Israelites, The Lord God of your fathers, the God of
Abraham, and the God of Isaac, and the God of Jacob,
sent me to you; this is my name forever, and this is my
title for all generations.)
16 Go thou, gather thou the elder men, *that is, (the)
judges,* of Israel, and thou shalt say to them, The Lord
God of your fathers appeared to me, (the) God of
Abraham, and God of Isaac, and God of Jacob, and he
said, I visiting have visited you, and I have seen all things
that befelled to you in Egypt;
17 and I said, that I *should* lead out you from the
affliction of Egypt (and I have decided that I will lead you

[4] In Hebrew, 'Gershom' sounds like the word for 'foreigner'.
[5] In Hebrew, 'Eliezer' sounds like the words for 'God helps me'.

out of your afflictions in Egypt), into the land of
Canaanites, and of Hittites, and of Amorites, and of
Perizzites, and of Hivites, and of Jebusites, to the land
flowing with milk and honey.
18 And they shall hear thy voice; and thou shalt enter,
and the elder men of Israel, to the king of Egypt, and thou
shalt say to him, The Lord God of Hebrews hath called
us; we shall go the way of three days into wilderness, that
we offer to our Lord God. (And they shall hear thy voice;
and then thou, and the elders of Israel, shall go to the
king of Egypt, and thou shalt say to him, The Lord God of
the Hebrews hath called us; let us make journey for three
days into the wilderness, so that we can offer our
sacrifices to the Lord our God.)
19 But I know, that the king of Egypt shall not deliver
you that ye go, but by strong hand; (But I know, that the
king of Egypt shall not let you go, unless compelled by a
strong hand;)
20 for I shall hold forth mine hand, and I shall smite
Egypt in all my marvels which I shall do in the midst of
them; after these things he shall deliver you. (and so I
shall stretch forth my hand, and I shall strike Egypt with
all the miracles which I shall do in their midst; and then
after these things he shall let you go.)
21 And I shall give grace to this people before [the]
Egyptians, and when ye shall go out, ye shall not go out
void;
22 but a woman shall ask of her neighbouress, and of
her that she is harboured with, silveren vessels, and
golden, and clothes, and ye shall put those upon your
sons and daughters, and ye shall make naked Egypt. (but
a woman shall go to her neighbour, and to her whom she
is harboured with, and shall ask for gold and silver
jewelry, and for clothes, and ye shall put those things on
your sons and your daughters, and so ye shall plunder
Egypt.)

CHAPTER 4

1 Moses answered, and said, *The commons* shall not
believe to me, neither they shall hear my voice; but they
shall say, The Lord appeared not to thee.
2 Therefore the Lord said to him, What is that that
thou holdest in thine hand? Moses answered, A rod, *that
is, a shepherd's staff.*
3 And the Lord said, Cast it forth into the earth (Throw
it down onto the ground); and he cast *it* forth, and it was
turned into a serpent, so that Moses fled.
4 And the Lord said, Hold forth thine hand, and take
the tail thereof; he stretched forth *his hand*, and held *it*,
and it was turned *again* into a rod. (And the Lord said,
Stretch forth thy hand, and take its tail; and he stretched
forth *his hand*, and took hold of *it*, and it turned *back* into
a staff.)
5 And the Lord said, (So) That they (shall) believe, that
the Lord God of thy fathers appeared to thee, (yea, the)
God of Abraham, God of Isaac, and God of Jacob.
6 And the Lord said again *to Moses*, Put thine hand
into thy bosom; and when he had put it into his bosom,
he brought forth it leprous, at the likeness of snow. (And
the Lord said *to Moses*, Put thy hand inside thy cloak;
and after he had put it inside his cloak, when he took it
out again, he brought it forth leprous, and as white as
snow.)
7 The Lord said, Again draw thine hand into thy
bosom; Moses again drew *(in) his hand*, and brought it
forth again, and it was like to the tother flesh. (And the
Lord said, Put thy hand inside thy cloak again; and Moses
put *his hand inside his cloak*, and when he took it out
again, once more it was like his other flesh.)
8 The Lord said, If they shall not believe to thee,
neither shall hear the word of the former sign, *either
miracle*, they shall believe to the word of the sign
following; (And the Lord said, If they do not believe thee,
nor accept the proof of the first sign, *or the first miracle*,
then they may believe the proof of the sign that
followeth;)
9 that if they believe not to these two signs, neither
hear thy voice, take thou water of the flood, and shedded
out it on the dry land, and whatever thing thou shalt draw
up of the flood, it shall be turned into blood. (but if they
do not believe these two signs, nor will listen to thy
voice, then take some water from the River, and pour it
out onto the dry land; and whatever water thou shalt
draw up out of the River, it shall be turned into blood,
when it falleth onto the ground.)
10 Moses said, Lord, I beseech (thee), I am not
eloquent, *that is, a fair speaker*, from yesterday and the
third day ago; and since thou hast spoken to thy servant, I
am of more hindered, and of slower tongue.
11 The Lord said to him, Who made the mouth of [a]
man, or who made a dumb man, and deaf, seeing, and
blind? whether not I? (And the Lord said to him, Who
gave speech to people, or who made anyone dumb, or
deaf, or seeing, or blind? was it not I?)
12 Therefore go thou, and I shall be in thy mouth, and I
shall teach thee what thou shalt speak.
13 And Moses said, Lord, I beseech *thee*, send whom
thou shalt.
14 And the Lord was wroth against Moses, and said, I
know, that Aaron, thy brother, of the lineage of Levi, is
eloquent, *that is, a fair speaker*; lo! he shall go out into
thy coming, and he shall see thee, and he shall be glad in
heart. (And the Lord was angry against Moses, and said, I
know, that thy brother Aaron, of the tribe of Levi, is
eloquent, *that is, a fair speaker*; lo! he is coming to meet
thee, and he shall see thee, and he shall be glad in his
heart.)
15 Speak thou to him, and put thou my words in his

mouth, and I shall be in thy mouth, and in his mouth;
and I shall show to you what ye ought to do.
16 He shall speak for thee to the people, and he shall
be thy mouth; forsooth thou shalt be to him in these
things, that pertain to God.
17 Also take thou this rod in thine hand, in which thou
shalt do miracles. (And take thou this staff in thy hand,
with which thou shalt do miracles.)
18 Moses went, and turned again to Jethro, his wife's
father, and said to him, I shall go, and turn again to my
brethren into Egypt, that I see, whether they live yet. To
whom Jethro said, Go thou in peace. (Then Moses went,
and returned to Jethro, his father-in-law, and said to him,
I shall go now, and return to my brothers in Egypt, so that
I can see if they be alive or not. To whom Jethro said,
Go in peace.)
19 Therefore the Lord said to Moses in Midian, Go
thou, and turn again into Egypt; for all they be dead that
sought thy life. (And so the Lord said to Moses in Midian,
Go thou, and return to Egypt, for all those who sought thy
life have now died.)
20 Moses took his wife, and his sons, and set them on
an ass, and he turned again into Egypt, and he bare the
rod of God in his hand. (And Moses took his wife, and
his sons, and put them on donkeys, and he returned to
Egypt, holding the staff of God in his hand.)
21 And the Lord said to him turning again into Egypt,
See, that thou do all the wonders, which I have put in
thine hand, before Pharaoh; I shall make hard his heart,
and he shall not deliver the people; (And the Lord said to
him as he returned to Egypt, See, that thou do all the
miracles before Pharaoh, which I have put in thy hand;
but I shall harden his heart, and he shall not let the
people go;)
22 and thou shalt say to him, The Lord saith these
things, My first begotten son is Israel (Israel is my first-
born son);
23 I said to thee, Deliver thou my son, that he serve
me, and thou wouldest not deliver him; lo! I shall slay thy
first begotten son. (I said to thee, Let my son go, so that
he can worship me, but thou wouldest not let him go; so
now I shall kill thy first-born son.)
24 And when Moses was in the way, in an inn, the
Lord came to him, and would slay him. (And when
Moses was on the way, at an inn, the Lord came to him,
intending to kill him.)
25 Zipporah took anon a most sharp stone, and
circumcised the rod of her son; and she touched Moses'
feet (with the bloody piece of skin), and said, Thou art an
husband of bloods to me. (But at once Zipporah took a
most sharp stone, and circumcised her son's rod; and she
touched Moses' feet with the bloody piece of skin, and
said, Thou art a husband in blood to me.)
26 And he let go him, after that she had said, Thou art
an husband of bloods to me, for [the] circumcision. (And
God let him go/And God let him live, after that she had
said, Thou art a husband in blood to me, because of the
rite of circumcision.)
27 Forsooth the Lord said to Aaron, Go thou into the
coming of Moses into desert; which went against Moses
into the hill of God, and kissed him. (And the Lord said to
Aaron, Go thou into the wilderness to meet Moses; and
so he went to meet Moses at God's mountain, and kissed
him.)
28 And Moses told to Aaron all the words of the Lord,
for which he had sent Moses (that he had sent Moses to
say); and *he told* (him about) the miracles, which the
Lord had commanded (him to perform).
29 And they came together, and gathered all the elder
men of the sons of Israel. (And they came, and gathered
together all the elders of the Israelites.)
30 And Aaron spake all the words, which the Lord had
said to Moses, and he did the signs before the people
(and then Moses did all the miracles before the people);
31 and the people believed; and they heard, that the
Lord had visited the sons of Israel, and that he had beheld
the torment of them; and they worshipped low(ly), *or
meekly, the Lord.* (and the people believed; and when
they had heard, that the Lord had visited the Israelites,
and that he had seen their torment, they lowly, *or
meekly*, worshipped *the Lord*.)

CHAPTER 5

1 After these things Moses and Aaron entered, and
said to Pharaoh, The Lord God of Israel saith these things,
Deliver thou my people, that it make sacrifice to me in
desert (The Lord God of Israel saith these things, Let my
people go, so that they can hold a Feast unto me in the
wilderness).
2 And Pharaoh answered, Who is the Lord, that I hear
his voice, and deliver Israel? I know not the Lord, and I
shall not deliver Israel. (And Pharaoh answered, Who is
the Lord, that I should listen to him, and let Israel go? I
do not know the Lord, and I will not let Israel go.)
3 They said, [The] God of Hebrews called us, that we
go the way of three days into wilderness, and that we
make sacrifice to our Lord God, lest peradventure
pestilence, or sword, befall to us. (And they said, The
God of the Hebrews hath told us that we should make
journey for three days into the wilderness, and that we
should offer our sacrifices to the Lord our God, lest
pestilence, or the sword, befall us.)
4 (And) The king of Egypt said to them, Moses and
Aaron, why stir ye (up) the people from their works? Go
ye to your charges (Get back to your work!).
5 And Pharaoh said, The people of the land is much;
ye see that the company hath increased; how much more
shall it increase, if ye shall give to them rest from works.

(And Pharaoh said, There be many of thy people in this
land; ye see how they have increased; how much more
shall they increase, if ye shall get them rest from their
work.)
6 Therefore Pharaoh commanded in that day to the
masters of works (And so that day Pharaoh commanded
to the taskmasters), and to the rent gatherers of the
people, and said,
7 Ye shall no more give straw to the people, to make
tilestones, as *ye have done* before; but go they, and
gather stubble; (No more shall ye give straw to the
people, to make the bricks, as *ye have done* before; but
let them go, and gather the stubble themselves;)
8 and ye shall set on them the measure of tilestones,
which they made before (but ye shall still require from
them the same number of bricks, which they made
before), neither ye shall abate anything; for they be idle,
and therefore they cry (out), and say, Go we, and make
we sacrifice(s) to our God;
9 be they oppressed by works, and fulfill they those
(let them be oppressed by their work, and make them
complete it), (so) that they assent not to false words.
10 Therefore the masters of the works and the rent
gatherers went out to the people, and said, Thus saith
Pharaoh, I give not to you straw (I shall not give you any
more straw);
11 go ye, and gather ye (it yourselves), if ye may find
(it) any where; neither anything shall be decreased of
your work (but your daily quota shall not be decreased).
12 And the people was scattered by all the land of
Egypt to gather straw. (And so the people scattered out
into all the land of Egypt to gather straw.)
13 And the masters of the works were busy, and said,
Fulfill ye your work each day, as ye were wont to do
(before), when the straw was given to you.
14 And they, that were (the) masters of the works of the
sons of Israel, were beaten of the rent gatherers of
Pharaoh, that said, Why fulfilled ye not the measure of
tilestones, as *ye did* before, neither yesterday, neither
today? (And they, who were the taskmasters of the
Israelites, were beaten by Pharaoh's rent gatherers, who
said to them, Why have ye not made the same number of
bricks as *ye did* before, not yesterday, nor today?)
15 And the sovereigns of the children of Israel came
(And the taskmasters of the Israelites came), and cried to
Pharaoh, and said, Why doest thou so against thy
servants?
16 Straw is not given to us, and tilestones be
commanded in like manner (Straw is not given to us, but
yet the same number of bricks be required from us as
before). Lo! we thy servants be beaten with scourges, and
it is done unjustly against thy people.
17 (But) Pharaoh said, Ye give attention to idleness, and
therefore ye say, Go we, and make we sacrifice(s) to the
Lord;
18 therefore go ye (now), and (get to) work; (for) straw
shall not be given to you, and ye shall yield the
customable number of tilestones (but ye shall yield the
same, *or the customary,* number of bricks, as before).
19 And the sovereigns of the children of Israel saw
themselves in evil, for it was said to them, Nothing shall
be decreased of tilestones by all days. (And the
taskmasters of the Israelites saw themselves in an evil
situation, for it was said to them, The number of bricks
that ye must produce each day will not be decreased.)
20 And they coming out from Pharaoh, met Moses and
Aaron, that stood even there against (who were standing
there, waiting for them),
21 and they said to them, The Lord see, and deem
(thee), for ye have made our odour, *or fame,* (to) stink
before Pharaoh, and his servants, *that is, ye have made
us abominable and hateful (to them)*; and ye have given
to him a sword, that he should slay us (with).
22 And Moses turned again to the Lord, and said, Lord,
why hast thou tormented this people? why sentest thou
me?
23 For since I entered to Pharaoh, that I should speak in
thy name, thou hast tormented thy people, and hast not
delivered them. (For since I went in to speak in thy name
to Pharaoh, he hath tormented thy people, and thou hast
not rescued them.)

CHAPTER 6

1 And the Lord said to Moses, Now thou shalt see,
what things I shall do to Pharaoh; for by [a] strong hand
he shall deliver them, *that is, the sons of Israel,* and in [a]
mighty hand he shall cast them out of his land (for with
my strong hand, I shall compel him to let them go, *that
is, the Israelites,* and under my mighty hand, he shall
throw them out of his land).
2 And the Lord spake to Moses, and said, I am the
Lord,
3 that appeared to Abraham, and to Isaac, and to
Jacob, I am Almighty God; and I showed not to them my
great name Adonai, *that is, Tetragrammaton.* (who
appeared to Abraham, and to Isaac, and to Jacob, I am
Almighty God; but I did not tell them my great *and holy*
name, Yahweh, *or Jehovah;*)
4 and I made [a] covenant with them, that I should give
to them the land of Canaan, the land of their pilgrimage,
in which they were comelings. (and I made a covenant
with them, that I would give them the land of Canaan, the
land where they lived as newcomers, *or as foreigners.*)
5 I heard the wailing of the sons of Israel, in which the
Egyptians oppressed them, and I had mind of my
covenant. (I have heard the wailing of the Israelites,
whom the Egyptians oppressed, and I have remembered
my covenant.)

6 Therefore say thou to the sons of Israel, I am the
Lord, that shall lead you out of the prison of the
Egyptians; and I shall deliver *you* from servage; and I
shall again-buy *you* in an arm straight out, and in great
dooms; (And so say thou to the Israelites, I am the Lord,
who shall lead you out of your Egyptian prison; and I
shall rescue *you* from your servitude, *or your slavery*; and
I shall buy *you* back, *that is, redeem you*, with an
outstretched arm, and with mighty acts of judgement;)
7 and I shall take you to me into a people, and I shall
be your God; and ye shall know, for I am your Lord God,
which have led you out of the prison of (the) Egyptians,
(and I shall make you my people, and I shall be your
God; and ye shall know, that I am the Lord your God,
who led you out of your Egyptian prison,)
8 and have led you into the land, on which I raised
[up] mine hand, that I should give it to Abraham, and to
Isaac, and to Jacob; and I shall give to you that land to be
had in possession (and I shall give you that land for a
possession); I [am] the Lord.
9 Therefore Moses told all things to the sons of Israel,
which assented not to him for the anguish of spirit, and
for the full hard work *by which they were troubled*. (And
so Moses told all these things to the Israelites, but they
assented not to him, because of the anguish of their spirit,
and all their hard labour, *or all their tribulation*.)
10 And the Lord spake to Moses, and said,
11 Enter thou, and speak to Pharaoh, king of Egypt, that
he deliver the children of Israel from his land. (Go thou,
and tell Pharaoh, the king of Egypt, that he must let the
Israelites go out from his land.)
12 Moses answered before the Lord, Lo! the children of
Israel hear not me; and how shall Pharaoh hear, mostly
since I am uncircumcised in lips? (Moses answered the
Lord, and said, Lo! the Israelites will not listen to me;
how then shall Pharaoh listen to me, especially since I
am such a poor speaker?)
13 And the Lord spake to Moses and to Aaron, and he
gave (them) behests to the sons of Israel, and to Pharaoh,
king of Egypt, that they should lead out the sons of Israel
from the land of Egypt. (Yea, the Lord spoke to Moses
and Aaron, and gave them his commands concerning the
Israelites, and Pharaoh, the king of Egypt, namely, that
they should lead the Israelites out of the land of Egypt.)
14 These be the princes of the houses by their families.
The sons of Reuben, the first begotten of Israel (Israel's
first-born); Hanoch, and Pallu, Hezron, and Carmi; these
be the kindreds of Reuben.
15 The sons of Simeon; Jemuel, and Jamin, and Ohad,
and Jachin, and Zohar, and Saul (and Shaul), the son of a
woman of Canaan; these be the kindreds of Simeon.
16 And these be the names of the sons of Levi by their
kindreds; Gershon, and Kohath, and Merari. Forsooth
the years of the life of Levi were an hundred and seven
and thirty.
17 The sons of Gershon; Libni, and Shimi, by their
kindreds.
18 The sons of Kohath; Amram, and Izhar, and Hebron,
and Uzziel; and the years of the life of Kohath were an
hundred and three and thirty.
19 The sons of Merari were Mahali and Mushi. These
were the kindreds of Levi by their families.
20 Forsooth Amram took a wife, Jochebed, the
daughter of his father's brother, and she childed to him
Aaron, and Moses, and Marie; and the years of the life of
Amram were an hundred and seven and thirty. (And
Amram took a wife, his father's sister Jochebed, and she
bare him Aaron, and Moses, and Miriam; and Amram
lived a hundred and thirty-seven years.)
21 Also the sons of Izhar were Korah (And the sons of
Izhar were Korah), and Nepheg, and Zichri.
22 Also the sons of Uzziel were Mishael (And the sons
of Uzziel were Mishael), and Elzaphan, and Zithri.
23 Soothly Aaron took a wife, Elisheba, the daughter of
Amminadab, the sister of Naashon, and she childed to
him Nadab, and Abihu, and Eleazar, and Ithamar.
24 Also the sons of Korah were Assir (And the sons of
Korah were Assir), and Elkanah, and Abiasaph; these
were the kindreds of Korah.
25 And soothly Eleazar, son of Aaron, took a wife of the
daughters of Putiel, and she childed Phinehas to him.
These be the princes of the families of Levi by their
kindreds.
26 This is (that) Aaron and Moses, to which the Lord
commanded, that they should lead out of the land of
Egypt the sons of Israel by their companies; (These be
that Aaron and Moses, to whom the Lord commanded,
that they should lead the Israelites out of the land of
Egypt by their companies, *or by their tribes*;)
27 these it be, that spake to Pharaoh, king of Egypt, that
they lead the sons of Israel out of Egypt; this is (that)
Moses and Aaron, (these be the men, who spoke to
Pharaoh, the king of Egypt, and told him to let them lead
the Israelites out of Egypt; these be that Moses and Aaron,)
28 in the day in which the Lord spake to Moses in the
land of Egypt. (on the day in which the Lord spoke to
Moses in the land of Egypt.)
29 And the Lord spake to Moses, and said, I am the
Lord; speak thou to Pharaoh, king of Egypt, all things
which I speak to thee. (Yea, the Lord spoke to Moses, and
said, I am the Lord; tell Pharaoh, the king of Egypt, all the
things that I say to thee.)
30 And Moses said before the Lord, Lo! I am
uncircumcised in lips; how shall Pharaoh hear me? (Lo! I
am such a poor speaker! how will Pharaoh listen to me?)

CHAPTER 7

1 And the Lord said to Moses, Lo! I have made thee

the god of Pharaoh (Lo! I have made thee like a god to
Pharaoh); and Aaron, thy brother, shall be thy prophet.
2 Thou shalt speak to Aaron all things which I
command to thee, and he shall speak to Pharaoh, that he
deliver the sons of Israel from his land. (Thou shalt tell
Aaron all the things which I command to thee, and he
shall tell Pharaoh to let the Israelites go out of his land.)
3 But I shall make hard his heart, and I shall multiply
my signs and marvels in the land of Egypt, (But I shall
harden his heart, and then I shall multiply my signs and
miracles in the land of Egypt,)
4 and he shall not hear you; and I shall send mine
hand on Egypt, and I shall lead out mine host, and my
people, the sons of Israel, from the land of Egypt by most
dooms; (but he shall not listen to you; and then I shall put
my hand upon Egypt, and with mighty acts of judgement
I shall lead out my army, yea, my people, the Israelites,
from the land of Egypt;)
5 and [the] Egyptians shall know, that I am the Lord,
which have held forth mine hand on Egypt, and have led
out of the midst of them the sons of Israel. (and then the
Egyptians shall know, that I am the Lord, when I have
stretched forth my hand against Egypt, and have led the
Israelites out of their midst.)
6 And so Moses did and Aaron; as the Lord
commanded, so they did. (And so Moses and Aaron did
as the Lord commanded; yea, so they did.)
7 Forsooth Moses was of fourscore years, and Aaron
of fourscore years and three, when they spake to Pharaoh.
8 And the Lord said to Moses and to Aaron,
9 When Pharaoh shall say to you, Show ye signs to us,
thou shalt say to Aaron, Take thy rod, and cast forth it
before Pharaoh, and be it turned into a serpent. (When
Pharaoh shall say to you, Show ye signs to us, thou shalt
say to Aaron, Take thy staff, and throw it down before
Pharaoh, and it shall be turned into a serpent.)
10 And so Moses and Aaron entered to Pharaoh, and
did as the Lord commanded; and Aaron took the rod, and
cast forth it before Pharaoh and his servants, the which
rod was turned into a serpent. (And so Moses and Aaron
came before Pharaoh, and did as the Lord commanded;
and Aaron took his staff, and threw it down before Pharaoh
and his servants, and the staff was turned into a serpent.)
11 Forsooth Pharaoh called forth wise men, and
witches, and they also did by enchantments of Egypt, and
by some privy things, in like manner; (And Pharaoh
called forth Egypt's wise men, and witches, and they did
likewise with their enchantments, and their secret words;)
12 and all casted forth their rods, which were turned
into dragons; but the rod of Aaron devoured their rods.
(and they all threw down their staffs, and they turned into
serpents; but Aaron's staff devoured their staffs.)
13 And the heart of Pharaoh was made hard, and he
heard not them, as the Lord commanded. (But Pharaoh's
heart was hardened, and he would not listen to them, as
the Lord had said.)
14 Forsooth the Lord said to Moses, The heart of
Pharaoh is made grievous, he will not deliver the people;
(And the Lord said to Moses, Pharaoh's heart is hardened,
and he will not let the people go;)
15 go thou to him early; lo! he shall go out to the
waters, and thou shalt stand in the coming of him on the
brink of the flood; and thou shalt take in thine hand the
rod, that was turned into a dragon, (and so go thou early
to him; lo! he shall go out to the waters, and thou shalt
meet him on the river bank; and thou shalt take in thy
hand the staff, that was turned into a serpent,)
16 and thou shalt say to him, The Lord God of Hebrews
sent me to thee, and said, Deliver thou my people, that it
make sacrifice to me in desert; and till to *this* present time
thou wouldest not hear. (and thou shalt say to him, The
Lord God of the Hebrews sent me to thee, and said, Let
my people go, so that they can worship me in the
wilderness; and until this time thou hast not listened to
him.)
17 Therefore the Lord saith these things, In this thou
shalt know, that I am the Lord; lo! I shall smite with the
rod, that is in mine hand, the water of the flood, and it
shall be turned into blood (lo! I shall strike the water of
this River with the staff, that is in my hand, and that water
shall be turned into blood);
18 and the fishes that be in the flood shall die; and the
waters shall wax rotten, and the Egyptians drinking the
water of the flood shall be tormented. (and the fish that
be in the River shall die; and the waters shall grow rotten,
and the Egyptians shall not be able to drink any water
from this River.)
19 Also the Lord said to Moses, Say thou to Aaron,
Take thy rod, and hold forth thine hand on the waters of
Egypt, and on the floods of them, and on the streams of
them, and on the marshes, and on all the lakes of waters,
that those be turned into blood; and blood be in all the
land of Egypt, as well in vessels of wood, as of stone.
(And the Lord said to Moses, Say thou to Aaron, Take thy
staff, and stretch forth thy hand over the waters of Egypt,
yea, over the rivers, and the streams, and the marshes,
and all the lakes, so that they all be turned into blood;
and then blood shall be in all the land of Egypt, and even
in wooden vessels, and in stone vessels.)
20 And Moses and Aaron did so, as the Lord
commanded; and Aaron raised the rod, and smote the
water of the flood before Pharaoh and his servants, which
water was turned into blood; (And Moses and Aaron did
as the Lord commanded; and Aaron raised up his staff,
and struck the water of the River before Pharaoh and his
servants, and the water was turned into blood;)
21 and [the] fishes, that were in the flood, died; and the
flood was rotten, and [the] Egyptians might not drink the

water of the flood; and blood was in all the land of Egypt.
(and the fish, that were in the River, died; and the River
was rotten, and the Egyptians could not drink the water of
the River; and blood was in all the land of Egypt.)
22 And the witches of [the] Egyptians did in like
manner by their enchantments; and the heart of Pharaoh
was made hard, and he heard not them, as the Lord
commanded. (And the Egyptian witches did likewise with
their enchantments; but Pharaoh's heart was hardened,
and he would not listen to them, as the Lord had said.)
23 And he turned away himself (And he turned himself
away), and entered into his house, neither he took it to
heart, yea, in this time.
24 Forsooth all [the] Egyptians digged water about the
flood, to drink; for they might not drink of [the] water of
the flood. (And then all the Egyptians dug about the River
for water to drink, for they could not drink the water out
of the River, *that is, out of the Nile*.)
25 And seven days were fulfilled, after that the Lord
smote the flood. (And then seven days passed, from when
the Lord struck the River.)

CHAPTER 8

1 Also the Lord said to Moses, Enter thou to Pharaoh,
and thou shalt say to him, The Lord saith these things,
Deliver thou my people, that it make sacrifice to me;
(And then the Lord said to Moses, Go to Pharaoh, and
thou shalt say to him, The Lord saith these things, Let my
people go, so they can worship me;)
2 soothly if thou wilt not deliver (them), lo! I shall
smite all thy terms, *or coasts*, with paddocks; (and if thou
wilt not let them go, lo! I shall cover all thy land with
frogs,)
3 and the flood shall boil out paddocks, that shall go
up, and enter into thine house, and into the closet of thy
bed, and on thy bed, and into the house(s) of thy
servants, and into thy people, and into thine ovens, and
into the remnants of thy meats; (and the River shall boil
out frogs, that shall go up, and enter into thy house, and
into thy bed-closet, and onto thy bed, and into thy
servants' houses, and onto thy people, and into thy
ovens, and even onto thy food;)
4 and the paddocks shall enter to thee, and to thy
people, and to all thy servants. (and the frogs shall jump
on thee, and on thy people, and on all thy servants.)
5 And the Lord said to Moses, Say thou to Aaron,
Hold forth thine hand on the floods, and on the streams,
and on the marshes; and bring out paddocks on the land
of Egypt. (And the Lord said to Moses, Say thou to Aaron,
Stretch forth thy hand over the rivers, and the steams, and
the marshes; and bring out frogs onto the land of Egypt.)
6 And Aaron held forth the hand on the waters of
Egypt; and paddocks went up, and covered the land of
Egypt. (And Aaron stretched forth his hand over the
waters of Egypt; and frogs went out, and covered the land
of Egypt.)
7 Forsooth and the witches did in like manner by their
enchantments; and they brought forth paddocks on the
land of Egypt. (And the witches did likewise with their
enchantments; and they also brought forth frogs onto the
land of Egypt.)
8 Forsooth Pharaoh called (for) Moses and Aaron, and
said to them, Pray ye the Lord, that he do away the
paddocks from me, and from my people; and I shall
deliver the people, that it make sacrifice to the Lord (and
then I shall let the people go, so that they can offer
sacrifices to the Lord).
9 And Moses said to Pharaoh, Ordain thou a time to
me, when I shall pray for thee, and for thy servants, and
for thy people, that the paddocks be driven away from
thee, and from thine house(s), and from thy servants, and
from thy people; and [they] dwell only in the flood. (And
Moses said to Pharaoh, Ordain thou a time for me, when
I shall pray for thee, and for thy servants, and for thy
people, so that the frogs be driven away from thee, and
from thy houses, and from thy servants, and from thy
people; and so that they live only in the River.)
10 And he answered, Tomorrow. And Moses said, I
shall do by thy word, (so) that thou know, that none is as
our Lord God;
11 and the paddocks shall go away from thee, and from
thine house(s), and from thy children, and from thy
servants, and from thy people; and they shall dwell only
in the flood (and they shall live only in the River).
12 And Moses and Aaron went out from Pharaoh. And
Moses cried to the Lord, for the promise of (the)
paddocks, which he had said to Pharaoh (And Moses
cried to the Lord, to take away the frogs which he had
brought upon Pharaoh).
13 And the Lord did by the word of Moses; and the
paddocks were dead from [the] houses, and from [the]
towns, and from [the] fields; (And the Lord did what
Moses asked; and the frogs were dead in the houses, and
in the towns, and in the fields;)
14 and they gathered them into great heaps, and the
land was rotten, *or corrupted with stink*. [and they gathered
them together into great heaps without number, and the earth
stank.]
15 Soothly Pharaoh saw that rest was given, and he
made grievous his heart, and he heard not them, as the
Lord commanded. (But when Pharaoh saw that the
trouble had ceased, he hardened his heart, and he would
not listen to them, as the Lord had said.)
16 And the Lord said to Moses, Speak thou to Aaron,
Hold forth thy rod, and smite the dust of the earth (Say
thou to Aaron, Stretch forth thy staff, and strike the dust
of the earth), and little flies, *or gnats*, be in all the land of
Egypt.

17 And they did so; and Aaron held forth the hand, and
held the rod, and smote the dust of [the] earth; and gnats
were made in men, and in work beasts; all the dust of the
earth was turned into gnats by all the land of Egypt. (And
they did so; and Aaron stretched forth the staff with his
hand, and struck the dust of the earth; and gnats came on
people, and on the work beasts; yea, all the dust of the
earth was turned into gnats in all the land of Egypt.)
18 And the witches did in like manner by their
enchantments, that they should bring forth gnats, and
they might not; and gnats were as well in men as in work
beasts. (And the witches did likewise with their
enchantments, so that they would also bring forth gnats,
but they could not do so; still, gnats covered all the
people, and the work beasts as well.)
19 And the witches said to Pharaoh, This is the finger of
God. And the heart of Pharaoh was made hard, and he
heard not them, as the Lord commanded (But Pharaoh's
heart was hardened, and he would not listen to them, as
the Lord had said).
20 And the Lord said to Moses, Rise thou (up) early,
and stand before Pharaoh, for he shall go out to the
waters; and thou shalt say to him, The Lord saith these
things, Deliver thou my people, that it make sacrifice to
me (The Lord saith these things, Let my people go, so that
they can worship me);
21 that if thou wilt not deliver the people (but if thou
wilt not let the people go), lo! I shall send into thee, and
into thy servants, and into thy people, and into thine
houses, all the kind(s) of flies; and the houses of the
Egyptians shall be full-filled with flies of diverse kinds,
and all the land in which they shall be.
22 And in that day I shall make wonderful the land of
Goshen, in which my people is, that flies be not there;
and that thou know that I am the Lord in the midst of
[the] earth; (But on that day I shall protect the land of
Goshen, where my people be, so that there shall be no
flies there; and so that thou shalt know that I, the Lord,
am in the midst of the land;)
23 and I shall set parting betwixt my people and thy
people; this sign shall be tomorrow (this miracle shall
come tomorrow).
24 And the Lord did so. And a most grievous fly, *that
is, (a) multitude of flies*, came into the house of Pharaoh,
and *into the houses* of his servants, and into all the land
of Egypt; and the land was corrupted of such flies (and
the land was ruined by such a multitude of flies).
25 And Pharaoh called (for) Moses and Aaron, and said
to them, Go ye, make ye sacrifice to the Lord your God,
in this land (Go ye, and offer your sacrifices to the Lord
your God, here in this land).
26 And Moses said, It may not be [done] so, for why
shall we offer to the Lord our God the abominations of
Egyptians; that if we shall slay before the Egyptians those
things which they worship, they shall throw us down
with stones. (And Moses said, It cannot be done so, for
we shall not offer to the Lord our God the abominations
of the Egyptians; and if, in front of the Egyptians, we kill
those things which they worship, they shall throw us
down with stones.)
27 We shall go the way of three days into wilderness,
and we shall make sacrifice to our Lord God, as he
commanded us. (We shall make a journey for three days
into the wilderness, and we shall offer sacrifices to the
Lord our God, as he commanded us.)
28 And Pharaoh said, I shall deliver you, that ye make
sacrifice to the Lord your God in desert (I shall let you go,
so that ye can offer sacrifices to the Lord your God in the
wilderness); nevertheless go ye not (any) further; (and)
pray ye for me.
29 And Moses said, I shall go out from thee, and I shall
pray (to) the Lord; and the fly, *that is, the multitude of
flies*, shall go away from Pharaoh, and from his servants,
and (from) his people, tomorrow; nevertheless do not
thou more deceive me, that thou deliver not the people
to make sacrifice to the Lord (but do not thou deceive me
again, and not allow the people to go, and offer sacrifices
to the Lord).
30 And Moses went out from Pharaoh, and prayed the
Lord,
31 the which did by the word of Moses (and he did
what Moses asked), and took away the flies from
Pharaoh, and from his servants, and from his people;
none (was) left, soothly not one.
32 And the heart of Pharaoh was made hard, so that he
delivered not the people, soothly neither in this time.
(But again Pharaoh's heart was hardened, and he would
not let the people go, yea, truly not at that time.)

CHAPTER 9

1 Forsooth the Lord said to Moses, Enter thou to
Pharaoh, and speak thou to him, (and say,) The Lord God
of Hebrews saith these things, Deliver thou my people,
that it make sacrifice to me (And the Lord said to Moses,
Go thou to Pharaoh, and tell him, The Lord God of the
Hebrews saith these things, Let my people go, so that
they can worship me;)
2 that if thou forsakest yet, and withholdest them, (but
if thou yet forsakest, and holdest onto them,)
3 lo! mine hand shall be on thy fields, (and) on the
horses, and asses, and camels, and oxen, and sheep, a
pestilence full grievous; (lo! my hand shall be upon thy
fields, and upon the horses, and donkeys, and camels,
and oxen, and sheep, with a horrible pestilence;)
4 and the Lord shall make a marvellous thing betwixt
the possessions of Israel and the possessions of the
Egyptians (and the Lord shall make a distinction between
the Israelites' possessions, and the Egyptians'

possessions), (so) that utterly nothing perish of these
things that pertain to the sons of Israel.
5 And the Lord ordained a time, and said, Tomorrow
the Lord shall do this word in the land (Tomorrow the
Lord shall do this thing in the land).
6 Therefore the Lord made this word in the tother day,
and all the living beasts of the Egyptians were dead;
forsooth utterly nothing perished of the beasts of the sons
of Israel. (And so the Lord brought this about the next
day, and all of the Egyptians' beasts died; but none of the
Israelites' beasts perished.)
7 And Pharaoh sent to see (what had happened), (for)
neither anything was dead of these things which Israel
wielded; and the heart of Pharaoh was made full
grievous, and he delivered not the people (but Pharaoh's
heart was hardened, and he would not let the people go).
8 And the Lord said to Moses and Aaron, Take ye *your*
hands full of ashes of a chimney, and Moses sprinkle it
into heaven before Pharaoh; (And the Lord said to Moses
and Aaron, Take ye some handfuls of ashes from a
chimney, and Moses toss it into the air before Pharaoh;)
9 and be there dust on all the land of Egypt; for why
botches shall be in men, and in work beasts, and swelling
bladders shall be in all the land of Egypt. (and let there be
dust in all the land of Egypt; and let it bring forth sores of
swelling boils on the people, and on the work beasts, in
all the land of Egypt.)
10 And they took ashes of a chimney, and they stood
before Pharaoh; and Moses sprinkled it into heaven; and
wounds of swelling bladders were made in men, and in
work beasts; (And so they took some ashes from a
chimney, and they stood before Pharaoh; and Moses
tossed it into the air; and sores of swelling boils were
made on the people, and on the work beasts;)
11 and the witches might not stand before Moses, for
the wounds, *or sores*, that were in them, and in all the
land of Egypt. (and the witches could not stand up before
Moses, because of the sores that were on them, and on
all the Egyptians.)
12 And the Lord made hard the heart of Pharaoh, and
he heard not them, as the Lord spake to Moses. (But the
Lord hardened Pharaoh's heart, and he would not listen
to them, as the Lord had said to Moses.)
13 Also the Lord said to Moses, Rise thou early, and
stand before Pharaoh, and thou shalt say to him, The
Lord God of Hebrews saith these things, Deliver thou my
people, that it make sacrifice to me; (And the Lord said to
Moses, Rise thou up early, and stand before Pharaoh, and
thou shalt say to him, The Lord God of the Hebrews saith
these things, Let my people go, so that they can worship
me;)
14 for in this time I shall send all my vengeances on
thine heart, and on thy servants, and on thy people, that
thou know, that none is like me in all [the] earth. (for at
this time I shall send all my plagues onto thee, and onto
thy servants, and onto thy people, so that thou know, that
there is no one like me in all the earth.)
15 For now I shall hold forth mine hand, and I shall
smite thee and thy people with pestilence, and thou shalt
perish from the earth; (And now I shall stretch forth my
hand, and I shall strike thee and thy people with
pestilence, and thou shalt perish from off the earth;)
16 forsooth therefore I have set thee, that I show my
strength in thee, and that my name be told (out) in each
land. (yea, I have kept thee alive, only so that I could
show my strength through thee, and so that my name
would be spoken of in every land.)
17 Yet thou withholdest my people, and wilt not
deliver it? (Yet still thou holdest onto my people, and wilt
not let them go!)
18 Lo! tomorrow, in this same hour (at this same hour),
I shall rain full much hail, what manner hail was not in
Egypt, from the day in which it was founded, till into this
present time.
19 Therefore send thou (a command) right now, and
gather (in) thy work beasts, and all things that thou hast in
the field; for (those) men, and work beasts, and all things
that be in fields withoutforth, and be not gathered (in) from
the fields, and [the] hail fall on those, they shall (all) die.
20 He that dreaded the word of the Lord (He who feared
the word of the Lord), of the servants of Pharaoh, made his
servants and (his) work beasts (to) flee into (their) houses;
21 soothly he that despised the Lord's word, left his
servants and *his* work beasts in the fields.
22 And the Lord said to Moses, Hold forth thine hand
into heaven, that hail be made in all the land of Egypt
(Stretch forth thy hand toward the heavens, so that hail
shall fall on all the land of Egypt), (yea,) on men, and on
work beasts, and on each herb of the field in the land of
Egypt.
23 And Moses held forth the rod into heaven (And
Moses stretched forth his staff toward the heavens); and
the Lord gave thunders, and hail, and lightnings running
about on (all) the land; and the Lord rained hail on the
land of Egypt;
24 and hail and fire meddled together were borne forth;
and it was of so much greatness, how great appeared
never before in all the land of Egypt, since that people
was made. (and hail and fire mixed, *or mingled*, together
were brought forth; yea, it was so great, that never had
such appeared before in all the land of Egypt, since that
people were made.)
25 And the hail smote in all the land of Egypt all (the)
things that were in the fields, from man till to work beast;
and the hail smote all the herb of the field, and brake all
the flax of the country;
26 only the hail felled not in the land of Goshen, where
the sons of Israel were. (and only in the land of Goshen,

where the Israelites lived, did no hail fall/was there no
hail.)
27 And Pharaoh sent, and called (for) Moses and Aaron,
and said to them, I have sinned also now (This time I
have sinned); the Lord is just, and I and my people be
wicked;
28 pray ye the Lord, that the thunders and hail of God
cease, and I shall deliver you, and dwell ye no more here
(and I shall let you go, and ye shall no longer remain
here).
29 Moses said, When I shall go out of the city, I shall
hold forth mine hands to the Lord, and [the] lightnings
and (the) thunders shall cease, and (the) hail shall not be,
(so) that thou know, that the earth is the Lord's;
30 forsooth I know, that thou and thy servants dread
not yet the Lord [God]. (but I know, that thou and thy
servants do not yet fear the Lord God.)
31 Therefore the flax and barley was hurt, for the barley
was green, and the flax had burgeoned then knops; (And
so the flax and the barley were destroyed, for the barley
was still green, and the flax had only then brought forth
knops, *or buds*;)
32 forsooth wheat and beans were not hurt, for those
were late *sown*. (but the wheat and the beans were not
destroyed, for they were *sown* late.)
33 And Moses went out from Pharaoh, and from the
city, and held forth his hands to the Lord, and (the)
thunders and (the) hail ceased, and [the] rain dropped no
more on the earth.
34 Soothly Pharaoh saw that the rain had ceased, and
the hail, and thunders, and he increased (his) sin; and the
heart of him, and of his servants, was made grievous,
(And when Pharaoh saw that the rain, and the hail, and
the thunder, had ceased, he increased his sin; and his
heart, and the hearts of his servants, were hardened,)
35 and his heart was made hard greatly; neither he let
go the sons of Israel, as the Lord commanded by the hand
of Moses. (yea, his heart was greatly hardened; and he
still would not let the Israelites go, as the Lord had said
through Moses.)

CHAPTER 10

1 And the Lord said to Moses, Enter thou to Pharaoh,
for I have made hard the heart of him, and of his servants,
that I do these signs of me in him (so that I can do my
miracles before him/so that I can do my miracles among
them);
2 and (so) that thou (can) tell in the ears of thy son(s),
and of thy sons' sons, how oft I all-brake the Egyptians,
and did signs in them (and did these miracles among
them); and (so) that ye know that I am the Lord.
3 Therefore Moses and Aaron entered to Pharaoh, and
said to him, The Lord God of (the) Hebrews saith these
things, How long wilt thou not be made subject to me?
Deliver thou my people, that it make sacrifice to me (Let
my people go, so that they can worship me);
4 else soothly if thou against-standest, and wilt not
deliver it, lo! I shall bring in tomorrow a locust, *that is, a
multitude of locusts*, into thy coasts, (or else, if thou
standest against me, *that is, if thou refusest me*, and wilt
not let them go, lo! tomorrow I shall bring a multitude of
locusts into thy land,)
5 that shall cover the over-part of the earth, neither
anything thereof shall appear, but that, that was left of the
hail shall be eaten *of (the) locusts*; for the locust(s) shall
gnaw all the trees that burgeon in [the] fields; (which
shall cover the face of the earth, so that none of it can be
seen; and what was left by the hail shall be eaten *by the
locusts*, for the locusts shall gnaw all the trees that grow
in the fields;)
6 and they shall full-fill thine houses, and *the houses*
of thy servants, and of all the Egyptians, (by) how great
thy fathers and thy grand-sires saw not, since they were
born on (the) earth, till into *this* present day. And Moses
turned away himself (And then Moses turned), and went
out from Pharaoh.
7 Forsooth the servants of Pharaoh said to him, How
long shall we suffer this offense? Deliver the men, that
they make sacrifice to their Lord God; seest thou not that
Egypt hath perished? (And Pharaoh's servants said to him,
How long shall we suffer this tribulation?/How long shall
this man bring trouble upon us? Let those people go, so
that they can worship the Lord their God; seest thou not
that Egypt hath been destroyed?)
8 And they again called Moses and Aaron to Pharaoh,
and he said to them, Go ye, and make ye sacrifice to your
Lord God; which be they, that shall go? (and he said to
them, Go ye, and worship the Lord your God; who be
they, who shall go?)
9 Moses said, We shall go with our little children and
(our) elders, and with (our) sons, and (our) daughters,
(and) with (our) sheep, and (our) great beasts; for it is the
solemnity of our Lord God (for it is a Feast unto the Lord
our God).
10 And Pharaoh answered, So the Lord be with you[6];
how therefore shall I deliver you, and your little children?
to whom is it doubt(ful), that ye think (not the) worst
things? (And Pharaoh answered, And may the Lord be
with you! but how can I let you, and your little children,
go? for who doubteth, that ye think, *or that ye plan*, to do
only the worst *things* against me?)
11 It shall not be done so; but go ye men only, and
make ye sacrifice to the Lord; for also ye asked this. And
anon they were cast out from the sight of Pharaoh. (Nay,
it shall not be done so! but only the men shall go, and

---

[6] *He said this in scorn, (or sarcastically,) understanding the contrary.*

worship the Lord; for this is what ye asked for. And at
once they were cast out from before Pharaoh.)
12 Forsooth the Lord said to Moses, Hold forth thine
hand on the land of Egypt, to a locust, *that is, (a)
multitude of locusts*, that it ascend on the land, and
devour all the herb which is left of the hail. (And the Lord
said to Moses, Stretch forth thy hand over the land of
Egypt, for a multitude of locusts to ascend upon the land,
and devour all the herbage that be left from the hail.)
13 And Moses held forth the rod on the land of Egypt
(And so Moses stretched out his staff over the land of
Egypt), and the Lord brought in a burning wind all that
day and night; and when the morrowtide was made, the
burning wind raised [up] (the) locusts,
14 which ascended on all the land of Egypt, and sat in
all the coasts of Egyptians (and settled on all the land of
Egypt); *and the locusts were* unnumberable, and such
were not before that time, neither shall come afterward.
15 And those covered all the face of the earth, and
wasted all things; therefore the herb of the earth was
devoured, and whatever (thing) of apples was in (the)
trees, which the hail had left, *it was devoured*; and utterly
no green thing was left in trees, and in herbs of the earth,
in all Egypt (and utterly nothing green was left on the
trees, or on the plants of the land, in all of Egypt).
16 Wherefore Pharaoh hasted, and called (for) Moses
and Aaron, and said to them, I have sinned against your
Lord God, and against you (I have sinned against the Lord
your God, and against you);
17 but now forgive ye the sin to me; also in this time
pray ye your Lord God, that he take away from me this
death. (but now forgive ye my sin; and also at this time
pray ye the Lord your God, that he take away this death
from me.)
18 And Moses went out of the sight of Pharaoh, and
prayed the Lord; (And Moses went out from before
Pharaoh, and prayed to the Lord;)
19 the which made a full strong wind to blow from the
west, and it took, and cast the locust(s) into the Red Sea[7];
soothly there (was) left not one, in all the coasts of Egypt.
(and the Lord made a strong wind to blow from the west,
and it took, and threw the locusts into the Red Sea; and
there was not one left in all the land of Egypt.)
20 And the Lord made hard the heart of Pharaoh, and
he let not go the sons of Israel. (But the Lord hardened
Pharaoh's heart, and still he would not let the Israelites go.)
21 Forsooth the Lord said to Moses, Hold forth thine
hand into heaven (Stretch forth thy hand toward the
heavens), and (let) darkness/es be on (all) the land of Egypt,
so thick that they may be groped.
22 And Moses held forth his hand into heaven, and
horrible darknesses were made in all the land of Egypt;
(And Moses stretched forth his hand toward the heavens,
and a horrible darkness came upon all the land of Egypt;)
23 *and* in three days no man saw his brother, neither
moved himself from that place in which he was.
Wherever the children of Israel dwelled, light was. (*and*
for three days no one saw their brother, nor moved
themselves from where they were. But there was light
wherever the Israelites were.)
24 And Pharaoh called Moses and Aaron, and said to
them, Go ye, make ye sacrifice to the Lord; only your
sheep and your great beasts dwell still; your little
children go with you. (And Pharaoh called for Moses and
Aaron, and said to them, Go ye, and worship the Lord;
your sheep and your great beasts must stay here, but
even your little children can go with you.)
25 And Moses said, Also thou shalt give to us offerings
and burnt sacrifices, which we shall offer to our Lord
God; (And Moses said, Then shalt thou give us the
offerings, and the burnt sacrifices, which we shall offer to
the Lord our God?)
26 (nay!) all the flocks shall go with us, for a claw shall
not dwell of those things, that be needful into the
worshipping of our Lord God, mostly since we know not
what oughteth to be offered, till we come to that place.
27 Forsooth the Lord made hard the heart of Pharaoh,
and he would not deliver them. (But the Lord hardened
Pharaoh's heart, and he would not let them go.)
28 And Pharaoh said to Moses, Go away from me, and
beware that thou see no more my face; in whatever day
thou shalt appear to me, thou shalt die. (And Pharaoh
said to Moses, Go away from me, and beware that thou
do not see my face again; for on whatever day thou shalt
appear before me, thou shalt die.)
29 Moses answered, Be it done so, as thou hast spoken;
I shall no more see thy face. (Moses answered, Let it be
done as thou hast spoken; I shall not see thy face again.)

CHAPTER 11

1 And the Lord said to Moses, Yet I shall touch Pharaoh
and Egypt with one vengeance, and after these things he
shall deliver you, and he shall constrain you to go out.
(And then the Lord said to Moses, Yet I shall strike Pharaoh
and Egypt with one more plague, and after these things he
shall let you go, yea, he shall compel you to go out *of his
land*.)
2 Therefore thou shalt say to all the people, that a man
ask of his friend, and a woman of her neighbouress, silver
vessel(s) and golden, and clothes; (And so thou shalt say to
all the people, that every man ask his friend, and every
woman her neighbour, for gold and silver jewelry, and for
clothes;)
3 forsooth the Lord shall give grace to his people before
the Egyptians. And Moses was a full great man in the land

[7] In Hebrew, 'the Sea of Reeds'; in Greek, 'the Red Sea'. (Gehman)

of Egypt, before the servants of Pharaoh and all the people;
4 and (at once) he said (to the king), The Lord saith
these things, At midnight I shall enter into Egypt;
5 and each first begotten thing in the land of Egyptians
shall die, from the first begotten of Pharaoh, that sitteth in
the throne of him, till to the first begotten of the
handmaid, which is at [the] quern; and all the first
engendered of beasts *shall die*; (and every first-born *son*
in the land of Egypt shall die, from the first-born of
Pharaoh, who sitteth on his throne, unto the first-born of
the slave-girl, who is at the hand-mill; and also all the
first-born *male* beasts *shall die*;)
6 and [a] great cry shall be in all the land of Egypt,
what manner cry was not before, neither shall be
afterward (nor shall ever be heard again).
7 Forsooth at all the children of Israel, a dog shall not
make (a) privy noise, from man till to beast; that ye know
by how great miracle the Lord parteth [the] Egyptians and
Israel. (And yet among all the Israelites, a dog shall not
even bark at a man or a beast; so that ye know by how
great a miracle the Lord separateth the Egyptians and the
Israelites.)
8 And all these thy servants shall come down to me,
and they shall pray (to) me, and shall say, Go out thou
(Go thou out), and all the people which is subject to
thee; (and) after these things we shall go out. And (then)
Moses full wroth went out from Pharaoh.
9 Forsooth the Lord said to Moses, Pharaoh shall not
hear you, that many signs be made in the land of Egypt
(For the Lord had said to Moses, Pharaoh shall not listen
to you, so that many miracles can be done in the land of
Egypt.)
10 Soothly Moses and Aaron made all the signs and
wonders, that be *here* written, before Pharaoh; and the
Lord made hard the heart of Pharaoh, neither he delivered
the sons of Israel from his land. (And Moses and Aaron
did all the miracles and wonders, that be written *here*,
before Pharaoh; but the Lord hardened Pharaoh's heart,
and he would not let the Israelites go out of his land.)

CHAPTER 12

1 Also the Lord said to Moses and Aaron in the land of
Egypt,
2 This month, the beginning of months to you, shall
be the first in the months of the year. (This month shall be
the beginning of months for you, yea, it shall become the
first month of the new year.)
3 Speak ye to all the company of the sons of Israel,
and say ye to them, In the tenth day of this month, each
man take a lamb by his families and houses; (Speak ye to
all the Israelites, and say ye to them, On the tenth day of
this month, each man take a lamb for his family, one for
each household;)
4 but if the number (of people) is less, that it may not
suffice to eat the lamb, he shall take (it with) his
neighbour, which is joined to his house, by the number
of souls, that may suffice to the eating of the lamb. (but if
the number of people in his family is too small to eat the
lamb, he shall eat it with his neighbour who is near to his
house, yea, with the number of souls who shall suffice to
eat all of the lamb.)
5 Forsooth the lamb shall be a male of one year,
without wem; by which custom ye shall take also a kid, *if
a lamb may not be had in good manner*; (And the lamb
shall be a male of one year, without blemish, *or without
fault*; for which rite ye may also take a goat kid, *if a lamb
cannot be had in good manner*;)
6 and ye shall keep him till to the fourteenth day of
this month; and all the multitude of the sons of Israel
shall offer him at eventide.
7 And they shall take of his blood, and they shall put
it on ever either (door-)post, and in the lintels, *or higher
thresholds*, of the houses, in which they shall eat him;
(And they shall take some of his blood, and they shall put
it on both door-posts, and on the lintels, *or the upper
thresholds*, of the houses, in which they shall eat the
lamb;)
8 and in that night they shall eat (the) flesh, roasted
with fire, and therf loaves, with the *herb* lettuce of the
field/with bitternesses of the field. (and on that night they
shall eat the flesh, roasted with fire, and unleavened
bread, and bitter herbs of the field.)
9 Ye shall not eat thereof any raw thing, neither
sodden in water, but roasted only by fire; ye shall devour
the head with the feet, and with the entrails thereof; (Ye
shall not eat any of it raw, or boiled in water, but only
that which is roasted in the fire; ye shall devour the head
with the feet, and all its entrails;)
10 neither anything thereof shall abide till to the
morrowtide; if any*thing thereof* is left (over), ye shall
burn *it* in the fire.
11 Forsooth thus ye shall eat him; ye shall gird your
reins, and ye shall have shoes in *your* feet, and ye shall
hold staves in *your* hands, and ye shall eat *it* hastily; for it
is pask, that is, the passing [forth] of the Lord. (And ye
shall eat it thus; ye shall gird up your reins, and ye shall
have shoes on *your* feet, and ye shall hold your staff in
your hand, and ye shall eat *it* hastily; for it is the
Passover, that is, the Passing Over of the Lord.)
12 And I shall pass through the land of Egypt in that
night, and I shall smite all the first engendered thing(s)/(all)
the first begotten thing(s) in the land of Egypt, from man till
to beast; and I the Lord shall make dooms in all the gods
of Egypt. (And I shall pass through the land of Egypt on
that night, and I shall strike down all the first-born in the
land of Egypt, from man unto beast; and I the Lord shall
execute judgement against all the gods of Egypt.)
13 Forsooth [the] blood shall be to you into (a) sign, in

the houses in which ye shall be; and I shall see the blood,
and I shall pass (over) you; neither a wound destroying
shall be in you, when I shall smite the land of Egypt. (And
the blood on the houses in which ye shall be, shall be a
sign of you; and I shall see the blood, and I shall pass
over you; and there shall be no destroying wound
inflicted upon you, when I shall strike the land of Egypt.)
14 Forsooth ye shall have this day into mind, and ye
shall make it solemn to the Lord in your generations, by
everlasting worshipping. (And ye shall remember this
day, and on it ye shall dedicate a Feast unto the Lord in
all your generations to come, by an everlasting rite.)
15 Seven days ye shall eat therf bread; in the first day
nothing dighted with sourdough shall be in your houses;
whoever shall eat anything dighted with sourdough, from
the first day till to the seventh day, that soul shall perish
from Israel. (For seven days ye shall eat unleavened
bread; from the first day nothing made with yeast shall be
in your houses; whoever shall eat anything made with
yeast, from the first day until the seventh day, that soul
shall perish from the midst of Israel.)
16 The first day shall be holy and solemn, and the
seventh day (also) shall be worshipful by the same
hallowing; ye shall not do any work in those days, except
these things that pertain to meat; (On the first day there
shall be a holy gathering, and on the seventh day there
shall also be a holy gathering; ye shall not do any work
on those days, except those things that pertain to the
preparation of meals;)
17 and ye shall keep (the feast of) therf bread. For in
that same day I shall lead out of the land of Egypt your
host; and ye shall keep this day in your generations by
everlasting custom. (and ye shall keep the Feast of
Unleavened Bread. For on that day I led your host out of
the land of Egypt; and ye shall remember this day in all
your generations to come, by an everlasting rite.)
18 In the first month, in the fourteenth day of the
month, at eventide, ye shall eat therf bread, till to the one
and twentieth day of the same month at eventide. (In the
first month, on the fourteenth day of the month, from the
evening on, ye shall eat unleavened bread, until the one
and twentieth day of the same month, in the evening.)
19 In seven days nothing dighted with sourdough shall
be found in your houses; if any eateth anything dighted
with sourdough, his soul shall perish from the company
of Israel, as well of comelings, *that be heathen men
converted to the faith of Jews,* as of them that be born in
the land. (Yea, for seven days nothing made with yeast
shall be found in your houses; if anyone eateth anything
made with yeast, they shall perish, *or be cut off,* from the
congregation of Israel, yea, this is for both newcomers,
that is, the heathen who be converted to the Jewish faith,
as well as for those who be born in the land.)
20 Ye shall not eat anything made with sourdough, and
ye shall eat therf bread in all your dwelling places.
21 Forsooth Moses called all the elder men of the sons
of Israel, and said to them, Go ye, and take ye a beast by
your families, and offer ye pask; (And so Moses called all
the elders of the Israelites, and said to them, Go ye, and
get ye a beast for your families, and offer ye the Passover;)
22 and dip ye a bundle of hyssop, in the blood which is
in the threshold, *either in a vessel beside the threshold,*
and sprinkle ye thereof on the lintel, and ever either
(door-)post; none of you shall go out at the door of his
house till the morrowtide. (and dip ye a bundle of hyssop
in the blood which is on the threshold, *or in a vessel
beside the threshold,* and sprinkle some of it on the lintel,
and on both door-posts; and then none of you shall go
out of the door of his house until the morning.)
23 For the Lord shall pass [forth] smiting the Egyptians;
and when he shall see the blood in the lintel, and in
ever either post (and when he shall see the blood on the
lintel, and on both door-posts), he shall pass (over) the
door of the house; and he shall not suffer the smiter to
enter into your houses, and to hurt *you.*
24 Keep thou this word; it shall be a lawful thing to thee
and to thy sons till into without end. (Do thou this thing;
yea, it shall be an everlasting rite for thee and for thy sons.)
25 And when ye shall enter into the land which the
Lord shall give to you, as he promised, ye shall keep
these ceremonies;
26 and when your sons shall say to you, What is this
religion? (What is the meaning of this rite?)
27 ye shall say to them, It is the sacrifice of the passing
(over) of the Lord, when he passed over the houses of the
sons of Israel in Egypt, and smote the Egyptians, and
delivered our houses (but spared our houses). And the
people was bowed, and worshipped.
28 And the sons of Israel went out (And the Israelites
went out), and did as the Lord commanded to Moses and
Aaron.
29 Forsooth it was done in the midst of the night, the
Lord smote all the first begotten thing(s) in the land of
Egypt, from the first begotten of Pharaoh, that sat in the
throne of him (who sat on his throne), till to the first
begotten of a captive woman, that was in (the) prison,
and all the first engendered of beasts.
30 And Pharaoh rose (up) in the night, and all his
servants, and all Egypt; and a great cry was made in Egypt;
for none house was, in which a dead man lay not (for there
was not one house in which there was not a dead son).
31 And when Moses and Aaron were called in the
night, Pharaoh said, Rise ye, and go ye out from my
people, both ye and the sons of Israel; go ye, offer ye to
the Lord, as ye say; (And when Moses and Aaron were
called for in the night, Pharaoh said, Rise ye up, and go
ye out from my people, both ye and the Israelites; go ye,
and worship ye the Lord, as ye say that ye want to do;)

32 (and) take ye your sheep and [your] great beasts, as
ye asked (for); and go ye, and (also) bless ye me.
33 And the Egyptians constrained the people to go out
of the land swiftly, and said, All we shall die! (And the
Egyptians compelled the people to swiftly go out of the
land, saying, Or else we shall all die!)
34 Therefore the people took meal sprinkled together,
before that it was dighted with sourdough (And so the
people took the meal, *or the flour,* before that any yeast
was added to it); and they bound *it* in mantles, and put *it*
on their shoulders.
35 And the sons of Israel did as the Lord commanded to
Moses; and they asked of the Egyptians silver vessels and
golden, and full much clothing. (And the Israelites did as
the Lord commanded to Moses; and they asked the
Egyptians for gold and silver jewelry, and for a great deal
of clothes.)
36 Forsooth the Lord gave grace to the people before the
Egyptians, that the Egyptians lent to them; and they made
bare the Egyptians. (And the Lord gave grace to the people
before the Egyptians, so that the Egyptians gave them all
these things; and so they plundered the Egyptians.)
37 And the children of Israel went forth from Rameses
into Succoth, almost six hundred thousand of footmen,
without little children and women; (And the Israelites
went forth from Rameses unto Succoth, almost six
hundred thousand men on foot, not counting the women
and the little children;)
38 but also the common people of males and of
females unnumberable went up with them; (and) sheep,
and oxen, and full many beasts of diverse kind *also.*
39 And they baked meal, which sprinkled together a
while ago they took from Egypt, and made therf loaves
baken under ashes; for the loaves might not be dighted
with sourdough, for [the] Egyptians compelled *them* to go
out, and suffered not *them* to make any tarrying, neither
it was leisure to make any stew. (And they baked the
meal, which they had taken from Egypt, and made
unleavened bread baked under ashes; for the loaves did
not have any yeast, for the Egyptians compelled *them* to
go out, and did not allow *them* to tarry, nor was there
time to even make any stew.)
40 Forsooth the dwelling of the sons of Israel, by which
they dwelled in Egypt, was of four hundred and thirty
years; (And the Israelites had lived in Egypt for four
hundred and thirty years;)
41 and when those *years* were fulfilled, all the host of
the Lord went out of the land of Egypt in the same day.
(and when those *years* were ended, all the Lord's army
went out of the land of Egypt on the same day.)
42 This night is worthy to be kept in the worshipping of
the Lord, when he led them out of the land of Egypt; all the
sons of Israel ought to keep this *night* in their generations.
(This night is worthy to be kept for worshipping the Lord,
when he led them out of the land of Egypt; all the Israelites
ought to keep watch on this *night* in all their generations.)
43 Also the Lord said to Moses and Aaron, This is the
religion of pask; each alien shall not eat thereof; (And the
Lord said to Moses and Aaron, This is the rite of the
Passover; each foreigner, *or each stranger,* shall not eat it;)
44 soothly each servant bought shall be circumcised,
and so he shall eat; (but each bought servant, *or slave,*
shall be circumcised first, and then he shall eat it;)
45 a comeling and a hired man shall not eat thereof;
(but the newcomer and the hired man shall not eat it;)
46 it shall be eaten in one house; neither ye shall bear
out the flesh thereof; neither ye shall break a bone thereof.
47 Each company of the sons of Israel shall make that
pask; (All the congregation of Israel shall keep this Feast;)
48 that if any pilgrim will pass into your faith and
worshipping, and make [the] pask of the Lord, each male
kind of him shall be circumcised *before the solemnity,*
and then he shall make *it* lawful(ly), and he shall be
together *with them* as a man born of the land; forsooth if
any man is not circumcised, he shall not eat thereof. (and
if any foreigner will join your faith and worshipping, and
he desire to keep the Lord's Passover, each male of them
shall be circumcised *before the Feast,* and then he shall
keep *it* lawfully, and he shall be like a man born in the
land; but if any man is not circumcised, he shall not eat it.)
49 The same law shall be to a man born of the land,
and to a comeling, that taketh your faith, the which is a
pilgrim with you. (The same law shall be for a man born
in the land, as for a newcomer, who taketh your faith,
yea, he who is a foreigner among you.)
50 And all the sons of Israel did as the Lord
commanded to Moses and Aaron.
51 And in the same day the Lord led out of the land of
Egypt the sons of Israel, by their companies. (And so on
that day the Lord led the Israelites out of the land of
Egypt, by their tribes.)

CHAPTER 13

1 And the Lord spake to Moses, and said,
2 Hallow thou to me each first begotten thing that
openeth the womb among the sons of Israel, as well of
men as of beasts (of men as well as of beasts), for why
(they) all be mine.
3 And Moses said to the people, Have ye mind of this
day, in which ye went out of Egypt, and of the house of
servage, for in [a] strong hand the Lord led you out of this
place, that ye eat no bread dighted with sourdough. (And
Moses said to the people, Remember ye this day, in
which ye went out of Egypt, and out of the house of
servitude, *or of slavery,* for by his strong hand the Lord
led you out of this place, and remember to not eat any
bread made with yeast *on this day.*)
4 Today ye go out, in the month of new fruits; (Go ye

out today, in the month of Abib;)
5 and when the Lord hath led thee into the land of
Canaanites, and of Hittites, and of Amorites, and of
Hivites, and of Jebusites, which land he swore to thy
fathers, that he should give to thee, a land flowing with
milk and honey, thou shalt hallow this custom of holy
things in this month (thou shalt keep this rite in this
month).
6 Seven days thou shalt eat therf loaves, and the
solemnity of the Lord shall be in the seventh day; (For
seven days thou shalt eat unleavened bread, and a Feast
unto the Lord shall be held on the seventh day;)
7 ye shall eat therf loaves seven days, nothing dighted
with sourdough shall appear at thee, neither in all thy
coasts. (ye shall eat unleavened bread for seven days, and
nothing made with yeast shall be seen among thee, not in
all thy land.)
8 And thou shalt tell to thy son in that day, and shalt
say, This it is that the Lord did to me, when I went out of
Egypt. (And thou shalt say to thy son on that day, This is
done because of what the Lord did for me, when I went
out of Egypt.)
9 And it shall be as a sign in thine hand, and as a
memorial before thine eyes, and that the law of the Lord
be ever[more] in thy mouth; for in a strong hand the Lord
led thee out of Egypt, and of the house of servage. (And it
shall be like a sign on thy hand, and as a reminder before
thine eyes, so that the Lord's law is always in thy mouth;
for by a strong hand the Lord led thee out of Egypt, and
out of the house of servitude, *or of slavery*.)
10 Thou shalt keep such a worshipping in time
ordained, from days into days, *that is, from year into
year*. (Thou shalt keep this rite in the time ordained, that
is, from year to year.)
11 And when the Lord hath brought thee into the land
of Canaanites, as he swore to thee, and to thy fathers, and
hath given it to thee,
12 thou shalt separate to the Lord all thing (of male
kind) that (first) openeth the womb, and that that is first in
thy beasts (thou shalt set aside for the Lord all the males
who first openeth the womb, and all the males that be
first in thy beasts); whatever thing thou hast of male kind,
thou shalt hallow *it* to the Lord.
13 Thou shalt (ex)change the first engendered of an ass
for a sheep, that if thou again-buyest *it* not, thou shalt slay
it; forsooth thou shalt again-buy with price all the first
begotten of a man of thy sons. (Thou shalt exchange the
first-born of a donkey for a sheep, and if thou buyest *it*
not back, then thou shalt kill *it*; but thou must buy back
all thy first-born sons.)
14 And when thy son shall ask thee tomorrow, and say,
What is this? thou shalt answer to him, In a strong hand
the Lord led us out of the land of Egypt, of the house of
servage (By a strong hand the Lord led us out of the land
of Egypt, out of the house of servitude, *or of slavery*);
15 for when Pharaoh was made hard *in heart*, and
would not deliver us, the Lord slew all the first begotten
thing in the land of Egypt, from the first begotten of man,
till to the first engendered of beasts; therefore I offer to
the Lord all thing of male kind that (first) openeth the
womb, and I (shall) again-buy all the first begotten things
of my sons. (for when Pharaoh's heart was hardened, and
he would not let us go, the Lord killed all the first-born
things in the land of Egypt, from the first-born of man,
unto the first-born of beasts; and so I offer to the Lord all
the things of male kind that first openeth the womb, and I
shall buy back all the first-born of my sons.)
16 Therefore it shall be as a sign in thine hand, and as a
thing hanged for mind before thine eyes, for in a strong
hand the Lord led us out of Egypt. (And so it shall be like
a sign on thy hand, and like a thing hung up as a
reminder before thine eyes, for by a strong hand the Lord
led us out of Egypt.)
17 Therefore when Pharaoh had sent out the people,
God led not them out by the way of the land of Philistines,
which is nigh; and areckoning lest peradventure it would
repent the people, if he had seen battles rise against him,
and the people would turn again into Egypt; (Now when
Pharaoh let the people go, God did not lead them out by
the way of the land of the Philistines, which was near;
reckoning that when they had seen battles rise up against
them, perhaps they would repent, *or would change their
minds*, and then the people would return to Egypt;)
18 but *God* led *the people* about by the way of desert,
which way is beside the Red Sea. And the sons of Israel
were armed, and went up from the land of Egypt. (but
God led *the people* out by the way of the wilderness,
which was towards the Red Sea. And so the Israelites
were armed, and went up from the land of Egypt.)
19 And Moses took the bones of Joseph with him, for he
had charged the sons of Israel, and had said, God shall visit
you, and bear ye out from hence my bones with you (and
at that time carry ye away my bones from here with you).
20 And they went forth from Succoth, and setted tents
in Etham (and pitched their tents at Etham), in the last
ends of the wilderness.
21 Forsooth the Lord went before them to show *them*
the way, by day in a pillar of cloud, and by night in a
pillar of fire, that he should be leader of the way in ever
either time (so that he would be their leader on the way
at all times);
22 the pillar of cloud failed never by day, neither the
pillar of fire by night, before the people. (and the pillar of
cloud never ceased from being in front of the people
during the day, nor the pillar of fire during the night.)

CHAPTER 14

1 Forsooth the Lord spake to Moses, and said,

2 Speak thou to the sons of Israel; turn they again, and
set they tents even against Pihahiroth, which is betwixt
Migdol and the sea, against Baalzephon; and in the sight
thereof ye shall set tents on the sea. (Speak thou to the
Israelites; tell them to turn back, and pitch their tents
before Pihahiroth, which is between Migdol and the Red
Sea, *or the Sea of Reeds*, east of Baalzephon; yea, in the
sight of it, ye shall pitch your tents by the sea.)
3 And Pharaoh shall say on the sons of Israel, They be
made strait in the land, the desert hath closed them
together. (And Pharaoh shall say of the Israelites, The
land is too narrow there for all of them, yea, the
wilderness hath enclosed them.)
4 And I shall make hard his heart, and he shall pursue
you, and I shall be glorified in Pharaoh, and in all his
host; and the Egyptians shall know that I am the Lord;
and they did so.
5 And it was told to the king of the Egyptians, that the
people had fled; and the heart of Pharaoh and of his
servants was changed on the people, and they said, What
would we do, that we let go Israel, that it should not
serve us? (And it was told to the king of the Egyptians,
that the people had fled; and Pharaoh's heart, and the
hearts of his servants, were turned against the people,
and they said, What have we done? we have let Israel go,
and now there is no one here to serve us!)
6 Therefore Pharaoh joined (up) the chariot, and took
with him all his people; (And so Pharaoh joined up his
chariot, and took all his people with him;)
7 and he took six hundred chosen chariots, and
whatever thing of chariots was in Egypt, and [the] dukes
of all the host. (and he took six hundred of the choicest
chariots, and whatever other chariots were in Egypt, and
all the leaders of his army.)
8 And the Lord made hard the heart of Pharaoh, king
of Egypt, and he pursued the sons of Israel; and they were
gone out in an high hand. (And the Lord hardened the
heart of Pharaoh, king of Egypt, and he pursued the
Israelites; and they went forth with great defiance.)
9 And when the Egyptians pursued the steps *of the
sons of Israel* before-going, they found them in tents on
the sea; (and) all the chivalry, and [the] chariots of
Pharaoh, and all the host were in Pihahiroth, against
Baalzephon. (And the Egyptians, yea, all the cavalry, and
the chariots, and all of Pharaoh's army, pursued the steps
of the Israelites who had gone forth before them; and
they found them in their tents by the Red Sea, by
Pihahiroth, and east of Baalzephon.)
10 And when Pharaoh had nighed, the sons of Israel
raised [up] their eyes, and they saw the Egyptians behind
them, and they dreaded greatly (and they greatly feared);
and they cried to the Lord,
11 and said to Moses, In hap sepulchres were not in
Egypt, therefore thou hast taken us away, that we shall
die in wilderness? what wouldest thou do this, that thou
leddest us out of Egypt? (and they said to Moses, Perhaps
there were no tombs, *or no graves*, in Egypt, and so thou
hast taken us away, so that now we can die here in this
wilderness? why hast thou done this, and led us out of
Egypt?)
12 Whether this is not the word that we spake to thee
in Egypt (Was this not what we said to thee in Egypt),
saying, Go away from us, (so) that we (can) serve the
Egyptians? for it is much better to serve them, than to die
in (the) wilderness.
13 And Moses said to the people, Do not ye dread,
stand ye, and see the great works of God, which he shall
do today; for ye shall no more see the Egyptians, which
ye see now, till into without end; (And Moses said to the
people, Do not ye fear, stand ye, and see the great works
of God, which he shall do today; for the Egyptians,
whom ye now see, soon ye shall never see them again;)
14 the Lord shall fight for you, and ye shall be still. (the
Lord shall fight for you, but ye must keep still/but ye must
be silent).
15 And the Lord said to Moses, What criest thou to me?
Speak thou to the sons of Israel, that they go forth; (And
the Lord said to Moses, Why criest thou to me? Speak
thou to the Israelites, so that they go forth;)
16 forsooth raise thou thy rod, and stretch forth thine
hand on the sea, and part thou it, that the sons of Israel
go in the midst of the sea, by dry place. (now raise thou
up thy staff, and stretch forth thy hand over the sea, and
part thou it, so that the Israelites can go through the midst
of the sea, on dry land.)
17 Forsooth I shall make hard the heart(s) of [the]
Egyptians, that they pursue you, and I shall be glorified in
Pharaoh, and in all the host of him, and in the chariots *of
him*, and in the knights of him; (But I shall harden the
hearts of the Egyptians, so that they pursue you, and I
shall be glorified in Pharaoh, and in all his army, and in
his chariots, and in his soldiers;)
18 and [the] Egyptians shall know that I am the Lord
God, when I shall be glorified in Pharaoh, and in the
chariots, and in the knights of him (and in his soldiers).
19 And the angel of the Lord, that went before the
castles, *or tents*, of Israel, took himself, and went behind
them; and the pillar of cloud *went* together with him, and
left the former things after the back, (And the angel of the
Lord, who went before the tents, *or the army*, of Israel,
took himself, and went behind them; and the pillar of
cloud *went* with him, yea, it also went from in front of
them, to behind their backs,)
20 and stood betwixt the castles of Egyptians and the
castles of Israel; and the cloud was dark *toward the
Egyptians*, and *it was* lightening the night *toward Israel*, so
that in all the time of the night, they might not [come] nigh
together to themselves. (and they stood between the tents,

or the army, of the Egyptians and the tents, *or the army,*
of Israel; and the cloud was dark *toward the Egyptians,*
but *it was* lighting the night *toward the Israelites,* so that
they could not come close to each other in all that night.)
21 And when Moses had stretched forth his hand on
the sea, the Lord took away the sea, the while a great
wind and a burning (one) blew in all the night, and
turned the sea into dryness; and the water was parted.
(And when Moses had stretched forth his hand over the
Red Sea, the Lord took away the sea, by a great burning
wind that blew all that night, and turned the sea into dry
land; and so the waters were parted.)
22 And the sons of Israel entered by the midst of the
dry sea; for the water was as a wall at the right side, and
the left side of them. (And the Israelites entered into the
midst of the sea on dry land; for the water was like a wall
on their right side, and on their left side.)
23 And the Egyptians pursued, and entered after them,
all the riding of Pharaoh, his chariots, and [his] knights,
by the midst of the sea. (And the Egyptians pursued them,
and entered into the midst of the sea after them, yea, all
the horses of Pharaoh, and his chariots, and his soldiers.)
24 And the watch of the morrowtide came then, and lo!
the Lord beheld on the castles of the Egyptians, by a pillar
of fire, and of cloud, and killed the host of them; (And the
morning watch came then, and lo! the Lord looked down
through the pillars of fire, and of cloud, on the army of
the Egyptians, and he panicked all the soldiers;)
25 and he destroyed the wheels of [the] chariots, and
those were borne into the depth (and he clogged up the
wheels of the chariots, and they turned with great
difficulty). Therefore the Egyptians said, Flee we (from)
Israel; for the Lord fighteth for them against us.
26 And the Lord said to Moses, Hold forth thine hand
on the sea, that the waters turn again to [the] Egyptians,
on the chariots, and on the knights of them. (And the
Lord said to Moses, Stretch forth thy hand over the sea,
so that the waters return onto the Egyptians, yea, onto
their chariots, and onto their soldiers.)
27 And when Moses had held forth his hand against the
sea, it turned again first in the morrowtide to the former
place (And Moses stretched forth his hand over the sea,
and early in the morning it returned to its former place);
and when the Egyptians fled, the waters came (up) against
them, and the Lord wrapped them (up) in the midst of the
flood.
28 And the waters turned again, and covered the
chariots, and [the] knights of all the host of Pharaoh,
which followed, and entered into the sea; soothly not
one of them was (left) alive. (And the waters returned,
and covered the chariots, and all the soldiers of Pharaoh's
army, who had followed the Israelites, and had entered
into the sea after them; truly not one of them was left
alive.)
29 Forsooth the sons of Israel went through the midst of
the dry sea, and the waters were to them as for a wall, on
the right side, and *on the* left side. (But the Israelites went
through the midst of the sea on dry land, and for them
the waters were like a wall, on their right side, and on
their left side.)
30 And in that day the Lord delivered Israel from the
hand of [the] Egyptians, and they saw the Egyptians dead
on the brink of the sea, (And on that day the Lord saved
Israel from the hands of the Egyptians, and they saw the
Egyptians lying dead on the seashore,)
31 and *they saw* the great hand, *or power/or might,*
which the Lord had used against the Egyptians; and the
people dreaded the Lord, and they believed to the Lord,
and to Moses his servant (and *they saw* the great power,
or the great might, which the Lord had used against the
Egyptians; and the people feared the Lord, and they
believed in the Lord, and in his servant Moses.)

CHAPTER 15

1 Then Moses sang, and the sons of Israel, this song to
the Lord; and they said, Sing we to the Lord, for he is
magnified gloriously; he hath cast down the horse and
the horseman into the sea. (Then Moses, and the
Israelites, sang this song to the Lord; Sing we to the Lord,
for he is gloriously magnified; he hath thrown down the
horse and the rider into the sea.)
2 My strength and my praising is the Lord; and he is
made to me into health. This is my God, and I shall
glorify him; the God of my father, and I shall enhance
him. (The Lord is my strength, and my praise; yea, he is
my salvation. This is my God, and I shall glorify him; the
God of my father, and I shall exult him.)
3 The Lord is a man-fighter, his name is Almighty;
(The Lord is a fighter, and his name is The Almighty;)
4 he casted down into the sea the chariots of Pharaoh,
and his host (he threw down Pharaoh's chariots, and his
army, into the sea). His chosen princes were drowned in
the Red Sea;
5 the deep waters covered them; they went down into
the depth as a stone (they went down into the depths like
a stone).
6 Lord, thy right hand is magnified in strength; Lord,
thy right hand smote the enemy.
7 And in the multitude of thy glory, thou hast put
down all thine adversaries; thou sentest thine ire, that
devoured them as stubble (thou sentest out thy anger,
that devoured them like stubble).
8 And (the) waters were gathered [together] in the
spirit of thy strong vengeance (And the waters were
gathered together with the blast of thy strong vengeance);
[the] flowing water stood, [the] deep waters were
gathered [together] in the midst of the sea.
9 The enemy said, I shall pursue (them), and I shall

(over)take (them); I shall part (the) spoils, (and) my soul,
that is, (my) will, shall be fulfilled. I shall draw out my
sword; mine hand shall slay them.
10 Thy spirit blew (Thou blewest with thy breath), and
the sea covered them; they were drowned as lead in (the)
great waters.
11 Lord, who is like thee in strong men, who is like
thee? *thou art* a great doer in holiness; fearful, and
praiseable, and doing miracles. (Lord, who is like thee
among the strong, yea, who is like thee? *thou art* a great
doer of holiness; fearful, and worthy of praise, and doing
miracles.)
12 Thou heldest forth thine hand (Thou hast stretched
forth thy right hand), and the earth devoured them;
13 thou were leader in thy mercy to thy people, which
thou again-boughtest; and thou hast borne him in thy
strength to thine holy dwelling place. (in thy mercy thou
were the leader of thy people, whom thou boughtest
back, *or ransomed,* and thou hast carried them by thy
strength to thy holy dwelling place.)
14 Peoples went up, and were wroth; sorrows held the
dwellers of Philistia. (The nations heard, and trembled in
fear; sorrows held the people of Palestina.)
15 Then the princes of Edom were troubled; trembling
held the strong men of Moab. All the dwellers of Canaan
dreaded, *or were encumbered* (All the people of Canaan
were in fear);
16 inward dread fall on them, and outward dread in the
greatness of thine arm. Be they made unmoveable as a
stone, till thy people pass, Lord; till thy people pass,
whom thou wieldedest. (inward fear fell upon them, and
outward fear of the greatness of thy power. They were
made immovable like a stone, until thy people passed by,
Lord; until thy people passed by, whom thou possessest.)
17 Thou shalt bring them in, and thou shalt plant them
in the hill of thine heritage; in the most steadfast dwelling
place which thou hast wrought, Lord; Lord, (in) thy
saintuary, which thine hands made steadfast. (Thou
bringest them in, and thou hast planted them on the
mountain of thy inheritance; in the most steadfast
dwelling place which thou hast wrought, Lord; yea, in
thy sanctuary, Lord, which thy hands have made firm.)
18 The Lord shall reign without end, *and over all
thing(s).*
19 Forsooth Pharaoh, on horse, entered with his
chariots and [his] horsemen into the sea, and the Lord
brought the waters of the sea on them; soothly the sons of
Israel went by the dry place (but the Israelites went on
dry ground), in [the] midst of the sea.
20 Therefore Marie (And Miriam), the prophetess, the
sister of Aaron, took a tympan in her hand, and all the
women went out after her with tympans and companies;
21 to which she sang before, and said, Sing we to the
Lord, for he is magnified gloriously; he hath cast down
into the sea the horse and the rider of him. (and she sang
before them, Sing we to the Lord, for he is gloriously
magnified; he hath thrown down the horse and his rider
into the sea.)
22 Forsooth Moses took Israel from the Red Sea, and
they went out into the desert of Shur; and they went three
days by the wilderness, and they found not water (and they
went three days in the wilderness, but found no water).
23 And they came into Marah, and they might not drink
the waters of Marah, for they were bitter; wherefore he
putted a covenable name to the place, and called it
Marah, *that is, bitterness.* (And they came to Marah, but
they could not drink the water there, for it was bitter; so
they put a suitable name to that place, and called it
Marah, *that is, Bitterness.*)
24 And the people grouched against Moses (And the
people grumbled against Moses), and said, What shall we
drink?
25 And Moses cried to the Lord, which showed to him
a tree; and when he had put that tree into the waters,
those (waters) were turned into sweetness. There the Lord
ordained commandments and dooms to the people, and
there he assayed the people (There the Lord ordained
commandments and judgements for the people, and he
tested, *or proved,* the people there),
26 and (he) said, If thou shalt hear the voice of thy Lord
God, and shalt do that that is rightful before him, and
shalt obey to his commandments, and shalt keep all his
behests, I shall not bring in on thee all the sickness,
which I have put in Egypt, for I am thy Lord Saviour (then
I shall not bring in on thee all the sickness, which I have
put on Egypt, for I am the Lord thy Saviour).
27 Forsooth the sons of Israel came into Elim, where
were twelve wells of water, and seventy palm trees, and
they setted tents beside the waters. (And the Israelites
came to Elim, where there were twelve wells of water,
and seventy palm trees, and they pitched their tents
beside the waters.)

CHAPTER 16

1 And they went forth from Elim, and all the multitude
of the sons of Israel came into the desert of Sin, which is
betwixt Elim and Sinai, in the fifteenth day of the second
month, after that they went out of the land of Egypt. (And
they went forth from Elim, and all the multitude of the
Israelites came into the wilderness of Sin, which is
between Elim and Sinai, on the fifteenth day of the second
month, after that they went out of the land of Egypt.)
2 And all the congregation of the sons of Israel
grouched against Moses (And all the Israelites grumbled
against Moses), and against Aaron, in the wilderness.
3 And the sons of Israel said to them, We would that
we had been dead by the hand of the Lord in the land of
Egypt, when we sat on the flesh pots, and ate loaves in

plenty; why led ye us into this desert, that ye should slay all the multitude with hunger? (And the Israelites said to them, We wish that we had died by the Lord's hand in the land of Egypt, when we sat by the flesh pots, and had plenty of loaves to eat; why did ye lead us into this wilderness, so that ye could kill all the multitude with hunger?)
4 Forsooth the Lord said to Moses, Lo! I shall rain to you loaves from heaven; the people go out, that it gather those things that suffice by each day; that I assay the people, whether it go in my law, or not. (And the Lord said to Moses, Lo! I shall rain down loaves from the heavens for you; have the people go out, and gather those things that suffice for each day; and I shall test, *or shall prove*, the people, and see if they go in my law, or not.)
5 Soothly in the sixth day, make they ready that that they shall bear in, and be it double over that they were wont to gather by each (other) day. (And on the sixth day, when they prepare what they bring in, it shall be double over what they were wont to gather on the other days.)
6 And Moses and Aaron said to all the sons of Israel, At eventide ye shall know that the Lord [hath] led you out of the land of Egypt;
7 and in the morrowtide ye shall see the glory of the Lord; for I heard your grouching against the Lord; soothly what be we, for ye grouch against us? (and in the morning ye shall see the glory of the Lord; for he hath heard your grumbling against him; and who be we, that ye grumble against us?)
8 And Moses said, The Lord shall give to you at eventide flesh to eat, and loaves in the morrowtide in plenty, for he [hath] heard your grouchings, by which ye grouched against him; for why, what be we? your grouching is not against us, but against the Lord. (And Moses said, The Lord shall give you flesh to eat in the evening, and plenty of loaves in the morning, for he hath heard your grumbling, by which ye grumbled against him; for who be we? yea, your grumbling is not against us, but against the Lord.)
9 And Moses said to Aaron, Say thou to all the congregation of the sons of Israel, Nigh ye before the Lord, for he [hath] heard your grouching (for he hath heard your grumbling).
10 And when Aaron spake to all the company of the sons of Israel, they beheld to the wilderness, and lo! the glory of the Lord appeared in a cloud.
11 Forsooth the Lord spake to Moses, and said,
12 I heard the grouchings of the sons of Israel (I heard the grumbling of the Israelites); speak thou to them, (and say,) At eventide ye shall eat flesh, and in the morrowtide ye shall be filled with loaves, and ye shall know that I am the Lord your God.
13 Therefore eventide was made, and curlews went up, and covered the castles; and in the morrowtide dew came before the face of the castles. (And so the evening came, and curlews flew in, and covered the tents; and in the morning dew lay all around the tents.)
14 And when it had covered the earth, a little thing, and as pounded with a pestle, in the likeness of an hoarfrost on the earth, appeared in the wilderness. (And when it had covered all the ground, there appeared in the wilderness a little thing, as if it was pounded with a pestle, and like hoarfrost on the ground.)
15 And when the sons of Israel had seen that, they said together, Man na? which signifieth, What is this? for they wist not what it was (And when the Israelites had seen it, they said to each other, Manna? which meaneth, What is this? for they did not know what it was). To whom Moses said, This is the bread which the Lord hath given you to eat.
16 This is the word which the Lord commanded, Each man gather thereof as much as it sufficeth to be eaten, omer by each head, by the number of your souls that dwell in the tabernacle, so ye shall take. (This is the thing which the Lord hath commanded, saying, Each of you gather as much of it as sufficeth to be eaten, yea, an omer for each soul, such ye shall gather by the number of souls who live in your tent.)
17 And the sons of Israel did so, and they gathered (it), one more, and another less;
18 and they meted [it] at the measure of omer; neither he that gathered more had more, neither he that made ready less found less, but all gathered by that that they might eat. (and they measured it at the measure of an omer per person, and he who gathered more did not have too much, nor he who gathered less had not enough, but they all gathered just what they could eat.)
19 And Moses said to them, No man leave thereof into the morrowtide; (And Moses said to them, No one leave any of it until the next morning;)
20 which heard not him, but some of them left *thereof* till to the morrowtide, and it began to boil with worms, and it was rotten; and Moses was wroth against them. (but some of them did not listen to him, and saved *some of it* for the next day, and it began to boil with worms, and it was rotten; and Moses was angry at them.)
21 Forsooth all they gathered in the morrowtide as much as sufficed to be eaten; and when the sun was hot, it was molten. (So every morning they all gathered as much as sufficed to be eaten; and when the sun was risen, it melted away.)
22 Soothly in the sixth day they gathered double meats, that is, two omers each man (And on the sixth day they gathered double the amount, that is, two omers for each person). Forsooth all the princes of the multitude came, and told (that) to Moses,
23 which said to them, This it is that the Lord spake, The rest of the sabbath is hallowed to the Lord; do ye whatever

thing (that) shall be wrought tomorrow, and seethe ye
those things that shall be sodden; soothly whatever thing
is residue, *or left over*, keep ye it till into the morrow.
(and he said to them, This is what the Lord hath said,
Tomorrow is the rest of the sabbath, that is holy, *or is
dedicated*, to the Lord; so do ye today whatever needeth to
be done, and boil ye those things that need to be boiled;
and whatever is left over, keep ye it for tomorrow.)
24 And they did so as Moses commanded (And so they
did as Moses commanded), and it was not rotten, neither
a worm was found therein.
25 And Moses said, Eat ye that in this day, for it is the
sabbath of the Lord, it shall not be found today in the field;
(And Moses said, Eat ye it today, for this is the sabbath of
the Lord, and no food shall be found in the field today;)
26 gather ye it in six days, forsooth the sabbath of the
Lord is in the seventh day, therefore *in that day* it shall
not be found. (gather ye it for six days, but the sabbath of
the Lord is on the seventh day, and so *on that day* it shall
not be found.)
27 The seventh day came, and *some* of the people went
out to gather, and they found not. (But the seventh day
came, and *some* people went out to gather food, but they
found it not.)
28 Forsooth the Lord said to Moses, How long will ye
not keep my commandments, and my law?
29 See ye that the Lord gave to you the sabbath, and for
that he hath given to you in the sixth day double meats;
each man dwell at himself, no man go out of his place in
the seventh day. (See ye that the Lord hath given you the
sabbath, and for that he hath given you double the food
on the sixth day; so everyone should stay at home, and
no one should go out of their place on the seventh day.)
30 And the people kept sabbath in the seventh day.
(And so the people kept the sabbath on the seventh day.)
31 And the house of Israel called the name thereof
man(na), which was white, as the seed of coriander, and
the taste thereof was as of flour (mixed) with honey.
32 Forsooth Moses said, This is the word which the
Lord commanded, Fill thou an omer thereof, and be it
kept into generations to coming afterward (and let it be
kept for the generations to come later), (so) that they
know (of) the bread with which I fed you in (the)
wilderness, when ye were led out of the land of Egypt.
33 And Moses said to Aaron, Take thou a vessel, and
put therein man(na), as much as an omer may take, and
put it before the Lord, to be kept into your generations,
(And Moses said to Aaron, Take thou a vessel, and put
manna in it, an omer of it, and put it before the Lord, to
be kept for all generations to come;)
34 as the Lord commanded to Moses; and Aaron put
that to be kept in the tabernacle. (so as the Lord
commanded to Moses, Aaron put the vessel of manna in
the Ark with the stone tablets, to be kept there *forever*.)
35 Forsooth the sons of Israel ate manna forty years, till
they came into the land habitable, *that is, able to be
inhabited*; they were fed with this meat, till they touched
the coasts of the land of Canaan. (And the Israelites ate
manna for forty years, until they came to the land where
they could live; yea, they were fed with this food, until
they reached the land of Canaan.)
36 Forsooth (an) omer is the tenth part of (an) ephah.

CHAPTER 17

1 Therefore all the multitude of the sons of Israel went
forth from the desert of Sin, by their dwellings, by the
word of the Lord, and setted tents in Rephidim, where was
no water to the people to drink. (And so all the Israelites
went forth from the wilderness of Sin, in stages, by the
word of the Lord, and pitched their tents in Rephidim,
where there was no water for the people to drink.)
2 Which *people* chided against Moses, and said, Give
water to us, that we drink. To whom Moses answered,
What chide ye against me, and why tempt ye the Lord?
(And the *people* complained to Moses, and said, Give us
some water to drink. To whom Moses answered, Why
do ye complain to me, and why do ye tempt the Lord?)
3 Therefore the people thirsted there for the
scarceness of water, and they grouched against Moses,
and said, Why madest thou us to go out of Egypt, (for) to
slay us, and our free children, and our beasts, for thirst?
(And so the people thirsted there for the scarceness of
water, and they grumbled against Moses, and said, Why
hast thou made us to go out of Egypt, in order to kill us,
and our children, and our beasts, with thirst?)
4 Forsooth Moses cried to the Lord, and said, What
shall I do to this people? yet a little, and it shall stone me
(What shall I do with these people? very soon they shall
all stone me!).
5 The Lord said to Moses, Go thou before the people,
and take with thee of the elder men of Israel, and take in
thine hand the rod, with the which thou hast smitten the
flood, and go; (The Lord said to Moses, Go thou before
the people, and take some of the elders of Israel with
thee, and take in thy hand the staff with which thou
struck the River, and go;)
6 lo! I shall stand there before thee, above the stone of
Horeb, and thou shalt smite the stone, and water shall go
out thereof, that the people drink. Moses did so before
the elder men of Israel; (lo! I shall stand there before thee,
by the rock at Mount Sinai, and thou shalt strike the rock,
and water shall come out of it, and then the people shall
have something to drink. Moses did this in the sight of
the elders of Israel;)
7 and he called the name of that place Temptation, for
the chiding of the sons of Israel, and for they tempted the
Lord, and said, Whether the Lord is in us, or nay? (and he
called the name of that place Massah and Meribah,

because of the complaining of the Israelites, and because
they tempted the Lord and said, Is the Lord with us, or
not?)
8 Forsooth Amalek came (And the Amalekites came),
and fought against Israel in Rephidim.
9 And Moses said to Joshua, Choose thou men, and
go out, and fight tomorrow against the men of Amalek;
lo! I shall stand in the top of the hill, and I shall have the
rod of God in mine hand. (And Moses said to Joshua,
Choose thou some men, and tomorrow go out, and fight
against the Amalekites; lo! I shall stand on the hill-top,
and I shall have God's staff in my hand.)
10 Joshua did as Moses spake, and he fought against
Amalek. Forsooth Moses, and Aaron, and Hur went up
on(to) the top of the hill;
11 and when Moses raised [up] his hands, Israel
overcame; forsooth if he let them down a little, Amalek
overcame.
12 Soothly Moses' hands were (made) heavy, therefore
they took a stone, and put (it) under him, on which *stone*
he sat. Forsooth Aaron and Hur sustained his hands, on
ever either side; and (so) it was done, that his hands were
not made weary, till to the going down of the sun.
13 And Joshua drove away Amalek and his people, in
the mouth of [the] sword, *that is, by the sharpness of the*
sword, Joshua killed the strong men of Amalek.
14 Forsooth the Lord said to Moses, Write thou this in a
book, for mind, and take (it) in(to) the ears of Joshua; for I
shall do away the mind of Amalek from under heaven.
(And the Lord said to Moses, Write thou about this in a
book to remember it, and tell it to Joshua; for I shall do
away all memory of the Amalekites from under heaven.)
15 And Moses builded an altar, and called the name
thereof, The Lord *is* mine enhancer, (And Moses built an
altar there, and called it Jehovahnissi,)
16 and he said, For (it is) the hand of the Lord alone,
and the battle of God shall be against Amalek (and God
shall fight against the Amalekites), from generation into
generation.

CHAPTER 18

1 And when Jethro, the priest of Midian, the ally,
either (the) father of the wife of Moses, had heard all
things which God had done to Moses, and to Israel his
people, for the Lord had led Israel out of the land of
Egypt, (And when Jethro, the priest of Midian, Moses'
father-in-law, had heard of all the things which God had
done for Moses, and for his people Israel, yea, that the
Lord had led Israel out of the land of Egypt,)
2 Jethro took Zipporah, Moses' wife, whom Moses
had sent again (whom Moses had sent back to him),
3 and his two sons, of which one was called Gershom,
for *the father at his birth* (had) said, I was a comeling in
an alien land (I was a newcomer in a foreign land),
4 forsooth the tother *was called* Eliezer, for *Moses at*
his birth (had) said, (For the) God of my father is mine
helper, and he delivered me from the sword of Pharaoh.
5 Therefore Jethro, ally of Moses, came, and the sons
of Moses and his wife *came* to Moses, into desert, where
Jethro set tents beside the hill of God; (And so Jethro,
Moses' father-in-law, came with Moses' wife and their
sons, into the wilderness, where Moses had pitched the
tents beside God's mountain;)
6 and he sent to Moses, and said, I Jethro, thine ally,
come to thee, and thy wife, and thy two sons with her.
(and he sent word to Moses, and said, I Jethro, thy father-
in-law, have come to thee, with thy wife, and thy two
sons with her.)
7 And Moses went out into the coming of his ally, and
worshipped, and kissed him, and they greeted themselves
together with peaceable words. And when Jethro had
entered into the tabernacle, (And Moses went out to meet
his father-in-law, and bowed before him, and kissed him,
and they greeted each other with friendly words. And
when Jethro had gone into the tent,)
8 Moses told to him all (the) things which God had
done to Pharaoh, and to the Egyptians, for Israel, and *he*
told to him all the travail that befell to them in the way,
of which the Lord had delivered them (and *he told him* of
all the tribulation that had befallen them on the way, and
how the Lord had saved them).
9 And Jethro was glad on all the goods which the Lord
had done to Israel, for he [had] delivered Israel from the
hand of [the] Egyptians. (And Jethro was glad for all the
good things that the Lord had done for Israel, for he had
saved Israel from the power of the Egyptians.)
10 And Jethro said, Blessed be the Lord, that delivered
you from the hand(s) of the Egyptians, and from the hand
of Pharaoh, the which *Lord* delivered his people from
(being under) the hand, (*or the power*,) of Egypt;
11 now I know that the Lord is great above all gods, for
they did proudly against them. (now I know that the Lord
is greater than all the gods, for what he hath done to
those who did so proudly against thee.)
12 Therefore Jethro, ally of Moses (And so Jethro,
Moses' father-in-law), offered burnt sacrifices and
offerings to God; and Aaron, and all the elder men of
Israel, came to eat bread with Jethro before God.
13 Forsooth in the tother day, Moses sat that he should
deem the people, which stood nigh to Moses, from the
morrowtide till to the eventide. (And the next day, Moses
sat down to judge the people, who stood about him, from
the morning until the evening.)
14 And when his ally had seen this, that is, all things
which he did in the people, he said, What is this that
thou doest in the people? why sittest thou alone, and all
the people abideth thee from the morrowtide till to
eventide? (And when his father-in-law had seen this, that

is, all the things which he did for the people, Jethro said,
What is this that thou doest for the people? why sittest
thou alone, and all the people waiteth for thee from the
morning until the evening?)
15 To whom Moses answered, The people cometh to
me, and asketh the sentence of God;
16 and when any strife befalleth to them, they come to
me, that I deem betwixt them (so that I can judge
between them), and show (them) the commandments of
God, and his laws.
17 And Jethro said, Thou doest a thing *that is* not good,
18 thou art wasted with a fond travail, both thou, and
this people that is with thee; the work is above thy
strengths, thou alone mayest not suffer it (thou cannot do
it all alone).
19 But hear thou my words, and *my* counsels, and the
Lord shall be with thee; be thou to the people in these
things that pertain to God, that thou tell (them) the things
that be said to the people; (But hear thou my words, and
my counsel, and the Lord shall be with thee; it is right to
represent the people before God, and to bring their
causes to him;)
20 and show to the people the ceremonies, and [the]
custom(s) of worshipping, and the way by which they
ought to go, and the work which they ought to do.
21 Forsooth purvey thou of all the people wise men, and
dreading God, in which is truth, and which hate avarice;
and ordain thou of them tribunes, and centurions, and
quinquagenaries, and deans [and ordain of them rulers upon
thousands, and rulers upon hundreds, and rulers upon fifty, and
rulers upon ten], (But find thou out of the people some
men who be wise, and who fear God, in whom is truth,
and who hate greed; and make thou them leaders of a
thousand, and of a hundred, and of fifty, and of ten,)
22 which shall deem the people in all time; soothly
whatever thing is greater, tell they to thee, and deem they
only [the] less(er) things, and be it easier to thee, when
the burden is parted into other men. (and they shall judge
their people at all times; but whatever case is hard, *or too
difficult*, let them tell that to thee, and judge they only the
simple cases, and so it shall be easier for thee, when the
burden is shared with these other men.)
23 If thou shalt do this, thou shalt fulfill the
commandment of God, and thou shalt be able to bear his
commandments; and all this people shall turn again with
peace to their places (and all these people shall return to
their places in peace).
24 And when these things were heard, Moses did all
things which Jethro counselled.
25 And when noble men of all Israel were chosen,
Moses ordained them princes of the people (And when
some noble men were chosen out of all Israel, Moses
ordained them the people's leaders), tribunes, and
centurions, and quinquagenaries, and deans [rulers upon
thousands, and rulers upon hundreds, and rulers upon fifties,
and rulers upon ten],
26 which deemed the people in all time; forsooth,
whatever thing was harder, they told to Moses, and they
deemed [the] easier things only. (who judged the people
at all times; but whatever case was hard, *or too difficult*,
they told it to Moses, and they judged only the easy, *or
the simple*, cases.)
27 And Moses let go his ally, which turned again, and
went into his land. (And then Moses let his father-in-law
go, and he returned to his own land.)

CHAPTER 19

1 In the third month of the going of Israel out of the
land of Egypt, in this day they came into the wilderness
of Sinai; (In the third month of Israel going out of the land
of Egypt, on this day they came into the Sinai Desert;)
2 for they went forth from Rephidim, and came till into
the desert of Sinai, and they setted tents in the same place;
and there Israel setted tents, even against the hill (and
Israel pitched their tents there, opposite the mountain).
3 Forsooth Moses went up into the hill to God; and
the Lord called him from the mount, and said, Thou shalt
say these things to the house of Jacob, and thou shalt tell
to the sons of Israel, (And Moses went up the mountain to
meet with God/And Moses went up God's mountain; and
the Lord called to him from the mount, and said, Thou
shalt say these things to the house of Jacob, and thou
shalt tell it to the Israelites,)
4 Ye *your*selves have seen what things I have done to
[the] Egyptians, how I bare you on the wings of eagles,
and took you to me (and brought you here to me).
5 Therefore if ye shall hear my voice, and shall keep
my covenant, ye shall be to me into a specialty of all
peoples (ye shall be special to me out of all peoples), *that
is, a thing loved excellently*; for all the earth is mine;
6 and ye shall be to me into a realm of priesthood,
and an holy folk; these be the words which thou shalt
speak to the sons of Israel. (and ye shall be my kingdom
of priests, and my holy nation; these be the words which
thou shalt say to the Israelites.)
7 Moses came, and when the greater men in birth of
the people were called together, he expounded all the
words which the Lord commanded *him*. (Moses came
back down, and when the men of great age, *that is, the
elders*, of the people were called together, he expounded
all the words which the Lord commanded *him to say*.)
8 And all the people answered together, (and said,) We
shall do all [the] things which the Lord hath spoken. And
when Moses had told the words of the people to the Lord,
9 the Lord said to him, Right now I shall come to thee
in the darkness of a cloud, (so) that the people hear me
speaking to thee, and believe to thee [into] without end
(and then they shall always believe thee). Therefore

Moses told the words of the people to the Lord,
10 which said to Moses (who said to Moses), Go thou
(back) to the people, and make them holy today and
tomorrow, and wash they their clothes,
11 and be they ready into the third day; for in the third
day the Lord shall come down before all the people on
the hill of Sinai. (and be they ready by the third day; for
on the third day the Lord shall come down on Mount
Sinai in the sight of all the people.)
12 And thou shalt set terms to the people, by compass;
and thou shalt say to them, Be ye ware, that ye go not up
into the hill, neither touch ye the ends thereof; each man
that shall touch the hill, shall die by death. (And thou
shalt set a boundary for the people, all around the
mountain; and thou shalt say to them, Beware, that ye go
not up onto the mountain, nor even touch its edges; for
anyone who shall touch the mountain, shall die.)
13 Hands shall not touch him, but he shall be
oppressed with stones, or he shall be pierced with darts;
whether it shall be a beast, or a man, it shall not live;
(but) when a clarion shall begin to sound, then go they
up into the hill. (No hands shall touch him, but he shall
be thrown down with stones, or shall be pierced with
arrows; whether it be a beast, or a person, they shall not
live; but when the trumpet shall begin to sound, then the
people can come up onto the mountain.)
14 And Moses came down from the hill to the people,
and hallowed it (And so Moses came down from the
mountain to the people, and hallowed them); and when
they had washed their clothes,
15 he said to them, Be ye ready into the third day (Be
ye ready by the third day); nigh ye not to your wives.
16 And now the third day was come, and the
morrowtide was clear; and, lo! thunders began to be
heard, and lightnings to shine, and a most thick cloud to
cover the mountain; and the sounding of a clarion made
noise full greatly, and the people dreaded, that was in the
tents (and the sounding of a trumpet made a very great
noise, and the people in their tents had great fear).
17 And when Moses had led them out into the coming
of God, from the place of the tents, they stood at the
roots of the hill. (And when Moses had led them out from
the place of the tents to meet with God, they stood at the
foot of the mountain.)
18 Forsooth all the hill of Sinai smoked, for the Lord
had come down thereon in fire; and the smoke thereof
went up as of a furnace, and all the hill was fearful; (And
all of Mount Sinai smoked, for the Lord had come down
on it in fire; and its smoke went up like that of a furnace,
and all the mountain fearfully shook;)
19 and the sound of a clarion increased little and little,
and it was holden forth longer (and longer). (And) Moses
spake, and the Lord answered him (with a clap of
thunder/by a voice),
20 and the Lord came down on the hill of Sinai, in that
top of the hill, and he called Moses to the top thereof.
And when he had gone up thither, (and the Lord came
down on Mount Sinai, onto the top of the mountain, and
he called Moses up to the top of it. And when he had
gone up there,)
21 the Lord said to him, Go thou down, and witness
thou to the people, lest peradventure it will pass [over] the
terms to see the Lord (lest they pass over the boundary to
see the Lord), and [a] full great multitude thereof perish;
22 and [the] priests, that nigh to the Lord, be they
hallowed, lest I smite them (or I shall strike them down).
23 And Moses said to the Lord, The common people
may not go up into the hill of Sinai; for thou hast
witnessed, and hast commanded, saying, Set thou terms
about the hill, and hallow it. (And Moses said to the Lord,
The common people cannot come up onto Mount Sinai;
for thou hast witnessed, and hast commanded, saying, Set
thou a *sacred* boundary all around the mountain, and
hallow it, and they have heard thee.)
24 To whom the Lord said, Go thou down, and (then)
thou shalt go up, and (bring) Aaron with thee; forsooth
the priests and the people pass not (over) the terms,
neither go they up to the Lord, lest peradventure he slay
them. (To whom the Lord said, Go thou down, and then
come back up, and bring Aaron with thee; but the priests
and the people must not pass over the boundary, nor let
them come up to the Lord, lest I kill them.)
25 Moses went down to the people, and told all things
to them. (And so Moses went down to the people, and
told all these things to them.)

CHAPTER 20

1 And the Lord spake all these words,
2 I am thy Lord God, that led thee out of the land of
Egypt, from the house of servage. (I am the Lord thy God,
who led thee out of the land of Egypt, from the house of
servitude, *or of slavery*.)
3 Thou shalt not have alien gods before me. (Thou
shalt not have foreign, or *other*, gods in place of
me/instead of me.)
4 Thou shalt not make to thee a graven image, neither
any likeness *of (any)thing* that is in heaven above, and
that is in (the) earth beneath, neither of those things that
be in waters under the earth; (Thou shalt not make a
carved image for thyself, nor any likeness *of anything* that
is in the heavens above, or on the earth beneath, or of
those things that be in the waters under the earth;)
5 thou shalt not bow down to them, neither worship
them; for I am thy Lord God, a strong(ly) jealous lover; I
visit the wickedness of (the) fathers in (the) children into
the third and fourth generation of them that hated me,
(thou shalt not bow down to them, nor worship them; for
I, the Lord thy God, am a jealous God; I punish the

children for the wickedness of their fathers, unto the third
and fourth generations of those who hate me,)
6 and I do mercy into thousands, to them that love
me, and keep my behests. (but I do mercy unto thousands,
to those who love me, and who keep my commandments.)
7 Thou shalt not take in vain the name of thy Lord
God, for the Lord shall not have him guiltless, that taketh
in vain the name of his Lord God. (Thou shalt not take
the name of the Lord thy God in vain, for the Lord shall
not hold guiltless he who taketh the name of the Lord his
God in vain.)
8 Have thou mind, that thou hallow the sabbath day;
(Remember to keep the sabbath day holy, *or sacred;*)
9 in six days thou shalt work, and do all thy works;
(for six days thou shalt work, and do all thy works;)
10 forsooth in the seventh day is the sabbath of thy
Lord God; thou shalt not do any work (on that day), thou,
and thy son, and thy daughter, and thy manservant, and
thine handmaid, thy work beast, and the comeling that is
within thy gates; (but on the seventh day is a sabbath of
the Lord thy God; thou shalt not do any work on that
day, thou, and thy son, and thy daughter, and thy male
slave, and thy slave-girl, and thy work beast, and the
newcomer who is within thy gates;)
11 for in six days God made (the) heaven(s) and (the)
earth, the sea, and all things that be in those, and rested
in the seventh day (and then he rested on the seventh
day); therefore the Lord blessed the sabbath day, and
hallowed it.
12 Honour thy father and thy mother, that thou be long
living on the land (so that thou can live a long life in the
land), which thy Lord God shall give to thee.
13 Thou shalt not slay. (Thou shalt not kill.)
14 Thou shalt not do lechery.
15 Thou shalt not do theft.
16 Thou shalt not speak false witnessing against thy
neighbour.
17 Thou shalt not covet the house of thy neighbour,
neither thou shalt desire his wife, nor his (man)servant,
nor his handmaid, nor *his* ox, nor *his* ass, neither
(anything of) all (the) things that be his. (Thou shalt not
covet thy neighbour's house, nor shalt thou desire his
wife, or his slave, or his slave-girl, or *his* ox, or *his*
donkey, or anything of all the things that be his.)
18 Forsooth all the people heard voices, (*that is, the
thunder,*) and saw lamps, *that is, shining lights,* and the
sound of a clarion, and the hill smoking; and they were
afeared, and shaken with inward dread, and stood afar,
(And all the people heard the thunder, and saw the
lightening, and heard the sound of the trumpet, and saw
the mountain smoking; and they were afraid, and shaken
with inward fear, and stood afar off,)
19 and (they) said to Moses, Speak thou to us, and we
shall hear; (but) the Lord speak not to us, lest peradventure
we die.
20 And Moses said to the people, Do not ye dread, for
God came to prove you, and that his dread should be in
you, and that ye should not do sin. (And Moses said to
the people, Do not ye fear/Fear not, for God came to
prove you, so that his fear would be in you, and then ye
shall not sin.)
21 And the people stood afar (off); and Moses nighed to
the darkness, wherein God was.
22 And the Lord said furthermore to Moses, Thou shalt
say these things to the sons of Israel, Ye saw that from
heaven I have spoken to you; (And the Lord also said to
Moses, Thou shalt say these things to the Israelites, Ye
have seen that I have spoken to you from heaven;)
23 ye shall not make gods of silver, neither ye shall make
to you gods of gold. (ye shall not make gods out of silver,
or gods out of gold, to be worshipped in addition to me.)
24 Ye shall make an altar of earth to me, and ye shall
offer thereon your burnt sacrifices, and peaceable
sacrifices, your sheep, and oxen; in each place in which
the mind of my name shall be, I shall come to thee, and I
shall bless thee. (Ye shall make an altar out of earth for
me, and ye shall offer on it your burnt sacrifices, and
your peace offerings, your sheep, and your oxen; and in
each place where I ask thee to remember my name, I
shall come to thee, and I shall bless thee.)
25 That if thou shalt make an altar of stone to me, thou
shalt not build it of stones hewn (And if thou make an
altar out of stones for me, thou shalt not build it out of
cut stones); for if thou shalt raise thy knife thereupon, *or
(any) other instrument wherewith blood may be shed
out,* it shall be polluted.
26 Thou shalt not go up by degrees to mine altar, lest
thy filth(hood) be showed. (Thou shalt not go up to my
altar by steps, lest thy nakedness should be shown.)

CHAPTER 21

1 These be the dooms, which thou shalt set forth to
them. (These be the laws, which thou shalt set forth to
them.)
2 If thou buyest an Hebrew servant, he shall serve
thee six years; in the seventh year he shall go out free,
without price; (If thou buyest a Hebrew slave, he shall
serve thee for six years; then in the seventh year he shall
go out free, without payment of any money;)
3 with what manner cloak he entered, with such cloak
go he out; if *he entered* having a wife, also the wife shall
go out together with him.
4 But if the lord *of a servant* gave a wife to him, and
she childed sons and daughters, the woman and her
children shall be her lord's; soothly the servant shall go
out with his own cloth. (But if the lord of *a slave* gave a
wife to him, and she bare him sons and daughters, the
woman and her children shall be her lord's; the slave

shall go out free with only his own cloak.)
5 And if the servant saith, I love my lord, and my wife,
and children, I will not go out free; (And if the slave saith,
I love my lord, and my wife, and my children, and I shall
not go out free;)
6 his lord *shall* bring him to [the] gods, *that is, (to the)
judges*; and he shall be set to the door, and to the posts;
and *his lord* shall pierce his ear with an awl, and he shall
be servant to him till into the world. (then his lord *shall*
bring him to the judges; and he shall put him up against
the door, or the door-post; and *his lord* shall pierce his ear
with an awl, and then he shall be his slave forevermore.)
7 If any man selleth his daughter into a servantess, she
shall not go out as handmaids were wont to go out; (If
any man selleth his daughter to be a slave-girl, she shall
not go out free like slaves can go out free;)
8 if she displeaseth in the eyes of her lord, to whom she
was betaken, he shall deliver her; soothly he shall not have
power, (or the right,) to sell *her* to an alien people, if he
forsaketh her. (yea, if she displeaseth in the eyes of her
lord, to whom she was delivered, then he shall sell her
back to her father; and he shall not have the power, or the
right, to sell *her* to a foreign people, if he forsaketh her.)
9 Forsooth if he weddeth her to his son, he shall do to
her by the custom of daughters (he shall treat her like a
daughter);
10 and if he take *with this handmaid* another woman,
or wife, to his son, he shall purvey to the (first) damsel, *or
handmaid*, weddings, and clothes, and he shall not deny
her the price of (her) chastity, *that is, the hour of yielding
debt.* (but if he get another wife, besides *this woman,* for
his son, he shall still give this young woman her
wedding, and her clothes, and he shall not deny her the
rights of her marriage bed.)
11 If he doeth not *to her* these three (things), she shall
go out freely without money. (And if he giveth *her* not
these three things, then she shall go out free without
payment of any money.)
12 He that smiteth a man, and will slay *him*, die he by
death; (He who striketh a man, and killeth *him*, shall be
put to death;)
13 forsooth if a man setteth not ambush, but God betook
him into his hands, I shall ordain a place to thee (I shall
ordain a place for thee), whither he oughteth to flee.
14 If any man slayeth his neighbour by before-casting,
and by ambush, draw thou him away from mine altar,
that he die (and put him to death).
15 He that smiteth his father, or his mother, die he by
death. (He who striketh his father, or his mother, shall be
put to death.)
16 He that curseth his father, or mother, die he by
death. (He who curseth his father, or his mother, shall be
put to death.)
17 He that stealeth a man, and selleth him, *if he is*
convicted of the guilt, die he by death (shall be put to
death).
18 If men chide, and the tother smite his neighbour
with a stone, or with the fist, and he is not dead, but lieth
in the bed,
19 if he riseth (up), and goeth forth on his staff, he that
smote (him) shall be innocent; so nevertheless that he
restore (to him for) his travails, and his costs in leaches
(and his expenses for physicians).
20 He that smiteth his servant, or handmaid, with a rod,
and they be dead in his hands, he shall be guilty of the
crime, *or hideous trespass.* (He who striketh his slave, or
his slave-girl, with a rod, and they die by his hands, he
shall be guilty of a crime, *or of a hideous trespass.*)
21 Soothly if the servant liveth over this beating one
day, or twain, *the smiter* shall not be subject to the pain
of death, for the servant is his *master's* chattel.
22 If men chide, and a man smiteth a woman with
child, and soothly he maketh the child dead-born, but the
woman liveth over *that smiting*, he shall be subject to the
harm (he shall be subject to a fine), as much as the
woman's husband asketh (for), and as the judges deem
(appropriate).
23 Soothly if the death of her followeth (And if her
death followeth), he shall yield life for life,
24 eye for eye, tooth for tooth, hand for hand, foot for
foot,
25 burning for burning, wound for wound, sore for sore.
26 If a man smiteth the eye of his servant, either of his
handmaid, and maketh them one-eyed, he shall deliver
them free for the eye which he put out (he shall let them
go out free for the eye which he hath put out).
27 Also if he smite out a tooth of his servant, or (of)
[his] handmaid, in like manner he shall deliver them free
(likewise he shall let them go out free).
28 If an ox smiteth with his horn either man, or
woman, and they be dead, the ox shall be thrown down
with stones, and his flesh shall not be eaten, and the lord
of the ox shall be guiltless. (If an ox striketh with his horn
a man, or a woman, unto the death, the ox shall be
thrown down with stones, and his flesh shall not be
eaten, but the lord of the ox shall be guiltless.)
29 That if the ox was an horn-putter from yesterday and
the third day ago, and men warned his lord, (yet) neither
the lord closed him, and he slayeth a man, or a woman,
both the ox shall be thrown adown with stones, and they
shall slay his lord; (But if the ox was a horn-putter from
yesterday and the third day ago, and men had warned his
lord, but his lord did not enclose him, and he killeth a
man, or a woman, the ox shall be thrown down with
stones, and they shall also kill his lord;)
30 that if the price be put to the lord, he shall give for his
life whatever he is asked. (but if a fine be put on the ox's
lord, he shall give whatever he is asked for, as the ransom

for his life.)
31 And if he smiteth with (his) horn a *man's* son, and
his daughter (And if the ox striketh with his horn a *man's*
son, or his daughter), his lord shall be subject to the same
sentence.
32 If the ox assaileth a manservant, and an handmaid,
the lord of the ox shall give thirty shekels of silver to the
lord of that servant; forsooth the ox shall be oppressed
with stones. (But if the ox assaileth a slave, or a slave-girl,
the ox's lord shall give thirty shekels of silver to their
lord, and the ox shall be thrown down with stones.)
33 If any man openeth a cistern, *or a pit*, and diggeth it,
and covereth it not, and an ox either an ass falleth into it,
(If anyone openeth a cistern, *or a well*, and diggeth it, and
covereth it not up, and an ox or a donkey falleth into it,)
34 the lord of the cistern shall yield the price of the
beasts (the lord of the cistern shall pay *the fair value* for
the beast); forsooth that that is dead shall be his.
35 If one man's ox woundeth the ox of another man,
and he is dead, they shall sell the quick ox, and they shall
part the price (If one person's ox woundeth another
person's ox, and it dieth, they shall sell the living ox, and
they shall evenly divide the price); soothly they shall part
betwixt them(selves) the carcass of the dead ox.
36 Forsooth if the lord knew, that his ox was a (horn)-
putter from yesterday and the third day ago, and kept not
him (and did not keep him in), he shall yield (another) ox
for (the dead) ox, and he shall take the whole dead carcass.

CHAPTER 22

1 If any man stealeth a sheep, or (an) ox, and slayeth,
or selleth (it), he shall restore five oxen for one ox, and
four sheep for one sheep.
2 And if a night thief breaking (into) an house, either
undermining (it), is found (out), and he taken is (made)
dead by a wound, *or hurt* (and when he is caught, he
dieth from a wound), the smiter shall not be guilty of *his*
blood, *or death*;
3 that if he did this when the sun was risen, he did
manslaying, and he shall die (but if the lord of the house
did this when the sun was up, he hath done
manslaughter, and he shall be put to death). If *a thief*
have not that, that he shall yield for [the] theft, he shall be
sold (to make recompense);
4 if that thing that he stole, is found quick at him, either
ox, either ass, either sheep, he shall restore the double. (if
what he stole, is found alive with him, either an ox, or a
donkey, or a sheep, he shall restore double what he stole.)
5 If a man harmeth a field, or a vinery, and suffereth his
beast, that it waste other men's things (If anyone harmeth
a field, or a vineyard, by allowing his beast to destroy
another person's things), he shall restore for the value of
[the] harm (done), (with) the best thing(s) (of) whatever he
hath in his (own) field, either in his (own) vinery.
6 If fire goeth out, and findeth, *or burneth*, ears of
corn, and catcheth heaps of corn, or corns standing in
(the) fields, he that kindled the fire shall yield (for) the
harm (he who kindled the fire shall make recompense for
the harm done).
7 If a man betaketh into keeping money to a friend, or
a vessel, and it is taken away by theft from him that
received *it*, if the thief is found, he shall restore the
double. (If anyone taketh money, or a vessel, to a friend
for safe keeping, and it is taken away by theft from him
who received *it*, if the thief is found, he shall restore
double what he stole.)
8 (But) If the thief is hid(den), *or unknown*, the lord of
the house *that received that good* shall be brought to the
gods, *that is, to (the) judges*, and he shall swear, that he
held not forth his hand into his neighbour's thing, to
defraud (and he shall swear, that he did not put forth his
hand to his neighbour's thing, to defraud him);
9 as well in ox, as in ass, and in sheep, and in cloth;
and in whatever thing may bring in harm, the cause of
ever either shall come to the judges, and if they deem
him *guilty*, he shall restore the double to his neighbour.
(and with any ox, or donkey, or sheep, or cloak, or
whatever thing which may be claimed by two people, the
case shall come to the judges, and whom they judge
guilty, he shall restore double to his neighbour.)
10 If any man betaketh to his neighbour ox, ass, sheep,
and all work beast to keeping, and it is dead, or is made
feeble, or is taken of enemies, and no man seeth this, (If
anyone taketh an ox, a donkey, a sheep, or any work
beast, to his neighbour for safe keeping, and it dieth, or is
hurt, or is taken by enemies, but no one seeth this,)
11 an oath shall be in the midst, that he held not forth
his hand to the impairing of his neighbour's thing; and
the lord *that owned that good* shall receive his oath, and
he *to whom it was taken* shall not be compelled to yield,
or restore it. (he shall make an oath before all, that he did
not put forth his hand to the impairment of his
neighbour's thing; and the lord *who owned that thing*
shall receive his oath, and then he *to whom the thing
was given* shall not be compelled to yield any
recompense for it, *or to restore it*.)
12 That if it is taken away by theft, he shall restore the
harm to the lord; (But if it is taken away by theft, he shall
yield recompense to its lord for it;)
13 if it is eaten of a beast (and if it is eaten by a wild
beast), he shall bring to the lord that that is slain, and he
shall not (have to) restore *it otherwise*.
14 He that asketh of his neighbour anything of these
foresaid things by borrowing, and it is enfeebled, either
dead, while the lord *thereof* is not present, he shall be
constrained to yield (for) it; (He who asketh to borrow
from his neighbour any of these *foresaid things*, and it is
enfeebled, or dead, while *its* lord is not present, he shall

be compelled to yield recompense for it;)
15 that if the lord is in presence, he shall not restore it,
mostly if it came hired, *that is, if to hire he took it*, for
meed of his work. (but if its lord was present, he shall not
have to restore it, and if it was hired, *that is, if he took it
to hire*, only the wages for its work shall be due.)
16 If a man deceiveth a virgin not yet wedded, and
sleepeth with her, he shall give dower to her (he shall
give her a dowry), and shall have her to wife.
17 If the father of the virgin will not give *her to him*, he
shall (still) give (the) money, by the manner of dower (in
the manner of a dowry), which virgins were wont to take.
18 Thou shalt not suffer witches to live.
19 He that doeth lechery with a beast, die he by death
(shall be put to death).
20 He that offereth to (any) gods, except to the Lord
alone, be he slain (shall be put to death).
21 Thou shalt not make sorrowful a comeling, neither
thou shalt torment him; for also ye were comelings in the
land of Egypt (for ye were also newcomers in the land of
Egypt).
22 Ye shall not harm a widow, and a fatherless or a
motherless child. (Ye shall not harm a widow, or a
fatherless or a motherless child.)
23 If ye hurt them, they shall cry to me, and I shall hear
the cry of them,
24 and my great vengeance shall have indignation *on
you*, and I shall smite you with sword (and I shall strike
you down with a sword), and your wives shall be
widows, and your sons shall be fatherless.
25 If thou givest money to loan to my poor people, that
dwelleth with thee, thou shalt not constrain him as an
extortioner *doeth*, neither thou shalt oppress him by
usuries. (If thou lendest money to anyone of my poor
people, who liveth with thee, thou shalt not compel him
like an extortioner *doeth*, nor shalt thou oppress him with
usury.)
26 If thou takest of thy neighbour a cloth to wed (If thou
takest a cloak from thy neighbour for a pledge), thou shalt
yield it (back) to him before the going down of the sun;
27 for that alone is the clothing of his flesh, with which
he is covered, neither he hath another, in which he shall
sleep; if he crieth to me, I shall hear him; for I am merciful.
28 Thou shalt not backbite [the] gods, *that is, (the)
priests, or (the) judges*, and thou shalt not curse the
prince of thy people (and thou shalt not curse the leaders
of thy people).
29 Thou shalt not tarry to offer to the Lord thy tithes,
and thy first fruits. Thou shalt give to me the first begotten
of thy sons (Thou shalt give me thy first-born sons);
30 also of [thine] oxen, and of (thy) sheep, thou shalt do
in like manner; seven days be he with his mother, in the
eighth day thou shalt yield him to me. (and thou shalt do
likewise with thy oxen, and with thy sheep; for seven days
let him be with his mother, then on the eighth day thou
shalt yield him to me.)
31 Ye shall be holy men to me; ye shall not eat the
flesh that is before-tasted of (other) beasts, but ye shall
cast it forth to hounds. (Ye shall be holy before me; ye
shall not eat the flesh of that which is killed by another
beast, but ye shall throw it to the hounds.)

CHAPTER 23

1 Thou shalt not receive a voice of leasing (Thou shalt
not spread a rumour, or a lie), (and) thou shalt not raise
thine hand, *that is, make (a) covenant, either (a) promise*,
that thou say false witnessing for a wicked man.
2 Thou shalt not follow a company to do evil, neither
thou shalt assent to the sentence of full many men in
doom, that thou go away from truth. (Thou shalt not
follow a crowd and do evil, nor shalt thou agree with the
sentence, *or the decree*, of a great many men in
judgement, and in doing so, go away from the truth.)
3 Also thou shalt not have mercy of a poor man in a
cause, *or doom*. (And thou shalt not favour a poor person
in his case, *or in its judgement*.)
4 If thou meetest thine enemy's ox, either his ass,
straying, lead it again to him. (If thou seest thy enemy's
ox, or his donkey, straying, lead it back to him.)
5 If thou seest that the ass of him that hateth thee
lieth under a burden, thou shalt not pass, but thou shalt
raise up *it* with him. (If thou seest that the donkey of
him who hateth thee lieth under a burden, thou shalt
not pass by, but thou shalt raise *it* up with him.)
6 Thou shalt not bow [away] *from truth* in the doom
of a poor man. (Thou shalt not turn away *from the truth*
in the judgement of a poor person.)
7 Thou shalt flee leasing. Thou shalt not slay an
innocent man, and just; for I am adversary to a wicked
man. (Thou shalt flee from lies. Thou shalt not kill the
innocent, or the just; for I am the adversary to the wicked.)
8 Take thou not gifts, that blind, yea, prudent men,
and destroy the words of just men. (Do not take gifts, *or
bribes*, that blind, yea, the prudent, and that destroy the
words of the just.)
9 Thou shalt not be dis-easeful of a pilgrim, for ye
know the souls of comelings, for also ye were pilgrims in
the land of Egypt. (Thou shalt not mis-treat a foreigner, for
ye know the souls of newcomers, for ye were foreigners
in the land of Egypt.)
10 Six years thou shalt sow thy land, and thou shalt
gather [the] fruits thereof;
11 forsooth in the seventh year thou shalt leave it, and
make it to rest, that the poor men of thy people eat, and
whatever is left ungathered, the beasts of the field eat it;
so thou shalt do in thy vinery, and in the place of thine
olive trees. (but in the seventh year thou shalt let it be,
and allow it to rest, and thy poor people shall get food

from it, and whatever is left ungathered, the beasts of the
field shall eat it; so shalt thou also do with thy vineyard,
and with the place of thy olive trees.)
12 Six days thou shalt work, and in the seventh day
thou shalt cease, that thine ox, and thine ass rest, and the
son of thine handmaid, and the comeling be refreshed.
(For six days thou shalt work, and on the seventh day
thou shalt rest, so that thy ox, and thy donkey, can also
rest, and so that the son of thy slave-girl, and the
newcomer, *or the foreigner*, can be refreshed.)
13 Keep ye all things, which I [have] said to you; and
ye shall not swear by the name of alien gods, neither it
shall be heard of your mouth. (Hold ye onto all the
things, that I have said to you; and ye shall not swear in
the name of foreign, *or other*, gods, nor shall it be heard
coming out of your mouths.)
14 In three times by all years ye shall hallow feasts to
me. (Three times each year ye shall dedicate Feasts to me.)
15 Thou shalt keep the solemnity of therf loaves; seven
days thou shalt eat therf bread, as I commanded to thee,
in the time of [the] month of new things, when thou
wentest out of Egypt; thou shalt not appear void in my
sight. (Thou shalt keep the Feast of Unleavened Bread;
for seven days thou shalt eat unleavened bread, as I
commanded to thee, at the time of the month of Abib,
when thou wentest out of Egypt; and thou shalt not
appear before me empty-handed.)
16 And *thou shalt keep* the solemnity of the month of
the first things of thy works, (of) whatever things thou hast
sown in the field. Also *thou shalt keep* the solemnity in
the going out of the year, when thou hast gathered all thy
fruits of the field. (And *thou shalt keep* the Feast of the
First Fruits[8] of thy works, with whatever things thou hast
sown in the field. And *thou shalt keep* the Feast of
Ingathering[9], when thou hast gathered in all thy fruits
from the field, in the going out of the year.)
17 (So) Thrice in the year all thy male kind shall appear
before thy Lord God.
18 Thou shalt not offer the blood of thy slain sacrifice
on sourdough; neither the fatness of my solemnity shall
dwell till to the morrowtide. (Thou shalt not offer the
blood of my slain sacrifice with anything made with
yeast; and the fat of my sacrifice for any Feast shall not
remain until the morning.)
19 Thou shalt bear the first things of the fruits of thy
land into the house of thy Lord God. Thou shalt not
seethe a kid in the milk of his mother.
20 Lo! I send mine angel, that shall go before thee, and
shall keep *thee* in the way, and shall lead *thee* to the
place which I have made ready to thee. (Lo! I shall send
an angel before thee, and he shall keep *thee* safe on the
way, and he shall lead *thee* to the place which I have
prepared for thee.)
21 Take thou heed to him, and hear thou his voice,
neither guess thou *him* to be despised, *or despisable*; for
he shall not forgive (thee), when thou sinnest, and my
name is in him (for my authority is with him).
22 For if thou hearest his voice, and doest all things
which I speak (But if thou listenest to his voice, and doest
all the things which I say to thee), I shall be (an) enemy to
thine enemies, and I shall torment them, that torment thee;
23 and mine angel shall go before thee, and he shall
lead in thee to Amorites (and he shall lead thee to the
Amorites), and Hittites, and Perizzites, and Canaanites,
and Hivites, and Jebusites, which I shall break, *or destroy*.
24 Thou shalt not honour the gods of them, neither thou
shalt worship them; thou shalt not do the works of them
(thou shalt not follow their rites), but thou shalt destroy
their gods, and thou shalt break the images of them.
25 And ye shall serve to your Lord God, (so) that I (can)
bless thy loaves, and thy waters, and do away sickness
from the midst of thee;
26 neither a woman unfruitful, neither barren, shall be
in thy land (no unfruitful, or barren, woman shall be in
thy land); (and) I shall fulfill the number of thy days.
27 I shall send my dread into thy before-going, and I
shall slay all the people, to which thou shalt enter (I shall
send the fear of me before thee, and I shall kill all the
people, unto whom thou shalt enter), and I shall turn the
backs of all thine enemies before thee;
28 and I shall send out before thee crabrones, *or
stinging flies*, that shall drive away (the) Hivite, and
Canaanite, and Hittite, before that thou enter.
29 (But) I shall not cast them out from thy face in one
year, lest the land be turned into wilderness, and beasts
increase against thee;
30 little and little I shall cast them out from thy sight, till
thou be increased, and wield the land.
31 Forsooth and I shall set thy terms from the Red Sea
till to the sea of Palestines, and from the desert till to the
flood (And I shall set thy borders from the Red Sea unto
the Sea of the Philistines, *or the Mediterranean Sea*, and
from the wilderness unto the *Euphrates* River). I shall
give (in)to your hands the dwellers of the land, and I shall
cast them out from your sight;
32 thou shalt not make bond of peace with them,
neither with their gods. (thou shalt not make a covenant
with them, nor with their gods.)
33 Dwell they not in thy land, lest peradventure they
make thee to do sin against me; if thou servest their gods,
which thing certainly shall be to thee into cause of
stumbling. (They shall not continue to live in thy land,
lest they make thee to sin against me; for if thou servest
their gods, that certainly shall become a cause of

[8] Also known as the Feast of the Harvest, and the Feast of Weeks.
[9] Also known as the Feast of Tabernacles, the Feast of Booths, and the Feast of Shelters.

stumbling for thee.)

CHAPTER 24

1 Also he said to Moses, Go thou up to the Lord, thou,
and Aaron, and Nadab, and Abihu, and [the] seventy
elder men of Israel; and ye shall worship afar, (And he
said to Moses, Come up to the Lord, thou, and Aaron,
Nadab, and Abihu, and the seventy elders of Israel; and
ye shall worship me from afar,)
2 and Moses alone go up to the Lord, and they shall
not nigh, neither the people shall go up with him. (and
then Moses shall come up alone to the Lord, but the
elders shall not come near, and let none of the common
people come up onto the mountain with you.)
3 Therefore Moses came, and told to the people all
the words and the dooms of the Lord; and all the people
answered with one voice, (and said,) We shall do all the
words of the Lord which he hath spoken. (And so Moses
came, and told the people all the words and the
judgements of the Lord; and all the people answered with
one voice, and said, We shall do all that the Lord hath
spoken.)
4 Forsooth Moses wrote (down) all the words of the
Lord; and he rose early, and builded an altar to the Lord
at the roots of the hill, and *he builded* twelve titles, *or
stones*, by twelve lineages of Israel. (And Moses wrote
down all the words of the Lord; and then he rose up early,
and built an altar to the Lord at the foot of the mountain,
and *he set up* twelve stones, for the twelve tribes of Israel.)
5 And he sent young men of the sons of Israel (to it),
and they offered burnt sacrifices, and peaceable sacrifices
to the Lord (and they offered burnt sacrifices, and peace
offerings to the Lord), (yea,) twelve calves/two calves.
6 And so Moses took half the part of the blood, and
put it into great cups; forsooth he shedded the residue
part on the altar. (And Moses took half of the blood, and
put it into great bowls, *or into great basins*; and he threw
the rest of it against the altar.)
7 And he took the book of the bond of peace, and read
[it], while the people heard; the which said, We shall do
all things that the Lord spake, and we shall be obedient.
(And he took the Book of the Covenant, and read it,
while all the people listened; and they said, We shall do
everything that the Lord spoke, and we shall be obedient.)
8 Forsooth Moses took the blood, and sprinkled it on
the people, and said, This is the blood of the bond of
peace (This is the blood of the covenant), which the Lord
covenanted with you on all these words.
9 And (then) Moses, and Aaron, and Nadab, and
Abihu, and seventy of the elder men of Israel went up,
10 and saw [the] God of Israel, (and) under his feet,
they saw as the work of a sapphire stone, and as heaven
when it is clear. (and they saw the God of Israel, and
under his feet *they saw* a pavement made out of sapphire
stones, yea, like the heavens when they be clear *blue*.)
11 And he sent not his hand on the lords of the sons of
Israel, that had gone far away (But he did not put his hand
upon the leaders of the Israelites, who were there before
him); and they saw God, and (then they) ate and drank.
12 Forsooth the Lord said to Moses, Come thou up to
me into the hill, and be thou there, and I shall give to
thee tables of stone, and the law, and commandments,
which I have written, that thou teach *them*. (And the Lord
said to Moses, Come thou up the mountain to me, and be
thou here, and I shall give thee the stone tablets on
which I have written the Law, yea, the commandments,
so that thou can teach *them* to the people.)
13 [And] Moses and Joshua, his minister, rose, and
Moses went up into the hill of God, (And Moses and
Joshua, his servant, arose, and Moses went up the
mountain to God,)
14 and said to the elder men, Abide ye here, till we
turn again to you; ye have Aaron and Hur with you, if
anything of question be made, ye shall tell [it] to them.
(and he said to the elders *as he left*, Wait here, until we
return to you; ye have Aaron and Hur with you, if any
question ariseth, ask ye it of them.)
15 And when Moses had gone up, a cloud covered the
hill (a cloud covered the mountain),
16 and the glory of the Lord dwelled upon Sinai, and
covered it with a cloud (for) six days; forsooth in the
seventh day (and on the seventh day), the Lord called (to)
him from the midst of the cloud;
17 forsooth the likeness of the glory of the Lord was as
fire burning on the top of the hill in the sight of the sons
of Israel. (and the glory of the Lord was like a fire burning
on the top of the mountain before all the Israelites.)
18 And Moses entered into the midst of the cloud, and
went up into the hill, and he was there forty days and
forty nights. (And Moses went up the mountain, and into
the midst of the cloud, and he was there for forty days
and forty nights.)

CHAPTER 25

1 And the Lord spake to Moses, and said,
2 Speak thou to the sons of Israel, that they take to me
the first fruits; of each man that offereth willfully, ye shall
take those [things]. (Tell thou the Israelites, that they
should bring me the first fruits; and from everyone who
willingly offereth them, ye shall receive those things.)
3 Forsooth these things it be, which ye shall take, gold,
and silver, and brass, (And these be the things which ye
shall receive from them, gold, and silver, and bronze,)
4 and jacinth, and purple, and red *silk* twice-dyed,
and bis, *that is, white silk*, [and] hairs of goats, (and
jacinth, and purple, and red *silk* twice-dyed, and fine
linen, and goats' hair,)
5 and skins of wethers made red, and skins of jacinth,

and wood of shittim, (and red rams' skins, and blue skins,
and shittim wood, *that is, acacia wood,*)
6 and oil to lights to be ordained, sweet smelling
spiceries into ointment, and incense of good odour, (and
oil to nourish the light/and oil to fuel the lanterns, and
sweet smelling spices for the ointment, and for the
incense of the sweetest aroma,)
7 onyx stones, and gems to adorn (the) ephod, *that is,
a chasuble*, and the rational, *that is, an ouch hanging on
the priest's breast, in which was written doom and truth.*
(and onyx stones, and gems to adorn the ephod, *that is, a
chasuble, or an apron-like garment*, and the breast-piece,
*that is, a pouch, or a pocket, hanging upon the priest's
breast, in which were carried the Urim and the
Thummim.*)
8 And they shall make a saintuary to me, and I shall
dwell in the midst of them, (And they shall make a
sanctuary for me, and I shall live there in their midst,)
9 by all the likeness of the tabernacle that I shall show
to thee, and of all the vessels of [the] adorning thereof.
10 And thus ye shall make it; join together an ark, *or a
coffer*, of the wood of shittim, whose length shall have
two cubits and an half, the breadth shall have one cubit
and an half, the height in like manner one cubit and an
half. (And ye shall make it thus; construct the Ark, *that is,
the Box for the tablets of the Law*, out of shittim wood, *or
acacia wood*, and it shall be two and a half cubits in
length, one and a half cubits in breadth, and one and a
half cubits in height.)
11 And thou shalt overgild it with cleanest gold within
and without; and thou shalt make a golden crown above
by compass, (And thou shalt gild it with pure gold within
and without; and thou shalt put a gold band all around it,)
12 and four golden rings, which thou shalt set by [the]
four corners of the ark; two rings be in [the] one side, and
two rings in the other side. (and *thou shalt make* four
gold rings, which thou shalt fasten to the four corners of
the Ark; two rings shall be on one side of it, and two
rings shall be on the other side.)
13 Also thou shalt make bars of the wood of shittim
(And thou shalt make bars out of shittim wood), and thou
shalt cover them with gold,
14 and thou shalt bring (them) in by the rings that be in
the sides of the ark, that it be borne in them, (and thou
shalt bring them in through the rings that be on the sides
of the Ark, so that the Ark can be carried with them,)
15 the which *bars* shall ever[more] be in the rings,
neither they shall any time be drawn out of them. (which
bars shall remain in the rings forevermore, and they shall
never be drawn out of them at any time.)
16 And thou shalt put into the ark the witnessing, *that
is, (the) law*, which I shall give to thee. (And thou shalt
put into the Ark the Witnessing, *that is, the tablets of the
Law*, which I shall give to thee.)
17 And thou shalt make a propitiatory[10] of cleanest gold;
that is, a table covering the ark [that is, a place of purchasing
mercy]; the length thereof shall hold two cubits and an half,
[and] the breadth shall hold one cubit and an half. (And
thou shalt make the mercy seat, *that is, a lid to cover the
Ark*, out of pure gold; its length shall be two and a half
cubits, and its breadth shall be one and a half cubits.)
18 Also thou shalt make on ever either side of God's
answering place, two cherubims of gold, and beaten out
with an hammer; (And thou shalt make for each end of
the propitiatory, *or the mercy seat*, two gold cherubim,
beaten out with a hammer;)
19 one cherub be on one side of God's answering
place, and the tother in the tother *side*; cover they ever
either side of the propitiatory, (one cherub shall be at one
end of the lid, and the other cherub shall be at the other
end of the lid; and the cherubim shall be made so that
they form one piece with the propitiatory,)
20 and hold they forth the(ir) wings, and cover they
God's answering place; and behold they themselves
together, while their faces be turned in to the propitiatory,
(and their wings shall be spread out, and they shall cover
the lid; and they shall face each other, but their faces
shall be turned down toward the propitiatory,)
21 with which the ark of the Lord shall be covered, in
which ark thou shalt put the witnessing, that is, the
(tablets of the) law, that I shall give to thee.
22 From thence I shall command, and I shall speak to
thee above the propitiatory, that is, from the midst of [the]
two cherubims, that shall be on the ark of witnessing, all
things which I shall command by thee to the sons of
Israel. (From there I shall command, and I shall speak to
thee from above the propitiatory, that is, from the midst
of the two cherubim, who shall be over the Ark of the
Witnessing, all the things which I shall command by thee
to the Israelites.)
23 Also thou shalt make a board of the wood of shittim,
having two cubits of length, and one cubit of broadness,
and one cubit and an half in height. (And thou shalt make
a table out of shittim wood, two cubits in length, one
cubit in breadth, and one and a half cubits in height.)
24 And thou shalt overgild the board with most pure
gold, and thou shalt make to it a golden brink about;
(And thou shalt gild the table with pure gold, and thou
shalt put a gold band all around it;)
25 and *thou shalt make* to that brink a crown raised
betwixt four fingers high, and *thou shalt make* on that
another little golden crown. (and *thou shalt make* a gold
rim four fingers high around that band, and *thou shalt* put
another gold band around the rim.)
26 And thou shalt make ready four golden rings, and
thou shalt put them in [the] four corners of the same

[10] Also known as 'God's answering place' and the 'mercy seat'.

board, by all the feet thereof. (And thou shalt make four
gold rings, and thou shalt fasten them to the four corners
of the table, by its legs.)
27 Under the crown shall be (the) golden rings, that the
bars be put through them, and so the table may be borne.
(And the gold rings shall be fastened near the rim, for the
bars to be put through, so that the table can be carried.)
28 Thou shalt make the bars of the wood of shittim, and
thou shalt compass *them* with gold to bear the board.
(Thou shalt make the bars out of shittim wood, and cover
them with gold, and thou shalt use them to carry the
table.)
29 And thou shalt make ready vessels of vinegar, and
vials, and censers, and cups of purest gold, in which
flowing sacrifices shall be offered. (And thou shalt make
out of pure gold the vessels for the vinegar, and the
censers, and the cups, and the basins, in which the wine
offerings shall be made.)
30 And thou shalt set on the board (the) loaves of
proposition, *or (the loaves) of setting forth*, (to be) in my
sight ever[more]. (And thou shalt put the showbread on
the table, to be there before me forevermore.)
31 And thou shalt make a candlestick beaten out with
an hammer, of cleanest gold, [and] *thou shalt make* the
shaft thereof, and [the] rods, and cups, and little roundels,
and lilies coming forth thereof. (And thou shalt make a
lamp-stand out of pure gold, beaten out with a hammer,
yea, *thou shalt make* its shaft, and the rods, and cups,
and little balls, and lilies, that shall all come forth from it.)
32 Six rods shall go out of the sides (of it), three (out) of
the one side, and three (out) of the other.
33 Three cups as in the manner of a nut by each rod,
and [the] little roundels together, and a lily, and in like
manner three cups at the likeness of a nut in the tother
rod, and (the) little roundels together, and a lily; this shall
be the work of (the) six rods, that shall be brought forth
[out] of the *candlestick* shaft. (And there shall be three
cups shaped like almonds, and little balls, and a lily
together on the first rod, and likewise three cups shaped
like almonds, and little balls, and a lily together on the
next rod; such shall be the metalwork for all six rods that
shall come forth from the shaft *of the lamp-stand*.)
34 Forsooth in that candlestick shall be four cups in the
manner of a nut, and little roundels and lilies by each
cup; (And on the shaft of the lamp-stand shall be four
cups shaped like almonds, and little balls, and lilies, by
all the cups;)
35 and the little roundels shall be under (each of) two
rods by three places, the which rods altogether be made
six, coming forth of (the) one shaft; (and a little ball shall
be under each pair of rods, that is, in three places, which
rods altogether be six, coming forth from the one shaft *of
the lamp-stand*;)
36 and therefore the little roundels and the rods thereof
shall be all beaten out with an hammer, of cleanest gold.
(and so all the little balls and its rods shall be made out of
pure gold, beaten out with a hammer.)
37 And thou shalt make seven lanterns, and thou shalt
set them on the candlestick, that they shine even against
each other. (And thou shalt make seven lanterns, and
thou shalt put them on the lamp-stand, so that they shine
toward the front.)
38 Also tongs to snuff the candles, and (the vessels)
where those snuffs, that be snuffed out, be quenched, be
made of cleanest gold. (And the tongs to snuff out the
candles, and the firepans, where those tongs shall be
quenched, shall be made out of pure gold.)
39 All the weight of the candlestick with all his vessels
shall have, *or weigh*, a talent of cleanest gold. (And the
lamp-stand and all its vessels shall be made out of one
talent of pure gold.)
40 Behold thou, and make all thing(s) by the exemplar,
which is showed to thee in the hill. (See that thou make
all these things by the example that was shown to thee
on the mountain.)

CHAPTER 26

1 Forsooth the tabernacle shall be made thus; thou
shalt make ten curtains of bis folded again, and of jacinth,
and of purple, and of red *silk* twice-dyed, made diverse
by embroidery work. (And the Tabernacle shall be made
thus; thou shalt make ten curtains out of finely woven
linen, and jacinth, and purple, and red *silk* twice-dyed,
and embroider them with cherubim.)
2 The length of one curtain shall have eight and twenty
cubits, the breadth shall be of four cubits; all the curtains[11]
shall be made of one measure. (The length of one curtain
shall be twenty-eight cubits, and the breadth shall be four
cubits; all the curtains shall have the same measurements.)
3 Five curtains shall be joined to themselves together,
and other five shall cleave together by like bond. (Five
curtains shall be joined to each other in one set, and
another five shall be joined together in another set.)
4 Thou shalt make small rings, *or eyelets*, of jacinth in
the sides, and in the heights of the curtains, that they may
be coupled together. (And thou shalt put small eyelets,
made out of jacinth, on the outer edge of one curtain in
each set, so that the two sets can be joined together.)
5 One curtain shall have fifty eyelets in ever either
part, so set in, that one eyelet come against *another*
eyelet, and that the one *curtain* may be shaped to the

[11] In the original text, throughout the rest of Exodus, "curtain/s" and "tent/s" are used interchangeably. To avoid confusion, and to enhance comprehension, only "curtain/s" will be used in this context. As well, "say/s" and "serge/s" are also used for "curtain/s"; they appear in this text where they appear in the original text.

tother. (Each set of curtains shall have fifty eyelets on an
outer edge, and one eyelet shall come together with
another eyelet, so that one *set of curtains* can be joined
to the other set *of curtains*.)
6 And thou shalt make fifty golden rings, by which the
veils of [the] curtains shall be joined, that one tabernacle
be made. (And thou shalt make fifty gold fasteners, with
which the two sets of curtains shall be joined together, and
so one Tabernacle shall be made out of all the curtains.)
7 Also thou shalt make eleven says to cover the
covering of the tabernacle; (And thou shalt make eleven
curtains out of goats' hair to make a tent over the
Tabernacle;)
8 the length of one say shall have thirty cubits, and the
breadth shall have four cubits; even measure shall be of
all the says. (the length of each curtain shall be thirty
cubits, and its breadth shall be four cubits; all these
curtains shall have the same measurements.)
9 Of which thou shalt join five by themselves, and
thou shalt couple six to themselves together, so that thou
double the sixth say in the front of the roof. (And thou shalt
join five together in one set, and the other six together in
another set; and thou shalt fold the sixth curtain of the
second set over double at the front of the Tabernacle.)
10 And thou shalt make fifty eyelets in the hem of [the]
one say, that it may be joined to the tother; and fifty
eyelets in the hem of the tother say, that it be coupled
with the tother; (And thou shalt make fifty eyelets on the
outer edge of the last curtain in the first set, and fifty
eyelets on the *joining* edge of the second set;)
11 *and thou shalt make* fifty fastenings, or buckles, of
brass, with which the (small) rings, *or eyelets*, of the
curtains shall be joined together, and *so* one covering be
made of all. (*and thou shalt make* fifty bronze fasteners,
with which the eyelets of the curtains shall be joined
together, and so one tent shall be made out of all of these
curtains.)
12 Soothly that that is left (over) in the says, that be
made ready to the covering, that is, (with the) one say
that is more, of the half thereof, thou shalt cover the
hinder part of the tabernacle; (And what is left over of the
tent curtains, that is, the half curtain that remaineth, shall
hang over the back part of the Tabernacle;)
13 and a cubit shall hang on [the] one part, and the
tother cubit on the tother part, which *cubit* is more in the
length of [the] says, and it shall cover ever either side of
the tabernacle. (and out of the length of the tent curtains,
one cubit shall hang over on one side, and another cubit
on the other side, and so both sides of the Tabernacle
shall be covered.)
14 And thou shalt make another covering to the roof, of
skins of wethers made red, and over this thou shalt make
again another covering of skins of jacinth. (And to cover
the tent thou shalt make a covering out of red rams' skins,
and another covering to be placed on top of that, out of
blue skins.)
15 Also thou shalt make [the] standing boards[12] of the
tabernacle, of the wood of shittim, (And thou shalt make
the upright boards for the Tabernacle out of shittim
wood, *or acacia wood*,)
16 which *boards* shall have each by themselves ten
cubits in length, and in breadth a cubit and an half. (each
board shall be ten cubits in length, and one and a half
cubits in breadth.)
17 Forsooth two indentings shall be in the sides of a
board, by which one board shall be joined to another
board; and in this manner all the boards shall be made
ready. (And there shall be two tenons on the bottom edge
of each board, so that the boards can stand upright, side-
by-side; and all the boards shall be prepared in this
manner.)
18 Of which boards twenty shall be in the midday side,
that goeth to the south; (Of which boards twenty shall be
on the south side, facing south;)
19 to the which boards thou shalt set forty silveren bases,
that two bases be set under each board, by two corners.
(for which boards thou shalt make forty silver bases, so that
two bases can be put under each board, to hold its tenons.)
20 And in the second side of the tabernacle, that goeth
to the north, shall be twenty boards, (And on the second
side of the Tabernacle, facing north, shall be twenty
boards,)
21 having forty silveren bases; two bases shall be set
under each board. (with forty silver bases; two bases shall
be put under each board, to hold its tenons.)
22 Soothly at the west coast of the tabernacle thou shalt
make six boards; (And for the west side, *or for the back*,
of the Tabernacle, thou shalt make six boards;)
23 and again *thou shalt make* twain other boards, that
shall be raised, *or set up*, in the corners on the back half
of the tabernacle; (and *thou shalt make* two other boards,
that shall be set up in the corners at the back of the
Tabernacle;)
24 and the boards shall be joined to themselves from
beneath till to above, and one joining shall withhold all
the boards. And like joining shall be kept to the two
boards, that shall be set in the corners, (and the boards
shall be joined to each other from the bottom to the top,
and the same joining shall hold all the boards together.
And like joining shall be used for the two boards, that
shall be put at the corners,)
25 and they shall be eight boards (al)together; the
silveren bases of them shall be sixteen, while two bases

[12] In the original text, throughout the rest of Exodus, "board/s" and "table/s" are used interchangeably to refer to construction materials. To avoid confusion, and to enhance comprehension, only "board/s" will be used in this context.

be reckoned by one board. (and so altogether there shall
be eight boards on the west side; and they shall have
sixteen silver bases, with two bases under each board, to
hold its tenons.)
26 Thou shalt make also five bars of [the] wood of
shittim, to hold together the boards in one side of the
tabernacle, (And thou shalt make five bars out of shittim
wood, *or acacia wood*, to hold together the boards on
one side of the Tabernacle,)
27 and five other bars in the other side, and of the same
number at the west coast; (and five other bars for the other
side, and the same number for the back, or the west side;)
28 the which bars shall be put through the middle (of
the) boards from the one end till to the other. (and a
middle bar, which shall be put in half-way up the boards,
to run from one end of the Tabernacle to the other.)
29 And thou shalt overgild those boards, and thou shalt
set golden rings in them, by the which *rings*, the bars shall
hold together the work of the boards, the which *bars* thou
shalt cover with golden plates. (And thou shalt gild those
boards with gold, and thou shalt fasten gold rings to them,
by which *rings* the bars shall hold the boards together,
and thou shalt cover those bars with gold plates.)
30 And thou shalt raise up the tabernacle, by the
exemplar that was showed to thee in the hill. (And thou
shalt set up the Tabernacle after the example that was
shown to thee on the mountain.)
31 Thou shalt make also a veil of jacinth, and purple,
and of red *silk* twice-dyed, and of bis folded again, by
embroidery work, and woven together by fair diversity;
(And thou shalt make the Veil out of jacinth, and purple,
red *silk* twice-dyed, and finely woven linen, and
embroider it with cherubim;)
32 which veil thou shalt hang before four pillars of the
wood of shittim; and soothly those pillars shall be overgilt;
and they shall have golden hooks[13], but the bases shall be
silver. (which Veil thou shalt hang on four pillars made
out of shittim wood; and those pillars shall be gilded with
gold, and they shall have gold hooks, and silver bases.)
33 Forsooth the veil shall be set in by the rings, within
which veil thou shalt set the ark of witnessing, whereby
the saintuary, and the saintuary of *saintuaries*, shall be
separated. (And the Veil shall be hung under the fasteners
of the Tabernacle, and thou shalt put the Ark of the
Witnessing behind the Veil; and the Veil shall separate
the Holy Place from the Most Holy Place, *or the Holy of
Holies.*)
34 And thou shalt set the propitiatory, *that is, a golden
table covering the ark of God*, on the ark of [the]
witnessing, into the holy of holy things; (And thou shalt set
the propitiatory, *that is, the gold lid, that covereth the Ark*,
onto the Ark of the Witnessing, in the Holy of Holies;)
35 and *thou shalt set* a board without the veil, and
against the board *thou shalt set* the candlestick in the
south side of the tabernacle; for the board shall stand in
the north side. (and *thou shalt put* the table outside the
Veil, and opposite the table *thou shalt put* the lamp-stand
on the south side of the Tabernacle; for the table shall
stand on the north side.)
36 Thou shalt make also a curtain in the entering of the
tabernacle, of jacinth, and purple, and of red *silk* twice-
dyed, and of bis folded again, by embroidery work. (And
thou shalt make a curtain for the entrance of the
Tabernacle, out of jacinth, and purple, and red *silk* twice-
dyed, and finely woven linen, and embroider it.)
37 And thou shalt overgild five pillars of [the] wood of
shittim, before which pillars the curtain shall be led, of
which pillars the hooks shall be of gold, and the bases of
brass. (And thou shalt make five pillars out of shittim
wood, to hang the curtain on, and thou shalt gild the
pillars with gold, and they shall have gold hooks, and
bronze bases.)

CHAPTER 27

1 Also thou shalt make an altar of the wood of shittim,
which shall have five cubits in length, and so many in
breadth, that is, square, and three cubits in height. (And
thou shalt make an altar out of shittim wood, *or acacia
wood*, which shall be five cubits in length, and as many
in breadth, that is, square, and three cubits in height.)
2 Forsooth horns shall be by [the] four corners thereof;
and thou shalt cover it with brass. (It shall have horns at
its four corners, and thou shalt cover it with bronze.)
3 And thou shalt make into the uses of the altar, pans
to receive [the] ashes, and tongs, and fleshhooks, and
firepans; thou shalt make all *these* vessels of brass. (And
thou shalt make for use with the altar, pans to receive the
ashes, and tongs, and fleshhooks, and firepans; thou shalt
make all *these* vessels out of bronze.)
4 And thou shalt make a brazen griddle in the manner
of a net, and by the four corners thereof shall be four
brazen rings, (And thou shalt make a bronze griddle,
fashioned like a net, and at its four corners shall be four
bronze rings,)
5 which *griddle* thou shalt put under the firepan of the
altar; and the griddle shall be till to the midst of the altar.
(and thou shalt put the griddle under the rim of the altar,
set-in half-way up the altar.)
6 And thou shalt make the two bars of the altar, of the
wood of shittim, the which bars thou shalt cover with
plates of brass; (And thou shalt make two bars out of
shittim wood for the altar, which bars thou shalt cover
with bronze plates;)

[13] In the original text, throughout the rest of Exodus, "hook/s" and "head/s" are used interchangeably. To avoid confusion, and to enhance comprehension, only "hook/s" will be used in this context.

7 and thou shalt lead in *the bars* by the rings, and they
shall be on ever either side of the altar, to bear (it). (and
thou shalt lead in *the bars* through the rings, and they
shall be on both sides of the altar, to carry it.)
8 Thou shalt make that *altar* not massive, but void,
and hollow within, as it was showed to thee in the hill.
(Thou shalt not make that *altar* solid, but empty, or
hollow within, as it was shown to thee on the mountain.)
9 Also thou shalt make a large porch of the tabernacle,
in the manner of a churchyard, in whose midday coast
against the south shall be curtains of bis folded again;
one side shall hold an hundred cubits in length, (And
thou shalt make the courtyard of the Tabernacle *in the
manner of a churchyard*, on whose south side facing
south shall be curtains made out of finely woven linen;
this side shall be a hundred cubits long,)
10 and twenty pillars, with so many brazen bases[14],
which pillars shall have silver hooks, and the holdings of
those[15]. (with twenty bronze pillars, and as many bronze
bases, and the pillars shall have silver hooks and bands.)
11 In like manner in the north side, by the length, shall
be curtains of an hundred cubits, twenty pillars, and
brazen bases of the same number; and the hooks of the
pillars, and the holdings of those, shall be of silver.
(Likewise on the north side shall be curtains a hundred
cubits long, with twenty bronze pillars, and as many
bronze bases, and the pillars shall have silver hooks and
bands.)
12 Forsooth in the breadth of the large porch, that
beholdeth to the west, shall be curtains by fifty cubits,
and ten pillars *shall be*, and as many bases. (And on the
breadth of the courtyard, facing west, shall be curtains
fifty cubits long, with ten pillars, and as many bases.)
13 In that breadth of the large porch, that beholdeth to
the east, shall be fifty cubits, (And the breadth of the
courtyard, facing east, shall be fifty cubits,)
14 in which the curtains of fifteen cubits shall be
assigned to one side, and three pillars, and so many bases;
(and on one side of the entrance there shall be curtains
fifteen cubits long, with three pillars, and as many bases;)
15 and in the other side shall be curtains holding fifteen
cubits, and three pillars, and so many bases. (and on the
other side of the entrance, there shall also be curtains
fifteen cubits long, with three pillars, and as many bases.)
16 Forsooth in the large entry of the porch shall be made
a curtain of twenty cubits, of jacinth, and purple, and of
red *silk* twice-dyed, and of bis folded again, by embroidery
work; it shall have four pillars, with so many bases. (And
at the entrance to the courtyard shall be a curtain twenty
cubits long, made out of jacinth, and purple, and red *silk*
twice-dyed, and finely woven linen, and embroidered; it
shall be hung on four pillars, with as many bases.)
17 All the pillars of the great porch by compass shall be
clothed with plates of silver, with hooks of silver, and
with bases of brass. (All the pillars around the courtyard
shall have silver bands, silver hooks, and bronze bases.)
18 The great porch shall occupy an hundred cubits in
length, fifty in breadth; the height *of the curtains* shall be
of five cubits; and it shall be made of bis folded again;
and it shall have brazen bases. (The courtyard shall be a
hundred cubits in length, fifty cubits in breadth, and five
cubits in height; *the curtains* shall be made out of finely
woven linen, and the bases made out of bronze.)
19 Thou shalt make of brass all the vessels of the
tabernacle, into all uses and ceremonies, as well (as) the
stakes thereof, as (also those) of the great entry. (Thou
shalt make out of bronze all the vessels for use in all the
ceremonies in the Tabernacle, as well as its pegs, and the
pegs for the courtyard.)
20 Command thou also to the sons of Israel, that they
bring to thee the cleanest oil of olive trees, and pounded
with a pestle, that a lantern burn ever[more] (And
command to the Israelites, that they bring thee the purest
olive oil, yea, pounded with a pestle, so that the lantern
shall burn forevermore)
21 in the tabernacle of witnessing without the veil,
which is hanged in the tabernacle of witnessing; and
Aaron and his sons shall set it, that it shine before the
Lord (from eventide) till (to) the morrowtide; it shall be
everlasting worshipping by their successions, *or after-
comings*, of the sons of Israel. (in the Tabernacle of the
Witnessing, outside the Veil which is hung in front of the
Witnessing; and Aaron and his sons shall set it, so that it
will shine before the Lord from the evening until the
morning; this is an everlasting command for their
successors, *or after-comers*, among the Israelites.)

CHAPTER 28

1 Also apply thou to thee, *or bring to thy presence*,
Aaron, thy brother, with his sons, from the midst of the
sons of Israel, that Aaron, Nadab, and Abihu, Eleazar,
and Ithamar, be set in priesthood to me. (And bring thou
into thy presence, Aaron, thy brother, and his sons, from
the midst of the Israelites, so that Aaron, and Nadab,
Abihu, Eleazar, and Ithamar, can serve as my priests.)
2 And thou shalt make an holy cloth to Aaron, thy
brother, into glory and fairness. (And thou shalt make
holy clothes for thy brother Aaron, for his glory and
beauty, *or for his glory and grandeur*.)
3 And thou shalt speak to all [the] wise men in heart,
which I have filled with the spirit of prudence, that they
make clothes to Aaron (so that they make clothes for

---

[14] In the original text, throughout the rest of Exodus, "foundament/s" and "base/s" are used interchangeably in reference to the pillars. To avoid confusion, and to enhance comprehension, only "base/s" will be used in this context.

[15] From the gloss for verse 38:10.

Aaron), in which he shall be hallowed, and shall minister
to me.
4 Forsooth these shall be the clothes, which they shall
make; they shall make a rational, *that is, an ouch upon
the breast, in which doom and truth shall be written*, and
a cloak on the shoulders, a coat, and a strait linen cloth, a
mitre, and a girdle; holy clothes to Aaron, thy brother,
and to his sons, that they be set in priesthood to me. (And
these shall be the clothes, which they shall make; they
shall make a breast-piece, *that is, a pouch, or a pocket,
upon the breast, in which shall be carried the Urim and
the Thummim*, and an ephod, a robe, and an
embroidered linen shirt, *or tunic*, a turban, and a sash;
these shall be the holy clothes for thy brother Aaron, and
for his sons, when they serve as my priests.)
5 And they shall take gold, and jacinth, and purple,
and red *silk* twice-dyed, and bis (and fine linen);
6 forsooth they shall make the cloak on the shoulders
of gold, and of jacinth, and of purple, and of red *silk*
twice-dyed, and of bis folded again, by embroidery work
of diverse colours [with needlework of diverse colours]. (and
they shall make the ephod out of gold, and jacinth, and
purple, red *silk* twice-dyed, and finely woven linen, and
embroider it with diverse colours.)
7 It shall have two hems joined to ever either side of
[the] highness, that they go into one. (It shall have two
shoulder straps, fastened to its top edges in the front, and
behind, to secure the ephod in place.)
8 That (the) weaving, and all [the] diversity of the work
shall be of gold, and of jacinth, and of purple, and of red
silk twice-dyed, and of bis folded again. (And its waistband
shall also be made out of gold, and jacinth, and purple,
and red *silk* twice-dyed, and finely woven linen, and it
shall be joined to the ephod to form one piece.)
9 And thou shalt take two stones of onyx, and thou
shalt grave in them the names of the sons of Israel, (And
thou shalt take two onyx stones, and thou shalt engrave
on them the names of the sons of Israel,)
10 six names in one stone, and six others in the tother
stone, by the order of their birth; (six names on one stone,
and six names on the other stone, in their birth order;)
11 by the work of a graver, and by the painting of a
man that adorneth with gems, thou shalt grave those
stones with the names of the sons of Israel; and thou shalt
enclose and compass with gold. (by the work of an
engraver, and by the painting of a man who adorneth
with gems, thou shalt engrave those stones with the
names of the sons of Israel; and thou shalt enclose and
encompass them with gold.)
12 And thou shalt set *those stones* in ever either side of
the cloak on the shoulders, (as) a memorial to the sons of
Israel; and Aaron shall bear the names of them before the
Lord on ever either shoulder, for remembering. (And thou
shalt fasten *those stones* on the two shoulder straps of the
ephod, as a reminder of the twelve tribes of Israel; Aaron
shall carry their names before the Lord on both
shoulders, so that I shall remember them.)
13 And thou shalt make (two) hooks (out) of (pure) gold,
14 and two little chains of cleanest gold, cleaving to
themselves together, which little chains thou shalt set in
the hooks. (and two little chains out of pure gold, which
shall be twisted like ropes, and which thou shalt fasten to
the hooks.)
15 Also thou shalt make the rational of doom by work
of diverse colours, after the weaving of the cloak on the
shoulder(s), of gold, jacinth, and purple, of red *silk* twice-
dyed, and of bis folded again. (And thou shalt make the
breast-piece of judgement like the weaving of the ephod,
out of gold, and jacinth, and purple, and red *silk* twice-
dyed, and finely woven linen, and embroider it.)
16 It shall be four-cornered, and double; it shall have
the measure of a palm of an hand, as well in the length,
as in breadth. (It shall be square, and folded over double;
its measurements, the length as well as the breadth, shall
be the palm of a hand.)
17 And thou shalt set therein four orders of stones; in the
first order shall be the stone sardius, topaz, and smaragdus;
(And thou shalt fasten to it four rows of stones; in the first
row shall be stones of sardius, topaz, and emerald;)
18 in the second order shall be carbuncle, sapphire,
and jasper; (in the second row shall be carbuncle,
sapphire, and jasper;)
19 in the third order shall be ligure, agate, and amethyst;
(in the third row shall be ligure, agate, and amethyst;)
20 and in the fourth order shall by crystallite, onyx, and
beryl; these shall be closed in gold, by their orders, (and in
the fourth row shall by crystallite, onyx, and beryl; they
shall all be enclosed in gold, and in their proper order,)
21 and shall have the names of the sons of Israel; these
shall be graved with twelve names; all the stones by
themselves, with the names of all the sons by themselves,
by [the] twelve lineages. (and shall have on them the
names of the sons of Israel; yea, they shall be engraved
with their twelve names; each of the stones shall have the
name of one of the sons, to represent the twelve tribes *of
Israel*.)
22 Thou shalt make in the rational chains cleaving to
themselves together of purest gold, (Thou shalt make
chains for the breast-piece out of pure gold, which shall
be twisted like ropes,)
23 and *thou shalt make* two golden rings, which thou
shalt set in ever either highness of the rational. (and *thou
shalt make* two gold rings, which thou shalt fasten to the
upper corners of the breast-piece.)
24 And thou shalt join the golden chains with the rings
that be in the margins thereof, (And thou shalt join these
gold chains to the rings that be fastened to the corners of
the breast-piece,)

25 and thou shalt couple the ends of the chains to the
two hooks in ever either side of the cloak on the
shoulder(s), that beholdeth the rational. (and the other
ends of these chains shall be joined to the two hooks,
that shall be fastened to the upper part of the front of the
two shoulder straps of the ephod.)
26 And thou shalt make two golden rings, which thou
shalt set in the highness of the rational, and in the hems
of the cloak on the shoulder(s), that be even against, and
behold the latter things thereof. (And thou shalt make two
gold rings, which thou shalt fasten to the lower corners of
the breast-piece, by the hem of the ephod, so that they be
opposite each other.)
27 Also and *thou shalt make* twain other golden rings,
that shall be set in ever either side of the cloak on the
shoulder(s) beneath, that beholdeth against the face of the
lower joining, that it may be set covenably with the cloak
on the shoulder(s). (And *thou shalt make* two more gold
rings, and fasten them to the lower part of the front of the
two shoulder straps of the ephod, near the seam, and
above the waistband.)
28 And the rational be bound by his rings with the rings
of the cloak on the shoulder(s), with a lace of jacinth, that
the joining made (may) craftily dwell, and that the rational
and the cloak on the shoulder(s) may not be separated
each from (the) other. (And the breast-piece shall be bound
by its rings to the rings of the ephod with a lace of jacinth,
so that the joining shall dwell secure, and the breast-piece
and the ephod shall not separate from each other.)
29 And Aaron shall bear the names of the sons of Israel
in the rational of doom on his breast, when he entereth
into the saintuary, a memorial before the Lord [into]
without end. (And so Aaron shall carry the names of the
tribes of Israel on the breast-piece of judgement on his
breast, when he entereth into the sanctuary, as a
reminder before the Lord forevermore.)
30 Forsooth thou shalt set in the rational of doom,
teaching and truth, which shall be in the breast of Aaron,
when he entereth before the Lord; and he shall bear the
doom of the sons of Israel in his breast in the sight of the
Lord ever[more]. (And thou shalt put in the breast-piece
of judgement the Urim and the Thummim, which shall
be on Aaron's breast, when he entereth before the Lord;
and he shall carry these symbols of the judgement of the
Israelites upon his breast before the Lord forevermore.)
31 And thou shalt make the coat of the cloak on the
shoulder(s) all of jacinth, (And thou shalt make the robe
to wear under the ephod out of jacinth,)
32 in whose middle above shall be an hood, *that is, an
hole for the head,* and a woven hem by compass thereof,
as it is wont to be done in the hems of clothes, lest it be
broken lightly. (in whose middle on top shall be a hole *for
the head,* with a hem woven all around it, as it is wont to
be done in the hems of clothes, lest it be easily broken.)
33 Forsooth beneath at the feet of the same coat, by
compass, thou shalt make as pomegranates, of jacinth, and
purple, and of red *silk* twice-dyed, and of bis folded again;
(And beneath, all around on the lower hem of the robe,
thou shalt put pomegranates made out of jacinth, and
purple, and red *silk* twice-dyed, and finely woven linen;)
34 while small bells be meddled in the midst, so that a
little gold bell be and a pomegranate, and again another
little bell of gold and a pomegranate. (with little bells
mixed, or mingled, in the midst thereof, so that there be a
little gold bell and a pomegranate, and another little gold
bell and a pomegranate, and so on, all around the hem.)
35 And Aaron shall be clothed with that coat, *or alb,* in
the office of his service, that the sound be heard, when he
entereth into the saintuary, and goeth out, in the sight of
the Lord; and that he die not. (And Aaron shall be clothed
with that robe, *or that alb,* when he ministereth, so that the
sound can be heard when he entereth into the sanctuary
before the Lord, and when he goeth out; and so that he
shall not die/and so that he shall not be killed.)
36 And thou shalt make a plate (out) of purest gold, in
which thou shalt grave by the work of a graver, The Holy
to the Lord (on which thou shalt engrave by the work of
an engraver, Holy to the Lord), *that is, the name of the
Lord, Tetragrammaton.*
37 And thou shalt bind that plate with a lace of jacinth,
and it shall be on the mitre, and it shall nigh [to] the
forehead of the bishop. (And thou shalt tie that plate to
the turban with a lace of jacinth, and it shall be on the
forehead of the High Priest.)
38 And Aaron shall bear the wickednesses of those
things that the sons of Israel shall offer, and hallow in all
their gifts *to God,* and in their free gifts *to men*; and the
plate shall ever[more] be in Aaron's forehead, that the
Lord be pleased to them. (And Aaron shall bear the
wickednesses done when the Israelites offer, and
dedicate, all their gifts *to the Lord*; and the plate shall
always be on his forehead, so that these gifts shall be
acceptable to the Lord.)
39 And thou shalt bind the coat of bis, (*that is, the linen
cloth,*) and the mitre of bis, and thou shalt make also a
girdle, by embroidery work. (And thou shalt make the
shirt, *or the tunic,* and the turban, *and the sash* out of fine
linen, and the sash shall be embroidered.)
40 Forsooth thou shalt make ready to Aaron's sons
linen coats, (*that is, linen clothes,*) and girdles, and
mitres, into glory and fairness. (And thou also shalt make
fine linen shirts, *or tunics,* and sashes, and *peaked* caps,
for Aaron's sons, for their glory and beauty, *or for their
glory and grandeur.*)
41 And thou shalt clothe Aaron, thy brother, with all
these, and his sons with him. And thou shalt (anoint
them, and make) sacred the hands of them all; and thou
shalt hallow them, that they be set in priesthood to me.

(And thou shalt clothe thy brother Aaron, and his sons,
with all these things. And thou shalt anoint them, and
consecrate them, and ordain, *or install*, them, so that they
can serve as my priests.)
42 Also thou shalt make to them linen breeches, that
they cover the flesh of their filth[hood], from the reins
unto their hips. (And thou shalt make linen breeches for
them, so that they cover their naked flesh, from their
reins unto their hips.)
43 And Aaron and his sons shall use those *breeches*,
when they shall enter into the tabernacle of witnessing,
or when they nigh to the altar, that they minister in the
saintuary, lest they be guilty of wickedness, and die; it
shall be a lawful thing everlasting to Aaron, and to his
seed after him. (And Aaron and his sons shall use those
breeches, whenever they shall enter into the Tabernacle
of the Witnessing, or when they approach the altar, to
minister in the sanctuary, lest they be guilty of
wickedness, and die; this shall be an everlasting law for
Aaron, and for his descendants after him.)

CHAPTER 29

1 But also thou shalt do this, that they be (made)
sacred to me in priesthood; take thou a calf of the drove,
and two rams without wem, (And thou shalt do this to
consecrate them as my priests; take a calf from the herd,
and two rams without blemish, *or without fault*,)
2 and therf loaves, and a cake without sourdough,
which be sprinkled (al)together with oil, and therf pastes
sodden in water, (and) balmed, *either fried*, with oil; thou
shalt make all these things of pure wheat flour, (and
unleavened bread, and cakes made without yeast, which
be sprinkled with oil, and unleavened wafers boiled in
water, and fried in oil; thou shalt make all these things
out of pure wheat flour,)
3 and thou shalt offer *them* put in a basket. Forsooth
thou shalt present the calf, and [the] two rams, (and thou
shalt put them in a basket, and offer them with the calf,
and the two rams.)
4 and Aaron and his sons, at the door of the
tabernacle of witnessing; and when thou hast washed the
father and his sons in water, (And thou shalt bring Aaron
and his sons to the entrance of the Tabernacle of the
Witnessing; and when thou hast washed the father and
his sons with water,)
5 thou shalt clothe Aaron with his clothes, that is, the
linen cloth, and coat, and the cloak on the shoulders, and
the rational, which thou shalt bind with a girdle. (thou
shalt clothe Aaron with his clothes, that is, the linen shirt,
or tunic, and the robe, and the ephod, and the breast-
piece, which thou shalt tie up with the sash.)
6 And thou shalt set the mitre on his head, and the holy
plate on the mitre, (And thou shalt put the turban on his
head, and the holy plate of consecration on the turban,)
7 and thou shalt shed the oil of anointing on his head;
and by this custom he shall be (made) sacred. (and thou
shalt pour the anointing oil on his head; and by this rite
he shall be consecrated.)
8 Also thou shalt present his sons, and thou shalt
clothe *them* with linen clothes, (And then thou shalt
present his sons, and thou shalt clothe *them* with linen
shirts, *or tunics*,)
9 and thou shalt gird Aaron and (each of) his sons with
a girdle; and thou shalt set mitres on them; and they shall
be my priests by everlasting religion. [And] After that
thou hast hallowed their hands, (and as with Aaron, thou
shalt gird each of his sons with a sash; and thou shalt put
the *peaked* caps on them; and they shall serve as my
priests by an everlasting law. And after that thou hast
consecrated them,)
10 also thou shalt present the calf before the tabernacle
of (the) witnessing; and Aaron and his sons shall put *their*
hands upon the calf's head;
11 and thou shalt slay it in the sight of the Lord, beside
the door of the tabernacle of witnessing. (and thou shalt
kill it before the Lord, at the entrance to the Tabernacle of
the Witnessing.)
12 And thou shalt take the blood of the calf, and thou
shalt put it with thy finger upon the corners of the altar.
Forsooth thou shalt shed the other blood *that is left*
beside the foundament of the altar (And thou shalt pour
out the rest of the blood at the foundation, *or at the base*,
of the altar).
13 And thou shalt take all the fatness that covereth the
entrails, and the caul of the maw, and the two kidneys,
and the fatness that is on them; and thou shalt offer *them*
(as) incense upon the altar.
14 Forsooth thou shalt burn without(forth) (of) the tents
the flesh of the calf, and the skin, and the dung, for it is
slain for sin. (But the calf's flesh, and its skin, and its dung,
thou shalt burn away from the tents, for it is a sin offering.)
15 Also thou shalt take one (of the) ram(s), on whose
head Aaron and his sons shall set (*their*) hands;
16 and when thou hast slain that ram, thou shalt take
(all) of his blood, and shalt shed it about the altar (and
thou shalt throw it against the sides of the altar).
17 Forsooth thou shalt cut that ram into small gobbets,
and thou shalt put his entrails washed, and his feet, upon
his flesh carved, and upon his head; (And then thou shalt
cut that ram into small pieces, and thou shalt wash its
entrails, and its feet, and put them on its carved flesh, and
on its head;)
18 and thou shalt offer *thus* all the ram into incense on
the altar; it is an offering to the Lord, the sweetest odour of
the slain sacrifice of the Lord. (and *so* thou shalt offer all
the ram as incense upon the altar; it is an offering to the
Lord, the sweetest aroma of the slain sacrifice to the Lord.)
19 And thou shalt take the tother ram, on whose head

Aaron and his sons shall set *their* hands;
20 and when thou hast offered that ram, thou shalt take
(some) of his blood, and thou shalt put it upon the last
part of the right ear of Aaron, and of his sons, and upon
the thumbs of their (right) hand, and (the big toes) of their
right foot; and thou shalt shed the blood on the altar by
compass (and thou shalt throw the rest of the blood
against the sides of the altar).
21 And when thou hast taken (some) of the blood, that
is on the altar, and (some) of the oil of anointing, thou
shalt sprinkle Aaron and his clothes, [and] his sons and
their clothes. And when they and their clothes be (made)
sacred (And when they and their clothes be consecrated),
22 thou shalt take the inner fatness of the ram, and the
tail, and the fatness that covereth the entrails, and the
caul of the maw, and the two kidneys, and the fatness
that is on them; and *thou shalt take* the right shoulder, for
it is the ram of consecration;
23 and *thou shalt take* a tender cake of one loaf,
sprinkled with oil, (and the) paste (that is) sodden in
water, and after(ward) fried in oil, (out) of the pannier of
therf loaves, which is set in the sight of the Lord. (and
thou shalt take one loaf of bread, and one cake of bread
sprinkled with oil, and one wafer boiled in water, and
then fried in oil, from the basket of unleavened bread,
which is put before the Lord.)
24 And thou shalt put all *these* things upon the hands
of Aaron (And thou shalt put all *these* things into the
hands of Aaron), and (those) of his sons, and thou shalt
hallow them, and raise them [up] (as a special gift) before
the Lord.
25 And thou shalt take all *these* things from their hands,
and thou shalt burn them on the altar, into burnt sacrifice,
(for) [the] sweetest odour in the sight of the Lord, for it is
the offering of the Lord. (And then thou shalt take all
these things out of their hands, and thou shalt burn them
upon the altar, for a burnt sacrifice, to make the sweetest
aroma before the Lord, for it is an offering to the Lord.)
26 Also thou shalt take the breast of the ram, by which
Aaron was hallowed, and thou shalt hallow it, raised [up]
before the Lord; and it shall turn into thy part. (And thou
shalt take the ram's breast, with which Aaron was
consecrated, and thou shalt hallow it, and raise it up
before the Lord; and it shall be thy portion.)
27 And thou shalt hallow also the breast (made) sacred,
and the shoulder which thou separatedest from the ram,
by which Aaron was hallowed, and his sons; (And thou
shalt also hallow the consecrated breast, and the shoulder
which thou separatedest from the ram, with which Aaron
and his sons were consecrated;)
28 and they shall turn into the part of Aaron, and of his
sons, by everlasting right, of the sons of Israel; for they be
the first things, and the beginning/s of the peaceable
sacrifices of them, which they offer to the Lord. (and they
shall belong to Aaron, and to his sons, by an everlasting
law, as a gift from the Israelites; for they be the first
things, and the beginnings of their peace offerings, which
they offer to the Lord.)
29 Forsooth the sons of Aaron shall have after him the
holy cloth(es), which Aaron shall use, that they be
anointed therein, and that their hands be (made) sacred.
(And the holy clothes which Aaron shall wear, shall
belong to his sons after him, and they shall be anointed,
and consecrated, in them.)
30 That of his sons, that shall be made bishop for him,
shall use that cloak (for) seven days, and which son shall
enter into the tabernacle of witnessing, that he minister in
the saintuary. (He of his sons, who shall be made the
High Priest after him, and shall enter into the Tabernacle
of the Witnessing to minister in the sanctuary, shall wear
those clothes for seven days.)
31 And soothly thou shalt take the wether of hallowing,
that is, the ram of consecration, and thou shalt seethe his
flesh in the holy place,
32 which flesh Aaron and his sons shall eat, and they
shall eat the loaves, that be in the basket, in the porch of
the tabernacle of witnessing, (and Aaron and his sons shall
eat the ram's flesh, and the loaves that be in the basket, at
the entrance to the Tabernacle of the Witnessing.)
33 that it be a pleasing sacrifice, and that the hands of
the offerers be hallowed. An alien shall not eat of these
things, for they be holy. (They shall eat those things that
be offered when they be consecrated. But a stranger, *that
is, any unqualified person,* shall not eat any of these
things, for they be holy.)
34 That if anything leaveth of the flesh hallowed, either
of the loaves, till to the morrowtide (And if anything is
left of the consecrated flesh, or of the loaves, until the
morning), thou shalt burn the remnants with fire; they
shall not be eaten, for they be hallowed.
35 Thou shalt do on Aaron, and on his sons, all things
which I commanded to thee. Seven days thou shalt (make)
sacred their hands, (Thou shalt do unto Aaron, and unto
his sons, all the things which I have commanded to thee.
For seven days thou shalt consecrate them.)
36 and thou shalt offer a calf for sin by each day (for) to
cleanse; and thou shalt cleanse the altar, when thou hast
offered the sacrifice of cleansing, and thou shalt anoint
the altar into [the] hallowing (of it). (And each day thou
shalt offer a calf as a sin offering for cleansing; and so
thou shalt cleanse the altar, when thou hast offered the
sacrifice of cleansing, and then thou shalt anoint the altar
with oil to consecrate it.)
37 Seven days thou shalt cleanse and hallow the altar,
and it shall be the holy of holy things; each man that shall
touch it shall be hallowed. (For seven days thou shalt
cleanse and consecrate the altar, and it shall be most holy;
anyone who is unclean who toucheth it, shall be harmed.)

38 This it is, that thou shalt do in the altar; two lambs of
one year continually by each day, (This is what thou shalt
offer on the altar; two lambs, one year old, each and
every day,)
39 one lamb in the morrowtide, and the tother in the
eventide;
40 *thou shalt do* in one lamb the tenth part of flour
sprinkled with oil, pounded, that shall have a measure, the
fourth part of hin, *that is, of two pounds,* and wine of the
same measure, to make (the flowing) sacrifice. (*thou shalt
offer* with the first lamb the tenth part of flour sprinkled
with oil from pounded olives, that hath a measure of the
fourth part of a hin, *that is, of two pounds,* and the same
amount of wine, to make the wine offering.)
41 Soothly thou shalt offer the tother lamb at eventide,
by the custom of the offering of the morrowtide, and by
those things, which we said, into the odour of sweetness;
(And thou shalt offer the other lamb in the evening, by
the same rite as the morning offering, and with those
things, which we said, to make the sweetest aroma;)
42 it is a sacrifice to the Lord by everlasting offering
into your generations, at the door of the tabernacle of
witnessing before the Lord, where I shall ordain that I
speak to thee; (it is a sacrifice to the Lord, yea, an offering
that shall be made by all your generations to come, at the
entrance to the Tabernacle of the Witnessing before the
Lord, where I have ordained that I shall speak to thee;)
43 and there I shall command to the sons of Israel; and
the altar shall be hallowed in my glory. (and I shall meet
with the Israelites there; and the place shall be hallowed,
or made holy, by my glory.)
44 And I shall hallow also the tabernacle of witnessing
with the altar, and Aaron and his sons, that they be set in
priesthood to me. (And I shall hallow the Tabernacle of
the Witnessing, and the altar, and also Aaron and his
sons, so that they can serve as my priests.)
45 And I shall dwell in the midst of the sons of Israel,
and I shall be God to them; (And I shall dwell in the
midst of the Israelites, and I shall be their God;)
46 and they shall know, that I am their Lord God,
which led them out of the land of Egypt, that I should
dwell among them; for I am their Lord God. (and they
shall know, that I am the Lord their God, who led them
out of the land of Egypt, so that I could live among them;
for I am the Lord their God.)

CHAPTER 30

1 Also thou shalt make an altar of the wood of shittim,
for to burn incense; (And thou shalt make an altar out of
shittim wood, *or acacia wood,* on which to burn incense;)
2 and the altar shall have a cubit of length, and
another cubit of breadth, that is four-cornered, and two
cubits in height; (and the) corners shall come forth of the
altar. (and the altar shall be one cubit in length, and one
cubit in breadth, that is, square, and two cubits in height;
and horns shall come forth from the altar.)
3 And thou shalt clothe it with cleanest gold, as well
the roof thereof, *that is, the higher part,* as the walls, and
[the] corners by compass thereof; and thou shalt make to
the altar a little golden crown by compass, (And thou
shalt cover it with pure gold, the top of it, and its walls,
and the horns on its corners; and thou shalt put a gold
band all around the altar,)
4 and two golden circles under the crown by all sides,
that bars be put into those rings, and *so* the altar be
borne. (and *thou shalt fasten* two gold rings under the
band on each side, so that bars can be put through those
rings, and the altar can be carried.)
5 Also thou shalt make the bars of the wood of
shittim, and thou shalt overgild them; (And thou shalt
make the bars out of shittim wood, and thou shalt gild
them with gold;)
6 and thou shalt set the altar against the veil, that
hangeth before the ark of witnessing, (and) before the
propitiatory, with which the witnessing is covered, where
I shall speak to thee. (and thou shalt put the altar outside
the Veil, that hangeth in front of the Ark of the
Witnessing, and in front of the propitiatory, *that is, the
mercy seat, or the lid,* that covereth the Ark of the
Witnessing, where I shall speak to thee.)
7 And Aaron shall burn thereon incense smelling
sweetly early (And early each day, Aaron shall burn
sweet smelling incense on it); when he shall array the
lanterns, he shall burn it;
8 and when he setteth the lanterns at eventide, he
shall burn everlasting incense before the Lord, into your
generations. (and when he setteth the lanterns in the
evening, he shall also burn everlasting incense on it
before the Lord, and so shall all your generations to come.)
9 Ye shall not offer thereon incense of (any) other
making, neither offering, nor slain sacrifice, neither ye
shall offer flowing offerings *thereon* (nor shall ye offer
any wine offerings *on it*).
10 And Aaron shall pray on the horns thereof once by
the year, in the blood which is offered for sin, and he
shall please (the Lord) thereon in your generations; it
shall be the holy of holy things to the Lord. (And once
every year Aaron shall put blood on its horns, from the
yearly sin offering, and for all your generations to come,
the priest shall cleanse, *or shall purify,* the altar in this
way; for it is most holy to the Lord.)
11 And the Lord spake to Moses, and said,
12 When thou shalt take the sum of the sons of Israel, all
by themselves shall give by the number (the) price for their
souls to the Lord, and vengeance shall not be in them,
when they be numbered. (When thou shalt take the sum of
the sons of Israel, *that is, when thou shalt register them,*
each one shall give a ransom for his life to the Lord, and so

vengeance shall not come upon them, as they be listed.)
13 Soothly each that passeth to the name(d), *that is, of*
twenty years, shall give this *price* (And each one who
passeth over to the named, *that is, he who is twenty*
years of age, or older, shall pay this *amount of money*),
half a shekel by the measure of the temple; a shekel hath
twenty half-pence; the half part of a shekel shall be
offered to the Lord.
14 He that is had in the number, from twenty years and
above, shall give *this* price; (He that is had in the
number, from twenty years of age and older, shall pay
this amount of money;)
15 a rich man shall not add to the half of a shekel, and
a poor man shall nothing abate (and a poor man shall not
pay less).
16 And thou shalt betake into the uses of the tabernacle
of witnessing the money taken, which is gathered of the
sons of Israel, that it be a mind of them before the Lord,
and he shall be merciful to their souls. (And thou shalt
use the money, which is gathered from the sons of Israel,
for the needs of the Tabernacle of the Witnessing; and it
shall be a reminder of them to the Lord, and so I shall be
merciful to their souls.)
17 And the Lord spake to Moses, and said,
18 Also thou shalt make a great vessel of brass with his
foundament, to wash in, and thou shalt set it betwixt the
tabernacle of witnessing and the altar; and when water is
put therein, (And thou shalt make a great bronze vessel,
with a bronze foundation, *or a bronze base,* to wash in,
and thou shalt set it between the Tabernacle of the
Witnessing and the altar; and when water is put in it,)
19 Aaron and his sons shall wash therein their hands
and their feet,
20 when they shall enter into the tabernacle of
witnessing, and when they shall nigh to the altar, that
they offer therein incense to the Lord, lest peradventure
they die; (whenever they shall go into the Tabernacle of
the Witnessing, or when they shall approach the altar to
offer incense on it to the Lord, otherwise they shall die/or
they shall be killed;)
21 it shall be a lawful thing everlasting to him and to
his seed by successions. (this shall be an everlasting law
for him and for his descendants by succession.)
22 And the Lord spake to Moses, and said,
23 Take to thee sweet smelling spiceries, of the first and
chosen myrrh, (equal to the weight of) five hundred
shekels; and of canel the half (and half as much canel),
that is, (the weight of) two hundred and fifty shekels;
[and] in like manner of calamus, *that is, a sweet smelling*
tree, small and full of knots, (the weight of) two hundred
and fifty shekels;
24 also of cassia five hundred shekels, in the weight of
[the] saintuary; the oil of olives trees, the measure of hin;
(and of cassia, the weight of five hundred shekels, all by
the measure of the sanctuary; and the oil of olives trees,
the measure of a hin, *that is, two pounds;*)
25 and thou shalt make the holy oil of anointing, an
ointment made by the craft of an ointment maker.
26 And thou shalt anoint thereof the tabernacle of
witnessing, and the ark of the testament, (And thou shalt
anoint with it the Tabernacle of the Witnessing, and the
Ark of the Witnessing,)
27 and the board with his vessels, [and] the candlestick,
and the purtenances thereof, (and) the altars of incense,
(and the table, and its vessels, and the lamp-stand, and its
purtenances, and the altar of incense,)
28 and of burnt sacrifice, and all the purtenance, that
pertaineth to the adorning of those things. (and the altar
of burnt sacrifice, and the purtenances of the altars, and
the great washing vessel, and its foundation, *or its base.*)
29 And thou shalt hallow all (these) things, and they
shall be the holy of holy things; he that shall touch those,
shall be hallowed *beforehand.* (And thou shalt hallow all
these things, and they shall be most holy; anyone who is
unclean who toucheth these things, shall be harmed.)
30 Thou shalt anoint Aaron, and his sons, and thou
shalt hallow them, that they be set in priesthood to me
(so that they can serve as my priests).
31 And thou shalt say to the sons of Israel, This oil of
anointing shall be holy to me into your generations. (And
thou shalt say to the Israelites, This anointing oil shall be
holy to me, for all your generations to come.)
32 The flesh of (a) man shall not be anointed thereof,
and by the making thereof ye shall not make another
such oil, for it is hallowed, and it shall be holy to you.
33 Whatever man maketh such oil, and giveth thereof
to an alien, he shall be put out of his people. (Whoever
maketh such an oil, or giveth it to anyone, shall be put
out, *or shall be cut off,* from his people.)
34 Forsooth the Lord said to Moses, Take to thee sweet
smelling spiceries, stacte, and onycha, galbanum of good
odour, and most pure (frank)incense, all these shall be of
even weight (and they all shall be of equal weight).
35 And thou shalt make (the) incense, made by the craft
of an ointment maker, meddled *together* diligently
(diligently mixed *together*), and pure, and most worthy of
hallowing.
36 And when thou hast pounded all *these* things into
(the) smallest powder, thou shalt put thereof before the
tabernacle of witnessing, in which place I shall appear to
thee; the made incense shall be to you the holy of holy
things. (And when thou hast pounded all *these* things into
the smallest powder, thou shalt sprinkle it in front of *the*
Ark of the Witnessing in the Tabernacle, where I shall
appear to thee; this incense shall be most holy to you.)
37 Ye shall not make such a making into your [own]
uses, for it is holy to the Lord. (Ye shall not make such
incense for your own uses, for it is holy to the Lord.)

38 Whatever man maketh like thing *to it*, that he use
the odour thereof, he shall perish from his people.
(Whoever maketh anything like *it*, so that he can have its aroma for himself, he shall perish, *or shall be cut off*, from the midst of his people.)

CHAPTER 31

1 And the Lord spake to Moses, saying,
2 Lo! I have called Bezaleel by name, the son of Uri,
son of Hur, of the lineage of Judah; (Lo! I have called by name Bezaleel, the son of Uri, the son of Hur, of the tribe of Judah;)
3 and I have filled him with the spirit of God, with
wisdom, and understanding, and knowing in all (manner of) work,
4 to find out, *or cast*, whatever thing may be made
subtly of gold, and silver, and brass, (to design whatever things may be made out of gold, and silver, and bronze,)
5 and marble, and gems, and of (the) diversity of
woods.
6 And I have given to him a fellow, Aholiab, the son of
Ahisamach, of the kindred of Dan; and I have put in their hearts the wisdom of each learned man, that they make all things which I have commanded to thee; (And I have given for fellowship to him, Aholiab, the son of Ahisamach, of the family, *or the tribe*, of Dan; and I have put wisdom in the heart of other learned men, so that they know how to make all the things which I have commanded to thee;)
7 the tabernacle of [the] bond of peace, and the ark of
witnessing, and the propitiatory, *or the table*, that is thereon, and all the vessels of the tabernacle; (the Tabernacle of the Covenant, *that is, the Tabernacle of the Witnessing*, and the Ark of the Witnessing, and the propitiatory, *that is the lid*, that covereth the Ark, and all the vessels of the Tabernacle;)
8 also the board, and the vessels thereof, the cleanest
candlestick with his vessels, and the altars of incense, (and the table, and its vessels, the lamp-stand of pure gold, and its vessels, and the altar of incense,)
9 and of burnt sacrifice, and all the vessels of them;
the great washing vessel with his foundament; (and the altar of burnt sacrifice, and all their vessels; the great washing vessel, and its foundation, *or its base*;)
10 [the] holy clothes in service to Aaron the priest, and
to his sons, that they be set in their office in holy things; (the holy clothes of ministry for Aaron the priest, and for his sons, to use when they serve as my priests;)
11 the oil of anointing, and the incense of sweet
smelling spiceries in the saintuary (the anointing oil, and the incense of sweet smelling spices for the sanctuary); they shall make all *these* things that I have commanded to thee.
12 And the Lord spake to Moses, saying,
13 Speak thou to the sons of Israel, and thou shalt say
to them, See ye that ye keep my sabbath, for it is a sign betwixt me and you in your generations; that ye know, that I am the Lord, which hallow[eth] you. (Speak thou to the Israelites, and thou shalt say to them, See ye that ye keep my sabbath, for it is a sign between me and you for all generations to come; so that ye know, that I am the Lord, who halloweth you.)
14 Keep ye my sabbath, for it is holy to you; he that
defouleth it, shall die by death (he who defileth it, must be put to death); (yea,) the soul of him, that doeth work in the sabbath, shall perish from the midst of his people.
15 Six days ye shall do work; in the seventh day is
sabbath, the holy rest to the Lord; each man that doeth work in this day shall die. (For six days ye shall do work; but on the seventh day is the sabbath of rest, which is holy to the Lord; any person who doeth work on this day must be put to death.)
16 The sons of Israel keep [the] sabbath, and hallow it
in their generations; it is a covenant everlasting (The Israelites shall keep the sabbath, and make it holy in all their generations; it is an everlasting covenant)
17 betwixt me and the sons of Israel, and it is a sign
everlasting; for in six days God made heaven and earth, and in the seventh day he ceased of work. (between me and the Israelites, and it is an everlasting sign; for in six days God made the heavens and the earth, and on the seventh day he ceased from all his work.)
18 And when he had [ful]filled to speak to Moses, the
Lord gave to Moses, in the hill of Sinai, two stone tables of witnessing, written with the finger of God. (And when he had finished speaking with Moses on Mount Sinai, the Lord gave Moses the two stone tablets of the Witnessing, *that is, the Law*, written with the finger of God.)

CHAPTER 32

1 Forsooth the people saw, that Moses made tarrying to
come down from the hill, and it was gathered together against Aaron, and said, Rise thou, and make gods to us, that shall go before us, for we wot not what is befallen to this man Moses, that led us out of the land of Egypt. (And the people saw, that Moses was very long in coming down from the mountain, and so they gathered together around Aaron, and said, Rise thou up, and make gods for us, that shall go before us, for we know not what hath befallen this man Moses, who led us out of the land of Egypt.)
2 And Aaron said to them, Take ye the golden earrings
from the ears of your wives (Take ye the gold earrings from the ears of your wives), (and) of your sons, and of your daughters, and bring ye them to me.
3 The people did those things, that he commanded,
and brought the earrings to Aaron;
4 and when he had taken those, he formed *them* by
work of melting, and he made of them a molten calf (and he made a calf out of the melted gold). And they said,

Israel, these be thy gods, that led thee out of the land of
Egypt.
5 And when Aaron had seen this thing, he builded an
altar before the calf, and he cried by the voice of a crier,
and said, Tomorrow is the solemnity of the Lord. (And
when Aaron had seen this thing, he built an altar before
the calf, and he cried by the voice of a crier, and said,
Tomorrow shall be a Feast to the Lord.)
6 And they rose (up) early, and offered burnt sacrifices,
and peaceable sacrifices (and peace offerings); and the
people sat (down) to eat and to drink, and (then) they rose
up to play, *or to scorn, for idolatry is (the) scorning of God.*
7 And the Lord spake to Moses, and said, Go thou, go
down, thy people hath sinned, whom thou leddest out of
the land of Egypt. (And the Lord spoke to Moses, and
said, Go thou, and go down now, for thy people, whom
thou leddest out of the land of Egypt, have sinned.)
8 They have gone away soon from the way that thou
showedest them, and they have made to them a molten
calf, and have worshipped it, and they have offered
sacrifices to it, and said, Israel, these be thy gods, that led
thee out of the land of Egypt. (So soon, *or so quickly*,
they have gone away from the way that thou showedest
them, and they have made for themselves a calf out of
melted gold, and have worshipped it, and they have
offered sacrifices to it, and have said, These be thy gods,
Israel, that led thee out of the land of Egypt.)
9 And again the Lord said to Moses, I see [well], that
this people is of hard noll; (And the Lord said to Moses,
now I clearly see, that this is a hard-headed, *or a
stubborn*, people;)
10 suffer thou me, that my strong vengeance be wroth
against them, and that I do away them; and I shall make
thee into a great folk. (allow me, that my strong anger
come forth in vengeance against them, and that I do them
away; and then I shall make a great nation to come forth
from thee.)
11 Forsooth Moses prayed the Lord his God, and said,
Lord, why is thy vengeance wroth against thy people,
whom thou hast led out of the land of Egypt in great
strength, and in a strong hand? (But Moses prayed to the
Lord his God, and said, Lord, why be thou so angry for
vengeance against thy people, whom thou hast led out of
the land of Egypt with great strength, and with a strong
hand?)
12 I beseech (thee), that [the] Egyptians say not, He led
them out fellily (He led them out with an evil intent), to
slay (*them*) in the hills, and to do *them* away from [the]
earth; (let) thine ire cease, and be thou quemeful on the
wickedness of thy people.
13 Have thou mind of Abraham, of Isaac, and of Israel,
thy servants, to which thou hast sworn by thyself, and
saidest, I shall multiply your seed as the stars of heaven,
and I shall give to your seed all the land of which I spake,
and ye shall wield it ever[more]. (Remember Abraham,
and Isaac, and Jacob, thy servants, to whom thou hast
sworn by thy own self, and saidest, I shall multiply your
descendants like the stars of the heavens, and I shall give
to your descendants all the land of which I spoke, and ye
shall possess it forevermore.)
14 And the Lord was pleased (with Moses' words), (so)
that he did not (do) the evil which he spake against his
people.
15 And Moses turned again from the hill, and bare in
his hand(s) (the) two tables of witnessing, written in either
side, (And then Moses turned, and went down from the
mountain, and carried in his hands the two tablets of the
Witnessing, written on both sides,)
16 and made by the work of God; and the writing of
God was graven in the tables. (and made by God's work;
and God's writing was engraved on the tablets.)
17 Forsooth Joshua heard the noise of the people crying
[out], and he said to Moses, (The) Yelling of fighting is
heard in the tents.
18 To whom Moses answered, It is not a cry of men
exciting to battle, neither the cry of *men* compelled to
fleeing, but I hear the voice(s) of singers.
19 And when Moses had nighed to the tents, he saw
the calf, and (the) dances; and he was wroth greatly, and
he threw out of his hand(s) the tables, and he brake them
at the roots of the hill. (And when Moses came close to
the tents, he saw the calf, and the people dancing; and he
was greatly angered, and he threw the tablets out of his
hands, and he broke them at the foot of the mountain.)
20 And he took the calf, which they had made, and he
burnt it, and brake it till (in)to powder, which he
sprinkled into the water, and gave thereof (to) drink to the
sons of Israel (and then he made the Israelites to drink it).
21 And Moses said to Aaron, What did this people to
thee, that thou hast brought in on them the greatest sin?
(And Moses said to Aaron, What did this people do to
thee, so that thou hast brought in on them this very great
sin?)
22 To whom he answered, My lord, be not thou wroth
(My lord, do not thou be angry), for thou knowest this
people, that it is inclined, *either ready*, to evil;
23 they said to me, Make thou gods to us, that shall go
before us, for we wot not, what hath befallen to this
Moses, that led us out of the land of Egypt. (they said to
me, Make thou gods for us, that shall go before us, for we
know not, what hath befallen this Moses, who led us out
of the land of Egypt.)
24 To whom I said, Who of you hath gold? They took
(And so they brought what they had), and gave (it) to me,
and I casted it forth into the fire, and this calf went out.
25 Therefore Moses saw the people, that it was made
bare; for Aaron had spoiled it for the shame of the
filth(hood) *of making of the idol*, and he had made the

people naked among (their) enemies. (And so Moses saw that the people were made bare; for Aaron had plundered them for the shame of the filthhood *of the making of the idol*, and he had made the people look foolish before their enemies.)

26 And Moses stood in the gate of the tents (And Moses stood at the gate of the tents, *or of the camp*), and said, If any man is of the Lord, be he joined to me; and all the sons of Levi were gathered to him.

27 To which he said, The Lord God of Israel saith these things, A man put his sword upon his hip, go ye, and turn ye again from gate unto gate by the middle of the tents, and each man slay his brother, his friend, and [his] neighbour, *which consented to this idolatry*. (To whom he said, The Lord God of Israel saith these things, Each man put his sword on his hip, and then go ye through the midst of the camp, from one gate to the other, and back again, and each man kill his brother, his friend, and his neighbour, *yea, all who consented to this idolatry*.)

28 And the sons of Levi did by the word of Moses, and as three thousand of men felled down in that day. (And the Levites obeyed Moses, and three thousand men fell down dead that day.)

29 And Moses said, Ye have hallowed your hands today to the Lord, each man in his son, and [his] brother, that blessing be given to you. (And Moses said, Today ye have consecrated yourselves to the Lord, each man against his son, and against his brother, and so a blessing hath been given to you.)

30 Soothly when the tother day was made, Moses spake to the people, (and said,) Ye have sinned the most sin (Ye have sinned this very great sin); I shall go up to the Lord, if in any manner I shall be able to beseech him for your felony.

31 And he turned again to the Lord, and said, Lord, I beseech *thee*, this people hath sinned a great sin, and they have made golden gods to them; (And he returned to the Lord, and said, Lord, I beseech *thee*, this people hath sinned a very great sin, and they have made gods out of gold for themselves;)

32 either forgive thou this guilt to them, either if thou doest not, do away me from thy book, which thou hast written. (and so either forgive thou them this guilt, or if thou shalt not, then do me away from thy book, which thou hast written.)

33 To whom the Lord answered, I shall do away from my book him that sinneth against me;

34 forsooth go thou, and lead this people, whither I spake to thee; mine angel shall go before thee; forsooth in the day of vengeance I shall visit also this sin of them (but on the day of vengeance, I shall punish them for their sin).

35 Therefore the Lord smote the people (And so the Lord struck the people with a plague), for the guilt of the calf, which Aaron (had) made.

CHAPTER 33

1 And the Lord spake to Moses, and said, Go, and go up from this place (Get up, and go forth from this place), thou, and thy people, that thou hast led out of the land of Egypt, into the land, which I have sworn to Abraham, and to Isaac, and to Jacob, saying, I shall give it to thy seed.

2 And I shall send thy before-goer, an angel, that I cast out Canaanite, and Amorite, and Hittite, and Perizzite, and Hivite, and Jebusite; (And I shall send an angel before thee, and I shall throw out the Canaanites, and Amorites, and Hittites, and Perizzites, and Hivites, and Jebusites;)

3 and that thou enter into the land flowing with milk and honey; for I will not go up with thee, for thou art a people of hard noll, lest peradventure I lose thee in the way. (and thou shalt enter into the land flowing with milk and honey; but I will not go up with thee, for thou art a hard-headed, *or a stubborn*, people, and I might destroy thee on the way.)

4 The people heard this worst word, and mourned, and none was clothed with his adorning, *that is, (his) precious clothes*, (as) by custom.

5 And the Lord said to Moses, Speak thou to the sons of Israel, (and say,) Thou art a people of hard noll; (at) once I shall go up in the midst of thee, and I shall do away thee; right now put thou away thine adorning, *that is, crowns which they made in(to) receiving of the law*, that I know, what I shall do to thee. (For the Lord had said to Moses, Speak thou to the Israelites, and say, Thou art a hard-headed, *or a stubborn*, people; and at once I shall go up into the midst of thee, and I shall do thee away; so right now, put away thy adornment, *that is, the crowns which they had made to wear when they received the Law*, and then I shall decide what I shall do to thee.)

6 Therefore the sons of Israel putted away their adorning, from the hill of Horeb (onwards). (And so, the Israelites put away their adornment, from that day at Mount Sinai, and forevermore.)

7 And Moses took the tabernacle, and set it far without the tents, and he called the name thereof the tabernacle of [the] bond of peace. And all the people that had any question, went out to the tabernacle of the bond of peace, without the tents. (And Moses took the Tabernacle, and set it up far away from the tents, and he called it the Tabernacle of the Covenant, *that is, the Tabernacle of the Witnessing*. And all the people, who had any question, went out to the Tabernacle of the Covenant, which was pitched far away from the camp.)

8 And when Moses went out to the tabernacle, all the people rose, and each man stood in the door of his tent, and they beheld after Moses, till he entered into the tent. (And when Moses went out to the Tabernacle, all the people rose up, and they all stood at the entrance to their

tents, and they watched Moses, until he entered into the
Tent.)
9 Soothly when he entered into the tabernacle of the
bond of peace, a pillar of cloud came down, and stood at
the door *of the tabernacle*; and the Lord spake with
Moses, (And when he entered into the Tabernacle of the
Covenant, *that is, the Tabernacle of the Witnessing*, a
pillar of cloud came down, and stood at the entrance *to
the Tabernacle*; and the Lord spoke with Moses,)
10 while all men saw that the pillar of cloud stood at the
door of the tabernacle; and they stood, and worshipped, at
the doors of their tabernacles. (while everyone saw that the
pillar of cloud stood at the entrance to the Tabernacle; and
they stood, and worshipped, at the entrance to their tents.)
11 Forsooth the Lord spake to Moses face to face, *that
is openly*, as a man is wont to speak with his friend; and
when Moses turned again into his tabernacle, Joshua, his
servant, the son of Nun, a young man, went not out of
the tabernacle (but when Moses returned to the camp, his
servant Joshua, a young man, the son of Nun, remained
in the Tabernacle).
12 Forsooth Moses said to the Lord, Thou commandest,
that I lead out this people, and thou hast not showed to
me, whom thou shalt send with me, namely since thou
saidest, I knew thee by name, and thou hast found grace
before me. (And Moses said to the Lord, Thou
commandest, that I lead out this people, but thou hast not
shown me, whom thou shalt send with me; yet thou hast
said to me, I know thee by name, and thou hast found
grace before me.)
13 Therefore if I have found grace in thy sight, show
thy face to me, that I know thee, and find grace before
thine eyes; behold thy people, and this folk. (And so, if I
have found grace before thee, show thy face to me, so
that I can know thee, and continue to find grace before
thee; and remember, *Lord*, that this nation is thy people.)
14 And God said, My face shall go before thee, and I
shall give rest to thee.
15 And Moses said, If thou thyself shalt not go before
us, lead thou not us out of this place; (And Moses said, If
thou shalt not go before *us*, then do not thou lead us out
of this place;)
16 for in what thing may we know, I and thy people, that
we have found grace in thy sight, if thou shalt not go with
us (unless thou shalt go with us), (and) that we be glorified
(out) of all (the) peoples that dwell on [the] earth?
17 Forsooth the Lord said to Moses, I shall do also this
word, that thou hast spoken; for thou hast found grace
before me, and I know thyself by name. (And the Lord said
to Moses, I shall do what thou hast asked; for thou hast
found grace before me, and I know thee by name.)
18 And Moses said, Lord, show thou thy glory to me.
19 God answered, I shall show all (my) good(ness) to
thee, and I shall call in the name of the Lord before thee,
and I shall do mercy to whom I will, and I shall be
merciful, *either goodly*, on whom it pleaseth me. (God
answered, I shall show all my goodness to thee, and I
shall declare the name of the Lord before thee, and I shall
do mercy to whom I will, and I shall be merciful, *or
forgiving*, to whom it pleaseth me.)
20 And again *God said*, Thou mayest not see my face,
for a man shall not see me, and live. (And then *God said*,
But thou cannot see my face, for no one can see me, and
live.)
21 And again *God said*, A place is with me, and thou
shalt stand upon a stone; (And *God said*, Here is a place
beside me, and thou shalt stand on a rock;)
22 and when my glory shall pass (by), I shall set thee in
the hole of the stone, and I shall cover thee with my right
hand, till that I pass (by);
23 and (then) I shall take away mine hand, and thou
shalt see mine hinder parts, forsooth thou mayest not see
my face.

CHAPTER 34

1 And afterward God said, Hew to thee two tables of
stone at the likeness of the former, and I shall write on
those tables those words, which the tables, that thou
brakest, had. (And afterward God said, Cut thou two
stone tablets like the first ones, and I shall write on these
tablets the same words which the first tablets had, that
thou hast broken.)
2 Be thou ready in the morrowtide, that thou go up
anon into the hill of Sinai; and thou shalt stand with me
on the top of the hill; (Be thou ready in the morning, and
come up at once onto Mount Sinai; and thou shalt stand
with me on the top of the mountain;)
3 no man go up with thee, neither any man be seen
by all the hill; and oxen and sheep be not fed against *the
hill.* (no one shall come up with thee, nor shall anyone
be seen on all the mountain; and no oxen or sheep shall
be fed near *the mountain.*)
4 Therefore Moses hewed two tables of stone, (in)
which manner the tables were before, and he rose by
night, and went up into the hill of Sinai, as the Lord
commanded to him; and he bare with him the tables. (And
so Moses cut two stone tablets, like the first tablets, and he
rose up early, and went up Mount Sinai, as the Lord
commanded to him; and he carried the tablets with him.)
5 And when the Lord had come down by a cloud,
Moses stood with him, and called inwardly the name of
the Lord; (And the Lord came down in a cloud, and Moses
stood with him, and the Lord proclaimed his own name;)
6 and when the Lord passed before him (yea, when
the Lord passed before him), he said, Lordshipper, Lord
God, merciful, and pious, patient, and of much mercy
doing, and soothfast,
7 which keepest covenant and mercy into thousands,

which doest away wickedness, and trespasses, and sins,
and no man by himself is innocent with thee, which
yieldest the wickedness of fathers to their sons, and to the
sons of their sons, into the third and the fourth
generation. (who keepest covenant and mercy with
thousands *of people*, who doest away wickedness, and
trespasses, and sins, but no one in themselves is innocent
with me, and who punishest their sons, and the sons of
their sons, to the third and fourth generations, for the
wickedness of their fathers.)
8 And hastily Moses was bowed low to [the] earth,
and worshipped, (And Moses hastily bowed down low to
the ground, and worshipped,)
9 and said, Lord, if I have found grace in thy sight,
(then) I beseech thee, that thou go with us, for the people
is of hard noll (for the people is hard-headed, *or is
stubborn*); and that thou do away our wickednesses and
sins, and wield us.
10 The Lord answered, I shall make (a) covenant, and in
(the) sight of all men I shall make signs, that were never
seen (before) on [the] earth, neither in any folks (nor in any
nation), (so) that this people, in whose midst thou art, see
the fearedful work of the Lord, that I shall make (for thee).
11 Keep thou all things, which I command to thee
today (Obey thou everything which I command to thee
today); I myself shall cast out before thy face (the)
Amorites, and Canaanites, and Hittites, and Perizzites,
and Hivites, and Jebusites.
12 Beware, lest any time thou join friendships with the
dwellers of that land, which friendships (shall) be into
falling to thee.
13 But also destroy thou their altars, break the images,
and cut thou down their [maumet] woods; (And also
destroy thou their altars, and break in pieces their images,
and cut thou down their idol woods, *or their sacred poles*;)
14 do not thou worship an alien God; a jealous lover is
the Lord's name, God is a fervent lover; (do not thou
worship any foreign, *or any other*, god; for the Lord's
name is Jealous, and he is a jealous God;)
15 make thou not (a) covenant with the men of those
countries, lest when they have done fornication, *that is,
idolatry*, with their gods, and have worshipped the
simulacra of them, any man call thee (someone call thee),
that thou eat (some) of the things offered to an idol.
16 Neither thou shalt take a wife of their daughters to
thy sons, lest after those daughters have done fornication,
that is, idolatry, they make also thy sons to do fornication
into their gods (they also make thy sons to do idolatry
with their gods).
17 Thou shalt not make to thee molten gods. (Thou
shalt not make gods for thyselves out of melted metal.)
18 Thou shalt keep the solemnity of therf loaves; seven
days thou shalt eat therf loaves, as I commanded to thee,
in the time of the month of new fruits; for in the month of
ver time thou wentest out of Egypt. (Thou shalt keep the
Feast of Unleavened Bread; for seven days thou shalt eat
unleavened bread, as I commanded to thee, at the time of
the month of Abib; for in the month of Abib thou wentest
out of Egypt.)
19 All thing of male kind that (first) openeth the womb
shall be mine, of all living beasts, as well of oxen, as of
sheep, it shall be mine. (All the males that first openeth
the womb shall be mine, yea, of people, and of all living
beasts, of oxen, as well as of sheep, they all be mine.)
20 Thou shalt again-buy with a sheep the first
engendered of an ass, else if thou givest not [the] price
therefore, it shall be slain. Thou shalt again-buy the first
begotten of thy sons; neither thou shalt appear void in my
sight. (Thou shalt buy back the first-born of a donkey with
a sheep, but if thou wilt not buy it back, it shall be killed.
Thou shalt buy back the first-born of thy sons; thou shalt
not appear empty-handed before me.)
21 Six days thou shalt work, in the seventh day thou
shalt cease to ear and to reap. (For six days thou shalt
work, but on the seventh day thou shalt cease to plow
and to harvest.)
22 Thou shalt make to thee the solemnity of weeks, in
the first things of fruits of thy ripe corn of wheat, and the
solemnity when all things be gathered *into barns*, when
the time of the year cometh again. (Thou shalt keep the
Feast of Weeks, with the first fruits of thy wheat harvest,
and also the Feast of Ingathering, when all things be
gathered *into the barns*, when that time of the year
cometh again.[16])
23 Each male kind of thee shall appear in three times of
the year in the sight of the Lord Almighty, thy God of
Israel. (All thy adult males shall appear before the Lord
Almighty, the God of Israel, three times each year.)
24 For when I shall take away (the) folks from thy face,
and I shall alarge thy terms, none shall set treasons to thy
land, while thou goest up (when thou goest up), and
appearest in the sight of thy Lord God, thrice in the year.
25 Thou shalt not offer on sourdough the blood of my
sacrifice, neither anything of the slain sacrifice of the
solemnity of pask shall abide unto the morrowtide. (Thou
shalt not offer the blood of my sacrifice with anything
made with yeast, nor shall anything of the slain sacrifice
of the Feast of Passover remain until the morning.)
26 (Each year) Thou shalt offer in the house of thy Lord
God the first of the fruits of thy land. Thou shalt not
seethe a kid in the milk of his mother (Thou shalt not boil
a goat-kid in its mother's milk).
27 And the Lord said to Moses, Write thou (down)
these words, by which I smote a bond of peace (by which
I make a covenant), both with thee and with Israel.
28 Therefore Moses was there with the Lord by forty

[16] See Exodus 23:16, and footnote #7.

days and forty nights, and he ate not bread, and drank
not water; and he wrote in [the] tables the ten words of
the bond of peace. (And so Moses was there with the
Lord for forty days and forty nights, and he ate no bread,
and drank no water; and he wrote on the tablets the Ten
Commandments of the covenant.)
29 And when Moses came down from the hill of Sinai,
he held *in his hand(s)* two tables of witnessing, and he
wist not that his face was horned *with wonderful shining
beams*, of the fellowship of God's word. (And when Moses
came down from Mount Sinai, he held *in his hands* the
two tablets of the Witnessing, and he did not know that
his face shone *with wonderful shining beams*, from his
time of fellowship and of speaking with the Lord.)
30 Forsooth Aaron and the sons of Israel saw (that)
Moses' face (was) horned, and they dreaded to nigh nigh,
(And Aaron and the Israelites saw that Moses' face shone,
and they were afraid to come near,)
31 and they were called of him, and they turned again,
as well Aaron as the princes of the synagogue; and after
that Moses spake, (but he called to them, and they came
over to him, Aaron as well as the leaders of the
congregation; and after that Moses had spoken with these
men,)
32 they came to him, yea all the sons of Israel; to which
he commanded all things, which he had heard of the
Lord in the hill of Sinai. (then all the other Israelites came
over to him; to whom he commanded all the things,
which he had heard from the Lord on Mount Sinai.)
33 And when the words were fulfilled (And when he
had finished speaking), he put a veil on his face;
34 and (when) he entered to the Lord, and spake with
him, and he did away that veil, till he went out; and then
he spake to the sons of Israel all things that were
commanded to him; (but when he went in before the
Lord, and spoke with him, he did away the veil, until he
went out again; and then he would tell the Israelites all
the things that were commanded to him;)
35 which saw that the face of Moses going out was
horned, but again he covered his face, if any time he
spake to them. (and they saw that Moses' face shone
whenever he went out, and so he covered his face any
time that he spoke to them.)

CHAPTER 35

1 Therefore when all the company of the sons of Israel
was gathered (together), Moses said to them, These things
it be, which the Lord commanded to be done.
2 Six days ye shall do work, the seventh day shall be
holy to you, the sabbath and the rest of the Lord; he that
doeth work in the sabbath shall be slain. (For six days ye
shall do work, but the seventh day shall be holy to you,
yea, the sabbath of rest, holy to the Lord; he who doeth
work on the sabbath shall be put to death.)
3 Ye shall not kindle fire in all your dwelling places by
the sabbath day. (Ye shall not kindle a fire in any of your
dwellings on the sabbath day.)
4 And Moses said to all the company of the sons of
Israel, This is the word which the Lord commanded, and
said,
5 Separate ye at you the first fruits to the Lord; each
willful man and of ready will offer them to the Lord, gold,
and silver, and brass, (Set ye aside among you the first
fruits to the Lord; yea, each willing person, and of ready
desire, shall offer to the Lord out of their gold, and silver,
and brass,)
6 and jacinth, and purple, and red *silk* twice-dyed,
and bis, and hairs of goats, (and jacinth, and purple, and
red *silk* twice-dyed, and fine linen, and goats' hair,)
7 and skins of rams made red, and (skins) of jacinth,
and [the] wood of shittim, (and red rams' skins, and blue
skins, and shittim wood, *or acacia wood*,)
8 and oil to the lights to be ordained, and (spices so)
that the ointment (can) be made, and (for) the incense
most sweet, (and oil to nourish the light/and oil to fuel
the lanterns, and spices to make the ointment, and the
most sweet incense,)
9 stones of onyx, and gems, to the adorning of the
cloak on the shoulders, and of the rational. (and onyx
stones, and gems, for the adornment of the ephod, and
the breast-piece.)
10 Whoever of you is wise, come he, and make that,
that the Lord commanded,
11 that is, the tabernacle, and the roof thereof, and the
covering; rings, and the buildings of boards, with [the]
bars, stakes, and bases; (that is, the Tabernacle, its tent,
and its coverings; its rings, and boards, and bars, and
pegs, and bases;)
12 the ark, and bars; the propitiatory, and the veil,
which is hanged before it; (the Ark, *that is, the Box for
the tablets of the Law*, and its bars; the propitiatory, *that
is, the mercy seat, or the lid for the Box*, and the Veil,
which is hung in front of it;)
13 the board, with bars, and vessels, and with [the]
loaves of setting forth; (the table, and its bars, and vessels,
and the loaves of proposition, *that is, the showbread*;)
14 the candlestick to sustain [the] lights, the vessels,
and lanterns thereof, and oil to the nourishing of fires;
(the lamp-stand to provide the light/the lamp-stand to
hold the lanterns, and its vessels, and its lanterns, and the
oil for the nourishing of the light;)
15 the altar of incense, and the bars; the oil of anointing,
and [the] incense of sweet smelling spiceries; the curtain at
the door of the tabernacle; (the altar of incense, and its
bars; the anointing oil, and the incense of sweet smelling
spices; the curtain at the Tabernacle's entrance;)
16 the altar of burnt sacrifice, and his brazen griddle,
with his bars, and vessels; the great washing vessel, and

his foundament; (the altar of burnt sacrifice, and its
bronze griddle, and its bars, and vessels; the great
washing vessel, and its foundation, *or its base*;)
17 the curtains of the large entry, with the pillars, and
their bases; the curtain in the doors of the porch; (the
curtains for the courtyard, and its pillars, and their bases;
and the curtain for the courtyard's entrance;)
18 the stakes of the tabernacle, and of the large entry,
with their cords; (the pegs for the Tabernacle, and for the
courtyard, and their cords;)
19 the clothes, whose use is in the service of the
saintuary; the clothes of Aaron the bishop, and of his
sons, that they be set in priesthood to me. (the clothes,
for ministering in the sanctuary; yea, the clothes for
Aaron the High Priest, and for his sons, when they serve
as my priests.)
20 And all the multitude of the sons of Israel went out
of the sight of Moses, (And then all the Israelites went out
from Moses' presence,)
21 and offered with most ready soul and devout the first
things to the Lord, to make the work of the tabernacle of
witnessing, whatever was needful to the adorning, and to
the holy clothes. (and they offered with most ready and
devout souls their first things to the Lord, for the building
of the Tabernacle of the Witnessing, yea, whatever was
needed for its adornment, and for the holy clothes.)
22 Men and women gave bands of the arms, and
earrings, and other rings, and ornaments of their arms
nigh the hand; each golden vessel was separated into the
gifts of the Lord. (Men and women gave arm bands, and
earrings, and other rings, and ornaments for their arms
nigh the hand, *that is, bracelets*; and each gold vessel
was set aside as a gift to the Lord.)
23 If any man had jacinth, and purple, and red *silk*
twice-dyed, bis, and the hairs of goats, skins of rams made
red, and (skins) of jacinth, *either blue*, (And anyone who
had jacinth, and purple, and red *silk* twice-dyed, and fine
linen, and goats' hair, and red rams' skins, and blue skins,)
24 (and) metals of silver, and of brass, they offered (it) to
the Lord, and [the] wood of shittim into diverse uses. (and
metals of silver, and brass, they offered it to the Lord, and
also shittim wood, *or acacia wood*, for diverse uses.)
25 But also women taught gave those things, which
they had spun, (of) jacinth, and purple, and vermilion,
and bis, (And all the skilled women gave those things
which they had spun out of jacinth, and purple, and red
silk twice-dyed, and fine linen,)
26 and the hairs of goats (and also out of goats' hair);
and they gave all (these) things by their own free will.
27 Forsooth (the) princes offered stones of onyx, and
gems, to the cloak on the shoulders, and to the rational,
(And the leaders offered onyx stones, and gems, for the
ephod, and the breast-piece,)
28 and sweet smelling spiceries, and oil to the lights to
be ordained, and to make ready the ointment, and to
make the incense of the sweetest odour. (and oil to
nourish the light/and oil to fuel the lanterns, and sweet
smelling spices to make the ointment, and the incense of
the sweetest aroma.)
29 All men and women offered gifts with devout
soul(s), (so) that the works should be made, which the
Lord commanded by the hand of Moses; all the sons of
Israel hallowed willful things to the Lord (yea, all the
Israelites willingly dedicated these things to the Lord).
30 And Moses said to the sons of Israel, Lo! the Lord
hath called Bezaleel by name, the son of Uri, the son of
Hur, of the lineage of Judah; (And Moses said to the
Israelites, Lo! the Lord hath called by name Bezaleel, the
son of Uri, the son of Hur, of the tribe of Judah;)
31 and the Lord hath filled him with the spirit of God,
of wisdom, and of understanding, and of knowing, and
with all doctrine, (and the Lord hath filled him with the
spirit of God, yea, with wisdom, and understanding, and
knowledge, and all doctrine,)
32 to find out and to make work in gold, and silver, and
brass, (to know how to do work in gold, and silver, and
brass,)
33 and in stones to be graven, and in work of
carpentry; whatever thing may be found craftily, (and to
engrave stones, and to do carpentry; yea, whatever thing
that can be done with craftsmanship,)
34 the Lord hath given in his heart; and *the Lord hath*
called Aholiab, the son of Ahisamach, of the lineage of
Dan; (the Lord hath put this in his heart; and *the Lord
hath* also called Aholiab, the son of Ahisamach, of the
tribe of Dan;)
35 the Lord [hath] taught both with wisdom, that they
make the works of a carpenter, of (a) stainer, and of (an)
embroiderer, of jacinth, and of purple, and of red *silk*
(twice-dyed), and of bis, and that they make all things,
and find all new things. (the Lord hath taught both of
them with wisdom, so that they know how to do the
work of a carpenter, and of a stainer, and of an
embroiderer with jacinth, and purple, and red *silk* twice-dyed, and fine linen, yea, so that they know how to make
all kinds of things, and to devise all kinds of new things.)

CHAPTER 36

1 Therefore Bezaleel, and Aholiab, and each wise
man, to whom the Lord gave wisdom and understanding,
that they know how to work craftily, made things that
were needful into the uses of the saintuary, and which
the Lord commanded to be made. (And so Bezaleel, and
Aholiab, and each wise man, to whom the Lord gave
wisdom and understanding, that they know how to work
with craftsmanship, made things that were needed for use
in the sanctuary, which the Lord commanded to be made.)
2 And when Moses had called them, and each learned

man, to whom the Lord had given wisdom and knowing,
and the which proffered themselves by their own (free)
will to make the work,
3 Moses betook to them all the gifts of the sons of
Israel. And when they were busy in their work each day,
the people offered *their* avows early. (Moses brought
them all the gifts of the Israelites. And while they were
busy with their work each day, the people continued to
bring their offerings each morning.)
4 Wherefore the workmen were compelled to come,
5 and they said to Moses, The people offereth more
than is needful. (and they said to Moses, The people
offereth more than is needed.)
6 Therefore Moses commanded to be cried by the
voice of a crier, Neither man nor woman offer more
anything in the work of [the] saintuary; and so it was
ceased from gifts to be offered, (And so Moses
commanded to be cried by the voice of a crier, No man
or woman need offer anything more for the work of the
sanctuary; and so they ceased from offering gifts,)
7 for the things offered sufficed, and were over-
abundant (and indeed were more than enough).
8 And all the wise men in heart, to fulfill the work of
the tabernacle, made ten curtains of bis folded again, and
of jacinth, and purple, and of red *silk* twice-dyed, by
diverse work, and by the craft of many colours. (And the
most skilled men, doing the work for the Tabernacle,
made ten curtains out of finely woven linen, and jacinth,
and purple, and red *silk* twice-dyed, and embroidered
them with cherubim.)
9 Of which curtains one had in length eight and
twenty cubits, and four cubits in breadth; one measure
was of all the curtains. (And each curtain was twenty-
eight cubits in length, and four cubits in breadth; all the
curtains had the same measurements.)
10 And he joined five curtains one to another, and he
coupled (the) other five to themselves together; (And they
joined five of the curtains to each other in one set, and
the other five curtains together in another set;)
11 and he made eyelets of jacinth in the hem of the one
curtain on ever either side, and in like manner in the hem
of the tother curtain, (and they made eyelets out of
jacinth on the outer edge of one curtain in each set,)
12 that the eyelets shall come together against
themselves, and they shall be joined together; (so that the
eyelets would be opposite each other, and they could be
joined together;)
13 wherefore he melted out also fifty golden rings, that
shall hold the eyelets of the curtains; and *so* one
tabernacle was made. (and they made fifty fasteners out
of melted gold, which they used to join together the
eyelets of the two sets of curtains; and *so* one Tabernacle
was made out of all the curtains.)
14 He made also eleven says of the hairs of goats, to
cover the roof of the tabernacle; (And they made eleven
curtains out of goats' hair, to make a tent over the
Tabernacle;)
15 one say had thirty cubits in length, [and] four cubits
in breadth; all the says were of one measure; (each of
these curtains was thirty cubits in length, and four cubits
in breadth; all of the curtains had the same measurements;)
16 of which says he joined (together) five by
themselves, and six others by themselves. (and they
joined five of these curtains together in one set, and the
other six together in another set.)
17 And he made fifty eyelets in the hem of one say, and
fifty in the hem of the tother say, that those should be
joined to themselves together; (And they made fifty
eyelets on the outer edge of the last curtain in the first set,
and fifty eyelets on the joining edge of the second set, so
that the two sets could be joined together;)
18 and *he made* fifty buckles of brass by which the roof
was fastened together, that one covering were made of all
the says. (and *they made* fifty bronze fasteners, which
they used to join together the eyelets of the two sets of
curtains, and so one tent was made out of all the curtains.)
19 He made also a covering of the tabernacle of the
skins of rams made red, and another veil above (that) of
the skins of jacinth. (And they made a covering for the
tent out of red rams' skins, and another covering to be
placed on top of that, out of blue skins.)
20 He made also [the] standing boards of the tabernacle,
of the wood of shittim; (And they made the upright boards
for the Tabernacle, out of shittim wood, *or acacia wood*;)
21 the length of one board was of ten cubits, and the
breadth held one cubit and an half. (each board was ten
cubits in length, and one and a half cubits in breadth; all
the boards had the same measurements.)
22 Two indentings were by each board, that the one
should be joined to the tother; so he made in all the
boards of the tabernacle. (And they made two tenons at
the bottom of each board, so that the boards could stand
upright, side-by-side; so they made all the boards for the
Tabernacle.)
23 Of which boards twenty were at the midday coast
against the south, (Of which boards twenty were on the
south side, facing south,)
24 with forty bases of silver; two bases were set under
one board on ever either side of the corners, where the
indentings, *or rabbetings*, of the sides were ended in the
corners. (with forty silver bases; two bases were put
under each board, to hold its tenons.)
25 And at the coast of the tabernacle that beholdeth to
the north, he made twenty boards, (And for the north side
of the Tabernacle, they made twenty boards,)
26 with forty bases of silver, two bases by each board.
(with forty silver bases, two bases for each board, to hold
its tenons.)

27 Forsooth against the west, he made six boards, (And
for the west side, *or the back of the Tabernacle*, they
made six boards,)
28 and twain other boards by each corner of the
tabernacle behind, (and two other boards that were set
up in the corners at the back of the Tabernacle,)
29 which were joined from beneath till to above, and
were borne into one joining (al)together; so he made on
ever either part by the corners, (and these boards were
joined to each other from the bottom to the top, and the
same joining held all the boards together; so they made
the two boards that were put at the corners,)
30 that they were eight boards (al)together, and they
had sixteen bases of silver, that is, two bases under each
board. (and so altogether, there were eight boards on the
west side, and they had sixteen silver bases, that is, two
bases under each board, to hold its tenons.)
31 He made also bars of the wood of shittim, five bars to
hold together the boards of the one side of the tabernacle,
(And they made bars out of shittim wood, five bars to
hold together the boards on one side of the Tabernacle,)
32 and five other bars to shape together the boards of
the tother side; and without these, he made five other
bars (for the boards) at the west coast of the tabernacle
against the sea. (and five other bars to hold together the
boards on the other side; and besides these, they made
five more bars for the boards at the back, *or at the far
end*, of the Tabernacle, on the west side.)
33 He made also another bar, that should come by the
middle (of the) boards, from corner till to corner. (And they
made the middle bar, that would run from one end of the
Tabernacle to the other end, half-way up the boards.)
34 Forsooth he overgilded the walls (made) of the
boards, and he melted out their silveren bases, and he
made their golden rings, by which the bars might be
brought in, and he covered those same bars with golden
plates. (And they gilded the walls made out of the boards
with gold, and they made their bases out of melted silver,
and their rings out of melted gold, through which the
bars could be brought in, and they covered those same
bars with gold plates.)
35 He made also a veil diverse and parted, of jacinth,
and purple, and red *silk* (twice-dyed), and bis folded again,
by the work of embroidery. (And they made the Veil out
of jacinth, and purple, and red *silk* twice-dyed, and finely
woven linen, and embroidered it with cherubim.)
36 *He made* also four pillars of shittim wood, which
pillars with the hooks he overgilded, and he melted out
their silveren bases. (And to support the Veil, *they made*
four pillars out of shittim wood, and they gilded the
pillars with gold, and made their hooks out of melted
gold, and their bases out of melted silver.)
37 He made also in the entering of the tabernacle a
curtain of jacinth, and purple, and red *silk* (twice-dyed),
and bis folded again, by the work of embroidery. (And for
the entrance to the Tabernacle they made a curtain out of
jacinth, and purple, red *silk* twice-dyed, and finely woven
linen, and embroidered it.)
38 And *he made* five pillars with their hooks, which he
covered with gold; and he melted out their brazen bases,
(and their holdings,) which he covered with gold. (And to
support the curtain, *they made* five pillars out of shittim
wood, with their hooks; and they covered their tops and
bands with gold, and made their bases out of
bronze./And to support the curtain, *they made* five pillars
out of shittim wood, which they covered with gold; and
they had gold hooks, and they covered their tops and
bands with gold, and made their bases out of bronze.)

CHAPTER 37

1 Forsooth Bezaleel made also an ark of the wood of
shittim, having two cubits and an half in length, and a
cubit and an half in breadth; forsooth the height was of
one cubit and an half; (Then Bezaleel made the Ark, *that
is, the Box for the tablets of the Law*, out of shittim wood,
or acacia wood, two and a half cubits in length, and one
and a half cubits in breadth, and one and a half cubits in
height;)
2 and he covered the ark with purest gold, within and
withoutforth. And he made to it a golden crown by
compass (And he put a gold band all around it),
3 and he melted out four golden rings, (to be set) by
the four corners thereof, two rings in one side, and two
rings in the other side. (and he made four rings out of
melted gold, to be fastened to its four corners, two rings
on one side, and two rings on the other side.)
4 And he made (its) bars (out) of the wood of shittim,
the which he covered with gold,
5 and which bars he put into the rings that were in the
sides of the ark, to bear it. (and he put the bars through the
rings that were fastened to the sides of the Ark, to carry it.)
6 He made also a propitiatory, *that is, God's
answering place*, of purest gold, of two cubits and an half
in length, and one cubit and an half in breadth. (And he
made the propitiatory, *that is, God's answering place, or
the lid for the Box*, out of pure gold, two and a half cubits
in length, and one and a half cubits in breadth.)
7 Also *he made* two cherubims (out) of gold, beaten
out with an hammer, which he set on ever either side of
the propitiatory, (And *he made* two gold cherubim,
beaten out with a hammer, which he put at either end of
the propitiatory,)
8 one cherub in the height of the one part, and the
tother cherub in the height of the tother part; two
cherubims, *one* in each highness of the propitiatory, (one
cherub at one end, and the other cherub at the other end;
two cherubim, but each joined with the lid to make one
piece,)

9 stretching out the wings, and covering the
propitiatory, and beholding themselves together, and that
propitiatory. (stretching out their wings, and covering the
propitiatory, and facing each other, but with their faces
turned down toward the *propitiatory.*)
10 He made also a board of the wood of shittim, in the
length of two cubits, and in the breadth of one cubit,
which board had a cubit and an half in height. (And he
made a table out of shittim wood, *or acacia wood,* two
cubits in length, and one cubit in breadth, and one and a
half cubits in height.)
11 And he compassed the table with cleanest gold, and
made to it a golden brink by compass; (And he covered
the table with pure gold, and put a gold band all around
it;)
12 and *he made* to that brink a golden crown, raised
betwixt of four fingers; and on the same crown he made
another golden crown. (and *he made* a gold rim four
fingers wide around that band, and then another gold
band around that rim.)
13 Also he melted out four golden rings, which he put
into the four corners, by all the feet of the table against
the crown, (And he made four rings out of melted gold,
which he fastened to the four corners of the table, by
each leg, close to the rim,)
14 and he put bars into the circles, *or rings,* that the
table might be borne. (and he put bars through the rings,
so that the table could be carried.)
15 And he made the bars (out) of the wood of shittim,
and compassed those with gold (and covered them with
gold).
16 And *he made* [the] vessels to diverse uses of the
board, vessels of vinegar, vials, and little cups, and
censers of pure gold, in which the flowing sacrifices shall
be offered. (And *he made* the vessels for diverse uses on
the table, yea, the vessels for vinegar, and the censers,
and the little cups, and the basins in which the wine
offerings could be made, all made out of pure gold.)
17 And he made a candlestick, beaten out with an
hammer, of cleanest gold, of whose stock, rods, cups,
and little roundels, and lilies came forth; (And he made
the lamp-stand out of pure gold, beaten out with a
hammer, from whose shaft its rods, and cups, and little
balls, and lilies came forth;)
18 six in ever either side (six on each side), three rods
on (the) one side, and three on the other side;
19 three cups in the manner of a nut by each rod, and
little roundels together, and lilies; and three cups at the
likeness of a nut in the tother rod, and little roundels
together, and lilies; forsooth the work of (the) six shafts
that came forth of the stock of the candlestick, was even.
(with three cups shaped like almonds, and little balls, and
a lily together on the first rod; and three cups shaped like
almonds, and little balls, and a lily together on the next
rod, and so on; all the work of the six rods that came
forth from the shaft of the lamp-stand, was the same.)
20 Soothly in that stock were four cups, in the manner
of a nut, and little roundels and lilies were by all the *cups;*
(And on the shaft were four cups, shaped like almonds,
and there were little balls, and lilies, by all the *cups;*)
21 and [the] little roundels were under the two shafts by
three places, which (al)together be made six shafts
coming forth of one stock; (and a little ball was under
each pair of rods, that is, in three places, and altogether
there were six rods coming forth from the one shaft;)
22 therefore the little roundels, *or balls,* and the shafts
thereof, were all beaten out with hammer, of purest gold.
(and so the little balls, and its rods, were all made out of
pure gold, beaten out with a hammer.)
23 He made also seven lanterns, with their snuffing
tongs, and the vessels where the snuffs be quenched, of
cleanest gold. (And he made seven lanterns, with their
snuffing tongs, and the firepans where those tongs be
quenched, out of pure gold.)
24 The candlestick with all his vessels weighed a talent
of gold. (The lamp-stand, and all its vessels, were made
out of one talent of pure gold.)
25 He made also the altar of incense, of the wood of
shittim, having a cubit by square, *that is, on each side
one cubit,* and two cubits in height, of whose corners
came forth horns. (And he made the altar of incense out
of shittim wood, one cubit square, *that is, one cubit on
each side,* and two cubits in height, out of whose corners
the horns came forth.)
26 And he covered it with cleanest gold, and the
griddle, and (the) walls, and the horns (thereof); and he
made to it a little golden crown by compass, (And he
covered it with pure gold, yea, its top, and its walls, and
its horns; and he put a gold band all around it,)
27 and two golden rings under the crown, by each side,
that [the] bars be put into those, and the altar may be
borne. (and he made two gold rings to be fastened under
the band, on each side of the altar, for bars to be put
through, so that the altar could be carried.)
28 Forsooth he made those bars (out) of the wood of
shittim, and covered *them* with golden plates.
29 He made also oil to the ointment of hallowing, and
[the] incense of sweet smelling spiceries, most clean, by
the work of (the) apothecary. (And he made the holy oil
for anointing, and the pure incense of sweet smelling
spices, by the work of an apothecary.)

CHAPTER 38

1 He made also the altar of burnt sacrifice of the wood
of shittim, of five cubits by square, and of three cubits in
height; (And he made the altar of burnt sacrifice out of
shittim wood, *or acacia wood,* five cubits square, and
three cubits in height;)

2 whose horns came forth [out] of the corners, and he
covered it with plates of brass. (whose horns came forth
out of the corners, and he covered it with bronze plates.)
3 And into the uses thereof he made ready of brass
diverse vessels, cauldrons, tongs, fleshhooks, hooks, and
firepans. (And he made diverse vessels out of bronze for
use with it, yea, the cauldrons, tongs, fleshhooks, hooks,
and firepans.)
4 He made also the brazen griddle thereof, in (the)
manner of a net (And he made its bronze griddle, which
was like a net), and a firepan under it, (in) the midst of
the altar.
5 And he melted out four rings, by so many ends of
the griddle, to put in the bars [for] to bear it; (And he
made four bronze rings, to fasten to the four corners of
the griddle, for the bars to be put through, to carry it;)
6 and he made those same bars of the wood of
shittim, and covered *them* with plates of brass. (and he
made those bars out of shittim wood, and covered *them*
with bronze plates.)
7 And he led *them* into the rings that stood forth in the
sides of the altar. Forsooth that altar was not firm, but
hollow of the building of the boards, and void within.
(And he put *them* through the rings that were fastened to
the sides of the altar. And that altar was not solid, but
hollow, having been built out of boards, and so was
empty within.)
8 He made also a great washing vessel of brass, with
his foundament, of the mirrors (of brass) of the women
that watched in the great street of the tabernacle. (And he
made a great bronze washing vessel, and its bronze
foundation, *or its bronze base*, out of the bronze mirrors
belonging to the women who served at the entrance to
the Tabernacle of the Witnessing.)
9 And *he made* the great porch, *or (the) great entry*, in
whose south coast were [the] curtains of bis folded again,
of an hundred cubits, (And *he made* the courtyard, on
whose south side were curtains made out of finely woven
linen, a hundred cubits long,)
10 (and) twenty brazen pillars with their bases; the
hooks of [the] pillars, and the holdings of those[17], were of
silver; (with twenty bronze pillars, and their bronze
bases; and the hooks of the pillars, and their bands, were
made out of silver;)
11 evenly at the north coast, the curtains, pillars, and
bases, and the hooks of (the) pillars, and the holdings of
those, were of the same measure, and work, and metal.
(likewise on the north side, the curtains, the pillars, the
bases, the hooks of the pillars, and their bands, all had
the same measurements, and work, and metal, as those
on the south side.)
12 Forsooth in that coast that beholdeth [to] the west
were curtains of fifty cubits, (and) ten brazen pillars with
their bases; and the hooks of (the) pillars, and the
holdings of those, were of silver. (And on the west side
were curtains fifty cubits long, with ten bronze pillars,
and their bronze bases; and the hooks of the pillars, and
their bands, were made out of silver.)
13 Soothly against the east he made ready curtains of
fifty cubits, (And the east side, where the entrance to the
Tabernacle was, was also fifty cubits long,)
14 of which curtains one side had fifteen cubits, of
three pillars with their bases; (and on one side of the
entrance, he made curtains fifteen cubits long, with three
pillars, and their bases;)
15 and in the other side, for he made the entering of
the tabernacle betwixt ever either, were curtains evenly
of fifteen cubits, three pillars, and so many bases. (and on
the other side of the entrance, he also made curtains
fifteen cubits long, with three pillars, and their bases.)
16 Bis folded again covered all the curtains of the great
entry. (And all the curtains of the courtyard were made
out of finely woven linen.)
17 The bases of the pillars were of brass; forsooth the
hooks of those pillars, and the holdings of them, were of
silver; but also he covered with silver (the heads of) the
pillars of the great entry. (The bases of the pillars were
made out of bronze; and the hooks of the pillars, and
their bands, were made out of silver; and the tops of the
pillars in the courtyard were also made out of silver.)
18 And in the entering thereof he made a curtain, by
embroidery work, of jacinth, purple, vermilion, *either red
cloth*, and of bis folded again, which curtain had twenty
cubits in length, and the height was of five cubits, by the
measure which all the curtains of the great entry had.
(And for the entrance to the courtyard he made a curtain
out of jacinth, and purple, and red *silk* twice-dyed, and
finely woven linen, and embroidered it; which curtain
was twenty cubits in length, and five cubits in height, the
same measurements as the courtyard curtains.)
19 Forsooth the pillars in the entering were four, with
brazen bases, and the hooks of (the) pillars, and the
holdings of those, were of silver; (And there were four
pillars at the entrance, with bronze bases, and the hooks
of the pillars, and their bands, were made out of silver;)
20 and he made [the] brazen stakes of the tabernacle,
and of the great entry, by compass. (and he made the
bronze pegs for the Tabernacle, and for the courtyard all
around it.)
21 These be the numbers (of the amounts of metals) of
the tabernacle of witnessing, that be numbered, by the
commandment of Moses, in the ceremonies, *that is,
services*, of Levites, by the hand of Ithamar, the son of
Aaron, [the] priest. (These be the numbers for the
amounts of the metals used in the Tabernacle of the
Witnessing, that be listed, by the commandment of

[17] From the gloss in copies G, Q, and X.

Moses, and made by the Levites, under the hand, *or under the authority*, of Ithamar, the son of Aaron, the priest.)
22 Which instruments Bezaleel, the son of Uri, [the] son of Hur, of the lineage of Judah, fulfilled; for the Lord commanded by Moses, (Which *Tabernacle, and its purtenances*, Bezaleel, the son of Uri, the son of Hur, of the tribe of Judah, made; all of which the Lord commanded to Moses *to be made*.)
23 while Aholiab, the son of Ahisamach, of the lineage of Dan, was joined fellow to him, and he himself was a noble craftsman of wood, and a tapicer, *that is, a weaver of diverse colours*, and an embroiderer of jacinth, purple, vermilion, and bis. (And Aholiab, the son of Ahisamach, of the tribe of Dan, was joined in fellowship with *Bezaleel*, and he himself was a noble craftsman of wood, and a tapicer, *that is, a weaver of diverse colours*, and an embroiderer in jacinth, and purple, and red *silk* twice-dyed, and fine linen.)
24 All the gold that was spended in the work of the saintuary, and that was offered in gifts, was of nine and twenty talents, and of seven hundred and thirty shekels, at the measure of the saintuary. (All the gold that was used for the work of the sanctuary, and that was offered in gifts, was twenty-nine talents, and seven hundred and thirty shekels, by the measure of the sanctuary.)
25 Forsooth the silver of (the) numbering of the people was an hundred hundreds, and a thousand and seven hundred and seventy (and five) shekels, at the weight of (the) saintuary, (And the silver gotten from the registering of the people was a hundred talents, and a thousand and seven hundred and seventy-five shekels, by the measure of the sanctuary,)
26 half a shekel by each head of all that passed (by) to (be) number(ed), from twenty years and above, of six hundred thousand and three thousand, and five hundred and fifty men. (half a shekel from each man who was registered, twenty years and older, that is, from six hundred and three thousand, and five hundred and fifty men.)
27 Furthermore there were an hundred talents of silver, of which the bases of the saintuary were melted out (al)together, and (the bases) of the entering, where the veil hangeth; an hundred bases were made of an hundred talents, for to each base was ordained a talent. (And furthermore there were a hundred talents of silver, out of which the bases, for the sanctuary, and for the entrance where the Veil hangeth, were melted out; one hundred bases were made out of one hundred talents, that is, one talent was used for each base.)
28 Forsooth (from out) of a thousand (and) seven hundred and seventy and five shekels, he made the hooks of [the] pillars, and covered the heads of the pillars with silver (and covered the tops of the pillars with silver).
29 Also of brass were offered two and seventy thousand talents, and four hundred shekels over. (And of bronze, there were offered seventy talents, and two thousand and four hundred shekels.)
30 Of which the bases in the entering of the tabernacle of witnessing were melted out, and the brazen altar, with his griddle, and all the vessels that pertain to the use thereof, (From which were melted out the bases for the entrance to the Tabernacle of the Witnessing, and the bronze altar, and its griddle, and all the vessels that pertain to its use,)
31 and the bases of the great entry, as well in the compass, as in the entering thereof, and the stakes of the tabernacle, and of the great entry by compass. (and the bases for the pillars all around the courtyard, and its entrance, and the pegs for the Tabernacle, and for all around the courtyard.)

CHAPTER 39

1 Forsooth of jacinth, and purple, vermilion, and bis, he made [the] clothes in which Aaron was clothed, when he ministered in [the] holy things, as the Lord commanded to Moses. (And they made out of jacinth, and purple, and red *silk* twice-dyed, and fine linen, the clothes in which Aaron was clothed, when he served in the Holy Place, as the Lord commanded to Moses.)
2 Therefore he made the cloak on the shoulders of gold, jacinth, and purple, and of red *silk* twice-dyed, and of bis folded again, by work of embroidery; (And so they made the ephod out of gold, and jacinth, and purple, and red *silk* twice-dyed, and finely woven linen, and embroidered it;)
3 also he cut (up) thin golden plates, and made (them very) thin into threads, that those may be folded again, with the warp of the former colours; (and they cut up thin gold plates, and made them into very thin threads, to be woven into the warp of the other colours;)
4 and *he made* twain hems coupled to themselves together, in ever either side of the ends; (and *they made* two shoulder straps, fastened in the front, and behind, to the top edges of the ephod, to secure it;)
5 and *he made* a girdle of the same colours, as the Lord commanded to Moses. (and *they made* the waistband out of the same things, and joined it to the ephod to form one piece, as the Lord commanded to Moses.)
6 And he made ready two onyx stones, bound and closed in gold, and graved by the craft of a worker in gems with the names of the sons of Israel; (And they prepared two onyx stones, bound and enclosed in gold, and engraved by the craft of a worker in gems with the names of the sons of Israel;)
7 six names in one stone, and six in the tother stone, by the order of their birth. And he set those stones in the side(s) of the cloak on the shoulders, into a memorial of the sons of Israel, as the Lord commanded to Moses. (six

names on one stone, and six on the other stone, in their
birth order. And they fastened those stones onto the two
shoulder straps of the ephod, as a reminder of the twelve
tribes of Israel, as the Lord commanded to Moses.)
8 He made also the rational, by work of embroidery,
by the work of the cloak on the shoulders, of gold,
jacinth, purple, and red *silk* twice-dyed, and of bis folded
again; (And they made the breast-piece, like the ephod,
out of gold, and jacinth, and purple, and red *silk* twice-
dyed, and finely woven linen, and embroidered it;)
9 *he made the rational* four-cornered, double, of the
measure of four fingers. (and *they made the breast-piece*
square, and folded over double, measuring four fingers
thick.)
10 And he set therein four orders of gems; in the first
order was sardius, topaz, smaragdus; (And they fastened
four rows of gems to it; in the first row was sardius,
topaz, and emerald;)
11 in the second order was carbuncle, sapphire, jasper;
(in the second row was carbuncle, sapphire, and jasper;)
12 in the third order was ligure, agate, amethyst; (in the
third row was ligure, agate, and amethyst;)
13 in the fourth order was crystallite, onyx, and beryl;
compassed and enclosed with gold, by their orders. (and
in the fourth row was crystallite, onyx, and beryl; all
encompassed and enclosed in gold, in their proper
order.)
14 And those twelve stones were graven with [the]
twelve names of the lineages of Israel, all the stones by
themselves, by the names of all the lineages by
themselves. (And those twelve stones were engraved with
the twelve names of the sons of Israel, each of the stones
had the name of one of the sons, representing the twelve
tribes *of Israel*.)
15 They made also in the rational, little chains, cleaving
to themselves together, of purest gold, (And for the
breast-piece, they made little chains out of pure gold, that
were twisted like ropes,)
16 and twain hooks, and so many rings of gold. (and
two gold hooks, and two gold rings.)
17 Forsooth they setted the rings on ever either side of
the rational, (And they fastened the rings to the upper
corners of the breast-piece,)
18 on which rings [the] two golden chains hanged,
which they setted in the hooks, that stood forth in the
corners of the cloak on the shoulders. (and they joined
the two gold chains to the rings, and then joined the
other ends of the chains to the two hooks, which they
fastened to the upper part of the front of the two shoulder
straps of the ephod.)
19 These accorded so to themselves, both before and
behind, (so) that the cloak on the shoulders, and the
rational, (And they made two gold rings, which they
fastened to the lower corners of the breast-piece, by the
hem of the ephod, so that they were opposite each
other;)
20 were knitted together, and fastened to the girdle,
(and two gold rings, which they fastened to the lower
part of the front of the two shoulder straps of the ephod,
near the seam, and above the waistband.)
21 and coupled full strongly with the rings, which *rings*
a lace of jacinth joined together, lest they were loosed,
and slacked, and were moved (away) each from (the)
other; as the Lord commanded to Moses. (And then the
breast-piece was bound by its rings to the rings of the
ephod, with a lace of jacinth, so that the joining would
stay secure, and the breast-piece and the ephod would
not separate from each other; all as the Lord commanded
to Moses.)
22 They made also a coat on the shoulders, *or alb*, all
of jacinth; (And they made the robe, *or the alb*, out of
jacinth,)
23 and the hood, *or the amice*, in the higher part, about
the midst, and a woven hem, by the compass of the
hood; (with a hole in the middle for the head, and with a
woven hem all around it, so that it would not tear;)
24 forsooth beneath at the feet *they made* pineapples of
jacinth, and purple, and vermilion, and bis folded again;
(and on the lower hem *they put* pomegranates made out
of jacinth, and purple, and red *silk* twice-dyed, and finely
woven linen;)
25 and *they made* little bells of purest gold, which they
setted betwixt the pomegranates, in the hem of the alb,
by compass; (and *they made* little bells out of pure gold,
which they put between the pomegranates, all around the
hem of the robe;)
26 a golden little bell, and a pineapple; with which the
bishop went adorned, when he was set in service, as the
Lord commanded to Moses. (a little gold bell, and a
pomegranate, and another little gold bell, and a
pomegranate, and so on, all around the hem; with which
the High Priest went adorned, when he was ministering,
as the Lord commanded to Moses.)
27 They made also coats of bis, (*that is, linen clothes*,)
by woven work, to Aaron and to his sons, (And they
made finely woven linen shirts, *or tunics*, for Aaron and
his sons,)
28 and mitres with small crowns of bis, and linen
clothes of bis; (and the turban, and the *peaked* caps, out
of fine linen, and breeches out of finely woven linen;)
29 forsooth *they made* a girdle of bis folded again, of
jacinth, purple, and vermilion, parted by (the) craft of
embroidery, as the Lord commanded to Moses. (and *they
made* sashes out of finely woven linen, and jacinth, and
purple, and red *silk* twice-dyed, and embroidered them,
as the Lord commanded to Moses.)
30 They made also a plate of holy worshipping, of
purest gold, and they wrote therein by the craft of a

graver in gems, The Holy of the Lord. (And they made the
plate of holy dedication, *or of consecration*, out of pure
gold, and they wrote on it by the craft of an engraver of
gems, Holy to the Lord.)
31 And they bound it with the mitre by a lace of
jacinth, as the Lord commanded to Moses. (And they
fastened it to the turban with a lace of jacinth, as the Lord
commanded to Moses.)
32 Therefore all the work of the tabernacle, and the
covering of the witnessing, was performed; and the sons
of Israel did all things which the Lord commanded to
Moses. (And so all the work for the Tabernacle of the
Witnessing, and the tent, and the coverings, was finished;
and the Israelites did all the things which the Lord
commanded to Moses.)
33 And they offered the tabernacle (to Moses), and the
roof, and all the purtenance(s), rings, boards, bars, and
pillars, and the bases; (And they brought the Tabernacle
to Moses, and the tent, and all its purtenances, yea, the
rings, the boards, the bars, and the pillars, and the bases;)
34 the covering of skins of rams made red, and another
covering of skins of jacinth; the veil, (the covering made
out of red rams' skins, and the other covering made out
of blue skins; the Veil,)
35 the ark, the bars, and the propitiatory; (the Ark, *that
is, the Box for the tablets of the Law*, and its bars, and the
propitiatory, *that is, the mercy seat, or the lid for the
Box*;)
36 the board with (its) vessels, and with the loaves of
setting forth; (the table, and its vessels, and the loaves of
proposition, *or the showbread*;)
37 the candlestick, lanterns, and the purtenances of
those, with [the] oil; (the lamp-stand, its lanterns, and its
purtenances, and the oil;)
38 the golden altar, and the ointment, and [the] incense
of sweet smelling spiceries; and the curtain in the
entering of the tabernacle; (the gold altar, and the
ointment, and the incense of sweet smelling spices; and
the curtain for the entrance to the Tabernacle;)
39 the brazen altar, [the] griddle, bars, and all the
vessels thereof; the great washing vessel, with his
foundament; (the bronze altar, its griddle, its bars, and all
its vessels; the great washing vessel, and its foundation,
or its base;)
40 the curtains of the great entry, and the pillars with
their bases; the curtain in the entering of the great porch,
and the cords, and the stakes thereof. Nothing of the
vessels failed, that was commanded to be made into [the]
service of the tabernacle, and into the roof of the bond of
peace. (the curtains for the courtyard, with its pillars, and
their bases; the curtain for the entrance to the courtyard,
and its cords, and its pegs. And also all the vessels that
were commanded to be made for use in the Tabernacle
of the Covenant, *that is, the Tabernacle of the
Witnessing*.)
41 Also the sons of Israel offered the clothes which the
priests, that is, Aaron and his sons, use in the saintuary,
(And the Israelites also offered the clothes which the
priests, that is, Aaron and his sons, were to use in the
sanctuary,)
42 as the Lord commanded (to Moses).
43 And after that Moses saw all those things fulfilled, he
blessed them. (And after that Moses had seen all of those
things that were made, he blessed them.)

CHAPTER 40

1 And the Lord spake to Moses, saying,
2 In the first month, in the first day of the month, thou
shalt raise the tabernacle of witnessing. (In the first
month, on the first day of the month, thou shalt raise up
the Tabernacle of the Witnessing.)
3 And thou shalt set the ark therein, and thou shalt
leave a veil before it. (And thou shalt put the Ark in it,
and thou shalt put the Veil in front of the Ark.)
4 And when the board is borne in, thou shalt set
thereon those things that be commanded justly, *either by
the law*. The candlestick shall stand with his lanterns,
(And when the table is brought in, thou shalt put on it
those things that be commanded by the law. And thou
shalt bring in the lamp-stand, and its lanterns,)
5 and the golden altar, wherein the incense is burnt
before the ark of witnessing. Thou shalt set a curtain in
the entering of the tabernacle; (and the gold altar, on
which the incense is burned before the Ark of the
Witnessing. And thou shalt hang the curtain at the
entrance to the Tabernacle;)
6 and before it *thou shalt set* the altar of burnt
sacrifice, (and in front of it, *thou shalt put* the altar of
burnt sacrifice,)
7 *(and) thou shalt set* the washing vessel betwixt the
altar and the tabernacle, which washing vessel thou shalt
fill with water.
8 And thou shalt (en)compass the great porch, and the
entering thereof, with curtains. (And thou shalt set up the
courtyard all around it, and hang up the curtain at its
entrance.)
9 And when thou hast taken the oil of anointing, thou
shalt anoint the tabernacle, with his vessels (thou shalt
anoint the Tabernacle, and all its vessels), (so) that those
be hallowed;
10 the altar of burnt sacrifice, and all the vessels
thereof;
11 the washing vessel, with his foundament. Thou
shalt anoint all things with the oil of anointing, that they
be holy of holy things. (and the washing vessel, and its
foundation, *or its base*. Thou shalt anoint all these things
with the anointing oil, so that they be consecrated, and
most holy.)

12 And thou shalt present Aaron and his sons to the
door of the tabernacle of witnessing (And thou shalt bring
Aaron and his sons to the entrance of the Tabernacle of
the Witnessing); and, when they be washed with water,
13 thou shalt clothe *them* in (the) holy clothes, that
they minister to me (so that they can serve as my priests),
14 (See verse 13 above.)
15 and (so) that the anointing of them profit into (an)
everlasting priesthood.
16 And Moses did all things that the Lord commanded.
17 Therefore in the first month of the second year, in
the first day of the month, the tabernacle was set. (And so
in the first month of the second year, on the first day of
the month, the Tabernacle was set up.)
18 And Moses areared it, and he set (up) the boards,
and bases, and bars, and he ordained [the] pillars;
19 and he stretched out the roof upon the tabernacle,
and he put a covering above (it), as the Lord
commanded. (and he stretched out the tent over the
Tabernacle, and he put the coverings over the tent, as the
Lord commanded.)
20 He put also the witnessing, *that is, the tables of the
law,* in the ark, and he set the bars within (the rings), and
God's answering place above (the ark). (And he put the
Witnessing, *that is, the tablets of the Law,* into the Ark,
that is, the Box for the tablets, and he set the bars within
the rings, and *he put* the propitiatory, *that is, the mercy
seat, or the lid,* on the Box.)
21 And when he had brought the ark into the
tabernacle, he hanged a veil before it, that he should
fulfill the commandment of the Lord. (And when he had
brought the Ark into the Tabernacle, he hung up the Veil
in front of it, as the Lord commanded him.)
22 He setted also the board in the tabernacle of
witnessing, at the north coast, without the veil, (And he
put the table in the Tabernacle of the Witnessing, on the
north side of the Tabernacle, in front of the Veil,)
23 and he ordained the loaves of setting forth (on the
table,) before (the Lord), as the Lord commanded to
Moses. (and he placed the loaves of proposition, *or the
showbread,* on the table, before the Lord, as the Lord
commanded to Moses.)
24 He set also the candlestick in the tabernacle of
witnessing, even against the board, in the south side,
(And he set the lamp-stand in the Tabernacle of the
Witnessing, opposite the table, on the south side of the
Tabernacle,)
25 and he set the lanterns by order, by the
commandment of the Lord. (and he set up the lanterns
before the Lord, as the Lord commanded him.)
26 He putted also the golden altar under the roof of
witnessing, *that is, of the tabernacle,* against the veil,
(And he put the gold altar in the Tent of the Witnessing,
that is, in the Tabernacle, in front of the Veil,)
27 and he burnt thereon incense of sweet smelling
spiceries, as the Lord commanded to Moses.
28 He set also a curtain in the entering of the
tabernacle, (And he hung up the curtain at the entrance
to the Tabernacle,)
29 and (set) the altar of burnt sacrifice in the porch (of
the tabernacle) of witnessing, and he offered there(on)
burnt sacrifice, and sacrifices, as the Lord commanded.
(and put the altar of burnt sacrifice by the entrance to the
Tabernacle of the Witnessing, and then he offered on it
the burnt sacrifice, and the sacrifices, as the Lord
commanded him.)
30 Also he ordained the washing vessel, betwixt the
tabernacle of witnessing and the altar, and filled it with
water. (And he put the washing vessel between the
Tabernacle of the Witnessing and the altar, and filled it
with water.)
31 And Moses, and Aaron, and his sons, washed their
hands and their feet therein,
32 when they entered into the tabernacle of the bond
of peace, and nighed to the altar, as the Lord commanded
to Moses. (whenever they entered into the Tabernacle of
the Covenant, *that is, the Tabernacle of the Witnessing,*
or when they approached the altar, as the Lord
commanded to Moses.)
33 He areared also the great porch, by compass of the
tabernacle and of the altar, and setted a curtain in the
entering thereof. (And he set up the courtyard, *that is, the
pillars and the curtains that enclosed the courtyard,* all
around the Tabernacle and the altar, and hung up a
curtain at its entrance.)
34 After that all things were perfectly made, a cloud
covered the tabernacle of witnessing, and the glory of the
Lord filled it; (And when all things were completed, a
cloud covered the Tabernacle of the Witnessing, and the
glory of the Lord filled it;)
35 neither Moses might enter into the tabernacle of the
bond of peace (and Moses could not go into the
Tabernacle of the Covenant, *that is, the Tabernacle of the
Witnessing*), while the cloud covered all things, and the
majesty of the Lord shined, for the cloud covered all
things.
36 If any time the cloud left the tabernacle, the sons of
Israel went forth by their companies; (And any time that
the cloud left the Tabernacle, the Israelites went forth on
their journey;)
37 (but) if the cloud hanged *there*above, they dwelled
in the same place;
38 for the cloud of the Lord rested on the tabernacle by
day, and fire (was on it) in the night, in the sight of the
people of Israel, by all their dwellings. (for the cloud of
the Lord rested on the Tabernacle by day, and a fire was
over it in the night, before the people of Israel, during all
of their journey.) ✡

LEVITICUS

CHAPTER 1

1 Forsooth the Lord called Moses, and spake to him
from the tabernacle of witnessing, saying, (And the Lord
called Moses, and spoke to him from the Tabernacle of
the Witnessing, saying,)
2 Speak thou to the sons of Israel, and thou shalt say
to them, A man of you, that offereth to the Lord a
sacrifice of beasts, that is, of oxen and of sheep, and
offereth slain sacrifices, (Speak thou to the Israelites, and
thou shalt say to them, A man of you, who offereth to the
Lord a sacrifice of beasts, that is, of oxen or of sheep, and
offereth slain sacrifices,)
3 if his offering is burnt sacrifice, and of the drove of
oxen, he shall offer a male beast without wem at the door
of the tabernacle of witnessing, to make the Lord pleased
to him. (if his offering is a burnt sacrifice, from the herd
of oxen, he shall offer a male beast without blemish, *or
without fault*, at the entrance to the Tabernacle of the
Witnessing, to gain the Lord's acceptance.)
4 And he shall set *his* hands on the head of the
sacrifice, and it shall be acceptable, and profiting into the
cleansing of him. (And he shall put *his* hands upon the
head of the sacrifice, and it shall be acceptable, and
profiting into his cleansing.)
5 And he shall offer a calf before the Lord, and the
sons of Aaron, [the] priests, shall offer the blood thereof,
and they shall shed it by compass of the altar, that is
before the door of the tabernacle. (And he shall offer a
calf before the Lord, and the priests, the sons of Aaron,
shall offer its blood, and they shall throw it against all the
sides of the altar, that is in front of the entrance to the
Tabernacle.)
6 And when the skin of the sacrifice is drawn away,
they shall cut the members into gobbets, (*or into pieces*);
7 and they shall put under the altar the fire, and they
shall make an heap of wood *ready* before; (and they shall
put a fire on the altar, and put wood on the fire;)
8 and they shall ordain above *that wood* those things
that be cut, that is, the head, and all things that cleave to
the maw, (and on top of *that wood* they shall put those
things that be cut, *or be carved*, that is, the head, and the
suet, *or the fat*,)
9 when the entrails and the feet be washed with
water; and the priest shall burn those on the altar, into
burnt sacrifice, and to sweet odour to the Lord. (and after
the innards and the feet be washed in water, the priest
shall burn all these things offered on the altar, for a burnt
sacrifice, to make the sweetest aroma to the Lord.)
10 That if the offering is of little beasts, a burnt sacrifice
of sheep, either of goats, he shall offer a male beast
without wem, (And if the offering is of small beasts, that
is, a burnt sacrifice of sheep, or of goats, he shall offer a
male beast without blemish, *or without fault*,)
11 and he shall offer that at the side of the altar that
beholdeth to the north, before the Lord. Soothly the sons
of Aaron shall pour the blood thereof on the altar by
compass (And the priests, the sons of Aaron, shall throw
its blood against all the sides of the altar),
12 and they shall part the members, the head, and all
things that cleave to the maw (and they shall cut the
members, the head, and the suet, *or the fat*), and they shall
put *them* on the wood, under which the fire shall be set;
13 soothly they shall wash in water the entrails and
[the] feet; and the priest shall burn all things offered on
the altar, into burnt sacrifice, and sweetest odour to the
Lord. (and they shall wash the innards and the feet in
water; and the priest shall burn all the things offered on
the altar, for a burnt sacrifice, to make the sweetest aroma
to the Lord.)
14 Forsooth if the offering of burnt sacrifice to the Lord
is of birds, of turtles, or of culvers birds, (And if the
offering to the Lord is a burnt sacrifice of birds, that is, of
turtledoves, or of young pigeons,)
15 the priest shall offer it at the altar; and when the
head is writhed to the neck, and the place of the wound
is broken, he shall make the blood run down on the brink
of the altar.
16 Soothly he shall cast forth the little bladder of the
throat, *or the crop*, and the feathers beside the altar, at
the east coast, in the place in the which the ashes be
wont to be cast out; (And he shall throw away the crop of
the throat, and the feathers, beside the altar, on the east
side, in the place where the ashes be poured out;)
17 and the priest shall break the wings thereof, and he
shall not carve it, neither part it with iron; and he shall
burn it on the altar, when fire is put under the wood; it is
a burnt sacrifice, and an offering of sweetest odour to the
Lord. (and the priest shall break its wings, but he shall not
carve it, or cut it, with anything made out of iron; and he
shall burn it on the altar, when fire is put under the
wood; yea, it is a burnt sacrifice, for an offering of the
sweetest aroma to the Lord.)

CHAPTER 2

1 When a soul, *that is, a poor man*, offereth an
offering of sacrifice to the Lord, [tried] flour *of wheat* shall
be his offering. And he shall pour oil thereon, and he
shall put incense, (When anyone offereth a grain offering
to the Lord, fine *wheat* flour shall be his offering. And he
shall pour oil on it, and he shall put frankincense on it,)
2 and he shall bear it to the sons of Aaron, [the]
priest(s), of the which sons one of them shall take an

handful of tried *wheat* flour, and of oil, and all the
incense; and he shall put these (as) a memorial on the
altar, into the sweetest odour to the Lord. (and he shall
take it to the priests, the sons of Aaron, of which priests
one of them shall take a handful of the fine *wheat* flour,
and some oil, and all the frankincense; and he shall burn
this on the altar as a token of the offering, to make the
sweetest aroma to the Lord.)
3 Forsooth that that is left of the sacrifice shall be
Aaron's and his sons', the holy of holy things of offerings
to the Lord. (And the rest of the grain offering shall be for
Aaron and his sons, a most holy thing, from the offerings
to the Lord.)
4 Forsooth when thou offerest a sacrifice baken in an
oven, of tried *wheat* flour, that is, loaves without
sourdough, sprinkled with oil, and therf bread sodden in
water, balmed with oil; (And if thou offerest an offering of
fine *wheat* flour baked in an oven, it shall be cakes made
without yeast, sprinkled with oil, or unleavened wafers,
boiled in water, and fried in oil;)
5 if thine offering is of tried *wheat* flour sprinkled with
oil, and without sourdough, *taken* of the frying pan, (if
thy offering is of fine *wheat* flour sprinkled with oil,
without any yeast, and cooked on a griddle,)
6 thou shalt part it in(to) small parts, and thou shalt
pour oil thereon.
7 Else if the sacrifice *is* taken of the griddle, evenly the
[tried] *wheat* flour shall be sprinkled with oil; (Or if the
offering *is* taken from the frying pan, the fine *wheat* flour
shall be sprinkled with oil;)
8 the which *wheat* flour thou shalt offer to the Lord,
and thou shalt betake it in(to) the hands of the priest.
And when he hath offered it,
9 he shall take a memorial of the sacrifice, and he shall
burn *it* on the altar, into odour of sweetness to the Lord.
(he shall take a token of the offering, and he shall burn *it*
on the altar, to make the sweetest aroma to the Lord.)
10 Soothly whatever thing is left, it shall be Aaron's and
his sons, the holy of holy things of the offerings to the Lord
(And whatever is left, it shall be for Aaron and his sons, a
most holy, *or sacred*, thing, from the offerings to the Lord.)
11 Each offering which is offered to the Lord, shall be
without sourdough, neither anything of sourdough, and
of honey, shall be burnt in the sacrifice of the Lord. (Each
offering which is offered to the Lord, shall be made
without yeast, yea, nothing of yeast, or of honey, shall be
burned as an offering to the Lord.)
12 Ye shall offer only the first fruits of those, and gifts;
soothly those shall not be put on the altar, into odour of
sweetness. (Ye shall offer the first fruits of your grain each
year to the Lord; but they shall not be put on the altar, to
make the sweetest aroma *to the Lord*.)
13 Whatever thing of sacrifice thou shalt offer, thou
shalt make it savory with salt, neither thou shalt take
away the salt of the bond of peace of thy God from thy
sacrifice; in each offering thou shalt offer salt. (With every
grain offering that thou shalt offer, thou shalt make it
savoury with salt, yea, thou shalt not fail to offer salt with
thy grain offering, for it representeth the covenant with
thy God; with every offering thou shalt offer salt.)
14 Forsooth if thou offerest a gift of the first things of
thy fruits to the Lord, of ears of corn yet green, thou shalt
scorch, *or singe*, them in fire, and thou shalt break them
in the manner of bruised corn; and so thou shalt offer thy
first fruits to the Lord,
15 and thou shalt pour oil thereupon, and thou shalt
put incense, for it is the offering of the Lord. (and thou
shalt pour oil on it, and thou shall put frankincense on it,
for it is a grain offering to the Lord.)
16 Of which the priest shall burn, into mind of the gift,
a part of the bruised corn, and of the oil, and all the
incense. (Of which the priest shall burn, as a token of the
offering, some of the bruised corn, some of the oil, and
all of the frankincense.)

CHAPTER 3

1 That if his offering is a sacrifice of peaceable things,
and he will offer of [the] oxen, he shall offer before the
Lord a male, either a female, without wem. (And if his
offering is a peace offering, and he will offer it from the
oxen, he shall offer before the Lord a male, or a female,
without blemish, *or without fault*.)
2 And he shall set *his* hand upon the head of his slain
sacrifice, which shall be offered in the entering of the
tabernacle; and the sons of Aaron, [the] priest(s), shall
pour the blood by compass of the altar. (And he shall put
his hand on the head of his sacrifice, and shall offer, *or
shall kill*, it at the entrance to the Tabernacle; and the
priests, the sons of Aaron, shall throw the blood against
all the sides of the altar.)
3 And they shall offer of the sacrifice of peaceable
things into offering to the Lord, the fatness that covereth
the entrails, and whatever thing of fatness is within; (And
they shall offer for the peace offering, as a burnt sacrifice
to the Lord, the fat that covereth the innards, and
whatever fat is within;)
4 *they shall offer* [the] two kidneys with the fatness by
which the guts called ileum be covered, and the caul of
the liver, with the little reins, (*or with the kidneys*).
5 And they shall burn those on the altar, into burnt
sacrifice, when fire is put under the wood, into offering of
the sweetest odour to the Lord. (And they shall burn them
on the altar, for a burnt sacrifice, when fire is put under the
wood, for an offering of the sweetest aroma to the Lord.)
6 Soothly if his offering is of sheep, and a sacrifice of
peaceable things, whether he offereth a male or a female,
they shall be without wem. (And if his offering for a
peace offering is a sheep, whether he offereth a male or a

female, they shall be without blemish.)
7 If he offer a lamb before the Lord,
8 he shall set his hand upon the head of his sacrifice,
that shall be offered in the porch of the tabernacle of
witnessing; and the sons of Aaron shall pour the blood
thereof by environ of the altar. (he shall put his hand on
the head of his sacrifice, that shall be offered in front of
the Tabernacle of the Witnessing; and the priests, the
sons of Aaron, shall throw its blood against all the sides
of the altar.)
9 And they shall offer of the sacrifice of peaceable
things a sacrifice to the Lord, the inner fatness, and all the
tail with the reins, and the fatness that covereth the
womb, and all the entrails, (And they shall offer for the
peace offering, as a burnt sacrifice to the Lord, the inner
fat, and all the tail by the kidneys, and the fat that
covereth the womb, and all the innards,)
10 and ever either little rein, with the fatness which is
beside the guts called (the) ileum, and the caul of the
maw, with the little reins. (and the two kidneys, with the
fat which is beside the haunches, and the caul of the
liver, with the kidneys.)
11 And the priest shall burn them upon the altar, into
the feeding, *or nourishing,* of the fire, and of the offering
to the Lord (for a burnt sacrifice to the Lord).
12 If his offering is a goat, and he offereth it to the Lord,
13 he shall set his hand on the head thereof, and he
shall offer it in the entry of the tabernacle of witnessing;
and the sons of Aaron shall pour the blood thereof by
compass of the altar. (he shall put his hand on its head,
and he shall offer it at the entrance to the Tabernacle of
the Witnessing; and the priests, the sons of Aaron, shall
throw its blood against all the sides of the altar.)
14 And they shall take thereof, into the feeding, *or
nourishing,* of the Lord's fire, the fatness that covereth the
womb, and that covereth all the entrails,
15 and the two little reins with the caul that is on those
beside the ileum, and the fatness of the maw, with the
entrails that cleave to the little reins.
16 And the priest shall burn those on the altar, into the
feeding, *or nourishing,* of the fire, and of sweetest odour
(to make the sweetest aroma); all the fatness shall be the
Lord's,
17 by everlasting right in generations, and in all your
dwelling places, neither in any manner ye shall eat
blood, neither fatness. (by an everlasting law for all your
generations, in all your dwelling places, for not in any
manner shall ye eat any blood, or fat.)

CHAPTER 4

1 And the Lord spake to Moses, and said,
2 Speak thou to the sons of Israel, When a soul, *that
is, a man,* hath done sin by ignorance, and hath done
anything of all the commandments of the Lord, which he
commanded that those shall not be done, (thou shalt
follow these ordinances); (Say thou to the Israelites,
When someone hath done sin by ignorance, and hath
done anything against any of the Lord's commandments,
which he commanded that should not be done, thou
shalt follow these ordinances;)
3 if a priest that is anointed, hath done sin, making the
people to trespass, he shall offer for his sin a calf without
wem to the Lord (he shall offer for his sin offering a calf
without blemish, *or without fault,* to the Lord).
4 And he shall bring it to the door of the tabernacle of
witnessing, before the Lord (And he shall bring it to the
entrance of the Tabernacle of the Witnessing, before the
Lord), and he shall put his hand on the head thereof, and
he shall offer it to the Lord.
5 And he shall take up of the blood of the calf, and
shall bring it into the tabernacle of witnessing. (And he
shall take some of the calf's blood, and shall bring it into
the Tabernacle of the Witnessing.)
6 And when he hath dipped his finger into the blood,
he shall sprinkle it seven times before the Lord, against the
veil of the saintuary (in front of the Veil of the sanctuary).
7 And he shall put of the same blood on the corners of
the altar of incense most acceptable to the Lord, which
altar is in the tabernacle of witnessing; soothly he shall
shed all the tother blood into the foundament of the altar
of burnt sacrifice in the entering of the tabernacle. (And
he shall put some of the blood on the horns of the altar of
sweet incense to the Lord, which altar is in the
Tabernacle of the Witnessing; and he shall pour out all
the other blood at the foundation, *or at the base,* of the
altar of burnt sacrifice at the entrance to the Tabernacle.)
8 And he shall offer for *his* sin the inner fatness of the
calf, as well it that covereth the entrails, as all things that
be within, (And for *his* sin offering, he shall offer the
inner fat of the calf, which covereth the innards, as well
as all the things that be within,)
9 (and the) two little reins, and the caul, which is on
them, beside [the] ileum, and the fatness of the maw,
with the little reins,
10 as it is offered of the calf of the sacrifice of
peaceable things (as it is offered from the calf for the
peace offering); and the priest shall burn those *things* on
the altar of (the) burnt sacrifice.
11 Soothly the priest shall bear out of the tents (And the
priest shall carry away from the tents, *or from the camp*),
the skin, and all the flesh, with the head, and the feet,
and [the] entrails, and the dung,
12 and the body *that* is left, into a clean place, where
[the] ashes be wont to be poured out; and he shall burn
those *things* upon the heap of wood, the which shall be
burnt in the place of ashes poured out (which shall be
burned in the place where the ashes be poured out).
13 That if all the company of the sons of Israel knoweth

not (And if all the congregation of the Israelites knoweth
not), and doeth by unknowing that that is against the
commandment of the Lord,
14 and afterward understandeth his sin, he shall offer a
calf for that sin, and he shall bring the calf to the door of
the tabernacle. (and afterward understand their sin, they
shall offer a calf for a sin offering, and they shall bring the
calf to the entrance, *or to the front*, of the Tabernacle.)
15 And the elder men of the people shall set hands on
the head thereof before the Lord; and when the calf is
offered in the sight of the Lord, (And the elders of the
people shall put their hands on its head before the Lord;
and when the calf is killed before the Lord,)
16 the priest that is anointed shall bear in of his blood
into the tabernacle of witnessing; (the anointed priest
shall bring some of its blood into the Tabernacle of the
Witnessing;)
17 and when he hath dipped his finger, he shall
sprinkle *the blood* seven times against the veil. (and
when he hath dipped his finger in it, he shall sprinkle *the
blood* in front of the Veil seven times before the Lord.)
18 And he shall put of the same blood in the horns of
the altar, which is before the Lord in the tabernacle of
witnessing; soothly he shall pour the blood that leaveth,
(*or the residue blood,*) beside the foundament of the altar
of burnt sacrifice, which is in the door of the tabernacle
of witnessing. (And he shall put some of the blood on the
horns of the altar, which is before the Lord in the
Tabernacle of the Witnessing; and he shall pour out the
blood that is left at the foundation, *or at the base*, of the
altar of burnt sacrifice, which is at the entrance to the
Tabernacle of the Witnessing.)
19 And he shall take all the fatness thereof, and shall
burn *it* on the altar;
20 and he shall do also of this calf, as he did before *of
the tother* (and so he shall do with this calf, as he did
before *with the other one*); and when the priest shall pray
for them, the Lord shall be merciful.
21 Forsooth he shall bear out [of the tents] that calf, and
he shall burn *it*, as *he did* also the former calf, for it is for
the sin of the multitude. (And he shall carry that calf out
away from the tents, and he shall burn *it*, as *he burned*
the other calf, for it is a sin offering for the multitude.)
22 If a prince sinneth, and doeth by ignorance one
thing of many, which is forbidden in the law of the Lord,
23 and afterward understandeth his sin, he shall offer to
the Lord a sacrifice, a goat buck, without wem (without
blemish, *or without fault*);
24 and he shall set his hand on the head thereof. And
when he hath offered it in the place, where [the] burnt
sacrifice is wont to be slain, before the Lord, for it is for
sin (for it is a sin offering);
25 the priest shall dip his finger in the blood of [the]
sacrifice for sin, and he shall touch *with his bloody finger*
the corners of the altar of burnt sacrifice, and he shall
pour the blood that leaveth, (*or the residue blood,*) at the
foundament thereof. (the priest shall dip his finger in the
blood of the sin offering, and he shall touch *with his
bloody finger* the horns of the altar of burnt sacrifice, and
he shall pour out the blood that is left at the foundation,
or at the base, of the altar.)
26 Soothly the priest shall burn the inner fatness above
the altar, as it is wont to be done in the sacrifice of
peaceable things (And the priest shall burn the inner fat
on *the altar*, as it is done for the peace offering), and the
priest shall pray for him, and for his sin, and it shall be
forgiven to him.
27 That if a soul, *that is, a singular man* (And if
anyone), of the people of the land sinneth by ignorance,
that he do anything of these [things] that be forbidden in
the law of the Lord, and trespasseth,
28 and knoweth his sin, he shall offer a she goat
without wem (he shall offer a she goat without blemish);
29 and he shall set his hand upon the head of the
sacrifice which is for [the] sin (and he shall put his hand
on the head of the sin offering,) and he shall offer it in the
place of [the] burnt sacrifice.
30 And the priest shall take of the blood *thereof* upon
his finger, and he shall touch the horns of the altar of
burnt sacrifice, and he shall pour the blood that is left at
the foundament of the *altar*. (And the priest shall take
some of *its* blood on his finger, and he shall touch the
horns of the altar of burnt sacrifice, and he shall pour out
the blood that is left at the foundation, *or at the base*, of
the *altar*.)
31 Soothly he shall take away all the inner fatness, as it
is wont to be done away of the sacrifices of peaceable
things, and he shall burn *it* on the altar, into odour of
sweetness to the Lord (And he shall take away all the
inner fat, as it is done away with the peace offering, and
he shall burn *it* on the altar, to make the sweetest aroma
to the Lord); and the priest shall pray for him, and it shall
be forgiven to him.
32 Soothly if he offereth of little beasts a sacrifice for
sin, that is, a sheep without wem, (And if he offereth a
small beast for his sin offering, that is, a sheep without
blemish, *or without fault*,)
33 he shall put his hand on the head thereof, and he
shall offer it in the place where the beasts of (the) burnt
sacrifices be wont to be slain.
34 And the priest shall take of the blood thereof in his
finger, and he shall touch *therewith* the horns of the altar
of burnt sacrifice, and he shall pour the blood that is left
at the foundament of the *altar*. (And the priest shall take
some of its blood with his finger, and he shall touch *with
it* the horns of the altar of burnt sacrifice, and he shall
pour out the blood that is left at the foundation, *or at the
base*, of the *altar*.)

35 And he shall do away all the inner fatness, as the
inner fatness of the ram, that is offered for peaceable
things, is wont to be done away, and the priest shall burn
it upon the altar of incense of the Lord (And he shall do
away all the inner fat, as the inner fat of the ram, that is
offered for the peace offering is done away, and the priest
shall burn *it* on the altar on top of, or along with, the
burnt sacrifices to the Lord); and the priest shall pray for
him, and for his sin, and it shall be forgiven to him.

CHAPTER 5

1 If a soul, *that is, (a) man,* sinneth, and heareth the
voice of an oath, and is (a) witness, *that is, (is) required to
bear witnessing of a thing that he knoweth,* for either he
saw, either is witting, if he showeth (it) not, *but hideth
the truth,* he shall bear his sin. (If someone taketh an
oath, for he is a witness, for either he saw, or heard, or
knoweth something, but if he hideth the truth, *and telleth
it not,* he sinneth, and he shall bear his sin.)
2 A person that toucheth any unclean thing, or which
is slain of a beast, either is dead by itself, either *toucheth*
any other creeping beast, and forgetteth his uncleanness,
he is guilty, and trespasseth. (A person who toucheth any
unclean thing, such as the dead body of an unclean beast
killed by another beast, or one which dieth naturally, or
the body of an unclean creeping beast, *that is, an
unclean reptile,* and forgetteth its uncleanness, he is
guilty, and trespasseth.)
3 And if he toucheth anything of the uncleanness of
man, by all the uncleanness by which he is wont to be
defouled (Or if he toucheth anything of the uncleanness
of man, by all the uncleanness by which he is wont to be
defiled), and he forgetteth it, and knoweth this afterward,
he shall be subject to that trespass.
4 A soul that sweareth (Anyone who maketh an oath),
and bringeth forth with his lips, that he should do either
evil, or well, and doeth *it* not, and confirmeth the same
thing with an oath, either with a word, and forgetteth
what he swore, or said, and afterward understandeth his
trespass,
5 do he penance for his sin,
6 and offer he of the flocks a female lamb, either a
goat, (for a sin offering); and the priest shall pray for him,
and for his sin.
7 But if he may not offer a beast, offer he two turtles,
either two birds of culvers to the Lord, one for [the] sin,
and the tother into burnt sacrifice. (And if he cannot offer
such a beast, offer he two turtledoves, or two young
pigeons to the Lord, one for a sin offering, and the other
for a burnt sacrifice.)
8 And he shall give those to the priest, which shall
offer the first for [the] sin, and shall fold again the head
thereof to the wings, so that it cleave to the neck, and be
not broken utterly. (And he shall give them to the priest,
who shall offer the first for a sin offering; and he shall
fold back its head to its wings, but it shall still cleave to
the neck, and not be broken completely off.)
9 And *the priest* shall sprinkle the wall of the altar, of
the blood thereof; soothly whatever is residue, he shall
make to drop down at the foundament of the altar, for it
is for sin. (And *the priest* shall sprinkle the side of the
altar with some of its blood; and whatever is left, he shall
pour out at the foundation, *or at the base,* of the altar, for
it is a sin offering.)
10 Soothly he shall burn the tother *bird* into burnt
sacrifice, as it is wont to be done; and the priest shall
pray for him, and for his sin, and it shall be forgiven to
him. (And he shall burn the other *bird* for a burnt
sacrifice, as it is wont to be done; and the priest shall
pray for him, and for his sin, and he shall be forgiven.)
11 That if his hand *for poverty* may not offer two turtles,
either two birds of culvers, he shall offer for his sin the
tenth part of ephah of tried *wheat* flour; he shall not put
oil into it, neither he shall put anything of incense, for it
is for sin. (But if *for poverty,* his hand cannot find two
turtledoves, or two young pigeons, to offer, he shall offer
the tenth part of an ephah of fine *wheat* flour for a sin
offering; he shall not put any oil on it, nor shall he put
any frankincense on it, for it is a sin offering.)
12 And he shall give it to the priest, which *priest* shall
take up an handful thereof, and shall burn it on the altar,
into mind of him that offered *it* (as a token that all of it
hath been offered to the Lord),
13 and *the priest* shall pray for him, and cleanse him;
forsooth the priest shall have the tother part into gift. (and
the priest shall pray for his cleansing, and he shall be
forgiven; and the priest shall have the other part for a gift,
as it is with the grain offering.)
14 And the Lord spake to Moses, and said,
15 If a soul, *that is, a man,* breaketh [the] ceremonies
by error, and sin in these things that be hallowed to the
Lord, he shall offer for his trespass (offering) a ram
without wem of the flocks, that may be bought for two
shekels, at the weight of the saintuary. (If someone
breaketh the ceremonies by error, and sin in those things
that be dedicated to the Lord, he shall offer for his
trespass offering a ram without blemish, *or without fault,*
from the flocks, that can be bought for two shekels, by
the measure of the sanctuary.)
16 And he shall restore that harm that he did, and he
shall put the fifth part *thereof* above (and he shall add a
fifth part to it), and he shall give it to the priest, which
priest shall pray for him, and (shall) offer the ram, and it
shall be forgiven to him.
17 A soul, *that is, a man,* that sinneth by ignorance
(Anyone who sinneth by ignorance), and doeth one of
these things that be forbidden in the law of the Lord, and
is guilty of [the] sin, and understandeth his wickedness,

18 he shall offer to the priest (for a trespass offering) a
ram without wem of the flocks, by the measure and
estimation, *or value*, of the sin; and the priest shall pray
for him, for he did (it) unwitting(ly), and it shall be
forgiven to him,
19 for by error he trespassed against the Lord.

CHAPTER 6

1 And the Lord spake to Moses, and said,
2 A soul, *that is, a man*, that sinneth, and despiseth
the Lord, and denieth to his neighbour a thing betaken to
his keeping, that was betaken to his faith, either taketh
masterfully a thing by violence, either maketh false
challenge, (Anyone who sinneth, and despiseth the Lord,
and denieth to his neighbour that a thing was given to his
keeping, that was given to him in faith, or who taketh a
thing by violence, or who maketh false challenge,)
3 either findeth a thing lost, and denieth it
furthermore, and forsweareth, and doeth any other thing
of many, in which things men be wont to do sin, (or who
findeth a lost thing, but denieth it forevermore, and
forsweareth, or who doeth any other thing of many
things, in which people be wont to sin,)
4 if it is convicted of the guilt, he shall yield whole all
things which he would get by fraud, (if he is convicted,
and found guilty, he shall give back whole everything
which he hath gotten by fraud,)
5 and furthermore (add) the fifth part to the lord, to
whom he did [the] harm. (and furthermore add a fifth part
to it, for the person to whom he did the harm.)
6 Soothly for his sin he shall offer a ram unwemmed
of the flock (And for his trespass offering, he shall offer a
ram without blemish of the flock), and he shall give that
ram to the priest, by the value and the measure of the
trespass;
7 and *the priest* shall pray for him before the Lord,
and it shall be forgiven to him, for all (the) things (in)
which he sinned in doing.
8 And the Lord spake to Moses, and said,
9 Command thou to Aaron, and to his sons, This is the
law of burnt sacrifice; it shall be burnt in the altar all
night till the morrow; fire *that is given from heaven* shall
be of the same altar. (Command thou to Aaron, and to his
sons, and say, This is the law for the burnt sacrifice; it
shall be burned on the altar all night until the morning;
and the fire on the altar shall be kept burning there.)
10 The priest shall be clothed with a coat, and with
linen breeches; and he shall take away the ashes, which
the fire devouring hath burnt out, and he shall put *those*
beside the altar; (The priest shall be clothed with a linen
robe, and with linen breeches; and he shall take away the
ashes, which the devouring fire hath burned out, and he
shall put *them* beside the altar;)
11 and he shall be spoiled of the former clothes, and he
shall be clothed with other (clothes), and he shall bear
those *ashes* out of the tents, and in a most clean place he
shall make *them* to be wasted, *or quenched*, till to a dead
spark. (and then he shall take off those clothes, and he
shall be clothed with other clothes, and he shall carry
those *ashes* away from the tents, to a most clean place.)
12 Forsooth [the] fire shall burn ever[more] in the altar,
which fire the priest shall nourish, putting wood under
(it), in the morrowtide by each day; and when [the] burnt
sacrifice is put above, *the priest* shall burn the inner
fatness of peaceable things. (And the fire shall burn
forevermore on the altar, which fire the priest shall
nourish, putting wood under it, each day in the morning;
and when the burnt sacrifice is put on it, *then the priest*
shall burn the inner fat of the peace offering on top of it.)
13 This is everlasting fire, that shall never fail in the
altar. (This is everlasting fire on the altar, that shall never
go out.)
14 This is the law of sacrifice, and of the flowing
offerings, which the sons of Aaron shall offer before the
Lord, and before the altar. (And this is the law for the
grain offering, which the priests, the sons of Aaron, shall
offer before the Lord, in front of the altar.)
15 The priest shall take an handful of tried wheat flour,
which is sprinkled with oil, and all the incense which is
put on the flour, and he shall burn it on the altar, into
mind of sweetest odour of the Lord. (The priest shall take
a handful of fine wheat flour, which is sprinkled with oil,
and all the frankincense which is put on it, and he shall
burn this token of the offering on the altar, to make the
sweetest aroma to the Lord.)
16 Forsooth Aaron with his sons shall eat the tother part
of [the] tried wheat flour, without sourdough; and he
shall eat *this* in the holy place of the great porch of the
tabernacle. (And Aaron and his sons shall eat the rest of
the fine wheat flour as bread made without yeast; and
they shall eat *this* in a holy place, the courtyard of the
Tabernacle.)
17 Soothly therefore it shall not be dighted with
sourdough, for a part thereof is offered into incense of the
Lord; it shall be holy of holy things, as (the) *offering(s)* for
sin and (for) trespass. (And so it shall not be prepared
with yeast, for a part of it is offered as incense to the
Lord; it shall be a most holy, *or sacred*, thing, like the sin
offering, and the trespass offering.)
18 Males only of the kindred of Aaron shall eat it; it is a
lawful thing and everlasting in your generations, of the
sacrifice of the Lord; each man that toucheth them shall
be hallowed. (Only males of Aaron's family shall eat it;
this is an everlasting law for all your generations, for the
sacrifices to the Lord; anyone else who toucheth them
shall be harmed by their holiness.)
19 And the Lord spake to Moses, and said,
20 This is the offering of Aaron, and of his sons, which

they ought (to) offer to the Lord, (each) in the day of his
anointing; they shall offer the tenth part of ephah of
[tried] *wheat* flour, into everlasting sacrifice, the half
thereof in the morrowtide, and the half thereof in the
eventide; (This is the offering from Aaron, and his sons,
which they ought to offer to the Lord, on the day of their
installation, *or their ordination*; they shall offer the tenth
part of an ephah of fine *wheat* flour, for a consecration
offering, half of it in the morning, and half of it in the
evening;)
21 which shall be sprinkled with oil in a frying pan,
and (then) it shall be fried.
22 Soothly the priest which is successor to his father,
shall offer it hot, into [the] sweetest odour to the Lord;
and all it shall be burnt in the altar. (And the priest who is
the successor to his father *as the High Priest*, shall
likewise offer it, to make the sweetest aroma to the Lord;
and all of it shall be burned on the altar.)
23 For all the sacrifice of priests shall be burnt with fire,
neither any man shall eat thereof. (For all of the grain
offering of a priest shall be burned with fire, no one shall
eat any of it.)
24 And the Lord spake to Moses, and said,
25 Speak thou to Aaron and to his sons, This is the law
of sacrifice for sin; it shall be offered before the Lord, in
the place where burnt sacrifice is offered; it is holy of
holy things. (Say thou to Aaron and his sons, This is the
law for the sin offering; it shall be offered before the Lord,
in the place where the burnt sacrifice is offered; it is a
most holy, *or sacred*, thing.)
26 The priest that offereth it, shall eat it in the holy
place, in the great porch of the tabernacle (in the
courtyard of the Tabernacle).
27 Whatever thing shall touch the flesh thereof, shall be
hallowed (shall be harmed by its holiness); if a cloak is
besprinkled with the blood thereof, it shall be washed in
the holy place.
28 Soothly the earthen vessel, in which it is sodden,
shall be broken; that if the vessel is of brass, it shall be
scoured, and washed with water. (Any clay vessel in which
it is boiled, shall be broken; but if the vessel is bronze, *or
is copper*, it shall be scoured, and washed in water.)
29 Each male of the priests' kin shall eat of the flesh
thereof; for it is holy of holy things (for it is a most holy
thing).
30 Soothly the sacrifice which is slain for sin, whose
blood is borne into the tabernacle of witnessing to
cleanse in the saintuary (whose blood is brought into the
Tabernacle of the Witnessing, for the cleansing *rite* in the
sanctuary), shall not be eaten, but it shall be burnt in (the)
fire.

CHAPTER 7

1 And this is the law of sacrifice for trespass; it is holy
of holy things. (And this is the law for the trespass
offering; it is a most holy, *or sacred*, thing.)
2 Therefore where burnt sacrifice is offered, also the
sacrifice for trespass shall be slain; the blood thereof shall
be shed by compass of the altar. (The trespass offering
shall be killed in the same place, where the burnt
sacrifice is killed; and its blood shall be thrown against all
the sides of the altar.)
3 They shall offer the tail thereof, and the fatness that
covereth the entrails,
4 the two little reins, and the fatness which is beside
the ileum, and the caul of the maw, with the little reins.
5 And the priest shall burn those on the altar; it is
incense of the Lord, for trespass (it is incense for the Lord,
it is a trespass offering).
6 Each male of the priests' kin shall eat these fleshes in
the holy place, for it is holy of holy things. (Any male of
the priests' kin can eat this flesh, but only in a holy place,
for it is a most holy, *or sacred*, thing.)
7 As a sacrifice is offered for sin, so and for trespass,
one law shall be of ever either sacrifice; it shall pertain to
the priest, that offereth it. (As for the sin offering, so for
the trespass offering, yea, one law shall be for both
offerings; and it shall belong to the priest who offereth it.)
8 The priest that offereth the beast of (a) burnt sacrifice
shall have the skin thereof.
9 And each sacrifice of [tried] *wheat* flour, that is
baken in an oven, and whatever is made ready in a
griddle, either in a frying pan, it shall be that priest's, of
whom it is offered, (And each offering of fine *wheat* flour,
that is baked in an oven, or is cooked in a frying pan, or
on a griddle, shall be the priest's, who offered it.)
10 whether it is sprinkled with oil, either dry. To all the
sons of Aaron even measure shall be parted, to each
[one] by themselves. (But all of the priests, the sons of
Aaron, shall receive an equal share of the uncooked grain
offerings, whether they be sprinkled with oil, or be dry.)
11 This is the law of the sacrifice of peaceable things,
which is offered to the Lord. (And this is the law for the
peace offerings which be offered to the Lord.)
12 If the offering is for the doing of thankings, they shall
offer loaves without sourdough sprinkled with oil, and
thin therf cakes, *that be* anointed with oil; and *they shall
offer* [tried] *wheat* flour baken, and little round loaves,
sprinkled altogether with the meddling of oil. (If the
offering is a thank offering, they shall offer bread made
without yeast and sprinkled with oil, and thin unleavened
wafers *that be* anointed with oil, and little round cakes of
fine *wheat* flour, mixed with oil.)
13 Also *they shall offer* loaves dighted with sourdough,
with the sacrifice of thankings which is offered for
peaceable things; (And *they shall offer* loaves made with
yeast, with the thank offering, which is a peace offering;)
14 of all one loaf shall be offered to the Lord for the

first fruits, and it shall be the priest's that shall pour the
blood of the sacrifice, (and one part of every offering
shall be offered to the Lord as a special contribution, and
it shall be the priest's who shall throw the blood of the
sacrifice against all the sides of the altar,)
15 whose flesh shall be eaten in the same day (whose
flesh shall be eaten on the same day), neither anything of
those shall dwell till the morrowtide.
16 If a man offereth a sacrifice by a vow, either by free
will, it shall be eaten in like manner in the same day; but
also if anything dwelleth into the morrow, it is leaveful to
eat *it*; (If someone offereth an offering to fulfill a vow, or
by free will, it shall be eaten in like manner on the same
day; and if anything dwelleth into the next day, it is
lawful to eat *it*;)
17 soothly [the] fire shall waste whatever thing the third
day shall find.
18 If any man eateth in the third day of the flesh of [the]
sacrifice of peaceable things (If anyone eateth the flesh of
the peace offering on the third day), his offering shall be
made void, neither it shall profit to the offerer; but rather,
whatever soul defouleth himself with such meat, he shall
be guilty of breaking of the law.
19 [The] Flesh that toucheth any unclean thing shall not
be eaten, but it shall be burnt by fire (but it shall be
burned in the fire); (then) he that is clean, shall eat it.
20 A polluted soul, *that is, a defouled man*, that eateth
of the flesh of the sacrifice of peaceable things, which is
offered to the Lord, shall perish from his peoples. (A
polluted soul, *that is, any defiled person*, who eateth the
flesh of the peace offering that is offered to the Lord, shall
be cut off from his people.)
21 And he that toucheth [the] uncleanness of man,
either of beast, either of all thing that may defoul, and
eateth of such fleshes, shall perish from his peoples. (And
anyone who toucheth the uncleanness of man, or of
beast, or of anything that can defile *someone*, and eateth
such flesh, shall be cut off from his people.)
22 And the Lord spake to Moses, and said,
23 Speak thou to the sons of Israel, Ye shall not eat the
inner fatness of a sheep, of an ox, and of a goat; (Say thou
to the Israelites, Ye shall not eat the inner fat of a sheep,
or of an ox, or of a goat;)
24 ye shall have into diverse uses the inner fatness of a
carcass dead by itself, and of that beast which is taken, *or
slain*, of a *ravenous* beast. (ye shall put into diverse uses
the inner fat of a beast that dieth naturally, or of a beast
which is killed by a *ravenous* beast, *but ye shall not eat it*.)
25 If any man eateth the inner fatness, that oughteth to
be offered into incense to the Lord, he shall perish from
his people. (If anyone eateth the inner fat, that ought to
be offered as incense to the Lord, he shall be cut off from
his people.)
26 Also ye shall not take in meat the blood of any
beast, as well of birds, as of beasts; (And ye shall not eat
the blood of any beast, or any bird, wherever ye shall live;)
27 each man that eateth blood shall perish from his
peoples. (anyone who eateth blood shall be cut off from
his people.)
28 And the Lord spake to Moses, and said,
29 Speak thou to the sons of Israel, He that offereth a
sacrifice of peaceable things to the Lord, offer he together
also a sacrifice, that is, the flowing offerings thereof. (Say
thou to the Israelites, He who offereth a peace offering
shall give part of it as a special gift to the Lord, *which the
priest shall receive*.)
30 He shall hold in his hands the inner fatness of the
sacrifice, and the breast; and when he hath hallowed
both *(of) these* (to be) offered to the Lord, he shall take
them to the priest,
31 the which shall burn the inner fatness upon the altar;
soothly the breast shall be Aaron's and his sons';
32 and the right shoulder of the sacrifices of peaceable
things shall turn into the first fruits of the priest. (and the
right shoulder of the peace offering shall be a special
contribution, given to the priest who killeth the offering.)
33 He that of Aaron's sons offereth the blood, and the
inner fatness, shall have also the right shoulder in his
portion. (Yea, the priest, of the sons of Aaron, who
offereth the blood, and the inner fat, shall also have the
right shoulder for his portion.)
34 For I have taken from the sons of Israel the breast of
raising, and the shoulder of separating, of their peaceable
sacrifices, and I have given *those* to Aaron the priest and
to his sons, by everlasting law, of all the people of Israel.
(For I have taken from the Israelites the breast of raising,
as a special gift, and the shoulder of separating, *as a
special contribution*, out of their peace offerings, and I
have given *them* to Aaron the priest, and to his sons, by
an everlasting law, from all the people of Israel.)
35 This is the anointing of Aaron, and of his sons, *that is,
(their portion of) the offering in the day of their anointing*,
in the ceremonies of the Lord, in the day wherein Moses
offered them, that they should be set in priesthood, (This
is the portion for Aaron, and for his sons, out of the
offerings given on the day of their installation, *or their
ordination*, in the ceremonies of the Lord, on the day
when they were presented to serve as priests,)
36 and which things the Lord commanded to be given
to them of the sons of Israel, by everlasting religion in
their generations. (and which things the Lord
commanded to be given to them by the Israelites, by an
everlasting law for all their generations.)
37 This is the law of burnt sacrifice, and of sacrifice for
sin, and for trespass, and for hallowing, and for the
sacrifices of peaceable things; (This then is the law for
burnt sacrifices, grain offerings, sin offerings, trespass
offerings, installation, *or ordination*, offerings, and peace

and thank offerings;)
38 which law the Lord ordained to Moses in the hill of
Sinai, when he commanded to the sons of Israel that they should offer their offerings to the Lord, in the desert of Sinai. (which law the Lord ordained to Moses on Mount Sinai, when he commanded to the Israelites that they should offer their sacrifices to the Lord, in the Sinai Desert.)

CHAPTER 8

1 And the Lord spake to Moses, and said,
2 Take thou Aaron with his sons, their clothes, and the
oil of anointing, a calf for sin, and two rams, a basket with therf loaves; (Take thou Aaron and his sons, their clothes, the anointing oil, a calf for the sin offering, two rams, and a basket of unleavened bread;)
3 and thou shalt gather together all the company to
the door of the tabernacle. (and gather together all the congregation at the entrance of the Tabernacle.)
4 Moses did as the Lord commanded; and when all
the company was gathered before the gates of the tabernacle (and when all the congregation was gathered together at the entrance to the Tabernacle),
5 Moses said, This is the word which the Lord
commanded to be done. (Moses said, This is what the Lord commanded to be done.)
6 And at once *Moses* offered, *or presented to (the)*
priest's office, Aaron and his sons; and when he had washed them,
7 he clothed (Aaron,) the bishop, with a linen shirt,
and girded him with a girdle, and clothed [him] with a coat of jacinth, and putted the cloak on the shoulders above, which *cloak on the shoulders* he bound with a girdle, (he clothed Aaron, the High Priest, with a linen shirt, *or with a linen robe*, and girded him with a sash, and clothed him with a robe, *or with an alb*, of jacinth, and put the ephod over it, which *ephod* he bound with a sash,)
8 and joined thereto the rational, wherein doctrine
and truth was. (and joined the breast-piece to it, in which was the Urim and the Thummim.)
9 And *Moses* covered *Aaron's* head with a mitre, and
upon the mitre, about the front, he put the golden plate, (made) sacred in the hallowing, as the Lord commanded to him. (And *Moses* covered *Aaron's* head with a turban, and on the turban, at the front, he put the gold plate, the sacred symbol of dedication, as the Lord commanded to him.)
10 And he took also the oil of anointing, with which he
anointed the tabernacle with all his purtenance; and when he had hallowed (them), (And he took the anointing oil, and he anointed the Tabernacle, and all its purtenances; and when he had consecrated, *or had dedicated*, them,)
11 and had sprinkled the altar seven times, he anointed
it, and hallowed with (the) oil all the vessels thereof, and the great washing vessel with his foundament (and the great washing vessel, and its foundation, *or its base*).
12 Which *oil* he shedded upon Aaron's head, and
anointed him, and hallowed (him). (And then he poured some of the oil on Aaron's head, and anointed him, and consecrated him.)
13 And his sons offered, *or presented*, Moses clothed
(them) with linen coats, and he girded them with girdles, and he set on *their heads* mitres, as the Lord commanded. (And then Aaron's sons were brought forth, and Moses clothed them with linen shirts, *or with linen robes*, and he girded them with sashes, and he put turbans, *or caps*, on *their heads*, as the Lord commanded.)
14 He offered also a calf for sin (And he brought forth
the calf for the sin offering); and when Aaron and his sons had put their hands on the head of that calf,
15 he offered it, and drew up [the] blood; [and] when
the finger was dipped in the blood *thereof*, he touched the corners of the altar by compass (he touched the horns all around the altar); (and) when the altar was cleansed and hallowed, Moses poured (out) the blood that was left at the altar's foot, (*or at its base*).
16 Soothly he burnt on the altar the inner fatness that
was on the entrails, and the caul of the maw, and the two little reins with their little fatnesses;
17 and he burnt without the tents the calf, with the
skin, the flesh, and the dung, as the Lord commanded. (and away from the tents, he burned the calf, and its skin, and its flesh, and its dung, as the Lord commanded.)
18 And he offered a ram into burnt sacrifice (And then
he offered the ram for the burnt sacrifice); and when Aaron and his sons had set their hands upon the head thereof,
19 he offered it, and he poured the blood thereof by
compass of the altar. (he offered it, and then he threw its blood against all the sides of the altar.)
20 And he cutted that ram into gobbets, and he burnt
with fire the head thereof, and the members, and the inner fatness, (And he cut, *or carved*, that ram into pieces, and he burned its head, and its members, and the inner fat,)
21 when the entrails and the feet were washed before;
and he burnt all the ram together upon the altar, for it was the burnt sacrifice of sweetest odour to the Lord, as the Lord commanded to him. (and when the entrails and the feet were washed in water, he burned the rest of the ram on the altar, for it was the burnt sacrifice to make the sweetest odour to the Lord, as the Lord commanded to him.)
22 He offered also the second ram, into the hallowing
of (the) priests; and Aaron and his sons putted their hands upon the head thereof. (And then he offered the second

ram, for the installation, *or the ordination*, of the priests; and Aaron and his sons put their hands on its head.)
23 And when Moses had offered that ram, he took of the blood, and touched *therewith* the last part of the right ear of Aaron, and the thumb of his right hand, and in like manner of his foot. (And when Moses had killed that ram, he took some of the blood, and touched *with it* the lobe of Aaron's right ear, and the thumb of his right hand, and the great toe of his right foot.)
24 He offered also the sons of Aaron. And when he had touched of the blood of the ram offered the last part of the right ears of all, and the thumbs of the right hand and foot, he poured the blood that was left upon the altar by compass. (And then he brought forth Aaron's sons. And when he had touched with the blood of the offered ram the lobes of their right ears, and the thumbs of their right hands, and the great toes of their right feet, he threw the rest of the blood against all the sides of the altar.)
25 Soothly he separated the inner fatness, and the tail, and all the fatness that covereth the entrails, and the caul of the maw, and the two reins with their fatnesses, and with the right shoulder (and the right shoulder).
26 Forsooth he took of the pannier of therf loaves, that was before the Lord, loaves without sourdough, and a cake sprinkled with oil, and he putted (those) loaves first sodden in water, and afterward fried in oil, on the inner fatness, and the right shoulder; (Then from the basket of unleavened bread, that was before the Lord, he took out a loaf made without yeast, and a cake sprinkled with oil, and a wafer, which was first boiled in water, and then fried in oil, and he put them on the inner fat, and on the right shoulder;)
27 and he betook all these things together to Aaron, and to his sons. And after that they [had] raised (up) those (things as a special gift) before the Lord,
28 again he took them of their hands, and burnt them upon the altar of burnt sacrifice, for it was the offering of hallowing, into the odour of sweetness of sacrifice, into his part to the Lord. (he took them out of their hands, and burned them on the altar on top of the burnt sacrifice, for it was an installation, *or an ordination*, offering, to make the sweetest aroma to the Lord.)
29 He took also the breast of the ram of consecration into his part, and raised it (up as a special gift) before the Lord, as the Lord commanded to him. (And he took the breast of the ram of installation, *or of ordination*, and raised it up as a special gift before the Lord, as the Lord commanded to him.)
30 And he took the ointment, and the blood that was in the altar, and he sprinkled *them* upon Aaron, and on his clothes, and upon his sons, and on their clothes. And when *Moses* had hallowed them in their clothing, (And he took some of the anointing oil, and some of the blood that was on the altar, and he sprinkled *it* on Aaron, and on his clothes, and on his sons, and on their clothes. And when *Moses* had consecrated them, and their clothing,)
31 he commanded to them, and said, Seethe ye the flesh before the tabernacle gates, and there eat ye it; also eat ye the loaves of hallowing, that be put in the basket, as God commanded to me, and said, Aaron and his sons shall eat those loaves; (he commanded to them, and said, Boil ye the flesh at the entrance to the Tabernacle, and eat ye it there; also eat ye the installation, *or the ordination*, loaves, that be put in the basket, as God commanded to me, and said, Aaron and his sons shall eat those loaves;)
32 soothly whatever thing is left of the flesh and of the loaves, [the] fire shall waste it.
33 Also ye shall not go out of the door of the tabernacle in seven days, till to the day in which the time of your hallowing shall be fulfilled; for the hallowing is ended in seven days, (And ye shall not go out of the entrance to the Tabernacle for seven days, until the day in which the time of your ordination is fulfilled; for the installation rites shall last for seven days,)
34 as it is done now in this present time, that the rightfulness of the sacrifice were fulfilled. (as it is done now at this present time, so that your sin is taken away.)
35 Ye shall dwell day and night in the tabernacle, and ye shall keep the keepings of the Lord (and ye shall do the commands of the Lord), (so) that ye die not; for so it is commanded to me.
36 And Aaron and his sons did all things, which the Lord spake by the hand of Moses.

CHAPTER 9

1 Forsooth when the eighth day was made, Moses called Aaron, and his sons, and the greater men in birth of Israel (and the men of great age in Israel, *that is, the elders*);
2 and he said to Aaron, Take thou of the drove a calf for sin, and a ram for burnt sacrifice, ever either without wem, and offer thou them before the Lord. (and he said to Aaron, Take thou a calf from the herd for a sin offering, and a ram for a burnt sacrifice, both without blemish, and offer thou them before the Lord.)
3 And thou shalt speak to the sons of Israel, Take ye a buck of goats for sin, and a calf, and a lamb, (both) of one year, and without wem, into burnt sacrifice, (And thou shalt say to the Israelites, Take ye a goat buck for a sin offering, and a calf and a lamb, both of one year, and without blemish, for a burnt sacrifice,)
4 (and) an ox and a ram for peaceable things; and offer ye them before the Lord, and offer ye [tried] *wheat* flour sprinkled with oil in the sacrifice of each *of them*; for today the Lord shall appear to you. (and an ox and a ram for peace offerings; and offer ye them before the Lord, and offer ye fine *wheat* flour sprinkled with oil

along with each offering; for today the Lord shall appear
to you.)
5 Therefore they took all things, which Moses
commanded, to the door of the tabernacle, where, when
all the multitude stood, (And so they took all these things,
which Moses commanded, to the entrance of the
Tabernacle, where, when all the multitude stood,)
6 Moses said, This is the word which the Lord
commanded (This is what the Lord commanded), do ye
it, and his glory shall appear to you.
7 And Moses said to Aaron, Nigh thou to the altar,
and offer thou for thy sin; offer thou burnt sacrifice, and
pray for thee, and for the people; and when thou hast
slain the sacrifice of the people, pray thou for them, as
the Lord commanded. (And Moses said to Aaron,
Approach thou to the altar, and offer thy sin offering, and
thy burnt sacrifice, and pray for thyself, and for the
people; and when thou hast killed the offering for the
people, pray thou for them, as the Lord commanded.)
8 And anon Aaron nighed to the altar, and offered a
calf for his sin; (And at once Aaron approached the altar,
and offered a calf for his own sin offering;)
9 whose blood his sons offered, *or brought*, to him, in
which blood Aaron dipped his finger, and he touched the
horns of the altar, and he poured the blood that was left
at the foundament *of the altar* (and he poured out the
blood that was left at the foundation, *or at the base, of
the altar*);
10 and he burnt upon the altar the inner fatness, and
the little reins, and the caul of the maw, (for the sin
offering,) as the Lord commanded to Moses.
11 Forsooth Aaron burnt with fire without the tents the
flesh and the skin thereof. (But Aaron burned its flesh and
its skin away from the tents.)
12 And he offered the beast of burnt sacrifice, and his
sons brought to him the blood thereof, which he shedded
by compass of the altar; (And then he offered the beast
for the burnt sacrifice, and his sons brought him its
blood, which he threw against all the sides of the altar;)
13 they offered also that sacrifice cut into gobbets, with
the head, and all the members; and he burnt by fire all
these things upon the altar, (and they gave him the
offering cut into pieces, with the head, and all its
members; and he burned all these things on the altar,)
14 when the entrails and the feet were washed before
with water. (and when the innards and the feet were
washed in water, they were also burned, on top of the
burnt sacrifice.)
15 And he offered and killed a buck of goats, for the sin
of the people (And then he brought forth and offered a
goat buck, for the people's sin offering); and when the
altar was cleansed, he made (the) burnt sacrifice,
16 and he added into the sacrifice flowing offerings,
that be offered together; (and he added the grain offering
to the sacrifice, that should be offered with it;)
17 and he burnt those on the altar, without the
ceremonies of [the] burnt sacrifice of the morrowtide.
(and he burned a handful of the grain offering on the
altar, in addition to the morning burnt sacrifice.)
18 He offered also an ox, and a ram, [the] peaceable
sacrifices of the people; and his sons offered to him the
blood, the which he poured by compass of the altar. (And
he offered the ox and the ram, for the peace offerings of
the people; and his sons brought him the blood, which
he threw against all the sides of the altar.)
19 Forsooth they putted on the breasts the inner fatness
of the ox, and the tail of the ram, and the little reins with
their fatnesses, and the caul of the maw.
20 And when the inner fatnesses were burnt upon the
altar,
21 Aaron separated the breasts, and the right shoulders
of them, and raised them (up as a special gift) before the
Lord, as Moses commanded.
22 And he stretched forth *his* hands to the people, and
blessed it; and so when the sacrifices for sin, and [the]
burnt sacrifices, and [the] peaceable sacrifices, were
fulfilled, Aaron came down *from the place of sacrificing.*
(And he stretched forth *his* hands to the people, and
blessed them; and when the sin offerings, the burnt
sacrifices, and the peace offerings, were finished, Aaron
came down *from the place for sacrificing.*)
23 Soothly Moses and Aaron entered into the
tabernacle of witnessing, and went out afterward, and
blessed the people; (And Moses and Aaron entered into
the Tabernacle of the Witnessing, and when they came
out afterward, they blessed the people;)
24 and the glory of the Lord appeared to all the
multitude. And lo! fire went out from the Lord, and
devoured the burnt sacrifice, and the inner fatnesses that
were upon the altar; and when the companies had seen
this thing, they praised the Lord, and felled on their faces
(and when the congregation saw this, they praised the
Lord, and fell on their faces).

CHAPTER 10

1 And when Nadab and Abihu, the sons of Aaron, had
taken censers, and putted fire (therein), and incense
[there]above, and offered before the Lord alien fire,
which thing was not commanded to them. (But then
Nadab and Abihu, Aaron's sons, took their censers, and
put fire in them, and some incense on it, and offered
unholy fire before the Lord, which they were not
commanded to do.)
2 And fire went out from the Lord, and devoured
them, and they were dead before the Lord.
3 And Moses said to Aaron, This thing it is that the
Lord spake (This is what the Lord meant when he said), I
shall be hallowed in them that nigh to me, and I shall be

glorified in the sight of all the people; which thing Aaron
heard, and was still.
4 Soothly when Moses had called Mishael and
Elzaphan, the sons of Uzziel, the brother of Aaron's
father, he said to them, Go ye, and take away your
brethren from the sight of [the] saintuary, and bear ye
them out of the tents (Go ye, and take away your cousins'
bodies from the sanctuary, and take ye them away from
the tents).
5 And anon they went, and took them, as they lay
clothed with linen coats, and casted them out, as it was
commanded to them. (And at once they went, and took
them, as they lay clothed in their linen shirts, *or in their
linen robes*, and cast them out, as it was commanded to
them.)
6 And Moses spake to Aaron, and to Eleazar and
Ithamar, the sons of Aaron, Do not ye make naked your
heads, and do not ye rend your clothes, lest peradventure
ye die, and (the) indignation *of God* rise upon all the
company; (but let) your brethren and all the house of
Israel bewail the burning which the Lord hath raised up.
(And Moses said to Aaron, and to Eleazar and Ithamar,
Aaron's sons, Do not ye make your heads naked, and do
not ye tear your clothes, lest ye die, and *God's*
indignation rise up against all the congregation; but let
your brothers and all the house of Israel bewail the
burning which the Lord hath raised up.)
7 But ye shall not go out of the gates of the tabernacle,
else ye shall perish; for the oil of holy anointing is on you
(But ye shall not leave the entrance to the Tabernacle, for
ye shall perish, for the Lord's anointing oil is upon you).
The which did all things by the behest of Moses.
8 Also the Lord said to Aaron, (And the Lord said to
Aaron,)
9 Thou and thy sons shall not drink wine, and all thing
that may make drunken, when ye shall enter into the
tabernacle of witnessing, lest ye die; for it is everlasting
behest into your generations, (Thou and thy sons shall
not drink wine, or anything that can make ye drunk,
when ye shall enter into the Tabernacle of the
Witnessing, lest ye die; this is an everlasting law for all
your generations,)
10 [and] that ye have knowing to make doom betwixt
holy thing and unholy, betwixt polluted thing and clean;
(so that ye can judge between holy and unholy things,
and between unclean, and clean things;)
11 and that ye teach the sons of Israel all my lawful
things (and that ye teach the Israelites all my laws), which
the Lord spake to them by the hand of Moses.
12 And Moses spake to Aaron, and to Eleazar and
Ithamar, his (two) sons that were left, Take ye the sacrifice
that (is) left of the offering of the Lord, and eat ye it
without sourdough, beside the altar, for it is holy of holy
things. (And Moses said to Aaron, and to Eleazar and
Ithamar, his two sons who were left, Take ye the grain
offering that is left of the offerings to the Lord, and eat it
without yeast, beside the altar, for it is a most holy, *or
sacred*, thing.)
13 Soothly ye shall eat in the holy place that that is given
to thee, and to thy sons, of the offerings of the Lord (out
of the offerings to the Lord), as it is commanded to me.
14 Also thou, and thy sons, and thy daughters with
thee, shall eat in the cleanest place the breast which is
offered, and the shoulder which is separated; for those be
kept to thee, and to thy free sons, of the healthful
sacrifices of the sons of Israel; (And thou, and thy sons,
and thy daughters with thee, shall eat in the cleanest
place the breast of the special gift, and the shoulder of
the special contribution; for they be kept for thee, and for
thy sons, out of the peace offerings of the Israelites;)
15 for they raised before the Lord the shoulder and the
breast, and the inner fatnesses that be burnt in the altar;
and pertain they to thee, and to thy sons, by everlasting
law, as the Lord commanded. (for they raised up before
the Lord the shoulder, and the breast, and the inner fat
that shall be burned on the altar; and they pertain to thee,
and to thy sons, by an everlasting law, as the Lord
commanded.)
16 Among these things when Moses sought the goat
buck that was offered for sin, he found *it* burnt, and he
was wroth against Eleazar and Ithamar, Aaron's sons, that
were left *alive*. And he said, (And then Moses inquired
about the goat buck for the sin offering, and he found that
it had already been burned, and he was angry with
Eleazar and Ithamar, Aaron's sons, who were left *alive*.
And he said,)
17 Why ate not ye the sacrifice for sin in the holy
place, the which sacrifice is holy of holy things, and it is
given to you, that ye bear the wickedness of the
multitude, and pray for it in the sight of the Lord; (Why
did ye not eat the sin offering in the holy place? this
offering is a most holy, *or sacred*, thing, and it is given to
you, so that ye carry the wickedness of the multitude, and
pray for them before the Lord;)
18 mostly since of the blood thereof is not borne in
within [the] holy things, and ye ought to eat it in the
saintuary, as it is commanded to me? (mostly since its
blood is not brought into the Holy Place, so ye ought to
eat it in the sanctuary, as it was commanded to me.)
19 And Aaron answered, Sacrifice for sin, and burnt
sacrifice is offered today before the Lord; soothly this
thing that thou seest, befelled to me (And Aaron
answered, The sin offering, and the burnt sacrifice, were
offered today before the Lord, but then this thing that
thou saw, befell to me); how might I eat it, either please
God in ceremonies, with (such a) sorrowful soul?
20 And when Moses had heard this, he received
satisfaction, *or covenable answer (or a suitable, or an*

acceptable, answer).

CHAPTER 11

1 And the Lord spake to Moses and Aaron, and said,
2 Say ye to the sons of Israel (Say ye to the Israelites),
Keep ye all things which I wrote to you, (so) that I (shall)
be your God. These be the beasts, which ye shall eat,
(out) of all the living beasts of (the) earth;
3 ye shall eat all things among beasts that have the
claw parted, and cheweth the cud; (ye shall eat all those
among the beasts that have a divided hoof, *or foot*, and
that chew the cud;)
4 soothly whatever thing cheweth cud, and hath a
claw, but parteth not it, as a camel, and other beasts (but
whatever beast cheweth the cud, and hath a hoof, *or a
foot*, but it is not divided, like a camel, and other beasts),
ye shall not eat it, and ye shall areckon *it* among unclean
things.
5 A coney, which cheweth (the) cud, and parteth not
the claw (but its foot is not divided), is unclean;
6 and an hare, for also he cheweth (the) cud, but
parteth not the claw (but its foot is not divided);
7 and a swine, that cheweth not the cud, though he
parteth the claw (though its hoof is divided).
8 Ye shall not eat the flesh of these *beasts*, neither ye
shall touch their dead bodies, for those be unclean to
you.
9 Also these things be that be engendered in waters,
and [it] is leaveful to eat; ye shall eat all things that have
fins and scales, as well in the sea, as in [the] fresh floods,
and standing waters; (And these things that be begotten
in waters, it is lawful for ye to eat; ye shall eat all the
things that have fins and scales, that be in the sea, as well
as those that be in fresh water rivers, and lakes, *and
ponds*;)
10 soothly whatever thing of them that be moved and
live in waters (but whichever of them that move and live
in water), (but) hath not fins and scales, shall be
abominable, and loathsome to you;
11 and ye shall not eat the flesh of those, and ye shall
eschew their bodies dead by themselves. (and ye shall
not eat their flesh, and ye shall shun their dead bodies.)
12 All things in [the] waters that have not fins and
scales, shall be polluted, (*that is, defiled, or unclean*).
13 These things be of (the) fowls which ye shall not eat,
and shall be eschewed of you (and shall be shunned by
you); an eagle, and a gripe, [and] an aliet,
14 and a kite, and a vulture by his kind;
15 and all the kind of ravens by his likeness;
16 a struthio, and a night crow, [and] a lari, *or a coot*,
and a hawk by his kind;
17 an owl, and a dipper (and a divedapper), and (a)
ciconia;
18 a swan, and a cormorant, and a pelican;
19 a falcon, [and] a jay by his kind; [and] a lapwing,
and a rearmouse, *or a bat*.
20 All thing of fowls that goeth on four feet, shall be
abominable to you; (All creatures with wings, *that is,
insects*, that go upon four feet, shall be abominable to
you;)
21 soothly whatever thing goeth on four feet, but hath
longer hips behind, by which it skippeth on the earth (by
which it leapeth upon the ground), ye shall eat;
22 as is a bruchus, *that is, the fruit of locusts before it
hath wings*, in his kind, and (an) accatus, *that is, the fruit
of locusts when it beginneth to have wings*, and (an)
ophimachus, [*that is, a foul enemy to serpents*,] and a
locust, all by their kind.
23 Forsooth whatever thing of birds (that) hath four feet
only, it shall be abominable to you; (But all other
creatures with wings that hath four feet, they shall be
abominable to you;)
24 and whoever toucheth their bodies dead by
themselves, shall be polluted, *or defouled*, and shall be
unclean till to eventide; (and whoever toucheth their
dead bodies, shall be polluted, *or defiled*, and shall be
unclean until the evening;)
25 and if it is need, that he bear any dead thing of
these, he shall wash his clothes, and he shall be unclean
till to the going down of the sun.
26 Soothly each beast that hath a claw, but parteth not
it, neither cheweth cud, shall be unclean; and whatever
thing toucheth it, shall be defouled. (And each beast that
hath a hoof, *or a foot*, but it is not parted, nor cheweth
the cud, shall be unclean; and whatever thing that
toucheth it, shall be defiled, *or unclean*.)
27 That that goeth on hands, of all beasts that go on
four feet, shall be unclean; he that toucheth their bodies
dead by themselves, shall be defouled till to eventide (he
who toucheth their dead bodies, shall be defiled, *or
unclean*, until the evening);
28 and he, that beareth such dead bodies, shall wash
his clothes, and he shall be unclean till to eventide; for
all these things be unclean to you.
29 Also these things shall be areckoned among
defouled things, of these things that be moved on earth
(of these things that move upon the ground); a weasel,
and a mouse, and a crocodile, each after his kind;
30 a migale, (and) a chameleon, and (a) stellion, and a
lacert, and a mouldwarp.
31 All these be unclean; he that toucheth their bodies
dead by themselves (he who toucheth their dead bodies),
shall be unclean till to eventide;
32 and that thing shall be defouled, on which anything
of their bodies dead by themselves falleth, as well a
vessel of wood, and a cloth, as skins, *or pilches*, either
hair-shirts; and in whatever thing work is made, it shall
be dipped in water, and those things shall be defouled till

to eventide, and so afterward they shall be cleansed. (and
anything shall be defiled, on which any of their dead
bodies falleth, yea, a vessel of wood, or a cloak, or skins,
or pilches, or hair-shirts, however they might be used; it
shall be dipped in water, and shall remain defiled until
the evening, and then it shall be clean again.)
33 Soothly a vessel of earth, in which anything of these
falleth within, shall be defouled, and therefore it shall be
broken. (And an earthen, *or a clay*, vessel, in which any
of these things falleth within, shall be unclean, and so it
shall be broken.)
34 Each meat, that ye shall eat, shall be unclean, if
water *of such a vessel* is poured out thereon; and each
flowing thing, that is drunken of such a vessel, shall be
unclean; (Any food that ye shall eat, shall be unclean, if
water *from such a vessel* is poured out onto it; and
anything that is drunk from such a vessel, shall be
unclean;)
35 and whatever thing of such dead bodies by
themselves shall fall upon (and anything that a dead body
of such a creature shall fall upon), it shall be unclean,
whether furnaces, or kettles standing upon three feet,
(and) they shall be destroyed, and shall be unclean.
36 Soothly wells and cisterns, and all the gatherings
together of waters, shall be clean. He that toucheth their
body dead by itself, shall be defouled (But whoever
toucheth their dead body shall be defiled, *or unclean*).
37 If it falleth upon (a) seed, it shall not defoul the seed;
38 soothly if any man sheddeth out [the] seed with
water, and afterward the water is touched with dead
bodies by themselves, it shall be defouled anon. (but if
anyone poureth out the seed with water, and afterward
the seed is touched by their dead bodies, at once it shall
be defiled, *or unclean*.)
39 If a beast is dead, which it is leaveful to you to eat (If
a beast dieth naturally, which it is lawful for you to eat),
he that toucheth the dead body thereof shall be unclean
till to eventide;
40 and he that eateth thereof anything, either beareth *it*,
shall wash his clothes, and shall be unclean till to
eventide.
41 All thing that creepeth upon earth, shall be
abominable, neither it shall be into meat. (All things that
creep upon the ground, shall be abominable, and shall
not be eaten.)
42 Whatever thing goeth upon the breast, and on four
feet, and hath many feet, either is drawn by the earth, ye
shall not eat *it*, for it is abominable. (Whatever thing
goeth on its breast, or hath many feet, or draweth itself
upon the ground, ye shall not eat *it*, for it is abominable.)
43 Do not ye defoul your souls, neither touch ye
anything of them, lest ye be unclean;
44 for I am your Lord God; be ye holy, for I am holy.
Defoul ye not your souls in each creeping thing that is
moved upon earth (Defile ye not your souls with any
creeping thing that moveth upon the ground);
45 for I am the Lord, that led you out of the land of
Egypt, that I should be to you into God; ye shall be holy,
for I am holy. (for I am the Lord, who led you out of the
land of Egypt, so that I could become your God; ye shall
be holy, for I am holy.)
46 This is the law of living beasts, and of fowls, and of
each living thing that is moved in water, and creepeth in
earth; (This is the law concerning living beasts, and birds,
and each living thing that moveth in water, and that
creepeth upon the ground;)
47 that ye know the differences of clean thing and
unclean (so that ye know the difference between clean
and unclean things), and that ye know what ye shall eat,
and what ye ought to forsake.

CHAPTER 12

1 And the Lord spake to Moses, and said,
2 Speak thou to the sons of Israel, and thou shalt say
to them, If a woman, when she hath received seed,
childeth a knave child, she shall be unclean by seven
days, by the days of her separating of corruptible blood,
that runneth from her by months; (Speak thou to the
Israelites, and thou shalt say to them, If a woman, when
she hath received seed, beareth a boy, she shall be
unclean for seven days, as she is in the days of her
separation for the corrupt blood that runneth from her
every month;)
3 and the young child shall be circumcised in the
eighth day. (and the young boy shall be circumcised on
the eighth day.)
4 Soothly she shall dwell three and thirty days in the
blood of her purifying; she shall not touch any holy thing,
neither she shall enter into the saintuary, till the days of
her cleansing be [ful]filled.
5 Soothly if she childeth a female, she shall be
unclean (for) two weeks, (as she is) by the custom of [the]
flowing (out) of unclean blood, and threescore and six
days she shall dwell in the blood of her cleansing.
6 And when the days of her cleansing, for a son, or for
a daughter, be fulfilled, she shall bring a lamb of one year
into burnt sacrifice, and a culver bird, either a turtle, for
sin, to the door of the tabernacle of witnessing; and she
shall give to the priest, (And when the days of her
cleansing, for a son, or for a daughter, be fulfilled, she
shall bring a lamb of one year for a burnt sacrifice, and a
young pigeon, or a turtledove, for a sin offering, to the
entrance of the Tabernacle of the Witnessing; and she
shall give *them* to the priest,)
7 which shall offer those before the Lord, and shall
pray for her, and so she shall be cleansed from the
flowing (out) of her blood. This is the law of a *woman*
that childeth male, or female (This is the law for a *woman*

who beareth a boy, or a girl).
8 That if her hand find not, neither she may offer a
lamb, she shall take two turtles, either two culver birds,
one into burnt sacrifice, and the tother for sin; and the
priest shall pray for her, and so she shall be cleansed.
(But if *because of poverty*, her hand cannot find a lamb
that she may offer, she shall take two turtledoves, or two
young pigeons, one for a burnt sacrifice, and the other for
a sin offering; and the priest shall pray for her, and then
she shall be clean.)

CHAPTER 13

1 The Lord spake to Moses and Aaron, and said,
2 A man in whose skin and flesh riseth diverse colour,
either (a) whelk, either as some shining thing, that is, a
wound of leprosy [that is to say, a plague of leprosy], he
shall be brought to Aaron the priest, either to one of any
of his sons (or to one of his sons);
3 and when he seeth the leprosy, *or meselry*, in the
skin, and the hair changed into white colour, and that the
species of leprosy *is* lower than the other skin and the
flesh, it is a wound of leprosy [it is a plague of leprosy], and
he shall be separated at the doom of the priest (and the
priest shall pronounce him to be unclean).
4 Soothly if the shining whiteness that is in the skin,
neither (it) is lower than the tother flesh, and the hairs be
of the former colour, the priest shall close him seven days
(then the priest shall enclose him for seven days);
5 and the priest shall behold him in the seventh day,
and soothly if the leprosy wax not further, neither passeth
the former terms in the flesh, again the priest shall close
him again seven other days; (and the priest shall examine
him on the seventh day, and if the leprosy hath not
grown, *or not spread*, nor it hath passed the original
borders in the flesh, the priest shall enclose him again for
seven more days;)
6 and he shall behold *him* in the seventh day; if the
leprosy is then dark, and waxeth not in the flesh, the
priest shall cleanse him, *that is, shall deem him to be
clean*, for it is a scab; and the man shall wash his clothes,
and he shall be clean. (and he shall examine *him* again
on the seventh day; if the leprosy is then dark, and hath
not grown, *or not spread*, in the flesh, the priest shall
pronounce him to be clean, for it is a scab; and the man
shall wash his clothes, and so he shall be clean.)
7 That if the leprosy waxeth again, after that he is seen
of the priest, and is yielded to cleanness, he shall be
brought again to the priest, (But if the leprosy groweth
again, *or spreadeth*, after that he was seen by the priest,
and was pronounced clean, he shall be brought again to
the priest,)
8 and he shall be deemed *to be* of uncleanness. (and
the priest shall pronounce him *to be* unclean.)
9 If the wound of leprosy is in a man [If the plague of
leprosy is in a man], he shall be brought to the priest,
10 and he shall see the man; and when white colour is
in the flesh, and it changeth the sight, *or former colour*,
of [the] hairs, and that flesh appeareth quick, *or waxing*
(and that flesh appeareth to be raw),
11 it shall be deemed the eldest leprosy, and grown to
the skin; therefore the priest shall defoul him, *that is,
deem him to be foul*, and the priest shall not close him
again, for it is of open uncleanness. (it shall be judged to
be an old leprosy, *or a chronic skin disease*, grown in the
skin; and so the priest shall pronounce him to be defiled,
or unclean, but he shall not enclose him again, for it is an
open uncleanness.)
12 But if the leprosy running about in the skin
flowereth out, (*or spreadeth*,) and covereth all the flesh,
from the head till to the feet, (on) whatever thing falleth
under the sight of (his) eyes;
13 the priest shall behold him, and he shall deem him
to be holden with the cleanest leprosy, for all the skin is
turned into whiteness, and therefore the man shall be
clean. (the priest shall examine him, and he shall
pronounce him to be clean, for all the skin hath turned
white, and so the man shall be clean.)
14 Soothly when quick flesh appeareth in him, he shall
be defouled (But when raw flesh appeareth on him, he
shall be pronounced defiled, *or unclean*,)
15 by the doom of the priest, and he shall be areckoned
among unclean men; for quick flesh is unclean, if it is
sprinkled with leprosy. (by the priest, and he shall be
reckoned among the unclean; for raw flesh is unclean, if
it is sprinkled with leprosy.)
16 That if the (raw) flesh is turned again into whiteness,
and covereth all the man, (But when the raw flesh
healeth, and turneth white, the man shall go to the
priest,)
17 the priest shall behold him, and shall deem that he
is clean. (and the priest shall examine him, and shall
pronounce that he is clean.)
18 The flesh and the skin, in which a botch is bred, and
is healed, (The flesh and the skin, in which a boil, *or a
sore*, is bred, and then is healed,)
19 and the place of the botch, *or a fell sore (or the
sore)*, appeareth white, either red, the man shall be
brought to the priest;
20 and when the priest seeth the place of the leprosy
(to be) lower than the other flesh, and the hairs turned
into whiteness, the priest shall defoul him, *that is, (shall)
deem him (to be) foul*, (the priest shall pronounce him to
be defiled, *or unclean)*; for the wound of leprosy is bred
in the botch [for a plague of leprosy is sprung in the botch].
21 That if the hair is of the former colour, and the sign
of the wound is some-deal dark, and is not lower than the
flesh beside, the priest shall close the man seven days;
(But if the hair is of the former colour, and the mark of

the plague is somewhat dark, and is not lower than the
flesh beside it, the priest shall enclose the man for seven
days;)
22 and soothly, if *his sore* waxeth, the priest shall deem
the man to be (a) leper; (and if *his sore* groweth, *or*
spreadeth, the priest shall pronounce him to be a leper;)
23 forsooth if it standeth in his place, it is a sign of a
botch, and the man shall be clean. (but if it standeth in its
place, it is the sign of a boil, *or of a sore*, and the priest
shall pronounce him to be clean.)
24 Flesh, and skin, which the fire hath burnt, and is
(now) healed, and hath a white, either red, sign of (a)
wound, the priest shall behold it (the priest shall examine
it),
25 and lo! if it is turned into whiteness, and the place
thereof is lower than the tother skin, the priest shall
defoul the man (the priest shall pronounce him to be
defiled, *or unclean*), for a wound of leprosy is bred in the
sign of (the) wound [for the plague of leprosy is sprung in the
fell wound].
26 That if the colour of [the] hairs is not changed,
neither the wound, *or soreness*, is lower than the tother
flesh, and that species of leprosy is some-deal dark, the
priest shall close the man seven days; (But if the colour of
the hairs is not changed, and the sore is not lower than
the other flesh, and that kind of leprosy is somewhat
dark, the priest shall enclose the man for seven days;)
27 and in the seventh day he shall behold *him*; if the
leprosy waxeth in the flesh, the priest shall defoul the
man, (*that is, shall deem him to be defiled, or unclean*);
(and on the seventh day he shall examine *him*; if the
leprosy hath grown, *or spread*, in the flesh, the priest
shall pronounce him to be defiled, *or unclean*;)
28 else if the whiteness standeth in his place, and is not
clear enough, it is a wound, *or soreness*, of burning, and
therefore the man shall be cleansed, for it is a sign of
burning. (but if the whiteness standeth in its place, and is
light in colour, it is a sore from a burn, and so the man
shall be clean, *that is, the priest shall pronounce him to*
be clean, for it is the mark of a burn.)
29 A man or a woman, in whose head or beard leprosy
burgeoneth, (A man or a woman, on whose head, or
chin, groweth leprosy,)
30 the priest shall see them; and if the place is lower
than the tother flesh, and the hair is white, and is subtler,
either smaller, than it is wont (to be), the priest shall
defoul them, for it is leprosy of the head, and of the beard
(the priest shall pronounce them to be defiled, *or*
unclean, for it is a leprosy of the head, or of the chin).
31 Else if he seeth the place of the wem, *or the sore*, (to
be) even with the nigh flesh, and the hair black, the priest
shall close them seven days (then the priest shall enclose
them for seven days),
32 and he shall see them in the seventh day; if the wem
waxeth not, and the hair is of his colour, and the place of
wound is even with the tother flesh, (and he shall
examine them on the seventh day; if the sore hath not
grown, *or not spread*, and the hair is its proper colour,
and the place of the sore is even with the other flesh,)
33 the man shall be shaven, without the place of the
wem, and he shall be closed again by seven other days.
(the man, or the woman, shall be shaved, except for the
place of the sore, and they shall be enclosed again for
another seven days.)
34 If in the seventh day the wound, *or soreness*, is seen
to have stand in his place, neither (it) is lower than the
tother flesh, the priest shall cleanse the man; and when
his clothes be washed, he shall be clean. (If on the
seventh day, the sore is seen to have stood in its place,
nor is it any lower than the other flesh, the priest shall
pronounce them to be clean; and when their clothes be
washed, they shall be clean.)
35 Else if after the cleansing, a spot waxeth again in the
skin, (But if, after they be pronounced clean, a spot
groweth again, *or spreadeth*, in the skin,)
36 the priest shall no more inquire, whether the hair is
changed into white colour, for apertly he is unclean. (the
priest shall inquire no more, whether the hair is changed
to white colour, or not, for they be openly unclean.)
37 Soothly if the spot standeth still, and the hairs be
black, know then the priest that the man is healed, and
trustily pronounce he the man clean. (But if the spot
standeth still, and the hairs be black, then let the priest
know that they be healed, and trustily pronounce he that
they be clean.)
38 A man or a woman, in whose skin whiteness
appeareth,
39 the priest shall behold them; if he perceiveth, that
whiteness some-deal dark shineth in the skin, know he,
that it is no leprosy, but a spot of white colour, and that
the man is clean. (the priest shall examine them; if he
perceiveth that a somewhat dark whiteness shineth in the
skin, know he, that it is not leprosy, but a spot of white
colour, and they be clean.)
40 A man of whose head the hairs float away, he is
bald, and clean; (A man from whose head the hairs float
away, he is bald, and is clean;)
41 and if the hairs fall from the forehead, he is bald,
and is clean;
42 else if in the baldness before, either in the baldness
behind (but if in the baldness at the front, or in the
baldness at the back), white either red colour is bred, *or*
is sprung up,
43 and the priest seeth this, he shall condemn the man,
without (any) doubt of (him having) leprosy, which is
bred in the baldness.
44 Therefore whoever is defouled with leprosy, and is
separated *from other men*, at the doom of the priest (by

the priest's pronouncement),
45 he shall have his clothes unsewed (he shall wear
torn clothes), and his head (shall be) bare, and his mouth
(shall be) covered with a cloth, [and] he shall cry himself
(to be) defouled, and vile;
46 in all the time that he is leprous and unclean, he
shall dwell alone, without the tents. (and in all the time
that he is leprous and unclean, he shall live alone, away
from the tents.)
47 A woollen cloth, either linen, (A woollen cloak, or a
linen one,)
48 that hath leprosy in the warp, either woof, either
certainly a skin, *or a pilch*, either whatever thing is made
of skin,
49 if it is corrupted with a white spot, either red, it shall
be areckoned (to be) leprosy, and it shall be showed to
the priest;
50 the which when he hath beheld (it), shall close it up
seven days (shall enclose it for seven days).
51 And again he shall behold it in the seventh day, and
if he perceiveth, that the leprosy therein hath waxed, it
shall be *deemed* [a] continual leprosy; he shall deem that
cloth defouled, and all thing(s) in which it is found; (And
he shall examine it again on the seventh day, and if he
perceiveth, that the leprosy in it hath grown, it shall be
judged an abiding leprosy; he shall judge that cloak to be
defiled, and all the things in which it is found;)
52 and therefore the cloth shall be burnt with flames of
fire. (and so the cloak shall be burned in the fire.)
53 And if the priest seeth that *the spot* hath waxed not,
(And if the priest seeth that *the spot* hath not grown, *or
not spread*,)
54 he shall command, and they shall wash that thing
wherein the leprosy is, and he shall close it again seven
other days (and he shall enclose it for another seven
days);
55 and when he seeth the former likeness not changed
again, nevertheless that neither the leprosy hath waxed,
he shall (still) deem that thing (to be) unclean, and he
shall burn *it* in fire, for the leprosy is shed in the over-part
of that cloth, either through[out] *it* all (for there is leprosy
on the outer part of that cloak, or on the inside of *it*).
56 Else if the place of [the] leprosy is darker, after that
the cloth is washed, he shall break away that dark place,
and he shall part it from the whole. (But if the place of
the leprosy is darker, after that the cloak is washed, he
shall tear away that dark place, and so he shall part it
from the whole.)
57 That if fleeing leprosy and unsteadfast appeareth
furthermore in these places, that were unwemmed
before, it oughteth to be burnt in fire; (But if a spreading
leprosy appeareth again in these places, that before were
without blemish, it ought to be burned in the fire;)
58 if it ceaseth, he shall wash the second time those
things that be clean, and they shall be clean. (but if it
ceaseth, he shall wash those things that be clean a
second time, and then they shall be clean.)
59 This is the law of leprosy of a cloth, woollen and
linen, of warp and woof, and of all purtenance of skin,
how it oughteth to be cleansed, either to be defouled.
(This is the law for leprosy in a cloak, woollen or linen,
and of warp and woof, and of all purtenances of skins,
and how they ought to be pronounced clean, or unclean.)

CHAPTER 14

1 And the Lord spake to Moses, and said,
2 This is the custom of a leprous man, when he shall
be cleansed, (*that is, when he shall be pronounced
clean*). He shall be brought to the priest,
3 the which *priest* shall go out of the tents, and when
he shall find that the leprosy is cleansed, (which *priest*
shall take him away from the tents, and examine him,
and if he shall find that the leprosy is healed,)
4 he shall command to the man that is (to be)
cleansed, that he offer for himself two quick sparrows,
which is leaveful to eat, and cedar wood, and vermilion,
that is, a red thread, and hyssop. (he shall command to
the man who is to be pronounced clean, that he offer for
himself two living sparrows, which be lawful to eat, and
cedar wood, and a red thread, and hyssop.)
5 And the priest shall command that one of the
sparrows be offered in an earthen vessel upon quick
waters; (And the priest shall command that one of the
sparrows be offered in an earthen, *or a clay*, vessel filled
with fresh water;)
6 soothly he shall dip the tother *sparrow* quick, with
the cedar wood, and with the red thread, and hyssop, in
the blood of the sparrow (that was) offered, (and then he
shall dip the other living *sparrow*, and the cedar wood,
and the red thread, and the hyssop, in the blood of the
sparrow that was offered,)
7 with which he shall sprinkle seven times him that
shall be cleansed, that he be purged rightfully; and he
shall deliver the quick sparrow, that it fly [away] into the
field. (with which he shall sprinkle seven times him who
shall be pronounced clean, so that by this rite he be
cleansed; and then he shall release the living sparrow, so
that it can fly away into the field.)
8 And when the man hath washed his clothes, he shall
shave all the hairs of his body, and he shall be washed in
water, and he shall be cleansed, and he shall enter into
the tents; so only that he dwell without his tabernacle by
seven days; (And when the man hath washed his clothes,
he shall shave off all the hair of his body, and he shall
wash in water, and so he shall be made clean, and then
he can return to the tents; but he must live outside his
own tent for seven days;)
9 and that in the seventh day (and then on the seventh

day), he (shall) shave (again) the hairs of the head, and his beard, and his brows, and the hairs of all his body. And when his clothes and his body be washed again,
10 in the eighth day he shall take two lambs without wem, and a sheep of one year without wem, and three dimes, *or three tenth parts,* of [tried] *wheat* flour, into sacrifice, which be sprinkled with oil, and (also take) by itself a sextary, *or a pint,* of oil. (on the eighth day he shall take two lambs without blemish, *or without fault,* and a sheep of one year without blemish, *or without fault,* and three tenths of an ephah of fine *wheat* flour for a grain offering, which shall be sprinkled with oil, and also a pint of oil.)
11 And when the priest that purgeth the man, hath set him and all his things before the Lord, in the door of the tabernacle of witnessing (at the entrance to the Tabernacle of the Witnessing),
12 he shall take a lamb, and shall offer it for trespass, and *shall (also) offer* the sextary of oil; and when all things be offered before the Lord, (he shall take the lamb for the trespass offering, and also the pint of oil; and when all these things be presented as a special gift before the Lord,)
13 he shall offer the lamb, where the sacrifice for sin and the burnt sacrifice is wont to be offered, that is, in the holy place; for as for sin, so and for trespass, the offering pertaineth to the priest; it is holy of holy things. (he shall offer the lamb, where the sin offering and the burnt sacrifice be offered, that is, in the holy place; for the trespass offering, like the sin offering, belongeth to the priest; it is a most holy, *or sacred,* thing.)
14 And the priest shall take of the blood of [the] sacrifice which is offered for trespass, and shall put on the last part of the right ear of him which is (to be) cleansed, and on the thumbs of the right hand and foot. (And the priest shall take some of the blood of the trespass offering, and shall put it on the lobe of the right ear of him who is to be pronounced clean, and on the thumb of his right hand, and the great toe of his right foot.)
15 And he shall put (some) of the pint of oil into his (own) left hand,
16 and the priest shall dip his right finger therein, and he shall sprinkle it seven times before the Lord.
17 Soothly he shall pour that that is left of the oil in the left hand, on the last part of the right ear of him which is (to be) cleansed, and on the thumbs of the right hand and foot, and on the blood which is shed for trespass, (And he shall put some of the oil that is still in his left hand, on the lobe of the right ear of him who is to be pronounced clean, and on the thumb of his right hand, and the great toe of his right foot, on top of the blood of the trespass offering,)
18 and (then pour the rest of the oil) on(to) his head.
19 And the priest shall pray for him before the Lord,
and shall make sacrifice for sin (and shall offer the sin offering);
20 then the priest shall offer the burnt sacrifice, and he shall put it in the altar with his flowing sacrifices, and the man shall be cleansed rightfully. (then the priest shall offer the burnt sacrifice, and he shall put it on the altar with the grain offering, and by this rite the man shall be made clean.)
21 That if he is poor, and his hand may not find those things that be said, he shall take for his trespass a lamb to [the] offering, that the priest pray for him, and the tenth part of [tried] *wheat* flour sprinkled (al)together with oil, into sacrifice, and a sextary of oil, (But if he is poor, and his hand cannot find those things that be said above, he shall take a lamb for his trespass offering, as a special gift to the Lord, for the priest who shall pray for him, and the tenth part of an ephah of fine *wheat* flour sprinkled with oil, for the grain offering, and a pint of oil,)
22 and two turtles, either two culver birds, of which one *shall* be for sin, and the tother into burnt sacrifice; (and two turtledoves, or two young pigeons, of which one *shall* be for a sin offering, and the other for a burnt sacrifice;)
23 and he shall offer those in the eighth day of his cleansing to the priest, at the door of the tabernacle of witnessing, before the Lord. (and he shall bring them on the eighth day of his cleansing to the priest, at the entrance to the Tabernacle of the Witnessing, before the Lord.)
24 And the priest shall take the lamb offered for trespass, and the sextary of oil, and shall raise (them up) together; (And the priest shall take the lamb for the trespass offering, and the pint of oil, and shall raise them up as a special gift before the Lord;)
25 and when the lamb is offered, he shall put of the blood thereof on the last part of the right ear of him that is (to be) cleansed, and on the thumbs of his right hand and foot. (and when the lamb is offered, he shall put some of its blood on the lobe of the right ear of him who is to be pronounced clean, and on the thumb of his right hand, and the great toe of his right foot.)
26 Soothly the priest (shall) put the part of (the) oil into his *own* left hand, (Then the priest shall put some of the oil into his *own* left hand,)
27 in which he shall dip the finger of his right hand, and he shall sprinkle it seven times against the Lord (and he shall sprinkle it seven times before the Lord);
28 and the priest shall touch the last part of the right ear of him that is (to be) cleansed, and the thumbs of the right hand and foot, in the place of [the] blood which is shed out for trespass. (and the priest shall put some of the oil on the lobe of the right ear of him who is to be pronounced clean, and on the thumb of his right hand, and the great toe of his right foot, that is, where the blood for the trespass offering was put.)

29 Soothly the priest shall put the tother part of [the]
oil, that is in his left hand, upon the head of the man that
is (to be) cleansed, that he please the Lord for him. (And
the priest shall put the rest of the oil, that is in his left
hand, on the head of the man that is to be pronounced
clean, so that he be made clean before the Lord.)
30 And he shall offer a turtle, or a culver bird, (And he
shall offer a turtledove, or a young pigeon,)
31 one for trespass, and the tother into burnt sacrifice,
with their flowing offerings. (one for a sin offering, and
the other for a burnt sacrifice, with the grain offering.)
32 This is the sacrifice of a leprous man, that may not
have all things into the cleansing of himself. (This is the
law for a leprous man, who may not have all the things
needed for the offering for his cleansing.)
33 And the Lord spake to Moses and Aaron, and said,
34 When ye have entered into the land of Canaan,
which I shall give to you into possession, if the wound of
leprosy is in the houses, (When ye have entered into the
land of Canaan, which I shall give to you for a
possession, if there is a plague of leprosy in a house,)
35 he shall go, whose the house (it) is, and shall tell to
the priest, and shall say, It seemeth to me, that as it were
a wound of leprosy is in mine house. (he shall go, whose
house it is, and shall say to the priest, It seemeth to me,
that a plague of leprosy is in my house.)
36 And the priest shall command, that they bear out of
the house all things, before that he enter into it, that he
may see whether it be leprosy, lest all things that be in
the house be made unclean (And the priest shall
command, that they carry everything out of the house,
before that he enter into it, so that he can see whether
there is leprosy, lest all the things that be in the house
should be pronounced unclean); and the priest shall enter
afterward, that he see the leprosy of the house.
37 And when he seeth in the walls thereof as little
valleys, *or crevices*, defouled with paleness, either with
redness, and lower than the tother higher part, (And
when he seeth little valleys, *or little crevices*, in its walls,
defiled with paleness, or with redness, and lower than
the other higher part,)
38 he shall go out at the door of the house, and anon
he shall close it by seven days. (he shall go out of the
door of the house, and at once he shall close it up for
seven days.)
39 And he shall turn again in the seventh day (And he
shall return on the seventh day), and shall see it; [and] if
he findeth that the leprosy hath increased,
40 he shall command that the stones be cast out, in
which the leprosy is, and that those stones be cast out of
the city into an unclean place. (he shall command that
the stones, on which the leprosy is found, be thrown out,
and that those stones be thrown into an unclean place
outside the city.)
41 Soothly *he shall command* that that house be razed
within by compass, and that the dust of the razing be
sprinkled without the city, in an unclean place,
42 and that other stones be put again for these, that be
taken away, and that the house be daubed with other
mortar.
43 But if after that the stones be taken away, and the
dust is borne out, and [with] other earth (it) is daubed
(and it is daubed with other mortar),
44 the priest entereth, and seeth the leprosy turned
again, and the walls sprinkled with spots, the leprosy is
then steadfastly dwelling, and the house is unclean; (the
priest entereth, and seeth that the leprosy hath returned,
and that the walls be sprinkled with spots, then the
leprosy is steadfastly dwelling, and the house is unclean;)
45 which house they shall destroy anon, and they shall
cast out of the city, into an unclean place, the stones
thereof, and the wood, and all the dust. (which house
they shall destroy at once, and its stones, and its wood,
and all of its dust, they shall throw into an unclean place
outside the city.)
46 He that entereth into the house, when it is shut (up),
shall be unclean till to eventide,
47 and he that sleepeth [in it,] and eateth anything
therein, he shall wash his clothes.
48 That if the priest entereth, and seeth that the leprosy
increased not in the house, after that it was daubed the
second time, the priest shall cleanse it; for health is yielded
[again] *thereto*. (But if the priest entereth, and seeth that
the leprosy hath not grown again, *or not spread*, in the
house, after that it was daubed the second time, the priest
shall pronounce it to be clean; for health hath been
restored to it, *that is, the plague hath been cured*.)
49 And to the cleansing thereof (And for its cleansing),
the priest shall take two sparrows, and cedar wood, and
vermilion, *that is, a red thread*, and hyssop.
50 And when one sparrow is offered in a vessel of
earth, on quick waters, (And when one sparrow is offered
in an earthen, *or a clay*, vessel, filled with fresh water,)
51 the priest shall take the cedar wood, and hyssop,
and the red thread, and the quick sparrow, and he shall
dip, *or wet*, all these things in the blood of the sparrow
offered, *or slain*, and in the quick waters; and he shall
sprinkle the house seven times; (the priest shall take the
cedar wood, and the hyssop, and the red thread, and the
living sparrow, and he shall dip all these things in the
blood of the slain sparrow, and in the fresh water; and he
shall sprinkle the house seven times;)
52 and he shall cleanse it as well in the blood of the
sparrow, as in the living waters, and in the quick
sparrow, and in the cedar wood, and in the hyssop, and
(the) red thread. (and so he shall cleanse the house with
the blood of the sparrow, and the fresh water, and the
living sparrow, and the cedar wood, and the hyssop, and

the red thread.)
53 And when he hath let go the sparrow to fly away
into the field freely, he shall pray for the house, and it
shall be cleansed rightfully. (And when he hath let the
sparrow go, to fly away freely into the field, he shall pray
for the house, and so by this rite it shall be made clean.)
54 This is the law of all leprosy, and of smiting, (This is
the law for all kinds of leprosy, and of scurf, *or of scales*,)
55 [and] of leprosy of clothes, and of houses,
56 [and] of the sign of (a) wound, and of little whelks
breaking out, [and] of spot shining, and in colours
changed into diverse spots, (and of the mark of a sore,
and of little whelks breaking out, and of shining spots,
and of colours changed into diverse spots,)
57 that it may be known, what is clean, or unclean. (so
that it can be pronounced what is clean, and what is
unclean.)

CHAPTER 15

1 And the Lord spake to Moses and Aaron, saying,
2 Speak ye to the sons of Israel, and say ye to them, A
man that suffereth the running out of seed, shall be
unclean; (Say thou to the Israelites, When a man suffereth
the running out of his seed, such an issue shall be
unclean;)
3 and then he shall be deemed to be subject to this
vice, when by all moments foul humour, *either moisture*,
cleaveth to his flesh, and groweth (al)together (or runneth
continually).
4 Each bed in which he sleepeth shall be unclean, and
wherever he sitteth.
5 If any man toucheth his bed, he shall wash his
clothes, and he shall be washed in water, and shall be
unclean till to eventide.
6 If a man sitteth where he sat, also that man shall
wash his clothes (that man shall wash his clothes), and he
shall be washed in water, and shall be unclean till to
eventide.
7 He that toucheth his flesh, shall wash his clothes,
and he shall be washed in water, and shall be unclean till
to eventide.
8 If such a man casteth out spittle upon him that is
clean, he shall wash his clothes, and he shall be washed
in water, and shall be unclean till to eventide.
9 The saddle on which he sitteth, shall be unclean;
and each man that toucheth whatever thing is under him
that suffereth the flowing out of seed, shall be defouled,
(*or unclean*), till to eventide.
10 He that beareth any of these things, shall wash his
clothes, and he shall be washed in water, and shall be
unclean till to eventide.
11 Each man, whom he that is such toucheth with
hands not washed before (Anyone, whom he who
suffereth such a passion, toucheth with his hands that
have not been washed), shall wash his clothes, and he
shall be washed in water, and shall be unclean till to
eventide.
12 An(y) earthen vessel that he toucheth, shall be
broken; but a wooden vessel shall be washed in water.
13 If he that suffereth such a passion, is healed, he shall
number seven days after his cleansing, and when his
clothes and all his body be washed in living waters, he
shall be clean. (When he, who suffereth such a passion,
is healed, he shall count seven days for his cleansing, and
after his clothes and all his body be washed in fresh
water, he shall be made clean.)
14 Forsooth in the eighth day he shall take two turtles,
or two culver birds, and he shall come in the sight of the
Lord at the door of the tabernacle of witnessing, and shall
give those to the priest; (Then on the eighth day, he shall
take two turtledoves, or two young pigeons, and he shall
come before the Lord at the entrance to the Tabernacle of
the Witnessing, and shall give them to the priest;)
15 and the priest shall make, *or offer*, one of them for
the man's sin, and the tother into burnt sacrifice (and the
priest shall offer one for a sin offering, and the other for a
burnt sacrifice); and the priest shall pray for him before
the Lord, that he be cleansed from the flowing out of his
seed.
16 A man from whom the seed of lechery, *either of
fleshly coupling*, goeth out, shall wash in water all his
body (shall wash all his body in water), and he shall be
unclean till to eventide.
17 He shall wash in water the cloak and (the) skin, *or
(the) pilch*, that he hath used, (*or worn*, at) that time, and
it shall be unclean till to eventide.
18 The woman with which he is coupled fleshly (The
woman with whom he is fleshly coupled), shall be
washed in water, and shall be unclean till to eventide.
19 A woman that suffereth the flowing out of blood,
when the month cometh again, *she* shall be separated by
seven days (*she* shall be set apart for seven days); each
man that toucheth her shall be unclean till to eventide,
20 and the place in which she sleepeth either sitteth in
the days of her separating, shall be defouled, (*or unclean*).
21 He that toucheth her bed shall wash his clothes, and
he shall be washed in water, and shall be unclean till to
eventide.
22 Whoever toucheth any vessel, *or thing*, upon which
she sitteth, he shall wash his clothes, and he shall be
washed in water, and shall be unclean till to eventide.
23 (See verse 22 above.)
24 If a man is coupled fleshly with her in the time of
blood that cometh, *or runneth, from her* by (the) months,
he shall be unclean by seven days, and each bed in
which he sleepeth shall be unclean. (If a man is fleshly
coupled with her at the time of blood that runneth *out
from her* by the month, he shall be unclean for seven

days, and each bed in which he sleepeth shall be
unclean.)
25 A woman that suffereth in many days the flowing
out of blood, not in the time of [the] months, either
which woman ceaseth not to flow out blood after the
blood of [the] months, shall be unclean as long as she
shall be subject to this passion, as if she is in the time of
[the] months. (A woman who suffereth for many days the
flowing out of blood, but not at the time of the month, or
which woman ceaseth not to flow out blood after the
blood of the month, shall be unclean for as long as she is
subject to this passion, just as she is at the time of the
month.)
26 Each bed in which she sleepeth, and whatever thing
she sitteth upon, shall be unclean.
27 Whoever toucheth her shall wash his clothes, and
he shall be washed in water, and shall be unclean till to
eventide.
28 If her blood standeth, and ceaseth to flow out, she
shall number seven days of her cleansing, (But when her
blood standeth, and ceaseth to flow out, she shall count
seven days for her cleansing,)
29 and in the eighth day she shall offer for herself to the
priest two turtles, either culver birds, at the door of the
tabernacle of witnessing; (and on the eighth day she shall
bring her offering of two turtledoves, or two young
pigeons, to the priest, at the entrance to the Tabernacle of
the Witnessing;)
30 and the priest shall offer one for her sin, and the
tother into burnt sacrifice (and the priest shall offer one
for a sin offering, and the other for a burnt sacrifice); and
the priest shall pray for her before the Lord, and for the
flowing out of her uncleanness.
31 Therefore ye shall teach the sons of Israel, that they
eschew uncleannesses, and that they die not for their
filths, when they defoul my tabernacle that is among
them. (And so ye shall teach the Israelites, that they must
shun uncleannesses, and not bring in their filths to defile
my Tabernacle that is among them, and so be put to
death because of that.)
32 This is the law of him that suffereth the flowing out
of seed, and (of him) that is defouled with fleshly
coupling, (This is the law for him who suffereth the
flowing out of seed, and for him who is defiled with
fleshly coupling,)
33 and *also of the woman* that is separated in the time
of (the) months, either that floweth out in continual
blood, and of the man that sleepeth with her. (and *also of
the woman* who is set apart at the time of the month, or
who floweth out with continual blood, and of the man
who sleepeth with her.)

CHAPTER 16

1 And the Lord spake to Moses, after the death of the
two sons of Aaron, when they offered alien fire (when
they offered unholy fire), and were slain,
2 and commanded to him and said, Speak thou to
Aaron, thy brother, that he enter not in all time into the
saintuary, which is within the veil before the propitiatory,
with which the ark is covered, that he die not; for I shall
appear in a cloud on God's answering place; (and
commanded to him and said, Tell thou thy brother
Aaron, that he must not enter into the sanctuary, which is
behind the Veil, to go before the propitiatory, *that is, the
mercy seat, or the lid*, which is on the Ark, *that is, the
Box for the tablets of the Law*, except at the appointed
time, so that he not die; for I shall appear there in a cloud
above the propitiatory, *or God's answering place*;)
3 no but he do these things before. He shall offer a
calf for sin, and a ram into burnt sacrifice; (and to enter
only after he hath first done these things. He shall bring a
calf for a sin offering, and a ram for a burnt sacrifice;)
4 he shall be clothed with a linen cloth, [and] he shall
hide his shamefast members with linen breeches; he shall
be girded with a linen girdle, [and] he shall put a linen
mitre on his head; for these clothes be holy, with them all
he shall be clothed, when he is washed. (and he shall be
clothed with a linen cloak, *or with a linen robe*, and he
shall hide his shameful members with linen breeches;
and he shall be girded with a linen sash, and put a linen
turban on his head; for these clothes be holy, and he
shall be clothed with all of them, after that he hath
washed himself.)
5 And he shall take of all the multitude of the sons of
Israel two kids for sin, and one ram into burnt sacrifice;
(And he shall take from all the multitude of the Israelites
two goat kids for a sin offering, and one ram for a burnt
sacrifice;)
6 and when he offereth a calf, and prayeth, for
himself, and for his house, (and after that he offereth the
calf, and prayeth *for cleansing* for himself, and for his
household, *or for his family*,)
7 he shall make (the) two goat bucks to stand before
the Lord, in the door of the tabernacle of witnessing (at
the entrance to the Tabernacle of the Witnessing);
8 and Aaron shall cast lot upon ever either, one lot to
the Lord, and another lot to the goat that shall be sent
out. (and Aaron shall cast lots over the two goats, one lot
for the Lord, and the other lot for the goat that shall be
sent out, *that is, the scapegoat for Azazel*.)
9 Whose lot goeth out to the Lord, he shall offer it for
sin; (Whichever lot goeth out for the Lord, he shall offer
that goat as a sin offering;)
10 soothly whose *lot goeth out* into the goat that shall
be sent out, he shall set him quick before the Lord, that
he send prayers on him, and send him out into
wilderness. (and whichever *lot goeth out* for the goat that
shall be sent out, *that is, the scapegoat for Azazel*, he

shall present him alive before the Lord, and send prayers
upon him, and then send him out into the wilderness, *to
Azazel*.)
11 When these things be done rightfully, he shall offer
the calf, and he shall pray for himself, and for his house,
and shall offer the calf. (When these things be done by
this rite, he shall bring forth the calf, and he shall pray *for
cleansing* for himself, and for his household, *or for his
family*, and then he shall kill the calf for a sin offering.)
12 And when he hath taken a censer, which he hath
[full-]filled of the coals of the altar, and he hath taken in
[his] hand the sweet smelling spicery made into incense,
he shall enter over the veil into the holy things; (And
when he hath taken a censer, which he hath filled full
with coals from the altar, and he hath taken in his hand
the sweet smelling spices made into incense, he shall go
into the Most Holy Place within the Veil;)
13 that when sweet smelling spiceries be put on the
fire, the cloud and vapour of those cover God's
answering place, *that is, the propitiatory*, which is on the
witnessing, *that is, on the ark with the tables of (the) law*,
and he die not. (so that when the sweet smelling spices
be put on the fire, their cloud and vapour cover the
propitiatory, *that is, the mercy seat, or the lid*, which is
on the Ark of the Witnessing, *that is, the Box containing
the tablets of the Law*, and so he shall not die.)
14 Also Aaron shall take of the calf's blood, and he
shall sprinkle seven times with his finger against God's
answering place, eastward. (And Aaron shall take some of
the calf's blood, and he shall sprinkle it with his finger
onto that lid, eastwards, and seven times in front of the
propitiatory, *that is, in front of the mercy seat*.)
15 And when Aaron hath slain the goat buck, *offered*
for [the] sin of the people, he shall bring in the blood
thereof within the veil, as it is commanded of the calf's
blood, that he sprinkle it even against God's answering
place, (And when Aaron hath killed the goat buck,
offered for the people's sin, he shall bring in its blood
within the Veil, as it is commanded of the calf's blood,
and sprinkle it on the propitiatory, and in front of it,)
16 and (so) he shall cleanse the saintuary from [the]
uncleanness of the sons of Israel, and from their
trespassings, and [from] all *their* sins. By this custom he
shall do in the tabernacle of witnessing (And by this
custom he shall do all of this in the Tabernacle of the
Witnessing), which is set among them, in the midst of
[the] filths of the habitation of them.
17 No man be in the tabernacle, when the bishop shall
enter into the saintuary, that he pray for himself, and for
his house, and for all the company of Israel, till he go out
of the tabernacle. (No one should be in the Tabernacle,
when the High Priest shall enter into the sanctuary, so
that he can pray for himself, and for his household, *or for
his family*, and for all the congregation of Israel, and until
that he go out of the Tabernacle.)
18 Soothly when he hath gone out to the altar which is
before the Lord, pray he for himself, and shed he on the
horns thereof, by compass, the blood *that is* taken of the
calf, and of the goat buck; (And when he hath gone out
to the altar which is before the Lord, pray he for himself,
and take he some of the calf's blood, and some of the
goat's blood, and put he it on the horns all around the
altar;)
19 and sprinkle he it seven times with his finger (and
with his finger sprinkle he some of the blood onto the
altar seven times), and (so) cleanse he, and hallow he the
altar from [the] uncleannesses of the sons of Israel.
20 After that he hath cleansed the saintuary, and the
tabernacle, and the altar, then offer he the living goat
buck; (And after that he hath cleansed the sanctuary, and
the Tabernacle, and the altar, then bring he forth the
living goat *for Azazel*;)
21 and when his ever either hand is put upon the head
thereof, acknowledge the priest all the wickednesses of
the sons of Israel, and all their trespasses and sins, which
sins the priest shall wish, *or will*, (on)to the goat('s) head,
and he shall send the goat out into desert by a man made
ready *thereto* (and then he shall send this goat, *that is,
the scapegoat*, out into the desert, *or into the wilderness*,
by a man ordained *for that task*).
22 And when the goat buck hath borne all their
wickednesses into (a) desert land, and he is let go there,
23 Aaron shall turn again into the tabernacle of
witnessing (Aaron shall return to the Tabernacle of the
Witnessing); and when the clothes be put off, in which
he was clothed before, when he entered into the
saintuary of God, and *those clothes* be left there,
24 he shall wash his flesh in the holy place, and he
shall be clothed in his own clothes, and after that he hath
gone out, and hath offered the burnt sacrifice of himself,
and of the people, he shall pray as well for himself, as for
the people; (he shall wash his flesh in a holy place, and
he shall be clothed in his own clothes, and after that he
hath gone out, and hath offered the burnt sacrifice for
himself, and for the people, he shall pray for himself, as
well as for the people;)
25 and he shall burn on the altar the inner fatness
which is offered for sin. (and he shall burn on the altar
the inner fat of the sin offering.)
26 Soothly he that let go the goat buck able to be sent
out, shall wash his clothes and his body with water, and
so he shall enter into the tents. (And he who drove the
scapegoat into the desert, *or into the wilderness, to
Azazel*, shall wash his clothes and his body in water, and
then he shall return to the tents.)
27 Forsooth they shall bear out of the tents the calf and
the goat buck, that were offered for sin, and whose blood
was brought into the saintuary, that the cleansing were

fulfilled; and they shall burn in fire as well the skins, as the flesh, and [the] dung of those *beasts.* (And they shall carry away from the tents the calf and the goat buck, that were the sin offerings, and whose blood was brought into the sanctuary, so that the cleansing is fulfilled; and they shall burn in the fire the skins, and the flesh, and the dung of those *beasts.*)

28 And whoever burneth those, he shall wash his clothes and flesh in water, and so he shall enter into the tents (and then he shall return to the tents).

29 And this shall be to you a lawful thing everlasting; in the seventh month, in the tenth day of the month, ye shall torment your souls, and ye shall not do any work, neither a man born in the land, neither a comeling that is a pilgrim among you. (And this shall be an everlasting law for you; in the seventh month, on the tenth day of the month, ye shall torment your souls, and ye shall not do any work, not someone born in the land, nor a newcomer who is a foreigner, *or a stranger,* among you.)

30 The delivering from sin, and the cleansing of you, shall be in this day (shall be on this day), (and) ye shall be cleansed before the Lord from all your sins;

31 for it is the sabbath of resting, and ye shall torment your souls by everlasting religion. (for it is a sabbath of rest for you, and ye shall torment your souls; this is an everlasting law.)

32 Soothly the priest shall cleanse, the which is anointed, and whose hands be hallowed, that he be set in priesthood for his father; and he shall be clothed in a linen stole, and in holy clothes, (And the priest, who is anointed, and consecrated, so that he can serve in the priesthood for his father, shall perform this rite of cleansing; he shall be clothed in holy linen clothes,)

33 and he shall cleanse the saintuary, and the tabernacle of witnessing (and he shall cleanse the sanctuary, and the Tabernacle of the Witnessing), and the altar, and the priests, and all the people.

34 And this shall be to you a lawful thing everlasting (And this shall be an everlasting law for you), that ye pray for the sons of Israel, and for all their sins, once in the year. Therefore Aaron did, as the Lord commanded to Moses.

CHAPTER 17

1 And the Lord spake to Moses, and said,

2 Speak thou to Aaron, and to his sons, and to all the sons of Israel (and to all the Israelites), and say thou to them, This is the word which the Lord commanded, and said,

3 Each man of the house of Israel shall be guilty of blood, *or (of) great sin,* if he slayeth an ox, or a sheep, either a goat, in the tents, either out of the tents (inside, or outside, the camp),

4 and offereth not an offering to the Lord at the door of the tabernacle of witnessing (and then bringeth it not as an offering to the Lord to the entrance of the Tabernacle of the Witnessing); (it is) as if he shedded (out) *man's* blood, (and) so he shall perish from the midst of his people.

5 Therefore the sons of Israel ought to offer their sacrifices to the priest, which they slay in the field, that those be hallowed to the Lord, before the door of the tabernacle of witnessing, and that they offer those peaceable sacrifices to the Lord. (And so the Israelites ought to bring to the Lord the sacrifices which they kill in the field; they shall bring them to the priest, at the entrance to the Tabernacle of the Witnessing, and offer them as peace offerings to the Lord.)

6 And the priest shall pour out the blood upon the altar of the Lord, at the door of the tabernacle of witnessing; and he shall burn the inner fatness into odour of sweetness to the Lord. (And the priest shall throw the blood against all the sides of the altar of the Lord, at the entrance to the Tabernacle of the Witnessing; and he shall burn the inner fat, to make the sweetest aroma to the Lord.)

7 And they shall no more offer their sacrifices to fiends, with which they did fornication, *that is, idolatry*; it shall be a lawful thing everlasting to them, and to their after-comers (this shall be an everlasting law for them, and for their after-comers).

8 And thou shalt say to them, A man of the house of Israel, and of the comelings that be pilgrims among you, that offereth a burnt sacrifice, either a slain sacrifice, (And thou shalt say to them, Any Israelite, or a newcomer who is a foreigner, *or a stranger,* among you, who offereth a burnt sacrifice, or a slain sacrifice,)

9 and bringeth it not to the door of the tabernacle of witnessing (and bringeth it not to the entrance of the Tabernacle of the Witnessing), that it be offered to the Lord, *he* shall perish from his people.

10 If any man of the sons of Israel, and of the comelings that be pilgrims among you, eateth any blood, I shall set fast my face against his soul, and I shall lose him from his people; (If any Israelite, or a newcomer who is a foreigner, *or a stranger,* among you, eateth any blood, I shall set my face firmly against that person, and I shall cut him off from his people;)

11 for the life of (the) flesh is in the blood, and I gave that *blood* to you, (so) that ye cleanse *therewith* upon mine altar for your souls, and (so) that the blood be *sprinkled* for [the] sin of the soul.

12 Therefore I said to the sons of Israel, Each living man of you shall not eat blood, neither *any* of the comelings that be pilgrims among you. (And so I said to the Israelites, None of you shall ever eat blood, nor shall *any* of the newcomers who be foreigners, *or strangers,* among you.)

13 Whatever man of the sons of Israel, or of the

comelings that be pilgrims with you, taketh a wild beast,
either a bird, which it is leaveful to eat (If any Israelite, or
a newcomer who is a foreigner among you, taketh a wild
beast, or a bird, which it is lawful to eat), whether by
hunting, whether by hawking, pour he out the blood
thereof, and cover it with earth;
14 for the life of [all] flesh is in (the) blood. Wherefore I
said to the sons of Israel, Ye shall not eat the blood of any
flesh, for the life of (all) flesh is in the blood, and
whoever eateth blood, shall perish.
15 A man that eateth a thing dead by itself, either taken
of a beast, as well of men born in the land, as of
comelings, he shall wash his clothes, and himself in
water, and he shall be defouled, (*or unclean,*) till to
eventide; and by this order, he shall be made clean;
(Anyone who eateth a thing that dieth naturally, or is
killed by a beast, of those born in the land, as well as
newcomers, he shall wash his clothes, and himself in
water, and he shall be defiled, *or unclean*, until the
evening; and by this rite, he shall be made clean;)
16 that if he washeth not his clothes, or his body, he
shall bear his wickedness. (but if he washeth not his
clothes, or his body, he shall bear his wickedness.)

CHAPTER 18

1 And the Lord spake to Moses, and said,
2 Speak thou to the sons of Israel, and thou shalt say
to them, I am your Lord God; (Speak thou to the
Israelites, and thou shalt say to them, I am the Lord your
God;)
3 ye shall not do by the custom of the land of Egypt,
in which ye dwelled; ye shall not do by the custom of the
land of Canaan, to which I shall bring you in, neither ye
shall go in the lawful things of them, *that is, in the(ir)
custom of worshipping* (nor shall ye follow their laws, *or
their custom of worshipping*).
4 Ye shall do my dooms, and ye shall keep my
behests, and ye shall go in them; I am your Lord God. (Ye
shall follow my laws, *or my judgements*, and ye shall
obey my commands, and ye shall walk in them; I am the
Lord your God.)
5 Keep ye my laws and dooms, which a man shall do,
and he shall live in those; I am your Lord God. (Obey ye
my laws and judgements, for those who follow them,
shall have life; I am the Lord your God.)
6 A man shall not nigh to a nigh *woman* of his blood,
that he show her filthhood (that he uncover her
nakedness/so that they have intercourse); I am the Lord.
7 Thou shalt not discover the filthhood of thy father,
and the filthhood of thy mother; she is thy mother, thou
shalt not show her filthhood. (Thou shalt not uncover thy
father's nakedness, that is, thy mother's nakedness; for
she is thy mother, and thou shalt not uncover her
nakedness.)
8 Thou shalt not uncover the filthhood of the wife of
thy father, for it is the filthhood of thy father. (Thou shalt
not uncover the nakedness of thy father's wife, for her
nakedness is for thy father alone.)
9 Thou shalt not show the filthhood of thy sister, of
father, either of mother (Thou shalt not uncover thy
sister's nakedness, that is, thy father's daughter, or thy
mother's daughter), which sister is begotten at home, *that
is, in wedlock*, either withoutforth, *that is, out of wedlock*.
10 Thou shalt not show the filthhood of the daughter of
thy son, either of thy niece, *that is, the daughter of thy
daughter*, for it is thy filthhood. (Thou shalt not uncover
the nakedness of thy son's daughter, or thy daughter's
daughter, for it is thy own nakedness, *that is, they be of
thy own flesh*.)
11 Thou shalt not show the filthhood of the daughter of
the wife of thy father, which she childed to thy father,
and she is thy sister. (Thou shalt not uncover the
nakedness of the daughter of thy father's wife, whom she
bare for thy father, for she is thy sister.)
12 Thou shalt not open the filthhood of thy father's
sister, for she is the flesh of thy father. (Thou shalt not
uncover the nakedness of thy father's sister, for she is of
thy father's flesh.)
13 Thou shalt not show the filthhood of the sister of thy
mother, for she is the flesh of thy mother. (Thou shalt not
uncover the nakedness of thy mother's sister, for she is of
thy mother's flesh.)
14 Thou shalt not show the filthhood of the brother of
thy father, neither thou shalt nigh to his wife, that is
joined to thee by affinity. (Thou shalt not uncover the
nakedness of thy father's brother, that is, thou shalt not
come near to his wife, for she is joined to thee by affinity.)
15 Thou shalt not show the filthhood of thy son's wife,
for she is the wife of thy son, neither thou shalt discover
her shame; and no man take his brother's wife. (Thou
shalt not uncover the nakedness of thy son's wife, for she
is thy son's wife, so thou shalt not uncover her nakedness;
and no man shall take his brother's wife *to bed*.)
16 Thou shalt not show the filth(hood) of thy brother's
wife, for it is the filthhood of thy brother. (Thou shalt not
uncover the nakedness of thy brother's wife, for her
nakedness is for thy brother alone.)
17 Thou shalt not show the filth(hood) of a woman, and
of her daughter; thou shalt not take the daughter of her
son, and the daughter of her daughter, that thou show her
shame; they be the flesh of her, and such lechery is
incest, *that is, lechery of them that be kin*. (Thou shalt
not uncover the nakedness of both a woman, and her
daughter; thou shalt not take her son's daughter, or her
daughter's daughter, and uncover their nakedness; for
they be of her flesh, and such lechery is incest, *that is,
lechery of them who be kin*.)
18 Thou shalt not take the sister of thy wife, to (the)

anguish of her, neither thou shalt show the filth(hood) of
her, while thy wife liveth yet. (Thou shalt not take thy
wife's sister *to bed*, and so cause thy wife anguish, nor
shalt thou uncover her sister's nakedness, while thy wife
yet liveth.)
19 Thou shalt not nigh to a woman that suffereth the
running of blood of month, neither thou shalt show her
filthhood. (Thou shalt not come near to a woman who
suffereth the running of the blood of the month, nor shalt
thou uncover her nakedness.)
20 Thou shalt not do lechery with thy neighbour's wife,
neither thou shalt be defouled with mixing [together] of
seed. (Thou shalt not do fleshly coupling with thy
neighbour's wife, and so be defiled with her.)
21 Thou shalt not give of thy seed, that it be offered to
the idol Moloch, neither thou shalt defoul the name of
thy God; I am the Lord. (Thou shalt not give any of thy
children to be offered to the false god Moloch, and so
defile the name of thy God; I am the Lord.)
22 Thou shalt not be meddled, [(or) mingled,] with a
man, by lechery of a woman, for it is abomination. (Thou
shalt not be mixed together with a man, like in fleshly
coupling with a woman, for it is an abomination.)
23 Thou shalt not do lechery with any beast, neither
thou shalt be defouled with it. A woman shall not lie
under a beast, neither shall be meddled, [(or) mingled,]
therewith, *that is, defouled by fleshly knowing thereof,*
for it is great sin. (Thou shalt not do lechery with any
beast, nor shalt thou be defiled with it. A woman shall
not lie under a beast, nor shall be mixed together with it,
that is, be defiled by fleshly knowing of it, for it is a great
sin.)
24 Be ye not defouled in all these things, in which all
folks, *either heathen men,* be defouled, which *folks* I
shall cast out before your sight, (Do not ye be defiled
with any of these things, in which all the nations, *or all
the heathen,* be defiled, which *nations* I shall throw out
before you,)
25 of whom the land is defouled, of which *land* I shall
visit the great sins (of them upon it), that it vomit, *or
throw* out, his dwellers. (by whom the land is defiled, of
which *land* I shall visit their great sins upon it, so that it
vomit, *or throw* out, its inhabitants.)
26 Keep ye my lawful things, and my dooms, that ye do
not any of all these abominations, as well a man born in
the land, as a comeling that is a pilgrim with you. (Obey
ye my laws, and my judgements, so that ye do not do any
of these abominations, yea, anyone born in the land, as
well as a newcomer who is a foreigner, *or a stranger,*
among you.)
27 For the dwellers of the land, that were before you,
did all (of) these abominations, and defouled that land.
28 Therefore beware, lest it cast out vilely you in the
same manner, when ye shall do such sins, as it casted out
vilely the folk, that was before you. (And so beware, lest
when ye shall do such sins, it vilely throw you out, in the
same manner as it hath vilely thrown out the people,
who were before you.)
29 Each man that shall do anything of these
abominations, shall perish from the midst of his people.
30 Keep ye my behests; do not ye do those things,
which they that were before you did, and be ye not
defouled in those; I am your Lord God. (Obey ye my
commands; do not ye do those things, which they who
were before you did, and be ye not defiled with them; I
am the Lord your God.)

CHAPTER 19

1 The Lord spake to Moses, and said,
2 Speak thou to all the company of the sons of Israel,
and thou shalt say to them, Be ye holy, for I am holy,
your Lord. God. (Speak thou to all the congregation of
the Israelites, and thou shalt say to them, Be ye holy, for I
am holy, the Lord your God.)
3 Each man dread his father, and his mother. Keep ye
my sabbaths; I am your Lord God. (Everyone honour his
father, and his mother. Keep ye my sabbaths; I am the
Lord your God.)
4 Do not ye be turned to idols, neither ye shall make
to you molten gods; I am your Lord God. (Do not ye turn
to idols; nor make ye gods out of metal for yourselves; I
am the Lord your God.)
5 If ye offer a sacrifice of peaceable things to the Lord,
that it be quemeful, (If ye offer a peace offering to the
Lord, so that it be acceptable,)
6 ye shall eat it in that day, in which it is offered, and
in the tother day (ye shall eat it on the day, on which it is
offered, and on the next day); soothly whatever thing is
left into the third day, ye shall burn it in (the) fire.
7 If any man eateth thereof after two days, he shall be
unholy, and guilty of unfaithfulness, *either wickedness;*
8 and he shall bear his wickedness, for he defouled
the holy thing of the Lord, and his soul shall perish from
his people.
9 When thou shalt reap the fruits of thy land, thou
shalt not cut till to the ground the corns of the land,
neither thou shalt gather the ears of corn that be left;
(When thou shalt harvest the fruits of thy land, thou shalt
not cut the corners of the land down to the ground, nor
shalt thou gather up all the ears of corn that be left;)
10 neither in thy vineyard thou shalt gather the raisins
and the grains falling down, but thou shalt leave them to
be gathered of poor men and of pilgrims; I am your Lord
God. (nor in thy vineyard shalt thou gather up all the
raisins and the grains that fall down, but thou shalt leave
them to be gathered up by the poor and by foreigners; I
am the Lord your God.)
11 Ye shall not do theft. Ye shall not lie, and no man

(shall) deceive his neighbour.
12 Thou shalt not forswear in my name, neither thou
shalt defoul the name of thy God; I am the Lord.
13 Thou shalt not make false challenge to thy
neighbour, neither thou shalt oppress him by violence.
The hire of thy workman shall not dwell with thee unto
the morrowtide. (Thou shalt not rob thy neighbour, nor
shalt thou oppress him with violence. The wages of thy
workman shall not abide with thee until the next
morning.)
14 Thou shalt not curse a deaf man, neither thou shalt
set an hurting before a blind man; but thou shalt dread
thy Lord God, for I am the Lord. (Thou shalt not curse the
deaf, nor shalt thou put a cause of stumbling in front of
the blind; but thou shalt fear the Lord thy God, for I am
the Lord.)
15 Thou shalt not do that, that is wicked, neither thou
shalt deem unjustly; behold thou not the person of a poor
man, neither honour thou the face of a mighty man;
deem thou justly to thy neighbour (simply judge thy
neighbour justly).
16 Thou shalt not be a slanderer, *that is, a false
accuser*, neither a privy backbiter in the people (nor a
backbiter in private among the people); thou shalt not
stand against the blood of thy neighbour; I am the Lord.
17 Thou shalt not hate thy brother in thine heart, but
reprove thou him openly, lest thou have sin on him.
(Thou shalt not hate thy brother in private, but rather,
reprove thou him openly, lest thou sin because of him.)
18 Thou shalt not seek vengeance, neither thou shalt be
mindful of the wrong of thy citizens (nor shalt thou
remember the wrong-doings of thy fellow citizens); thou
shalt love thy friend as thyself; I am the Lord.
19 Keep ye my laws (Obey ye my laws). Thou shalt not
make thy beasts to engender with the beasts of another
kind. Thou shalt not sow a field with diverse seed. Thou
shalt not be clothed in a cloak which is woven of two
things.
20 If a man sleepeth with a woman by fleshly knowing
of seed, which woman is an handmaid, *or bond*, yea, a
noble *woman of kin*, and nevertheless is not again-
bought by price, neither rewarded with freedom, she
shall be beaten [both shall be scourged], and they shall not
die, for she was not free. (If a man sleepeth with a
woman by fleshly knowing of seed, which woman is a
slave-girl, *or a bondwoman*, and betrothed to another, but
nevertheless not bought back with money, or rewarded
with freedom, she shall be beaten/both of them shall be
scourged, but they shall not die, for she was not free.)
21 Soothly the man for his trespass shall offer a ram to
the Lord, at the door of the tabernacle of witnessing; (And
the man shall bring a ram for a trespass offering to the
Lord, to the entrance of the Tabernacle of the Witnessing;)
22 and the priest shall pray for him, and for his trespass,
before the Lord; and the Lord shall be merciful to him,
and the sin shall be forgiven.
23 When ye have entered into the land *of promise*, and
have planted therein apple trees, ye shall do away the first
fruits; (for three years) the apples which those trees bring
forth shall be unclean to you, neither ye shall eat of them.
24 Forsooth in the fourth year all the fruit of the trees
shall be hallowed and be praiseable to the Lord; (But in
the fourth year, all the fruit of the trees shall be declared
holy, and shall be given as a gift to the Lord;)
25 forsooth in the fifth year ye shall eat the fruits, and
ye shall gather (the) apples, which those trees bring forth;
I am your Lord God (I am the Lord your God).
26 Ye shall not eat flesh with [the] blood. Ye shall not
make vain divining, neither ye shall keep (mind of)
dreams (nor shall ye remember, or think upon, dreams);
27 neither ye shall clip the hair round, neither ye shall
shave the beard; (nor shall ye round off the ends of your
hair, nor shall ye shave off your beard;)
28 and on dead men ye shall not cut your flesh, neither
ye shall make to you any figures, *either marks in your
flesh*; I am the Lord. (and ye shall not cut your flesh in
mourning for the dead, nor shall ye make any tattoos on
yourself, *that is, any marks in your flesh*; I am the Lord.)
29 Set thou not thy daughter to do lechery for hire, and
the land be defouled, and be [full-]filled with sin. (Do not
thou allow thy daughter to go awhoring for hire, so that
the land be defiled, and it be filled full with sin.)
30 Keep ye my sabbaths, and dread ye my saintuary
(and honour my sanctuary); I am the Lord.
31 Bow ye not to astrologers, neither ask ye anything of
false diviners, that ye be defouled by them; I am your
Lord God. (Do not ye turn to astrologers, nor ask ye
anything of those who claim to contact the dead, so that
ye be defiled by them; I am the Lord your God.)
32 Rise thou before an hoar head, and honour thou the
person of an eld man, and dread thou thy Lord God (and
fear thou the Lord thy God); I am the Lord.
33 If a comeling dwelleth in your land, and abideth
among you, despise ye not him, (If a newcomer liveth in
your land, and abideth among you, do not ye despise
him,)
34 but be he among you as a man born in the land; and
ye shall love him as yourself, for also ye were comelings
in the land of Egypt; I am your Lord God. (but let him be
among you like anyone born in the land; and ye shall
love him like yourself, for ye were once newcomers in
Egypt; I am the Lord your God.)
35 Do not ye do any wicked thing in doom, in rule, in
weight, and in measure; (Do not ye do any wicked thing
in judgement, in rule, in weight, or in measure;)
36 the balance be just, and the weights be even, the
bushel be just, and the pint be even; I am your Lord God,
that led you out of the land of Egypt. (let the balances be

true, and the weights be equal, the bushels be true, and
the pints be equal; I am the Lord your God, who led you
out of Egypt.)
37 Keep ye all my behests, and all my dooms, and do
ye them; I am the Lord. (Obey ye all my commands, and
all my laws, *or judgements*, and do ye them; I am the
Lord.)

CHAPTER 20

1 And the Lord spake to Moses, and said,
2 Speak thou these things to the sons of Israel, If any
man of the sons of Israel, and of the comelings that dwell
in Israel, giveth of his seed to the idol Moloch, die he by
death; the people of the land shall stone him. (Say thou
these things to the Israelites, If any Israelite, or a
newcomer who liveth in Israel, giveth his children to the
false god Moloch, he shall be put to death; the people of
the land shall stone him.)
3 And I shall set fast my face against him, and I shall
cut away him from the midst of my people, for he gave of
his seed to Moloch, and defouled my saintuary, and
defouled mine holy name. (And I shall set my face
against him, and I shall cut him off from the midst of my
people, for he gave his children to Moloch, and defiled
my sanctuary, and defiled my holy name.)
4 That if the people of the land is negligent, and little
chargeth (for) my behest, and suffereth the man that gave
of his seed to Moloch, neither will slay him, (But if the
people of the land be negligent, and care little for my
command, and consent to the man who gave his children
to Moloch, and indeed will not kill him,)
5 I shall set my face on that man, and on his kindred,
and I shall cut him down, and all that consented to him,
that they should do fornication, *that is, idolatry*, with
Moloch, from the midst of their people. (I shall set my
face against that man, and against his kindred, and I shall
cut off him, and all who consented to him, yea, they who
would do fornication, *that is, idolatry*, with Moloch, from
the midst of their people.)
6 If a man boweth to astrologers, and to false diviners,
and doeth fornication with them, I shall set my face
against him, and I shall slay him from the midst of his
people (and I shall cut him off from the midst of his
people).
7 Be ye hallowed, and be ye holy, for I am holy, your
Lord God (the Lord your God).
8 Keep ye my behests, and do ye those, for I am the
Lord that halloweth you. (Obey ye my commands, and
do ye them, for I am the Lord who maketh you holy.)
9 Therefore he that curseth his father, either mother,
die he by death; if a man curseth his father and mother,
his blood be on him. (He who curseth his father, or his
mother, shall be put to death; if a man curseth his father,
or his mother, his blood be on him.)
10 If a man doeth lechery with another man's wife, and
doeth adultery with his neighbour's wife, both the
adulterer and the adulteress die they by death. (If a man
doeth lechery with another man's wife, yea, if he doeth
adultery with his neighbour's wife, both the adulterer and
the adulteress shall be put to death.)
11 If a man sleepeth with his step-dame, and showeth
his father's shame, both they die by death; their blood be
on them. (If a man sleepeth with his step-mother, and
uncovereth her nakedness, which is for his father alone,
they both shall be put to death; their blood be on them.)
12 If any man sleepeth with his son's wife, ever either
die, for they have wrought great sin (they both shall be
put to death, for they have done a great sin); their blood
be on them.
13 If a man sleepeth with a man, by lechery of a
woman, ever either hath wrought unleaveful thing, die
they by death; their blood be on them. (If a man sleepeth
with a man, like in fleshly coupling with a woman, they
both have done an unlawful thing, and they both shall be
put to death; their blood be on them.)
14 He that weddeth over his wife her mother, hath
wrought great sin; he shall be burnt quick with them, and
so great unleaveful doing shall not dwell in the midst of
you. (He who taketh both his wife and her mother *to
bed*, hath done a great sin; he shall be burned alive with
them, and so a great unlawful doing shall not remain in
the midst of you.)
15 He that doeth lechery with a great beast, or *with* a
little (beast), die he by death (shall be put to death), also
slay ye the beast.
16 A woman that lieth under any beast, be *she* slain
together with it; their blood be on them.
17 He that taketh his sister, his father's daughter, or his
mother's daughter, and seeth her filth(hood), and she
seeth the shame of her brother, they have wrought an
unleaveful thing, both shall be slain in the sight of their
people; for they showed together their filth(hood), and
they shall bear together their wickedness. (He who taketh
to bed his sister, his father's daughter, or his mother's
daughter, and seeth her nakedness, and she seeth her
brother's nakedness, they both have done an unlawful
thing, and they both shall be cut off in the presence of
their people; for they uncovered their nakedness to each
other, and so they shall bear their wickedness together.)
18 If a man doeth fleshly knowing with a woman in the
flowing of blood of the month, and showeth her
filth(hood), and she openeth the well of her blood, both
they shall be slain from the midst of their people. (If a
man doeth fleshly knowing with a woman during the
flowing out of the blood of the month, and uncovereth
her nakedness, and she openeth the well of her blood to
him, they both shall be cut off from the midst of their
people.)

19 Thou shalt not discover the filth(hood) of thy
mother's sister, and of thy father's sister; he, that doeth
this, shall make naked the shame of his flesh, and both
they shall bear their wickedness. (Thou shalt not uncover
the nakedness of thy mother's sister, or of thy father's
sister; he, who doeth this, shall make naked his own kin's
flesh, and they both shall bear their wickedness.)
20 He that doeth fleshly knowing with the wife of his
father's brother, either of his mother's brother, and
showeth the filth(hood) of his kin, both they shall bear
their sin, [and] they shall die without free children. (He
who doeth fleshly knowing with the wife of his father's
brother, or the wife of his mother's brother, and
uncovereth the nakedness of his kin, they both shall bear
their sin, and they shall die without any children.)
21 He that weddeth his brother's wife, doeth an
unleaveful thing; he showed his brother's filth(hood),
[and] he shall be without free children. (He who weddeth
his brother's wife, doeth an unlawful thing; he uncovered
her nakedness which is for his brother alone, and they
shall die without any children.)
22 Keep ye my laws and my dooms, and do ye those,
lest the land, into which ye shall enter and dwell in, cast
out vilely also you (also vilely throw you out).
23 Do not ye go in the lawful things, *that is, in
worshipping and in the manner of living of them,* of the
nations, which I shall cast out before you, for they did all
these things, and I had abomination of them. (Do not ye
follow the laws, *and the customs,* of the nations which I
shall throw out before you, for they did all these things,
and I found them abominable.)
24 Forsooth I spake to you, Wield ye their land, that I
shall give to you into heritage, that land flowing with
milk and honey; I am your Lord God, that parted you
from other peoples. (But I said to you, Take ye their land,
that I shall give to you for an inheritance, that land
flowing with milk and honey; I am the Lord your God,
who separated you from other peoples.)
25 Therefore also ye part a clean beast from an
unclean, and a clean bird from an unclean, lest ye defoul
your souls in beasts, and in birds, and in all things that be
moved in earth, and which things I showed to you to be
defouled. (And so ye shall separate a clean beast from an
unclean one, and a clean bird from an unclean one, lest
ye defile your souls with beasts, and birds, and with all
the things that move upon the earth, and which things I
showed you to be defiled, *or unclean.*)
26 Ye shall be holy to me, for I the Lord am holy, and I
separated you from other peoples, (so) that ye shall be
mine.
27 A man either a woman, in which is an unclean spirit
[of witchcraft] speaking in the womb, either a spirit of
false divining, die they by death (shall be put to death);
men shall oppress them with stones; their blood be on
them.

CHAPTER 21

1 And the Lord said to Moses, Speak thou to [the]
priests, the sons of Aaron, and thou shalt say to them, A
priest be not defouled in the dead men of his citizens (A
priest shall not be defiled with the dead among his fellow
citizens),
2 no but only in his kinsmen, and nigh of blood, that
is, on father, and mother, and son, and daughter, and
brother, (only with his own relatives, and next of kin, that
is, with his father, and mother, and son, and daughter,
and brother,)
3 and sister, (who is) a virgin, that is not wedded to
man;
4 but neither he shall be defouled in the prince of his
people. (but he shall not be defiled even with the ruler of
his people.)
5 Priests shall not shave their head, neither beard,
neither they shall make (any) carvings in their fleshes;
6 they shall be holy to their God, and they shall not
defoul his name; for they offer incense of the Lord, and
the loaves of their God, and therefore they shall be holy.
(they shall be holy to their God, and they shall not defile
his name; for they offer incense to the Lord, and the
loaves to their God, and so they shall be holy.)
7 A priest shall not wed (for) a wife a corrupt woman,
and a foul whore, neither *he shall wed* her that is
forsaken of the husband, for he is hallowed to his God,
(A priest shall not wed for a wife any corrupt woman, or
a foul whore, nor *shall he wed* she who is forsaken by
her husband, for he is holy to his God,)
8 and offereth the loaves of setting forth; therefore be
he holy, for I am the holy Lord that halloweth you. (and
offereth the loaves of proposition; and so regard him as
holy, for I am holy, the Lord who maketh you holy.)
9 If the daughter of a priest is taken in defouling of
virginity, and defouleth the name of her father, she shall
be burnt in fire. (If a priest's daughter is caught in defiling
her own virginity, and so defileth her father's name, she
shall be burned in the fire.)
10 The bishop, that is the most priest among his
brethren, upon whose head the oil of anointing is
poured, and whose hands be (made) sacred in
priesthood, and he is clothed in holy clothes, shall not
discover his head, he shall not tear his clothes, (The High
Priest, who is the highest priest among his brothers, on
whose head the anointing oil was poured, who is
consecrated in priesthood, and who is clothed in holy
clothes, shall not uncover his head, and he shall not tear
his clothes,)
11 and utterly he shall not enter [in] to any dead man;
and he shall not be defouled on his father, and mother
(yea, he shall not even be defiled for his father, or his

mother),
12 neither he shall go out of [the] holy places, lest he
defoul the saintuary of the Lord, for the oil of holy
anointing of his God is on him; I am the Lord. (nor shall
he go out of the holy place, lest he defile the Lord's
sanctuary, for the holiness of the anointing oil of his God
is upon him; I am the Lord.)
13 He shall wed to wife a virgin; (He shall wed a virgin
for his wife;)
14 he shall not take a widow, and a forsaken woman,
and a foul *woman*, and (a) whore, but a virgin of his
people; (he shall not wed a widow, or a forsaken woman,
or a defiled *woman*, or a whore, but only a virgin out of
his people;)
15 meddle he not the generation of his kin to the
common people of his folk, for I am the Lord, that
halloweth him. (and so he shall not mix together, *or
dishonour*, any of the generation of his kin among the
common people, for I am the Lord, who maketh him holy.)
16 And the Lord spake to Moses, and said,
17 Speak thou to Aaron; a man of thy seed, by families,
that hath a wem, *that is, a notable foulness*, shall not
offer bread to his God, (Say thou to Aaron, A man of thy
seed, among thy families, who hath a blemish, *that is, a
notable foulness*, shall not offer the bread, or the loaves,
to his God,)
18 neither shall nigh to his service; (nor,) if he is blind;
if he is crooked; if he is either of little, either of great, or
wrong nose; (nor shall he come to do his service; nor, as
well, if he is blind, or lame; or too small, or too big;)
19 if he is of broken foot, either hand; (if he hath a
crippled, *or deformed*, hand or foot;)
20 if he hath a botch, *or a bulge, on his back*; either if
he is bleary-eyed; if he hath white colour, *or a pearl*, in
his eye, that hindereth his sight; if he hath (a) continual
scab; if he hath a dry scab in his body (if he hath a dry
scab on his body); either if he be bruised in (the) privy
members.
21 Each man of the seed of Aaron the priest, that hath a
wem (who hath any blemish, *or any fault*), shall not nigh
to offer sacrifices to the Lord, neither *to offer* loaves to his
God;
22 nevertheless he shall (still) eat the loaves that be
offered in the saintuary,
23 so only that he enter not within the veil; he shall not
nigh to the altar, for he hath a wem, and he shall not
defoul my saintuary; I am the Lord, that hallow them. (so
only that he not come within the Veil; he shall not
approach the altar, for he hath a blemish, *or a fault*, and
he shall not defile my sanctuary; I am the Lord who
maketh them holy.)
24 Therefore Moses spake to Aaron, and to his sons,
and to all Israel, all things that were commanded to him.
(And so Moses spoke to Aaron, and to his sons, and to all
the Israelites, all that was commanded to him.)

CHAPTER 22

1 And the Lord spake to Moses, and said,
2 Speak thou to Aaron and to his sons, that they
beware of these things of the sons of Israel, which things
be hallowed, *or offered*; and that they defoul not the
name of the things hallowed to me, which they offer; I
am the Lord. (Say thou to Aaron and to his sons, that they
must treat with respect those things which the Israelites
offer, *or dedicate*, to me, so that they do not defile my
holy name; I am the Lord.)
3 Say thou to them, and to the after-comers of them,
Each man of your kindred, that nigheth to those things
that be hallowed, and which things the sons of Israel
offered to the Lord, in whom is uncleanness, *he* shall
perish before the Lord; I am the Lord. (Say thou to them,
and to their after-comers, Anyone of your kindred, who is
unclean, but still cometh near those things that be
dedicated, yea, which things the Israelites have offered to
the Lord, *he* shall never again be allowed to come before
the Lord; I am the Lord.)
4 A man of the seed of Aaron that is leprous, either
suffereth (the) flowing out of seed, shall not eat of these
things, that be hallowed to me, till he be healed. He that
toucheth an(y) unclean thing on a dead body, and from
whom the seed as of lechery goeth out (or from whom
the seed of lechery goeth out),
5 and that toucheth a creeping beast, and whatever
unclean thing, whose touching is foul, (or who toucheth
a creeping beast, or whatever unclean thing, whose
touching is foul,)
6 he shall be unclean till to eventide, and he shall not
eat these things that be hallowed to me; but when he
hath washed his flesh in water,
7 and the sun hath gone down, then he shall be
cleansed, and shall eat hallowed things, for it is his meat.
(and the sun hath gone down, then he shall be clean, and
he can eat the dedicated things, *or the sacred offerings*,
for this is his food.)
8 He shall not eat a thing dead by itself, and taken of a
beast, neither he shall be defouled in those things; I am
the Lord. (He shall not eat anything that dieth naturally,
or that is killed by a beast, so that he be not defiled with
those things; I am the Lord.)
9 They shall keep my behests, that they be not subject
to sin, and die in the saintuary, when they have defouled
it; I am the Lord that hallow(eth) you. (They shall obey
my commands, so that they be not subject to sin, and
then die in the sanctuary, when they have defiled it; I am
the Lord who maketh you holy.)
10 Each alien shall not eat of things hallowed; the hind
that is a stranger, and the hired man of the priest, shall
not eat of those things. (No one not of the priestly family

shall eat any of the dedicated things; yea, even a visitor to
the priest, or his hired man, shall not eat those things.)
11 Soothly these *servants*, that the priest hath bought,
and he that is a born servant of his house, shall eat of
those things. (But those *slaves*, whom the priest hath
bought, or he who is a slave born in his house, can eat
those things.)
12 If the priest's daughter is wedded to any man of the
people, she shall not eat of these things that be hallowed,
and of the first fruits (or of the first fruits);
13 soothly if she is a widow, either forsaken, and
turneth again without free children to her father's house,
she shall be sustained by the meats of her father, as a
damsel was wont (to be); each alien hath not power to
eat of those things. (but if she is a widow, or forsaken,
and returneth to her father's house without any children,
she shall be sustained by her father's food, as any young
woman is wont to be; but no foreigner, *or stranger*, can
eat those things.)
14 He that eateth by ignorance of hallowed things,
shall add to (it) the fifth part with that that he ate, and he
shall give it to the priest in the saintuary, (He who eateth
any of the dedicated things in ignorance, shall add the
fifth part to what he ate, and he shall give it to the priest
in the sanctuary,)
15 and they shall not defoul the hallowed things of the
sons of Israel, which they offer to the Lord,
16 lest peradventure they suffer the wickedness of their
trespass, when they have eaten the hallowed things; I am
the Lord that hallow them.
17 The Lord spake to Moses, and said,
18 Speak thou to Aaron, and to his sons, and to all the
sons of Israel, and thou shalt say to them, A man of the
house of Israel, and of the comelings that dwell with
them, that offereth his offering to the Lord, and either
payeth avows, either offereth by his free will, whatever
thing he offereth into burnt sacrifice of the Lord
(whatever thing he offereth for a burnt sacrifice to the
Lord),
19 that it be offered by you, it shall be a male without
wem, of oxen, and of sheep, and of goats; (that it be
acceptable, ye shall offer a male without blemish, *or
without fault*, of the oxen, or the sheep, or the goats;)
20 if it hath a wem (but if it hath a blemish, *or a fault*),
ye shall not offer *it*, neither it shall be acceptable.
21 A man that offereth a sacrifice of peaceable things to
the Lord, and either payeth avows, either offereth by free
will, as well of oxen as of sheep, he shall *offer a beast*
without wem, that it be acceptable; no wem shall be
therein. (A man who offereth a peace offering to the Lord,
whether he payeth a vow, or offereth by free will,
whether of oxen or of sheep, he shall *offer a beast*
without blemish, so that it be acceptable; yea, no blemish
shall be upon it.)
22 If it is blind, if it is broken, if it hath a wound or a
scar, if it hath whelks, either (a) scab, either (a) dry scab,
ye shall not offer those *beasts* to the Lord, neither ye shall
burn (any) of those *beasts* upon the altar of the Lord.
23 A man may offer willfully a sheep and an ox (that
hath anything) superfluous and diminished, that is,
having a member superfluous, either failing a member;
but a vow may not be paid of these beasts. (Someone
may make a freewill offering of a sheep or of an ox that
hath something superfluous, or something missing, that
is, that hath an extra member, or is missing a member;
but a vow cannot be satisfied with these beasts.)
24 Ye shall not offer to the Lord any beast, whose privy
members be broken, either bruised, either cut, and taken
away, and utterly ye shall not do these things in your
land (yea, ye shall never offer such a beast in your land).
25 Of the hand of an alien ye shall not offer loaves to
your God, and whatever other thing he will give, for all
(*their*) things be corrupt and defouled; ye shall not
receive those. (Ye shall not offer loaves to your God from
the hand of a foreigner, *or of a stranger*, or any other
thing that he shall give you, for all *their* things be
corrupted and defiled; ye shall not take them.)
26 And the Lord spake to Moses, and said,
27 When an ox, sheep, and goat be brought forth *of the
mother's womb*, in seven days those shall be under the
teat of their mother; soothly in the eighth day, and from
thenceforth, those may be offered to the Lord, (When an
ox, a sheep, or a goat be brought forth *from the mother's
womb*, they shall be under their mother's teat for seven
days; but on the eighth day, and from thenceforth, they
can be offered to the Lord,)
28 whether that is a cow, whether a sheep; those shall
not be offered in one day with their fruits. (but whether it
is a cow, or a sheep, thou shalt not offer them on the
same day with their young.)
29 If ye offer to the Lord a sacrifice for the doing of
thankings, that it may be pleasant [that it may be pleasable],
(If ye offer a sacrifice of a thank offering to the Lord, so
that it shall be acceptable,)
30 ye shall eat it in the same day in which it is offered;
anything *thereof* (ye) shall not leave into the morrowtide
of the tother day; I am the Lord. (ye shall eat it on the same
day in which it is offered; ye shall not leave anything *of it*
into the morning of the next day; I am the Lord.)
31 Keep ye my behests, and do ye those (Obey my
commandments, and do them); I am the Lord.
32 Defoul ye not mine holy name, that I be hallowed in
the midst of the sons of Israel; I am the Lord, that
hallow(eth) you, (Do not ye defile my holy name, I shall
be hallowed in the midst of the Israelites; I am the Lord,
who maketh you holy,)
33 and led you out of the land of Egypt, that I should be
to you into God (so that I could become your God); I am

the Lord.

CHAPTER 23

1 And the Lord spake to Moses and said,
2 Speak thou to the sons of Israel, and thou shalt say
to them, These be the fairs, *that is, holidays/holy days,* of
the Lord, which ye shall call holy. (Speak thou to the
Israelites, and thou shalt say to them, These be the Feasts,
or the Festivals, that is, the Holy Days, to honour the
Lord, which ye shall call holy.)
3 Six days ye shall do work, the seventh day shall be
called holy, for it is the rest of the sabbath; ye shall not
do any work therein (ye shall not do any work on it); it is
the sabbath of the Lord in all your dwelling places.
4 These be the holy fairs, *either solemnities,* of the
Lord, which ye ought to hallow in their times. (These be
the Feasts, *or the Festivals,* to honour the Lord, yea, the
holy gatherings, which ye ought to proclaim at their
proper time.)
5 In the first month, in the fourteenth day of the
month, at eventide, is [the] pask of the Lord; (In the first
month, on the fourteenth day of the month, in the
evening, is the Lord's Passover;)
6 and in the fifteenth day of this month is the
solemnity of therf loaves of the Lord; seven days ye shall
eat therf loaves; (and on the fifteenth day of this month is
the Feast of Unleavened Bread to honour the Lord; for
seven days ye shall eat unleavened bread, *that is, bread
made without yeast;*)
7 the first day shall be most solemn and holy to you;
ye shall not do any servile work therein, (on the first day
there shall be a holy gathering; ye shall not do any daily
work on it,)
8 but ye shall offer sacrifice in fire to the Lord seven
days; soothly the seventh day shall be more solemn and
holier, and ye shall not do any servile work therein. (but
for seven days ye shall offer burnt sacrifices to the Lord;
and on the seventh day there shall be another holy
gathering, and ye shall not do any daily work on it.)
9 And the Lord spake to Moses and said,
10 Speak thou to the sons of Israel, and thou shalt say
to them, When ye have entered into the land which I
shall give to you, and have reaped [the] corn, ye shall
bear handfuls of ears of corn, the first fruits of your ripe
corn, to the priest (ye shall take, *or shall bring in,* some
sheaves, the first fruits of your harvest, to the priest);
11 and the priest shall raise up a bundle before the
Lord, that it be acceptable for you, in the tother day of
the sabbath, *that is, of (the) pask;* and the priest shall
hallow that bundle; (and the priest shall raise up, *or shall
wave,* the sheaf as a special gift before the Lord, so that
you gain acceptance; yea, on the day after the sabbath,
that is, the day after the Passover, the priest shall
dedicate that sheaf;)
12 and the same day, wherein the handful is hallowed,
a lamb of one year without wem shall be slain into burnt
sacrifice of the Lord; (and on the same day in which the
sheaf is dedicated, *or is waved,* a lamb of one year,
without blemish, shall be killed for a burnt sacrifice to the
Lord;)
13 and [the] flowing offerings shall be offered
therewith, two tenth parts of [tried] wheat flour sprinkled
(al)together with oil, into incense of the Lord, and
sweetest odour, and [the] flowing offerings of wine, the
fourth part of hin. (and the grain offering shall be offered
with it, that is, two tenths of an ephah of fine wheat flour
altogether sprinkled with oil, as incense to the Lord, to
make the sweetest aroma, and also the wine offering, the
fourth part of a hin.)
14 Ye shall not eat a loaf, neither cake, nor pottage of
the corn, till to the day in which ye shall offer thereof to
your God; it is a behest everlasting in your generations,
and [in] all your dwelling places (this is an everlasting law
for all your generations, in all your dwelling places).
15 Therefore ye shall number from the tother day of the
sabbath, in which ye offered handfuls of the first fruits,
seven full weeks, (And so ye shall count seven full weeks
from the day after the sabbath, *that is, after the Passover,*
in which ye offered the sheaves as a special gift,)
16 till to the tother day of (the) filling of the seventh
week, that is (in all), fifty days; and so ye shall offer [a]
new sacrifice to the Lord, (until the day after the filling of
the seventh week, that is in all, fifty days; and then ye
shall offer a new grain offering to the Lord,)
17 of all your dwelling places, two loaves of the first
fruits, of two tenth parts of [tried] (*wheat*) flour, dighted
with sourdough, which loaves ye shall bake into the first
fruits to the Lord. (brought from all your dwelling places,
as a special gift, two loaves made out of two tenths of an
ephah of fine *wheat* flour, and baked with yeast, *or with
leaven;* these shall be the first fruits, given to the Lord.)
18 And ye shall offer with the loaves seven lambs of
one year without wem, and one calf of the drove, and
two rams; and these shall be in(to) burnt sacrifice, with
their flowing offerings, into the sweetest odour to the
Lord. (And ye shall offer with the loaves seven lambs of
one year, and one calf from the herd, and two rams, all
without blemish, *or without fault;* and these shall be for a
burnt sacrifice, with the proper grain offering, and the
proper wine offering, to make the sweetest aroma to the
Lord.)
19 Ye shall make also a goat buck for sin, and two
lambs of one year, [the] sacrifices of peaceable things. (Ye
shall also offer a goat buck for a sin offering, and two
lambs of one year for a peace offering.)
20 And when the priest hath raised those (up, *or waved
them*), with the loaves of the first fruits, (as a special gift)
before the Lord, those shall fall into the priest's use (they

shall belong to the priest).
21 And ye shall call this day most solemn, and most
holy; ye shall not do therein any servile work; it shall be
a lawful thing everlasting in all your dwellings, and
generations. (And on this day there shall be a holy
gathering; ye shall not do any daily work on it; this shall
be an everlasting law for all your generations, in all your
dwelling places.)
22 Forsooth after that ye have reaped the corn of your
land, ye shall not cut it till to the ground, neither ye shall
gather the ears of corn that abide, but ye shall leave those
to poor men and pilgrims; I am the Lord your God. (And
when ye harvest your land, ye shall not cut the corners of
the land down to the ground, nor shall ye gather up all
the ears of corn that be left, but ye shall leave them for
the poor and for foreigners; I am the Lord your God.)
23 And the Lord spake to Moses, and said,
24 Speak thou to the sons of Israel, In the seventh
month, in the first day of the month, shall be [a] sabbath,
(a) memorial to you, sounding with trumps, and it shall
be called holy; (Say thou to the Israelites, In the seventh
month, on the first day of the month, shall be a sabbath
day of rest for you, and there shall be a holy gathering,
with the sounding of trumpets;)
25 ye shall not do any servile work therein (ye shall not
do any daily work on it), and ye shall offer (a) burnt
sacrifice to the Lord.
26 And the Lord spake to Moses, and said,
27 In the tenth day of this seventh month, the day of
cleansings shall be most solemn, and it shall be called
holy; and ye shall torment your souls to God, and ye
shall offer burnt sacrifice to the Lord; (And on the tenth
day of this seventh month, shall be the most solemn Day
of Cleansing, *or Day of Atonement*, and there shall be a
holy gathering; and ye shall torment your souls before
God, and ye shall offer a burnt sacrifice to the Lord;)
28 ye shall not do any work in the time of this day, for
it is the day of cleansing, that your Lord God be merciful
to you. (ye shall not do any work on this day, for it is the
Day of Cleansing, *that is, the Day of Atonement*, so that
the Lord your God shall be merciful to you.)
29 Each man which is not tormented in this day, shall
perish from his peoples, (Anyone who shall not torment
himself on this day, shall be cut off from among his
people,)
30 and I shall do away from his people that man that
doeth anything of work *in that day*; (and I shall do away
from his people anyone who doeth any work *on that day*;)
31 therefore ye shall not do anything of work in that
day; it shall be a lawful thing everlasting to you in all
your generations and dwellings; (and so ye shall not do
any work on that day; this shall be an everlasting law for
you for all your generations, in all your dwelling places;)
32 it is the sabbath of resting. Ye shall *therein* torment
your souls from the ninth day of the month; from the
eventide till to (the next) eventide ye shall hallow your
sabbaths. (it is the sabbath day of rest, *and on it* ye shall
torment your souls; yea, on the ninth day of the month,
from the evening until the next evening, ye shall keep
your sabbath holy, *that is, keep this sacred day of rest.*)
33 And the Lord spake to Moses, and said,
34 Speak thou to the sons of Israel, From the fifteenth
day of this seventh month shall be the fairs of
tabernacles, in seven days to the Lord; (Say thou to the
Israelites, From the fifteenth day of this seventh month,
and for seven days, shall be the Feast of Tabernacles[1], to
honour the Lord;)
35 the first day shall be called most solemn and most
holy, ye shall not do any servile work therein; (on the first
day there shall be a holy gathering, ye shall not do any
daily work on it;)
36 and seven days ye shall offer burnt sacrifices to the
Lord, and the eighth day shall be most solemn and most
holy; and ye shall offer burnt sacrifice to the Lord, for it is
the *day* of company, and of gathering; ye shall not do any
servile work therein. (and for seven days ye shall offer
burnt sacrifices to the Lord, and then on the eighth day
there shall be another holy gathering; and on it ye shall
offer a burnt sacrifice to the Lord, for it is the *day* of
congregation, yea, of gathering together; ye shall not do
any daily work on it.)
37 These be the fairs of the Lord, which ye shall call
most solemn and most holy; and in them ye shall offer
offerings to the Lord, burnt sacrifices, and flowing
offerings, by the custom of each day, (These be the
Feasts, *or the Festivals*, to honour the Lord, which shall
be holy gatherings for you; and at them ye shall offer
burnt sacrifices to the Lord, and peace offerings, and
grain offerings, and sacrifices, and wine offerings, by the
custom of each day,)
38 besides the sabbaths of the Lord, and your gifts, and
that that ye offer by avows, either that that ye give by free
will to the Lord. (besides the Lord's sabbaths, and your
gifts, and what ye offer by vows, and those free will
offerings that ye give to the Lord.)
39 Therefore from the fifteenth day of the seventh
month, when ye have gathered all the fruits of your land,
ye shall hallow the fairs of the Lord seven days; in the
first day and the eighth day shall be (a) sabbath, *that is,
rest.* (And so from the fifteenth day of the seventh month,
when ye have gathered in all the fruits of your land, and
for seven days, ye shall keep this Feast to honour the
Lord; on the first day, and on the eighth day, shall be a
sabbath, *that is, a day of rest.*)
40 And ye shall take to you in the first day fruits of the

[1] Also known as the Feast, *or Festival*, of Booths, or of Shelters, or of Ingathering.

fairest tree(s), and [the] branches of palm trees, and the
branches of a thick-boughed tree, and sallows of the
running stream, and ye shall be glad before your Lord
God; (And on the first day ye shall take the fruits of the
fairest trees, and the branches of palm trees, and the
branches of thick-boughed trees, and of willows from the
banks of the streams, and ye shall rejoice before the Lord
your God;)
41 and ye shall hallow his solemnity seven days in the
year; it shall be a lawful thing everlasting in your
generations. In the seventh month ye shall hallow the
feast days, (and ye shall dedicate this Feast to honour the
Lord for seven days each year; this shall be an everlasting
law for all your generations. In the seventh month ye
shall dedicate these feast days,)
42 and ye shall dwell in shadowing places seven days;
each man that is of the kin of Israel, shall dwell in (these)
tabernacles, (and ye shall live in tents, or booths, or
shelters, for seven days; everyone who is of the kin of
Israel, shall live in these simple shelters,)
43 that your after-comers learn, that I made the sons of
Israel to dwell in tabernacles, when I led them out of the
land of Egypt; I am your Lord God. (so that your after-
comers learn, that I made the Israelites to live in simple
shelters, when I led them out of the land of Egypt; I am
the Lord your God.)
44 And Moses spake of the solemnities of the Lord to
the sons of Israel. (And so Moses spoke to the Israelites
about the Feasts, *or the Festivals*, to honour the Lord.)

CHAPTER 24

1 And the Lord spake to Moses, and said,
2 Command thou to the sons of Israel, that they bring
to thee oil of olives, most pure oil, and bright, to the
lanterns to be ordained continually, (Command thou to
the Israelites, that they bring thee olive oil, yea, most
pure and bright oil, for the lanterns to be continually
ordained, *or fueled*,)
3 without the veil of (the) witnessing, in the tabernacle
of [the] bond of peace; and Aaron shall array those
lanterns from eventide till to eventide before the Lord, by
religion and custom everlasting in your generations;
(which be outside the Veil of the Witnessing, in the
Tabernacle of the Witnessing; and Aaron *and his
descendants* shall array those lanterns from evening until
morning before the Lord, by an everlasting law and
custom, for all your generations;)
4 those lanterns shall be set ever[more] upon a
cleanest candlestick in the sight of the Lord. (these
lanterns shall be set forevermore on the lamp-stand of
pure gold before the Lord.)
5 Also thou shalt take [tried] wheat flour (And thou
shalt take fine wheat flour), and thou shalt bake thereof
twelve loaves, which shall have each by themselves two
tenth parts (of an ephah),
6 of which thou shalt set six on ever either side, on a
full clean board before the Lord; (of which thou shalt put
six in a row, on both sides of the clean table, before the
Lord;)
7 and thou shalt set clearest incense upon those
loaves, that the loaves be into mind of [the] offering of
the Lord; (and thou shalt sprinkle pure frankincense on
those loaves, as a token of the bread offered to the Lord
as a food offering;)
8 by each sabbath those shall be changed before the
Lord, and shall be taken of the sons of Israel by
everlasting bond of peace; (on each sabbath they shall be
changed before the Lord, and shall be received from the
Israelites, by an everlasting covenant;)
9 and they shall be Aaron's and his sons', that they eat
those (things) in the holy place, for it is (the most) holy of
holy things, of the sacrifices of the Lord, by (an)
everlasting law.
10 Lo! forsooth the son of a woman of Israel, whom she
childed of an Egyptian, went out among the sons of
Israel, and he chided in the tents with a man of Israel,
(Lo! the son of an Israelite woman, whom she bare by an
Egyptian man, went out among the Israelites, and he
quarreled in the tents, *or in the camp*, with an Israelite,)
11 and when he had blasphemed the name of the Lord,
and had cursed the Lord, he was brought to Moses;
soothly his mother was called Shelomith, the daughter of
Dibri, of the lineage of Dan (of the tribe of Dan);
12 and they sent him into prison, till they knew what
the Lord commanded.
13 And the Lord spake to Moses, and said,
14 Lead out the blasphemer without the tents, and all
men that heard *him*, set they their hands upon his head,
and all the people stone him. (Lead out the blasphemer
away from the tents, and all those who heard *him*, put
they their hands upon his head, and let all the people
stone him.)
15 And thou shalt speak to the sons of Israel, (and say,)
A man that curseth his God, shall bear his sin,
16 and he that blasphemeth the name of the Lord, die
he by death; all the multitude of the people shall oppress
him with stones; whether he that blasphemed the name
of the Lord is a citizen, or a pilgrim, die he by death. (and
he who blasphemeth the Lord's name, shall be put to
death; all the multitude of the people shall stone him;
yea, whether he who blasphemed the Lord's name is a
citizen, or a foreigner, he shall be put to death.)
17 He that smiteth and slayeth a man, die he by death;
(He who striketh and killeth a man, shall be put to death;)
18 he that smiteth a beast, yield one in his stead, that is,
life for life.
19 If a man giveth a wem to any of his citizens (If a man
giveth a wound, *or an injury*, to any of his fellow citizens),

as he did, so be it done to him;
20 he shall restore breaking for breaking, eye for eye,
tooth for tooth; what manner wem he gave, he shall be
compelled to suffer such a wem (what manner wound, *or
injury*, he gave, he shall be compelled to suffer such a
wound, *or injury*).
21 He that smiteth a work beast, yield he another; he
that smiteth a man, shall die. (He who striketh down a
work beast, give he another in its place; he who striketh
down a man, shall be put to death.)
22 Even doom be among you, whether a pilgrim either
a citizen sinneth, for I am your Lord God. (Let equal
justice be among you, whether a foreigner or a fellow
citizen sinneth, for I am the Lord your God.)
23 And Moses spake to the sons of Israel, and they
brought forth out of the tents him that blasphemed, and
oppressed him with stones. And the sons of Israel did, as
the Lord commanded to Moses. (And Moses spoke to the
Israelites, and they brought out him who blasphemed
away from the tents, and stoned him. And so the
Israelites did, as the Lord commanded to Moses.)

CHAPTER 25

1 And the Lord spake to Moses in the hill of Sinai, and
said (And the Lord spoke to Moses on Mount Sinai, and
said,)
2 Speak thou to the sons of Israel, and thou shalt say
to them, When ye have entered into the land which I
shall give to you, the earth keep the sabbath of the Lord
(the land shall keep sabbaths to the Lord);
3 six years thou shalt sow thy field, and six years thou
shalt cut thy vineyard, and thou shalt gather the fruits
thereof;
4 forsooth in the seventh year shall be the sabbath of
the earth, of [the] resting of the Lord (but the seventh year
shall be a sabbath of rest for the land, yea, a sabbath to
the Lord); thou shalt not sow the field, and thou shalt not
cut the vineyard,
5 thou shalt not reap those things which the earth
bringeth forth freely, and thou shalt not gather the grapes
of thy first fruits, as vintage; for it is the year of resting of
the land; (thou shalt not harvest those things which the
land bringeth forth freely, and thou shalt not gather the
grapes of thy first fruits, as vintage; for it is a year of rest
for the land;)
6 but those *fruits* shall be to you into meat, to thee,
and to thy servant, and to thine handmaid, and to thine
hired man, and to the comeling that is a pilgrim with
thee; (but those *fruits* shall be food for you, yea, for thee,
and for thy slave, and for thy slave-girl, and for thy hired
man, and for the newcomer who is a foreigner, *or a
stranger*, among thee;)
7 all things that come forth, shall give meat to thy
work beasts, and [thy] small beasts. (all things that come
forth, shall be food for thy work beasts, and thy small
beasts.)
8 Also thou shalt number to thee seven weeks of years
(And thou shalt count seven sabbaths of years to thee),
that is, seven times seven, which (al)together make nine
and forty years;
9 and thou shalt sound with a clarion in the seventh
month, in the tenth day of the month, in the time of
propitiation, *that is, (in the time of) mercy*, in all your
land. (and thou shalt sound with a trumpet in the seventh
month, on the tenth day of the month, that is, on the Day
of Cleansing, *or the Day of Atonement*, in all your land.)
10 And thou shalt hallow the fiftieth year, and thou
shalt call it remission, *or forgiveness*, to all the dwellers
of thy land; for *that* year is [the] jubilee, *that is, the joyful
year*; a man shall turn again to his possession, and each
man shall go again to his first family, (And thou shalt
hallow the fiftieth year, and thou shalt proclaim
remission, *or forgiveness*, for all the inhabitants of thy
land; for *that* is the Jubilee Year, *that is, the Year of
Restoration*; a man shall return to his possession, and
each man shall go back to his first family,)
11 for it is the jubilee, and the fiftieth year (for the
fiftieth year is the Jubilee Year). Ye shall not sow, neither
ye shall reap *those* things, that come forth freely in the
field, and ye shall not gather (in) the first fruits of [the]
vintage,
12 for (it is) the hallowing of [the] jubilee; but anon ye
shall eat things taken away; (for it is the Jubilee, and it
shall be holy to you; ye shall only eat things taken from
off the land;)
13 in the year of jubilee, all men go again to their
possessions. (and in the Jubilee Year, everyone shall
return to their possessions.)
14 When thou shalt sell anything to thy citizen(ry),
either shalt buy of him, make thou not sorry, (*or heavy*,)
thy brother, (When thou shalt sell anything to a fellow
citizen, or thou shalt buy anything from him, do not thou
oppress one another,)
15 but by the number of the years of [the] jubilee thou
shalt buy of him (but by the number of the years since the
Jubilee, thou shalt buy from him), and by the reckoning
of fruits, (*or by the annual harvests*,) he shall sell to thee.
16 (That is,) By as much as more years dwell after the
jubilee, by so much also the price shall increase, and by
as much as thou numberest less of time, by so much and
the buying shall cost less (by so much the buying, *or the
purchasing*, shall cost less); for he shall sell to thee the
time of (the) fruits.
17 Do not ye torment men of your lineages, but each
man dread his God; for I am your Lord God. (Do not ye
torment anyone in your tribes, but each person fear his
God; for I am the Lord your God.)
18 Do ye my behests, and keep ye my dooms, and

fulfill ye those, that ye may dwell in (t)his land without
any dread, (Do ye my commands, and obey ye my
judgements, and fulfill ye them, so that ye shall live in
this land without any fear,)
19 and that the earth bring forth his fruits to you (and so
that the land shall bring forth its harvest for you), which
ye shall eat till to fullness, and dread not the assailing of
any man.
20 That if ye say (And if ye say to me), What shall we
eat in the seventh year, if we sow not, neither gather (in)
our fruits?
21 (For an answer,) I shall give my blessing to you in
the sixth year, and it shall make [the] fruits of three years;
22 and ye shall sow in the eighth year, and ye shall eat
eld fruits till to the ninth year; (yea,) till new things come
forth, ye shall eat the eld things.
23 Also the land shall not be sold into without end, for
it is mine, and ye be my comelings, and [my] tenants;
24 wherefore all the country of your possession shall be
sold under the condition of again-buying. (and so all the
land of your possession shall be sold under the condition
of being able to buy it back.)
25 If thy brother is made poor, and selleth his little
possession, and his nigh kinsmen will, he may again-buy
that that he sold (he can buy back what he hath sold);
26 soothly if he hath no nigh kinsman, and he may find
[the] price to again-buy, (and if he hath no one near of
kin, but he findeth the money to buy it back,)
27 the fruits shall be reckoned from that time in which
he sold *it*, and he shall yield that that is left to the buyer,
and he shall receive so his possession *again* (and so he
shall receive his possession *back again*).
28 That if his hand findeth not, that he yield the price,
the buyer shall have that that he bought, till to the year of
jubilee; for in that year each selling shall go again to the
lord, and to the first wielder. (But if his hand findeth not,
so that he can pay the price, the buyer shall have what he
bought, until the Jubilee Year; then in that year each
parcel of land which hath been purchased, shall return to
its original owner.)
29 He that selleth his house, within the walls of a city,
shall have license to again-buy (it), till one year be [full-
]filled; (He who selleth his house, within the walls of a
city, shall have license to buy it back, until one year is
fulfilled;)
30 if he again-buyeth (it) not, and the circle of the year
is passed, the buyer shall wield it, and his heirs into
without end, and it shall not be able to be again-bought,
yea, in the jubilee. (but if he buyeth it not back, and the
circle of the year is passed, the buyer, and his heirs, shall
own it forever, and it shall not be able to be bought back,
yea, even in the Jubilee Year.)
31 Forsooth if the house is in a town that hath not
walls, it shall be sold by the law of [the] fields; soothly if
it is not again-bought in the jubilee, it shall turn again to
the lord *thereof* (and even if it is not bought back, in the
Jubilee Year it shall return to *its* original owner).
32 The houses of [the] deacons, that be in [the] cities,
may ever[more] be again-bought; (But the houses of the
Levites, that be in the cities, can be bought back
forevermore;)
33 if those be not again-bought, those shall turn again
in the jubilee to the lords (*thereof*); for the houses of the
cities of deacons be for (their) possessions (forevermore)
among the sons of Israel; (and even if they be not bought
back, they shall still return to their original owners in the
Jubilee Year; for the houses in the Levite cities shall be
their possessions among the Israelites forevermore;)
34 forsooth the suburbs of them shall not be sold, for it
is (their) everlasting possession.
35 If thy brother is made poor, and feeble in power,
and thou receivest him as a comeling, and a pilgrim (and
thou receivest him like a newcomer, or like a foreigner),
and he liveth with thee,
36 take thou not usuries of him, neither more than thou
hast given; dread thou thy God, that thy brother may live
with thee. (receive thou not usury, *or interest*, from him,
nor any more than thou hast given to him; fear thou thy
God, and let thy brother live with thee.)
37 Thou shalt not give to him thy money (in)to usury
(Thou shalt not charge him interest for thy money), and
thou shalt not ask over *that that thou lendest*, (for)
increases of (thy) fruits;
38 I am your Lord God, that led you out of the land of
Egypt, that I should give to you the land of Canaan, and
that I should be your God. (I am the Lord your God, who
led you out of the land of Egypt, so that I could give you
the land of Canaan, and so that I would become your
God.)
39 If thy brother compelled by poverty selleth himself
to thee, thou shalt not oppress him by servage of servants
(thou shalt not make him thy slave),
40 but he shall be as an hired man and (as) a tenant; till
to the year of jubilee he shall work with thee (he shall
work for thee until the Jubilee Year),
41 and afterward he shall go out with his free children,
and he shall turn again to his kindred, and to the
possession of his fathers. (and then he shall go out free
with his children, and he shall return to his family, and to
his inheritance from his fathers.)
42 For they be my servants, and I led them out of the
land of Egypt; they shall not be sold by the condition of
servants; (For they be my slaves, and I led them out of
Egypt; and they shall not be sold into *human* slavery;)
43 torment thou not them by thy power, but dread thou
thy Lord. (so do not thou torment him with thy power,
but rather, fear thou thy God.)
44 A servant and (a) handmaid be to you of [the]

nations that be in your compass, and of [the] comelings
the which be pilgrims with you, (For your slaves and your
slave-girls, buy thou them from the nations that be all
around you, and from the newcomers who be foreigners,
or strangers, among you,)
45 either they that be born of *comelings* in your land;
ye shall have these (as) servants, and by right of heritage
ye shall leave them to your after-comers, and ye shall
wield *them* without end; (or they who be born to
newcomers in your land; ye shall have them as your
slaves, and by right of inheritance ye shall leave them to
your after-comers, and so ye shall own *them* forever;)
46 soothly oppress ye not by power your brethren, the
sons of Israel. (but with your power, do not ye oppress
your own brothers, the Israelites.)
47 If the hand of a comeling or of a pilgrim waxeth
strong at you, and thy brother is made poor, and selleth
himself to *that comeling*, either to any of his kin, (And if
a newcomer, or a foreigner who liveth with you, groweth
rich, and thy brother is made poor, and selleth himself to
that newcomer, or to any of his kin,)
48 he may be again-bought after the selling; he that will
of his brethren, again-buy him; (he can be bought back
after that he is sold; yea, he of his brothers who will do
so, should buy him back;)
49 both his father's brother, and the son of his father's
brother, and *his* kinsman, and his ally. Else if also he
shall be able, he shall again-buy himself, (or his father's
brother, or the son of his father's brother, or *another of
his* kin, *should buy him back*. Or if he is able, he should
buy himself back,)
50 while the years be reckoned only from the time of
his (original) selling till into the year of jubilee; and while
the money, for which he was sold, is reckoned by the
number of years, and while the hire of an hired man is
reckoned. (while the years be reckoned from the time
when he first sold himself until the Jubilee Year; and
while the price, for which he can be bought back, be
reckoned by the wages for a hired man.)
51 If more years be that dwell till to the jubilee, by
these years he shall yield also the price; (If there be more
years that remain until the Jubilee Year, he shall pay the
value of those years;)
52 if few years be (and even if there be only a few years
left), he shall (still) set reckoning with him by the number
of the(se) years; and (so) he shall yield (money) to the
buyer (for) that that is left of [the] years,
53 while those years, in which he served before, be
reckoned for hires; (and) *a stranger* shall not torment *an
home-born man* violently in thy sight. (while those years,
in which he served before, shall be reckoned as for a
hired man; never let *a foreigner, or a stranger*, violently
torment *a man born in the land* before thee.)
54 That if he may not be again-bought by this *manner*,
he shall go out with his free children in the year of
jubilee; (And even if he is not bought back in this
manner, he shall still go out free with his children in the
Jubilee Year;)
55 for the sons of Israel be my servants, which I led out
of the land of Egypt. I am your Lord God; (for the
Israelites be my slaves, whom I led out of Egypt. I am the
Lord your God;)

CHAPTER 26

1 ye shall not make to you an idol, and a graven
image (nor a *carved* image), neither ye shall raise up
titles, *that is, altars for idolatry*, neither ye shall set (up) a
noble stone in your land, that ye worship it; for I am your
Lord God.
2 Keep ye my sabbaths, and dread ye at my saintuary
(and honour my sanctuary); I am the Lord.
3 If ye go in my behests, and keep my
commandments, and do those,
4 I shall give to you rain in their times, and the earth
shall bring forth his fruit, and [the] trees shall be filled
with apples; (I shall give you rain at the proper time, and
the land shall bring forth its harvest, and the trees shall be
filled with fruit;)
5 the threshing of ripe corns shall take (you until) the
vintage, and the vintage shall occupy (you until) the seed
time, and ye shall eat your bread in fullness, and ye shall
dwell in your land without dread (and ye shall live in
your land without any fear).
6 I shall give peace in your coasts; ye shall sleep, and
none shall be that shall make you afeared; I shall do
away evil beasts from you, and a sword shall not pass by
your terms.
7 Ye shall pursue your enemies, and they shall fall
before you;
8 five of your men shall pursue an hundred aliens, and
an hundred of you *shall pursue* ten thousand; your
enemies shall fall by sword in your sight (your enemies
shall fall by the sword before you).
9 I shall behold you, and I shall make *you* to increase;
ye shall be multiplied; and I shall make steadfast my
covenant with you;
10 ye shall eat the eldest of (the) eld things, and (then)
ye shall cast away the eld things, when [the] new things
shall come above (when the new things shall come forth);
11 I shall set my tabernacle in the midst of you, and my
soul shall not cast you away;
12 I shall go among you, and I shall be your God, and
ye shall be a people to me (and ye shall be my people).
13 I am your Lord God, that led you out of the land of
Egyptians, that ye should not serve them (any more), and
I have broken the chains off your nolls, that ye should go
upright. (I am the Lord your God, who led you out of the
land of the Egyptians, so that ye would no longer serve

them, and I have broken the chains from off your necks,
so that ye could walk upright.)
14 That if ye hear not me, neither do all my behests,
(But if ye will not listen to me, nor do all my commands,)
15 and if ye forsake my laws, and despise my dooms,
that ye do not those things that be ordained of me, and
that ye bring follily my covenant to nought, (and if ye
forsake my laws, and despise my judgements, so that ye
do not do those things that be ordained by me, but ye
foolishly break my covenant,)
16 also I shall do these things to you; I shall visit you
swiftly in neediness, and in burning, which shall torment
your eyes, and waste your lives; in vain ye shall sow
seed, that shall be devoured of enemies; (then I shall do
these things to you; I shall swiftly visit you with want, *or
with need*, and with burning, which shall torment your
eyes, and shall waste your lives; ye shall sow your seed
in vain, for it shall be devoured by your enemies;)
17 I shall set my face against you, and ye shall fall
before your enemies, and ye shall be subjects to them
that hate you (and ye shall be made subject to them who
hate you); (and) ye shall flee, while no man pursueth you.
18 But if neither so ye obey to me (And if ye shall still
not obey me), I shall increase your chastising sevenfold
for your sins;
19 and I shall all-break the pride of your hardness, and I
shall give to you heaven above as iron, and the earth as
brass; (and I shall break in pieces all of your hard-headed
pride; and I shall make the heavens above you like iron,
and the earth beneath you like bronze;)
20 your travail shall be wasted in vain, neither the earth
shall bring forth fruit, neither [the] trees shall give apples.
(all your labour shall be in vain, the land shall not bring
forth any harvest, nor shall the trees give forth any fruit.)
21 If ye go contrary to me, neither will hear me (and
will not listen to me), I shall increase your wounds, *either
vengeances*, till into sevenfold for your sins;
22 I shall send out into you *cruel* beasts of the field (I
shall send *cruel* wild beasts among you), that shall waste
you, and your beasts, and shall bring all things to
fewness, and your (by)ways shall be forsaken.
23 That if neither so ye will receive doctrine, *either
chastising*, but go contrary to me, (And if ye will still not
receive chastising, *or discipline*, but continue to go
contrary to me,)
24 also I shall go adversary against you, and I shall
smite you seven times for your sins; (then I shall also be
your adversary/then I shall also go contrary to you, and I
shall strike you seven times for your sins;)
25 and I shall bring in on you the sword, venger of my
bond of peace (the avenger of my covenant); and when
ye flee into [your] cities, I shall send pestilence in[to] the
midst of you, and ye shall be betaken in(to) the hands of
[your] enemies,
26 after that I have broken the staff of your bread, so
that ten women shall bake their loaves in one oven, and
(they shall) yield, *or deliver*, those loaves at weight; and
ye shall eat (them), and (yet) ye shall not be fulfilled.
27 But if neither by these things ye will hear me, but go
against me, (And if, in spite of all these things, ye still will
not listen to me, but continue to go against me,)
28 and I shall go against you in contrary strong
vengeance, and I shall chastise you by seven vengeances
for your sins, (then I also shall be contrary, and go against
you with strong vengeance, and I shall chastise you seven
times for your sins,)
29 so that ye (shall) eat the flesh of your sons, and of
your daughters;
30 I shall destroy your high things, and I shall break
your simulacra (I shall destroy your high places, *or your
hill shrines*, and I shall break your idols); ye shall fall
betwixt the fallings of your idols, and my soul shall have
you abominable,
31 in so much that I shall turn your cities into
wilderness, and make your saintuaries forsaken, neither I
shall receive more the sweetest odour; (in so much that I
shall turn your cities into wilderness, and make your
sanctuaries forsaken, nor shall I receive from you any
more the sweetest aroma;)
32 and I shall destroy your land, and your enemies
shall be astonished thereon, when they shall be dwellers
thereof; (and I shall destroy your land, and your enemies,
when they become its inhabitants, shall be astonished *at
what hath happened there*;)
33 forsooth I shall scatter you into folks, *or into heathen
men*, and I shall draw out of the sheath the sword after
you (yea, I shall scatter you among the heathen, and I
shall draw the sword out of its sheath, and come after
you), and your land shall be forsaken, and your cities
shall be cast down.
34 Then his sabbaths shall please the earth, in all the
days of his wilderness; when ye be in the land of (your)
enemies, it shall keep sabbath, (Then the land shall enjoy
its sabbaths, in all the days of its wilderness; while ye be
in the land of your enemies, it shall keep the sabbaths,
that is, the land shall take rest,)
35 and it shall rest in the sabbaths of his wilderness, for
it rested not in your sabbaths, when ye dwelled therein.
(yea, it shall rest on its sabbaths in its time of wilderness,
for it did not rest on your sabbaths, when ye still lived
there.)
36 And I shall give dread in their hearts, that shall abide
of you, in the countries of your enemies; the sound of a
leaf flying shall make them afeared, and so they shall flee
it as a sword; they shall fall, while none pursueth, (And I
shall put fear in the hearts of those who be left of you, in
the countries of your enemies; the sound of a leaf flying
in the wind shall make them afraid, and they shall flee it

like a sword; they shall fall, when no one pursueth them,)
37 and all they shall fall upon their brethren, as men
fleeing battles (*out of fear*); no man of you shall be hardy
to against-stand (your) enemies; (and they all shall fall upon
their brothers, like men fearfully fleeing from battle; not
one of you shall be hardy to stand against your enemies;)
38 ye shall perish among heathen men, and the land of
(your) enemies shall waste you.
39 That if some of these *Jews* dwell (And those *Jews*
who shall still remain), they shall fail in their
wickednesses, in the land of their enemies; and they shall
be tormented for the sins of their fathers, and for their
own sins,
40 till they acknowledge their wickednesses, and have
mind of their evils (and remember their evil-doing), by
which they trespassed against me, and went contrary to
me.
41 Therefore and I shall go against them (And so I shall
go against them), and I shall bring them into the land of
their enemies, till the uncircumcised soul of them be
ashamed; then they shall pray for (the forgiveness of)
their wickedness,
42 and I shall have mind of my bond of peace, that I
covenanted with Jacob, Isaac, and with Abraham; also I
shall be mindful of the land, (and I shall remember my
covenant, which I made with Jacob, and Isaac, and
Abraham; and I shall remember the land,)
43 which, when it is left of them, shall please to itself in
his sabbaths, and shall suffer wilderness for them;
forsooth they shall pray for their sins, for they casted
away my dooms, and despised my laws; (which, when it
is rid of them, shall enjoy its sabbaths, and shall become
a wilderness without them; and they shall pray for *the
forgiveness of* their sins, for they threw away my
judgements, and despised my laws;)
44 nevertheless, yea, when they were in the land of
(their) enemies, I casted not them away utterly (I did not
utterly throw them away), neither I despised them, so that
they were wasted, and that I made void my covenant
with them; for I am the Lord God of them.
45 And I shall have mind of my former bond of peace
(And I shall remember my covenant with their ancestors),
when I led them out of the land of Egypt, in the sight of
heathen men, that I should be their God; I am the Lord
God.
46 These be the behests, and dooms, and laws, which
the Lord gave betwixt himself and the sons of Israel, in
the hill of Sinai, by the hand of Moses. (These be the
commands, and judgements, and laws, which the Lord
gave between himself and the Israelites, on Mount Sinai,
through Moses.)

CHAPTER 27

1 And the Lord spake to Moses and said,
2 Speak thou to the sons of Israel, and thou shalt say
to them, A man that maketh a (special) vow, and
promiseth his soul to God, he shall give the price under
(the) value, *either appraising thereof.* (Speak thou to the
Israelites, and thou shalt say to them, A person who
maketh a special vow, and promiseth his life to God, to
fulfill the vow, he shall pay the price of the value, *or of
the appraisal, of his life.*)
3 If it is a male, from the twentieth year till to the
sixtieth year, he shall give fifty shekels of silver, at the
measure of the saintuary (by the measure of the
sanctuary),
4 if it is a woman, *she shall give* thirty shekels;
5 forsooth from the fifth year till to the twentieth year,
a male shall give twenty shekels, a woman *shall give* ten
shekels;
6 from one month till to the fifth year, five shekels
shall be given for a male, three shekels for a woman;
7 a male of sixty years and over shall give fifteen
shekels, a woman shall give ten shekels.
8 If it is a poor man, and [he] may not yield the value,
he shall stand before the priest, and as much as the priest
appraiseth, and seeth that the poor man may yield, so
much he shall give (that much he shall give).
9 Soothly if any man avoweth a beast, that may be
offered to the Lord, it shall be holy,
10 and it shall not be able to be changed, that is,
neither a better for a worse, neither an evil for a good;
and if he changeth it, both that, that is changed, and that,
for which it is changed, shall be hallowed to the Lord.
(and he shall not be able to exchange it for another, that
is, neither a better for a worse, nor a bad one for a good
one; and if he exchangeth it, both that, which is
exchanged, and that, for which it is exchanged, shall be
holy to the Lord.)
11 Soothly if any man avoweth an unclean beast, that
may not be offered to the Lord, it shall be brought before
the priest,
12 and the priest shall deem whether it is good either
evil (and the priest shall decide whether it is good or
bad), and he shall set the price;
13 (for) which price, if he that offereth (it) will not give
(it), he shall add the fifth part over the value (to buy it
back).
14 If a man avoweth his house, and halloweth it to the
Lord, the priest shall behold, whether it is good either
evil, and by the price which is ordained of him, it shall
be sold; (If a man voweth his house, and dedicateth it to
the Lord, the priest shall look at it, and decide if it is good
or bad, *that is, he shall determine its value*, and it shall
be sold for the price which is ordained by him;)
15 soothly if he that avowed will again-buy it, he shall
give the fifth part of the value above, and he shall have
the house. (and if he who vowed it will buy it back, he

shall add the fifth part above its value, and then he shall
have the house.)
16 That if a man avoweth the field of his possession,
and halloweth it to the Lord, the price shall be deemed
by the measure of [the] seed (And if a man voweth the
field of his possession, and dedicateth it to the Lord, its
value shall be determined by the measure of its seed); if
the field is sown with thirty bushels of barley, it shall be
sold for fifty shekels of silver.
17 If he avoweth the field anon from the year of [the]
beginning of the jubilee, as much as it may be worth, by
so much it shall be appraised; (If he voweth the field from
the beginning of the Jubilee Year, it shall be worth as
much as it shall be appraised for;)
18 but if *it be* after some part of time, the priest shall
reckon, *either determine*, the money by the number of
the years that be left till to the jubilee, and it shall be
withdrawn of the price. (but if *it be* after some time, the
priest shall determine its value by the number of years
that be left until the Jubilee, and that shall be deducted
from the price.)
19 That if he that avowed will again-buy the field, he
shall add the fifth part of the money *that (it) is* appraised
(for), and he shall wield it; (And if he, who vowed the
field, will buy it back, he shall add a fifth part to the
value *that it is* appraised for, and then it shall be his;)
20 but if he will not again-buy it, but it is sold to any
other man, he that avowed it shall never be able to again-
buy it; (but if he will not buy it back, and it is sold to
another man, then he who vowed it shall never be able
to buy it back;)
21 for when the day of jubilee cometh, that field shall
be hallowed to the Lord, and the possession hallowed
pertaineth to the right of priests. (for when the Jubilee
Year cometh, that field shall be holy to the Lord, and
dedicated possessions belong to the priests.)
22 If the field is bought, and is not of the possession of
greater men, *that is, of ancestors*, and it is hallowed to
the Lord, (If a field is bought, and it is not part of a
person's ancestral land, and it is holy to the Lord,)
23 the priest shall determine the price by the number of
years till to the jubilee, and he that avowed the field shall
give *the price thereof* to the Lord; (the priest shall
determine its value by the number of years until the
Jubilee, and he who vowed the field shall pay *its value* to
the Lord;)
24 forsooth in the jubilee it shall turn again to the
former lord that sold it, and he shall have it into the
heritage of his possession. (but in the Jubilee Year it shall
return to the original owner who sold it, and it shall be in
the inheritance of his possession.)
25 All the appraising, *or value*, shall be weighed by the
shekel of the saintuary (shall be made with the shekel of
the sanctuary); a shekel hath twenty halfpence.
26 No man may hallow and avow the first engendered
things that pertain to the Lord, whether it is (an) ox, or (a)
sheep, (for) they be the Lord's *part*.
27 That if the beast is unclean *that is avowed*, he that
offered it shall again-buy it after the value *that it is
appraised to*, and he shall add to (it) the fifth part of the
price; (or) if he will not again-buy it, it shall be sold to
another man, for as much as it is *appraised*. (And if the
beast *that is vowed* is unclean, he who offered it can buy
it back for the value *that it is appraised for*, and he shall
add to it the fifth part of its value; or if he will not buy it
back, it shall be sold to another man, for the value that it
is *appraised for*.)
28 All thing that is hallowed to the Lord, whether it is
man, or beast, (or) whether (the) field of his heritage, it
shall not be sold, neither it shall be able to be again-
bought; whatever thing is hallowed once, it shall be holy
of holy things to the Lord, (Everything that is dedicated to
the Lord, whether it is a man, or a beast, or the field of
his inheritance, shall not be sold, nor shall it be able to
be bought back; once something is dedicated, it shall be
a most holy thing to the Lord,)
29 and each hallowing which is offered of man, shall
not be again-bought, but it shall die by death. (yea, even
a man who is dedicated to the Lord, shall not be able to
be bought back, but he shall be put to death.)
30 All the tithes of [the] earth, whether of fruits *of corn*,
whether of apples of trees, be the Lord's *part*, and be
hallowed to him; (All the tithes from the land, whether
grain, or the fruits of trees, be the Lord's *portion*, and be
holy to him;)
31 soothly if any man will again-buy his tithes, he shall
add to (them) the fifth part of those; (and if anyone will
buy back his tithes, he shall add the fifth part to their
value;)
32 (yea,) of all the tithes of sheep, and of oxen, and of
goats, that pass under the shepherd's rod, whatever thing
cometh to the tenth *part*, it shall be hallowed to the Lord
(it shall be holy to the Lord);
33 it shall not be chosen, neither good, neither evil;
neither it shall be changed for another; if any man
changeth it, both that, that is changed, and that, for
which it is changed, shall be hallowed to the Lord, and it
shall not be again-bought. (it shall not be chosen from out
of the whole, neither good, nor bad; nor shall it be
exchanged for another; if anyone exchangeth it, both
that, which is exchanged, and that, for which it is
exchanged, shall be holy to the Lord, and shall not be
bought back.)
34 These be the commandments which the Lord
commanded to Moses, and to the sons of Israel, in the
hill of Sinai. (These be the commandments which the
Lord commanded to Moses, and to the Israelites, on
Mount Sinai.) ✡

NUMBERS

CHAPTER 1

1 And the Lord spake to Moses in the desert of Sinai,
in the tabernacle of the bond of peace[1], in the first day of
the second month, in the tother year of their going out of
Egypt, and said, (And the Lord spoke to Moses in the
Sinai Desert, in the Tabernacle of the Covenant, *that is,
the Tabernacle of the Witnessing,* on the first day of the
second month, in the second year of their going out of
Egypt, and said,)
2 Take ye the sum, *or the number,* of all the
congregation of the sons of Israel, by their kindreds, and
families, and all their names each by themselves,
whatever thing of male kind, (Take ye the sum, *or the
number,* of all the congregation of the people of Israel, by
their kindreds, and families, and list, *or register,* all their
names, whoever is a male,)
3 from the twentieth year and above, of all the strong
men of Israel (from twenty years of age and older, of all
the strong men in Israel); and thou and Aaron shall
number them by their companies.
4 And the princes of the lineages (And the leaders of
the tribes), and of the families, in their kindreds, shall be
with you,
5 of which *princes,* these be the names (of which
leaders, these be the names); of Reuben, Elizur, the son
of Shedeur;
6 of Simeon, Shelumiel, the son of Zurishaddai;
7 of Judah, Nahshon, the son of Amminadab;
8 of Issachar, Nethaneel, the son of Zuar;
9 of Zebulun, Eliab, the son of Helon;
10 soothly of the sons of Joseph; of Ephraim, Elishama,
the son of Ammihud; of Manasseh, Gamaliel, the son of
Pedahzur;
11 of Benjamin, Abidan, the son of Gideoni;
12 of Dan, Ahiezer, the son of Ammishaddai;
13 of Asher, Pagiel, the son of Ocran;
14 of Gad, Eliasaph, the son of Deuel;
15 of Naphtali, Ahira, the son of Enan.
16 These *were* the noblest princes of the multitude, by
their lineages, and kindreds, and the heads of the host(s)
of Israel, (These *were* the noblest leaders of the
multitude, by their tribes, and kindreds, and the heads of
the armies of Israel,)
17 the which princes Moses and Aaron took, with all
the multitude of the common people. (which leaders
Moses and Aaron took, along with all the multitude of
the common people.)
18 And they gathered (them together) in the first day of
the second month, and they told them, (*or they totalled
them,*) by kindreds, and houses, and families, and heads,
and names of each by themselves, from the twentieth
year and above, (And they gathered them together on the
first day of the second month, and they listed, *or they
registered,* them by their kindreds, and houses, and
families, and heads, and their names, from twenty years
of age and older,)
19 as the Lord commanded to Moses, (and so he
numbered them there in the Sinai Desert).
20 And of Reuben, the first begotten of Israel, were
numbered, in the desert of Sinai, by their generations,
and families, and houses, and by the names of all the
heads, all thing that is of male kind, from twenty years
and above, of men going forth to battle, (And so the sons
of Reuben, the first-born of Israel, were listed by their
generations, and families, and houses of their kindreds,
with the names of all who were twenty years of age and
older, and all the men who could go forth to battle
numbered)
21 six and forty thousand and five hundred.
22 Of the sons of Simeon, by their generations, and
families, and houses of their kindreds, were numbered, by
the names and heads of all, all that is of male kind, from
twenty years and above, of men going forth to battle,
(The sons of Simeon were listed by their generations, and
families, and houses of their kindreds, with the names of
all who were twenty years of age and older, and all the
men who could go forth to battle numbered)
23 nine and fifty thousand and three hundred.
24 Of the sons of Gad, by generations, and families,
and houses of their kindreds, were numbered, by the
names of all, from twenty years and above, all men that
went forth to battle, (The sons of Gad were listed by their
generations, and families, and houses of their kindreds,
with the names of all who were twenty years of age and
older, and all the men who could go forth to battle
numbered)
25 five and forty thousand (and) six hundred and fifty.
26 Of the sons of Judah, by generations, and families,
and houses of their kindreds, by the names of all, from
twenty years and above, all men that might go [forth] to
battles, (The sons of Judah were listed by their generations,
and families, and houses of their kindreds, with the names
of all who were twenty years of age and older, and all the
men who could go forth to battle numbered)
27 were numbered four and seventy thousand and six
hundred. (seventy-four thousand and six hundred.)
28 Of the sons of Issachar, by their generations, and

[1] In Numbers, the Tabernacle is often called 'the tabernacle of the bond of peace', that is, 'the Tabernacle of the Covenant'; in the rest of the Wycliffe Old Testament, it is usually referred to as 'the tabernacle of (the) witnessing'.

families, and houses of their kindreds, by the names of
all, from twenty years and above, all men that went forth
to battles, (The sons of Issachar were listed by their
generations, and families, and houses of their kindreds,
with the names of all who were twenty years of age and
older, and all the men who could go forth to battle
numbered)
29 were numbered four and fifty thousand and four
hundred. (fifty-four thousand and four hundred.)
30 Of the sons of Zebulun, by generations, and
families, and houses of their kindreds, were numbered,
by the names of all, from twenty years and above, all
men that might go forth to battles, (The sons of Zebulun
were listed by their generations, and families, and houses
of their kindreds, with the names of all who were twenty
years of age and older, and all the men who could go
forth to battle numbered)
31 seven and fifty thousand and four hundred.
32 Of the sons of Joseph, of the sons of Ephraim, by
generations, and families, and houses of their kindreds,
were numbered, by the names of all, from twenty years
and above, all men that might go forth to battles, (The
sons of Joseph, those of the sons of Ephraim, were listed
by their generations, and families, and houses of their
kindreds, with the names of all who were twenty years of
age and older, and all the men who could go forth to
battle numbered)
33 forty thousand and five hundred.
34 Forsooth of the sons of Manasseh, by their
generations, and families, and houses of their kindreds,
were numbered, by the names of all, from twenty years
and above, all men that might go forth to battles, (And
the sons of Manasseh were listed by their generations,
and families, and houses of their kindreds, with the
names of all who were twenty years of age and older,
and all the men who could go forth to battle numbered)
35 two and thirty thousand and two hundred.
36 Of the sons of Benjamin, by generations, and
families, and houses of their kindreds, were numbered,
by the names of all, from twenty years and above, all
men that might go forth to battles, (The sons of Benjamin
were listed by their generations, and families, and houses
of their kindreds, with the names of all who were twenty
years of age and older, and all the men who could go
forth to battle numbered)
37 five and thirty thousand and four hundred.
38 Of the sons of Dan, by generations, and families,
and houses of their kindreds, were numbered, by the
names of all, from twenty years and above, all men that
might go forth to battles, (The sons of Dan were listed by
their generations, and families, and houses of their
kindreds, with the names of all who were twenty years of
age and older, and all the men who could go forth to
battle numbered)
39 two and sixty thousand and seven hundred.
40 Of the sons of Asher, by generations, and families,
and houses of their kindreds, were numbered, by the
names of all, from twenty years and above, all men that
might go forth to battles, (The sons of Asher were listed
by their generations, and families, and houses of their
kindreds, with the names of all who were twenty years of
age and older, and all the men who could go forth to
battle numbered)
41 forty thousand and a thousand and five hundred.
42 Of the sons of Naphtali, by generations, and
families, and houses of their kindreds, were numbered,
by the names of all, from twenty years and above, all
men that might go forth to battles, (The sons of Naphtali
were listed by their generations, and families, and houses
of their kindreds, with the names of all who were twenty
years of age and older, and all the men who could go
forth to battle numbered)
43 three and fifty thousand and four hundred.
44 These men it be, which Moses and Aaron and the
twelve princes of Israel numbered, each by their houses
and kindreds. (These be the men, whom Moses and
Aaron and the twelve leaders of Israel listed, *or
registered,* each by the house of his kindred.)
45 And all men of the sons of Israel, by their houses,
and families, from twenty years and above, that might go
forth to battles, (And all the men of the Israelites, by their
houses, and families, from twenty years of age and older,
who could go forth to battle,)
46 were all together six hundred thousand and three
thousand men, and five hundred and fifty. (were
altogether six hundred thousand and three thousand and
five hundred and fifty men.)
47 Soothly the deacons[2] in the lineage of their families
were not numbered with them. (But the Levites, in the
tribe of their families, were not listed with them.)
48 And the Lord spake to Moses, and said, (For the
Lord spoke to Moses, and said,)
49 Do not thou number the lineage of Levi, neither set
thou the sum of them with the sons of Israel; (Do not
thou list, *or register,* the tribe of Levi, nor take thou the
sum of them among the Israelites;)
50 but thou shalt ordain them upon the tabernacle of
(the) witnessing, and upon all the vessels thereof, and
upon whatever thing pertaineth to [the] ceremonies,
either sacrifices. They shall bear the tabernacle, and all
the purtenances thereof, and they shall be in the service
of it, and they shall set [their] tents by compass of the
tabernacle (and they shall pitch their tents around the
Tabernacle).

[2] Often in the Wycliffe Old Testament, where the "Later Version" has 'deacon' or 'deacons', the "Early Version" has 'Levite' or 'Levites'.

51 When men shall go forth, *or be removed*, the
deacons shall take down the tabernacle; when the tents
shall be set (up), they shall set it up (again). Whoever of
strangers nigheth (to it), he shall be slain (he shall be put
to death).
52 Soothly the sons of Israel shall set tents, each man
by *his* companies, and his fellowships, and his host; (And
the other Israelites shall pitch their tents, each man in *his*
company, and his fellowship, and his army;)
53 forsooth the deacons shall set their tents by compass
of the tabernacle, lest indignation be made on the
multitude of the sons of Israel; and they shall (stand)
watch in the keepings of the tabernacle of witnessing.
(but the Levites shall pitch their tents around the
Tabernacle, lest my indignation come upon all the
multitude of the Israelites; and they shall keep charge of
the Tabernacle of the Witnessing.)
54 Therefore the sons of Israel did by all things which
the Lord commanded to Moses. (And so the Israelites did
all the things that the Lord commanded to Moses.)

CHAPTER 2

1 And the Lord spake to Moses and to Aaron, and said,
2 All men of the sons of Israel shall set tents by the
companies, signs, and banners, and houses of their
kindreds, by compass of the tabernacle of [the] bond of
peace. (All the men of the Israelites shall pitch their tents
by the companies, signs, and banners, and houses of their
kindreds, around the Tabernacle of the Covenant, *that is,
the Tabernacle of the Witnessing*.)
3 At the east Judah shall set tents, by the companies of
his host; and Nahshon, the son of Amminadab, shall be
prince of the sons of Judah; (On the east side, the sons of
Judah shall pitch their tents, by the companies of its
army; and Nahshon, the son of Amminadab, shall be the
leader of the sons of Judah;)
4 and all the number of fighters of his kindred, four
and seventy thousand and six hundred. (and the number
of all the fighters in his army, was seventy-four thousand
and six hundred.)
5 Men of the lineage of Issachar setted tents beside
him, of which the prince was Nethaneel, the son of Zuar;
6 and all the number of his fighters, four and fifty
thousand and four hundred. (and the number of all the
fighters in his army, was fifty-four thousand and four
hundred.)
7 Eliab, the son of Helon, was prince of the lineage of
Zebulun;
8 all the host of fighters of his kindred, seven and fifty
thousand and four hundred. (and the number of all the
fighters in his army, was fifty-seven thousand and four
hundred.)
9 (So) All that were numbered in the tents of Judah,
were an hundred thousand and fourscore thousand and
six (thousand) and four hundred; and they shall go out
first by their companies.
10 In the tents of the sons of Reuben, at the south coast,
Elizur, the son of Shedeur, shall be prince; (On the south
side, the sons of Reuben shall pitch their tents, and
Elizur, the son of Shedeur, shall be their leader;)
11 and all the host of his fighters, that were numbered,
six and forty thousand and five hundred. (and the number
of all the fighters in his army, was forty-six thousand and
five hundred.)
12 Men of the lineage of Simeon setted tents beside
him, of which the prince was Shelumiel, the son of
Zurishaddai;
13 and all the host of his fighters, that were numbered,
nine and fifty thousand and three hundred. (and the
number of all the fighters in his army, was fifty-nine
thousand and three hundred.)
14 Eliasaph, the son of Reuel, was prince in the lineage
of Gad;
15 and all the host of his fighters, that were numbered,
five and forty thousand and six hundred and fifty. (and
the number of all the fighters in his army, was forty-five
thousand and six hundred and fifty.)
16 All that were numbered of the tents of Reuben (So
all who were numbered in the tents of Reuben), (were) an
hundred thousand and fifty thousand and one thousand
and four hundred and fifty; they shall go forth in the
second place by their companies.
17 Soothly the tabernacle of witnessing shall be raised
up by the offices of deacons, and by their companies; as
it shall be raised up *by them*, so it shall be taken down *by
them*; all they shall go forth by their places and orders.
(The Tabernacle of the Witnessing shall be raised up by
the companies of the Levites; it shall be raised up *by
them*, and it shall be taken down *by them*; and they all
shall go forth in their proper place and order.)
18 The tents of the sons of Ephraim shall be at the west
coast, of which the prince was Elishama, the son of
Ammihud; (On the west side, the sons of Ephraim shall
pitch their tents, and Elishama, the son of Amnmihud,
shall be their leader;)
19 and all the host of his fighters, that were numbered,
forty thousand and five hundred. (and the number of all
the fighters in his army, was forty thousand and five
hundred.)
20 And with them was the lineage of the sons of
Manasseh, of which the prince was Gamaliel, the son of
Pedahzur;
21 all the host of his fighters, that were numbered, *were*
two and thirty thousand and two hundred. (and the
number of all the fighters in his army, was thirty-two
thousand and two hundred.)
22 In the lineage of the sons of Benjamin, the prince
was Abidan, the son of Gideoni;

23 and all the host of his fighters, that were numbered,
were five and thirty thousand and four hundred. (and the
number of all the fighters in his army, was thirty-five
thousand and four hundred.)
24 (So) All men that were numbered in the tents of
Ephraim were an hundred thousand and eight thousand
and one hundred; they shall go forth in the third *place* by
their companies.
25 At the north coast the sons of Dan setted tents, of
which the prince was Ahiezer, the son of Ammishaddai;
(And on the north side, the sons of Dan shall pitch their
tents, and Ahiezer, the son of Ammishaddai, shall be
their leader;)
26 all the host of his fighters, that were numbered, *were*
two and sixty thousand and seven hundred. (and the
number of all the fighters in his army, was sixty-two
thousand and seven hundred.)
27 And men of the lineage of Asher setted tents beside
him, of which the prince was Pagiel, the son of Ocran;
28 and all the host of his fighters, that were numbered,
were one and forty thousand and five hundred. (and the
number of all the fighters in his army, was forty-one
thousand and five hundred.)
29 Of the lineage of the sons of Naphtali, the prince
was Ahira, the son of Enan; (In the tribe of the sons of
Naphtali, the leader was Ahira, the son of Enan;)
30 and all the host of his fighters, (that were
numbered), were three and fifty thousand and four
hundred. (and the number of all the fighters in his army,
was fifty-three thousand and four hundred.)
31 (So) All that were numbered in the tents of Dan were
an hundred thousand and seven (thousand) and fifty
thousand and six hundred; they shall go forth the last.
32 This is the number of the sons of Israel, by the
houses of their kindreds, and by companies of the host
parted, six hundred thousand and three thousand five
hundred and fifty. (And so the number of the Israelites, by
the houses of their kindreds, and by the companies of
each of their separate armies, was six hundred thousand
and three thousand and five hundred and fifty.)
33 Soothly the deacons were not numbered among the
sons of Israel; for God commanded so to Moses. (But the
Levites were not listed, *or were not registered*, among the
Israelites; for God had so commanded to Moses.)
34 And the sons of Israel did by all things which the
Lord commanded; they setted tents by their companies,
and they went forth by the families, and houses of their
fathers. (And the Israelites did all the things that the Lord
commanded; they pitched their tents by their companies,
and they went forth by their families, and the houses of
their fathers.)

CHAPTER 3

1 These be the generations of Aaron and of Moses, in
the day in which the Lord spake to Moses, in the hill of
Sinai. (These be the generations of Aaron and of Moses,
on the day in which the Lord spoke to Moses, on Mount
Sinai.)
2 And these be the names of the sons of Aaron; his
first engendered, Nadab (Nadab, his first-born); afterward,
Abihu, and Eleazar, and Ithamar;
3 these be the names of Aaron's sons, (the) priests,
that were anointed, and whose hands were [ful]filled and
hallowed, that they should be set in priesthood. (these be
the names of Aaron's sons, the priests, who were
anointed, and consecrated, so that they could be
installed, *or ordained*, in the priesthood.)
4 Nadab and Abihu [died], when they offered alien
fire in the sight of the Lord, in the desert of Sinai, (and
they) were dead without free children; and Eleazar and
Ithamar were set in priesthood before Aaron their father.
(But then Nadab and Abihu were killed, when they
offered unholy fire before the Lord, in the Sinai Desert,
and they died before having any children; and so Eleazar
and Ithamar were ordained in the priesthood in the sight
of their father Aaron.)
5 And the Lord spake to Moses, saying,
6 Present thou the lineage of Levi, and make it to
stand in the sight of Aaron, the priest, that they minister
to him; (Present thou the tribe of Levi, and make them to
stand before Aaron, the priest, to serve him;)
7 and (to stand) watch, and that they keep whatever
thing pertaineth to the religion of the multitude, before
the tabernacle of witnessing; (and to keep charge, and to
do whatever thing pertaineth to the service of the
multitude, in the Tabernacle of the Witnessing;)
8 and that they keep (charge of) the vessels of the
tabernacle, and serve in the service of it.
9 And thou shalt give by free gift the Levites to Aaron
and to his sons, to whom they be given (out) of the sons
of Israel. (And thou shalt give the Levites as a gift to
Aaron and his sons, to whom they be given from all the
Israelites.)
10 Soothly thou shalt ordain Aaron and his sons on the
religion of priesthood; a stranger that nigheth for to
minister, shall die. (And thou shalt ordain Aaron and his
sons to serve in the priesthood; a stranger who cometh
near to try to minister, shall be put to death.)
11 And the Lord spake to Moses, saying,
12 I have taken the Levites (out) of the sons of Israel for
each first engendered (male) thing that openeth the
womb in the sons of Israel; and the Levites shall be mine,
13 for each first engendered (male) thing is mine; since
the time I smote the first engendered (male) thing in the
land of Egypt, I have hallowed to me whatever (male)
thing is born first in Israel (I have consecrated to myself
whatever male is first-born in Israel); from man unto beast
they be mine; I am the Lord.

14 And the Lord spake to Moses in the desert of Sinai,
and said,
15 Number thou the sons of Levi by their fathers'
houses, and by their families, each male from one month
and above (every male one month of age and older).
16 [And] Moses numbered *them*, as the Lord
commanded.
17 And the sons of Levi were found, by their names,
Gershon, and Kohath, and Merari;
18 the sons of Gershon *were* Libni, and Shimei;
19 the sons of Kohath *were* Amram, and Izhar, Hebron,
and Uzziel;
20 and the sons of Merari *were* Mahli, and Mushi.
21 Of Gershon were two families, (they) of Libni, and
(they) of Shimei;
22 of which the people of male kind was numbered,
from one month and above, seven thousand and five
hundred. (of whom the number of the males, who were
one month of age and older, was seven thousand and five
hundred.)
23 These shall set tents behind the tabernacle at the
west part, (They shall pitch their tents behind the
Tabernacle, on the west side,)
24 under the prince Eliasaph, the son of Lael. (and their
leader shall be Eliasaph, the son of Lael.)
25 And they shall have the keepings in the tabernacle
of [the] bond of peace, the tabernacle itself, and the
covering thereof, (and) the tent that is drawn before the
gates of the covering of the witnessing of the bond of
peace; (And they shall keep charge of the Tabernacle of
the Covenant, that is, the Tabernacle itself, and its
coverings, and the curtain which is hung at the entrance
to the Tabernacle of the Covenant;)
26 and the curtains of the great entry, also the tent that
is hanged in the entering of the great entry of the
tabernacle, and whatever thing pertaineth to the use of
the altar, the cords of the tabernacle, and to all the
service thereof. (and the curtains for the courtyard all
around the Tabernacle, and the curtain that is hung at the
entrance to the courtyard, and whatever pertaineth to the
use of the altar, and all the other things in the service
thereof.)
27 The kindred of Kohath shall have the peoples of
Amram, and of Izhar, and of Hebron, and of Uzziel;
these be the families of Kohathites,
28 numbered by their names, all of male kind, from
one month and above, eight thousand and six hundred.
They shall have the keepings of the saintuary, (and the
number of all the males, from one month of age and
older, was eight thousand and six hundred. They shall
keep charge of the holy things of the sanctuary,)
29 and they shall set their tents at the south coast
thereof; (and they shall pitch their tents on *its* south side;)
30 and the prince of them shall be Elizaphan, the son of
Uzziel. (and their leader shall be Elizaphan, the son of
Uzziel.)
31 And they shall keep (charge of) the ark, and the
table, and the candlestick, the altars, and the vessels of
the saintuary in which it is served, and the veil, and all
such manner purtenance. (And they shall keep charge of
the Ark, *that is, the Box containing the tablets of the Law*,
and the table, and the lamp-stand, and the altars, and the
vessels of the sanctuary with which they shall serve, *or
they shall minister*, and the Veil, and all the other things
in the service thereof.)
32 Soothly the prince of princes of Levites shall be
Eleazar, the son of Aaron, the priest; and he shall be
upon the keepers of the keeping of the saintuary. (And
the leader of the leaders of the Levites shall be Eleazar,
the son of Aaron, the priest; and he shall be over those in
charge of the sanctuary.)
33 And soothly of Merari shall be the peoples of Mahli,
and of Mushi,
34 numbered by their names, all the male kind, from
one month and above, six thousand and two hundred;
(and the number of all the males, from one month of age
and older, was six thousand and two hundred;)
35 the prince of them *shall be* Zuriel, the son of
Abihail; they shall set their tents in the north coast. (their
leader *shall be* Zuriel, the son of Abihail; and they shall
pitch their tents on the north side of the Tabernacle.)
36 And under the keeping of them shall be the tables of
the tabernacle, and the bars, and the pillars, and the
foundaments of those, and all things that pertain to such
adorning, (And the sons of Merari shall be in charge of
the tables of the Tabernacle, and the bars, and the pillars,
and their foundations, *or their bases*, and all the things in
the service thereof,)
37 and the pillars of the great entry by compass (and
the pillars all around the courtyard), with their bases, and
the stakes with *their* cords.
38 Forsooth Moses, and Aaron with his sons, shall set
their tents before the tabernacle of [the] bond of peace,
that is, at the east coast, and shall have the keeping of the
saintuary, in the midst of the sons of Israel; whatever
alien nigheth *thereto*, he shall die. (And Moses, and
Aaron with his sons, shall pitch *their* tents in front of the
Tabernacle of the Covenant, that is, on the east side, and
they shall be in charge of the sanctuary, on behalf of the
Israelites; and any stranger who cometh near *to it*, shall
be put to death.)
39 All the Levites, which Moses and Aaron numbered,
by the commandment of the Lord, by their families, in
male kind, from one month and above, were two and
twenty thousand. (And the number of all the Levites,
whom Moses and Aaron listed, *or registered*, by the
Lord's command, by their families, all the males from one
month of age and older, was twenty-two thousand.)

40 And the Lord said to Moses, Number thou the first
begotten of male kind of the sons of Israel, from one
month and above (from one month of age and older); and
thou shalt have the sum, *or the number,* of them;
41 and thou shalt take the Levites to me for all the first
begotten of the sons of Israel; I am the Lord; and *thou
shalt take* their beasts (to me) for all the first begotten of
the sons of Israel. (and thou shalt give me the Levites in
place of all the first-born sons of the Israelites; I am the
Lord; and *thou shalt give* me the beasts of the Levites in
place of all the first-born male beasts of the Israelites.)
42 And as the Lord commanded, Moses numbered the
first begotten (male) children of the sons of Israel;
43 and the males were by their names, from one month
and above, two and twenty thousand two hundred and
seventy and three. (and the number of the males, listed
by their names, from one month of age and older, was
twenty-two thousand and two hundred and seventy-
three.)
44 And the Lord spake to Moses, and said,
45 Take thou the Levites for the first begotten of the
sons of Israel, and take the beasts of the Levites for the
beasts of them, and the Levites shall be mine; I am the
Lord. (Now give me the Levites in place of all the first-
born sons of the Israelites, and the beasts of the Levites in
place of the first-born male beasts of the Israelites, and so
the Levites shall be mine; I am the Lord.)
46 Forsooth in the price of two hundred and seventy
and three *persons,* that pass the number of the Levites, of
the first begotten (sons) of the sons of Israel, (And as
payment to buy back the two hundred and seventy-three
persons, of the first-born sons of the Israelites, who
surpass the number of the Levites,)
47 thou shalt take five shekels by each head, at the
measure of the saintuary (thou shalt take five shekels for
each one, by the measure of the sanctuary); a shekel hath
twenty halfpence;
48 and thou shalt give the money to Aaron and to his
sons, the price of them that be *numbered* above (the
number of the Levites). (and thou shalt give this money to
Aaron and to his sons, as payment for those who be
listed, or registered, above the number of the Levites.)
49 Therefore Moses took the money of them that were
numbered above, and which they had again-bought of
the Levites, (And so Moses took the money for the first-
born sons of the Israelites, who surpassed the number of
the Levites, and so had to be bought back, *or ransomed,
or redeemed,*)
50 for the first begotten (sons) of the sons of Israel, a
thousand three hundred and sixty and five of shekels, by
the weight of the saintuary; (in all, a thousand and three
hundred and sixty-five shekels, by the measure of the
sanctuary;)
51 and he gave that *money* to Aaron and to his sons, by
the word that the Lord commanded to him.

CHAPTER 4

1 And the Lord spake to Moses and to Aaron, and
said,
2 Take thou the sum, *or the number,* of the sons of
Kohath, from the midst of (the) Levites, by their houses
and families,
3 from the thirtieth year and above unto the fiftieth
year, of all that enter, that they stand and minister in the
tabernacle of the bond of peace. (from thirty years of age
up to fifty years old, of all who enter to serve in the
Tabernacle of the Covenant.)
4 This is the religion of the sons of Kohath; Aaron and
his sons shall enter into the tabernacle of the bond of
peace, and into the holy of holy things, (This is the
service of the sons of Kohath; Aaron and his sons shall
enter into the Tabernacle of the Covenant, and into the
Most Holy Place, *or the Holy of Holies,*)
5 when the tents shall be moved; and they shall do
down the veil that hangeth before the gates, and they
shall wrap in it the ark of witnessing; (when the tents
shall be moved; and they shall take down the Veil that
hangeth before the Ark, and they shall wrap the Ark of
the Witnessing, *that is, the Box containing the tablets of
the Law,* in it;)
6 and they shall cover *it* again with a veil of jacinthine
skins, and they shall stretch forth above (that) a mantle all
of jacinth, and they shall lead in [the] bearing staves. (and
they shall wrap *it* with a leather cover, and put a blue
mantle over that, and then put in the carrying bars.)
7 Also they shall wrap the board of proposition, *that
is, (of) setting forth,* in a mantle of jacinth, and they shall
put therewith [the] censers, and spoons of gold, little
cups, and great cups to flowing sacrifices to be shed
(out); loaves shall ever[more] be in the board. (And they
shall wrap the table of proposition, *that is, the table of
setting forth,* in a blue mantle, and they shall put the
censers, and the gold saucers, and the little cups, and the
great cups for the wine offerings upon it; and loaves shall
be on the table forevermore.)
8 And they shall stretch forth thereabove a red mantle,
which they shall cover again with a covering of
jacinthine skins, and they shall lead in the bearing staves.
(And they shall spread a red mantle over them, and put a
leather cover over that, and then put in the carrying bars.)
9 They shall take also a mantle of jacinth with which
they shall cover the candlestick, with his lanterns, and
tongs, and snuffers, and all the oil vessels that be needful
to the lanterns to be ordained; (And they shall take a blue
mantle with which they shall cover the lamp-stand, with
its lanterns, and tongs, and snuffers, and all the oil vessels
that be needed for the lanterns to be lit;)
10 and upon all these things they shall put a covering

of jacinthine skins, and they shall bring, *or lead,* in the
bearing staves. (and they shall wrap all these things in a
leather cover, and then put it on a carrying bar, *or a*
carrying pole.)
11 Also they shall wrap the golden altar in a cloth of
jacinth; and they shall stretch forth above it a covering of
jacinthine skins, and they shall lead in [the] bearing
staves. (And they shall wrap the gold altar in a blue
mantle; and they shall wrap that in a leather cover, and
then put in the carrying bars.)
12 They shall wrap in a mantle of jacinth all the vessels
in which it is ministered in the saintuary, and they shall
stretch forth above *it* a covering of jacinthine skins, and
they shall lead in the bearing staves. (And they shall wrap
all the vessels with which they minister in the sanctuary
in a blue mantle, and they shall wrap that in a leather
cover, and then put it on a carrying bar, *or a carrying*
pole.)
13 But also they shall cleanse the altar from (all) ashes,
and (then) they shall wrap it in a cloth of purple.
14 And they shall put with it all the vessels which they
use in the service thereof, that is, the resets of fire, the
tongs, and fleshhooks, and other hooks, and the censers,
or the pans of coals; they shall cover all the vessels of the
altar (al)together in a veil of jacinthine skins, and they
shall lead in the bearing staves. (And they shall put on the
altar all the vessels which they use in its service, that is,
the fire receptacles, the tongs, and fleshhooks, and other
hooks, and the censers, or the pans, for the coal; and they
shall cover all the vessels of the altar with a leather cover,
and then put in the carrying bars.)
15 And when Aaron and his sons have wrapped the
saintuary, and all [the] vessels thereof, in the moving of
tents, then the sons of Kohath shall enter, that they bear
the things wrapped, and touch not the vessels of the
saintuary, lest they die. These be the burdens of the sons
of Kohath in the tabernacle of [the] bond of peace, (And
when Aaron and his sons have wrapped up the
sanctuary, and all its vessels, in the moving of the tents,
then the sons of Kohath shall enter to carry the things that
be wrapped up, but they must not touch the sanctuary
vessels, or they shall die/for if they touch them, then they
must be put to death. These be the loads for the sons of
Kohath in the Tabernacle of the Covenant.)
16 on which Eleazar, the son of Aaron, (the) priest,
shall be; to whose care the oil pertaineth (with which) to
ordain (the) lanterns, and the incense which is made by
craft, and the sacrifice which is offered ever[more], *that*
is, in each day, and the oil of anointing, and whatever
thing pertaineth to the adorning of the tabernacle, and of
all vessels that be in the saintuary. (And Eleazar, the son
of Aaron, the priest, shall be in charge of the oil to fuel
the lanterns, and the incense which is made by craft, and
the offering which is offered forevermore, *that is, on each*
day, and the oil of anointing, for he is in charge of
whatever pertaineth to the service of the Tabernacle, and
of all the vessels that be in the sanctuary.)
17 And the Lord spake to Moses and to Aaron, and
said,
18 Do not ye lose, *or destroy,* the people of Kohath
from the midst of the Levites; (Do not ye allow the
people of Kohath to be done away from the midst of the
Levites;)
19 but do ye this thing to them, that they live, and die
not, if they touch the holy of holy things. Aaron and his
sons shall enter, and they shall dispose the works of all
the sons of Kohath, and they shall part (to each) what
who oughteth to bear. (but do ye this thing for them, so
that they shall live, and not die, when they approach the
most holy things. Aaron and his sons shall enter, and
they shall direct the works of all *the sons of Kohath,* and
they shall assign to each what he ought to carry.)
20 Other men see not by any curiosity those things that
be in the saintuary, before that those be wrapped; else
they shall die. (And let not other people who be curious
see those things that be in the sanctuary, before that they
be wrapped up; for if they do, then they shall die/then
they must be put to death.)
21 And the Lord spake to Moses, and said,
22 Take thou the sum, *or the number,* also of the sons
of Gershon, by their houses, and families, and kindreds;
(Take thou also the sum, *or the number,* of the sons of
Gershon, by their houses, and families, and kindreds;)
23 number thou *them* from thirty years and above unto
fifty years, all that enter and serve in the tabernacle of the
bond of peace. (make thou a list of *them* from thirty years
of age up to fifty years old, all who enter to serve in the
Tabernacle of the Covenant.)
24 This is the office of the sons of Gershonites, (This is
the service of the sons of the Gershonites,)
25 that they bear the curtains of the tabernacle, and the
roof, *or covering,* of the bond of peace, another covering,
and the veil of jacinth that shall be above all things, and
the tent that hangeth in the entry of the tabernacle of the
bond of peace; (that they carry the curtains of the
Tabernacle, and the Tent of the Tabernacle of the
Covenant, another cover, the leather cover that shall be
on top of it, and the curtain that hangeth in the entrance
to the Tabernacle of the Covenant;)
26 and the curtains of the great entry, and the veil in
the entry, that is before the tabernacle (by compass). (and
the curtains of the courtyard, that is all around the
Tabernacle, and the curtain at the entrance to the
courtyard.)
27 When Aaron commandeth and his sons, the sons of
Gershon shall bear all things that pertain to the altar, the
cords, and the vessels, *or instruments,* of their service;
and all *they* shall know, to what charge they ought to be

bound. (And when Aaron and his sons command, the
sons of Gershon shall carry all the things that pertain to
the altar, and the cords, and the vessels, *or the
instruments*, of their service; and *they* all shall know,
what each of them ought to carry.)
28 This is the office of the families of Gershonites, in
the tabernacle of [the] bond of peace (This is the service
of the Gershonite families in the Tabernacle of the
Covenant); and they shall be under the hand of Ithamar,
the son of Aaron, [the] priest.
29 Also thou shalt number the sons of Merari, by the
families and houses of their fathers,
30 from thirty years and above unto fifty years, all that
enter to the office of their service, and to the adorning of
the bond of peace of witnessing. (from thirty years of age
up to fifty years old, all who enter to serve in the
Tabernacle of the Covenant, *that is, in the Tabernacle of
the Witnessing*.)
31 These be their charges; they shall bear the tables of
the tabernacle, and the bars thereof, the pillars, and their
foundaments (and their foundations, *or their bases*);
32 also the pillars of the great entry by compass, with
their foundaments, and their stakes, and their cords (and
the pillars all around the courtyard, with their bases, and
their stakes, and their cords); and they shall take all the
instruments and the purtenance of *the tabernacle*, by
number, and so they shall bear *them*.
33 This is the office of the family of Merarites, and the
service in the tabernacle of the bond of peace (These be
the duties of the Merarite family, in their service in the
Tabernacle of the Covenant); and they shall be under the
hand of Ithamar, the son of Aaron, the priest.
34 Therefore Moses and Aaron and the princes of the
synagogue, numbered the sons of Kohath, by the
kindreds, and houses of their fathers, (And so Moses and
Aaron and the leaders of the congregation, listed, *or
registered*, the Kohathites, by the kindreds, and houses of
their fathers,)
35 from thirty years and above unto the fiftieth year, all
that enter to the service of the tabernacle of [the] bond of
peace; (from thirty years of age up to fifty years old, all
who entered to serve in the Tabernacle of the Covenant;)
36 and they were found (to be) two thousand (and)
seven hundred and fifty.
37 This is the number of the people of Kohath, which
entereth into the tabernacle of [the] bond of peace; Moses
and Aaron numbered these, by the word of the Lord, by
the hand of Moses. (This is the number of the people of
Kohath, who served in the Tabernacle of the Covenant;
Moses and Aaron listed them, obeying the word of the
Lord, spoken by Moses.)
38 And the sons of Gershon were numbered, by the
kindreds and houses of their fathers,
39 from thirty years and above unto fifty years, all that
enter that they serve in the tabernacle of [the] bond of
peace; (from thirty years of age up to fifty years old, all
who entered to serve in the Tabernacle of the Covenant;)
40 and they were found (to be) two thousand (and) six
hundred and thirty.
41 This is the people of Gershonites, that Moses and
Aaron numbered, by the kindreds and houses, by the
word of the Lord.
42 And the sons of Merari were numbered, by the
kindreds, and houses of their fathers,
43 from thirty years and above unto fifty years, all that
enter to fulfill the customs, *or the services*, of the
tabernacle of the bond of peace; (from thirty years of age
up to fifty years old, all who entered to serve in the
Tabernacle of the Covenant;)
44 and they were found (to be) three thousand and two
hundred.
45 This is the number of the sons of Merari, which
Moses and Aaron numbered, by the commandment of
the Lord, by the hand of Moses. (This is the number of
the Merarites, whom Moses and Aaron listed, *or
registered*, by the Lord's command, spoken by Moses.)
46 All that were numbered of the Levites, and which
Moses and Aaron and the princes of Israel made to be
numbered, by the kindreds, and houses of their fathers,
47 from thirty years and above unto fifty years, and
entered to the service of the tabernacle, and to bear the
charges thereof, (from thirty years of age up to fifty years
old, and entered to serve in the Tabernacle, and to carry
its loads,)
48 were (al)together eight thousand (and) five hundred
and fourscore.
49 By the word of the Lord Moses numbered them,
each man by his office and his charges (each one
according to his service and his loads), as the Lord
commanded to him.

CHAPTER 5

1 And the Lord spake to Moses, and said,
2 Command thou to the sons of Israel, that they cast
out of the tents each leprous man, and that floweth out
the seed, and that is defouled upon a dead body;
(Command thou to the Israelites, that they throw out of
the tents, *that is, out of the camp*, any person who is
leprous, and he who floweth out the seed, and anyone
who is defiled by contact with a dead body;)
3 cast ye out of the tents, as well a male as a female,
lest they defoul those, when they dwell with you. (throw
ye out of the camp, a female as well as a male, lest they
defile all the tents, where I live among you.)
4 And the sons of Israel did so (And the Israelites did
so); and they putted them out of the tents, as the Lord
spake to Moses.
5 And the Lord spake to Moses, and said,

6 Speak thou to the sons of Israel (Say thou to the
Israelites), When a man either a woman hath done any of
all (of) the sins that be wont to fall to men, and have
broken by negligence the behest of the Lord, and have
trespassed,
7 they shall acknowledge their sin, and they shall
yield that head, *or debt*, and (add) the fifth part above (it),
(and give it) to him against whom they (have) sinned.
8 But if none there is that shall receive *that*, they shall
give it to the Lord, and it shall be the priest's *part*, besides
the ram that is offered for cleansing, that it be a quemeful
sacrifice. (But if there is no one who can receive *that
payment*, then they shall give it to the Lord, and it shall
be the priest's *portion*, besides the ram for making
amends, which is offered to make amends for them.)
9 Also all the first fruits, which the sons of Israel offer
(which the Israelites offer), pertain to the priest;
10 and whatever thing is offered of each man in the
saintuary, which a man hallowed, and gave to the hands
of the priest, it shall be the priest's part. (and whatever
thing is offered by anyone in the sanctuary, which a
person hath dedicated, and put into the hands of the
priest, it shall be the priest's portion.)
11 And the Lord spake to Moses, and said,
12 Speak thou to the sons of Israel (Speak thou to the
Israelites), and thou shalt say to them, If a man's wife hath
erred, and hath despised her husband,
13 and hath slept with another man, and the husband
may not take, *either prove* this, but the adultery is hid,
and may not be proved by witnesses, for she is not found
in lechery; (and hath slept with another man, but her
husband cannot prove it, for the adultery is hidden, *or is
done in secret*, and so cannot be proved by witnesses, for
she was not found in lechery;)
14 (or) if the spirit of jealousy stirreth the husband
against his wife, which is either defouled, either she is
impeached by false suspicion, (or if the spirit of jealousy
stirreth a husband against his wife, and she is either truly
defiled, or is impeached by false suspicion,)
15 the man shall bring her to the priest, and he shall
offer an offering for her, the tenth part of a measure
called (a) saton of barley meal; he shall not pour oil
thereupon, neither he shall put incense *thereto*, for it is
the sacrifice of jealousy, and an offering inquiring (about)
adultery. (the husband shall bring her to the priest, and
he shall offer an offering for her, the tenth of a measure
called a seah of barley meal, *that is, the tenth of an
ephah*; he shall not pour oil on it, nor shall he put
incense *on it*, for it is an offering for jealousy, and an
offering to inquire about adultery.)
16 Therefore the priest shall offer her, and shall set *her*
before the Lord; (And so the priest shall bring her forth,
and shall put *her* before the Lord;)
17 and he shall take holy water in an earthen vessel,
and he shall put into it a little earth of the pavement of
the tabernacle. (and he shall pour some holy water into
an earthen, *or a clay*, vessel, and he shall put into it a
little dust, *or a little dirt*, from the floor of the Tabernacle,
to make the water bitter.)
18 And when the woman standeth in the sight of the
Lord, the priest shall uncover her head, and he shall put
upon her hands the sacrifice of remembering, and the
offering of jealousy. Soothly he shall hold (in his hand)
the most bitter waters, in which he hath gathered
together curses with cursing. (And when the woman
standeth before the Lord, the priest shall uncover her
head, and he shall put in her hands the offering of
remembrance, which is the offering for jealousy. And he
shall hold in his hand this most bitter water, into which
he shall gather together curses.)
19 And he shall conjure her, and say, If an alien man
slept not with thee, and if thou art not defouled in
forsaking the bed of thine husband, these bitter waters
shall not harm thee, into which I have gathered together
curses; (And he shall adjure her, and say, If thou hath not
slept with a stranger, and if thou art not defiled by
forsaking thy husband's bed, then this most bitter water,
into which I shall gather together curses, shall not harm
thee;)
20 else if thou bowedest away from thine husband, and
art defouled, and hast lain with another man, (but if thou
hast turned away from thy husband, and art defiled, and
hast lain with another man,)
21 thou shalt be subject to these cursings; the Lord give
thee into cursing, and into ensample of all men in his
people; *the Lord* make thine hip to wax rotten, and thy
womb (to) swell, and be it broken; (then thou shalt be
subject to these curses; yea, let the Lord make thee a
curse, and an example to all among his people; *and may
the Lord* make thy hip to grow rotten, and thy womb to
swell, and let it be broken;)
22 *(yea, let) these* cursed waters enter into thy womb,
and while thy womb swelleth, thine hip wax rotten. And
the woman shall answer, Amen! amen!
23 And the priest shall write these curses in a little
book, and he shall do away those curses with the bitterest
waters (and then he shall wash them off into this most
bitter water),
24 into which he gathered (those) curses, and he shall
give to her *the waters* to drink. And when she hath
drunk those waters, (into which he shall gather together
these curses, and then he shall give her *this water* to
drink. And when she hath drunk the water,)
25 the priest shall take (out) of her hand the sacrifice of
jealousy (the priest shall take from her hand the offering
for jealousy), and he shall raise it [up] before the Lord,
and he shall put it on the altar;
26 so only that he take before an handful of that

sacrifice that is offered, and burn it upon the altar, and so
give (for to) drink to the woman the most bitter waters.
(so only that first he take a handful of the offering that is
offered, and burn it on the altar, and then afterward give
the woman this most bitter water to drink.)
27 And when she hath drunk those waters, if she is
defouled, and is guilty of adultery, for her husband is
despised *of her* (for her husband was despised *by her*),
the waters of cursing shall pass through her, and while
her womb is swollen, her hip shall wax rotten, and the
woman shall be into cursing and into ensample to all the
people.
28 That if she is not defouled, she shall be harmless,
and shall bring forth free children. (But if she is not
defiled, she shall be without harm, and shall bring forth
children.)
29 This is the law of jealousy, if a woman boweth away
from her husband, and is defouled, (This is the law of
jealousy, when a woman turneth away from her husband,
and is defiled,)
30 and the husband is stirred with the spirit of jealousy,
and bringeth her into the sight of the Lord, and the priest
doeth to her by all things that be written (here), (or when
her husband is stirred with the spirit of jealousy, *or of
suspicion*, and he bringeth her before the Lord, and the
priest doeth to her by all the things that be written here;)
31 the husband shall be without sin, and she shall
receive her wickedness. (then the husband shall be
without sin, and she, if guilty, shall bear her wickedness.)

CHAPTER 6

1 And the Lord spake to Moses, and said,
2 Speak thou to the sons of Israel, and thou shalt say
to them, When a man either a woman maketh a vow, that
they be hallowed, and they will hallow themselves to the
Lord, (Say thou to the Israelites, When a man or a woman
maketh a vow, that they will become a Nazarite, and they
will consecrate, *or will dedicate*, themselves to the Lord,)
3 they shall abstain from wine, and from all thing that
may make drunken; they shall not drink vinegar of wine,
and of anything able to make drunken, and whatever
thing is pressed out of the grape; they shall not eat fresh
grapes and dry, (they shall abstain from wine, and from
all things that can make them drunk; they shall not drink
wine vinegar, or any other thing that is able to make
them drunk, or whatever is pressed out of the grape; they
shall not eat fresh grapes, or dried grapes,)
4 all [the] days in which they be hallowed by a vow to
the Lord; they shall not eat whatever thing may be of the
vinery, from the rind till to the little grains that be in the
midst of the grape.
5 All the time of his separating, *or of his avow
holding*, a razor shall not pass upon his head, unto the
day(s) be fulfilled in which he is hallowed to the Lord; he
shall be holy, and the hair of his head shall wax. (All the
time of his separation, *or of the keeping of his vow*, a
razor shall not pass over his head, until the days be
fulfilled in which he is consecrated, *or is dedicated*, to
the Lord; he shall be holy, and his head hair shall grow.)
6 In all the time of his hallowing (In all the time of his
consecration, *or his dedication*), he shall not enter upon a
dead body,
7 and soothly he shall not be defouled upon the dead
body of his father and of his mother, of brother and of
sister, for the hallowing of his God is upon his head; (yea,
he shall not even be defiled with the dead body of his
own father or his mother, or his brother or his sister, for
the consecration of his God is upon his head;)
8 each day of his separating, *or avowing*, shall be holy
to the Lord.
9 But if any man is dead suddenly before him, the
head of his hallowing shall be defouled, which he shall
shave anon in the same day of his cleansing, and again in
the seventh day; (But if anyone is suddenly dead before
him, the hair of his consecration shall be defiled, and he
shall shave it off on the day of his cleansing, that is, on
the seventh day afterward;)
10 forsooth in the eighth day he shall offer two turtles,
either two birds of a culver, to the priest, in the entering
of the bond of peace of witnessing. (then on the eighth
day, he shall offer two turtledoves, or two young pigeons,
to the priest, at the entrance to the Tabernacle of the
Covenant, *that is, the Tabernacle of the Witnessing*.)
11 And the priest shall make, *or offer*, one for sin, and
the tother into burnt sacrifice; and the priest shall pray for
him, for he sinned upon a dead body, and he shall
hallow his head in that day. (And the priest shall offer
one of the birds for a sin offering, and the other for a
burnt sacrifice, and so the priest shall make amends for
him, for he sinned through contact with a dead body; and
then he shall consecrate his head again on that day.)
12 And he shall hallow to the Lord the days of his
separating, and he shall offer a lamb of one year for his
sin, so nevertheless that the former days be made void,
for his hallowing is defouled. (And he shall rededicate
the days of his separation to the Lord, and he shall offer a
one-year-old lamb for his sin, nevertheless the former
days shall be made void, for the hair of his consecration
was defiled.)
13 This is the law of hallowing. When the days shall
be fulfilled, which he deemed *to fulfill* by a vow, *the
priest* shall bring him to the door of the tabernacle of
[the] bond of peace, (This is the law of consecration, *or of
dedication*/This is the law for the Nazarite. And when
the days shall be fulfilled, which he committed *to fulfill*
by a vow, *the priest* shall bring him to the entrance of the
Tabernacle of the Covenant,)
14 and he shall offer his offering to the Lord, a lamb of

one year without wem, into burnt sacrifice, and a sheep
of one year without wem, for sin, and a ram without
wem, (as) a peaceable sacrifice; (and he shall offer his
offering to the Lord, a one-year-old lamb without
blemish, *or without fault*, for a burnt sacrifice, and a one-
year-old sheep without blemish, for a sin offering, and a
ram without blemish, for a peace offering;)
15 also a basket of therf loaves, that be sprinkled
(al)together with oil, and cakes sodden in water, and after
anointed with oil, without sourdough, and [the] flowing
sacrifices of all *these* by themselves; (and a basket of
unleavened bread, that is sprinkled with oil, and cakes
made without yeast, boiled in water, and anointed with
oil, and the grain and wine offerings for all of *these*;)
16 which the priest shall offer before the Lord, and he
shall make, *or offer these*, as well for sin as into burnt
sacrifice. (which the priest shall offer before the Lord, and
he shall offer *these* for his sin offering, and for his burnt
sacrifice.)
17 Soothly he shall offer the ram (as) a peaceable
sacrifice to the Lord, and he shall offer therewith a basket
of therf loaves, and flowing sacrifices, that be due by
custom. (And he shall offer the ram as a peace offering to
the Lord, and he shall offer a basket of unleavened bread
with it, and the grain and wine offerings, that be due by
custom.)
18 Then the Nazarite, *or he that is hallowed*, shall be
shaven from the hair of his hallowing, before the door of
the tabernacle of [the] bond of peace; and *the priest* shall
take his hairs, and he shall put them upon the fire, which
is put under the sacrifice of peaceable things. (Then the
Nazarite, *that is, he who is consecrated*, shall shave off
the hair of his consecration, at the entrance to the
Tabernacle of the Covenant; and *the priest* shall take his
hair, and he shall put it on the fire which is under the
peace offering.)
19 And *he shall take* the shoulder sodden of the ram,
and one therf cake from the basket, and one [thin] therf
cake first sodden in water and afterward fried in oil, and
he shall betake *them* into the hands of the Nazarite, after
that his head is shaven. (And *he shall take* the boiled
shoulder of the ram, and one unleavened cake from the
basket, and one thin unleavened wafer first boiled in
water and then fried in oil, and he shall put *them* into the
hands of the Nazarite, after that he hath shaved his head.)
20 And the priest shall raise (up) in the sight of the Lord
the things taken again of him. And those things hallowed
shall be the priest's *part*, as the breast which is
commanded to be separated, and the hip. After these
things the Nazarite may (again) drink wine. (And then the
priest shall take these things from him, and raise them up
as a special gift before the Lord. And these consecrated
things shall be the priest's *portion*, including the special
gift of the breast, and the special contribution of the leg.
And after these things be done, the Nazarite can drink
wine again.)
21 This is the law of the Nazarite, when he hath
avowed his offering to the Lord, in the time of his
consecration, *or hallowing*, besides these things which
his hand findeth. By this that he [hath] avowed in soul,
or in will, so he shall do, to the perfection of his
hallowing. (This is the law for the Nazarite, when he hath
vowed his offering to the Lord, at the time of his
consecration, besides these things which his hand
findeth. By this that he hath vowed with his soul, *or with
his will*, so he shall do, to the perfection, *or the
completion*, of his dedication.)
22 And the Lord spake to Moses and said,
23 Speak thou to Aaron and to his sons, (and say,) Thus
ye shall bless the sons of Israel (Thus shall ye bless the
Israelites), and ye shall say to them,
24 The Lord bless thee, and keep thee;
25 the Lord show his face to thee, and have mercy
upon thee;
26 the Lord turn his cheer to thee, and give peace to
thee. (the Lord turn his face to thee, and give peace to
thee.)
27 They shall call inwardly my name on the sons of
Israel, and I shall bless them. (Yea, they shall call my
name upon, *or over*, the Israelites, and I shall bless them.)

CHAPTER 7

1 And it was done in the day in which Moses fulfilled,
or ended, the tabernacle, and areared it, and anointed it,
and hallowed it with all the vessels, *or instruments*,
thereof, and the altar *he hallowed* in like manner, and the
vessels thereof. (And it was done on the day in which
Moses finished the Tabernacle, and raised it up, that he
anointed it, and consecrated it, *or dedicated it*, and all of
its vessels, *or its instruments*, and the altar, and its vessels.)
2 And the princes of Israel, and the heads of families,
that were, by all lineages, the sovereigns of them that
were numbered, (And the leaders of Israel, that is, the
heads of the families, who were, by all the tribes, the
rulers of those who were listed, *or were registered*,)
3 offered gifts before the Lord, six wains covered, with
twelve oxen; two dukes offered one wain, and each
offered one ox. And they offered those *wains* before the
tabernacle. (brought their offerings before the Lord, in six
covered wagons, with twelve oxen; two leaders, *or two
chief men*, offered one wagon, and each offered one ox.
And they brought those *wagons* to the front of the
Tabernacle.)
4 Soothly the Lord said to Moses,
5 Take thou of them, that they serve in the service of
the tabernacle, and betake thou those things to the
deacons, by the order of their service. (Receive thou
these gifts from them, to use in service for the Tabernacle,

and give thou them to the Levites, according to the order
of their service.)
6 And so when Moses had taken the wains, and the
oxen, he betook them to the deacons. (And so when
Moses had received the wagons, and the oxen, he gave
them to the Levites.)
7 He gave two wains and four oxen to the sons of
Gershon, after that (that) they had need (of).
8 He gave four other wains and eight oxen to the sons
of Merari, by their offices and religion (for their duties
and their service), under the hand of Ithamar, the son of
Aaron, the priest.
9 Forsooth he gave not wains and oxen to the sons of
Kohath, for they serve in the saintuary, and bear the
charges with their own shoulders. (But he did not give
any wagons or oxen to the sons of Kohath, for they serve
in the sanctuary, and carry the loads with their own
shoulders.)
10 Therefore the dukes offered, in the hallowing of the
altar, in the day in which it was anointed, their offering to
the Lord, before the altar. (And so the leaders offered, for
the dedication of the altar, on the day in which it was
anointed, their offering to the Lord, before the altar.)
11 And the Lord said to Moses, All the dukes by
themselves offer they gifts, by all days by themselves, into
the hallowing of the altar. (And the Lord said to Moses,
Have all the leaders offer their gifts, one by one, in the
days that follow, for the dedication of the altar.)
12 Nahshon, the son of Amminadab, (the prince) of the
lineage of Judah, offered his offering in the first day; and
(he offered) (On the first day, Nahshon, the son of
Amminadab, the leader of the sons of Judah, offered)
13 a silver vessel *to prove incense and such things*, in
the weight of an hundred and thirty shekels, a basin of
silver, having seventy shekels by the weight of the
saintuary, ever either full of [tried] flour sprinkled
(al)together with oil, into sacrifice; (a silver vessel,
weighing a hundred and thirty shekels, and a silver basin,
weighing seventy shekels, by the measure, *or the
standard*, of the sanctuary, and each full of fine flour
sprinkled with oil, for a grain offering;)
14 a spoon of ten golden shekels, full of incense. (and a
gold saucer, weighing ten shekels, full of incense.)
15 *He offered* an ox of the drove, and a ram, and a
lamb of one year, into burnt sacrifice; (*And he offered* an
ox from the herd, and a ram, and a one-year-old lamb, for
a burnt sacrifice;)
16 and a buck of (the) goats, for sin. (and a goat buck,
for a sin offering.)
17 And *he offered* in the sacrifice of peaceable things,
twain oxen, five rams, five goat bucks, five lambs of one
year. This is the offering of Nahshon, the son of
Amminadab. (And for a peace offering, *he offered* two
oxen, five rams, five goat bucks, and five one-year-old
lambs. This was the offering of Nahshon, the son of
Amminadab.)
18 In the second day, Nethaneel, the son of Zuar, duke
of the lineage of Issachar, offered (On the second day,
Nethaneel, the son of Zuar, the leader of the sons of
Issachar, offered)
19 a silver vessel *to prove incense and such things*,
weighing an hundred and thirty shekels, a silver basin,
having seventy shekels by the weight of the saintuary,
ever either full of [tried] flour sprinkled (al)together with
oil, into sacrifice; (a silver vessel, weighing a hundred
and thirty shekels, and a silver basin, weighing seventy
shekels, by the measure of the sanctuary, and each full of
fine flour sprinkled with oil, for a grain offering;)
20 a golden spoon, having ten shekels, full of incense;
(a gold saucer, weighing ten shekels, full of incense;)
21 an ox of the drove, and a ram, and a lamb of one
year, into burnt sacrifice; (an ox from the herd, and a
ram, and a one-year-old lamb, for a burnt sacrifice;)
22 and a buck of (the) goats, for sin. (and a goat buck,
for a sin offering.)
23 And in the sacrifice of peaceable things *he offered*
twain oxen, five rams, five goat bucks, five lambs of one
year. This was the offering of Nethaneel the son of Zuar.
(And for a peace offering, *he offered* two oxen, five rams,
five goat bucks, and five one-year-old lambs. This was the
offering of Nethaneel the son of Zuar.)
24 In the third day (On the third day), Eliab, the son of
Helon, the prince of the sons of Zebulun, offered
25 a silver vessel *to prove incense and such things*,
weighing an hundred and thirty shekels, a silver basin,
having seventy shekels at the weight of [the] saintuary,
ever either full of [tried] flour sprinkled (al)together with
oil, into sacrifice; (a silver vessel, weighing a hundred
and thirty shekels, and a silver basin, weighing seventy
shekels, by the measure of the sanctuary, and each full of
fine flour sprinkled with oil, for a grain offering;)
26 a golden spoon, weighing ten shekels, full of incense;
(a gold saucer, weighing ten shekels, full of incense;)
27 an ox of the drove, and a ram, and a lamb of one
year, into burnt sacrifice; (an ox from the herd, and a
ram, and a one-year-old lamb, for a burnt sacrifice;)
28 and a buck of (the) goats, for sin. (and a goat buck,
for a sin offering.)
29 And in the sacrifice of peaceable things *he offered*
twain oxen, five rams, five goat bucks, five lambs of one
year. This is the offering of Eliab, the son of Helon. (And
for a peace offering, *he offered* two oxen, five rams, five
goat bucks, and five one-year-old lambs. This was the
offering of Eliab, the son of Helon.)
30 In the fourth day (On the fourth day), Elizur, the son
of Shedeur, the prince of the sons of Reuben, offered
31 a silver vessel *to prove incense and such things*,
weighing an hundred and thirty shekels, a silver basin,

having seventy shekels at the weight of [the] saintuary,
ever either full of [tried] flour sprinkled (al)together with
oil, into sacrifice; (a silver vessel, weighing a hundred
and thirty shekels, and a silver basin, weighing seventy
shekels, by the measure of the sanctuary, and each full of
fine flour sprinkled with oil, for a grain offering;)
32 a golden spoon weighing ten shekels, full of incense;
(a gold saucer, weighing ten shekels, full of incense;)
33 an ox of the drove, and a ram, and a lamb of one
year, into burnt sacrifice; (an ox from the herd, and a
ram, and a one-year-old lamb, for a burnt sacrifice;)
34 and a buck of (the) goats, for sin. (and a goat buck,
for a sin offering.)
35 And into [the] sacrifice of peaceable things *he
offered* twain oxen, five rams, five goat bucks, five lambs
of one year. This was the offering of Elizur, the son of
Shedeur. (And for a peace offering, *he offered* two oxen,
five rams, five goat bucks, and five one-year-old lambs.
This was the offering of Elizur, the son of Shedeur.)
36 In the fifth day (On the fifth day), Shelumiel, the son
of Zurishaddai, the prince of the sons of Simeon, offered
37 a silver vessel *to prove incense and such things,*
weighing an hundred and thirty shekels, a silver basin,
having seventy shekels at the weight of [the] saintuary,
ever either full of [tried] flour sprinkled (al)together with
oil, into sacrifice; (a silver vessel, weighing a hundred
and thirty shekels, and a silver basin, weighing seventy
shekels, by the measure of the sanctuary, and each full of
fine flour sprinkled with oil, for a grain offering;)
38 a golden spoon, weighing ten shekels, full of incense;
(a gold saucer, weighing ten shekels, full of incense;)
39 an ox of the drove, and a ram, and a lamb of one
year, into burnt sacrifice; (an ox from the herd, and a
ram, and a one-year-old lamb, for a burnt sacrifice;)
40 and a buck of (the) goats, for sin. (and a goat buck,
for a sin offering.)
41 And into [the] sacrifice of peaceable things *he
offered* twain oxen, five rams, five goat bucks, five lambs
of one year. This was the offering of Shelumiel, the son
of Zurishaddai. (And for a peace offering, *he offered* two
oxen, five rams, five goat bucks, and five one-year-old
lambs. This was the offering of Shelumiel, the son of
Zurishaddai.)
42 In the sixth day (On the sixth day), Eliasaph, the son
of Deuel, the prince of the sons of Gad, offered
43 a silver vessel *to prove incense and such things,*
weighing an hundred and thirty shekels, a silver basin,
having seventy shekels at the weight of [the] saintuary,
ever either full of [tried] flour sprinkled (al)together with
oil, into (a) sacrifice; (a silver vessel, weighing a hundred
and thirty shekels, and a silver basin, weighing seventy
shekels, by the measure of the sanctuary, and each full of
fine flour sprinkled with oil, for a grain offering;)
44 a golden spoon, weighing ten shekels, full of incense;
(a gold saucer, weighing ten shekels, full of incense;)
45 an ox of the drove, and a ram, and a lamb of one
year, into burnt sacrifice; (an ox from the herd, and a
ram, and a one-year-old lamb, for a burnt sacrifice;)
46 and a buck of (the) goats, for sin. (and a goat buck,
for a sin offering.)
47 And into (the) sacrifice of peaceable things *he
offered* two oxen, five rams, five goat bucks, five lambs of
one year. This was the offering of Eliasaph, the son of
Deuel. (And for a peace offering, *he offered* two oxen,
five rams, five goat bucks, and five one-year-old lambs.
This was the offering of Eliasaph, the son of Deuel.)
48 In the seventh day (On the seventh day), Elishama,
the son of Ammihud, the prince of the sons of Ephraim,
offered
49 a silver vessel *to prove incense and such things,*
weighing an hundred and thirty shekels, a silver basin,
having seventy shekels at the weight of [the] saintuary,
ever either full of [tried] flour sprinkled (al)together with
oil, into sacrifice; (a silver vessel, weighing a hundred
and thirty shekels, and a silver basin, weighing seventy
shekels, by the measure of the sanctuary, and each full of
fine flour sprinkled with oil, for a grain offering;)
50 a golden spoon, weighing ten shekels, full of incense;
(a gold saucer, weighing ten shekels, full of incense;)
51 an ox of the drove, and a ram, and a lamb of one
year, into burnt sacrifice; (an ox from the herd, and a
ram, and a one-year-old lamb, for a burnt sacrifice;)
52 and a buck of (the) goats, for sin. (and a goat buck,
for a sin offering.)
53 And into (the) sacrifice of peaceable things *he
offered* twain oxen, five rams, five goat bucks, five lambs
of one year. This was the offering of Elishama, the son of
Ammihud. (And for a peace offering, *he offered* two oxen,
five rams, five goat bucks, and five one-year-old lambs.
This was the offering of Elishama, the son of Ammihud.)
54 In the eighth day (On the eighth day), Gamaliel, the
son of Pedahzur, the prince of the sons of Manasseh,
offered
55 a silver vessel *to prove incense and such things,*
weighing an hundred and thirty shekels, a silver basin,
having seventy shekels at the weight of [the] saintuary,
ever either full of [tried] flour sprinkled (al)together with
oil, into sacrifice; (a silver vessel, weighing a hundred
and thirty shekels, and a silver basin, weighing seventy
shekels, by the measure of the sanctuary, and each full of
fine flour sprinkled with oil, for a grain offering;)
56 a golden spoon, weighing ten shekels, full of incense;
(a gold saucer, weighing ten shekels, full of incense;)
57 an ox of the drove, and a ram, and a lamb of one
year, into burnt sacrifice; (an ox from the herd, and a
ram, and a one-year-old lamb, for a burnt sacrifice;)
58 and a buck of (the) goats, for sin. (and a goat buck,
for a sin offering.)

59 And into (the) sacrifices of peaceable things *he*
offered twain oxen, five rams, five goat bucks, five lambs
of one year. This was the offering of Gamaliel, the son of
Pedahzur. (And for a peace offering, *he offered* two oxen,
five rams, five goat bucks, and five one-year-old lambs.
This was the offering of Gamaliel, the son of Pedahzur.)
60 In the ninth day (On the ninth day), Abidan, the son
of Gideoni, the prince of the sons of Benjamin, offered
61 a silver vessel *to prove incense and such things,*
weighing an hundred and thirty shekels, a silver basin,
having seventy shekels at the weight of [the] saintuary,
ever either full of [tried] flour sprinkled (al)together with
oil, into sacrifice; (a silver vessel, weighing a hundred
and thirty shekels, and a silver basin, weighing seventy
shekels, by the measure of the sanctuary, and each full of
fine flour sprinkled with oil, for a grain offering;)
62 a golden spoon, weighing ten shekels, full of incense;
(a gold saucer, weighing ten shekels, full of incense;)
63 an ox of the drove, and a ram, and a lamb of one
year, into burnt sacrifice; (an ox from the herd, and a
ram, and a one-year-old lamb, for a burnt sacrifice;)
64 and a buck of (the) goats, for sin. (and a goat buck,
for a sin offering.)
65 And into the sacrifice of peaceable things *he offered*
twain oxen, five rams, five goat bucks, five lambs of one
year. This was the offering of Abidan, the son of
Gideoni. (And for a peace offering, *he offered* two oxen,
five rams, five goat bucks, and five one-year-old lambs.
This was the offering of Abidan, the son of Gideoni.)
66 In the tenth day (On the tenth day), Ahiezer, the son
of Ammishaddai, the prince of the sons of Dan, offered
67 a silver vessel *to prove incense and such things,*
weighing an hundred and thirty shekels, a silver basin,
having seventy shekels at the weight of [the] saintuary,
ever either full of [tried] flour sprinkled (al)together with
oil, into sacrifice; (a silver vessel, weighing a hundred
and thirty shekels, and a silver basin, weighing seventy
shekels, by the measure of the sanctuary, and each full of
fine flour sprinkled with oil, for a grain offering;)
68 a golden spoon, weighing ten shekels, full of incense;
(a gold saucer, weighing ten shekels, full of incense;)
69 an ox of the drove, and a ram, and a lamb of one
year, into burnt sacrifice; (an ox from the herd, and a
ram, and a one-year-old lamb, for a burnt sacrifice;)
70 and a buck of (the) goats, for sin. (and a goat buck,
for a sin offering.)
71 And into (the) sacrifices of peaceable things *he*
offered twain oxen, five rams, five goat bucks, five lambs
of one year. This was the offering of Ahiezer, the son of
Ammishaddai. (And for a peace offering, *he offered* two
oxen, five rams, five goat bucks, and five one-year-old
lambs. This was the offering of Ahiezer, the son of
Ammishaddai.)
72 In the eleventh day (On the eleventh day), Pagiel,
the son of Ocran, the prince of the sons of Asher, offered
73 a silver vessel *to prove incense and such things,*
weighing an hundred and thirty shekels, a silver basin,
having seventy shekels at the weight of [the] saintuary,
ever either full of [tried] flour sprinkled (al)together with
oil, into sacrifice; (a silver vessel, weighing a hundred
and thirty shekels, and a silver basin, weighing seventy
shekels, by the measure of the sanctuary, and each full of
fine flour sprinkled with oil, for a grain offering;)
74 a golden spoon, weighing ten shekels, full of incense;
(a gold saucer, weighing ten shekels, full of incense;)
75 an ox of the drove, and a ram, and a lamb of one
year, into burnt sacrifice; (an ox from the herd, and a
ram, and a one-year-old lamb, for a burnt sacrifice;)
76 and a buck of (the) goats, for sin. (and a goat buck,
for a sin offering.)
77 And into (the) sacrifice of peaceable things *he*
offered twain oxen, five rams, five goat bucks, five lambs
of one year. This was the offering of Pagiel, the son of
Ocran. (And for a peace offering, *he offered* two oxen,
five rams, five goat bucks, and five one-year-old lambs.
This was the offering of Pagiel, the son of Ocran.)
78 In the twelfth day (And on the twelfth day), Ahira,
the son of Enan, the prince of the sons of Naphtali,
offered
79 a silver vessel *to prove incense and such things,*
weighing an hundred and thirty shekels, a silver basin,
having seventy shekels at the weight of [the] saintuary,
ever either full of [tried] flour sprinkled (al)together with
oil, into sacrifice; (a silver vessel, weighing a hundred
and thirty shekels, and a silver basin, weighing seventy
shekels, by the measure of the sanctuary, and each full of
fine flour sprinkled with oil, for a grain offering;)
80 a golden spoon, weighing ten shekels, full of incense;
(a gold saucer weighing ten shekels, full of incense;)
81 an ox of the drove, and a ram, and a lamb of one
year, into burnt sacrifice; (an ox from the herd, and a
ram, and a one-year-old lamb, for a burnt sacrifice;)
82 and a buck of (the) goats, for sin. (and a goat buck,
for a sin offering.)
83 And into (the) sacrifice of peaceable things *he*
offered twain oxen, five rams, five goat bucks, five lambs
of one year. This was the offering of Ahira, the son of
Enan. (And for a peace offering, *he offered* two oxen, five
rams, five goat bucks, and five one-year-old lambs. This
was the offering of Ahira, the son of Enan.)
84 These things were offered of the sons of Israel, in the
hallowing of the altar, in the day in which it was
hallowed; silver vessels *to prove incense and such things*
twelve, silver basins twelve, golden spoons twelve;
(These were the things that were offered by the leaders of
Israel, for the dedication of the altar, on the day in which
it was anointed; twelve silver vessels, twelve silver
basins, and twelve gold saucers;)

85 so that one vessel *to prove incense and such things*
had an hundred and thirty shekels of silver, and one
basin had seventy shekels, that is, in common, two
thousand and four hundred shekels of all the vessels of
silver, by the weight of [the] saintuary; (and each silver
vessel weighed a hundred and thirty silver shekels, and
each silver basin weighed seventy silver shekels, so that
altogether, all the silver dishes weighed two thousand
and four hundred shekels, by the measure of the
sanctuary;)
86 golden spoons twelve, full of incense, weighing ten
shekels, by (the) weight of the saintuary, that is,
(al)together, an hundred and twenty shekels of gold;
(twelve gold saucers, full of incense, each weighing ten
shekels, by the measure of the sanctuary, so that
altogether, all the gold of the dishes weighed a hundred
and twenty shekels;)
87 oxen of the drove into burnt sacrifice twelve, twelve
rams, twelve lambs of one year, and the flowing sacrifices
of those, twelve bucks of (the) goats for sin; (twelve oxen
from the herd, twelve rams, and twelve one-year-old
lambs, each with their grain offerings, for the burnt
sacrifice, and twelve goat bucks, for the sin offering;)
88 the sacrifices of peaceable things, four and twenty
oxen, sixty rams, sixty goat bucks, sixty lambs of one
year. These things were offered in the hallowing of the
altar, when it was anointed. (and for the peace offering,
four and twenty oxen, sixty rams, sixty goat bucks, and
sixty one-year-old lambs. These were the things that were
offered for the dedication of the altar when it was
anointed.)
89 And when Moses entered into the tabernacle of [the]
bond of peace, to ask counsel of God's answering place,
he heard the voice *of God* speaking to him from (above)
the propitiatory, which was on the ark of (the) witnessing,
betwixt [the] two cherubims, from whence also God
spake to Moses. (And when Moses entered into the
Tabernacle of the Covenant, to ask for counsel from God,
he heard the voice *of God* speaking to him from above
the propitiatory, *that is, from above the lid,* which was on
top of the Ark of the Witnessing, *that is, the Box
containing the tablets of the Law,* from between the two
cherubim, that is where God spoke to Moses.)

CHAPTER 8

1 And the Lord spake to Moses, and said,
2 Speak thou to Aaron, and thou shalt say to him,
When thou hast set (up the) seven lanterns, the
candlestick (should) be raised (up) in the south part;
therefore command thou this, that the lanterns behold
even against the north to the board of [the] loaves of
setting forth, (so that) those lanterns shall shine against
that part that the candlestick beholdeth to. (Speak thou to
Aaron, and thou shalt say to him, When thou putteth the
lanterns onto the lamp-stand, put them so that their light
shineth out towards the front.)
3 And Aaron did so, and he putted the lanterns upon
the candlestick (and he put the lanterns on the lamp-
stand), as the Lord commanded to Moses.
4 Soothly this was the making of the candlestick; *it
was* of gold beaten out with hammers, as well the middle
stalk, as all the things that came forth on ever either side
of the rods; by the sample which the Lord showed to
Moses, so he wrought the candlestick. (And this was the
making of the lamp-stand; *it was* made of gold, beaten
out with hammers, the middle stem, as well as all of its
branches; by the example, *or the pattern,* which the Lord
had shown to Moses, so he made the lamp-stand.)
5 And the Lord spake to Moses, and said,
6 Take thou the Levites from the midst of the sons of
Israel; and thou shalt cleanse them by this custom. (Take
thou the Levites from the midst of the Israelites; and thou
shalt cleanse, *or shalt purify,* them by this rite.)
7 Be they sprinkled with (the) water of cleansing, *or of
purification,* and shave they all the hairs of their flesh.
And when they have washed their clothes and be
cleansed,
8 take they an ox of the droves, and the flowing
sacrifice thereof, [tried] flour sprinkled (al)together with
oil; forsooth thou shalt take another ox of the drove for
sin; (take they an ox from the herd, and its grain offering
of fine flour sprinkled with oil; and thou shalt take
another ox from the herd for a sin offering;)
9 and thou shalt present the Levites before the
tabernacle of the bond of peace (and thou shalt bring the
Levites before the Tabernacle of the Covenant), when all
the multitude of the sons of Israel is called together.
10 And when the Levites be *presented* before the Lord,
the sons of Israel shall set their hands upon them;
11 and Aaron shall offer, (*or shall present,*) the Levites
in the sight of the Lord, (*as*) a gift of the sons of Israel, that
they serve in the service of him. (and Aaron shall offer
the Levites before the Lord, *as* a special gift from the
Israelites, to serve in the Lord's service.)
12 Also the Levites shall set their hands upon the heads
of the oxen, of which oxen thou shalt make, *or ordain,*
one for sin, and the tother into burnt sacrifice of the Lord,
that thou pray for them. (And the Levites shall put their
hands on the heads of the oxen, of which oxen thou shalt
ordain one for a sin offering, and the other for a burnt
sacrifice to the Lord, to make amends for the Levites.)
13 And thou shalt ordain the Levites in the sight of
Aaron, and of his sons, and thou shalt (make) sacred
them (that be) offered to the Lord (and thou shalt
consecrate, *or shalt dedicate, those* who be offered to the
Lord);
14 and thou shalt separate *them* from the midst of the
sons of Israel, (so) that they be mine.

15 And afterward enter they into the tabernacle of [the]
bond of peace, that they serve me; and so thou shalt
cleanse and hallow them, into an offering of the Lord,
(And afterward they shall enter into the Tabernacle of the
Covenant to serve me; and so thou shalt cleanse, *or shalt
purify*, and dedicate them, as an offering to the Lord,)
16 for by free gift they be given to me (out) of the sons
of Israel. I have taken them for the first begotten things
that open each womb in Israel; (for they be given to me
as a special gift from all the Israelites. I have taken them
in place of the first-born males that open every womb in
Israel;)
17 for all the first begotten things of the sons of Israel
be mine, as well of men as of beasts (for all the first-born
males of the Israelites be mine, of people as well as of
beasts), (yea,) from the day in which I smote each first
engendered (male) thing in the land of Egypt, I [have]
hallowed them to me.
18 And I took the Levites for all the first begotten (sons)
of the sons of Israel; (And I took the Levites in place of all
the first-born sons of the Israelites;)
19 and I gave them by free gift to Aaron and to his sons,
from the midst of the people, that they serve me for
Israel, in the tabernacle of the bond of peace, and that
they pray for them, lest vengeance be in the people, if
they be hardy to nigh to the saintuary. (and I gave them
as a gift to Aaron and to his sons, out of the midst of the
people, to serve me for all the Israelites, in the
Tabernacle of the Covenant, and to make amends for
them, lest vengeance come upon the people, if they be
fool-hardy enough to come near to the sanctuary.)
20 And Moses and Aaron, and all the multitude of the
sons of Israel, did upon the Levites those things that the
Lord commanded to Moses. (And so Moses and Aaron,
and all the multitude of the Israelites, did with the Levites
those things that the Lord commanded to Moses.)
21 And (so) *the Levites* were cleansed, and they washed
their clothes; and Aaron raised, *or presented*, them in the
sight of the Lord, and he prayed for them, that they shall
be cleansed (and he made amends for them, to purify
them),
22 and should enter to their offices into the tabernacle
of [the] bond of peace, before Aaron and his sons (and
then they entered into the Tabernacle of the Covenant to
perform their service, before Aaron and his sons); as the
Lord commanded to Moses of the Levites, so it was done.
23 And the Lord spake to Moses, and said,
24 This is the law of [the] Levites; from five and twenty
years and above they shall enter, for to minister in the
tabernacle of [the] bond of peace; (This is the law for the
Levites; from twenty-five years of age and older, they
shall serve in the Tabernacle of the Covenant;)
25 and when they have filled the fiftieth year of age,
they shall cease to serve.
26 And they shall be the ministers of their brethren in
the tabernacle of [the] bond of peace, that they keep
(watch on) those things that be betaken to them; soothly
they shall not do those works, *as they did before*; thus
thou shalt dispose [the] Levites in their keepings. (And
afterward, they shall help their brothers in the Tabernacle
of the Covenant, and do those tasks that be assigned to
them; but they shall not do the work *that they did before*;
thus thou shalt ordain the Levites in their duties.)

CHAPTER 9

1 And the Lord spake to Moses, in the desert of Sinai
(And the Lord spoke to Moses, in the Sinai Desert), in the
second year after they went out of the land of Egypt, in
the first month, and said,
2 The sons of Israel make they pask in his time, (Have
the Israelites observe the Passover at this time,)
3 *that is*, in the fourteenth day of this month, at
eventide, by all the ceremonies and justifyings thereof.
(*that is*, on the fourteenth day of this month, in the
evening, with all of its ceremonies and its customs.)
4 And Moses commanded to the sons of Israel, that
they should make pask; (And so Moses commanded to
the Israelites to observe the Passover;)
5 which made *pask* in his time, in the fourteen day of
the month, at eventide, in the hill of Sinai; by all things
that the Lord commanded to Moses, the sons of Israel
did. (and so they observed *the Passover* at this time, on
the fourteen day of the month, in the evening, in the
Sinai Desert; all the things that the Lord commanded to
Moses, the Israelites did.)
6 Lo! forsooth some men (that were) unclean on the
soul of (a) man, that might not make pask in that day,
nighed to Moses and to Aaron, (But some men, who were
unclean from contact with the dead body of someone,
and so could not observe the Passover on that day, came
to Moses and Aaron,)
7 and said to them, We be unclean on the soul of (a)
man; why be we defrauded, that we may not offer an
offering to the Lord in his time, among the sons of Israel?
(and said to them, We be made unclean from contact
with the dead body of someone; but must we be denied,
so that we cannot offer an offering to the Lord at this
time, among the Israelites?)
8 To which Moses answered, Stand ye *aside, or
abideth*, that I take counsel, what the Lord commandeth
of you. (To whom Moses answered, Wait ye here, until I
take counsel, what the Lord commandeth of you.)
9 And the Lord spake to Moses, and said,
10 Speak thou to the sons of Israel, A man of your folk
that is unclean upon a soul, either is in the way far (off)[3],

[3] *In Latin books it is added, 'in your folk', but this is not in Hebrew.*

make he pask to the Lord (Say thou to the Israelites,
Anyone of your people who is made unclean from
contact with a dead body, or is on the way afar off, shall
observe the Passover to the Lord)
11 in the second month, in the fourteenth day of the
month, at eventide; with therf loaves and lettuces of the
field he shall eat it. (in the second month, on the
fourteenth day of the month, in the evening; yea, they
shall eat it with unleavened bread and field lettuce, *or
bitter herbs*.)
12 They shall not leave anything thereof till to the
morrowtide, and they shall not break a bone thereof; they
shall keep all the custom of pask (they shall follow all the
customs, *or all the rites*, of the Passover).
13 Forsooth if any man is clean, and is not in the way,
and nevertheless made not [the] pask, that man shall be
destroyed from his peoples, for he offered not sacrifice to
the Lord in his time *set, or covenable (time)*; he shall bear
his sin. (But if anyone is clean, and is not away, and
nevertheless did not observe the Passover, that person
shall be cut off from his people, for he did not offer an
offering to the Lord at the *set, or the appointed,* time; he
shall bear his sin.)
14 Also if a pilgrim and a comeling is with you, make
he pask to the Lord, by the ceremonies and the justifyings
thereof; the same behest shall be with (all of) you, as well
to a comeling as to a man born in the land. (And if a
foreigner or a newcomer is with you, let him observe the
Passover to the Lord, with all of its ceremonies and its
customs, *or its rites*; the same law shall apply to all of
you, to a newcomer, as well as to someone born in the
land.)
15 Therefore in the day in which the tabernacle was
raised, a cloud covered it; soothly as the likeness of fire
was on the tent, *that is, (the) tabernacle,* from (the)
eventide till to the morrowtide. (And on the day in which
the Tabernacle was raised up, a cloud came and covered
it; and a brightness like fire was over the Tent, *that is, the
Tabernacle,* from the evening until the morning.)
16 Thus it was done continually, a cloud covered it by
day, and as the likeness of fire by night. (Thus it was
done continually, that a cloud stood over it by day, and a
brightness like fire during the night.)
17 And when the cloud that covered the tabernacle was
taken away, then the sons of Israel went forth; and in the
place where the cloud stood, there they setted tents. (And
when the cloud that covered the Tabernacle lifted up,
and moved away, then the Israelites went forth; and in
the place where the cloud stopped, there they pitched
their tents.)
18 At the commandment of the Lord they went forth,
and at his commandment they setted (up) the tabernacle.
In all the days in which the cloud stood upon the
tabernacle, they dwelled in the same place. (At the Lord's
command they went forth, and at his command they put
up the Tabernacle. And all the days in which the cloud
stood over the Tabernacle, they remained in the same
place.)
19 And if it befelled that it dwelled much time upon the
tabernacle, the sons of Israel were in the watches of the
Lord, and they went not forth, (And if it befell that it
stayed a long time over the Tabernacle, the Israelites kept
watch for the Lord, and they did not go forth,)
20 in how many ever days the cloud was upon the
tabernacle. At the commandment of the Lord they raised
[the] tents, and at his commandment they did them
down. (for however many days the cloud stood over the
Tabernacle. At the Lord's command they raised the tents,
and at his command they did them down.)
21 If the cloud was *standing upon the tabernacle* from
the eventide unto the morrowtide, and anon in the
morrowtide had left, *or gone thence*, they went forth; and
if, after a day and a night, the cloud had gone away, they
scattered, *either did down*, the tents. (If the cloud *stood
over the Tabernacle* from the evening until the morning,
and then in the morning had left, *or had gone away*, they
went forth at once; or if, after only a day, or only a night,
the cloud went away, then they scattered, *or did down*,
the tents, and they moved on.)
22 Whether in two months, either in one month, either
in longer time, *the cloud* had been upon the tabernacle,
the sons of Israel dwelled in the same place, and went
not forth; but anon as it had gone away, they moved the
tents. (Or when for one month, or two months, or for an
even longer time, *the cloud* stood over the Tabernacle,
the Israelites remained in the same place, and they went
not forth; but as soon as it had gone away, then they
moved the tents.)
23 By the word of the Lord they setted (up) their tents,
and by his word they went forth; and they were in the
watches of the Lord, by his commandment, by the hand
of Moses. (By the word of the Lord they pitched their
tents, and by his word they went forth; they kept watch
for the Lord's command, spoken by Moses.)

CHAPTER 10

1 And the Lord spake to Moses, and said,
2 Make to thee two silver trumps (Make for thyself two
silver trumpets), beaten out with hammers, by which
thou mayest call together the multitude, when the tents
shall be moved.
3 And when thou shalt sound with trumps, all the
company shall be gathered to thee at the door of the
tabernacle of the bond of peace. (And when thou shalt
sound with the trumpets, all the multitude shall be
gathered to thee at the entrance to the Tabernacle of the
Covenant.)
4 If thou shalt trump *with one trump*, the princes and

the chief men of the multitude of Israel shall come to
thee; (If thou shalt sound *with one trumpet*, the leaders
who be the chief men of the multitude of Israel shall
come to thee;)
5 but if a longer, and a parted trumping *of two trumps*
shall sound, they that be at the east coast shall move *their*
tents first (then they who be on the east side shall move
their tents first).
6 Forsooth in the second sound[ing], and in like noise
of the trump, they that dwell at the south coast shall raze
their tents (they who live on the south side shall take
down their tents); and by this manner, (the) other men
shall (also) do (so), when the trumps shall sound into
going forth.
7 Forsooth when the people shall be gathered
together, (a) simple cry of trumps shall be, and the trumps
shall not sound partingly. (And when the people should
gather together, there shall be a simple cry of the
trumpets, and they shall not sound separately.)
8 The sons of Aaron, [the] priest(s), shall sound with
[the] trumps, and this shall be a lawful thing everlasting in
your generations (and this shall be an everlasting law in
all your generations).
9 If ye shall go out of your land to battle against the
enemies that fight against you, ye shall cry with trumps
sounding, and the bethinking of you shall be before your
Lord God, that ye be delivered from the hands of your
enemies. (If ye shall go out of your land to do battle
against the enemies who fight against you, ye shall cry
with sounding trumpets, and then the remembrance of
you shall be before the Lord your God, and ye shall be
delivered from the hands of your enemies.)
10 If any time ye shall have a feast, and holidays, and
calends, *that is, the first day of the month*, ye shall sing in
trumps upon the burnt sacrifices, and [the] peaceable
sacrifices, that those be to you into remembering of your
God; I am your Lord God. (And at the times that ye have
feasts, and holidays, and calends, *that is, the first day of
the month*, ye shall sing with trumpets over the burnt
sacrifices, and the peace offerings, so that they bring forth
a remembrance of you before your God; I am the Lord
your God.)
11 In the second year, in the second month, in the
twentieth day of the month, the cloud was raised [up]
from the tabernacle of [the] bond of peace. (Now in the
second year, in the second month, on the twentieth day
of the month, the cloud lifted up from the Tabernacle of
the Covenant.)
12 And the sons of Israel went forth by their companies
from the desert of Sinai; and the cloud rested in the
wilderness of Paran. (And the Israelites went forth by
their companies from the Sinai Desert; and the cloud
stopped in the wilderness of Paran.)
13 And the sons of Judah by their companies, of which
the prince was Nahshon (of whom the leader was
Nahshon), the son of Amminadab,
14 moved first tents, by the Lord's commandment,
made in the hand of Moses. (moved their tents first, at the
Lord's command, spoken by Moses.)
15 In the lineage of the sons of Issachar the prince was
Nethaneel, the son of Zuar.
16 In the lineage of (the sons of) Zebulun the prince
was Eliab, the son of Helon.
17 And the tabernacle was taken down, which the sons
of Gershon and Merari bare, and they went forth.
18 And (then) the sons of Reuben went forth by their
companies and order, of which the prince was Elizur, the
son of Shedeur.
19 Forsooth in the lineage of the sons of Simeon the
prince was Shelumiel, the son of Zurishaddai.
20 Soothly in the lineage of (the sons of) Gad the prince
was Eliasaph, the son of Deuel.
21 And the sons of Kohath went forth, and bare the
saintuary; and they raised the tabernacle till to the
coming of them. (And then the sons of Kohath went forth,
carrying the sacred vessels; and the Tabernacle was set
up by the time that they had arrived.)
22 Also the sons of Ephraim, by their companies,
moved *their* tents, in whose host the prince was
Elishama, the son of Ammihud. (And then the sons of
Ephraim, by their companies, moved *their* tents, in whose
army the leader was Elishama, the son of Ammihud.)
23 Forsooth in the lineage of the sons of Manasseh the
prince was Gamaliel, the son of Pedahzur.
24 And in the lineage of (the sons of) Benjamin the
duke was Abidan, the son of Gideoni. (And in the tribe of
Benjamin the leader was Abidan, the son of Gideoni.)
25 (And) The sons of Dan, by their companies, went
forth the last of all the tents, in whose host the prince was
Ahiezer, the son of Ammishaddai.
26 Soothly in the lineage of the sons of Asher the
prince was Pagiel, the son of Ocran.
27 And in the lineage of the sons of Naphtali the prince
was Ahira, the son of Enan.
28 These be the tents and the goings forth of the sons of
Israel, by their companies, when they went forth.
29 And Moses said to Hobab, the son of Raguel, of
Midian, his ally, *either, (that is, the) father of his wife*,
We (shall) go forth to the place which the Lord shall give
to us; come thou with us, that we do well to thee (come
thou with us, and we shall treat thee well), for the Lord
[hath] promised good things to Israel.
30 To whom he answered, I shall not go with thee, but
I shall turn again into my land, in which I was born. (To
whom he answered, I shall not go with thee, but I shall
return to my own land, where I was born.)
31 And Moses said, Do not thou forsake us, for thou
knowest in which places we ought to set tents (for thou

knowest where it is best for us to pitch our tents), and
thou shalt be our leader;
32 and when thou shalt come with us, whatever thing
shall be (the) best of the riches that the Lord shall give to
us, we shall give to thee.
33 And therefore they went forth from the hill of the
Lord the way of three days; and the ark of the bond of
peace of the Lord went before them, by those three days,
and purveyed the places of their tents. (And so they went
forth from *Mount Sinai*, the Lord's mountain, the way of
three days; and the Ark of the Covenant of the Lord, *that
is, the Ark of the Witnessing*, always went ahead of them,
to find a good place for their tents.)
34 And the cloud of the Lord was upon, *or over*, them
by day, when they went forth.
35 And when the ark was raised (up), Moses said, Rise
thou (up), Lord, and thine enemies be scattered, and they
that hate thee, flee from thy face;
36 forsooth when the ark was put down, he said, Lord,
turn again to the multitude of the host of Israel. (and
when the Ark was put down, he said, O Lord, return to
the multitudes of Israel's armies!)

CHAPTER 11

1 In the meantime grouching of the people, as of men
sorrowing for travail, rose against the Lord. And when
Moses had heard this thing, he was wroth; and the fire of
the Lord was kindled upon them, and devoured the last
part of the tents. (In the meantime, the grumbling of the
people, yea, the people complaining about their travail,
or their troubles, rose up against the Lord. And when
Moses had heard this, he was very angry; and the Lord's
fire was kindled upon them, and devoured the last part of
the camp.)
2 And when the people had cried to Moses, Moses
prayed [to] the Lord, and the fire was quenched.
3 And he called the name of that place Burning (And
they called that place Taberah), for the fire of the Lord
was kindled against them (there).
4 And the common people of men and women, that
had gone up with them, burnt with desire of flesh (burnt
with desire for flesh), and they sat, and wept, with the
sons of Israel joined together with them, and said, Who
shall give us flesh to eat?
5 We think upon the fish that we ate in Egypt freely
(We remember all the fish that we ate in Egypt); gourds,
and melons, and leeks, and onions, and garlic come into
our mind(s);
6 our soul is dry; our eyes behold none other thing
than manna. (but now our bodies be all dried up, and
there is nothing to see but this manna!)
7 Soothly manna was as the seed of coriander, of the
colour of bdellium, *which is white, and (as) bright as
crystal.*
8 And the people went about, and gathered it, and
brake *it* with a quernstone, either pounded *it* in a mortar,
and seethed *it* in a pot (and boiled *it* in a pot); and made
thereof little cakes of the (same) savour as of bread made
with oil.
9 And when [the] dew came down in the night upon
the tents, also manna came down together *therewith*.
10 Then Moses heard the people weeping by families,
and each of them by the doors of their tents; and the
strong vengeance of the Lord was wroth greatly, but also
the grouching was seen (as) unsufferable to Moses. (And
Moses heard all the people crying with their families, by
the entrances to their tents; and the Lord was greatly
angered, and provoked to take strong vengeance, and
Moses also thought that the grumbling was insufferable.)
11 And he said to the Lord, Why hast thou tormented
thy servant? why find I not grace before thee? and why
hast thou put the burden of all this people onto me? (And
he said to the Lord, Why hast thou so tormented thy
servant? why do I not find grace before thee? and why
hast thou put the burden of all of these people onto me?)
12 whether I have conceived all this multitude, either
have begotten it, that thou say to me, Bear thou them in
thy bosom, as a nurse is wont to bear a little young child,
and bear thou *this people* into the land for the which
thou swore to their fathers? (have I conceived all this
multitude, or have I begotten them, so that now thou can
say to me, Carry thou them in thy bosom, like a nurse is
wont to carry about a young child, and carry thou *these
people* into the land for which thou swore to their fathers?)
13 whereof be meats to me, that I feed so great a
multitude? They weep before me, and say, Give us flesh,
that we eat; (where shall I find enough meat, so that I can
feed so great a multitude? They weep before me, and say
to me, Give us flesh, so that we can eat it;)
14 I may not alone sustain all this people, for it is
grievous to me. (I cannot sustain all these people alone,
for this is too heavy a burden for me/for they be too
heavy a burden for me.)
15 If in other manner it seemeth to thee, I beseech thee,
that thou slay me, and that I find grace in thine eyes, that
I be not punished, *or travailed*, with so great evils. (If it
seemeth to thee otherwise, then I beseech thee, that thou
kill me, and so I shall receive grace from thee, and I shall
no longer be punished, *or travailed*, with such great evil.)
16 And the Lord said to Moses, Gather thou to me
seventy men of the elder men of Israel, whom thou
knowest to be (the) eld(er) men, and (the) masters of the
people; and thou shalt lead them to the door of the
tabernacle of [the] bond of peace (and thou shalt bring
them to the entrance to the Tabernacle of the Covenant),
and thou shalt make them to stand there with thee,
17 that I come down, and speak to thee; and I shall take
away of thy spirit, and I shall give to them, that they

sustain with thee the burden of the people, and not thou
alone be grieved. (and I shall come down, and speak
with thee; and I shall take away some of the spirit that is
upon thee, and I shall give it to them, so that they can
help sustain the burden of the people along with thee,
and so that not only thou be travailed.)
18 And thou shalt say to the people, Be ye hallowed;
tomorrow ye shall eat flesh; for I heard you say, Who
shall give us the meats of flesh? it was well to us in Egypt;
that the Lord give you flesh, (And thou shalt say to the
people, Be ye purified; for tomorrow ye shall eat some
flesh; for I heard you say, Who shall give us flesh to eat?
yea, it was well with us in Egypt; and so the Lord shall
give you flesh to eat,)
19 and ye (shall) eat (it) not *only* one day, either twain,
either five, either ten, soothly neither twenty *days*,
20 but till to a month of days, till it go out by your
nostrils, and turn into loathing; for *by your grouching* ye
have put away the Lord, which is in the midst of you, and
ye wept before him, and said, Why went we out of
Egypt? (but for a whole month of days, until it go out of
your nostrils, and it turn loathsome to you; for *by your
grumbling* ye have rejected the Lord, who is in the midst
of you, and ye have cried before him, and have said,
Why did we go out of Egypt?)
21 And Moses said to the Lord, Six hundred thousand
of footmen be of this people, and thou sayest, I shall give
them to eat flesh an whole month. (And Moses said to the
Lord, Six hundred thousand footmen be among these
people, and thou sayest, I shall give all of them flesh to
eat for a whole month?)
22 Whether the multitude of sheep and of oxen shall *be
able to* be slain, that it may suffice *(to) this people* to
meat (that it can suffice for enough food *for these
people*), either whether all the fishes of the sea shall be
gathered together, that those [ful]fill them?
23 To whom the Lord answered, Whether the Lord's
hand is unmighty? right now thou shalt see, whether my
word shall be fulfilled in work. (To whom the Lord
answered, Is the Lord's hand unmighty, *or without
power*? thou shalt see right now, if my word shall be
fulfilled in work, or not.)
24 Therefore Moses came, and told the people the
words of the Lord; and he gathered seventy men of the
elders of Israel, which he made (to) stand about the
tabernacle.
25 And the Lord came down by a cloud, and spake to
Moses, and took away of the spirit that was in Moses, and
gave (it) to the seventy men; and when the spirit had
rested in them, they prophesied, and moreover they
ceased not. (And the Lord came down in a cloud, and
spoke to Moses, and then took away some of the spirit
that was on Moses, and gave it to the seventy men; and
when the spirit had rested on them, they prophesied, and
they did not cease.)
26 Forsooth two men dwelled still in the tents, of which
men one was called Eldad, and the tother Medad, on
which the spirit rested; for also they were described, *or
ordained/or chosen*, and they went not out to the
tabernacle. And when they prophesied in the tents, (But
two men still remained in the tents, one of whom was
called Eldad, and the other Medad, and the spirit also
rested on them; for they were also chosen, but they did
not go out to the Tabernacle. And when they prophesied
in the tents,)
27 a young man ran, and told to Moses, and said, Eldad
and Medad prophesy in the tents.
28 Anon Joshua, the son of Nun, the servant of Moses,
and chosen of many, said, My lord Moses, forbid thou
them. (At once Joshua, the son of Nun, Moses' servant,
and chosen out of many, said, My lord Moses, forbid
thou them.)
29 And Moses said, What, hast thou envy for me? who
giveth, *whether not God*, that all the people prophesy,
and that God give his spirit to them? (And Moses said,
Why, hast thou envy for me? O that God would give his
spirit to everyone, and make all the people prophesy!)
30 And Moses turned again, and the elder men in birth
of Israel, into the tents. (And then Moses, and the elders
of Israel, returned to the camp.)
31 Forsooth a wind went forth from the Lord, and it took
(hold of a multitude of) curlews, and brought *them* over
the sea, and he left them in the tents, in journey, as much
as may be performed in one day, by each part of the tents
by compass; and they flew in the air by two cubits in
height above the earth. (And a wind went forth from the
Lord, and it took hold of a multitude of curlews, *or of
quails*, and brought *them* over the sea, and it left them
about the camp, as much as can be performed in one day's
journey, by each part of the camp all around; and they
flew in the air by two cubits in height above the ground.)
32 Therefore the people rose (up) in all that day, and
(all) that night, and into the tother day, and gathered a
multitude of curlews; he that *gathered* little, gathered ten
cors; and they dried those *curlews* by compass of the
tents (and they dried those *quails* all around the tents).
33 Yet (while the) flesh was in their teeth, and such
meat failed them not; and lo! the wrath of the Lord was
raised against his people, and he smote it with a full great
vengeance (and he struck them with a very great plague).
34 And that place was called The Sepulchres of
Covetousness, *or Lust*, for there they buried the people
that desired flesh. (And so that place was called
Kibrothhattaavah, for they buried the people there who
lusted after flesh.)
35 Soothly they went forth from The Sepulchres of
Covetousness, *or Lust*, and came into Hazeroth, and
dwelled there. (Then they went forth from

Kibrothhattaavah, and came to Hazeroth, and stayed
there.)

CHAPTER 12

1 And Marie spake and Aaron against Moses, for his
wife (was) a woman of Ethiopia, (And Miriam and Aaron
spoke against Moses, for his wife was an Ethiopian
woman,)
2 and they said, Whether God spake his will only by
Moses? whether he spake not also to us in like manner?
And when the Lord had heard this, he was wroth greatly
(he was greatly angered);
3 for Moses was the mildest man, over all men that
dwelled in earth. (for Moses was the humblest man, more
humble than any other man who lived upon the face of
the earth.)
4 And suddenly the Lord spake to Moses and to Aaron
and to Marie, (and said,) Go out ye three alone to the
tabernacle of the bond of peace. And when they were
gone in, (And suddenly the Lord spoke to Moses and
Aaron and Miriam, and said, Ye three go out alone to the
Tabernacle of the Covenant. And when they had gone
out to it,)
5 the Lord came down in a pillar of cloud, and he
stood in the entering of the tabernacle, and called Aaron
and Marie. And when they had gone forth, (the Lord
came down in a pillar of cloud, and he stood at the
entrance to the Tabernacle, and called Aaron and
Miriam. And when they had come forth,)
6 he said to them, Hear ye my words; if any among
you is a prophet of the Lord, I shall appear to him in
revelation, either I shall speak to him by a dream.
7 And he said, And my servant Moses is not such, the
which is most faithful in all mine house; (Then he said,
But my servant Moses is not such a prophet, for he alone
is most faithful in all my household;)
8 for I speak to him mouth to mouth, and he seeth
God openly, and not by dark speeches, *either dark
likenesses*, and figures. Why therefore dreaded ye not to
backbite my servant Moses? (and I speak with him face to
face, and he seeth God openly, and not only through
riddles. Yea, he hath even seen my form, *or my figure*!
So why do ye not fear to backbite my servant Moses?)
9 And the Lord was wroth against them, and he went
away.
10 And the cloud went away, that was on the
tabernacle, and lo! Marie appeared shining with leprosy
(and lo! Miriam had become leprous), white as snow.
And when Aaron beheld her, and saw her besprinkled
with leprosy,
11 he said to Moses, My lord, I beseech thee, put thou
not this sin upon us, which we did follily (for we acted
foolishly),
12 (and) that this *woman* be not made as dead, and as a
dead born thing that is cast out of the mother's womb; lo!
now the half of her flesh is devoured, *or over-covered*,
with leprosy (lo! now half of her flesh hath been
devoured by the leprosy!).
13 And Moses cried to the Lord, and said, Lord, I
beseech thee, heal thou her.
14 To whom the Lord answered, If her father had spit
into her face, whether she ought not to be full-filled with
shame, namely seven days? Therefore be she separated
out of the tents by seven days, and afterward she shall be
called again (And so let her be set apart from the tents for
seven days, and then she shall be called back again).
15 And so Marie was excluded, *or put*, out of the tents
by seven days; and the people was not moved from that
place, till Marie was called again. (And so Miriam was
sent away from the tents for seven days; and the people
did not move from that place, until Miriam was called
back again.)
16 And the people went forth from Hazeroth, when the
tents were set in the desert of Paran. (And then the
people went forth from Hazeroth, and pitched their tents
in the wilderness of Paran.)

CHAPTER 13

1 And there the Lord spake to Moses, and said,
2 Send thou men, that shall behold the land of
Canaan, which I shall give to the sons of Israel; of each
lineage *send thou* one man of the princes. (Send thou
some men, to look over the land of Canaan, which I shall
give to the Israelites; *send thou* one of the leaders from
each tribe.)
3 Moses did that that the Lord commanded, and sent
from the desert of Paran (the) princes, (the) men of which
these be the names. (Moses did what the Lord
commanded, and sent from the wilderness of Paran
twelve of their leaders, of which these be their names.)
4 Of the lineage of Reuben, Shammua, the son of
Zaccur.
5 Of the lineage of Simeon, Shaphat, the son of Hori.
6 Of the lineage of Judah, Caleb, the son of
Jephunneh.
7 Of the lineage of Issachar, Igal, the son of Joseph.
8 Of the lineage of Ephraim, Oshea, the son of Nun.
(Of the tribe of Ephraim, Hoshea, *or Joshua*, the son of
Nun.)
9 Of the lineage of Benjamin, Palti, the son of Raphu.
10 Of the lineage of Zebulun, Gaddiel, the son of Sodi.
11 Of the lineage of Joseph, of the generation of
Manasseh, Gaddi, the son of Susi. (Of the tribe of Joseph,
that is, of the tribe of Manasseh, Gaddi, the son of Susi.)
12 Of the lineage of Dan, Ammiel, the son of Gemalli.
13 Of the lineage of Asher, Sethur, the son of Michael.
14 Of the lineage of Naphtali, Nahbi, the son of
Vophsi.

15 Of the lineage of Gad, Geuel, the son of Machi.
16 These be the names of [the] men, which Moses sent
to behold the land of Canaan; and Moses called Oshea,
the son of Nun, Joshua. (These be the names of the men,
whom Moses sent to look over the land of Canaan; and
Moses called Hoshea, the son of Nun, Joshua.)
17 Therefore Moses sent them to behold the land of
Canaan, and said to them, Go ye up by the south coast;
and when ye come [in]to the hills, (And so Moses sent
them to look over the land of Canaan, and he said to
them, Go ye up by the Negeb, *or by the southern part*,
and when ye come into the hill country,)
18 behold ye the land, what manner land it is; and
behold ye the people which is the dweller thereof,
whether it is strong, either feeble, few in number, either
many; (look over the land, and see what it is like; and
look over the people who live there, whether they be
strong, or feeble, and few in number, or many;)
19 *whether* that land is good, either evil (or bad); what
manner cities be there, walled, either without walls;
20 *whether* the land is fat, either barren, *whether it is*
full of woods, either without trees. Be ye comforted, and
bring ye to us of the fruits of that land. Soothly then the
time was, when [the] grapes first ripe might be eaten.
(*whether* the land is fertile, or barren, *whether it is* full of
woods, or without trees. Be ye strengthened, *that is, be
ye of good courage*, and bring ye to us some of the fruits
of that land. For it was then the time when the first ripe
grapes could be eaten.)
21 And when they had gone up, they espied the land,
from the desert of Zin till to Rehob, as men enter to
Hamath. (And so when they had gone up, they spied out
the land, from the wilderness of Zin unto Rehob, as
people go to Hamath.)
22 And they went up to the south *coast*, and came into
Hebron, where Ahiman, and Sheshai, and Talmai, the
sons of Anak, were; for Hebron was made seven years
before Tanis, the city of Egypt. (And they went up by the
Negeb, *or by the southern part*, and came to Hebron,
where Ahiman, and Sheshai, and Talmai, the sons of the
giants, were living; for Hebron was built seven years
before Tanis, the city of Egypt.)
23 And they went to the strand of [the] cluster, and they
cutted down a scion with his grapes, which two men
bare with a bearing staff; also they took of [the]
pomegranates, and of the figs of that place, (And they
went to the Eshcol Valley, and cut down a branch with
all of its grapes, which two men had to carry on a
carrying bar, *or a carrying pole*; and they also took
pomegranates and figs from that place,)
24 which is called Nahal-eshcol, *that is, the strand of
(the) grape(s), or the strand of (the) cluster*, for the sons of
Israel bare a cluster from thence. (which they called
Nahal-eshcol, *that is, the Eshcol Valley, or the Valley of
the Cluster of Grapes*, for the Israelites carried a cluster of
grapes from there.)
25 And the spyers of the land [turned again], when they
had compassed all the country(side), after forty days (And
the spies returned, when they had gone about all the
countryside, yea, after forty days)
26 they came to Moses and Aaron, and to all the
company of the sons of Israel, into the desert of Paran,
which is in Kadesh. And *the spyers* spake to them, and
showed the fruits of the land to all the multitude, (they
came back to Moses and Aaron, and to all the company
of the Israelites, at Kadesh in the wilderness of Paran.
And *the spies* spoke to them, and to all the multitude,
and showed them the fruits of the land,)
27 and they told, and said (and they spoke to Moses,
and said), We came to the land, to which thou sentest us,
which land truly floweth with milk and honey, as it may
be known by these fruits;
28 but it hath most strong dwellers, and great cities,
and walled (but it hath very strong inhabitants, and great
walled cities); we saw there the kindred of (the) Anakim,
that is, (of the) giants;
29 Amalek dwelleth *there* in the south; Hittites, and
Jebusites, and Amorites *dwell* in the hilly places; forsooth
Canaanites dwell beside the sea, and beside the floods of
Jordan. (and the Amalekites live *there* in the south; and
the Hittites, and Jebusites, and Amorites *live* in the hill
country; and the Canaanites live by the Mediterranean
Sea, and along the Jordan River.)
30 Among these things, *or sayings*, Caleb peaced the
grouching of the people, that was made against Moses,
and said, Go we up, and wield we the land, for we be
able to get it. (Then after these words, Caleb tried to calm
the grumbling of the people, and said, No matter! We
shall go up, and take the land, for we be well able to get
it.)
31 Soothly the other *spyers*, that were with him, said,
We be not able to go up to this people, for it is stronger
than we. (But the other *spies* who went with him said,
We shall not be able to go up against these people, for
they all be stronger than us!)
32 And they spake evil of the land which they had
beheld, to the sons of Israel, and said, The land that we
compassed devoureth his dwellers; the people that we
beheld is of large stature; (And so, they gave a bad report
about the land which they had seen, to the Israelites, and
said, The land which we went about shall eat up anyone
who shall go there to live; and the people, who we saw
there, be of very large stature;)
33 there we saw some wonders against kind, of the
sons of Anak, of the kind of giants, to which we were
comparisoned, and were seen as locusts. (yea, we saw
some wonders against kind there, the sons of Anak, who
be giants, and compared to them, we felt as small as

locusts, *or like grasshoppers.*)

CHAPTER 14

1 Therefore all the company cried, and wept in that
night,
2 and all the sons of Israel grouched against Moses
and Aaron, and said, We would that we had been dead
in Egypt, either that we were dead in this wilderness; we
would that we perished, (and all the Israelites grumbled
against Moses and Aaron, and said, We wish that we had
died in Egypt, or that we had already died here in this
wilderness; yea, we wish that we were dead,)
3 and that the Lord lead us not into this land, lest we
fall by sword, and our wives and our free children be led,
or taken, prisoners; whether it is not better to us to turn
again into Egypt? (is it not better for us to return to Egypt?)
4 And they said one to another, Ordain we a duke, *or
a leader*, to us, and turn we again into Egypt. (And they
said to one another, Let us choose a *new* leader, and let
us return to Egypt.)
5 And when this was heard, Moses and Aaron fell
down low to the earth (Moses and Aaron fell down on
the ground), before all the multitude of the sons of Israel.
6 And soothly Joshua, the son of Nun, and Caleb, the
son of Jephunneh, which also compassed the land, rent
their clothes, (And truly Joshua, the son of Nun, and
Caleb, the son of Jephunneh, two of the spies who had
gone throughout the land, tore their clothes,)
7 and they spake thus to all the multitude of the sons
of Israel, (and said,) The land which we compassed is full
good; (and they spoke thus to all the multitude of the
Israelites, and said, The land which we went about is
very good;)
8 if the Lord is merciful to us, he shall lead us into it,
and he shall give *us* the land flowing with milk and
honey.
9 Do not ye rebel against the Lord, neither dread ye
the people of this land, for we be able to devour them so
as bread; all their help hath passed away from them, the
Lord is with us, do not ye dread. (Do not ye rebel against
the Lord, nor fear ye the people of this land, for we be
able to eat them up like a piece of bread; all their help
hath passed away from them, yea, the Lord is with us, do
not ye fear.)
10 And when all the multitude cried (out), and would
have oppressed them with stones, the glory of the Lord
appeared upon the roof of the bond of peace, while all
the sons of Israel saw. (But when all the multitude
shouted, and would have killed them with stones, the
glory of the Lord appeared over the Tabernacle of the
Covenant, before all the Israelites.)
11 And the Lord said to Moses, How long shall this
people backbite me, *or mis-deem me*? How long shall
they not believe to me, in (spite of) all the signs which I
have done before them? (And the Lord said to Moses,
How long shall these people backbite me, *or mis-judge
me*? How long shall they not believe me, *or not trust in
me*, in spite of all the miracles which I have done before
them?)
12 Therefore I shall smite them with pestilence, and I
shall waste *them*; soothly I shall make thee prince upon a
greater folk, and stronger than is this. (And so I shall
strike them with a pestilence, *or a plague*, and I shall
destroy *them*; and then I shall make thee the leader of a
greater, and of a stronger, nation than these people be.)
13 And Moses said to the Lord, [The] Egyptians hear
not, from whose middle thou leddest out this people,
(And Moses said to the Lord, But then the Egyptians, from
whose midst thou leddest out these people, shall hear of
it,)
14 and (they shall tell it to) the dwellers of this land,
which heard that thou, Lord, art in this people (who have
heard that thou, Lord, art with these people), and art seen
face to face, and that thy cloud defendeth them, and that
thou goest before them in a pillar of cloud by day, and in
a pillar of fire by night,
15 that thou hast slain so great a multitude as (if they be
just) one man, and (then they shall) say,
16 He might not bring this people into the land for
which he swore to give to them, therefore he killed them
in (the) wilderness; (Because he could not bring these
people into the land which he had sworn to give them,
and so he killed all of them in this wilderness;)
17 therefore (let) the strength of the Lord be magnified,
or made great, as thou hast sworn, (saying of thyself),
18 [The] Lord (is) patient, and of much mercy, doing
away wickedness and trespasses, and leaving no man
unguilty, (*or innocent*,) which visitest the sins of (the)
fathers into (the) sons into the third and fourth generation
(and who visitest the sins of the fathers upon the children
into the third and fourth generations),
19 (so) I beseech thee, forgive thou the sin of this thy
people, after the greatness of thy mercy, as thou were
merciful to them going out of Egypt till to this place.
20 And the Lord said, I have forgiven to them, by thy
word. (And the Lord said, I now forgive them, because of
thy words.)
21 *And as soothly (as)* I live; and the glory of the Lord
shall be filled in all [the] earth; (*But as truly as* I live, the
glory of the Lord shall fill all the earth;)
22 nevertheless all [the] men that saw my majesty, and
my signs, (*and wonders*,) which I did in Egypt and (here)
in the wilderness, and [have] tempted me now by ten
times, and obeyed not to my voice,
23 shall not see the land for which I swore to their
fathers, neither any of them that backbited me, shall see
it.
24 I shall lead my servant Caleb, that was full of

another spirit and followed me, into this land, which he
compassed, and his seed shall wield it. (But I shall lead
my servant Caleb, who was full of another spirit and
followed me, into this land, which he went about, and
his descendants shall possess it.)
25 For Amalek and Canaanites dwell in the valleys,
tomorrow move ye [the] tents, and turn ye again into the
wilderness by the way of the Red Sea. (For the
Amalekites and the Canaanites live in these valleys,
tomorrow move ye your tents, and return ye to the
wilderness by way of the Red Sea.)
26 And the Lord spake to Moses and to Aaron, and
said,
27 How long groucheth this worst multitude against
me? I have heard the *grouching* plaints of the sons of
Israel. (How long grumbleth this worst multitude against
me? I have heard all the *grumbling* and the complaints of
the Israelites.)
28 Therefore say thou to them, (As) I live, saith the
Lord; as ye spake while I heard, so I shall do to you;
29 your carrions, *or dead bodies*, shall lie in this
wilderness. All ye that be numbered, from twenty years
and above, and have grouched against me, (all your
corpses shall lie here in this wilderness. All ye who be
listed, *or registered*, from twenty years of age and older,
and have grumbled against me,)
30 shall not enter into the land, upon which I have
raised (up) mine hand, that I should make you to dwell
there (where I would have you live), except Caleb, the
son of Jephunneh, and Joshua, the son of Nun.
31 Forsooth I shall lead in your little children, of which
ye said that they should be preys, *either ravens*, to (thine)
enemies, that they see the land which displeased you.
(But I shall lead in your little children, they of whom ye
said would become your enemies' spoils, so that they can
have the land which hath so displeased you.)
32 Forsooth your carrions shall lie in the wilderness;
(But your corpses shall lie here in this wilderness;)
33 your sons shall be walkers-about in the desert by
forty years, and they shall bear your fornication, till the
carrions of their fathers be wasted in (the) desert, (your
sons shall be wanderers in this wilderness for forty years,
and they shall bear your punishment, until their fathers'
corpses be wasted in this wilderness,)
34 by the number of forty days, in which ye beheld the
land; a year shall be reckoned for a day, and by forty
years ye shall receive (the penalty for) your wickedness,
or be punished for your grouching, and ye shall know my
vengeance. (yea, for the forty days in which ye looked
the land over, a year shall be reckoned for a day, and so
for forty years ye shall receive the penalty for your
wickedness, *and shall be punished for your grumbling*,
and then ye shall know my vengeance.)
35 For as I spake, so I shall do to all this worst
multitude, that rose (up) together against me; it shall fail
(they shall fail), and shall die in this wilderness.
36 Therefore all the men which Moses had sent to see
the land, and which turned again, and made all the
multitude to grouch against him, and depraved the land,
(And so all the men whom Moses had sent to look over
the land, and returned, and then had made all the
multitude to grumble against him, and to despise the
land,)
37 that it was evil, were dead, and smitten in the sight
of the Lord[4]. (by saying that it was evil, were then struck
by the Lord with a pestilence, *or a plague*, and died.)
38 Soothly (only) Joshua, the son of Nun, and Caleb,
the son of Jephunneh, lived, of all the men, that went to
see the land (who went to see the land).
39 And Moses spake all these words to all the sons of
Israel, and the people mourned greatly. (And Moses
spoke all these words to all the Israelites, and the people
greatly mourned.)
40 And, lo! they rose in the morrowtide first, and they
went up into the top of the hill, and said, We be ready to
go up to the place, of which the Lord spake, for we have
sinned. (And lo! they rose up early the next morning, and
left to go up into the heights of the hill country, saying,
See, now we be ready to go up to the place, of which the
Lord hath spoken, and we confess, that we have sinned.)
41 To whom Moses said, Why over-pass ye the word of
the Lord, that shall not befall to you into prosperity? (To
whom Moses said, Why pass ye over the word of the
Lord? this shall not befall to you into any prosperity, *or
any success, but only evil.*)
42 Do not ye go up, for the Lord is not with you, lest ye
fall before your enemies. (Do not ye go up, for the Lord is
not with you, and ye shall fall before your enemies.)
43 Amalek and Canaanites be before you, by the sword
of which ye shall fall, for ye would not assent to the Lord,
neither the Lord shall be with you. (The Amalekites and
the Canaanites be before you, by whose sword ye shall
fall, for ye would not assent to the Lord, and so the Lord
shall not be with you.)
44 And they were made dark, *that is, blinded in their
sin*, and went up into the top of the hill; forsooth the ark
of the testament of the Lord and Moses went not away
from the tents. (But they were blinded by their sin, and
they went up anyway into the heights of the hill country;
but neither the Ark of the Covenant of the Lord, *that is,
the Ark of the Witnessing*, nor Moses, left the camp.)
45 And Amalek came down, and Canaanites, that
dwelled in the hill, and he smote the children of Israel,
and he cutted them down, and pursued them (till) to
Hormah. (And the Amalekites, and the Canaanites, who

[4] *That is, suddenly and horribly, by the sentence of the Lord, (and) to the dread of (the) other men.*

lived in that hill country, came down, and they struck the
Israelites, and they cut them down, and pursued them as
far as Hormah.)

CHAPTER 15

1 And the Lord spake to Moses, and said,
2 Speak thou to the sons of Israel (Speak thou to the
Israelites), and thou shalt say to them, When ye have
entered into the land of your habitation, which I shall
give to you,
3 and ye shall make an offering to the Lord into burnt
sacrifice, either a peaceable sacrifice, and ye pay avows,
either offer gifts by free will, either in your solemnities ye
burn odour of sweetness to the Lord, of oxen, either of
sheep; (and ye shall make an offering to the Lord for a
burnt sacrifice, or a peace offering, or ye pay vows, or
freely offer gifts, or at your feasts, *or your festivals*, ye
make the sweetest aroma to the Lord, by burning oxen,
or sheep;)
4 whoever offereth the slain sacrifice, shall offer a
sacrifice of flour, the tenth part of (an) ephah, sprinkled
(al)together with oil, which oil shall have a measure (of)
the fourth part of (a) hin; (whoever offereth a burnt
sacrifice, shall also offer a grain offering, the tenth of an
ephah, sprinkled with oil, which oil shall be a quarter of
a hin;)
5 and he shall give wine to [the] flowing sacrifices to
be poured (out), *of the same measure*, into burnt
sacrifice, and slain sacrifice. (and he shall add *the same*
measure of wine, for the wine offering to be poured out,
with the burnt sacrifice.)
6 By each lamb and ram shall be the sacrifice of [tried]
flour, of two tenth parts, which shall be sprinkled
(al)together with oil, of the third part of (a) hin; (With
each lamb and each ram shall be a grain offering of fine
flour of two tenths of an ephah, which shall be sprinkled
with a third of a hin of oil;)
7 and he shall offer wine to the flowing sacrifice, of
the third part of the same measure, into odour of
sweetness to the Lord. (and he shall offer wine of the
same measure, for the wine offering, *that is, a third of a*
hin, to make the sweetest aroma to the Lord.)
8 Forsooth when thou makest a burnt sacrifice, either
an offering, of oxen, that thou [ful]fill a vow, either
peaceable sacrifice[s], (And when thou makest a burnt
sacrifice, or a sacrifice, of an ox, so that thou fulfill a vow,
or a peace offering,)
9 thou shalt give, by each ox, three tenth parts of tried
flour, sprinkled (al)together with oil, which shall have the
half measure of (a) hin; (thou shalt give, with each ox, a
grain offering of fine flour, three tenths of an ephah,
sprinkled with half a hin of oil;)
10 *and thou shalt give* wine to [the] flowing sacrifice to
be poured (out), of the same measure, into offering of the
sweetest odour to the Lord. (*and thou shalt give* wine of
the same measure, *that is, half a hin*, for the wine offering
to be poured out, to make an offering of the sweetest
aroma to the Lord.)
11 So ye shall do by each ox, and ram, and lamb, and
kid; (So ye shall do with each ox, and ram, and lamb, and
goat kid;)
12 (See verse 11 above.)
13 as well men born in the land, as pilgrims, shall offer
sacrifices by the same custom; (people born in the land,
as well as foreigners, *or strangers*, shall offer these
offerings by the same custom;)
14 (See verse 13 above.)
15 (See verse 16 below.)
16 one commandment and doom shall be, as well to
you as to [the] comelings of the land. (one law and one
custom shall be for you, and for all the newcomers in the
land.)
17 And the Lord spake to Moses, and said,
18 Speak thou to the sons of Israel, and thou shalt say
to them, When ye come into the land which I shall give
to you,
19 and ye eat of the loaves of that country, ye shall
separate a little cake of your pastes to the Lord (ye shall
set apart a little cake, as a contribution to the Lord);
20 as ye shall separate the first fruits of *your* cornfloors,
(as ye shall set apart the first fruits from *your* threshing
floors,)
21 so ye shall give the first fruits also of *your* sowls to
the Lord. (so ye shall also give the first fruits of *your*
dough to the Lord.)
22 That if by ignorance ye pass (over) any of those
things which the Lord spake to Moses, (And if, by
ignorance, ye forget to do any of these things which the
Lord spoke to Moses,)
23 and [hath] commanded by him to you, from the day
in which he began to command (to Moses), and over
(and thereafter),
24 and the multitude hath forgotten to do *this*, it shall
offer a calf of the drove, (for) burnt sacrifice into sweetest
odour to the Lord, and the sacrifices thereof, and (the)
flowing offerings, as the ceremonies thereof ask; and *it*
shall offer a buck of (the) goats for sin. (but the multitude
hath forgotten to do *this*, they shall offer a calf from the
herd, for a burnt sacrifice, to make the sweetest aroma to
the Lord, with its grain and wine offerings, as such
ceremonies require; and *they shall offer* a goat buck for a
sin offering.)
25 And the priest shall pray for all the multitude of the
sons of Israel, and it shall be forgiven to them, for they
sinned not willfully. And nevertheless they shall offer
incense to the Lord for themselves, and for their sin, and
their error; (And the priest shall make amends for all the
multitude of the Israelites, and it shall be forgiven to

them, for they did not sin willfully, *or intentionally*. And
they have now offered incense to the Lord for
themselves, yea, a sin offering for *their* error;)
26 and it shall be forgiven to all the people of the sons
of Israel, and to the comelings that be pilgrims among
them, for it is the sin of all the multitude by ignorance.
(and so it shall be forgiven to all the people of the
Israelites, and to the foreigners who be newcomers
among them, for it is a sin of ignorance by all the
multitude.)
27 That if a soul sinneth unwittingly, it shall offer a
[she] goat of one year for his sin; (And if someone sinneth
unwittingly, he shall offer a one-year-old she goat, for his
sin offering;)
28 and the priest shall pray for that soul, for it sinned
unwittingly before the Lord; and the priest shall get
forgiveness to it, and the sin shall be forgiven to him.
(and the priest shall make amends for that person, for he
sinned unwittingly before the Lord; and so the priest shall
get forgiveness for him, and his sin shall be forgiven.)
29 As well to men born in the land, as to comelings,
one law shall be of all that sin unwittingly. (Yea, for men
born in the land, as well as for newcomers, one law shall
be for all who sin unwittingly, *or unintentionally*.)
30 Forsooth a man that doeth any sin by pride, shall
perish from the people, whether he be a citizen, either a
pilgrim, for he was rebel against the Lord; (But anyone
who doeth any sin by pride, shall be cut off from the
people/shall be put to death, whether he is a citizen, or a
foreigner, for he rebelled against the Lord;)
31 for he despised the word of the Lord, and made void
his commandment; therefore he shall be done away (and
so he shall be cut off/and so he shall be put to death), and
shall bear his own wickedness.
32 Soothly it was done, when the sons of Israel were in
wilderness, and they had found a man gathering wood in
the sabbath day, (And it was done, when the Israelites
were still in the wilderness, and they found a man
gathering wood on the sabbath day,)
33 they brought him to Moses, and to Aaron, and to all
the multitude;
34 the which closed, *or put*, him into prison, and they
knew not what they should do to him. (and they enclosed
him in prison, and they did not know what they should
do with him.)
35 And the Lord said to Moses, This man die by death;
all the company oppress him with stones without the
tents. (And the Lord said to Moses, This man must be put
to death; take him away from the tents, and have all the
people kill him with stones.)
36 And when they had led him withoutforth, they killed
him with stones, and (so) he was dead, as the Lord
commanded (to Moses).
37 Also the Lord said to Moses,
38 Speak thou to the sons of Israel, and thou shalt say
to them, that they make to them hems by (the) four
corners of *their* mantles, and fasten they in them laces of
jacinth; (Speak thou to the Israelites, and thou shalt say to
them, beginning now, and forevermore, they shall put
tassels on the four corners of *their* mantles, and fasten a
blue ribbon to the tassels;)
39 and when they see those, have they mind of all the
commandments of the Lord, lest they follow their [own]
thoughts and their eyes, doing fornication by diverse
things. (and when they see those things, they shall
remember all the Lord's commands, lest they follow their
own thoughts, and their own eyes, and do idolatry with
diverse things;)
40 but more be they mindful of the behests of the Lord,
and do they those, and be they holy to their God. (yea,
let them remember the Lord's commands, and do they
them, and be they holy, yea, consecrated to their God.)
41 I am your Lord God, which led you out of the land
of Egypt, that I should be your God. (I am the Lord your
God, who led you out of the land of Egypt, so that I could
be your God.)

CHAPTER 16

1 Forsooth Korah, the son of Izhar, the son of Kohath,
the son of Levi, and Dathan and Abiram, the sons of
Eliab, and On, the son of Peleth, of the sons of Reuben,
2 rose against Moses, and (with them) others of the
sons of Israel, two hundred men and fifty, princes of the
synagogue, and which were called by their names in the
time of counsel. (rose up against Moses, and with them
were other Israelites, two hundred and fifty men, leaders
of the synagogue, who were called by their names at the
times of gathering together.)
3 And when these stood against Moses and Aaron,
they said, Suffice it to you, for all the multitude is of holy
men, and the Lord is in them; why be ye raised up
presumptuously on the people of the Lord? (And when
they stood against Moses and Aaron, they said, Suffice it
to you, for all the multitude be holy men, and the Lord is
with them; why be ye so *presumptuously* raised up over
the Lord's people?)
4 And when Moses had heard this, he fell down low
upon his face (he fell down on the ground).
5 And he spake to Korah, and to all the multitude; he
said, Early the Lord shall make known which *men* pertain
to him, and he shall apply, *or draw*, to him holy men;
and they which he hath chosen, shall nigh to him. (And
he spoke to Korah, and to all the multitude, and said,
Early tomorrow the Lord shall make known which *man*
pertaineth to him, for he shall draw to himself the man
who is holy; and he whom he hath chosen, shall be near
to him.)
6 Therefore do ye this thing; each man take his censer,

thou Korah, and all thy counsel; (And so do ye this thing;
each man take his censer, thou Korah, and all thy
company, *or all thy people*;)
7 and tomorrow when fire is taken up, put ye incense
above before the Lord (and tomorrow put fire in them,
and put ye incense on it before the Lord), and whomever
the Lord chooseth, he shall be holy. Ye sons of Levi be
much raised (up).
8 And again Moses said to Korah, Ye sons of Levi,
hear.
9 Whether it is little to you (Is it such a small thing for
you), that (the) God of Israel [hath] separated you from all
the people, and hath joined *you* to himself, (so) that ye
should serve him in the service of the tabernacle, and
that ye should stand before the multitude of the people,
and serve him, (yea, serve Almighty God)?
10 Made he therefore thee, and all thy brethren the
sons of Levi (with thee), to nigh to himself, that ye
challenge to you also (the) priesthood, (Yea, he made
thee, and all thy brothers, *or thy kinsmen*, the Levites,
with thee, just for that, to be near him; but now ye seek
the priesthood for yourselves as well,)
11 and (for that,) all thy gathering together stand against
the Lord? For why, what is Aaron, that ye grouch against
him? (and for that, all thy company now stand against the
Lord! For what is Aaron, that ye should grumble against
him?)
12 Therefore Moses sent to call Dathan and Abiram,
the sons of Eliab; which answered, We come not. (And
so Moses sent for Dathan and Abiram, the sons of Eliab;
but they answered, We shall not come *to thee*.)
13 Whether is it little to thee, that thou leddest us out of
the land that flowed with milk and honey, to slay us in
the desert, no but also thou be lord of us? (Is it such a
small thing for thee, that thou leddest us out of the land
of Egypt which flowed with milk and honey, to kill us
here in the wilderness, but must thou also be our lord
and master?)
14 Verily thou hast brought us into the land that
floweth with streams of milk and honey, and [thou] hast
given to us possession of fields, and of vineyards[5];
whether also thou wilt put out our eyes? We come not *to
thee* (We shall not come *to thee*).
15 And Moses was wroth greatly, and said to the Lord,
Behold thou not the sacrifices of them; thou knowest that
I took never of them a little ass, neither I tormented any
of them. (And Moses was greatly angered, and said to the
Lord, Do not thou receive any of their offerings, *Lord*; for
thou knowest that I never took a solitary donkey from
them, nor did I torment any of them.)
16 And Moses said to Korah, Thou and all thy
congregation stand asides half before the Lord, and Aaron
tomorrow by himself. (And Moses said to Korah,
Tomorrow, thou, and all thy company, *or all thy people*,
come and stand here before the Lord, and also Aaron, by
himself.)
17 Take ye all by yourselves your censers, and put ye
incense in those (All of you shall take your censers, and
put ye incense in them), and offer ye to the Lord, twain
hundred and fifty censers; and Aaron hold he his censer
(also).
18 And (so the next day) when they had done this,
while Moses and Aaron stood *there*,
19 and they had gathered all the multitude to the door
of the tabernacle against them, the glory of the Lord
appeared to all. (and Korah had gathered all the
multitude against them at the entrance to the Tabernacle,
the glory of the Lord appeared to all of them.)
20 And the Lord spake to Moses and to Aaron, and
said,
21 Be ye separated from the midst of this congregation,
that I lose them suddenly. (Be ye set apart from the midst
of this company, *or of these people*, so that I can quickly
destroy them.)
22 The which fell down low upon their face(s), and
said, Most strong God of the spirits of all flesh, whether
thy wrath shall be fierce against all men, for one man
sinneth?
23 And the Lord said to Moses,
24 Command thou to all the people, that it be
separated from the tabernacles of Korah, and of Dathan,
and of Abiram. (Command thou to all the people, that
they move away from the tents of Korah, and Dathan,
and Abiram.)
25 And Moses rose (up), and went to Dathan and
Abiram; and while the elder men of Israel followed him,
26 he said to the company, Go ye away from the
tabernacles of the wicked men, and do not ye touch
those things that pertain to them, lest ye be wrapped in
the sins of them. (he said to the people, Go ye away from
the tents of these wicked men, and do not ye touch those
things that pertain to them, lest ye be wrapped up in their
sins.)
27 And when they had gone away from their tents by
compass, Dathan and Abiram went out, and stood in the
entry of their tents, with their wives, and their free
children, and with all the multitude. (And when they had
gone away from their tents all around, Dathan and
Abiram went out, and stood at the entrance to their tents,
with their wives, and their children, and with all their
multitude.)
28 And Moses said, In this ye shall know that the Lord
sent me, that I should do all things which ye see, and that
I brought them not forth of mine own heart. (And Moses
said, By this ye shall know that the Lord hath sent me, to

[5] They said this in scorn, to signify that Moses (had) deceived the people by false promises.

do all these things which ye see, and that I did not bring
them forth from my own heart.)
29 If they perish by customable death of men, and
wound, *either pestilence*, visit them, by which also other
men be wont to be visited, the Lord sent not me; (If these
men die by the customary deaths of people, or if a
wound, *or a pestilence*, visit them, by which other
people be wont to be visited, then the Lord did not send
me;)
30 but if the Lord doeth a new thing, that the earth
open his mouth, and swallow them, and all things that
pertain to them, and they go down quick into hell, ye
shall know that they blasphemed the Lord. (but if the
Lord doeth a new thing, yea, and the earth open its
mouth, and swallow them, and all things that pertain to
them, and they go down alive into hell, *or to Sheol*, then
ye shall know that they blasphemed against the Lord.)
31 Therefore anon as he ceased to speak, the earth was
broken under their feet, (And so as soon as he ceased to
speak, the ground broke up under their feet,)
32 and the earth opened his mouth, and devoured
them, with their tabernacles, and all their chattel; (and
the earth opened its mouth, and swallowed them, and
their tents, and all their possessions;)
33 and they went down quick, into hell, and *were*
covered with earth, and they perished from the midst of
the multitude. (and they went down alive into hell, *or to
Sheol*, and then they *were* covered with earth, and so
they perished from the midst of the multitude.)
34 And soothly all Israel that stood about, fled from the
cry of men perishing, and said, Lest peradventure the
earth swallow also us. (And all the Israelites who stood
about, fled from the cry of the people as they perished,
saying, Lest the earth swallow us as well.)
35 But also fire went out from the Lord, and killed (the)
twain hundred and fifty men that offered incense.
36 And the Lord spake to Moses, and said,
37 Command thou to Eleazar, the son of Aaron, [the]
priest, that he take, *or gather up*, the censers that lie in
the burning, and that he scatter the fire hither and thither;
for those *censers* be hallowed (for those censers be holy),
38 in the deaths of (these) sinners; and that he bring
forth those *censers* into plates, and nail them to the altar,
for incense is offered in those to the Lord, and those be
hallowed, that the sons of Israel see them for a sign and a
memorial. (even without the deaths of these sinners; and
that he make those *censers* into plates, and then nail
them to the altar, for incense was offered in them to the
Lord, and so they be holy; and then the Israelites shall
see them as a sign and as a reminder.)
39 Therefore Eleazar, the priest, took the brazen
censers, in which they, which the burning had devoured
had offered, and he beat out those censers into plates,
and nailed them to the altar; (And so Eleazar, the priest,
took the bronze censers, with which they, whom the
burning had devoured, had made an offering to the Lord,
and he beat those censers into plates, and then nailed
them to the altar;)
40 that the sons of Israel should have *those censers
with them* afterward, by which they should remember
this great vengeance of God, lest any alien, and which is
not of the seed of Aaron, nigh to offer incense to the
Lord; lest he suffer, as Korah suffered, and all his
multitude, while the Lord spake to Moses. (so that the
Israelites would have *those censers with them* afterward,
by which they would remember *this great vengeance of
God*, lest any stranger, who is not of Aaron's
descendants, come near to offer incense to the Lord; for
then he would suffer, like Korah and all his fellows had
suffered; all of this was done as the Lord commanded to
Eleazar, through Moses.)
41 Forsooth all the multitude of the sons of Israel
grouched in the day following against Moses and Aaron,
and said, Ye have slain the people of the Lord. (But on
the following day all the multitude of the Israelites
grumbled against Moses and Aaron, and said, Ye have
killed the people of the Lord.)
42 And when dissension (a)rose, and the noise
increased, Moses and Aaron fled to the tabernacle of the
bond of peace (Moses and Aaron fled to the Tabernacle
of the Covenant); and after that they entered into it, a
cloud covered the tabernacle, and the glory of the Lord
appeared.
43 (See verse 42 above.)
44 And the Lord said to Moses and Aaron,
45 Go ye away from the midst of this multitude, also
now I shall do away them. And when they lay in the
earth, (Go ye away from the midst of this multitude, for I
shall now destroy them. And when they lay on the
ground,)
46 Moses said to Aaron, Take thy censer, and when the
fire is taken up from (off) the altar, cast thou incense
above, and go thou forth soon to the people, that thou
pray for them; for now wrath is gone out from the Lord,
and the vengeance is fierce. (Moses said to Aaron, Take
thy censer, and when thou hast taken fire from off the
altar, cast thou incense on it, and quickly go forth to the
people, and make amends for them; for anger hath now
gone out from the Lord, and the plague hath begun.)
47 And when Aaron had done this, and had run to the
midst of the multitude, which the burning wasted then,
he offered incense; (And Aaron did this, and ran to the
midst of the multitude, who were already dying from the
plague, and he offered the incense;)
48 and he stood betwixt the dead men and the living,
and he prayed for the people, and the vengeance ceased.
(and he stood there among the living and the dead, and
made amends for the people, and then the plague

ceased.)
49 Soothly they that were slain were fourteen thousand
of men and seven hundred, without them that perished in
the dissension of Korah. (But fourteen thousand and
seven hundred people died from the plague, besides
those who had perished in the rebellion of Korah.)
50 And Aaron turned again to Moses, to the door of the
tabernacle of the bond of peace, after that the perishing
of men ceased. (And then Aaron returned to Moses, at
the entrance to the Tabernacle of the Covenant, after that
the plague had ceased.)

CHAPTER 17

1 And the Lord spake to Moses, saying,
2 Speak thou to the sons of Israel, and take thou rods,
by their kindreds, by each kindred one rod, *take thou* of
all the princes of the lineages twelve rods; and thou shalt
write the name of each *lineage* upon his rod; (Speak thou
to the Israelites, and take thou staffs, from their kindreds,
one staff from each kindred, *yea, take thou* twelve staffs
from all the leaders, *or all the chief men*, of the tribes;
and thou shalt write the name of each *leader* on his staff;)
3 soothly the name of Aaron shall be *written* in the
lineage of Levi, and one rod shall contain all the families
of Levi. (and Aaron's name shall be *written* on the staff of
Levi; yea, one staff shall be for the head of each family.)
4 And thou shalt put those rods in the tabernacle of
[the] bond of peace, before the witnessing, where I shall
speak with thee; (And thou shalt put those staffs in the
Tabernacle of the Covenant, before the *Ark of the*
Witnessing, *that is, the Box containing the tablets of the*
Law, where I speak with thee;)
5 the rod of him shall burgeon, whom I shall choose
of them *to the office of priesthood*; and I shall *thereby*
refrain, *or quench*, from me the complainings, *or*
grouchings, of the sons of Israel, by which they grouch
against you. (and the staff of him shall sprout, whom I
shall choose out of them *for the office, or for the duties,*
of the priesthood; and I shall *thereby* quench the
complaints, *or the grumblings*, of the Israelites, by which
they grumble against you.)
6 And Moses spake to the sons of Israel; and all the
princes gave to him rods, by all their lineages; and the
rods were twelve, without the rod of Aaron. (And Moses
spoke to the Israelites; and each leader from each tribe
gave him a staff; and so there were twelve staffs, and
Aaron's staff was among them.)
7 And when Moses had put those rods before the
Lord, in the tabernacle of witnessing, (And when Moses
had put those staffs before the Lord, in the Tabernacle of
the Witnessing,)
8 he went again in the day following, and found that
the rod of Aaron, in the house of Levi, had burgeoned;
and when [the] knops were great, the blossoms had
broken out, which were alarged in (the) leaves, and were
formed into almonds. (he went back on the following
day, and found that Aaron's staff, for the house of Levi,
had sprouted; and first the buds grew great, and then the
blossoms broke out, and enlarged themselves amid the
leaves, and then they were formed into almonds.)
9 Therefore Moses brought forth all the rods from the
sight of the Lord to all the sons of Israel; and they saw,
and received each his rod. (And so Moses brought out all
the staffs from before the Lord to all the Israelites; and
they looked at all of them, and then each man received
back his own staff.)
10 And the Lord said to Moses, Bear thou again the rod
of Aaron into the tabernacle of witnessing, that it be kept
there into a token of the rebel sons of Israel, and that
their complainings, *or grouchings*, cease from me, lest
they die. (And the Lord said to Moses, Bring thou back
Aaron's staff into the Tabernacle of the Witnessing, so
that it can be kept there as a sign, *or as a warning*, to all
the rebellious Israelites, so that their complaints, *or their*
grumblings, cease, or else they shall die.)
11 And Moses did, as the Lord commanded.
12 Soothly the sons of Israel said to Moses, Lo! we be
wasted, all we have perished; (And the Israelites said to
Moses, Lo! we be destroyed, and we all shall perish;)
13 whoever nigheth to the tabernacle of the Lord, he
dieth; whether we shall all be done away unto the death?
(whoever cometh near to the Tabernacle of the Lord, he
dieth; we all shall be done away unto death!)

CHAPTER 18

1 And the Lord said to Aaron, Thou, and thy sons, and
the house of thy father with thee, shall bear the
wickedness of the saintuary; and thou and thy sons
together shall suffer the sins of your priesthood (but only
thou and thy sons shall bear the sins of your priesthood).
2 But also take thou with thee thy brethren of the
lineage of Levi, and the sceptre, *or power*, of thy father,
and be they ready, that they minister to thee. Forsooth
thou and thy sons shall minister in the tabernacle of
witnessing; (And also take with thee thy brothers from the
tribe of Levi, thy father's tribe, and be they ready to serve
thee. But thou and thy sons shall minister in the
Tabernacle of the Witnessing;)
3 and the deacons shall (stand) watch at thy
commandments, and at all the works of the tabernacle; so
only that they nigh not to the vessels of the saintuary, and
to the altar, lest both they die, and ye, and (you all) perish
together. (and the Levites shall do thy commands, and all
their work in the Tabernacle; but they must not go near
the vessels of the sanctuary, lest both they and ye die,
and all of you perish together.)
4 Soothly be they with thee, and (stand) watch they in
the keepings of the tabernacle, and in all the ceremonies

thereof. An alien shall not be meddled with you. (Yea, be they with thee, and do their duties in the Tabernacle, and at all of its ceremonies. But do not let a foreigner, *or a stranger*, be mixed in with you.)

5 (Stand) Watch ye in the keeping of the saintuary, and in the service of the altar, lest indignation rise upon the sons of Israel. (Do ye all your duties in the sanctuary, and in the service of the altar, lest indignation rise upon the Israelites.)

6 Lo! I have given to you your brethren, the deacons, from the midst of the sons of Israel, and I have given you them (as) a free gift to the Lord, that they serve in the services of the tabernacle. (Lo! I have given you your brothers, the Levites, from among the Israelites, and I have given them to you as a free gift for the Lord, in their service to the Tabernacle.)

7 Soothly thou and thy sons, keep your priesthood; and all things that pertain to the adorning of the altar, and be within the veil, shall be ministered by [the] priests; if any stranger nigheth *thereto*, he shall be slain. (Thou and thy sons, do your priestly duties; and all the things in the service of the altar, and that be within the Veil, shall be the priests' responsibility; if any stranger nigheth *thereto*, he shall be put to death.)

8 The Lord spake to Aaron, Lo! I have given to thee the keeping of my first fruits; I have given to thee, and to thy sons, all things that be hallowed of the sons of Israel, for [the] priest's office (to be) everlasting lawful things. (And the Lord spoke to Aaron, and said, Lo! I give thee the special contributions given to me, for thy own use; I give thee, and thy sons, all the things that be hallowed by the Israelites, by an everlasting law, for the office, *or the use*, of the priest.)

9 Therefore thou shalt take these things of those things that be hallowed, and be offered to the Lord; each offering, and sacrifice, and whatever thing is yielded, (*or offered,*) to me for sin and for trespass, and cometh into (the) holy of holy things, shall be thine and thy sons (shall be for thee and thy sons).

10 Thou shalt eat it in the saintuary; males only shall eat thereof, for it is hallowed to the Lord. (Thou shalt eat it in the sanctuary; only males can eat it, for it is dedicated, *or consecrated*, to the Lord.)

11 Soothly I have given to thee, and to thy sons and thy daughters, by everlasting right, the first fruits which the sons of Israel avow and offer; he that is clean in thine house(hold), shall eat those things. (And I have also given to thee, and to thy sons and thy daughters, by an everlasting right, the first fruits which the Israelites vow and offer; anyone who is clean in thy family, can eat those things.)

12 I have given to thee all the marrow, *or the best*, of (the) oil, and of (the) wine, and of (the) wheat, whatever thing of the first fruits (that) they shall offer to the Lord.

13 All the beginnings of fruits which the earth bringeth forth, and be brought (in) to the Lord, shall fall into thine uses; he that is clean in thine house(hold), shall eat of those (things).

14 All things that the sons of Israel yield by a vow, shall be thine. (Everything that the Israelites give by a vow, shall be yours.)

15 Whatever thing cometh first forth of the womb of all flesh, which they offer to the Lord, whether it is of men, either of beasts, it shall be of thy right; so only that thou take price for the first begotten child of man, and that thou make each beast that is unclean to be bought again; (Whatever thing of all flesh that cometh forth first from the womb, whether it is of men, or of beasts, which they offer to the Lord, shall be thy right to have; so only that thou take payment *in exchange, or as redemption*, for the first-born of man, and that thou make each beast that is unclean to be bought back;)

16 whose again-buying shall be after one month, for five shekels of silver, by the weight of [the] saintuary (whose redemption shall be after one month, for five shekels of silver, by the measure of the sanctuary); a shekel hath twenty halfpence.

17 Forsooth thou shalt not make the first engendered of an ox, and of sheep, and of goat, to be again-bought, for those be hallowed to the Lord; only thou shalt pour the blood of those upon the altar, and thou shalt burn the inner fatness into sweetest odour to the Lord. (But thou shalt not allow the first-born of an ox, or of a sheep, or of a goat, to be bought back, for they be holy to the Lord; thou must throw their blood against the altar, and thou shalt burn their inner fatness to make the sweetest aroma to the Lord.)

18 Soothly the flesh shall fall into thine use, as the breast hallowed and the right shoulder, shall be thine. (But their flesh shall be for thy use, like the breast for the special gift, and the right shoulder, be for thee.)

19 I have given to thee, and to thy sons and thy daughters, by everlasting right, all the first fruits of the saintuary, which the sons of Israel offer to the Lord; it is (an) everlasting covenant of salt before the Lord, to thee, and to thy sons (with thee, and with thy sons).

20 And the Lord said to Aaron, Ye shall not wield anything *of heritage* in the land of Israel, neither ye shall have part among them; I am thy part and thine heritage, in the midst of the sons of Israel. (And the Lord said to Aaron, Ye shall not possess any *inheritance* in the land of Israel, nor shall ye have any portion among them; for I am thy portion, and thy inheritance, among the Israelites.)

21 Soothly, I gave to the sons of Levi all the tithes of Israel into possession, for the service by which they serve me in the tabernacle of [the] bond of peace; (Truly, I have given to the sons of Levi all of the tithes of Israel for a

possession, for the service which they do in the
Tabernacle of the Covenant, *that is, the Tabernacle of the*
Witnessing;)
22 that the sons of Israel nigh no more to the tabernacle
of [the] bond of peace, neither do deadly sin. (so that the
Israelites no longer come near to the Tabernacle of the
Covenant, and so do sin, and then must die.)
23 To the sons alone of Levi, serving me in the
tabernacle, and bearing the people's sins, it shall be a
lawful thing everlasting in your generations. (This is only
for the sons of Levi, who serve me in the Tabernacle, and
who bear the people's sins; and this shall be an
everlasting law in all your generations.)
24 They shall wield none other thing, and they shall be
satisfied with the offering of tithes, which I separated into
[the] uses and necessaries of them. (They shall possess
nothing else, and they shall be satisfied with the offering
of the tithes which I set apart for their uses and their
necessities.)
25 And the Lord spake to Moses and said,
26 Command thou, and announce to the deacons,
When ye have taken tithes of the sons of Israel, which I
gave to you, offer ye the first fruits of those to the Lord,
that is, the tenth part of the tenth, (Command thou, and
say to the Levites, When ye have received the tithes of
the Israelites, which I gave to you, offer ye the first fruits
of those tithes to the Lord, that is, a tithe of the tithe,)
27 that it be areckoned to you into [the] offering of the
first fruits, as well of the cornfloors, as of the presses; (so
that it shall be counted for you as though it be an offering
of the first fruits, yea, from the threshing floor, and from
the winepress;)
28 and of all things of which ye take *tithes*, offer ye the
first fruits to the Lord, and give ye *those* to Aaron, the
priest.
29 All (the) things which ye shall offer of (the) tithes,
and shall separate into the gifts of the Lord (and shall set
apart for a gift to the Lord), shall be the best, and all the
choice things.
30 And thou shalt say to them, If ye offer to the Lord all
the [more] clean and better things of tithes, it shall be
areckoned to you, as if ye gave the first fruits of the
cornfloor, and of the press. (And thou shalt say to them,
When ye have offered to the Lord all the more clean and
better things of the tithes, it shall be counted for you, like
the first fruits from the threshing floor, and from the
winepress.)
31 And ye shall eat those *tithes* in all your places, as
well ye as your families, for it is the price for the service,
for which ye serve in the tabernacle of witnessing. (And
ye shall eat those *tithes* in all your dwelling places, ye as
well as your families, *or your households*, for it is the
payment for the service which ye do, in the Tabernacle of
the Witnessing.)
32 And ye shall not do sin on this thing, and reserve
[the] noble things and [the] fat to you, lest ye defoul the
offerings of the sons of Israel, and ye die. (And ye shall
not do sin with these things, and take the noble and the
fat things for yourselves, lest ye defile the offerings of the
Israelites, for then ye shall die/for then ye must be put to
death.)

CHAPTER 19

1 And the Lord spake to Moses and to Aaron, and
said,
2 This is the religion of sacrifice, which the Lord
ordained. Command thou to the sons of Israel, that they
bring to thee a red cow of whole *colour*, in which is no
wem, neither she hath borne (a) yoke. (This is the law of
sacrifice, which the Lord hath ordained. Command thou
to the Israelites, that they bring to thee a red cow of
whole *colour*, in which there is no blemish, *or fault*, nor
hath she ever borne a yoke.)
3 And ye shall betake her to Eleazar, the priest, that
shall offer *her*, led out of the tents, in the sight of all men.
(And ye shall give her to Eleazar, the priest, and when
she is led away from the tents, he shall offer her in the
sight of all the people.)
4 And he shall dip his finger in the blood thereof, and
shall sprinkle (it) seven times against the gates of the
tabernacle. (And he shall dip his finger in her blood, and
he shall sprinkle it seven times towards the front of the
Tabernacle.)
5 And he shall burn that cow, while all men see; and
he shall give as well the skin, and the flesh thereof, as the
blood, and the dung, to [the] burning. (And then a man
shall burn that cow, in front of Eleazar; and he shall put
its skin, and flesh, and blood, and dung, in the fire.)
6 Also the priest shall put cedar wood (And the priest
shall put cedar wood), and hyssop, and red thread dyed
twice, into the fire, that burneth the cow.
7 And then at the last, when the priest's clothes and
his body be washed, he shall enter into the tents, and he
shall be defouled, *or unclean*, till to eventide. (And then,
after the priest hath washed his clothes, and his body, he
shall return to the tents, but he shall be defiled, *or*
unclean, until the evening.)
8 But also he that burnt the cow, shall wash his
clothes, and *his* body, and he shall be unclean till to
eventide. (And the man who burned the cow, shall also
wash his clothes, and his body, and he shall also be
unclean until the evening.)
9 Soothly a clean man shall gather the ashes of the
cow, and he shall pour them out without the tents, in a
place most clean, that those *ashes* be to the multitude of
the sons of Israel into keeping, and into water of
sprinkling; for that cow is burnt for sin. (And a man who
is clean shall gather up the cow's ashes, and he shall

pour them out away from the tents, in a most clean place,
so that those *ashes* can be used for the multitude of the
Israelites to make the water of cleansing, *or of
purification*; for that cow is burnt as a sin offering.)
10 And when he that bare out the ashes of the cow,
hath washed his clothes, he shall be unclean till to
eventide. And the sons of Israel, and the comelings that
dwell among them, shall have, *or hold*, this (to be) holy
by (an) everlasting law.
11 He that toucheth a dead body of a man, and is
unclean for this by seven days, (He who toucheth
someone's dead body, is made unclean by this for seven
days,)
12 shall be sprinkled of this water in the third [day], and
in the seventh day; and so he shall be cleansed. If he is
not sprinkled in the third day, he shall not be able to be
cleansed in the seventh day. (and he shall be sprinkled
with the water of cleansing, *or of purification*, on the
third day, and on the seventh day; and then he shall be
clean again. If he is not sprinkled on both the third day,
and on the seventh day, he shall not be made clean.)
13 Each that toucheth the dead body by itself of (a)
man's soul, and is not sprinkled with this meddling (*of
water and ashes*), defouleth the tabernacle of the Lord,
and he shall perish from Israel; for he is not sprinkled
with the water of cleansing, he shall be unclean, and his
filth shall dwell upon him. (Anyone who toucheth a dead
body, and is not sprinkled with this mixture *of water and
ashes*, defileth the Tabernacle of the Lord, and he shall be
cut off, *or be put out*, from Israel; and because he is not
sprinkled with the water of cleansing, he shall remain
unclean, and his filth shall remain upon him.)
14 This is the law of a man that dieth in the tabernacle;
all that enter into his tent, and all the vessels that be
there, shall be defouled by seven days. (This is the law
for anyone who dieth in a tent; all who enter into his
tent, and all the vessels that be there, shall be defiled, *or
unclean*, for seven days.)
15 A vessel that hath not a covering, neither a binding
above, shall be unclean. (Any open vessel there, that hath
not a cover, or a lid on top of it, shall be unclean.)
16 If any man toucheth the dead body of a man slain in
the field, either dead by himself, either a bone of him,
either his sepulchre, he shall be unclean by seven days.
(If anyone toucheth the dead body of someone killed in
the field, *that is, outside*, or who hath died naturally, or
who toucheth one of their bones, or their grave, *or their
tomb*, they shall be unclean for seven days.)
17 And they shall take of the ashes of the burning, and
of the sin (offering), *that is, of the cow offered for sin*, and
they shall put quick waters into a vessel, upon those
ashes; (And they shall take some of the ashes from the
burning of that sin offering, *that is, some of the ashes of
the cow offered for sin*, and they shall put those ashes
into a vessel with fresh water;)
18 in which when a clean man hath dipped hyssop, he
shall sprinkle therewith the tent, and all the purtenance of
the household, and the men also defouled with such
defouling (and also anyone defiled with such defilement).
19 And in this manner a clean man shall cleanse an
unclean *thing*, in the third (day) and in the seventh day;
and he shall be cleansed in the seventh day. And he
shall wash himself, and his clothes, and he shall be
unclean till to eventide. (And in this manner a clean man
shall sprinkle an unclean *thing* on the third day, and on
the seventh day; and it shall be clean on the seventh day.
And then he shall wash himself, and his clothes, but he
shall be unclean until the evening.)
20 If any man is not cleansed by this custom, (*or rite*,)
the soul of him shall perish from the midst of the church
(that person shall be cut off, *or shall be put out*, from
among the congregation); for he defouleth the saintuary
of the Lord, and he is not sprinkled with the water of
cleansing.
21 This behest shall be a lawful thing everlasting. Also
he that shall sprinkle the waters (of cleansing) shall wash
his clothes; each man that toucheth the waters of
cleansing, shall be unclean till to eventide. (This rule
shall be an everlasting law. He who shall sprinkle the
water of cleansing shall wash his clothes; and anyone
who toucheth the water of cleansing shall be unclean
until the evening.)
22 Whatever thing an unclean man toucheth, he shall
make unclean; and a soul that toucheth any of these
things *defouled* so, shall be unclean till to eventide.
(Whatever thing an unclean person toucheth, they shall
make that unclean; and anyone who toucheth any of
these things that be so *defiled*, shall be unclean until the
evening.)

CHAPTER 20

1 And the sons of Israel and all the multitude came
into the desert of Zin, in the first month. And the people
dwelled in Kadesh; and Marie was dead there, and
buried in the same place. (And so the Israelites and all
the multitude came into the wilderness of Zin, in the first
month. And the people stayed in Kadesh; and Miriam
died there, and was buried there.)
2 And when the people had need to water (And when
the people needed water), they went together against
Moses and Aaron;
3 and they were turned into dissension, *that is, rebelty
and striving (that is, rebellion and strife)*, and said, We
would that we had perished among our brethren before
the Lord.
4 Why have ye led out the church of the Lord into
wilderness, that both we and our beasts die (here)? (Why
have ye led out the Lord's congregation into this

wilderness, so that both we and our beasts shall die
here?)
5 Why have ye made us to go up from Egypt, and
have brought us into *this* worst place, which may not be
sown, which neither bringeth forth fig trees, nor vines,
neither pomegranates; furthermore and it hath not water
to drink? (and furthermore there is no water to drink!)
6 And when the multitude was left, Moses and Aaron
entered into the tabernacle of [the] bond of peace, and
they fell down low upon the earth, and they cried to
God, and said, Lord God, hear the cry of this people, and
open to them thy treasure, a well of quick water, that
when they be filled, the grouching of them cease. And
the glory of the Lord appeared upon them; (And they left
the multitude, and Moses and Aaron entered into the
Tabernacle of the Covenant, and they fell down on the
ground, and they cried out to God, and said, Lord God,
hear the cry of these people, and open thy treasure to
them, yea, a well of fresh water, so that when they be
filled, their grumbling shall cease. And the glory of the
Lord appeared above them;)
7 and the Lord spake to Moses, and said,
8 Take the rod *of Aaron*, and gather together the
people, thou, and Aaron thy brother; and speak ye to the
stone before them, and it shall give out waters. And
when thou hast led water out of the stone, all the
multitude shall drink, and their beasts thereof. (Take the
staff, and gather together the people, thou, and thy
brother Aaron; and speak ye to the stone before them,
and it shall give out water. And when thou hast led out
water from the stone, all the multitude and their beasts
shall drink it.)
9 Therefore Moses took the rod that was in the sight of
the Lord, as the Lord commanded to him, (And so Moses
took the staff from before the Lord, as the Lord
commanded him,)
10 when the multitude was gathered before the stone;
and he said to them, Hear ye, rebel[s], and unbelieveful;
whether we may bring out of this stone water to you?
(and when the multitude was gathered in front of the
stone, Moses said to them, Listen, ye rebels and
unbelievers; must we get water out of this stone for you?)
11 And when Moses had raised his hand, and had
smitten the flint twice with the rod, most large waters
went out, so that the people drank, and their beasts. (And
when Moses had raised up his hand, and had struck the
rock twice with the staff, a great deal of water came out,
so that the people drank, and also their beasts.)
12 And the Lord said to Moses and to Aaron, For ye
believed not to me, that ye should hallow me before the
sons of Israel (For ye did not believe me, and uphold my
holiness before the Israelites), ye shall not lead these
peoples into the land which I shall give to them.
13 This is the water of against-saying; there the sons of
Israel strived against the Lord, and he was hallowed in
them. (This is the water of Meribah; there the Israelites
complained against the Lord, but he was still holy before
them.)
14 In the meantime Moses sent messengers from
Kadesh to the king of Edom, the which (messengers) said,
Israel thy brother, sendeth these things to thee. Thou
knowest all the travail that hath taken us,
15 how our fathers went down into Egypt, and we
dwelled there much time, and (the) Egyptians tormented
us, and our fathers (as well);
16 and how we cried to the Lord, and he heard us, and
sent an angel that [hath] led us out of Egypt. And lo! we
be set in the city of Kadesh, that is in thine uttermost
coasts (that is on thy most distant border),
17 and we beseech thee that it be leaveful to us to pass
through thy land; we shall not go by thy fields, neither by
thy vineries, neither we shall drink waters of thy wells;
but we shall go in the common way, and we shall not
bow to the right side, neither to the left side, till we pass
thy terms. (and we beseech thee that it be lawful for us to
pass through thy land; we shall not go into thy fields, or
into thy vineyards, and we shall not drink any water from
thy wells; but we shall go on the common way, and we
shall not turn to the right side, or to the left side, till we
go out again over thy border.)
18 To whom Edom answered, Ye shall not pass by me,
else I shall be armed, and come against thee. (To whom
the Edomites answered, Ye shall not pass through our
land, and if ye try, we shall be armed, and shall come out
against thee.)
19 And the sons of Israel said, We shall go by the way
commonly used, and if we and our beasts drink thy
waters, we shall give that that is just; no hardness shall be
in the price, only pass we in haste (we will have no
difficulty to pay you for it; but just let us quickly pass
through thy land).
20 And he answered, Ye shall not pass *by me*. And
anon he went out against *Israel*, with a multitude without
number, and [with a] strong hand/and with strong power,
(And they answered, Ye shall not pass *through our land*.
And at once the Edomites went out against *Israel*, in a
multitude without number, and with mighty power,)
21 neither he would assent *to Israel* beseeching, that he
should grant passage by his coasts. (for they would not
agree to *Israel's* beseeching, to grant them passage
through their land.)
22 Wherefore Israel turned away from him. And when
Israel had moved their tents from Kadesh, they came into
the hill of Hor, (And so Israel turned, and went by
another way. And when they had moved on from
Kadesh, they came to Mount Hor,)
23 which is in the ends of the land of Edom (which is
near Edom's border); where the Lord spake to Moses, and

said,
24 Aaron (shall) go to his people; for he shall not enter
into the land which I gave to the sons of Israel, for he was
unbelieveful to my word, at the waters of against-saying.
(Aaron shall now go to his people, *that is, he shall die*;
for he shall not enter into the land which I gave to the
Israelites, for he did not believe my word at the waters of
Meribah.)
25 Take thou Aaron, and his son with him, and thou
shalt lead them into the hill of Hor; (Take thou Aaron, and
his son with him, and lead thou them up onto Mount Hor;)
26 and when thou hast made naked the father of his
cloth (and when thou hast made stripped the father of his
priestly cloak, *or robe*), thou shalt clothe therewith
Eleazar, his son, and Aaron shall be gathered (to his
people), and shall die there.
27 And Moses did as the Lord commanded; and they
ascended into the hill of Hor, before all the multitude
(and they went up onto Mount Hor, in the sight of all the
multitude).
28 And when Moses had made naked Aaron of his
clothes, he clothed with those Eleazar, his son. Soothly
when Aaron was dead in the top of the hill, Moses came
down with Eleazar. (And when Moses had stripped Aaron
of his priestly clothes, he clothed Aaron's son Eleazar
with them. And then, after that Aaron had died there on
the mountain-top, Moses came down with Eleazar.)
29 Soothly all the multitude saw that Aaron was dead,
and it wept upon him thirty days, by all their families.
(And all the multitude saw that Aaron had died, and all
the families wept over him for thirty days.)

CHAPTER 21

1 And when [the] Canaanite, the king of Arad, that
dwelled at the south, had heard this, that is, that Israel
came by the way of [the] spyers (that the Israelites came
by the way of Atharim), he fought against them; and (the)
Canaanite was the overcomer, and he led away (as) prey
(some of) the men of Israel.
2 And Israel bound himself by a vow to the Lord, and
said, If thou shalt betake this people in(to) mine hand, I
shall do away their cities. (And the Israelites bound
themselves with a vow to the Lord, and said, If thou shalt
deliver these people into our hands, we shall do away
their cities.)
3 And the Lord heard the prayers of Israel, and betook
to them the Canaanites; and Israel killed him, and
destroyed his cities; and Israel called the name of that
place Hormah, *that is, cursing*. (And the Lord heard the
prayers of the Israelites, and delivered the Canaanites
unto them; and the Israelites killed them, and destroyed
their cities; and the Israelites called the name of that
place Hormah, *that is, Cursing*.)
4 Soothly Israel went forth from the hill of Hor, by the
way that leadeth to the Red Sea, that they would compass
the land of Edom; and it began to annoy the people, of
the way and [of the] travail. (And the Israelites went forth
from Mount Hor, by the way that leadeth to the Red Sea,
to by-pass the land of Edom; and the way, and all the
tribulation, began to vex the people.)
5 And the people spake against the Lord, and Moses,
and said, Why leddest thou us out of Egypt, that we
should die in wilderness? bread faileth, waters be not;
our soul loatheth now on this meat most light. (And the
people spoke against the Lord, and Moses, and said, Why
leddest thou us out of Egypt, so that we would die here in
this wilderness? bread faileth us, waters be not; and our
souls now loathe this most light food*, yea, this manna*!)
6 Wherefore the Lord sent fired serpents/fiery adders
into the people; at the wounds of which serpents, and
(after) the deaths of full many men, (And so the Lord sent
poisonous snakes among the people; and they bit many
of them, and after many people had died,)
7 they came to Moses, and said, We have sinned, for
we spake against the Lord, and thee; pray thou (the Lord),
that he take away from us the serpents (pray thou to the
Lord, that he take these snakes away from us). And
Moses prayed for the people;
8 and the Lord said to him, Make thou a [brazen]
serpent, and set thou it in a perch; he that is smitten and
beholdeth it, shall live. (and the Lord said to him, Make
thou a bronze snake, and put it up on a pole; he who is
struck, *or is bitten*, and seeth it, shall live.)
9 Therefore Moses made a serpent of brass, and setted
(it) in a perch; and (those) men (who were) hurt, and
beholding it, were healed. (And so Moses made a bronze
serpent, and put it up on a pole; and those who were
bitten, and looked at it, were healed.)
10 And the sons of Israel went forth, and setted tents in
Oboth; (And the Israelites went forth, and pitched their
tents at Oboth;)
11 from whence they went forth, and setted tents in
Iyeabarim, in the wilderness that beholdeth Moab,
against the east coast. (and they went forth from there,
and pitched their tents in Iyeabarim, in the wilderness on
Moab's eastern border.)
12 And they moved from thence, and came to the
strand of Zared; (And they went from there, and came to
the valley of the Zared River;)
13 which they left, and setted tents against (the) Arnon,
which is in the desert, and it appeareth in the coasts of
Amorites. Forsooth (the) Arnon is the term of Moab, and
parteth Moabites and Amorites. (and they left there, and
pitched their tents on the north side of the Arnon River,
which is in the wilderness, that goeth into the land of the
Amorites. The Arnon River is the border of Moab, and it
separateth the Moabites and the Amorites.)
14 Wherefore it is said in the book of battles of the

Lord, As he did in the Red Sea, so he shall do in the
strands of (the) Arnon; (And so it is said in the Book of the
Battles of the Lord, As he did at the Red Sea, so he also
did at the Arnon River,)
15 the hard rocks of the strands were bowed down, that
they shall rest in Ar, *or abide there*, and should lie in the
coasts of Moabites. (and from the cliffs of the river, down
to the city of Ar, that sitteth on the border of Moab.)
16 From that place (they went to where) the well
appeared, of which the Lord spake to Moses, Gather thou
together the people, and I shall give water to it. (From
there they went to Beer, *that is, The Well*, of which the
Lord spoke to Moses, and said, Gather thou the people
together, and I shall give them water.)
17 Then Israel sang this song, The *water of the* well,
ascend up; they sang together, (Then Israel sang this
song, Go ye up, *water of the* well; yea, we sing to thee,)
18 The well which the princes digged, and the dukes of
the multitude made ready, in the giver of the law, and in
their staves (The well from the Giver of the Law, which
the leaders dug, yea, which the leaders of the multitude
brought forth with their staffs). And (then) they went forth
from the wilderness to Mattanah,
19 from Mattanah to Nahaliel, from Nahaliel into
Bamoth;
20 Bamoth is a valley in the country of Moab, in the
top of Pisgah, that beholdeth against the desert. (and from
Bamoth to the valley in the country of Moab, below the
top of Mount Pisgah, that looketh towards Jeshimon, *that
is, towards the wilderness*.)
21 Soothly Israel sent messengers to Sihon, king of
Amorites, and said, (And the Israelites sent messengers to
Sihon, the king of the Amorites, and they said,)
22 I beseech thee, that it be leaveful to me to pass
through thy land; we shall not bow into thy fields, and
vineries; we shall not drink waters of thy wells; we shall
go in the king's way, till we pass (by) thy terms. (We
beseech thee, that it be lawful for us to pass through thy
land; we shall not go into thy fields, or into thy vineyards;
we shall not drink any water from thy wells; we shall go
on the king's highway, until we go out again over thy
border.)
23 Which would not grant that Israel should pass
through his coasts, but rather, when his host was
gathered, he went out against *Israel*, into desert. And he
came into Jahaz, and fought against Israel; (But Sihon
would not allow the Israelites to pass through his land,
but rather, when his host was gathered together, he went
out into the wilderness against them. And he came into
Jahaz, and fought against the Israelites;)
24 of whom he was smitten in the sharpness of sword,
and his land was wielded *of Israel* from (the) Arnon unto
(the) Jabbok, and Ammon's sons, *or his host*; for the
coasts of Ammonites were holden with strong help, *or
power*. (but Sihon and the Amorites were struck down by
the sharpness of the *Israelites'* swords, and his land was
taken *by them*, from the Arnon River to the Jabbok River,
that is, up to the land of the Ammonites; for the border of
the Ammonites was strongly defended.)
25 Therefore Israel took all his cities, and dwelled in
the cities of Amorites, that is, in Heshbon, and in his
towns. (And so the Israelites took all the cities of the
Amorites, and lived in them, that is, in Heshbon, and its
towns.)
26 The city of Heshbon was Sihon's, king of Amorites,
which Sihon fought against the king of Moab, and took
all the land that was of his lordship, till to (the) Arnon.
(The city of Heshbon was Sihon's, the king of the
Amorites, who had fought against the king of Moab, and
had taken all the land that was under his rule, unto the
Arnon River.)
27 Therefore it is said in proverb, Come ye into
Heshbon, be it builded (again), and (re)made, the city of
Sihon; (And so it is said in a proverb, Come ye into
Heshbon, let Sihon's city be rebuilt, and be remade;)
28 fire went out of Heshbon, flame went out of the city
of Sihon, and devoured (the city of) Ar of (the) Moabites,
and the dwellers of the high *places* of (the) Arnon (and
the inhabitants of the high *places* of the Arnon River).
29 Moab, woe to thee! thou, people of Chemosh, hast
perished; it gave the sons thereof into flight, and the
daughters into captivity to Sihon, king of Amorites;
(Moab, woe to thee! O people of Chemosh, now ye have
perished; thy god hath given his sons into flight, and his
daughters into captivity to Sihon, the king of the
Amorites;)
30 the yoke, *or lordship*, of them perished (their yoke,
or their rule, hath now ended), from Heshbon unto
Dibon; the weary men came into Nophah, and unto
Medeba.
31 And so Israel dwelled in the land of (the) Amorites.
32 And Moses sent men that should espy Jaazer, whose
towns they took, and wielded the dwellers. (And Moses
sent men to spy out Jaazer, and then they took it, and its
towns, and drove out all of its inhabitants.)
33 And they turned themselves (And then they turned),
and went up by the way of Bashan. And Og, the king of
Bashan, with all his people, came against them, to fight in
Edrei.
34 And the Lord said to Moses, Dread thou not him, for
I have betaken him, and all his land, and all his people,
in thine hand; and thou shalt do to him as thou didest to
Sihon, king of Amorites, the dweller of Heshbon. (And
the Lord said to Moses, Do not thou fear him, for I have
delivered him, and all his land, and all his people, into
thy hands; and thou shalt do to him as thou didest to
Sihon, the king of Amorites, and the inhabitants of
Heshbon.)

35 Therefore they smote Og with his sons, and all his
people, unto [the] death; and they wielded his land. (And
so they struck down Og and his sons, and all his people,
unto the death; and then they occupied his land.)

CHAPTER 22

1 And the sons of Israel went forth, and setted tents in
the field places of Moab, where Jericho is set, over
Jordan. (And the Israelites went forth, and pitched their
tents on the plains of Moab, across the Jordan River,
opposite Jericho.)
2 Soothly Balak, the son of Zippor, saw all things that
Israel had done to (the) Amorites,
3 and that men of Moab dreaded Israel, and they
might not bear the assailing of Israel. (and that the
Moabites feared the Israelites, for they could not survive
an assault from Israel.)
4 And he said to the greater men in birth of Midian,
So this people shall do away all men that dwell in our
coasts, as an ox is wont to do away an herb till to the
roots. Forsooth he, *that is, Balak*, was king in that time in
Moab. (And the Moabites said to the men of great age,
that is, the elders, of Midian, These people shall do away
all the men who live in our land, as easily as an ox is
wont to do away grass unto its roots. And he, *that is,
Balak*, was king at that time in Moab.)
5 Therefore he sent messengers to Balaam, the son of
Beor, a false diviner, that dwelled (in Pethor) on, *or nigh*,
the flood of the land of the sons of Amaw, that they
should call him, and should say, Lo! a people went out of
Egypt, which people covered the face of the earth, and
sitteth against me. (And so he sent messengers to Balaam,
the son of Beor, a false diviner, who lived at Pethor, near
the Euphrates River, in the land of the sons of Amaw, and
instructed the messengers to say to him, Lo! a people
went out of Egypt, which people covered the face of the
earth, and now they be ready to come against me.)
6 Therefore come thou, and curse this people, that is
stronger than I, if in any manner I may smite and drive
him out of my land; for I know, that he is blessed whom
thou blessest, and he is cursed whom thou hast cursed.
(And so come thou, and curse these people who be
stronger than I, and then I may be able to fight against
them, and drive them out of my land; for I know that he
is blessed whom thou blessest, and he is cursed whom
thou cursest.)
7 The elder men of Moab and the elder men of
Midian went forth, having in *their* hands the price of false
divining; and when they had come to Balaam, and had
told to him all the words of Balak, (The elders of Moab
and of Midian went forth, having in *their* hands the
payment for the curse; and when they had come to
Balaam, and had told him all of Balak's words,)
8 he answered, Dwell ye here tonight, and I shall
answer *to Balak* whatever thing the Lord shall say to me.
And the princes of Moab dwelled at Balaam (And so the
leaders of Moab stayed that night with Balaam).
9 God came, and said to him, What will these men
with thee? (And God came, and said to him, Who be
these men with thee?)
10 Balaam answered, Balak, the son of Zippor, king of
Moabites, sent (them) to me, and (he) said,
11 Lo! a people that is gone out of Egypt hath covered
the face of the earth; come thou, and curse them, if in
any manner I may fight *with them* (for then I may be able
to fight *against them*), and drive them away.
12 And God said to Balaam, Do not thou go with them,
neither curse thou the people, for it is blessed (for they be
blessed/for *on the contrary*, they should be blessed).
13 And *Balaam* rose early, and said to the princes, Go
ye into your land (Go ye back to your land), for God hath
forbade me to come with you.
14 The princes turned again (So the leaders returned),
and said to Balak, Balaam would not come with us.
15 Again Balak sent many more, and nobler, men, than
he had sent before;
16 which said (who said), when they had come to
Balaam, Balak, the son of Zippor, saith thus, Tarry thou
not to come to me,
17 (for I am) ready to honour thee; and whatever thing
thou wilt, I shall give to thee; come thou, and curse this
people (so then come thou, and curse these people).
18 Balaam answered, Though Balak shall give to me his
house full of silver and of gold, I shall not be able to
change the word of my God, that I speak either more or
less. (But Balaam answered, Even if Balak should give me
all the gold and silver in his house, I could not change
the word of my God, so that I speak something else,
either more or less.)
19 I beseech *you*, that ye dwell here also in this night
(But I beseech *you*, stay ye here this night), (so) that I may
know what the Lord shall answer again to me.
20 Therefore the Lord came to Balaam in that night,
and said to him, If these men (have) come to call thee,
rise thou, and go with them, so only that thou do that that
I shall command to thee (but do only what I shall
command thee to do).
21 (So) Balaam rose early, and when his she ass was
saddled, he went forth with them.
22 And God was wroth *with Balaam*. And the angel of
the Lord stood in the way against Balaam, that sat upon
the she ass, and had two servants with him. (But God was
angry *with Balaam for going*. And so the angel of the
Lord stood in the way against Balaam, who rode on his
donkey, and had his two servants with him.)
23 The (she) ass saw the angel standing in the way,
with sword drawn, and the (she) ass turned herself from
the way, and went by the field (And the donkey saw the

angel standing in the way, with his sword drawn, and she
turned herself from the way, and went into a field). And
when Balaam beat her, and would lead *her* again to the
path,
24 the angel stood in the straitness of two walls with
which the vineries were (en)compassed. (the angel stood
in the narrowness between two walls which went all
around, *or enclosed*, the vineyards on either side.)
25 And the female ass saw the angel, and she went
herself nigh to the wall, and she hurtled the foot of the
sitter *upon her*; and he beat again *her*. (And the female
donkey saw the angel again, and she brought herself near
to the wall, and hurtled the foot of *her* rider against it;
and so he beat *her* again.)
26 And nevertheless the angel went to a strait place,
where was no going out of the way, neither to the right
side, nor to the left, and stood against Balaam
(Nevertheless the angel went to a narrow place, where
there was no going out of the way, neither to the right
side, nor to the left, and stood before Balaam.)
27 And when the (she) ass saw the angel standing
(there), she felled down under the feet of the sitter *upon
her*, the which was wroth full greatly (who then was
greatly angered), and (once more) he beat her sides with
a staff.
28 And the Lord opened the mouth of the (she) ass, and
she spake, (And the Lord opened the donkey's mouth,
and she said), What have I done to thee? why smitest
thou me, lo! now the third time?
29 Balaam answered, For thou hast dis-served (me), and
hast scorned me; I would that I had a sword to slay thee.
30 And the (she) ass said, Whether I am not thy beast
upon which thou were wont to ride ever[more] till into
this present day? say thou, what like thing *to this* I did
ever to thee? And Balaam said, Never *thus thou
servedest me*. (And the donkey said, Am I not the beast
upon which thou were always wont to ride until this
present day? say thou, what thing like *this* have I ever
done to thee before? And Balaam said, Never *before hast
thou served me thus*.)
31 Anon the Lord opened the eyes of Balaam, and he
saw the angel standing in the way, holding a drawn
sword in *his* hand; and Balaam worshipped him lowly
into the earth. (And at once the Lord opened Balaam's
eyes, and he saw the angel standing in the way, holding a
drawn sword in *his* hand; and Balaam worshipped, *or
honoured*, him lowly on the ground.)
32 To whom the angel said, Why hast thou thrice
beaten thine ass? I came (here) to be (an) adversary to
thee, for thy way is wayward, and contrary to me;
33 and if the (she) ass had not bowed away from the
way, and given place to the against-stander, I had slain
thee, and the (she) ass should have lived. (and if the
donkey had not turned aside from the way, and given
place to the one who stood against thee, I would have
already killed thee, but the donkey would have lived.)
34 Balaam said, I have sinned, not witting that thou
stoodest against me; and now, if it displeaseth thee that I
go, I shall turn again. (And Balaam said, I have sinned,
not knowing that thou stoodest against me; and now, if it
displeaseth thee I shall turn back/I shall go back home.)
35 The angel said, (Nay,) Go thou with these men, but
beware, that thou speak not [any] other thing than (what)
I shall command to thee. Therefore Balaam went with the
princes (And so Balaam went forth with Balak's leaders).
36 And when Balak heard *that Balaam was nigh*, he
went out into the coming of him, in (Ar,) the city of
Moabites, which is set in the last coast of (the) Arnon.
(And when Balak heard *that Balaam was near*, he went
out to meet him, at Ar, the city of the Moabites, which is
set on their most distant border, by the Arnon River.)
37 And Balak said to Balaam, I sent messengers to call
thee; why camest thou not anon to me? whether for I
may not yield meed to thy coming? (And Balak said to
Balaam, I sent messengers to call thee; why did thou not
come at once to me? did you think that I would not
reward thee for coming?)
38 To whom Balaam answered, Lo! I am present, (but)
whether I shall be able to speak (any) other thing than
that, that God shall put in my mouth? (To whom Balaam
answered, Lo! I am present, but do not think that I shall
speak anything, other than what God himself shall put in
my mouth!)
39 Therefore they went forth together, and they came
into a city, which was in the last coast of his realm
(which was Kiriathhuzoth, *that is, the City of Huzoth*).
40 And when Balak had slain sheep, and oxen, he sent
(part of them as) gifts to Balaam and the princes that were
with him.
41 Forsooth when the morrowtide was made, Balak led
Balaam (up) to the high places of Baal (Balak led Balaam
up to Bamoth Baal, *that is, the Heights of Baal*), and
(there) he beheld (unto) the last part of the people, *that is,
(he saw) all the host (of the Israelites) till to the last part.*

CHAPTER 23

1 And Balaam said to Balak, Build thou here to me
seven altars, and make thou ready so many calves, and
rams of the same number. (And Balaam said to Balak,
Build thou here seven altars for me, and prepare seven
calves, and the same number of rams.)
2 And when Balak had done by the word of Balaam,
they putted a calf and a ram together on the altar. (And
when Balak had done what Balaam had asked, they
offered a calf and a ram on each altar.)
3 And (then) Balaam said to Balak, Stand thou (here) a
little while beside thy burnt sacrifice, while I go, if in hap
the Lord (shall) meet (with) me; and I shall tell thee

whatever thing he shall command. And when he had
gone [away] swiftly (And when he had quickly gone
away by himself),
4 God came to him; and Balaam spake to him, and
said, I have raised up seven altars, and I have put a calf
and a ram above *each of them* (and I have put a calf and
a ram on *each of them*).
5 Forsooth the Lord putted a word in his mouth, and
said, Turn again to Balak, and thou shalt speak these
things. (And the Lord put a word in his mouth, and said,
Return to Balak, and thou shalt say these things *to him.*)
6 He turned again, and found Balak standing beside
his burnt sacrifice, and all the princes of Moabites. (And
he returned, and found Balak standing beside his burnt
sacrifice, he and all the leaders of the Moabites.)
7 And when his parable was taken, he said, Balak, the
king of Moabites, brought me from Aram, from the hills
of the east; and he said, Come thou, and curse Jacob;
haste thou, and curse Israel. (And when he had received
his prophecy, he said, Balak, the king of the Moabites,
brought me from Syria, yea, from the hills of the east; and
he said, Come thou, and curse Jacob; hurry thou, and
curse Israel.)
8 How shall I curse, whom God hath cursed not? (But
how can I curse, whom God hath not cursed?) by what
reason shall I loathe, whom God loatheth not?
9 From the highest flints I shall see him, and from the
little hills I shall behold him; the people shall dwell
alone, and it shall not be reckoned among heathen men.
(From the highest rocks I shall see them, and from the
little hills I shall behold them; these people shall live
alone, and they shall not be counted among the heathen.)
10 Who may number the dust, *that is, the kindred*, of
Jacob, and *who may* know the number of the generation
of Israel? My life die in the death of just men, and my
last things be made like them! (O let me die like the
righteous die, and let my ending be made like theirs!)
11 And Balak said to Balaam, What is this that thou
doest? I called thee, that thou shouldest curse mine
enemies, and on the contrary, thou blessest them.
12 To whom Balaam answered, Whether I may speak
(any) other thing, no but that that the Lord commandeth?
13 Therefore Balak said to Balaam, Come with me into
another place, from whence thou mayest see a part of
Israel, and thou mayest not see all; from thence curse
thou him. (And so Balak said to Balaam, Come with me
to another place, from where thou can see a part of the
Israelites, but thou cannot see all of them; and curse thou
them from there.)
14 And when he had led Balaam into an high place, on
the top of the hill of Pisgah, he builded *there* seven altars
to Balaam, and when calves and rams were put above
them, (And so when he had led Balaam to the Field of
Zophim, *that is, to the Field of the Watchers*, on top of
Mount Pisgah, he built seven altars for Balaam, and when
a calf and a ram were offered on each altar,)
15 Balaam said to Balak, Stand here beside thy burnt
sacrifice, while I go *to meet with the Lord.*
16 And when the Lord had met with Balaam, and had
put a word in his mouth, he said, Turn again to Balak
(Return to Balak), and thou shalt say these things to him.
17 He turned again, and found Balak standing beside
his burnt sacrifice, and the princes of Moabites with him.
To whom Balak said, What hath spoken the Lord? (And
he returned, and found Balak standing beside his burnt
sacrifice, and the leaders of the Moabites with him. And
Balak said to him, What hath the Lord said?)
18 And when his parable was taken (And when he had
received his prophecy), he said, Stand thou (up), Balak,
and harken; hear, thou son of Zippor.
19 God is not a man, that he (can) lie, neither he is as
the son of a man, that he (can) be changed; therefore he
hath said, and shall he not do it? he hath spoken, and
shall he not fulfill it?
20 I am brought *hither by the Lord* to bless; (and) I may
not forbid, *or hinder,* (the) blessing.
21 None idol is in Jacob, neither simulacrum is seen in
Israel; his Lord God is with him, and the sound of the
victory of a king is in him. (There is no idolatry in Jacob,
no false god is seen in Israel; the Lord their God is with
them, and they hear the shout of the victory of their
King.)
22 The Lord God led him out of Egypt, whose strength
is like an unicorn; (The Lord God led them out of Egypt,
whose strength is like a wild ox;)
23 false divining by (the) chittering of birds is not in
Jacob, neither false divining is in Israel. In his times, *(that
is,) when, where, and how God will,* it shall be said to
Jacob and to Israel, What the Lord hath wrought! (false
divining by the twittering of birds is not in Jacob, yea,
false divining is not in Israel. In his own timing, *that is,
when, where, and how God desireth it,* it shall be said of
Jacob, and of Israel, What the Lord hath wrought!/Yea, at
this time, it can be said of Jacob, and of Israel, What the
Lord hath wrought!)
24 Lo! the people shall rise together as a lioness, and *it*
shall be raised as a lion (Lo! the people shall rise up like a
lioness, and *they* shall be raised up like a lion); the lion
shall not rest, till he devour [the] prey, and drink the
blood of them that be slain.
25 And Balak said to Balaam, Neither curse thou,
neither bless thou him. (And Balak said to Balaam, If thou
wilt not curse them, at least do not thou bless them!)
26 And Balaam said, Whether I said not to thee, that
whatever thing God commanded to me, I would do that?
27 And Balak said to him, Come, and I shall lead thee
to another place, if in hap it pleaseth God that from
thence thou curse him (perhaps it shall please God that

thou curse them from there).
28 And when Balak had led him out on(to) the top of
the hill of Peor, that beholdeth the wilderness, (And
when Balak had led Balaam to the top of Mount Peor,
that overlooketh Jeshimon, *that is, the wilderness,*)
29 Balaam said to Balak, Build here seven altars to me,
and make ready so many calves, and rams of the same
number. (Balaam said to Balak, Now also build seven
altars here for me, and prepare seven calves, and the
same number of rams.)
30 Balak did as Balaam said, and he put the calves and
the rams, by all the altars. (And Balak did as Balaam said,
and he put a calf and a ram on each of the altars.)

CHAPTER 24

1 And when Balaam saw that it pleased the Lord that
he should bless Israel, he went not as he had gone
before, that he should seek false divining by chittering of
birds, but he (ad)dressed his face against the desert, (And
when Balaam saw that it pleased the Lord when he
blessed Israel, he went not as he had gone before, to seek
out false divining by the twittering of birds, but he
directed his face towards the wilderness,)
2 and he raised up his eyes, and he saw Israel
dwelling in tents by his lineages (and he raised up his
eyes, and he saw the Israelites living in their tents, tribe
by tribe). And when the Spirit of God fell upon him,
3 and when the parable was taken (and when he had
received his prophecy), he said, Balaam, the son of Beor,
said, (yea,) a man, whose eye is stopped, said,
4 the hearer of God's words said, which beheld the
revelation of Almighty God, which falleth down, and his
eyes be opened so, (yea, the hearer of God's words said,
who beheld the revelation of Almighty God, and who
falleth down, but his eyes still be open,)
5 How fair be thy tabernacles, Jacob, and thy tents,
Israel!
6 as valleys full of trees, and moist gardens beside
floods, as tabernacles which the Lord hath set (up), as
cedar trees beside waters; (like valleys full of trees, and
watered gardens beside the river, like aloes planted by
the Lord, and cedar trees beside the water;)
7 water shall flow (out) of his bucket, and his seed
shall be into many waters, *that is, peoples.* The king of
him shall be taken away for Agag, and the realm of him
shall be done away. (water shall flow out of his bucket,
and his descendants shall be like many waters, *that is,
they shall become many people.* His king shall be greater
than Agag, and his kingdom shall prevail.)
8 God led him out of Egypt, whose strength is like an
unicorn; the sons of Israel shall waste, *or devour,* (the)
heathen men, their enemies; and they shall break the
bones of them, and pierce (them through) with (their)
arrows.
9 He rested, and slept as a lion, and as a lioness,
whom no man shall dare raise. He that blesseth thee,
shall be blessed; and he that curseth, shall be areckoned
into cursing. (He rested, and slept like a lion, and like a
lioness, whom no man shall dare raise up. He who
blesseth thee, shall be blessed; and he who curseth *thee*,
shall be cursed.)
10 And Balak was wroth against Balaam, and he said,
when his hands were wrung together, I called thee to
curse mine enemies, whom, on the contrary, thou hast
blessed thrice (but who, instead, thou hast now blessed
three times!).
11 Turn again to thy place; forsooth I deemed to
honour thee greatly, but the Lord deprived thee from
[thine] honour (that was) disposed. (Return to thy place; I
had intended to greatly reward thee, but the Lord hath
now deprived thee of the reward which I had ordained
for thee.)
12 Balaam answered to Balak, Whether I said not to thy
messengers, which thou sentest to me, (Balaam answered
to Balak, Did I not say to thy messengers, whom thou
sentest to me,)
13 Though Balak shall give to me his house full of
silver and of gold, I shall not be able to pass [over] the
word of my Lord God, that I bring forth of mine heart
anything, either of good or of evil, but whatever thing the
Lord shall say, I shall speak that? (Even if Balak shall give
me all the gold and silver in his house, I shall not change
the word of the Lord my God, so that I bring forth
something out of my own heart, either good or bad, nay,
but whatever thing the Lord shall say, that I shall speak?)
14 Nevertheless I shall go to my people, and I shall
give counsel to thee, what thy people shall do in the last
time to this people. (Nevertheless, I shall now return to
my people, but first I shall give thee counsel, what these
people shall do to thy people in the days to come.)
15 Therefore when a parable was taken (And so when
he had received his prophecy), he said again, Balaam, the
son of Beor, said, (yea,) a man, whose eye is stopped,
said,
16 the hearer of God's words said, which knoweth the
doctrine of the Highest, and seeth the revelation of
Almighty God, which falleth down, and hath open eyes
(yea, the hearer of God's words said, who knoweth the
doctrine of the Highest, and seeth the revelation of
Almighty God, and who falleth down, but his eyes still be
open,)
17 I shall see him, but not now; I shall behold him, but
not nigh; a star shall be born of Jacob, and a rod shall rise
(out) of Israel; and he shall smite the dukes of Moab, and
he shall waste all the sons of Seth; (I shall see him, but
not now; I shall behold him, but not near; a star shall be
born in Jacob, and a sceptre shall rise up out of Israel;
and he shall strike down Moab's leaders, and he shall

destroy all the sons of strife;)
18 and Idumea shall be his possession, the heritage of
Seir shall befall to his enemies; soothly Israel shall do
strongly, (and Edom shall become his possession, yea,
the inheritance of Seir shall befall to their enemies; and
Israel shall be victorious,)
19 of Jacob shall be he that shall be lord, and shall lose
the relics, *or (the) remnants*, of the city. (for out of Jacob
shall come he who shall be their lord, and he shall
destroy those who last remain in the city of Ar.)
20 And when he had seen Amalek, he took a parable,
and said, Amalek is the beginning of heathen men,
whose last things shall be lost. (And *in a vision* he saw
the Amalekites, and when he had received his prophecy,
he said, Amalek was the first in all the heathen, but its
end shall be utter destruction.)
21 Also he saw Kenites, and when a parable was taken,
he said, Soothly thy dwelling place is strong, but if thou
shalt set thy nest in a stone, (And he also saw the Kenites,
and when he had received his prophecy, he said, Thy
dwelling place is strong, and thou shalt set thy nest in a
stone,)
22 and shalt be chosen of the generation of Kenites,
how long shalt thou be able to dwell? soothly Assur shall
take thee. (and shalt be the chosen of the generation of
Kenites, but how long shalt thou be able to live there? for
Assyria shall take thee captive.)
23 And when a parable was taken, *or showed to him*,
he said again (And when he had received his prophecy,
he said), Alas! who shall live, when the Lord shall do
these things?
24 They shall come in great ships from Italy (They shall
come in great ships from Chittim), (and) they shall
overcome Assyria, and they shall destroy Eber, and at the
last also they themselves shall perish.
25 And Balaam rose, and turned again into his place;
and Balak went again by the way in which he came. (And
then Balaam rose up, and returned to his home; and
Balak returned by the way by which he came.)

CHAPTER 25

1 Soothly in that time Israel dwelled in Shittim (And so
the Israelites lived in Shittim); and the people did
fornication with the daughters of Moab;
2 which daughters called them to their sacrifices, and
they ate (the sacrificial food), and worshipped the gods of
those daughters;
3 and Israel made sacrifice to Baalpeor. And the Lord
was wroth, (and the Israelites sacrificed to Baal of Peor.
And the Lord was angry against them,)
4 and said to Moses, Take thou all the princes of the
people, and hang them against the sun in gibbets, that my
strong vengeance be turned away from Israel. (and said to
Moses, Take thou all the leaders of the people, and hang
them up on gallows out in the sun, so that my strong
vengeance be turned away from Israel.)
5 And Moses said to the judges of Israel, Each man
slay his neighbours, that made sacrifice to Baalpeor. (And
Moses said to the judges of Israel, Each one of you kill his
neighbours, yea, they who sacrificed to Baal of Peor.)
6 And lo! one of the sons of Israel entered before his
brethren to an whore of Midian, in the sight of Moses,
and of all the company of the sons of Israel, which wept
before the gates of the tabernacle. (And lo! one of the
Israelites brought a woman of Midian into his tent, in the
sight of Moses, and all the congregation of the Israelites,
who were mourning at the entrance to the Tabernacle.)
7 And when Phinehas, the son of Eleazar, the son of
Aaron, the priest, had seen this *unshamefast doing* (had
seen this *shameful thing*), he rose (up) from the midst of
the multitude; and when he had taken a sword,
8 he entered after the man of Israel into the
whorehouse, and sticked through both together, that is,
the man and the woman, in the places of engendering.
And the vengeance ceased from the sons of Israel, (he
went into that bawdy house, after the man of Israel, and
stuck his sword through both of them together, that is, the
man and the woman, in their places of begetting. And so
the plague that had attacked the Israelites was stopped,)
9 and four and twenty thousand of men were slain.
(but by then, twenty-four thousand people had already
died.)
10 And the Lord said to Moses,
11 Phinehas, the son of Eleazar, son of Aaron, (the)
priest, hath turned away my wrath from the sons of Israel;
for he was moved against them by my fervent love, (and
so for) that, I myself (did) not do away the sons of Israel
in my great ferventness *of vengeance*. (Phinehas, the son
of Eleazar, the son of Aaron, the priest, hath turned away
my anger from the Israelites; for he was moved against
them by his fervent love for me, and because of that, I
did not do away all the Israelites in my great fervour *for
vengeance*.)
12 Therefore speak thou to him, Lo! I give to him the
peace of my covenant, (And so tell thou him, that lo! I
now give him my covenant of peace,)
13 and it shall be an everlasting covenant of
priesthood, as well to himself as to his seed; for he loved
fervently for his God, and he hath cleansed the great
trespass of the sons of Israel. (and it shall be an
everlasting covenant of priesthood, with him as well as
with his descendants; because he fervently loved for his
God, and he made amends for the great trespass of the
Israelites.)
14 Forsooth the name of the man of Israel, that was
slain with the woman of Midian, was Zimri, the son of
Salu, duke, of the kindred and lineage of Simeon (a
leader, of the kindred and the tribe of Simeon).

15 Soothly the woman of Midian that was slain together
with the whoreling, was called Cozbi, the daughter of
Zur, the noblest prince of (the) Midianites.
16 And the Lord spake to Moses, and said,
17 Midianites feel you enemies, and smite ye them;
(Regard ye the Midianites as your enemies, and strike ye
them down;)
18 for also they have done enemy-like against you, and
deceived you by treasons, by the idol of Peor, and by
their sister Cozbi, daughter of the duke of Midian, which
daughter was slain in the day of vengeance, for the
sacrilege of Peor. (for they were like an enemy to you,
and they deceived you with treasons, first in the matter at
Peor, and then with their sister Cozbi, the daughter of a
leader of Midian, which daughter was killed during the
plague, on the day of vengeance for the sacrilege at
Peor.)

CHAPTER 26

1 After that the blood of (the) guilty men was shed out,
the Lord said to Moses and to Eleazar, the priest, [the] son
of Aaron,
2 Reckon ye all the number of the sons of Israel, from
twenty years and above (from twenty years of age and
older), by their houses, and *their* kindreds, (yea,) all (the)
men that be able to go forth to battles.
3 And so Moses and Eleazar, the priest, spake in the
field places of Moab, over Jordan, against Jericho, (And
so Moses and Eleazar, the priest, spoke on the plains of
Moab, across the Jordan River, opposite Jericho,)
4 to them that were of twenty years and above (to
those who were twenty years of age and older), as the
Lord commanded; of which this is the number.
5 Reuben, the first begotten of Israel (Reuben, Israel's
first-born); the son of him *was* Hanoch, of whom *came*
the family of Hanochites; and Pallu, of whom *came* the
family of Palluites;
6 and Hezron, of whom *came* the family of
Hezronites; and Carmi, of whom *came* the family of
Carmites.
7 These were the families of the generation of Reuben,
of which families (all) the number was found (to be) three
and forty thousand (and) seven hundred and thirty.
8 The son of Pallu *was* Eliab;
9 the sons of him *were* Nemuel, and Dathan, and
Abiram. These were Dathan and Abiram, [the] princes of
the people, that rose against Moses and Aaron, in the
rebelty of Korah, when they rebelled against the Lord
(These were that Dathan and Abiram, the leaders of the
people, who rose up against Moses and Aaron, in the
rebellion of Korah, when they rebelled against the Lord);
10 and the earth opened his mouth, and devoured
Korah, and full many *men* died, when the fire burnt two
hundred men and fifty; and a great miracle was done,
(and the earth opened its mouth, and devoured Korah,
and a great many died, when the fire burned up two
hundred and fifty men; and a great miracle was done,)
11 that when Korah perished, his sons perished not.
(that when Korah died, his sons did not die.)
12 The sons of Simeon by their kindreds; Nemuel, of
him *was* the family of Nemuelites; Jamin, of him the
family of Jaminites; Jachin, of him the family of Jachinites;
13 Zerah, of him the family of Zarhites; Shaul, of him
the family of Shaulites.
14 These were the families of Simeon, of which all the
number was two and twenty thousand and two hundred.
15 The sons of Gad by their kindreds; Zephon, of him
the family of Zephonites; Haggi, of him the family of
Haggites; Shuni, of him the family of Shunites;
16 Ozni, of him the family of Oznites; Eri, of him the
family of Erites;
17 Arod, of him the family of Arodites; Areli, of him the
family of Arelites.
18 These were the families of Gad, of which all the
number was forty thousand and five hundred.
19 The sons of Judah *were* Er and Onan, which both
were dead in the land of Canaan. (The sons of Judah
were Er and Onan, and both of them died in the land of
Canaan.)
20 And the sons of Judah were *these* by their kindreds;
Shelah, of whom *came* the family of Shelanites; Pharez,
of him the family of Pharzites (Perez, of him the family of
Perezites); Zerah, of him the family of Zarhites.
21 Soothly the sons of Pharez *were* Hezron (And the
sons of Perez *were* Hezron), of him the family of
Hezronites; and Hamul, of him the family of Hamulites.
22 These were the families of Judah, of which all the
number was seventy thousand and five hundred.
23 The sons of Issachar by their kindreds; Tola, of him
the family of Tolaites; Pua, of him the family of Punites;
24 Jashub, of him the family of Jashubites; Shimron, of
him the family of Shimronites.
25 These were the kindreds of Issachar (These were the
families of Issachar), of which (all) the number was four
and sixty thousand and three hundred.
26 The sons of Zebulun by their kindreds; Sered, of him
the family of Sardites; Elon, of him the family of Elonites;
Jahleel, of him the family of Jahleelites.
27 These were the kindreds of Zebulun (These were the
families of Zebulun), of which (all) the number was sixty
thousand and five hundred.
28 The sons of Joseph by their kindreds were Manasseh
and Ephraim.
29 Of Manasseh was born Machir, of him the family of
Machirites. Machir begat Gilead, of him, the family of
Gileadites.
30 Gilead had *these* sons; Jeezer, of him the family of
Jeezerites; and Helek, of him the family of Helekites;

31 and Asriel, of him the family of Asrielites; and
Shechem, of him the family of Shechemites;
32 and Shemida, of him the family of Shemidaites; and
Hepher, of him the family of Hepherites.
33 Soothly Hepher was the father of Zelophehad, that
had not sons, but only daughters; of which these were
the names; Mahlah, and Noah, and Hoglah, and Milcah,
and Tirzah.
34 These were the families of Manasseh, and (all) the
number of them was two and fifty thousand and seven
hundred.
35 Soothly the sons of Ephraim by their kindreds were
these; Shuthelah, of him the family of Shuthalhites;
Becher, of him the family of Bachrites; Tahan, of him the
family of Tahanites.
36 Soothly the son of Shuthelah was Eran, of him the
family of Eranites.
37 These were the kindreds of the sons of Ephraim
(These were the families of Ephraim), of which (all) the
number was two and thirty thousand and five hundred.
These were the sons of Joseph, by their families.
38 The sons of Benjamin in their kindreds (These were
the families of Benjamin); Bela, of him the family of
Belaites; Ashbel, of him the family of Ashbelites; Ahiram,
of him the family of Ahiramites;
39 Shupham, of him the family of Shuphamites;
Hupham, of him the family of Huphamites.
40 The sons of Bela, (were) Ard and Naaman; of Ard,
the family of Ardites; of Naaman, the family of Naamites.
41 These were the sons of Benjamin by their kindreds
(These were the families of Benjamin), of which (all) the
number was five and forty thousand and six hundred.
42 The sons of Dan by their kindreds; Shuham, of him
the family of Shuhamites. These were the kindreds of
Dan by their families (These were the families of Dan);
43 (and) all (of them) were Shuhamites, of which (all)
the number was four and sixty thousand and four
hundred.
44 The sons of Asher by their kindreds (These were the
families of Asher); Jimna, of him the family of Jimnites;
Jesui, of him the family of Jesuites; Beriah, of him the
family of Beriites.
45 The sons of Beriah; Heber, of him the family of
Heberites; and Malchiel, of him the family of
Malchielites.
46 Soothly the name of the daughter of Asher was
Serah.
47 These were the kindreds of the sons of Asher (These
were the families of Asher), and (all) the number of them
was four and fifty thousand and four hundred.
48 The sons of Naphtali by their kindreds; Jahzeel, of
him the family of Jahzeelites; Guni, of him the family of
Gunites;
49 Jezer, of him the family of Jezerites; (and) Shillem, of
him the family of Shillemites.
50 These were the kindreds of the sons of Naphtali by
their families (These were the families of Naphtali), of
which (all) the number was five and forty thousand and
four hundred.
51 This is the sum of the sons of Israel, that were
numbered (who were listed, *or registered*), six hundred
thousand and a thousand (and) seven hundred and thirty.
52 And the Lord spake to Moses, and said,
53 The land shall be parted to these, by the number of
names into their possessions; (The land shall be divided
into possessions for these tribes, according to the number
of names listed;)
54 thou shalt give the greater part to [the] more men,
and the less(er) part to [the] fewer men; possession shall
be given to all by themselves, as they be numbered now;
(thou shalt give the larger part to the larger group of
people, and the smaller part to the smaller group of
people; a possession shall be given to each by
themselves, as they now be numbered, *that is, in
proportion to their number*;)
55 so only that (the) lot part the land to lineages and to
families.
56 Whatever thing befalleth by lot, either more (men),
either fewer men, take that.
57 Also this is the number of the sons of Levi by their
families; Gershon, of whom *is* the family of Gershonites;
Kohath, of him the family of Kohathites; Merari, of him
the family of Merarites.
58 These were the families of Levi; the family of Libni,
the family of Hebron, the family of Mahli, the family of
Mushi, the family of Korah. And soothly Kohath begat
Amram,
59 which had a wife, Jochebed, the daughter of Levi,
which daughter was born to him in Egypt. This *Jochebed*
engendered to her husband Amram, (his two) sons, Aaron
and Moses, and Marie, the sister of them. (who had a
wife, Jochebed, who was the daughter of Levi, and she
was born to him in Egypt. This *Jochebed* bare for her
husband Amram, his two sons, Aaron and Moses, and
their sister, Miriam.)
60 Nadab, and Abihu, and Eleazar, and Ithamar were
begotten of Aaron;
61 of which Nadab and Abihu were dead, when they
had offered alien fire before the Lord. (and Nadab and
Abihu died, when they offered unholy fire before the
Lord.)
62 And all that were numbered *of this lineage* were
three and twenty thousand of male kind, from a month
and above, which were not numbered among the sons of
Israel, neither possession was given to them with other
men. (And all who were listed, *or registered, in this tribe*
were twenty-three thousand males, from one month of
age and older, but they were not listed with the other

Israelites, nor was any possession given to them among
the other people.)
63 This is the number of the sons of Israel, that be
described of Moses and Eleazar, [the] priest, in the field
places of Moab, over Jordan, against Jericho; (These were
all the Israelites listed by Moses and Eleazar, the priest,
on the plains of Moab, across the Jordan River, opposite
Jericho;)
64 among which none of them was that were
numbered before of Moses and Aaron, in the desert of
Sinai; (and there was not one among them who had been
registered by Moses and Aaron before, in the Sinai
Desert;)
65 for the Lord before-said, that all should die in the
wilderness; and none of them dwelled *alive*, but Caleb,
Jephunneh's son, and Joshua, the son of Nun. (for the
Lord had said before, that they would all die in the
wilderness; and so none of them remained *alive*, but
Caleb, Jephunneh's son, and Joshua, the son of Nun.)

CHAPTER 27

1 Soothly the daughters of Zelophehad, the son of
Hepher, son of Gilead, son of Machir, son of Manasseh,
that was the son of Joseph, nighed (came near); of which
daughters these be the names; Mahlah, and Noah, and
Hoglah, and Milcah, and Tirzah.
2 And they stood before Moses, and Eleazar, the
priest, and before all the princes of the people, at the
door of the tabernacle of [the] bond of peace; and said,
(And they stood before Moses, and Eleazar, the priest,
and before all the leaders of the people, at the entrance
to the Tabernacle of the Covenant; and they said,)
3 Our father was dead in the desert, neither he was in
the rebelty that was raised against the Lord under Korah,
but he was dead in his sin; he had no male sons [he had
not male children]. (Our father died in the wilderness, and
he was not in the rebellion that was raised against the
Lord under Korah, but he died in his own sin; and he had
no sons.)
4 Why is his name taken away from his family, for he
hath no son? Give ye possession to us among our father's
kinsmen. (But why should his name be done away from
his family, simply because he hath no son? Give ye to us
a possession, *that is, some property*, among our father's
kinsmen.)
5 And Moses told their cause to the doom of the Lord;
(And Moses brought their case to the judgement of the
Lord;)
6 the which said to Moses, (and the Lord said to
Moses,)
7 The daughters of Zelophehad ask a just thing; give
thou possession to them among their father's kinsmen,
and be they successors to him into heritage. (The
daughters of Zelophehad ask for a just thing; give thou
them some property among their father's kinsmen, and
let them be the successors of his inheritance.)
8 Forsooth thou shalt speak these things to the sons of
Israel, When a man is dead without son, the heritage
shall go to his daughter; (And thou shalt speak these
words to the Israelites, When a man is dead without a
son, the inheritance shall go to his daughter;)
9 if he hath no daughter, he shall have (as) his heirs
his brethren; (if he hath no daughter, his brothers shall be
his heirs;)
10 that and if brethren be not, ye shall give the heritage
to the brethren of his father; (and if he hath no brothers,
ye shall give the inheritance to his father's brothers;)
11 soothly if he have no brethren of his father, the
heritage shall be given to them that be next to him. And
this shall be holy by everlasting law to the sons of Israel,
as the Lord commanded to Moses. (and if his father hath
no brothers, the inheritance shall be given to them who
be next to him. And this shall be holy by an everlasting
law to the Israelites, as the Lord commanded to Moses.)
12 Also the Lord said to Moses, Go (thou) up into this
hill of Abarim, and behold thou from thence the land,
which I shall give to the sons of Israel. (And then the Lord
said to Moses, Go thou up onto this Mount Abarim, and
from there behold thou the land, which I have given to
the Israelites.)
13 And when thou hast seen it, also thou shalt go to thy
people, as thy brother Aaron went; (And when thou hast
seen it, then thou also shalt go to thy people, *that is, thou
shalt die*, like thy brother Aaron did;)
14 for thou offendedest me in the desert of Zin, in the
against-saying of the multitude, neither thou wouldest
hallow me before *the people*, upon the waters. These be
the waters of against-saying in Kadesh, in the desert of
Zin. (for thou offendedest me in the wilderness of Zin,
when the people spoke against me, and thou didest not
uphold my holiness before *the people*, there at the
waters. These be the waters of Meribah at Kadesh, in the
wilderness of Zin.)
15 To whom Moses answered,
16 The Lord God of the spirits of all flesh, purvey a
man, that he be on this multitude, (May the Lord God of
the spirits of all people purvey a man who shall be over
these people,)
17 and that may go out (and who can go out), and enter
in before them, and lead them out, and lead them in, lest
the people of the Lord be as sheep without (a) shepherd.
18 And the Lord said to Moses, Take thou Joshua, the
son of Nun, a man in whom the spirit of God is (a man in
whom is the spirit of God), and put thine hand upon him;
19 and he shall stand before Eleazar, the priest, and
before all the multitude. And thou shalt give to him
behests, in the sight of all men (And thou shalt give him
his orders, *or his commission*, in the sight of all the

people),
20 and a part of thy glory, that all the synagogue of the
sons of Israel hear him. (and some of thy authority, so
that all the congregation of the Israelites shall listen to
him, *and shall follow him*.)
21 If anything shall be worthy to be done for this *man,*
Joshua, Eleazar, the priest, shall counsel the Lord; he
shall go out, and shall go in, at the word of Eleazar; he,
and all the sons of Israel with him, and the tother
multitude. (And if anything shall be worthy to be done for
this *man, Joshua,* Eleazar, the priest, shall ask counsel
from the Urim and the Thummim, before the Lord; he
shall go out, and shall go in, at the word of Eleazar; he,
and all the multitude of the Israelites.)
22 Moses did as the Lord commanded, and when he
had taken Joshua, he set him before Eleazar, the priest;
and before all the multitude of the people;
23 and when he had put his hands upon his head, he
rehearsed all things that the Lord commanded. (and when
he had laid his hands upon his head, he repeated all the
things that the Lord had commanded.)

CHAPTER 28

1 Also the Lord said to Moses, (And the Lord said to
Moses,)
2 Command thou to the sons of Israel, and thou shalt
say to them, Offer ye by their times mine offering, and
loaves, and incense of sweetest odour. (Command thou
to the Israelites, and thou shalt say to them, At the
appointed times, offer ye my food offerings, to make the
incense of the sweetest aroma.)
3 These be the sacrifices which ye ought to offer; two
lambs of one year, without wem, each day, into
everlasting burnt sacrifice. (These be the offerings which
ye ought to offer; two one-year-old lambs, without
blemish, *or without fault*, for a continual, *or a daily*,
burnt sacrifice.)
4 Ye shall offer one lamb early, and the tother at
eventide. (Ye shall offer one lamb in the morning, and
the other in the evening.)
5 The tenth part of (an) ephah of tried flour, that shall
be sprinkled with purest oil, and have it the fourth part of
(a) hin. (And the grain offering of the tenth of an ephah of
fine flour, that shall be sprinkled with a quarter of a hin of
most pure oil.)
6 It is (the) continual burnt sacrifice, which ye offered
in the hill of Sinai, into odour of sweetest incense to the
Lord. (This is the continual, *or the daily*, burnt sacrifice,
which ye first offered at Mount Sinai, to make the incense
of the sweetest aroma to the Lord.)
7 And (for the wine offering,) ye shall offer the fourth
part of (a) hin of wine, by each lamb, in the saintuary of
the Lord. (And for the wine offering, ye shall offer a
quarter of a hin of wine with each lamb, in the sanctuary
of the Lord.)
8 And ye shall offer in like manner the tother lamb at
eventide, by all the custom of the morrow sacrifice, and
of the moist sacrifices thereof, an offering of sweetest
odour to the Lord. (And ye shall offer in like manner the
other lamb in the evening, with all the customs, *or all the*
rites, of the morning offering, with its grain and wine
offerings, to make an offering of the sweetest aroma to
the Lord.)
9 Soothly in the sabbath day ye shall offer two lambs
of one year, without wem, and two tenth parts of tried
flour sprinkled (al)together with oil, in sacrifice, (And on
the sabbath day, ye shall offer an offering of two one-
year-old lambs, without blemish, *or without fault*, with its
grain offering of two tenths of an ephah of fine flour
sprinkled with oil, and its wine offering,)
10 and the moist sacrifices that be poured (out) by
custom, by all sabbaths, into everlasting burnt sacrifice.
(on every sabbath, besides the continual, *or the daily*,
offering, and its wine offering.)
11 Soothly in the calends, that is, in the beginnings of
months, ye shall offer burnt sacrifice to the Lord, twain
calves of the drove, one ram, seven lambs of one year,
without wem, (And on the calends, that is, at the
beginning of every month, ye shall offer a burnt sacrifice
to the Lord, two calves from the herd, one ram, and
seven one-year-old lambs, all without blemish, *or*
without fault,)
12 and three tenth parts of [tried] flour sprinkled
(al)together with oil, in the sacrifice, by each calf, and
two tenth parts of [tried] flour sprinkled (al)together with
oil, by each ram; (and for the grain offering, three tenths
of an ephah of fine flour sprinkled with oil, with each
calf, and two tenths of an ephah of fine flour sprinkled
with oil, with each ram;)
13 and the tenth part of the tenth of [tried] flour
sprinkled (al)together with oil, in the sacrifice, by each
lamb; it is burnt sacrifice of sweetest odour, and of
incense to the Lord. (and the tenth part of an ephah of
fine flour sprinkled with oil, with each lamb; this is a
burnt sacrifice to make the incense of the sweetest aroma
to the Lord.)
14 Soothly the moist sacrifices of wine, that shall be
poured (out) by all the slain sacrifices, shall be these; the
half part of (a) hin by each calf, the third part by a ram,
the fourth part by a lamb; this shall be the burnt sacrifices
by each month, that come one after another while the
year turneth about. (And the wine offerings, that shall be
poured out with all the burnt sacrifices, shall be these;
half a hin with each calf, the third of a hin with the ram,
and a quarter of a hin with each lamb; all these shall be
the burnt sacrifices for all the months, that come one after
the other, while the year turneth about.)
15 Also a buck of (the) goats shall be offered to the Lord

for sins, into everlasting burnt sacrifice, with his moist
offerings. (And a goat buck shall be offered to the Lord
for a sin offering, besides the continual, *or the daily*,
burnt sacrifice, with its wine offering.)
16 Soothly in the first month, in the fourteenth day of
the month, shall be pask, *either (the) passing (over)*, of
the Lord; (And in the first month, on the fourteenth day of
the month, shall be the Passover of the Lord;)
17 and in the fifteenth day shall be the solemnity of
therf loaves. By seven days ye shall eat therf loaves; (and
on the fifteenth day shall be the Feast of Unleavened
Bread. For seven days ye shall eat only unleavened
bread, *that is, bread made without yeast*;)
18 of which the first day shall be worshipful and holy;
ye shall not do any servile work therein. (and on the first
day there shall be a holy gathering; ye shall not do any
daily work on it.)
19 And ye shall offer burnt sacrifice to the Lord, two
calves, one ram, seven lambs of one year, without wem;
(And ye shall offer a burnt sacrifice to the Lord, two
calves, one ram, and seven one-year-old lambs, all
without blemish, *or without fault*;)
20 and the sacrifices of each by itself of [tried] flour,
which be sprinkled (al)together with oil, three tenth parts
by each calf, and two tenth parts by a ram, (and with
each offering its grain offering of fine flour sprinkled with
oil, that is, three tenths of an ephah with each calf, and
two tenths of an ephah with the ram,)
21 and the tenth part of the tenth by each lamb, that is,
by seven lambs. (and the tenth of an ephah with each of
the seven lambs.)
22 And *ye shall offer* one buck of (the) goats for sin,
that cleansing be made for you, (And *ye shall offer* one
goat buck for a sin offering, to make amends for you,)
23 besides the burnt sacrifice of the morrowtide, which
ye shall offer ever[more]. (besides the morning burnt
sacrifice, which ye shall offer continually, *or daily*.)
24 So ye shall do by each day of [the] seven days, into
the nourishing of (the) fire, and into the sweetest odour to
the Lord, that shall rise of the burnt sacrifice, and of the
moist sacrifices of each *offering*. (So ye shall offer on
each of the seven days, by the nourishing of the fire, to
make the sweetest aroma to the Lord, besides the daily
burnt sacrifice, with its wine offering.)
25 Also the seventh day shall be most solemn and holy
to you; ye shall not do any servile work therein. (And on
the seventh day, there shall also be a holy gathering; ye
shall not do any daily work on it.)
26 Also the day of the first fruits, when ye shall offer
new fruits to the Lord, when the weeks shall be fulfilled,
shall be worshipful and holy; ye shall not do any servile
work therein. (And on the Day of Firstfruits, *that is, the
Feast of Weeks, or the Harvest Festival*, when ye shall
offer your new grain to the Lord, yea, when the weeks
shall be fulfilled, there shall be a holy gathering; ye shall
not do any daily work on it.)
27 And ye shall offer burnt sacrifice to the Lord, into
sweetest odour; two calves of the drove, one ram, and
seven lambs of one year, without wem; (And ye shall
offer a burnt sacrifice, to make the sweetest aroma to the
Lord; two calves from the herd, one ram, and seven one-
year-old lambs, all without blemish;)
28 and in the sacrifices of those *ye shall offer* three
tenth parts of tried flour sprinkled (al)together with oil, by
each calf, two tenth parts by the rams, (and with each
offering *ye shall offer* its grain offering of fine flour
sprinkled with oil, that is, three tenths of an ephah with
each calf, two tenths of an ephah with each ram,)
29 the tenth part of the tenth by the lambs, which be all
together seven lambs. (and the tenth part of an ephah
with each of the seven lambs.)
30 And *ye shall offer* a buck of (the) goats (for sin),
which is offered for cleansing, (And *ye shall offer* one
goat buck for a sin offering, to make amends for you,)
31 besides [the] burnt sacrifice everlasting, and the
moist sacrifices thereof; ye shall offer all things without
wem, with their moist sacrifices. (besides the continual,
or the daily, burnt sacrifice, with its grain and wine
offerings; and ye shall offer all these things without
blemish.)

CHAPTER 29

1 Forsooth the first day of the seventh month shall be
holy, and worshipful to you; ye shall not do any servile
work therein, for it is the day of sounding, and of trumps.
(On the first day of the seventh month, there shall be a
holy gathering; ye shall not do any daily work on it, for it
is the day of the sounding of trumpets *for the New Year's
Festival*.)
2 And ye shall offer burnt sacrifice, into sweetest
odour to the Lord, one calf of the drove, one ram, and
seven lambs of one year, without wem; (And ye shall
offer a burnt sacrifice, to make the sweetest aroma to the
Lord, one calf from the herd, one ram, and seven one-
year-old lambs, all without blemish, *or without fault*;)
3 and in the sacrifice of those *ye shall offer* three tenth
parts of tried flour sprinkled (al)together with oil, by each
calf, two tenth parts by a ram, (and with each offering *ye
shall offer* its grain offering of fine flour sprinkled with
oil, that is, three tenths of an ephah with each calf, two
tenths of an ephah with the ram,)
4 one tenth part by a lamb, which (al)together be
seven lambs. (and one tenth of an ephah with each of the
seven lambs.)
5 And *ye shall offer* a buck of (the) goats, which is
offered for sin, into the cleansing of the people, (And *ye
shall offer* one goat buck for the sin offering, to make
amends for the people/to make amends for you,)

6 without [the] burnt sacrifice of the beginning of
months, with his sacrifices, *and without* the everlasting
burnt sacrifice, with customable flowing offerings; and by
the same ceremonies, *or customs*, ye shall offer incense,
into sweetest odour to the Lord. (besides the burnt
sacrifice for the beginning of the month, *or the calends*,
with its grain offering, *and besides* the continual, *or the
daily*, burnt sacrifice, with its grain and wine offerings;
yea, with the same ceremonies, *and customs, or rites*, ye
shall offer this incense of the sweetest aroma to the Lord.)
7 Also the tenth day of this seventh month shall be
holy and worshipful to you, and ye shall torment your
souls; ye shall not do any servile work therein. (And there
shall also be a holy gathering on the tenth day of this
seventh month, *the Day of Atonement*, and ye shall
torment your souls; ye shall not do any daily work on it.)
8 And ye shall offer burnt sacrifice to the Lord, into
sweetest odour; one calf of the drove, one ram, seven
lambs of one year, without wem. (And ye shall offer a
burnt sacrifice, to make the sweetest aroma to the Lord;
one calf from the herd, one ram, and seven one-year-old
lambs, all without blemish, *or without fault*.)
9 And in the sacrifices of those *ye shall offer* three
tenth parts of [tried] flour sprinkled (al)together with oil,
by each calf, two tenth parts by a ram, (And with each
offering *ye shall offer* its grain offering of fine flour
sprinkled with oil, that is, three tenths of an ephah with
each calf, two tenths of ephah with each ram,)
10 the tenth part of the tenth by each lamb, that be
(al)together seven lambs. (and the tenth part of an ephah
with each of the seven lambs.)
11 And *ye shall offer* a buck of (the) goats for sin,
without these things that be wont to be offered for sin
into cleansing, and everlasting burnt sacrifice in the
sacrifice, and flowing offerings of those things. (And *ye
shall offer* one goat buck for the sin offering, besides the
goat that is offered as a sin offering to make amends, and
the continual, *or the daily*, burnt sacrifice, with its grain
and wine offerings.)
12 Forsooth in the fifteenth day of the seventh month,
that shall be holy and worshipful to you, ye shall not do
any servile work [in it], but ye shall hallow the solemnity
to the Lord by seven days; (On the fifteenth day of the
seventh month, there shall also be a holy gathering, and
ye shall not do any daily work on it, but ye shall
celebrate the Feast of Tabernacles, *or the Festival of
Booths, or of Shelters*, to the Lord, for seven days;)
13 and ye shall offer burnt sacrifice, into sweetest
odour to the Lord, thirteen calves of the drove, two rams,
fourteen lambs of one year, without wem. (and ye shall
offer a burnt sacrifice, to make the sweetest aroma to the
Lord, thirteen calves from the herd, two rams, and
fourteen one-year-old lambs, all without blemish, *or
without fault*.)
14 And in the moist sacrifices of those *ye shall offer*
three tenth parts of tried flour sprinkled (al)together with
oil, by each calf, that be (al)together thirteen calves, and
ye shall offer two tenth parts to two rams together, that is,
one tenth part to one ram, (And with each offering *ye
shall offer* its grain offering of fine flour sprinkled with
oil, that is, three tenths of an ephah with each of the
thirteen calves, and two tenths of an ephah with each of
the two rams,)
15 and the tenth part of the tenth to each lamb, which
be (al)together fourteen lambs. (and the tenth part of an
ephah with each of the fourteen lambs.)
16 And *ye shall offer* a buck of (the) goats for sin,
without [the] everlasting burnt sacrifice, and the sacrifice,
and [the] moist offering thereof. (And *ye shall offer* one
goat buck for the sin offering, besides the continual, *or
the daily*, burnt sacrifice, with its grain and wine
offerings.)
17 In the tother day ye shall offer twelve calves of the
drove, two rams, fourteen lambs of one year, without
wem. (On the *second* day, ye shall offer twelve calves
from the herd, two rams, and fourteen one-year-old
lambs, all without blemish.)
18 And ye shall hallow rightfully the sacrifices, and
[the] moist offerings of all, by the calves, and rams, and
lambs. (And ye shall offer the proper grain and wine
offerings, with each of the calves, and the rams, and the
lambs.)
19 And *ye shall offer* a buck of (the) goats for sin,
without the everlasting burnt sacrifice, and the sacrifice,
and the moist offering thereof. (And *ye shall offer* one
goat buck for the sin offering, besides the continual, *or
the daily*, burnt sacrifice, with its grain and wine
offerings.)
20 In the third day, ye shall offer eleven calves, two
rams, fourteen lambs of one year, without wem. (On the
third day, ye shall offer eleven calves, two rams, and
fourteen one-year-old lambs, all without blemish.)
21 And ye shall hallow rightfully the sacrifices, and the
moist offerings of all *these*, by the calves, and rams, and
lambs. (And ye shall offer the proper grain and wine
offerings, with each of the calves, and the rams, and the
lambs.)
22 And *ye shall offer* a buck of (the) goats for sin,
without (the) everlasting burnt sacrifice, and the sacrifice,
and [the] moist offering thereof. (And *ye shall offer* one
goat buck for the sin offering, besides the continual, *or
the daily*, burnt sacrifice, with its grain and wine
offerings.)
23 In the fourth day, ye shall offer ten calves, two rams,
fourteen lambs of one year, without wem. (On the fourth
day, ye shall offer ten calves, two rams, and fourteen one-
year-old lambs, all without blemish.)
24 And ye shall hallow rightfully the sacrifices, and the

moist offerings of all, by the calves, and rams, and lambs.
(And ye shall offer the proper grain and wine offerings,
with each of the calves, and the rams, and the lambs.)
25 And *ye shall offer* a buck of (the) goats for sin,
without the everlasting burnt sacrifice, and the sacrifice,
and the moist offering thereof. (And *ye shall offer* one
goat buck for the sin offering, besides the continual, *or
the daily*, burnt sacrifice, with its grain and wine
offerings.)
26 In the fifth day, ye shall offer nine calves, two rams,
fourteen lambs of one year, without wem. (On the fifth
day, ye shall offer nine calves, two rams, and fourteen
one-year-old lambs, all without blemish.)
27 And ye shall hallow rightfully the sacrifices, and
[the] moist offerings of all, by the calves, and rams, and
lambs. (And ye shall offer the proper grain and wine
offerings, with each of the calves, and the rams, and the
lambs.)
28 And *ye shall offer* a buck of (the) goats for sin,
without [the] everlasting burnt sacrifice, and the sacrifice,
and [the] moist offering thereof. (And *ye shall offer* one
goat buck for the sin offering, besides the continual, *or
the daily*, burnt sacrifice, with its grain and wine
offerings.)
29 In the sixth day, ye shall offer eight calves, two
rams, fourteen lambs of one year, without wem. (On the
sixth day, ye shall offer eight calves, two rams, and
fourteen one-year-old lambs, all without blemish.)
30 And ye shall hallow rightfully the sacrifices, and
[the] moist offerings of all, by the calves, and rams, and
lambs. (And ye shall offer the proper grain and wine
offerings, with each of the calves, and the rams, and the
lambs.)
31 And *ye shall offer* a buck of (the) goats for sin,
without [the] everlasting burnt sacrifice, and the sacrifice,
and [the] moist offering thereof. (And *ye shall offer* one
goat buck for the sin offering, besides the continual, *or
the daily*, burnt sacrifice, with its grain and wine
offerings.)
32 In the seventh day, ye shall offer seven calves, two
rams, fourteen lambs of one year, without wem. (On the
seventh day, ye shall offer seven calves, two rams, and
fourteen one-year-old lambs, all without blemish.)
33 And ye shall hallow rightfully the sacrifices, and
[the] moist offerings of all, by the calves, and rams, and
lambs. (And ye shall offer the proper grain and wine
offerings, with each of the calves, and the rams, and the
lambs.)
34 And *ye shall offer* a buck of (the) goats for sin,
without [the] everlasting burnt sacrifice, and the sacrifice,
and [the] moist offering thereof. (And *ye shall offer* one
goat buck for the sin offering, besides the continual, *or
the daily*, burnt sacrifice, with its grain and wine
offerings.)
35 In the eighth day, which is most solemn, ye shall not
do any servile work (therein), (On the eighth day, there
shall also be a holy gathering, and ye shall not do any
daily work on it;)
36 and ye shall offer burnt sacrifice, into sweetest
odour to the Lord, one calf, one ram, seven lambs of one
year, without wem. (and ye shall offer a burnt sacrifice, to
make the sweetest aroma to the Lord, one calf, one ram,
and seven one-year-old lambs, all without blemish.)
37 And ye shall hallow rightfully the sacrifices, and
[the] moist offerings of all, by the calves, and rams, and
lambs. (And ye shall offer the proper grain and wine
offerings, with each of the calves, and the rams, and the
lambs.)
38 And *ye shall offer* a buck of (the) goats for sin,
without [the] everlasting burnt sacrifice, and the sacrifice,
and [the] moist offering thereof. (And *ye shall offer* one
goat buck for the sin offering, besides the continual, *or
the daily*, burnt sacrifice, with its grain and wine
offerings.)
39 Ye shall offer these things to the Lord, in your
solemnities, without *your* avows, and your willful
offerings, in the burnt sacrifice(s), in sacrifice(s), in the
moist offering(s), and in peaceable sacrifices. (Ye shall
offer these things to the Lord, at your feasts, besides *your*
vows, your freewill offerings, the burnt sacrifices, the
grain offerings, the wine offerings, and the peace
offerings.)
40 And Moses told to the sons of Israel all things which
the Lord commanded to him. (And Moses told the
Israelites everything that the Lord commanded him.)

CHAPTER 30

1 And he spake to the princes of the lineages of the
sons of Israel, This is the word, which the Lord
commanded, (And he spoke to the leaders of the tribes of
the Israelites, and said, This is what the Lord
commanded,)
2 If any of men maketh a vow to the Lord, either
bindeth himself by an oath, he shall not make void, *or
false*, his word, but he shall fulfill all thing that he
promised. (If anyone maketh a vow to the Lord, or
bindeth himself with an oath, he shall not make his word
void, *or false*, but he shall fulfill everything that he
promised.)
3 If a woman that is in the house of her father, and is
yet in the age of a young damsel, avoweth anything,
either bindeth herself by an oath (or bindeth herself with
an oath),
4 (and) her father knoweth the avow, that she
promised, and the oath, by which she bound her soul,
and he is still, she shall be guilty of that oath, if she break
it; whatever thing she promised, and swore, she shall
fulfill in work. (and her father knoweth of the vow, which

she promised to do, or the oath, with which she hath
bound her soul, and he is silent, she shall be bound by
that oath, if she break it, and whatever thing that she hath
promised, or hath sworn, to do, she shall fulfill it, *or shall
do it.*)
5 Forsooth if her father against-said (*it*), anon as he
heard (as soon as he heard it), both (her) vows, and her
oaths shall be (made) void, and she shall not be holden
bound to the promise, for her father against-said *it.*
6 If she hath an husband, and *she* avoweth anything,
and a word going out of her mouth (or with a word going
out of her mouth), (at) once bindeth her soul with an
oath,
7 in what day her husband heareth this, and against-
saith it not, she shall be guilty, *or bound,* to that vow; she
shall yield, whatever thing she promised. (from the day
that her husband heareth of it, and saith nothing against
it, she shall be bound by that vow; she shall yield
whatever thing that she hath promised.)
8 But if the husband heareth *it,* and anon against-saith
(*it*), and maketh void all her promises, and (the) words by
which she bound her soul, the Lord shall be merciful to
her. (But if her husband heareth of *it,* and at once saith
against *it,* and maketh void all of her promises, or the
words with which she bound her soul, then the Lord shall
be merciful to her.)
9 A widow, and a woman forsaken of her husband,
shall yield, whatever thing they avow. (Regarding a
widow, or a woman forsaken by her husband, both shall
yield whatever thing they have vowed.)
10 When a wife in her husband's house bindeth herself
by a vow, and an oath (or with an oath),
11 if her husband heareth it, and is still, and against-
saith not her promise, she shall yield, whatever thing she
promised. (if her husband heareth of it, and is silent, and
saith nothing against her promise, she shall yield
whatever that she hath promised.)
12 Soothly if the husband against-said anon, she shall
not be holden guilty of the promise, for *her* husband
against-said it anon, and the Lord shall be merciful to her.
(But if her husband said against *it* at once, she shall not
be held to the promise, for *her* husband said against it at
once, and so the Lord shall be merciful to her.)
13 If she avoweth, and bindeth herself by an oath, that
she torment her soul by fasting, either by abstinence of
other things, it shall be in the doom of her husband, that
she do that, either do it not. (If she voweth, or bindeth
herself with an oath, that she torment her soul with
fasting, or by abstaining from other things, it shall be her
husband who shall decide whether she must do it, or
not.)
14 That if the husband heareth it, and he is still, and
delayeth the sentence in[to] the tother day, she shall yield
whatever thing she avowed and promised, for he was
still, (and said not against it,) anon as he heard. (But if her
husband heareth of it, and he is silent, and delayeth his
judgement into the next day, she shall yield whatever
that she hath vowed, or hath promised, for he was silent,
and said nothing against it, as soon as he heard of it.)
15 Soothly if her husband against-said *her avow, and
her oath,* after that he knew *thereof,* he shall bear his
wickedness. (But if her husband saith against *her vow, or
her oath,* sometime after that he hath learned *of it,* he
shall bear her wickedness, *that is, the penalty for not
fulfilling the vow.*)
16 These be the laws, which the Lord ordained to
Moses, betwixt the husband and the wife, (and) betwixt
the father and the daughter, which is yet in the age of a
young damsel, or that yet dwelleth in her father's house
unmarried.

CHAPTER 31

1 And the Lord spake to Moses, and said,
2 Venge thou first the sons of Israel of (the) Midianites,
and so thou shalt be gathered to thy people. (First take
thou vengeance for the Israelites upon the Midianites,
and then thou shalt be gathered to thy people, *that is,
thou shalt die.*)
3 And anon Moses said, Arm ye (some) men of you to
battle, that be able to take of the Midianites the
vengeance of the Lord. (And at once Moses said to the
people, Arm ye some men of you for battle, so that we
can take the vengeance of the Lord upon the Midianites.)
4 (Out) Of each lineage be chosen a thousand men of
Israel, that shall be sent (in)to battle.
5 And of each lineage they gave a thousand, that is,
twelve thousand of men, ready to battle; (And so from
each tribe they gave a thousand men, that is, twelve
thousand men in all, ready for battle;)
6 which Moses sent forth with Phinehas, the son of
Eleazar, the priest. And Moses betook to them [the] holy
vessels, and trumps to make sound (and the trumpets
with which to sound the battle-cry).
7 And when they had fought against (the) Midianites,
and had overcome *them,* Israel killed all the males (the
Israelites killed all their adult males),
8 and the kings of them, Evi, and Rekem, and Zur, and
Hur, and Reba, five princes of the folk of them. Also
Israel killed with sword Balaam, the son of Beor. (and
their kings, Evi, and Rekem, and Zur, and Hur, and Reba,
the five Midianite kings. And the Israelites also killed
with the sword Balaam, the son of Beor.)
9 And Israel took the women of them, and their little
children, and all their beasts, and all the purtenance of
their household; whatever they might have, they spoiled,
that is, they destroyed; (And the Israelites took captive
the Midianite women, and their little children, and
carried off all their beasts, and all their household things;

yea, whatever the Midianites possessed, they took;)
10 the flame burnt as well the cities, as (the) little
towns, and castles. (and the flame burned up the cities, as
well as the little towns, and the tents, *or the camps.*)
11 And they took prey, and all things which they had
taken, as well of men as of beasts, (And they took the
spoils, and all the things which they had captured, of
men and of beasts,)
12 and they brought to Moses, and to Eleazar, the
priest, and to all the multitude of the sons of Israel.
Soothly they bare other useable things to their tents,
standing in the field places of Moab, beside (the) Jordan,
against Jericho. (and they brought it all to Moses, and to
Eleazar, the priest, and to all the multitude of the
Israelites. Yea, they carried all the useable things back to
the tents, pitched there on the plains of Moab, across the
Jordan River, opposite Jericho.)
13 [And] Moses and Eleazar, the priest, and all the
princes of the synagogue, went out into the coming of
them, without the tents. (And Moses and Eleazar, the
priest, and all the leaders of the congregation, went out to
meet them, away from the tents.)
14 And Moses was wroth to the princes of the host, to
the tribunes, and the centurions [(to the) leaders of
thousands, and governors of hundreds], that came from the
battle; (And Moses was angry with the leaders of the
army, yea, with the tribunes, *that is, the leaders of a
thousand men,* and the centurions, *that is, the leaders of
a hundred men,* who came back from the battle;)
15 and he said to *them,* Why kept ye (all) [the] women
(alive)?
16 whether it be not these that deceived the sons of
Israel, at the suggestion of Balaam, and made you to do
trespass against the Lord, upon the sin of Peor, wherefore
also the people was slain? (was it not they who deceived
the Israelites, at Balaam's suggestion, and made you to
trespass against the Lord with your sin at Peor, after
which so many of the people then perished with the
plague?)
17 And therefore slay ye all the men, whatever is of
male kind, and the little children (And so kill ye all the
men, yea, whoever is a male, and all the little children);
and strangle ye the women that have known men fleshly;
18 soothly keep ye to you the young damsels, and all
women virgins, (but you can keep for yourselves the
young girls, and all the women who still be virgins,)
19 and dwell ye without the tents seven days. He that
slayeth a man, or toucheth a slain man, shall be cleansed
in the third [day], and the seventh day; (and then stay ye
away from the tents for seven days. He who killeth a
man, or toucheth a dead man, must cleanse both himself,
and his captives, on the third day, and on the seventh
day;)
20 and of all the prey, whether it is cloth, or vessel, and
anything made ready to things pertaining to use, of the
skins and hairs of goats, and wood, it shall be cleansed.
(and all the spoils, whether it is a cloak, or a vessel, or
anything made out of skin, or of goat hair, or of wood,
must also be made clean, *or purified.*)
21 And Eleazar, the priest, spake thus to the men of the
host that fought, This is the commandment of the law,
which the Lord commanded to Moses,
22 The gold, and silver, and brass, and iron, and tin,
and lead,
23 and all thing that may pass by (the) flame, shall be
purged by fire; soothly whatever thing may not suffer fire,
shall be hallowed with the water of cleansing. (and all
the things that can pass through the flame, shall be
purified by fire; but whatever thing cannot survive the
flame, shall be made clean with the water of cleansing, *or
of purification.*)
24 And ye shall wash your clothes in the seventh day,
and ye shall be cleansed; and afterward ye shall enter
into the tents. (And ye shall wash your clothes on the
seventh day, and then ye shall be clean; and afterward ye
can return to the tents.)
25 And the Lord said to Moses,
26 Take ye the sum, *or the number,* of those things that
be taken, from man till to beast, thou, and Eleazar, [the]
priest, and all the princes of the common people.
27 And thou shalt part evenly the prey betwixt them
that fought and went out to battle, and betwixt all the
other multitude. (And thou shalt evenly divide the spoils
between those who went out to the battle and fought,
and all the *other* multitude.)
28 And thou shalt separate a part to the Lord, of them
that have fought, and were in battle, one soul of five
hundred, as well of men, as of oxen, and of asses, and of
sheep. (And thou shalt take a tribute, *or a tax,* for the
Lord, from those who fought, and were in the battle, one
soul out of five hundred, of people, and of oxen, and of
donkeys, and of sheep.)
29 And thou shalt give that part to Eleazar, the priest,
for those be the first fruits of the Lord. (And thou shalt
give that portion to Eleazar, the priest, for they be the first
fruits, *or a special contribution,* for the Lord.)
30 Also of the half part of the sons of Israel, thou shalt
take the fiftieth head of men, and of oxen, and of asses,
and of sheep, and of all living beasts; and thou shalt give
those to the deacons, that (stand) watch in the keepings
of the tabernacle of the Lord. (And from the half portion
given to the Israelites, thou shalt take the fiftieth head of
people, and of oxen, and of donkeys, and of sheep, yea,
of all the living beasts; and thou shalt give them to the
Levites, who keep charge of the Tabernacle of the Lord.)
31 And Moses and Eleazar did, as the Lord
commanded.
32 Forsooth the prey which the host had taken, was six

hundred and five and seventy thousand of sheep, (And
the spoils which the army had captured, were six
hundred and seventy-five thousand sheep,)
33 of oxen, two and seventy thousand, (and seventy-
two thousand oxen,)
34 of asses, sixty thousand and a thousand; (and sixty-
one thousand donkeys;)
35 the souls of the persons of women kind, that knew
not men, were two and thirty thousand. (and thirty-two
thousand *young* women, who knew not men.)
36 And the half part (that) was given to them that were
in the battle, of sheep three hundred seven and thirty
thousand, and five hundred; (And so the half portion of
the sheep, that was given to them who were in the battle,
was three hundred and thirty-seven thousand, and five
hundred;)
37 of which six hundred five and seventy sheep were
numbered into the part of the Lord; (of which six hundred
and seventy-five sheep were paid as the tribute, *or the
tax*, to the Lord;)
38 and of six and thirty thousand oxen, two and
seventy oxen; (and of the thirty-six thousand oxen,
seventy-two oxen were paid as the tribute, *or the tax*, to
the Lord;)
39 and of thirty thousand asses and five hundred, one
and sixty asses; (and of the thirty thousand and five
hundred donkeys, sixty-one donkeys were paid as the
tribute, *or the tax*, to the Lord;)
40 (and) of [the] sixteen thousand persons of men, two
and thirty persons befelled into the part of the Lord. (and
of the sixteen thousand women, *that is, the virgins*, thirty-
two persons were paid as the tribute, *or the tax*, to the
Lord.)
41 And Moses betook the number of the first fruits of
the Lord to Eleazar, the priest, as it was commanded to
him, (And Moses gave the tribute of the first fruits, *or the
special contribution*, for the Lord, to Eleazar, the priest,
as the Lord had commanded him,)
42 of the half part of the sons of Israel, which he parted
to them that were in battle. (out of the half portion for the
Israelites, which he had separated for them who were in
the battle.)
43 And of the half part that befelled to the tother
multitude, that is, of three hundred seven and thirty
thousand sheep and five hundred, (And out of the half
portion that befell to the rest of the people, that is, of the
three hundred and thirty-seven thousand and five
hundred sheep,)
44 and of six and thirty thousand oxen, (and of the
thirty-six thousand oxen,)
45 and of thirty thousand asses and five hundred, (and
of the thirty thousand and five hundred donkeys,)
46 and of sixteen thousand women, (and of the sixteen
thousand virgins,)
47 Moses took the fiftieth head, and he gave them to
the deacons, that (stood) watch in the tabernacle of the
Lord, as the Lord commanded. (Moses took the fiftieth of
each, and he gave them to the Levites, who kept charge
of the Tabernacle of the Lord, as the Lord commanded.)
48 And when the princes of the host, and the tribunes,
and the centurions had nighed to Moses, [And when the
princes of the host were gone to Moses, and the leaders of
thousands, and rulers of hundreds,] (And then the leaders of
the army, the tribunes, and the centurions, came to
Moses,)
49 they said, We thy servants have told, (*or totalled*,)
the number of fighters, which we had under our hand, *or
power*, and soothly not one failed; (and they said, We thy
servants have counted up again the number of the
fighters, that we have under our command, and not one
of them is missing;)
50 for which cause we offer, *or bring*, to thee free gifts
of the Lord, all by ourselves, that that we might find of
gold in the prey, girdles for the women's middles, and
bands of the arms, and rings, and ornaments of the arm
nigh the hand, and bands of the necks of women, that
thou pray the Lord for us. (for which reason, we now
freely bring to thee gifts for the Lord, from each of us, of
that which we found in the spoils, yea, gold, and girdles
for the women's middles, and arm bands, and rings, and
bracelets, and women's necklaces, and we also ask that
thou pray to the Lord for us.)
51 And Moses and Eleazar, the priest, took all the gold
in diverse kinds, (And so Moses and Eleazar, the priest,
received all these diverse things of gold,)
52 by the weight of the saintuary, sixteen thousand
seven hundred and fifty shekels, of the tribunes, and the
centurions [of the leaders of thousands, and rulers of
hundreds]. (by the measure of the sanctuary, sixteen
thousand and seven hundred and fifty shekels, from the
tribunes, and the centurions.)
53 For that that each man ravished in the prey, was his
own; (For the spoils that each man had taken from the
battle, was his own;)
54 and they bare *the gold* taken into the tabernacle of
witnessing, into mind of the sons of Israel, before the
Lord. (and they took *the gold*, and brought it into the
Tabernacle of the Witnessing, so that the Lord would
remember the Israelites, *and would protect them*.)

CHAPTER 32

1 Soothly the sons of Reuben and of Gad had many
beasts, and cattle without number was to them, in work
beasts. And when they had seen Jazer and Gilead, to be
covenable lands to beasts to be fed, (Now the sons of
Reuben and of Gad had many beasts, and of work beasts,
they had cattle without number. And so when they had
seen that Jazer and Gilead had suitable lands, where

beasts could be pastured,)
2 they came to Moses, and to Eleazar, the priest, and
to the princes of the multitude (and to the leaders of the
multitude), and said,
3 Ataroth, and Dibon, and Jazer, and Nimrah,
Heshbon, and Elealeh, and Shebam, and Nebo, and
Beon,
4 (that is,) the land which the Lord smote in the sight
of the sons of Israel, is of most plenteous country to the
pasture of beasts (is very fine land for pasturing beasts);
and we thy servants have full many beasts;
5 and we pray thee, if we have found grace before
thee, that thou give to us thy servants that *country* into
possession, and make not us to pass [over] Jordan. (and
we pray thee, that if we have found grace before thee,
that thou give to us thy servants this *land* for our
possession, and do not make us cross over the Jordan
River to live.)
6 To whom Moses answered, Whether your brethren
shall go to battle, and ye shall sit here?
7 Why mis-turn ye the thoughts of the sons of Israel,
that they dare not pass (over) into the place, which the
Lord shall give to them? (Why would ye want to
discourage the Israelites, so that they dare not cross over
to the place, which the Lord shall give them?)
8 Whether your fathers did not so, when I sent them
from Kadeshbarnea to espy the land, (This is just what
your fathers did, when I sent them from Kadeshbarnea to
spy out the land,)
9 and when they came to the valley of Cluster, when
all the country was compassed, they turned into fear the
heart of the sons of Israel, that they entered not into the
coasts, which the Lord had given to them. (and they went
as far as the Eshcol Valley, and then when all the land
was surveyed, they came back, and turned the hearts of
the Israelites to fear, so that they would not enter into the
land, which the Lord had given them.)
10 And the Lord therefore was wroth (And so the Lord
was angry), and he swore, saying,
11 These men that went up from Egypt, from twenty
years *of age* and above, shall not see the land which I
promised under an oath to Abraham, Isaac, and Jacob,
and [they] would not follow me, (These men who went
up from Egypt, from twenty years *of age* and older, shall
not see the land which I promised under an oath to
Abraham, Isaac, and Jacob, for they would not follow
me,)
12 except Caleb, (the) Kenezite, the son of Jephunneh,
and Joshua, the son of Nun; these *twain* fulfilled my will.
13 And the Lord was wroth against Israel, and led him
about the desert by forty years (And so the Lord was
angry with the Israelites, and led them about in the
wilderness for forty years), till all the generation was
wasted, that had done (this) evil in the sight of the Lord.
14 And Moses said, Lo! ye the increasings, and
nourished children, of sinful men, have risen (up) for
your fathers, that ye should increase the strong
vengeance of the Lord against Israel. (And Moses said,
Lo! now ye, the increasings, and nourished children, of
sinful men, have taken your fathers' place, and ye would
provoke the strong vengeance of the Lord against Israel
once again.)
15 That if ye will not follow the Lord, in the wilderness
he shall (again) forsake the people, and ye shall be [the]
cause of the death of all (these) men. (For if ye will not
follow the Lord, he shall again forsake the people in the
wilderness, and ye shall be responsible for the death of
all these people.)
16 And they went nigh, and said, We shall make
sheepfolds, and stables of beasts, and *we shall make*
strengthened cities to our little children. (And they came
near, and said to him, We shall make sheepfolds, and
stables for our beasts, and *we shall make* our cities safe
and strong for our little children.)
17 Forsooth we ourselves shall be armed *to defense*,
and shall be girded *with arms to assailing*, and shall go to
battle before the sons of Israel, till we bring them into
their places; (but) our little children, and whatever thing
we may have, shall be in strengthened cities, for the
treasons of the dwellers (*hereabout*). (And then we
ourselves shall be armed *for defense*, and shall be girded
for assault, and we shall go forth to battle at the front of
the Israelites, until we have brought them into their land;
but our little children, and whatever things we have, shall
stay here safe in our cities, made strong against the
treasons of the inhabitants *hereabout*.)
18 We shall not turn again into our houses, till the sons
of Israel wield their heritage; (We shall not return to our
houses, until the Israelites possess their inheritance;)
19 and we shall not ask (for) anything over Jordan, for
we have now our possession in the east coast thereof.
(and we shall not ask for anything on the west side of the
Jordan River, for now we have received our possession
here on the east side of the river.)
20 To whom Moses said, If ye do that, that ye promise,
be ye made ready, and go ye to (the) battle before the
Lord;
21 and each fighting man be armed, and pass he [over]
Jordan (and cross he over the Jordan River, and remain
there), till the Lord destroy his enemies,
22 and all the land be made subject to him; then ye
shall be made guiltless with God, and with Israel, and ye
shall wield the countries, which ye will, before the Lord.
(and all the land be made subject to him; then ye shall
have fulfilled your obligation to God, and to Israel, and
ye shall possess the land, which ye desire, in the sight of
the Lord.)
23 But if ye do not that, that ye say, it is no doubt to

any man, that not ye sin against God; and know ye, that
your sin shall take (hold of) you. (But if ye do not do what
ye say ye will, no one shall have any doubt, but that ye
have sinned against God; and know ye, that your sin
shall catch up with you.)
24 Therefore build ye cities to your little children, and
folds, and stables to *your* sheep, and to beasts; and
[ful]fill ye that, that ye have promised. (And so build ye
cities for your little children, and folds for *your* sheep,
and stables for *your* beasts; but then fulfill ye, what ye
have promised to do.)
25 And the sons of Gad and of Reuben said to Moses,
We be thy servants; we shall do that, that our lord
commandeth.
26 We shall leave our little children, and (our) women,
and our sheep, and (our) beasts, in the cities of Gilead;
27 forsooth all we thy servants shall go ready to battle,
as thou, (my) lord, speakest. (but we thy servants all shall
go forth, ready for battle, as thou, my lord, sayest.)
28 Therefore Moses commanded to Eleazar, the priest,
and to Joshua, the son of Nun, and to the princes of the
families, by the lineages of Israel, (And so Moses
commanded to Eleazar, the priest, and to Joshua, the son
of Nun, and to the leaders of the families, of the tribes of
Israel,)
29 and he said to them, If the sons of Gad, and the sons
of Reuben, go all armed with you [over Jordan], to (do)
battle before the Lord, and the land be made subject to
you, give ye to them Gilead into possession; (and he said
to them, If the sons of Gad, and the sons of Reuben, all
go armed with you across the Jordan River, to do battle
before the Lord, and the land be made subject to you,
give ye to them Gilead for their possession;)
30 but if they will not pass (over) with you (armed,) into
the land of Canaan, take they then places to dwell among
you. (but if they do not cross over with you, ready for
battle, then they shall take places to live among you, in
the land of Canaan.)
31 And the sons of Gad and the sons of Reuben
answered, As the Lord hath spoken to his servants, so we
shall do;
32 we shall go armed before the Lord, into the land of
Canaan, and we acknowledge, that we have taken now
possession over Jordan. (we all shall go armed before the
Lord, into the land of Canaan, and we acknowledge, that
we have now received our possession, here on the
eastern side of the Jordan River).
33 And so Moses gave to the sons of Gad, and of
Reuben, and to half the lineage of Manasseh, the son of
Joseph, the realm of Sihon, king of Amorites, and the
realm of Og, king of Bashan, and their land(s), with their
cities, by compass.
34 Therefore the sons of Gad builded Dibon, and
Ataroth, and Aroer,
35 and Atroth, Shophan, and Jaazer, and Jogbehah,
36 and Bethnimrah, and Bethharan, strengthened cities;
and folds to their beasts. (and Bethnimrah, and
Bethharan, all of them fortified cities, with folds for their
beasts.)
37 Soothly the sons of Reuben builded Heshbon, and
Elealeh, and Kiriathaim,
38 and Nebo, and Baalmeon, when the names were
turned, and *they builded* Shibmah; and they putted
names to the cities, which they had builded. (and Nebo,
and Baalmeon, whose name they changed, and Shibmah;
these were the names of the cities that they built.)
39 Soothly the sons of Machir, the son of Manasseh,
went into Gilead, and destroyed it, and they killed (the)
Amorite, the dweller thereof (and they killed the
Amorites, who lived there).
40 Therefore Moses gave the land of Gilead to (the sons
of) Machir, the son of Manasseh, the which *Machir*
dwelled therein. (And so Moses gave the land of Gilead
to the sons of Machir, and that is where the Machirites
lived.)
41 Soothly Jair, the son of Manasseh, went, and
occupied the towns thereof, which he called Havothjair,
that is, the towns of Jair.
42 Also Nobah went, and took Kenath, with his towns,
and called it, by his name, Nobah. (And Nobah went
forth, and took Kenath and its towns, and called it
Nobah, after himself.)

CHAPTER 33

1 These be the dwellings of the sons of Israel, that
went out of the land of Egypt, by their companies, in the
hand of Moses and Aaron; (These be the dwelling places
of the Israelites, after they went out of the land of Egypt,
by their companies, *or their tribes*, under the hand of
Moses and Aaron;)
2 which *dwellings* Moses described by the places of
(the) tents, that were changed by commandment of the
Lord. (and Moses wrote down each place where they
pitched their tents, by the Lord's command.)
3 Therefore the sons of Israel went forth in an high
hand from Rameses, in the first month, in the fifteenth
day of the first month, in the tother day of pask, *that is, in
the morrow of the offering of the lamb of pask*, while all
[the] Egyptians saw, (And so the Israelites went forth
defiantly from Rameses, in the first month, on the
fifteenth day of the first month, on the day after the first
Passover, *that is, in the morning after the offering of the
lamb of the first Passover*, while all the Egyptians
watched,)
4 and (while) the Egyptians buried their first begotten
(male) children, which the Lord had slain; for the Lord
took vengeance also upon their gods. (and while the
Egyptians buried their first-born sons, whom the Lord had

killed; and the Lord also took vengeance upon their gods,
and their animals.)
5 *The sons of Israel* (first) setted tents in Succoth, (*The*
Israelites first pitched their tents at Succoth,)
6 and from Succoth they came into Etham, which is in
the last coasts of the wilderness; (and from Succoth they
went to Etham, which is on the edge of the wilderness;)
7 from thence they went forth, and came against
Pihahiroth, which beholdeth Baalzephon, and setted
tents before Migdol. (and they went forth from Etham,
and turned back near Pihahiroth, east of Baalzephon, and
pitched their tents near Migdol.)
8 And they went forth from Pihahiroth, and they
passed through the midst of the sea into wilderness, and
they went three days by the desert of Etham, and setted
tents in Marah. (And they went forth from Pihahiroth, and
they passed through the midst of the Red Sea to the
wilderness, and went for three days in the wilderness of
Etham, and pitched their tents at Marah.)
9 And they went forth from Marah, and came into
Elim, where (there) were twelve wells of water, and
seventy palm trees; and there they setted tents (and they
pitched their tents at Elim).
10 But also they went forth from thence, and setted
tents on the Red Sea. (And they went forth from Elim, and
pitched their tents by the Red Sea.)
11 And they went forth from the Red Sea, and setted
tents in the desert of Sin (and pitched their tents in the
wilderness of Sin),
12 from whence they went forth, and came into
Dophkah. (and they went forth from the wilderness of
Sin, and pitched their tents at Dophkah.)
13 And they went forth from Dophkah, and setted tents
in Alush (and pitched their tents at Alush).
14 And they went forth from Alush, and setted tents in
Rephidim, where water failed to the people (for) to drink
(where there was no water for the people to drink).
15 And they went forth from Rephidim, and setted tents
in the desert of Sinai (and pitched their tents in the Sinai
Desert).
16 But also they went out of the wilderness of Sinai,
and came to the Sepulchres of Covetousness, *or Lust*.
(And they went forth from the Sinai Desert, and came to
Kibrothhattaavah.)
17 And they went forth from the Sepulchres of
Covetousness, *or Lust*, and setted tents in Hazeroth. (And
they went forth from Kibrothhattaavah, and pitched their
tents at Hazeroth.)
18 And from Hazeroth they came into Rithmah. (And
they went forth from Hazeroth, and pitched their tents at
Rithmah.)
19 And they went forth from Rithmah, and setted tents
in Rimmonparez (and pitched their tents at
Rimmonparez);
20 from whence they went forth, and came into Libnah.
(and they went forth from Rimmonparez, and pitched
their tents at Libnah.)
21 And from Libnah they setted tents in Rissah. (And
they went forth from Libnah, and pitched their tents at
Rissah.)
22 And they went forth from Rissah, and came into
Kehelathah (and pitched their tents at Kehelathah);
23 from whence they went forth, and setted tents in the
hill of Shapher. (and they went forth from Kehelathah,
and pitched their tents on Mount Shapher.)
24 And they went forth from the hill of Shapher, and
they came into Haradah; (And they went forth from
Mount Shapher, and pitched their tents at Haradah;)
25 from thence they went forth, and setted tents in
Makheloth. (and they went forth from Haradah, and
pitched their tents at Makheloth.)
26 And they went forth from Makheloth, and came into
Tahath (and pitched their tents at Tahath).
27 From Tahath they setted tents in Tarah; (And they
went forth from Tahath, and pitched their tents at Tarah;)
28 from whence they went forth, and setted tents in
Mithcah. (and they went forth from Tarah, and pitched
their tents at Mithcah.)
29 And from Mithcah they setted tents in Hashmonah.
(And they went forth from Mithcah, and pitched their
tents at Hashmonah.)
30 And they went forth from Hashmonah, and came
into Moseroth (and pitched their tents at Moseroth);
31 and from Moseroth they setted tents in Benejaakan.
(and they went forth from Moseroth, and pitched their
tents at Benejaakan.)
32 And they went forth from Benejaakan, and came
into the hill of Gidgad (and pitched their tents at
Horhaggidgad);
33 from whence they went forth, and setted tents in
Jotbathah. (and they went forth from Horhaggidgad, and
pitched their tents at Jotbathah.)
34 And from Jotbathah they came into Ebronah. (And
they went forth from Jotbathah, and pitched their tents at
Ebronah.)
35 And they went forth from Ebronah, and setted tents
in Eziongaber (and pitched their tents at Eziongaber);
36 from thence they went forth, and came into the
desert of Zin; this is Kadesh. (and they went forth from
Eziongaber, and pitched their tents in the wilderness of
Zin; that is, Kadesh.)
37 And they went forth from Kadesh, and they setted
tents in the hill of Hor, in the last coasts of the land of
Edom. (And they went forth from Kadesh, and they
pitched their tents on Mount Hor, on the border of
Edom.)
38 And Aaron, the priest, ascended into the hill of Hor,
for the Lord commanded, and there he was dead, in the

fortieth year of the going out of the sons of Israel from
Egypt, in the fifth month, in the first day of the month;
(And Aaron, the priest, went up on Mount Hor, as the
Lord commanded, and he died there, in the fortieth year
of the going out of the Israelites from Egypt, in the fifth
month, on the first day of the month;)
39 when he was of an hundred and three and twenty
years *old*.
40 And (the) Canaanite, the king of Arad, that dwelled
at the south (who lived in the south), in the land of
Canaan, heard that the sons of Israel came *thither.*
41 And they went forth from the hill of Hor, and setted
tents in Zalmonah; (And they went forth from Mount Hor,
and pitched their tents at Zalmonah;)
42 from thence they went forth, and came into Punon.
(and they went forth from Zalmonah, and pitched their
tents at Punon.)
43 And they went forth from Punon, and setted tents in
Oboth (and pitched their tents at Oboth).
44 And from Oboth they came into Iyeabarim, *that is,*
into the wilderness of Abarim, which is in the ends of
Moabites. (And they went forth from Oboth, and pitched
their tents at Iyeabarim, *that is, in the wilderness of*
Abarim, which is on the border of Moab.)
45 And they went forth from Iyeabarim, and they setted
tents in Dibon of Gad; (And they went forth from
Iyeabarim, *or Iyim,* and they pitched their tents at
Dibongad;)
46 from whence they went forth, and setted tents in
Almon of Diblathaim, (and they went forth from
Dibongad, and pitched their tents at Almon of
Diblathaim,)
47 And they went forth from Almon of Diblathaim, and
they came to the hills of Abarim, against Nebo (and they
pitched their tents in the Abarim mountains, near Nebo).
48 And they went forth from the hills of Abarim, and
passed to the field places of Moab, over Jordan, against
Jericho. (And they went forth from the Abarim mountains,
and came to the plains of Moab, across the Jordan River,
opposite Jericho.)
49 And there they setted tents, from Bethjesimoth till to
Abelshittim, in the plainer places of Moabites, (And they
pitched their tents there, from Bethjesimoth to
Abelshittim, on the plains of Moab,)
50 where the Lord spake to Moses, (and said,)
51 Command thou to the sons of Israel, and say thou to
them, When ye have passed (over) Jordan (When ye have
crossed over the Jordan River), and have entered into the
land of Canaan,
52 destroy ye all the dwellers of that country; break ye
the titles, *that is, altars,* and drive ye to powder the
images, and destroy ye all high things, (destroy ye all the
inhabitants of that country; break ye up their titles, *that is,*
their altars, and drive ye into powder their images, and
destroy ye all their high places of worship, *or the hill*
shrines,)
53 and cleanse ye (out) the land, and (kill ye) all the
men dwelling therein. For I have given to you that *land*
into possession (For I have given you that *land* for a
possession),
54 which ye shall part to you by lot; to more men *in*
number ye shall give larger land, and to fewer men *in*
number straiter, *or less,* land, as the lot falleth to all men,
so [the] heritage shall be given; the possession shall be
parted to lineages and families. (which ye shall divide
among yourselves by lot; to those greater *in number* ye
shall give more land, and to those fewer *in number,* less
land, as the lot falleth to all, so the inheritance shall be
given; the possession shall be divided among tribes and
families.)
55 But if ye will not slay the dwellers of the land, they,
that abide, shall be to you as *nails* in the eyes, and as
spears in the sides; and they shall be adversaries to you in
the land of your habitation; (But if ye do not kill all the
inhabitants of the land, they, who remain, shall be to you
like *nails* in your eyes, and like spears in your sides; and
they shall be your adversaries in the very land where you
live;)
56 and whatever thing I (had) thought to do to them, I
shall do to you.

CHAPTER 34

1 And the Lord spake to Moses, and said,
2 Command thou to the sons of Israel, and thou shalt
say to them, When ye have entered into the land of
Canaan, and it befall into possession to you by lot, it shall
be ended by these ends. (Command thou to the Israelites,
and thou shalt say to them, When ye have entered into
the land of Canaan, and it become your possession by
lot, it shall have these borders.)
3 The south part shall begin at the wilderness of Zin,
which is beside Edom, and it shall have (as) the terms
against the east, the saltiest sea, (The southern border
shall begin in the wilderness of Zin, which is beside
Edom, and its east end shall be the Salt Sea, *that is, the*
Dead Sea,)
4 the which *terms* shall compass the south coast by
the going up *of the hill* Scorpion, so that those *terms* pass
into Zin, and come to the south, unto Kadeshbarnea;
from whence the terms shall go forth to the town, Addar
by name, and they shall stretch forth unto Azmon; (the
southern border shall then go along the ascent *of Mount*
Akrabbim, and then down through Zin, as far south as
Kadeshbarnea; from there the border shall go west to
Hazaraddar, and then to Azmon;)
5 and the term shall go by compass from Azmon unto
the strand of Egypt, and it shall be ended by the brink of
the great sea. (and then the border shall go west from

Azmon to the River of Egypt, *that is, the Nile*, and then
continue to the shore of the Great Sea, *that is, the
Mediterranean Sea*.)
6 Soothly the west coast shall begin at the great sea,
and it shall be closed by that end. (The western border
shall begin, and end, at the Mediterranean Sea.)
7 Soothly at the north coast, the terms shall begin at
the great sea, and they shall come unto the highest hill,
(The northern border shall begin at the Mediterranean
Sea, and it shall go forth to Mount Hor,)
8 from which *hill* those terms shall come into Hamath,
unto the terms of Zedad; (from which *mountain* the
border shall go forth to the Hamath Pass, and then to
Zedad;)
9 and the coasts shall go unto Ziphron, and to the
town of Enan. These shall be the terms in the north part.
(and then the border shall go to Ziphron, and to
Hazarenan. This shall be the northern border.)
10 From thence they shall mete the coasts against the
east coast, from the town (of) Enan to Shepham; (From
there the eastern border shall run from Hazarenan to
Shepham;)
11 and from Shepham the terms shall go down into
Riblah, against the well of Ain; from thence those *terms*
shall come against the east to the sea of Chinnereth; (and
from Shepham, the border shall go down to Riblah, east
of Ain; from there the border shall go forth to the eastern
shore of the Sea of Galilee, *that is, Lake Galilee*;)
12 and those *terms* shall stretch forth till to (the) Jordan,
and at the last those shall be closed with the saltiest sea.
Ye shall have this land by his coasts in compass. (and the
border shall then go south along the Jordan River, and
end at the Salt Sea, *that is, the Dead Sea*. Ye shall have
all the land within these borders.)
13 And Moses commanded to the sons of Israel, and
said, This shall be the land which ye shall wield by lot,
and which the Lord commanded to be given to the nine
lineages, and to the half lineage; (And Moses
commanded to the Israelites, and said, This shall be the
land which ye shall possess by lot, and which the Lord
commanded to be given to the nine tribes, and to the half
tribe;)
14 for the lineage of the sons of Reuben, by their
families, and the lineage of the sons of Gad, by their
kindred and number, and half the lineage of Manasseh,
(for the tribes of the sons of Reuben, and of the sons of
Gad, and half of the tribe of the sons of Manasseh,)
15 that is, two lineages and an half, have taken their
part over Jordan, against Jericho, at the east coast. (that is,
two and a half tribes, family by family, have received
their portion here on the eastern side of the Jordan River,
opposite Jericho.)
16 And the Lord said to Moses,
17 These be the names of [the] men that shall part the
land to you (These be the names of the men who shall
divide the land for you), Eleazar, the priest, and Joshua,
the son of Nun,
18 and of each lineage, one prince; (and one leader
from each tribe;)
19 of which these be the names; of the lineage of
Judah, Caleb, the son of Jephunneh;
20 of the lineage of Simeon, Shemuel, the son of
Ammihud;
21 of the lineage of Benjamin, Elidad, the son of
Chislon;
22 of the lineage of the sons of Dan (of the lineage, *or
the tribe*, of Dan), Bukki, the son of Jogli;
23 of the sons of Joseph, of the lineage of Manasseh,
Hanniel, the son of Ephod;
24 (and) of the lineage of Ephraim, Kemuel, the son of
Shiphtan;
25 of the lineage of Zebulun, Elizaphan, the son of
Parnach;
26 of the lineage of Issachar, duke Paltiel, the son of
Azzan;
27 of the lineage of Asher, Ahihud, the son of Shelomi;
28 of the lineage of Naphtali, Pedahel, the son of
Ammihud.
29 These men it be, to which the Lord commanded,
that they should part to the sons of Israel the land of
Canaan. (These be the men, whom the Lord commanded,
to divide up the land of Canaan for the Israelites.)

CHAPTER 35

1 And the Lord spake these things to Moses, in the
field places of Moab, above Jordan, against Jericho, (And
the Lord spoke these things to Moses, on the plains of
Moab, across the Jordan River, opposite Jericho,)
2 Command thou to the sons of Israel, that they give
to the deacons, of their possessions, cities to dwell in,
and the suburbs of those by compass, (Command thou to
the Israelites, that they give to the Levites, out of their
possessions, cities to live in, and the suburbs around
them,)
3 that they dwell in the cities, and the suburbs be to
beasts, and work beasts; (so that they can live in those
cities, and that the suburbs can be for their beasts, and
their work beasts;)
4 which *suburbs* shall be stretched forth from the
walls of the cities withoutforth by compass, in the space
of a thousand paces;
5 against the east *coast* shall be two thousand cubits,
and against the south in like manner shall be two
thousand *cubits*, and at the sea that beholdeth to the west
shall be the same measure, and the north coast shall be
ended by even term. And the cities shall be in the midst,
and the suburbs withoutforth. (that is, the eastern border
shall be two thousand cubits out from the city, and the

southern border shall also be two thousand cubits out,
and the western border shall be the same measure out, as
shall be the northern border. And the cities shall be in
the midst, and the suburbs shall be all around them.)
6 Forsooth of those cities which ye shall give to [the]
deacons, six shall be separated into [the] helps of
fugitives, *either of fleeing men,* that he that shedded
blood, flee to those; (And of the cities which ye shall give
to the Levites, six shall be set apart for fugitives, *or for
those who flee,* so that anyone who sheddeth out blood,
can flee to them;)
7 and besides these six *cities, ye shall give to the
deacons* (*ye shall give to the Levites*), (an)other two and
forty cities, that is, altogether eight and forty, with their
suburbs.
8 And (of) those cities that shall be given (out) of the
possession of the sons of Israel, more *cities* shall be taken
away from them that have more, and fewer *from them*
that have less; all *the sons of Israel* by themselves shall
give by the measure of their heritage, cities to the
deacons (each *tribe* of *the Israelites* shall give cities to the
Levites, according to the size of their inheritance).
9 (And) The Lord said to Moses,
10 Speak thou to the sons of Israel, and thou shalt say
to them, When ye have passed [over] Jordan (When we
have crossed over the Jordan River), in[to] the land of
Canaan,
11 deem ye which cities ought to be into the helps of
fugitives which not willfully have shed blood. (decide ye
which cities ought to be for the help of those who flee,
who have not intentionally shed blood.)
12 In which *cities* when the fleer hath fled, the kinsman
of him that is slain, shall not be able to slay him, till he
stand in the sight of the multitude, and the cause of him
be deemed. (In which *cities* to where a fleer hath fled,
the next-of-kin of him who is killed, shall not be able to
kill the one who fleeth, until he standeth before the
multitude, and his case is tried.)
13 Forsooth of those cities that be separated to the
helps of fugitives, (And of those cities that shall be set
apart for the help of fleeing men,)
14 three shall be beyond (the) Jordan, (*that is, on the
eastern side of the river,*) and three in the land of Canaan;
15 as well to the sons of Israel as to comelings, and
pilgrims; that he flee to those cities, that shedded blood
not willfully. (for the Israelites, as well as for newcomers,
and foreigners, *or strangers*; so that anyone, who did not
intentionally shed blood, can flee to one of those cities.)
16 If any man smiteth a man with (a thing of) iron, and
he that is smitten is dead, *the smiter* shall be guilty of
manslaying, and he shall die. (If anyone striketh someone
with a thing of iron, and he who is struck dieth, *the
striker* shall be guilty of manslaughter, and he must be
put to death.)
17 If he casteth a stone, and *a man* is dead by the
stroke *thereof,* the caster shall be punished in like
manner. (If anyone throweth a stone, and *someone* dieth
by the stroke *of it,* the stone-thrower must be put to
death.)
18 If *a man* smitten with a staff dieth, he shall be
venged by the blood of the smiter. (If *someone* struck
with a staff dieth, he shall be avenged by the death of the
person who struck him.)
19 The nigh kinsman of him that is slain shall slay the
manslayer; anon as he taketh (hold of) the manslayer, he
shall slay *him.* (The next-of-kin of him who is killed, shall
kill the man-killer; as soon as he catcheth the man-killer,
he shall kill *him.*)
20 If by hatred a man hurtleth, *either shoveth,* a man,
either casteth anything into him by ambushings, (If in
hatred anyone hurtleth, *or pusheth,* someone, or
intentionally throweth something into him,)
21 either when he was enemy *to him,* smite him with
his hand, and he is dead, the smiter shall be guilty of
manslaying. The kinsman of him that is slain, anon as he
findeth him, *that is, the slayer,* shall slay him. (or when
he was an enemy *to him,* he striketh him with his hand,
and he dieth, the striker shall be guilty of manslaughter.
The next-of-kin of him who is killed, as soon as he
findeth the killer, shall kill him.)
22 That if by sudden case, and without hatred and
enmities, a man doeth anything of these; (But if, on the
spur of the moment, *or by accident,* and without any
hatred or enmities, someone doeth any of these things;)
23 (This verse is omitted in the original text.)
24 and this is proved, the people hearing (and this is
proven before the people), and the question of the blood,
or death, is discussed betwixt the smiter and the kinsman
of him that is slain,
25 the innocent (man) shall be delivered from the hand
of the venger (of the blood), and by sentence *of judges* he
shall be led again into the city, to which he fled, and he
shall dwell there, till the great priest die, which is
anointed with [holy] oil. (the guiltless person, *that is, he
who killed unintentionally,* shall be rescued from the
hand of the avenger of the blood, and by the sentence *of
the judges* he shall be brought again to the city, to which
he fled, and he shall live there until the High Priest, who
is anointed with holy oil, hath died.)
26 If the slayer is found without the coasts of the cities
that be assigned to exiled men, (But if the killer is found
anywhere outside the cities of refuge,)
27 and he is slain of him that is venger [of the blood],
he that slayeth him shall be without guilt; (and he is
killed by him who is the avenger of the blood, he who
killeth him shall be without guilt;)
28 for the exiled man ought (to) sit in the city till to the
death of the bishop; forsooth after that that *bishop* is

dead, the manslayer shall turn again into his land. (for the
exiled person ought to remain in the city until the death
of the High Priest; but after that the *High Priest* is dead,
the man-killer can return to his own land.)
29 These shall be everlasting and lawful things in all
your dwellings. (These shall be everlasting laws wherever
you shall live.)
30 A manslayer shall be punished under witnesses; no
man shall be condemned at the witnessing of one man.
(A man-killer shall be found guilty, and put to death, only
after the testimony of two or more witnesses; no one shall
be put to death after the testimony of only one person.)
31 Ye shall not take price of him which is guilty of
blood, *or death*, anon and he shall die. (Ye shall not take
payment from anyone who is guilty of murder, so that he
can live, but he must be put to death at once.)
32 Men exiled, and fugitives, shall not be able to turn
again in any manner into their cities, before the death of
the bishop, (Exiled people, and fugitives, shall not be
able to return to their own cities, for any reason, before
the death of the High Priest,)
33 lest ye defoul the land of your habitation, which is
defouled by the (shedding of the) blood of innocent men;
and it may not be cleansed in (any) other manner, no but
by the blood of him, that shedded the blood of another
man.
34 And so your possession shall be cleansed, for I shall
dwell with you; for I am the Lord, that dwell among the
sons of Israel. (And so the land, in which I live with you,
shall be made clean, *or purified*; for I am the Lord, who
liveth among the Israelites.)

CHAPTER 36

1 Soothly and the princes of the families of Gilead, the
son of Machir, son of Manasseh, of the generation of the
sons of Joseph, nighed, and spake to Moses before the
princes of Israel, (And the leaders of the families of
Gilead, the son of Machir, the son of Manasseh, of the
families of the sons of Joseph, came, and spoke to Moses
before the leaders of Israel,)
2 and said, The Lord commanded to thee our lord,
that thou shouldest part the land by lot to the sons of
Israel (that thou shouldest divide up the land by lot to the
Israelites), and that thou shouldest give to the daughters
of Zelophehad, our brother, the possession due to their
father.
3 And if men of another lineage shall take to wives
these *daughters*, their possession shall follow *them*, and it
shall be translated to another lineage, and *so it* shall be
decreased from our heritage; (But if men from another
tribe shall take these *daughters* as wives, their possession
shall follow *them*, and it shall be transferred to another
tribe, and so *it* shall be taken away from our inheritance;)
4 and so it shall be done, that when the jubilee, *that
is, the fiftieth year of remission*, cometh, the parting of
lots be confounded, *or fail*, and that the possession of
other men pass to other men (and that the possession of
some men shall pass to other men). (and then it shall be
done, that when the Jubilee cometh, *that is, the fiftieth
Year of Remission, or the Year of Restoration or
Forgiveness*, their possession shall be transferred to the
possession of the tribe to whom they go, and so it shall
be taken away from our inheritance forevermore.)
5 Moses answered to the sons of Israel, and said, for
the Lord commanded (it), The lineage of the sons of
Joseph hath spoken rightfully, (And Moses answered to
the Israelites, by the Lord's command, and said, The tribe
of the sons of Joseph hath spoken rightly, *or correctly*,)
6 and this law is announced of the Lord on the
daughters of Zelophehad; be they wedded to which men
they will, (but) only to the men of their lineage; (and so
this is the Lord's command for Zelophehad's daughters;
let them be wedded to whichever men they want, as long
as they be men of their own tribe;)
7 lest the possession of the sons of Joseph be meddled
from lineage into lineage. For all men shall wed wives of
their lineage and kindred; (lest the possession of the
Israelites be mixed, *or mingled*, from tribe to tribe. For
all men shall only wed wives of their own tribe and
kindred;)
8 and each daughter, that shall have the heritage (who
shall have an inheritance), shall be (a) wife to one man of
the kindred of her father,
9 and [the] lineages be not meddled to themselves,
but dwell so, as those be parted of the Lord. (and so the
tribes shall not be mixed, *or mingled*, among themselves,
but shall remain as they were separated by the Lord./and
so the inheritance, *or the possession*, shall not pass from
one tribe to another, but each tribe shall keep its own
inheritance unto itself.)
10 And the daughters of Zelophehad did, as it was
commanded to them.
11 And Mahlah, and Tirzah, and Hoglah, and Milcah,
and Noah, were wedded to the sons of their father's
brother(s),
12 of the family of Manasseh, that was the son of
Joseph; and (so) the possession that was given to them,
dwelled in the lineage (stayed in the tribe), and in the
family, of their father.
13 These be the commandments and dooms, which the
Lord commanded, by the hand of Moses, to the sons of
Israel, in the field places of Moab, above (the) Jordan,
against Jericho. (These be the commandments and the
laws, which the Lord commanded, through Moses, to the
Israelites, on the plains of Moab, across the Jordan River,
opposite Jericho.) ✡

DEUTERONOMY

CHAPTER 1

1 These be the words which Moses spake to all Israel
over (the) Jordan, in the wilderness of the field, (over)
against the Red Sea, betwixt Paran, and Tophel, and
Laban, and Hazeroth, where is full much gold, (These be
the words which Moses spoke to all Israel, east of the
Jordan River, in the wilderness, in the field opposite the
Red Sea, *or the Sea of Reeds*, between Paran on one side,
and Tophel, Laban, Hazeroth, and Dizahab on the other,)
2 by eleven days *journey* from Horeb by the way of
the hill of Seir, till to Kadeshbarnea. (eleven days *journey*
from Mount Sinai, by way of the hill country of Seir, *or of
Edom*, unto Kadeshbarnea.)
3 In the fortieth year, in the eleventh month, in the
first day of the month, Moses spake to the sons of Israel
all things which the Lord commanded to him that he
should say to them, (In the fortieth year, in the eleventh
month, on the first day of the month, Moses spoke to the
Israelites all the things which the Lord commanded to
him that he should say to them,)
4 after that he had smitten, *or killed*, Sihon, the king of
Amorites, that dwelled in Heshbon, and Og, the king of
Bashan, that dwelled in Ashtaroth, and in Edrei,
5 over (the) Jordan (east of the Jordan River), in the
land of Moab. And Moses began to declare the law, and
to say,
6 Our Lord God spake to us in Horeb, and said, It
sufficeth to you that ye have dwelled in this hill; (The
Lord our God spoke to us on Mount Sinai, and said, It
now sufficeth for you that ye have stayed on this
mountain long enough;)
7 turn ye again, and come ye to the hill (country) of
(the) Amorites, and to (the) other places that be next to it;
and to the places of fields, and of hills, and to [the] lower
places against the south, and beside the brink of the sea,
to the land of Canaanites, and of Lebanon, till to the great
flood Euphrates (unto the great Euphrates River).
8 Lo, he saith, I have given to you *that land*; enter ye,
and have it in possession, on which the Lord swore to
your fathers, Abraham, Isaac, and Jacob, that he should
give that land to them, and to their seed after them.
9 And I said to you in that time, I may not alone
sustain you, (And I said to you at that time, I cannot carry
all of you by myself,)
10 for your Lord God hath multiplied you, and ye be
full many today, as the stars of heaven; (for the Lord your
God hath multiplied you, and today, ye be as many as
the stars in the heavens;)
11 (may) the Lord God of your fathers add to this
number many thousands, and bless you, as he spake (as
he said he would do).
12 I may not alone sustain, *or bear*, your causes, and
your burdens, and (your) strives;
13 give ye of you men wise, and witting, whose
conversation is proved in your lineages, that I set them
princes to you. (choose ye wise men from among you,
with knowledge, *or understanding*, whose lives, *or
reputation*, is proven among your tribes, so that I can
make them your leaders.)
14 Then ye answered to me, (and said,) The thing is
good which thou wilt do.
15 And I took of your lineages men wise, and noble;
and I ordained them *to be your* princes, *your* tribunes,
and centurions, and quinquagenaries, and deans, which
shall teach you all things. (And so I took from your tribes
wise and noble men; and I ordained them *to be your*
leaders, yea, *your* tribunes, and centurions, and
quinquagenaries, and deans, and they shall be your
authorities.)
16 And I commanded to them, and said, Hear ye *the
people*, and deem ye that that is just, whether he be a
citizen, or a pilgrim. (And I commanded to them, and
said, Listen ye to *the people*, and judge ye them justly, *or
rightly*, whether they be citizens, or foreigners.)
17 No difference shall be *in doom* of persons; ye shall
hear so a little man, *that is, poor*, as a great man, neither
ye shall take *heed* to the person of any man, for it is the
doom of God. That if anything seemeth hard to you, tell
ye that to me, and I shall hear it. (No difference shall be
in the judging of persons; ye shall hear the poor, just like
the rich, nor shall ye take *heed* of anyone's rank, *or
status*, for judgement cometh from God. And if anything
seemeth hard to you, tell ye that to me, and I shall hear it.)
18 And I commanded (*to you*) all things which ye
ought to do.
19 Forsooth we went forth from Horeb, and passed by
a fearedful desert, and greatest wilderness, which ye saw,
by the way of the hill of Amorites, as our Lord God
commanded to us. And when we had come into
Kadeshbarnea, (And we went forth from Mount Sinai, and
passed through a fearful desert, yea, a great and a vast
wilderness, which ye saw, by way of the hill country of
the Amorites, as the Lord our God commanded to us.
And when we had come to Kadeshbarnea,)
20 I said to you, Ye be come to the hill (country) of
(the) Amorites, which your Lord God shall give to you;
21 see thou, *Israel*, the land that the Lord God shall
give to thee; go thou up, and wield it, as our Lord God
spake to thy fathers; dread thou not, neither in thine heart
be thou anything aghast (fear thou not, nor let thy hearts
be afraid of anything).
22 And all (of) ye nighed to me, and ye said, Send we

men, that shall behold the land (who shall spy out the
land), and shall tell us by what way we ought to go up
thither, and to which cities we ought to go.
23 And when the word pleased to me, I sent of you
twelve men, of each lineage one. (And I agreed, and I
sent out twelve men of you, one from each tribe.)
24 And when they had gone *forth*, and had gone up
into the hilly places, they came unto the valley of Cluster;
and when they had beheld the land, (And when they had
gone *forth*, and had gone up into the hill country, they
came to the Eshcol Valley; and when they had spied out
the land,)
25 they took (some) of the fruits thereof, to show the
plenty *of it*, and they brought *those fruits* to us, and said,
The land is good that our Lord God shall give to us.
26 And ye would not go up *thither*, but ye were
unbelieveful to the word of our Lord God. (But ye would
not go up *there*, for ye did not believe the word of the
Lord our God.)
27 And ye grouched in your tabernacles, and ye said,
The Lord hateth us, and therefore he led us out of the
land of Egypt, that he should betake us in the hand of
Amorites, and do away *us*. (And ye grumbled in your
tents, and ye said, The Lord hateth us, and so he led us
out of the land of Egypt, so that he could deliver us into
the hands of the Amorites, and do *us* away.)
28 Whither shall we ascend? the messengers made
afeared our heart, and said, A greatest multitude is, and
larger in stature than we; the cities be great, and walled
till to heaven; we saw there the sons of Anakim, *that is,*
giants. (Why should we go up there? the messengers
made our hearts afraid when they said, There is a great
multitude there, and they be larger in stature than us, and
the cities be great, and walled unto the heavens; *yea,*
they said, We saw the sons of the Anakim, *that is, the*
sons of the giants, there!)
29 And I said to you, Have ye no dread (Do not ye be
afraid), nor be ye aghast;
30 the Lord God himself, which is your leader (who is
your leader), shall fight for you, as he did in Egypt, while
all men saw (it).
31 And ye saw in the wilderness, thy Lord God bare
thee, as a man is wont to bear his little son, in all the way
by which ye went, till ye came to this place. (And ye saw
in the wilderness, how the Lord thy God carried thee,
like a man is wont to carry his little son, all the way by
which ye went, until ye came to this place.)
32 And soothly neither so ye believed to your Lord
God, (But still ye would not trust the Lord your God,)
33 that went before you in the way (who went before
you on the way), and measured the place in which ye
ought to set your tents, and he showed in the night the
way to you by fire, and in the day by a pillar of cloud.
34 And when the Lord had heard the voice of your
words, he was wroth, and swore, and said, (And when
the Lord heard what you said, he was angry, and swore,
and said,)
35 None of the men of this worst generation shall see
the good land, which I promised under an oath to your
fathers,
36 except Caleb, the son of Jephunneh; forsooth he shall
see it, and I shall give to him the land upon which he
hath trodden, and to his sons, for he followed the Lord.
37 Neither *the Lord's* indignation against the people is
to be marveled (at), since the Lord was wroth also to me
for you, and said, Neither thou shalt enter thither, (Nor
was *the Lord's* anger against the people to be marveled
at, since, because of you, he was also angry at me, and
said, Nor shalt thou enter in there either,)
38 but Joshua, the son of Nun, thy servant, he shall
enter *into that land* for thee; excite, and strengthen thou
him, and he shall part the land by lot to Israel (encourage
thou him, and he shall divide the land by lot to Israel).
39 Your little children, of which ye said, that they
should be led prisoners, and the sons that know not
today the diversity of good and of evil, they shall enter
thither; and I shall give to them the land, and they shall
wield it. (Your little children, of whom ye said, that they
would be led away as prisoners, and thy sons and
daughters who know not today the diversity of good and
evil, they shall enter in *there*; yea, I shall give the land to
them, and they shall take it.)
40 Soothly turn ye again, and go ye into the wilderness,
by the way of the Red Sea. (So now turn ye around, and
go ye back to the wilderness, by way of the Red Sea, *or*
the Sea of Reeds.)
41 And ye answered to me, We have sinned to the
Lord; we shall go up, and we shall fight, as our Lord God
commanded. And when ye were arrayed with armours,
and went into the hill, (And ye answered to me, and said,
We have sinned against the Lord; but now we shall go
up, and we shall fight, as the Lord our God commanded.
And when ye were arrayed with arms, *or with weapons*,
and were about to go up to the hill country,)
42 the Lord said to me, Say thou to them, Do not ye go
up, neither fight ye, for I am not with you, lest ye fall
before your enemies.
43 (So) I spake *this to you*, and ye heard me not; but ye
were adversaries to the commandment of the Lord, and
swelling with pride, went up into the hill (country).
44 Therefore Amorites went out, that dwelled in the
hills, and he came against *you*, and pursued you, as bees
be wont to pursue, and he killed you down from Seir
unto Hormah. (And so the Amorites, who lived in the
hills, came out, and they went against *you*, and pursued
you, as bees be wont to pursue *their prey*, and they killed
you at Hormah, in Seir, *or in Edom*.)
45 And when ye turned again, and wept before the

Lord, he heard not you, neither would assent to your
voice; (And when ye returned, and wept before the Lord,
he would not listen to you, nor assent to your pleadings;)
46 therefore ye sat in Kadesh by much time. (and so ye
sat there in Kadesh for a long time.)

CHAPTER 2

1 And we went forth from thence, and came into the
wilderness that leadeth to the Red Sea, as the Lord said to
me; and we compassed the hill of Seir in long time. (And
we went forth from there, and came to the wilderness
that leadeth to the Red Sea, as the Lord said to me; and we
marched around the hill country of Seir for a long time.)
2 And (then) the Lord said to me,
3 It sufficeth to you to compass this hill; go ye against
the north. (It sufficeth for you to have gone around these
hills long enough; now go ye to the north.)
4 And command thou to the people, and say, Ye shall
pass by the terms of your brethren, the sons of Esau, that
dwell in Seir, and they shall dread you. Therefore see ye
diligently, (And command thou to the people, and say,
Ye shall pass by the borders, *or the territory*, of your
brothers, the sons of Esau, who live in Seir, and they shall
fear you. And so see ye diligently,)
5 that ye be not moved against them; for I shall not
give to you of their land as much as the step of one foot
may tread, for I have given the hill of Seir into the
possession of Esau. (that ye go not against them; for I
shall not give you any of their land, not as much as the
step of one foot can tread, for I have given the hill
country of Seir to the sons of Esau for a possession.)
6 Ye shall buy of them meats for money, and ye shall
eat; and ye shall draw, and drink water bought. (Ye shall
buy food from them with your money, and then ye shall
eat; and ye shall buy some water, and drink it.)
7 Thy Lord God hath blessed thee in all the works of
thine hands; he hath known thy way, how thou hast
passed this most wilderness, by forty years; and thy Lord
God dwelled with thee, and nothing failed to thee. (The
Lord thy God hath blessed thee in all the works of thy
hands; he hath known thy way, how thou hast passed
through this great wilderness for forty years; and the Lord
thy God hath been with thee, and thou hast lacked
nothing.)
8 And when we had passed by our brethren, the sons
of Esau, that dwelled in Seir, by the way of the field of
Elath, and of Eziongaber, we came to the way that
leadeth into the desert, (*or the wilderness*,) of Moab.
9 And the Lord said to me, Fight thou not against
Moabites, neither begin thou battle against them; for I
shall not give to thee anything of their land, for I have
given Ar into possession to the sons of Lot (for I have
given Ar to the sons of Lot for a possession).
10 Emim were the first dwellers thereof, a great people,
and strong, and so high, (The Emims were the first
inhabitants there, a great and strong people, and so tall,)
11 that they were believed *to be* as giants, of the
generation of Anakim, and they were like the sons of
Anakim; forsooth Moabites call them Emim (but the
Moabites call them the Emims).
12 Soothly Horims dwelled before in Seir, and when
they were put out, and were done away, the sons of Esau
dwelled *there*, as Israel did in the land of his possession,
which the Lord gave to him. (And the Horims lived there
before in Seir, and when they were put out, and were
done away, then the sons of Esau lived *there*, like the
Israelites did in the land of their possession, which the
Lord gave to them.)
13 Therefore we rose up, that we should pass the strand
of Zered, and we came to it. (And so we rose up, and
went out, and crossed over the Zered River.)
14 Soothly the time in which we went from
Kadeshbarnea till to the passing of the strand of Zered,
was of eight and thirty years (And the time it took us to
go from Kadeshbarnea until we crossed over the Zered
River, was thirty-eight years), till all the generation of
fighting men was wasted from their tents, as the Lord had
sworn;
15 whose hand was against them, (so) that they should
perish from the midst of their tents.
16 Soothly after that all the fighters had fallen down,
(And when all the fighting men had died,)
17 the Lord spake to me, and said,
18 Thou shalt pass today the coasts of Moab, (by) the
city, Ar by name, (Today, thou shalt cross over the border
of Moab, by the city of Ar,)
19 and thou shalt nigh into the coasts of the sons of
Ammon; be thou ware that thou fight not against them,
nor be moved to battle; for I shall not give to thee of the
land of the sons of Ammon, for I have given it to the sons
of Lot into possession. (and thou shalt come near to the
land of the Ammonites; be thou careful that thou do not
fight against them, nor go into battle with them; for I shall
not give thee any of the land of the Ammonites, for I have
given it to the sons of Lot for a possession.)
20 It is reckoned the land of giants, and giants
inhabited therein sometime, which giants Ammonites call
Zamzummims; (It is reckoned the land of giants, and
giants lived there sometime ago, whom the Ammonites
called the Zamzummims;)
21 a much people, and great, and of noble length, as
Anakim, which the Lord did away from the face of them,
and made them to dwell (*there*) for those *giants*, (a great
and numerous people, and as tall as the Anakim, whom
the Lord did away from there, and then allowed the
Ammonites to live *there* instead of those *giants*,)
22 as he did to the sons of Esau, that dwelled in Seir,
and did away Horims, and gave to them the land of

Horims, which *the sons of Esau* wield till into present time.
(as he did for the sons of Esau, who lived in Seir, for he did
away the Horims, and gave the land of the Horims to *the
sons of Esau*, which they possess unto this present time.)
23 Also men of Cappadocia putted out Avims, that
dwelled in Hazerim, till to Gaza; which went out from
Cappadocia, and did away Avims, and dwelled *there* for
them. (And the men of Caphtor put out the Avims, who
lived in Hazerim, unto Gaza; yea, they went out from
Caphtor, and did away the Avims, and lived *there* in their
place.)
24 Rise ye, and pass ye the strand of Arnon; lo! I have
betaken in(to) thine hand Sihon, king of Heshbon, of
Amorites; and his land begin thou to wield, and smite
thou battle against him. (So rise ye up, and cross ye over
the Arnon River; lo! I have delivered Sihon, the king of
Heshbon, of the Amorites, and his land, into thy hands;
now begin thou to possess it, and make thou battle
against him.)
25 Today I shall begin to send thy dread, and thy fear
into the peoples that dwell under all heaven (Today I
shall begin to put the dread and the fear of thee into all
the peoples who live under heaven), (so) that when thy
name is heard, they dread, and tremble, by the manner of
women travailing of child, and be holden with sorrow.
26 Therefore I sent messengers from the wilderness of
Kedemoth to Sihon, king of Heshbon; and I said with
peaceable words (and I said with these words of peace),
27 We shall pass through thy land, we shall go in the
common way; we shall not bow neither to the right side,
nor to the left side. (We desire to pass through thy land,
and we shall go by the common way; we shall not turn to
the right, nor to the left.)
28 Sell thou us meats for price, that we eat; give thou
us water for money, and so we shall drink. Only it is *that
we ask of thee* that thou grant passage to us, (Sell thou
food to us for money, so that we can eat; and sell thou
water *to us* for money, so that we can drink. All that *we
ask of thee* is that thou grant passage to us,)
29 as the sons of Esau did, that dwell in Seir, and the
Moabites, that dwell in Ar, till we come to (the) Jordan,
and pass to the land which our Lord God shall give to us.
(as the sons of Esau did, who live in Seir, and the
Moabites, who live in Ar, until we come to the Jordan
River, and then cross over to the land which the Lord our
God shall give to us.)
30 And Sihon, king of Heshbon, would not give
passage to us; for thy Lord God made hard his spirit, and
made firm *in evil* the heart of him, that he should be
betaken into thine hands, as thou seest now. (But Sihon,
the king of Heshbon, would not grant us passage; for the
Lord thy God made his spirit hard, and his heart firm *in
evil*, so that he would be delivered into thy hands, as
thou now seest *that he is*.)
31 And the Lord said to me, Lo, I have begun to betake
to thee Sihon, and his land; begin thou to wield it. (And
the Lord said to me, Lo! I have now begun to deliver unto
thee Sihon, and his land; begin thou to possess it.)
32 And Sihon went out against us with all his people,
to battle in Jahaz (to do battle at Jahaz).
33 And our Lord God betook him to us, and we have
smitten him (and we struck him down), with his sons,
and all his people.
34 And we took in that time all the cities, when the
dwellers of those cities, men, and women, and children,
were slain; we left not in them anything, (And we took all
their cities at that time, and the inhabitants of those cities,
the men, and women, and children, were all killed; we
left nothing in them,)
35 except beasts that fell into the part of men taking
prey (except for the beasts which we took as prey), *and
except* (for the) spoils of the cities which we (also) took.
36 From Aroer, which is on the brink of the strand of
Arnon, from the town which is set in the valley, unto
Gilead, no town was, nor city, that escaped our hands.
Our Lord God betook all to us; (From Aroer, which is on
the bank of the Arnon River, and from the town which is
set in the valley, unto Gilead, there was no town, or city,
that escaped our hands. The Lord our God delivered all
of them to us;)
37 except the land of the sons of Ammon, to which
land we nighed not, and all things that lie to the strand of
Jabbok, and *except* the cities of the mountains, and all the
places from which our Lord God forbade us. (except for
the land of the Ammonites, which land we did not even
come near to, and all the places that be along the Jabbok
River, and *except* for the cities in the mountains, and all
the places to which the Lord our God forbade us to go.)

CHAPTER 3

1 And so we turned, and went up by the way of
Bashan; and Og, the king of Bashan, went out against us
with his people, to fight in Edrei (to fight us at Edrei).
2 And the Lord said to me, Dread thou not him, for he
is betaken into thine hand (Do not thou fear him, for he is
delivered into thy hands), with all his people, and his
land; and thou shalt do to him, as thou didest to Sihon,
king of Amorites, that dwelled in Heshbon.
3 Therefore our Lord God betook in our hands also
Og, the king of Bashan, and all his people; and we have
smitten him unto death, (And so the Lord our God also
delivered Og, the king of Bashan, into our hands, with all
his people; and we struck down all of them, unto the
death,)
4 and we wasted all his cities in one time; no town
there was *of his* that escaped us; *we destroyed* sixty
cities, all the country of Argob, of the realm of Og in
Bashan. (and we destroyed all his cities at that time; there

was no town *of his* that escaped us; *we destroyed* sixty
cities, all the region of Argob, the kingdom of Og in
Bashan.)
5 All the cites were strengthened with most high
walls, and with gates and bars; without towns
unnumberable, that had no walls (besides the
innumerable towns, that had no walls).
6 And we did away those men, as we did to Sihon,
king of Heshbon; and we destroyed each city *of that
land*, and the men, and the women, and (the) little
children;
7 and we took by prey beasts, and spoils of the cities.
(and for prey, we took beasts, and spoils, from all the cities.)
8 And we took in that time the land from the hand of
the two kings of Amorites, that were beyond (the) Jordan,
from the strand of Arnon unto the hill of Hermon, (And
so at that time we took from the hands of the two kings of
the Amorites, all the land which was east of the Jordan
River, from the Arnon River unto Mount Hermon,)
9 which *hill* Sidonians call Sirion, and Amorites call
Shenir. (which *mountain* the Sidonians call Mount Sirion,
and the Amorites call Mount Shenir.)
10 *And we took* all the cities that were set in the plain,
and all the land of Gilead, and of Bashan, unto Salchah
and Edrei, cities of the realm of Og, in Bashan. (*And we
took* all the cities that were set there on the plain, and all
the land of Gilead, and of Bashan, unto Salchah and
Edrei, cities in the kingdom of Og, in Bashan.)
11 For Og alone, king of Bashan, was left of the
generation of giants; and his iron bed is showed, which is
in Rabbath, of the sons of Ammon, and it hath nine cubits
of length, and four cubits of breadth, at the measure of a
cubit of a man's hand. (For only Og, the king of Bashan,
was left of the generation of the giants; and his iron bed
is on display in the city of Rabbath, of the Ammonites,
and it is nine cubits in length, and four cubits in breadth,
at the measure of one cubit equal to a man's hand.)
12 And we wielded in that time the land, from Aroer,
which is on the brink of the strand of Arnon, unto the half
part of the hill of Gilead; and I gave his cities to Reuben
and to Gad. (And so we took the land from Aroer, which
is on the bank of the Arnon River, unto half of the hill
country of Gilead; and I gave its cities to the tribes of
Reuben and of Gad.)
13 And I gave the tother part of Gilead, and all Bashan,
of the realm of Og, to the half lineage of Manasseh, and
all the country of Argob. All Bashan was called the land
of giants. (And I gave the other part of Gilead, and all of
Bashan, which was Og's kingdom, that is, all the region
of Argob, to half of the tribe of Manasseh. Previously, all
of Bashan was called the land of the giants.)
14 Jair, the son of Manasseh, wielded all the country of
Argob, unto the land of Geshuri and of Maachathi; and
he called (the towns there) by his name Bashanhavothjair,
that is, the towns of Jair, till into this present day. (Jair,
the son of Manasseh, took all the region of Argob, unto
the borders of the Geshurites and the Maachathites; and
he called the towns there Bashanhavothjair, *that is, the
towns of Jair*, after his own name, and they still be called
that unto this present day.)
15 Also I gave Gilead to Machir; (And I gave Gilead to
Machir;)
16 and to the lineages of Reuben and of Gad I gave the
land of Gilead, till to the strand of Arnon, (that is, unto)
the middle of the strand, and of the ends till to the strand
of Jabbok, which is the term of the sons of Ammon. (and
to the tribes of Reuben and of Gad I gave the land of
Gilead, unto the middle of the Arnon River in the south,
and up to the Jabbok River in the north, which is the
border with the Ammonites.)
17 And *I gave to them* the plain of the wilderness, unto
(the) Jordan, and the terms of Chinnereth unto the sea of
(the) desert, the which is the most salt(y) sea, at the roots
of the hill of Pisgah, against the east. (And *on the west, I
gave them* the plain, *or the Arabah*, unto the Jordan
River, from the Sea of Galilee, *or Lake Galilee*, in the
north, down to the Salt Sea, *or the Dead Sea*, in the
south, and to the foot of Ashdothpisgah, *or Mount
Pisgah*, on the east.)
18 And I commanded to you in that time, and said,
Your Lord God giveth to you this land into heritage; all
ye strong men, (And I commanded to you at that time,
and said, The Lord your God hath given you this land for
an inheritance; all ye strong men,)
19 without (your) wives, and little children, and beasts,
be ye made ready, and go ye before your brethren, the
sons of Israel. For I know that ye have many beasts, and
those shall dwell in the cities that I have given to you,
20 till the Lord give rest to your brethren, as he hath
given to you, and *till* they also wield the land which *the
Lord* shall give to them beyond (the) Jordan; then each
man shall turn again into his possession that I have given
to you. (until the Lord give rest to your brothers, as he
hath given to you, and *until* they also take the land which
the Lord shall give them on the other side of the Jordan
River; then each man can return to his possession that I
have given you.)
21 Also I commanded to Joshua in that time, and said,
Thine eyes have seen what things your Lord God did to
these two kings; so he shall do to all the realms, to which
thou shalt go; (And I commanded to Joshua at that time,
and said, Thine eyes have seen what the Lord your God
did to these two kings; so he shall do to all the kingdoms
into which thou shalt go;)
22 dread thou not them; [the Lord our God shall fight
for us]. (do not thou fear them; for the Lord your God
shall fight for you.)
23 And I prayed the Lord in that time, and said, (And I

prayed to the Lord at that time, and said,)

24 Lord God, thou hast begun to show to *me* thy servant thy greatness, and thy full strong hand, for none other God there is, either in heaven, either in earth, that may do thy works, and may be comparisoned to thy strength (for there is no other god, either in heaven, or on earth, who can do thy works, and whose strength can be compared to thy strength).

25 Therefore I shall pass, and shall see this best land beyond (the) Jordan, and this noble hill, and Lebanon. (And so I shall cross over, and shall see this best land beyond the Jordan River, and this noble hill country, and the *mountains of* Lebanon.)

26 And the Lord was wroth to me for you, neither he heard me, but he said to me, It sufficeth to thee; speak thou no more of this thing to me. (But because of you, the Lord was angry with me, and he would not listen to me, and he said to me, It sufficeth for thee; speak thou no more of this thing to me.)

27 Go thou up into the highness of Pisgah, and cast about thine eyes to the west, and north, and south, and east, and behold, for thou shalt not pass this Jordan. (Go thou up onto the top of Mount Pisgah, and cast thine eyes to the west, and the north, and the south, and the east, and see it all, for thou shalt not cross over the Jordan River.)

28 Command thou to Joshua, and strengthen thou him, and comfort him; for he shall go before this people, and he shall part to them the land, which thou shalt see. (Then command thou to Joshua, and strengthen thou him, and encourage him; for he shall lead this people across to take the land, which thou shalt *only* see.)

29 And we dwelled in the valley against the temple of Bethpeor. (And so we stayed in the valley opposite the town of Bethpeor.)

CHAPTER 4

1 And now, thou Israel, hear the behests and dooms which I teach thee, that thou do those, and live, and that thou enter and wield the land which the Lord God of your fathers shall give to you. (And now, O Israel, listen to the statutes and laws, *or judgements*, which I shall teach thee, so that thou do them, and live, and so that thou can enter and take the land which the Lord God of your fathers shall give to you.)

2 Ye shall not add to the word which I speak to you, neither ye shall take away from it; keep ye the commandments of your Lord God (obey the commandments of the Lord your God), which I command to you.

3 Your eyes saw all things which the Lord did against Baalpeor; how he all-brake all the worshippers of him from the midst of you. (Your own eyes saw all the things which the Lord did at Mount Peor; how he destroyed all the worshippers of Baal of Peor in the midst of you.)

4 Forsooth ye that cleave(d) to your Lord God live all till into (this) present day. (But all of ye who cleaved to the Lord your God still be alive unto this present day.)

5 Ye know that I taught you the behests and the rightwisenesses, as my Lord God commanded to me; so ye shall do *them* in the land that ye shall wield, (Ye know that I have taught you all the statutes and the laws, *or the judgements*, as the Lord my God commanded to me; and ye shall do *them* in the land that ye shall take,)

6 and ye shall keep, and fulfill *them* in work. For this is your wisdom and understanding before [the] peoples, that all men hear these behests, and say, Lo! a wise people and an understanding (one)! a great folk! (and ye shall obey them, and fulfill *them* in work. For this shall show your wisdom and understanding to the other peoples, and when the other peoples hear of these statutes, they shall say, Lo! a wise people, a people of understanding! yea, a great nation!)

7 None other nation is so great, that hath Gods nighing to itself, as our God is ready to all our beseechings. (No other nation, no matter how great, hath gods so near to it, as our God is to us.)

8 For what other folk is so noble, that it hath ceremonies, and just dooms, and all the law, which I shall set forth today before your eyes? (For what other nation is so noble, that it hath statutes, and judgements, and all the law/s, which I shall set forth today before your eyes?)

9 Therefore keep thyself, and thy soul busily; forget thou not the words which thine eyes have seen, and fall they not down from thine heart, in all the days of thy life. Thou shalt teach those (to) thy sons, and thy sons' sons. (And so guard thyself, and thy soul; forget thou not the things which thine eyes have seen, and fall they not down from thy heart, all the days of thy life. Thou shalt teach them to thy sons and thy daughters, and to thy children's children.)

10 *Tell thou to them* (about) the day in which thou stoodest before thy Lord God in Horeb, when the Lord spake to me, and said, Gather thou the people to me, that it hear my words, and that it learn for to dread me in all time in which it liveth in (the) earth, and teach his sons. (*Tell thou them* about the day in which thou stoodest before the Lord thy God at Mount Sinai, when the Lord spoke to me, and said, Gather thou the people to me, so that they can hear my words, and that they learn to fear me/and that they learn to revere me, in all the time in which they live on the earth, and that they also teach their sons and their daughters this.)

11 And ye nighed to the root of the hill, that burnt till to heaven; and darknesses, and cloud, and mist were therein. (And ye came near, and stood at the foot of the mountain, that burned unto the heavens; and darkness, and cloud, and mist were on that mountain.)

12 And the Lord spake to you from the midst of [the]

fire; ye heard the voice of his words, and utterly ye saw
no form, *or shape.* (And the Lord spoke to you from the
midst of the fire; ye heard him speaking *to you*, but truly
ye saw no shape, *or form.*)
13 And he showed to you his covenant, which he
commanded that ye should do, and [the] ten words,
which he wrote in two tables of stone. (And he told you
his covenant, which he commanded that ye should do,
and the Ten Words, *that is, the Ten Commandments*,
which he wrote on two tablets of stone.)
14 And he commanded to me in that time, that I should
teach you ceremonies and dooms (that I should teach
you the statutes and laws, *or judgements*), which ye
ought to do in the land which ye shall wield.
15 Therefore keep ye busily your minds; ye saw not
any likeness in the day in which the Lord spake to you in
Horeb, from the midst of the fire; (And so guard ye your
minds; for ye saw not any form, *or figure*, on the day in
which the Lord spoke to you on Mount Sinai, from the
midst of the fire;)
16 lest peradventure ye be deceived, and make to you
a graven likeness, either an image of male, either female;
(lest ye be deceived, and make for yourselves an idol, a
carved image of a man, or a woman,)
17 or a likeness of all beasts that be on earth, either of
birds flying under heaven, (or a likeness of any beast that
is on the earth, or of any bird flying in the sky,)
18 either of creeping beasts that be moved in the earth,
either of fishes that dwell under the earth in waters; (or of
any creeping beast that moveth on the ground, or of any
fish that liveth in the waters under the earth;)
19 lest peradventure, when thine eyes be raised up to
heaven, thou see the sun, and the moon, and all the stars
of heaven, and thou be deceived by error, and worship
those *things*, and honour them, the which things thy Lord
God made of nought, into the service of all folks that be
under heaven. (lest, when thine eyes be raised up to the
heavens, and thou see the sun, and the moon, and all the
stars in the sky, *that is, the host of heaven*, thou be
deceived by error, and thou worship those *things*, and
honour them, which things the Lord thy God made out of
nothing, for the service of all the peoples who be under
heaven.)
20 Forsooth the Lord took you, and led you out of the
iron furnace, *or strong tribulation*, of Egypt, that he
should have a people of heritage, as it is in [the] present
day. (But the Lord took you, and led you out of the iron
furnace, *that is, out of thy strong tribulation*, in Egypt, so
that he would have a people of inheritance, as ye be to
this present day.)
21 And the Lord was wroth against me for your words,
and swore that I should not pass (the) Jordan, and that I
should not enter into the best land, which he shall give to
you. (But because of you, the Lord was angry with me,
and he swore that I would not cross over the Jordan
River, and that I would not enter into that best land,
which he shall give to you.)
22 Lo! I die in this land; I shall not pass (the) Jordan; ye
shall pass it, and shall wield the noble land. (Lo! I shall
die here in this land; I shall not cross over the Jordan
River, but ye shall cross over it, and ye shall possess the
noble land.)
23 Be ye ware, lest any time thou forget the covenant of
thy Lord God, which he made with thee, and lest thou
make to thee a graven likeness of those things which the
Lord hath forbidden *thee* to make. (Be ye careful, lest any
time thou forget the covenant of the Lord thy God, which
he made with thee, and lest thou make for yourselves a
carved image, *or an idol*, of those things which the Lord
hath forbidden *thee* to make.)
24 For thy Lord God is a fire wasting; a jealous God. (For
the Lord thy God is a wasting fire; yea, a jealous God.)
25 If ye beget sons, and sons of sons, and ye dwell in
the land, and ye be deceived, and make to you any
likeness, *or image* (and make for yourselves any likeness,
or idol), and do evil before your Lord God, (so) that ye
stir him to great wrath,
26 I call (to) witness today heaven and earth, that ye
shall perish soon from the land, that ye shall wield, when
ye have passed (the) Jordan; ye shall not live long time
therein, but the Lord shall do away you, (I call heaven
and earth to witness against you today, that ye soon shall
perish from the land that ye shall take, when ye have
crossed over the Jordan River; ye shall not live a long
time in it, but the Lord shall do you away,)
27 and he shall scatter you *abroad* among all heathen
men, and ye shall dwell few (in number) among the
nations, to which the Lord shall lead you.
28 And there ye shall serve to gods, that be made by
men's hands, to tree and to stone (And there ye shall
serve gods, that be made by the hands of men, out of
wood and stone), (gods) that neither see, neither hear,
neither eat, neither smell.
29 And when thou hast sought there thy Lord God,
thou shalt find him (But if thou shalt seek the Lord thy
God there, thou shalt find him); if nevertheless thou
seekest him with all thy heart, and with all the tribulation
of thy soul.
30 After that all things have found thee, that be before-
said, soothly in the last time, thou shalt turn again to thy
Lord God, and thou shalt hear his voice. (And when all
these things have found thee, that be spoken of before,
thou shalt finally return to the Lord thy God, and thou
shalt listen to his voice, *and obey him*.)
31 For thy Lord God is a merciful God; he shall not
forsake thee, neither he shall do *thee* away utterly,
neither he shall forget the covenant, in which he swore to
thy fathers. (For the Lord thy God is a merciful God; he

shall not forsake thee, nor shall he utterly do *thee* away,
nor shall he forget the covenant, which he swore to thy
fathers.)
32 Ask thou (them) of [the] eld days, *or times*, that were
before thee, from the day in which thy Lord God made of
nought man upon (the) earth, *ask thou* from the one end
of heaven unto the tother end thereof, *that is, take heed
to all things that ever were done*, if such a thing was
done any time, (Ask thou them about the days of old, *or
the former times*, that were before thee, from the day in
which the Lord thy God made a man out of nothing on
the earth, *ask thou* from one end of heaven unto the
other, *that is, take heed of all the things that were ever
done*, if at any time such a thing was ever done,)
33 either if it was ever known, that a people heard the
voice of God speaking from the midst of the fire, as thou
hast heard and seen; (or was it ever made known, if any
other people heard the voice of God speaking to them
from the midst of the fire, as thou hast heard, and yet still
lived?)
34 *either* if that God went in, and took to himself a folk
from the midst of nations, by temptations, miracles, and
great wonders, by battle, and strong hand, and arm
stretched forth, and horrible sights, by all things which
your Lord God did for you in Egypt, in sight of thine eyes;
(*or* if any god went in, and took for himself a people from
the midst of another nation, by temptations, and miracles,
and great wonders, and by battle, and by a strong hand,
and an outstretched arm, and terrible sights, yea, by all
the things which the Lord your God did for you in Egypt,
in the sight of thine own eyes?)
35 that thou shouldest know, that the Lord himself is
God, and none other is, besides (this) one. (so that thou
wouldest know, that the Lord himself is God, and there is
no other besides him.)
36 From heaven he made thee to hear his voice, that he
should teach thee; and in [the] earth he showed to thee
his full great fire (and on the earth he showed thee his
very great fire), and thou heardest his words from [the]
midst of the fire;
37 for he loved thy fathers, and chose their seed after
them. And he led thee out of Egypt, and went before
thee in his great strength,
38 that he should do away the greatest nations, and
stronger than thou, in thine entering, and that he should
lead thee in, and should give to thee their land into
possession (and should give thee their land for a
possession), as thou seest in (this) present day.
39 Therefore know thou today, and think in thine heart,
that the Lord himself is God in heaven above, and in
earth beneath, and none other is. (And so know thou
today, and take to thy heart, that the Lord himself is God
in heaven above, and on the earth beneath, and there is
no other.)
40 Keep thou his behests, and his commandments,
which I command to thee, that it be well to thee, and to
thy sons after thee, and that thou dwell much time upon
the land, which thy Lord God shall give to thee. (Obey
thou his statutes, and his commandments, which I
command to thee, that it be well with thee, and with thy
children after thee, and so that thou live a long time on
the land, which the Lord thy God shall give to thee.)
41 Then Moses separated three cities beyond (the)
Jordan at the east coast, (Then Moses set apart three cities
east of the Jordan River,)
42 that he flee to those, that slayeth his neighbour not
willfully, and was not (an) enemy (*to him*) before one and
the tother day, and that he may flee to some of these
cities; (so that anyone might flee to them, who did not
willfully, *or intentionally*, kill his neighbour, and was not
an enemy *to him* the day before, and so that he might
escape to one of these cities, and live;)
43 Bezer in the wilderness, which is set in the field
land, of the lineage of Reuben; and Ramoth in Gilead,
which is in the lineage of Gad; and Golan in Bashan,
which is in the lineage of Manasseh. (Bezer in the
wilderness, which is set on the plains, for the tribe of
Reuben; and Ramoth in Gilead, for the tribe of Gad; and
Golan in Bashan, for the tribe of Manasseh.)
44 This is the law which Moses setted forth before the
sons of Israel,
45 and these be the witnessings, and ceremonies, and
the dooms, which he spake to the sons of Israel, when
they went out of Egypt, (and these be the testimonies, and
statutes, and the laws, *or the judgements*, which he spoke
to the Israelites, when they went out of Egypt,)
46 beyond (the) Jordan, in the valley against the temple
of Bethpeor, in the land of Sihon, king of Amorites, that
dwelled in Heshbon, whom Moses killed. And the sons
of Israel went out of Egypt, (east of the Jordan River, in
the valley opposite the town of Bethpeor, in the land of
Sihon, the king of the Amorites, who lived in Heshbon.
Moses and the Israelites defeated him, after they went out
of Egypt,)
47 and wielded his land, and the land of Og, king of
Bashan, two kings of Amorites, that were beyond (the)
Jordan, at the rising of the sun; (and they took his land,
and also the land of Og, the king of Bashan, the two
kings of the Amorites, who lived on the east side of the
Jordan River;)
48 from Aroer, which is set on the brink of the strand of
Arnon, till to the hill of Sion, which is Hermon; (from
Aroer, which is set on the bank of the Arnon River, unto
Mount Sirion, that is, Mount Hermon;)
49 *and they wielded* all the plain beyond (the) Jordan,
at the east coast, unto the sea of (the) wilderness, and
unto the roots of the hill of Pisgah. (*and they took* all the
plain, *or the Arabah*, east of the Jordan River, unto the

Dead Sea, and the foot of Mount Pisgah.)

CHAPTER 5

1 And Moses called all Israel, and said to him, Hear,
thou Israel, the ceremonies and dooms, which I speak
today in your ears; learn ye them, and fulfilleth in deed.
(And Moses called all the Israelites, and said to them,
Hear, O Israel, the statutes and laws, *or judgements*,
which I speak today in your ears; learn ye them, and do
ye them.)
2 Our Lord God made a bond of peace with us in
Horeb; (The Lord our God made a covenant with us at
Mount Sinai;)
3 he made not covenant with our fathers, but with us
that be present, and live. (he did not make the covenant
with our fathers, but with us who be alive, and present
here today.)
4 Face to face he spake to us in the hill, from the
midst of the fire. (Face to face he spoke to you on the
mountain, from the midst of the fire.)
5 I was (a) reconciler and a mediator betwixt God and
you in that time, that I should tell to you his words, for ye
dreaded the fire, and ye went not up into the hill. And he
said, (I was a reconciler and a mediator between God
and you at that time, to tell you his words, for ye feared
the fire, and ye would not go up the mountain. And he
said,)
6 I am thy Lord God, that led thee out of the land of
Egypt, from the house of servage. (I am the Lord thy God,
who led thee out of the land of Egypt, from the house of
servitude, *or of slavery*.)
7 Thou shalt not have alien Gods in my sight. (Thou
shalt not have *any* foreign, *or other*, gods before me.)
8 Thou shalt not make to thee a graven image, neither
a likeness of all things that be in heaven above, and that
be in earth beneath, and that be in waters under (the)
earth; (Thou shalt not make a carved image, *or an idol*,
for thyself, nor a likeness of anything that be in the
heavens above, or on the earth beneath, or in the waters
under the earth;)
9 thou shalt not praise them, nor worship *them*; for I
am thy Lord God, a jealous God; and I yield the
wickedness of (the) fathers into the sons, into the third
and the fourth generation to them that hate me (and I put
the punishment of the fathers upon the children, into the
third and the fourth generations of those who hate me),
10 and I do mercy into many thousands to them that
love me, and keep my behests. (but I do mercy to the
many thousands who love me, and keep my
commandments.)
11 Thou shalt not mis-take the name of thy Lord God in
vain, for he shall not be unpunished, that taketh the name
of God in a vain thing. (Thou shalt not take the name of
the Lord thy God in vain, for no one shall go unpunished,
who taketh the name of God in vain.)
12 Keep thou the sabbath day that thou hallow it, as thy
Lord God commanded to thee. (Keep thou the sabbath
day holy, as the Lord thy God commanded thee.)
13 In six days thou shalt work, and do all thy works;
14 the seventh day is the day of sabbath, that is, the rest
of thy Lord God. Thou shalt not do therein anything of
work; thou, and thy son, and thy daughter, thy servant,
and thine handmaid, and thine ox, and thine ass, and all
thy work beasts, and the pilgrim that is within thy gates;
that thy servant rest and thine handmaid, as also thou.
(the seventh day is the day of sabbath, that is, the rest of
the Lord thy God. Thou shalt not do any work on it; thou,
and thy son, and thy daughter, thy slave, and thy slave-
girl, and thy ox, and thy donkey, and all thy work beasts,
and the foreigner, *or the stranger*, who is within thy gates;
so that thy slave and thy slave-girl can rest, as thou doeth.)
15 Have mind, that also thyself servedest in Egypt, and
thy Lord God led thee out from thence, in a strong hand,
and in an arm stretched forth (Remember, that thou were
slaves in Egypt, and that the Lord thy God led thee out
from there, with a strong hand, and an outstretched arm);
therefore he commanded to thee, that thou shouldest
keep the sabbath day.
16 Honour thy father and thy mother, as thy Lord God
commanded to thee, that thou live in long time, and that
it be well to thee, in the land which thy Lord God shall
give to thee. (Honour thy father and thy mother, as the
Lord thy God commanded thee, so that thou live a long
time, and that it be well with thee, in the land which the
Lord thy God shall give thee.)
17 Thou shalt not slay. (Thou shalt not kill.)
18 Thou shalt not do lechery.
19 Thou shalt not do theft.
20 Thou shalt not speak false witnessing against thy
neighbour.
21 Thou shalt not covet thy neighbour's wife, nor his
house, nor his field, nor his servant, nor his handmaid,
nor his ox, nor ass, and all things, *that is, nothing of all
the things*, that be his. (Thou shalt not covet thy
neighbour's wife, nor his house, nor his field, nor his
slave, nor his slave-girl, nor his ox, nor his donkey, nor
anything that be his.)
22 The Lord spake these words to all your multitude, in
the hill, from the midst of the fire, and of the cloud, and
of the mist, with great voice, and he added to (it) nothing
more; and he wrote those *words* in two tables of stone,
which he gave to me. (The Lord spoke these words to all
the multitude of you, on the mountain, from the midst of
the fire, and of the cloud, and of the mist, with a great
voice, and he added nothing more to it; and he wrote
those *words* on two stone tablets, which he gave to me.)
23 And after that ye heard the voice from the midst of
the darknesses, and ye saw the hill burn, all ye princes of

the lineages, and the greater men in birth, nighed to me,
(And after that ye heard the voice from the midst of the
darkness, and ye saw the mountain burning with fire, all
ye leaders of the tribes, and the men of great age, *that is,
the elders*, came to me,)
24 and ye said, Lo! our Lord God hath showed to us his
majesty and greatness; we heard his voice from [the]
midst of the fire, and we have proved today that a man
liveth, God speaking with man. (and ye said, Lo! the Lord
our God hath shown us his majesty and his greatness; we
heard his voice from the midst of the fire, and we have
proven today that a person can live, even after God hath
spoken with him.)
25 Why therefore shall we die, and shall this greatest fire
devour us? For if we hear more the voice of our Lord God,
we shall die. (And so why should we risk death again? for
this great fire shall devour us! Yea, if we hear the voice of
the Lord our God again, surely we shall all die!)
26 What is each man, that he hear the voice of God
living, that speaketh from [the] midst of the fire, as we
have heard, and that he may live? (For what person hath
ever heard the voice of the living God, speaking from the
midst of the fire, as we have, and still lived to tell about it?)
27 Rather nigh thou, and hear thou all things which our
Lord God shall say to thee; and thou shalt speak to us,
and we shall hear, and do those *words*. (Instead, thou go
near, and listen thou to all the things that the Lord our
God shall say to thee; and thou shalt tell us, and we shall
hear, and do those *things*.)
28 And when the Lord had heard this, he said to me, I
have heard the voice of the words of this people, which
they have spoken to thee; they have spoken well all
things. (And when the Lord had heard this, he said to me,
I have heard the words of these people, that they have
spoken to thee; and they have spoken all things well.)
29 Who shall give that they have such soul, that they
dread me, and keep all my commandments in all time,
that it be well to them, and to the sons of them, [into]
without end? (O that they would have such a soul, that
they would fear me at all times/that they would revere me
at all times, and obey all my commandments, so that it
would be well with them, and with their children,
forevermore!)
30 Go thou, and say to them, Turn ye again into your
tents. (Go thou, and say to them, Return ye to your tents.)
31 Soothly stand thou here with me, and I shall speak
to thee all [the] commandments, and ceremonies, and
dooms, which thou shalt teach them, that they do those
in the land which I shall give to them into possession.
(But thou stand here with me, and I shall tell thee all the
commandments, and statutes, and laws, *or judgements*,
which thou shalt teach them, so that they can do them in
the land which I shall give them for a possession.)
32 Therefore keep ye (And so obey ye), and do ye those
things, which the Lord God hath commanded to you; ye
shall not bow away, neither to the right side, nor to the
left side,
33 but ye shall go by the way which your Lord God
commanded, that ye live, and that it be well to you (so
that ye can live, and it shall be well with you), and that
your days be lengthened in the land of your possession.

CHAPTER 6

1 These be the commandments, ceremonies, and
dooms, which your Lord God commanded that I should
teach you, and that ye do them in the land to which ye
pass over to wield; (These be the commandments, and
statutes, and laws, *or judgements*, which the Lord your
God commanded that I should teach you, so that ye would
do them in the land to which ye shall cross over to take;)
2 that thou dread thy Lord God, and keep all his
commandments, and behests, which I command to thee,
and to thy sons, and to the sons of thy sons, in all the
days of thy life, that thy days be lengthened. (that thou
fear the Lord thy God/that thou revere the Lord thy God,
and obey all his commandments, and statutes, which I
command to thee, and to thy sons and daughters, and to
thy children's children, in all the days of thy life, so that
thy days be lengthened.)
3 Thou Israel, hear, and keep, that thou do those
things which the Lord commanded to thee, and that it be
well to thee, and thou be multiplied more, as the Lord
God of thy fathers hath promised, to give to thee a land
flowing with milk and honey. (Hear, O Israel, and obey,
that thou do those things which the Lord commanded
thee, and that it be well with thee, and thou be greatly
multiplied in the land flowing with milk and honey, as
the Lord God of thy fathers promised thee.)
4 Thou Israel, hear, thy Lord God is one God. (Hear,
O Israel, the Lord thy God is one God.)
5 Thou shalt love thy Lord God of all thine heart, and
of all thy soul, and of all thy strength. (Thou shalt love the
Lord thy God with all thy heart, and with all thy soul, and
with all thy strength.)
6 And these words which I command to thee today,
shall be in thine heart;
7 and thou shalt tell those to thy sons, and thou shalt
think upon them, sitting in thine house, and going in the
way (and going on the way), lying down, and rising (up).
8 And thou shalt bind those as a sign in thine hand;
and those shall be, and shall be moved before thine eyes;
(And thou shalt bind them upon thy hands for a sign; and
they shall be before thine eyes forevermore;)
9 and thou shalt write them in the lintel, and in the
doors of thine house. (and thou shalt write them on the
lintels, and on the door-posts of thy houses.)
10 And when thy Lord God hath brought thee into the
land, for which he swore to thy fathers, to Abraham,

Isaac, and Jacob, and he hath given to thee great cities,
and best, which thou buildedest not (and he hath given
thee the best and the greatest cities, yea, which thou hast
not built),
11 houses full of all riches, which thou madest not, and
cisterns, which thou diggedest not, (and) vineyards, and
olive places, which thou plantedest not, and *when* thou
hast eaten, and art full-filled (and art filled full),
12 beware diligently, lest thou forget the Lord, that led
thee out of the land of Egypt, from the house of servage.
(be careful, lest thou forget the Lord, who led thee out of
the land of Egypt, from the house of servitude, *or of
slavery*.)
13 Thou shalt dread thy Lord God (Thou shalt fear the
Lord thy God/Thou shalt revere the Lord thy God), and
thou shalt serve him alone, and thou shalt swear by his
name.
14 Ye shall not go after alien gods, of all (the) heathen
men that be in your compass/that be about you; (Ye shall
not follow foreign, *or other*, gods, the gods of the
heathen who be all around you;)
15 for God is a fervent lover, thy Lord God is in the
midst of thee, lest any time the strong vengeance/the
fierceness of thy Lord God be wroth against thee, and do
away thee from the face of the earth. (for God is a jealous
lover, the Lord thy God who is in the midst of thee, lest
any time the Lord thy God be angry with thee, and in his
strong vengeance he do thee away from off the face of
the earth.)
16 Thou shalt not tempt thy Lord God, as thou
temptedest *him* in the place of tempting. (Thou shalt not
tempt the Lord thy God, as thou temptedest *him* at
Massah.)
17 Keep thou the commandments of thy Lord God, and
the witnessings, and ceremonies, which he hath
commanded to thee; (Obey thou the commandments of
the Lord thy God, and his testimonies, and statutes,
which he hath commanded to thee;)
18 and do thou that that is pleasing and good in the
sight of the Lord, that it be well to thee (so that it shall be
well with thee), and that thou enter, and wield the best
land, of which the Lord swore to thy fathers,
19 that he should do away all thine enemies before
thee, as he hath spoken. (and that he would do away all
thy enemies before thee/and that thou would do away all
thy enemies before thee, as he hath promised.)
20 And when thy son shall ask thee tomorrow, *that is,
in time to coming*, and shall say, What will these
witnessings, and ceremonies, and dooms to themselves,
which our Lord God commanded to us? (And when thy
son, *or thy daughter*, shall ask thee tomorrow, *that is, in
the time to come*, and shall say, What is the meaning of
these testimonies, and statutes, and laws, *or judgements*,
which the Lord our God hath commanded us *to obey*?)
21 thou shalt say to him, We were Pharaoh's servants
in Egypt, and the Lord led us out of Egypt, in a strong
hand; (thou shalt say to them, We were Pharaoh's slaves
in Egypt, and the Lord led us out of Egypt, with a strong
hand;)
22 and he did miracles, and great wonders, and worst,
that is, most painful vengeances, in Egypt, against
Pharaoh, and all his house, in our sight. (and he did
miracles, and wonders, yea, the greatest and the worst, in
Egypt, against Pharaoh, and all his household, right
before our eyes.)
23 And he led us out thereof, that he should give *to us*
led in, the land of which he swore to our fathers. (And he
led us out of there, to lead *us* into the land which he had
promised to our fathers, that he would give us.)
24 And the Lord commanded to us, that we do all these
lawful things, and dread our Lord God, that it be well to
us, in all the days of our life, as it is today. (And the Lord
commanded us, to obey all these laws, and to fear the
Lord our God/and to revere the Lord our God, so that it
would be well with us, all the days of our life, as it is
today.)
25 And he shall be merciful to us, if we shall do and
keep all his behests, before our Lord God, as he
commanded to us. (And he shall be merciful to us, if we
shall obey all these commandments, before the Lord our
God, as he commanded us.)

CHAPTER 7

1 When thy Lord God hath led thee into the land, into
which thou shalt enter to wield, and hath done away
many folks before thee, (the) Hittites, and Girgashites,
and Amorites, Canaanites, and Perizzites, Hivites, and
Jebusites; seven folks, of much greater number than thou
art, and stronger than thou;
2 and *when* thy Lord God hath betaken them to thee,
thou shalt smite them unto death, thou shalt not make
with them a bond of peace, neither thou shalt have
mercy upon them, (and *when* the Lord thy God hath
delivered them unto thee, thou shalt strike them down
unto the death, thou shalt not make a covenant, *or a
peace treaty*, with them, nor shalt thou have mercy on
them,)
3 neither thou shalt fellowship marriages with them;
thou shalt not give thy daughter to his son, neither thou
shalt take his daughter to thy son (nor shalt thou take his
daughter for thy son);
4 for she shall deceive thy son, that he follow not me,
that he serve more alien gods; and *then* the fierce
vengeance of the Lord shall be wroth, and shall do away
thee soon. (for she shall deceive thy son, so that he shall
not follow me, and moreover, so that he serve foreign, *or
other*, gods; and *then* the Lord shall be angry, and with
fierce vengeance he shall swiftly do thee away.)

5 But rather thou shalt do these things to them;
destroy ye their altars, and break ye their molten images
of metal, and cut ye down *their* woods, and burn ye their
graven images. (But rather thou shalt do these things to
them; destroy ye their altars, and break ye up their metal
idols, and cut ye down their sacred groves, *or poles*, and
burn ye up their carved idols.)
6 For thou art an holy people to thy Lord God; thy
Lord God chose thee, that thou be a special people to
him, of all peoples that be on earth. (For thou art a holy
people to the Lord thy God; the Lord thy God chose thee
to be his special people, out of all the peoples that be on
the earth.)
7 Not for ye overcame in number all folks, the Lord is
joined to you, and chose you, since ye be fewer than all
peoples; (The Lord is not joined to you, or chose you,
because ye were greater in number than all the other
nations, since ye be fewer than all the other peoples;)
8 but for the Lord loved you, and kept the oath which
he swore to your fathers; and he led you out in [a] strong
hand, and again-bought *you* from the house of servage,
from the house of Pharaoh, king of Egypt. (but because
the Lord loved you, and kept the oath which he swore to
your fathers; and he led you out with a strong hand, and
bought you back, *that is, redeemed, or ransomed, you*,
from the house of servitude, *or of slavery*, from the hand,
or the power, of Pharaoh, the king of Egypt.)
9 And thou shalt know, that thy Lord God himself is a
strong God, and faithful, and keepeth covenant and
mercy to them that love him, and to them that keep his
commandments, into a thousand generations; (And thou
shalt know, that the Lord thy God himself is a strong
God, and faithful, and keepeth covenant and mercy with
those who love him, and with those who obey his
commandments, unto a thousand generations;)
10 and he yieldeth anon to them that hate him, so that
he destroy them, and defer, *or tarry*, no longer; restoring,
or yielding, anon to them that that they deserve. (but that
he yieldeth at once to those who hate him, to destroy
them, and to defer, *or to tarry*, no longer; yea, swiftly
yielding to them what they deserve.)
11 Therefore keep thou the commandments, and
ceremonies, and dooms, which I command to thee today,
that thou do *them*. (And so obey thou the
commandments, and statutes, and laws, *or judgements*,
which I command to thee today, yea, do thou *them*.)
12 If after that thou hearest these dooms, thou keepest,
and doest them, thy Lord God shall keep to thee
covenant, and mercy, which he swore to thy fathers. (If
after that thou hearest these laws, *or these judgements*,
thou obeyest, and doest them, then the Lord thy God
shall keep the covenant with thee, which he swore to thy
fathers, and show his mercy to thee.)
13 And he shall love thee, and multiply *thee*, and he
shall bless the fruit of thy womb, and the fruit of thy land,
thy wheat, and thy vintage, thine oil, and thy droves of
beasts, and the flocks of thy sheep, on the land for which
he swore to thy fathers, that he should give it to thee.
(And he shall love thee, and multiply *thee*, and he shall
bless the fruit of thy womb, and the fruit of thy land, yea,
thy corn, and thy wine, thy oil, and thy herds of beasts,
and the flocks of thy sheep, in the land which he swore
to thy fathers, that he would give thee.)
14 Thou shalt be blessed among all peoples; none
barren of ever either kind shall be with thee, as well in
men, as in thy flocks. (Thou shalt be blessed among all
peoples; there shall be no barren among thee, male or
female, in people, as well as in thy flocks.)
15 The Lord shall do away from thee all ache (The Lord
shall take away all thy aches and pains); and he shall not
bring to thee the full evil sicknesses of Egypt, that thou
hast known, but to all thine enemies *these sicknesses
shall come*.
16 And thou shalt devour, *that is, destroy*, all [the]
peoples, which thy Lord God shall give (over) to thee;
thine eye shall not spare them, neither thou shalt serve
their gods, lest they be into the falling of thee (lest they
be thy downfall).
17 If thou sayest in thine heart, These folks be more
than I, how may I do away them? (If thou sayest in thy
heart, These nations, *or these peoples*, be more than I,
how can I do them away?)
18 do not thou dread, but have thou mind, what things
thy Lord God did to Pharaoh, and all the Egyptians; (do
not thou fear, but remember, what things the Lord thy
God did to Pharaoh, and to all the Egyptians;)
19 *he did to them* the greatest vengeances, which thine
eyes saw, and miracles, and great wonders, and the
strong hand, and an arm stretched out, that thy Lord God
should lead thee out *(from) thence*; so he shall do to all
peoples which thou dreadest. (*he did to them* the greatest
vengeances, which thine eyes saw, and miracles, and
great wonders, with a strong hand, and an outstretched
arm, so that the Lord thy God could lead thee out *from
there*; so shall he do to all the peoples whom thou fearest.)
20 Furthermore and thy Lord God shall send venomous
flies into them, till he do away, and destroy all men, that
fled (from) thee, and they shall not be able to be hid.
(And furthermore, the Lord thy God shall send venomous
flies into them, until he do away, and destroy, all those
who fled from thee, and they shall not be able to hide
from them.)
21 Thou shalt not dread them, for thy Lord God is in
the midst of thee, a great God, and fearful. (Thou shalt
not fear them, for the Lord thy God is in the midst of
thee, yea, a great and fearful God.)
22 He himself shall waste these nations in thy sight,
(by) little and little, and by parts; thou shalt not be able to

do away them (al)together (but thou shalt not be able to
completely do them away), lest peradventure [the] beasts
of the earth be multiplied against thee;
23 and thy Lord God shall give them *to thee* in thy sight,
and he shall slay them, till they be done away utterly.
(and the Lord thy God shall give them over *to thee*, and
he shall kill them, until they be utterly done away.)
24 And he shall betake their kings into thine hands, and
thou shalt destroy their names under heaven; none shall
be able to against-stand thee, till thou all-break them.
25 Thou shalt burn in fire their graven images; thou
shalt not covet the silver and gold, of which *those images*
be made, neither thou shalt take of those anything to
thee, lest thou offend therefore, for it is abomination of
thy Lord God. (Thou shalt burn their carved images with
fire; thou shalt not covet the silver and gold, which be on
those idols, nor shalt thou take it for thyself, lest thou be
caused to stumble because of it, for they be abominations
to the Lord thy God.)
26 Neither thou shalt bring anything of the idol into
thine house, lest thou be made cursed, as also that *idol* is;
thou shalt loathe *it* as filth, and thou shalt have *it* as
defouling, and as filths of abomination, for it is cursed.
(Nor shalt thou bring any idol into thy house, lest thou be
cursed, like that *idol* is cursed; thou shalt loathe *it* like
filth, and thou shalt see *it* as defiled, and like the filths of
abominations, for it is cursed.)

CHAPTER 8

1 Be thou ware diligently (Be thou careful), that thou
do each commandment which I command to thee today,
(so) that ye may live, and be multiplied, and that ye enter,
and wield the land, for which the Lord swore to your
fathers.
2 And thou shalt have mind of all the way, by which
thy Lord God led thee by forty years, in (the) desert, that
he should torment thee, and should assay thee; and that
those things that were treated in thy soul should be
known, whether thou wouldest keep his commandments,
either nay. (And thou shalt remember all the way, by
which the Lord thy God led thee for forty years, in the
wilderness, to humble thee, and to try, *or to test*, thee; so
that those things that were treated in thy soul could be
known, whether thou wouldest obey his commandments,
or not.)
3 And he tormented thee with neediness, and he gave
to thee meat, manna *to eat*, which thou knewest not, and
thy fathers *knew not*, that he should show to thee, that a
man liveth not in bread alone, but in each word that
cometh out of the Lord's mouth. (And so he humbled
thee with neediness, *or with want*, and he gave thee
food, manna *to eat*, which thou knewest not, nor thy
fathers *knew*, to show thee, that a man liveth not by
bread alone, but by each word that cometh out of the
mouth of the Lord.)
4 Thy cloak, with which thou were covered, failed not
for eldness, and thy foot was not bruised underneath, lo!
the fortieth year is (lo! this is the fortieth year);
5 that thou think in thine heart, for as a man teacheth
his son, so thy Lord God hath taught thee, (so that thou
remember in thy heart, that like a man teacheth his son,
so the Lord thy God hath taught thee,)
6 that thou keep the commandments of thy Lord God,
and go in his ways, and dread him. (and that thou obey
the commandments of the Lord thy God, and go in his
ways, and fear him/and revere him.)
7 For thy Lord God shall lead thee into a good land,
into the land of rivers, and of *standing* waters, and of
wells, in whose fields and mountains the depths of floods
break out; (For the Lord thy God shall lead thee into a
good land, a land of rivers, and ponds, and springs, and
underground streams, gushing forth onto its fields and
mountains;)
8 into the land of wheat, of barley, and of vines, in
which land fig trees, and pomegranates, and olives come
forth; into the land of oil, and honey;
9 where thou shalt eat thy bread without neediness,
and thou shalt use the plenty of all things; of which land
the stones be iron, and metals of tin be digged (out) of the
hills thereof; (where thou shalt eat thy bread without any
neediness, *or want*, and thou shalt make use of the plenty
of all things; in which land the stones be made out of
iron, and brass can be dug out of its hills;)
10 that when thou hast eaten, and art full-filled, thou
bless thy Lord God for the best land which he hath given
to thee. (so that when thou hast eaten, and art filled full,
thou shalt bless the Lord thy God for this best land which
he hath given thee.)
11 Therefore keep thou, and beware, lest any time thou
forget thy Lord God, and despise his commandments,
and dooms, and ceremonies, which I command to thee
today; (And so remember thou, and be careful, lest any
time thou forget the Lord thy God, and fail to obey his
commandments, and laws, *or judgements*, and statutes,
which I command to thee today;)
12 lest after that thou hast eaten, and art full-filled (and
art filled full), (and) hast builded fair houses, and hast
dwelled in them,
13 and hast droves of oxen (and hast herds of oxen),
and flocks of sheep, and plenty of silver, and of gold, and
of all things,
14 thine heart be *then* raised, and thou think not upon
thy Lord God, that led thee out of the land of Egypt, and
from the house of servage, (*then* thy heart be raised up,
and thou forget the Lord thy God, who led thee out of the
land of Egypt, and from the house of servitude, *or of
slavery*,)
15 and he was thy leader in the great wilderness and

fearful, in which wilderness was a serpent burning with
blast, and a scorpion, and (a) dipsas, *that is, an adder,
that maketh them whom he stingeth to die for thirst*, and
utterly no waters *were in the desert*, the which Lord
brought out streams of the hardest stone, (for he was thy
leader in the great and fearful wilderness, in which
wilderness there were poisonous serpents, and scorpions,
and dipsas, *that is, snakes that make those that they sting
to die from thirst*, and when there *was* utterly no water *in
that wilderness*, the Lord brought forth streams out of the
hardest stone,)
16 and he fed thee with manna (there) in the wilderness,
which *manna* thy fathers knew not. And after that the
Lord had tormented thee, and proved thee, at the last he
had mercy on thee (And after that the Lord had humbled
thee, and had tested thee, finally he had mercy on thee),
17 lest thou wouldest say in thine heart, My strength,
and the might of mine hand, hath given all these things to
me. (lest thou shouldest say in thy heart, My own
strength, and the might of my own hand, hath given me
all these things.)
18 But think thou upon thy Lord God, that he hath
given strengths to thee (to become prosperous), that he
should fulfill his covenant, of which he swore to thy
fathers, as this present day showeth. (But rather,
remember the Lord thy God, that it is he who hath given
thee the power to become prosperous, in order to fulfill
his covenant which he swore to thy fathers, as he doeth
in this present day.)
19 Forsooth if thou forgettest thy Lord God, and
followest alien gods, and worshippest them in (thine)
heart, and honourest [them] *withoutforth*, lo! now I
before-say to thee, that thou shalt perish utterly; (But if
thou forgettest the Lord thy God, and followest foreign,
or other, gods, and worshippest them *inwardly*, and
honourest them *outwardly*, lo! I now say to thee
beforehand, *that is, I warn thee*, that thou shalt utterly
perish;)
20 as [the] heathen men *perished*, which the Lord did
away in thine entering, so also ye shall perish, if ye shall
be unobedient to the voice of your Lord God. (as the
heathen *shall perish*, whom the Lord shall do away when
thou shalt enter *into the land*, so also ye shall perish, if ye
do not obey the voice of the Lord your God.)

CHAPTER 9

1 Hear thou, Israel; thou shalt pass (the) Jordan today,
that thou wield the most nations, and stronger than thou;
great cities, and walled till to heaven; (Hear, O Israel;
thou shalt cross over the Jordan River today, to take over
nations greater and stronger than thou; yea, great cities,
that be walled unto the heavens;)
2 a great people, and high; the sons of Anakim, which
thyself hast seen, and heard, which no man may against-stand in the contrary part. (a great and tall people; the
sons of the Anakim, *that is, the giants*, whom thou hast
seen, and heard, and whom no one can stand against.)
3 Therefore thou shalt know today that thy Lord God
himself shall pass before thee; *he is* a fire devouring and
wasting, that shall all-break them, and he shall do them
away, and destroy *them* before thy face swiftly, as he
spake to thee. (And so know thou today that the Lord thy
God himself shall go ahead of thee; *he is* a devouring and
wasting fire, and he shall all-break them before thy face,
and then ye shall do them away, and swiftly destroy
them, as he promised thee.)
4 Say thou not in thine heart, when thy Lord God hath
done them away in thy sight, For my rightwiseness the
Lord hath brought me in *hither*, that I should wield the
land; since these nations be done away for their
wickednesses. (But when the Lord thy God hath done
them away before thee, do not thou say in thy heart,
Because of my righteousness, the Lord hath brought me
here, so that I could take this land; since these nations
shall be done away because of their own wickednesses.)
5 For not for thy rightwiseness, and for the equity of
thine heart thou shalt enter, that thou wield their land;
but for they did wickedly, they were done away (by thy
Lord God), when thou enteredest, and that the Lord
should [ful]fill his word which he promised under an oath
to thy fathers, to Abraham, Isaac, and Jacob. (For it is not
because of thy own righteousness, or the integrity of thy
own heart, that thou shalt enter to take their land; but
they shall be done away before thee by the Lord thy God,
because they did wickedly, and so that the Lord would
fulfill his word which he promised under an oath to thy
fathers, to Abraham, Isaac, and Jacob.)
6 Therefore know thou that not for thy rightwisenesses
thy Lord God hath given to thee this best land into
possession, since thou art a people of most hard noll.
(And so know thou that the Lord thy God hath not given
thee this best land for a possession because of thy own
righteousness, since thou art a most stubborn, *or a stiff-necked*, people.)
7 Have thou (in) mind, and forget not (Remember, and
do not forget), how in the wilderness thou stirredest thy
Lord God to great wrath; (and) from that day in which
thou wentest out of Egypt till to this place, thou hast
striven ever[more] against the Lord.
8 For why also in Horeb, thou stirredest him (to wrath),
and he was wroth, and would have done thee away,
(Yea, also at Mount Sinai, thou stirredest him to anger,
and he was so angry that he would have done thee away;)
9 and when I went up into the hill, that I should take
(the) two tables of stone, the tables of (the) covenant
which the Lord made with you, and I abode in the hill
forty days and forty nights, and I ate not bread, and I
drank not water. (and when I went up the mountain, so

that I could receive the two stone tablets, the tablets of
the covenant which the Lord made with you, I stayed on
the mountain for forty days and forty nights, and I ate no
bread, and I drank no water.)
10 And the Lord gave to me two tables of stone, ever
either written with God's finger, and containing all the
words which he spake to you in the hill, from the midst
of the fire, when the company of people was gathered
together. (And the Lord gave me the two stone tablets,
each written with the finger of God, and containing all
the words which he spoke to you from the midst of the
fire, when the congregation of the people was gathered
together there at the mountain.)
11 And when forty days and so many nights had
passed, the Lord gave to me (the) two tables of stone,
(the) tables of the bond of peace; (And so when forty days
and as many nights had passed, the Lord gave me the two
stone tablets, the tablets of the covenant;)
12 and he said to me, Rise thou, and go down from
hence soon, for thy people, that thou hast led out of
Egypt, have forsaken swiftly the way that thou showedest
to them, and they have made to them[selves] a molten
calf. (and he said to me, Rise thou up, and quickly go
down from here, for thy people, whom thou hast led out
of Egypt, have already forsaken the way that thou hast
shown them, and they have cast *an idol* for themselves,
yea, a metal calf.)
13 And again the Lord said to me, I see that this people
is of an hard noll; (And again the Lord said to me, I see
that this people be stubborn/be stiff-necked;)
14 suffer thou me, that I all-break him, and do away his
name from under heaven; and I shall ordain thee on a
folk which is greater and stronger than this folk. (allow
me to all-break them, and do away their name from
under heaven; and then I shall ordain thee upon a nation
which shall be greater and stronger than this nation.)
15 And when I came down from the hill burning, and I
held with either hand the two tables of the bond of peace,
(And when I came down from the burning mountain, and
I held in my hands the two tablets of the covenant,)
16 and I saw, that ye had sinned to your Lord God, and
had made to you a molten calf, and that ye had forsaken
swiftly the way of God that he had showed to you, (and I
saw that ye had sinned against the Lord your God, and
had cast *an idol*, yea, a metal calf, for yourselves, and
that ye had already forsaken the way of God that he had
shown you,)
17 then I threw down the tables from mine hands, and I
brake those tables in your sight. (then I threw down the
tablets from my hands, and I broke those tablets in front
of you.)
18 And I felled down before the Lord as before, in forty
days and forty nights, and I ate not bread, and drank not
water, for all your sins which ye did against the Lord, and
stirred him to great wrath; (And I fell down before the
Lord as I did before, for forty days and forty nights, and I
ate no bread, and drank no water, for all your sins which
ye did against the Lord, and so had stirred him to such
great anger;)
19 for I dreaded the indignation and the wrath of *the
Lord*, by which he was stirred against you, and would do
you away. And the Lord heard me also in this time
praying for you (But once again the Lord listened to me
praying for you).
20 Also the Lord was wroth greatly against Aaron, and
would have all-broken him, and I prayed in like manner
for him. (And the Lord was also greatly angered with
Aaron, and would have killed him, and I prayed for him
in like manner.)
21 Forsooth I took your sin which ye made, that is, the
calf, and burnt *it* in fire, and I all-brake *it* into gobbets,
and drove (it) utterly into dust, and I cast it forth into *the*
strand, that came down from the hill. (And I took that
sinful thing which ye had made, that is, *the idol of* the
calf, and I burned *it* with fire, and I broke it all up into
pieces, and drove it down utterly into dust, and then I
threw it forth into *the* river that came down from the
mountain.)
22 Also in the burning, and in the temptation *at the
waters of against-saying*, and in the Sepulchres of
Covetousness, ye stirred the Lord (to wrath); (And ye also
stirred the Lord to anger at Taberah, and at Massah, and
at Kibrothhattaavah;)
23 and when I sent you from Kadeshbarnea, and said,
Go ye up, and wield ye the land which I have given to
you, and ye despised the commandment of your Lord
God, and ye believed not to him, neither ye would hear
his voice; (and again when the Lord sent you out from
Kadeshbarnea, saying, Go ye up, and take ye the land
which I have given you, and ye disobeyed the command
of the Lord your God, and ye did not trust him, nor
would ye listen to his voice;)
24 but ever[more] ye were rebel, from the day in which
I began to know you. (but ye were always rebellious
against the Lord, yea, from the day in which I first began
to know you.)
25 And I lay before the Lord forty days and forty nights,
in which I besought him meekly, that he should not do
away you, as he menaced. (And so for forty days and
forty nights I lay before the Lord, in which time I meekly
besought him not to destroy you, as he had threatened.)
26 And I prayed *him*, and said, Lord God, destroy not
thy people, and thine heritage, which thou again-
boughtest in thy greatness, which thou leddest out of
Egypt in (a) strong hand. (And I prayed to *him*, and said,
Lord God, do not destroy thy people, and thy
inheritance, whom thou hast bought back, *or hast
redeemed, or ransomed*, by thy great power, and whom

thou hast led out of Egypt with thy strong hand.)
27 Have thou mind of thy servants, of Abraham, Isaac,
and Jacob; behold thou not the hardness of this people,
and the wickedness, and the sin *thereof,* (Remember thy
servants, Abraham, Isaac, and Jacob; do not thou look
upon the stubbornness of this people, and their
wickedness, and their sin,)
28 lest peradventure the dwellers of the land, out of
which thou leddest us, say, The Lord might not bring
them into the land which he promised to them, and he
hated them; therefore he led them out that he should slay
them in (the) wilderness; (lest the inhabitants of the land,
out of which thou hast led us, shall say, The Lord could
not bring them into the land that he promised them, and
because he hated them, he hath led them out so that he
could kill them in the wilderness;)
29 and *Lord,* they be thy people, and thine heritage,
which thou leddest out in thy great strength, and in thine
arm stretched forth. (but *Lord,* they be thy people, and
thy inheritance, whom thou hast led out with thy great
strength, and thy outstretched arm.)

CHAPTER 10

1 In that time the Lord said to me, Hew thou two
tables of stone to thee, as the former were; and go thou
up to me into the hill. And thou shalt (also) make an ark,
either a coffer, of wood, (And at that time the Lord said to
me, Cut thou two stone tablets, like the first ones; and
then come thou up to me on the mountain. And thou
shalt also make an Ark, *or a Box,* out of wood,)
2 and I shall write in the tables, the words that were in
these tables which thou brakest before; and thou shalt put
those tables into the ark. (and I shall write on these
tablets the words that were on the first tablets which thou
hast broken; and thou shalt put these tablets into the Ark,
or the Box.)
3 Therefore I made an ark of the wood of shittim, and
when I had hewn the two tables of stone, at the likeness
of the former tables, I went up into the hill, and I had the
tables in *mine* hands. (And so I made the Ark out of
shittim wood, *or acacia wood,* and when I had cut the
two stone tablets, like the first tablets, I went up the
mountain, with the *tablets* in *my* hands.)
4 And he wrote in the tables, by that that he had
written before, the ten words, which the Lord spake to
you in the hill, from the midst of the fire, when the
people was gathered, and the Lord gave the *tables* to me.
(And he wrote on the tablets, what he had written before,
the Ten Words, *that is, the Ten Commandments,* which
the Lord spoke to you on the mountain, from the midst of
the fire, when the people was gathered there, and then
the Lord gave those *tablets* to me.)
5 And I turned again from the hill, and came down,
and I put the tables into the ark that I had made, which
tables be there hitherto, as the Lord commanded to me.
(And I turned, and came down from the mountain, and I
put the tablets into the Ark that I had made, as the Lord
commanded to me, and they still be there to this day.)
6 And the sons of Israel moved *their* tents from
Beeroth of the sons of Jaakan into Mosera, where Aaron
was dead, and buried, (and) for whom his son Eleazar
was set in priesthood. (And the Israelites moved *their*
tents from Beeroth of the sons of Jaakan to Mosera, where
Aaron died, and was buried, and his son Eleazar took his
place in the priesthood.)
7 From thence they came into Gudgodah; from which
place they went forth, and setted tents in Jotbathah, in the
land of waters and of strands. (And from Mosera, they
came to Gudgodah; and from Gudgodah they went forth,
and pitched their tents at Jotbathah, a land of many rivers.)
8 In that time I separated the lineage of Levi, that it
should bear the ark of the bond of peace of the Lord, and
it should stand before him in service, and should bless in
his name, into this present day. (At that time the Lord set
apart the tribe of Levi to carry the Ark of the Covenant of
the Lord, and to stand before him in service, *that is, to
minister to him,* and to bless in his name, *which they
continue to do* unto this present day.)
9 For which thing Levi had no part, neither possession
with his brethren, for the Lord himself is his possession,
as thy Lord God promised to him. (That is why the
Levites have no part, nor possession, with their brothers,
for the Lord himself is their possession, as the Lord thy
God promised them.)
10 And I stood in the hill as *I did* before, forty days and
forty nights, and the Lord heard me also in this time, and
he would not lose thee. (And I stayed on the mountain
like *I did* before, for forty days and forty nights, and once
again the Lord listened to me, and he consented not to
destroy thee.)
11 And he said to me, Go thou, and go before this
people, that it enter, and wield the land which I swore to
their fathers, that I should give to them. (And he said to
me, Go thou, and lead this people, so that they enter
now, and take the land which I swore to their fathers, that
I would give them.)
12 And now, Israel, what asketh thy Lord God of thee,
but that thou dread thy Lord, and go in his ways, and that
thou love him, and serve thy Lord God in all thine heart,
and in all thy soul (and that thou love him, and serve the
Lord thy God with all thy heart, and with all thy soul);
13 and that thou keep the commandments of thy Lord
God, and the ceremonies of him, which I command to
thee today, that it be well to thee. (and that thou obey the
commandments of the Lord thy God, and his statutes,
which I command to thee today, so that it be well with
thee.)
14 Lo! heaven is of thy Lord God, and heaven of

heaven; the earth and all things that be therein *be his*;
(Lo! all of heaven is the Lord thy God's, yea, the Heaven
of Heavens, *that is, the Highest Heaven*; and the earth,
and all the things that be in it, also *be his*;)
15 and nevertheless the Lord was joined (*by fervent*
affection) to thy fathers, and he loved them, and he chose
their seed after them, and you of all folks, as it is proved
today. (yet nevertheless the Lord was joined *by fervent*
affection to thy fathers, and he loved them, and he chose
their descendants after them, that is, you, out of all the
nations, as ye be this day.)
16 Therefore circumcise ye the prepuce, *that is, the*
uncleanness, of your heart, and no more make ye hard
your noll (and no more be ye stubborn, *or stiff-necked*).
17 For your Lord God himself is God of gods, and Lord
of lords, a great God, and mighty, and fearful, which
taketh not a person, neither gifts, *but justly he deemeth*
rich and poor. (For the Lord your God himself is God of
gods, and Lord of lords, the great God, and mighty, and
fearful, who respecteth not a person's rank, *or status*, nor
accepteth any gift, *or bribe*, *but justly judgeth the rich*
and the poor.)
18 He maketh doom to the fatherless, and motherless,
and to the widow; he loveth a pilgrim, and giveth to him
lifelode and clothing. (He getteth justice for the fatherless
or the motherless child, and the widow; he loveth the
foreigner, *or the stranger*, and giveth him sustenance and
clothing.)
19 And therefore love ye pilgrims, for also ye were
comelings in the land of Egypt. (And so love ye
foreigners, *or strangers*, for ye were also newcomers in
the land of Egypt.)
20 Thou shalt dread thy Lord God, and thou shalt serve
him alone, and thou shalt cleave to him, and thou shalt
swear in his name. (Thou shalt fear the Lord thy
God/Thou shalt revere the Lord thy God, and thou shalt
serve him alone, and thou shalt cleave to him, and thou
shalt swear by his name.)
21 He is thy praising, and thy God, that made to thee
these great works, and fearful, which thine eyes have
seen. (He is thy praise, and thy God, who did for thee
these great and fearful things, which thine eyes have
seen.)
22 In seventy men thy fathers went down into Egypt,
and lo! now thy Lord God hath multiplied thee as the
stars of heaven. (For only seventy men of thy fathers went
down to Egypt, but lo! now the Lord thy God hath made
thee as innumerable as the stars in the heavens.)

CHAPTER 11

1 Therefore love thy Lord God, and keep thou his
commandments, and ceremonies, and dooms, and his
behests, in all time. (And so love the Lord thy God, and
obey thou his commandments, and statutes, and laws, *or*
judgements, and his orders, *or his charges*, for all time.)
2 Know ye today those things which your sons know
not, *which* sons have not seen the doctrine, (*or*
discipline,) of your Lord God, *nor* his great works, and
his strong hand, and his stretched (out) arm, (Know ye
today those things which your children know not, for
they have not seen the discipline of the Lord your God,
nor his greatness, and his strong hand, and his
outstretched arm,)
3 his miracles, and his works, which he did in the
midst of Egypt, to Pharaoh, [the] king, and to all his land,
4 and to all the host of the Egyptians, and to their
horses, and cars; how the waters of the Red Sea covered
them, when they pursued you, and the Lord did away
them till into present day; (and to all the army of the
Egyptians, and to their horses, and chariots; how the
waters of the Red Sea covered them, when they pursued
you, and the Lord did them away, and so things remain
unto this present day;)
5 and which things the Lord did to you in (the)
wilderness, till ye came to this place; (and what the Lord
did for you in the wilderness, until ye came to this place;)
6 and to Dathan and Abiram, the sons of Eliab, that
was the son of Reuben, which the earth swallowed,
when his mouth was opened, with their house(hold)s,
and tabernacles, and all the chattel that they had, in the
midst of Israel. (and to Dathan and Abiram, the sons of
Eliab, who was Reuben's son, who, when the earth
opened its mouth, were swallowed up with their families,
and their tents, and all their substance, in the midst of all
Israel.)
7 Your eyes saw all the great works of the Lord, which
he did,
8 that ye keep all his behests which I command today
to you, and that ye may enter, and wield the land, (and
so obey ye all his commandments which I command to
you today, so that ye can enter, and take the land,)
9 to which ye shall enter, and ye live therein much
time; which land, flowing with milk and honey, the Lord
promised under an oath to your fathers and their seed. (to
which ye shall enter; and so that ye can live a long time
in the land, which the Lord promised by an oath to your
fathers and their descendants, yea, a land flowing with
milk and honey.)
10 For the land, to which thou shalt enter to wield, is
not as the land of Egypt, out of which thou wentest,
where when the seed is sown in the manner of gardens,
moist waters be led *thereto* (where when the seed is
sown, water must be brought *to it*, like in a garden);
11 but *the land that Israel shall wield* is hills, and
fields, and it abideth rains from heaven, (but *the land*
which Israel shall possess is a land of mountains, and
valleys, and it receiveth rain from the heavens,)
12 which land thy Lord God beholdeth, and his eyes be

therein (and his eyes be upon it), from the beginning of
the year unto the end thereof.
13 Therefore if ye shall obey to my behests which I
command today to you, that ye love your Lord God, and
serve him in all your heart, and in all your soul; (And so
if ye will obey my commandments which I command to
you today, that ye love the Lord your God, and serve him
with all your heart, and with all your soul;)
14 he shall give to your land rain timely and late, that
ye gather wheat, and wine, and oil, (he shall give rain on
your land, timely and late, so that ye can gather corn, and
wine, and oil,)
15 (and) hay of the fields to feed beasts, that ye both eat
and be full-filled. (and hay from the fields to feed your
beasts, so that ye shall eat and be filled full.)
16 Be ye ware, lest peradventure your heart be
deceived, and ye go away from the Lord, and serve alien
gods, and worship them; (Be ye careful, lest your heart be
deceived, and ye go away from the Lord, and serve
foreign, *or other*, gods, and worship them;)
17 and the Lord *therefore* be wroth, and close heaven,
and rain come not down, neither the earth give his fruit,
and ye perish swiftly from the full good land that the Lord
shall give to you. (and *so* the Lord be angry, and close up
the heavens, and the rain come not down, nor the earth
give its fruit, and ye swiftly perish from the very good
land which the Lord shall give you.)
18 Put ye these my words in your hearts and in your
souls, and hang ye them up for a token, *or a sign*, in your
hands, and set ye them betwixt your eyes. (Put ye these
my words in your hearts and in your souls, and bind ye
them for a sign upon your hands, and set ye them before
your eyes forevermore.)
19 Teach ye your sons, (so) that they think upon those
words, when thou sittest in thine house, and goest in the
way (and goest on the way), and liest down, and risest up.
20 Thou shalt write those *words* upon the (door-)posts,
and the gates of thine house(s),
21 that the days of thee and of thy sons be multiplied in
the land which the Lord swore to thy fathers, that he
should give to them, as long as heaven is above (the)
earth. (so that the days of thee and of thy sons, can be
multiplied in the land which the Lord swore to thy fathers
to give them, for as long as the heavens be above the
earth.)
22 For if ye keep the behests which I command to you,
and do those (For if ye obey all these commandments
which I command to you, and do them), that ye love
your Lord God, and go in all his ways, and cleave to him,
23 the Lord shall destroy all these heathen men before
your face, and ye shall wield those folks that be greater
and stronger than ye.
24 Each place which your foot shall tread, shall be
yours; from the desert, and from Lebanon, and from the
great flood Euphrates unto the west sea, shall be your
terms. (Every place where your feet shall tread, shall be
yours; from the wilderness to the mountains of Lebanon,
and from the great Euphrates River unto the Great Sea, *or
the Mediterranean Sea*, shall be yours.)
25 None shall stand against you; your Lord God shall
give your outward dread and *your* inward dread upon
each land that ye shall tread, as he spake to you. (No one
shall stand against you; the Lord your God shall put the
fear of you and the dread of you upon every land where
ye shall tread, as he promised you.)
26 Lo! I set forth in your sight today blessing and
cursing; (Lo! I set before you today the choice of a
blessing and a curse;)
27 blessing, if ye obey to the behests of your Lord God,
which I command to you today; (a blessing, if ye obey
the commandments of the Lord your God, which I
command to you today;)
28 cursing, if ye hear not the behests of your Lord God,
but go away from the way which I show now to you, and
go after alien gods, which ye know not. (and a curse, if
ye hear not the commandments of the Lord your God,
and ye go away from the way which I now show to you,
and follow foreign, *or other*, gods, which ye do not know.)
29 Soothly when thy Lord God hath brought thee into
the land, to which to inhabit thou goest, thou shalt set
(the) blessing upon the hill Gerizim, (and the) cursing
upon the hill Ebal, (And when the Lord thy God hath
brought thee into the land, to which thou goest to
inhabit, thou shalt proclaim the blessing from Mount
Gerizim, and the curse from Mount Ebal,)
30 which *hills* be beyond (the) Jordan, after the way
that goeth to the going down of the sun, in the land of
Canaanites, that dwell in the field places against Gilgal,
which is beside the valley going and entering far. (which
mountains be on the western side of the Jordan River, on
the way that leadeth to the going down of the sun, in the
land of the Canaanites, who live on the plains near
Gilgal, which is close to the sacred trees of Moreh.)
31 For ye shall pass (the) Jordan, that ye wield the land
which your Lord God shall give to you, and that ye have
and wield that land. (For ye shall cross over the Jordan
River to possess the land which the Lord your God shall
give to you, and ye shall take that land and have it.)
32 Therefore see ye, that ye fulfill the ceremonies and
dooms, which I shall set today in your sight. (And so see
ye, that ye fulfill the statutes and laws, *or judgements*,
which I shall set before you today.)

CHAPTER 12

1 These be the behests and dooms (These be the
statutes and laws, *or judgements*), which ye ought to do,
in the land which the Lord God of thy fathers shall give
to thee, that thou wield it, in all (the) days in which thou

shalt go upon [the] earth.
2 Destroy ye all the places wherein [the] heathen men
which ye shall wield, worshipped their gods, on high
mountains, and little hills, and under each tree full of
boughs.
3 Destroy ye their altars, and break their images; and
burn ye the (sacred) woods with fire, and all-break ye the
idols; destroy ye their names from (all) the places.
4 Ye shall not do so to your Lord God; (Ye shall not
worship the Lord your God in those ways;)
5 but ye shall come to the (one) place which your
Lord God (shall) choose (out) of all your lineages, that he
put his name there, and dwell therein;
6 and ye shall come *thither*, and offer in that place
your burnt sacrifices, and slain sacrifices, the tithes, and
first fruits of your hands, and avows, and gifts, and the
first engendered things of your oxen, and of (your) sheep.
(and ye shall come *there*, and offer in that place your
burnt sacrifices, and slain sacrifices, your tithes, and the
first fruits of your hands, and your vows, and gifts, and
the first-born *males* of your oxen, and of your sheep.)
7 And ye and your houses shall eat there in the sight
of your Lord God; and ye shall be glad in all things to
which ye put the hand, in which your Lord God hath
blessed you. (And ye and your households, *or your
families*, shall eat there before the Lord your God; and ye
shall be glad in all the things to which ye put your hands,
because the Lord your God hath blessed you.)
8 Ye shall not do there those things which we do here
today, each man that that seemeth rightful to himself.
9 For unto the time that is now, ye came not to (the)
rest, and to [the] possession, which the Lord God shall
give to you.
10 Ye shall pass (the) Jordan (Ye shall cross over the
Jordan River), and ye shall dwell in the land which your
Lord God shall give to you, that ye rest from all (your)
enemies about, and that ye dwell without any dread.
11 In the place which your Lord God (shall) choose that
his name be therein. Thither ye shall bear all things, which
I command *to you*, burnt sacrifices, and sacrifices, and
the tithes, and the first fruits of your hands, and whatever
is the best thing in gifts, which ye avow to the Lord.
12 There ye shall eat before your Lord God, ye, and
your sons, and daughters, your menservants, and
womenservants, and the deacons, that dwell in your
cities; for they have none other part and possession
among you. (And ye shall eat there before the Lord your
God, ye, and your sons, and your daughters, your slaves,
and your slave-girls, and the Levites who live in your
cities, because the Levites have no other portion or
possession among you.)
13 Be thou ware lest thou offer thy burnt sacrifices in
each place that thou seest, (Be thou careful, lest thou
offer thy burnt sacrifices in any place that thou seest,)
14 but in that place which the Lord [shall] choose in
one of thy lineages, thou shalt offer sacrifices, and thou
shalt do whatever things I command to thee. (but rather,
only at that place which the Lord shall choose in one of
thy tribes, shalt thou offer thy sacrifices, and thou shalt do
whatever I command thee.)
15 For if thou wilt eat, and the eating of flesh delighteth
thee, slay thou, and eat, by the blessing of thy Lord God,
that he hath given to thee in thy cities, whether it is
unclean, *that is, spotted, either wemmed*, and feeble,
either clean, and without wem, *that is, whole in each
member*, (that) which is leaveful to be offered, thou shalt
eat *those*, as (of) a capret, and an hart; (But if thou art
hungry, and the eating of flesh delighteth thee, kill thou,
and eat, whatever he hath given thee, wherever thou may
live, with the blessing of the Lord thy God; yea, whether
ye be clean, or unclean, ye can eat it, as you would eat
the meat of a gazelle, or a deer;)
16 only without eating of [the] blood, which thou shalt
shed out as water upon the earth. (but thou shalt not eat
the blood; thou shalt pour it out like water onto the
ground.)
17 Thou shalt not be able to eat in thy cities the tithes
of thy wheat, (of) thy wine, and of thine oil, nor the first
engendered things of thy droves, and of thy sheep, and
all things which thou hast avowed, and wilt offer by free
will, and the first fruits of thine hands; (Thou shalt not eat
in thy cities the tithes of thy corn, or thy wine, or thy oil,
or the first-born of thy herds, or of thy sheep, or anything
which thou hast vowed, or wilt offer by free will, or the
first fruits of thy hands;)
18 but thou shalt eat those things before thy Lord God,
in the place which thy Lord God choose, thou, and thy
son, and thy daughter, thy manservant, and thy
womanservant, and the deacon that dwelleth in thy cities
(but thou shalt eat those things before the Lord thy God,
in the place which the Lord thy God shall choose, thou,
and thy son, and thy daughter, thy slave, and thy slave-
girl, and the Levite who liveth in thy cities); and thou
shalt be glad, and thou shalt be fulfilled before thy Lord
God in all (the) things to which thou holdest forth thine
hand (to do).
19 Be thou ware lest thou forsake the deacon in all
time, in which thou livest in (the) earth. (Be thou careful,
lest thou forget the Levite at any time in which thou livest
on the earth.)
20 When thy Lord God hath alarged thy terms, as he
spake to thee (When the Lord thy God hath enlarged thy
borders, as he hath promised thee), and thou wilt eat
(some) flesh, which thy soul desireth,
21 forsooth if the place is far, which thy Lord God
choose, that his name be there, thou shalt slay of thine
oxen, and sheep, which thou hast, as the Lord
commanded to thee; and thou shalt eat in thy cities as it

pleaseth thee. (but if the place is too far from thee, which
the Lord thy God shall choose, that his name be there,
thou shalt kill some of thy oxen, or of thy sheep, which
thou hast, as the Lord commanded thee; and thou shalt
eat *it* in thy cities as it pleaseth thee.)
22 As (the meat of) a capret and an hart is eaten, so
thou shalt eat those; both a clean man and an unclean
(man) shall eat *thereof* in common. (Thou shalt eat it, like
thou would the meat of a gazelle, or a deer; both a clean
person and an unclean person shall eat *it* in common.)
23 Only eschew thou this, that thou eat not (the) blood;
for the blood *of those beasts* is for the life, and therefore
thou oughtest not eat the life with fleshes (and so thou
ought not to eat the life with the flesh, *or with the meat*),
24 but thou shalt pour *it* out as water upon the earth,
(but thou shalt pour *it* out like water onto the ground,)
25 that it be well to thee, and to thy sons after thee (that
it be well with thee, and with thy children after thee),
when thou hast done that, that pleaseth in the sight of the
Lord.
26 Soothly thou shalt take that that thou hast avowed,
and hallowed to the Lord, and thou shalt come to the
place which the Lord choose; (And thou shalt take what
thou hast vowed, and dedicated to the Lord, and thou
shalt come to the place which the Lord shall choose;)
27 and thou shalt offer there thine offerings, and flesh,
and blood, upon the altar of thy Lord God; thou shalt
pour (out) in the altar the blood of the sacrifices; but thou
shalt eat the flesh. (for thy burnt sacrifice, thou shalt offer
both the flesh, and the blood, on the altar of the Lord thy
God; and for thy peace offering, thou shalt pour the blood
of the offering on the altar, but thou shalt eat its flesh.)
28 Keep thou and hear all things which I command to
thee, that it be well to thee, and to thy sons after thee,
[into] without end, when thou hast done that, that is good
and pleasing in the sight of thy Lord God. (Hear thou and
obey all the things which I command to thee, so that it be
well with thee, and with thy children, forevermore, when
thou hast done what is good and pleasing in the sight of
the Lord thy God.)
29 When thy Lord God hath destroyed before thy face
[the] folks, to which thou shalt enter and wield (When the
Lord thy God hath destroyed the nations before thy face,
to whom thou shalt enter in to take), and *when* thou hast
wielded those folks, and hast dwelled in their land,
30 be thou ware lest thou follow them, after that they
be destroyed, when thou enterest, and thou seek their
ceremonies, and say, As these folks worshipped their
gods, so and I shall worship. (be thou careful, after that
thou hast entered, and they be destroyed, lest thou follow
them; do not thou seek out their ceremonies, saying, As
these nations worshipped their gods, so we shall worship
our God.)
31 Thou shalt not do in like manner to thy Lord God
(Thou shalt not worship the Lord thy God in like
manner); for they did (un)to their gods all the
abominations which the Lord loatheth, and they offered
(up) their sons and their daughters, and they burnt them
with fire.
32 Do thou to the Lord this thing only which I
command to thee, neither add thou anything, neither
abate. (Do thou to the Lord only the things which I
command to thee, neither add thou anything, nor abate
thou anything.)

CHAPTER 13

1 If a prophet riseth in the midst of thee, either he that
saith himself to have seen a dream, and he before-saith a
sign, and a wonder to come after, (When a prophet riseth
up in the midst of thee, or him who saith that he hath
seen a dream, and he speaketh of a sign, or a wonder,
before that it cometh,)
2 and this thing that he said befalleth, and he saith to
thee, Go we, and follow we alien gods, which thou
knowest not, and serve we them, (and what he said
befalleth, and then he saith to thee, Now let us go, and
follow foreign, *or other*, gods, which thou knowest not,
and let us serve them,)
3 thou shalt not hear the words of that prophet, either
of that dreamer; for your Lord God assayeth you, that he
know openly whether ye love him, either nay, in all your
heart, and in all your soul. (thou shalt not listen to the
words of that prophet, or of that dreamer; for the Lord
your God trieth, *or testeth*, you, to clearly know whether
ye love him, or not, with all your heart, and with all your
soul.)
4 Follow ye your Lord God, and dread ye him; keep
ye his commandments, and hear ye his voice; ye shall
serve him, and ye shall cleave to him. (Follow ye the
Lord your God, and fear ye him; obey ye his
commandments, and listen ye to his voice; ye shall serve
him, and ye shall cleave to him.)
5 And that prophet, either (that) feigner of dreams,
shall be slain; for he spake (so) that he should turn you
away from your Lord God, that led you out of the land of
Egypt, and again-bought you from the house of servage
(and bought you back, *or redeemed, or ransomed, you*,
from the house of servitude, *or of slavery*), (so) that he
make thee to err from the way that thy Lord God
commanded to thee; and *in (the) killing of him* thou shalt
do away evil from the midst of thee.
6 If thy brother, the son of thy mother, either thy son,
either thy daughter, either the wife which is in thy
bosom, either thy friend, whom thou lovest as thy (own)
soul, will counsel thee, and saith privily, Go we and
serve alien gods, which thou knowest not, and thy fathers
know not (will counsel thee, and saith privately, Let us
go, and serve foreign, *or other*, gods, which thou

knowest not, nor thy fathers *knew*),
7 (the gods) of all the folks about, that be nigh either
far, from the beginning unto the end of the land,
8 assent thou not to him, neither hear thou him,
neither thine eye spare him, that thou have mercy *of him*,
and hide him, (assent thou not to him, nor listen thou to
him, nor thine eye spare him, so that thou have mercy *on*
him, or that thou hide him,)
9 but anon thou shalt slay him. Thine hand be first
upon him, and after thee, all the people put to (the) hand.
(but at once thou shalt kill him. Thy hand be the first upon
him, and after thee, the hands of all the other people.)
10 He shall be oppressed with stones, and shall be
slain; for he would draw thee away from thy Lord God,
that led thee out of the land of Egypt, from the house of
servage, (He shall be killed with stones; for he tried to
draw thee away from the Lord thy God, who led thee out
of the land of Egypt, from the house of servitude, *or of*
slavery,)
11 that all Israel hear *this* and dread, and do no more
anything like this thing. (then all Israel shall hear of this,
and be afraid, and never again do anything *evil* like this.)
12 If thou hearest any men saying in one of thy cities,
which thy Lord God shall give thee to dwell in,
13 The sons of Belial went out from the midst of thee,
and turned away the dwellers of the city, and said, Go
we, and serve alien gods, which ye knew not, (The sons
of Belial went out from thy midst, and turned away that
city's inhabitants, for they said, Let us go, and serve
foreign, *or other*, gods, which ye knew not,)
14 inquire thou busily, and when the truth of the thing
is beholden diligently, if thou findest that this thing is
certain, that is said, and that this abomination is done
indeed, (carefully inquire thou, and when the truth of the
thing is diligently seen, if thou findest that it is certain
that this was said, and that this abomination was indeed
done,)
15 anon thou shalt smite the dwellers of that city with
the sharpness of sword (at once thou shalt strike the
inhabitants of that city with the sharpness of the sword),
and thou shalt destroy that city, and all things that be
therein, unto the beasts.
16 Also whatever thing of purtenance of household is
found there, thou shalt gather it together in [the] midst of
the streets thereof, and thou shalt burn it with that city, so
that thou waste all things before thy Lord God, and it be a
burial everlasting; it shall no more be builded. (And
whatever thing of purtenance of household is *found*
there, thou shalt gather it together in the middle of its
streets, *or in the town square*, and thou shalt burn all
those things along with that city, so that thou destroy all
those things before the Lord thy God, and it shall be an
everlasting burial; *that city* shall never be rebuilt.)
17 And nothing of that cursing shall dwell in thine
hand, that the Lord be turned away from the wrath of his
strong vengeance, and have mercy upon thee, and
multiply thee, as he swore to thy fathers. (And then
nothing of what be cursed shall be found in thy hands,
and the Lord shall turn away from the anger of his strong
vengeance, and shall have mercy on thee, and shall
multiply thee, as he promised to thy fathers.)
18 When thou hast heard the voice of thy Lord God,
thou shalt keep all his behests which I command to thee
today, that thou do that thing that is pleasing in the sight
of thy Lord God. (When thou hast heard the voice of the
Lord thy God, thou shalt obey all his commandments
which I command to thee today, so that thou do what is
right before the Lord thy God.)

CHAPTER 14

1 Be ye the sons of your Lord God; ye shall not cut
you(rselves), neither ye shall make baldness (upon
yourselves), upon a dead man, (Ye be the children, *or the*
people, of the Lord your God; ye shall not cut yourselves,
nor shall ye make yourselves bald, when mourning for a
dead person,)
2 for thou art an holy people to thy Lord God, and he
chose thee that thou be to him into a special people, of
all the folks that be upon earth. (for thou art a holy
people to the Lord thy God, and he chose thee that thou
be to him a special people, out of all the nations, *or all*
the peoples, that be upon the earth.)
3 Eat ye not those things that be unclean.
4 This is a beast which ye shall eat (These be the
beasts which ye shall eat); an ox, and a sheep, and a goat,
5 an hart, a capret, a wild ox, (a) tragelaph, *that is, a*
beast in part like a goat buck, and in part like an hart, a
pygarg, an ostrich, a camelopard. (a deer, a gazelle, a
wild ox, *or a buffalo*, a tragelaph, *that is, a beast in part*
like a goat buck, and in part like a deer, an antelope, an
ostrich, and a giraffe.)
6 Ye shall eat each beast that parteth the claw into two
parts, and cheweth the cud. (Ye may eat any beast which
hath a divided hoof, *or foot*, and cheweth the cud.)
7 And ye shall not eat these *beasts*, of them that chew
the cud, and part not the claw; a camel, an hare, and a
coney; for these chew the cud, and part not the claw,
they shall be unclean to you; (But ye shall not eat those
beasts, which chew the cud, but do not have a divided
hoof, *or foot*; such as a camel, a hare, and a rock-badger;
for these chew the cud, but do not have a divided hoof,
or foot, and so they shall be unclean to you;)
8 also a swine, for it parteth the claw, and cheweth
not the cud, shall be unclean (and a pig, for it hath a
divided hoof, but it cheweth not the cud, and so it shall
be unclean); ye shall not eat the flesh of them, and ye
shall not touch *their* dead bodies.
9 Ye shall eat these things, of all that dwell in waters

(Of all the things that live in water, these ye shall eat); eat
ye those things that have fins and scales;
10 eat ye not those things that be without fins and
scales, for those be unclean.
11 Eat ye all clean birds;
12 (but) eat ye not unclean birds, that is, an eagle, and
a gripe, and an aliet,
13 an heron, and a vulture, and a kite by his kind,
14 and all thing of ravens' kind,
15 and a struthio, and a night crow, and a lari, and an
hawk by his kind,
16 a falcon, and a swan, and a ciconia,
17 and a dipper, a porphyrio, and a rearmouse, a
cormorant,
18 and a calidris, all in their kind; also a lapwing and a
bat.
19 And all thing that creepeth, and hath fins, shall be
unclean, and shall not be eaten. (And all insects that both
creep and fly, shall be unclean, and shall not be eaten.)
20 Eat ye all thing (that creepeth,) and that is clean; (But
ye can eat all clean insects.)
21 but whatever thing is dead by itself, eat ye not
thereof. Give thou (it as) *meat* to the pilgrim that is
within thy gates, that he eat (it), either sell thou (it as)
meat to him, for thou art an holy people of thy Lord God.
Thou shalt not seethe a kid in his mother's milk.
(Whatever thing that dieth a natural death, ye shall not
eat. Give thou it as *food* to the foreigner, *or the stranger*,
who is within thy gates, so that he can eat it, or sell thou
it to him for food, but thou art a holy people of the Lord
thy God, and thou shalt not eat it. And thou shalt not
boil a kid in his mother's milk.)
22 Thou shalt separate the tenth part of all thy fruits that
come forth in the land by each year; (Thou shalt set aside
the tenth part of all thy produce that cometh forth from
the land each year;)
23 and thou shalt eat (it) in the sight of thy Lord God, in
the place which he choose, that his name be called
therein; thou shalt offer the tithe of thy wheat, of wine,
and oil, and the first engendered things of thy droves, and
of thy sheep, that thou learn to dread thy Lord God in all
time. (and thou shalt eat it before the Lord thy God, in
the place which he shall choose, that his name be called
there; thou shalt offer a tenth of thy corn, and of thy
wine, and of thy oil, and the first-born *male* things of thy
herds, and of thy sheep, so that thou learn to fear the
Lord thy God/so that thou learn to revere the Lord thy
God for all time.)
24 But when the way is longer, and the place that thy
Lord God choose *is far*, and he hath blessed, *or
increased*, thee, and thou mayest not bring all these
things to that place, (But when the way is too long, and
the place that the Lord thy God shall choose *is too far
from thee*, and he hath blessed thee, but thou cannot
bring all these things to that place,)
25 thou shalt sell all *these* things, and shalt turn *them*
into price, and thou shalt bear them in thine hand, and
thou shalt go to the place which thy Lord God choose;
(then thou shalt sell all *these* things, and shalt turn *them*
into money, and thou shalt carry it in thy hand, and thou
shalt go to the place which the Lord thy God shall choose;)
26 and thou shalt buy of the same money whatever
thing pleaseth to thee, either of droves, either of sheep;
also *thou shalt buy* wine, and cider, and all things that
thy soul desireth; and thou shalt eat (it) before thy Lord
God, and thou shalt make feast, thou, and thine house,
(and thou shalt buy with that money whatever pleaseth
thee, from the herds, or the sheep; and *thou shalt buy*
wine, or cider, or anything else that thy soul desireth; and
thou shalt eat it before the Lord thy God, and thou shalt
make a feast, thou, and thy household, *or thy family*,)
27 and the deacon that is within thy gates; be thou
ware lest thou forsake him, for he hath not other part in
thy possession. (and the Levite who is within thy gates;
be thou careful, lest thou forget him, for he hath no
portion or possession among thee.)
28 In the third year thou shalt separate another tithe of
all things that grow to thee in that year, and thou shalt
keep it within thy gates. (And in the third year thou shalt
set aside a tenth of all the things that grow for thee in that
year, and thou shalt keep it within thy gates.)
29 And the deacon shall come, that hath none other
part nor possession with thee, and the pilgrim, and the
fatherless, either motherless child, and the widow, that
be within thy gates, and they shall eat, and be fulfilled,
that thy Lord God bless thee, in all the works of thine
hands which thou shalt do. (And the Levite shall come,
who hath no portion or possession among thee, and the
foreigner, *or the stranger*, and the fatherless or the
motherless child, and the widow, yea, they who be
within thy gates, and they shall eat, and be fulfilled, and
then the Lord thy God shall bless thee, in all the work of
thy hands which thou shalt do.)

CHAPTER 15

1 In the seventh year thou shalt make (a) remission, (In
the seventh year thou shalt make a forgiveness of debts,)
2 that shall be fulfilled by this order. To whom
anything is owed, of his friend, either neighbour, and
brother, he shall not be able to ask (for) *it*, for it is the
year of remission, *or forgiveness*, of the Lord. (that shall
be fulfilled in this way. To whom anything is owed, to
his friend, or his neighbour, or his brother, he shall not
be able to ask for *it*, for it is the Year of Remission, *or the
Year of Forgiveness*, of the Lord.)
3 Thou shalt ask it of a pilgrim, *that is, a stranger, or
he that is not of the faith of (the) Jews*, and of a comeling;
thou hast no power to ask (for) it of a citizen and of a

neighbour; (Thou shalt ask for it from a foreigner, *that is, from a stranger, or from he who is not of the faith of the Jews*, and a newcomer; but thou hast no power to ask for it from a citizen, or from a neighbour.)
4 and utterly a needy man and a beggar shall not be
among you, that thy Lord God bless thee, in the land which he shall give to thee into possession. (And there shall never be a needy person, or a beggar, among you, and then the Lord thy God shall bless thee, in the land which he shall give to thee for a possession,)
5 If nevertheless thou shalt hear the voice of thy Lord
God, and shalt keep all things which he commanded, and which I command today to thee, (if only thou shalt hear the voice of the Lord thy God, and shalt obey all the things which he commanded, and which I command to thee today,)
6 he shall bless thee, as he promised. Thou shalt lend
to many folks, and thou shalt not take borrowing of any man; thou shalt be lord of full many nations, and no man shall be lord of thee. (yea, then he shall bless thee, as he promised. Thou shalt lend to many nations, but thou shalt not borrow from anyone; thou shalt be lord of a great many nations, but no one shall be thy lord.)
7 If one of thy brethren that dwell within the gates of
thy city, in the land which thy Lord God shall give to thee, cometh to poverty, thou shalt not make hard thine heart, neither thou shalt withdraw thine hand (from him),
8 but thou shalt open it to the poor man, and thou
shalt lend him whatso(ever) thou seest him have need to. (but thou shalt open it to the poor, and thou shalt lend to them whatever thou seest that they have need of.)
9 Be thou ware lest peradventure [a] wicked thought
creep (in) privily to thee, and thou say in thine heart, The seventh year of remission, (*or of forgiveness,*) nigheth; and thou turn away thine eyes from thy poor brother, and thou wilt not give to him the loan that he asketh (for); lest he cry against thee to the Lord, and it be made to thee into sin (lest he cry to the Lord against thee, and thou be judged to be guilty of sin).
10 But thou shalt give to him, and thou shalt not do
anything falsely in relieving his needs, that thy Lord God bless thee in all time, and in all things to which thou shalt put to *thine* hand. (But thou shalt give to him, and thou shalt not do anything falsely when relieving his need, so that the Lord thy God shall bless thee for all time, and in all the things to which thou shalt put *thy* hand.)
11 Poor men shall not fail (to be) in the land of thy
dwelling; therefore I command to thee, that thou open thy hand to thy brother needy (and) poor, that live with thee in the land. (There shall always be poor people in the land of thy dwelling; and so I command thee, that thou open thy hands to thy brothers and sisters who be needy and poor, who live with thee in the land.)
12 When thy brother, an Hebrew man, either an
Hebrew woman, is sold to thee, and hath served thee six years, in the seventh year thou shalt deliver him free (in the seventh year thou shalt set them free).
13 And thou shalt not suffer him (to) go away *from thee*
void, to whom thou hast given freedom; (And when thou shalt set them free, thou shalt not allow them to go away empty-handed *from thee*;)
14 but thou shalt give him lifelode in the way, of thy
flocks, and of thy cornfloor, and of thy presser, in which thy Lord God hath blessed thee. (but thou shalt give them sustenance for the way, out of thy flocks, and from thy threshing floor, and thy winepress, yea, out of all in which the Lord thy God hath blessed thee.)
15 Have thou mind that also thou servedest in the land
of Egypt, and thy Lord God delivered thee, and therefore I command now (this) to thee. (Remember that thou were slaves in the land of Egypt, and the Lord thy God set thee free, and so now I command this to thee.)
16 But *if* he say, I will not go out, for he loveth thee,
and thine house(hold), and he feeleth that it is well to him with thee, (But *if thy slave* saith, I will not leave thee, for I love thee, and thy family, and he feeleth that it is good for him to be with thee,)
17 thou shalt take an awl, and thou shalt pierce (it
through) his ear in(to) the door of thine house, and (then) he shall serve thee till into the world; also thou shalt do in like manner to an handmaid (and thou shalt treat a slave-girl in the same manner).
18 Thou shalt not turn away from them thine eyes,
when thou shalt deliver them free, for by the hire of an hired man they served thee by six years; that thy Lord God bless thee, in all the works which thou doest. (Thou shalt not turn away thine eyes from them, when thou shalt set them free, for they have served thee for six years at half the cost, *or at half the wages*, of a hired servant; and then the Lord thy God shall bless thee, in all the works which thou doest.)
19 Of the first engendered things that be born in thy
droves, and in thy sheep, whatever is of male kind, thou shalt hallow to thy Lord God (Of the first-born of thy herds, and of thy sheep, whatever is male, thou shalt dedicate to the Lord thy God). Thou shalt not work with the first engendered thing of oxen, and thou shalt not shear the first engendered things of sheep.
20 Thou shalt eat those by all years in the sight of thy
Lord God, thou, and thine house, in the place which the Lord choose. (Rather, year after year, thou shalt eat them before the Lord thy God, thou, and thy household, *or thy family*, in the place which the Lord shall choose.)
21 And if it have a wem (But if it hath a blemish, *or a*
fault), either is crooked, either (is) blind, either is foul, either (is) feeble in any part, it shall not be offered to thy Lord God;
22 but thou shalt eat it within the gates of thy city, both

a clean man and an unclean (man) shall eat of those in
like manner, as of a capret, and of an hart. (but thou shalt
eat it within the gates of thy city, both a clean person and
an unclean person shall eat it, like they would a gazelle,
or a deer.)
23 Only thou shalt keep this, that thou eat not the
blood of those, but shed it out as water into the earth.
(But thou shalt not eat any of their blood, but thou shalt
pour it out like water onto the ground.)

CHAPTER 16

1 Keep thou the month of new fruits, and of the
beginning of summer, that thou make pask to thy Lord
God; for in this month thy Lord God led thee out of Egypt
in the night. (Observe thou the month of Abib, at the
beginning of summer, and keep thou the Passover to the
Lord thy God; for in this month the Lord thy God led thee
out of Egypt in the night.)
2 And thou shalt offer pask to thy Lord God, of sheep,
and of oxen, in the place which thy Lord God choose,
that his name dwell there. (And thou shalt offer the
Passover to the Lord thy God, yea, a sheep, or an ox, in
the place which the Lord thy God shall choose, that his
name shall be there.)
3 Thou shalt not eat therein bread dighted with
sourdough; in seven days thou shalt eat bread of
affliction, (that is) without sourdough, for suddenly, *either*
hastily, thou wentest out of Egypt, that thou have mind of
the day of thy going out of Egypt, in all the days of thy
life. (Thou shalt not eat it with any bread made with
yeast; yea, for seven days thou shalt eat the bread of
affliction, that is, bread made without yeast, for suddenly,
or hastily, thou wentest out of Egypt, so that thou shalt
remember the day of thy going out of Egypt, all the days
of thy life.)
4 Nothing dighted with sourdough shall appear in all
thy coasts by seven days, and of the flesh of that that is
offered in the eventide, (*that is, of the lamb of the pask*,)
shall not dwell in the first day in the morrowtide.
(Nothing made with yeast shall appear in all thy land for
seven days, and none of the flesh of what is offered in the
evening, *that is, of the Passover lamb*, shall remain past
the first day, into the next morning.)
5 Thou shalt not be able to offer pask in each of thy
cities which thy Lord God shall give to thee, (Thou shalt
not offer the Passover in all the cities which the Lord thy
God shall give thee,)
6 but in the place which thy Lord God choose, that his
name dwell there; thou shalt offer pask in the eventide, at
the going down of the sun, when thou wentest out of
Egypt. (but only in the place which the Lord thy God
shall choose, that his name shall be there; thou shalt offer
the Passover there in the evening, at the going down of
the sun, the time when thou wentest out of Egypt.)
7 And thou shalt seethe (*thy offering*), and eat (*it*), in
the place which thy Lord God hath chosen, and thou
shalt rise in the morrowtide of *the second day*, and thou
shalt go into thy tabernacles (and then thou shalt return to
thy tents).
8 Six days thou shalt eat therf bread; and in the
seventh day, for it is the gathering of thy Lord God, thou
shalt not do work. (Six days thou shalt eat unleavened
bread; and on the seventh day, there shall be a holy
gathering to the Lord thy God, and thou shalt not do any
work on it.)
9 Thou shalt number to thee seven weeks, from that
day in which thou settedest a sickle into the corn; (Thou
shalt count seven weeks, from that day on which thou
puttest the sickle to the corn;)
10 and thou shalt hallow the feast day(s) of weeks to
thy Lord God, a willful offering of thine hand, which thou
shalt offer by the blessing of thy Lord God. (and then
thou shalt keep the Feast of Weeks, *or the Harvest*
Festival, to the Lord thy God, and thou shalt offer a
freewill offering, in proportion to the blessing given thee
by the Lord thy God.)
11 And thou shalt eat before thy Lord God, thou, and
thy son, and thy daughter, and thy servant, and thine
handmaid, and the deacon that is within thy gates, and
the comeling, and the fatherless, either motherless child,
and the widow, that dwell with you, in the place which
thy Lord God choose, that his name dwell there. (And
thou shalt eat before the Lord thy God, thou, and thy son,
and thy daughter, and thy slave, and thy slave-girl, and
the Levite who is within thy gates, and the newcomer,
and the fatherless or the motherless child, and the
widow, yea, all who live with you, in the place which the
Lord thy God shall choose, that his name is there.)
12 And thou shalt have mind for thou were (a) servant
in Egypt, and thou shalt keep and do those things that be
commanded. (And thou shalt remember that thou were
slaves in Egypt, and thou shalt obey and do those things
that be commanded.)
13 And thou shalt hallow the solemnity of tabernacles
by seven days, when thou hast gathered thy fruits of thy
cornfloor, and of the presser. (And thou shalt keep the
Feast of Tabernacles, *or the Festival of Booths, or of*
Shelters, for seven days, when thou hast gathered in the
produce from thy threshing floor, and from thy winepress.)
14 And thou shalt eat in thy feast, thou, and thy son,
and thy daughter, and thy manservant, and thine
handmaid, also the deacon, and the comeling, and the
fatherless, either motherless child, and the widow, that
be within thy gates. (And thou shalt be glad at thy feast,
or thy festival, thou, and thy son, and thy daughter, and
thy slave, and thy slave-girl, and the Levite, and the
newcomer, and the fatherless or the motherless child,
and the widow, yea, all who be within thy gates.)

15 By seven days thou shalt hallow feasts to thy Lord
God, in the place which the Lord choose; and thy Lord
God shall bless thee, in all thy fruits, and in all the work
of thine hands, and thou shalt be in gladness. (For seven
days thou shalt keep this feast to the Lord thy God, in the
place which the Lord shall choose; and the Lord thy God
shall bless thee, with all thy fruits, and with all the work
of thine hands, and thou shalt be glad, *or be happy*.)
16 In three times by the year all thy male kind shall
appear in the sight of thy Lord, in the place which he
choose, in the solemnity of therf loaves, and in the
solemnity of weeks, and in the solemnity of tabernacles.
A man shall not appear void before the Lord; (Three
times a year all thy males shall appear before the Lord thy
God, in the place which he shall choose, at the Feast of
Unleavened Bread, and at the Feast of Weeks, and at the
Feast of Tabernacles. A man shall not appear empty-
handed before the Lord;)
17 but each man shall offer after that that he hath, by
the blessing of his Lord God, that he gave to him. (but
each man shall offer what he hath, in proportion to the
blessing which the Lord his God hath given him.)
18 Thou shalt ordain judges, and exactors, in all thy
gates which thy Lord God shall give to thee, by each of
thy lineages, that they deem the people by just doom,
(Thou shalt ordain judges, and exactors, in all thy gates
which the Lord thy God shall give thee, in each of thy
tribes, and they shall judge the people with fair
judgements,)
19 and bow they not into the other part *for favour,
either gift*. Thou shalt not take a person, neither gifts, for
why gifts blind the eyes of wise men, and change the
words of just men (Thou shalt not show favour to anyone,
nor take a bribe, *or a gift*, for bribes blind the eyes of the
wise, and change the words of the just).
20 Thou shalt pursue justly that that is just, that thou
live, and wield the land which thy Lord God shall give to
thee. (Thou shalt only pursue what is right, *or just*, so that
thou can live, and possess the land which the Lord thy
God shall give thee.)
21 Thou shalt not plant a wood, and each tree (or any
tree), by the altar of thy Lord God; (Thou shalt not plant a
sacred grove, or put up a pole, beside the altar of the
Lord thy God;)
22 neither thou shalt make to thee, and ordain an
image; which things thy Lord God hateth. (nor shalt thou
set up a sacred pillar, or an idol, for thee to worship; the
Lord thy God hateth all these things.)

CHAPTER 17

1 Thou shalt not offer to thy Lord God an ox and a
sheep in which is a wem, either anything of vice/either
anything of reproof, for it is abomination to thy Lord
God. (Thou shalt not offer to the Lord thy God an ox or a
sheep which hath a blemish, *or a fault*, for that is an
abomination to the Lord thy God.)
2 And when a man either a woman, that do evil in the
sight of thy Lord God, be found with thee, within one of
thy gates which thy Lord God shall give to thee, and they
break the covenant of God,
3 that they go and serve alien gods, and worship
them, the sun, and the moon, and all the knighthood of
heaven, which things I commanded not; (and go and
serve foreign, *or other*, gods, and worship them, or the
sun, and the moon, and all the host of heaven, which
things I would never command;)
4 and this is told to thee, and thou hearest (of) it, and
inquirest diligently, and thou findest that it is sooth, and
that (such an) abomination is done in Israel;
5 thou shalt lead out the man and the woman, that did
that most cursed thing, to the gates of thy city, and they
shall be oppressed with stones (until they die). (thou shalt
lead out the man, or the woman, who did this most
cursed thing, to the gates of thy city, and they shall be
killed with stones.)
6 He that shall be slain, shall perish in the mouth of
twain, either of three witnesses; no man be slain, for one
man saith witnessing against him. (He who shall be put to
death, shall die only after the testimony of two, or three,
witnesses; no one shall die because one person saith
witnessing against them.)
7 The hand of the witnesses shall first slay him, and at
the last the hand of the other people shall be put to, *for to
throw him down with stones*, that thou do away evil from
the midst of thee. (The hands of the witnesses shall be the
first to stone them, and then the other people shall put
their hands to it, *and they shall throw their stones*, so that
thou do away evil from the midst of thee.)
8 If thou perceivest, that hard and doubtful doom is
with thee (If thou perceivest, that there is a hard and
difficult judgement before thee), betwixt blood and
blood, cause and cause, leprosy and not leprosy, and
thou seest that the words of [the] judges within thy gates
be diverse *in their deeming*; rise thou, and go up to the
place that thy Lord God hath chosen;
9 and thou shalt come to the priests of the kin of Levi,
and to the judge that is in that time, and thou shalt ask of
them, which shall show to thee the truth of [the] doom.
(and thou shalt come to the levitical priests, and to the
judge then in office, and thou shalt ask them, and they
shall tell thee the correct judgement and sentence.)
10 And thou shalt do, whatever thing they say, that be
sovereigns in the place which the Lord choose (who be
the rulers in the place which the Lord shall choose), and
(who) teach thee by the law of the Lord;
11 thou shalt follow the sentence of them; thou shalt
not bow *therefrom* to the right side, either to the left.
12 For that man shall die, that is proud, and will not

obey to the behest of the priest, that ministereth in that time to thy Lord God, and to the sentence of the judge, and thou shalt do away evil from the midst of Israel; (And the person shall die, who is proud, and will not obey the decision of the priest, who ministereth at that time to the Lord thy God, or the sentence of the judge, and so thou shalt do away evil from the midst of Israel;)
13 and all the people shall hear, and dread, that no man from thenceforth swell with pride. (and all the people shall hear, and have fear, so that henceforth no one should swell with pride.)
14 When thou hast entered into the land, which thy Lord God shall give to thee, and wieldest it, and dwellest therein, and sayest, I shall ordain a king on me, as all nations by compass have (and sayest, We shall ordain a king over us, like all the nations around us have);
15 thou shalt ordain him, whom thy Lord God chooseth, (out) of the number of thy brethren. Thou shalt not be able to make king a man of another folk, which *man* is not thy brother (Thou shalt not ordain a man from another nation to be your king, yea, a *man* who is not thy brother, *that is, thy kinsman*).
16 And when the king is ordained, he shall not multiply horses to him(self), neither he shall lead again the people into Egypt, neither he shall be raised *into pride, or tyranny,* by the number of knights, mostly since the Lord commanded to you, that ye turn no more again by the same way. (And when the king is ordained, he shall not multiply horses unto himself, nor shall he lead the people back to Egypt, in order to add to his horses, for the Lord hath commanded that ye never go back there.)
17 The king shall not have many wives, that draw his mind *to lusts*, neither *he shall have* great weights of silver and of gold. (The king shall not have many wives, who would draw away his mind *to lust, or too much fleshliness,* nor *shall he have* great quantities of silver and gold.)
18 Forsooth after that he hath set in the throne of his realm, he shall write to himself, *that is, shall make to be written*, the deuteronomy, *that is, declaration*, of this law in a book, and he shall take (the) exemplar of (the) priests of the kin of Levi; (And after that he hath sat on the throne of his kingdom, he shall have written for himself the deuteronomy, *or the declaration*, of this law in a book, and his copy shall be made from the original held by the levitical priests;)
19 and he shall have *it* with him, and he shall read it in all the days of his life, that he learn to dread his Lord God, and to keep his words and his ceremonies, that be commanded in the law; (and he shall have *it* with him, and he shall read it all the days of his life, so that he can learn to fear the Lord his God/so that he can learn to revere the Lord his God, and obey all his words and his statutes, that be commanded in the law;)
20 neither his heart be raised into pride on his brethren, neither bow he into the right side, either left side, that he reign long time, he and his sons on Israel. (and then his heart shall not be raised up in pride above his brothers, *or his kinsmen*, nor shall he turn from these commandments to the right, or to the left, and then he and his sons shall reign a long time over Israel.)

CHAPTER 18

1 Priests and deacons, and all men that be of the same lineage, shall have no part and heritage with the tother people of Israel, for they shall eat the sacrifices of the Lord, and the offerings of him; (The levitical priests, and all the men who be of the tribe of Levi, shall have no part or inheritance with the other people of Israel, for they shall eat the burnt sacrifices, and the other offerings, to the Lord;)
2 and they shall not take any other thing of the possession of their brethren; for the Lord himself is their heritage, as he spake to them. (and they shall have no possession among their brothers; for the Lord himself is their inheritance, as he promised them.)
3 This shall be the doom of (the) priests, *that is, the thing justly given, either granted,* of the people, and of them that offer sacrifices (This shall be the priest's due, *that is, the thing rightly given* from the people, yea, from those who offer sacrifices); whether they offer an ox, either a sheep, they shall give to the priest the shoulder, and the paunch,
4 the first fruits of wheat, and of wine, and of oil, and a part of wools of the shearing of sheep. (the first fruits of thy corn, and of thy wine, and of thy oil, and a part of the wools from the shearing of thy sheep.)
5 For thy Lord God hath chosen him (out) of all thy lineages, that he stand and minister to the name of the Lord (that he stand to minister in the name of the Lord), he and his sons, [into] without end.
6 If a deacon goeth out of one of thy cities of all Israel, in which he dwelleth (If a Levite goeth out of any of thy cities in Israel, in which he liveth), and will come and desireth the place which the Lord (shall) choose,
7 he shall minister in the name of his Lord God, as all his brethren deacons, that shall stand in that time before the Lord. (then he shall minister in the name of the Lord his God, like all of his fellow Levites, who stand before the Lord at that time.)
8 He shall take the same part of meats, that also other *deacons shall take*; besides that that is due to him in his city, by succession, *either heritage*, of (his) father. (He shall receive the same portion of food, that other *Levites receive*; besides what is due to him in his own city, by succession, *either inheritance*, from his father.)
9 When thou hast entered into the land which thy Lord God shall give to thee, be thou ware lest thou wilt follow the abominations of those folks;

10 none be found in thee that cleanseth his son, either
his daughter, and leadeth by the fire, either that asketh
questions of diviners that divine about the altars, and that
taketh heed to dreams, and (to) chittering of birds; neither
any witch be (*among you*), (let none be found among
thee who maketh his son, or his daughter, to pass
through the fire, or who asketh questions of diviners who
divine about the altars, or who taketh heed to dreams, or
to the twittering of birds; and let there be no witch *found
among you*,)
11 neither any enchanter *or tregetour, (that is, he who
deceiveth men's eyes so that a thing seem that which it is
not)*; neither a man take counsel of them that have a fiend
speaking within them, neither of false diviners, neither
seek of dead men the truth (nor let anyone take counsel
from them who have a fiend speaking within them, or
from false diviners, nor seek they to learn the truth from
the dead).
12 For the Lord hath abomination of all these things,
and for such wickednesses he shall do away them in
thine entering. (For the Lord hath abomination for all
these things, and for such wickednesses, he shall drive
them all out before thee.)
13 Thou shalt be perfect, and without filth, with thy
Lord God.
14 These heathen men, whose land thou shalt wield,
hear them that work by chittering of birds, and false
diviners; but thou art taught in other manner of thy Lord
God. (These heathen, whose land thou shalt possess,
listen to those who portend by the twittering of birds, and
to false diviners; but thou art taught in another way, by
the Lord thy God.)
15 Thy Lord God shall raise a prophet of thy folk, and
of thy brethren, as me, *to thee*, (and) thou shalt hear him;
(The Lord thy God shall raise up a prophet like me, *for
thee*, from thy nation, *or thy people*, yea, one of thy
brothers, *or one of thy kinsmen*, and thou shalt listen to
him;)
16 as thou askedest of thy Lord God in Horeb, when
the company was gathered together, and thou saidest, I
shall no more hear the voice of my Lord God, and I shall
no more see this greatest fire, lest I die. (as thou askedest
of the Lord thy God at Mount Sinai, when the
congregation was gathered together, and thou saidest,
We shall not hear again the voice of the Lord our God,
and we shall not see this great fire again, lest we die.)
17 And the Lord said to me, They have spoken well all
things (They have spoken all things well).
18 I shall raise to them a prophet, like thee, of the midst
of their brethren, and I shall put my words in his mouth,
and he shall speak to them all things, which I shall
command to him. (I shall raise up for them a prophet, like
thee, from the midst of their brothers, *or of their kinsmen*,
and I shall put my words in his mouth, and he shall speak
to them all the things, that I shall command to him.)
19 And I shall be venger of him, that will not hear his
words, which he shall speak in my name. (And I shall
take vengeance upon anyone, who shall not obey the
words, which he shall speak in my name.)
20 Soothly a prophet shall be slain, which is depraved
with pride, and will speak in my name those things,
which I commanded not to him, that he should say,
either by the name of alien gods. (And the prophet who is
depraved with pride, and shall speak in my name those
things, which I did not command him to say, or shall
speak in the name of foreign, *or other*, gods, that prophet
must be put to death.)
21 That if thou answerest by privy thought, How may I
understand the word, which the Lord spake not? (And if
thou ask within thyselves, How can we know that the
Lord did not speak this word?)
22 thou shalt have this sign, or token, (*to know a false
prophet from a true prophet*,) if that that that prophet
saith before in the name of the Lord, cometh not, the
Lord spake it not, but he feigned it through (the) pride of
his soul, and therefore thou shalt not dread him. (thou
shalt have this sign, *to know a false prophet from a true
prophet*; If what that prophet saith beforehand in the
name of the Lord, cometh not, then the Lord did not
speak it, but *the false prophet* feigned *his prophecy*
through the pride of his soul, and so thou shalt not fear
him.)

CHAPTER 19

1 When thy Lord God hath destroyed the folks, whose
land he shall give to thee, and thou hast wielded it, and
hast dwelled in the cities, and in [the] houses thereof;
2 thou shalt separate three cities to thee in the midst of
the land, which thy Lord God shall give to thee into
possession. (thou shalt set apart three cities for thee in the
midst of the land, which the Lord thy God shall give thee
for a possession.)
3 Thou shalt make ready diligently the way, and thou
shalt part evenly into three parts all the province(s) of thy
land, that he that is exiled for manslaying, have nigh (at)
hand whither he may escape. (Thou shalt diligently make
ready the way, and thou shalt evenly divide all the
provinces of thy land into three parts, so that anyone who
is exiled for manslaughter, shall have a place close at
hand to which they can escape.)
4 This shall be the law of a manslayer fleeing, whose
life shall be kept. If a man smiteth unwittingly his
neighbour, and which is proved to have not had any
hatred against him yesterday, and the third day ago, (This
shall be the law for anyone fleeing manslaughter, whose
life shall be saved. If anyone unwittingly, *or
unintentionally*, striketh down his neighbour, and is
proved to have not had any hatred against him yesterday,

and the third day ago,)
5 but to have gone simply with him into the wood to
hew down trees, and in the felling down of trees the ax
flieth from his hand, and the iron slideth from the helve,
and smiteth, and slayeth his friend; this man shall flee to
one of the foresaid cities, and shall live; (but simply to
have gone into the woods with him to cut down some
trees, and in the felling down of the trees, the ax flieth
out of his hand, and the iron slideth from the helve, and
striketh, and killeth his friend; this person shall flee to
one of the foresaid cities, and shall be safe there;)
6 lest peradventure the next kinsman of him, whose
blood is shed out, be pricked with sorrow, and pursue,
and (over)take him, if the way is longer, and slay his life,
that is not guilty of death; for it is showed that he had not
any hatred before against him that is slain. (lest the next
of kin of him whose blood is shed out, be pricked with
sorrow, and he pursue the killer, and overtake him,
because the way is long, and then take the life of him
who is truly not guilty of murder; for it was shown that he
had no hatred before against that person who was killed.)
7 Therefore I command to thee, that thou separate
three cities of even space betwixt themselves. (And so I
command thee to set apart three cities with even space
between them.)
8 Forsooth when thy Lord God hath alarged thy terms,
as he swore to thy fathers, and hath given to thee all the
land which he promised to them;
9 if nevertheless thou keepest his commandments,
and doest those things which I command to thee today,
that thou love thy Lord God, and go in his ways in all
time (so that thou love the Lord thy God, and go in his
ways at all times), (then) thou shalt add to thee three
other cities, and (so) thou shalt double the number of the
foresaid cities,
10 that guiltless blood be not shed out in the midst of
the land which thy Lord God shall give to thee to have in
possession, lest thou be guilty of blood. (so that innocent
blood be not shed out in the midst of the land which the
Lord thy God shall give thee to have for a possession,
and that thou be guilty of shedding that innocent blood.)
11 Forsooth if any man hateth his neighbour, and
setteth ambushes to his life, and riseth up *against him
privily*, and smiteth him, and he is dead (and he dieth),
and *the manslayer* fleeth to one of the foresaid cities,
12 the elder men of that city shall send (for), and take
him from the place of refuge; and they shall betake *him*
into the hand of the next kinsman of *him*, whose blood is
shed out, and he shall die, (the elders of that city shall
send for him, and shall bring him back from the place of
refuge; and they shall deliver *him* into the hands of the
next of kin of *him* whose blood was shed out, and he
shall die/and he shall be put to death,)
13 and thou shalt not have mercy upon him; and thou
shalt do away guilty blood from Israel, that it be well to
thee. (and thou shalt not give him any mercy; and so thou
shalt do away from Israel the guilt for innocent blood, so
that it be well with thee.)
14 Thou shalt not take, and turn over, the terms of thy
neighbour, which the former men set in thy possession,
which thy Lord God shall give to thee in the land, which
land thou shalt take to be wielded. (Thou shalt not take
away, or turn over, thy neighbour's boundary *stones*,
which the people in former times put there in thy
possession, which the Lord thy God shall give thee, in
the land which thou shalt take for thyselves.)
15 One witness shall not stand against any man,
whatever thing it is of sin, and of wickedness; but each
word shall stand in the mouth of twain, either of three
witnesses. (One witness shall not convict anyone,
whatever his sin, or wickedness; but each charge must be
established by the testimony of two, or three, witnesses.)
16 If a false witness standeth against a man, and
accuseth him of breaking of the law,
17 both they, of whom the cause is, shall stand before
the Lord, in the sight of priests, and of judges, that be in
those days. (then both of the people who be in dispute,
shall stand before the Lord, in the sight of the priests, and
the judges, who then be in office.)
18 And when they seeking *the cause* most diligently
(And if, after they have studied the case most diligently),
(they) have found that the false witness said a lie against
his brother,
19 they shall yield to him, as he thought to have done
to his brother; and (*so*) thou shalt do away evil from the
midst of thee,
20 that other men hear, and have dread, and be no
more hardy to do such things (so that other people can
hear, and have fear, and no more be so fool-hardy to do
such things). Thou shalt not have mercy on him,
21 but thou shalt ask life for life, eye for eye, tooth for
tooth, hand for hand, foot for foot.

CHAPTER 20

1 If thou goest out to battle against thine enemies, and
thou seest a multitude of knights, and of chariots, and a
greater multitude of the adversary('s) host than (what)
thou hast, thou shalt not dread them; for thy Lord God is
with thee, that led thee out of the land of Egypt. (If thou
goest out to battle against thy enemies, and thou seest a
multitude of horsemen, and of chariots, and a greater
multitude of the adversary's army than what thou hast,
thou shalt not fear them; for the Lord thy God is with
thee, who led thee out of the land of Egypt.)
2 Soothly when the battle nigheth now, the priest shall
stand before the battle array, and thus he shall speak to
the people (and he shall speak to the people thus),
3 Thou, Israel, hear today, ye have battle against your

enemies; your heart dread not, be ye not afeared; do not
ye give stead, dread ye not them; (Hear, O Israel, today
ye shall do battle against your enemies; but do not let
your heart fear, and do not be afraid; do not ye give place
to panic, and do not ye fear them;)
4 for your Lord God is in the midst of you, and he
shall fight for you against *your* adversaries, that he deliver
you from peril. (for the Lord your God is in your midst,
and he shall fight for you against *your* adversaries, so that
he can save you from peril.)
5 But the leaders shall cry by all the companies, while
the host shall hear, (*and shall say,*) Who is the man that
hath builded a new house, and hath hallowed not it? go
he and turn again into his house, lest peradventure he die
in battle, and another man hallow it. (Then the leaders of
the army shall say, in the hearing of all the people, Who
is the man who hath built a new house, and hath not yet
dedicated it? go he back, and return to his house, lest he
die in the battle, and another man dedicate it.)
6 Who is the man that (hath) planted a vinery, and
hath not yet made it to be common, and of which it is
leaveful to all men to eat? go he, and turn again into his
house, lest peradventure he die in battle, and another
man be set in his office. (Who is the man who hath
planted a vineyard, and hath not yet made it to be
common, and therefore lawful for all men to eat of it? go
he back, and return to his house, lest he die in the battle,
and another man enjoy its fruits.)
7 Who is the man that hath espoused a wife, and hath
not (yet) taken her *by fleshly knowing*? go he, and turn
again into his house, lest peradventure he die in battle,
and another man take her. (Who is the man who hath
espoused a wife, and hath not yet taken her *in fleshly
knowing*? go he back, and return to his house, lest he die
in the battle, and another man take her.)
8 When these things be said, *the leaders of the host*
shall add to (them) other things, and they shall speak to
the people, *and say,* Who is a fearful man, and of
dreadful heart? go he, and turn again into his house, lest
he make his brethren's hearts to dread, as he is aghast by
dread. (When these things be said, *the leaders of the
army* shall add other things, and they shall say to the
people, Who is fearful, and hath a heart full of dread? go
he back, and return to his house, lest he make his
kinsmen's hearts to fear, just like his is filled with fear.)
9 And when the dukes of the host be still, and have
made (an) end of speaking, each *chieftain of thy host*
shall make ready his companies to battle. (And when the
leaders of the army have finished speaking, they shall
appoint a leader, *or a chief man,* for each company.)
10 If any time thou shalt go to a city to overcome it,
first thou shalt proffer peace to it. (Now anytime that thou
shalt go to attack a city, thou shalt first make an offer of
peace to them, *that is, thou shalt give them a chance to
surrender.*)
11 If the city receiveth *thy (offer of) peace,* and openeth
to thee the gates, all the people that is therein shall be
saved, and it shall serve thee under tribute. (If the city
accepteth *thy offer of peace, and they surrender,* and
they open the gates to thee, then all the people who be
there shall become your slaves, and shall serve thee.)
12 But if they will not make bond of peace with thee,
and begin battle against thee, thou shalt fight against it.
(But if they will not make peace with thee, but begin
battle against thee, then thou shalt fight against them.)
13 And when thy Lord God hath betaken it in(to) thine
hands, thou shalt smite by the sharpness of sword all
thing of male kind that is therein, (And when the Lord thy
God hath delivered them into thy hands, thou shalt strike
down, *or shalt kill,* with the sharpness of the sword, all
the males who be there,)
14 without women, and young children, beasts, and
other things that be in the city. Thou shalt part all the
prey to the host, and thou shalt eat of the spoils of thine
enemies, which *spoils* thy Lord God hath given to thee.
(but not the women, and the young children, and the
beasts, and the other things that be in the city. Thou shalt
divide all the prey among the army, and thou shalt eat
the spoils of thy enemies, which *spoils* the Lord thy God
hath given thee.)
15 Thus thou shalt do to all the cities, that be full far
from thee, and be not of these (nigh) cities which thou
shalt take into possession. (Thus thou shalt do, to all the
cities that be far away from thee, but not to the cities that
be near, which thou shalt take for a possession.)
16 But of these cities that shall be given to thee, thou
shalt not suffer any to live, but thou shalt slay by the
sharpness of sword; (But in these cities that shall be given
to thee *by the Lord,* thou shalt not allow anyone to
remain alive, but thou shalt kill them all by the sharpness
of the sword;)
17 that is to say, Hittites, and Amorites, and Canaanites,
and Perizzites, and Hivites, and Jebusites, as thy Lord
God hath commanded to thee;
18 lest peradventure they teach you to do all the
abominations, which they have wrought (un)to their
gods, and ye do sin against your Lord God (and then ye
sin against the Lord your God).
19 When thou hast besieged a city by long time, and
thou hast compassed it with strongholds that thou
overcome it, thou shalt not cut down the trees, of which
men may eat/of which fruit may be eaten, neither thou
shalt waste the country(side) about with axes; for it is a
tree, and not a man, neither it may increase the number
of fighters against thee. (When thou hast besieged a city
for a long time, and thou hast surrounded it with
strongholds so that thou can overcome it, thou shalt not
cut down the trees, from which men can eat/whose fruit

can be eaten, nor shalt thou destroy all the countryside
about with axes; for it is a tree, and not a man, and it
cannot increase the number of fighters against thee.)
20 And if any of them be not apple trees, but be wild,
and able into other uses, cut them down, and make of
them engines, till thou take the city that fighteth against
thee. (But if any of them be not apple trees, *or other
kinds of fruit* trees, but be wild, and good for other uses,
then cut them down, and make engines, *or bulwarks*, out
of them, until thou take the city that fighteth against thee.)

CHAPTER 21

1 When the carrion of a man slain is found in the land
which thy Lord God shall give to thee, and he that is
guilty of his death is unknown, (When the corpse of a
slain man is found in the land which the Lord thy God
shall give to thee, and he who is guilty of his death is
unknown,)
2 the greater men in birth and thy judges shall go out,
and they shall mete from the place of the carrion the
spaces of all the cities about; (the men of great age, *that
is, the elders*, and the judges shall go out, and they shall
measure the distance from the corpse to all the cities
thereabouts;)
3 and which city they see to be nearer *that carrion*,
than another, the elder men of that city shall take of [the]
drove a cow calf, that hath not drawn yoke, neither hath
cut the earth with a (plow)share; (and whichever city they
see to be nearer *to that corpse*, than any other, the elders
of that city shall take a cow calf from the herd, that hath
not yet worn a yoke, nor hath cut the earth with a
plowshare;)
4 and they shall lead that cow calf to a sharp stony
valley, that was never eared, nor received seed; and in
that valley they shall cut the head off the cow calf. (and
they shall lead that cow calf to a valley of sharp stones,
that was never plowed, nor received seed; and in that
valley they shall cut off the head of the cow calf.)
5 And the priests, the sons of Levi, shall nigh, which
thy Lord God chose, that they minister to him, and bless
in his name, and all the cause shall hang at their word;
and whatever thing is clean either unclean, be it deemed
by them. (And the levitical priests shall come forth,
whom the Lord thy God hath chosen to minister to him,
and bless in his name, and all the cases shall hang on
their words; and whatever thing is clean or unclean, shall
be judged, *or determined*, by them.)
6 And the greater men in birth of that city shall come
to the slain man, and they shall wash their hands on the
cow calf, that was slain in the valley; (And the men of
great age, *that is, the elders*, of the city that is nearest to
the slain man shall come, and they shall wash their hands
over the cow calf, that was killed in the valley;)
7 and they shall say, Our hands shed not out this
blood, neither our eyes have seen *who shed it*.
8 Lord, be merciful to thy people Israel, whom thou
hast again-bought, and areckon thou not innocent blood
in the midst of thy people Israel. And the guilt of blood
shall be done away from them. (Lord, be merciful to thy
people Israel, whom thou hast bought back, *or hast
redeemed*, and put thou not the guilt of innocent blood
on thy people Israel. And so the guilt for the innocent
blood shall be done away from them.)
9 Forsooth thou shalt be alien, *or unguilty*, from the
blood of the innocent which is shed, when thou hast
done that that the Lord commanded. (And so thou shalt
be free from any guilt for the innocent blood which is
shed, when thou hast done what the Lord commanded.)
10 If thou goest out to battle against thine enemies, that
thy Lord God betaketh them in thine hand, and thou
leadest (back) prisoners, (When thou goest out to battle
against thy enemies, and the Lord thy God delivereth
them into thy hands, and thou takest some prisoners,)
11 and thou seest in the number of those prisoners a
fair woman, and thou lovest her, and will have *her to*
wife (and will have *her for your* wife),
12 thou shalt bring her into thine house; which *woman*
shall shave her hair, and she shall cut her nails about,
(thou shalt bring her into thy house; and this *woman* shall
shave off her hair, and she shall pare her nails,)
13 and she shall put away the cloth, wherein she was
taken, and she shall sit in thine house, and she shall
beweep her father and her mother by a month (and she
shall put away the clothes in which she was taken
prisoner, and she shall sit in thy house, and she shall
weep for her father and her mother for a full month); and
afterward thou shalt enter to her, and thou shalt sleep
with her, and she shall be thy wife.
14 But if afterward she sitteth not in thy soul, *that is, (if
she) pleaseth not thy will*, thou shalt deliver her free,
neither thou shalt be able to sell *her* for money, neither
oppress by power, for thou madest her low. (But if
afterward she sitteth not right with thy soul, *that is, if she
pleaseth not thy will*, thou shalt set her free, and thou
shalt not be able to sell *her* for money, nor oppress her
by force, for thou hast made her low.)
15 If a man hath two wives, one loved, and another
hateful, and he begetteth of her free children, and the son
of the odious wife is the first begotten, (If a man hath two
wives, one loved, and the other hated, and he begetteth
children with them, and the son of the hated wife is the
first-born,)
16 and the father will part his chattel betwixt his sons,
he shall not be able to make the son of the loved wife his
first begotten son, and set him before the son of the
hateful wife, (and the father will divide his possessions
between his sons, he shall not be able to make the son of
the loved wife his first-born son, and set him before the

son of the hated wife,)
17 but he shall know the son of the hateful wife to be
his first begotten son, and he shall give to that son all
things double of those things that he hath; for this son is
the beginning of his free children, and the first
engendered things be due to him. (but he shall
acknowledge the son of the hated wife to be his first-born
son, and he shall give double to that son of all the things
that he hath; for this son is the first of his children, and
the rights of the first-born *son* be due to him.)
18 If a man beget a son (who is a) rebel, and a froward
(boy), that heareth not the behest of his father and
mother, and he is chastised, and despiseth to obey *to
them,* (If a man beget a son who is rebellious, and
froward, who obeyeth not his father or his mother, and
after that he is chastised, he still despiseth to obey *them,*)
19 they shall take him, and lead him to the elder men
of that city, and to the gate of doom, (*or of judgement*);
20 and they shall say to them, This our son is
overthwart, and (a) rebel; he despiseth to hear our
behests, *or admonishings,* he giveth attention to
gluttonies, and to lechery, and to feasts. (and they shall
say to them, Our son here is froward and rebellious; he
despiseth to hear our commands, *or our admonishments,*
and he only giveth attention to gluttonies, and to lechery,
and to feasts.)
21 The people of the city shall oppress him with stones,
and he shall die, (so) that ye do away evil from the midst
of you, and that all Israel hear (of) it, and dread.
22 When a man doeth a sin which is worthy to be
punished by death, and he is deemed to (be put to)
death, and is hanged in a gibbet (and is hanged on a
gallows),
23 his carrion shall not dwell in the tree, but it shall be
buried in the same day; for he that hangeth in the tree/for
he that hangeth in the cross is cursed of God, and thou
shalt not defoul thy land which thy Lord God gave thee
into possession. (his corpse shall not remain on the
gallows, but it shall be buried on the same day; for he
who hangeth on a tree is cursed by God, and thou shalt
not defile thy land which the Lord thy God shall give
thee for a possession.)

CHAPTER 22

1 Thou shalt not see thy brother's ox, either sheep,
erring, and shalt pass *thereby,* but thou shalt bring it
again to thy brother. (Thou shalt not see thy brother's ox,
or sheep, go astray, and pass *by it,* but thou shalt bring it
back to thy brother, *that is, thy kinsman.*)
2 And if thy brother is not nigh, neither thou knowest
him, thou shalt lead *those beasts* into thine house (thou
shalt bring *those beasts* back to thy house), and those
shall be with thee, as long as thy brother seeketh them,
and till he receive *them* (back again).
3 In like manner thou shalt do of thy brother's ass, and
of his cloth, and of each thing of thy brother, that was
lost; if thou findest it, be thou not negligent, as of an alien
thing. (In like manner thou shalt do with thy brother's
donkey, and *his* cloak, and with anything else of thy
brother's, that was lost; if thou findest it, be thou not
negligent, that is, do not just pass by it.)
4 If thou seest that the ass, either the ox, of thy brother
hath fallen in the way, thou shalt not despise (it), but thou
shalt raise (it up) with him. (If thou seest that thy brother's
donkey, or his ox, hath fallen down along the way, thou
shalt not just ignore it, but thou shalt help him lift it up
again.)
5 A woman shall not be clothed in a man's cloak,
neither a man shall use a woman's cloak; for he that
doeth these things is abominable before God.
6 If thou goest in the way, and findest a bird's nest in a
tree, either in the earth, and *findest* the mother sitting on
the birds, either [the] eggs, thou shalt not hold the mother
with the children, (If thou goest on the way, and findest a
bird's nest in a tree, or on the ground, and *findest* the
mother bird sitting on her young, or the eggs, thou shalt
not take hold of both the mother bird and her children,)
7 but thou shalt suffer *the mother* [to] go, and shalt
hold the sons taken, that it be well to thee, and that thou
live in long time. (but thou shalt allow *the mother bird* to
go free, and shalt only take her children, so that it be well
with thee, and that thou live a long time.)
8 When thou buildest a new house, thou shalt make a
wall of the roof by compass, lest blood be shed out in
thine house, and thou be guilty, if another man slideth
(off), and falleth into a ditch. (When thou buildest a new
house, thou shalt make a wall all around the roof, lest
blood be shed out on thy house, and thou be guilty, if
someone slideth off, and falleth into a ditch.)
9 Thou shalt not sow thy vinery with another seed,
lest both the seed which thou hast sown, and those things
that come forth of the vinery, *that is, the fruit of the
vinery,* be defouled[1] together. (Thou shalt not sow thy
vineyard with another seed, lest both the seed which
thou hast sown, and those things that come forth of the
vineyard, *that is, the fruit of the vineyard,* be defiled.)
10 Thou shalt not ear with an ox and an ass together.
(Thou shalt not plow with an ox and a donkey together.)
11 Thou shalt not be clothed in a cloth, which is woven
together of wool and of flax. (Thou shalt not be clothed
in a cloak, which is woven with wool and flax together.)
12 Thou shalt make little cords by four corners in the
hems of thy mantle, with which thou art covered. (Thou
shalt put tassels on the four corners of the hem of thy
mantle, with which thou art covered.)

[1] *The Hebrew word here signifieth both defouling (defiling) and hallowing.*

13 If a man weddeth a wife, and afterward hateth her,
14 and seeketh occasions by which he may leave her,
and he putteth against her the worst name, and saith, I
have taken this wife, and I have entered to her, and I
found not her a virgin (and I did not find her a virgin);
15 (then) the father and mother of her shall take her,
and they shall bear with them the tokens of her virginity
to the elder men of the city, that be in the gate (who be at
the gate);
16 and her father shall say, I gave my daughter (for a)
wife to this man, and for (that) he hateth her,
17 he putteth to her the worst name, that he saith, I
found not thy daughter a virgin (he hath put on her the
worst name, for he saith, I did not find thy daughter to be
a virgin); and lo! these be the tokens of the virginity of my
daughter; (and) they shall spread forth a cloth before the
elder men of the city.
18 And the elder men of that city shall take the man,
and shall beat him,
19 and furthermore they shall condemn him in an
hundred shekels of silver, which he shall give to the
father of the damsel, for he defamed her by the worst
name *that may be* upon a virgin of Israel; and he shall
have her to wife, and he shall not be able to forsake her,
in all his lifetime. (and furthermore they shall fine him a
hundred shekels of silver, which he shall give to the
young woman's father, for he defamed her with the worst
name *that can be put* on a virgin of Israel; and he shall
have her for his wife, and he shall not be able to divorce
her, all the days of his life.)
20 That if it is *found* sooth, that (that) he putteth against
her, and virginity is not found in the damsel, (But if what
he hath put against her is *found* to be true, and no proof
of the young woman's virginity is found,)
21 they shall cast her out of her father's gates; and men
of that city shall oppress *her* with stones, and she shall
die, for she did [an] unleaveful thing in Israel, that she did
lechery in her father's house; and *so* thou shalt do away
evil from the midst of thee. (then they shall bring her to
the door of her father's house; and men of that city shall
kill *her* with stones, and she shall die, for she did an
unlawful thing in Israel, she did lechery in her father's
house; and *so* thou shalt do away evil from the midst of
thee.)
22 If a man sleepeth with the wife of another man, ever
either shall die, that is, the adulterer, and the adulteress;
and *thus* thou shalt do away evil from Israel.
23 If a man espouseth a damsel (who is a) virgin, and
an*other* man findeth her in the city, and doeth lechery
with her,
24 thou shalt lead ever either to the gate of that city,
and they shall be killed with stones (and both of them
shall be killed with stones); the damsel *shall be stoned*,
for she cried not, when she was in the city; the man *shall
be stoned*, for he defouled his neighbour's wife; and *thus*
thou shalt do away evil from the midst of thee.
25 But if a man findeth in the field a damsel, which is
espoused (who is espoused), and he taketh (hold of) her,
and doeth lechery with her, he alone shall die;
26 the damsel shall suffer nothing of evil, neither is
guilty of death; for as a thief riseth against his brother,
and slayeth him, so and the damsel suffered; (the young
woman shall not suffer any punishment, nor is she guilty
of anything deserving of death; for like a thief riseth
against his brother, *or his kinsman*, and killeth him, so
this young woman also hath suffered;)
27 she was alone in the field, she cried, and none was
present, that should deliver her. (for she was alone in the
field, and she cried, but no one was present, who could
save her.)
28 If a man findeth a damsel (who is a) virgin, that hath
no spouse, and taketh, and doeth lechery with her, and
the thing cometh to the doom, (If a man findeth a young
woman who is a virgin, who hath no spouse, and he
taketh hold of her, and doeth lechery with her, and the
thing cometh to be known,)
29 he that slept with her shall give to the father of the
damsel fifty shekels of silver, and he shall have her to
wife, for he made her low; he shall not be able to forsake
her, in all the days of his life. (he who slept with her shall
give the young woman's father fifty shekels of silver, and
he shall have her for his wife, for he made her low; he
shall not be able to divorce her, all the days of his life.)
30 A man shall not take his father's wife, neither he
shall show her private(s).

CHAPTER 23

1 A gelding when his stones be broken, either cut
away, and his rod cut off, he shall not enter into the
church of the Lord. (When a man is made a gelding, *or a
eunuch*, that is, if his stones, *or his ballocks*, be broken,
or cut off, or if his rod is cut off, he shall no longer be
part of the Lord's congregation.)
2 A child born of whoredom shall not enter into the
church of the Lord, unto the tenth generation.
3 Ammonites and Moabites, yea after the tenth
generation, shall not enter into the church of the Lord
(into) without end; (The Ammonites and the Moabites,
even after the tenth generation, shall not be part of the
Lord's congregation, yea, forevermore;)
4 for they would not come to you with bread and
water in the way, when ye went out of Egypt; and for
they hired against thee Balaam, the son of Beor, of
Mesopotamia of Syria, that he should curse thee;
(because they would not come to you with bread and
water on the way, when ye went out of Egypt; and
because they hired against thee Balaam, the son of Beor,
from Pethor in Mesopotamia, to curse thee;)

5 and thy Lord God would not hear Balaam (but the
Lord thy God would not listen to Balaam), and God
turned his curse into thy blessing, for he loved thee.
6 Thou shalt not make peace with them, neither thou
shalt seek good things to them (nor shalt thou seek good
things for them), in all the days of thy life (and) into
without end.
7 Thou shalt not loathe a man of Idumea, for he is thy
brother, neither of a man of Egypt, for thou were a
comeling in the land of him. (Thou shalt not despise an
Edomite, for he is thy brother, nor an Egyptian, for thou
were newcomers in his land.)
8 They that be born of them, shall enter in the third
generation into the church of the Lord. (They who be
born of them, from the third generation onward, can be
part of the Lord's congregation.)
9 When thou shalt go out into battle against thine
enemies, thou shalt keep thee from all evil thing (thou
shalt keep thyself from all evil things).
10 If a man is among you, that is defouled in his night
sleep, he shall go out of *your* tents; and he shall not turn
again (If there is a man among you, who is defiled during
his night's sleep, he shall go away from *your* tents; and
he shall not return)
11 before that he be washed in water at the eventide,
and after the going down of the sun, he shall turn again
into the tents. (until he is washed in water in the evening,
and then, after the going down of the sun, he shall return
to the camp.)
12 Thou shalt have a place without the tents, to which
thou shalt go out to (do the) needful things of (man)kind;
13 and thou shalt bear a little stake in thy girdle; and
when thou hast set, thou shalt dig about, and thou shalt
cover with earth things voided out, where thou art
relieved. (and thou shalt bring a little peg in thy belt; and
after that thou hast squatted down, thou shalt dig about,
and thou shalt cover with earth the things voided out,
where thou art relieved.)
14 For thy Lord God goeth in (the) midst of the tents,
that he deliver thee, and betake thine enemies to thee,
that thy tents be holy, and nothing of filth appear in
them, lest *for uncleanness* he forsake thee. (For the Lord
thy God goeth in the midst of thy tents, to keep thee safe,
and to deliver thy enemies to thee, so thy tents must be
kept holy, and nothing of filth appear in them, otherwise
he shall leave thee *because of thy uncleanness*.)
15 Thou shalt not take a servant (back) to his lord,
which fleeth to thee; (Thou shalt not take a slave, who
hath fled to thee, back to his master;)
16 he shall dwell with thee in the place that pleaseth
him, and he shall abide in one of thy cities; and make
thou not him sorry, *or heavy* (and do not thou mistreat
him).
17 None whore/No strumpet shall be of the daughters
of Israel, neither a lecher of the sons of Israel.
18 Thou shalt not offer the hire of an whorehouse,
neither the price of a dog, in the house of thy Lord God,
(for) whatever thing it is that thou hast avowed; for ever
either is abomination before thy Lord God. (Thou shalt
not offer the wages of a common whore, or the fee of a
male prostitute, in the House of the Lord thy God, to
fulfill thy vow; for both of them be abominable before the
Lord thy God.)
19 Thou shalt not lend to thy brother to usury, money,
neither fruits, neither any other thing, (Thou shalt not
lend money, or fruits, or any other thing, to thy brother,
that is, thy kinsman, and charge him interest,)
20 but (thou mayest) to an alien. For thou shalt lend to
thy brother without usury that that he needeth, that thy
Lord God bless thee in all thy work in the land to which
thou shalt enter to wield. (but thou mayest do so to a
foreigner, *or a stranger*. For thou shalt lend to thy brother
what he needeth without charging interest, and then the
Lord thy God shall bless thee in all thy work in the land
to which thou shalt enter to take.)
21 When thou makest a vow to thy Lord God, thou
shalt not tarry to yield *it*, for thy Lord God shall ask that
of thee; and if thou tarriest, it shall be reckoned to thee
into sin. (When thou makest a vow to the Lord thy God,
thou shouldest not delay in fulfilling *it*, for the Lord thy
God shall ask for that *of thee*; and if thou delayest, it shall
be reckoned unto thee as a sin.)
22 If thou wilt not promise, thou shalt be without sin. (If
thou maketh no vow, thou hast not sinned.)
23 Forsooth thou shalt keep (*thy word*), and do that that
went out once of thy lips, as thou promisedest to thy Lord
God, and hast spoken with thine own will and thy
mouth. (But once *thy vow* hath gone out of thy lips, thou
shalt keep *thy word*, and do it, as thou promisedest to the
Lord thy God, and hast spoken with thy own will and thy
own mouth.)
24 If thou enterest into the vineyard of thy neighbour, eat
thou (some) grapes, as much as [it] pleaseth thee; but bear
thou none out with thee (but carry none away with thee).
25 If thou enterest into the corn (field) of thy friend,
thou shalt break off the ears of the corn, and rub them
together with thine hands; but thou shalt not reap them
with a sickle.

CHAPTER 24

1 If a man taketh a wife, and hath her, and she findeth
not grace before his eyes for some vileness, *or
uncleanness*, he shall write a little book of forsaking, and
he shall give (*it*) in her hand, and he shall deliver her
from his house. (When a man taketh a wife, and hath her,
and she findeth not favour before him, because of some
vileness, *or uncleanness*, in her, he shall write up a bill of
divorce, and he shall give *it* to her, and he shall put her

out of his house.)
2 And when she goeth out *from him,* and weddeth
another husband,
3 and he also hateth her, and giveth to her a little
book of forsaking, and delivereth *her* from his house,
either certainly he is dead, (and he also hateth her, and
giveth her a bill of divorce, and putteth *her* out of his
house, or if he should die,)
4 the former husband shall not be able to receive her
again into wife, for she is defouled, and made
abominable before the Lord (the first husband shall not
be able to take her back *again* to be his wife, for she is
defiled, and made abominable before the Lord); lest thou
make thy land to do sin, which thy Lord God hath given
thee to wield.
5 When a man hath taken (of) late a wife, he shall not
go forth to battle, neither anything of the common needs
shall be enjoined to him, but he shall give attention
without blame to his house(hold), that he be glad in one
year with his wife. (When a man hath recently taken a
wife, he shall not go forth to battle, nor anything of the
common needs shall be required from him, but he shall
give attention to his family for one year without blame,
so that he can be happy with his wife.)
6 Thou shalt not take instead of a wed the lower and
the higher quernstone *of thy brother,* for he hath put his
life to thee. (Thou shalt not take in place of a pledge the
lower or the higher millstone *of thy brother,* for then he
hath given thee his life, *that is, his livelihood.*)
7 If a man is taken, *that is, convicted in doom,* busily
ambushing to steal his brother of the sons of Israel, and
when he hath sold him, taketh price, he shall be slain;
and *thus* thou shalt do away evil from the midst of thee.
(If a man hath kidnapped his brother, yea, one of the
Israelites, and maketh him his slave, or selleth him into
slavery, he shall be put to death; and *so* thou shalt do
away evil from the midst of thee.)
8 Keep thou diligently, lest thou run into the sickness
of leprosy, but thou shalt do whatever things that the
priests of the kin of Levi teach thee, by that that I
commanded to them, and fulfill thou it diligently. (Be
thou careful, when thou hast run into the sickness of
leprosy, that thou do whatever the levitical priests tell
thee to do, yea, what I have commanded to them, and
which thou must obey *in order to recover.*)
9 Have ye mind what things your Lord God did to
Marie, in the way, when ye went out of Egypt.
(Remember what the Lord your God did to Miriam, on
the way, when ye went out of Egypt.)
10 When thou shalt ask of thy neighbour anything that
he oweth to thee, thou shalt not enter into his house, that
thou take away *from him* a wed; (When thou shalt ask
thy neighbour for what he oweth thee, thou shalt not
enter into his house, to take away a pledge *from him;*)
11 but thou shalt stand withoutforth, and he shall bring
forth *to thee* that that he hath.
12 And if he is poor, his wed shall not abide by night
with thee (his pledge shall not stay with thee all night),
13 but anon thou shalt yield *his wed* to him before the
going down of the sun, that he sleep in his cloth, and
bless thee, and thou have rightwiseness before thy Lord
God. (but at once thou shalt yield *his pledge* back to him,
yea, before the going down of the sun, so that he can
sleep in his own cloak, and bless thee, and then thou
shalt have righteousness before the Lord thy God.)
14 Thou shalt not deny the hire of thy brother (who is)
needy and poor, either of the comeling that dwelleth
with thee in thy land, and is within thy gates; (Thou shalt
not withhold the wages of thy servant who is needy and
poor, whether he be a fellow Israelite, or a newcomer
who dwelleth with thee in thy land, within thy gates;)
15 but in the same day thou shalt yield to him the price
of his travail, before the going down of the sun, for he is
poor, and sustaineth thereof his life; lest he cry against
thee to the Lord, and it be reckoned to thee into sin. (but
thou shalt yield to him the wages for his work on the
same day, before the going down of the sun, for he is
poor, and sustaineth his life with them; lest he cry against
thee to the Lord, and it be reckoned unto thee as a sin.)
16 The fathers shall not be slain for the sons, neither
the sons for the fathers, but each man shall die for his
own sin.
17 Thou shalt not *waywardly* turn, *or mis-deem,* the
doom of the comeling, or of the fatherless, either
motherless child; neither thou shalt take away instead of
a wed the cloth of a widow. (Thou shalt not *waywardly*
turn, *or pervert,* justice for the newcomer, or for the
fatherless or the motherless child; nor shalt thou take
away the cloak of a widow in place of a pledge.)
18 Have thou mind (Remember), that thou servedest in
Egypt, and thy Lord God delivered thee from thence;
therefore I command to thee that thou do this thing.
19 When thou reapest corn in thy field, and forgettest,
and leavest a reap, thou shalt not turn again to take it, but
thou shalt suffer that a comeling, and a fatherless, either
motherless child, and a widow take it away, that thy Lord
God bless thee in all the work of thine hands. (When
thou reapest corn in thy field, and forgettest, and leavest
a sheaf, thou shalt not return to get it, but thou shalt
allow the newcomer, the fatherless or the motherless
child, and the widow, to take it, so that the Lord thy God
may bless thee in all the work of thy hands.)
20 If thou gatherest the fruits of olives, whatever thing
leaveth in the trees, thou shalt not turn again to gather *it,*
but thou shalt leave it to a comeling, a fatherless, either
motherless [child], and to a widow. (When thou gatherest
the fruits of olives, whatever thing be left in the trees,
thou shalt not return to gather *it,* but thou shalt leave it

for the newcomer, the fatherless or the motherless child,
and the widow.)
21 If thou gatherest grapes of thy vinery, thou shalt not
gather [the] raisins that leave, but those shall fall into the
uses of the comeling, of the fatherless, either motherless
[child], and of the widow. (When thou gatherest grapes
from thy vineyard, thou shalt not gather the raisins that be
left, but they shall be left for the newcomer, the fatherless
or the motherless child, and the widow.)
22 Have thou mind, that also thou servedest in Egypt
(Remember, that thou were slaves in Egypt), and
therefore I command to thee, that thou do this thing.

CHAPTER 25

1 If a cause is betwixt any men, and they ask (the)
judges, they shall give the victory of rightwiseness to him,
whom they perceive to be just, and they shall condemn
him of wickedness, whom *they perceive to be* wicked.
2 And if they see him that hath sinned, (to be) worthy
of beatings, they shall cast *him* (face) down, and they
shall make him to be beaten before them; and the
manner of the beatings shall be for the measure of the sin
(and the number of beatings, *or strokes*, shall correspond
to the measure of the sin),
3 so only that they pass not the number of forty
strokes, lest thy brother be rent vilely before thine eyes,
and go *then* away (and *then* go away).
4 Thou shalt not bind the mouth of the ox treading
(out) thy fruits in the cornfloor. (Thou shalt not bind the
mouth of the ox threshing thy grains on the threshing
floor.)
5 When brethren dwell together, and one of them is
dead without free children, the wife of the dead *brother*
shall not be wedded to another man, but his brother shall
take her, and he shall raise (up) the seed of his brother.
6 And he shall call her first begotten son by his name,
that is, of the dead brother, (so) that his name be not
done away from Israel.
7 And if he will not take the wife of his brother, which
is due to him by law, the woman shall go to the gate of
the city; and she shall ask the greater men in birth, and
she shall say *to them*, My husband's brother will not raise
the seed of his brother in Israel, neither he will take me
into marriage (and she shall say to the men of great age,
that is, the elders, My husband's brother will not raise up
his brother's descendants in Israel, nor will he take me
into marriage).
8 And at once they shall make him to be called, and
they shall ask him. If he answer, *and say*, I will not take
her to wife (And If he answer, *and say*, I will not take her
for a wife);
9 the woman shall go to him before the elder men of
Israel, and she shall take his shoe off from his foot (and
she shall take off the shoe from his foot), and she shall
spit into his face, and she shall say *to them*, Thus it shall
be done to the man, that buildeth not his brother's house;
10 and his name shall be called in Israel, The house of
the man unshod (The house of the unshod, *or the
shoeless*, man).
11 If two men have strife betwixt themselves, and one
beginneth to strive against another, and the wife of the
one man will deliver her husband from the hand of the
stronger man, and she putteth forth her hand, and
holdeth him by his privy members (and taketh hold of
him by his private parts),
12 thou shalt cut off her hand, neither thou shalt be
bowed on her with any mercy (nor shalt thou show her
any mercy).
13 Thou shalt not have in thy bag diverse weights, a
greater *to buy with*, and a less(er) *to sell with*,
14 neither a bushel more and a (bushel) less shall be in
thine house. (nor shall a larger bushel and a smaller
bushel be in thy house.)
15 Thou shalt have a just weight and true, and an even
bushel and true shall be to thee, that thou live in much
time on the land which thy Lord God shall give to thee.
(Thou shalt have true and just weights, and there shall be
a true and just bushel with thee, so that thou can live a
long time on the land which the Lord thy God shall give
thee.)
16 For the Lord shall have him abominable that doeth
these things, and he loatheth, *either curseth*, all
unrightfulness.
17 Have mind what things Amalek did to thee in the
way (Remember what the Amalekites did to thee on the
way), when thou wentest out of Egypt;
18 how he came to thee, and killed the last men of
thine host, that sat *behind* weary, when thou were dis-
eased with hunger and travail, and he dreaded not God.
(how they came to thee, when thou were hungry and
tired, and killed the last men of thy army, who were
weary and lagged *behind*, for they had no fear of God.)
19 Therefore when thy Lord God hath given rest to
thee, and hath made subject to thee all (the) nations
(round) about, in the land that he promised to thee, thou
shalt do away Amalek's name from under heaven (thou
shalt do away the name of the Amalekites from under
heaven); be thou ware lest thou forget this.

CHAPTER 26

1 And when thou hast entered into the land which thy
Lord God shall give to thee to wield, and thou hast gotten
it, and hast dwelled therein,
2 thou shalt take the first fruits of all thy fruits, and
thou shalt put *them* in a basket; and thou shalt go to the
place which thy Lord God (shall) choose, that his name
be inwardly called there.
3 And thou shalt go to the priest, that shall be in those

days, and thou shalt say to him, I acknowledge today
before thy Lord God, that I have entered into the land,
which he swore to our fathers, that he should give it to us
(that he would give to us).
4 And the priest shall take the basket (out) of thine
hand, and he shall set it (down) before the altar of thy
Lord God.
5 And thou shalt say in the sight of thy Lord God, (A)
Syrian pursued (was) my father, that went down into
Egypt, and was a pilgrim there in fewest number; and he
increased into a great folk, and strong, and of multitude
without number. (And thou shalt say before the Lord thy
God, A wandering Syrian was my father, who went down
into Egypt, and he, with a few others, were foreigners
there; but they increased into a great and strong nation,
and into a multitude without number.)
6 And [the] Egyptians tormented us, and pursued us,
and *they* putted *upon us* most grievous burdens.
7 And we cried to the Lord God of our fathers, which
heard us (who heard us), and he beheld our meekness,
and our travail, and our anguish;
8 and he led us out of Egypt in a mighty hand, and in
an arm stretched out, in great dread, and in miracles, and
in great wonders, (and he led us out of Egypt with a
mighty hand, and an outstretched arm, with great and
fearful miracles, and with great wonders,)
9 and he led *us* into this place; and he hath given to
us a land flowing with milk and honey.
10 And therefore I offer now to thee the first fruits of
the fruits of the land which (thou,) the Lord, gave to me.
And thou shalt leave them in the sight of thy Lord God.
And when thy Lord God is worshipped, (And so now I
offer the first fruits of the fruits of the land which thou, O
Lord, hath given me. And thou shalt leave them before
the Lord thy God. And when thou hast worshipped the
Lord thy God,)
11 thou shalt eat in all the goods which thy Lord God
gave to thee, and to thine house, thou, and the deacon,
and the comeling that is with thee. (thou shalt make joy
for all the good things which the Lord thy God hath given
thee, and thy family, thou, and also the Levite, and the
newcomer who is with thee.)
12 When thou hast fulfilled the tithe of all thy fruits, in
the third year of thy tithes, thou shalt give (them) to the
deacon, and to the comeling, and to the fatherless, either
the motherless child, and to the widow, that they eat
within thy gates, and be full-filled. (When thou hast taken
the tithe of all thy fruits in the third year, which is the
tithe-year, thou shalt give them to the Levite, and the
newcomer, and the fatherless or the motherless child,
and the widow, so that they can eat it within thy gates,
and be filled full.)
13 And thou shalt speak in the sight of thy Lord God,
and say, I have taken away that that is hallowed of mine
house, and I gave it to the deacon, and to the comeling,
and to the fatherless, either motherless child, and to the
widow, as thou commandedest to me; I passed not (over)
thy commandments, I forgot not thy behest. (And thou
shalt say before the Lord thy God, I have brought forth
from my house what was dedicated to thee, and I have
given it to the Levite, and the newcomer, and the fatherless
or the motherless child, and the widow, as thou hast
commanded me; I have not passed over thy
commandments, I have not forgotten thy charge, *or thy
orders*.)
14 I ate not of those things in my mourning, neither I
separated them in(to) any uncleanness, neither I spended
of those anything in burying of a dead body (I did not eat
any of it while mourning, I did not put any of it aside for
unclean uses, and I did not spend any of it for burying a
dead body). I obeyed to the voice of my Lord God, and I
did all things as thou commandedest to me.
15 Behold thou from thy saintuary, from the high dwelling
place of heaven, and bless thou thy people Israel, and the
land which thou hast given to us, as thou hast sworn to
our fathers, the land flowing with milk and honey.
16 Today *Israel*, thy Lord God commanded to thee, that
thou do these behests and dooms, that thou keep and
fulfill *them* of all thine heart, and of all thy soul. (Today
Israel, the Lord thy God hath commanded thee, that thou
obey these statutes and laws, *or judgements*, that thou
keep and fulfill *them* with all thy heart, and with all thy
soul.)
17 Thou hast chosen the Lord today, that he be God to
thee, and that thou go in his ways, and that thou keep his
ceremonies, and his behests, and his dooms, and obey to
his commandment. (Thou hast chosen the Lord today, that
he be thy God, and that thou go in his ways, and that thou
keep his statutes, and his commandments, and his laws,
or his judgements, and obey his bidding, *or his orders*.)
18 Lo! the Lord hath chosen thee today, that thou be a
special people to him, as he hath spoken to thee, and that
thou keep all his commandments; (Lo! the Lord hath
chosen thee today, that thou be a special people to him,
as he hath promised thee, and also that thou obey all his
commandments;)
19 and he shall make thee higher than all folks, which
he made into his praising, and name, and glory; that thou
be an holy people to thy Lord God, as he hath spoken to
thee. (and he shall grant thee more favour than all the
nations which he hath made, to bring him praise, and
fame, and glory/and thou shalt bring him praise, and
fame, and glory; and thou shalt be a holy people to the
Lord thy God, as he promised thee.)

CHAPTER 27

1 And Moses commanded, and the elder men, to the
people of Israel, and said, Keep ye each commandment

which I command to you today. (And Moses, with the
elders of Israel, commanded to the people, and said, Obey
ye each commandment which I command to you today.)
2 And when ye have passed (the) Jordan (And when
ye have crossed over the Jordan River), into the land
which thy Lord God shall give to thee, thou shalt raise
(up) great stones, and thou shalt make them plane with
chalk,
3 that thou may write in them all the words of this
law, when (the) Jordan is passed, that thou enter into the
land which thy Lord God shall give to thee, the land
flowing with milk and honey, as he promised to thy
fathers. (so that thou can write on them all the words of
this law, when the Jordan River is crossed over, and thou
enter into the land that the Lord thy God shall give thee,
the land flowing with milk and honey, as he promised to
thy fathers.)
4 Therefore when thou hast passed (the) Jordan, raise
thou up the stones which I command today to thee, in
the hill of Ebal; and thou shalt make them plane with
chalk. (And so when thou hast crossed over the Jordan
River, raise thou up these stones on Mount Ebal, as I
command to thee today, and thou shalt make them plane
with chalk.)
5 And there thou shalt build an altar to thy Lord God,
of stones which iron touched not, (And thou shalt build
an altar there to the Lord thy God, out of stones which
iron hath not touched,)
6 and of stones unformed and unpolished; and thou
shalt offer thereon burnt sacrifices to thy Lord God; (yea,
of unformed and unpolished stones; and thou shalt offer
burnt sacrifices on it to the Lord thy God;)
7 and thou shalt offer peaceable sacrifices, and thou
shalt eat there, and thou shalt make feast before thy Lord
God. (and thou shalt offer peace offerings, and thou shalt
eat them there, and thou shalt make a feast before the
Lord thy God.)
8 And thou shalt write plainly and clearly on the stones
all the words of this law. (And thou shalt write all the
words of this law, clearly and plainly upon those stones.)
9 And Moses and the priests of the kindred of Levi
said to all Israel, Israel, take heed thou, and hear; today
thou art made the people of thy Lord God; (And Moses
and the levitical priests said to all Israel, O Israel, take
heed thou, and listen; today thou art made the people of
the Lord thy God;)
10 thou shalt hear his voice, and thou shalt do the
commandments, and his rightwisenesses, which I
command to thee today. (thou shalt listen to his voice,
and thou shalt do his commandments, and his statutes,
which I command to thee today.)
11 And Moses commanded to the people in that day,
and said,
12 These men shall stand upon the hill of Gerizim to
bless the Lord, when (the) Jordan they have over-passed;
Simeon, Levi, Judah, Issachar, Joseph, and Benjamin.
(These tribes shall stand on Mount Gerizim, when ye
have crossed over the Jordan River, and the blessings be
proclaimed upon the people; Simeon, Levi, Judah,
Issachar, Joseph, and Benjamin.)
13 And even against, these men shall stand in the hill of
Ebal to curse; Reuben, Gad, and Asher, Zebulun, Dan,
and Naphtali. (And opposite them, these tribes shall stand
on Mount Ebal, when the curses be proclaimed; Reuben,
Gad, and Asher, Zebulun, Dan, and Naphtali.)
14 And the deacons shall pronounce, and shall say with
high voice to all the men of Israel, (And then the Levites
shall pronounce, and shall say with a loud voice to all the
Israelites,)
15 Cursed is the man that maketh a graven image and
molten, abomination of the Lord, the work of the hands
of craftsmen, and shall set it in a privy place; and all the
people shall answer, and say, Amen! (Cursed is anyone
who maketh a carved or a cast idol, an abomination to
the Lord, the work of the hands of craftsmen, and then
shall set it up in a secret place; and all the people shall
answer, and say, Amen!)
16 He is cursed that honoureth not, *or despiseth*, his
father and mother; and all the people shall say, Amen!
(Cursed is anyone who honoureth not his father or his
mother; and all the people shall say, Amen!)
17 Cursed is he that over-beareth, *or undoeth*, the terms
of his neighbour; and all the people shall say, Amen!
(Cursed is anyone who turneth over, *or moveth*, his
neighbour's boundary stones; and all the people shall
say, Amen!)
18 Cursed is he that maketh a blind man to err in the
way; and all the people shall say, Amen! (Cursed is
anyone who leadeth a blind man astray; and all the
people shall say, Amen!)
19 He is cursed that perverteth the doom of a comeling,
of a fatherless, either motherless child, and of a widow;
and all the people shall say, Amen! (Cursed is anyone
who withholdeth justice, *or their rights*, from the
newcomer, the fatherless or the motherless child, and the
widow; and all the people shall say, Amen!)
20 Cursed is (he) that sleepeth with his father's wife,
and showeth the private(s) of his bed; and all the people
shall say, Amen!
21 Cursed is he that sleepeth with any beast; and all the
people shall say, Amen!
22 Cursed is he that sleepeth with his sister, the
daughter of his father, either of his mother; and all the
people shall say, Amen!
23 Cursed is he that sleepeth with his wife's mother;
and all the people shall say, Amen!
24 Cursed is he that slayeth privily his neighbour; and
all the people shall say, Amen! (Cursed is anyone who

secretly killeth his neighbour; and all the people shall
say, Amen!) Cursed is he that sleepeth with his
neighbour's wife; and all the people shall say, Amen!
25 Cursed is he that taketh gifts, that he smite the life of
innocent blood; and all the people shall say, Amen!
(Cursed is anyone who taketh money, *or a reward*, to kill
an innocent person; and all the people shall say, Amen!)
26 Cursed is he that abideth not in the words of this
law, neither fulfilleth them in work (nor fulfilleth them
with deeds); and all the people shall say, Amen!

CHAPTER 28

1 Forsooth if thou hearest the voice of thy Lord God,
that thou do and keep all his commandments, which I
command to thee today, thy Lord God shall make thee
higher than all folks that live in earth. (But if thou hearest
the voice of the Lord thy God, and do and obey all of his
commandments, which I command to thee today, the
Lord thy God shall raise thee up higher, *that is, shall
grant thee more favour*, than all the other nations who
live on the earth.)
2 And all these blessings shall come [up]on thee, and
shall take thee; if nevertheless thou hearest his behests.
(And all these blessings shall come to thee, and shall
overtake thee, if thou but obeyest his commands.)
3 Thou *shalt be* blessed in [the] city, and blessed in
the field;
4 blessed *shall be* the fruit of thy womb, and the fruit
of thy land, and the fruit of thy beasts, the flocks of thy
great beasts, and the folds of thy sheep (yea, the herds of
thy great beasts, and the flocks of thy sheep);
5 blessed *shall be* thy barns, and blessed *shall be* thy
remnants, (*or that which thou hast stored up*);
6 thou shalt be blessed entering in, and going out.
7 The Lord shall give thine enemies to fall in thy sight,
that shall rise against thee; by one way they shall come
against thee, and by seven ways they shall flee from thy
face. (The Lord shall make thy enemies, who shall rise up
against thee, to fall down before thee; they shall come
out against thee by one way, but they shall flee from thee
by seven ways.)
8 The Lord shall send out blessing(s) upon thy cellars,
and upon all the works of thine hands; and he shall bless
thee in the land which thou hast taken (and he shall bless
thee in the land which he is giving thee).
9 The Lord shall raise thee to himself into an holy
people, as he swore to thee, if thou keepest the behests
of thy Lord God, and goest in his ways. (The Lord shall
raise thee up into a holy people to himself, as he swore
to thee, if thou but obeyest the commandments of the
Lord thy God, and goest in his ways.)
10 And all the peoples of *other* lands shall see, that the
name of the Lord is inwardly called upon thee, and they
shall dread thee. (And all the peoples of *other* lands, shall
see that thou art called by the name of the Lord, and they
shall fear thee.)
11 The Lord shall make thee to be plenteous in all
goods (The Lord shall make thee to be plenteous in all
good things), (yea,) in the fruit of thy womb, and in the
fruit of thy beasts, (and) in the fruit of thy land, which the
Lord swore to thy fathers, that he would give to thee.
12 The Lord shall open his best treasure, heaven, that
he give rain to thy land in his time; and he shall bless all
the works of thine hands; and thou shalt lend to many
folks, and of no man thou shalt take borrowing. (The Lord
shall open his treasure house, the heavens, and give rain
to thy land at the proper time; and he shall bless all the
works of thy hands; and thou shalt lend to many nations,
but thou shalt not borrow from anyone.)
13 The Lord God shall set thee into the head, and not
into the tail, and ever[more] thou shalt be above, and not
beneath (The Lord God shall make thee the head, and not
the tail, and thou shalt always be above, and never
beneath); if nevertheless thou hearest the commandments
of thy Lord God, which I command to thee today, and
keepest, and doest *them*,
14 and bowest not away from them, neither to the right
side, neither to the left side, neither followest alien gods
(nor followest foreign, *or other*, gods), nor worshippest
them.
15 That if thou wilt not hear the voice of thy Lord God,
that thou keep and do all his behests, and ceremonies,
which I command to thee today, all these cursings shall
come upon thee, and shall take thee. (But if thou wilt not
listen to the voice of the Lord thy God, and obey all his
commandments, and statutes, which I command to thee
today, all these curses shall come to thee, and shall
overtake thee.)
16 Thou shalt be cursed in (the) city, and cursed in (the)
field.
17 Cursed *shall be* thy barn, and cursed *shall be* thy
remnants, (*or that which thou hast stored up*).
18 Cursed *shall be* the fruit of thy womb, and the fruit
of thy land, the droves of thine oxen (the herds of thy
oxen), and the flocks of thy sheep.
19 Thou shalt be cursed going in, and cursed going out.
20 The Lord shall send upon thee hunger, and thirst,
and blaming, into all the works which thou shalt do, till
he all-break thee, and lose *thee* swiftly, for thy full
wicked findings, in which thou hast forsaken me. (The
Lord shall send hunger, and thirst, and rebuke upon thee,
in all the things which thou shalt do, until he hath all-
broken thee, and swiftly destroyed thee, for thy full
wicked doings in which thou hast forsaken me.)
21 The Lord *shall* join pestilence to thee, till he waste
thee from (off) the land, to which thou shalt enter to wield.
22 The Lord shall smite thee with neediness, with fever,
and cold, with burning, and heat, with corrupt air, and

mildew, *either rust*; and he shall pursue *thee* till thou
perish.
23 Heaven, that is above thee, be it brazen; and the
earth, that thou treadest on, be it iron. (The heavens, that
be above thee, shall become as hard as brass; and the
earth, which thou treadest upon, shall become as hard as
iron.)
24 The Lord give dust for rain to thy land, and ash
come down from heaven upon thee, till thou be all-
broken. (The Lord shall give dust to thy land instead of
rain, and ashes shall come down upon thee from the sky,
until thou be all-broken.)
25 The Lord give thee (to) falling before thine enemies;
by one way go thou [out] against them, and by seven ways
flee thou *from them*, and be thou scattered by all the
realms of [the] earth; (The Lord shall cause thee to fall
before thy enemies; thou shalt go out against them by one
way, but thou shalt flee *from them* by seven ways, and
thou shalt be scattered into all the kingdoms of the earth;)
26 and thy dead body be it into meat to all birds of
heaven, and to beasts of the earth, and none be that *may*
drive *them* away. (and thy dead bodies shall be food for
all the birds of the air, and all the beasts of the earth, and
there shall be no one who *can* drive *them* away.)
27 The Lord smite thee with the botch of Egypt, and *the*
Lord smite the part of (the) body whereby ordures, *or*
turds, be voided out; also *the Lord smite thee* with scab,
and itching, so that thou mayest not be cured. (The Lord
shall strike thee with the boils of Egypt, and *he shall*
strike the part of the body where the ordures, *or the*
turds, be voided out; and *he shall also strike thee* with
scabs, and itching, from which thou can never be cured.)
28 The Lord smite thee with madness, and blindness,
and wildness of thought; (The Lord shall strike thee with
madness, and blindness, and wildness of thought;)
29 and grope thou in midday, as a blind man is wont to
grope in darknesses; and (ad)dress he not thy ways; in all
time suffer thou false challenge, and be thou oppressed
by violence, neither have thou any that shall deliver thee.
(and thou shalt grope in midday, like a blind man is wont
to grope in the darkness; and the Lord shall not direct thy
ways; at all times, *or continuously*, thou shalt be violently
attacked and robbed, but thou shalt have no one to save
thee.)
30 Take thou a wife, and another man sleep with her;
build thou an house, and dwell thou not therein; plant
thou a vinery, and gather thou not grapes thereof. (Thou
shalt take a wife, but another man shall sleep with her;
thou shalt build a house, but thou shalt not live in it; and
thou shalt plant a vineyard, but thou shalt not gather its
grapes.)
31 Thine ox be offered before thee, and eat thou not
thereof; thine ass be ravished in thy sight, and be it not
yielded *again* to thee; thy sheep be given to thine
enemies, and none be that help thee *to recover them.*
(Thy ox shall be slaughtered before thee, but thou shalt
not eat any of it; thy donkey shall be stolen from thee,
and it shall not be given *back* to thee; thy sheep shall be
given over to thy enemies, and no one shall help thee *to*
recover them.)
32 Thy sons and thy daughters be given to another
people, while thine eyes see, and fail at the sight of them
all day; and no strength be in thine hand (*to help them*).
(Thy sons and thy daughters shall be given to another
people, while thou seest it, and then thine eyes shall fail
for not being able to see thy children all day long; and
there shall be no strength in thy hands *to help them.*)
33 A people whom thou knowest not, eat (up) the fruits
of thy land, and all thy travails; and ever[more] be thou
suffering false challenges, and *be thou* oppressed in all
days, *or all time*, (A people, whom thou knowest not,
shall eat up the fruits of thy land, and thou shalt suffer
false challenges forevermore, and *thou shalt* be
oppressed for all time,)
34 and be thou wondering at the fearfulness of those
things which thine eyes shall see. (and thou shalt wonder
at the fearfulness of those things which thine eyes shall
see.)
35 The Lord smite thee with the worst botch in the
knees, and in the hinder parts of the leg; and thou may
not be healed from the sole of thy foot till to thy top/unto
the noll. (The Lord shall strike thee with the worst boils
on your knees, and on the back part of your legs; and
thou shalt never be able to be healed, from the sole of
thy feet unto the top of thy head.)
36 And the Lord shall lead thee, and thy king, whom
thou shalt ordain on thee, into a folk which thou knowest
not, thou, and thy fathers; and thou shalt serve there to
alien gods, to tree, and to stone. (And the Lord shall bring
thee, and thy king, whom thou shalt ordain over thee, to
a nation whom thou knowest not, neither thou, nor thy
fathers; and thou shalt serve foreign, *or other*, gods there,
yea, gods made out of wood and stone.)
37 And thou shalt be lost, *or forgotten*, into a proverb,
and into a fable, to all peoples, to whom the Lord shall
bring thee in. (And thou shalt become a proverb, and a
fable, to all the people into whom the Lord shall bring
thee.)
38 Thou shalt cast much seed into the earth, and thou
shalt gather *again* little; for locusts shall devour all things.
39 Thou shalt plant, and dig a vinery, and thou shalt
not drink the wine *of it*, neither thou shalt gather thereof
anything; for it shall be wasted with worms. (Thou shalt
plant a vineyard, and dig it, but thou shalt not drink the
wine *of it*, nor shalt thou gather anything from it; for it
shall be wasted by worms.)
40 Thou shalt have olive trees in all thy coasts, and
thou shalt not be anointed with (the) oil *of them*; for they

shall fall down, and perish. (Thou shalt have olive trees in
all thy land, but thou shalt not be anointed with *their* oil;
for they shall all fall down, and perish.)
41 Thou shalt beget sons and daughters, and thou shalt
not use them (but thou shalt not have them near); for they
shall be led into captivity.
42 Rust, *or mildew*, shall waste all thy trees and the
fruits of thy land.
43 A comeling, that dwelleth with thee in the land,
shall go up upon thee, and he shall be the higher;
forsooth thou shalt go down, and shalt be the lower. (A
newcomer, who shall live with thee in the land, shall go
up over thee, and he shall be higher; but thou shalt go
down, and shalt be lower.)
44 He shall lend to thee, and thou shalt not lend to
him; he shall be into the head, and thou shalt be into the
tail. (He shall lend to thee, but thou shalt not lend to him;
he shall be the head, and thou shalt be the tail.)
45 And all these cursings shall come upon thee, and
shall pursue thee, and take thee, till thou perish; for thou
heardest not the voice of thy Lord God, neither keptest
his commandments and ceremonies, which he
commanded to thee. (And all these curses shall come
upon thee, and they shall pursue thee, and shall overtake
thee, until thou die; for thou heardest not the voice of the
Lord thy God, nor obeyed his commandments and
statutes, which he commanded to thee.)
46 And signs, and great wonders shall be in thee, and
in thy seed, till into without end; (And these signs, and
great wonders, shall be upon thee, and upon thy
descendants, forevermore;)
47 for thou servedest not thy Lord God in joy and
gladness of heart, for the abundance of all things *that
God sent thee*. (for thou servedest not the Lord thy God
with joy and gladness in your heart, for the abundance of
all the good things *that God hath sent thee*.)
48 Thou shalt serve thine enemy, whom God shall send
to thee, in hunger, and thirst, and in nakedness, and in
poverty of all things; and he shall put an iron yoke on thy
noll, till he all-break thee. (And so thou shalt serve thy
enemy, whom God shall send against thee, in hunger,
and thirst, and nakedness, and in the poverty of all things;
and he shall put an iron yoke upon thy neck, until he all-
break thee.)
49 The Lord shall bring on thee a folk from far place,
and from the last ends of [the] earth, into the likeness of
an eagle flying with rush, of which folk thou mayest not
understand their language; (The Lord shall bring against
thee a nation from a far place, and from the last ends of
the earth, like an eagle flying swiftly *to its prey*, of which
nation thou shalt not understand their language;)
50 a folk most greedy asker *this shall be* (*they shall be* a
nation, *or a people*, of fierce countenance), that shall not
give reverence to an eld man, neither have mercy upon a
little child.
51 And it shall devour the fruit of thy beasts, and the
fruits of thy land, till thou perishest, and *this folk* shall not
leave to thee wheat, wine, and oil, *nor* droves of oxen,
and flocks of sheep, till he lose thee, (And they shall
devour the fruit of thy beasts, and the fruit of thy land,
until thou diest, and *this nation* shall not leave thee any
corn, or wine, or oil, *or* herds of oxen, or flocks of sheep,
until they have completely destroyed thee,)
52 and all-break [thee] in all thy cities (and have all-
broken thee in all thy cities), and till thy firm and high
walls be destroyed, in which thou haddest trust in all thy
land. Thou shalt be besieged within thy gates in all thy
land, which thy Lord God shall give to thee.
53 And thou shalt eat the fruit of thy womb, and the
flesh of thy sons, and of thy daughters, which thy Lord
God shall give to thee, in the anguish, and in the
destroying, by which thine enemies shall oppress thee.
(And thou shalt eat the fruit of thy womb, yea, the flesh of
thy sons, and of thy daughters, whom the Lord thy God
hath given thee, amidst the anguish and the destruction
with which thy enemies shall oppress thee.)
54 A man delicate of life, and full lecherous, shall have
envy greatly to his brother, and to his wife that lieth in his
bosom, (and also toward the remnant of his children, that
he hath left,) (A delicate and tender man among you,
shall be stingy toward his brother, and toward his wife
who lieth in his bosom, and even toward the remnant of
his children, who be left,)
55 lest he give to them of the flesh of his sons which he
shall eat; for he hath none other thing in [the] besieging,
and (the) poverty, by which thine enemies shall waste
thee within all thy gates. (lest he give them any of the
flesh of his other children which he shall eat; for he hath
nothing left amidst the anguish and the destruction, with
which thy enemies shall oppress thee within all thy gates.)
56 A tender woman and delicate, that might not go
upon the earth, neither set a step of [the] foot, for *her*
most softness and tenderness, shall have envy to her
husband that lieth in her bosom, on the flesh of her son,
and daughter, (A delicate and tender woman, who,
because of *her* great softness and tenderness, need not
walk, nor even put a step of her foot upon the ground,
shall be stingy toward her husband who lieth in her
bosom, and toward her son and her daughter,)
57 and on the filth of [the] skins, *wherein the child is
wrapped in the mother's womb*, that go out of the midst
of her hip bones, *or loins*, and on [the] free children that
be born in the same hour. They shall eat those *children*
privily, for the scarcity of all things in besieging and
destroying, by which thine enemy shall oppress thee
within thy gates. (and she shall keep for herself all the
filthy skins, *in which the child is wrapped in its mother's
womb*, that goeth out of the midst of her hip bones, and

the children who be born at that same hour. And she
shall secretly eat those skins, and those *children*, for the
scarcity of all things amidst the anguish and the
destruction, with which thy enemies shall oppress thee
within thy gates.)
58 No but thou shalt keep and do all the words of this
law, that be written in this volume, *either book*, and shalt
dread his glorious name and fearful, that is, thy Lord
God, (No, unless thou obey and do all the words of this
law, that be written in this book, and fear his glorious and
fearful name, that is, The Lord Thy God,)
59 the Lord shall increase thy wounds, *or torments*, and
the wounds of thy seed; great wounds and continual,
sicknesses worst and everlasting. (the Lord shall send
more and more plagues upon thee, and upon thy
descendants; yea, great and continual plagues, and the
worst and everlasting sicknesses.)
60 And he shall turn into thee all the torments of Egypt,
which thou dreadedest, and those shall cleave to thee.
(And he shall bring in upon thee all the diseases of Egypt,
which thou hast feared, and they shall cleave to thee.)
61 Furthermore the Lord shall bring upon thee also all
the sorrows and wounds, that be not written in the book
of this law, till he all-break thee. (And furthermore, the
Lord shall bring in upon thee all the other sicknesses and
plagues, that be not written down in this Book of the
Law, until he hath all-broken thee.)
62 And ye shall dwell few in number, that were before
as the stars of heaven for multitude, for thou heardest not
the voice of thy Lord God. (And ye shall be few in
number, who before were like the stars in the heavens in
multitude, for thou did not obey the Lord thy God.)
63 And as the Lord was glad before upon you, and did
well to you, and multiplied you; so he shall be glad to
lose you, and to destroy you, that ye be taken away from
the land, to which thou shalt enter to wield. (And so
before, the Lord was glad about you, and did good to
you, and multiplied you; but now, he shall be glad to
utterly destroy you, and ye shall be taken away from the
land, which thou shalt enter to take.)
64 The Lord shall scatter thee into all peoples, from [the]
highness of the earth unto the coasts thereof; and thou
shalt serve there to alien gods, which thou knowest not,
and thy fathers *knew not*, to trees and stones. (The Lord
shall scatter thee among all the peoples, from the heights
of the earth unto the coasts of the sea; and there thou
shalt serve other gods, which thou knowest not, and thy
fathers *knew not*, yea, *gods* made out of wood and stone.)
65 Also thou shalt not (have) rest in those folks, neither
rest shall be (given) to the step of thy foot. For the Lord
shall give to thee there a fearful heart, and eyes failing,
and a soul wasted with privy sorrow. (And thou shalt not
have rest among these nations, nor shall thy footsteps
have rest. For the Lord shall give thee there a fearful
heart, and failing eyes, and a soul wasted with secret
sorrows.)
66 And thy life shall be as hanging before thee; thou
shalt dread night and day, and thou shalt not trust to thy
life. (And thy life shall be seen as hanging in doubt before
thee; thou shalt have fear day and night, and thou shalt
have no security, *or assurance*, in all thy life.)
67 In the morrowtide thou shalt say, Who shall give the
eventide to me? and in the eventide *thou shalt say*, Who
shall give the morrowtide to me? for the dread of thine
heart, by which thou shalt be made afeared, and for those
things which thou shalt see with thine eyes.
68 The Lord shall lead thee again by ships into Egypt,
by the way of which he said to thee, Thou shouldest no
more see it. There thou shalt be sold to thine enemies,
into menservants and womenservants; and none shall be
that shall deliver thee. (And the Lord shall bring thee
back to Egypt by ships, by the very way of which I had
said to thee, Thou shalt not go that way again. And there
thou shalt try to sell thyselves to thy enemies, as slaves
and slave-girls; but no one will want to buy thee.)

CHAPTER 29

1 These be the words of the bond of peace, which the
Lord commanded to Moses, that he should make with the
sons of Israel in the land of Moab, besides the bond of
peace, which he covenanted with them in Horeb. (These
be the words of the covenant, which the Lord
commanded to Moses, that he should make with the
Israelites in the land of Moab, in addition to the covenant
which he made with them on Mount Sinai.)
2 And Moses called all Israel, and said to them, Ye
have seen all (the) things which the Lord did before you
in the land of Egypt, to Pharaoh, and to all his servants,
and to all his land;
3 the great temptations which thine eyes have seen
(the great plagues which thou hast seen), (and) those
signs, and the great wonders.
4 And the Lord gave not to you an heart
understanding, and eyes seeing, and ears that may hear,
till into this present day. (But unto this present day, the
Lord hath not given you a heart to understand with, or
eyes to see with, or ears to hear with.)
5 He led you by forty years through desert; your
clothes were not broken, neither the shoes of your feet
were wasted by eldness; (He led you for forty years
through the wilderness; yet your clothes did not wear
out, nor were your shoes wasted with oldness;)
6 ye ate not bread, neither ye drank wine and cider,
that ye should know that he is your Lord God. (ye ate no
bread, and ye drank no wine or cider, *but ye survived
through his provision*, so that ye would know that he is
the Lord your God.)
7 And ye came to this place; and Sihon, the king of

Heshbon went out, and Og, the king of Bashan, and they
came to us to battle. And we smote them, (And ye came
to this place; and Sihon, the king of Heshbon, and Og,
the king of Bashan, came out, and they went against us in
battle. And we struck them down,)
8 and we took away their land, and we gave it to
possession, to Reuben, and to Gad, and to the half
lineage of Manasseh. (and we took away their land, and
we gave it for a possession to Reuben, and to Gad, and to
half of the tribe of Manasseh.)
9 Therefore keep ye the words of this covenant, and
fulfill ye them, that ye understand all things which ye
shall do. (And so keep ye the words of this covenant, and
fulfill ye them, so that ye shall prosper in everything
which ye shall do.)
10 All ye stand today before your Lord God, your
princes, and lineages, and the greater men in birth, and
your teachers or doctors, (with) all the people of Israel,
(Ye all stand here today before the Lord your God, yea,
the leaders of the tribes, and the men of great age, *that is,*
the elders, and your officers, with all the people of Israel,)
11 your free children, and your wives, and the
comelings that dwell with thee in the tents, besides the
hewers of wood, *and besides* they that bear water; (yea,
your children, and your wives, and the newcomers who
live with thee in the tents, as well as the hewers of wood,
and the bearers of water;)
12 that thou go into the bond of peace of thy Lord God,
and in the oath which thy Lord God smiteth with thee,
(that thou enter into the covenant of the Lord thy God, and
accept the oath which the Lord thy God striketh with thee,)
13 that he raise thee up into a people to himself, and
that he be thy Lord God, as he spake to thee, and as he
swore to thy fathers, Abraham, Isaac, and Jacob. (so that
he can raise thee up into a people unto himself, and that
he be the Lord thy God, as he promised thee, and as he
swore to thy fathers, Abraham, Isaac, and Jacob.)
14 And not to you alone I make this bond of peace, and
confirm these oaths, (And it is not with you alone do I
make this covenant, and confirm this oath,)
15 but to all men (but with all *Israelites*), present and
absent.
16 For ye know how we dwelled in the land of Egypt,
and how we passed by the midst of nations; which ye
passed (by), (For ye know how we lived in the land of
Egypt, and how, when we passed through the midst of
the nations,)
17 and saw abominations and filths, that is, their idols,
(of) wood and stone, silver and gold, which they
worshipped. (we saw their abominations and filths, that
is, their idols, and false gods, made out of wood and
stone, and silver and gold, which they worshipped.)
18 Lest peradventure among you be man either
woman, family either lineage, whose heart is turned
away today from your Lord God, that he go, and serve
the gods of those folks; and a root burgeoning gall and
bitterness be among you; (Lest there be among you a
man or a woman, a family or a tribe, whose heart today is
turned away from the Lord your God, so that they go,
and serve the gods of those nations; and there be a root
burgeoning gall and bitterness among you;)
19 and when he hath heard the words of this oath, he
bless himself in his heart, and say, Peace shall be to me,
and I shall go in the depravity of mine heart; and *lest* the
drunken take the thirsty, (and so when he hath heard the
words of this oath, he bless himself in his heart, and say,
There shall still be peace for me, yea, even though I go in
the depravity of my heart; but such thinking shall destroy
everything;)
20 and the Lord forgive not to him, but then full greatly
his strong vengeance be fierce, and his fervour burst out
against that man, and all the curses that be written in this
book rest upon him; and *the Lord* do away his name from
under heaven, (for the Lord shall not forgive him, but his
strong vengeance shall be greatly fierce, and his fervour
shall burst out against that person, and all the curses that
be written in this book shall rest upon him; and *the Lord*
shall do away his name from under heaven,)
21 and waste him into perdition from all the lineages of
Israel, by the curses that be contained in the book of this
law, and of the bond of peace. (yea, he shall bring him
out of all the tribes of Israel, and shall bring him down
into perdition, according to all the curses of the
covenant, that be contained in this Book of the Law.)
22 And the generation following shall see, and the sons
that shall be born afterward, and pilgrims that shall come
from [a]far, seeing the vengeances of that land, and the
sicknesses by which the Lord tormented that land, (And
the generation following, and the descendants who shall
be born afterward, and the foreigners who shall come
from afar, shall all see the plagues that be in the land, and
the sicknesses with which the Lord hath tormented it,)
23 burning *that land* with brimstone, and heat of the
sun, so that it be no more sown, neither bring forth any
green thing, into ensample of [the] destroying of Sodom,
and Gomorrah, of Admah, and of Zeboiim, which the
Lord destroyed in his wrath, and strong vengeance.
(burning up *that land* with brimstone, and the heat of the
sun, so that it can no more be sown, nor bring forth any
green thing, following the examples of the destruction of
Sodom, and Gomorrah, and Admah, and Zeboiim, all of
which the Lord destroyed in his anger, and his strong
vengeance.)
24 And all folks shall say, Why did the Lord so to this
land? What is the great wrath of his strong vengeance?
(And all the nations shall say, Why hath the Lord done so
to this land? What is the reason for his great anger and
strong vengeance?)

25 and they shall answer, For they forsook the covenant
of the Lord, which he covenanted with their fathers,
when he led them out of the land of Egypt,
26 and they served alien gods, and worshipped them,
which they knew not, and to which they were not given;
(and they served foreign, *or other*, gods, and worshipped
them, which they knew not, and which he had not given
them;)
27 therefore the strong vengeance of the Lord was
wroth against this land, that he brought in upon it all the
curses that be written in this book; (and so with strong
vengeance the Lord was angry against this land, and he
brought in on it all the curses that be written in this book;)
28 and he casted them out of their land, in wrath and
strong vengeance, and in full great indignation; and he
casted forth them into an alien land, as it is proved today.
(and he threw them out of their land, in his anger and
strong vengeance, and very great indignation; and he
threw them forth into a foreign land, where they still be
today.)
29 *Diverse* things *be* hid, *or privy*, of our Lord God,
that is, in his before-knowing, which things be showed to
us, and to our sons (into) without end, that we do all the
words of this law. (Some things *be* hid, *or known only*,
by the Lord our God, *that is, in his foreknowing*, but
other things be shown to us, and to our descendants into
without end, so that we can do all the words of this law.)

CHAPTER 30

1 Therefore when all these come upon thee, blessing
either cursing, which I have set forth in thy sight, and *if*
thou art led by repentance of thine heart among all folks,
into which thy Lord God hath scattered thee, (And so
when all these things have come upon thee, the blessing
and the curse which I have set forth before thee, *if* thou
art led by the repentance of thy heart, when thou be
among all the nations into which the Lord thy God hath
scattered thee,)
2 and *if* thou turnest again to him, and obeyest to his
behests, as I have commanded to thee today, with thy
sons, in all thine heart, and in all thy soul, (and *if* thou,
and thy sons and thy daughters, turn back to him, and
obey his commands, as I have commanded thee today,
with all thy heart, and with all thy soul,)
3 thy Lord God shall lead thee again from thy
captivity, and shall have mercy on thee, and again he
shall gather thee from all peoples, into which he hath
scattered thee before. (then the Lord thy God shall have
mercy on thee, and he shall bring thee back from thy
captivity, yea, he shall gather thee again from all the
peoples into whom he hath scattered thee.)
4 If thou art scattered to the ends of heaven, from
thence thy Lord God shall draw thee; (Even if thou art
scattered unto the ends of the heavens, the Lord thy God
shall gather thee back from there;)
5 and he shall take *thee*, and bring thee into the land
which thy fathers wielded (and he shall bring thee back
to the land which thy fathers possessed); and thou shalt
hold it, (*or possess it*,) and he shall bless thee, and shall
make thee to be of more number than thy fathers were.
6 Thy Lord God shall circumcise thine heart, and the
heart of thy seed, that thou love thy Lord God in all thine
heart, and in all thy soul, and thou mayest live. (The Lord
thy God shall circumcise thy hearts, and the hearts of thy
descendants, so that thou shalt love the Lord thy God
with all thy heart, and with all thy soul, and that thou
mayest live.)
7 Forsooth the Lord shall turn all these cursings on
thine enemies, and on them that hate *thee*, and pursue
thee.
8 Soothly thou shalt turn again, and shalt hear the
voice of thy Lord God, and shalt do all the behests which
I command to thee today; (And thou shalt return, and
hear the voice of the Lord thy God, and shalt do all the
commands which I command to thee today;)
9 and thy Lord God shall make thee to be plenteous,
in all the works of thine hands, in the children of thy
womb, and in the fruit of thy beasts, and in (the)
abundance of thy land, and in (the) largeness of all
things. For the Lord shall turn again, that he have joy
upon thee in all goods, as he joyed in thy fathers (For the
Lord shall again have joy over thee, and shall be good to
thee, as he had joy over thy fathers);
10 if nevertheless thou hearest the voice of thy Lord
God, and keepest his behests and his ceremonies, that be
written in this (book of the) law, and *if* thou turn again to
thy Lord God in all thine heart, and in all thy soul. (if
nevertheless thou hearest the voice of the Lord thy God,
and obey his commandments and his statutes, that be
written in this Book of the Law, and *if* thou return to the
Lord thy God with all thy heart, and with all thy soul.)
11 This commandment which I command to thee
today, is not (too far) above thee, neither it is set far *from
thee* (nor is it set too far away *from thee*),
12 neither it is set in heaven, that thou say, Who of us
may go up to heaven, that he bring it to us, and we hear
it, and fulfill *it* in work? (nor is it set in the heavens, so
that thou sayest, Who shall go up to the heavens for us,
and bring it down, so that we can hear it, and fulfill *it*
with our deeds?)
13 neither *it is set* beyond the sea, that thou complain,
and say, Who of us may pass over the sea, and bring it
hither to us, that we may hear, and do that that is
commanded *to us*? (nor *is it set* beyond the sea, so that
thou can complain, and say, Who of us shall cross over
the sea, and bring it back here to us, so that we can hear
it, and do what is commanded *to us*?)
14 But the word is full nigh thee, in thy mouth, and in

thine heart, that thou do it. (But the word is very near to
thee, yea, *it is* in thy mouth, and in thy heart, so that thou
can do it.)
15 Behold thou, that today I have set forth in thy sight
life and good, and, on the contrary, death and evil;
16 that thou love thy Lord God, and go in his ways, and
keep his behests, and *his* ceremonies, and *his* dooms;
and that thou live, and he multiply thee, and bless thee in
the land to which thou shalt enter to wield. (so that thou
can love the Lord thy God, and go in all his ways, and
obey his commandments, and *his* statutes, and *his* laws,
or his judgements; and so that thou shalt live, and that he
multiply thee, and bless thee in the land to which thou
shalt enter to take.)
17 But if thine heart is turned away, and thou wilt not
hear, and thou art deceived by error, and worshippest
alien gods, and servest them, (But if thy heart is turned
away, and thou wilt not listen, *and obey*, and thou art
deceived by error, and worshippest foreign, *or other*,
gods, and servest them,)
18 I before-say to thee today, that thou shalt perish, and
thou shalt dwell little time in the land, to which thou
shalt enter to wield, when thou shalt pass (the) Jordan. (I
say to thee today, before the time, *or ahead of time*, that
thou shalt die, and *thou* shalt live only a short time in the
land, which thou shalt enter to take, when thou shalt
cross over the Jordan River.)
19 I call today heaven and earth to witness, *that is,
angels and men*, that I have set forth to you life and
death, good and evil, blessing and cursing; therefore
choose thou life, that both thou live and thy seed, (I call
heaven and earth, *that is, the angels and men*, to witness
today, that I have set forth before you life and death,
good and evil, blessing and curses; and so choose thou
life, so that both thou and thy descendants shall live,)
20 and that thou love thy Lord God, and obey to his
voice, and cleave to him, for he is thy life, and the length
of thy days; that thou dwell in the land, for which the
Lord swore to thy fathers, Abraham, Isaac, and Jacob, that
he should give it to them. (and that thou love the Lord thy
God, and obey his voice, and cleave to him, for he is thy
life, and the length of thy days; and so that thou can live
in the land which the Lord swore to thy fathers, Abraham,
Isaac, and Jacob, that he would give them.)

CHAPTER 31

1 And so Moses went, and spake all these words to all
Israel,
2 and said to them, I am today of an hundred and
twenty years, I may no further go out and go in, most(ly)
since also the Lord said to me, Thou shalt not pass this
Jordan. (and said to them, Today I am a hundred and
twenty years old, and I can no longer go out and come
in, and the Lord hath said to me, Thou shalt not cross
over this Jordan River.)
3 Therefore thy Lord God shall pass before thee (And
so the Lord thy God shall cross over before thee); he shall
do away these folks in thy sight, and thou shalt wield
them; and this Joshua shall go before thee, (in the lead,)
as the Lord spake.
4 And the Lord shall do to them as he did to Sihon,
and to Og, the kings of (the) Amorites, and to their land;
and he shall do them away.
5 Therefore when the Lord hath betaken to you also
them (And so when the Lord hath also delivered them to
you), ye shall do in like manner to them, as I have
commanded to you.
6 Do ye manly, and be ye comforted (Be ye strong, and
be ye encouraged); do not ye dread in heart, neither dread
ye at the sight of them, for thy Lord God himself is thy
leader, and he shall not leave thee, neither forsake thee.
7 And Moses called Joshua, and said to him before all
the multitude of the sons of Israel, Be thou comforted,
and be thou strong (Be thou encouraged, and be thou
strong); for thou shalt lead this people into the land that
the Lord swore that he shall give to their fathers; and thou
shalt part it by lot.
8 And the Lord himself, which is your leader (And the
Lord himself, who is your leader), shall be with thee, he
shall not leave [thee], neither forsake thee; do not thou
dread *outward(ly)*, neither dread thou *in heart*.
9 Therefore Moses wrote this law, and betook it to the
priests, the sons of Levi, that bare the ark of the bond of
peace of the Lord, and to all the elder men of Israel. (And
so Moses wrote this law, and gave it to the levitical
priests, who carried the Ark of the Covenant of the Lord,
and to all the elders of Israel.)
10 And Moses commanded to them, and said, After
seven years, in the year of remission, (*or release*,) in the
solemnity of tabernacles, (And Moses commanded to
them, and said, After seven years, in the Year of
Restoration, *or the Year of Forgiveness*, at the Feast of
Tabernacles,)
11 when all men of Israel shall come together, that they
appear in the sight of their Lord God, in the place which
the Lord choose, thou shalt read the words of this law
before all Israel, while they hear, (when all the people of
Israel shall come together, so that they can come before
the Lord their God, in the place which the Lord shall
choose, thou shalt read the words of this law before all
Israel, while they hear,)
12 and while all the people is gathered together, as
well to men, as to women, to little children, and to
comelings that be within thy gates; that they hear, and
learn, and dread your Lord God, and keep and [ful]fill all
the words of this law; (and while all the people is
gathered together, men and women, and little children,
and the newcomers who be within thy gates; so that they

can listen, and learn, and fear the Lord your God/and
revere the Lord your God, and obey and fulfill all the
words of this law;)
13 also that the sons of them, that now know not, may
hear, and that they dread their Lord God in all days in
which they live in the land to which ye shall go to get,
when (the) Jordan is passed. (and also so that their
children, who now do not know, can listen, and learn to
fear the Lord their God/and learn to revere the Lord their
God, in all the days in which they live in the land to
which ye shall go to get, after that ye have crossed over
the Jordan River.)
14 And the Lord said to Moses, Lo! the days of thy
death be nigh; call thou Joshua, and stand ye in the
tabernacle of witnessing, that I command to him (and
stand ye together in the Tabernacle of the Witnessing, so
that I can give him his charge, *or his commission*).
Therefore Moses and Joshua went, and they stood in the
tabernacle of (the) witnessing;
15 and the Lord appeared there in a pillar of cloud, that
stood in the entering of the tabernacle (that stood at the
entrance to the Tabernacle).
16 And the Lord said to Moses, Lo! thou shalt sleep
with thy fathers, and this people shall rise up, and it shall
do fornication, *or idolatry, going* after alien gods in the
land, into which it shall enter, that it dwell therein; there
it shall forsake me, and shall make void the bond of
peace, which I covenanted with it. (And the Lord said to
Moses, Lo! soon thou shalt sleep with thy fathers, *that is,
thou shalt die*, and then this people shall rise up, and
they shall do fornication, *or idolatry, going* after foreign,
or other, gods in the land, into which they shall enter, to
live there; and they shall forsake me there, and they shall
make void, *or shall break*, the covenant, which I made
with them.)
17 And my strong vengeance shall be wroth against
that people in that day, and I shall forsake it, and I shall
hide my face from it, and it shall be into devouring; all
evils and tormentings shall find it, so that it say in that
day, Verily for the Lord is not with me, these evils have
found me. (And my strong vengeance shall be stirred
against them in that day, and I shall forsake them, and I
shall hide my face from them, and they shall be
devoured; and many evils and torments shall find them,
so that they say on that day, Truly these evils have found
us, because the Lord is not with us.)
18 Soothly I shall hide my face, and cover it in that day,
for all the evils which *this people* hath done, for it hath
followed alien gods. (And I shall hide my face, and cover
it on that day, for all the evils which *this people* hath
done, for they have followed foreign, *or other*, gods.)
19 Now therefore write ye to you this song, and teach
ye the sons of Israel, that they hold *it* in mind, and sing *it*
in mouth; and that this song be to me for a witnessing
among the sons of Israel. (And so now write down this song
for you, and teach ye it to the Israelites, so that they can
remember *it*, and sing *it* with their mouths; and so that
this song can be a witness for me against the Israelites.)
20 For I shall lead him into the land, for which I swore to
his fathers, flowing with milk and honey; and when they
have eaten, and be full-filled, and be made fat, they shall
turn to alien gods, and they shall serve them; and they
shall backbite me, and shall make void my covenant. (For
I shall lead them into the land, for which I swore to their
fathers, a land flowing with milk and honey; and when
they have eaten, and be filled full, and be made fat, then
they shall turn to foreign, *or to other*, gods, and they shall
serve them; and they shall backbite me, and they shall
make void, *or shall break*, my covenant.)
21 After that many evils and tormentings have found
them, this song shall answer to him for (a) witnessing,
which song no forgetting shall do away from the mouth
of thy seed. For I know the thoughts thereof today, what
things it shall do, before that I bring it into the land which
I promised to it. (And after that many evils and torments
have found them, this song shall speak against them as a
witness, which no forgetting shall do away from the
mouths of their descendants. For I know their thoughts
today, and what things they shall do, before that I bring
them into the land which I promised them.)
22 Therefore Moses wrote the song, and he taught it to
the sons of Israel. (And so Moses wrote down this song,
and he taught it to the Israelites.)
23 And the Lord commanded to Joshua, the son of Nun,
and said, Be thou comforted (Be thou encouraged), and be
thou strong; for thou shalt lead the sons of Israel into the
land which I promised (*them*), and I shall be with thee.
24 Therefore after that Moses had written the words of
this law in a book, and fulfilled *them* (and finished *them*),
25 he commanded to the Levites that bare the ark of the
bond of peace of the Lord, and said, (he commanded to
the Levites who carried the Ark of the Covenant of the
Lord, and said,)
26 Take ye this book (of the law), and put ye it in the
side of the ark of the bond of peace of your Lord God,
that it be there against thee into witnessing. (Take ye this
Book of the Law, and put ye it beside the Ark of the
Covenant of the Lord your God, to be a witness there
against thee.)
27 For I know thy striving, and thy most hard noll; yet
while I lived and entered with you, ye did ever[more]
strivingly against the Lord; how much more when I shall
be dead. (For I know thy defiance, *or thy rebellious
nature*, and thy stiff neck/and thy stubbornness; yet while
I lived and went with you, ye often defied the Lord; so
then how much more, after that I am dead?)
28 Gather ye to me all the greater men in birth, and
teachers [and doctors], by your lineages, and I shall speak

to them, hearing these words, and I shall call (to witness)
against them heaven and earth. (Gather ye to me all the
men of great age, *that is, the elders,* of your tribes, and
the officers, and I shall speak to them, and they shall hear
all these words, and I shall call heaven and earth to
witness against them.)
29 For I know, that after my death, ye shall do
wickedly, and shall bow away soon from the way which I
commanded to you; and evils shall come to you in the
last time(s), when ye have done evil in the sight of the
Lord, that ye stir him to wrath by the works of your hands.
(For I know, that after my death, ye shall do wickedly, and
shall soon turn away from the way which I commanded
to you; and evils shall come to you in the days to come,
when ye have done evil in the sight of the Lord, and so
stir him to anger with the works of your hands.)
30 Therefore while all the company of the sons of Israel
heard, Moses spake the words of this song, and he
fulfilled *it* unto the end. (And so while all the
congregation of the Israelites listened, Moses spoke the
words of this song, and he spoke *every word of it,* from
the beginning unto the end.)

CHAPTER 32

1 Ye heavens, hear what things I shall speak; the earth
hear the words of my mouth.
2 My teaching wax (al)together as rain; my speech
flow out as dew, as soft rain upon herb, and as drops
upon grass. (My teaching shall fall like drops of rain; my
speech shall flow out like the dew, like showers on the
herbs, and raindrops on the grass.)
3 For I shall inwardly call the name of the Lord; give
ye glory to our God. (For I shall call out loud the name of
the Lord; give ye glory to our God.)
4 The works of God be perfect, and all his ways be
dooms (and all his ways be just); God is faithful, and
without any wickedness; he *is* just and rightful.
5 They sinned against him, and (they be) not his sons,
(they be) in the filths *of idolatry;* (they be a) depraved and
wayward generation.
6 Whether thou yieldest these things to the Lord, thou
fond people and unwise? Whether he is not thy father,
that wielded thee, and made, and formed thee of nought?
(Did thou yield these things to the Lord, thou foolish and
unwise people? Is he not thy father, who made thee, and
formed thee out of nothing, and wieldeth thee?)
7 Have thou mind of eld days, think thou (on) all
generations; ask thy father, and he shall tell to thee, *ask*
thy greater men, and they shall say to thee. (Remember
the days of old, and think thou on all the generations; ask
thy father, and he shall tell thee, *ask* the men of great age,
that is, thy elders, and they shall say to thee.)
8 When the highest parted folks, when he separated
the sons of Adam, he ordained the terms of peoples by
the number of the sons of Israel. (When the Most High
God divided the nations, when he separated the sons of
man, he ordained the borders of the peoples according to
the number of the sons of God.)
9 Forsooth the part of the Lord is his people; Jacob is
the little part of his heritage. (But the Lord's portion was
his own people; Jacob was the portion of his inheritance.)
10 The Lord found him in a desert land, in the place of
horror, *either hideousness,* and of waste wilderness; the
Lord led him about, and taught *him,* and he kept him as
the apple of his eye. (The Lord found them in a desert
land, in a howling, wasted wilderness; and the Lord led
them about, and taught *them,* and kept them as the apple
of his eye.)
11 As an eagle stirring his birds to fly, and flying above
them, he spreaded forth his wings, and took them *into his*
protection, and he bare them in his shoulders. (Like an
eagle stirring his young to fly, and flying above them, he
spread out his wings, and took them up, and he carried
them upon his shoulders.)
12 The Lord alone was his leader, and none alien god
was with him. (The Lord alone was their leader, and no
other god was with him.)
13 The Lord ordained him on an high land, that he
should eat the fruits of fields, that he should suck honey
of a stone, and oil of the hardest rock; (The Lord ordained
them upon the highlands, and they ate the fruits of the
fields, and sucked honey out of the stones, and oil out of
the hardest rock,)
14 butter of the drove, and milk of sheep, with the
fatness of lambs, and of rams, of the sons of Bashan; and
that he should eat kids with [the] marrow, *or tried flour,*
of wheat, and he should drink the clearest blood, *or*
wine, of the grape. (and *they ate* butter from the herds,
and milk from the sheep, and the fatness of lambs, and
rams from the sons of Bashan, and goats, and the
marrow, *or the fine flour,* of wheat; and they drank the
clearest blood, *that is, the purest wine,* of the grapes.)
15 The beloved *people* was made fat, and (they) kicked
against (God); made fat withoutforth, made fat within,
and alarged; he forsook God his maker, and went away
from God his health/from God his saviour. (And Jeshurun
was made fat, and rebellious; made fat withoutforth,
made fat within, yea enlarged; and they forsook God
their Maker, and went away from God their
salvation/from God their Saviour.)
16 They stirred God to wrath in alien gods *that they*
praised, they stirred him to wrathfulness in their
abominations, *that is, their own findings.* (They provoked
God to anger with foreign, *or other,* gods *that they*
praised, and they stirred him to rage with their
abominable doings.)
17 They offered to fiends, *or devils,* and not to God, to
gods which they knew not, (to) new *gods,* and fresh(ly)

came up *by their findings*, which their fathers
worshipped not. (They offered to fiends, *or to devils*, and
not to God, to gods which they knew not, to new *gods*
which they discovered *in their searching*, that their
fathers did not worship.)
18 Thou hast forsaken God that begat thee, and thou
hast forgotten thy Lord creator/the Lord thy maker. (Thou
hast forsaken the God who begat thee, and thou hast
forgotten the Lord thy Creator/the Lord thy Maker.)
19 The Lord saw *that*, and he was stirred to wrathfulness;
for his sons, and daughters stirred him *to vengeance*. (The
Lord saw *this*, and he was stirred to rage; yea, his sons
and his daughters, stirred him *to vengeance*.)
20 And the Lord said, I shall hide my face from them,
and I shall behold their last things; for this is a wayward
generation, and unfaithful sons *they be*. (And the Lord
said, I shall hide my face from them, and then I shall see
what will happen to them; for this is a wayward
generation, *they be* unfaithful children.)
21 They have stirred me to wrath in *worshipping* him
that was not God, and they have moved me to vengeance
in their vain idols; and I shall stir them (to wrath) in him,
that is not a people, and I shall stir them to ire in a fond
folk. (They have stirred me to jealousy by *worshipping*
what was not God, and they have moved me to
vengeance with their vain idols; and so I shall stir them to
jealousy, with those who be not a people, and I shall stir
them to anger, with a nation of fools.)
22 Fire is kindled in my strong vengeance, and it shall
burn unto the last things of hell; and it shall devour the
land with his fruit, and it shall burn the foundaments of
hills (and it shall devour the land with its fruit, and it shall
burn the very roots, *or the foundations*, of the mountains).
23 I shall gather evils on them, and I shall [ful]fill mine
arrows in them. (I shall gather one evil after another upon
them, and I shall send all my arrows against them/and I
shall spend all my arrows against them.)
24 They shall be wasted with hunger, and birds shall
devour them with most bitter biting; I shall send into
them the teeth of beasts, with the strong vengeance of
(those) drawing upon (the) earth, and of serpents. (They
shall be wasted with hunger, and fever, and terrible
sicknesses; I shall send into them the teeth of beasts, and
the poisonous bites of serpents which draw themselves
upon the ground/through the dust.)
25 Sword withoutforth, and dread within, shall waste
them; a young man and a virgin together, a sucking child
with an eld man.
26 And I said, Where be they now? I shall make the
mind of them to cease of *all* men (I shall make the
memory of them to vanish, *or to cease*, from *all* people).
27 But I delayed, *or tarried*, for the wrath of (their)
enemies, lest peradventure their enemies should be
proud, and say, Our high hand, and not the Lord('s), did
all these things.
28 It is a folk without counsel, and without prudence,
or wariness; (They be a nation without counsel, and
without wisdom, *or without caution*;)
29 I would that they savoured, and understood, and
purveyed the last things. (O that they considered, and
understood this, and gave some thought to their end.)
30 How pursued one *of (their) enemies* a thousand *of
Jews*, and twain drove away ten thousand? Whether not
therefore for their God had sold them, *forsaking them*,
and the Lord had enclosed them altogether *in their
enemies' hands*? (How could just one *of their enemies*
pursue a thousand *Jews*, and two drive away ten
thousand? Was it not because their God had *forsaken
them*, and had sold them out to their enemies, yea, the
Lord had given them up *into the hands of their enemies*?)
31 For our God is not as the gods of them, and our
enemies be judges (of this). (For our enemies have no
god like our God, ours is strong, and they know that their
gods be weak.)
32 The vine of them *is* of the vine of Sodom, and of the
suburbs of Gomorrah; the grape of them *is* the grape of
gall, and the cluster *is* most bitter. (Their vines *be* like the
vines of Sodom, and like those grown in the suburbs of
Gomorrah; their grapes *be* grapes of gall, and their
clusters *be* most bitter.)
33 The gall of dragons is the wine of them, and the
venom of adders, that may not be healed. (The gall of
dragons is their wine, yea, the cruel venom of adders.)
34 Whether these things be not hid with me, and be
sealed (up) in my treasuries, (*or in my storehouses*)?
35 Vengeance is mine, and I shall yield (it) to them in
time, (so) that the foot of them slide; the day of perdition
is nigh, and the times hasten to be present.
36 The Lord shall deem his people, and he shall do
mercy in his servants; the *people* shall see that the hand
of *(the) fighters* is sick, *or feeble*, and also men (en)closed
failed, and the remnant people, *or left*, be wasted. (The
Lord shall judge his people, and he shall do mercy to his
servants; for he shall see that the hands of *their fighters*
be feeble, *or weak*, and that the enclosed men have
failed, and that the remnant, *that is, the people who were
left*, now is gone.)
37 And they shall say, Where be their gods, in which
they had trust? (And then the Lord shall say, Where be
your gods, in which ye had trust?)
38 Of whose sacrifices they ate the fatnesses, and they
drank the wine of flowing sacrifices, rise they and help
you, and defend they you in (time of) need. (Yea, the
gods which ate the fat of your offerings, and which drank
the wine of your wine offerings, now let them rise up and
help you, and defend they you in your time of need!)
39 See, *or understand*, ye, that I am *God* alone, and
none other God is except me; I shall slay, and I shall

make to live; I shall smite, and I shall make whole; and
none is that may deliver from mine hand. (See ye, *that is,*
understand ye, that I am *God* alone, and there is no other
god except me; I shall kill, and I shall make to live; I shall
strike down, and I shall make whole; no one can rescue
anyone out of my hands.)
40 And I shall raise up mine hand to heaven, and I shall
say, I live without end. (And I shall raise up my hand to
heaven, and I shall say, As surely as I live forever,)
41 If I shall whet my sword as lightning, and mine hand
shall take doom, I shall yield vengeance to mine
enemies, and I shall requite to them that hate me. (I shall
whet my sword with lightning, and my hand shall make
judgement, I shall yield vengeance to my enemies, and I
shall requite to them who hate me.)
42 I shall full-fill mine arrows with blood, and my sword
shall devour (the) fleshes of the blood of them *that be* slain,
and of the captivity, of the head(s) of (the) enemies made
naked. (I shall fill my arrows full of blood, and my sword
shall devour the flesh of the blood of them *who be* killed,
and of the captives, yea, the very heads of the enemies.)
43 Folks, praise ye the people of him, for he shall
venge the blood of his servants, and he shall yield
vengeance to the enemies of them (Nations, praise ye
him with his people, for he shall avenge the blood of his
servants, and he shall yield vengeance to their enemies);
and he shall be merciful to the land of his people.
44 Therefore Moses came, and spake all the words of
this song in the ears of the people; both he and Joshua,
the son of Nun. (And so Moses came, and spoke all the
words of this song to the people; both he and Joshua, the
son of Nun.)
45 And Moses fulfilled all these words, and spake to all
Israel, (And when Moses finished speaking all these
words, to all Israel,)
46 and said to them, Put ye your hearts into all the
words which I witness to you today, that ye command to
your sons, to keep, and to do those, and to fulfill all
things that be written in the book of this law; (he said to
them, Put ye into your hearts all the words which I
witness to you today, so that ye command to your
children to obey them, and to do them, and to fulfill all
the things that be written in this Book of the Law;)
47 for not in vain *these things* be commanded to you,
but that all men should live in *doing* those *things*; which
if ye shall do (them), *then* ye shall abide, and shall
continue long time in the land, to which ye shall enter to
wield, when (the) Jordan *ye have* over-passed. (for *these*
things be not commanded to you in vain, but so that all
of you should live by doing them; which if ye shall do
these things, *then* ye shall live, and shall continue a long
time in the land, which ye shall enter to take, when *ye*
have crossed over the Jordan River.)
48 And the Lord spake to Moses in the same day, and
said, (And the Lord spoke to Moses on that same day, and
said,)
49 Go thou up into this hill Abarim, *that is, passing,*
into the hill of Nebo, which is in the land of Moab, (over)
against Jericho; and see thou the land of Canaan, which I
shall give to the sons of Israel to hold, (Go thou up to the
Abarim Mountains, *that is, to The Passages,* yea, onto
Mount Nebo, which is in the land of Moab, opposite, *or*
east of, Jericho; and see thou the land of Canaan, which I
shall give to the Israelites for their possession,)
50 and die thou *there* in *this* hill. Into which *hill* thou
shalt go up, and thou shalt be joined to thy peoples, as
Aaron, thy brother, was dead in the hill of Hor, and was
put to his peoples. (and then thou shalt die *there* on *that*
mountain. Yea, thou shalt go up onto this *mountain,* and
thou shalt join thy people, like when thy brother Aaron
died on Mount Hor, and he joined his people.)
51 For ye trespassed against me, in the midst of the
sons of Israel, at the Waters of Against-saying, in Kadesh,
of the desert of Zin; and ye hallowed not me among the
sons of Israel. (For both of you trespassed against me,
before the Israelites, at the waters of Meribah-Kadesh, in
the wilderness of Zin; for ye did not uphold my holiness
among the Israelites.)
52 Opposite (thee), thou shalt see the land, and thou
shalt not enter into it, which I shall give to the sons of
Israel. (And thou shalt look across, and see the land, but
thou shalt not enter into it, yea, the land which I shall
give to the Israelites.)

CHAPTER 33

1 This is the blessing, with which Moses, the man of
God, blessed the sons of Israel before his death; (This is
the blessing, with which Moses, the man of God, blessed
the Israelites before his death;)
2 and said, The Lord came from Sinai, and he rose to
us from Seir; he appeared from the hill of Paran, and
thousands of saints with him; a law of fire in his right
hand. (and he said, The Lord came from Sinai, and he
rose up like the sun to us from Seir, *or Edom*; he
appeared from Mount Paran, and thousands of saints, *or*
holy ones, or angels, were with him; a Law of fire was in
his right hand.)
3 He loved peoples; all saints be in his hand, and they
that nigh to his feet shall take of his doctrine. (He loved
the people; all the saints be in *the palm of* his hand, and
they who sit at his feet shall receive his doctrine, *or his*
teaching.)
4 Moses commanded the law to us, the heritage of the
multitude of Jacob. (Yea, the Law which Moses commanded
to us, the inheritance of the multitude of Jacob.)
5 And the king shall be at the most rightful, when
princes of the people be gathered together with the
lineages of Israel. (And then the King was there in

Jeshurun, when the leaders of the people were gathered
together with the tribes of Israel.)
6 Reuben live, and die not, and be he little in number.
(May *the tribe of* Reuben live, and not die out, but be
they few in number.)
7 This is the blessing of Judah; Lord, hear thou the
voice of Judah, and bring in him to his people; his hands
shall fight for him, and the helper of him, shall be against
his adversaries. (This is the blessing for *the tribe of* Judah;
Lord, hear thou the voice of Judah, and unite them again
with the other tribes; thy hands shall fight for them, and
thou shalt be their helper against their adversaries.)
8 Also he said to Levi, Thy perfection and thy teaching
is of an holy man, whom thou hast proved in temptation,
and hast deemed at the Waters of Against-saying; (And he
said of *the tribe of* Levi, *Lord,* may thy Thummim and thy
Urim be with them, thy holy servants, whom thou hast
proved at Massah, and hast judged at the waters of
Meribah;)
9 which *Levi* said to his father and to his mother, I
know not you, and to his brethren, I know not them; and
knew not his sons. These kept thy speech, and these kept
thy covenant; (yea, the *Levites* said to their fathers and
their mothers, We do not know you, and to their
brothers, We do not know you; and they did not even
know their own sons and daughters. They obeyed thy
words, and they kept thy covenant.)
10 O! Jacob, they kept thy dooms, and thy law, O!
Israel; they shall put incense in thy strong vengeance, and
burnt sacrifice on thine altar. (They shall teach Jacob thy
precepts, and Israel thy Law; they shall put incense and
burnt offerings upon thy altar.)
11 Lord, bless thou the strength of him, and receive
thou the works of his hands; smite thou the backs of his
enemies, and they that hate him, rise they not. (Lord,
bless thou their strength, and receive thou the works of
their hands; strike thou the backs of their enemies, and
they who hate them, let them never rise up again.)
12 And he said to Benjamin, The most loved of the
Lord shall dwell trustily in him; he shall dwell all day as
in a chamber, and he shall rest betwixt the shoulders of
the Lord. (And he said of *the tribe of* Benjamin, The
beloved of the Lord shall dwell trustily in him; they shall
live all day long like in a secure place, and they shall rest
between the shoulders of *the Lord.*)
13 Also he said to Joseph, His land *is* of the Lord's
blessing; of the apples of heaven, and of the dew, and of
water lying beneath; (And he said of *the tribe of* Joseph,
Their land *is* blessed by the Lord, with precious fruits
watered from the heavens above, and from the streams
flowing beneath;)
14 of the apples of the fruits of the sun, and moon; (with
precious fruits, ripened by the sun, over the months;)
15 [and] of the top of eld mountains, and of the apples of
everlasting little hills; (with precious fruits, from the tops of
the old mountains, and from the everlasting little hills;)
16 and of the fruits of the land, and of the fullness
thereof. The blessing of him that appeared in the bush
come upon the head of Joseph, and upon the foretop,
that is, the crown of the head, of the Nazarite, *or (the)*
holy (one), among his brethren. (with the fruits, *and other*
crops, of the land, in all its fullness. May these blessings
of him who appeared in the bush come upon Joseph's
head, yea, upon the tribe of him who was separated from
his brothers/who was the leader of his brothers.)
17 As the first engendered of a bull is the fairness of
him; the horns of an unicorn be the horns of him; in
those he shall winnow folks, till to the terms of [the]
earth. These be the multitudes of Ephraim, and these be
the thousands of Manasseh. (His fairness is like the first-
born of a bull; his horns be like the horns of a wild ox;
and with them he shall winnow the nations, unto the
ends of the earth. Such shall be the multitudes of
Ephraim, and the thousands of Manasseh.)
18 And he said to Zebulun, Zebulun, be thou glad in
thy going out, and Issachar, in thy tabernacles. (And he
said of *the tribes of* Zebulun, and *of* Issachar, Zebulun,
be thou prosperous abroad, and Issachar, *be thou*
prosperous in thy tents, *or at home.*)
19 They shall call peoples to the hill, [and] there they
shall offer sacrifices of rightfulness; which shall suck the
flowing(s) of the sea as milk, and hid treasures of gravel.
(They shall call the peoples to the mountain, and there
they shall offer the right sacrifices; they shall suck *up* the
wealth of the sea like milk, and they shall dig up hidden
treasures out of the gravel.)
20 And he said to Gad, Gad *is* blessed in broadness; he
rested as a lion, and he took *from his adversary* the arm
and the noll. (And he said of *the tribe of* Gad, Gad *is*
blessed in their broad places; they rest like a lion, but
they tear off the arms and the tops of the heads *of their*
adversaries.)
21 And he saw his *princehood,* that he was kept a
teacher in his part; the which was with (the) princes of
the people, and he did the rightfulnesses of the Lord, and
his doom with Israel. (And they chose the best land for
themselves, a ruler's portion, when the leaders of the
people were gathered together; and they did the justice
of the Lord, and his laws, *or his judgements,* with Israel.)
22 Also he said to Dan, Dan, a whelp of a lion, shall
flow largely from Bashan. (And he said of *the tribe of*
Dan, Dan *is* a whelp of a lion, leaping out from Bashan.)
23 And he said to Naphtali, Naphtali shall use
abundance, and he shall be full with blessings of the
Lord; and he shall wield the sea[2] and the south. (And he

[2] For the Sea of Galilee, as to the south part thereof, felled in the lot of Naphtali.

said of *the tribe of* Naphtali, Naphtali shall have great
abundance, and they shall be full of the Lord's blessings;
they shall take the land southward from Lake Galilee.)
24 Also he said to Asher, Asher, be blessed in sons, and
please he his brethren; dip he his foot in oil. (And he said
of *the tribe of* Asher, Asher is the most blessed of the
tribes; may they be the favourite among their brothers, *or*
their kinsmen, and may they bathe their feet in oil.)
25 Iron and brass (be) the shoe(s) of him; as the day of
thy youth, so and thine eld (age). (May thy gates be made
out of iron and brass; and thy old age be like the days of
thy youth.)
26 None other god is as the God of the most rightful;
the rider of heaven is thine helper; clouds run about by
the glory of him. (There is no other god like the God of
Jeshurun; the Rider of heaven is thy helper, riding upon
the clouds in his glory/riding through the clouds in his
glory.)
27 His dwelling place is above, and his arms
everlasting be beneath; he shall cast out from thy face the
enemy, and he shall say *to them*, Be thou all-broken. (His
dwelling place is above, but his everlasting arms be
beneath; he shall throw out the enemy from before us,
and he shall say *to us*, Destroy them all!)
28 Israel shall dwell trustily and alone; the eye of Jacob
is in the land of wheat, and of wine; and (the) heavens
shall be dark with dew. (And then Israel shall live secure
and alone; the tribes of Jacob *shall be* in the land of corn,
and of wine; and the skies shall be dark with dew.)
29 Blessed art thou, Israel; thou people that art saved in
the Lord, who is like thee? The shield of thine help and
the sword of thy glory is thy God; thine enemies shall
deny thee, and thou shalt tread their necks. (Blessed art
thou, O Israel; who is like thee? the people who art saved
by the Lord! Thy God is the shield of thy help, and the
sword of thy glory; thy enemies shall beg thee for mercy,
but thou shalt tread upon their necks!)

CHAPTER 34

1 Therefore Moses went up from the field places of
Moab upon the hill of Nebo, into the top of Pisgah, (over)
against Jericho. And the Lord showed to him all the land
of Gilead, till to Dan, (And so Moses went up from the
plains of Moab to Mount Nebo, and then to the top of
Mount Pisgah, opposite, *or east of*, Jericho. And the Lord
showed him all the land of Gilead, unto Dan,)
2 and all Naphtali, and the land of Ephraim and of
Manasseh, and all the land of Judah, unto the last, *or*
furtherest, sea; (and all of Naphtali, and the land of
Ephraim and of Manasseh, and all the land of Judah, as
far west as the Great Sea, *or the Mediterranean Sea*;)
3 and the south part, and the breadth of the field of
Jericho, of the city of Palms, till to Zoar. (and the south
part, *or the Negeb*, and the breadth of the plain of
Jericho, yea, from the City of Palms, unto Zoar.)
4 And the Lord said to him, This is the land for which
I swore to Abraham, Isaac, and Jacob; and I said, I shall
give it to thy seed; (now) thou hast seen it with thine
eyes, and thou shalt not pass to it (but thou shalt not cross
over to it).
5 And Moses, the servant of the Lord, was dead there,
in the land of Moab, for the Lord commanded. (And then
Moses, the servant of the Lord, died there, in the land of
Moab, as the Lord had said.)
6 And *the Lord* buried him in a valley of the land of
Moab, (over) against Bethpeor; and no man knew his
sepulchre unto this day. (And *the Lord* buried him in a
valley of the land of Moab, opposite the town of Bethpeor;
but unto this day, no one knoweth the place of his burial.)
7 Moses was of an hundred and twenty years when he
died; his eye dimmed not, neither his teeth were stirred.
(Moses was a hundred and twenty years old when he
died; but his eyes had not dimmed, and his strength had
not diminished.)
8 And the sons of Israel bewept him thirty days in the
field places of Moab; and the days of wailing of men
bemourning Moses were fulfilled. (And the Israelites
wept for him on the plains of Moab for thirty days; and
then the days of the wailing of the people mourning for
Moses were finished.)
9 Soothly Joshua, the son of Nun, was full-filled with
the spirit of wisdom, for Moses had put his hands upon
him; and the sons of Israel obeyed to Joshua, and did as
the Lord commanded to Moses. (And Joshua, the son of
Nun, was filled full with the spirit of wisdom, for Moses
had put his hands upon him; and the Israelites obeyed
Joshua, and did what the Lord commanded to Moses.)
10 And a prophet rose no more in Israel (*such*) as
Moses, whom the Lord knew face to face, (And never
again did a prophet ever arise in Israel such as Moses,
yea, whom the Lord knew face to face,)
11 in all the miracles, and great wonders, which the
Lord sent, *or did*, by him, that he should do in the land of
Egypt to Pharaoh, and to all his servants, and to all his
land, (and so *thou should always remember* all the
miracles, and the great wonders, which the Lord sent him
to do in the land of Egypt, to Pharaoh, and to all his
servants, and to all his land,)
12 and all the strong hand, *or power*, and the great
marvels, which Moses did before all Israel. (yea, to
remember the strong hand of Moses, and the great
marvels which he did before all Israel.)

Here endeth (the) Pentateuch, see now the prologue of Joshua.[3] ✡

[3] This rubric appears in one copy of the Later Version.

JOSHUA

CHAPTER 1

1 And it was done after the death of Moses, the
servant of the Lord, that the Lord spake to Joshua, the son
of Nun, the servant of Moses, and said to him,
2 Moses, my servant is dead; rise thou, and pass [over]
this Jordan, thou, and all the people with thee, into the
land which I shall give to the sons of Israel. (My servant
Moses is dead; rise thou up, and cross over the Jordan
River to the other side, thou, and all the people with
thee, into the land which I shall give to the Israelites.)
3 I shall give to you each place which the step of your
foot shall tread, as I spake to Moses,
4 from the desert and Lebanon till to the great flood
[of] Euphrates; all the land of Hittites, unto the great sea
against the going down of the sun, shall be your term.
(from the wilderness and Lebanon unto the great Euphrates
River; yea, all the Hittites' land, unto the Great Sea, *that
is, the Mediterranean Sea*, in the west, shall be your land.)
5 None shall be able to against-stand you in all the
days of thy life; as I was with Moses, so I shall be with
thee; I shall not leave, neither I shall forsake thee. (No
one shall be able to stand against you all the days of thy
life; as I was with Moses, so I shall be with thee; I shall
not leave thee, nor shall I abandon thee.)
6 Be thou comforted, and be thou strong; for thou
shalt part by lot to this people the land, for which I swore
to thy fathers, that I should give it to them. (Be thou
encouraged, and be thou strong; for thou shalt divide up
by lot the land to this people, which I swore to thy
fathers, that I would give them.)
7 Therefore be thou comforted, and be thou full
strong, that thou keep and do all the law, which Moses,
my servant, commanded to thee; bow thou not from it to
the right side, either to the left side, that thou understand
all things which thou doest. (And so be thou encouraged,
and be thou strong, so that thou obey and do all the law,
which my servant Moses commanded to thee; turn thou
not from it to the right, or to the left, so that thou shalt
prosper in all things wherever thou goest.)
8 The book of this law depart not from thy mouth, but
thou shalt think therein in days and nights, that thou keep
and do all things that be written therein; then thou shalt
(ad)dress thy way, and thou shalt understand it. (Let not
this Book of the Law depart from thy mouth, but think
thou on it day and night, so that thou obey and do all the
things that be written in it; then thou shalt make thy way
prosperous, and be successful.)
9 Lo! I command to thee; be thou comforted, and be
thou strong; do not thou dread, nor be thou afeared; for
thy Lord God is with thee in all things, to which thou
goest. (Lo! I command thee; be thou encouraged, and be
thou strong; do not thou fear, nor be thou afraid; for the
Lord thy God is with thee in all things, to which thou
goest.)
10 And Joshua commanded to the princes of the
people, and said, (And Joshua commanded to the leaders
of the people, and said,)
11 Pass ye through the midst of the castles, and
command ye to the people, and say ye, Make ye ready
meats to you; for after the third day ye shall pass [over]
(the) Jordan, and ye shall enter [in] to wield the land,
which your Lord God shall give to you. (Go ye through
the midst of the tents, *or the camp*, and command ye to
the people, and say ye, Prepare ye food for yourselves;
for in three days ye shall cross over the Jordan River, and
ye shall go in to take the land, which the Lord your God
shall give you.)
12 Also Joshua said to men of Reuben, and to men of
Gad, and to the half lineage of Manasseh, (And Joshua
said to the men of Reuben, and the men of Gad, and the
men of *the eastern* half of the tribe of Manasseh[1],)
13 Have ye mind of the word which Moses, the servant
of the Lord, commanded to you, and said, Your Lord God
hath given to you rest, and all the land; (Remember what
Moses, the servant of the Lord, commanded to you,
saying, The Lord your God hath given rest to you, and
hath given you all of this land;)
14 your wives, and your sons, and your beasts shall
dwell in the land that Moses gave to you beyond (the)
Jordan, (*that is, on the east side of the river*); but pass ye
(over) armed, all (the) strong in hand, before your
brethren; and fight ye for them,
15 till the Lord give rest to your brethren, as he gave
also to you, and till also they wield the land which your
Lord God shall give to them; and so turn ye again into
the land of your possession, and ye shall dwell in that
land which Moses, [the] servant of the Lord, gave to you
over Jordan, against the rising of the sun. (until the Lord
give rest to your kinsmen, as he also gave to you, and
until they also take the land which the Lord your God
shall give them; and then ye shall return to the land of
your possession, and ye shall live in that *land* which
Moses, the servant of the Lord, gave you on this east side
of the Jordan River, near to the rising of the sun.)
16 And they answered to Joshua, and said, We shall do
all things which thou commandest to us, and we shall go,
whither ever thou sendest us;
17 as we obeyed in all things to Moses, so we shall

---

[1] The tribe of Manasseh divided in two after the defeat of Sihon and Og; one half settled on the eastern side of the Jordan River, and the other half on the western side.

obey also to thee; only thy Lord God be with thee, as he
was with Moses. (as we obeyed Moses in all things, so
shall we also obey thee; only may the Lord thy God be
with thee, as he was with Moses.)
18 Die he that against-saith thy word, and obeyeth not
to all thy biddings, which thou commandest to him; only
be thou comforted, and do thou manly (only be thou
encouraged, and be thou strong).

CHAPTER 2

1 Therefore Joshua, the son of Nun, sent from Shittim
two men, spyers in huddles, and said to them, Go ye, and
behold ye the land, and the city of Jericho. Which went,
and entered into the house of a woman whore, Rahab by
name, and rested at her. (And so Joshua, the son of Nun,
secretly sent out two spies from Shittim, and said to them,
Go ye, and look ye over the land, and the city of Jericho.
And they went, and entered into the house of a whore-
woman, Rahab by name, and stayed with her.)
2 And it was told, and said to the king of Jericho, Lo!
men of the sons of Israel have entered hither by night, to
espy the land. (And it was told to the king of Jericho, Lo!
some men of the Israelites have come in here by night, to
spy out the land.)
3 Therefore the king of Jericho sent to Rahab the
whore, and said, Bring out the men, that came to thee,
and that entered into thine house; for they be spyers (for
they be spies), and they came to behold all the land.
4 And the woman took the men, and hid *them*, and
said, I acknowledge, that they came to me, but I wist not
of whence they were; (But *earlier*, the woman had taken
the men, and had hid *them*, and so she said, I
acknowledge, that they came to me, but I knew not
where they came from;)
5 and when the gate was closed in darknesses, and
they went out together, I know not whither they went
(and tonight before the *city* gate was closed, they went
out together, but I do not know where they went); pursue
ye *them* soon, and ye shall overtake them.
6 Forsooth she (had) made the men to go up into the
solar of her house, and she (had) covered them with
stubble, *or sheaves*, of flax, that was there.
7 And they, that were sent, followed them by the way
that leadeth to the fords of (the) Jordan; and when they
were gone out, anon the gate was closed. (And they, who
were sent there, followed after them by the way that
leadeth to the crossings of the Jordan River; and when
they were gone out, at once the *city* gate was closed.)
8 [And] They that were hid, slept not yet, and lo! the
woman went up to them,
9 and said, I know that the Lord hath betaken to you
this land; for your fearedfulness is fallen into us, and all
the dwellers of the land be abashed. (and she said, I
know that the Lord hath delivered this land to you; for we
all be afraid of you, and all the inhabitants of the land be
greatly panicked.)
10 We have heard, that the Lord hath dried up the
waters of the Red Sea at your entering, when ye went out
of Egypt; and what things ye did to the two kings of
Amorites, that were beyond (the) Jordan, to Sihon and
Og, which ye killed; (We have heard, that the Lord dried
up the waters of the Red Sea, *or the Sea of Reeds*, before
you, when ye went out of Egypt; and what ye did to the
two kings of the Amorites, who were on the eastern side of
the Jordan River, that is, to Sihon and Og, whom ye killed;)
11 and we heard these things, and we dreaded, and our
heart was sick, and spirit dwelled not in us at your
entering; for the Lord your God himself is God in heaven
above, and in earth beneath (and on the earth below).
12 Now therefore swear ye to me by the Lord God, that
as I did mercy with you, so and ye do with the
house(hold) of my father; and give ye to me a very sign,
(And so now swear ye to me by the Lord God, that as I
did mercy with you, so ye shall also do mercy with my
family; and give ye to me a true sign,)
13 that ye (shall) save my father, and my mother, and
my brethren, and [my] sisters, and all things that be
theirs, and (shall) deliver our lives from death.
14 Which answered to her, Our life be for you into
death, if nevertheless thou betrayest not us; and when the
Lord hath betaken to us the land, we shall do mercy and
truth with thee. (And they answered to her, Our lives be
for yours unto death, if thou betrayest us not; and when
the Lord hath delivered the land to us, we shall show
mercy and faithfulness to thee.)
15 Then she let them down from the window by a
cord; for her house was joined to the *town* wall.
16 And she said to them, Go ye up to the hilly places,
lest peradventure the men turning again meet you; and
be ye hid there three days, till they come again; and so ye
shall go by your way. (And she said to them, Go ye up to
the hills, lest as the men return, they come upon you; and
be ye hid there for three days, until they return; and then
ye can go on your way.)
17 Which said to her, We shall be guiltless of this oath,
by which thou hast charged us,
18 if, when we enter into the land, this red cord is not
(shown as) a sign, and thou bindest it not in the window,
by which thou lettest us down; and thou gatherest not
into thine house thy father, and mother, and brethren,
and all thy kindred;
19 the blood of him shall be on his head, that goeth out
at the door of thine house, and we shall be guiltless;
forsooth the blood of all men that be in the house with
thee, shall turn into our head (shall be on our heads), if
any man toucheth them.
20 That if thou wilt betray us, and bring forth into the
midst this word, we shall be clean of this oath, by which

thou hast charged us. (But if thou wilt betray us, and bring forth this word into the midst/and make known our agreement, then we shall be released from this oath, by which thou hast charged us.)
21 And she answered, As ye have spoken, so be it done. And she let go them, that they should go forth (And she let them go, so that they could go forth), and (then) she hanged the red cord in her window.
22 And they went forth, and came into the hilly places, and dwelled there three days, till they turned again that (had) pursued *them*; for they sought *them* by each way, and found not them. (And they went forth, and came to the hills, and stayed there for three days, until they who had pursued *them* returned; for they had sought *them* every place that they could think of, but could not find them anywhere.)
23 And when *the seekers* entered into the city *again*, the spyers turned again, and came down from the hill; and when they had passed [over] (the) Jordan, they came to Joshua, the son of Nun; and they told to him all things that befelled to them, (And after that *those who had sought them* had entered into the city *again*, the spies returned, and came down from the hills; and when they had crossed back over the Jordan River, they came to Joshua, the son of Nun; and they told him everything that had happened to them,)
24 and said, The Lord hath betaken all the land into our hands, and all the dwellers thereof be cast down by dread. (and they said, The Lord hath delivered all the land into our hands, and all of its inhabitants be greatly afraid of us.)

CHAPTER 3

1 Therefore Joshua rose by night, and moved thence the tents; and they went out of Shittim, and came to (the) Jordan, he and all the sons of Israel (he and all the Israelites), and dwelled there three days.
2 And when those days were passed, criers/beadles went through the midst of the tents,
3 and began to cry, When ye see the ark of [the] bond of peace of your Lord God, and the priests of the generation of Levi bearing it, also *then* rise ye, and follow the before-goers; (and began to cry, When ye see the Ark of the Covenant of the Lord your God, and the levitical priests carrying it, *then* ye shall rise up, and follow them;)
4 and a space of two thousand cubits be betwixt you and the ark, (so) that ye may see (it from) [a]far, and (so that ye can) know by which way ye shall enter, for ye have not gone before by it (for ye have not gone this way before); and be ye ware, that ye nigh not to the ark.
5 And Joshua said to the people, Be ye hallowed, for tomorrow the Lord shall make marvels among you.
6 And Joshua said to the priests, Take ye the ark of the bond of peace of the Lord, and go ye before the people. The which fulfilled the behests of Joshua, and they took *the ark*, and went before *the people*. (And Joshua said to the priests, Take ye the Ark of the Covenant of the Lord, and go ye before the people. And they obeyed Joshua's commands, and they took *the Ark*, and went before *the people*.)
7 And the Lord said to Joshua, Today I shall begin to enhance thee before all Israel (Today I shall begin to magnify thee before all Israel), (so) that they know, that as I was with Moses, so I am also with thee.
8 Forsooth command thou to the priests, that bear the ark of [the] bond of peace, and say thou to them, When ye have entered into a part of the water of (the) Jordan, stand ye therein. (And command thou to the priests, who carry the Ark of the Covenant, and say thou to them, When ye have entered into a part of the water of the Jordan River, stand ye there.)
9 And Joshua said to the sons of Israel, Nigh ye hither, and hear ye the word of your Lord God. (And Joshua said to the Israelites, Come ye here, and hear ye the word of the Lord your God.)
10 And again he said, In this ye shall know that the Lord God living is in the midst of you (And he said, By this ye shall know that the living God is in the midst of you); and he shall destroy in your sight (the) Canaanites, Hittites, Hivites, and Perizzites, and Girgashites, and Jebusites, and Amorites.
11 Lo! the ark of the bond of peace of the Lord of all earth shall go before you through Jordan. (Lo! the Ark of the Covenant of the Lord of all the earth shall go before you across the Jordan River.)
12 Make ye ready twelve men of the twelve lineages of Israel, by each lineage one man. (Make ye ready twelve men of the twelve tribes of Israel, one man out of each tribe.)
13 And when the priests, that bear the ark of [the] bond of peace of the Lord God of all earth (who carry the Ark of the Covenant of the Lord God of all the earth), have set the steps of their feet in the waters of (the) Jordan, the waters that be lower shall run down, and shall fail; soothly the waters that come from above shall stand together in one gathering, *or (in) a certain place.*
14 Therefore the people went out of their tabernacles for to pass over (the) Jordan; and the priests that bare the ark of [the] bond of peace went before the people. (And so the people went out of their tents to cross over the Jordan River; and the priests who carried the Ark of the Covenant went before the people.)
15 And when the priests entered into (the) Jordan, and their feet were dipped in the part of [the] water; forsooth (the) Jordan had filled the brinks of his trough in the time of ripe corn (for the Jordan River was filled to the brim of its trough at that time of harvest);
16 the waters (that) went down (from above halted), and stood in one place, and waxed great at the likeness

of an hill, and appeared far from the city that was called
Adam, till to the place of Zaretan; soothly the waters that
were lower went down into the sea of (the) wilderness,
which is now called the dead sea, till the waters failed
utterly. Forsooth the people went through (the) Jordan;
(the waters, that went down from above, stood in one
place, and grew great like a hill, going back as far away
as the city called Adam, which is close to the city of
Zaretan; and the waters that were lower, *or below*, went
down into the Sea of the Wilderness, which is now called
the Dead Sea, until there was no water. And then the
people crossed over opposite Jericho;)
17 and the priests, that bare the ark of the bond of
peace of the Lord, stood girded on the dry earth in the
midst of (the) Jordan, and all the people passed [over]
through the dry trough. (and the priests, who carried the
Ark of the Covenant of the Lord, stood firmly on the dry
earth in the midst of the Jordan River, until all the people
had crossed over through the dry trough.)

CHAPTER 4

1 And when *the sons of Israel* were passed over *(the)*
Jordan, the Lord said to Joshua, (And when *all the Israelites*
had crossed over the Jordan River, the Lord said to Joshua,)
2 Choose thou twelve men, by each lineage one man,
(Choose thou twelve men, one man out of each tribe,)
3 and command thou to them, that they take from the
midst of the trough of (the) Jordan, where the feet of [the]
priests stood, twelve hardest stones; the which thou shalt
set in [the] place of the tents, where ye shall set (the) tents
in this night. (and command thou to them, that they take
out of the middle of the trough, *or the river bed*, of the
Jordan River, twelve stones, from where the feet of the
priests had firmly stood; which thou shalt put in the place
of the camp, where ye shall pitch the tents tonight.)
4 And Joshua called (the) twelve men, which he had
chosen of the sons of Israel, of each lineage one man;
(And Joshua called the twelve men, whom he had chosen
out of the Israelites, one man out of each tribe;)
5 and he said to them, Go ye before the ark of your
Lord God to the midst of (the) Jordan, and bear ye from
thence in your shoulders each man one stone, by the
number of the sons of Israel, (and he said to them, Go ye
before the Ark of the Lord your God into the middle of
the Jordan River, and each man carry ye out from there a
stone on his shoulders, one for each of the tribes of Israel,)
6 that it be a sign betwixt you. And when your sons
shall ask you tomorrow, *that is, in time to coming*, and
shall say, What will these stones be mean(ing)? (that shall
become a sign for all of you. And so when your sons and
daughters shall ask you tomorrow, *that is, in the time to*
come, and shall say, What mean ye by these stones?)
7 ye shall answer to them, The waters of (the) Jordan
failed before the ark of [the] bond of peace of the Lord,
when the ark passed over (the) Jordan; therefore these
stones be set into mind of the sons of Israel, till into
without end. (ye shall answer to them, The waters of the
Jordan River stopped flowing before the Ark of the
Covenant of the Lord, when the Ark crossed over the
Jordan River; and so these stones be here to help the
Israelites to remember this forevermore.)
8 Therefore the sons of Israel did as Joshua
commanded to them, and bare from the midst of the
trough of (the) Jordan twelve stones, as the Lord
commanded to him, by the number of the sons of Israel,
unto the place in which they setted tents (one for each of
the tribes of Israel, unto the place where they pitched
their tents); and there they putted those stones.
9 Also Joshua putted (an)other twelve stones in the
midst of the trough of (the) Jordan, where the priests (had)
stood, that bare the ark of [the] bond of peace of the Lord
(who carried the Ark of the Covenant of the Lord); and
those stones be there unto this present day.
10 Forsooth the priests, that bare the ark, stood in the
midst of (the) Jordan, till all things were [ful]filled, which
the Lord commanded, that Joshua should speak to the
people (that Joshua should tell the people to do), as
Moses had said to him. And the people hasted, and
passed *over (the) Jordan.*
11 And when all men had passed [over], also the ark of
the Lord passed [over], and (then) the priests went before
the people (again).
12 Also the sons of Reuben, and of Gad, and half the
lineage of Manasseh, went armed before the sons of
Israel, as Moses commanded to them. (And the sons of
Reuben, and of Gad, and of *the eastern* half of the tribe
of Manasseh, went armed before the Israelites, as Moses
had commanded them to do.)
13 And forty thousand of fighters went by their
companies, and by *their* gatherings, on the plain and field
places of the city of Jericho. (And forty thousand fighting
men went by their companies, over the plains and fields,
near the city of Jericho.)
14 In that day the Lord magnified Joshua before all Israel,
that they should dread him, as they dreaded Moses, while
he lived yet. (On that day the Lord magnified Joshua
before all Israel, so that they would fear him, like they
had feared Moses/so that they would revere him, like
they had revered Moses, while he was yet alive.)
15 And the Lord said to Joshua,
16 Command thou to the priests that bear the ark of
[the] bond of peace, that they go up from (the) Jordan.
(Command thou to the priests who carry the Ark of the
Covenant, that they come up from the Jordan River.)
17 And Joshua commanded to them, and said, Go ye
up from (the) Jordan. (And Joshua commanded to them,
and said, Come ye up from the Jordan River.)
18 And when they had gone up, bearing the ark of [the]

bond of peace of the Lord, and had begun to tread on the
dry earth, the waters turned again into their trough, and
flowed again, as they were wont (to) before. (And when
they had come up, carrying the Ark of the Covenant of
the Lord, and had begun to tread on the dry earth, the
waters returned to their place, and flowed again, as they
were wont to before.)
19 And the people went up from (the) Jordan in the
tenth day of the first month, and they setted tents in
Gilgal, against the east coast of the city of Jericho. (And
the people went up from the Jordan River on the tenth
day of the first month, and they pitched their tents in
Gilgal, east of the city of Jericho.)
20 Also Joshua putted in Gilgal the twelve stones,
which they had taken from the trough of (the) Jordan.
21 And he said to the sons of Israel, When your sons
shall ask tomorrow their fathers, and shall say to them,
What will these stones be mean(ing)? (And he said to the
Israelites, When your sons and daughters shall ask their
fathers tomorrow, and shall say to them, What mean ye
by these stones?)
22 ye shall teach them, and say, We passed this Jordan
by the dry bottom, (ye shall teach them, and say, We
crossed over the Jordan River on dry land,)
23 for our Lord God dried the waters thereof in our
sight, till that we over-passed it, as he did before in the
Red Sea, which he dried while we passed [over], (for the
Lord our God dried up its waters before us, until we had
crossed over it, like he did before at the Sea of Reeds,
which he dried up so we could cross over it,)
24 that all the peoples of (the) earth learn, or *know*, (of)
the full strong might of the Lord, and that ye dread your
Lord God in all time. (so that all the peoples of the earth
can learn, or *come to know*, of the strong might, *or the
powerful hand*, of the Lord, and so that ye shall fear the
Lord your God forevermore/and so that ye shall revere
the Lord your God forevermore.)

CHAPTER 5

1 Therefore after that all the kings of Amorites heard,
that dwelled over (the) Jordan at the west coast, and all the
kings of Canaan, that wielded the nigh places of the great
sea, that the Lord had dried the flowings of (the) Jordan
before the sons of Israel, till they passed over, the heart of
them failed, and the spirit dwelled not in them, dreading
the entering of the sons of Israel. (And so when all the
kings of the Amorites, who lived on the west side of the
Jordan River, and all the kings of Canaan, who possessed
the lands near the Mediterranean Sea, heard that the Lord
had dried up the flowings of the Jordan River before the
Israelites, until they had crossed over, their hearts failed,
and there was no more spirit, *or courage*, left in them, for
they all feared the coming of the Israelites.)
2 In that time the Lord said to Joshua, Make to thee
knives of stone (Make thou some stone knives), and
circumcise thou the sons of Israel the second time.
3 Joshua did those things which the Lord commanded,
and he circumcised the sons of Israel in the hill of
prepuces (and he circumcised the male Israelites at the
Hill of the Foreskins).
4 And this is the cause of the second circumcision; all
the people of male kind, that went out of Egypt, all the
men fighters *of them*, were dead in (the) desert by the full
long compasses of (the) way, (And this is the reason for
the second circumcision; all the males, who went out of
Egypt, yea, all their fighting men, who had died in the
wilderness on the very long journey on the way,)
5 the which all were circumcised. But the *other*
people that was born in desert by forty years, in the way
of the full broad wilderness, was uncircumcised, (were all
circumcised. But the *other* males, those who were born
in the wilderness, were uncircumcised.)
6 till they (all) were wasted, that heard not the voice of
the Lord, and to which he swore before, that he should
(not) show to them the land flowing with milk and honey.
(Yea, for forty years, they went on the way of the very
broad wilderness, until all of them had died who had not
obeyed the voice of the Lord, and to whom he had sworn
before, that he would not let them see the land flowing
with milk and honey.)
7 The sons of them came afterward into the place of
[the] fathers, and they were circumcised of Joshua; which,
as they were born, were in prepuce, neither any man had
circumcised them in the way. (Their sons came afterward
into the place of their fathers, and they were the ones
whom Joshua circumcised; for they all had foreskins, as
when they were born, for no one had circumcised them
on the way.)
8 And after that they all were circumcised, they
dwelled in the same place of their tents, till they were
healed.
9 And the Lord said to Joshua, Today I have taken
away from you the shame of Egypt. And (so) the name of
the place was called Gilgal[2], unto this present day.
10 And the sons of Israel dwelled in Gilgal, and made
pask in the fourteenth day of the month at eventide, in
the field places of Jericho; (And the Israelites stayed at
Gilgal, and kept the Passover on the fourteenth day of the
month in the evening, on the plains of Jericho;)
11 and they ate of the fruits of the land in the tother
day, therf loaves, and pottage of the same year, *either
corns singed, and rubbed in the hand.* (and they ate of
the fruits of the land on the next day, unleavened bread,
and pottage of that year, *or corns singed, and then
rubbed by hand.*)

---

[2] "Gilgal" sounds like the Hebrew for "removed" or "taken away". (Good News Bible)

12 And (the) manna failed after that they ate of the fruits
of the land; and the sons of Israel used no more that meat
(and no longer did the Israelites receive that food), but they
ate of the fruits of (the) present year of the land of Canaan.
13 And when Joshua was in the field of the city of
Jericho, he raised up his eyes, and saw a man standing
(over) against him, and holding a drawn sword; and
Joshua went out to him, and said, Art thou with us, either
(with) our adversary?
14 To whom he answered, Nay, but I am (the) prince of
the host of the Lord, and now I (have) come. Joshua
felled low to the earth, and worshipped, and said, What
speaketh my Lord to his servant? (And Joshua fell down
onto the ground, and honoured *him*, and said, What saith
my lord to his servant?)
15 (And) He said, Unlace thy shoes from (off) thy feet,
for the place, in which thou standest, is holy. And Joshua
did, as it was commanded to him.

CHAPTER 6

1 Forsooth Jericho was (en)closed and warded, for the
dread of the sons of Israel (for fear of the Israelites), and
no man durst enter, either go out.
2 And the Lord said to Joshua, Lo! I have given into
thine hands Jericho, and the king thereof, and all the
strong men *of it*. (And the Lord said to Joshua, Lo! I have
given Jericho into thy hands, and its king, and all the
strong men *there*.)
3 All ye fighters, compass the city once by the day; so
ye shall do in six days (so ye shall do for six days).
4 And in the seventh day, the priests shall take seven
clarions, which be used in the jubilee; and they shall go
before the ark of [the] bond of peace; and seven times ye
shall compass the city, and the priests shall trump with
the clarions. (And on the seventh day, the priests shall
take seven trumpets, which be used on the Jubilee; and
they shall go before the Ark of the Covenant; and seven
times ye shall go around the city, and the priests shall
blow the trumpets.)
5 And when the voice of the trump shall sound
longer, and more by whiles, and shall sound in your ears,
all the people shall cry together with (the) greatest cry;
and the walls of the city shall fall all-down (and the city
walls shall all fall down), and all (the) men shall enter by
the place, against which they stand.
6 Therefore Joshua, the son of Nun, called the priests,
and said to them, Take ye the ark of the bond of peace,
and seven other priests take *they* seven clarions of the
jubilee years, and go they before the ark of the Lord.
(And so Joshua, the son of Nun, called the priests, and
said to them, Take ye the Ark of the Covenant, and seven
other priests take *they* seven trumpets used in the Jubilee
years, and go they before the Ark of the Lord.)
7 Also Joshua said to the people, Go ye, and compass
ye the city, and go ye armed before the ark of the Lord.
(And Joshua said to the people, Go ye, and go ye around
the city, and go ye armed before the Ark of the Lord.)
8 And when Joshua had ended these words, and the
seven priests trumped with seven trumps before the ark
of the bond of peace of the Lord, (And when Joshua had
finished speaking, the seven priests blew the seven
trumpets before the Ark of the Covenant of the Lord,)
9 and all the people armed went before, and the
tother common people *of fighters* followed the ark, and
all things sounded with the trumps. (and all the armed
men went before them, and the other common people *of
fighting men* followed the Ark, and everything echoed
with the sound of the trumpets.)
10 And Joshua commanded to the people, and said, Ye
shall not cry, neither your voice shall be heard, neither any
word shall go out of your mouth, till the day come, in
which I shall say to you, Cry ye, and (then) make ye noise.
11 Therefore the ark of the Lord compassed the city
once by the day, and it turned again into the tents, and
dwelled there. (And so they took the Ark of the Lord
around the city once that day, and then they returned to
their tents, *or the camp*, and stayed there.)
12 Therefore while Joshua rose early *in the
morrowtide*, [the] priests took the ark of the Lord; (And
the next day, Joshua rose up early *in the morning*, and
the priests again carried the Ark of the Lord;)
13 and seven of the priests *took* seven clarions, which
were used in the jubilee, and *the priests* went before the
ark of the Lord, and trumped; and the people went armed
before them. And the tother common people followed
the ark, and sounded with trumps. (and seven of the
priests *took up* seven trumpets, which were used on the
Jubilee, and *they* went before the Ark of the Lord, and
blew the trumpets; and the armed men went before them.
And the other common people followed the Ark, the
trumpets sounding as they went.)
14 And they compassed the city in the second day
once, and turned again into the tents; so they did six
days. (And they went around the city once on the second
day, and then they returned to their tents; and so they did
for six days.)
15 And in the seventh day they rose early, and
compassed the city, as it was ordained, seven times. (And
on the seventh day they all rose up early, and went
around the city, as it was ordained, seven times.)
16 And when in the seventh compass, the priests
sounded with clarions, Joshua said to all Israel, Cry ye,
for the Lord hath betaken the city to us; (And on the
seventh time around, when the priests blew the trumpets,
Joshua said to all Israel, Shout ye, for the Lord hath
delivered the city to us;)
17 and this city be cursed, *either destroyed*, and all
things that be therein be *hallowed* to the Lord. (Let)

Rahab the whore alone live, with all the men that be with
her in the house; for she hid the messengers which we
sent (for she hid the spies that we sent).
18 And be ye ware, lest ye touch anything of these
[things] that be forbidden to you, and ye be guilty of
trespassing; and all the tents of Israel be under sin, and be
troubled (for then all the tents of Israel would be under
sin, and we would be in great trouble).
19 For whatever thing is of gold, and of silver, and of
brazen vessels, and of iron (vessels), be it hallowed to the
Lord, and be it kept in his treasuries.
20 Then while all the people cried, and the trumps
sounded, after that the sound sounded in the ears of the
multitude, the walls felled down anon; and each man
went up by the place that was against him. And they
took the city, (Then while the trumpets sounded, and
were heard in the ears of the multitude, all the people
shouted, and the walls fell down at once; and each man
advanced straight ahead. And they took the city,)
21 and they killed all things that were therein, from
man unto woman, (and) from a young child unto an eld
man; also they killed by sharpness of sword, oxen, sheep,
and asses (and they killed by the sharpness of their
swords, all the oxen, and the sheep, and the donkeys).
22 Forsooth Joshua said to [the] two men, that were
sent (as) spyers, Enter ye into the house of the woman
whore, and bring ye forth her, and all things that be hers,
as ye made steadfast to her by an oath. (And Joshua said
to the two men, who were sent as spies, Go ye into the
house of the whore-woman, and bring ye her forth, and
all the things that be hers, as ye made steadfast to her,
that is, as ye promised her, by your oath.)
23 And the young men entered in, and they led out
Rahab, and her father, and mother, and all her brethren,
and all the purtenance of her, and kindred; and they
made them to dwell without the tents of Israel. (And the
young men went in, and they led out Rahab, and her
father, and her mother, and all her brothers, and sisters,
yea, all her family, and all who belonged to her; and they
let them live outside Israel's camp.)
24 And the men of Israel burnt the city, and all things
that were found therein, except [the] gold, and silver, and
brazen vessels, and iron (vessels), which they hallowed
into the treasury of the Lord (which they put in the Lord's
treasury).
25 Soothly Joshua made Rahab the whore to live, and
her father's house(hold), and all things that she had; and
they dwelled in the midst of Israel, unto this present day;
for she hid the messengers, which Joshua sent to espy
Jericho. (And Joshua spared the lives of Rahab the whore,
and her family, and all who belonged to her; and her
descendants have lived in the midst of Israel unto this
present day; for she hid the men, whom Joshua sent to
spy out Jericho.)
26 In that time Joshua prayed heartily, and said, Cursed
before the Lord be the man, that raiseth up and buildeth
(again) the city of Jericho! Lay he the foundaments thereof
in his first engendered son, and put he the gates thereof
in the last of his free children. (And at that time Joshua
heartily prayed, and said, Cursed be the man before the
Lord, who raiseth up and buildeth again this city of
Jericho! May he lay its foundations at the cost of the life
of his first-born son, and may he put up its gates at the
cost of the life of his last child.)
27 Therefore the Lord was with Joshua, and his name
was published in each land. (And so the Lord was with
Joshua, and his name was made known throughout the
land.)

CHAPTER 7

1 Forsooth the sons of Israel brake the commandment,
and mis-took of the cursed thing; for Achan, the son of
Carmi, the son of Zabdi, [the] son of Zerah, of the lineage
of Judah, took something of the cursed thing; and the
Lord was wroth against the sons of Israel. (But one of the
Israelites disobeyed the *Lord's* command, and took some
of the cursed things; for Achan, the son of Carmi, the son
of Zabdi, the son of Zerah, of the tribe of Judah, took
some of the cursed things; and so the Lord was angry
with the Israelites.)
2 And when Joshua sent men from Jericho against Ai,
which is beside Bethaven, at the east coast of the city of
Bethel, he said to them, Go ye up, and espy the land.
Which [ful]filled the commandments, and espied Ai;
(And when Joshua sent men from Jericho to Ai, which is
beside Bethaven, to the east of the city of Bethel, he said
to them, Go ye up, and spy out the land. And they
fulfilled his commands, and spied out Ai;)
3 and they turned again, and said to him, All the
people go not up thither, but two either three thousand of
men go, and do away the city (and they returned, and
said to him, All the people do not need to go up there,
but only two or three thousand men need to go, and do
away the city); why shall all the people be travailed in
vain against (such) full few enemies?
4 Therefore three thousand of fighters ascended,
which turned the backs anon, and were smitten of the
men of Ai; (And so three thousand fighting men went up,
who at once turned their backs, after they were attacked
by the men of Ai;)
5 and six and thirty men of them were slain; and the
adversaries pursued them from the (city) gate unto
Shebarim; and they felled down fleeing by (the) low
places. And the heart of the people dreaded *much*, and it
was made unsteadfast at the likeness of water (And the
people's hearts were full of fear, and they were made as
unstable as water).
6 And Joshua rent his clothes, and he fell down low to

the earth before the ark of the Lord, unto the eventide, as
well he, as all the elder men of Israel; and they casted
powder on their heads. (And Joshua tore his clothes, and
he fell down onto the ground before the Ark of the Lord,
until the evening, he, as well as all the elders of Israel;
and they threw powder on their heads.)
7 And Joshua said, Alas! alas! Lord God, what
wouldest thou lead this people over the flood Jordan, that
thou shouldest betake us in the hand of Amorites, and
should lose *us*? I would, that as we began, we had
dwelled beyond (the) Jordan. (And Joshua said, Alas! alas!
Lord God, why didest thou lead this people over the
Jordan River, so that thou couldest deliver us into the
hands of the Amorites, and so destroy *us*? Oh how I
wish, that we had stayed on the other side of the Jordan!)
8 My Lord God, what shall I say, seeing Israel turning
the backs to his enemies? (My Lord God, what can I say,
after seeing the men of Israel turn their backs to their
enemies?)
9 Canaanites, and all the dwellers of the land shall
hear *this*, and they shall be gathered together, and shall
compass us, and they shall do away our name from [the]
earth; and what shalt thou do to thy great name? (The
Canaanites, and all the inhabitants of this land, shall hear
of this, and they shall be gathered together, and shall
surround us, and they shall do away our names from the
earth; and then what shalt thou do for thy great name?)
10 And the Lord said to Joshua, Rise thou up; why liest
thou low in the earth? (why liest thou there on the ground?)
11 Israel hath sinned, and hath broken my covenant;
they have taken of the cursed thing(s), and they have stolen
of it, and lied, and hid among their vessels. (*Someone in*
Israel hath sinned, and hath broken my covenant; he hath
taken some of the cursed things, yea, he hath stolen it,
and lied about it, and hid it among his own possessions.)
12 And *therefore* Israel may not stand before his
enemies, and he shall flee them, for it is defouled with
cursing; I shall no more be with you, till that ye destroy
him that is guilty of this trespass. (And *so* the men of
Israel cannot stand before their enemies, and they shall
flee from them, for they be defiled with curses; I shall no
longer be with you, unless and until ye destroy him who
is guilty of this trespass.)
13 Rise thou (up), hallow the people, and say thou to
them, Be ye hallowed against tomorrow (Hallow thyselves
for tomorrow); for the Lord God of Israel saith these
things, O thou Israel! cursing is in the midst of thee; thou
shalt not be able to stand before thine enemies, till he
that is defouled by this trespass, be done away from thee.
14 And ye shall come (forth) early, all men by your
lineages; and whatever lineage the lot shall find, it shall
come by his families (it shall come by its families); and
the family *shall come* by (its) houses, and the house *shall
come* by (its) men.
15 And whoever shall be taken with this trespass, he
shall be burnt with fire with all his chattel, for he brake
the covenant of the Lord, and did unleaveful thing in
Israel. (And whoever shall be taken with this trespass, he
shall be burned with fire along with all his possessions,
for he broke the covenant of the Lord, and did an
unlawful thing in Israel.)
16 Therefore Joshua rose early, and setted in order
Israel by his lineages; and the lineage of Judah was
found; (And so Joshua rose up early, and put Israel in
order, tribe by tribe; and the tribe of Judah was found;)
17 and when that lineage was brought forth by his
families, the family of Zerah was found. And Joshua
brought forth it by men, *either houses*, and found Zabdi;
(and when that tribe was brought forth by its families, the
family of Zerah was found. And Joshua brought forth that
family by its men, *or its households*, and found Zabdi;)
18 whose house he parted into all men by themselves;
and he found Achan, the son of Carmi, [the] son of Zabdi,
[the] son of Zerah, of the lineage of Judah.
19 And Joshua said to Achan, My son, give thou glory
to the Lord God of Israel, and acknowledge thou, and
show to me what thou hast done; hide thou it not.
20 And Achan answered to Joshua, and said to him,
Verily (Truly), I have sinned before the Lord God of
Israel, and I have done thus and thus;
21 for among the spoils I saw a red mantle full good,
and two hundred shekels of silver, and a golden rule of
fifty shekels; and I coveted *those*, and took away, and I
hid those in the earth, against the midst of my tabernacle;
and I covered the silver with the earth delved. (for among
the spoils I saw a fine red mantle, and two hundred
shekels of silver, and a gold bar weighing fifty shekels;
and I coveted *them*, and took them away, and I hid them
in a hole in the ground, in the middle of my tent; and I
put the silver underneath it all.)
22 Then Joshua sent servants, the which ran to his
tabernacle, and found all these things hid in the same
place, and the silver together; (Then Joshua sent some
servants, who ran to his tent, and found all these things
hidden there, and the silver underneath it all;)
23 and they took *these things* away from the tent, and
they brought them to Joshua, and to all the sons of Israel
(and to all the Israelites); and they casted them forth
before the Lord.
24 Then Joshua took Achan, the son of Zerah, and the
silver, and the mantle, and the golden rule, and his sons,
and daughters, *his* oxen, asses, and sheep, and the
tabernacle itself, and all the purtenance of his household;
and all Israel with Joshua; and they led them to the valley
of Achor; (Then Joshua took Achan, the son of Zerah, and
the silver, and the mantle, and the gold bar, and his sons,
and daughters, and *his* oxen, and donkeys, and sheep,
and the tent itself, and all the purtenance of his

household; and all Israel went with Joshua; and they led
them to the valley of Achor;)
25 where Joshua said, For thou hast troubled us, the
Lord shall full out trouble thee in this day. And all Israel
stoned him; and all things that were his, were wasted by
fire. (where Joshua said, For thou hast brought forth
trouble upon us, the Lord shall now bring trouble upon
thee. And then all Israel stoned him; and all his things
were destroyed by fire.)
26 And they gathered upon him a great heap of stones,
the which abide there still into this day. And the strong
vengeance of the Lord was turned away from Israel; and
the name of that place is called the valley of Achor unto
this day.

CHAPTER 8

1 And the Lord said to Joshua, Neither dread thou, nor
be thou afeared; take with thee all the multitude of
fighting men, and rise thou, and go up into the city of Ai;
lo, I have betaken into thine hand the king thereof, and
the people, and the city, and the land.
2 And thou shalt do to the city of Ai, and to the king
thereof, as thou didest to Jericho, and the king thereof;
soothly ye shall take to you the prey (but this time ye can
take the prey for yourselves), and all [the] living beasts;
(and this time,) set thou ambushes, *either ambushments,*
to the city behind it.
3 And Joshua rose, and all the host of fighting men with
him, for to go up into Ai; and by night he sent (away) thirty
chosen thousand of strong men; (And so Joshua, and all his
army of fighters, rose up to go into Ai; and he chose thirty
thousand strong men, and sent them away in the night;)
4 and he commanded to them, and said, Set ye
ambushments behind the city, and go ye not further; and
all ye shall be ready (and all of ye be ready to fight);
5 forsooth I, and the tother multitude which is with
me, shall come on the contrary side against the city; and
when they shall go out against us, as we did before, we
shall flee, and turn the backs, (and I, and the other
multitude who be with me, shall come on the opposite
side toward the city; and when they shall go out against
us, we shall turn our backs, and flee, as we did before,)
6 till they pursue us, and be drawn away further from
the city; for they shall guess, that we shall flee them as
we did before. Then while we shall flee, and while they
pursue,
7 ye shall rise from the ambushments, and shall waste
the city; and your Lord God shall betake it into your
hands. (ye shall rise up from ambush, *or from lying in
wait,* and shall destroy the city; and the Lord your God
shall deliver it into your hands.)
8 And when ye have taken *it,* burn ye it; (yea,) do ye
all things, as I have commanded to you.
9 And Joshua let go them, and they went to the place
of [the] ambushments, and sat betwixt Bethel and Ai, at
the west coast of the city of Ai. Forsooth Joshua dwelled
in that night in the midst of the people. (And Joshua let
them go, and they went to the place of ambush, and sat
between Bethel and Ai, to the west of the city of Ai. But
Joshua stayed that night in the midst of his people.)
10 And he rose (up) early, and numbered his fellows,
and he went up with the elder men in the front of the
host (and he went up with the elders at the front of the
army), and was compassed with the help of (his) fighters.
11 And when they had come, and had gone up against
the city, they stood at the north coast of the city, betwixt
the which city and them a valley was in the midst. (And
they came toward the city, and arrived at the north side
of it, and there was a valley between them and the city.)
12 And Joshua had chosen five thousand men, and he
had set them in [the] ambushments betwixt Bethel and
Ai, in the west part of the same city. (And Joshua chose
five thousand men, and he put them in ambush between
Bethel and Ai, on the west side of the city.)
13 And all the tother host dressed the battle array to the
north, so [that] the last men of the multitude reached to
the west coast of the city. Then Joshua went in that night,
and stood in the midst of [the] valley;
14 and when the king of Ai had seen this, he hasted
(and rose up) early, and went out with all the host of the
city, and he dressed (the) battle array against the desert;
and he wist not that ambushments were hid behind his
back. (and when the king of Ai had seen this, he
hastened, and rose up early, and went out of the city with
all of his army, and he directed the battle array toward
the wilderness; but he did not know that men were
hidden in ambush behind his back.)
15 Forsooth Joshua and all the multitude of Israel gave
place, feigning dread, and fleeing (away) by the way of
(the) wilderness;
16 and the men cried together, and with gladness
stirred themselves together (and with gladness stirred
themselves up), and they pursued the men of Israel. And
when they had gone away from the city,
17 and soothly not one had (been) left in the city of Ai
and Bethel, that pursued not Israel, and they left the cities
open, as they had broken out, (and truly there was no
one left in the city of Ai, who did not pursue Israel, and
they left the city wide open, when they had broken out,)
18 the Lord said to Joshua, Raise up the shield that is in
thine hand, against the city of Ai; for I shall give it to
thee. And when Joshua had raised up his banner against
the city of Ai, [the Lord said to Joshua, Heave up thy sword
that is in thine hand, against the city of Ai; for to thee I shall
take it (for I shall deliver it to thee). And when he had heaved
up the sword over against the city,]
19 the ambushments, that were hid, rose up anon; and
they went to the city, and took [it], and burnt it. (those in

ambush, who were hid, rose up at once; and they went
into the city, and took it, and set it afire.)
20 Forsooth the men of the city, that pursued Joshua,
beheld, and saw the smoke of the(ir) city ascend till to
(the) heaven(s); and they might no more flee hither and
thither; most(ly) since they that had feigned flight, and
went to (the) wilderness, withstood strongliest against the
pursuers (now strongly withstood their pursuers).
21 And Joshua saw, and all Israel, that the city was
taken, and that the smoke of the city went up; and he
turned again, and killed the men of Ai. (And Joshua, and
all of Israel, saw that the city was taken, and that the
smoke of the city went up; and then they turned, and
killed the men of Ai.)
22 And also those men that had taken and burnt the
city, went out of the city against their enemies, and they
began to smite the middle men of their enemies (And
those men who had taken and set the city afire, now
came out of the city against their enemies, and they
began to strike down the enemies who were in their
midst); and when their adversaries were slain behind and
before, so that no man of so great [a] multitude was saved,
23 they took also the king of Ai living (they took the
king of Ai alive), and they brought *him* to Joshua.
24 Therefore, when all the men were slain, that pursued
Israel fleeing to desert, and had fallen by sword in the
same place, the sons of Israel turned again, and destroyed
the city *of Ai.* (And so, when all the men were killed, that
Israel had pursued fleeing to the desert, and they had
fallen by the sword in that place, then the Israelites
turned back, and completely destroyed the city *of Ai.*)
25 Forsooth they that felled down in the same day,
from man till to woman, were twelve thousand of men,
all men of the city of Ai. (And they who fell that day,
from the men unto the women, were twelve thousand
people, yea, all the inhabitants of the city of Ai.)
26 For Joshua withdrew not his hand, which he had
directed on high holding up his banner [that in height he
put up holding the sword (that he had put on high holding up
his sword)], till that all the dwellers of Ai were slain.
27 And the sons of Israel parted to themselves the work
beasts (And the Israelites divided among themselves the
work beasts), and the prey of the city, as the Lord
commanded to Joshua;
28 and Joshua burnt that city (and Joshua burned down
that city), and made it an everlasting burial.
29 And he hanged the king thereof in a gibbet, till to
the eventide, and the going down of the sun. And Joshua
commanded, and they putted down his dead body from
the cross; and they casted forth *him* in that entering of the
city, and gathered on him a great heap of stones, which
heap dwelleth till into present day. (And he hanged its
king upon a gallows, *or a tree*, until the evening, and the
going down of the sun. And then Joshua commanded,
and they took down his dead body from the tree; and
they threw *him* forth at the entrance to the city gate, and
gathered upon him a great heap of stones, which heap
remaineth there until this present day.)
30 Then Joshua builded an altar to the Lord God of
Israel in the hill of Ebal, (Then Joshua built an altar to the
Lord God of Israel on Mount Ebal,)
31 as Moses, the servant of the Lord, commanded to
the sons of Israel, and (as) it is written in the book of
Moses' law, an altar of stones unpolished, that iron hath
not touched. And he offered thereon burnt sacrifices to
the Lord, and he offered *also* peaceable sacrifices; (as
Moses, the servant of the Lord, commanded to the
Israelites, and as it is written in the Book of the Law by
Moses, yea, an altar of unpolished stones that iron hath
not touched. And he offered on it burnt sacrifices to the
Lord, and *also* peace offerings;)
32 and he wrote on the stones the Deuteronomy of
Moses' law, *not all the book, but the ten behests only*,
which he had declared before the sons of Israel. (and he
wrote on the stones the Deuteronomy of the Law by Moses,
not all the book, but only the Ten Commandments,
which he had declared before the Israelites.)
33 And all the people, and the greater men in birth, and
dukes, and judges, stood on either side of the ark, in the
sight of (the) priests and deacons, that bare the ark of the
bond of peace of the Lord; as a comeling, so and a man
born in the land; the half part of them *stood* beside the
hill Gerizim, and the half part of them *stood* beside the
hill Ebal, as Moses, the servant of the Lord, commanded.
And Joshua first blessed the people of Israel. (And all the
people, and the men of great age, *that is, the elders*, and
the leaders, and the judges, *and the officers*, stood on
either side of the Ark, before the priests and the Levites,
who carried the Ark of the Covenant of the Lord; a
stranger as well as someone born in the land; half of
them *stood* facing Mount Gerizim, and half of them *stood*
facing Mount Ebal, as Moses, the servant of the Lord, had
commanded. And first Joshua blessed the people of Israel.)
34 And (then) after these things he read all the words of
blessing and of cursing, and all things that were written in
the book of (the) law.
35 Joshua left nothing untouched of these things that
Moses commanded; but he declared all things before all
the multitude of Israel, to women, and little children, and
to comelings that dwelled among them. (Joshua left
nothing untouched of those things that Moses
commanded; yea, he declared everything before all the
multitude of Israel, including the women, and the little
children, and the newcomers, *or the foreigners*, who
lived among them.)

CHAPTER 9

1 And when these things were heard, all the kings

beyond (the) Jordan, that dwelt in hilly places, and in
plain places, in coasts of the sea, and in the brink of the
great sea, and they that dwelt beside Lebanon, (the)
Hittite, and Amorite, Canaanite, and Perizzite, Hivite,
and Jebusite, (And when these things were heard, all the
kings west of the Jordan River, who lived in the hill
country, and on the plains, and by the sea coasts, and at
the shore of the Mediterranean Sea, and they who lived
beside Lebanon, yea, the Hittites, and Amorites,
Canaanites, and Perizzites, Hivites, and Jebusites,)
2 were (all) gathered together to fight against Joshua
and Israel, with one will, and with the same accord.
3 And they that dwelt in Gibeon, heard (of) all the
things that Joshua had done to Jericho, and to Ai;
4 and they thought fellily, and took to themselves
meats, and putted eld sackcloths on asses, and wine
bottles broken, and sewed (up)/and patched, (and they
thought out things craftily, and then took some food for
themselves, and put old sackcloths upon their donkeys,
and wine bottles that were broken and then sewed up, or
patched,)
5 and full eld shoes, the which were sewed together
with old patches, to show their oldness; and these men
were clothed with full old clothes; also the loaves, which
they bare for lifelode in the way, were hard and broken
into gobbets (and the bread, which they carried for
sustenance on the way, was hard and broken into pieces).
6 And they went to Joshua, that dwelled then in tents
in Gilgal (who lived then in the camp at Gilgal); and they
said to him, and to all Israel together, We [have] come
from a far land, and we covet to make peace with you.
7 And the men of Israel answered to them, and said,
Lest peradventure ye dwell in the land, which is due to
us by heritage, and we may not make bond of peace with
you. (And the Israelites answered, and said to them,
Agreed, unless ye live in the land that is due to us by
inheritance, and then we cannot make a covenant with
you.)
8 And they said to Joshua, We be thy servants. To
whom Joshua said, What men be ye, and from whence
came ye?
9 They answered, (We) Thy servants came from a full
far land in the name of thy Lord God; for we have heard
the fame of his power, and all (the) things which he did
in Egypt,
10 and to the two kings of Amorites beyond (the)
Jordan; to Sihon king of Heshbon, and to Og king of
Bashan, that were in Ashtaroth. (and to the two kings of
the Amorites east of the Jordan River; that is, to Sihon, the
king of Heshbon, and to Og, the king of Bashan, who
lived in Ashtaroth.)
11 And the elder men and all the dwellers of our land
said to us, Take ye meats in your hands, for the full long
way; and go ye to them, and say ye, We be your servants;
make ye bond of peace with us. (And the elders and all
the citizens of our land said to us, Take ye food with you,
for the very long way; and go ye to them, and say ye, We
be your servants; make ye a covenant with us.)
12 And we took hot loaves, when we went out of our
houses to come to you; (but) now they be made dry and
broken, for great eldness;
13 we filled new bottles of wine (and we filled new
bottles with wine); (but) now they be broken and unsewed;
(and) the clothes and (the) shoes, with which we be
clothed, and which we have on our feet, be broken and
well nigh wasted, from the length of (the) long way.
14 Then they took of [the] meats of these men, and they
asked not counsel of the Lord. (And they took some food
from these men, but they did not ask any counsel from
the Lord.)
15 And Joshua made peace with them. And when the
bond of peace was made, he promised, that they should
not be slain; and the princes of the multitude swore to
them. (And so Joshua made peace with them. And when
the covenant was made, he promised, that they would
not be killed; and the leaders of the multitude swore to
them as well. And they went away.)
16 And after three days of the bond of peace made, the
men of Israel heard, that those men dwelled in nigh
place, and that they should be soon among those men.
(And three days after that the covenant was made, the
Israelites heard that those men lived nearby, and that they
would soon be among them.)
17 And the sons of Israel moved their tents, and came
in the third day into the cities of them (And the Israelites
moved their camp, and came on the third day into their
cities), of which cities these be the names; Gibeon, and
Chephirah, and Beeroth, and Kiriathjearim.
18 And Israel destroyed not them, for the princes of the
multitude had sworn to them in the name of the Lord
God of Israel. Therefore all the common people
grouched against the princes of Israel; (But Israel did not
destroy them, for the leaders of the multitude had sworn
to them in the name of the Lord God of Israel. And so all
the common people grumbled against Israel's leaders;)
19 and the princes answered to them, We swore to
them in the name of the Lord God of Israel, and therefore
we may not touch them; (and the leaders answered to
them, and said, We swore to them in the name of the
Lord God of Israel, and so we cannot touch them;)
20 but we shall do this thing to them; be they kept that
they live, lest the ire of the Lord be stirred against us, if
we forswear us to them; (but we shall do this to them; let
them be kept alive, lest the Lord's anger be stirred up
against us, if we break our oath to them;)
21 but so live they, that they hew trees, and bear
waters, into the uses of all the multitude (but let them
live, so that they can cut wood, and carry water, for the

use of all the multitude of Israel). And while they spake
these things,
22 Joshua called (for the) Gibeonites, and said to them,
Why would ye deceive us by fraud, (so) that ye said, We
dwell full far from you, since ye be in the midst of us?
(We live far away from you, when truly ye live right here
in the midst of us?)
23 Therefore ye shall be under cursing, and none shall
fail of your generation, hewing trees and bearing waters,
into the house of my God. (And so because ye did this,
ye shall all be cursed, and none of your generation shall
ever be free, from cutting wood and carrying water, for
the House of my God/for God's household, *or his family*.)
24 Which answered, It was told to us thy servants, that
thy Lord God promised to Moses, his servant, that he
should betake to you all the land, and should lose all the
dwellers thereof; therefore we dreaded greatly, and
purveyed to our lives, and we were compelled by your
dread, and we took this counsel. (And they answered, It
was told to us thy servants, that the Lord thy God
promised to his servant Moses, that he would deliver all
the land to you, and would destroy all of its inhabitants;
and so we greatly feared, and purveyed for our own lives,
and we were compelled by our fear of you, and so we
did this thing.)
25 Now forsooth we be in thine hand; do thou to us
that, that seemeth rightful and good to thee. (And so now
we be in thy hands; do thou to us what seemeth right and
good to thee.)
26 Therefore Joshua did, as he said, and delivered them
from the hands of the sons of Israel, that they should not
be slain. (And so Joshua did, as he said, and delivered
them from the hands of the Israelites, and they were not
killed.)
27 And in that day Joshua deemed them to be into the
service of all the people, and of the altar of the Lord, and
to hew trees, and to bear waters, till into present time, in
the place which the Lord had chosen. (And on that day,
Joshua decreed them to be in the service of all the people
of Israel, and of the altar of the Lord, and to cut wood,
and to carry water, yea, even until this present time, in
the place which the Lord had chosen.)

CHAPTER 10

1 And when Adonizedek, king of Jerusalem, had
heard these things, that is, that Joshua had taken Ai, and
had destroyed it; for as *Joshua* had done to Jericho and to
the king thereof, so he did to Ai and to the king thereof;
and that (the) men of Gibeon had fled (over) to Israel, and
were bound in peace with them (and had made a
covenant with them),
2 *Adonizedek* dreaded greatly (*Adonizedek* greatly
feared); for Gibeon was a great city, and one of the king's
cities, and greater than the city of Ai, and all the fighters
thereof were most strong.
3 Therefore Adonizedek, king of Jerusalem, sent to
Hoham, king of Hebron, and to Piram, king of Jarmuth,
and to Japhia, king of Lachish, and to Debir, king of
Eglon, and said,
4 Ascend ye to me, and help me (Come ye up to me,
and help me), (so) that we (can) fight against Gibeon, for
it was yielded to Joshua, and to the sons of Israel.
5 Therefore (the) five kings of (the) Amorites, the king
of Jerusalem, the king of Hebron, the king of Jarmuth, the
king of Lachish, (and) the king of Eglon, were gathered
(together), and ascended together with their hosts; and
setted tents against Gibeon (and pitched their tents
opposite Gibeon), and fought against it.
6 Soothly the dwellers of the city of Gibeon sent to
Joshua, that dwelled then in tents at Gilgal, and said to
him, Withdraw not thine hands from the help of thy
servants; go up soon, and deliver us, and [bring] help; for
all the kings of Amorites, that dwelled in the hilly places,
came together against us. (And the inhabitants of the city
of Gibeon sent to Joshua, who then lived in the camp at
Gilgal, and said to him, Do not thou withdraw thy hands
from helping thy slaves; come up soon, and help us, and
rescue us; for all the kings of the Amorites, who live in
the hill country, have come up together against us.)
7 And Joshua went up from Gilgal, (he) and all the
host of fighters with him, the most strong men.
8 And the Lord said to Joshua, Dread thou not them
(Do not thou fear them), for I have given them into thine
hands; and none of them shall be able to against-stand
thee.
9 Therefore Joshua felled suddenly on them, and went
up all that night from Gilgal; (And so Joshua fell suddenly
upon them, after going up all that night from Gilgal;)
10 and the Lord troubled them from the face of Israel,
and all-brake (them) with great vengeance in Gibeon.
And *Joshua* pursued them by the way of the ascending of
Bethhoron, and smote till to Azekah and Makkedah. (and
the Lord confounded them before the Israelites, and
destroyed them with great vengeance in Gibeon. And
Joshua pursued them by way of the ascent to Bethhoron,
and struck them down unto Azekah and Makkedah.)
11 And when they fled the sons of Israel, and were in
the going down of Bethhoron, the Lord sent great stones
upon them from heaven, till they came to Azekah; and
many more were dead by the hailstones, than they which
the sons of Israel killed with sword. (And when they fled
from the Israelites, and were on the descent from
Bethhoron, the Lord sent great hailstones upon them from
the heavens, until they came to Azekah; and many more
died from the hailstones, than they whom the Israelites
killed with their swords.)
12 Then Joshua spake to the Lord, in the day in which
he betook Amorites in the sight of the sons of Israel; and

Joshua said before the people, Sun, be thou not moved
against Gibeon, and the moon, against the valley of
Ajalon. (And Joshua spoke to the Lord, on the day in
which he delivered the Amorites into the hands of the
Israelites; and Joshua said before the people, Sun, stand
thou still over Gibeon, and Moon, stand thou still over
the Ajalon Valley.)
13 And the sun and the moon stood, unto the time the
folk *of God* had venged themselves of their enemies.
Whether this is not written in the book of just men? And
so the sun stood in the midst of heaven, and it hasted not
to go down in the space of a day; (And so the sun and the
moon stood still, until the time that the people *of God*
had avenged themselves upon their enemies. Is this not
written in the Book of Jashar? And so the sun stood still
in the midst of the heavens, and it hastened not to go
down in the space of a day;)
14 so long a day was not before and afterward (there
was never so long a day, before or afterward); for the
Lord obeyed to the voice of a man, and he fought for
Israel.
15 And Joshua turned again, with all Israel, into the
tents of Gilgal. (And then Joshua, and all Israel, returned
to their tents in Gilgal.)
16 For the five kings fled, and hid themselves in the
den of the city of Makkedah. (But those five kings had
escaped, and hid themselves in the cave at Makkedah.)
17 And it was told to Joshua, that the five kings were
found hid in the den of the city of Makkedah. (And
Joshua was told that the five kings were found hiding in
the cave of Makkedah.)
18 And Joshua commanded to fellows, and said,
Wallow ye great stones to the mouth of the den, and put
ye witting men, that shall keep the (en)closed kings; (And
Joshua commanded to his men, and said, Roll ye some
great stones to the mouth of the cave, and put ye some
able men there who shall keep the kings enclosed;)
19 soothly do not ye stand, but pursue ye the enemies,
and slay ye all the last of (the) fleers; and suffer ye not
them to enter into the strongholds of their cities (and do
not allow them to enter into the strongholds of their
cities), the which enemies your Lord God hath betaken
in(to) your hands.
20 Then when the adversaries were beaten with great
vengeance, and were almost wasted unto the death, they
that might flee Israel, entered into the strengthened cities.
(And so when their adversaries were beaten with a great
vengeance, and were almost destroyed unto the death,
the few who escaped from the Israelites, entered into
their strengthened cities.)
21 And all the host turned again whole, and in whole
number to Joshua, into Makkedah, where the tents were
then; and no man was hardy to grouch against the sons of
Israel (and no one was fool-hardy enough to grumble
against the Israelites).
22 And Joshua commanded, and said, Open ye the
mouth of the den (Open ye the mouth of the cave), and
bring forth to me the five kings that be hid(den) therein.
23 And the servants did, as it was commanded to them;
and they brought forth to Joshua the five kings from the
den; the king of Jerusalem, the king of Hebron, the king
of Jarmuth, the king of Lachish, and the king of Eglon.
24 And when they were led out to Joshua, he called all
the men of Israel, and said to the princes of the host, that
were with him, Go ye, and set your feet on the necks of
these kings. And when they had gone, and treaded the
necks of *the kings* subject to their feet (And when they
had come, and put their feet on the necks of *those kings*),
25 again Joshua said to *Israel*, Do not ye dread, neither
be ye afeared, be ye comforted, and be ye strong; for so
the Lord shall do to all your enemies, against which ye
shall fight. (Joshua said to *the people of Israel*, Fear ye
not, nor be ye afraid, but be ye encouraged, and be ye
strong; for so shall the Lord do to all of your enemies,
whom ye shall fight against.)
26 And Joshua smote those kings (And Joshua struck
those kings), and killed them, and he hanged them (up)
on five trees; and they were hanged unto the eventide.
27 And when the sun went down, he commanded to
fellows, that they should put them down from the
gibbets; and when they were put down, they casted forth
them into the den, in which they were hid; and they
putted great stones on the mouth thereof, which stones
dwell till to [the] present time. (And when the sun went
down, he commanded to his men, that they should take
them down from the gallows, *or the trees*; and when they
had taken them down, they threw them forth into the
cave in which they were hidden; and they put great
stones on the mouth of it, which stones remain there unto
this present time.)
28 In the same day, Joshua took Makkedah, and smote
by the sharpness of sword, and killed the king thereof,
and all the dwellers thereof; he left not therein, namely,
(any) little relics; and he did to the king of Makkedah, as
he had done to the king of Jericho. (On the same day,
Joshua took Makkedah, and struck it with the sharpness
of their swords, and killed its king, and all of its
inhabitants; he left nothing of value, *or any remnant,*
there; and so he did to the king of Makkedah, as he had
done to the king of Jericho.)
29 And Joshua passed (forth) with all Israel from
Makkedah into Libnah, and he fought against it,
30 which *city* the Lord betook, with the king thereof, in
the hand of Israel; and men of Israel smote that city by
the sharpness of sword, and all the dwellers thereof, and
they left not therein anything of value, *or relics*; and they
did to the king of Libnah as they had done to the king of
Jericho. (which *city* the Lord delivered, with its king, into

the hands of the Israelites; and the men of Israel struck
that city, and all its inhabitants, with the sharpness of
their swords, and they left nothing of value, *or any
remnant*, there; and so they did to the king of Libnah as
they had done to the king of Jericho.)
31 From Libnah, Joshua passed (forth) with all Israel,
into Lachish; and when the host was ordained by
compass, he fought against it.
32 And the Lord betook Lachish in the hand of the sons
of Israel; and Joshua took Lachish in the second day, and
smote (it) by the sharpness of sword, and each man, that
was therein, as he had done to Libnah. (And the Lord
delivered Lachish into the hands of the Israelites; and
Joshua took Lachish on the second day, and struck it with
the sharpness of their swords, and killed every person
who was there, as he had done in Libnah.)
33 In that time (At that time), Horam, king of Gezer,
went up to help Lachish; whom Joshua smote, with all
his people, till to [the] death.
34 And Joshua passed from Lachish into Eglon, and
compassed it, and overcame it in the same day; (And
then Joshua went forth from Lachish into Eglon, and
surrounded it, and overcame it on the same day;)
35 and he smote by the sharpness of sword all men that
were therein, (as) by all things that he had done to Lachish.
(and he struck all who were there with the sharpness of
their swords, just as he had done in Lachish.)
36 Also Joshua went up with all Israel from Eglon into
Hebron, and he fought against Hebron,
37 and he took (it), and smote it by the sharpness of
(the) sword; and the king thereof, and all the cities of that
country, and all men that dwelled therein; he left not any
things of value, *or relics*, therein (he left nothing of value,
or any remnant, there); as he had done to Eglon so he did
also to Hebron, and wasted by (the) sword all things that
were therein.
38 From thence Joshua turned (again) into Debir, and
took, and wasted it; (From there Joshua returned to Debir,
and took it, and destroyed it;)
39 and he smote by (the) sharpness of (the) sword the
king thereof, and all the towns about it; and he left not
any things of value, *or relics*, therein (and he left nothing
of value, *or any remnant*, there); as he had done to
Hebron, and to Libnah, and to their kings, so he did to
Debir, and to the king thereof.
40 And so Joshua smote all the land of the hills, and of
the south, and of the field, and Ashdod, with their kings;
he left not therein any relics, (*or anything of value*), but
he killed all thing(s) that might breath, as the Lord God of
Israel commanded to him; (And so Joshua struck down all
the people of the hill country, and of the lands of the
south, and of the plains, and of the springs, and all their
kings; he left nothing of value, *or any remnant*, there, but
he killed everything that lived, as the Lord God of Israel
commanded to him;)
41 from Kadeshbarnea unto Gaza, and all the land of
Goshen, unto Gibeon,
42 Joshua took, and wasted with one fierceness all the
kings, and their countries; for the Lord God of Israel
fought for him. (Joshua took, and destroyed all the kings,
and their lands, with one fierceness; for the Lord God of
Israel fought for Israel.)
43 And Joshua turned again with all Israel to the place
of (their) tents in Gilgal. (And then Joshua returned with
all the Israelites to their camp in Gilgal.)

CHAPTER 11

1 And when Jabin, king of Hazor, had heard these
things, he sent to Jobab, king of Madon, and to the king
of Shimron, and to the king of Achshaph;
2 forsooth to the kings of the north, that dwelled in the
hilly places, and in the plain against the south of
Chinneroth, and in the field places, and (in the) countries
of Dor, beside the sea, (and to the kings of the north, who
lived in the hill country, and those on the plain to the
south of the Sea of Galilee, *or Lake Galilee*, and in the
valley, and in the countryside of Dor, on the west,)
3 and to (the) Canaanite from the east and (the) west,
and to (the) Amorite, and Hittite, and Perizzite, and (the)
Jebusite in the mountains, and to (the) Hivite, that
dwelled at the roots *of the hill* of Hermon (who lived at
the foot of Mount Hermon), in the land of Mizpeh.
4 And (they) all went out with their companies, a full
much people, as the gravel which is in the brink of the
sea (like the gravel, *or the sand*, which is at the seashore),
and horses, and chariots, of great multitude.
5 And all these kings came together at the waters of
Merom, to fight against Israel.
6 And the Lord said to Joshua, Dread thou not them,
for tomorrow, in this same hour, I shall betake all these
men to be wounded in the sight of Israel; thou shalt hock
the horses of them, and thou shalt burn the chariots by
fire. (And the Lord said to Joshua, Do not thou fear them,
for tomorrow, at this same hour, I shall make all these
men to be killed before the army of Israel; and thou shalt
hock their horses, and thou shalt burn up their chariots
with fire.)
7 And Joshua came, and all his host with him, against
them suddenly, at the waters of Merom, and felled on
them. (And so Joshua, and all his army, suddenly came
against them, at the waters of Merom, and fell upon them.)
8 And the Lord betook them into the hands of (the
host of) Israel; which smited them, and pursued (them) till
to Great(er) Sidon, and the waters of Misrephothmaim
(and Misrephothmaim on the west), and to the field of
Mizpeh, which is at the east part thereof.
9 And Joshua smote so all them, that he left no things
of them (And Joshua so struck down all of them, that he

left nothing of them); and he did as the Lord commanded
to him; he hocked their horses, and burnt their chariots.
10 And he turned again anon, and took Hazor, and
smote by sword the king thereof (And at once he turned
his army, and then took Hazor, and struck down its king
with his sword); for Hazor held by eld time the
princehood among all these realms.
11 And he smote all persons that dwelled there, he left
not any relics, (*or anything of value*,) therein, but he
wasted all things till to (the) death; also he destroyed that
city by burning. (And he struck down all he people who
lived there, he left nothing of value, *or any remnant*,
there, but he destroyed everything unto the death; and he
burned down that city *to the ground*.)
12 And he took all (the) cities by compass, and the
kings of them, and smote (them), and did (them) away, as
Moses, the servant of the Lord, commanded to him,
13 without [the] cities that were set in the great hills,
and in [the] little hills; and Israel burnt (not) the other
cities; flame wasted only one city, Hazor, the strongest.
(but the men of Israel did not burn down the cities that
were set in the great hills, or in the little hills; their fire
burned down only one city, Hazor, the strongest.)
14 And (then) the sons of Israel parted to themselves all
the prey, and the work beasts of these cities, when all the
men of them were slain.
15 As the Lord commanded to his servant Moses, so
Moses commanded to Joshua, and Joshua fulfilled all
things; neither soothly he passed (over) one word of all
the behests, that the Lord commanded to Moses (he did
not pass over one word of all the commands, that the
Lord had commanded to Moses).
16 And so Joshua took all the land of the hills, and of
the south (And so Joshua took all the hill country, and the
land of the south), [and] the land of Goshen, and the
plain(s), and the west coast, and the hill of Israel, and the
field places thereof;
17 and the part of the hill that ascendeth to Seir till to
Baalgad, by the plain of Lebanon under the hill of
Hermon (and from Mount Halak that goeth up to Seir
unto Baalgad, by the plain of Lebanon under Mount
Hermon); Joshua took, and smote, and killed all the kings
of those *places*.
18 Joshua fought much time against these kings;
19 there was no city, which betook not itself to the sons
of Israel, except (the) Hivites that dwelled in Gibeon; he
took all (the other) men by battle. (there was no city
which made peace with the Israelites, except the Hivites
who lived in Gibeon; the Israelites took all the other
cities in battle.)
20 For it was the sentence of the Lord, that the hearts of
them should be made hard, and that they should fight
against Israel, and should fall, and [they] should not
deserve any mercy, and should perish (but should
perish), as the Lord commanded, to Moses.
21 Joshua came in that time, and killed (the) Anakim,
that is, (the) giants, from the hilly places of Hebron, and
of Debir, and of Anab (from the hill country of Hebron,
and Debir, and Anab), and from all the hill (country) of
Judah, and of Israel, and did away their cities.
22 He left not any man of the generation of Anakim in
the land of the sons of Israel, without the cities of Gaza,
and Gath, and Ashdod (except in the cities of Gaza, and
Gath, and Ashdod), in which alone they were left.
23 Then Joshua took all the land, as the Lord spake to
Moses, and he gave it into (a) possession to the sons of
Israel, by their parts and lineages (and he gave it to the
Israelites for a possession, a portion to each tribe); and
(so) the land rested from battles.

CHAPTER 12

1 These be the (two) kings which the sons of Israel
have smitten, and wielded their lands, beyond (the)
Jordan, at the east, from the strand of Arnon unto the hill
of Hermon, and all the east coast that beholdeth the
wilderness. (These be the two kings whom the Israelites
struck down, and took over their lands, east of the Jordan
River, from the Arnon River unto Mount Hermon, and all
the land to the east that looketh toward the wilderness.)
2 Sihon, the king of Amorites, that dwelled in Heshbon,
was lord from Aroer, which is set on the brink of the strand
of Arnon, and of the middle part in the valley, and of half
Gilead, till to the strand of Jabbok, which is the term of
the sons of Ammon; (There was Sihon, the king of the
Amorites, who lived in Heshbon, and who ruled half of
Gilead, from Aroer, which is set on the banks of the
Arnon River, and from the middle part of the valley, unto
the Jabbok River, which is the border of the Ammonites;)
3 and from the wilderness unto the sea of Chinneroth,
against the east, and unto the sea of (the) desert, which is
the saltiest sea, at the east coast, in the way that leadeth
to Bethjeshimoth, and from the south part that lieth under
Ashdoth, unto Pisgah. (and from the wilderness unto the
eastern side of the Sea of Galilee, *or Lake Galilee*, and
unto the eastern side of the Salt Sea, *that is, the Dead
Sea*, on the way that leadeth to Bethjeshimoth, and from
the south that lieth under Mount Pisgah/and from the
south that lieth under Ashdothpisgah.)
4 The term of Og, king of Bashan, of the relics of
Rephaim, *that is, giants*, that dwelled in Ashtaroth and in
Edrei, (And there was Og, the king of Bashan, of the
remnant of the Rephaim, *that is, of the giants*, who lived
in Ashtaroth and in Edrei,)
5 and he was lord in the hill of Hermon, and in Salcah,
and in all Bashan, till to the terms of Geshurites and
Maachathites, and of the half part of Gilead, and to the
term of Sihon, king of Heshbon. (and he ruled Mount
Hermon, and Salcah, and all of Bashan, unto the borders

of the Geshurites and the Maachathites, and also ruled half
of Gilead, unto the border of Sihon, the king of Heshbon.)
6 Moses, the servant of the Lord, and the sons of
Israel, smited them (all); and Moses gave the land of them
into (a) possession to Reubenites, and to Gadites, and to
half the lineage of Manasseh (and Moses gave their lands
for a possession to the Reubenites, and the Gadites, and
to *the eastern* half of the tribe of Manasseh).
7 These be the kings of the land, which Joshua and the
sons of Israel smited beyond (the) Jordan, at the west
coast, from Baalgad in the field of Lebanon, till to the hill
whose part ascendeth into Seir; and Joshua gave it into (a)
possession to the lineages of Israel, to each his own part,
(And these be the kings of the lands, whom Joshua and
the Israelites struck down west of the Jordan River, from
Baalgad in the valley of Lebanon, unto Mount Halak,
which leadeth up to Seir; and Joshua gave it all for a
possession to the tribes of Israel, to each their own
portion,)
8 as well in hilly places, as in plain and field places; in
Ashtoreth, and in [the] wilderness, and in the south, was
(the) Hittites, and Amorites, Canaanites, and Perizzites,
Hivites, and Jebusites. (in the hill country, and on the
plains, *or on the Arabah*, and in the valley, and by the
springs, and in the wilderness, and in the south, *or in the
Negeb*; these lands had been inhabited by the Hittites,
and Amorites, Canaanites, and Perizzites, Hivites, and
Jebusites.)
9 The king of Jericho, one; the king of Ai, which is at
the side of Bethel, one (which is beside Bethel, one);
10 the king of Jerusalem, one; the king of Hebron, one;
11 the king of Jarmuth, one; the king of Lachish, one;
12 the king of Eglon, one; the king of Gezer, one;
13 the king of Debir, one; the king of Geder, one;
14 the king of Hormah, one; the king of Arad, one;
15 the king of Libnah, one; the king of Adullam, one;
16 the king of Makkedah, one; the king of Bethel, one;
17 the king of Tappuah, one; the king of Hepher, one;
18 the king of Aphek, one; the king of Lasharon, one;
19 the king of Madon, one; the king of Hazor, one;
20 the king of Shimronmeron, one; the king of
Achshaph, one;
21 the king of Taanach, one; the king of Megiddo, one;
22 the king of Kedesh, one; the king of Jokneam of
Carmel, one;
23 the king of Dor and of the province of Dor, one (the
king of Dor on the coast of Dor, one); the king of (the)
folks of Gilgal, one;
24 the king of Tirzah, one; all the kings, one and thirty.

CHAPTER 13

1 Joshua was eld and of great age; and the Lord said to
him, Thou hast waxed eld, and art of long time; and the
most large land is left, that is not yet parted by lot (and
much of the land is left, that hath not yet been taken);
2 that is, all the terms of Philistines, and all Geshuri,
(that is, all the land of the Philistines, and of the
Geshurites,)
3 from the troubled flood that moisteth Egypt, till to
the terms of Ekron against the north; (this is) the land of
Canaan, which is parted into (the) five little kings of
Philistines, (that is,) of Gaza, and of Ashdod, of Ashkelon,
of Gath, and of Ekron. Forsooth at the south be Avites,
(from the Nile River, *or the Shihor*, that watereth Egypt,
unto the border of Ekron to the north; this is the land of
Canaan, and it is divided among the five kings of the
Philistines, that is, he of Gaza, and he of Ashdod, and he
of Ashkelon, and he of Gath, and he of Ekron; and there
also be the Avites to the south;)
4 all the land of Canaan, and Mearah of Sidonians, till
to Aphek, and to the terms of Amorites, (all the land of
the Canaanites, and Mearah of the Sidonians, unto
Aphek, and to the border of the Amorites;)
5 and the coasts of him; and the country of Lebanon
against the east, from Baalgad, under the hill of Hermon,
till thou enterest into Hamath, (and the land of the
Gebalites; and the country of Lebanon to the east, from
Baalgad, under Mount Hermon, until thou enterest into
Hamath,)
6 of all men that dwelled in the hill, from the Lebanon
till to the waters of Misrephothmaim, and all men of
Sidon; I am, that shall do away them from the face of the
sons of Israel; therefore come it into the part of (the)
heritage of Israel, as I commanded to thee. (of all those
who live in the hill country, from Lebanon unto
Misrephothmaim, and all those of Sidon; I am he, who
shall do them away from before the Israelites; and so
divide it all up for the inheritance of the Israelites, as I
commanded to thee.)
7 And thou now part the land into (a) possession to the
nine lineages, and to the half lineage of Manasseh, (And
now divide thou up the land for a possession for the nine
tribes, and for *the western* half of the tribe of Manasseh.)
8 with which lineage(s) Reuben, and Gad, wielded the
land, which land Moses, the servant of the Lord, gave to
them beyond the flowings of (the) Jordan, at the east
coast; (For the tribes of Reuben, and Gad, and *the eastern*
half of the tribe of Manasseh, took the land, which land
Moses, the servant of the Lord, gave them beyond the
flowings of the Jordan River, on the east side;)
9 from Aroer, that is set in the brink of the strand of
Arnon (that is, from Aroer, that is set on the banks of the
Arnon River), in [the] midst of the valley, and all the field
places of Medeba, unto Dibon,
10 and all the cities of Sihon, king of Amorites, that
reigned in Heshbon, till to the terms of the sons of
Ammon, (and all the cities of Sihon, the king of the
Amorites, who reigned in Heshbon, unto the border of

the Ammonites,)
11 and of Gilead, and to the terms of Geshurites, and of
Maachathites, and all the hill of Hermon, and all Bashan,
till to Salcah; (and also Gilead, and the lands of the
Geshurites, and of the Maachathites, and all of Mount
Herman, and all of Bashan, unto Salcah;)
12 all the realm of Og in Bashan, that reigned in
Ashtaroth, and in Edrei; he was of the relics of Rephaim,
that is, of giants; and Moses smote them, and did away
them. (and all the kingdom of Og in Bashan, who reigned
in Ashtaroth, and in Edrei; he was of the remnant of the
Rephaim, *that is, of the giants*; and Moses struck them
down, and did *them* away.)
13 And the sons of Israel would not destroy Geshurites,
and Maachathites; and they dwelled in the midst of
Israel, till into [the] present day. (But the Israelites did not
destroy the Geshurites, or the Maachathites; and they live
in the midst of the Israelites, unto this present day.)
14 Soothly he gave not (any) possession to the lineage
of Levi, but [the] sacrifices, and [the] slain sacrifices of the
Lord God of Israel; that is his heritage, as *God* spake to
him (that is their inheritance, as *God* said to them).
15 Therefore Moses gave (a) possession to the lineage
of the sons of Reuben, by their kindreds;
16 and their term was from Aroer, that is in the brink of
the strand of Arnon, and in the middle valley of the same
strand, (and) all the plain *also* that leadeth to Medeba,
(and their land was from Aroer, that is on the banks of the
Arnon River, through the valley from the middle of that
river, and all the plain that leadeth to Medeba,)
17 and to Heshbon, and all the towns of them, that be
in the field places; and Dibon, and Bamothbaal, and the
city of Bethbaalmeon,
18 and Jahaza, and Kedemoth, and Mephaath,
19 and Kiriathaim, and Sibmah, and Zarethshahar in
the hill of the valley(,)
20 (and) of Bethpeor, and of Ashdothpisgah, and
Bethjeshimoth; (and Bethpeor, and Mount Pisgah, and
Bethjeshimoth;)
21 (and) all the field cities, and all the realms of Sihon,
king of Amorites, that reigned in Heshbon, whom Moses
smote, with his princes (of) Midian, Evi, and Rekem, and
Zur, and Hur, and Reba, the dukes of Sihon, dwellers of
the land. (and all the field cities, and all the kingdoms of
Sihon, the king of the Amorites, who reigned in
Heshbon, whom Moses struck down together with the
Midianite leaders, that is, Evi, and Rekem, and Zur, and
Hur, and Reba, who were Sihon's surrogates, and who
lived in the land.)
22 And the sons of Israel killed by (the) sword, Balaam,
the false diviner, the son of Beor, with other men slain
there.
23 And the term of the sons of Reuben *was* made the
flood of Jordan (And the western border of the sons of
Reuben was the Jordan River); this is the possession of
(the) men of Reuben, by their kindreds, (yea,) of (their)
cities and towns.
24 And Moses gave a possession to the lineage of Gad,
and to his sons, by their kindreds, of the which
possession this is the parting;
25 *he gave* the terms of Jazer, and all the cities of
Gilead, and the half part of the land of the sons of
Ammon, unto Aroer that is against Rabbah; (their territory
included Jazer, and all the cities of Gilead, and half of the
land of the Ammonites, unto Aroer, that is east of Rabbah;)
26 and from Heshbon unto Ramath of Mizpeh, and
Betonim, and Mahanaim, unto the terms of Debir (unto
the border of Lodebar);
27 and in the valley *he gave to them* Betharam, and
Bethnimrah, and Succoth, and Zaphon, *that was* the tother
part of the realm of Sihon, the king of Heshbon; and the
end of that term is (the) Jordan, unto the last part of the sea
of Chinnereth over (the) Jordan, at the east coast (and the
border was the Jordan River, unto the last part of the Sea
of Galilee, *or Lake Galilee*, east of the Jordan River).
28 This is the possession of the sons of Gad, by their
families, (yea,) the cities and the towns of them.
29 Moses gave also (a) possession to the half lineage of
Manasseh, and to his sons (and to their sons), by their
kindreds, of which possession this is the beginning; (And
Moses also gave a possession to *the eastern* half of the
tribe of Manasseh, and to their sons, by their families, of
which possession this is the beginning;)
30 *he gave* Mahanaim, and all (of) Bashan, and all the
realms of Og, king of Bashan, and all the towns of Jair,
that be in Bashan, (that is,) sixty cities;
31 and half the part of Gilead, and Ashtaroth, and
Edrei, the cities of the realm of Og, king of Bashan; he
gave (this) to the sons of Machir, the sons of Manasseh,
and to half the part of the sons of Machir, by their
kindreds. (and half of Gilead, and Ashtaroth, and Edrei,
the cities of the kingdom of Og, the king of Bashan; he
gave this to half of the sons of Machir, the son of
Manasseh, by their families.)
32 Moses parted this possession in the field places of
Moab over (the) Jordan, against Jericho, at the east coast.
(And so Moses divided up this possession in the plains of
Moab, near Jericho, on the eastern side of the Jordan
River.)
33 Forsooth Moses gave no possession to the lineage of
Levi; for the Lord God himself of Israel is the possession
of the kindred of Levi, as the Lord said to him. (But Moses
gave no possession, *or portion*, to the tribe of Levi; for
the Lord God of Israel himself is the possession of the
Levite families, as the Lord said to them.)

CHAPTER 14

1 This is the possession that the sons of Israel wielded

in the land of Canaan, which land(s) Eleazar the priest,
and Joshua, the son of Nun, and the princes of the
families of the lineages of Israel gave to them, (These be
the possessions which the Israelites took in the land of
Canaan, which lands Eleazar the priest, and Joshua, the
son of Nun, and the leaders of the families of the tribes of
Israel gave to them,)
2 and *these (men)* parted all things by lot, as the Lord
commanded in the hand of Moses (as the Lord
commanded by Moses), to the nine lineages, and to the
half lineage.
3 For Moses had given to the two lineages and to the
half lineage (their) possession(s) over (the) Jordan; without
the Levites, that took nothing of the land among their
brethren; (For Moses had already given the two tribes and
the half tribe on the eastern side of the Jordan River their
possessions; and without the Levites, who took nothing
of the land among their kinsmen;)
4 but the sons of Joseph were parted into two
lineages, (that) of Manasseh, and (that) of Ephraim, and
were heirs into the place of them. And the Levites took
none other part in the land, no but cities to dwell in, and
the suburbs of those to their work beasts and their sheep
to be fed in. (for Joseph's sons were divided into two
tribes, that of Manasseh, *which itself was divided into
two parts*, and that of Ephraim, and they were heirs in
their places. And the Levites took no portion of the land,
but only some cities to live in, and their suburbs for their
work beasts and their sheep to be fed in.)
5 As the Lord commanded to Moses, so the sons of
Israel did, and they parted the land. (As the Lord
commanded to Moses, so the Israelites did, and they
divided up the land.)
6 And so the sons of Judah went to Joshua in Gilgal;
and Caleb, the son of Jephunneh, of Kenaz, spake to him,
(and said,) Thou knowest, what the Lord spake to Moses,
the man of God, of me and of thee in Kadeshbarnea
(Thou knowest, what the Lord said to Moses, the man of
God, about you and me at Kadeshbarnea).
7 I was of forty years (I was forty years old), when
Moses, the servant of the Lord, sent me from
Kadeshbarnea, that I should behold the land, and I told to
him that, that seemed sooth to me.
8 And my brethren, that went up with me,
discomforted the heart(s) of the people, and nevertheless
I followed my Lord God. (And my kinsmen, who went up
with me, discomforted the hearts of the people, but
nevertheless, I followed the Lord my God.)
9 And Moses swore in that day, and said, The land,
that thy foot hath trodden, shall be thy possession, and
(that) of thy sons (into) without end; for thou followedest
thy Lord God.
10 Soothly the Lord granted life to me, as he promised,
till into present day. Forty years and five be, since the
Lord spake this word to Moses, when Israel went through
wilderness. Today I am of fourscore years and five, (And
the Lord granted life to me, as he promised, unto this
present day. Forty-five years be, since the Lord said this
word to Moses, when Israel went through the wilderness.
And today I am eighty five years old,)
11 and I am as mighty (now), as I was mighty in that
time, when I was sent (out) to espy; the strength of that
time dwelleth stably in me till to this day, as well to fight,
as to go (yea, the strength of that time remaineth in me
unto this day, to fight, as well as to go about my daily life).
12 Therefore give thou to me this hill, which the Lord
promised to me, while also thou heardest, in which hill
be Anakim, and great cities, and strengthened; if in hap
the Lord is with me, and I may do them away, as he
promised to me. (And so give thou to me this hill, which
the Lord promised me, while also thou heardest it, on
which hill be the Anakim, *that is, the giants*, and great
and strengthened cities; and if the Lord be with me, then
I shall be able to do them away, as he promised me.)
13 And Joshua blessed Caleb, and he gave to him
Hebron into (a) possession. (And Joshua blessed Caleb,
and he gave Hebron to him for a possession.)
14 And from that time Hebron was of Caleb (And from
that time Hebron belonged to Caleb), the son of
Jephunneh, of Kenaz, unto this present day; for he
followed the Lord God of Israel.
15 The name of Hebron was called before Kiriatharba.
Arba, the greatest (man), was set there in the land of
Anakim; and the land ceased from battles. (Hebron was
called Kiriatharba before. And Arba had been the
greatest man there in the land of the Anakim, *or of the
giants*. And so the land ceased from battles.)

CHAPTER 15

1 Then this was the part of the sons of Judah, by their
kindreds; from the term of Edom till to the desert of Zin
against the south (from the border of Edom in the desert of
Zin southward), and till to the last part of the south coast,
2 the beginning thereof from the height of the saltiest
sea (its beginning was the end of the Salt Sea, *that is, the
Dead Sea*), and from the arm thereof, that beholdeth to
the south.
3 And it goeth out against the ascending of Scorpion
(And it goeth out to Maalehacrabbim), and passeth into
Zin; and it ascendeth into Kadeshbarnea, and cometh
into Hezron, and it ascendeth to Adar, and compasseth
Karkaa;
4 and from thence it passeth into Azmon, and cometh
to the strand of Egypt; and the terms thereof shall be the
great sea; this shall be the end of the south coast. (and
from there it passeth into Azmon, and cometh to the
River of Egypt, *that is, the Nile River, or the Shihor*; and
its end, *or its limit*, shall be the Mediterranean Sea; this

shall be the southern border.)
5 And from the east the beginning shall be the saltiest
sea, unto the last parts of (the) Jordan (And on the east the
beginning shall be the Salt Sea, or *the Dead Sea,* unto the
last parts of the Jordan River), and those parts that behold
(to) the north, from the arm of the sea unto the same
flood of (the) Jordan.
6 And the term ascendeth into Bethhogla, and passeth
from the north into Betharabah; and it ascendeth to the
stone of Bohan, (who was) [the] son of Reuben,
7 and it goeth unto the terms of Debir, from the valley
of Achor against the north; and it beholdeth Gilgal,
which is on the contrary part of the ascending of
Adummim, from the south part of the strand; and it
passeth the waters, that be called the well of the sun; and
the outgoings thereof shall be to the well of Rogel. (and it
goeth unto Debir, from the Achor Valley, and turneth to
the north; and it beholdeth Gilgal, which is on the
opposite side of the ascent of Adummim, south of the
river, *or the valley*; and it passeth the waters of
Enshemesh; and its end, *or its limit,* shall be Enrogel.)
8 And it goeth up by the valley of the son of Hinnom,
by the side of (the) Jebusites, at the south; this is
Jerusalem; and from thence it up-raiseth itself to the top
of the hill, that is against Hinnom at the west, in the
height of the valley of Rephaim, against the north; (And it
goeth up by the Hinnom Valley, on the south side of the
Jebusites; that is Jerusalem; and from there it raiseth itself
up to the top of the hill, west of the Hinnom Valley,
which is at the northern end of the Rephaim Valley;)
9 and it passeth forth from the top of the hill to the
well of the water(s) of Nephtoah, and it cometh unto the
towns of the hill of Ephron; and it is bowed into Baalah,
that is Kiriathjearim, *that is, the city of woods*;
10 and it compasseth from Baalah against the west,
unto the hill of Seir, and it passeth by the side of the hill
of Jearim to the north in Chesalon (and it goeth west from
Baalah to Mount Seir, and it passeth by the north side of
Mount Jearim, which is Chesalon), and (then) it goeth
down into Bethshemesh; and it passeth forth into Timnah,
11 and it cometh against the parts of the north by the
side of Ekron; and it is bowed to Shicron, and it passeth
the hill of Baalah (and it goeth by Mount Baalah); and it
cometh into Jabneel,
12 and it is closed with the end of the great sea, against
the west. These be the terms of the sons of Judah, by
compass in their families. (and it endeth with the
Mediterranean Sea, as its western border. This is the course
of the borders of the sons of Judah, family by family.)
13 And *Joshua* gave to Caleb, the son of Jephunneh, (a)
part in the midst of the sons of Judah, as the Lord
commanded to him, *this part called* Kiriatharba, of the
father of Anak; that is Hebron. (And *Joshua* gave to
Caleb, the son of Jephunneh, a portion in the midst of the
sons of Judah, as the Lord commanded him, and that was
the city of Arba, who was the father of the Anakim, *or of
the giants*; this is Hebron.)
14 And Caleb did away from *thence* (the) three sons of
Anak, Sheshai, and Ahiman, and Talmai, of the
generation of Anak.
15 And Caleb went up from thence, and he came to the
dwellers of Debir, that was called before Kiriathsepher,
that is, the city of letters (that before was called
Kiriathsepher, *that is, the City of Letters*).
16 And Caleb said, I shall give Achsah, my daughter,
(for a) wife to him that shall smite Kiriathsepher, and shall
take it.
17 And Othniel, the son of Kenaz, the younger brother
of Caleb, took the city: and Caleb gave Achsah, his
daughter, (for a) wife to him.
18 And when she went together (with him), her
husband counselled her, that she should ask of her father
a field (that she should ask for a field from her father);
and (so) she sighed, as she sat upon the ass; and Caleb
said to her, What hast thou *in thy mind*?
19 And she answered, Give thou a blessing to me; thou
hast given to me the south land and dry (thou hast given
me the dry south land); join thou also thereto a moist
land. And (so) Caleb gave to her the moist land, above
and beneath.
20 This is the possession of the lineage of the sons of
Judah, by their families.
21 And the cities from the last parts of the sons of
Judah, beside the terms of Edom (beside the border with
Edom), from the south were *these cities*; Kabzeel, and
Eder, and Jagur,
22 Kinah, and Dimonah, Adadah,
23 and Kedesh, and Hazor, and Ithnan,
24 and Ziph, and Telem, and Bealoth,
25 and Hazor, Hadattah, and Kerioth, (and) Hezron,
this is Hazor,
26 Amam, Shema, and Moladah,
27 and Hazargaddah, and Heshmon, (and) Bethpalet,
28 and Hazarshual, and Beersheba, and Bizjothjah,
29 and Baalah, and Iim, and Azem,
30 and Eltolad, and Chesil, and Hormah,
31 and Ziklag, and Madmannah, and Sansannah,
32 Lebaoth, and Shilhim, and Ain, and Rimmon; all the
cities, nine and twenty, and the towns of those.
33 And in the field places, Eshtaol, and Zoreah, and
Ashnah,
34 and Zanoah, and Engannim, and Tappuah, and
Enam,
35 and Jarmuth, Adullam, Socoh, and Azekah,
36 and Sharaim, Adithaim, and Gederah, and
Gederothaim; fourteen cities, and the towns of those;
37 Zenan, and Hadashah, and Migdalgad,
38 Dilean, and Mizpeh, (and) Joktheel,

39 Lachish, and Bozkath, and Eglon,
40 Cabbon, and Lahmam, and Kithlish,
41 and Gederoth, and Bethdagon, and Naamah, and
Makkedah; sixteen cities, and the towns of those,
42 Libnah, and Ether, and Ashan,
43 Jiphtah, and Ashnah, and Nezib,
44 and Keilah, and Achzib, and Mareshah; nine cities,
and the towns of those;
45 Ekron, with his towns and villages; (Ekron, and its
towns and villages;)
46 from Ekron till to the sea, all that go to Ashdod, and
the towns thereof; (and from Ekron to the west, all the
cities close to Ashdod, and its towns;)
47 Ashdod with his towns and villages; Gaza with his
towns and villages, till to the strand of Egypt; and the
great sea is the term thereof; (Ashdod, and its towns and
villages; Gaza, and its towns and villages, unto the River
of Egypt, *that is, the Nile*; and the Mediterranean Sea is
its border;)
48 and in the hill (country), Shamir, and Jattir, and
Socoh,
49 and Dannah, (and) Kiriathsannah, this is Debir,
50 Anab, and Eshtemoh, and Anim,
51 Goshen, and Holon, and Giloh; eleven cities, and
the towns of those;
52 Arab, and Dumah, and Eshean,
53 and Janum, and Bethtappuah, and Aphekah,
54 Humtah, and Kiriatharba, this is Hebron, and Zior;
nine cities, and the towns of those;
55 Maon, and Carmel, and Ziph, and Juttah,
56 Jezreel, and Jokdeam, and Zanoah,
57 and Cain, Gibeah, and Timnah; ten cities, and the
towns of those;
58 Halhul, and Bethzur, and Gedor,
59 Maarath, and Bethanoth, and Eltekon; six cities, and
the towns of those;
60 Kiriathbaal, this is Kiriathjearim, *the city of (the)
woods*, and Rabbah; two cities, and the towns of those;
61 in the desert, Betharabah, Middin, and Secacah,
62 Nibshan, and the city of Salt, and Engedi; six cities,
and the towns of those; *the cities* were (all) together an
hundred and fifteen.
63 Soothly the sons of Judah might not do away
Jebusites, the dweller(s) of Jerusalem; and Jebusites
dwelled with the sons of Judah in Jerusalem unto this
present day. (But the sons of Judah could not do away the
Jebusites, the inhabitants of Jerusalem; and so the
Jebusites live with the sons of Judah in Jerusalem unto
this present day.)

CHAPTER 16

1 And the lot, *either part*, of the sons of Joseph felled
from (the) Jordan against Jericho, and to the waters
thereof, from the east; (that) is, (to) the wilderness, that
goeth up from Jericho to the hill of Bethel,
2 and it goeth out from Bethel into Luz, and it passeth
the term of Archi (to) Ataroth, (and it goeth out from
Bethel to Luz, and then it passeth the border of the
Archites at Atarothaddar,)
3 and it goeth down to the west, beside the term of
Japhleti, unto the terms of the lower Bethhoron, and of
Gezer; and the countries thereof be ended with the great
sea, (and it goeth down to the west, beside the border of
the Japhletites, unto the border of Lower Bethhoron, and
Gezer; and their land endeth at the Mediterranean Sea,)
4 which *countries* Manasseh and Ephraim, the sons of
Joseph, wielded. (which *lands the tribes of western*
Manasseh and of Ephraim, the sons of Joseph, took.)
5 And the term of the sons of Ephraim, by their
families, and the possession of them was made against
the east, (from) Atarothaddar till to the higher Bethhoron.
(And the border of the possession of the sons of Ephraim,
by their families, on the east, went from Atarothaddar
unto Upper Bethhoron.)
6 And the coasts go out into the sea; for Michmethah
beholdeth the north, and it compasseth the terms against
the east in Taanathshiloh, and it passeth from the strand
of Janohah; (And then the border goeth out to the west, to
Michmethah in the north, and then out to the east of
Taanathshiloh, and passeth by it on the east to Janohah;)
7 and it goeth down from Janohah into Ataroth(addar),
and into Naarath, and it cometh into Jericho; and it goeth
out to (the) Jordan(;)
8 (and it goeth forth) from Tappuah, and passeth
against the sea into the valley of the place of reeds; and
the goings out thereof be unto the saltiest sea. This is the
possession [of the lineage] of the sons of Ephraim, by
their families; (and from Tappuah it goeth west by the
Kanah River; and its end, *or its limit*, is the Mediterranean
Sea. This is the possession of the tribe of the sons of
Ephraim, by their families;)
9 and the cities and the towns of those be separated to
the sons of Ephraim, in the midst of the possession of the
sons of Manasseh.
10 And the sons of Ephraim killed not Canaanites, that
dwelled in Gezer; and Canaanites dwelled (as a) tributary
in the midst of Ephraim till to this day. (And the sons of
Ephraim did not kill the Canaanites who lived in Gezer;
and so the Canaanites live as tributaries in the midst of
the Ephraimites unto this present day/and so the
Canaanites live in the midst of the Ephraimites, and pay
them tribute, *or taxes*, unto this present day.)

CHAPTER 17

1 Forsooth (a) lot felled to the lineage of Manasseh, for
he is the first engendered son of Joseph; *(that is, a) lot
felled* to Machir, the first engendered son of Manasseh, to
the father of Gilead (the father of Gilead), that was a

warrior, and he had [the] possession (of) Gilead and Bashan.
2 And *(a) lot felled* to the others of the sons of Manasseh, by their families; to the sons of Abiezer, and to the sons of Helek, and to the sons of Asriel, and to the sons of Shechem, and to the sons of Hepher, and to the sons of Shemida; these be the sons of Manasseh, the son of Joseph, the male children, by their families.
3 But to Zelophehad, the son of Hepher, son of Gilead, son of Machir, son of Manasseh, there were not sons, but daughters alone (but only daughters); of which these be the names, Mahlah, and Noah, and Hoglah, and Milcah, and Tirzah.
4 And they came in the sight of Eleazar, [the] priest, and of Joshua, [the] son of Nun, and of the princes, and said, The Lord commanded by the hand of Moses, that (a) possession should be given to us in the midst of our brethren. And Joshua gave to them (a) possession, by the commandment of the Lord, in the midst of the brethren of their father. (And they came before Eleazar, the priest, and Joshua, the son of Nun, and the leaders, and said, The Lord commanded by Moses, that a possession should be given to us in the midst of our kinsmen. And Joshua gave them a possession, by the commandment of the Lord, in the midst of their father's brothers.)
5 And ten cords, *that is, lands measured by ten cords,* felled to Manasseh, without the land of Gilead and Bashan, beyond (the) Jordan; (And ten cords, *that is, the lands measured by ten cords,* fell to Manasseh, besides the land of Gilead and Bashan, on the eastern side of the Jordan River;)
6 for the daughters of Manasseh wielded (a) heritage in the midst of the sons of him. For the land of Gilead felled into the part of the sons of Manasseh, that were left *alive.* (for Manasseh's daughters received an inheritance in the midst of his sons. For the land of Gilead fell into the portion for the rest of Manasseh's sons.)
7 And the term of Manasseh was from Asher to Michmethah, that beholdeth Shechem, and *it* goeth forth to the right side, beside the dwellers of the well (of) Tappuah; (And the territory of *western* Manasseh went from Asher to Michmethah, which is east of Shechem, and *it* goeth forth to the right side, beside the inhabitants of Entappuah;)
8 for the land of Tappuah, which is beside the terms of Manasseh, and of the sons of Ephraim, felled in the lot of Manasseh. (for the land of Tappuah fell in the lot of Manasseh, but Tappuah itself was on the border of Manasseh, and belonged to the sons of Ephraim.)
9 And the term of the valley of the place of reeds goeth down in the south of the strand of the cities of Ephraim, that be in the midst of the cities of Manasseh. The term of Manasseh is from the north of the strand, and the going(s) out thereof goeth to the sea; (And the border goeth down to the Kanah River, and then south of the river; the cities there belonged to Ephraim, even though they be in the midst of the cities of Manasseh. The border of Manasseh is along the north side of the river, and its end, *or its limit,* is the Mediterranean Sea;)
10 so that the possession of Ephraim is from the south, and the possession of Manasseh is from the north, and the sea closeth ever either; and those *possessions* be joined to themselves in the lineage of Asher from the north, and in the lineage of Issachar from the east. (so the possession of Ephraim is from the south side of the river, and the possession of *western* Manasseh is from the north side of the river, and the Mediterranean Sea closeth, *or endeth,* both; and the tribe of Asher is to the north, and the tribe of Issachar is to the east.)
11 And the heritage of Manasseh was in Issachar and in Asher, Bethshean, and the towns thereof, and Ibleam, with his towns, and the dwellers of Dor, with her cities, and the dwellers of Endor, with her towns, and also the dwellers of Taanach, with her towns, and the dwellers of Megiddo, with her towns, and the third part of the city (of) Naphath[3]. (And Manasseh had possessions within Issachar and Asher, Bethshean, and its towns, and Ibleam, and its towns, and the inhabitants of Dor, and its towns, and the inhabitants of Endor, and its towns, and the inhabitants of Taanach, and its towns, and the inhabitants of Megiddo, and its towns, and the third part of the city of Naphath.)
12 And the sons of Manasseh might not destroy these cities, but Canaanites began to dwell in this land. (And the sons of Manasseh could not destroy these cities, and so the Canaanites continued to live in this land.)
13 And after that the sons of Israel had waxed strong, they made subject (these) Canaanites, and they made them tributaries to themselves, and they killed them not. (And after the Israelites had grown strong, they made these Canaanites to pay tribute, *or taxes,* to them, but they did not kill them.)
14 And the sons of Joseph spake to Joshua, and said, Why hast thou given to me land into (a) possession of (only) one lot and [one] part, since I am of so great multitude, and the Lord hath blessed me, *that is, hath alarged me in children*? (And Joseph's sons, *that is, the sons of Ephraim and of Manasseh,* spoke to Joshua, and said, Why hast thou given us the land of only one lot, yea, only one portion for a possession, since we be of so great a multitude, and the Lord hath blessed us, *that is, hath enlarged us, with so many children*?)
15 To whom Joshua said, If thou art a much people, go

[3] The Hebrew meaning of this phrase, "and the third part of the city (of) Naphath", is unclear; other possibilities include: "even the three countries, *or regions*", "even the three heights", and "and the third is Naphath, *that is, the hills of Dor*".

thou up into the wood, and cut down to thee spaces in the land of Perizzites, and of Rephaim, for the possession of the hill of Ephraim is (too) strait to thee. (To whom Joshua said, If thou be so many people, and the possession of the hill country of Ephraim is too small for thee, go thou up into the woods, and cut down space for thyselves in the land of the Perizzites, and of the Rephaim, *or of the giants*.)
16 To whom the sons of Joseph answered, We may not ascend to the hilly places, since Canaanites, that dwell in the land of the field, use iron chariots; in which land Bethshean, with his towns, and Jezreel, wielding the middle valley, be set. (To whom Joseph's sons answered, The hill country is still not large enough; and also, the Canaanites, who live there in the land of the valley, have iron chariots; yea, all those who live in Bethshean, and its towns, and who live in the Jezreel Valley.)
17 And Joshua said to the house of Joseph, and of Ephraim, and of Manasseh (And Joshua said to the house of Joseph, that is, to the tribes of Ephraim, and of Manasseh), Thou art [a] much people, and of great strength; thou shalt not have (only) one lot,
18 but thou shalt pass to the hill, and thou shalt cut down to thee trees; and thou shalt cleanse spaces to dwell in (but thou shalt go into the hill country, and thou shalt cut down the trees; and thou shalt clear out space for thyselves to live in). And thou shalt be able to go forth further, when thou hast destroyed (the) Canaanites, whom thou sayest to have iron chariots, and to be most strong.

CHAPTER 18

1 And all the sons of Israel were gathered in Shiloh, and there they setted fast the tabernacle of witnessing; and the land was subject to them. (And all the Israelites were gathered in Shiloh, and they set up the Tabernacle of the Witnessing there; and the land was made subject to them.)
2 And (yet) seven lineages of the sons of Israel *dwelt* there, that had not yet taken their possessions.
3 To the which Joshua said, How long fade ye, or wallow through sloth, and enter not to wield the land, which the Lord God of your fathers hath given to you?
4 Choose ye (out) of each lineage three men, (so) that I send them, and they go, and compass the land; and that they describe the land by the number of each multitude (and they set the borders of the land, suitable for the number of each multitude), and (then) bring to me that, that ye have described.
5 Part ye the land to you into seven parts (Divide ye up the land among you into seven parts); Judah be in his terms at the south coast, and the house of Joseph at the north;
6 describe ye the middle land betwixt them into seven parts; and then ye shall come to me, that I send lot to you
here before your Lord God; (describe ye *in writing, or survey*, the borders for seven divisions of the land in the middle between them; and then come ye back to me, and I shall cast, *or throw*, lots for you here before the Lord your God;)
7 for the part of Levites is not among you, but the priesthood of the Lord, this is the heritage of them. For Gad, and Reuben, and the half lineage of Manasseh, have taken now their possession(s) beyond (the) Jordan, at the east coast, which Moses, the servant of the Lord, gave to them. (and the Levites shall have no portion among you, for the priesthood of the Lord is their inheritance. And Gad, and Reuben, and half of the tribe of Manasseh have now taken their possessions on the eastern side of the Jordan River, which Moses, the servant of the Lord, gave them.)
8 And when the men had risen up to go, to describe the land, Joshua commanded to them, and said, Compass ye the land, and describe it, and turn again to me, that I send lot to you here in Shiloh, before your Lord God. (And when the men had risen up to go, to describe *in writing, or to survey*, the borders of the land, Joshua commanded to them, and said, Go ye around the land, and describe it *in writing*, and then return to me, and I shall throw lots for you, before the Lord your God, here in Shiloh.)
9 And so they went forth, and compassed that land, and parted it into seven parts, writing it (all) in a book; and they turned again to Joshua, into the tents in Shiloh (and then they returned to Joshua, to the camp at Shiloh).
10 And Joshua sent lots before the Lord God in Shiloh, and he parted the land to the sons of Israel, into seven parts. (And Joshua threw lots before the Lord God in Shiloh, and he divided up the land into seven portions, for the Israelites.)
11 And the first lot of the sons of Benjamin, by their families, went up, that they should wield the land betwixt the sons of Judah and the sons of Joseph. (And the first lot went out to the sons of Benjamin, by their families, that they should possess the land between the sons of Judah and the sons of Joseph.)
12 And the term of them was against the north from (the) Jordan, and it passed by the side of Jericho at the north coast; and it ascended from thence against the west to the hilly places, and it came to the wilderness of Bethaven; (And their border at the north went out from the Jordan River, and it passed by the northern side of Jericho; and it went up from there to the west to the hill country, and it came to the wilderness of Bethaven;)
13 and it passed beside Luz to the south; that is Bethel; and (then) it goeth down into Atarothaddar, into the hill (country) which is at the south of Lower Bethhoron;
14 and it is bowed, and it compasseth against the sea, at the south of the hill that beholdeth Bethhoron against

the north; and the outgoings thereof be into Kiriathbaal,
which is called also Kiriathjearim, the city of the sons of
Judah; this is the great coast against the sea, at the west.
(and then it is turned, and it goeth to the west, southward
from the hill country that beholdeth Bethhoron; and its
end, *or its limit,* is Kiriathbaal, which is also called
Kiriathjearim, the city of the sons of Judah; this is the
western border.)
15 And from the south, by the part of Kiriathjearim, the
term goeth out against the sea, and cometh till to the well
of (the) waters of Nephtoah; (And in the south, from the
edge of Kiriathjearim, the border goeth out toward the
west, and cometh unto the well of the waters of
Nephtoah;)
16 and it goeth down into the part of the hill that
beholdeth the valley of the sons of Hinnom, and it is
against the north coast, in the last part of the valley of
Rephaim; and Ge Hinnom, *that is, the valley of Hinnom,*
goeth down by the side of Jebusites, at the south, and
cometh to the well of Rogel, (and it goeth down to the
edge of the hill that beholdeth the Hinnom Valley, north
of the Rephaim Valley, and then goeth down the Hinnom
Valley, to the south side of the Jebusites, and cometh to
Enrogel,)
17 and it passeth to the north, and it goeth out to
Enshemesh, *that is, the well of the sun,* and it passeth unto
the little hills that be against the going up of Adummim
(and it passeth by Geliloth, that faceth the ascent of
Adummim); and it goeth down to Even Bohan, *that is, the
stone of Bohan,* (that was named for) the son of Reuben,
18 and passed by the side of the north to the field
places; and it goeth down into the plain, (and passed by
the north side of the Arabah; and then it goeth down into
the Arabah,)
19 and it passeth forth against the north to Bethhoglah;
and the outgoings thereof be against the arm of the
saltiest sea, from the north, and the end of (the) Jordan is
at the south coast, (and it passeth forth toward the north
to Bethhoglah; and its end, *or its limit,* is at the northern
arm of the Dead Sea, at the southern end of the Jordan
River; this is the southern border;)
20 which is the term thereof from the east (the Jordan
River is its eastern border). This is the possession of the
sons of Benjamin, by their terms in compass, and by their
families;
21 and the cities thereof were Jericho and Bethhoglah,
and the valley of Keziz (and Emekkeziz),
22 Betharabah, and Zemaraim, and Bethel,
23 and Avim, and Parah, and Ophrah,
24 the town of Chepharhaammonai, and Ophni, and
Geba; twelve cities, and the towns of those;
25 Gibeon, and Ramah, and Beeroth,
26 and Mizpeh, and Chephirah, and Mozah,
27 and Rekem, Irpeel, and Taralah,
28 and Zela, Eleph, and Jebus, which is Jerusalem,
Gibeath, and Kiriath(jearim); fourteen cities, and the
towns of those; this is the possession of the sons of
Benjamin, by their families.

CHAPTER 19

1 And the second lot of the sons of Simeon went out,
by their families; and the heritage of them, in the midst of
the possession of the sons of Judah, (And the second lot
went out to the sons of Simeon, by their families; and
their inheritance, in the midst of the possession of the
sons of Judah,)
2 was Beersheba, and Sheba, and Moladah,
3 and Hazarshual, and Balah, and Azem,
4 and Eltolad, and Bethul, and Hormah,
5 and Ziklag, and Bethmarcaboth, and Hazarsusah,
6 and Bethlebaoth, and Sharuhen; thirteen cities[4], and
the towns of those;
7 Ain, and Remmon, and Ether, and Ashan; four cities,
and the towns of those;
8 all the towns by compass of these cities, unto
Baalath(beer) Ramath, against the south coast, were
seventeen cities. This is the heritage of the sons of
Simeon, by their families, (and so all the cities with the
towns around them, unto Baalathbeer, or Ramah, in the
south, were seventeen altogether. This is the inheritance
of the sons of Simeon, by their families,)
9 in the possession and part of the sons of Judah, for it
was more (than Judah had need of); and therefore the
sons of Simeon had (a) possession in the midst of the
heritage thereof (and so the sons of Simeon had *their*
possession in the midst of Judah's inheritance).
10 And the third lot of the sons of Zebulun felled, by
their families; and the term of (the) possession of the sons
of Zebulun was made unto Sarid; (And the third lot fell to
the sons of Zebulun, by their families; and the border of
the possession of the sons of Zebulun was made unto
Shadud;)
11 and it goeth up from the sea, and from Maralah; and
it cometh into Dabbasheth, unto the strand that is against
Jokneam; (and it goeth up to the west to Maralah; and it
cometh to Dabbasheth, and to the river east of Jokneam;)
12 and it turneth again from Sarid, against the east, into
the coasts of Chislothtabor (and it turneth again from
Shadud, toward the east, to the border of Chislothtabor);
and it goeth out to Daberath; and it goeth up against
Japhia;
13 and from thence it passeth forth to the east coast to
Gittahhepher, and to Ittahkazin; and it goeth out into
Remmonmethoar, and Neah;
14 and it compasseth to the north, and to Hannathon;

---

[4] In verse 2, the Hebrew text adds, "and Sheba", making *fourteen* cities.

and the goings out thereof be the valley of Jiphthahel
(and its end, *or its limit*, is the Jiphthahel Valley),
15 and Kattath, and Nahallal, and Shimron, and Idalah,
and Bethlehem; twelve cities, and the towns of those.
16 This is the heritage of the lineage of the sons of
Zebulun, by their families, and the cities and towns of
those. (This is the inheritance of the tribe of the sons of
Zebulun, by their families, and their cities and towns.)
17 The fourth lot went out to Issachar, by his families;
(The fourth lot went out to the sons of Issachar, by their
families;)
18 and the heritage thereof was Jezreel (and its
inheritance was Jezreel), and Chesulloth, and Shunem,
19 and Haphraim, and Shihon, and Anaharath,
20 and Rabbith, and Kishion, (and) Abez,
21 and Remeth, and Engannim, and Enhaddah, and
Bethpazzez.
22 And the term thereof cometh unto Tabor, and
Shahazimah, and Bethshemesh; and the outgoings
thereof were (the) Jordan; sixteen cities, and the towns of
those. (And its border cometh unto Tabor, and
Shahazimah, and Bethshemesh; and its end, *or its limit*,
was the Jordan River; sixteen cities, and their towns.)
23 This is the possession of the sons of Issachar, by
their families, the cities and the towns of those.
24 And the fifth lot felled to the lineage of the sons of
Asher, by their families;
25 and the term of them was Helkath (and its border
was made unto Helkath), and Hali, and Beten, and
Achshaph,
26 and Alammelech, and Amad, and Misheal; and it
cometh till to Carmel of the sea, and Shihor, and Libnath
(and it goeth unto Carmel on the west, and Shihorlibnath);
27 and it turneth again, against the east, to Bethdagon;
and it passeth unto Zebulun, and to the valley of
Jiphthahel, against the north, in[to] Bethemek, and Neiel;
and it goeth out to the left side to Cabul (and it goeth out
on the north side to Cabul),
28 and Hebron, and Rehob, and Hammon, and Kanah,
unto Great(er) Sidon;
29 and it turneth again into Ramah, unto the strongest
city Tyre, and unto Hosah; and the outgoings thereof
shall be into the sea, from the part of Achzib, (and it
turneth again at Ramah, and goeth to the strengthened
city of Tyre, and to Hosah; and its ends, *or its limits*, on
the west were Mahalab, and Achzib,)
30 and Ummah, and Aphek, and Rehob; two and
twenty cities, and the towns of those.
31 This is the possession of the sons of Asher, by their
families, the cities, and (the) towns of those.
32 The sixth lot of the sons of Naphtali felled, by their
families; (The sixth lot fell to the sons of Naphtali, by
their families;)
33 and the term began from Heleph, and Allon, and
Zaanannim, and Adami, which is Nekeb, and Jabneel, till
to Lakum; and the outgoing(s) of them till to (the) Jordan;
(and the border began from Heleph, and Allon, and
Zaanannim, and Adami, which is Nekeb, and Jabneel,
unto Lakum; and its end, *or its limit*, was the Jordan River;)
34 and the term turneth again, against the west, into
Aznoth of Tabor; and from thence it goeth out into
Hukkok, and it passeth into Zebulun, against the south,
and into Asher, against the west, and into Judah, at (the)
Jordan, against the rising of the sun; (and the border
turneth again, on the west, into Aznothtabor; and from
there it goeth out to Hukkok, and it passeth into Zebulun,
on the south, and into Asher, on the west, and into Judah,
at the Jordan River, on the east;)
35 of the strongest city Ziddim, Zer, and Hammath, and
Rakkath, Chinnereth, (and their strengthened cities were
Ziddim, Zer, and Hammath, and Rakkath, and
Chinnereth,)
36 and Adamah, and Ramah, Hazor,
37 and Kedesh, and Edrei, Enhazor,
38 and Iron, and Migdalel, Horem, and Bethanath, and
Bethshemesh; nineteen cities, and the towns of those.
39 This is the possession of the lineage of the sons of
Naphtali, by their families, the cities, and the towns of
those.
40 The seventh lot went out to the lineage of the sons
of Dan, by their families;
41 and the term of the possession thereof was Zorah,
and Eshtaol, and Irshemesh, *that is, the city of the sun*,
(and the border of its possession was Zorah, and Eshtaol,
and Irshemesh, *that is, the City of the Sun*,)
42 Shaalabbin, and Ajalon, and Jethlah,
43 Elon, and Thimnathah, and Ekron,
44 Eltekeh, Gibbethon, and Baalath,
45 Jehud, and Beneberak, and Gathrimmon,
46 and Mejarkon, and Rakkon, with the term that
beholdeth Joppa, and is closed with that end. (and
Mejarkon, and Rakkon, and the border was opposite
Joppa; but the sons of Dan lost this land.)
47 And (so) the sons of Dan went up, and fought
against Leshem; and they took it, and they smote it by the
sharpness of (the) sword, and they had it in possession,
and dwelled therein; and they called the name thereof
Leshem, Dan, by the name of Dan, their father (and they
renamed Leshem, Dan, after Dan, the name of their
forefather).
48 This is the possession of the lineage of Dan, by their
families, the cities, and the towns of those.
49 And when they had fulfilled to part the land by lot
to all men by their lineages, the sons of Israel gave (a)
possession to Joshua, the son of Nun, in the midst of
them,
50 by the commandment of the Lord, the city which he
asked (for), Timnathserah, in the hill (country) of Ephraim;

and he builded the city, and dwelled therein (and lived
there).
51 These be the possessions which Eleazar, the priest,
and Joshua, the son of Nun, and the princes of the families,
and of the lineages of the sons of Israel (and the heads of
the families of the tribes of the Israelites), parted by lot in
Shiloh, before the Lord, at the door of the tabernacle of
(the) witnessing; and (so) they parted the land.

CHAPTER 20

1 And the Lord spake to Joshua, and said,
2 Speak thou to the sons of Israel, and say thou to
them, Separate ye (out) the cities of fugitives, *either of
men exiled for (the) unwillful shedding of blood*, of
which cities I spake to you by the hand of Moses, (Speak
thou to the Israelites, and say thou to them, Ordain ye the
cities of refuge *for those who be exiled for the unwillful,
or the unintentional, shedding of blood*, of which cities I
spoke to you by Moses,)
3 that whoever slayeth unwittingly a man, flee to
those cities; that when he hath fled to one of those cities,
he may escape the ire of the neighbour, which is venger
of blood. (so that whoever unwittingly killeth someone,
can flee to those cities; so that when he hath fled to one
of these cities, he can escape the anger of the neighbour,
who avengeth the blood.)
4 And he shall stand before the gates of the city, and he
shall speak to the elder men of that city those things that
shall prove him(self) innocent; and so they shall receive
him, and they shall give to him a place to dwell *in*.
5 And when the venger of blood pursueth him, they *of
that city* shall not betake him into the hands of the
venger; for unwittingly he killed his neighbour (for he
killed his neighbour unwittingly, *or unintentionally*), and
he is not proved (to be) his enemy before the second day
either the third day.
6 And he shall dwell in that city, till he stand before
the doom, and yield, *or show*, the cause of his deed.
And he that killed *a man*, dwell *in that city*, till the great
priest die, which is in that time; then the manslayer shall
turn again, and he shall enter into his city, and house,
from which he fled. (And he shall remain in that city,
until he stand before the judge, and show the reason for
his deed. And he who killed *someone*, shall stay *in that
city*, until the High Priest die, who is in office at that
time; then the man-killer shall return, and he shall enter
into his city, and into his house, from which he fled.)
7 And they ordained Kedesh in Galilee, of the hill of
Naphtali, and Shechem in the hill of Ephraim, and
Kiriatharba, that is Hebron, in the hill of Judah. (And they
ordained Kedesh in Galilee, in the hill country of Naphtali,
and Shechem in the hill country of Ephraim, and
Kiriatharba, that is Hebron, in the hill country of Judah.)
8 And beyond (the) Jordan, against the east coast of
Jericho (And on the eastern side of the Jordan River, east
of Jericho), they ordained Bezer, that is set in the field
wilderness of the lineage of Reuben, and Ramoth in
Gilead, of the lineage of Gad, and Golan in Bashan, of
the lineage of Manasseh.
9 These cites were ordained to all the sons of Israel,
and to the comelings that dwell among them, that he that
killed unwittingly a man, should flee to those cities; and
he should not die in the hand of the neighbour, coveting
to venge the blood shed out, till he stood before the
people, to declare his cause. (These cities were ordained
to all the Israelites, and to the newcomers who live
among them, so that he who unwittingly killed someone,
could flee to them; and so that he would not die at the
hand of the neighbour, coveting to avenge the blood
shed out, until he first had stood before the people to
declare his case.)

CHAPTER 21

1 And the princes of the families of Levi nighed to
Eleazar, the priest, and to Joshua, the son of Nun, and to
the dukes of the kindreds, by all the lineages of the sons
of Israel; (And the leaders of the families of Levi came to
Eleazar, the priest, and to Joshua, the son of Nun, and to
the leaders of the families, of all the tribes of the Israelites;)
2 and they spake to them in Shiloh, *a city* of the land
of Canaan, and they said, The Lord commanded by the
hand of Moses, that cities should be given to us to dwell
in, and the suburbs of those for *our* work beasts to be fed
in. (and they spoke to them in Shiloh, *a city* in the land of
Canaan, and they said, The Lord commanded by Moses,
that we should be given cities to live in, and also their
suburbs for *our* work beasts to be fed in.)
3 And the sons of Israel gave of their possessions, by
commandment of the Lord, cities and the suburbs of
those. (And so the Israelites gave to the Levites out of
their possessions, by the command of the Lord, the
following cities and their suburbs.)
4 And the lot went out into the family of Kohath, of
the sons of Aaron, the priest, of the lineages of Judah, and
of Simeon, and of Benjamin, thirteen cities; (And the lot
went out to the Kohathite families, that is, to the Levites
of the sons of Aaron, the priest, thirteen cities from the
tribes of Judah, and Simeon, and Benjamin;)
5 and to the others of the sons of Kohath, that is, to
the deacons that were left (over), of the lineages of
Ephraim, and of Dan, and of the half lineage of
Manasseh, ten cities. (and to the rest of the Kohathite
families, that is, to the Levites of the lower degree, ten
cities from the tribes of Ephraim, and Dan, and *the
western* half of the tribe of Manasseh.)
6 And lot went out to the sons of Gershon, that they
should take of the lineages of Issachar, and of Asher, and
of Naphtali, and of the half lineage of Manasseh in

Bashan, thirteen cities in number; (And the lot went out
to the Gershonites, that they should receive from the
tribes of Issachar, and Asher, and Naphtali, and from the
eastern half of the tribe of Manasseh in Bashan, thirteen
cities in number;)
7 and to the sons of Merari, by their families, of the
lineages of Reuben, and of Gad, and of Zebulun, twelve
cities. (and for the Merarites, by their families, from the
tribes of Reuben, and Gad, and Zebulun, twelve cities.)
8 And the sons of Israel gave to the deacons cities,
and their suburbs, as the Lord commanded by the hand
of Moses; and all gave by lot. (And so the Israelites gave
to the Levites these cities, and their suburbs, as the Lord
commanded by Moses; and all gave by lot.)
9 (Out) Of [*the*] *possessions* of the lineages of the sons
of Judah, and of Simeon, Joshua gave (these) cities;
10 to the sons of Aaron, by the families of Kohath, of
the kin of Levi (to the sons of Aaron, who were of the
Kohathite families of the Levites), of the which cities
these be the names; for the first lot went out to them;
11 Kiriatharba, of the father of Anak, which is called
Hebron, in the hill of Judah, and the suburbs thereof by
compass; (Kiriatharba, that is, the City of Arba, who was
the father of the Anak, *that is, the Anakim*, in the hill
country of Judah, which is now called Hebron, and the
suburbs around it;)
12 soothly he gave the fields and towns thereof to
Caleb, son of Jephunneh, to have in possession. (and he
gave its fields and towns to Caleb, the son of Jephunneh,
to have for a possession.)
13 Therefore *Joshua* gave to the sons of Aaron, the
priest, Hebron, *to be* a city of refuge, and the suburbs
thereof, and Libnah with his suburbs (and Libnah with its
suburbs),
14 and Jattir, and Eshtemoa,
15 and Holon, and Debir,
16 and Ain, and Juttah, and Bethshemesh, with their
suburbs; nine cities, of [the] two lineages, as it is said
(nine cities, from these two tribes).
17 And (out) of the lineage of the sons of Benjamin, *he
gave* Gibeon, and Geba,
18 and Anathoth, and Almon, with their suburbs; four
cities.
19 All the cities together of the sons of Aaron, the
priest, *were* thirteen, with their suburbs. (All the cities
given to the sons of Aaron, the priest, *were* thirteen cities,
with their suburbs.)
20 But to the others, by the families of the sons of
Kohath, of the kin of Levi, this possession was given; (out)
of the lineage of Ephraim, (And to the rest of the Kohathite
families, that is, to the Levites of the lower degree, these
possessions were given; from the tribe of Ephraim,)
21 the city of refuge, Shechem, with his suburbs, in the
hill of Ephraim, and Gezer, (Shechem, the city of refuge,
with its suburbs, in the hill country of Ephraim, and
Gezer,)
22 and Kibzaim, and Bethhoron, with their suburbs;
four cities;
23 also (out) of the lineage of Dan, Eltekeh, and
Gibbethon, (and from the tribe of Dan, Eltekeh, and
Gibbethon,)
24 and Aijalon, and Gathrimmon, with their suburbs;
four cities;
25 soothly of the half lineage of Manasseh (and from
the *western* half of the tribe of Manasseh), Taanach and
Gathrimmon, with their suburbs; two cities.
26 All the cities were ten, and their suburbs, that were
given to the sons of Kohath, of the lower degree. (So all
the cities that were given to the rest of the Kohathite
families, that is, to the Levites of the lower degree, were
ten cities, with their suburbs.)
27 Also to the sons of Gershon, of the kin of Levi,
Joshua gave (out) of the half lineage of Manasseh, cities
of refuge, Golan in Bashan, and Beeshterah, with their
suburbs; two cities. (And to the Gershonites, of the
Levites, from *the eastern* half of the tribe of Manasseh,
Joshua gave a city of refuge, Golan in Bashan, and
Beeshterah, with their suburbs; two cities.)
28 And (out) of the lineage of Issachar, *he gave* Kishon,
and Dabereh,
29 and Jarmuth, and Engannim, with their suburbs; four
cities.
30 (And out) Of the lineage of Asher, *he gave* Mishal,
and Abdon,
31 and Helkath, and Rehob, with their suburbs; four
cities.
32 Also (out) of the lineage of Naphtali (And from the
tribe of Naphtali), *he gave* the city of refuge, Kedesh in
Galilee, and Hammothdor, and Kartan, with their
suburbs; three cities.
33 All the cities of the families of Gershon *were* thirteen,
with their suburbs. (So all the cities given to the Gershonite
families *were* thirteen cities, with their suburbs.)
34 Soothly to the sons of Merari, deacons of the lower
degree, by their families, was given Jokneam, (out) of the
lineage of Zebulun, and Kartah, (And to the Merarites,
Levites of the lower degree, by their families, from the
tribe of Zebulun, *he gave* Jokneam, and Kartah,)
35 and Dimnah, and Nahalal; four cities, with their
suburbs.
36 And (out) of the lineage of Gad, *he gave* the city of
refuge, Ramoth in Gilead, and Mahanaim,
37 and Heshbon, and Jazer; four cities, with their
suburbs.
38 And (out) of the lineage of Reuben, beyond (the)
Jordan, against Jericho (And from the tribe of Reuben, on
the eastern side of the Jordan River, near Jericho), *he gave*
the city of refuge, Bezer in the wilderness of Mizar, and

Jahazah,
39 and Kedemoth, and Mephaath; four cities, with their
suburbs.
40 (So) All the cities *given to the sons* of Merari, by
their families and kindreds, *were* twelve (cities).
41 And so all the cities of (the) Levites, in the midst of
[the] possession(s) of the sons of Israel, were eight and
forty (cities), with their suburbs;
42 and all (these) *cities* were parted by families. (and all
these *cities* were divided up among the families.)
43 And the Lord gave to Israel all the land that he
swore himself to give to their fathers, and they had it in
possession, and dwelled therein (and lived there).
44 And peace was given of the Lord into all nations
about; and none of [the] enemies were hardy to
withstand the sons of Israel, but all *men* were driven into
their lordship. (And the Lord gave them peace with all
the nations about; and none of their enemies was fool-
hardy enough to stand against the Israelites, indeed, the
Lord brought all these *people* under their rule.)
45 Forsooth neither one word, that he promised himself
to give to *Israel*, was void, but all *his words* were fulfilled
in works. (And so not one thing that the Lord had
promised to give *Israel* was left void, *or undone*, but
rather, all of *his words* were fulfilled with deeds.)

CHAPTER 22

1 In the same time Joshua called the men of Reuben,
and the men of Gad, and half the lineage of Manasseh,
(At that time Joshua called the men of Reuben, and the
men of Gad, and *the eastern* half of the tribe of
Manasseh,)
2 and said to them, Ye have done all things which
Moses, the servant of the Lord, commanded to you, also
ye [have] obeyed to me in all things;
3 neither ye have left your brethren in much time till
into present day, and ye kept the commandment of your
Lord God. (nor have ye ever left your brothers, *or your
kinsmen*, unto this present day, and ye have obeyed the
commandments of the Lord your God.)
4 Therefore for your Lord God hath given rest and
peace to your brethren, as he promised, turn ye again,
and go ye into your tabernacles, and into the land of your
possession, which *land* Moses, the servant of the Lord,
gave to you beyond (the) Jordan; (And so for the Lord
your God hath given rest and peace to your kinsmen, as
he promised, now return ye, and go ye back to your
tents, *or your homes*, in the land of your possession,
which *land* Moses, the servant of the Lord, gave you on
the east side of the Jordan River;)
5 so only that ye keep busily, and [ful]fill in work the
commandment and [the] law, which law Moses, the
servant of the Lord, commanded to you; that ye love your
Lord God, and go in all his ways, and keep his behests,
and cleave to him, and serve *him* in all your heart, and in
all your soul. (so only that ye busily obey, and fulfill in
deeds, the commandments and the law, which law
Moses, the servant of the Lord, commanded to you; yea,
that ye love the Lord your God, and go in all his ways,
and obey his commands, and cleave to him, and serve
him with all your heart, and with all your soul.)
6 And Joshua blessed them, and let go them, which
turned again into their tabernacles. (And so Joshua
blessed them, and let them go, and they returned to their
tents, *or their homes*.)
7 Soothly Moses had given (a) possession in Bashan to
the half lineage of Manasseh; and therefore to the half
lineage that (was) left [over], Joshua gave (a) part among
their other brethren beyond (the) Jordan, at the west coast
thereof. And when *Joshua* let them go into their
tabernacles, and had blessed them, (Now Moses had
given a possession in Bashan, *that is, on the eastern side
of the Jordan River*, to half of the tribe of Manasseh; and
so to the other half *of this tribe*, Joshua gave a portion
among their other kinsmen, on the western side of the
Jordan River. And before *Joshua* let them go back to their
tents, *or their homes*, he blessed them,)
8 he said to them, With much cattle and riches turn ye
again to your seats (and he said to them, Return ye to
your homes with much cattle and riches); with silver and
gold, and brass, and iron, and with much clothing; (and)
part ye the prey of [the] enemies with your brethren.
9 And the sons of Reuben, and the sons of Gad, and
the half lineage of Manasseh turned again, and went from
the sons of Israel from Shiloh, which is set in the land of
Canaan, that they should enter into Gilead, the land of
their possession, which they got by [the] commandment
of the Lord in the hand of Moses. (And so the sons of
Reuben, and the sons of Gad, and the *eastern* half of the
tribe of Manasseh went away from the Israelites at Shiloh,
which is in the land of Canaan, to return to Gilead, the
land of their possession, which they got by the Lord's
command, through Moses.)
10 And when they had come to the terms of (the) Jordan,
into the land of Canaan, they builded beside (the) Jordan
an altar of (the) greatest sight. (And when they had come
to Geliloth, by the Jordan River, *in the region of Gilgal*,
they built a great altar there by the river for all to see.)
11 And when the sons of Israel had heard this, and
certain messengers had told (this) to them, that the sons
of Reuben, and of Gad, and the half lineage of Manasseh,
had builded an altar in the land of Canaan, on the heaps
of (the) Jordan, against the sons of Israel, (And when the
Israelites had heard of this, and certain messengers had
told them, that the sons of Reuben, and of Gad, and of
the *eastern* half of the tribe of Manasseh, had built an
altar on the bank of the Jordan River, facing the Israelites
in the land of Canaan,)

12 all they came together in Shiloh (they all came
together in Shiloh), (so) that they should go up, and fight
against them.
13 And in the meantime, they sent to them into the
land of Gilead, Phinehas, the priest, the son of Eleazar,
(And in the meantime, they sent Phinehas, the priest, the
son of Eleazar, to those tribes in the land of Gilead,)
14 and ten princes with him; of each lineage one
prince. (and ten leaders with him; one leader from each
tribe.)
15 The which came to the sons of Reuben, and of Gad,
and to the half lineage of Manasseh, into the land of
Gilead, and they said to them, (And they came to the sons
of Reuben, and of Gad, and of the *eastern* half of the tribe
of Manasseh, in the land of Gilead, and they said to them,)
16 All the people of the Lord sendeth *to you, (and*
asketh) these things; What is this trespassing? Why have
ye forsaken the Lord God of Israel, and have builded a
cursed altar, and have gone away from the worshipping
of him?
17 Whether the sin of Peor is little to you, of which we
(still) be not clean till to this day, and many of the people
felled down (there)?
18 And today ye have forsaken the Lord, and tomorrow,
that is, in time to coming (that is, in the time to come),
the ire of him shall be fierce against all Israel.
19 That if ye guess that the land of your possession is
unclean, pass ye (over) to the land, in which the
tabernacle of the Lord is, and dwell ye among us, only
that ye go not away from the Lord, and from our
fellowship, by an altar builded beside the altar of our
Lord God. (But if ye think that the land of your possession
is unclean, then come ye back here to the land where the
Tabernacle of the Lord is, and live ye among us, so only
that ye go not away from the Lord, and from our
fellowship, with an altar built in addition to the altar of
the Lord our God.)
20 Whether not Achan, the son of Zerah, passed the
commandment of the Lord, and his ire felled on all the
people of Israel? And he was one man; and we would
that he alone had perished in his trespass. (Did not
Achan, the son of Zerah, pass over the Lord's command,
and then the Lord's anger fell on all the people of Israel?
And Achan was but one man; and we wish that he alone
had perished for his trespass.)
21 And the sons of Reuben, and of Gad, and of half the
lineage of Manasseh, answered to the princes of the
message of Israel, (And the sons of Reuben, and of Gad,
and of the *eastern* half of the tribe of Manasseh, answered
to the leaders of the families of Israel, and said,)
22 The strongest Lord God himself of Israel knoweth,
and Israel shall understand altogether; (The most strong
Lord God of Israel himself knoweth, and Israel must also
understand;)
23 if we builded this altar for intent of trespassing, *that
is, of idolatry,* the Lord keep not us, but punish he us in
this present time; and if we did by that mind, that we
should put thereon burnt sacrifice[s], and sacrifice(s), and
peaceable sacrifices, he seek, and deem; (that if we have
built this altar with the intention of trespassing, *that is, for
idolatry,* the Lord should not allow us to live, and he
should punish us right now; yea, if we did it for this
purpose, so that we could put on it burnt sacrifices, and
sacrifices, and peace offerings, *or grain offerings,* let him
seek it out, and judge us right now;)
24 and not more, *rather, (that) we did it* with this
thinking and treating, that we should say *thus,* (If) Your
sons *hereafter* shall say to our sons, What is to you and to
the Lord God of Israel? *or, What claim (have) ye to be of
his people*?
25 O! ye sons of Reuben, and ye sons of Gad, the Lord
hath set a term, the flood Jordan, betwixt us and you; and
therefore ye have no part in the Lord; and by this
occasion your sons shall turn away our sons from the
dread of the Lord. (*and they say,* O! ye sons of Reuben,
and ye sons of Gad, the Lord hath set a border, the Jordan
River, between us and you; and so ye have no part in the
Lord; and in this way your sons and daughters shall turn
away our sons and daughters from the fear of the
Lord/from reverence for the Lord.)
26 Therefore we guessed (it) better, and we said, Build
we an altar to us, not into burnt sacrifices, neither to
sacrifices to be offered, (And so we thought about it, and
we said to each other, Let us build an altar for ourselves,
not for burnt sacrifices, nor for sacrifices to be offered,)
27 but into witnessing betwixt us and you, and betwixt
our children and your generation, that we serve the Lord,
and that it be of our right to offer burnt sacrifices, and
sacrifices, and peaceable sacrifices; and that your sons
say not tomorrow to our sons, No part in the Lord is to
you. (but as a witness between us and you, and between
our children and your children, that we serve the same
Lord, and that it be our right to offer burnt sacrifices, and
sacrifices, and peace offerings, *or grain offerings*; and so
your children shall not be able to say to our children
tomorrow, and the next day, There is no part for you in
the Lord.)
28 And if *your sons* will say this, *our sons* shall answer
(to) them, Lo! the altar of the Lord, which our fathers
made, not into burnt sacrifices, neither into slain
sacrifices, but into our and your witnessing everlasting
(not for burnt sacrifices, nor for slain sacrifices, but for an
everlasting witness between us and you).
29 Far be this trespass from us, that we go away from
the Lord, and forsake his steps, by an altar builded to
burnt sacrifices, and slain sacrifices, and sacrifices of
praising to be offered *thereon,* besides the altar of the
Lord our God, that is builded before his tabernacle. (So

let this trespass be far from us, that we would ever go
away from the Lord, and forsake to follow his steps, with
an altar built for burnt sacrifices, and slain sacrifices, and
grain offerings to be offered *on it*, in addition to the altar
of the Lord our God, that standeth before his Tabernacle.)
30 And when these things were heard, Phinehas, [the]
priest, and [the] princes of the message of Israel, that
were with him, were pleased; and they received gladly
the words of the sons of Reuben, and of Gad, and of the
half lineage of Manasseh. (And when these words were
heard, Phinehas, the priest, and the leaders of the families
of Israel who were with him, were pleased; and they
gladly received the words of the sons of Reuben, and of
Gad, and of the *eastern* half of the tribe of Manasseh.)
31 And Phinehas, the priest, the son of Eleazar, said to
them, Now we know, that the Lord is with you; for ye be
alien, *or guiltless*, from this trespassing, and ye have
delivered the sons of Israel from the hand, *or punishing*,
of the Lord.
32 And Phinehas turned again with the princes from the
sons of Reuben and of Gad, from the land of Gilead to
the coast of Canaan, to the sons of Israel; and he told
these things to them.
33 And the word pleased to all men hearing *it*; and the
sons of Israel praised God, and said, that they would no
more ascend against them, and fight, and do away the
land of their possession. (And this word pleased all who
heard *it*; and the Israelites praised God, and agreed that
they would talk no more about going up against the sons
of Reuben, and of Gad, and fighting them, and destroying
the land of their possession.)
34 And the sons of Reuben and the sons of Gad called
the altar, which they had builded, Our Witnessing that
the Lord Himself is God.

CHAPTER 23

1 And when much time was passed after that the Lord
had given peace to Israel, and when all nations about
were subjected (and when all the nations about were
made subject to them); and when Joshua was now of
long life, and of full eld age,
2 Joshua called all Israel, and the greater men in birth,
and the princes, and dukes, and masters, and he said to
them, I have elded, and I am of full great age; (he called
all Israel, and the men of great age, *that is, the elders*,
and the leaders, and the judges, and the officers, and he
said to them, I have now grown old, and I am of a very
great age;)
3 and ye behold all things which your Lord God hath
done to all nations about, how he hath fought for you.
(and ye see all the things which the Lord your God hath
done to all the nations about, yea, how he hath fought for
you.)
4 And now for he hath parted to you by lot all the
land, from the east part of (the) Jordan unto the great sea,
and many nations be left yet, (And now, for I have
divided up for you by lot, all the land of the nations that I
have destroyed, as well as those that still be left, from the
Jordan River in the east, unto the Mediterranean Sea in
the west,)
5 your Lord God shall destroy them (and the Lord
your God shall destroy all those who remain), and he
shall take them away from your face; and ye shall wield
their land, as he promised to you.
6 Only be ye comforted, and be ye busy, that ye keep
all things that be written in the book of Moses' law, and
bow ye not away from those things, neither to the right
side, neither to the left side, (So be ye strengthened/So be
ye encouraged, and be ye busy, that ye obey all the
things that be written in the Book of the Law by Moses,
and turn ye not away from those things, neither to the
right, nor to the left,)
7 lest after that ye have entered to the heathen men,
that shall be among you, ye swear in the name of their
gods, and serve those gods, and worship them. (lest that
ye be mixed, *or mingled*, with the heathen, who be
among you, and ye swear in the name of their gods, and
serve those gods, and worship them.)
8 But cleave ye to your Lord God (So cleave ye only
to the Lord your God), the which thing ye have done
unto this day;
9 and then the Lord God shall do away in your sight
great folks, and strongest; and none shall be able to
against-stand you. (for the Lord God hath done away
from before you great and strong nations, and none hath
been able to stand against you.)
10 One of you shall pursue a thousand men of
enemies, for your Lord God shall fight for you, as he hath
promised. (Yea, one of you can pursue a thousand of the
enemies, for the Lord your God fighteth for you, as he
promised you that he would.)
11 Be ye ware before most diligently of this thing only,
that ye love your Lord God. (But be ye ware, that ye do
this thing most diligently, that ye love the Lord your God.)
12 That if ye will cleave to the errors of these folks that
dwell among you, and will meddle marriages with them,
and couple friendships, (But if ye cleave to the errors of
these people who live among you, and will mix
marriages with them, and couple friendships,)
13 know ye right now, that the Lord your God shall not
do away them before your face, but they shall be to you
into a ditch, and into a snare, and into hurting of your
side, and into stakes in your eyes, till your Lord God take
away you, and destroy you from this best land, which he
gave to you. (then know ye right now, that the Lord your
God shall not do them away from before your face, but
they shall be for you a ditch, and a snare, and a hurting to
your side, and stakes in your eyes, until the Lord your

God shall take you away, and destroy you from off this best land, which he gave to you.)
14 Lo! I enter today into the way of all (the) earth, *for soon I shall die, as each man shall*; and ye shall know with all (*your*) soul, that of all [the] words which the Lord promised himself to give to you, not one passed (away) in vain. (Lo! I go today the way of all people upon the earth, *for soon I shall die, as each person shall*; and ye know with all *your* soul, that of all the things which the Lord promised to give you, not one thing hath been left void, *or undone*.)
15 Therefore as he [ful]filled in work that, that he promised, and all things befelled by prosperity, so he shall bring on you whatever thing of evils he menaced, till he take away you, and destroy (you) from this best land, which he gave to you. (And so as he hath fulfilled with deeds what he promised, and all things have befallen with prosperity, so he shall also bring upon you whatever evil things that he threatened, until he shall take you away, and destroy you from off this best land, which he gave to you.)
16 For ye brake the covenant of your Lord God, which he made with you, and served alien gods, and worshipped them, soon and swiftly the strong vengeance of the Lord shall rise onto you; and ye shall be taken away from this best land, which he gave to you. (For if ye break the covenant of the Lord your God, which he made with you, and serve foreign, *or other*, gods, and worship them, then the strong vengeance of the Lord shall soon rise up against you; and ye shall swiftly be taken away from off this best land, which he gave to you.)

CHAPTER 24

1 And Joshua gathered all the lineages of Israel into Shechem; and he called the greater men in birth, and the princes, and judges, and masters; and they stood in the sight of the Lord. (And Joshua gathered all the tribes of Israel into Shechem; and he called the men of great age, *that is, the elders*, and the leaders, and the judges, and the officers; and they stood before the Lord.)
2 And Joshua spake thus to the people, The Lord God of Israel saith these things, Your fathers dwelled at the beginning beyond the flood *Euphrates*, (that is,) Terah, the father of Abraham and Nachor, and they served alien gods. (And Joshua spoke to the people thus, The Lord God of Israel saith these things, Long ago your forefathers lived on the other side of the *Euphrates* River, that is, Terah, and his sons Abraham and Nachor, and they served foreign, *or other*, gods.)
3 Therefore I took your father Abraham from the coasts of Mesopotamia, and I brought him into the land of Canaan; and I multiplied his seed, and I gave Isaac to him;
4 and again, I gave to Isaac, Jacob, and Esau; of which I gave to Esau the hill of Seir, to have in possession; and Jacob and his sons went down into Egypt. (and to Isaac I gave Jacob and Esau; and I gave Esau the hill country of Seir, to have for a possession; and Jacob and his sons went down into Egypt.)
5 And I sent Moses and Aaron, and I smote Egypt with many signs and wonders, and I led you
6 and your fathers out of Egypt. And ye came to the (Red) Sea, and (the) Egyptians pursued your fathers with chariots, and multitude of knights (and many soldiers), (yea,) unto the Red Sea.
7 And the sons of Israel cried to the Lord, and he put darknesses betwixt you and [the] Egyptians; and he brought the sea (down) on them, and (it altogether) covered them. Your eyes have seen all (the) things, which I did in Egypt. And ye dwelled in wilderness much time (And then ye lived in the wilderness, *or in the desert*, a long time).
8 And I brought you into the land of Amorites, that dwelled beyond (the) Jordan; and when they fought against you, I betook them into your hands, and ye had their land in possession, and ye killed them. (And I brought you into the land of the Amorites, who lived on the east side of the Jordan River; and when they fought against you, I delivered them into your hands, and ye had their land for a possession, and ye killed them.)
9 And Balak, the son of Zippor, the king of Moab, rose (up), and fought against Israel; and he sent (for), and called (on) Balaam, the son of Beor, that he should curse you.
10 And I would not hear him, but on the contrary by Balaam I blessed you, and I delivered you from the hands of Balak. (But I would not listen to him, and on the contrary, I blessed you by Balaam, and I rescued you from Balak's hands.)
11 And ye passed [over] (the) Jordan (And ye crossed over the Jordan River), and came to Jericho; and men of that city fought against you, Amorites, and Perizzites, and Canaanites, Hittites, and Girgashites, and Hivites, and Jebusites; and I betook them (all) into your hands.
12 And I sent flies with venomous tongues before you, and I casted them out of their places; (yea,) I killed [the] two kings of (the) Amorites, not in thy sword, nor in thy bow (but not with thy sword, or with thy bow).
13 And I gave to you the land in which ye travailed not, and cities which ye builded not, (so) that ye should dwell in those, and vineries (and vineyards), and places of olive trees, which ye planted not.
14 Now therefore dread ye the Lord, and serve ye him with perfect heart and most true; and do ye away the gods, to which your fathers served in Mesopotamia, and in Egypt; and serve ye the Lord. (And so now fear ye the Lord, and serve ye him with a perfect and a most true heart; and do ye away the gods whom your forefathers served in Mesopotamia, and in Egypt; and serve ye the Lord.)
15 But if it seemeth evil to you, that ye serve the Lord,

choosing is given to you; choose ye to you today that,
that pleaseth, whom ye ought most to serve; whether to
gods, which your fathers served in Mesopotamia,
whether to the gods of Amorites, in whose land ye dwell;
forsooth I, and mine house, shall serve the Lord. (But if it
seemeth onerous to you, that ye serve the Lord, choosing
is given to you; choose ye today what pleaseth you,
whom ye ought most to serve; whether the gods, which
your fathers served in Mesopotamia, or the gods of the
Amorites, in whose land ye live; but I, and my house,
shall serve the Lord.)
16 And all the people answered, and said, Far be it
from us that we forsake the Lord, and serve alien gods
(and serve foreign, *or other*, gods).
17 Our Lord God himself led us and our fathers out of
the land of Egypt, from the house of servage, and did
great signs in our sight; and he kept us (safe) in all the
way, by which we went, and in all peoples, by which we
passed; (The Lord our God himself led us and our fathers
out of the land of Egypt, from the house of servitude, *or
of slavery*, and did great miracles before us; and he kept
us safe on all the way, by which we went, and among all
the peoples, through whom we passed;)
18 and he casted out all folks, Amorites, the dwellers of
the land, into which we entered. Therefore we shall serve
the Lord, for he is our Lord God. (and he threw out the
Amorites, and all the other people, who lived in the land,
into which we entered. And so we shall serve the Lord,
for he is the Lord our God.)
19 And Joshua said to the people, Ye may not serve the
Lord; for God is holy, and a strong fervent lover, and he
forgiveth not your trespasses and sins. (But Joshua said to
the people, Ye shall not be able to serve the Lord; for
God is holy, and a jealous God, and he will not forgive
your trespasses and sins.)
20 If ye forsake the Lord, and serve alien gods (Yea, if
ye forsake the Lord, and serve foreign, *or other*, gods),
the Lord shall turn himself (away) *from you*, and he shall
torment (you), and destroy you, (even) after that he hath
given good things to you.
21 And the people said to Joshua, It shall not be so, as
thou speakest, but we shall serve the Lord.
22 And Joshua said to the people, Ye be witnesses (to
yourselves), that ye have chosen the Lord to you, that ye
serve him. And they answered, *We be* witnesses. (And
Joshua said to the people, Ye be your own witnesses, that
ye have chosen the Lord for yourselves, and that ye shall
serve him. And they answered, *We be* our own witnesses.)
23 Therefore, he said, now do ye away alien gods from
the midst of you (And so now, he said, do ye away
foreign, *or other*, gods from your midst), and bow ye your
hearts to the Lord God of Israel.
24 And the people said to Joshua, We shall serve the
Lord our God, and we shall be obedient to his behests
(and we shall obey his commands).
25 Therefore Joshua smote a bond of peace in that day,
and setted forth to the people commandments and
dooms in Shechem. (And so Joshua struck a covenant
that day, and set forth for the people commandments and
laws in Shechem.)
26 And he wrote all these words in the book of God's
law. And he took a great stone, and putted it under an
oak, that was in the saintuary of the Lord. (And he wrote
all these words in the Book of the Law of God. And he
took a great stone, and he set it up under the oak, *or by
the pole*, that was there in the sanctuary of the Lord.)
27 And he said to all the people, Lo! this stone shall be
to you into witnessing, that ye [have] heard all the words
of the Lord, which he spake to you, lest peradventure ye
would deny (*it*) afterward, and lie to your Lord God. (And
he said to all the people, Lo! this stone shall be your
witness, that ye have heard all the words of the Lord,
which he spoke to you, lest ye would deny *it* afterward,
and lie to the Lord your God.)
28 And Joshua let go the people, each man into his
possession. (And then Joshua let the people go, each man
back to his possession/each person back to their own
place.)
29 And after these things Joshua, the son of Nun, the
servant of the Lord, died, an hundred years eld and ten
(and he was a hundred and ten years old).
30 And they buried him in the coasts of his possession,
in Timnath of Serah, which is set in the hill of Ephraim,
from the north part of the hill (of) Gaash. (And they
buried him on his land, in Timnath Serah, which is set in
the hill country of Ephraim, north of Mount Gaash.)
31 And Israel served the Lord in all the days of Joshua,
and of the elder men, that lived (a) long time after Joshua,
and which elder men knew all the works of the Lord,
which he had done in Israel (which he had done for Israel).
32 Also the bones of Joseph, the which the sons of
Israel bare from Egypt, they buried in Shechem, in a part
of the field, the which field Jacob bought of the sons of
Hamor, the father of Shechem, for an hundred young
sheep; and that field was into (a) possession of the sons of
Joseph. (And Joseph's bones, which the Israelites had
brought from Egypt, they buried in Shechem, in a part of
the field, which Jacob had bought from the sons of Hamor,
the father of Shechem, for a hundred young sheep; for
that field became a possession of Joseph's sons.)
33 Also Eleazar, the son of Aaron, the priest, died; and
Phinehas and his sons buried him in Gibeah, which was
given to him in the hill of Ephraim. (And Eleazar, the son
of Aaron, the priest, died; and Phinehas and his sons
buried him on a hill, which had been given to Phinehas,
in the hill country of Ephraim.) ✡

JUDGES

CHAPTER 1

1 After the death of Joshua the sons of Israel
counselled with the Lord, and said, Who shall go up
before us against Canaanites, and shall be duke of the
battle? (After Joshua's death the Israelites counselled with
the Lord, and asked, Who shall go out first against the
Canaanites, and shall be our leader in the battle?)
2 And the Lord said, Judah shall go up (in the lead); lo!
I have given the land into his hands.
3 And Judah said to Simeon, his brother, Go thou up
with me in(to) my lot, and fight thou against Canaanites,
that I go with thee in thy lot (and then I shall go with thee
into thy lot). And (so) Simeon went with him;
4 and Judah went up (in the lead). And the Lord
betook (the) Canaanites and Perizzites into their hands,
and they killed in Bezek ten thousand men.
5 And they found Adonibezek in Bezek, and they
fought against him, and they overcame Canaanites, and
Perizzites.
6 And Adonibezek fled, whom they pursued, and took
(hold of), and they cut off the ends of his hands and of his
feet.
7 And Adonibezek said, Seventy kings, when the ends
of their hands and of their feet were cut away, gathered
remnants of meats under my board (gathered scraps of
food under my table); as I have done, so God hath
yielded to me. And they brought him into Jerusalem, and
there he died.
8 Then the sons of Judah fought against Jerusalem, and
they took it, and they smote it by the sharpness of sword,
and they betook all the city to burning. (Then the sons of
Judah fought against Jerusalem, and they took it, and they
struck down the people of Jerusalem with their sharp
swords, and they burned down all the city.)
9 And afterward they went down, and fought against
Canaanites, that dwelled in the hilly places (who lived in
the hill country), and at the south, (and) in [the] wild
fields.
10 And Judah went against Canaanites, that dwelled in
Hebron, whose name was by eld time Kiriatharba (And
Judah went out against the Canaanites, who lived in
Hebron, whose name in olden times was Kiriatharba);
and Judah killed Sheshai, and Ahiman, and Talmai.
11 And from thence he went forth, and he came to the
dwellers of Debir, whose eld name was Kiriathsepher,
that is, the city of letters. (And from there he went forth,
and he came to the inhabitants of Debir, whose old name
was Kiriathsepher, *that is, the City of Letters.*)
12 And Caleb said, I shall give Achsah, my daughter,
(for a) wife to him that shall smite Kiriathsepher, and shall
waste it.
13 And when Othniel, the son of Kenaz, the younger
brother of Caleb, had taken it, Caleb gave Achsah, his
daughter, (for a) wife to him.
14 And her husband stirred her, going in the way, that
she should ask of her father a field; and when she had
sighed, sitting on the ass, Caleb said to her, What hast
thou? (And her husband stirred her up, going on the way,
to ask for a field from her father; and when she sighed,
sitting on the donkey, Caleb said to her, What is the
matter?)
15 And she answered, Give thou [a] blessing to me, for
thou hast given a dry land to me; give thou *to me* also a
moist land with waters (now give thou also *to me* some
land with abundant water). And (so) Caleb gave to her
the moist land above, and the moist land beneath.
16 Forsooth the sons of (the) Kenite, the father of
Moses' wife, ascended from the city of Palms with the
sons of Judah, into the desert of his lot, which desert is at
the south of Arad; and [they] dwelled with him. (And the
sons of the Kenite, Moses' father-in-law, went up from the
City of Palms with the sons of Judah, into the wilderness
of Judah, which wilderness is south of Arad; and they
lived among the people there.)
17 And Judah went with Simeon, his brother; and they
smote altogether Canaanites, that dwelled in Zephath,
and they killed him; and the name of that city was called
Hormah, *that is, cursing, either perfect destroying, for
that city was destroyed utterly.* (And Judah went with his
brother Simeon; and they struck down the Canaanites
who lived in Zephath, and they killed them all; and the
name of that city was called Hormah, *that is, Cursed, or
Completely Destroyed, for that city was utterly
destroyed.*)
18 And Judah took Gaza with his coasts, and Askelon
(with his terms), and Ekron with his terms. (And Judah
took Gaza, and Askelon, and Ekron, along with their
land.)
19 And the Lord was with Judah, and he had in
possession the hilly places; and he might not do away the
dwellers of the valley, for they were plenteous in iron
chariots, (*full of weapons,*) sharp as scythes. (And the
Lord was with Judah, and they took possession of the hill
country; but they could not do away the inhabitants in
the valley, for they had plentiful iron chariots, *full of
weapons,* sharp as scythes.)
20 And *the sons of Israel* gave Hebron to Caleb, as
Moses had said, and Caleb did away from it (the) three
sons of Anak. (And *the Israelites* gave Hebron to Caleb,
as Moses had said, and Caleb did away from it the three
sons of the Anakim, *or of the giants.*)
21 But the sons of Benjamin did not (do) away

Jebusites, the dweller(s) of Jerusalem; and Jebusites
dwelled with the sons of Benjamin in Jerusalem unto this
present day. (But the Benjaminites did not do away the
Jebusites, the inhabitants of Jerusalem; and so the
Jebusites lived with the Benjaminites in Jerusalem unto
this present day.)
22 Also the house of Joseph went up into Bethel, and
the Lord was with them.
23 For when they besieged the city (And when they
besieged Bethel), that was called Luz before,
24 they saw a man going out of the city, and they said
to him, Show thou to us the entering of the city (Show us
how to enter the city), and we shall do mercy with thee.
25 And when he had showed to them, they smote the
city by sharpness of sword; and they delivered that man
and all his kindred. (And when he had shown them, they
struck down *the people of* that city with their sharp
swords; and they saved that man and all his family.)
26 And when he was delivered, he went into the land
of Hittites, and builded there a city, and called it Luz;
which is called so till into *this* present day (which it is
still called unto *this* present day).
27 Also Manasseh did not away Bethshean and
Taanach with their towns, and the dwellers of Dor, and
Ibleam, and Megiddo, with their towns; and Canaanites
began to dwell with them. (And Manasseh did not do
away Bethshean and Taanach with their towns, and the
inhabitants of Dor, and Ibleam, and Megiddo, with their
towns; and so the Canaanites began to live with them.)
28 Soothly after that Israel was strengthened, he made
them tributaries, *either to pay tribute,* and would not do
away *them.* (And after that Israel was made strong, they
made them all tributaries, *that is, they forced them to pay
tribute, or taxes,* and did not do *them* away.)
29 Soothly Ephraim killed not Canaanites that dwelled
in Gezer, but dwelled with him. (And Ephraim did not
kill the Canaanites who lived in Gezer, but they lived
with them.)
30 Zebulun did not away the dwellers of Kitron, and of
Nahalol; but Canaanites dwelled in the midst of him, and
was made tributary to him. (Zebulun did not do away the
inhabitants of Kitron, and of Nahalol; but the Canaanites
lived in their midst, and were made to pay tribute, *or
taxes,* to them.)
31 Also Asher did not away the dwellers of Accho (And
Asher did not do away the inhabitants of Accho), and of
Sidon, of Ahlab, and of Achzib, and of Helbah, and of
Aphik, and of Rehob;
32 and Asher dwelled in the midst of Canaanites, the
dweller(s) of that land, and Asher killed not him. (and so
the Asherites lived in the midst of the Canaanites, the
inhabitants of that land, and they did not kill them.)
33 Naphtali did not away the dwellers of Bethshemesh,
and of Bethanath; and he dwelled among Canaanites, the
dweller(s) of the land; and Bethshemesh and Bethanath
were (made) tributaries to him. (And the Naphtalites did
not do away the inhabitants of Bethshemesh, and of
Bethanath; and they lived among the Canaanites, the
people of the land; and the people of Bethshemesh and
of Bethanath were made to pay tribute, *or taxes,* to them.)
34 And Amorites held strait the sons of Dan in the hill,
and he gave not place to them to go down to [the] plainer
places; (And the Amorites held back the Danites in the
hill country, and would not allow them to come down
into the valley;)
35 and he dwelled in the hill of Heres, *which is
interpreted, Witnessing,* (and) in Aijalon, and in
Shaalbim. And the hand of the house of Joseph was
made heavy, and he was made tributary to him. (and they
lived on Mount Heres, *which is translated, Witnessing,*
and in Aijalon, and in Shaalbim. But then the hand of the
house of Joseph was made heavy upon them, and the
Amorites were made to pay tribute, *or taxes,* to them.)
36 And the term of Amorites was from the ascending of
Scorpion, and from the stone, and [the] higher places.
(And the border of the Amorites was from the going up of
Akrabbim, and from Sela, up to the higher places.)

CHAPTER 2

1 And the angel of the Lord went up from Gilgal to the
place of Weepers (And the angel of the Lord went up
from Gilgal to Bochim), and said, I led you out of Egypt,
and I brought *you* into the land, for which I swore to your
fathers, and promised, that I should not make void my
covenant with you into without end;
2 so only that ye should not smite (a) bond of peace
with the dwellers of this land, and that ye destroy their
altars; and you would not hear my voice. Why did ye
(do) these things? (so only that ye should not make a
covenant with the people of this land, and that ye destroy
their altars; but you would not listen to me. Why did ye
do this?)
3 Wherefore I would not do them away from your
face (And so I shall not take them away from you), (so)
that ye have them (as) enemies, and that their gods be to
you into falling.
4 And when the angel of the Lord spake these words
to all the sons of Israel, they raised [up] their voice, and
wept; (And when the angel of the Lord spoke these words
to all the Israelites, they raised up their voice, and wept;)
5 and the name of the place was called, the place of
Weepers, *either of tears*; and they offered there sacrifices
to the Lord. (and so the name of that place was called
Bochim, *or Tears*; and they made sacrifices, *or offerings,*
there to the Lord.)
6 Then Joshua let go the people; and the sons of Israel
went forth, each man into his possession, that they
should get it. (Then Joshua let the people go; and the

Israelites went forth, each man to get, *or to take*, his
possession.)
7 And they served the Lord in all the days of Joshua,
and of the elder men that lived after him long time, and
knew all the great works of the Lord, which he had done
with Israel. (And they served the Lord in all the days of
Joshua, and of the elders who lived a long time after him,
and who knew of all the great works of the Lord, which
he had done for Israel.)
8 Forsooth Joshua, [the] son of Nun, [the] servant of
the Lord, was dead of an hundred years and ten; (But
then Joshua, the son of Nun, the Lord's servant, died,
when he was a hundred and ten years old;)
9 and they buried him in the ends of his possession, in
Timnath of Heres, in the hill (country) of Ephraim, at the
north coast of the hill Gaash (on the north side of Mount
Gaash).
10 And all that generation was gathered to their fathers;
and other men *of Israel* rose up, that knew not the Lord,
and the works which he had done with Israel. (And all
that generation died; and other men rose up, who did not
know the Lord, and the works which he had done for
Israel.)
11 And the sons of Israel did evil in the sight of the
Lord, and they served Baalim and Ashtaroth; (And the
Israelites did evil before the Lord, and they served the
Baalim and the Ashtaroth;)
12 and forsook the Lord God of their fathers, that led
them out of the land of Egypt; and they followed alien
gods, the gods of peoples, that dwelled in the compass of
them, and worshipped those gods, and they stirred the
Lord to great wrath, (and deserted the Lord God of their
fathers, who led them out of the land of Egypt; and they
followed foreign, *or other*, gods, the gods of the peoples,
who lived all around them, and they worshipped those
gods, and they stirred the Lord to great anger,)
13 and *they* forsook him, and served Baal and
Ashtaroth.
14 And the Lord was wroth against Israel, and he
betook them into the hands of ravishers, the which took
them, and sold them to enemies, that dwelled by
compass (who lived all around them); and they might not
against-stand their adversaries;
15 but whither ever they would go, the hand of the
Lord was on them, *that is, to torment them*, as he spake
and swore to them; and they were tormented greatly. (but
wherever they went, the Lord's hand was against them, *to
torment them*, as he had said, and had sworn to them,
that he would do; and they were greatly tormented.)
16 And the Lord raised judges, that delivered them
from the hands of destroyers, (And then the Lord raised
up judges, who delivered them from the hands of their
destroyers,)
17 but they would not hear them, and they did
fornication, *that is, idolatry*, with alien gods, and
worshipped them. Soon they forsook the way, by which
their fathers entered; and they heard the commandments
of the Lord, and did all things contrary. (but they would
not listen to them, and they did fornication, *that is,
idolatry*, with foreign, *or other*, gods, and worshipped
them. And soon they deserted the way, by which their
fathers went; and they heard the commandments of the
Lord, but they did all things to the contrary.)
18 And when the Lord raised up judges in their days,
he was bowed by mercy, and he heard the wailings of
them that were tormented, and he delivered them from
the slaying of *their* destroyers.
19 Soothly after that the judge was dead, they turned
again, and did many things greater *in evil* than their
fathers did; and they followed alien gods, and served
them, and worshipped them; they left not their own
findings, and the hardest way by which they were wont
to go. (But after that the judge died, they returned *to their
old ways*, and did many things even greater *in evil* than
what their fathers did; and they followed foreign, *or
other*, gods, and served them, and worshipped them;
they did not cease from doing whatever they wanted to
do, and the stubborn, *or willful*, ways by which they
were wont to go.)
20 And the strong vengeance of the Lord was wroth
against Israel, and he said, For this people hath made
void my covenant which I covenanted with their fathers,
and (for they) have despised to hear my voice;
21 also I shall not do away the folks, which Joshua left,
and was dead; (yea, I shall not do away the nations,
which Joshua left alive, when he died;)
22 that in them I assay Israel (so that through them I can
test Israel), (to see) whether they keep the way of the
Lord, and go therein, as their fathers kept *it*, either nay.
23 Therefore the Lord left *alive* all these nations, and he
would not destroy them soon (and he would not soon
destroy them), neither he betook *them* into the hands of
Joshua.

CHAPTER 3

1 These be the folks which the Lord left *alive*, that in
them he should teach Israel, and all men that knew not
the battles of Canaanites; (These be the nations which the
Lord left *alive*, so that through them he would teach the
Israelites, all those who had not been part of the battles
for Canaan;)
2 and that afterward the sons of them should learn to
fight with enemies, and to have custom of battle. (and so
that through them their sons would learn to fight with
their enemies, and know the ways of battle.)
3 *He left (alive the)* five princes of the Philistines, and
all Canaanites, and the people of Sidon, and Hivites that
dwelled in the hill Lebanon, from the hill Baalhermon till

to the entering of Hamath. (*He left alive the* five rulers of
the Philistines, and all the Canaanites, and the people of
Sidon, and the Hivites who lived on Mount Lebanon,
from Mount Baalhermon unto Hamath Pass.)
4 And he left them, that in them he should assay
Israel, (to see) whether they would hear the behests of the
Lord, which he commanded to their fathers by the hand
of Moses, either nay. (Yea, he left them *alive*, so that
through them he could test Israel, to see whether they
would listen to the Lord's commands, which he
commanded to their fathers through Moses, or not.)
5 And so the sons of Israel dwelled in the midst of
Canaanites, of Hittites, and of Amorites, and of Perizzites,
and of Hivites, and of Jebusites, (And so the Israelites
lived in the midst of the Canaanites, the Hittites, and the
Amorites, and the Perizzites, and the Hivites, and the
Jebusites,)
6 and they wedded wives, the daughters of them; and
the sons of Israel gave their daughters to their sons, and
they served to their gods (and they served their gods).
7 And the sons of Israel did evil in the sight of the
Lord, and forgat their Lord God, and served Baalim, and
Asheroth. (And the Israelites did evil before the Lord, and
forgot the Lord their God, and served the Baalim, and the
Asheroth.)
8 And the Lord was wroth against Israel, and he
betook them into the hands of Chushanrishathaim, king
of Mesopotamia, and they served him eight years.
9 And they cried to the Lord, and he raised to them a
saviour, and (he) delivered them, that is, Othniel, the son
of Kenaz, and the younger brother of Caleb. (And they
cried to the Lord, and he raised up a saviour for them,
and he delivered them; that was Othniel, the son of
Kenaz, Caleb's younger brother.)
10 And the spirit of the Lord was in him, and he
deemed Israel. And he went out to battle, and the Lord
betook into his hand Chushanrishathaim, king of Syria
(the king of Mesopotamia); and *Othniel* oppressed him.
11 And the land rested forty years; and (then) Othniel,
the son of Kenaz, died.
12 Forsooth the sons of Israel added to do evil in the
sight of the Lord (And the Israelites did more evil before
the Lord); and he strengthened against them Eglon, the
king of Moab, for they did evil in the sight of the Lord.
13 And the Lord coupled to him the sons of Ammon
and Amalek; and he went, and smote Israel (and he went,
and struck Israel), and had in possession the city of
Palms.
14 And the sons of Israel served Eglon, the king of
Moab, eighteen years. (And the Israelites served Eglon,
the king of Moab, for eighteen years.)
15 And afterward they cried to the Lord; and he raised
to them a saviour, Ehud by name, the son of Gera, son of
Benjamin, the which Ehud used ever either hand for the
right hand. And the sons of Israel sent by him gifts, *that
is, (the) tribute*, to Eglon, king of Moab; (And they cried
to the Lord; and he raised up a saviour for them, named
Ehud, the son of Gera, the son of Benjamin, and he used
either hand for the right hand. And the Israelites sent him
to take the tribute, *that is, the taxes*, to Eglon, the king of
Moab;)
16 [the] which Ehud made to him(self) a sword carving
on ever either side, of the length of the palm of an hand;
and he was girded therewith under the say, *that is, a
knight's mantle*, in the right hip. (and Ehud made for
himself a sword sharp on both sides, the length of the
palm of a hand; and he was girded with it under his say,
that is, under his knight's mantle, on the right hip.)
17 And he brought gifts to Eglon, king of Moab; and
Eglon was full fat. (And he brought the tribute, *or the
taxes*, to Eglon, the king of Moab; and Eglon was very
fat.)
18 And when he had given gifts to the king, he
followed forth *after* his fellows that came with him; (And
when he had given the tribute to the king, he went away
with his fellows who had come with him;)
19 and he turned again from Gilgal, where (the graven)
idols were, and he said to the king, O king, I have a privy
word to thee (but he turned back at Gilgal, where the
carved stones were, and when he had come before the
king, he said, O king, I have a private word for thee).
And the king commanded silence. And when all men
were gone out, that were about him,
20 Ehud entered (un)to him; and the king sat alone in a
summer parlour. And Ehud said, I have the word of God
to thee (And Ehud said, I have a word from God for thee).
The which rose at once from his throne.
21 And Ehud held forth his left hand, and took his
sword from his right hip; and he put it into the king's
womb so strongly,
22 that the pommel, *either hilt*, followed the iron in(to)
the wound, and was holden strait in the thickest fatness
within; and Ehud drew not out the sword, but so as he
had smitten *Eglon* (but as he had so struck *Eglon*), he left
it in his body; and at once by the privates of (man)kind,
the turds of the womb burst out.
23 Forsooth when the doors of the parlour were closed
most diligently, and fastened with lock, (And when he
had quietly closed the parlour doors, and fastened them
with a lock,)
24 Ehud went out by a porch (Ehud went out by the
porch). And (soon after) the king's servants entered, *not
into the parlour, but into the porch*, and they saw the
doors of the parlour closed, and they said, In hap he
purgeth the womb in the summer parlour.
25 And they abode so long, till they were ashamed; and
they saw that no man opened the door, and they took the
key, and they opened (it), and they found their lord lying

dead on the earth. (And they waited so long for him, that
they were embarrassed; and when they saw that no one
opened the door, they took the key, and they opened it,
and they found their lord lying dead on the floor.)
26 And while they were troubled, Ehud fled out, and
passed the place of (the graven) idols, from whence he
turned again (and passed the place of the carved stones,
where he had turned back); and he came into Seirath.
27 And anon he sounded with a clarion in the hill of
Ephraim; and the sons of Israel came down with him, and
he went in the front. (And at once he sounded with a
trumpet in the hill country of Ephraim; and the Israelites
came down with him, and he went at the front.)
28 Which said to them, Follow ye me, for the Lord hath
betaken our enemies, (the) Moabites, into our hands.
And they came down after him, and occupied the fords
of (the) Jordan (River), that led over into Moab. And they
suffered not any man to pass [over],
29 but they smote in that time about ten thousand
Moabites, all mighty men and strong; no man of them
might escape. (but they struck down at that time about
ten thousand Moabites, all of them strong and mighty
men; yea, not one of them could escape.)
30 And Moab was made low in that day under the
hand of Israel, and the land rested eighty years. (And
Moab was made low on that day under the hand of
Israel, and then the land rested for eighty years.)
31 After him was Shamgar, the son of Anath, that smote
of Philistines six hundred men with a goad of (an) ox
(who struck down six hundred Philistines with an ox's
goad); and he also defended Israel.

CHAPTER 4

1 And the sons of Israel added to do evil in the sight of
the Lord, after the death of Ehud. (And the Israelites did
more evil before the Lord, after the death of Ehud.)
2 And the Lord betook them into the hands of Jabin,
king of Canaan, that reigned in Hazor; and he had a duke
of his host, Sisera by name; and he dwelled in Harosheth
of heathen men. (And the Lord delivered them into the
hands of Jabin, the king of Canaan, who reigned in
Hazor; and he had a leader of his army, who was named
Sisera; and he lived in Harosheth of the heathen.)
3 And the sons of Israel cried to the Lord; for Jabin had
nine hundred iron chariots, *full of weapons*, sharp as
scythes, and twenty years he oppressed Israel greatly.
(And the Israelites cried to the Lord; for Jabin had nine
hundred iron chariots, *full of weapons*, sharp as scythes,
and for twenty years he greatly oppressed Israel.)
4 And Deborah was a prophetess, the wife of
Lapidoth, the which Deborah deemed the people *of
Israel* in that time;
5 and she sat under a palm tree, that was called by her
name, betwixt Ramah and Bethel, in the hill of Ephraim;
and the sons of Israel went up to her at each doom. (and
she sat under a palm tree, that was named after her,
between Ramah and Bethel, in the hill country of
Ephraim; and the Israelites went up to her for
judgements.)
6 And she sent, and called Barak, the son of Abinoam,
of Kedesh of Naphtali, and she said to him, The Lord
God of Israel commanded to thee, (and said,) Go thou,
and lead an host into the hill of Tabor, and thou shalt
take with thee ten thousand of fighters of the sons of
Naphtali and of the sons of Zebulun. (And she sent, and
called for Barak, the son of Abinoam, of Kedesh of
Naphtali, and she said to him, The Lord God of Israel
commanded to thee, and said, Go thou, and lead an
army to Mount Tabor, and thou shalt take with thee ten
thousand fighting men of the Naphtalites and of the
Zebulunites.)
7 And I shall bring to thee, in the place of the strand of
Kishon, Sisera, the prince of Jabin's host, and his chariots,
and all the multitude; and I shall betake them in thine
hand. (And I shall bring to thee, at the Kishon River,
Sisera, the leader of Jabin's army, and his chariots, and all
the multitude; and I shall deliver them into thy hands.)
8 And Barak said to her, If thou comest with me, I
shall go; if thou wilt not come with me, I shall not go.
9 And she said to him, Soothly I shall go with thee;
but in this time the victory shall not be areckoned to
thee; for Sisera shall be betaken into the hand of a
woman (for Sisera shall be delivered into the hand of a
woman). And so Deborah rose, and went with Barak into
Kedesh.
10 And when Zebulun and Naphtali were called, Barak
ascended with ten thousand of fighters (Barak went up
with ten thousand fighting men), and had Deborah in his
fellowship.
11 Forsooth Heber of (the) Kenites had parted
(company) some time (ago) from other Kenites his
brethren, [the] sons of Hobab, the father of Moses' wife;
and he had set forth tabernacles till to the valley, which is
called Zaanaim, and was beside Kedesh (and he pitched
his tent in the Zaanaim Valley, which was beside
Kedesh).
12 And it was told to Sisera, that Barak, the son of
Abinoam, had gone up into the hill of Tabor. (And Sisera
was told that Barak, the son of Abinoam, had gone up to
Mount Tabor.)
13 And Sisera gathered nine hundred iron chariots, *full
of weapons*, carving as scythes, and all the host, from
Harosheth of heathen men to the strand of Kishon. (And
Sisera gathered his nine hundred iron chariots, *full of
weapons*, sharp as scythes, and all his army, from
Harosheth of the heathen unto the Kishon River.)
14 And Deborah said to Barak, Rise thou up, for this is
the day, in which the Lord hath betaken Sisera into thine

hands; lo! the Lord is thy leader. And so Barak came
down from the hill of Tabor, and ten thousand of fighters
with him (And so Barak came down from Mount Tabor,
and had ten thousand fighting men with him).
15 And the Lord made afeared Sisera, and all his
chariots, and all the multitude, by the sharpness of sword,
at the sight of Barak, in so much that Sisera leaped down
off the chariot, and fled on foot. (And when they saw
Barak, and all of his sharp swords, the Lord made Sisera,
and all those in his chariots, and all those in his
multitude, greatly afraid, in so much that Sisera leapt
down off the chariot, and fled away on foot.)
16 And Barak pursued the chariots fleeing, and the
host, till to Harosheth of heathen men (And Barak
pursued the fleeing chariots, and the army, unto
Harosheth of the heathen); and all the multitude of [the]
enemies felled down till to death.
17 And Sisera fled, and came to the tent of Jael, the
wife of Heber (the) Kenite; for peace was betwixt Jabin,
king of Hazor, and betwixt the house of Heber (the)
Kenite (for there was peace between Jabin, the king of
Hazor, and the house of Heber the Kenite).
18 Therefore Jael went out into the coming of Sisera,
and said to him, My lord, enter thou to me, enter thou to
me; dread thou not. And he entered into her tabernacle,
and he was covered of her with a mantle (And he went
into her tent, and she covered him with a cloak).
19 And he said to her, I beseech *thee*, give me a little
water, for I thirst greatly (for I have a great thirst). And
she opened a bottle of milk, and gave (it) to him to drink,
and (then she) covered him (up again).
20 And Sisera said to her, Stand thou before the door of
the tabernacle, and when any man cometh, and asketh
thee, and saith, Whether any man is here? thou shalt
answer, No man is *here*. (And Sisera said to her, Stand
thou before the door of the tent, and if anyone cometh,
and asketh thee, and saith, Is there anyone here? thou
shalt answer, No one is *here*.)
21 And so Jael, the wife of Heber, took a nail of the
tabernacle, and she took also an hammer; and she
entered privily, and with silence she put the nail upon
the temple of his head, and she fastened *the nail* smitten
with the hammer into his brain, unto the earth; and he
slept, and died together, and he failed *life*, and was dead.
(And then Jael, Heber's wife, got a tent peg, and she also
got a hammer; and she quietly entered, and silently put
the peg on the temple of his head, and struck it with the
hammer into his brain, and she fastened *the other end of
the peg* into the ground; and so he died in his sleep, yea,
his *life* failed, and he died.)
22 And lo! Barak (had) followed Sisera, and came (up to
the tent); and Jael went out into his coming, and said to
him, Come, and I shall show to thee the man whom thou
seekest. And when he had entered to her, he saw Sisera
lying dead, and a nail fastened into his temples (and a
tent peg fastened into his temple).
23 Therefore in that day (And so on that day), God
made low Jabin, the king of Canaan, before the sons of
Israel;
24 which increased each day, and with strong hand
they oppressed Jabin, the king of Canaan, till they did
him away.

CHAPTER 5

1 And Deborah and Barak, the son of Abinoam, sang
in that day, and said,
2 Ye *men* of Israel, that have willfully offered your
lives to peril (who have willingly offered your lives to
peril), bless ye the Lord.
3 Ye kings, hear; ye princes, perceive with ears (ye
princes, listen!); I am, I am *the woman*, that shall sing to
the Lord; I shall sing to the Lord God of Israel.
4 Lord, when thou wentest out from Seir, and
passedest by the countries of Edom (and passedest by the
countryside of Edom), the earth was moved, and (the)
heavens and (the) clouds dropped with waters;
5 (the) hills flowed from the face of the Lord, and Sinai
from the face of the Lord God of Israel.
6 In the days of Shamgar, the son of Anath, in the days
of Jael, [the] paths rested (the ways were empty), and they
that entered by those (ways), went [away] by paths out of
the way.
7 Strong men in Israel ceased, and rested, till Deborah
(a)rose, a mother in Israel.
8 The Lord chose new battles, and he destroyed the
gates of (their) enemies; shield and spear appeared not in
forty thousand of Israel. (They chose new gods, and then
there was war at the gates; but shields and spears did not
appear among the forty thousand of Israel.)
9 Mine heart loveth the princes of Israel; ye that
offered you(rselves) to peril by your own will, bless ye
the Lord; (My heart loveth the leaders of Israel; ye who
willingly offered yourselves to peril, bless ye the Lord;)
10 speak ye, that ascend on shining asses, and sit above
in doom, and go in the way. (speak ye, who ride on
shining donkeys, and sit in judgement, and go on the
way.)
11 Where the chariots were hurled down (al)together,
and the host of [the] enemy's was strangled, there the
Lord's rightwiseness be told out, and *his* mercy among
the strong men of Israel; then the Lord's people came
down to the gates, and got the princehood. (Where the
chariots were altogether hurled down, and the enemy's
army was strangled, there the Lord's righteousness be
told out, and *his* mercy among the strong men of Israel;
then the Lord's people came down to the gates, and got
the victory.)
12 Rise, rise thou, Deborah, rise thou, and speak a

song; rise thou, Barak, and thou, son of Abinoam, take
thy prisoners. (Rise, rise thou, Deborah, rise thou up, and
sing a song; rise thou up, Barak, thou son of Abinoam,
and take thy prisoners.)
13 The remnants of the people be saved; the Lord
fought against strong men of Ephraim. (The remnant of
the people were saved; the Lord's people fought against
the strong men.)
14 He did away them into Amalek, and after him from
Benjamin into thy peoples, thou Amalek. Princes of
Machir and of Zebulun went down, that led the host to
fight. (From out of Ephraim, they came into the valley,
behind the tribe of Benjamin and its people. The leaders
of Machir and of Zebulun went down, they who led the
army to fight.)
15 The dukes of Issachar were with Deborah, and
followed the steps of Barak, that gave himself to peril, as
into a ditch headlong, and into hell (like headlong into a
ditch, and down into hell). (Yea,) While Reuben was
parted against himself; the strife of great hearted men was
found.
16 Why dwellest thou betwixt twain ends (Why stayest
thou by the stalls), (so) that thou (mayest) hear the
hissings of (the) flocks? (Yea,) While Reuben was parted
against himself, the strife of great hearted men was found.
17 Gilead rested beyond (the) Jordan, and Dan gave
attention to ships. Asher dwelled in the brink of the sea,
and dwelled in havens (Asher stayed by the seashore, and
lived in safe coves).
18 And Zebulun and Naphtali offered their lives to the
death, in the country of Meromei, *that is interpreted,*
high. (And Zebulun and Naphtali offered their lives unto
the death, in the high places of the countryside.)
19 Kings came, and fought; kings of Canaan fought in
Taanach, beside the waters of Megiddo; and nevertheless
they took nothing by prey (but they took nothing of prey).
20 From heaven, it was fought against them (They
fought against them from the heavens); (the) stars dwelled
in their order, and in their course, and they fought against
Sisera.
21 The strand of Kishon drew (away) their dead bodies,
the strand of Kedumim, the strand of Kishon. My soul,
tread thou (down the) strong men. (The Kishon River
drew away their dead bodies, yea, the ancient river, the
Kishon River. My soul, tread thou forth with strength.)
22 The horsehoofs fell away, while the strongest of
enemies fled with rush (while the strongest of the
enemies fled away with haste), and (then) felled
headlong.
23 Curse ye the land of Meroz, said the angel of the
Lord, curse ye the dwellers of him, for they came not to
the help of the Lord, into the help of the strongest of him.
(Curse ye the land of Meroz, said the angel of the Lord,
curse ye its inhabitants, for they came not to the Lord's
help, nor to the help of his strongest men.)
24 Blessed among women be Jael, the wife of Heber
(the) Kenite; blessed be she in her tabernacle (blessed be
she in her tent).
25 *To Sisera* asking (for) water she gave milk, and in a
basin of princes she gave him butter.
26 She put the left hand to the nail, and her right hand
to *the* smith's hammer; and she smote Sisera, and sought
in his head a place of wound, and she pierced strongly
his temple. (Then she put a tent peg in her left hand, and
the smith's hammer in her right hand; and she sought a
place on his head for the wound, and then she struck
down Sisera, when she strongly pierced his temple.)
27 He felled betwixt her feet, (and) he failed, and died;
he was weltered before her feet, and he lay without life,
and wretchedful.
28 His mother beheld by a window, and yelled (out);
and she spake from the solar, Why tarrieth his chariot to
come again? Why tarry the feet of his four-horsed carts?
29 One wiser than [the] other wives of him answered
these words to the mother of her husband,
30 In hap now he parteth spoils, and the fairest of
women is chosen to him; clothes of diverse colours be
given to Sisera into prey, and diverse array of household
is gathered to adorn necks. (Perhaps now he parteth the
spoils, and the fairest of the women be chosen for him;
yea, clothes of diverse colours be given to Sisera for prey,
and a diverse array of things be gathered to adorn the
victor's neck.)
31 Lord, all thine enemies perish so; soothly, they that
love thee, shine so, as the sun shineth in his strength.
And the land rested forty years. (Lord, may all thy
enemies so perish; and may they who love thee, shine
like the sun shineth in its strength. And then the land
rested for forty years.)

CHAPTER 6

1 Forsooth the sons of Israel did evil in the sight of the
Lord, and he betook them into the hand of Midian seven
years. (And the Israelites did *more* evil before the Lord,
and he delivered them into the hands of the Midianites
for seven years.)
2 And Israel was oppressed of them greatly; and Israel
made ditches, and dens to themselves in hills, and most
strong places to fight against *Midian.* (And Israel was
greatly oppressed by them; and in the hills they made
ditches, and caves, and strongholds for themselves, from
which to fight against *the Midianites.*)
3 And when Israel had sown, Midian ascended, and
Amalek (was with them), and others of the nations of the
east;
4 and they setted *their* tents beside *the sons of Israel,*
and they wasted all things that were in herbs, *either*
green corn, unto the entering of Gaza, and utterly they

left not in Israel anything pertaining to life, not sheep, not
oxen, not asses (and they left not utterly any beast alive in
Israel, not sheep, nor oxen, nor donkeys).
5 For they and all their flocks came with their
tabernacles, and at the likeness of locusts they full-filled
all things, and a multitude of men and of camels was
without number (yea, they were a multitude without
number of men and of camels), and they wasted
whatever thing(s) they touched.
6 And Israel was made low greatly in the sight of
Midian (And Israel was brought greatly low before the
Midianites). And Israel cried to the Lord,
7 and asked (for) help against (the) Midianites;
8 and he sent to them a man, a prophet, and he spake
to them, (and said,) The Lord God of Israel saith these
things, I made you to go up from Egypt, and I led you out
of the house of servage,
9 and I delivered *you* from the hand of Egyptians, and
of all [the] enemies that tormented you (and from all of
the enemies who tormented you); and I casted them out
at your entering, and I gave to you the land of them;
10 and I said, I am the Lord your God; dread ye not the
gods of Amorites, in whose land ye dwell; and ye would
not hear my voice. (and I said, I am the Lord your God;
fear ye not, *or do not ye worship*, the gods of the
Amorites, in whose land ye live; but ye would not listen
to me.)
11 And (then) an angel of the Lord came, and sat under
an oak, that was in Ophrah, and it pertained to Joash, the
father of the family of Abiezrites. And when Gideon, the
son of Joash, threshed, and purged wheat in a presser,
that he should flee Midian (And when Gideon, the son of
Joash, threshed, and purged wheat in a winepress, to
hide it from the Midianites),
12 an angel of the Lord appeared to him (the angel of
the Lord appeared to him), and said, The Lord be with
thee, thou strongest of men.
13 And Gideon said to him, My lord, I beseech, if the
Lord is with us, why then have all these evils taken us?
Where be the marvels of him, which our fathers told, and
said, The Lord hath led us out of Egypt? For now he hath
forsaken us, and hath betaken us into the hand of Midian.
(And Gideon said to him, My lord, I beseech thee, if the
Lord is with us, then why have all these evils overtaken
us? Where be his miracles, which our fathers told us
about? Yea, they said, The Lord led us out of Egypt. But
now, he hath deserted us, and hath delivered us into the
hands of the Midianites.)
14 And the Lord beheld to him, and said, Go thou in
this strength of thee, and thou shalt deliver Israel from the
hand of Midian; (and) know thou, that I have sent thee.
15 And Gideon answered (to the angel), and said, My
lord, I beseech, in what thing shall I deliver Israel? (My
lord, I beseech thee, how can I save Israel?) Lo! my family
is the lowest in Manasseh, and I am the least in the house
of my father.
16 And the Lord said to him, I shall be with thee, and
thou shalt smite Midian as one man. (And the Lord said
to him, I shall be with thee, and thou shalt strike down all
of the Midianites like one man.)
17 And Gideon said, If I have found grace before thee,
give to me a sign, that thou, that speakest to me, *art sent
of God's part*; (And Gideon said to the angel, If I have
found grace before thee, give me a sign, that thou, who
speakest to me, *art sent from God*;)
18 go thou not away from hence, till I turn again to
thee, and bring (a) sacrifice, and offer (it) to thee. Which
answered, I shall abide thy coming (And he answered, I
shall wait for thee).
19 And so Gideon went in, and seethed a kid, and took
therf loaves of a bushel of meal, and (he put) the flesh in
a pannier; and he put the broth of the flesh in a pot, and
he bare all these things (to) under the oak, and offered
those to him.
20 To whom the angel of the Lord said, Take thou the
flesh, and the therf loaves, and put them on that stone,
and pour the broth above. And when he had done so, (To
whom the angel of the Lord said, Take thou the flesh, and
the unleavened bread, and put them on that stone, and
pour the broth upon it. And when he had done so,)
21 the angel of the Lord held forth the end of the staff,
which he held in the hand (which he held in his hand),
and he touched the fleshes, and the therf loaves; and fire
ascended from the stone, and wasted the fleshes, and
[the] therf loaves. And the angel of the Lord vanished
from his eyes.
22 And Gideon saw that he was an angel of the Lord,
and he said, Lord God, alas to me, for I saw the angel of
the Lord face to face. (And Gideon saw that he was the
angel of the Lord, and he said, Lord God, alas for me, for
I have seen the angel of the Lord face to face.)
23 And the Lord said to him, Peace be with thee; dread
thou not (fear not), thou shalt not die.
24 Then Gideon builded there an altar to the Lord, and
he called it the Peace of the Lord, (and it is there) unto
this present day. And when he was yet in Ophrah, which
is of the family of Abiezrites, (Then Gideon built an altar
there to the Lord, and he called it Jehovahshalom, and it
is there unto this present day, in Ophrah, which is of the
family of the Abiezrites.)
25 the Lord said to him in that night, Take thou thy
father's bull, and another bull of seven years, and thou
shalt destroy the altar of Baal, that is thy father's, and cut
thou down the wood, which is about the altar; (And then
the Lord said to him that night, Take thou thy father's
bull, and another bull that is seven years old, and destroy
thou the altar of Baal, that is thy father's, and cut thou
down the pole *of idolatry*, which is beside the altar;)

26 and thou shalt build an altar to thy Lord God in the
highness of this stone, on which thou puttedest (the)
sacrifice before; and thou shalt take the second bull, and
thou shalt offer (a) burnt sacrifice on the heap of trees,
which thou cuttedest down of the wood. (and thou shalt
build an altar to the Lord thy God on top of this stone, on
which before thou hast put the sacrifice; and thou shalt
take the second bull, and thou shalt offer a burnt sacrifice
on the heap of wood from the pole *of idolatry* which
thou hast cut down.)
27 Therefore Gideon took ten men of his servants, and
did as the Lord commanded to him. And Gideon
dreaded the house of his father (And Gideon feared his
father's family), and the men of that city, and (so) he
would not do (it) by day, but he fulfilled all things by
night.
28 And when men of that city had risen early, they saw
the altar of Baal destroyed, and the wood cut down, and
the tother bull put on the altar, that was builded. (And
when the men of that city had risen in the morning, they
saw that the altar of Baal had been destroyed, and the
pole *of idolatry* had been cut down, and the other bull
put on the altar that Gideon had built there.)
29 And they said together, Who hath done this? And
when they inquired (of) the doer of the deed, it was said,
Gideon, the son of Joash, did all these things.
30 And they said to Joash, Bring forth thy son hither,
that he die, for he hath destroyed the altar of Baal, and
hath cut down the wood *about it.* (And they said to Joash,
Bring thy son here, so that we can kill him, for he hath
destroyed the altar of Baal, and hath cut down the pole *of
idolatry* that was beside it.)
31 To whom Joash answered, Whether ye be the
vengers of Baal, that ye fight for him? he that is (the)
adversary of him, die he, before the morrow light come;
if he is God, venge he himself of him that hath cast down
his altar (yea, if he is a god, avenge he himself upon him
who hath thrown down his altar).
32 From that day Gideon was called Jerubbaal, for-thy
that Joash had said, Baal take vengeance of him that hath
cast down his altar. (So from that day, Gideon was called
Jerubbaal, *or Let Baal contend,* for Joash had said, Let
Baal himself take vengeance upon him who hath thrown
down his altar.)
33 Therefore all Midian, and Amalek, and the peoples
of the east were gathered together, and they passed over
(the) Jordan, and setted tents in the valley of Jezreel. (And
so all the Midianites, and the Amalekites, and the peoples
of the east were gathered together, and they passed over
the Jordan River *to the west side,* and pitched their tents
in the Jezreel Valley.)
34 Forsooth the spirit of the Lord clothed, *or full-filled,*
Gideon; and he sounded with a clarion, and called
together the house of Abiezer, that it should follow him.
(And the spirit of the Lord filled Gideon *full;* and he
sounded with a trumpet, and called out all the house of
Abiezer to follow him.)
35 And he sent messengers into all Manasseh, and he
followed Gideon (and they followed Gideon); and *he
sent* other messengers into Asher, and to Zebulun, and to
Naphtali, and they (also) came to him.
36 And Gideon said to the Lord, If thou makest safe
Israel by mine hand, as thou hast spoken, (And Gideon
said to the Lord, If thou wilt save Israel by my hand, as
thou hast said,)
37 I shall put this fleece of wool in the cornfloor; if the
dew is in the fleece alone, and dryness is in all the earth,
I shall know, that thou shalt deliver Israel by mine hand,
as thou hast spoken. (*for me to be certain of that,* I shall
put this fleece of wool on the threshing floor; and
tomorrow, if dew is found only on the fleece, and the
ground all around it is dry, then I shall know *for sure* that
thou shalt save Israel by my hand, just as thou hast said.)
38 And it was done so. And he rose by night (And he
rose up early), and when the fleece was wrung out, he
(had) filled a basin (full) with dew;
39 and (then) he said again to the Lord, Thy strong
vengeance be not wroth against me, if I assay yet once
(again), and seek a sign in the fleece (and seek a sign with
the fleece); I pray, that the fleece alone be dry, and that
all the earth (around it) be moist with dew.
40 And (so) the Lord did in that night, as Gideon asked;
and dryness was in the fleece alone, and dew was in all
the earth (and the next day, the fleece was dry, but there
was dew on the ground all around it).

CHAPTER 7

1 Then Jerubbaal, which also is Gideon, rose by night,
and all the people with him, and came to the well which
is called Harod. And the tents of Midian were in the
valley, at the north coast of the high hill. (Then Jerubbaal,
that is Gideon, and all the people with him, rose up
early, and they came to the well which is called Harod.
And the tents of the Midianites were pitched in the valley
to the north of Mount Moreh.)
2 And the Lord said to Gideon, (Too) Much people is
with thee, and Midian shall not be betaken into the hands
thereof, lest Israel have glory against me, and say, I am
delivered by my strengths. (And the Lord said to Gideon,
Too many people be with thee, and the Midianites shall
not be delivered into their hands, lest the people of Israel
take the glory from me, and say, We were saved by our
own strength.)
3 Speak thou to the people, and preach thou, while all
men hear, (and say,) He that is fearedful, and dreadful,
turn again. And (so) they (who were afraid) went away
from the hill of Gilead, and (in all) two and twenty
thousand of men turned again from the people; and only

ten thousand (still) dwelled (there).
4 And the Lord said to Gideon, Yet the people is (too)
much; lead thou them to the waters, and there I shall
prove them, and he (shall) go with thee, of whom I shall
say, that he (should) go; and turn he again, whom I shall
forbid to go.
5 And when the people had gone down to the waters,
the Lord said to Gideon, Thou shalt separate them by
themselves that lap (up the) waters with hand and tongue,
as dogs be wont to lap (it up); and those, that drink with
knees bowed, shall be in the tother part.
6 And so the number of them, that lapped (up the)
waters, by the hand casting (it) to the mouth, was three
hundred men; and all the tother multitude drank
kneeling.
7 And the Lord said to Gideon, In three hundred men,
that lapped waters, I shall deliver you, and I shall betake
Midian in thine hand; and all the tother multitude turn
again into their place. (And the Lord said to Gideon, With
the three hundred men who lapped up the water, I shall
save you, and I shall deliver the Midianites into thy
hands; and all the other multitude should return to their
homes.)
8 And [so] when they had taken meats and trumps for
the number of them, he commanded all the tother
multitude to go (back) to their tabernacles; and Gideon,
with (those) three hundred men, gave himself to [the]
battle. And the tents of Midian were beneath in the
valley (And the tents of the Midianites were pitched
below him in the valley).
9 In the same night the Lord said to him, Rise thou
(up), and go down into their tents, for I have betaken
them in thine hand (for I have delivered them into thy
hands);
10 and if thou dreadest to go alone, Phurah, thy
servant, go down with thee. (and if thou fearest to go
down alone, let thy servant Phurah go down with thee.)
11 And when thou shalt hear what they speak, then
thine hands shall be strengthened, and thou shalt go
down securer to the tents of [the] enemies. Therefore he
went down, and Phurah, his servant (And so he, and his
servant Phurah, went down), into the part of [the] tents,
where the watches of (the) armed men were.
12 And Midian, and Amalek, and all the peoples of the
east lay spread abroad in the valley, as the multitude of
locusts; and the camels were unnumberable, as gravel
that lieth in the brink of the sea. (And the Midianites, and
the Amalekites, and all the peoples of the east lay spread
abroad in the valley, like a multitude of locusts; and their
camels were innumerable, like the gravel, *or the sand*,
that lieth at the seashore.)
13 And when Gideon had come *down*, a man told (of)
a dream to his neighbour, and he told by this manner
that, that he had seen, (saying,) I saw a dream, and it
seemed to me, that as a barley loaf, baken under ashes,
was wallowed, and it came down into the tents of
Midian; and when it had come to a tabernacle, it smote
it, and destroyed it, and made it even utterly to the earth.
(And when Gideon had come *down*, a man told his
neighbour about a dream that he had, and he told in this
manner what he had seen, saying, I had a dream, and it
seemed to me, that a barley loaf, baked under ashes, was
rolled down into the tents of the Midianites; and when it
came to a tent, it struck it, and destroyed it, and made it
utterly even to the ground.)
14 That man answered, to whom he spake (And that
man to whom he spoke, answered), This is none other
thing, no but the sword of Gideon, [the] son of Joash, a
man of Israel; for the Lord God hath betaken Midian, and
all [the] tents thereof, into the hands of Gideon.
15 And when Gideon had heard the dream, and the
interpreting thereof, he worshipped *the Lord*, and turned
again to the tents of Israel, and said, Rise ye (up); for the
Lord hath betaken into our hands the tents of Midian (for
the Lord hath delivered the host, *or the army*, of the
Midianites into our hands).
16 And he parted the three hundred men into three
parts, and he gave them trumps in their hands, and empty
pots, and lamps (with lamps), *that is, (with) burning
brands, either torches, that might not lightly be
quenched*, in the midst of the pots.
17 And he said to them, Do ye this thing which ye see
me do; I shall enter into a part of the tents, and follow ye
that, that I do.
18 When the trump in my hand shall sound, sound ye
also all about the tents, and cry ye together, To the Lord,
and to Gideon.
19 And Gideon entered, and the three hundred men
that were with him, into a part of the tents, when the
watches of midnight began; and when the keepers were
raised, they began to sound with trumps, and to beat
together the pots among themselves (and after the guards
had changed, they began to sound with the trumpets, and
to beat the pots together).
20 And when they sounded in three places by compass,
and had broken the pots, they held [the] lamps in their
left hands, and [the] sounding trumps in their right hands;
and they cried, The sword of the Lord, and of Gideon;
21 and they stood all in their place, about the tents of
their enemies. And so all the tents were troubled; and
they cried [out], and yelled, and fled; (and they all stood
in their places, about the tents of their enemies. And all
the army was troubled, and many of the enemies cried
out, and yelled, and fled away;)
22 and nevertheless the three hundred men continued,
sounding with trumps. And the Lord sent sword in all the
tents, and they killed themselves by death each other;
and they (who were left) fled till to Bethshittah, (in

Zererath), and by the side, from Abelmeholah into
Tabbath. (but the three hundred men continued sounding
with the trumpets. And the Lord set each man in the
camp against his neighbour, and they killed each other
with their swords; and those who were left fled to
Bethshittah in Zererath, and to Abelmeholah Ridge by
Tabbath.)
23 And men of Israel cried together, of Naphtali, and of
Asher, and of all Manasseh, and they pursued Midian;
and the Lord gave victory to the people of Israel in that
day. (Then the men of Israel from Naphtali, and Asher,
and from both parts of Manasseh, were called out, and
they pursued the Midianites; and the Lord gave victory to
the people of Israel on that day.)
24 And Gideon sent messengers into all the hill
(country) of Ephraim, and said, Come ye down against
the coming of Midian, and occupy ye the waters till to
Bethbarah and (the) Jordan. And all Ephraim cried (And
all the men of Ephraim were called out), and before-
occupied the waters of the Jordan until Bethbarah.
25 And *Ephraim* killed two *chief* men of Midian, Oreb
and Zeeb; *he killed* Oreb in the stone of Oreb, and Zeeb
in the presser of Zeeb; and Ephraim pursued Midian, and
they bare the heads of Oreb and of Zeeb to Gideon, over
the floods of Jordan. (And *the Ephraimites* killed the two
chief men of the Midianites, Oreb and Zeeb; *they killed*
Oreb at the stone of Oreb, and Zeeb at the winepress of
Zeeb; and they pursued the Midianites, and brought the
heads of Oreb and Zeeb to Gideon, on the other side of
the Jordan River.)

CHAPTER 8

1 And the men of Ephraim said to Gideon, What is
this thing, that thou wouldest do, that thou calledest not
us, when thou wentest to battle against Midian? And they
chided *with him* strongly, and well nigh they did *to him*
violence. (And the men of Ephraim said to Gideon, What
is this that thou hast done, that thou did not call us when
thou wentest to battle against the Midianites? And they
strongly complained to *him*, and they almost did violence
to him.)
2 To whom he answered, And what such thing might I
have done, what manner thing ye have done? (But he
answered to them, Could I have done such a thing as ye
have done?) Whether a raisin of Ephraim is not better
than the vintages of Abiezer?
3 And the Lord hath betaken into your hands the
princes of Midian, Oreb and Zeeb. What such thing
might I have done, what manner thing ye have done?
(For the Lord hath delivered Oreb and Zeeb, the princes
of the Midianites, into your hands. Could I have done
such a thing as ye have done?) And when he had spoken
this thing, the spirit of them rested, by which they
swelled against him.
4 And when Gideon had come to (the) Jordan, he
passed it with three hundred men, that were with him;
and for weariness they might not pursue *them* that fled.
(And when Gideon had come to the Jordan River, he
crossed over it with the three hundred men who were
with him; and for weariness they might not pursue *those*
who had fled before them.)
5 And he said to the men of Succoth, I beseech (thee),
give ye (some) loaves to the people, that is with me; for
they failed greatly (for they faint now), (so) that we may
then pursue Zebah and Zalmunna, (the) kings of Midian.
6 And the princes of Succoth answered *in scorn*, (and
said,) In hap the palms of the hands of Zebah and of
Zalmunna be in thine hands, and therefore thou askest,
that we give (some) loaves to thine host.
7 To whom Gideon said, Therefore, when the Lord
shall betake Zebah and Zalmunna into mine hands, and
when I shall turn again (as an) overcomer in peace, I shall
rend your flesh with thorns and briars of the desert. (To
whom Gideon said, And so, when the Lord shall deliver
Zebah and Zalmunna into my hands, and when I shall
return to you in victory, I shall tear, *or shall cut*, your
flesh with thorns and briars from the desert.)
8 And Gideon went up from thence, and came into
Penuel; and he spake like things to men of that place, to
whom also they answered, as the men of Succoth had
answered (and they answered him just like the men of
Succoth had answered him).
9 And so he said to them, When I shall turn again (as
an) overcomer in peace (When I shall return to you in
victory), I shall destroy this tower.
10 Forsooth Zebah and Zalmunna rested with all their
host; for fifteen thousand men (were) left of all the
companies of the peoples of the east, when an hundred
and twenty thousand of fighters and of men drawing out
sword were slain. (And Zebah and Zalmunna were in
Karkor with their army; and fifteen thousand men were
all who were left of the companies of the peoples of the
east, for a hundred and twenty thousand fighting men
drawing out swords had been killed.)
11 And Gideon ascended by the way of them that
dwelled in tabernacles at the east coast of Nobah and of
Jogbehah, and smote the tents of [the] enemies, that were
secure, and supposed not anything of adversity.
12 And Zebah and Zalmunna fled, whom Gideon
pursued, and (he) took (hold of them), when all their host
was troubled.
13 And he turned again from battle before the rising of
the sun, (And Gideon returned from the battle by way of
the Ascent of Heres,)
14 and he took (hold of) a young man of the men of
Succoth; and he asked him the names of the princes, and
of the elder men of Succoth; and he described (to
Gideon) seven and seventy men in number.

15 And he came to Succoth, and said to them, Lo, (here
be) Zebah and Zalmunna! of which ye upbraided me (of
whom ye upbraided me), and said, In hap the hands of
Zebah and of Zalmunna be in thine hands, and therefore
thou askest, that we give (some) loaves to (thy) men, that
be weary and failed.
16 Therefore Gideon took the elder men of the city,
and thorns and briars of (the) desert, and he rent with
those, and all-brake the men of Succoth; (And so Gideon
took hold of the city elders, and some thorns and briars
from the desert, and he tore, *or cut*, them with those, and
broke the men of Succoth all to pieces;)
17 also he destroyed the tower of Penuel, when the
dwellers of the city were slain. (and he also destroyed the
tower of Penuel, and killed the inhabitants of that city.)
18 And he said to Zebah and Zalmunna, What manner
men were they, that ye killed in Tabor? Which
answered, *They were* like thee, and one of them was as
the son of a king (and one of them was like a king's son).
19 To whom Gideon said, They were (all) my brethren,
the sons of my mother; (as) the Lord liveth, if ye had
saved them, I would not slay you.
20 And he said to Jether, his first begotten son, Rise
thou (up), and slay them. And Jether drew not his sword;
for he dreaded, for he was yet a boy (But Jether would
not draw out his sword; for he was afraid, for he was still
a boy).
21 And Zebah and Zalmunna said (to Gideon), Rise
thou (up thyself), and fall on us; for thou art by the age
and strength of [a] man. (So) Gideon rose (up), and killed
Zebah and Zalmunna, and (then he) took the ornaments,
and (the) bells, with which the necks of (the) kings'
camels be wont to be made fair.
22 And all the men of Israel said to Gideon, Be thou
lord of us, thou, and thy son, and the son of thy son; for
thou deliveredest us from the hand of Midian.
23 To whom he said, I shall not be lord of you, neither
my son shall be lord on you, but the Lord shall be lord on
you. (To whom he said, I shall not rule over you, nor
shall my son rule over you, but the Lord shall rule over
you.)
24 And Gideon said to them, I ask one asking of you,
give ye to me the earrings of your prey; for Ishmaelites
were wont to have golden earrings.
25 Which answered, We shall give (you them) most
gladly. And they spreaded forth a mantle on the earth,
and casted forth therein [the] earrings of the prey;
26 and the weight of the earrings that he asked (for) was
a thousand and seven hundred shekels of gold, without
[the] ornaments, and brooches, and cloak of purple,
which the kings of Midian were wont to use, and besides
[the] golden bands of camels (and without the gold bands
for the camels).
27 And Gideon made thereof (an) ephod, *that is, a
priest's cloak*, and he put it in his city (of) Ophrah; and all
Israel did fornication, *that is idolatry*, therein (therewith);
and it was made to Gideon, and to all his house, into
falling.
28 But Midian was made low before the sons of Israel,
and they might no more raise up their nolls; and the land
rested forty years, in which Gideon was sovereign.
29 And so Jerubbaal, the son of Joash, went, and
dwelled in his house;
30 and he had seventy sons, that went out of his thigh,
for he had many wives.
31 And a concubine, *that is, (the) secondary wife*, of
him, whom he had in Shechem, engendered to him a
son, Abimelech by name.
32 And Gideon, the son of Joash, died in [a] good eld
[age], and was buried in the sepulchre of Joash, his father,
in Ophrah, of the family of Abiezrites.
33 And after that Gideon was dead, the sons of Israel
turned away, and they did fornication, *that is, idolatry*,
with Baalim; and they smote (a) bond of peace with
Baal(berith), that he should be to them into God (and
they made a covenant with Baalberith, so that he would
be their god),
34 neither Israel had mind of their Lord God, that had
delivered them from the hand of all their enemies by
compass/about; (and the people of Israel did not
remember the Lord their God, who had delivered them
from the hands of all their enemies around them;)
35 neither they did mercy to the family of Jerubbaal,
that is, Gideon, after all the good things that he did to
Israel. (nor were they grateful, *or loyal*, to Jerubbal's
family, after all the good that he had done for Israel.)

CHAPTER 9

1 Forsooth Abimelech, the son of Jerubbaal, went into
Shechem to the brethren of his mother; and he spake to
them, and to all the kindred of the house of his mother,
and said, (And Abimelech, the son of Jerubbaal, went
into Shechem to his mother's brothers *and her kinsmen*;
and he spoke to them, and to all the kindred of the house
of his mother, and said,)
2 Speak ye to all the men of Shechem, (and say,) What
is better to you, that seventy men, all the sons of
Jerubbaal, be lords of you, whether that one man be lord
to you? and also behold, that I am your bone, and your
flesh. (Say ye to all the men of Shechem, What is better
for you, that seventy men, all the sons of Jerubbaal, rule
over you, or that one man rule over you? and also
remember, that I am your own flesh and blood.)
3 And the brethren of his mother spake of him all
these words to all the men of Shechem; and they bowed
their hearts after Abimelech, and said, He is our brother.
(And his mother's kinsmen spoke all these words about
him to all the men of Shechem; and they turned their

hearts to Abimelech, and said, He is our kinsman.)
4 And they gave to him seventy pieces of silver (out)
of the temple of Baalberith; and he hired to him thereof
men poor and having no certain dwelling (and with it he
hired men to join him who were poor, and who had no
certain dwelling), and they followed him.
5 And he came into the house of his father in Ophrah,
and killed his brethren the sons of Jerubbaal, seventy
men, on one stone. And Jotham, the youngest son of
Jerubbaal, was left, and hid. (And he came to his father's
house in Ophrah, and killed his brothers the sons of
Jerubbaal, seventy men, on one stone. But Jotham, the
youngest son of Jerubbaal, was left alive, for he had hid
himself.)
6 And all the men of Shechem, and all the families of
the city of Millo, were gathered together, and they went,
and made Abimelech king, beside the oak that stood in
Shechem.
7 And when this thing was told to Jotham, he went,
and stood in the top of the hill Gerizim (and stood on the
top of Mount Gerizim), and cried (out) with (a) voice
raised [up], and said, Ye men of Shechem, hear me, so
that God (may) hear you.
8 Trees went to anoint a king on them (The trees went
to anoint a king over themselves); and they said to the
olive tree, Command thou to us.
9 Which answered, Whether I may forsake my fatness,
which both Gods and men use, and come, that I be
advanced among trees? (Which answered, Can I forsake
my rich oil, which is used to honour both gods and men,
and go that I be advanced over the other trees?)
10 And the trees said to the fig tree, Come thou, and
take the realm on us (Come thou, and take the kingdom,
and reign over us). Which answered to them,
11 Whether I may forsake my sweetness, and *my* full
sweet fruits, and go that I be advanced among other
trees? (Can I forsake my sweetness, and *my* full sweet
fruits, and go that I be advanced over the other trees?)
12 Also the trees spake to the vine, (and said,) Come
thou, and command to us.
13 Which answered, Whether I may forsake my wine,
that gladdeth God and men, and be advanced among
other trees? (Which answered, Can I forsake my wine,
that gladdeneth both the gods and people, and go that I
be advanced over the other trees?)
14 And all the trees said to the rhamn, *or the thieve-thorn*, Come thou, and be lord on us (Come thou, and be
lord over us).
15 Which answered to them, If ye make me verily king
to you, come, and rest ye under my shadow; and, if ye
will not, fire go out of the rhamn, and devour the cedars
of Lebanon. (Which answered to them, If ye truly shall
make me king over you, come, and rest ye under my
shadow; but if ye will not, then let fire go out of the
rhamn, and devour Lebanon's cedars.)
16 Now therefore, if rightfully and without sin ye have
made Abimelech king on you, and if ye have done well
with Jerubbaal, and with his house, and if ye have
yielded while to the benificences of him, (And so now, if
rightfully and without sin ye have made Abimelech king
over you, and if ye have done the right thing with
Jerubbaal, and with his household, and if ye have yielded
to him according to his good deeds,)
17 that fought for you, and gave his life for perils, that
he should deliver you from the hand of Midian; (yea, he
who fought for you, and gave, *or risked*, his life to perils,
so that he could save you from the hands of the
Midianites;)
18 and ye have risen now against the house of my
father, and have slain his sons, seventy men, on one
stone, and have made Abimelech, [the] son of his
handmaid, king on the dwellers of Shechem, for he is
your brother; (and ye have risen up now against my
father's household, *or his family*, and have killed his
sons, seventy men, on one stone, and have made
Abimelech, the son of his slave-girl, king over the
inhabitants of Shechem, for he is your kinsman;)
19 therefore if ye have done rightfully, and without sin
with Jerubbaal and his house, today be ye glad in
Abimelech, and be he glad in you; (and so if ye have
done rightfully, and without sin with Jerubbaal and with
his household, *or his family*, today, then be ye happy
with Abimelech, and let him be happy with you;)
20 but if ye have done waywardly, (may) fire go out
from Abimelech, and waste the dwellers of Shechem, and
the city of Millo; and (may) fire go out from the men of
Shechem, and from the city of Millo, and devour
Abimelech.
21 And when Jotham had said these things, he fled, and
went into Beer, and dwelled there, for dread of
Abimelech, his brother (in fear of his brother Abimelech).
22 And Abimelech reigned on Israel three years. (And
Abimelech reigned over Israel for three years.)
23 And the Lord sent the worst spirit betwixt Abimelech
and the dwellers of Shechem, which began to hold him
abominable, (And the Lord sent the worst spirit between
Abimelech and the inhabitants of Shechem, who began
to hold him abominable,)
24 and to areckon the felony of [the] slaying of the
seventy sons of Jerubbaal, and the shedding out of their
blood, into Abimelech their brother, and into [the] other
princes of Shechem, that had helped him. (and to reckon
the felony of the slaughter of the seventy sons of
Jerubbaal, yea, the shedding out of their blood, unto their
brother Abimelech, and unto those other men of
Shechem, who had helped him.)
25 And men of Shechem set ambushments against the
king in the highness of hills; and while they abode his

coming, they haunted thefts, and took preys of men
passing thereforth; and it was told to Abimelech. (And so
the men of Shechem set men in ambush against the king
in the highness of the hills; and while they waited for
him, they robbed, and took plunder, from those who
passed by; and this was told to Abimelech.)
26 And Gaal, the son of Ebed, came with his brethren,
and passed into Shechem; at whose entering the dwellers
of Shechem were raised, (And Gaal, the son of Ebed,
came with his kinsmen, and went into Shechem; at
whose entry, the inhabitants of Shechem were raised up,
and turned to him,)
27 and went out into [the] fields, and wasted vineries,
and trode grapes; and with companies of singers made,
they entered into the temple of their God, and among
meats and drinks they cursed Abimelech, (and they went
into the fields, and emptied out their vineyards, and trod
down the grapes at the winepress, and made merry; and
they entered into the temple of their god, and over food
and drink they cursed Abimelech,)
28 while Gaal, *the* son of Ebed, cried, Who is this
Abimelech? And what is Shechem, that we serve him?
Whether he is not the son of Jerubbaal, and made Zebul,
his servant, prince on the men of Hamor, the father of
Shechem? Why therefore shall we serve him? (while
Gaal, *the* son of Ebed, cried, Who is this Abimelech?
And why should we Shechemites serve him? Is he not
the son of Jerubbaal? Is not Zebul but his servant? Yea,
we should serve the men of Hamor, the father of
Shechem! Why do we serve him?)
29 Would God, (that) some man would give this people
(to be) under mine hand, and (then) I should do away
Abimelech from the midst *of Shechem*. And it was said
to Abimelech, Gather thou the multitude of an host, and
come thou (And then he said to Abimelech, *as if he were
there*, Gather thou the multitude of thy army, and come
thou out, *if thou darest*).
30 For when the words of Gaal, the son of Ebed, were
heard, Zebul, the prince of the city was full wroth; (And
when the words of Gaal, the son of Ebed, were heard,
Zebul, the leader of the city was very angry;)
31 and he sent privily messengers to Abimelech, and
said, Lo! Gaal, the son of Ebed, is come into Shechem
with his brethren, and he exciteth the city to fight against
thee; (and he sent messengers privately, *or secretly*, to
Abimelech, and said, Lo! Gaal, the son of Ebed, is come
into Shechem with his kinsmen, and he exciteth, *or
rouseth*, the city to fight against thee;)
32 therefore rise thou by night (and so rise thou up
tonight), with the people that is with thee, and be thou
hid in the field;
33 and first in the morrowtide, when the sun riseth, fall
thou upon the city; and when Gaal goeth out with his
people against thee, do thou to him that that thou mayest.
34 And so Abimelech rose with all his host by night,
and set ambushments beside Shechem, in four places.
(And so Abimelech and all his army rose up that night,
and set men in ambush beside Shechem, in four places.)
35 And Gaal, the son of Ebed, went out (the next
morning), and stood in the entering of the gate of the city
(and stood at the entrance to the city gate). And
Abimelech, and all the host with him, rose (up) from the
place of [the] ambushments.
36 And when Gaal had seen the people, he said to
Zebul, Lo! a multitude cometh down from the hills. To
whom Zebul answered, Thou seest the shadows of hills
as the heads of men, and thou art deceived by this error.
37 And again Gaal said, Lo! a people cometh down
from the midst of the earth, and one company cometh by
the way that beholdeth the oak. (And Gaal said again, Lo!
many people cometh down from the midst of the land,
and one company, *or one group*, cometh along the road
of the Soothsayers' Oak.)
38 To whom Zebul said, Where is now thy mouth, by
which thou speakest, Who is Abimelech, that we serve
him? (And then Zebul said to him, Now where is thy
mouth, by which thou speakest, and saith, Who is this
Abimelech, that we should serve him?) Whether this is
not the people, whom thou despisedest? Go thou out,
and fight against him.
39 Therefore Gaal went (out), while the people of
Shechem abode; and he fought against Abimelech. (And
so Gaal led out the men of Shechem; and they fought
against Abimelech.)
40 And pursued him fleeing, and constrained him to
flee into the city; and full many of the part of Gaal felled
down, unto the gate of the city. (And Abimelech fought
back, and pursued after them, and sent them *fleeing*; and
a great many of Gaal's men were killed, all the way back
to the city gate.)
41 And (then) Abimelech sat in Arumah; and Zebul put
Gaal and his fellows out of the city of Shechem, and he
suffered them not to dwell therein (and he did not allow
them to stay there).
42 Therefore in the day following, the people went out
into the field (And on the following day, the people came
out into the open); and when this thing was told to
Abimelech,
43 he took his host, and parted it in three companies,
and he set ambushments in the fields; and he saw that the
people went out of the city, and he rose, and felled upon
them with his company, (he took his army, and divided it
into three companies, *or three groups*, and he set men in
ambush in the fields; and when he saw the people go out
of the city, he rose up, and attacked them with his
company,)
44 and (he) besieged them and fought against the (men
of the) city. And two companies went about openly by

the field (And the other two companies went about
openly in the field), and pursued their adversaries.
45 And Abimelech fought against that city *all that day,*
the which he took, when the dwellers thereof were slain,
and that city was destroyed, so that he sprinkled abroad
salt therein (and then he sprinkled salt on it).
46 And when they, that dwelled in the tower of
Shechem, had heard this, they entered into the temple of
their god Berith, where they had made [a] bond of peace
with him; and of that *idol* the place took the name, the
which place was full strong. (And when they, who lived
in the tower of Shechem, had heard this, they entered
into the temple of their god Berith, where they had made
a covenant with him; and that place took the name of
that *idol*, and it was well-fortified.)
47 And Abimelech heard that (all) [the] men of the
tower of Shechem were gathered together (there),
48 and he went up into the hill of Zalmon with all his
people (and so he went up to Mount Zalmon with all his
people); and with an ax taken, he cut down a bough of a
tree, and he bare it, put upon his shoulder, and he said to
his fellows, Do ye at once this thing, that ye see me do.
49 Therefore with strife they cutted down boughs of the
trees, and followed the duke; the which compassed the
tower and burnt it up; and so it was done, that with
smoke and fire a thousand men were slain, men and
women together, of the dwellers of the tower of
Shechem. (And so they cut off the boughs of the trees,
and then followed their leader; and they surrounded the
temple, and then burned it down; and so it was, that with
smoke and fire, a thousand people were killed, men and
women together, all those of the tower of Shechem.)
50 And Abimelech went forth from thence, and came
to the city of Thebez, which he compassed, and besieged
with an host. (And then Abimelech went forth from there,
and came to the city of Thebez, which he surrounded,
and besieged with his army.)
51 And the tower was high in the midst of the city, to
which men and women fled together, and all the princes
of the city, while the gate was closed full strongly; and
they stood on the roof of the tower by [the] turrets. (And
the tower there was high in the middle of the city, to
which all the men and women, and all the city leaders
fled, and then the gate was securely closed; and they
stood on the roof of the tower by the turrets.)
52 And Abimelech came beside the tower, and fought
strongly *against it*, and he nighed to the door, and
endeavoured him to put fire under it (and he came up to
the door, and endeavoured to put fire under it);
53 and lo! a woman casted from above a gobbet of a
millstone, and hurtled to the head of Abimelech, and it
brake his noll. (and lo! a woman threw a piece of a
millstone down from above, and hurtled it onto
Abimelech's head, and it broke, *or it cracked*, his skull.)
54 And he called anon his squire, and said to him,
Draw out thy sword, and slay me, lest peradventure it be
said, that I am slain of a woman. Which performed the
commandments, and killed Abimelech; (And he called
out at once to his squire, and said to him, Draw out thy
sword, and kill me, lest it be said that I was killed by a
woman. And he followed the order, and killed
Abimelech;)
55 and when Abimelech was dead, all (the) men of
Israel that were with him turned again to their places.
56 And God yielded to Abimelech the evil that he did
against his father, for he killed his seventy brethren.
57 Also that evil was yielded to [the] men of Shechem,
(for) that (that) they wrought, and (so) the curse of Jotham,
the son of Jerubbaal, came upon them.

CHAPTER 10

1 After Abimelech rose a duke in Israel, Tola, the son
of Puah, son of Dodo; *Tola was* a man of Issachar, that
dwelled in Shamir, of the hill of Ephraim; (After
Abimelech, a leader arose in Israel, that is Tola, the son
of Puah, the son of Dodo; *and Tola was* a man of
Issachar, who lived in Shamir, in the hill country of
Ephraim;)
2 and he deemed Israel three and twenty years, and
(then) he died, and was buried in Shamir.
3 His successor was Jair, a man of Gilead, that
deemed Israel two and twenty years;
4 and he had thirty sons, sitting upon thirty colts of
she-asses, and they were princes of thirty cities, the
which be called by their father's name, Havothjair, *that
is, the cities of Jair,* unto this present day, in the land of
Gilead.
5 And (then) Jair died, and was buried in a place that
is called Camon.
6 Forsooth the sons of Israel joined new sins to eld
sins, and did evil in the sight of the Lord, and served to
the idols of Baalim, and to Ashtaroth, and to the gods of
Syria, and of Sidon, and of Moab, and of the sons of
Ammon, and of Philistines; and they left the Lord, and
worshipped not him (and did not worship him).
7 And the Lord was wroth against them, and he
betook them into the hands of Philistines, and of the sons
of Ammon.
8 And all *the sons of Israel* that dwelled beyond (the)
Jordan in the land of Amorites, that is, in Gilead, were
tormented and oppressed greatly by eighteen years, (And
all *the Israelites* who lived on the eastern side of the
Jordan River, in the land of Amorites, that is, in Gilead,
were tormented and greatly oppressed for eighteen
years,)
9 in so much that the sons of Ammon, when they had
passed [over] (the) Jordan, wasted Judah, and Benjamin,
and Ephraim; and Israel was tormented greatly. (in so

much that the Ammonites, when they had crossed over
the Jordan River, attacked Judah, and Benjamin, and
Ephraim; and so Israel was greatly tormented.)
10 And they cried to the Lord, and said, We have
sinned to thee, for we forsook our God, and served
Baalim. (And they cried to the Lord, and said, We have
sinned against thee, for we deserted our God, and served
the Baalim.)
11 To whom the Lord said, Whether not the Egyptians,
and Amorites, and the sons of Ammon, and Philistines,
12 and Sidonians, and Amalek, and Canaan (and
Maonites), have (all) oppressed you, and ye cried to me,
and I delivered you from their hands?
13 And nevertheless ye have forsaken me, and
worshipped alien gods; therefore I shall not add to, that I
deliver you [any] more (and so I shall not do anything
more to save you again).
14 Go ye, and call (on) [the] gods which ye have
chosen; deliver they you in the time of anguish (let them
save you in your time of anguish).
15 And the sons of Israel said to the Lord, We have
sinned; yield thou to us whatever thing pleaseth to thee;
only deliver us now. (And the Israelites said to the Lord,
We have sinned; yield thou to us *later* whatever pleaseth
thee; but right now, please save us!)
16 And they said these things, and casted forth from
their coasts all the idols of alien gods, and served the
Lord; which had ruth, *either compassion*, on (all) the
wretchednesses of them.
17 And so the sons of Ammon cried together, *each
moving (the) other to battle against Israel*, and setted
tents in Gilead, and the sons of Israel were gathered
against them, and setted tents in Mizpeh. (But then the
Ammonites cried together, *each moving the other to
battle against Israel*, and pitched their tents at Gilead; and
the Israelites gathered themselves together against them,
and pitched their tents at Mizpeh.)
18 And the princes of Gilead said each to his
neighbours, He, that beginneth first of us to fight against
the sons of Ammon, shall be duke of the people of
Gilead. (And the people and the rulers of Gilead said to
each other, He of us who first beginneth to fight against
the Ammonites, shall be the leader of all the people of
Gilead.)

CHAPTER 11

1 And so in that time Jephthah, a man of Gilead, was a
full strong man, and a fighter, the son of a woman whore,
the which Jephthah was born of Gilead. (Now at that
time Jephthah, a Gileadite, was a very strong man, and a
fighter, the son of a whore-woman, and his father was
Gilead.)
2 And Gilead had a wife, of whom he had sons,
which after that they increased (and after they had grown
up), casted out Jephthah, and said, Thou mayest not be
(an) heir in the house of our father, for thou art born of
another mother.
3 And (so) he fled (from) his brethren, and eschewed
them, and dwelled in the land of Tob; and poor men
were gathered to him, and followed him as a prince.
4 (And) In those days the sons of Ammon fought
against Israel;
5 and when they continued sharply (*their enmities*),
the greater men in birth of Gilead, went to take into the
help of themselves Jephthah from the land of Tob; (and
when they continued *their sharp enmities*, the men of
great age, *that is, the elders*, of Gilead went to get
Jephthah from the land of Tob to help them;)
6 and they said to him, Come thou, and be our prince,
and fight against the sons of Ammon.
7 To which he answered, Whether not ye it be, that
hated me, and threw me out of the house of my father,
and now ye have come to me, and were compelled by
need? (To whom he answered, Was it not ye, who hated
me, and threw me out of my father's house? but now ye
have come to me, yea, compelled by need!)
8 And the princes of Gilead said to Jephthah,
Therefore for this cause we came now to thee, that thou
go with us, and fight against the sons of Ammon; and that
thou be the duke of all men that dwell in Gilead. (And
the leaders of Gilead said to Jephthah, Yea, for this
reason we have now come to thee, so that thou go with
us, and fight against the Ammonites; and that thou be the
leader of all who live in Gilead.)
9 And Jephthah said to them, Whether ye came verily,
or without fraud, to me, that I fight for you against the
sons of Ammon, and if the Lord shall betake them into
mine hands, shall I be your prince? (And Jephthah said to
them, Did ye come truthfully, *or without deception*, to
me, so that if I fight for you against the Ammonites, and if
the Lord shall deliver them into my hands, then I shall be
your leader?)
10 The which answered to him, The Lord himself, that
heareth these things, is mediator and witness, that we
shall fulfill our promises *to thee*. (And they answered to
him, The Lord himself, who heareth these things, is our
mediator and witness, that we shall fulfill our promises *to
thee*.)
11 And so Jephthah went with the princes of Gilead,
and all the people made him their prince; and Jephthah
spake all his words (again) before the Lord in Mizpeh.
12 And he sent messengers to the king of the sons of
Ammon, which messengers should say of his person
(which messengers were to say for him), What is to me
and to thee, for thou hast come against me to waste my
land?
13 To the which messengers the king answered, For
Israel, when he ascended from Egypt, took away my land,

from the coasts of Arnon unto Jabbok, and to (the) Jordan,
now therefore yield it to me *again* with peace. (To which
messengers the king answered, For Israel, when they
came up from Egypt, took away my land, from the Arnon
River unto the Jabbok *River*, and unto the Jordan River;
and so now peacefully, *or without any need for fighting*,
return thou these lands to me.)
14 By the which messengers Jephthah sent again, and
commanded to them, that they should say to the king of
Ammon,
15 Jephthah saith these things, Israel took not the land
of Moab, neither the land of the sons of Ammon;
(Jephthah saith these things, Nay! Israel did not take the
land of Moab, nor the land of the Ammonites;)
16 but when they went up from Egypt, Israel went by
the wilderness unto the Red Sea, and came into Kadesh;
17 and he sent messengers to the king of Edom, and
said, Suffer thou me, that I go through thy land (and they
sent messengers to the king of Edom, saying, Allow us to
go through thy land); the which king would not assent to
the prayers of Israel. Also Israel sent to the king of Moab,
and he despised to give Israel passage; and so Israel
dwelled in Kadesh,
18 and he compassed by the side the land of Edom,
and the land of Moab; and he came to the east coast of
the land of Moab, and setted tents beyond Arnon, neither
he would enter into the terms of Moab; for Arnon is the
end of the land of Moab. (and they went around by the
borders of the land of Edom, and the land of Moab; and
they came to the east side of the land of Moab, and
pitched their tents on the other side of the Arnon River,
for they would not enter into the land of Moab; for the
Arnon River is the border of the land of Moab.)
19 And so Israel sent messengers to Sihon, king of
Amorites, that dwelled in Heshbon; and they said to him,
Suffer thou, that I pass through thy land unto the river.
(And so Israel sent messengers to Sihon, the king of the
Amorites, who lived in Heshbon; and they said to him,
Allow us to pass through thy land to the river.)
20 And he despised the words of Israel, and suffered
not him (to) pass by his terms, but with a multitude
without number gathered together, Sihon went out
against Israel (at Jahaz), and against-stood him strongly.
(But he scorned Israel's request, and would not allow
them to pass through his land; and with a multitude
without number gathered together, Sihon went out
against the people of Israel at Jahaz, and strongly stood
against them.)
21 And the Lord betook Sihon with all his host into the
hands of Israel; and Israel smote him, and had in
possession all the land of Amorites, the dweller(s) of that
country, (And the Lord delivered Sihon with all his army
into the hands of Israel; and Israel struck them down, and
had in possession all the land of the Amorites, the
inhabitants of that country,)
22 and all the coasts thereof, from (the) Arnon unto
(the) Jabbok, and from the wilderness unto (the) Jordan.
23 Therefore the Lord God of Israel destroyed Amorites,
fighting against him for his people Israel. And wilt thou
now have in possession his land? (And so the Lord God
of Israel destroyed the Amorites, fighting against them for
his people Israel. And now wilt thou take possession of
their land?)
24 Whether not those things which Chemosh, thy god,
had in possession, be due to thee by right? Soothly those
things which the Lord our God (the) overcomer hath
gotten, shall fall into our possession; (Be not those things
which Chemosh, thy god, had in possession, by rights be
due to thee? And likewise, those things which the Lord
our God the Overcomer hath taken, they shall be ours;)
25 but in hap thou art better than Balak, the son of
Zippor, king of Moab, either thou mayest say, that Balak
strived against Israel, and fought against him, (but
perhaps thou art better than Balak, the son of Zippor, the
king of Moab, or thou mayest say, that Balak contended
against Israel, and fought against them,)
26 when Israel dwelled in Heshbon, and in towns
thereof, and in Aroer, and in towns thereof, and in all
cities beyond (the) Jordan, by three hundred years. Why
in so much time assayed ye nothing on this asking again?
(when Israel lived in Heshbon, and its towns, and in
Aroer, and its towns, and in all the cities on the eastern
side of the Jordan River, for three hundred years. Why
have ye done nothing to try to take them back in all this
time?)
27 Therefore not I do sin against thee, but thou doest
evil against me, and bringest in battles not just to me; the
Lord, (the) judge of this day, deem betwixt the sons of
Israel and betwixt the sons of Ammon. (And so I do not
sin against thee, but thou doest evil against me, and
bringest in battles not just, *or fair*, to me; the Lord is the
judge, and he shall judge this very day between the
Israelites and the Ammonites.)
28 And the king of the sons of Ammon would not
assent to the words of Jephthah, which he sent by the
messengers.
29 Therefore the spirit of the Lord was made upon
Jephthah, and he compassed Gilead, and Manasseh,
Mizpeh and Gilead (and then back to Mizpeh of Gilead);
and he passed (over) from thence to the sons of Ammon,
30 and he made a vow to the Lord, and said, If thou
shalt betake the sons of Ammon into mine hands,
31 whoever goeth out first of the doors of mine house,
and cometh against me turning again with peace from the
sons of Ammon, I shall offer him (up as a) burnt sacrifice
to the Lord. (whoever first goeth out of the doors of my
house, and cometh to meet me when I return in victory
over the Ammonites, I shall offer him up as a burnt

sacrifice to the Lord.)
32 And Jephthah went to the sons of Ammon, to fight
against them, which the Lord betook into his hands;
33 and he smote from Aroer till that he came into
Minnith, (yea,) twenty cities, and (even) unto Abel, which
is set about with vineries, with full great vengeance; and
the sons of Ammon were made low of the sons of Israel.
(and he struck down, *or overcame*, from Aroer until that
he came unto Minnith, twenty cities, and even unto
Abelkeramim, with very great vengeance; and the
Ammonites were made low before the Israelites.)
34 And when Jephthah turned again into Mizpeh, (to)
his house, his one begotten daughter came to meet him
with tympans, and crowds dancing; for he had not other
free children. (And when Jephthah returned to Mizpeh, to
his house, his only daughter came to meet him with
tambourines, and people dancing; and he had no other
children.)
35 And when he saw her, he rent his clothes, and said,
Alas! my daughter, thou hast troubled me, and thou art
troubled; for I opened my mouth to the Lord, and I may
do none other thing. (And when he saw her, he tore his
clothes, and said, Alas! my daughter, thou hast brought
woe upon me, and woe upon thyself; for I opened my
mouth to the Lord, and I may do no other thing.)
36 To whom she answered, My father, if thou
openedest thy mouth to the Lord, do to me whatever
thing thou promisedest, while vengeance and victory of
thine enemies be granted to thee (for vengeance and
victory over thy enemies have been granted to thee by
the Lord).
37 And she said to her father, Give thou to me only this
thing, which I beseech; suffer thou me that in two months
I compass [the] hills (allow me for two months to go
about the hills), and bewail my maidenhood with my
fellows.
38 To whom he answered, Go thou. And he suffered
her in two months (And he allowed her to go away for
two months). And when she had gone forth with her
fellows, and her play-frères, she bewept her maidenhood
in the hills.
39 And when two months were fulfilled, she turned
again to her father, and he did to her as he (had) avowed;
and she knew no man *fleshly*, (*that is, she died a virgin*).
From that time a custom came in Israel, and that custom
is kept (to this day),
40 that after the end of the year the daughters of Israel
come together, and bewail the daughter of Jephthah of
Gilead (for) four days.

CHAPTER 12

1 And, lo! dissension (a)rose in Ephraim; for they, that
passed toward the north (who crossed over to Zaphon),
said to Jephthah, Why wentest thou to battle against the
sons of Ammon, and wouldest not call us, (so) that we
should go with thee. Therefore we shall burn (down)
thine house.
2 To which he answered, Great strife was to me and
to my people against the sons of Ammon, and I called
you, that ye should give help to me, and you would not
do *so*. (To whom he answered, There was great strife
between me and my people and the Ammonites, and I
called on you, to give me help, but ye would not do *so*.)
3 Which thing I saw, and putted my life in mine
hands; and I passed (forth) to the sons of Ammon, and the
Lord betook them into mine hands; what have I (done
that I) deserved, that ye rise together against me into
battle? (so what have I done that I deserve that ye rise up
against me in battle?)
4 Therefore when all the men of Gilead were called to
Jephthah, he fought against Ephraim; and [the] men of
Gilead smote Ephraim; for he said (for they said), Gilead
is fugitive, *either exiled*, from Ephraim, and in the midst
of Ephraim, and of Manasseh.
5 And the men of Gilead occupied the fords of (the)
Jordan, by which Ephraim should turn again. And when
a man, fleeing of the number of Ephraim, had come to
the fords, and had said, I beseech, that ye suffer me pass;
men of Gilead said to him, Whether thou art a man of
Ephraim? And when he had said, I am not (And when a
man, fleeing from the Ephraimites, had come to the
crossing, and had said, I beseech thee, that ye allow me
to cross over; the men of Gilead said to him, Art thou a
man of Ephraim? And when he had said, I am not),
6 they asked him, Say thou therefore Shibboleth,
which is interpreted, an ear of corn. Which answered,
Sibboleth, and he might not bring forth (the word for) an
ear of corn by the same letter. And anon they took and
strangled him in that passing (over) of (the) Jordan; and
two and forty thousand men of Ephraim felled down in
that time. (they said to him, Then say thou Shibboleth,
which is translated, an ear of corn. And he answered,
Sibboleth, and he could not bring forth the word for an
ear of corn. And at once they took and strangled him at
that crossing of the Jordan River; and forty-two thousand
men of Ephraim were killed at that time.)
7 And so Jephthah, a man of Gilead, deemed Israel six
years; and (then) he died, and was buried in his city (of)
Gilead.
8 Ibzan of Bethlehem, that had thirty sons, and so
many daughters, deemed Israel after Jephthah; (And Ibzan
of Bethlehem, who had thirty sons, and as many
daughters, judged, *or ruled*, Israel after Jephthah;)
9 which daughters he sent out, and gave *them* to
husbands, and he took wives to his sons of the same
number, and he brought *them* into his house; and Ibzan
deemed Israel seven years; (which daughters he sent
away, and gave *them* to husbands, and he found the

same number of wives for his sons, and he brought *them*
into his household, *or his family*; and Ibzan judged Israel
for seven years;)
10 and (then) he died, and was buried in Bethlehem.
11 Whose successor was Elon of Zebulun; and he
deemed Israel ten years;
12 and he was dead, and buried in Zebulun. (and then
he died, and was buried in Aijalon, in the land of
Zebulun.)
13 After him Abdon, the son of Hillel, of Pirathon,
deemed Israel;
14 the which Abdon had forty sons, and of them were
thirty sons, going upon seventy colts of she-asses, and
Abdon deemed Israel eight years; (and Abdon had forty
sons, who in turn had thirty sons, and they all went upon
seventy colts of female donkeys; and Abdon judged, *or
ruled*, Israel for eight years;)
15 and (then) he died, and was buried in Pirathon, in
the land of Ephraim, in the hill (country) of Amalek.

CHAPTER 13

1 And again the sons of Israel did evil in the sight of
the Lord, and he betook them in[to] the hands of [the]
Philistines (for) forty years.
2 Forsooth a man was of Zorah, of the kindred of Dan
(And there was a man of Zorah, of the tribe of Dan),
Manoah by name, and he had a barren wife.
3 To which wife an angel of the Lord appeared, and
said to her, Thou art barren, and without free children;
but thou shalt conceive, and bear a son.
4 Therefore be thou ware, lest thou drink wine, and
cider (or cider), neither eat thou any unclean thing;
5 for thou shalt conceive, and bear a son, whose head
a razor shall not touch; for he shall be a Nazarite, *that is,
holy* of God, from his young age, and from the mother's
womb (for he shall be a Nazarite, *that is, holy* to God,
from his mother's womb); and he shall begin to deliver
Israel from the hand of [the] Philistines.
6 And when she had come to her husband, she said to
him, A man of God came to me, and he had an angel's
cheer, and he was full fearedful (and he had the face of
an angel, and he was most frightening); and when I had
asked him, who he was, and from whence he came, and
by what name he was called, he would not say to me;
7 but he answered thus, Lo! thou shalt conceive, and
bear a son; (but) be thou ware, that thou drink no wine
nor cider, neither eat any unclean thing; for the child
shall be a Nazarite, *that is, holy* of the Lord, from his
young age, and from the mother's womb, till to the day
of his death (for the child shall be a Nazarite, *that is, holy*
to the Lord, from his mother's womb, until the day of his
death).
8 Therefore Manoah prayed the Lord, and said, Lord, I
beseech, that the man of God, whom thou sentest, come
again, and teach us, what we ought to do of the child,
that shall be born (what we ought to do with the child,
who shall be born to us).
9 And the Lord heard Manoah praying; and the angel
of the Lord appeared again to his wife sitting in the field;
forsooth Manoah, her husband, was not with her.
10 And when she had seen the angel, she hasted, and
ran to her husband, and told to him, and said, Lo! the
man whom I saw before, (hath) appeared to me (again).
11 Which rose (And he arose), and followed his wife;
and he came to the man, and said to him, Art thou he,
that hast spoken to the woman? And he answered, I am.
12 To whom Manoah said, When thy word shall be
fulfilled, what wilt thou, that the child do, either from
what thing shall he keep himself? (and from what things
should he keep himself?)
13 And the angel of the Lord said to Manoah, Abstain
he himself from all things which I spake to thy wife. (And
the angel of the Lord said to Manoah, Thy wife should
abstain from all the things which I spoke to her about.)
14 And eat he not whatever thing cometh forth of the
vine, drink he not wine, and cider, eat he not any
unclean thing, and fulfill he; and keep that, that I
commanded to him. (She should not eat anything that
cometh forth from the vine, nor should she drink wine, or
cider, or eat any unclean thing; she must fulfill, and obey
what I have commanded to her.)
15 Therefore Manoah said to the angel of the Lord, I
beseech, that thou assent to my prayers, and we array to
thee, *that is, make ready to meat*, a kid of the goats. (And
then Manoah said to the angel of the Lord, I beseech
thee, that thou assent to my prayers, and let us prepare *a
meal* for thee, yea, a goat kid.)
16 To whom the angel of the Lord answered, Though
thou (shalt) constrain me, I shall not eat thy bread; but if
thou wilt make (a) burnt sacrifice, offer thou it to the
Lord. And Manoah knew not, that it was an angel of the
Lord (For Manoah did not know that he was an angel of
the Lord).
17 And Manoah said to him, What name is to thee, that
if thy word be fulfilled, we (can) honour thee?
18 To whom he answered, Why askest thou my name,
which is hid, *either unknown*?
19 Therefore Manoah took a goat kid, and flowing
sacrifices (and the proper grain offering), and he put
(them) upon a stone, and he offered them to the Lord that
doeth wonderful things. And he and his wife beheld.
20 And when the flame of the altar ascended into
heaven, the angel of the Lord ascended together in the
flame (the angel of the Lord went up in the flame). And
when Manoah and his wife had seen this, they felled low
to the earth.
21 And the angel of the Lord appeared no more to
them. And at once Manoah understood, that he was the

angel of the Lord.
22 And he said to his wife, We shall die by death, for
we have seen the Lord.
23 To whom the woman answered, If the Lord would
slay us, he would not have taken of our hands burnt
sacrifices, and moist sacrifices, but neither he would have
showed all these things to us, neither have said to us (of)
those things, that be to coming. (To whom the woman
answered, If the Lord intended to kill us, he would not
have received out of our hands the burnt sacrifice, and
the grain offering, nor would he have shown all these
things to us, nor would he have told us of the things to
come.)
24 And so she childed a son, and called his name
Samson; and the child increased (in age), and the Lord
blessed him.
25 And the spirit of the Lord began to be with him in
the tents of Dan, betwixt Zorah and Eshtaol.

CHAPTER 14

1 Therefore (And so in time, when he was a grown
man,) Samson went down into Timnath, and he saw there
a woman of the daughters of (the) Philistines;
2 and he went up, and he told this to his father and
mother, and said, I saw a woman in Timnath of the
daughters of Philistines, and I beseech, that ye take her
(to be) a wife to me (and I beseech thee, that ye get her
for a wife for me).
3 To whom his father and mother said, Whether there
is no woman among the daughters of thy brethren, and in
all my people, for thou wilt take a wife of the Philistines,
that be uncircumcised? And Samson said to his father,
Take thou this (for a) *wife* to me, for she hath pleased
mine eyes. (To whom his father and mother said, Is there
no woman among the daughters of thy kinsmen, or
among all our people, that thou must take a wife of the
Philistines, yea, of those who be uncircumcised? And
Samson said to his father, Get thou her for a *wife* for me,
for she hath pleased my eyes.)
4 But his father and mother knew not, that this thing
was done of the Lord (that this thing was done by the
Lord); and that he sought occasions against [the]
Philistines; for in that time (the) Philistines were lords of
Israel.
5 Therefore Samson went down with his father and
mother into Timnath; and when they had come to the
vineries of the city, a fierce and roaring whelp of a lion
appeared, and ran to Samson (and ran at Samson).
6 And the spirit of the Lord felled into Samson, and he
rent the lion into gobbets, as if he had rent a kid, and
utterly he had nothing in his hand; and he would not
show this to his father and mother. (And the spirit of the
Lord fell upon Samson, and he tore the lion into pieces,
like tearing up a goat kid, and he had utterly nothing in
his hands; but he did not tell what he had done to either
his father or his mother.)
7 And (so) he went down, and spake to the woman,
that pleased his eyes.
8 And after some days he turned [again] to take her;
and he went aside to see the lion's carrion (and he went
aside to see the lion's carcass); and lo! a swarm of bees
was in the lion's mouth, and (also) an honeycomb.
9 And when Samson had taken the comb in his hands,
he ate it in the way; and he came to his father and
mother, and gave them part thereof, and they ate;
nevertheless he would not show to them, that he had
taken that honey of the lion's mouth. (And when Samson
had taken the comb in his hands, he ate some honey on
the way; and he came to his father and mother, and gave
them part of it, and they ate it; but he did not tell them,
that he had taken the honey out of the lion's mouth.)
10 And so his father went down to the woman, and
made a feast to his son Samson; for so young men were
wont to do. (And so his father went down to see the
woman, and Samson gave a feast there, as young men
were wont to do.)
11 Therefore when the citizens of that place had seen
him, they gave to him thirty fellows, which should be
with him.
12 To which Samson spake, I shall put forth to you a
problem, *that is, a doubtful word and privy,* and if ye
solve it to me within (the) seven days of the feast, I shall
give to you thirty linen clothes, and coats of the same
number; (To whom Samson said, I shall put forth a
problem, *or a riddle,* to you, and if ye solve it for me
within the seven days of the feast, I shall give you thirty
linen clothes, and the same number of coats;)
13 soothly if ye may not solve (it), ye shall give to me
thirty linen clothes, and coats of the same number (and
the same number of coats). Which answered to him, Set
forth the problem, (so) that we hear *it.*
14 And he said to them, Meat went out of the eater,
and sweetness went out of the strong. And by three days
they might not solve the proposition, *that is, the
reason(ing) set forth* (And for three days, they could not
solve the riddle).
15 And when the seventh day came, they said to the
wife of Samson, Gloss thine husband, and counsel him,
that he show to thee what the problem signifieth. That if
thou wilt not do it, we shall burn thee and the house of
thy father. Whether therefore ye called us to [the]
weddings, that ye should rob us? (And when the fourth
day came, they said to Samson's wife, Flatter thy
husband, and counsel him, so that he show thee what the
answer is. And if thou wilt not do this, we shall burn
down thee and thy father's house as well. Or have ye
only called us to the wedding, so that ye could rob us?)
16 And she shedded tears at Samson, and complained,

and said, Thou hatest me, and lovest *me* not, therefore
thou wilt not expound to me the problem, which thou
hast put forth to the sons of my people. And he
answered, I would not say *this thing* to my father and
mother, and shall I be able to show it to thee? (And so
she shed tears before Samson, and complained, and said,
Thou hatest me, and lovest *me* not, and so thou wilt not
expound the riddle to me, which thou hast put forth to
the sons of my people. And he answered, If I would not
even tell *it* to my father or my mother, then why would I
tell it to thee?)
17 Therefore by seven days of the feast she wept upon
him; and at the last in the seventh day, he told it to her
clearly, when she was dis-easeful to him. And anon she
told it to her citizens. (And so for the remainder of the
seven days of the feast, she wept before him; and at last
on the seventh day, he told her the answer, after that she
had made his life miserable. And at once she told it to
her fellow citizens.)
18 And they said to him in the seventh day before the
going down of the sun, What is sweeter than honey, and
what is stronger than a lion? And he said to them, If ye
had not eared, *or busied you,* in my cow calf, *that is, my*
wife, ye had not found (out) my proposition. (And so on
the seventh day, before the going down of the sun, they
said to him, What is sweeter than honey, and stronger
than a lion? And he said to them, If ye had not busied
yourselves with my cow calf, *that is, with my wife,* ye
would not have solved my riddle.)
19 Therefore the spirit of the Lord felled into him; and
he went down to Ashkelon, and killed there thirty men,
whose clothes he took away, and he gave to them that
solved the problem; and he was full wroth, and went up
into his father's house. (And then the spirit of the Lord fell
upon him; and he went down to Ashkelon, and killed
thirty men there, whose clothes he took away, and he
gave them to those who had solved his riddle; and he
was very angry, and went back to his father's house.)
20 Forsooth his wife took (as) an husband, one of the
friends and privy keepers of her. [Forsooth the wife of him
took an husband, one of his friends and wooers.]

CHAPTER 15

1 But a little time after, when the days of wheat
harvest nighed, Samson came, and would visit his wife,
and he brought to her a goat kid; and when he would
enter into her bed by custom, her father forbade him,
2 and said, I guessed that thou haddest hated her, and
therefore I gave her to thy friend; but she hath a sister,
which is younger and fairer than she, be she [a] wife to
thee for her (let her be your wife instead!).
3 To whom Samson answered, From this day *forth* no
blame shall be in me against [the] Philistines, for I shall
do evils to you. (To whom Samson answered, From this
day *forth,* none of the Philistines can blame me, though I
shall do much evil to you.)
4 And he went, and took three hundred foxes, and he
joined together their tails to tails, (one to one,) and he
bound fire brands in (the) middle *of the tails* (and he tied
torches in the middle *of their tails*),
5 which he kindled with fire, and (then) let them (go),
that they should run about hither and thither (so that they
would run about here and there); which went at once
into the corns of [the] Philistines, by which kindled, both
the corns borne now together, and (those) yet standing in
the stubble, were (all) burnt, in so much that the flame
(also) wasted (the) vineries, and (the) places of (the) olive
trees.
6 And the Philistines said, Who did this thing? To
whom it was said, Samson, the husband of (the) Timnite's
daughter, for he took away Samson's wife, and gave her
to another man. And (so) the Philistines went up, and
burnt (up) both the woman and her father.
7 To the which *Philistines* Samson said, Though ye
have done this thing, nevertheless yet I shall ask *and take*
vengeance of you, and then I shall rest. (To which
Philistines Samson said, Because ye have done this thing,
now I shall take vengeance on all of you, and then I shall
rest.)
8 And he smote them with great wound, so that they
wondered, and (they fled so fast, that they) putted the
hinder part of the hip on the thigh; and he went down,
and dwelled in the den of the stone of Etam. (And he
struck them down, hip and thigh, with a great slaughter;
and then he went, and lived in the cave in the Rock of
Etam.)
9 Then the Philistines went up into the land of Judah,
and they setted tents in the place, that was called
afterward Lehi, *that is, a cheek*[*bone*], where their host
was spread abroad. (Then the Philistines went up into the
land of Judah, and they pitched their tents at the place,
that later was called Lehi, *that is, Jawbone,* where their
army was spread out over all the land.)
10 And men of the lineage of Judah said to them, Why
have ye gone up against us? The which answered, We
come that we bind Samson (And they answered, We
have come so that we can bind up Samson), and yield to
him (for) those things the which he [hath] wrought against
us.
11 Therefore three thousand of men of Judah went
down to the den of the flint of Etam; and they said to
Samson, Knowest thou not, that [the] Philistines
command to us, *that is, they have lordship on us*? (And
so three thousand men of Judah went down to the cave
in the Rock of Etam; and they said to Samson, Knowest
thou not, that the Philistines command, or *rule,* over us?)
Why wouldest thou do this thing *to them*? To whom he
said, As they did to me, so I did to them.

12 They said, We come to bind thee, and to betake
thee into the hands of Philistines. To whom Samson
answered, Swear ye, and promise ye to me, that ye slay
not me. (And they said to him, We have come to bind
thee up, and to deliver *thee* into the hands of the
Philistines. To whom Samson answered, Swear ye, and
promise ye to me, that ye shall not kill me.)
13 And they said, We shall not slay thee, but we shall
betake *thee* bound *to them*. And (so) they bound him with
two new cords, and took him from the stone of Etam.
14 And when they had come to the place *that is called*
Cheek[bone], and the Philistines crying high had run (out)
to him, the spirit of the Lord felled into him, and as sticks
be wont to be wasted at the hot tasting of fire, so and the
bonds, with which he was bound, were scattered and
loosed. (And when they had come to the place *that now
is called* Lehi, *or Jawbone*, and the Philistines came
running toward him, and shouting, the spirit of the Lord
fell upon him, and as sticks be wont to be wasted with the
hot tasting of the fire, so the bonds, with which he was
bound, were scattered and loosed from off his hands.)
15 And when he had found a cheek[bone], *that is, the
nether cheekbone*, of an ass, that *there* lay, he took it,
and killed therewith a thousand men; (And when he had
found a jawbone, *that is, the lower jawbone*, of a
donkey, that lay *there*, he took it, and killed a thousand
men with it;)
16 and he said, With the cheek[bone] of an ass, *that is,
with the nether cheek[bone] of a colt of she-asses*, I have
done away Philistines, and I have killed therewith a
thousand men. (and he said, With the jawbone of a
donkey, *that is, with the lower jawbone of the colt of a
female donkey*, I have done away the Philistines, and I
have killed a thousand men with it.)
17 And when he had high cried these words, and had
fully ended them, he threw away from his hand the
nether cheekbone; and he called the name of that place
Ramathlehi, *that is to say, the Raising (up) of a
cheekbone*. (And after that he had sung these words, and
had finished them, he threw away the lower jawbone
from his hand; and he named that place Ramathlehi, *that
is to say, the Raising up of a jawbone*.)
18 And (then) he thirsted greatly, and cried to the Lord,
and said, Thou, *Lord*, hast given into the hand of thy
servant this greatest health and victory (Thou, *Lord*, hast
given thy servant this great victory); and lo! I die for thirst,
and I shall fall into the hands of uncircumcised men.
19 Therefore the Lord opened a wang tooth in the
cheekbone of the ass, and waters went out thereof, and
when he had drunken he refreshed his spirit, and
received strengths; therefore the name of that place was
called the Well of the inwardly caller of the cheekbone,
unto this present day. (And so the Lord opened a molar
tooth in the jawbone of the donkey, and water went out
of it, and when he had drunk, it refreshed his spirit, and
he received strength; and so the name of the spring there
in Lehi is called Enhakkore, *or the Spring of the Caller*,
unto this present day).
20 And Samson deemed Israel in the days of [the]
Philistines (for) twenty years.

CHAPTER 16

1 Also Samson went into Gaza, and he saw there a
woman whore, and he entered to her. (And one day
Samson went to Gaza, and he saw a whore-woman there,
and he slept with her.)
2 And when the Philistines had seen this, and it was
published among them, that Samson had entered into the
city, they compassed him (about), (and with) the keepers
set in the gates of the city; and the Philistines (were)
abiding there all that night privily, that in the morrowtide
they should kill Samson going out. (And when the
Philistines had seen this, and it was published among
them, that Samson had come into the city, they
surrounded him, and had guards set at the city gates; for
the Philistines had decided to secretly wait there all that
night, so that in the morning they could kill Samson
when he came out.)
3 And Samson slept till to midnight (But Samson
stayed only until midnight); and (then) he rose up to go
(from) thence, and he took both the closings, *or the
leaves*, of the (city) gate, with the posts and the lock; and
he bare *those gates* upon his shoulders, to the top of the
hill that beholdeth Hebron.
4 (And) After these things Samson loved a woman that
dwelled in the valley of Sorek, and she was called Delilah.
5 And the princes of the Philistines came to her, and
said, Deceive thou him, and learn thou of him, in what
thing he hath so great strength, and how we may
overcome him, and torment *him when he is* bound; the
which thing if thou doest, we shall give to thee, each
man, a thousand and an hundred pieces of silver. (And
the rulers of the Philistines came to her, and said,
Deceive thou him, and learn thou from him, by what
thing he hath so great strength, and how we can
overcome him, and torment *him when he is* bound; and
if thou doest that, each one of us shall give thee a
thousand and a hundred pieces of silver.)
6 Then Delilah spake to Samson, (and said,) I beseech
thee, say thou to me, wherein is thy greatest strength, and
what is that thing, with which if thou were bound, thou
mayest not break (it)?
7 To whom Samson answered, If I be bound with
seven cords of moist sinews not yet dry, I shall be (made
as) feeble as other men.
8 And the princes of [the] Philistines brought to her
seven cords, as he had said; with which she bound him,
9 while ambushments were hid at her, and abided in a

closet the end of the thing. And she cried to him,
Samson, the Philistines be upon thee! And he brake those
bonds, as if a man breaketh a thread of hards (of flax),
thrown with spittle, when it hath touched the heat of fire;
and (so) it was not *yet* known wherein his strength was.
(while the ambushers were hid with her, and waited in a
closet for the end of it all. And she cried to him, Samson,
the Philistines be upon thee! And he broke those bonds,
like a man breaketh a flaxen thread, thrown with spittle,
when it hath touched the heat of the fire; and so it was
not *yet* known where his strength lay.)
10 And Delilah said to Samson, Lo! thou hast scorned
me, and thou hast spoken false(ly); nevertheless now
show thou to me, with what thing thou shouldest be
bound.
11 To whom he answered, If I be bound with new
cords, that were not yet in work, I shall be feeble, and
like other men (I shall be made as feeble as other men).
12 With the which Delilah bound him again, and she
cried, Samson, the Philistines be upon thee! the while
ambushments were made ready in a closet (while the
ambushers were waiting in the closet). And Samson
brake his bonds as (if they were the) threads of (spider)
webs.
13 And Delilah said again to him, How long shalt thou
deceive me, and speak false(ly)? Show thou to me, with
what thing thou shalt be bound. To whom Samson
answered, he said, If thou pleatest (the) seven gobbets of
(the) hair of mine head with a strong bond (To whom
Samson answered, and said, If thou pleatest the seven
locks of the hair of my head into thy loom),
14 and fastenest (in)to the earth a nail bound about
with these hairs, I shall be (made) feeble. And when
Delilah had done this, she said to him, Samson, the
Philistines be upon thee! And he rose from sleep, and he
drew out the nail, with the hairs and a strong bond *tied
thereto.* (and tightenest the hair, bound in the loom, with
a peg, I shall be made as feeble as other men. And when
Delilah had done this, she said to him, Samson, the
Philistines be upon thee! And he arose from sleep, and
he drew out the peg, with his hair *tightly tied to it,* in a
strong bond.)
15 And Delilah said to him, How sayest thou, that thou
lovest me, since thine inward affection is not with me?
By three times thou hast lied to me, and wouldest not say
to me, wherein is thy most strength (where thy great
strength lieth).
16 And when she was dis-easeful to him, and cleaved
to him continually by many days, and to him gave no
space to rest, his life failed, and was made weary unto the
death. (And when she had made his life miserable, and
continually cleaved to him for many days, and gave him
no time for any rest, his strength, *or his resolve,* failed,
and he was made weary unto the death.)
17 (And) Then he opened the truth of the thing, and
said to her, Iron came never yet upon mine head (No
iron hath ever yet touched my head), for I am a Nazarite,
that is, hallowed to the Lord, from my mother's womb; if
mine head be shaven, my strength shall go away from
me, and I shall fail, and I shall be (made as feeble) as
other men.
18 And she saw that he [had] acknowledged to her all
his will, *either heart*; and she sent to the princes of
Philistines, and commanded, Go ye up yet (at) once, for
now he hath opened his heart to me. The which went
up, the money taken *with them* that they promised. (And
she saw that he had spoken to her with all his heart; and
she sent for the rulers of the Philistines, saying, Come ye
up at once, for he hath now opened up all his heart to
me. And they came to her immediately, bringing the
money that they had promised.)
19 And she made him sleep upon her knees, and to lay
his head in her bosom; and (then) she called (for) a
barber, and he shaved (the) seven (locks of the) hairs of
him; and (then) she began to shove him away, and to put
him (off) from her; for at once the strength went away
from him.
20 And she said, Samson, the Philistines be upon thee!
And he rose (up) from sleep, and said in his soul, I shall
go out, as I did before, and I shall shake me *from these
bonds*; and he knew not, that the Lord had gone away
from him.
21 And when the Philistines had taken him, anon they
put out his eyes, and led *him* bound with chains to Gaza,
and they closed him in prison, and made him to grind.
(And when the Philistines had taken hold of him, at once
they put out his eyes, and led *him* bound with chains to
Gaza, and there they enclosed him in prison, and made
him to grind with a wheel.)
22 And then his hairs began to grow again;
23 and [the] princes of (the) Philistines came together to
offer great sacrifices to Dagon, their god, and *they made
feasts* and ate, saying, Our god hath betaken Samson, our
enemy, into our hands.
24 And the people seeing also this thing praised their
god (And the people seeing this thing also praised their
god), and said the same things, (Yea,) Our god hath
betaken our adversary into our hands, which did away
our land, and killed full many men.
25 And they were glad(dened) by *(the) making of* feasts,
and then when they had eaten, they commanded that
Samson should be called, and (to) play before them; the
which was led out of (the) prison, and played before
them; and they made him stand betwixt two pillars.
26 And Samson said to the boy that governed his steps,
Suffer thou me, that I touch the pillars on which all the
house standeth (Allow me to touch the pillars on which
the whole house standeth), (so) that I (may) be bowed

upon those, and rest a little.
27 And the house was full of men and of women, and
(all) the princes of the Philistines were there, and about
three thousand of men and of women (and also about
three thousand men and women), beholding from the
roof, and from the solar, (while) Samson (was) playing.
28 And he called inwardly the Lord, and said, My Lord
God, have mind on me, and my God, yield thou now to
me the former strength, that I venge me of mine enemies,
and that I take one vengeance for the loss of *my* two
eyes. (And he inwardly called upon the Lord, and said,
Lord my God, remember me, and my God, yield thou
now to me the former strength, so that I can avenge
myself on my enemies, and so that I can now take one
vengeance for the loss of *my* two eyes.)
29 And he took both [the] pillars, on which the house
stood, and he held the one of those in his right hand, and
the tother in his left hand; (And he took hold of both of
the pillars, on which the house stood, and he held onto
one of them with his right hand, and the other one with
his left hand;)
30 and he said, My life die with the(se) Philistines! And
when the pillars were shaken (al)together strongly, the
house felled upon all the princes, and upon the multitude
that was there; and Samson dying killed many more, than
he alive had slain before. (and he said, Let me die with
these Philistines! And when the pillars were altogether
strongly shaken, the house fell on all the rulers, and on
all the multitude of people who were there; and in dying,
Samson killed many more than he had killed when he
was alive.)
31 And his brethren and all his kindred came down,
and took his body, and they buried it betwixt Zorah and
Eshtaol, in the sepulchre of Manoah, his father; and he
deemed Israel twenty years. (And his brothers and all his
kindred came down, and took away his body, and they
buried it between Zorah and Eshtaol, in the tomb of his
father Manoah; and he had ruled Israel for twenty years.)

CHAPTER 17

1 In that time was a man, that was called Micah, of the
hill of Ephraim. (At that time there was a man, who was
called Micah, of the hill country of Ephraim.)
2 And he said to his mother, Lo! I have a thousand
and an hundred pieces of silver, which thou separatedest
to thee, and on which thou cursedest, while I heard; and
those be with me. To whom she answered, Blessed be
my son of the Lord. (And he said to his mother, Thou
haddest a thousand and a hundred pieces of silver that
were taken from thee, and I heard thou curse him who
robbed thee; lo! I was the one who took them. And she
quickly said, May the Lord bless my son!)
3 Therefore he yielded those to his mother; and she
said to him, I hallowed and avowed this silver to the
Lord, that my son receive (it out) of mine hand, and make
(with it) a graven image and a molten image; and now I
give it to thee. (And so he gave the silver back to his
mother; and she said, I now hallow and vow this silver to
the Lord, to protect my son from the curse, and I ask that
ye, my son, have a carved idol, and a cast image, made
from it; and now I give it to thee.)
4 Therefore he yielded to his mother; and she took
two hundred pieces of (the) silver, and gave those to a
workman of silver, that he should make of those a graven
image and (a) molten (image), that was (to be put) in the
house of Micah. (And so he gave the silver back to his
mother; and she took two hundred pieces of the silver,
and gave them to a craftsman of silver, so that he could
make them into a carved idol, and a cast image; and they
were put in Micah's house.)
5 And Micah also separated a little house, *or an*
oratory, therein to God; and made (an) ephod, and
teraphim, *that is, a priest's cloak, and idols*; and he filled
the hand of one of his sons, and he was made a priest to
him (and he consecrated, *or dedicated*, one of his sons,
and he became his priest).
6 In those days was no king in Israel, but each man
did that, that seemed rightful to himself. (In those days
there was no king in Israel, but each person did what
seemed right to himself.)
7 Also another young waxing man was of Bethlehem
of Judah, of the kindred of Judah, and he was a deacon,
and dwelled there. (And there was a young man of
Bethlehem in Judah, of the tribe of Judah, and he was a
Levite, and lived there.)
8 And he went out of the city of Bethlehem, and
would be a pilgrim, wherever he found (it) profitable to
himself. And when he made journey, and had come into
the hill of Ephraim, and had bowed [down] a little into
the house of Micah, (And he went out of the city of
Bethlehem, and would be a visitor, wherever he found it
profitable for himself. And when he had made a journey,
and had come to the hill country of Ephraim, and had
rested a little at Micah's house,)
9 Micah asked him, From whence comest thou?
Which answered, I am a deacon of Bethlehem of Judah,
and I go, that I dwell where I may, and *where* I see that it
is profitable to me. (Micah asked him, Where comest
thou from? And he answered, I am a Levite of Bethlehem
in Judah, and I go, so that I can live where I may, and
where I see that it is profitable for me.)
10 And Micah said, Dwell thou with me, and be thou
to me a father and priest; and I shall give to thee by each
year ten pieces of silver, and a double clothing, and those
things that be necessary to lifelode. [And] He assented,
(And Micah said, Stay thou with me, and be thou a father
and a priest to me; and each year I shall give thee ten
pieces of silver, and thy clothes, and thy food, *or*

sustenance. And he agreed,)
11 and dwelled with that man; and he was to that man
as one of his sons. (and lived with that man; and he was
like one of his sons to that man.)
12 And Micah filled his hand (And Micah consecrated,
or dedicated, him), and he had the young man (become
his) priest, (and abide) with him,
13 and he said, Now I know, that God shall do well to
me, having a priest of the kin of Levi. (and he said, Now I
know that God shall make things go well for me, for I
have my own priest of the tribe of Levi.)

CHAPTER 18

1 In those days was no king in Israel; and the lineage
of Dan sought (a) possession to itself, to dwell therein; for
till to that day it had not taken heritage among other
lineages. (In those days there was no king in Israel; and
the tribe of Dan sought a possession for themselves to
live in; for unto that day they had not taken their
inheritance among the other tribes.)
2 Therefore the sons of Dan sent five (of) the strongest
men of their generation, and family, from Zorah and
Eshtaol, that they should espy the land, and behold
diligently (so that they could spy out the land, and
carefully look it over). And they said to them, Go ye, and
behold the land. And when they going forth had come
into the hill (country) of Ephraim, and had entered into
the house of Micah, they rested there.
3 And they knew the voice of the young waxing
deacon; and they rested in his place, and said to him,
Who brought thee hither? What doest thou here? For
what cause wouldest thou come hither? (And they knew
the voice of the young Levite; and they rested there
before him, and said to him, Who hath brought thee
here? What doest thou here? For what reason wouldest
thou come here?)
4 The which answered, Micah hath given to me these
things and these, and he hath hired me for meed, that I
be priest to him. (And he answered, Micah hath given
these things, and other things to me, and he hath hired
me for money, to be his priest.)
5 And they prayed him, that he should counsel with
the Lord, and that they might know (so that they could
know), whether they went in the way of prosperity, and
that the thing *of their purpose* should have effect.
6 Which answered to them, Go ye with peace, the
Lord beholdeth your way, and the journey whither ye go.
(And he answered to them, Go ye in peace, the Lord
watcheth over your way, and the journey on which ye
go/and where ye go on the journey.)
7 Then those five men went forth, and came to Laish;
and they saw the people dwelling therein without any
dread, by the custom of Sidonians, secure and restful, for
no man utterly against-stood them, and they were full
rich, and *dwelled* far from Sidon, and were parted from
all men. (Then those five men went forth, and came to
Laish; and they saw the people living there without any
fear, by the custom of the Sidonians, secure and at rest,
for there was utterly no one who stood against them, and
they were very rich, and *lived* far away from Sidon, and
were separated from all people.)
8 And they turned again to their brethren in Zorah and
Eshtaol; and they answered *to (their) brethren,* asking
what they had done, (And they returned to their kinsmen
in Zorah and Eshtaol; and they answered *to their
kinsmen,* who were asking what they had done,)
9 and said, Rise ye, and go we up to them *of Laish,* for
we have seen the land full rich and plenteous; do not ye
be negligent, do not ye cease, (but) go we forth, and have
we it into possession (and let us take the land);
10 no travail shall be *to us*; we shall enter to secure
men, into a full large country; and the Lord shall betake
to us a place, wherein is not poverty of anything of those
things that be brought forth in (all) [the] earth. (it shall not
be any great effort *for us*; for we shall go to a people who
be very complacent and naive, and into a very large
country; and the Lord shall deliver a place to us, where
nothing is lacking of anything, of that which be brought
forth in all the earth.)
11 Therefore six hundred men girded with armours of
battle went forth of the kindred of Dan, that is, from
Zorah and Eshtaol. (And so six hundred men of the
Danites, girded with arms, *or with weapons,* for battle,
went forth from Zorah and Eshtaol.)
12 And they went up, and dwelled in Kiriathjearim of
Judah, the which place took from that time the name of
[the] Tents of Dan (the which place from that time took
the name of Mahanehdan), and it is behind the back of
Kiriathjearim.
13 From thence they passed into the hill (country) of
Ephraim; and when they had come to the house of
Micah,
14 the five men, that were sent before to behold the
land of Laish, said to their other brethren, Know ye, that
ephod, and teraphim, and a graven image, and a molten
image is in (one of) these houses; see ye what pleaseth
you. (the five men, who were sent before to spy out the
land of Laish, said to their other kinsmen, Know ye, that
an ephod, and teraphim, and a carved idol, and a cast
image be in one of these houses? see ye what pleaseth
you.)
15 And when they had bowed a little *aside,* they
entered into the house of the young deacon, that was in
the house of Micah (they entered into the young Levite's
home, that is, into Micah's house), and they greeted him
with peaceable words.
16 And six hundred men stood before the door, so as
they were armed. (And the six hundred armed men stood

outside, in front of the door.)
17 And they, that entered into the house of the young
man, enforced to take away the graven image, and the
ephod, and teraphim, and the molten image; and the
priest stood before the door, while six hundred full strong
(armed) men abode not far (from) *thence.* (And they, who
had entered into the young man's home, that is, into
Micah's house, endeavoured to take away the carved
idol, and the ephod, and the teraphim, and the cast
image; and the priest stood outside the door, with the six
hundred very strong armed men, who waited not far from
there.)
18 Therefore they that entered took the graven image,
ephod, and idols, and the molten image; to whom the
priest said, What do ye? (And so they who entered took
the carved idol, and the ephod, and the teraphim, *or the
other idols*, and the cast image; and the priest said to
them, What be ye doing?)
19 To whom they answered, Be thou still, and put thy
finger on thy mouth, and come with us, that we have
thee (for a) father and (a) priest. What is better to thee,
that thou be priest in the house of one man, either (a
priest) in a lineage and (a) family of Israel? (What is better
for thee, that thou be a priest in the house of one man, or
a priest in a tribe and a family of Israel?)
20 And when he had heard this, he assented to their
words, and he took the ephod, and idols, and the graven
image, and went forth with them. (And when he had
heard this, he agreed with what they said, and he himself
took hold of the ephod, and the carved idol, and the
teraphim, and the cast image, and went away with them.)
21 And when they went forth, and had made their little
children, and their work beasts, and all thing that was
precious, to go before them; (And so they all went forth,
and made their little children, and their work beasts, and
all the things that were precious to them, to go before
them;)
22 and when they were now far from the house of
Micah, [the] men that dwelled in the houses of Micah
cried together, and followed (after them), (and when they
had gone some distance from Micah's house, Micah
gathered together the men who lived in the houses
nearby; and they followed after the Danites,)
23 and began to cry after the back(s) (of them). Which
when they had beheld, [they] said to Micah, What wilt
thou to thee? why criest thou? (and shouted at them
behind their backs. And when the Danites had seen
them, they said to Micah, What is the matter with thee?
why shoutest thou at us?)
24 Which answered, Ye have taken away my gods,
which I made to me, and the priest, and what dwelleth
over? and ye say, What is (it) to thee? (And Micah
answered, Ye have taken away my gods, which I had
made for me, and my priest, and now what do I have left?
and ye say, What is the matter with thee?)
25 And the sons of Dan said to him, Beware, lest thou
speak [any] more to us, and men stirred in soul come to
thee, and thou perish with all thine house.
26 And so (the sons of) Dan went forth in the journey
begun. And Micah saw, that they were stronger than he,
and [he] turned again into his house (and so he returned
to his house, *along with all of his neighbours*).
27 Forsooth six hundred men took the priest, and the
things which we before-said, and came into Laish to the
people resting and secure; and they smited them by the
sharpness of sword, and betook the city to burning, (And
the six hundred men took the priest, and all the things
which we spoke of, and came into Laish to the people
there, who were secure and at rest, *yea, without a care in
the world*; and they struck them down with their sharp
swords, and burned down the city,)
28 while no man utterly gave help (*to them*), for they
dwelled far from Sidon, and had not anything of
fellowship and cause with any men. And the city was set
in the country(side) of Bethrehob; the which city Dan
builded again, and dwelled therein; (while utterly no one
gave *them* any help, for they lived far from Sidon, and
the city was set in the countryside of Bethrehob, and they
had nothing of fellowship, or dealings, with anyone. And
then the Danites rebuilt the city, and lived there;)
29 and the name of the city was called Dan, by the
name of their father (after the name of their father), whom
Israel had begat, the which city was called Laish before.
30 And Dan setted there the graven image (And the
Danites set up Micah's idol), and Jonathan, the son of
Gershom, [the] son of Moses, and Jonathan's sons, (*were*)
the priests, in the lineage of Dan, till into the day of their
captivity.
31 And the idol of Micah dwelled with them, in all
[the] time that the house of God was in Shiloh. (And
Micah's idol stayed with them, all the time that the
House of God was in Shiloh.)

CHAPTER 19

1 In those days was no king in Israel. A man was a
deacon, dwelling in the side of the hill of Ephraim, the
which took a (secondary) wife of Bethlehem of Judah. (In
those days there was no king in Israel. And there was a
man who was a Levite, living far back, *or deep*, in the hill
country of Ephraim, who took a secondary wife, *or a
concubine*, of Bethlehem in Judah.)
2 And she did fornication on him, and turned again
into the house of her father in Bethlehem, and she
dwelled at him four months. (And she did fornication
against him/And she was angry with him, and returned to
her father's house in Bethlehem, and she stayed with him
for four months.)
3 And her husband followed her, and he would be

reconciled to her, and to speak fair *with her*, and to lead
her again with him; and he had in *his* company a servant,
and twain asses (And then her husband came to her, to
be reconciled with her, and to speak kindly *to her*, and to
bring *her* home again with him; and he had in *his*
company a servant, and two donkeys). And she received
him, and brought him into her father's house; and when
his wife's father had heard this, and saw him, he ran
gladly to him, and embraced the man.
4 And the husband of the daughter dwelled in the
house of his wife's father (for) three days, and ate and
drank at home with him.
5 And the fourth day, the deacon rose by night, and
would have gone forth; whom his wife's father held, and
said to him, Taste thou first a little bread, and comfort thy
stomach, and so thou shalt go forth. (And on the fourth
day, the Levite rose early, and desired to go home; but
his wife's father took hold of him, and said to him, Eat
thou first a little bread, and comfort thy stomach, and
then thou shalt go forth.)
6 And they sat together, and ate, and drank. And the
father of the damsel said to his daughter's husband, I
beseech thee, that thou dwell here today (I beseech thee,
that thou stay here today), and that we be glad together.
7 And he rose, and began to desire to go; and
nevertheless, his wife's father held him again meekly, and
made him to dwell with him. (And the Levite rose up,
and desired to go; but his wife's father meekly held onto
him again, and made him stay there with him.)
8 And when the morrowtide was made, the deacon
made him(self) ready to go (on) his way; to whom his
wife's father said again, I beseech thee, that thou take a
little meat, and make thee strong till the day increase, and
afterward go thou forth. Then they ate together (And so
they ate together again).
9 And the young man rose to go forth with his wife,
and with the servant; to whom the father of his wife
spake again, Behold thou, that the day is far forth gone
toward the [sun] going down, and it nigheth to the
eventide; dwell thou with me also today, and lead thou
with me a glad day, and tomorrow thou shalt go forth,
that thou go into thine house. (And then the young man
rose up to go forth with his concubine, and with his
servant; but his wife's father spoke to him again, and
said, See thou, that the day hath gone far toward the sun
going down, and it nigheth to the evening; stay thou here
with me also this night, and have thou a happy evening
with me, and tomorrow thou shalt go forth, and go to thy
house.)
10 (But) The daughter's husband would not assent to
his words; but he went forth at once, and came (over)
against Jebus, which by another name is called Jerusalem;
and he led with him two asses charged, and his
[secondary] wife (and he went with his two laden
donkeys, and his concubine, *and his servant*).
11 And now they were beside Jebus, and the day was
changed into night. And the servant said to his lord,
Come thou, I beseech *thee*, bow we [down] to the city of
Jebus, and dwell we therein (let us turn in to the city of
Jebus, and stay we there).
12 To whom his lord answered, I shall not enter into
the city of an alien folk, which is not of the sons of Israel,
but I shall pass forth into Gibeah; (To whom his lord
answered, I shall not go into the city of a foreign people,
who be not Israelites, but I shall go forth to Gibeah;)
13 and when I shall come thither, we shall dwell
therein, or else in the city of Ramah.
14 Therefore they passed Jebus, and took the way
begun. And the sun went down to them beside Gibeah,
which is in the lineage of Benjamin (And the sun went
down on them when they reached Gibeah, which is in
the tribe of Benjamin);
15 and (so) they turned (in) to Gibeah, that they would
dwell there. Whither when they had entered, they sat in
the street of the city, and no man would receive them to
harbour (but no one would give them any lodging).
16 And lo! an eld man turned again from the field, and
from his work in the eventide, and appeared to them,
which also himself was of the hill of Ephraim, and he
dwelled a pilgrim in Gibeah. And men of that country
were of the sons of Benjamin. (And lo! an old man
returned from the field, from his work in the evening, and
appeared before them, and he was also from the hill
country of Ephraim, but now he lived in Gibeah. But men
of that place were Benjaminites.)
17 And when the eld man raised up his eyes, he saw a
man sitting with his fardels in the street of the city; and
he said to him, From whence comest thou? and whither
goest thou?
18 Which answered to him, We went forth from
Bethlehem of Judah, and we go to our place, which is in
the side of the hill of Ephraim (which is deep in the hill
country of Ephraim), from whence we went (out) to
Bethlehem; and now we go to the house of God, and no
man will receive us under his roof,
19 and we have provender and hay into meat of *our*
asses, and bread and wine into mine uses, and of thine
handmaid, and of the servant which is with me; we have
no need to anything, but to harbour. (and we have
provender and hay for food for *our* donkeys, and bread
and wine for my use, and for my concubine, and for the
servant who is with me; yea, we have no need of
anything, except lodging.)
20 To whom the eld man answered, Peace be with
thee; I shall give (thee) all things, that be needful; only, I
beseech, dwell thou not in the street (only, I beseech
thee, do not thou stay in the street).
21 And he brought him into his house, and gave meat

to the asses; and after that they washed their feet, he
received them into feast. (And he brought them into his
house, and gave him food for the donkeys; and after that
they had washed their feet, he gave them dinner.)
22 (And) While they ate, and refreshed their bodies
with meat and drink after the travail of their way, men of
that city came, the sons of Belial, *that is, (them) without
(a) yoke*, and they compassed the old man's house (and
they surrounded the old man's house), and began to
knock on the doors; and they cried to the lord of the
house, and said, Lead out the man that entered into thine
house, (so) that we (can) misuse him.
23 And the eld man went out to them, and said, Do not
ye, brethren, do not ye do this evil; for the man hath
entered into mine harbour (for the man hath only entered
into my house for lodging); and cease ye of this folly.
24 I have a *daughter* virgin, and this man hath a
[secondary] wife; and I shall bring out them to you, that
ye make low them, and fulfill your lust (I have a daughter
who is a virgin, and this man hath a concubine; and I
shall bring them out to you, so that ye can make them
low, and fulfill your lust); only, I beseech you, that ye
work not this cursedness against kind with this man.
25 (But) They would not assent to his words; the which
thing the man seeing, he led out his [secondary] wife to
them, and he betook to them her to be defouled. And
when they had misused her all night, they let go her in
the morrowtide. (But they would not assent to his words;
and the Levite seeing that, he brought out his concubine
to them, and he gave her over to them to be defiled. And
when they had misused her all that night, they let her go
in the morning.)
26 And when the darknesses *of night* departed, the
woman came to the door of the house, where her lord
dwelled, and there she felled down.
27 And when the morrowtide was made, the man
(a)rose, and opened the door, for to go forth (on) his
journey; and lo! his [secondary] wife lay at the door, her
hands spread abroad in the threshold (and lo! his
concubine lay at the door, with her hands spread abroad
on the threshold).
28 And he guessed her to rest (there), and spake to her,
(and said,) Rise thou, and go we. And when she
answered nothing, he understood that she was dead; and
he took her, and put on the ass, and turned again into his
house (and he took her, and put her on the donkey, and
returned to his house).
29 And when he entered into that house, he took a
sword, and parted into twelve parts and gobbets, the
dead body of the (secondary) wife, (together) [with her
bones,] and sent (them) into all the terms of Israel. (And
when he had entered into his house, he took a sword, *or
a knife*, and cut the flesh and bones of the dead body of
his concubine into twelve parts, *or pieces*, and then he
sent them into all the corners of Israel.)
30 And when all men had heard this, they cried, Never
such a thing was done in Israel (And when all the people
had heard of this, they cried, Such a thing was never
done in Israel), from that day in which our fathers
ascended from Egypt, till into [the] present time; say ye
(the) sentence, and deem ye in common, what is needed
to be done (to avenge this horrible deed).

CHAPTER 20

1 Therefore all the sons of Israel went [out], and were
gathered together as one man, from Dan till to
Beersheba, and (also) from the land of Gilead, to the Lord
in Mizpeh (before the Lord at Mizpeh);
2 and all the corners of peoples, and all the lineages of
Israel, came together into the church of the people of God,
four hundred thousand of footmen fighters. (and all the
chief men of the people, of all the tribes of Israel, came
together to a gathering of the people of God, yea, to four
hundred thousand footmen who were ready to fight.)
3 And it was not hid from the sons of Benjamin, that
the sons of Israel had gone up into Mizpeh.
4 And the deacon, [the] husband of the (secondary)
wife *that was* slain, was asked, how so great felony was
done; and he answered, I came with my (secondary) wife
into Gibeah of Benjamin, and I turned thither. (And the
Levite, the husband of the concubine *who was* murdered,
was asked, How was this great felony done? and he
answered, I came with my concubine to Gibeah in
Benjamin, and I turned in there.)
5 And lo! [the] men of that city compassed in the night
the house, in which I dwelled (And lo! the men of that
city surrounded the house where I stayed that night), and
they would slay me, and they travailed my (secondary)
wife with unbelieveful madness of lechery; and at the last
she was dead.
6 And I took, and cut her into gobbets (And I took her,
and I cut her into pieces), and I sent those parts of her
into all the terms of your possession; for so great (a)
felony and so grievous (a) sin/and so great (a) sin was
never done in Israel.
7 *Now* all ye sons of Israel (who) be present; deem ye,
what ye ought to do.
8 And all the people stood, and answered as by the
word of one man, (and said,) We shall not go hence into
our tabernacles (We shall not go back to our tents),
neither any of us shall enter into his house;
9 but we shall do this thing in common against
Gibeah.
10 Ten men be chosen of an hundred, of all the
lineages of Israel, and an hundred of a thousand, and a
thousand of ten thousand, that they bear meats to the
host, and that we, fighting against Gibeah of Benjamin,
may yield to it for the trespass that that it deserveth. (Let

ten men be chosen out of a hundred, out of all the tribes
of Israel, and a hundred out of a thousand, and a
thousand out of ten thousand, to carry food for the army,
and the rest of us, fighting against Gibeah in Benjamin,
yield to them what they deserve for this trespass.)
11 And (so) all the people, as one man, came together
to the city (came together against the city *of Gibeah*), by
the same thought and (of) one counsel.
12 And (the sons of) Israel sent messengers to all the
lineage of Benjamin, and they said, Why so great felony
is found in you? (And the Israelites sent messengers to all
the tribe of Benjamin, and they said, Why is so great a
felony found among you?)
13 Betake ye the men of Gibeah, that did this
wickedness, that they die, and evil be done away from
Israel. Which would not hear the commandment of their
brethren, the sons of Israel, (Deliver ye *unto us* the men
of Gibeah, who did this wickedness, so that they can die,
and that this evil be done away from Israel. But they
would not listen to the command of their kinsmen, the
Israelites,)
14 but men of all the cities, that were of the part of
Benjamin, came together into Gibeah, to help them, and
to fight against all the people of Israel.
15 And twenty-six thousand were found of Benjamin,
of men drawing out sword, besides the dwellers of
Gibeah, which were seven hundred strongest men, (And
there were twenty-six thousand Benjaminites, men
drawing out the sword, besides the inhabitants of
Gibeah, who were seven hundred of the strongest men,)
16 fighting so with the left hand as with the right hand,
and casting so stones with slings at a certain thing, that
they might smite also an hair, and the stroke of the stone
should not be borne [away] into the tother part. (fighting
with their left hand like with their right hand, and
throwing stones with slings with such certainty, that they
could strike a hair, and yet the stroke of the stone would
never be borne aside into some other place.)
17 Also of the men of Israel, without the sons of
Benjamin, were found four hundred thousand drawing
out sword, and ready to battle. (And the Israelites,
without the Benjaminites, were four hundred thousand
men drawing out swords, and ready for battle.)
18 Which rose, and came into the house of God, that is
in Shiloh; and they counselled with God, and said, Who
shall be prince in our host of the battle against the sons of
Benjamin? To whom the Lord answered, Judah be your
duke. (And they rose up, and came into the House of
God, that was in Bethel; and they counselled with God,
and said, Who should be the leader of our army in the
battle against the Benjaminites? To whom the Lord
answered, Judah should be your leader.)
19 And anon the sons of Israel rose early, and setted
tents against Gibeah. (And so early in the morning the
Israelites rose up, and then pitched their tents opposite
Gibeah.)
20 And from thence they went out to battle against
Benjamin, and Israel began to fight against Gibeah.
21 And the sons of Benjamin went out of Gibeah, and
killed of the sons of Israel in that day two and twenty
thousand men.
22 And again (the next day,) the sons of Israel trusted in
their own strength, and in (the) number of (their) people,
and they dressed [the] battle array, in the same place in
which they (had) fought before;
23 so nevertheless that they went up before *to the
house (of God)*, and they wept before the Lord unto [the]
night, and they counselled with him, and said, Shall I go
forth more to fight against the sons of Benjamin, my
brethren, either nay? To whom he answered, Ascend ye
to them, and begin ye the battle. (for they had gone up
the evening before *to the House of God*, and they had
wept before the Lord into the night, and had counselled
with him, and had said, Should we go forth again to fight
against our kinsmen, the Benjaminites, or not? To whom
he answered, Go ye up to them, and make ye the battle.)
24 And (so) when the sons of Israel had gone forth to
battle in the tother day against Benjamin,
25 the sons of Benjamin brake out from the gates of
Gibeah, and came to (the sons of) Israel; *and the sons of
Benjamin* were wild against Israel by so fierce slaying
(*and the Benjaminites* were so wild against the Israelites
with such fierce slaughter), that they threw down
eighteen thousand men of Israel drawing out (the) sword.
26 Wherefore all the sons of Israel came (again) into the
house of God, and they sat, and wept before the Lord,
and they fasted in that day unto the eventide; and they
offered to the Lord burnt sacrifices, and peaceable
sacrifices (and they offered to the Lord burnt sacrifices,
and peace offerings),
27 and they asked *the Lord* of their state. In that time,
the ark of the bond of peace of God was there (For at that
time, the Ark of the Covenant of the Lord was there);
28 and Phinehas, the son of Eleazar, the son of Aaron,
was sovereign of the *Lord's* house. Then they counselled
(with) the Lord, and said, Shall we go out more to battle
against the sons of Benjamin, our brethren, either shall
we rest? To whom the Lord said, Go ye up against them,
for tomorrow I shall betake (the sons of) Benjamin into
your hands. (and Phinehas, the son of Eleazar, the son of
Aaron, was the ruler of the *Lord's* House. And again they
counselled with the Lord, and said, Should we go out
again to do more battle against our kinsmen the
Benjaminites, or should we cease? To whom the Lord
said, Go ye up against them, for tomorrow I shall deliver
the Benjaminites into your hands.)
29 And the sons of Israel setted ambushments by
compass of the city of Gibeah; (And so the Israelites set

men in ambush all around the city of Gibeah;)
30 and the third time, as once and twice before, they
brought forth the host against (the sons of) Benjamin.
31 But also then the sons of Benjamin brake out from
the city boldly, and they pursued further the adversaries
fleeing, so that they wounded of Israel, as they did in the
first day, and the second, and they killed by two paths
Israel turning (their) backs; of the which paths one was
straight out into Bethel, and the tother into Gibeah. And
Benjamin threw down about thirty men *of Israel*; (And
then the Benjaminites broke out boldly from the city, and
again they pursued their adversaries, and made them to
flee; and they struck the Israelites, like they did on the
first day, and on the second; and on two paths they killed
the Israelites who had turned their backs to them; of the
which paths one went straight out to Bethel, and the
other into Gibeah. And so the Benjaminites threw down
about thirty more men *of Israel*;)
32 for they guessed to destroy *Israel* as they did before;
and by craft, Israel took counsel, feigning them to flee
(but the Israelites had taken counsel, and by a carefully
thought-out plan, feigned themselves to flee), (so) that
they should draw (away the sons of) Benjamin from the
city, and that they as fleeing should bring forth (the sons
of) Benjamin to the foresaid paths.
33 Therefore all the sons of Israel rose (up out) of their
seats, and setted battle array in the place which is called
Baaltamar. And the ambushments, that were about the
city, began to open themselves little and little, and to go
forth from the west part of the city. (And so all the
Israelites rose up out of their places, and made the battle
array in the place which is called Baaltamar. And the
men in ambush, who were all around the city, began to
open themselves up little by little, and to go forth from
the west part of the city.)
34 But also other ten thousand of men of all Israel
excited the dwellers of the city to battles; and the battle
was made grievous against the sons of Benjamin, and
they understood not, that perishing nighed to them on
each part. (And another ten thousand Israelites attacked
the inhabitants of the city; and the battle was made
grievous, *or very hard*, against the Benjaminites, and they
did not understand, that death nighed to them on every
side.)
35 And the Lord smote Benjamin in the sight of the
sons of Israel, and Israel killed of them in that day five
and twenty thousand and an hundred men, and all these
were warriors and men drawing out sword. (And the Lord
struck down the Benjaminites before the Israelites, and
on that day the Israelites killed twenty-five thousand and
a hundred men of them, and they were all warriors and
men drawing out the sword.)
36 Soothly the sons of Benjamin began to flee, when
they saw, that they were the lower. And the sons of
Israel saw this, and gave to them place to flee, that they
should come to the ambushments made ready, which
they had set beside the city. (And the Benjaminites began
to flee, when they saw, that they were losing. And the
Israelites saw this, and gave them a place to which to flee,
so that they would come to the men who were waiting in
ambush, that they had positioned outside the city.)
37 And when these ambushments had risen up
suddenly from [the] hid places, and Benjamin gave (their)
backs to the slayers, they entered into the city, and they
smote it by sharpness of sword. (And when those set in
ambush had suddenly risen up from their hiding places,
and the Benjaminites had given their backs to the killers,
the Israelites entered into the city, and struck down the
people with their sharp swords.)
38 Soothly the sons of Israel had given a sign to them
which they had set in ambushments, that after that they
had taken the city, they should kindle (a) fire, and that by
smoke ascending on high, they should show the city (to
be) taken. (And the Israelites had arranged a sign, *or a
signal*, from those whom they had set in ambush, which
was that after they had taken the city, they would kindle a
fire, and that by the smoke going up on high, they would
show that the city had been taken.)
39 And when the sons of Israel set in that battle saw
this; for the sons of Benjamin guessed them to flee, and
they followed busilier, when thirty men of their host were
slain; (And so the Israelites set in the battle saw this; but
the Benjaminites guessed them to flee, and they followed
them more busily, for they had already killed thirty
Israelites;)
40 and they saw as a pillar of smoke go up from the
city. And also Benjamin beholding behind, when he saw
his city taken, and the flames be borne on high, (yea, the
Israelites saw the pillar of smoke go up from the city.
And then the Benjaminites looking behind, also saw that
their city had been taken, and the flames of it to be borne
up on high.)
41 they that feigned to flee before, turned their face to
Benjamin, and more strongly withstood him. And when
the sons of Benjamin had seen this thing, (And then they
who had feigned to flee before, now turned their faces to
the Benjaminites/now turned to face the Benjaminites,
and strongly stood against them. And when the
Benjaminites had seen this,)
42 they were turned into flight, and they began to go to
the way of desert; while also adversaries pursued them
there; but also they, that had burnt the city, came against
them. (they turned to flight, *yea, to run away*, and they
started on the way to the wilderness; but their adversaries
pursued them there; and then also they, who had burned
down the city, came out against them.)
43 And so it was done, that Benjamin was slain of
enemies on each part, neither there was any rest of men

dying; and they felled, and were cast down at the east
coast of the city of Gibeah. (And so it was done, that the
Benjaminites were killed by their enemies on every side,
nor was there any ceasing of men dying; and they fell,
and were thrown down on the east side of the city of
Gibeah.)
44 Forsooth they (of Benjamin), that were slain in the
same place, were eighteen thousand of men, all strongest
fighters. (And the Benjaminites, who were killed at that
place, were eighteen thousand, very strong fighting men.)
45 And when they that (were) left *alive* of Benjamin
had seen this, they fled into (the) wilderness, and they
went to the stone, whose name is Rimmon (and they
went to the Rock of Rimmon). And in that flight *the sons
of Israel* went openly *after (them),* into diverse places
(unto Gidom), and they killed of them five thousand men;
and when (the sons of) Benjamin fled further, they
pursued them, and killed also of them (an)other two
thousand men.
46 And so it was done, that all that felled down of (the
sons of) Benjamin in diverse places, were five and twenty
thousand, fighters most ready to battles. (And so it was
done, that all of the Benjaminites who fell down in
diverse places that day, were twenty-five thousand
fighting men, all ready for battle.)
47 And so six hundred men (were) left of all the
number of Benjamin, that might escape, and flee into
wilderness; and they sat in the stone of Rimmon four
months. (And so only six hundred men escaped, and
were left *alive*, of all the number of Benjamin, and they
fled into the wilderness; and they sat at the Rock of
Rimmon for four months.)
48 And the sons of Israel went out, and they smote with
sword all the remnants of the city, from men unto work
beasts; and (then) devouring flame wasted all the cities
and (the) towns of Benjamin.

CHAPTER 21

1 Also the sons of Israel had sworn in Mizpeh, and
said, None of us shall give to the sons of Benjamin a wife
of his daughters. (At Mizpeh the Israelites had sworn, and
said, None of us shall give any of his daughters for a wife
to the Benjaminites.)
2 And all came to the house of God in Shiloh, and they
sat in the sight of him till to eventide, and they raised their
voice, and began to weep with great yelling, (And now
when they all came to Bethel in the presence of God,
they sat before him until the evening, and they raised up
their voices, and began to weep with great yelling,)
3 and said, Lord God of Israel, why is this evil done in
thy people, that today one lineage be taken away of us?
(and they said, Lord God of Israel, why is this evil done
among thy people, that today one tribe was taken away
from us?)
4 Soothly in the tother day they rised early, and
builded an altar, and offered there burnt sacrifices and
peaceable sacrifices, (And the next day they rose up
early, and built an altar there, and offered burnt
sacrifices, and peace offerings,)
5 and said, Who of all the lineages of Israel went not
up into the host of the Lord? For when they were in
Mizpeh, they had bound themselves with a full great
oath, that they that failed (to go up) *thence* should be
(made) dead. (and they said, Who out of all the tribes of
Israel did not go up to the gathering unto the Lord? For
when they were in Mizpeh, they had bound themselves
with a very great, *or a very solemn*, oath, that anyone
who failed to go up *there* should be put to death.)
6 And the sons of Israel were led by penance on their
brother Benjamin, and began to say, One lineage of Israel
is taken away; (And the Israelites felt great remorse, *or
regret*, over their kinsmen the Benjaminites, and said
again, Today one of Israel's tribes was taken from us;)
7 whereof shall they take wives? certainly all we have
sworn in common, that we shall not give our daughters
to them. (where shall they get wives? for we have all
sworn in common, that we shall not give any of our
daughters to them.)
8 Then they said, Who is it of all the lineages of Israel,
that went not up to the Lord in Mizpeh? And lo! the
dwellers of Jabesh of Gilead were found, that they were
not in that host. (And again they said, Who is it out of all
of Israel's tribes, who did not go up unto the Lord at
Mizpeh? And lo! the inhabitants of Jabesh of Gilead were
found, that they had not been in that gathering.)
9 Also in that time, when they were in Shiloh, none of
them was found there. (And there at Bethel, when the
men were numbered, *or were listed*, none of the sons of
Jabesh of Gilead was found to be there.)
10 Therefore they sent ten thousand (of the) strongest
men, and commanded to them, Go ye, and smite the
dwellers of Jabesh of Gilead by the sharpness of sword,
as well the wives as the little children of them. (And so
they sent twelve thousand of their strongest men, and
commanded to them, Go ye, and strike down the people
of Jabesh of Gilead with thy sharp swords, and their
wives as well as their little children.)
11 And this thing shall be to you, that ye shall keep;
slay ye all of male kind, and the women that have known
men fleshly; reserve ye the virgins/but keep ye the
maidens. (And this word shall be to you, that ye shall
obey; kill ye all the males, and the women who have
fleshly known men; but reserve ye the virgins/but keep ye
the maidens.)
12 And four hundred virgins, that knew not the bed of
(a) man, were found (among the people) of Jabesh of
Gilead; and they brought them to the tents in Shiloh, into
the land of Canaan.

13 And Israel sent messengers to the sons of Benjamin,
that were in the stone of Rimmon; and they commanded
to them, that they should receive those women in peace.
(And then the Israelites sent messengers to the
Benjaminites, who were at the Rock of Rimmon; and they
agreed to make peace.)
14 And the sons of Benjamin came (back) in that time,
and the daughters of Jabesh of Gilead were given to them
to wives; for they found none other women, which they
should give *to them* in like manner. (And then the
Benjaminites came back, and the daughters of Jabesh of
Gilead were given to them for wives; but they found no
other women, whom they could give *to them* in like
manner.)
15 And all Israel sorrowed greatly, and did penance on
the slaying of one lineage of Israel. (And all Israel greatly
sorrowed, and had great remorse, *or regret*, over the
killing of one of the tribes of Israel.)
16 And the greater men in birth said, What shall we do
to the other men, that have not taken wives? All the
women in the lineage of Benjamin have fallen down,
(And the men of great age, *that is, the elders*, said, What
shall we do for the other men who have not received
wives? For all the women in the tribe of Benjamin have
been killed,)
17 and it is to us to purvey with great care and great
study, that one lineage be not done away from Israel.
(and it is for us to find a way, so that one tribe be not
done away from Israel.)
18 We may not give our daughters to them, for we be
bound with an oath and cursing, by which we said, Be he
cursed that giveth of his daughters (for) a wife to
Benjamin.
19 And they took counsel, and said, Lo! the solemnity
of the Lord is in Shiloh, (after) the year's turning about,
that is set at the north coast of the city of Bethel, and at
the east coast of the way that goeth from Bethel to
Shechem, and at the south of the city of Lebonah. (And
they took counsel, and said, Lo! the Feast of the Lord
shall soon be in Shiloh, after the year's turning about,
yea, that *city* which is north of the city of Bethel, and to
the east on the way that goeth from Bethel to Shechem,
and to the south of the city of Lebonah.)
20 And they commanded to the sons of Benjamin, and
said, Go ye, and be ye hid in [the] vineries; (And they
commanded to the Benjaminites, and said, Go ye, and be
ye hid there in the vineyards;)
21 and when ye see [the] daughters of Shiloh go forth
by custom to lead dances, go ye out of the vineries
suddenly, and ravish ye them, each man one wife, and
go ye into the land of Benjamin. (and when ye see the
daughters of Shiloh come out to dance, quickly go ye out
of the vineyards, and seize ye them, each man one wife,
and then go ye back to the land of Benjamin.)
22 And when the fathers and brethren of them shall
come, and begin to complain and plead against you, we
shall say to them, Have ye mercy of them; for we took
not from a man his wife in battle, neither ye gave (them)
to them, (so) why ye shall be blamed in time. (And when
their fathers and their brothers shall come to you, and
begin to complain and plead against you, ye shall say to
them, Have ye mercy on us; for we did not take a wife
from any man in battle, nor did ye give them to us, and
so ye shall not be blamed for breaking the oath.)
23 And the sons of Benjamin did as it was commanded
to them, and by their number they ravished wives to
them, each man one wife, of them that led (the) dances.
And they went into their possession, and builded cities,
and dwelled in those. (And the Benjaminites did as it was
commanded to them, and by their number they seized
wives for themselves, each man one wife, out of those
who led the dances. And then they went back to their
possessions, and builded cities, and lived in them.)
24 And the sons of Israel turned again, by their lineages
and families, into their tabernacles. (And the Israelites
returned, by their tribes and families, to their
inheritances, *or their possessions*.)
25 In those days was no king in Israel, but each man
did that thing, that seemed rightful to himself. (In those
days there was no king in Israel, but each person did
what seemed right to himself.) ✡

RUTH

CHAPTER 1

1 In the days of one judge, when judges were
sovereigns *in Israel*, hunger was made in the land; and a
man of Bethlehem of Judah went to be a pilgrim in the
country of Moab, with his wife and [his] two free sons. (In
the days of the judges, when they were the rulers *in
Israel*, there was hunger in the land; and a man of
Bethlehem of Judah went to live in the country of Moab,
with his wife and their two sons.)
2 He was called Elimelech, and his wife (was) Naomi,
and his two sons, the one *was called* Mahlon, and the
tother Chilion, Ephrathites of Bethlehem of Judah; and
they entered into the country of Moab, and they dwelled
there (and they went to the country of Moab, and they
lived there).
3 And Elimelech, the husband of Naomi, died, and
she (was) left with her sons;
4 and they took wives of Moab, of which wives one
was called Orpah, the tother Ruth. And the sons dwelled
there ten years (And the sons lived there for ten years),
5 and both died, that is, Mahlon and Chilion; and the
woman (was) left, and was made bare of her two free
sons, and her husband. (and then both of them died, that
is, Mahlon and Chilion; and so the woman was bereaved
of her two sons, and her husband.)
6 And she rose to go with ever either wife of her sons
into her country from the country of Moab; for she had
heard, that the Lord had beheld his people, and had
given meats to them. (And she rose up to go with the
wives of both of her sons back to her country from the
country of Moab; for she had heard, that the Lord had
looked *kindly* again upon his people, and had given
them food.)
7 And so she went out from the place of her
pilgrimage with ever either wife of her sons; and now
when she was set in the way of turning again into the
land of Judah, (And so she went out from the place where
she lived with the wives of both of her sons; and now
when she was set on the way, returning to the land of
Judah,)
8 she said to them, Go ye (again) into the house of
your mother; the Lord do mercy with you, as ye did with
the dead men, and with me;
9 the Lord give to you to find rest in the houses of
[the] husbands which ye shall take. And she kissed them.
And they began to weep with (a) high voice,
10 and to say, We shall go with thee to thy people.
11 To whom she answered, My daughters, turn ye
again, why come ye with me? I have no more sons in my
womb, that ye may hope husbands of me (To whom she
answered, My daughters, return ye *home*, why come ye
with me? I have no more sons in my womb, that ye may
have any hope of husbands from me;)
12 my daughters of Moab, turn ye again, and go (my
daughters of Moab, return ye, and go *home*); for now I
am made eld, and I am not able to the bond of marriage;
yea, though I might conceive in this night, and bear sons,
13 though ye will abide till they waxed, and [ful]fill the
years of marriage, ye shall sooner be eld women than ye
shall be wedded; I beseech (thee), my daughters, mourn
ye not, for your anguish oppresseth me the more, and the
hand of the Lord is gone out against me.
14 Therefore, when the voice was raised (up), again
they began to weep. And Orpah kissed her mother-in-
law, and turned again, and Ruth abode with her mother-
in-law (And Orpah kissed her mother-in-law, and
returned *home*, but Ruth stayed with her mother-in-law).
15 To whom Naomi said, Lo! thy kinswoman turned
again to her people, and to her gods; go thou with her.
16 And Ruth answered, Be thou not against me, that I
forsake thee, and go away; whither ever thou shalt go, I
shall go, and where thou shalt dwell, I shall dwell
together (with thee); thy people is my people, and thy
God is my God; (And Ruth answered, Be thou not against
me, that I should desert thee, and go away from thee;
wherever thou shalt go, I shall go, and where thou shalt
live, I shall live with thee; thy people is my people, and
thy God is my God;)
17 what land shall receive thee dying, I shall die
therein *also*, and there I shall take place of burying; God
do to me these things, and add these things, if death
alone shall not part me and thee. (whatever land shall
receive thee when thou diest, I shall die there *also*, and
that shall be the place where I am buried; yea, God do to
me terrible things, and add other things as well, if
anything but death separate me and thee.)
18 Therefore Naomi saw, that Ruth had deemed with
steadfast soul to go with her, and she would not be
against her, neither counsel further turning again to her
countrymen (and so she would not be against her, nor
further counsel her to return to *her own people*).
19 And (so) they went forth together, and came into
Bethlehem; and when they entered into the city, swift
fame (a)rose with all men, and women said, This is that
Naomi.
20 To whom she said, Call ye not me Naomi, *that is,
fair*, but call ye me Mara, *that is, bitter*; for Almighty God
hath filled me greatly with bitterness. (To whom she said,
Do not ye call me Naomi, *or Delightful*, *or Pleasant*, but
call ye me Mara, *or Bitter*; for Almighty God hath filled
me with great bitterness.)
21 I went out full, and the Lord led me again void; why

therefore call ye me Naomi, whom the Lord hath made
low, and (whom) Almighty God hath tormented?
22 Therefore Naomi came with Ruth of Moab, the wife
of her son, from the land of her pilgrimage, and turned
again into Bethlehem, when barley was reaped first. (And
so Naomi came with Ruth the Moabite, her son's wife,
from the land where she had lived, and returned to
Bethlehem with her, when the barley was first harvested.)

CHAPTER 2

1 Forsooth (there was) a mighty man and a man of
great riches, Boaz by name, (who) was (a) kinsman of
Elimelech.
2 And Ruth of Moab said to her mother-in-law, If thou
commandest, I shall go into the field, and I shall gather
ears of corn that flee the hands of (the) reapers, wherever
I shall find grace of an husbandman merciful in me
(wherever I shall find favour from a farmer, who is
merciful to me). To whom she answered, Go, my
daughter.
3 Therefore she went, and gathered ears of corn after
the backs of (some) reapers. And it befelled, that Boaz
was (the) lord of that field, (he) that was of the kindred of
Elimelech.
4 And lo! (one day) Boaz came from Bethlehem. And
he said to his reapers, The Lord be with you. And they
answered to him, The Lord bless thee.
5 And Boaz said to the young man that was chief over
the reapers, Who is this damsel?
6 And he answered, This is the woman of Moab, that
came with Naomi from the country of Moab;
7 and she prayed, that she should gather ears of corn
leaving behind, and follow the steps of [the] reapers; and
from the morrowtide till now she standeth in the field,
and soothly neither at a moment she turned again home.
(and she prayed us, that she could gather some ears of
corn that were left behind, and follow the steps of the
reapers; and so from the morning until now she standeth
in the field, and not for a moment hath she purposed to
return home.)
8 And Boaz said to Ruth, Daughter, hear thou; go thou
not into another field to gather, neither go (thou) away
from this place, but be thou joined to my damsels,
9 and follow thou where they reap; for I [have]
commanded to my young men, that no man be dis-
easeful to thee; but also if thou thirstest, go to the fardels,
and drink waters, of which my young men drink (and if
thou thirstest, go and drink from the water jars, which my
young men have filled).
10 And she felled on her face, and worshipped on the
earth; and she said to him, Whereof is this to me, that I
should find grace before thine eyes, that thou wouldest
know me, a strange woman? (And she fell on her face,
and honoured him on the ground; and she said to him,
Whereof is this to me, that I should find favour in thine
eyes, and that thou wouldest acknowledge me, who is
but a stranger?)
11 To whom Boaz answered, All things be told to me,
that thou hast done to thy mother-in-law after the death of
thine husband (All things have been told to me, what
thou hast done for thy mother-in-law after the death of
thy husband), and that thou hast forsaken thy father and
thy mother, and the land that thou were born in, and
thou art come to a people, that thou hast not known
before.
12 The Lord yield to thee for thy work, and receive
thou full meed of the Lord God of Israel, to whom thou
camest, and under whose wings thou fleddest. (May the
Lord reward thee for thy good deeds, yea, may thou
receive thy full reward from the Lord God of Israel, to
whom thou hast come, and under whose wings thou hast
fled.)
13 And she said, My lord, I have found grace before
thine eyes, and thou hast comforted me, and thou hast
spoken to the heart of thine handmaid, which am not like
one of thine handmaids. (And she said, My lord, for I
have found favour in thine eyes, and thou hast spoken to
the heart of thy servantess, though I am not equal to one
of thy servantesses, yea, thou hast greatly comforted me.)
14 And Boaz said to her, When the hour of eating is,
come thou hither, and eat bread, and wet thy morsel in
vinegar. Therefore she sat at the side of [the] reapers; and
he directed to her pottage, and she ate, and was filled;
and she took the remnants. (And Boaz said to her, When
it is time to eat, come thou here, and eat bread, and wet
thy morsel in the vinegar. And so she sat beside the
reapers; and Boaz passed her some roasted grain, and she
ate, and was fulfilled; and she took up the remnants.)
15 And she rose from thence to gather the ears of corn,
by custom. And Boaz commanded to his young men, and
said, Also if she will reap with you, forbid ye not her,
(And then she rose up from there to gather the ears of
corn again, as was her custom. And Boaz commanded to
his young men, and said, Yea, if she will reap with you,
forbid ye her not,)
16 and also cast ye forth to her handfuls of purpose
(and also throw ye forth to her some handfuls on
purpose), and suffer ye those to abide, that she gather
those without shame; and no man reprove her gathering
them.
17 Therefore she gathered in the field till to eventide;
and she beat with a rod, and shook out those things that
she had gathered; and she found of barley as the measure
of (an) ephah (and she found that she had about a bushel
of barley).
18 Which she bare, and turned again into the city, and
showed to her mother-in-law; furthermore she brought
forth, and gave to her the remnants of her meat, with

which meat she was (ful)filled. (Which she carried, and
returned to the city, and showed to her mother-in-law;
and she also brought forth, and gave her the remnants of
her food, with which food she was fulfilled.)
19 And her mother-in-law said to her, Where hast thou
gathered *this* today, and where hast thou done (all) this
work? Blessed be he, that had mercy on thee. And Ruth
told to her mother(-in-law) with whom she (had) wrought;
and she said that the man's name was called Boaz.
20 To whom Naomi answered, Blessed be he of the
Lord, for he [hath] kept also to dead men the same grace,
which he gave to the quick. And again she said, He is our
kinsman. (To whom Naomi answered, May the Lord
bless him; yea, the Lord hath given the same favour to
the living, as to the dead. And she said to Ruth, He is our
kinsman.)
21 And Ruth said, Also he commanded this thing to
me, that so long I should be joined to his reapers, till all
his corns were reaped. (And Ruth said, And he also
commanded this to me, that I should be joined to his
reapers, until all his grain was harvested.)
22 To whom her mother-in-law said, My daughter, it is
better, that thou go out to reap with his damsels, lest in
another field any man against-stand thee.
23 And so Ruth was joined to the damsels of Boaz; and
so long she reaped with them, till both the barley and the
wheat were closed in the barns. (And so Ruth was joined
to Boaz's young women; and she worked with them,
until all the barley and the wheat were harvested, and
enclosed in the barns.)

CHAPTER 3

1 And after that Ruth had turned (again) to her mother-
in-law, she heard of her, My daughter, I shall seek rest to
thee, and I shall purvey that it be well to thee. (And
sometime later, when Ruth had returned to her mother-
in-law, Naomi said to her, My daughter, I shall seek rest
for thee, and I shall purvey that it be well with thee.)
2 This Boaz, to whose damsels thou were joined (to)
in the field, is our kinsman, and in this night he
winnoweth the cornfloor of barley (and tonight he
thresheth barley at his threshing floor).
3 Therefore be thou washed, and anointed, and be
thou clothed with more honest clothes, and go thou
down into the cornfloor; the man see not thee, till he
have ended to eat and to drink. (And so be thou washed,
and anointed, and be thou clothed with more
honourable, *or more decent*, clothes, and then go thou
down to the threshing floor; but do not let the man see
thee until he hath finished eating and drinking.)
4 Forsooth when he goeth to sleep, mark thou the
place in which he sleepeth; and thou shalt come, and
uncover the cloak, with which he is covered, from the
part of the feet, and thou shalt cast thee down, and thou
shalt lie there. Forsooth he shall say to thee, what thou
oughtest to do.
5 And Ruth answered, Whatever thing thou
commandest to me, I shall do.
6 And she went down into the cornfloor (And she
went down to the threshing floor), and did all things
which her mother-in-law commanded to her.
7 And when Boaz had eaten and (had) drunk, and was
made more glad, and had gone to sleep beside the
mound of sheaves, Ruth came, and hid herself; and when
the cloth was uncovered from his feet, she casted down
herself (and she turned back the cloak over his feet, and
lay herself down).
8 And lo! now at midnight, the man dreaded, and was
troubled (And lo! at midnight, the man was startled, *or
was afraid*, and he woke up from his sleep); and he saw a
woman lying at his feet;
9 and he said to her, Who art thou? She answered, I
am Ruth, thine handmaid; stretch forth thy cloth on thy
servantess, for thou art nigh of kin. (and he said to her,
Who art thou? She answered, I am Ruth, thy servantess;
stretch forth thy cloak over thy servantess, for thou art my
next of kin.)
10 And he said, Daughter, thou art blessed of the Lord,
and thou hast overcome the former mercy with the latter
(and now thou hast surpassed thy earlier proof of family
devotion, *or loyalty*, with this one); for thou followedest
not young men, poor either rich.
11 Therefore, do not thou dread, but whatever thing
thou shalt say to me, I shall do to thee; for all the people
that dwelleth within the gates of my city know, that thou
art a woman of virtue. (And so, do not thou fear, but
whatever that thou shalt ask of me, I shall do for thee; for
all the people who liveth within the gates of my city
know, that thou art a woman of virtue.)
12 And I forsake not, that I am of nigh kin, but another
man is nearer kin than I; (And I do not deny, that I am
your close kin, but another man is a closer kin than I;)
13 (so) rest thou here this night, and when the
morrowtide is made, if the man will hold thee to wife by
right of nigh kin (if the man will make thee his wife by
right of next of kin), (then) the thing is well done; and if
he will not, (then) I shall take thee without any doubt, (as)
the Lord liveth; (so) sleep thou till the morrowtide.
14 Therefore she slept at his feet till to the going away
of [the] night, and then she rose (up), before that men
should know each other. And Boaz said to her, Be thou
ware lest any man know, that thou camest hither.
15 And again he said, Stretch forth thy mantle with
which thou art covered, and hold thou with ever either
hand. And while she stretched forth and held, he meted
six measures of barley, and putted on her; and she bare,
and entered into the city, (And then he said, Stretch forth
thy mantle with which thou art covered, and hold thou it

with both hands. And while she stretched it forth and held it, he measured, *or counted*, out six measures of barley, and put it on her *mantle*; and she carried it, and went into the city,)
16 and came to her mother-in-law. Which said to Ruth,
What hast thou done, daughter? And Ruth told to her all things, which the man had done to her. (and came *home* to her mother-in-law. And *Naomi* said to Ruth, What happened, my daughter? And Ruth told her all the things, that the man had done for her.)
17 And Ruth said, Lo! he gave to me six measures of
barley; and he said, I will not that thou turn again void to thy mother-in-law. (And Ruth added, Lo! he gave me six measures of barley; for he said, I will not have it that thou return empty-handed to thy mother-in-law.)
18 And Naomi said, Abide, daughter, till we see what
issue the thing shall have (And Naomi said, Just wait, *or have patience*, daughter, until we see what shall happen); for the man shall not cease, no but he [ful]fill those things which he spake.

CHAPTER 4

1 Therefore Boaz ascended to the gate, and sat there
(And so Boaz went up to the gate, and sat down there); and when he had seen the kinsman pass forth, of whom the word was had, Boaz said to him, Bow thou a little, and sit here; and he called him by his name. And he turned (back), and sat (down).
2 And Boaz took ten elder men of the city, and he said
to them, Sit ye down here. And while they sat (And when they had sat down),
3 Boaz spake to the kinsman, (and said,) Naomi, that
turned again from the country of Moab, sold, *that is, is in purpose to sell, for it was not yet sold*, the part of the field of our brother Elimelech, (Boaz said to his kinsman, *Our kinswoman* Naomi, who hath returned from the country of Moab, is selling the portion of the field, that was Elimelech's, our kinsman,)
4 which thing I would that thou hear; and I would say
to thee before all men sitting, and greater in birth of my people. If thou wilt have in possession the field by right of nigh kin, buy thou, and have thou in possession; soothly if it displeaseth thee, show thou this same thing to me, that I know what I ought to do; for none is nigh in kin, besides thee which art the former, and besides me which am the second. And the man answered, I shall buy the field. (which thing I desire that thou hear about; and I say it to thee before all the men sitting *here*, and of great age, *that is, the elders*, of my people. If thou wilt have the field for a possession by right of next of kin, buy thou it, and have thou it for a possession; but if it displeaseth thee, tell thou this to me, so that I know what I ought to do; for no one is next of kin, besides thee, who art the first by right, and I, who am the second. And the man answered, I shall buy the field.)
5 To whom Boaz said, When thou hast bought the
field (out) of the hand of the woman, thou oughtest also to take to wife Ruth of Moab, that was the wife of the dead man, that thou raise the name of thy kinsman in his heritage. (To whom Boaz then said, And when thou hast bought the field from the hand of the woman, thou ought also to take for a wife Ruth the Moabite, who was the wife of the dead man, so that thou can raise up the name of thy kinsman on his inheritance, *that is, on his land*.)
6 And he answered, I forsake the right of nigh kin; for
I ought not to do away the heritage of mine own family; use thou my privilege, the which I acknowledge me to want gladly. (And the man answered, If that be so, then I forsake the right of next of kin; for I ought not to take away any inheritance from my own family; use thou my privilege, though I acknowledge that I truly had wanted *that land*.)
7 Forsooth this was the custom by eld time in Israel
among kinsmen, that if a man gave his right to another man, that the granting were steadfast, the man should unlace his shoe, and give it to his kinsman; this thing was (the) witnessing of (such) a gift in Israel.
8 Therefore Boaz said to his kinsmen, Take off thy
shoe from thee; and he unlaced it anon from his foot (and at once he unlaced his shoe and took it off his foot).
9 And Boaz said to the greater men in birth, and to all
the people, Ye be witnesses today, that I have taken in possession all things that were of Elimelech, and of Chilion, and of Mahlon, by the gift of Naomi; (And Boaz said to the men of great age, *that is, the elders*, and to all the people there, Ye be my witnesses today, that I have taken in possession all the things that were Elimelech's, and Chilion's, and Mahlon's, by purchasing them from Naomi;)
10 and that I have taken into wedlock Ruth of Moab,
the wife of Mahlon, that I raise up the name of the dead man in his heritage; lest his name be done away from his family, and from his brethren, and his people. Ye, he said, be witnesses of this thing. (and that I have also taken into wedlock Ruth of Moab, the wife of Mahlon, so that I can raise up the name of the dead man on his inheritance, *that is, on his land*; lest his name be done away from his family, and from his kinsmen, and from his people. Ye be my witnesses of this, he said.)
11 All the people, that was in the gate, answered, and
the greater men in birth, (and said,) We be witnesses; the Lord make this woman, that entereth into thine house, as Rachel and Leah, that builded the house of Israel, that she be ensample of virtue in Ephratah, and have a solemn name in Bethlehem; (And all the people, and the men of great age, *or the elders*, who were there at the city gate, answered, We be thy witnesses; may the Lord make this woman, who entereth into thy house, like Rachel and

Leah, who built the house of Israel, and may she be an
example of virtue in Ephratah, and have a famous name
in Bethlehem;)
12 and thine house be made as the house of Pharez,
whom Tamar childed to Judah, of the seed which the
Lord shall give to thee of this damsel. (and may thy house
be made like the house of Perez, whom Tamar bore for
Judah, through the children, *or the descendants*, whom
the Lord shall give thee by this young woman.)
13 Then Boaz took Ruth, and he took her to wife (and
he made her his wife); and he entered to her, and the
Lord gave to her, that she conceived, and childed a son.
14 And women said to Naomi, Blessed be the Lord,
which suffered not, that an heir failed to thy family, and
his name were called in Israel; (And the women said to
Naomi, Blessed be the Lord, who hath not left thy family
without an heir; may his name be known in all of Israel;)
15 and that thou have (him), that shall comfort thy soul,
and nourish thine eld age. For *a child* is born of thy
daughter-in-law, that shall love thee, and he is better to
thee, than if thou haddest seven sons. (and that thou have
him, who shall comfort thy soul, and nourish thy old age.
For *a child* is born of thy daughter-in-law, who loveth
thee, yea, she hath done more for thee than if thou
haddest seven sons.)
16 And Naomi putted the child, whom she received, in
her bosom (And Naomi took the child, and put him in
her bosom); and she did the office of a nurse, and of a
bearer-about.
17 And [the] women neighbours thanked her, *or joyed
together with her*, and said, A son is born to Naomi; and
they called his name Obed. This is the father of Jesse,
the father of David.
18 These be the generations of Pharez; Pharez begat
Hezron; (For these be the descendants of Perez; Perez
begat Hezron;)
19 Hezron begat Ram; Ram begat Amminadab;
20 Amminadab begat Nahshon; Nahshon begat
Salmon;
21 Salmon begat Boaz; Boaz begat Obed;
22 Obed begat Jesse; Jesse begat David the king. (Obed
begat Jesse; and Jesse begat David, the king of Israel.) ✡

1ST SAMUEL

CHAPTER 1

1 There was a man of Ramathaim in Zophim, of the
hill (country) of Ephraim, and his name was Elkanah, the
son of Jeroham, son of Elihi, son of Tohu, son of Zuph, of
Ephraim.
2 And Elkanah had two wives; the name to the one
was Hannah, and the name of the second *was* Peninnah;
and sons were to Peninnah; but Hannah had none free
children. (And Elkanah had two wives; the name of the
first was Hannah, and the name of the second *was*
Peninnah; and Peninnah had children, but Hannah had
no children.)
3 And that man went up from his city in the days *that
were* ordained, to worship and to offer sacrifice to the
Lord of hosts in Shiloh. And [the] two sons of Eli were
there, Hophni and Phinehas, priests of the Lord.
4 Then the day came, and Elkanah offered, and he
gave parts to Peninnah, his wife (and he gave portions to
his wife Peninnah), and to all his sons and daughters;
5 forsooth he gave sorrowfully one part, *either double*,
to Hannah, for he loved Hannah; forsooth the Lord had
closed her womb. (and sorrowfully he gave only one
special portion to Hannah; for he loved Hannah, but the
Lord had closed up her womb.)
6 And (*Peninnah,*) her enemy tormented her, and
anguished (her) greatly, in so much that she upbraided
her, that the Lord had closed (up) her womb.
7 And so Peninnah did each year, when the time
came that they went up into the house of the Lord; and
so she stirred Hannah. And then she wept, and took no
meat. (And Peninnah did so each year, when the time
came that they went up to the House of the Lord; and so
she tormented Hannah. And then Hannah wept, and ate
no food.)
8 Therefore Elkanah, her husband, said to her,
Hannah, why weepest thou, and why eatest thou not,
and why is thine heart tormented? Whether I am not
better to thee than be ten sons? (Am I not better to thee
than ten sons?)
9 Soothly Hannah rose, after that she had eaten and
drunk in Shiloh. And the while Eli [the priest] was on his
great seat before the posts of the house of the Lord, (And
Hannah rose up, after that she had eaten and drunk in
Shiloh. And while Eli the priest was on his great throne,
beside the door of the House of the Lord,)
10 and when she was in bitter *sorrow of* soul, she
prayed (to) the Lord, and wept largely (and greatly wept);
11 and she made a vow to the Lord, and said, Lord God
of hosts, if thou beholdest, and seest the torment of thy
servantess, and if thou hast mind of me, and forgettest not
thine handmaid, and givest a son to thy servantess, I shall
give him to the Lord all the days of his life, and a razor
shall not come upon his head.
12 And it was done, when she multiplied her prayers
before the Lord, that Eli espied her mouth.
13 Forsooth Hannah spake in her heart, and only her
lips were moved, and utterly her voice was not heard.
Therefore Eli guessed her drunken, (And Hannah spoke
in her heart, so that only her lips moved, but her voice
was not heard. And so Eli guessed that she was drunk.)
14 and he said to her, How long shalt thou be drunken?
Avoid thou a little the wine, by which thou art moist (Be
thou done with the wine, by which thou art made drunk).
15 Hannah answered, and said, Nay, my lord, for I am
an unhappy woman; I have not drunk wine, neither
anything that may make drunken, but I have poured out
my soul in the Lord's sight (but I have poured out my
soul before the Lord);
16 guess thou not thine handmaid as one of the
daughters of Belial, for of the multitude of my sorrow and
of my mourning I have spoken unto this present time.
(think thou not that thy servantess is one of the daughters
of Belial, for until this present time I have spoken out of
the multitude of my sorrow, and of my mourning.)
17 Then Eli said to her, Go thou in peace, and (the)
God of Israel give to thee the asking that thou hast prayed
him (for).
18 And she said, I would that thine handmaid find
grace in thine eyes. And the woman went into her way,
and ate, and her cheers were no more changed diversely.
(And she said, I desire that thy servantess find favour in
thine eyes. And the woman went her way, and ate, and
her face was no longer sad.)
19 And they rised (up) early, and worshipped before the
Lord; and they turned again, and came into their house in
Ramah. And Elkanah knew Hannah, his wife; and the
Lord thought on her (and the Lord remembered her).
20 And it was done after the compass of days, Hannah
conceived, and childed a son, and called his name
Samuel; for she had asked him of the Lord (for she had
asked for him from the Lord).
21 And her husband Elkanah went up, and all his
house, to offer a solemn sacrifice, and his avow to the
Lord. (And then as before, her husband Elkanah, and all
his household, *or his family*, went up to offer the annual
sacrifice to the Lord, and to renew his vow.)
22 And Hannah went not up *to that solemnity* (But
Hannah did not go up *to that feast*), for she had said to
her husband, I shall not go (up), till the young child be
weaned, and till I lead him *thither*, and he appear before
the sight of the Lord, and dwell there continually.
23 And Elkanah, her husband, said to her, Do thou that

that seemeth good to thee, and dwell thou still till thou
have weaned him; and I beseech, that the Lord [ful]fill his
word. Therefore the woman abode, and gave milk to her
son, till the time (that) she removed him from the milk.
24 And (then) she brought him with her, after that she
had weaned him, with three calves, and three bushels of
meal, and an amphora, *either a pot*, of wine; and she
brought him to the house of the Lord in Shiloh. And the
child was yet full young.
25 And they sacrificed a calf, and they offered the child
to Eli.
26 And Hannah said, My lord, I beseech thee, (as) thy
soul liveth; I am the woman, that stood before thee here,
and prayed (to) the Lord;
27 for this child I prayed (I prayed for this child), and
the Lord gave to me mine asking which I asked (of) him;
28 therefore and I have given him to the Lord in all
[the] days, in which he is given to the Lord. And they
worshipped there the Lord. (and so I am lending him to
the Lord; yea, for all his days, he shall be lent to the Lord.
And then they worshipped the Lord there.)

CHAPTER 2

1 And Hannah worshipped, and said, Mine heart fully
joyed in the Lord, and mine horn is raised in my God; my
mouth is alarged on mine enemies, for I was glad in thine
health. (And Hannah worshipped, and said, My heart full
out joyeth in the Lord, and my head is raised up to my
God; my mouth is enlarged upon my enemies, *or harshly
speaketh about them*, and I am happy for thy help.)
2 None is holy as the Lord is; for none other is, except
thee, and none is strong as our God. (No one is as holy
as the Lord is; for there is no other, except thee, and no
one is as strong as our God.)
3 Do not ye multiply to speak high things, and have
glory *therein*; eld things go away from your mouth; for
God is Lord of knowings, and thoughts be made ready to
him. (Do not ye continue to speak proud things, and
have glory *in it*; let not proud words come out of your
mouth; for God is the Lord of all knowledge, and he
judgeth all that people do.)
4 The bow of strong men is overcome, and feeble
men be girded with strength.
5 Men full-filled before, setted themselves to hire for
loaves, and hungry men be filled; while the barren
woman childed full many, and she that had many sons,
was *made* sick. (Men filled full before, now hire
themselves out to work for loaves, and hungry men be
filled; while the barren woman bare a great many, and
she who had many sons, was *made* feeble, *or weak*.)
6 The Lord slayeth, and quickeneth; he leadeth forth
to hells, and bringeth again. (The Lord killeth, and
maketh alive; he leadeth down to Sheol, *or into the
grave*, and bringeth up again.)
7 The Lord maketh poor, and he maketh rich; he
maketh low, and he raiseth up.
8 He raiseth a needy man from powder, and he raiseth
a poor man from drit, that he sit with princes, and hold
the seat of glory; for the ends of [the] earth be of the Lord,
and he hath set the world on those. (He raiseth up the
needy from the dust, and he raiseth up the poor from the
dirt, so that they sit with princes, and have seats, *or
places*, of honour; for the ends of the earth be the Lord's,
and he hath set the world upon them.)
9 He shall keep the feet of his saints, and wicked men
shall be still (al)together in darknesses; for a man shall not
be made strong in his own strength. (He shall guard the
footsteps of his saints, and the wicked shall be still, *or
shall be silent*, in the darkness; for no one shall be made
strong by their own strength.)
10 [The] Adversaries of the Lord shall dread him, and
from (the) heavens he shall thunder upon them; the Lord
shall deem the ends of [the] earth, and he shall give
lordship to his king, and he shall enhance the horn, *that
is, (the) power*, of his Christ. (The Lord's adversaries shall
fear him, and he shall thunder upon them from heaven;
the Lord shall judge the ends of the earth, and he shall
give lordship to his king, yea, he shall enhance the horn,
that is, the power, of his anointed king.)
11 And Elkanah went into Ramah, into his house; and
the child was (a) servant in the sight of the Lord before
the face of Eli the priest.
12 Forsooth the sons of Eli *were* the sons of Belial, and
they knew not the Lord,
13 neither the office of (the) priests to the people; but
whoever had offered sacrifice, the servant of the priest
came, while the fleshes were in seething, and he had a
fleshhook with three teeth in his hand;
14 and he sent it into the great vessel of stone, either
into the cauldron, either into the pot, either into the pan;
and whatever thing the fleshhook raised, the priest took
that to himself; so they did to all Israel of men coming
into Shiloh. (and he sent it into the great stone vessel, or
the cauldron, or the pot, or the pan; and whatever thing
the fleshhook raised up, *or caught hold of*, the priest took
that for himself; and so they did to all Israel who came to
Shiloh.)
15 Yea, before that they burnt the inner fatness, the
priest's servant came, and said to the offerer, Give thou
flesh to me/Give to me the flesh, that I seethe it to the
priest; for I shall not take of thee sodden flesh, but raw.
(Yea, before that they burned the inner fatness, the
priest's servant came, and said to the offerer, Give thou to
me the flesh, so that I can roast it for the priest; for I shall
not take boiled flesh from thee, but only raw meat.)
16 And he that offered said to him, Be first the inner
fatness burnt today after the custom, and take thou *then*
to thee how much ever thy soul desireth. The which

answered, and said to him, Nay, but thou shalt give it
now; for else I shall take it by violence. (And if he who
offered said to him, First let the inner fatness be burned
today, after the custom, and *then* take thou for thyself
however much thy soul desireth, the servant would
answer, and say, No, thou shalt give it to me now; or else
I shall take it by force.)
17 Therefore the sin of the young men was full grievous
before the Lord; for they withdrew men from the sacrifice
of the Lord (for they drew people away, *or discouraged
them*, from sacrificing to the Lord).
18 Forsooth Samuel, a child girded with a linen cloth (a
boy wearing a linen cloak), ministered before the face of
the Lord.
19 And his mother made to him a little coat, the which
(s)he brought *to him* in the days ordained *to offer*, and she
went up with her husband, that he would offer a solemn
offering, and his avow. (And his mother made a little coat
for him, which she brought *to him* in the days ordained *for
offering*, when she went up each year with her husband,
when he offered a solemn sacrifice, and renewed his vow.)
20 And Eli blessed Elkanah and his wife; and said, The
Lord yield to thee seed of this woman, for the gift which
thou hast given to the Lord. And they went into their
place *again*. (And Eli blessed Elkanah and his wife; and
said, May the Lord give thee children from this woman,
for the loan which thou hast lent to the Lord. And then
they went home *again*.)
21 Therefore the Lord visited Hannah, and she
conceived, and childed three sons and two daughters.
And the child Samuel was magnified at the Lord (But
their boy Samuel grew up in the presence of the Lord).
22 And Eli was full eld, and he heard all the things that
his sons did in all Israel, and how they slept with women,
that waited at the door of the tabernacle. (And Eli grew
very old, and he heard of all the *improper* things that his
sons did to all Israel, and how they slept with the
women, who served at the entrance to the Tabernacle of
the Witnessing.)
23 And he said to them, Why do ye such things, (yea,)
the worst things, which I hear of (from) all the people?
24 Do not ye, my sons; it is not a good fame, that I
hear, that ye make the Lord's people to do trespass. (Do
not ye do this, my sons; for it is not a good report that I
hear, that ye make the Lord's people to trespass.)
25 If a man sinneth against a man, God may be pleased
to him *by prayers and sacrifices*; but if a man sinneth
against the Lord, who shall pray for him? And they heard
not the voice of their father, for God would slay them. (If
a man sinneth against another man, God may make him
appeased by *prayers and sacrifices*; but if a man sinneth
against the Lord, who shall pray for him? But they would
not listen to their father, for God had decided to kill them.)
26 Forsooth the child Samuel profited, and increased,
and pleased both God and men. (And the boy Samuel
grew, and learned, and pleased both God and men.)
27 Soothly a man of God came to Eli, and said to him,
The Lord saith these things, Whether I was not showed
apertly to the house of thy father, when he was in Egypt,
in the house of Pharaoh? (And a man of God came to Eli,
and said to him, The Lord saith these things, Was I not
openly showed to thy father's family, when they were in
Egypt, in Pharaoh's house?)
28 And I chose him of all the lineages of Israel *to be* a
priest to me, that he should go up to mine altar, and
should burn incense to me, and that he should bear
before me a priest's cloak; and I gave to the house of thy
father all things of the sacrifices of the sons of Israel. (And
I chose him out of all the tribes of Israel *to be* my priest,
so that he could go up to my altar, and burn incense to
me, and that he would wear the ephod; and I gave to thy
father's family all of the sacrifices of the Israelites.)
29 Why hast thou cast away with the heel my sacrifice,
and my gifts, which I [have] commanded to be offered in
the temple; and thou honouredest more thy sons than
me, that ye eat the principal parts of each sacrifice of
Israel my people? (Why hast thou kicked away my
sacrifice, and my gifts, which I commanded to be offered
in the Temple; and why hast thou honoured thy sons
more than me, so that ye eat the principal, *or the
choicest*, parts of each offering from my people Israel?)
30 Therefore the Lord God of Israel saith these things, I
speaking spake, that thine house, and the house of thy
father, should minister in my sight till into without end;
now forsooth the Lord saith, Far be this from me; but
whoever honoureth me, I shall glorify him; forsooth they
that despise me, shall be unnoble. (And so the Lord God
of Israel saith these things, Before I said, that thy family,
and thy father's family, shall serve before me
forevermore; but now the Lord saith, Far be this from me;
yea, whoever honoureth me, I shall glorify him; but they
who despise me, shall be despised.)
31 Lo! [the] days come, and I shall cut away thine arm,
or thy power, and the arm of the house of thy father, that
an eld man be not in thine house (so that no man shall
grow old in thy family).
32 And thou shalt see thine enemy in the temple, in all
the prosperities of Israel (amidst all of Israel's prosperity);
and an eld man shall not be in thine house in all days.
33 Nevertheless I shall not utterly take away of thee a
man from mine altar, but that thine eyes fail, and thy soul
fail/and thy life languish; and a great part of thine house
shall die, when it shall come to man's age. (And I shall
not utterly take away all of thy men from my altar, but he
who is left, his eyes shall fail, and his soul shall fail/and
his life shall languish; and a great part of thy family shall
die, when they come to a man's age.)
34 Forsooth this shall be [the] sign, that shall come to

thy two sons, Hophni and Phinehas; both they shall die in one day (they shall both die on the same day).
35 And I shall raise to me a faithful priest, that shall do by mine heart and my soul; and I shall build to him a faithful house, and he shall go before my Christ in all days. (And I shall raise up a faithful priest for me, one who shall do according to my heart and my soul; and I shall build him a faithful family, and he shall go before my anointed king in all his days.)
36 Forsooth it shall come, that whoever [still] dwelleth in thine house, that he come to bow for himself, in an half-penny of silver, and a cake of bread, and say, I beseech, suffer thou me to one part of the priest(s') (offices), that I eat a morsel of bread. (And it shall come, that whoever still remaineth in thy family, he shall come to beg for himself, for a half-penny of silver, and for a cake of bread, and he shall say, I beseech thee, allow me to hold one of the priests' offices, so that I can get a morsel of bread to eat.)

CHAPTER 3

1 Forsooth the child Samuel ministered to the Lord before Eli, and the word of the Lord was precious; in those days was none open revelation (for in those days there was no open revelation).
2 Therefore it was done in a day, Eli lay in his bed, and his eyes dimmed, and he might not see; (And so it was done one night, when Eli lay on his bed, and his eyes had dimmed, and he could not see;)
3 the lantern of the Lord was not yet quenched. And Samuel slept in the temple of the Lord, where the ark of God was. (and Samuel also slept in the Temple of the Lord, where the Ark of God was. And one morning, before that the lantern of God was quenched,)
4 And the Lord called Samuel; and he answered and said, Lo! I./Lo! I *am ready.* (the Lord called to Samuel; and he answered and said, Lo! I *am here.*)
5 And he ran to Eli, and said to him, Lo! I; for thou calledest me. And Eli said, I called not thee; turn thou again and sleep. And he went and slept. (And he ran to Eli, and said to him, Lo! I *am here*; for thou hast called me. And Eli said, I did not call thee; return thou, and go to sleep. And so he went and slept again.)
6 And the Lord added again to call Samuel; and Samuel rose (up), and went to Eli, and said, Lo! I *(am) here*; for thou calledest me. And Eli answered, I called not thee, my son; turn thou again and sleep (And Eli answered, I did not call thee, my son; return thou, and go back to sleep).
7 Forsooth Samuel knew not yet the Lord, neither the word of the Lord was showed to him. (For Samuel did not yet know the Lord, and the word of the Lord was not yet shown to him.)
8 And the Lord added, and called yet Samuel the third time; the which rose up and went to Eli, and said, Lo! I; for thou calledest me. Then Eli understood, that the Lord had called the child; (And the Lord added, and called to Samuel yet the third time; and he rose up and went to Eli, and said, Lo! I *am here*; for thou hast called me. Then Eli understood, that the Lord had called the child;)
9 and Eli said to Samuel, Go thou and sleep; and if he calleth thee afterward, thou shalt say, Speak thou, Lord, for thy servant heareth. Then Samuel went and slept in his place.
10 And the Lord came, and stood, and called as he had called the second time (and called *to him* as he had called the other times, saying), Samuel, Samuel. And Samuel said, Speak thou, Lord, for thy servant heareth.
11 And the Lord said to Samuel, Lo! I (shall) make a word, *that is, (I shall do) a thing signified by a word,* in Israel, which word whoever shall hear, both his ears shall ring, *that is, he shall be astonished for wonder and dread.*
12 In that day I shall raise up against Eli all (the) things that I have spoken upon his house; I shall begin (it), and I shall end (it).
13 For I before-said to him, that I should deem his house without end for the wickedness thereof; for he knew, that his sons did unworthily, and he chastised not them. (For I said to him before, that I would judge his family forevermore for its wickedness; and he knoweth, that his sons have done unworthily, and yet he hath not chastised them.)
14 Therefore I have sworn to the house of Eli, that the wickedness of his family, *or his house,* shall not be cleansed with sacrifices and gifts till into without end.
15 And then Samuel slept till the morrowtide, and he opened the doors of the house of the Lord; and Samuel dreaded to show the revelation to Eli.
16 Therefore Eli called Samuel, and said, Samuel, my son. And he answered and said, I am ready (And he answered, I am here).
17 And Eli asked him, What is the word that the Lord hath spoken to thee? I pray thee, hide it not from me; God do to thee these things, and increase these things, if thou hidest from me a word of all [the] words that be said to thee.
18 And Samuel showed to him all the words, and hid not (anything) from him. And Eli answered, He is the Lord; do he that, that is good in his eyes.
19 Forsooth Samuel increased (And so Samuel grew up), and the Lord was with him, and none of all his words felled into [the] earth, *that is, (were) in vain, for all was (ful)filled.*
20 And all Israel from Dan to Beersheba knew, that faithful Samuel was a prophet of the Lord. (And all Israel knew, from Dan to Beersheba, that truly Samuel was a prophet of the Lord.)
21 And the Lord added to appear again in Shiloh, for the Lord was showed to Samuel in Shiloh by the word of

the Lord;

CHAPTER 4

1 and the word of Samuel came to all Israel. And it
was done in those days (the) Philistines came together into
battle; for Israel went out against the Philistines into battle,
and setted tents beside the stone of help (and pitched their
tents at Ebenezer). And the Philistines came into Aphek,
2 and made ready (the) battle array against Israel. And
when the battle was begun, Israel turned the(ir) backs to
[the] Philistines; and as four thousand of men were slain
in that battle everywhere by fields; and the people *of
Israel* turned again to their tents. (and prepared the battle
array against Israel. And when the battle was begun,
Israel turned their backs to the Philistines; and about four
thousand men were killed that day in that battle, in every
part of the field; and then the people *of Israel* returned to
their tents.)
3 And the greater men in birth of Israel said, Why hath
the Lord smitten us today before the Philistines? Bring
we to us from Shiloh the ark of the bond of peace of the
Lord, and come it into the midst of us, that it save us from
the hand of our enemies. (And the men of great age, *that
is, the elders*, of Israel, said, Why did the Lord let us be
defeated today by the Philistines? Let us bring the Ark of
the Covenant of the Lord from Shiloh, and have it come
here into our midst, so that it can save us from the hand
of our enemies.)
4 Therefore the people sent into Shiloh, and they took
from thence the ark of the bond of peace of the Lord of
hosts, that sat on cherubim. And Hophni and Phinehas,
the two sons of Eli, were with the ark of the bond of
peace of the Lord. (And so the people sent to Shiloh, and
they brought from there the Ark of the Covenant of the
Lord of hosts, who sitteth above, *or upon*, the cherubim.
And Hophni and Phinehas, the two sons of Eli, came
with the Ark of the Covenant of the Lord.)
5 And when the ark of [the] bond of peace of the Lord
had come into the tents (And when the Ark of the
Covenant of the Lord came to the camp), all Israel cried
[out] with [a] great cry, and the earth sounded.
6 And the Philistines heard the voice of their cry, and
they said, And what is this voice of great cry in the tents
of Hebrews? And they knew, that the ark of [the] bond of
peace of the Lord had come into the tents of Israel. (And
the Philistines heard the sound of their cry, and they said,
And what is this sound of a great cry from the Hebrews'
tents? And then they knew, that the Ark of the Covenant
of the Lord had come to Israel's camp.)
7 And the Philistines dreaded, and said, God is come
into their tents; and they wailed, and said, Woe to us! for
so great out-joying was not there yesterday, and the third
day passed; (And the Philistines were afraid, and said,
God hath come to their tents; and they wailed, and said,
Woe to us! for there was not so great rejoicing there
yesterday, or the third day ago;)
8 woe to us! who shall keep us from the hand of these
high gods? these be the gods, that smited Egypt with all
vengeance in desert. (woe to us! who shall save us from
the power of these high gods? these be the gods, who
struck down the Egyptians with all that slaughter in the
wilderness.)
9 Philistines, be ye comforted, and be ye men, serve
ye not to the Hebrews, as they have served to you; be ye
comforted, and fight ye *against Israel*. (Philistines, take ye
courage, and be ye men, otherwise ye shall serve as
slaves to the Hebrews, like they have served you; yea, be
ye of good courage, and fight ye *against Israel*.)
10 Then the Philistines fought, and Israel was
overcome, and each man fled into his tabernacle; and a
full great vengeance was made, and thirty thousand of
(the) footmen of Israel felled down. (Then the Philistines
fought, and Israel was overcome, and each man fled into
his tent; and there was a great slaughter, and thirty
thousand of the footmen of Israel fell down.)
11 And the ark of God was taken; and, the two sons of
Eli, Hophni and Phinehas, were dead. (And the Ark of
God was taken; and Eli's two sons, Hophni and Phinehas,
were killed.)
12 And a man of Benjamin ran from the battle array, and
came into Shiloh in that day, with his cloth rent, and with
his head besprinkled with dust; (And a man of Benjamin
ran from the battle array, and came into Shiloh that day,
with his cloak torn, and with his head covered with dirt;)
13 and when he was come, Eli sat upon a seat, and
beheld against the way; for his heart was dreading for the
ark of the Lord (and when he arrived, Eli sat on a seat,
looking toward the road; for his heart was fearing for the
Ark of the Lord). And after that that man had entered, he
told (what had happened) to *the men of* the city, and
(then) all the city yelled.
14 And Eli heard the sound of the cry, and he said,
What is the sound of this noise? (And Eli heard all the
yelling, and he said, What is the meaning of this noise?)
And the man hasted, and came, and told to Eli.
15 And Eli was of fourscore years and eighteen, and his
eyes (had) dimmed/his eyes (had) darkened, and he might
not see.
16 And the man said to Eli, I am *he* that came from the
battle, and I am *he* that fled today from the battle array.
To whom Eli said, My son, what is there done? (My son,
what is done there?)
17 And he that told answered, and said, Israel hath fled
before the Philistines, and a great falling is made in the
people *of Israel*; furthermore and thy two sons, Hophni
and Phinehas, be dead, and the ark of God is taken. (And
he who had given the report answered him, and said,
Israel hath fled before the Philistines, and a great number

of the people *of Israel* have fallen; and furthermore thy
two sons, Hophni and Phinehas, were killed, and the Ark
of God was taken.)
18 And when he named the ark of God, Eli felled (off)
from the seat backward beside the door, and was dead
(and he died); for his neck was broken. For he was an eld
man, and of great age; and he deemed Israel forty years.
19 And his daughter-in-law, Phinehas' wife, was with
child, and nigh the child bearing; and when the message
was heard/and when she (had) heard by the messenger,
that the ark of God was taken, and that her father-in-law
was dead, and (also) her husband, she bowed herself
down, and childed; for sudden sorrows felled into her
(for suddenly her pains came upon her).
20 And in that moment of her death, (*the*) *women* that
stood about her said to her, Dread thou not, for thou hast
childed a son. And she answered not to them, neither
she took heed. (And at the moment of her death, *the
women* who stood about her said to her, Fear thou not,
for thou hast borne a son. But she did not answer them,
nor take any heed.)
21 And she called the child Ichabod, *that is, without
glory*, and said, The glory of the Lord is translated from
Israel, for the ark of God is taken; and for her father-in-
law and for her husband (And she called the child
Ichabod, *that is, Without glory*, and said, Now the glory
of the Lord hath been taken away from Israel; for the Ark
of God was taken, and her father-in-law, and her
husband, were dead;)
22 she said, The glory of God is translated from Israel/is
taken from Israel, for the ark of God is taken. (and she
said again, The glory of God hath been taken away from
Israel, for the Ark of God hath been taken *from us*.)

CHAPTER 5

1 And the Philistines took the ark of God, and bare it
away from the stone of help into Ashdod. (And the
Philistines took the Ark of God, and carried it away from
Ebenezer unto Ashdod.)
2 And the Philistines took the ark of God, and brought
it into the temple of Dagon, and setted it beside Dagon.
3 And when men of Ashdod had risen early in the
tother day, lo! Dagon lay low in the earth before the ark
of the Lord. And they took Dagon, and restored him in
his place. (And when the men of Ashdod had risen early
the next day, lo! Dagon lay low on the ground before the
Ark of the Lord. And they took Dagon, and restored him
to his place.)
4 And again they rose early in the tother day, and they
found Dagon lying on his face upon the earth before the
ark of the Lord. And the head of Dagon, and the two
palms of his hands, were broken off, (and were lying)
upon the threshold; and the stock alone of Dagon (was)
left in his place. (And they rose up early the next day, and
they found Dagon lying on his face on the ground before
the Ark of the Lord. And the head of Dagon, and the two
palms of his hands, were broken off, and were lying on the
threshold; and only Dagon's body was left in its place.)
5 For this cause the priests of Dagon, and all that enter
into his temple, tread not upon the threshold of Dagon in
Ashdod unto this day.
6 Forsooth the hand of the Lord was made grievous
upon [the] men of Ashdod, and he destroyed them, and
he smote Ashdod and the coasts thereof in the privier
part of [the] buttocks/in the more privy part of their tail
ends.
7 And men of Ashdod saw such a vengeance, and
they said, The ark of God of Israel dwell not with us; for
his hand is hard on us, and on Dagon our god. (And
when the men of Ashdod saw such vengeance taken
upon themselves, they said, The Ark of the God of Israel
must not remain among us; for his hand is hard upon us,
and upon our god Dagon.)
8 And they sent, and gathered all the wise men, *either
princes*, of Philistines to them, and said, What shall we
do of the ark of God of Israel? And the men of Gath
answered, The ark of God of Israel be led about; and they
led about the ark of God of Israel. (And they sent for, and
gathered together, all the princes of the Philistines, and
said to them, What shall we do with the Ark of the God
of Israel? And the men answered, The Ark of the God of
Israel should be taken to Gath; and so they took the Ark
of the God of Israel *there*.)
9 And while they led it about, the hand of the Lord was
made upon all the cities *about*, of full great slaughter; and
he smote men of each city, from a little man till to the
more, and the lower entrails of them waxed rotten, and
came forth; and men of Gath took counsel, and they
made to themselves seats of skins, *either cushions*. (And
after they took it there, the hand of the Lord was made
upon all the city with a full great slaughter; and he struck
the men of the city, from a small, *or a low*, man unto a
great man, and their lower entrails grew rotten, and came
forth; and the men of Gath took counsel together, and
then they made leather cushions for themselves.)
10 Therefore they sent the ark of the Lord into Ekron.
And when the ark of the Lord had come into Ekron, men
of Ekron cried [out], and said, They have brought to us the
ark of God of Israel, that he slay us and our people. (And
so they sent the Ark of the Lord to Ekron. And when the
Ark of the Lord had come to Ekron, the men of Ekron cried
out, and said, They have brought the Ark of the God of
Israel to us, so that now he will kill us and our people!)
11 Then they sent, and gathered together all the wise
men, *either princes*, of Philistines; which said, Deliver ye
the ark of God of Israel, and turn it again into his place,
and slay not us with our people. For dread of death was
made in all [the] cities, and the hand of the Lord was full

grievous. (And they sent for, and gathered together, all
the princes of the Philistines; and they said, Send the Ark
of the God of Israel away, and let it return to its own
place, so that it shall not kill us and our people. For the
fear of death was made in all the city, and the hand of the
Lord was very grievous there.)
12 And the men, that were not dead (who did not die),
were smitten in the privy parts of their buttocks, and the
yelling of each city went up into heaven.

CHAPTER 6

1 Therefore the ark of the Lord was in the country of
[the] Philistines (for) seven months;
2 and after these things the Philistines called together
[the] priests and false diviners, and said, What shall we
do of the ark of God? Show ye to us, how we shall send it
into his place. (and after these things the Philistines called
together the priests and the false diviners, and asked,
What shall we do with the Ark of God? Tell us how we
should send it back to its own place?)
3 Which said, If ye send again the ark of God of Israel,
do not ye deliver it void, but yield ye to him that thing,
that ye owe for [the] sin; and then ye shall be healed, and
ye shall know, why his hand goeth not away from you.
(Who said, If ye return the Ark of the God of Israel, do
not ye send it back without a gift, but send ye it back
with what ye owe for your sin; and then ye shall be
healed, and ye shall know why his hand goeth not away
from you now.)
4 And they said, What is it, that we ought to yield to
him for (the) trespass? And they answered to them, By the
number of the provinces of (the) Philistines, ye shall
make five golden arses, and five golden mice; for one
vengeance was to all (of) you, and to your wise men,
either princes.
5 And ye shall make the likeness of your arses, and
the likeness of [the] mice that destroyed your land; and
ye shall give glory to [the] God of Israel, if in hap he
withdraw his hand from you, and from your gods, and
from your land.
6 Why make ye heavy your hearts, as Egypt and
Pharaoh grieved their heart(s)? Whether not after that he
was smitten, then he delivered God's people, and they
went forth? (Why be ye stubborn, *or stiff-necked,* like
Egypt and Pharaoh were stubborn, *or stiff-necked*? For
after God had struck them, did they not let God's people
go, and they went away?)
7 Now therefore take ye, and make a new wain, and
join ye therein two kine having calves, on which kine no
yoke was put; and close ye their calves at home. (And so
now take ye, and make ready a new wagon, and join ye
it up to two cows who have calves, on which cows no
yoke was ever put; and enclose ye their calves at home.)
8 And ye shall take the ark of the Lord, and ye shall
set (it) in the wain; and ye shall put in a little coffer at the
side of the ark the golden vessels, which ye have paid to
the Lord for *your* trespass; and deliver ye the ark, that it
go forth. (And ye shall take the Ark of the Lord, and ye
shall put it on the wagon; and ye shall put the gold
vessels, that ye send to the Lord for *your* trespass, in a
small box at the side of the Ark; and then let the Ark go
forth as it will.)
9 And ye shall behold *it,* and soothly if it goeth up
against Bethshemesh by the way of his coasts, the Lord
hath then done to you this great evil; but if it go not
thither, we shall know that the hand of the Lord touched
not us, but this thing hath fallen to us by hap. (And ye shall
watch *it,* and truly if it goeth up toward Bethshemesh by
the way of its coasts, then the Lord hath done this great
evil to you; but if it go not *there,* then we shall know that
the hand of the Lord did not touch us, and that this thing
hath befallen to us all by happenstance, *or chance.*)
10 Then they did in this manner; and they took two
kine that gave milk to their calves, and they joined *them*
to the wain; and they (en)closed their calves at home.
11 And they put the ark of God upon the wain, and the
little coffer, (*or the small box,*) that had the gold mice,
and the likeness of (their) arses.
12 And the kine went straightly by the way that leadeth
to Bethshemesh; and those kine went in one way going
and lowing, and they bowed not neither to the right side
nor to the left side; but also the wise men of Philistines
followed unto the coasts of Bethshemesh (and the princes
of the Philistines followed them to the border of
Bethshemesh).
13 Forsooth (the) men of Bethshemesh reaped wheat in
the valley, and they lifted up their eyes, and saw the ark,
and they were joyful, when they had seen it.
14 And the wain came into the field of Joshua of
Bethshemesh, and stood there. And a great stone was
there; and they cutted the wood of the wain, and putted
the kine on that wood, (as) a burnt sacrifice to the Lord.
15 And the deacons took down the ark of God, and the
little coffer that was beside it, wherein the golden vessels
were; and they putted those upon the great stone. And the
men of Bethshemesh offered burnt sacrifices, and offered
slain sacrifices in that day to the Lord. (And the Levites
took down the Ark of God, and the small box that was
beside it, which held the gold vessels; and they put them
on the great stone. And the men of Bethshemesh offered
burnt sacrifices, and slain sacrifices, to the Lord that day.)
16 And [the] five princes of Philistines saw, and turned
again into Ekron in that day. (And the five princes of the
Philistines saw it, and then returned to Ekron that day.)
17 Soothly these be the golden arses, which the
Philistines yielded to the Lord for *their* trespass; Ashdod
yielded one; Gaza one; Askelon one; Gath one; Ekron
one;

18 and *the Philistines yielded* golden mice by the
number of cities of Philistines of [the] five provinces, from
a walled city unto an unwalled town, and unto the great
stone that was called Abel, on which they putted the ark
of the Lord, the which stone was there unto that day in
the field of Joshua of Bethshemesh. (and *they also gave*
gold mice by the number of the Philistines' cities
governed by the five princes, from a walled city unto an
unwalled town. And the great *stone that was called*
Eben, on which they put the Ark of the Lord, is there unto
this day, in the field of Joshua of Bethshemesh.)
19 Forsooth the Lord smote of the men of Bethshemesh,
for they had seen the ark of the Lord, and he smote of the
people seventy men, and fifty thousand of the poor-all[1].
And the people mourned, for the Lord had smitten the
people with [a] great vengeance. (But the Lord struck down
the men of Bethshemesh, because they had looked inside
the Ark of the Lord, and so he struck down seventy men of
the people there. And the people mourned, for the Lord
had struck down the people with such a great slaughter.)
20 And men of Bethshemesh said, Who shall now
stand in the sight of the Lord God of this holy thing, and
to whom shall it go up from us? (And the men of
Bethshemesh said, Who can now stand before the Lord,
yea, this holy God, and to whom shall we send *this Ark*
away from us?/and to whom shall he go away from us?)
21 And they sent messengers to the dwellers of
Kiriathjearim, and said, The Philistines have brought
again the ark of the Lord; come ye down, and lead it
again to you. (And they sent messengers to the
inhabitants of Kiriathjearim, who said, The Philistines
have returned the *Ark* of the Lord; come ye down, and
take it away with you.)

CHAPTER 7

1 Therefore men of Kiriathjearim came, and led again
the ark of the Lord, and brought it into the house of
Abinadab in Gibeah. And they hallowed Eleazar his son,
that he should keep the ark of the Lord. (And so some
men of Kiriathjearim came, and took the Ark of the Lord,
and they brought it to the house of Abinadab on the hill.
And they consecrated his son Eleazar, so that he could be
in charge of the Ark of the Lord.)
2 And it was done, from which day the ark of the Lord
dwelled in Kiriathjearim, (that the) days were multiplied;
for the twentieth year was now, *after that Samuel began
to teach the people*; and all Israel rested after the Lord
(and all Israel cried out to the Lord *for help*).
3 And Samuel spake to all the house of Israel, and
said, If in all your heart ye turn again to the Lord, do ye
away alien gods (do ye away foreign, *or other*, gods),
(the) Baalim, and (the) Ashtaroth, from the midst of you;
and make ye ready your hearts to the Lord, and serve ye
him alone; and (then) he shall deliver you from the hand
of the Philistines.
4 Therefore the sons of Israel did away Baalim and
Ashtaroth, and served the Lord alone. (And so the
Israelites did away the Baalim and the Ashtaroth, and
served the Lord alone.)
5 And Samuel said, Gather ye all Israel into Mizpah,
that I pray the Lord for you (and I shall pray to the Lord
for you).
6 And they came together into Mizpeh, and drew
water, and poured it out in the Lord's sight; and they
fasted in that day, and said, Lord, we have sinned to thee
(and said, Lord, we have sinned against thee). And
Samuel deemed the sons of Israel in Mizpeh.
7 And the Philistines heard that the sons of Israel were
gathered together in Mizpeh; and the princes of
Philistines went up to Israel. And when the sons of Israel
had heard this, they dreaded of the face of (the)
Philistines. (And the Philistines heard that the Israelites
were gathered together in Mizpeh; and the princes of the
Philistines came up against Israel. And when the Israelites
had heard this, they feared to face the Philistines.)
8 And they said to Samuel/And Israel cried to Samuel,
Cease thou not to cry for us to our Lord God, that he save
us from the hand of Philistines. (And the Israelites cried to
Samuel, Cease thou not to cry out to the Lord our God
for us, so that he will save us from the hands of the
Philistines.)
9 And Samuel took one sucking lamb, and offered it
whole into burnt sacrifice to the Lord (And Samuel took a
sucking lamb, and offered it whole for a burnt sacrifice to
the Lord). And Samuel cried to the Lord for Israel; and
the Lord heard him.
10 And it was done, when Samuel offered the burnt
sacrifice, that the Philistines began (to do) battle against
Israel. And the Lord thundered with great thunder in that
day upon the Philistines, and made them afeared; and
they were slain of the sons of Israel (and they fled in
panic before the Israelites).
11 And the sons of Israel went out of Mizpeh, and
pursued the Philistines, and smote them unto the place
that was under Bethcar.
12 And Samuel took one stone, and put it betwixt
Mizpeh, and Shen; and he called the name of that place
The stone of help (and he called the name of that place
Ebenezer). And he said, Hitherto the Lord hath helped us.
13 And the Philistines were made low, and they added
no more to come into the terms of Israel (And so the
Philistines were humbled, and they did not come any
more into the land of Israel). And so the hand of the Lord

[1] Hebrews understand thus the number of men slain here; they say that only seventy men were smitten, which were of so great (a) reputation, that they were (each) comparisoned to (almost) one thousand of the common people.

was made [up]on (the) Philistines in all the days of Samuel.
14 And the cities which the Philistines had taken from
Israel, were yielded again to Israel, from Ekron unto Gath,
and the coasts of Gath; and the Lord delivered Israel from
the hand of (the) Philistines; and peace was betwixt Israel
and Amorites (and there was peace between Israel and
the Amorites).
15 And Samuel deemed Israel all the days of his life,
that is, till to the ordaining and confirming of Saul;
16 and he went by each year, and compassed Bethel,
and Gilgal, and Mizpeh, and he deemed Israel in the
foresaid places.
17 And he turned again into Ramah, for his house was
there; and he deemed Israel there, and he builded there
also an altar to the Lord. (And then he returned to Ramah,
for his house was there; and he judged Israel there, and
he also built an altar there to the Lord.)

CHAPTER 8

1 And it was done, when Samuel waxed eld, he set
his sons *to be* judges of Israel. (And it was done, when
Samuel grew old, he made his sons *to be* judges in Israel.)
2 And the name of his first begotten son was Joel, and
the name of the second was Abiah, that were judges in
Beersheba (and they were judges in Beersheba).
3 And his sons went not in his ways, but they bowed
after avarice, and they took gifts, and perverted doom
(and perverted justice, *or judgement*).
4 Therefore all the greater men in birth of Israel were
gathered together, and came to Samuel into Ramah. (And
so all the men of great age, *that is, the elders,* of Israel
gathered together, and came to Samuel in Ramah.)
5 And they said to him, Lo! thou hast waxed eld, and
thy sons go not in thy ways; ordain thou a king to us, that
he deem us, as also all *other* nations have. (And they said
to him, Lo! thou hast grown old, and thy sons do not go
in thy ways; ordain thou a king for us, so that he can
judge, *or can rule,* us, like all the *other* nations have.)
6 And the word displeased in the eyes of Samuel, for
they had said, Give thou to us a king, that he deem us.
And Samuel prayed to the Lord. (And this request
displeased Samuel, for they had said, Give thou a king to
us, so that he can judge us. And Samuel prayed to the
Lord.)
7 And the Lord said to Samuel, Hear thou the voice of
the people in all things that they speak to thee; for they
have not cast away thee (for they have not thrown thee
away), but me, (so) that I reign not upon them.
8 By all the works that they have done, from the day
in which I led them out of Egypt unto this day, as they
have forsaken me, and they have served alien gods, so
they do also to thee (and they have served foreign, *or
other,* gods, and now they also do to thee).
9 Now therefore hear thou their voice; nevertheless
witness thou to them; and before-say thou to them the
right of the king, that shall reign upon them (and tell thou
them, the rights of the king who shall reign over them).
10 Then Samuel said all the words of the Lord to the
people, that had asked of him a king (who had asked him
for a king);
11 and he said, This shall be the right of the king, that
shall command to you; he shall take your sons, and he
shall set them in his chariots; and he shall make them to
himself riders, and before-goers of his carts (and he shall
make them to be his horsemen, *or his riders,* and to run
before his chariots);
12 and he shall ordain to him tribunes, *that is,
sovereigns of a thousand,* and centurions, *that is,
sovereigns of an hundred,* and earers/tillers of his fields,
and reapers of his corns, and smiths of his armours, and
(smiths) of his chariots. (and he shall ordain his tribunes,
that is, the rulers of a thousand, and his centurions, *that
is, the rulers of a hundred,* and the tillers of his fields, and
the reapers of his harvest, and the smiths of his arms, *or
of his weapons,* and the smiths of his chariots.)
13 Also he shall make your daughters (to be) makers of
his ointments, and his fire-makers (and his cooks), and
(his) bakers/his makers of bread.
14 And he shall take your fields, and your vineries (and
your vineyards), and the best places of olives, and he
shall give *those* to his servants.
15 But also he shall take the tenth part of your corns,
and (of) the rents of your vineries, that he give those to
his chamberlains, and [to his] servants.
16 And he shall take away your servants, and *your*
handmaids, and *your* best young men, and *your* asses,
and he shall set these in his work. (And he shall take
away your servants, and your servantesses, and *your* best
young men, and *your* donkeys, and he shall make them
do his bidding/and he shall make them work for him.)
17 Also he shall take the tenth part of your flocks; and
ye shall be his servants.
18 And ye shall cry in that day from the face of your
king, whom ye have chosen to you; and the Lord shall
not hear you in that day; for ye [have] asked (for) a king
to you. (And ye shall cry out on that day because of your
king, whom ye have chosen for yourselves; but the Lord
shall not hear you on that day; for ye have asked for a
king for yourselves.)
19 Soothly the people would not hear the voice of
Samuel, but they said, Nay, for a king shall be on us; (But
the people would not listen to Samuel, and they said, No!
let a king rule over us;)
20 and (then) we also shall be as all folks (and then we
shall be like all the other nations), and our king shall
deem us, and he shall go out before us, and he shall fight
our battles for us.
21 And Samuel heard all the words of the people, and

he spake them in the ears of the Lord.
22 And the Lord said to Samuel, Hear thou their voices,
and ordain thou a king upon them. And Samuel said to
the men of Israel, Each man go into his city (Now
everyone go home).

CHAPTER 9

1 And there was a man of Benjamin, that was called
Kish, the son of Abiel, the son of Zeror, the son of
Bechorath, the son of Aphiah, the son of a man *that was
called* Benjamin (a Benjamite), a strong man in bodily
might.
2 And to him was a son, Saul by name, chosen and
good(ly); and no man of the sons of Israel was better than
he; (and) from the shoulder(s) and above, he appeared
over all the people.
3 And the she-asses of Kish, the father of Saul, were
lost (And one day the female donkeys of Kish, Saul's
father, went missing). And Kish said to Saul his son, Take
with thee one of the servants, and rise thou, and go seek
the she-asses.
4 And when they had gone forth by the hill (country)
of Ephraim, and by the land of Shalisha, and they had not
found them, they passed forth also by the land of Shalim,
and they were not *there*; but also *they passed* by the land
of Benjamin, and yet they found (them) not.
5 And when they had come into the land of Zuph, and
had not found (them), Saul said to his servant that was
with him, Come thou, and turn we again; lest
peradventure my father hath left (off caring about) the
female asses, and is busy for us (and is now concerned
about us).
6 And the servant said to him, Lo! a man of God is in
this city, a noble man; all thing that he speaketh, cometh
without (a) doubt. Now therefore go we thither, if
peradventure he show to us of our way, for which we
came (And so now let us go there, perhaps he can show
us the way that we should go).
7 And Saul said to his servant, Lo! we shall go (there);
(but) what shall we bear to the man of God? Bread hath
failed in our scrips, and we have no present, that we
(can) give to the man of God, neither any other thing.
8 Again the servant answered to Saul, and said, Lo!
the fourth part of a stater, *that is, a shekel,* of silver is
found (here) in mine hand; give we *it* to the man of God,
that he show to us our way (so that he will show us the
way that we should go).
9 Sometime in Israel each man going to counsel with
God spake thus, Come ye, and go we to the seer; for he,
that is said now a prophet, was called sometime a seer (for
he, who now is called a prophet, before was called a seer).
10 And Saul said to his servant, Thy word is the best;
come thou, go we. And they went into the city, in which
the man of God was (And they went to the city, where
the man of God was).
11 And when they went up into the highness of the city,
they found damsels going out to draw water, and they said
to the damsels, Whether the seer is here? (Is the seer here?)
12 And the damsels answered, and said to them, He is
here; lo! he is before thee; haste thou now, for today he
came into the city; for today is sacrifice of the people in
the high place. (And the young women answered, and
said to them, He is here; lo! he is ahead of thee; haste
thou now, for he came into the city today; for there is a
sacrifice by all the people at the hill shrine today.)
13 Ye shall enter into the city, and at once ye shall find
him, before that he ascend into the high place to eat; for
the people shall not eat till he come, for he shall (first)
bless the sacrifice, and afterward they shall eat that be
called (and then afterward they who be called shall eat).
Now therefore go ye up, for today ye shall find him.
14 And they went up into the city. And when they
went into the midst of the city, Samuel appeared going
out against them, that he should go up into the high place
(Samuel appeared coming out toward them, as he went
on his way up to the hill shrine).
15 And the day before that Saul came, the Lord (had)
made (a) revelation in the ear of Samuel, and said,
16 In this same hour which is now, tomorrow, I shall
send to thee a man of the land of Benjamin, and thou
shalt anoint him duke upon my people Israel (and thou
shalt anoint him the ruler over my people Israel), and he
shall save my people from the hand(s) of (the) Philistines;
for I have beheld my people, forsooth their cry hath
come to me.
17 And when Samuel had beheld Saul, the Lord said to
Samuel, Lo! the man, (of) whom I said to thee; this man
shall be lord of my people.
18 And Saul nighed to Samuel in the midst of the gate,
and said, I pray thee, show thou to me, where is the
house of the seer?
19 And Samuel answered to Saul, and said, I am the
seer; go thou up before me into the high place, that thou
eat with me today, and I shall deliver thee in the
morrowtide, and I shall show to thee all things that be in
thine heart. (And Samuel answered Saul, and said, I am
the seer; go thou up before me, *or ahead of me,* to the
hill shrine, and thou shalt eat with me today, and in the
morning I shall let thee go, after that I show thee all the
things that be in thy heart.)
20 And be thou not busy of the female asses, which
thou lostest the third day ago, for those be found; and
whose shall be all the best things of Israel, whether not to
thee, and to all the house of thy father? (And be thou not
concerned about the female donkeys, which went
missing three days ago, for they be found; and now I ask
thee, who shall be regarded as the very best in Israel,
whether not thee, and all of thy father's family?)

21 And Saul answered, and said, Whether I am not a
son of Benjamin, of the least lineage of Israel, and my
kindred is the last among all the families of the lineage of
Benjamin? Why therefore hast thou spoken to me this
word? (And Saul answered, Am I not a Benjaminite, yea,
of the smallest tribe of Israel, and is not my kindred, *or
my family*, the least among all the families of the tribe of
Benjamin? Why then hast thou spoken such a word to
me?)
22 And so Samuel took Saul, and his servant, and led
them into the chamber of three orders (of seats, *or
benches*), and he gave to them a place in the beginning
of them that were called, (*or bidden to the meat*); for they
were as thirty men. (And then Samuel took Saul, and his
servant, and led them into a chamber with three rows of
seats, *or benches*, and he gave them a place at the head
of those who were called, *or were bidden to the meal*;
for there were about thirty men there.)
23 And Samuel said to the cook, Give thou the part
which I gave to thee (Bring thou out the portion which I
gave thee), and commanded, that thou shouldest keep (it)
by itself with thee.
24 And the cook took up a shoulder, and he set it
before Saul. And Samuel said, Lo! that, that hath (been)
left, take before thee, and eat; for of (this) purpose it was
kept to thee, when I called the people *hither*. And Saul
ate with Samuel that day. (And the cook took up a
shoulder, and he put it before Saul. And Samuel said, Lo!
that which was kept, take for thyself, and now eat it; for it
was kept for thee for this purpose, when I called the
people *here*. And so Saul ate with Samuel that day.)
25 And they came down from the high place into the
city; and Samuel spake with Saul in the solar, and Saul
arrayed a bed in the solar (for himself), and slept. (And
then they came down from the hill shrine into the city;
and Samuel spoke with Saul on the roof, and then Saul
arrayed a bed for himself on the roof, and slept.)
26 And when they had risen early, and the day began
to be clear, Samuel called Saul into the solar, and said,
Rise thou up, that I deliver thee (Samuel called to Saul on
the roof, and said, Rise thou up, so that I can let thee go).
And Saul rose up, and both went out, that is, he, and
Samuel.
27 And when they went down in(to) the last part of the
city, Samuel said to Saul, Say thou to the servant, that he
go before us, and pass [forth]; forsooth stand thou [still] a
little, that I show to thee the word of the Lord (but thou
stand here for a little while, so that I can tell thee the
word of the Lord).

CHAPTER 10

1 Forsooth Samuel took a vessel of oil, and he poured
it out on the head of Saul, and kissed him, and said, Lo!
the Lord hath anointed thee into prince on his heritage
(Lo! the Lord anointeth thee to be the prince, *or the ruler*,
over his people Israel);
2 when thou shalt go from me today, thou shalt find
two men beside the sepulchre of Rachel, in the ends of
Benjamin, in midday; and they shall say to thee, The
female asses be found, which thou wentest to seek; and
while the asses be left (off caring about), thy father is
(now) busy for you, and saith, What shall I do of my son?
(when thou shalt go away from me today, thou shalt find
two men beside the sepulchre of Rachel, at Zelzah, in the
territory of Benjamin; and they shall say to thee, The
female donkeys, which thou wentest to seek, be found;
and the female donkeys be no more cared about, but thy
father is now concerned about you, and saith, What shall
I do about my son?)
3 And when thou hast gone from thence, and hast
passed (forth) further, and hast come to the oak of Tabor,
three men, going up to God into Bethel (going up to
Bethel to worship God), shall find thee there, one man
bearing three kids, and another man bearing three cakes
of bread, and another man bearing a gallon of wine.
4 And when they have greeted thee, they shall give to
thee two loaves, and thou shalt take *those* of their hand
(and thou shalt take *their loaves*).
5 After these things thou shalt come into the hill of the
Lord, where is the standing place, *that is, the forcelet*, of
Philistines; and when thou shalt enter into the city, there
thou shalt have meeting thee a flock, *or a company*, of
prophets, coming down from the high place, and a
psaltery, and a tympan, and a pipe, and an harp before
them, and them prophesying. (After these things thou
shalt come to the Hill of the Lord, where the stronghold
of the Philistines is; and when thou shalt enter into the
city, there thou shalt meet a group of prophets, coming
down from the hill shrine, with a lute, and a drum, and a
pipe, and a harp going before them, and them
prophesying.)
6 And the Spirit of the Lord shall at once fall into thee,
and thou shalt prophesy with them, and thou shalt be
changed into another man.
7 Therefore when all these signs befall to thee, do
thou, whatever things thine hand findeth, for the Lord is
with thee.
8 And thou shalt go down before me into Gilgal; for I
shall come down to thee, to offer an offering, and
sacrifice peaceable sacrifices; by seven days thou shalt
abide, till I come to thee, and show thee what thou shalt
do. (And thou shalt go down before me to Gilgal; for I
shall come down to thee, to offer a burnt sacrifice, and to
sacrifice some peace offerings; thou shalt wait there for
seven days, until I come to thee, and show thee what
thou shalt do.)
9 Therefore when Saul had turned away his shoulder
to go from Samuel, God exchanged another heart to Saul

(God gave Saul another heart), and all these signs came
in that day.
10 And Saul and his servant came to the foresaid hill,
and lo! a company of prophets were meeting with him
(and lo! a group of prophets met him); and the Spirit of
the Lord fell *at once* upon Saul, and he prophesied in the
midst of the prophets.
11 And all men, that knew Saul yesterday and the third
day ago, saw that he was with the prophets, and that he
prophesied, and they said together, What thing hath
befallen to the son of Kish? Whether also Saul is among
[the] prophets? (Is Saul now also among the prophets?)
12 And one man answered to another, and said, And
who is the father of them? Therefore it was turned into a
proverb, Whether also Saul is among the prophets? (And
one man answered to another, and said, But who is their
father? And so it was turned into a proverb, Is Saul now
also among the prophets?)
13 And Saul ceased to prophesy, and he came to an
high place (and he came to the hill shrine).
14 And the brother of Saul's father said to him, and to
his servant, Whither went ye? And they answered, To
seek [the] she-asses; and when we found them not, we
came to Samuel.
15 And the brother of Saul's father said to him, Show
thou to me what Samuel said to thee. (And the brother of
Saul's father said to him, Tell thou to me what Samuel
said to thee.)
16 And Saul said to his uncle, Samuel showed to us,
that the she-asses were found. But he showed not to his
uncle of the word of the realm, that Samuel spake to him.
(And Saul said to his uncle, Samuel told us that the
female donkeys were found. But he did not tell his uncle
what Samuel had said to him about the kingdom/about
becoming king.)
17 And Samuel called together the people to the Lord
in Mizpeh; (And Samuel called the people together to the
Lord at Mizpeh;)
18 and he said to the sons of Israel, The Lord God of
Israel saith these things, I led Israel out of the land of Egypt,
and I delivered you from the hand of (the) Egyptians, and
from the hand of all the kings that tormented you.
19 And today ye have cast away your Lord God, which
alone saved you from all your evils and [your] tribulations
(who alone saved you from all your evils and your
tribulations); and ye [have] said (to him), Nay, but ordain
thou a king upon us. Now therefore stand ye before the
Lord by your lineages, and by (your) families.
20 And Samuel set together all the lineages of Israel,
and [the] lot felled upon the lineage of Benjamin.
21 And he set together the lineage of Benjamin, and the
families thereof; and (the) lot felled upon the family of
Matri, and it came unto Saul, the son of Kish. Therefore
they sought him, and he was not found there.
22 And after these things they counselled with the Lord,
whether Saul should come thither. And the Lord
answered, Lo! he is hid among (the) vessels.
23 Therefore they ran, and took him from thence; and
he stood in the middle of the people, and [he] was higher
than all the people from the shoulder[s] and above.
24 And Samuel said to all the people, Certainly ye see
whom the Lord hath chosen; for none in all the people is
like him (for there is no one like him among all the
people). And all the people cried, and said, (Long) Live
the king!
25 And Samuel spake to the people (concerning) the
law of the realm, and he wrote it in a book, and put it up
before the Lord. And Samuel delivered all the people,
each man into his house (And then Samuel sent all the
people back to their homes);
26 but also Saul went into his house in Gibeah; and a
part of the host went with him, whose hearts God had
touched. (and Saul also went home, back to Gibeah; and
a part of the army went with him, whose hearts God had
touched.)
27 And the sons of Belial said, Whether this man may
save us? And they despised him, and brought not gifts,
that is, presents, to him; and he let (it go) as though he
heard (it) not. (But the sons of Belial said, Can this man
truly save us? And they despised him, and did not bring
him any gifts; but he held his peace.)

CHAPTER 11

1 And it was done as after a month, Nahash of
Ammon went up, and began to fight against Jabesh of
Gilead. And all the men of Jabesh said to Nahash, Have
thou us bound in peace (Make thou a covenant, or a
bond of peace, with us), and we shall serve thee.
2 And Nahash of Ammon answered to them, In this I
shall smite (a) bond of peace with you, that I put out the
right eyes of all you, and that I put you to be reproof in
all Israel. (And Nahash of Ammon answered to them,
Only in this shall I strike a covenant with you, that I put
out all of your right eyes, and that I bring reproach, *or
disgrace*, upon all Israel.)
3 And the elder men of Jabesh said to him, Grant thou
to us seven days, that we send messengers to all the
coasts of Israel; and if none be that defend us, we shall go
out to thee. (And the elders of Jabesh said to him, First
grant thou us seven days, so that we can send messengers
into all the coasts of Israel; and if there be none who will
defend us, then we shall come out to thee.)
4 Then messengers came into Gibeah of Saul, and
spake these words, while the people heard; and all the
people raised (up) their voice, and wept.
5 And lo! Saul came from the field, and he followed
[the] oxen; and he said, What hath the people, for it
weepeth? (and he said, What maketh the people weep?)

And they told to him the words of the men of Jabesh.
6 And the Spirit of the Lord fell at once into Saul,
when he had heard these words, and his fierce wrath was
greatly stirred.
7 And he took ever either ox, and he cut *them* into
gobbets, and he sent those into all the coasts of Israel, by
the hands of messengers; and he said, Whoever goeth not
out, and followeth not Saul and Samuel, so it shall be
done to his oxen. Therefore the dread of the Lord went
into the people (And so the fear of the Lord went into the
people), and they went out as one man.
8 And Saul numbered them in Bezek; and three
hundred thousand were there of the sons of Israel; and of
the men of Judah were thirty thousand. (And Saul
counted, *or registered*, them in Bezek; and there were
three hundred thousand of the sons of Israel; and thirty
thousand of the men of Judah.)
9 And they said to the messengers that came, Thus ye
shall say to the men that be in Jabesh of Gilead,
Tomorrow shall be health to you, when the sun is hot
(Tomorrow, help shall come to you, when the sun is hot).
Then the messengers came, and told to the men of
Jabesh; the which were glad,
10 and said *to Ammon*, Early we shall go out to you,
and ye shall do to us all that pleaseth to you.[2] (and they
said *to the Ammonites*, Early in the morning, we shall
come out to you, and then ye can do to us all that
pleaseth you.)
11 And it was done, when the morrowtide came, Saul
ordained the people into three parts; and he entered into
the middle (of the) tents (of Ammon) in the waking of the
morrowtide, and he smote Ammon till the day was hot;
forsooth the residues were scattered, so that twain together
were not left in them. (And it was done, when the morning
came, Saul divided the people into three parts, *or groups*;
and they entered into the midst of the tents of the
Ammonites during the morning watch, and they struck
down the Ammonites until the day was hot; and the rest of
them scattered, so that two of them were not left together.)
12 And the people said to Samuel, Who is this, that
said, Saul shall not reign upon us? Give ye (up) the men,
and we shall slay them.
13 And Saul said, No man shall be slain in this day, for
today the Lord hath made health in Israel. (And Saul said,
No one shall be killed on this day, for today the Lord
hath given victory to Israel.)
14 And Samuel said to the people, Come ye, and go we
into Gilgal, and renew we there the realm (and let us
renew our loyalty to the kingdom there).
15 And all the people went into Gilgal, and there they
made Saul king before the Lord in Gilgal; and they
offered *there* peaceable sacrifices before the Lord. And
Saul was glad there, and all the men of Israel greatly.
(And all the people went to Gilgal, and there in Gilgal
they made Saul king before the Lord; and they offered
peace offerings *there* before the Lord. And Saul and all
the men of Israel were exceedingly glad there.)

CHAPTER 12

1 Forsooth Samuel said to all Israel, Lo! I [have] heard
your voice by all (the) things which ye spake to me, and I
[have] ordained a king upon you;
2 and now the king goeth before you. And I have
waxed eld and hoary; and my sons be with you; also I
have lived before you from my young waxing age unto
this day.
3 And lo! I am ready; speak ye to me before the Lord,
and before the christ of him/before his anointed, *or king*;
whether I have taken any man's ox, either his ass; if I
have falsely challenged any man; if I have oppressed any
man; if I have taken gift of any man's hand; I shall despise
it today, and I shall restore (it) to you. (And lo! I am
ready; speak ye to me before the Lord, and before his
anointed king; have I taken any man's ox, or his donkey;
have I falsely challenged any man; have I oppressed any
man; have I taken a gift from any man's hand? yea, if I
have, I shall despise it today, and I shall restore it to you.)
4 And they said, Thou hast not falsely challenged us,
neither thou hast oppressed *us*, neither thou hast taken
any thing of any man's hand.
5 And he said to them, The Lord is witness against
you, and his christ, *or king*, is witness in this day (and his
anointed *king* is a witness this day); for ye have not found
anything in mine hand. And they said, He is witness.
6 And Samuel said to the people, The Lord, that made
Moses and Aaron, and that led your fathers out of the
land of Egypt, is present; (And Samuel said to the people,
The Lord, who made Moses and Aaron, and who led
your fathers out of the land of Egypt, is present here;)
7 now therefore stand ye, that I strive by doom against
you before the Lord, of all the mercies of the Lord, which
he did with you, and with your fathers. (and so now
stand ye up, so that I can strive in judgement against you
before the Lord, and remind you of all the Lord's mercies,
which he did for you, and for your fathers.)
8 How that Jacob entered into Egypt, and your fathers
cried to the Lord; and the Lord sent Moses and Aaron,
and led your fathers out of Egypt, and hath set them in
this place.
9 Which forgat their Lord God; and he betook them
into the hand of Sisera, master of the chivalry of Hazor,
and in the hand of Philistines, and in the hand of the king
of Moab; and they fought against them. (Who then forgot
the Lord their God; and he delivered them into the hands
of Sisera, the master of Hazor's cavalry, *or his army*, and

[2] They said this in scorn, for they knew that help shall come to them in the morrow.

into the hands of the Philistines, and into the hands of the
king of Moab; and they fought against them.)
10 And after this your fathers cried to the Lord, and
said, We have sinned, for we forsook the Lord, and
served (the) Baalim and (the) Ashtaroth; now therefore
deliver thou us from the hand of our enemies, and we
shall serve thee.
11 And the Lord sent Jerubbaal, *that is Gideon*, and
Bedan, *that is, Samson*, and Barak, and Jephthah, and
Samuel, and delivered you from the hand of your enemies
by compass, (or all about); and then ye dwelled securely.
12 And ye saw, that Nahash, the king of the sons of
Ammon, came against you; and ye said to me,
counselling you to ask none other king than God, Nay,
but a king shall command to us; when your Lord God
reigned in you. (And then ye saw, that Nahash, the king
of the Ammonites, came against you; and ye said to me,
when I counselled you to ask for no other king than God,
Nay, but a king shall command us; when the Lord your
God then reigned over you.)
13 Now therefore your king is ready, whom ye have
chosen and asked (for); lo! the Lord hath given to you a
king (lo! the Lord hath given you a king).
14 If ye dread the Lord, and serve him, and hear his
voice, and wrath not the mouth of the Lord; ye and your
king, that commandeth to you, shall follow your Lord
God. (If ye fear the Lord/If ye revere the Lord, and serve
him, and listen to his voice, and do not rebel against the
Lord's commands, then ye and your king, who
commandeth you, shall follow the Lord your God.)
15 Forsooth if ye hear not the voice of the Lord, but
wrath his word, the hand of the Lord shall be on you, and
on your fathers. (But if ye do not listen to the Lord's
voice, and rebel against his commands, the hand of the
Lord shall be against you, and against your fathers.)
16 But also now stand ye, and see this great thing, that
the Lord shall do in your sight.
17 Whether (the) harvest of wheat is not today? I shall
inwardly call (upon) the Lord, and he shall give voices,
that is, thunders, and rains; and ye shall know, and see,
for ye asking a king upon you, ye have done grievous evil
to yourself in the sight of the Lord (and ye shall know,
and see, that in asking for a king *to rule* over you, ye
have done grievous evil to yourselves before the Lord).
18 And Samuel cried to the Lord, and the Lord gave
thunders and rains in that day. And all the people
dreaded greatly the Lord and Samuel; (And Samuel cried
to the Lord, and the Lord gave thunder and rain that day.
And all the people greatly feared the Lord and Samuel;)
19 and all the people said to Samuel, Pray thou for thy
servants to thy Lord God, that we die not; for we [have]
added evil to all our sins, that we ask a king to us. (and
all the people said to Samuel, Pray thou for thy servants
to the Lord thy God, so that we shall not die; for we have
added this evil to all our sins, that we asked for a king
over us.)
20 And Samuel said to the people, Dread ye not; ye
have done all this evil; nevertheless go ye not away from
(following) the back of the Lord, but serve ye the Lord in
all your heart (but serve ye the Lord with all your heart);
21 and do not ye bow after vain things, that shall not
profit you, neither they shall deliver you; for those be vain
things. (and do not ye worship false gods, that shall not
profit you, nor can they save you; for they be false gods.)
22 And *then* the Lord shall not forsake his people for
his great name; for the Lord hath sworn to make you a
people to himself. (And *then* the Lord shall not forsake
his people for the sake of his great name; for the Lord
hath sworn to make you his own people.)
23 And this sin be far from me against the Lord, that I
cease to pray for you; and I shall teach you a rightful way
and a good. (And let this sin against the Lord be far from
me, that I would ever cease to pray for you; yea, indeed, I
shall teach you the good and the right way.)
24 Therefore dread ye the Lord, and serve ye him in
truth, and of all your heart; for ye saw those great things,
that he hath done to you; (And so fear ye the Lord/And so
revere ye the Lord, and serve ye him in truth, and with all
your heart; for ye have seen all the great things which he
hath done for you;)
25 that if ye continue in malice, both ye and your king
shall perish (al)together. (but if ye continue in malice, *or
in wickedness*, both ye and your king shall altogether
perish.)

CHAPTER 13

1 Saul was a son of one year, *that is, as innocent and
clean of sin as a child of one year*, when he began to
reign; and he reigned upon Israel two (and twenty) years.
(Saul was fifty years old when he began to reign; and he
reigned over Israel for twenty-two years.)
2 And Saul chose to him three thousand *men* of Israel,
and two thousand *of them* were with Saul in Michmash,
(and) in the hill (country) of Bethel; and a thousand were
with (his son) Jonathan in Gibeah of Benjamin; soothly he
sent again the tother people each man into his tabernacle
(and he sent the rest of the people back to their tents).
3 And Jonathan smote the station, *that is, (the)
forcelet, either stronghold*, of (the) Philistines, that was in
Geba. And when (the) Philistines had heard (of) this,
Saul sounded with a clarion in all the land, and said,
Hebrews, hear. (And Jonathan struck the station, *that is,
the fortress, or the stronghold*, of the Philistines, that was
in Geba; and all the Philistines heard about it. And Saul
sounded with a trumpet in all the land, and said, Hebrew
men, hear this!)
4 And all Israel heard such a fame, (that) Saul smote
the station of Philistines; and Israel raised up himself

against the Philistines; then the people cried after Saul in
Gilgal. (And all Israel heard the report, that Saul had
struck the Philistines' station; and also that the people of
Israel were loathed by all the Philistines. And the people
came together in Gilgal to follow Saul.)
5 And the Philistines were gathered together to fight
against Israel; thirty thousand of chariots, and six
thousand of knights, and the tother common people, as
gravel which is full much in the brink of the sea (and the
common people, as innumerable as the sand which is on
the seashore); and they went up, and setted their tents in
Michmash, at the east coast of Bethaven.
6 And when [the] men of Israel had seen, that they
were set in straitness, for (this) the people was tormented,
(and) they hid themselves in dens (and they hid
themselves in caves), and in privy places, and in stones,
and in ditches, and in cisterns.
7 Soothly (some of the) Hebrews passed (over) Jordan,
into the land of Gad and of Gilead. And when Saul was
yet in Gilgal, all the people was afeared that followed
him (And when Saul was still in Gilgal, all the people
who followed him were afraid).
8 And seven days he abode Samuel by [the] covenant,
and Samuel came not into Gilgal; and the people went
away from Saul. (And for seven days he waited for
Samuel, as by their pact, but Samuel did not come to
Gilgal; and then the people began to go away from Saul.)
9 Therefore Saul said, Bring ye to me (a) burnt
sacrifice, and peaceable offerings (and peace offerings);
and he offered (the) burnt sacrifice.
10 And when he had ended offering the burnt sacrifice,
lo! Samuel came; and Saul went out against him, to greet
him (and Saul went out to greet him).
11 And Samuel said to Saul, What hast thou done? Saul
answered, Lo! for I saw that the people went away from
me, and thou camest not by the days of (our) covenant;
and the Philistines were gathered together in Michmash;
12 I said, Now (the) Philistines shall come down to me
in(to) Gilgal, and I have not pleased the face of the Lord;
(and so) I was compelled by need, and I offered (a) burnt
sacrifice to the Lord.
13 And Samuel said to Saul, Thou hast done follily, and
thou hast not kept the behests of thy Lord God, which he
commanded to thee (Thou hast done foolishly, and thou
hast not obeyed the command of the Lord thy God,
which he commanded to thee); and if thou haddest not
done this thing, right now the Lord had made ready thy
realm upon Israel [into] without end;
14 but thy realm shall not rise further. The Lord hath
sought a man to himself after his heart; and the Lord hath
commanded to him, that he should be duke on his
people, for thou keptest not those things which the Lord
commanded. (but now thy kingdom shall not endure.
And the Lord shall seek another man for himself after his
own heart; and the Lord shall command him, that he
should be the ruler over his people, for thou hast not
kept, *or obeyed*, what the Lord commanded to thee.)
15 And Samuel rose, and went up from Gilgal into
Gibeah of Benjamin; and the people that (were) left went
up after Saul against the people that fought against them;
and they came from Gilgal into Gibeah, in the hill of
Benjamin. And Saul numbered the people, that were
found with him, as six hundred men. (And Samuel rose up,
and went away from Gilgal to Gibeah of Benjamin; and
the people who were left went up with Saul to fight against
their enemies; and they came from Gilgal to Gibeah of
Benjamin. And Saul counted the people who were found
with him, and there were about six hundred men.)
16 And Saul, and Jonathan his son, and the people that
was found with them, was in Gibeah of Benjamin; and
the Philistines sat together in Michmash. (And Saul, and
his son Jonathan, and the people who were found with
them, were in Gibeah of Benjamin; and the Philistines sat
together in Michmash.)
17 And three companies went out of the Philistines'
tents to take prey; one company went against the way of
Ophrah, to the land of Shual (one group went toward
Ophrah, in the land of Shual);
18 and another company entered by the way of
Bethhoron; and the third company turned itself to the
way of the term in the land of Diba; and that term
nigheth to the valley of Zeboim against the desert. (and
the second group went by the way of Bethhoron; and the
third group turned toward the way of the border at Wadi
Abu Diba; and that border overlooketh the Zeboim
Valley and the wilderness.)
19 And none ironsmith was found in all the land of
Israel; for the Philistines were wary, *either eschewed*, lest
peradventure the Hebrews made sword either spear.
(And no ironsmith was found in all the land of Israel; for
the Philistines forbade them, lest the Hebrews made for
themselves swords or spears.)
20 Therefore all Israel went down to the Philistines, that
each man should sharpen his share, and his pickax, and
his ax, and his cutting hook; (And so all Israel needed to
go down to the Philistines, where each man could
sharpen his plowshare, and his pickax, and his ax, and
his cutting hook;)
21 for all the edges of their shares were blunt, and of
their pickaxes, and of their three-toothed forks, and of
axes, unto a prick to be amended. (for all the edges of
their plowshares, their pickaxes, their three-toothed forks,
and their axes, were blunt, and needed sharpening.)
22 And when the day of battle came, no sword nor
spear was found in the hand of all the people that was
with Saul and Jonathan, except Saul, and Jonathan his
son. (And so when the day of battle came, no sword or
spear was found in the hands of all the people who were

with Saul and Jonathan, except Saul, and his son Jonathan.)
23 Forsooth the station of Philistines went out, that it
should pass into Michmash. (And the Philistines' garrison
went out to the Michmash Pass.)

CHAPTER 14

1 And it befelled in a day, that Jonathan, the son of
Saul, said to his squire, a young man, Come thou, and
pass we (over) to the station of the Philistines, which is
beyond that place; soothly he showed not this same thing
to his father. (And it befell one day, that Saul's son
Jonathan, said to the young man who was his squire,
Come thou, and go we over to the Philistines' station, *or
post*, which is beyond that place over there; but he did
not tell this to his father.)
2 And Saul dwelled in the last part of Gibeah, under a
pomegranate tree, that was in the field of Gibeah; and the
people as of six hundred men was with him. (And Saul
remained in the last part of Gibeah, under a pomegranate
tree, that was in Migron; and the people who were with
him were about six hundred men.)
3 And Ahiah, the son of Ahitub, [the] brother of
Ichabod, the son of Phinehas, that was engendered of Eli,
the priest of the Lord in Shiloh, bare the ephod, *that is,
the priest's cloak*; but also the people knew not whither
Jonathan had gone (and the people did not know that
Jonathan had gone).
4 And betwixt the goings up, by which Jonathan
endeavoured to pass to the station of (the) Philistines,
were stones standing forth on ever either side, and scars
broken before, by the manner of teeth, on each side (and
broken scarps on each side, like teeth); (the) name to the
one was Bozez, and (the) name to the tother was Seneh;
5 one scar was standing forth to the north (over)
against Michmash, and the tother scar to the south (over)
against Gibeah. (one scarp was to the north, facing
Michmash, and the other scarp was to the south, facing
Gibeah.)
6 And Jonathan said to his young squire, Come thou,
pass we (over) to the station of these uncircumcised men,
if in hap the Lord do (battle) for us; for it is not hard to the
Lord to save, either in many, either in few (for it is not
hard for the Lord to keep a man safe, yea, either a few, or
many).
7 And his squire said to him, Do thou all things that
please thy soul; go whither thou covetest, I shall be with
thee, wherever thou wilt.
8 And Jonathan said, Lo! we pass (over) to these men;
and when we appear to them,
9 if they speak thus to us, Dwell ye (Stay ye), till we
come to you; stand we in our place, and go we not up to
them.
10 And if they say, Go ye up to us; go we up to them,
for the Lord hath betaken them into our hands; this shall
be a sign to us. (But if they say, Come ye up to us; then
we shall go up to them, for the Lord hath delivered them
into our hands; this shall be a sign to us.)
11 Therefore ever either appeared to the station of
Philistines (And so they both appeared before the
Philistines' station); and the Philistines said, Lo! the
Hebrews go out of [the] caves, in which they were hid.
12 And men of the station spake to Jonathan and to his
squire, and said, Go ye up to us, and we shall show to
you a thing. And Jonathan said to his squire, Ascend we,
follow thou me; for the Lord hath betaken them into the
hands of Israel. (And the men of the station said to
Jonathan and his squire, Come ye over to us, and we
shall show you a thing or two. And Jonathan said to his
squire, Go we up *to them*, follow thou me; for the Lord
hath delivered them into the hands of Israel.)
13 And Jonathan went up, creeping on hands and feet,
and his squire after him; and when they had seen the face
of Jonathan, some felled down before Jonathan, his
squire killed others, and followed him (and when they
were face to face with Jonathan, he killed some, and his
squire killed some others, following his master).
14 And the first wound was made, which Jonathan and
his squire smote, as of twenty men, in the middle part of
land, which a pair of oxen was wont to ear in the day.
(And so the first attack was made, in which Jonathan and
his squire killed about twenty men, in the middle part of
a field which a pair of oxen could plow in a day.)
15 And a miracle was done in the *Philistines'* tents, and
by their fields, but also all the people of the *Philistines'*
station that went out to take prey, dreaded, and their tents
were troubled; and it befelled as a miracle of God. (And
so terror spread across that field, and among the
Philistines' host, *or army*, and all the people at the
Philistines' station who went out to take prey were afraid,
and the army was greatly troubled; and so it befell as a
miracle of God.)
16 And the espyers of Saul beheld *this doing*, that were
in Gibeah of Benjamin, and lo! a multitude *of the
Philistines* was cast down, and fleeing away hither and
thither. (And Saul's watchmen, who were in Gibeah of
Benjamin, beheld *this event*, and lo! many *Philistines*
were thrown down, and others fled away here and there.)
17 And Saul said to the people that were with him,
Seek *ye*, and see ye, who went away from us. And when
they had sought, it was found, that Jonathan and his
squire were not present.
18 And Saul said to Ahiah, Bring hither the ark of the
Lord; for the ark of God was there in that time with the
sons of Israel. (And Saul said to Ahiah, Bring the ephod
here; for at that time Ahiah carried the ephod before the
Israelites.)
19 And when Saul spake to the priest, a great noise
(a)rose in the tents of the Philistines; and it increased little

and little, and it sounded more clearly. And Saul said to
the priest, Withdraw thine hand (And Saul said to the
priest, Hold back thy hand!).
20 Therefore Saul cried, and all the people that was
with him; and they came unto the place of battle, and, lo!
the sword of each man was turned to his neighbour, and
a full great slaying was. (And then Saul and all the people
who were with him cried together; and they came to the
place of the battle, and, lo! the sword of each man was
turned against his neighbour, and there was a very great
slaughter.)
21 But also the Hebrews that were with (the) Philistines
yesterday and the third day ago, and had gone up with
them in(to) their tents, turned again to be with the men of
Israel, that were with Saul and Jonathan.
22 Also all the men of Israel, that had hid themselves in
the hill (country) of Ephraim, heard that the Philistines
had fled; and they fellowshipped themselves with their
men in [the] battle, and as ten thousand of men were
with Saul (and about ten thousand men were with Saul).
23 And the Lord saved Israel in that day (And the Lord
saved Israel that day). And the battle came till to Bethaven.
24 And men of Israel were fellowshipped to themselves
in that day; forsooth Saul swore to the people, and said,
Cursed be the man that eateth bread till to eventide, till I
venge me of mine enemies. And all the people ate no
bread. (And the men of Israel felt faint that day; for Saul
had commanded to the people, and said, Cursed be the
man who eateth any food before evening, until I avenge
myself upon my enemies. And so all the people ate no
food.)
25 And all the common people of the land came into a
forest, in which was honey on the face of (the) earth
(where there was honey on the ground).
26 And so the people entered into the forest, and
flowing honey appeared (there); and no man put his hand
to his mouth *thereof*, for the people dreaded the oath (but
no man put his hand to his mouth, for the people feared
the oath/for the people feared Saul's curse).
27 And Jonathan heard not, when his father forbade
this to the people (But Jonathan did not hear his father
forbid this to the people); and (so) Jonathan held forth the
end of a little rod, that he held in his hand, and he
dipped it into an honeycomb; and he turned his hand to
his mouth, and his eyes were (en)lightened, (*that is, he
felt refreshed*).
28 And (at once) one of the people answered, and said,
Thy father bound the people with an oath, and said,
Cursed be the man that eateth bread today (Cursed be the
man who eateth any food today). And (so) the people was
faint.
29 And (then) Jonathan said, My father hath troubled
the land; ye see, that mine eyes be enlightened (ye see,
that I am refreshed), for I tasted a little of this honey;
30 how much more if the people had eaten (some) of
the prey of their enemies, that they found; whether not
greater vengeance had been made in [the] Philistines?
(would not a greater slaughter have been done to the
Philistines?)
31 Therefore they smote [the] Philistines in that day
from Michmash into Aijalon. And the people was made
full weary; (And so they struck down the Philistines that
day from Michmash to Aijalon. But the people were
made faint;)
32 and (so) the people turned to [the] prey, and took
sheep and oxen, and calves; and they killed *these beasts*
upon the earth (and they killed *these beasts* on the
ground); and (then) the people ate *the flesh* with (the)
blood (still in it).
33 And they told to Saul, and said, that the people
eating with blood had sinned to the Lord. And Saul said,
Ye have trespassed; wallow ye anon to me a great stone.
(And they told Saul, and said, The people have sinned
against the Lord, eating the flesh with the blood! And
Saul said, Ye have all trespassed; roll ye a great stone
over to me at once.)
34 And Saul said, Go ye forth abroad into the common
people, and say ye to them, that each man (should) bring
to me his ox and his wether, (*or his ram*); and slay ye
those upon this stone, and (then) eat ye them, and (so) ye
shall not do sin to the Lord, (by) eating them with (the)
blood. And so all the people brought each man an ox in
his hand unto the night, and they killed them there (And
so into the night each man brought forth an ox, and they
killed them there).
35 And Saul builded there an altar to the Lord; and then
first he began to build an altar to the Lord. (And Saul built
an altar there to the Lord; and this was the first altar that
he built to the Lord.)
36 And Saul said, Fall we upon the Philistines in the
night, and waste we/destroy we them till the morrowtide
shine; and leave we not of them a man (alive). And the
people said, Do thou all thing that seemeth good to thee
in thine eyes. And the priest said, Nigh we hither to God.
37 And Saul counselled with the Lord, and said,
Whether I shall pursue the Philistines? whether thou shalt
betake them into the hands of Israel? And the Lord
answered not to him in that day. (And Saul counselled
with the Lord, and asked, Shall I pursue the Philistines?
wilt thou deliver them into the hands of Israel? But the
Lord did not answer him that day.)
38 And Saul said, Bring ye hither all the corners, *or the
uttermost parties*, of the people (Bring ye here all the
chieftains, *or the chief men*, of the people), and know ye,
and see ye, by whom this sin hath fallen today.
39 The Lord the saviour of Israel liveth; for (even) if it is
done by Jonathan my son, he shall die without again-
drawing. At which *oath* no man of all the people against-

said him. (As the Lord liveth, yea, the saviour, *or the*
deliverer, of Israel; for even if it is done by my son
Jonathan, he shall die without any drawing back, *or*
without delay. At which *oath* no one of all the people
answered anything back to him.)
40 And he said to all Israel, Be ye separated into one
part, and I with my son Jonathan shall be in the tother
part. And the people answered to Saul, Do thou that,
that seemeth good to thine eyes (Do thou what seemeth
good in thine eyes).
41 And Saul said to the Lord God of Israel, Lord God of
Israel, give thou doom, what is it, that thou answerest not
today to thy servant? If this wickedness is in me, either in
Jonathan, my son, make thou showing *thereof*; either if
this wickedness is in thy people, give thou holiness. And
Jonathan was taken, and Saul, *by lot*; forsooth the people
went out. (And Saul said to the Lord God of Israel, Lord
God of Israel, give thou judgement, why is it that thou
hast not answered thy servant today? If this wickedness is
in me, or in my son Jonathan, let the lot be Urim; but if
this wickedness is in thy people, let it be Thummim. And
by lot Jonathan and Saul were indicted; and the people
were absolved.)
42 And Saul said, Send ye lot betwixt me and Jonathan
my son (And Saul said, Cast ye the lot/Throw ye the lot
between me and my son Jonathan). And Jonathan was
taken.
43 And Saul said to Jonathan, Show thou to me, what
thou didest. And Jonathan showed to him, and said, I
tasting tasted a little of honey in the end of the rod, that
was in mine hand; and lo! I die. (And Saul said to
Jonathan, Tell thou to me, what thou didest. And
Jonathan said to him, I tasted a little honey using the end
of the rod that was in my hand; and lo! now I must die.)
44 And Saul said, God do to me these things, and add
these things, for thou, Jonathan, shalt (indeed) die by
death.
45 And the people said to Saul, Therefore whether
Jonathan shall die, that did this great health in Israel? this
is unleaveful; the Lord liveth; none hair of his head shall
fall into the earth; for he hath wrought with God today.
Therefore the people delivered Jonathan, that he died
not. (And the people said to Saul, Should Jonathan truly
die, he who hath won this great victory for Israel? Nay!
this is unlawful; as the Lord liveth, there shall not fall to
the ground one hair of his head, for he hath worked with
God today. And so the people delivered Jonathan, so that
he did not die.)
46 And Saul went away, and he pursued not the
Philistines; and the Philistines went into their places.
47 And Saul, when his realm was stabled upon Israel,
fought by compass against all his enemies (And Saul,
when his kingdom was established upon Israel, fought
against all his enemies all around), (yea,) against Moab,
and the sons of Ammon, and Edom, and against the kings
of Zobah, and against the Philistines; and whither ever he
turned him[self], he overcame (them).
48 And when his host was gathered together, he smote
Amalek; and delivered Israel from the hand of his
destroyers. (And then when his army was gathered
together, he killed the Amalekites; and so he saved Israel
from the hands of their destroyers.)
49 And the sons of Saul were Jonathan, and Ishui, and
Melchishua; the names of his two daughters *be these*, the
name of the first engendered daughter was Merab, and
the name of the younger was Michal.
50 And the name of Saul's wife was Ahinoam, the
daughter of Ahimaaz; and the name of the prince of his
chivalry *was* Abner (and the name of the leader of his
cavalry, *or of his army*, *was* Abner), the son of Ner, the
brother of the father of Saul.
51 And Kish was the father of Saul; and Ner, the son of
Abiel, was the father of Abner.
52 Soothly mighty battle was against Philistines in all
the days of Saul; for whomever Saul saw (to be) a strong
man, and shapely to battle, he fellowshipped to himself
that man. (And there was great battle against the
Philistines in all the days of Saul; and whenever Saul saw
a strong man, ready for battle, he took that man into his
own service.)

CHAPTER 15

1 And Samuel said to Saul, The Lord sent me, that I
should anoint thee into king on his people Israel (The
Lord hath sent me to anoint thee king upon his people
Israel); now therefore hear thou the voice of the Lord.
2 The Lord of hosts saith these things, I have brought
to mind whatever things Amalek hath done to Israel; how
Amalek against-stood Israel in the way, when Israel went
up from Egypt. (The Lord of hosts saith these things, I
have remembered all the things that the Amalekites did to
Israel; how they opposed Israel on the way, when Israel
came up from Egypt.)
3 Now therefore go thou, and slay Amalek, and destroy
thou all his things; spare thou not him, nor covet thou
anything of his things; but slay thou from man unto
woman, and little child, and sucking, ox, and sheep, and
camel, and ass. (And so now go thou, and kill the
Amalekites, and destroy thou all of their things; spare thou
not any of them, nor covet thou any of their things; but kill
thou every man and woman, and little child, and suckling,
yea, *every* ox, and sheep, and camel, and donkey.)
4 And so Saul commanded the people *to be gathered*
together, and he numbered them as lambs, two hundred
thousand of footmen, and ten thousand of men of Judah.
(And so Saul commanded the people *to be gathered*
together, and he counted, *or registered*, them in Telaim,
and there were two hundred thousand footmen, and also

ten thousand men of Judah.)
5 And when Saul came to the city of Amalek, he made
ready ambushments in the (dry bed of the) strand. (And
when Saul came to the Amalekite city/And when Saul
came to the city of Amalek, he prepared an ambush in
the dry riverbed.)
6 And Saul said to (the) Kenites, Go ye, depart ye, and
go ye away from Amalek, lest peradventure I wrap thee
in with them; for thou didest mercy with all the sons of
Israel, when they went up from Egypt. And Kenites
departed from the midst of Amalek (And so the Kenites
departed from the midst of the Amalekites).
7 And Saul smote Amalek, from Havilah, till thou
come to Shur, which is even against Egypt. (And Saul
struck down the Amalekites, from Havilah until thou
come to Shur, which is on the border with Egypt.)
8 And Saul took Agag alive, the king of Amalek; and
he killed by sharpness of sword all the common people.
(And Saul took Agag, the king of Amalek, alive; but they
killed all the common people with the sharpness of their
swords.)
9 And Saul and the people spared Agag (But Saul and
his people spared Agag), and the best (of the) flocks of
(the) sheep, and of (the) great beasts, and (they kept the)
clothes, and (the) rams, and all things that were fair; and
they would not destroy those; but whatever thing was
vile, and reprovable, they destroyed that thing.
10 Forsooth the word of the Lord was made to Samuel,
and said,
11 It repenteth me, that I made Saul king; for he hath
forsaken me, and hath not fulfilled my words in work.
And Samuel was sorry, and he cried to the Lord in all that
night. (I repent, *that is, I regret,* that I made Saul king; for
he hath deserted me, and hath not fulfilled my words in
deeds. And Samuel was angry, and he cried out to the
Lord all that night.)
12 And (then) when Samuel had risen up by night to go
early to Saul, it was told to Samuel, that Saul had come
into Carmel, and had raised up to him a sign of victory
(and had raised up a victory monument for himself there);
and that he had turned again *from Amalek,* and had
passed forth, and had gone down into Gilgal.
13 Then Samuel came to Saul, and Saul offered burnt
sacrifice to the Lord of the chief things of the preys,
which he had brought from Amalek. And the while
Samuel came to Saul, Saul said to him, Blessed be thou
of the Lord, I have [ful]filled the word of the Lord. (And
when Samuel came to Saul, Saul was offering a burnt
sacrifice to the Lord of the chief things of the prey which
he had taken from the Amalekites. And when Samuel
came over to Saul, Saul said to him, Blessed be thou of
the Lord! I have fulfilled the word of the Lord.)
14 And Samuel said, And what is this voice of flocks
(But what is this sound of the flocks), that soundeth in
mine ears, and of (the) great beasts, which I hear?
15 And Saul said, They brought those from Amalek
(They were taken from the Amalekites); for the people
spared the best sheep and (the best) great beasts, that
those should be offered to thy Lord God; and we killed
the tother beasts.
16 And Samuel said to Saul, Suffer thou me (Allow me),
and I shall show to thee what things the Lord hath spoken
to me in this night. And Saul said to Samuel, Speak thou.
17 And Samuel said, Whether not, when thou were
little in thine own eyes, thou were made head in the
lineages of Israel, and the Lord anointed thee into king on
Israel; (And Samuel said, Was it not, when thou were
small, *or insignificant,* in thy own eyes, thou were made
the head of all the tribes of Israel, and did not the Lord
anoint thee king upon Israel?)
18 and the Lord sent thee into the way, and said, Go
thou, and slay the sinners of Amalek, and thou shalt fight
against them till to the slaying of them. (and the Lord sent
thee on the way, and said, Go thou, and kill those
sinners, the Amalekites, and thou shalt fight against them
until they all be slaughtered.)
19 Why therefore heardest thou not the voice of the
Lord, but thou were turned to the prey (but instead, thou
took that prey), and (so) didest evil in the eyes of the
Lord?
20 And Saul said to Samuel, Yes, I heard the voice of
the Lord, and I have gone in the way, by which the Lord
sent me, and I have brought Agag, the king of Amalek,
and I have killed Amalek. (And Saul said to Samuel, Yes,
I did listen to the Lord's voice, and I have gone on the
way where he sent me, and I have brought Agag, the king
of the Amalekites here, and I have killed all the other
Amalekites.)
21 Forsooth the people took of the prey, sheep and
oxen, the first fruits/the chief fruits of those things that be
slain, that they make sacrifice to their Lord God in Gilgal.
(But the people kept of the prey, sheep and oxen, the first
fruits/the chief fruits of those things that should be killed,
to offer as a sacrifice to the Lord their God here in Gilgal.)
22 And Samuel said, Whether the Lord will burnt
sacrifices, either slain sacrifices, and not more, *rather,*
that men obey to the voice of the Lord? (And Samuel
said, Desireth the Lord burnt sacrifices, and slain
sacrifices, or *rather,* that people obey his voice?) Forsooth
obedience *to him* is better than sacrifices, and to take heed
to his word is more than to offer the inner fatness of rams;
23 for it is as the sin of maumetry to fight against *God's
behest,* and it is as the wickedness of idolatry to not
assent *to God's behest.* Therefore for that, that thou
castedest away the word of the Lord, the Lord casted thee
away, that thou be not king. (for it is like the sin of
idolatry to fight against *God's command,* and it is like the
wickedness of idolatry to not assent *to God's command.*

And so because thou hast thrown away the word of the
Lord, the Lord hath thrown thee away, so that thou not
be king.)
24 And Saul said to Samuel, I have sinned, for I have
broken the word of the Lord, and thy words; and I
dreaded the people, and obeyed to the voice of them;
(And Saul said to Samuel, I have sinned, for I have
disobeyed the word of the Lord, and thy words; for I
feared the people, and obeyed their voice;)
25 but now, I beseech thee, bear thou my sin, and turn
thou again with me, (so) that I (can) worship the Lord.
26 And Samuel said to Saul, I shall not turn again with
thee, for thou castedest away the word of the Lord, and
the Lord hath cast away thee, that thou be not king upon
Israel. (And Samuel said to Saul, I shall not return with
thee, for thou hast thrown away the word of the Lord,
and so the Lord hath thrown thee away, so that thou not
be king upon Israel.)
27 And Samuel turned to go away; soothly Saul took the
end of the mantle of Samuel, which also was rent (and
Saul took hold of the end of Samuel's mantle, and it tore).
28 And Samuel said to him, The Lord hath cut the
realm of Israel from thee today (The Lord hath torn away
the kingdom of Israel from thee today), and he hath given
it to thy neighbour, (who is) better than thou;
29 certainly the Overcomer in Israel shall not spare
them that will not obey to him, and he shall not be
bowed by repentance; for he is not man, *that is,
changeable*, that he do repentance, (for he is not a man,
that is, that he change his mind).
30 And Saul said, I have sinned; but now honour thou
me before the elder men of my people, and before Israel,
and turn thou again with me, that I worship thy Lord God
(and return thou with me, so that I can worship the Lord
thy God).
31 Therefore Samuel turned again, and followed Saul,
and Saul worshipped the Lord.
32 And Samuel said, Bring ye to me Agag, the king of
Amalek. And Agag, most fat (and) trembling, was
brought to him. And Agag said, Whether thus departeth
bitter death? (And Samuel said, Bring ye to me Agag, the
king of the Amalekites. And Agag, most fat and
trembling, was brought to him. And Agag said, Hath
bitter death thus departed, *that is, May I live*?)
33 And Samuel said, As thy sword hath made women
without free children, so thy mother shall be without free
children among women. And Samuel hewed Agag into
gobbets before the Lord in Gilgal.
34 And (then) Samuel went into Ramah; and Saul went
up into his house in Gibeah.
35 And Samuel saw no more Saul unto the day of his
death; nevertheless Samuel bewailed Saul, for it repented
the Lord, that he had ordained Saul king upon Israel.
(And Samuel never again saw Saul until his dying day;
nevertheless Samuel bewailed Saul, and the Lord
repented, *that is, he regretted*, that he had made Saul
king upon Israel.)

CHAPTER 16

1 And the Lord said to Samuel, How long bewailest
thou Saul, since I have cast him away, that he reign not
upon Israel(?); fill thine horn with oil, and come, that I
send thee to Jesse of Bethlehem; for among his sons I
have purveyed a king to me (for I have chosen myself a
king from among his sons).
2 And Samuel said, How shall I go? for Saul shall hear
(of it), and he shall slay me. And the Lord said, Thou
shalt take a calf of the drove in thy hand (Thou shalt take
a calf from the herd with thee), and thou shalt say, I came
to make sacrifice to the Lord.
3 And thou shalt call Jesse to the sacrifice, and I shall
show to thee (and I shall tell thee), what thou shalt do;
and thou shalt anoint whomever I shall show to thee.
4 Then Samuel did, as the Lord spake to him; and he
came into Bethlehem, and the elder men of the city
wondered, and came to him, and said, Whether thine
entry be peaceable? (Hast thou come in peace?/Is all well?)
5 And he said, It is peaceable; I came to make
sacrifice to the Lord; be ye hallowed, and come ye with
me, that I make sacrifice. Therefore he hallowed Jesse,
and his sons, and called them to the sacrifice. (And he
said, Yea, I have come in peace/all is well; I have come
to offer a sacrifice to the Lord; be ye hallowed, and then
come ye with me, and make ye also the sacrifice. Then
he hallowed Jesse, and his sons, and invited them to the
sacrifice.)
6 And when they had entered, he saw Eliab, and said,
in his heart, Whether before the Lord is his christ? (Is this
the Lord's anointed?)
7 And the Lord said to Samuel, Behold thou not his
cheer (Look thou not at his face), neither the highness of
his stature; for I have cast him away, and I deem not by
man's sight; for man seeth those things that be open, but
the Lord beholdeth the heart.
8 And Jesse called Abinadab, and brought him before
Samuel; and he said, Neither the Lord hath chosen this
(and he said, The Lord hath not chosen this man either).
9 And Jesse brought forth Shammah; of whom Samuel
said, Also the Lord hath not chosen this (man).
10 And so Jesse brought forth his seven sons before
Samuel (And so Jesse brought forth seven of his sons
before Samuel); and Samuel said to Jesse, The Lord hath
chosen none of these.
11 And Samuel said to Jesse, Whether thy sons be now
filled? And Jesse answered, Yet there is another little
child, and he pastureth sheep. And Samuel said to Jesse,
Send ye, and bring him *hither*; for we shall not sit to
meat, before that he come hither. (And Samuel said to

Jesse, Be these all thy sons? And Jesse answered, There is
still another young boy, and he pastureth the sheep. And
Samuel said to Jesse, Send ye for him, and bring him *here*;
for we shall not sit to the meal, before that he come here.)
12 Therefore Jesse sent, and brought him (And so Jesse
sent for him, and brought him forth); soothly he was
ruddy, and fair in sight, and of seemly face. And the Lord
said, Rise thou, and anoint him; for it is he.
13 Therefore Samuel took the horn of oil, and anointed
him in the midst of his brethren; and the Spirit of the Lord
was directed into David from that day forth. And (then)
Samuel rose up, and went into Ramah.
14 And so the Spirit of the Lord went away from Saul,
and a wicked spirit of the Lord travailed Saul (and then a
wicked spirit from the Lord tormented him).
15 And the servants of Saul said to him, Lo! an evil
spirit of the Lord travaileth thee; (And Saul's servants said
to him, Lo! an evil spirit from the Lord tormenteth thee;)
16 our lord the king command, and thy servants, that
be before thee, shall seek a man, that can sing with an
harp, and when the evil spirit of the Lord taketh thee, he
harp with his hand, and thou bear it more easily. (let our
lord the king command, and then thy servants, who be
before thee, shall seek out a man who can play a harp,
and so when the evil spirit from the Lord taketh hold of
thee, he shall play his harp, and then thou shalt be able
to bear it more easily.)
17 And Saul said to his servants, Purvey ye to me some
man singing well (Find ye some man for me who can
play well), and bring ye him to me.
18 And one of his servants answered and said, Lo! I saw
a son of Jesse of Bethlehem, cunning to sing (who
knoweth how to play), and (a) most strong man, and a
man able to (do) battle, and prudent in words, and a fair
man; and the Lord is with him.
19 Therefore Saul sent messengers to Jesse, and said,
Send thou to me David thy son, that is keeping thy
beasts. (And so Saul sent messengers to Jesse, and said,
Send thou to me thy son David, who is keeping watch
over thy sheep.)
20 And so Jesse took an ass charged with loaves, and a
gallon of wine, and a goat kid; and he sent those by the
hand of David his son to Saul. (And so Jesse took a
donkey loaded with loaves, and a gallon of wine, and a
goat kid; and he sent them to Saul with his son David.)
21 And David came to Saul, and stood before him; and
Saul loved him greatly (and Saul greatly loved him), and
he was made his squire.
22 And Saul sent to Jesse, and said, (Let) David stand in
my sight, for he hath found grace in mine eyes.
23 Then whenever the evil spirit of the Lord travailed
Saul (And whenever the evil spirit from the Lord
tormented Saul), David took his harp, and harped with
his hand, and Saul was comforted, and he had *it* more
lightly; for (then) the evil spirit went away from him.

CHAPTER 17

1 Soothly the Philistines gathered together their
companies into battle, and came together in Shochoh of
Judah, and they setted tents betwixt Shochoh and
Azekah, in the coasts of Dammim (in Ephesdammim).
2 And Saul and the men of Israel were gathered
together, and came into the valley of Terebinth, and they
dressed (the) battle array to fight against [the] Philistines.
(And Saul and the men of Israel were gathered together,
and came into the Elah Valley, and they directed the
battle array to fight against the Philistines.)
3 And the Philistines stood above the hill on this part,
and Israel stood on the hill on the tother part of the
valley, that was betwixt them. (And the Philistines stood
on a hill on one side, and Israel stood on a hill on the
other side, and the valley was between them.)
4 And a man in the midst, *that is, a strong man, and
hardy, that goeth before the host, and is ready to fight
against one of the enemies in singular battle, (that is,
man-to-man,)* went out of the Philistines' tents, Goliath
by name, of Gath, of six cubits high and a span; (And a
champion went out from the Philistines' camp, whose
name was Goliath, and was from Gath, and he was six
cubits and a span in height;)
5 and a brazen basinet on his head; and he was
clothed with a mailed habergeon; and the weight of his
habergeon was five thousand shekels of brass; (and he
had a bronze helmet on his head; and was clothed with a
breastplate of mail; and the weight of his breastplate was
equal to five thousand brass shekels;)
6 and he had on his thighs brazen boots, and a brazen
shield covered his shoulders. (and he wore bronze boots up
to his thighs, and a bronze shield covered his shoulders.)
7 Forsooth the shaft of his spear was as the beam of
webs (And his spear shaft was like a weaver's beam); and
the iron of his spear weighed six hundred shekels of iron;
and his squire went before him.
8 And he stood, and cried (out) against the companies
of (the) armed men of Israel, and said to them, Why came
ye ready to (do) battle? Whether I am not a Philistine, and
ye be the servants of Saul? Choose ye a man of you, and
come he down to a singular battle, (*that is, man-to-man*);
9 if he may fight with me, and slay me, we shall be
your servants; forsooth if I have the mastery, and slay
him, ye shall be bond (ye shall be our bondsmen, *or our
slaves*), and serve us.
10 And the Philistine said, I have said shame today to
the companies of Israel; give ye [to me] a man, and begin
he singular battle with me. (And the Philistine said, I have
shamed Israel's companies this day; now give ye to me a
man, and let him fight with me man-to-man.)
11 Soothly Saul and all men of Israel heard such words

of the Philistine, and they were astonished, and dreaded
greatly (and were greatly afraid).
12 Forsooth David was the son of a man of Ephrath, of
whom it is said before, of Bethlehem of Judah, to whom
the name was Jesse, and he had eight sons; and in the
days of Saul, Jesse was an old man, and of great age
among men. (And David was the son of a man of
Ephrath, of whom it was spoken of before, of Bethlehem
in Judah, whose name was Jesse, and he had eight sons;
and Jesse was an old man in the days of Saul, and of great
age among men.)
13 And the three eldest sons of Jesse went after Saul
into battle; and the names of his three sons, that went to
battle (who went to battle), *were* Eliab, the first begotten,
and the second, Abinadab, and the third, Shammah.
14 And David was the youngest. Then while the three
eldest sons followed Saul,
15 David went, and turned again from Saul, that he
should keep the flock of his father in Bethlehem. (David
returned home from Saul, so that he could care for his
father's flock in Bethlehem.)
16 Forsooth the Philistine came forth in the
morrowtide, and [at] eventide; and stood by forty days.
[Forsooth the Philistine came forth early, and at even, standing
(and) reproving the children of Israel (for) forty days.]
17 And Jesse said to David his son, Take thou to thy
brethren meat made of meal, the measure of ephah, and
these ten loaves, and run thou in to the tents to thy
brethren; (And Jesse said to his son David, Take thou to thy
brothers this meal of *roasted* grain, an ephah in measure,
and these ten loaves, and run thou to thy brothers' camp;)
18 and thou shalt bare to the tribune these ten small
cheeses; and thou shalt visit thy brethren, whether they
do rightly (and see if all is well), and learn thou, with
which men they be ordained.
19 Forsooth Saul, and they, and all the sons of Israel in
the valley of Terebinth fought against the Philistines.
(Now Saul, and David's brothers, and all the Israelites
were in the Elah Valley fighting against the Philistines.)
20 And so David rose (up) early, and he betook the
flock to a keeper, and he went charged, as Jesse
commanded to him; and he came to the place of Magal,
and to the host, the which host went out to the fight, and
it cried [out] in the fighting (and he came to the place of
the circle of the camp, and to the army, who were going
out to the battle, and were shouting out the war-cry).
21 For Israel had ordained (the) battle array; and even
against them, the Philistines were ready also (and
opposite them, the Philistines were also ready).
22 Then David left the vessels, that he had brought,
under the hand of a keeper at the fardels, and he ran to
the place of [the] battle, and he asked, if all things were
done rightly with his brethren (and he asked his brothers
if all was well).
23 And when he spake yet to them, that bastard
appeared, Goliath by name, the Philistine of Gath, and
he went up from the tents of the Philistines; and while he
spake these same words, David heard. (And while he
spoke to them, that champion appeared, Goliath by
name, the Philistine of Gath, and he went up from the
Philistines' camp; and when he spoke the same words as
before, then David heard them.)
24 And when all the men of Israel had seen the man,
they fled from his sight, and dreaded him greatly (and
were greatly afraid of him).
25 And each man of Israel said *to (the) other*, Whether
thou hast seen this man that hath gone up? forsooth he
went up to say shame, or reproof, to Israel; therefore the
king shall make rich with great riches the man that slayeth
that Philistine; and the king shall give his daughter to that
man, and shall make the house of his father without
(having to pay) tribute in Israel (and he shall let his
father's family be exempt from paying any taxes in Israel).
26 And David spake to the men that stood with him,
and said, What shall be given to the man that slayeth this
Philistine, and doeth away shame from Israel? for who is
this Philistine uncircumcised, that despiseth the battle
arrays of God living? (for who is this uncircumcised
Philistine who despiseth the battle arrays of the living
God?)
27 Forsooth the people told to him the same word, and
said, These things shall be given to the man that slayeth
him.
28 And when Eliab, his more brother/the elder brother
of David, had heard this, while he spake with other men,
he was wroth against David, and said, Why camest thou
hither, and why hast thou left those few sheep in desert,
(and why hast thou left those few sheep back in the
wilderness)? I know thy pride, and the waywardness of
thine heart; for thou camest down to see the battle.
29 And David said, What have I done? Whether it is
not *but* a word? (Did I not just ask a question?)
30 And David went thence a little from him to another
man; and David said the same word, and the people
answered to him the word as they did before (and David
asked the same question, and the people gave him the
same answer).
31 And the words were heard, that David spake, and
they were told before Saul. And when David was brought
to Saul,
32 David spake to him *thus*, The heart of any man fall
not down *in him*, for I thy servant shall go, and fight
against the Philistine. (David spoke *thus* to him, Let not
any man's heart fall down *because of that man*, for I, thy
servant, shall go, and fight against the Philistine.)
33 And Saul said to David, Thou mayest not against-
stand this Philistine, neither fight against him, for thou art
a child (for thou art but a boy, *that is, a young man*);

forsooth this man is a warrior from his young waxing age.
34 And David said to Saul, Thy servant kept his father's
flock, and (when) a lion came, also a bear/either a bear,
and took away a ram from the midst of the flock;
35 I pursued, and killed them, and I ravished it from
their mouth; and they rose against me, and I took their
nether jowl, and I strangled, and killed them. (I pursued
him, and killed him, and I delivered the ram out of his
mouth; and when he rose up against me, I took his lower
jaw, and I strangled him, and killed him dead.)
36 For I thy servant killed both the lion and the bear;
therefore and this Philistine uncircumcised shall be as
one of them. Now I shall go, and I shall do away the
shame/the reproof of the people; for who is this Philistine
uncircumcised, that was hardy to curse the host of God
living? (For I thy servant, killed both the lion and the
bear; and so this uncircumcised Philistine shall be like
one of them. And now I shall go, and I shall do away the
people's shame, *or their reproof*; for who is this
uncircumcised Philistine, who was fool-hardy enough to
curse the army of the living God?)
37 And again David said, The Lord that delivered me
from the mouth of the lion, and from the hand, *that is,
(the) power*, of the bear, he shall deliver me from the
hand of this Philistine. And Saul said to David, Go thou,
and the Lord be with thee.
38 And Saul clothed David with his clothes, and he set
a brazen basinet on his head, and clothed him with an
habergeon.
39 Therefore David was girded with his sword on his
cloak, and began to assay if he might go armed; for he
had not [the] custom. And David said to Saul, I may not
go thus, for I have not the uses *of it*. And David put away
(all) those [things],
40 and he took his staff, that he had ever[more] in his
hands. And he chose to him five full clear *round* stones,
that is, hard, plain, and round, of the strand (And he
chose out of the stream for himself five hard, round, plain
stones); and he put those into his shepherd's script, that
he had with him; and he took a sling in his hand, and he
went forth against the Philistine.
41 Soothly the Philistine went, going and nighing
against David; and his squire went before him. (And the
Philistine came forth toward David; and his squire went
before him.)
42 And when the Philistine had beheld David, and saw
him, he despised David; forsooth David was a young
waxing man, ruddy, and fair in sight.
43 And the Philistine said to David, Whether I am a
dog, for thou comest to me with a staff? And the
Philistine cursed David in his gods; (And the Philistine
said to David, Am I but a dog, that thou comest to me
with a staff? And the Philistine cursed David by his gods;)
44 and he said to David, Come thou to me, and I shall
give thy flesh to the fowls of the air, and to [the] beasts of
the earth.
45 And David said to Goliath, Thou comest to me with a
sword and (a) spear, and (a) shield; but I come to thee in
(the) name of the Lord of hosts, (the) God of the companies
of Israel, to whom thou hast said reproof today.
46 And the Lord shall give thee in(to) mine hand, and I
shall slay thee, and I shall take thine head from thee; and
today I shall give the dead bodies of the tents of
Philistines to the fowls of (the) heaven(s), and to the
beasts of the earth (and today I shall give the dead bodies
of the Philistine's host, *or army*, to the birds of the air,
and to the beasts of the earth); (so) that all the earth (shall)
know, that the Lord God is in Israel,
47 and that all this church know, that the Lord saveth
not in sword neither in spear; for the battle is his, and he
shall betake you into our hands. (and so that all this
congregation shall know, that the Lord saveth not by
sword or by spear; for the battle is his, and he shall
deliver you into our hands.)
48 Therefore when the Philistine had risen (up), and
came, and nighed against David (and came toward
David), David hasted, and ran to (the) battle against the
Philistine.
49 And David put his hand in his scrip, and he took out
a stone, and he casted it with his sling, and led [it] about,
and smote the Philistine in the forehead; and the stone
was fastened in his forehead, and he felled down into his
face on the earth. (And David put his hand into his bag,
and he took out a stone, and he led it about, and threw it
with his sling, and hit the Philistine in the forehead; and
the stone stuck in his forehead, and he fell down on his
face on the ground.)
50 And David had the mastery against the Philistine in
a sling and a stone, and he killed the Philistine smitten.
And when David had no sword in his hand, (And so
David had the mastery against the Philistine with a sling
and a stone, and he struck down the Philistine, and killed
him. And when David had no sword in his hand,)
51 he ran, and stood on the Philistine, and took (hold
of) his sword; and David drew out the sword of his
sheath, and killed him, and cut off his head (and David
drew the sword out of its sheath, and killed him, and cut
off his head). And the Philistines saw, that the strongest of
them was dead, and they fled.
52 And the sons of Israel and of Judah rose up together,
and cried [out], and pursued the Philistines, till the time
they came into the valley, and unto the gate(s) of Ekron.
And the wounded men of the Philistines fell down in the
way of Shaaraim, and unto Gath, and unto Ekron (And
the wounded men of the Philistines fell down on the way
to Shaaraim, and unto Gath, and unto Ekron).
53 And the sons of Israel turned again, after that they
had pursued the Philistines, and they assailed their tents.

(And the Israelites returned, after that they had pursued
the Philistines, and they looted their camp.)
54 Forsooth David took the head of the Philistine, and
brought it into Jerusalem; soothly he putted his armours
in the tabernacle of the Lord (but he put Goliath's arms,
or his weapons, in his own tent).
55 Forsooth in that time in which Saul saw David going
out against the Philistine, he said to Abner, [the] prince of
his chivalry, Abner, of what generation is this young
man? And Abner said, King, thy soul liveth, I know not.
(Now at the time when Saul saw David going out against
the Philistine, he said to Abner, the leader of his cavalry,
or his army, Abner, whose son is this young man? And
Abner said, O king, as thy soul liveth, I do not know.)
56 And the king said, Ask thou, whose son this boy is.
57 And when David had come again, when the
Philistine was slain, Abner took David, and brought him
in, having in the hand the head of the Philistine, before
Saul. (And when David had come back, after the Philistine
was killed, Abner took David, and brought him in before
Saul, with the head of the Philistine still in his hand.)
58 And Saul said to him, Of what generation art thou,
young man? And David said, I am the son of thy servant,
Jesse of Bethlehem.

CHAPTER 18

1 And it was done, when David had ended to speak to
Saul, the soul of Jonathan was glued together to the soul
of David, *that is, (they were) joined together by the glue
of charity, (or of love,) that may not be broken,* and
Jonathan loved him as his own soul (and Jonathan loved
him as much as he loved his own life).
2 And Saul took David in that day, and granted not to
him, that he should turn again into the house of his
father. (And from that day on, Saul kept David with him,
and would not allow him to return to his father's house.)
3 And Jonathan and David made a bond of peace; for
Jonathan loved David as his own soul; (And Jonathan and
David made a covenant; for Jonathan loved David as
much as he loved his own life;)
4 for why Jonathan unclothed himself from the coat
that he was clothed in, and he gave it to David, and his
other clothes, unto his sword and his bow, and unto his
girdle.
5 And David went forth to all things, to whatever
things Saul sent him, and he governed himself prudently;
and Saul setted him over the men of battle, and he was
accepted in the eyes of all the people, and mostly in the
sight of the servants of Saul (and even before Saul's
officers).
6 Forsooth when David turned again, when the
Philistine was slain, and bare the head of the Philistine
into Jerusalem, women went out of all the cities of Israel,
and sang, and led dances, against the coming of king Saul,
in tympans of gladness, and in trumps. (And when David
returned, when the Philistine was killed, and carried the
Philistine's head into Jerusalem, women came out from
all the cities of Israel, and sang, and danced, and greeted
King Saul with joyful tambourines, and trumpets.)
7 And the women sang, playing, and saying, Saul hath
slain a thousand, and David ten thousand. (And the
women sang to one another as they danced, saying, Saul
hath killed thousands, but David *hath killed* tens of
thousands.)
8 And Saul was wroth greatly, and this word
displeased before him; and he said, They have given ten
thousand to David, and but one thousand to me; what
leaveth to him, no but the realm alone? (And Saul was
greatly angered, for these words displeased him; and he
said, They have given tens of thousands to David, but
only thousands to me; what is left for him now, but only
the kingdom itself?)
9 Therefore Saul beheld David not with rightful eye,
from that day and afterward. (And so from that day on,
Saul did not look kindly upon David.)
10 Soothly after the tother day, a wicked spirit of God
assailed Saul (And the next day, a wicked spirit from God
tormented Saul), and he prophesied in the midst of his
house. And David harped with his hand, as by all days
before; and Saul held a spear,
11 and (then he) cast it, and guessed that he might
preen David with the wall, *that is, pierce (right through
him) with the spear, so that it should pass into the wall;*
and David bowed [aside] from his face the second time
(and twice David veered away from the spear that Saul
threw at him).
12 And Saul dreaded David, (*or feared him,*) for the
Lord was with David, and had gone away from him.
13 Then Saul removed David from himself (Then Saul
removed David from his household), and made him (a)
chieftain upon a thousand men; and David went out and
he came in before the people.
14 And David did wisely in all his ways, and the Lord
was with him;
15 and so Saul saw that David was full prudent/was full
wise, and he began to beware of David.
16 And all Israel and Judah loved David; for he went in
and out before them.
17 And Saul said to David, Lo! mine elder daughter
Merab, I shall give her (for a) wife to thee; only be thou a
strong man, and fight thou the Lord's battles. Forsooth
Saul areckoned, and said, Mine hand be not in him, but
the hand of Philistines be on him (But Saul reckoned, and
said to himself, My hand shall not be upon him, but the
hands of the Philistines shall be upon him).
18 And David said to Saul, Who am I, either what is my
life, either (what is) the family of my father in Israel, that I
(should) be made the son-in-law of the king?

19 And when the time came that Merab, the daughter
of Saul, should have been given wife to David, she was
given wife to Adriel Meholathite. (But when the time
came that Merab, Saul's daughter, should have been
given for a wife to David, instead she was given for a
wife to Adriel the Meholathite.)
20 Forsooth David loved Michal, the [tother] daughter
of Saul; and it was told to Saul, and it pleased him.
21 And Saul said, I shall give her to him, that it be to
him into cause of stumbling, and the hand of Philistines
be upon him. Therefore Saul said to David, In (wedding
one of my) two daughters thou shalt be my son-in-law
today. (And Saul said, I shall give her to him, so that she
shall become a cause of stumbling to him, and so that the
hands of the Philistines shall be upon him. And so Saul
said to David, By wedding my *younger* daughter, on that
day thou shalt become my son-in-law.)
22 And Saul commanded to his servants, (and said,)
Speak ye privily to David, as if it were me unwitting
(Speak ye privately to David, as if I did not know it), and
say ye *to him*, Lo! thou pleasest the king, and all his
servants love thee; now therefore be thou [the] husband
of the king's daughter.
23 And the servants of Saul spake all these words in the
ears of David. And David said, Whether it seem little to
you (for) *me* to be the king's son-in-law? Forsooth I am a
poor man, and a feeble (I am but a poor and feeble man).
24 And the servants told to Saul, and said, David spake
such words.
25 Soothly Saul said, Thus speak ye to David, The king
hath no need to gifts for spousals, no but only to an
hundred prepuces, *that is, men's rods uncircumcised*, of
the Philistines, that vengeance be made of the king's
enemies. Certainly Saul thought to betake David into the
hands of Philistines. (And Saul said, Speak ye thus to
David, and say, The king hath no need for wedding gifts,
but only for a hundred prepuces, *that is, the rods of a
hundred uncircumcised men*, of the Philistines, so that
vengeance be taken upon the king's enemies. For Saul
intended to deliver David into the hands of the Philistines.)
26 And when the servants of Saul had told to David the
words, which Saul had said, the word pleased in the eyes
of David, that he should be made the king's son-in-law.
And after a few days, (And when Saul's servants told
David what Saul had said, it pleased him, that he could
become the king's son-in-law. And so, after a few days,)
27 David rose up, and went into Ekron, with the men
that were with him, and he killed of Philistines two
hundred men; and David brought their prepuces, and he
numbered those to the king, that he should be the king's
son-in-law. And so Saul gave Michal, his daughter, wife
to him. (David rose up, and went to Ekron, with the men
who were with him, and he killed two hundred of the
Philistine men; and David brought their foreskins, and he
counted those out to the king, so that he could be made
the king's son-in-law. And so Saul gave Michal, his
daughter, for a wife to him.)
28 And Saul saw, and understood, that the Lord was
with David. Certainly Michal, Saul's daughter, loved
David,
29 and Saul began more to dread David (and then Saul
began to fear David even more); and (so) Saul was made
(an) enemy to David in all days.
30 And the princes of (the) Philistines went out *to fight*;
but from the beginning of their going out, David bare
himself more wisely than all the men of Saul; and the
name of David was made full solemn (and David's name
became very famous).

CHAPTER 19

1 Soothly Saul spake to Jonathan, his son, and to all
his servants, that they should slay David;
2 certainly Jonathan, the son of Saul, loved David
greatly. And Jonathan showed to David, and said, Saul,
my father, seeketh to slay thee; wherefore, I beseech, keep
thyself *tomorrow* early; and thou shalt dwell privily, and
thou shalt be hid. (but Jonathan, Saul's son, greatly loved
David. And Jonathan told David, My father Saul seeketh
to kill thee; and so, I beseech thee, be careful tomorrow
morning; remain thou in secret, and be thou hid.)
3 And I shall go out, and stand beside my father in the
field, wherever he shall be; and I shall speak of thee to
my father, and whatever thing I shall see/and whatever
thing I shall understand *of him*, I shall tell thee (and
whatever I shall learn *from him*, I shall tell thee).
4 Then Jonathan spake good things of David to Saul,
his father, and said to him, King, do thou not sin against
thy servant David, for he hath not sinned to thee, and his
works be full good to thee; (Then Jonathan spoke good
things about David to his father Saul, and said to him, O
king, do not thou sin against thy servant David, for he
hath not sinned against thee, and his works be very good
towards thee;)
5 and he putted his life in his hand, and he killed the
Philistine. And the Lord made great help to all Israel;
thou sawest, and were glad; why therefore sinnest thou in
guiltless blood, and wilt slay David, that is without guilt?
(and he put his life in his hands, and he killed the
Philistine. And the Lord won a great victory for all Israel;
thou sawest this, and wast glad; and so why sinnest thou
against innocent blood, and wilt kill David, who is
without guilt?)
6 And when Saul had heard this, he was pleased with
the speaking of Jonathan, and he swore, (As) The Lord
liveth, for David shall not be slain.
7 And so Jonathan called David, and showed to him
all these words (and told him all these things). And
Jonathan brought in David to Saul, and he was before

him as [he was] yesterday and the third day ago.
8 Forsooth (the) battle was moved again; and David
went out, and fought against the Philistines, and he smote
them with a great wound/with great fierceness, and they
fled from his face.
9 And the evil spirit of the Lord was made upon Saul
(And then again an evil spirit from the Lord came upon
Saul); and he sat in his house, and held a spear; certainly
David harped with his hand.
10 And Saul enforced to preen, *that is pierce*, with the
spear *(right through)* David in(to) the wall; and David
bowed [aside] from the face of Saul; and the spear
without hurt *of David* was fixed into the wall; and David
fled, and so he was saved in that night. (And Saul
endeavoured to preen David with the spear, *that is, to
pierce right through him*, into the wall; but David veered
away from the spear thrown by Saul; and it was fixed into
the wall without hurting *him*; and David fled, and so he
was saved that night.)
11 Therefore Saul sent his knights in the night into the
house of David, that they should keep him, and that he
should be slain in the morrowtide. And when Michal, the
wife of David, had told this to David, and said, If thou
savest not thee in this night, thou shalt die tomorrow;
(And so Saul sent his sergeants in the night to David's
house, to keep watch over him, and then to kill him in
the morning. And Michal, David's wife, told this to
David, and said, If thou savest not thyself this night, thou
shalt die tomorrow;)
12 and she let him down by a window. And David
went, and fled thence, and (so) he was saved.
13 And Michal took an image (And Michal took an
idol), and laid it on the bed of David, and she put a rough
goatskin at the head thereof, and covered it with clothes.
14 Forsooth Saul sent sergeants, that should ravish
David, and it was answered, that he was sick. (Then
when Saul's sergeants entered to take hold of David, she
said that he was sick.)
15 And again Saul sent messengers, that they should
see David, and he said, Bring ye him to me in the bed,
that he be slain. (And Saul sent the men back to see
David for themselves, and he said, Bring ye him to me in
his bed, and then I shall kill him myself!)
16 And when the messengers had come, a simulacrum
was found on the bed, and skins of goat at the head
thereof. (And when the men had come in, they found the
idol on the bed, with a goatskin at its head.)
17 And Saul said to Michal, Why scornedest thou me
so (Why hast thou so scorned me), and deliveredest mine
enemy, (so) that he fled? And Michal answered to Saul,
For he spake to me, and said, Deliver thou me, (or) else I
shall slay thee.
18 Forsooth David fled, and was saved; and he came to
Samuel into Ramah, and told to him all things which Saul
had done to him; and he and Samuel went, and dwelled
in Naioth.
19 And it was told to Saul of men (And some men told
this to Saul), saying *to him*, Lo! David is in Naioth in
Ramah.
20 Therefore Saul sent men-slayers, that they should
ravish *(from) thence* David; and when they had seen the
company of prophets prophesying, and Samuel standing
over them, the Spirit of the Lord was made in them, and
they also began to prophesy. (And so Saul sent some
men-killers to take hold of David *there*; and when they
had seen the group of prophets prophesying, and Samuel
standing at their head, the Spirit of the Lord was made
upon them, and they also began to prophesy.)
21 And when this was told to Saul, he sent also other
messengers; soothly and they prophesied. And again
Saul sent the third messengers, and they prophesied.
(And when this was told to Saul, he sent other men; and
they also prophesied. And a third time Saul sent even
more men, and they also prophesied.)
22 And Saul was wroth with irefulness; and he also
went into Ramah (and then he went to Ramah), and he
came unto the great cistern which is in Sechu, and he
asked, and said, In what place be Samuel and David?
And it was said to him, Lo! they be in Naioth in Ramah.
23 And he went (thither) into Naioth in Ramah; and the
Spirit of the Lord was made also on him (And he went on
toward Naioth in Ramah; and the Spirit of the Lord was
also made upon him); and he went (on), and entered, and
prophesied, till the while he came into Naioth in Ramah.
24 And Saul also unclothed him(self) of his clothes, and
he prophesied with other men before Samuel, and he
prophesied naked all that day and night. Wherefore a
common saying went out, Whether and Saul be among
[the] prophets? (And so a *common* saying went out, Is
Saul now also among the prophets?)

CHAPTER 20

1 Forsooth David fled from Naioth, which is in
Ramah, and came and spake before Jonathan (and came
and said to Jonathan), What have I done? what is my
wickedness, and what is my sin against thy father, for
(that) he seeketh my life?
2 And Jonathan said to him, Far be it from thee, thou
shalt not die, for my father shall not do anything great
either little, no but he show first to me; therefore, (would)
my father (have) kept privy from me this word only,
forsooth it shall not be. And again he swore to David.
(And Jonathan said to him, Far be it from thee, thou shalt
not die, for my father shall not do anything great or small,
no but first he tell it to me; would my father have only
kept secret this word from me? no, it is not so. And again
he swore to David.)
3 And David said, Truly thy father knoweth, that I

have found grace in thine eyes, and he shall say,
Jonathan know not this, lest peradventure he be sorry;
certainly the Lord liveth, and thy soul liveth, for, that I say
so, I and death be parted only by one degree. (And David
said, Truly thy father knoweth that I have found favour in
thy sight, and he shall say, I will not let Jonathan know
this, lest he become angry, *or upset*; truly, as the Lord
liveth, and as thy soul liveth, I say that I and death be
separated by only one degree.)
4 And Jonathan said to David, Whatever thing thy soul
shall say to me, I shall do it to thee. (And Jonathan said to
David, Whatever thou shalt ask me, I shall do it for thee.)
5 And David said to Jonathan, Lo! calends be
tomorrow, *that is the feast of the new moon*, and by
custom I am wont to sit by the king to eat; therefore suffer
thou me, that I be hid in the field till to [the] eventide of
the third day (but instead, allow me to hide in the field
until the evening of the third day).
6 And if thy father beholdeth, and asketh after me,
thou shalt answer to him, David prayed me, that he might
go at once into Bethlehem, his city, for solemn sacrifices
be *now* there to all [the] men of his lineage (for *now* is
the time of the annual sacrifice there for all the men of
his family).
7 If he saith, Well, peace shall be to thy servant;
forsooth if he is wroth, know thou, that his malice is
filled. (And if he saith, Fine, then peace shall be to thy
servant; but if he is angry, then know thou, that he is
determined to harm me.)
8 Therefore do thou mercy into thy servant, for thou
hast made me thy servant to make with thee (a) bond of
peace of the Lord; but if any wickedness is in me, slay
thou me, and bring thou not in me to thy father. (And so
do thou mercy with me, thy servant, for thou hast made a
covenant with me before the Lord; but if there is any
wickedness in me, then thou kill me, and do not bring
me in to thy father.)
9 And Jonathan said, Far be this from me, for it may
not be done, that I tell (it) not to thee, if I know certainly,
that the malice of my father is filled against thee. (And
Jonathan said, Far be this from me, for it will not be
done, that I do not tell it to thee, if I know with certainty,
that my father is determined to harm thee.)
10 And David answered to Jonathan, Who shall tell me,
if in case thy father answereth hard [to thee] anything of
me? (And David asked Jonathan, Who shall tell me, if thy
father saith anything hard to thee about me?)
11 And Jonathan said to David, Come thou, and go we
forth into the field. And when they both had gone into
the field,
12 Jonathan said (out loud) to David, Thou Lord God of
Israel, if I inquire the sentence of my father tomorrow,
either in the next day after (O Lord God of Israel, if I
inquire about my father's thoughts tomorrow, or the next
day), and any good thing be *said* of thee, (David,) and I
send not at once to thee, and make it known to thee,
13 God do these things to Jonathan, and add these
(other) things. And if the malice of my father continue
against thee, I shall show it to thine ear (I shall tell it to
thee), and I shall deliver thee, (so) that thou go in peace;
and the Lord be with thee, as he was with my father.
14 And if I live, do thou the mercies of the Lord to me;
forsooth if I am dead, (And while I live, do thou the
Lord's mercies to me; but if I should die,)
15 take thou not away thy mercy from mine house unto
without end; and if I do it not, when the Lord shall draw
out by the root the enemies of David, each man from the
land, take he away Jonathan from his house, and seek the
Lord of the hand of the enemies of David. (take thou not
away thy mercy from my family forevermore; and even
when the Lord shall draw out David's enemies by the
root, yea, each man from the land, let the Lord call David
to account, if he and his household, *or his family*, no
longer be my friends.)
16 Therefore Jonathan made [a] bond of peace with the
house of David, and the Lord sought (it) of the hand of
[the] enemies of David. (And so Jonathan made a
covenant with the house of David, saying, Let the Lord
seek *justice for me* at the hands of David's enemies.)
17 And Jonathan added to swear steadfastly to David,
for he loved him; for he loved so David, as his own soul.
(And Jonathan added to steadfastly swear to David, for he
loved him; yea, he loved David as much as his own life.)
18 And Jonathan said to David, Tomorrow is the first
day of the month, that is solemn (and that is a feast day),
and thou shalt be sought (after);
19 and thy sitting shall be asked (of) till after the morrow.
Therefore thou shalt go down hastily, and thou shalt come
into a place, where thou shalt be hid in the day, when it
is leaveful to work (while this business is at hand); and
thou shalt sit beside the stone, that is called Ezel.
20 And I shall shoot three arrows beside that stone, and
I shall cast (those) as (if) exercising, *either playing* me at a
sign. (And I shall shoot three arrows toward that stone,
and I shall shoot them as if I were aiming at a mark, *or at
a target*.)
21 I shall send my child, and I shall say to him, Go
thou, and bring to me the arrows. If I say to the child, Lo!
the arrows be on this side (of) thee, take thou those; *then*
come thou to me, for peace is to thee, and nothing is of
evil, the Lord liveth. (And I shall send my boy, and I shall
say to him, Go thou, and bring me the arrows. Now if I
say to the boy, Lo! the arrows be on this side of thee, take
thou them; *then* come thou to me, for all is well for thee,
and nothing is of evil, as the Lord liveth.)
22 But if I speak thus to the child, Lo! the arrows be
beyond thee; go thou in peace, for the Lord hath
delivered thee. (But if I speak thus to the boy, Lo! the

arrows be beyond thee; then go thou away *to save thy own life*, for the Lord hath sent thee away.)
23 Certainly of the word that thou and I have spoken,
that is, of the bond of peace betwixt us and our heirs (that is, of the covenant between us and our heirs), the Lord be *witness* betwixt me and thee till into without end.
24 Therefore David was hid in the field; and the
calends/the solemn feast came, and the king sat to eat bread (and the king sat down to eat his meal).
25 And when the king had set on his chair (as) by
custom, which chair was beside the wall, Jonathan rose, and sat *after Abner*, and Abner sat at the side of Saul, and the place of David appeared void (and David's place was empty).
26 And Saul spake not anything in that day; for he
thought, that in hap it befelled to him, that he was not clean, neither purified. (And Saul did not say anything about David that day; for he thought perhaps it befell that David was not clean, or purified.)
27 And when the second day after the calends had
shined, again the place of David appeared void. And Saul said to Jonathan his son, Why cometh not the son of Jesse, neither yesterday, neither today, to eat? (And when the second day came after that the new moon had shone, again David's place was empty. And Saul said to his son Jonathan, Why cometh not the son of Jesse to eat, not yesterday, or today?)
28 And Jonathan answered to Saul, He prayed me
meekly that he should go into Bethlehem (He humbly asked me if he could go to Bethlehem);
29 and he said, Suffer thou me, for solemn sacrifice is
(now) in my city; one of my brethren [hath] called me; now therefore, if I [have] found grace in thine eyes, I shall go soon, and I shall see my brethren (I shall go swiftly, and I shall see my brothers); for this cause he cometh not to the table of the king.
30 And Saul was wroth against Jonathan, and said to
him, Thou son of the woman willfully ravishing a man (Thou son of the woman who willfully robbeth a man), whether I know not, that thou lovest the son of Jesse into thy [own] confusion, and into the confusion of thy shameful mother?
31 For in all the days in which the son of Jesse liveth on
[the] earth, thou shalt not be stablished, neither thy realm (thou shalt not be secure, nor shall thy kingdom); therefore right now/at once send thou, and bring him to me, for he is the son of death.
32 And Jonathan answered to Saul his father, and said,
Why shall he die? what hath he done?
33 And Saul took a spear, that he should smite him,
and Jonathan understood, that it was determined of his father, that David should be slain (and Jonathan understood that his father was determined to kill David).
34 Then Jonathan rose (up) from the table in full fierce
wrath, and he ate not bread in the second day of calends (and he ate nothing on the second day of the feast); for he was sorry for David, for his father had shamed him.
35 And when the morrowtide had shined, Jonathan
came into the field, and a little child with him, by the covenant made of David. (And when the morning came, Jonathan went into the field, and had a young boy with him, as by the pact which he had made with David.)
36 And Jonathan said to his child, Go thou, and bring
to me the arrows that I shoot. And when the child had run forth, he shot another arrow beyond the child. (And Jonathan said to his boy, Go thou, and bring me back the arrows that I shoot. And as the boy ran forth, he shot the arrows beyond the boy.)
37 Therefore when the child came to the place of the
arrow that Jonathan had shot, Jonathan cried behind the back of the child, and said, Lo! the arrow is not there, certainly it is beyond thee. (And so when the boy came to the place where the arrows were that Jonathan had shot, Jonathan cried behind the boy's back, and said, Lo! the arrows be not there, but they be beyond thee.)
38 And Jonathan cried again behind the back of the
child, Haste thou swiftly, stand thou not. Soothly the child gathered up the arrows of Jonathan, and brought *them* to his lord, (And Jonathan cried again behind the back of the boy, Run thou quickly, do not thou stand still. And the boy gathered up the arrows of Jonathan, and brought *them* back to his lord,)
39 and utterly the child knew not what was done; for
only Jonathan and David knew the thing. (and utterly the boy could not understand what had happened; but Jonathan and David knew what the words really meant.)
40 Then Jonathan gave his bow and arrows to the child,
and said to him, Go thou, bear *these* into the city. (Then Jonathan gave his bow and arrows to the boy, and said to him, Go thou, carry *these* back to the city.)
41 And when the child had gone, David rose from the
place that went to the south; and he felled low upon the earth, and worshipped the third time, and they kissed themselves together, and wept together; but David wept more. (And when the boy had gone, David rose up from a place toward the south; and he fell low on the ground, and bowed three times, and then they kissed one another, and wept together; but David wept more.)
42 Then Jonathan said to David, Go thou in peace;
whatever things we both have sworn in the name of the Lord, and said, The Lord be betwixt me and thee, and betwixt my seed and thy seed, till into without end, *be steadfast, (or certain)*. And David rose up, and went forth, but and Jonathan went into the city.

CHAPTER 21

1 Forsooth David came into Nob to Ahimelech, the
priest; and Ahimelech wondered, for David had come

(and Ahimelech wondered why David had come there);
and he said to David, Why art thou alone, and no man is
with thee?
2 And David said to Ahimelech the priest, The king
hath commanded to me a word, and said, No man know
this thing, for which thou art sent from me, and what
manner behests I have given to thee; for I said also to my
young men, that they should go into that and that place
(and so I said to my young men, that they should go to
such and such a place);
3 now therefore if thou hast anything at hand, either
five loaves (even five loaves), give thou (them) to me,
either whatever thing thou findest.
4 And the priest answered to David, and said to him, I
have not lay, *that is, common,* loaves at hand, but only
holy bread; whether the young men be clean, and mostly
of women? (And the priest answered David, and said to
him, I do not have any lay loaves, *or common bread*, at
hand, only holy bread; thy young men, be they clean, at
least from women?)
5 And David answered to the priest, and said to him,
And soothly if it is done of women, we have abstained us
from yesterday and the third day ago, when we went out,
and the vessels, *that is, (the) bodies,* of the young men
were clean; certainly this way is defouled, but and it shall
be hallowed today in the vessels. (And David answered
the priest, and said to him, If it is asked of women, we
have abstained ourselves from yesterday and the third
day ago, when we went out, and so the young men's
bodies be clean; truly, that way is defiled, but their
bodies remain pure.)
6 Therefore the priest gave to him hallowed bread, for
none other bread was there, but only loaves of setting
forth, that were taken away from the face of the Lord, that
hot loaves shall be set forth. (And so the priest gave him
the consecrated bread, for there was no other bread
there, but only the loaves of setting forth, *that is, the
loaves of proposition, or the showbread,* which had been
taken away from before the Lord, and replaced with fresh
hot loaves.)
7 And a man of the servants of Saul was there that
day, within in the tabernacle of the Lord; and his name
was Doeg of Idumea, the mightiest man of the
herds(men) of Saul.
8 And David said to Ahimelech, If thou hast here at
hand (a) spear, either (a) sword, give it to me; for I took
not with me my sword, neither mine armours (nor my
own arms, *or my own weapons*); for why the king's word
constrained me *to go in haste*.
9 And the priest said, Lo! the sword of Goliath (the)
Philistine, whom thou killedest in the valley of Terebinth,
is wrapped in a cloth *next* after [the] ephod; if thou wilt
take this, take it; for (t)here is none other except that.
And David said, None other is like this, give thou it to
me. (And the priest said, Lo! the sword of Goliath the
Philistine, whom thou killedest in the Elah Valley, is
wrapped in a cloth behind the ephod; if thou wilt have it,
then take it; for there is nothing else here except that.
And David said, There is no other like it, give it to me.)
10 And so David rose up, and fled in that day from the
face of Saul, and came to Achish, the king of Gath.
11 And the servants of Achish said to him, when they
had seen David, Whether this is not David, [the] king of
the land? Whether they sang not to him by quires/by
carols, and said, Saul smote a thousand, and David smote
ten thousand? (Did they not sing about him as they
danced, saying, Saul struck down thousands, but David
struck down tens of thousands?)
12 And David took these words in his heart, and he
dreaded greatly of the face of Achish, king of Gath. (And
David took these words to heart, and so he greatly feared
King Achish of Gath.)
13 And David changed his mouth before Achish, and
felled down betwixt their hands, and he painted on the
doors of the gate, and his dribbles, *that is, spittles,* flowed
down into his beard.
14 And Achish said to his servants, See ye the mad
man? (See ye not that the man is mad?) why brought ye
him to me?
15 whether mad men fail to us? why have ye brought in
him, that he should be mad, while I am present? Deliver
ye him from hence, lest he enter into mine house. (do we
not have enough mad men here already? why have ye
brought him in, so that he can be deranged right in front
of me! Get ye him away from here, lest he enter into my
house, *and touch things*!)

CHAPTER 22

1 Therefore David went from thence, and fled into the
den of Adullam (And so David went from there, and fled
to the cave of Adullam); and when his brethren, and all
the house of his father had heard this, they came down
thither to him.
2 And all men that were set in anguish, and oppressed
with other men's debt, and in bitter soul, came together
to him; and he was made the prince of them, and as four
hundred men were with him. (And all men who were set
in anguish, and were oppressed with owing debt to other
men, and were bitter in soul, came together to him; and
so about four hundred men were with him.)
3 And David went forth from thence into Mizpeh, that
is in Moab; and he said to the king of Moab, I pray, dwell
my father and my mother with you, till I know what thing
God shall do to me. (And David went forth from there to
Mizpeh, which is in Moab; and he said to the king of
Moab, I pray thee, let my father and my mother stay with
you, until I know what God shall do for me.)
4 And he left them *there* before the face of the king of

Moab; and they dwelled at him in all the days, that David
was in stronghold. (And so he left them *there* with the
king of Moab; and they stayed with him all the days that
David was in his stronghold.)
5 And Gad, the prophet, said to David, Do not thou
dwell in the forcelet, *or the stronghold;* go thou forth,
and go into the land of Judah. And David went forth, and
came into the forest of Hareth.
6 And Saul heard, that David appeared, and the men
that were with him. And when Saul dwelled in Gibeah,
and was in a wood that is in Ramah, and he held a spear
in his hand, and all his servants stood about him, (And
Saul heard that David, and the men who were with him,
had appeared. And Saul then lived in Gibeah, and was
in a forest that is in Ramah, and he held a spear in his
hand, and all his servants stood about him,)
7 he said to his servants that stood nigh [to] him, Ye
sons of Benjamin, hear me now; whether the son of Jesse
shall give to all you fields and vineries, and he shall make
all you chieftains upon thousands, and upon hundreds of
men? (and he said to his officers who stood about him, Ye
sons of Benjamin, hear me now; will the son of Jesse give
all of you fields and vineyards, and will he make all of you
chieftains over thousands, and chieftains over hundreds?)
8 For all ye have sworn, *either conspired,* together
against me, and none is that telleth to me; mostly since
also my son hath joined (in a) bond of peace with the son
of Jesse; none is of you, that sorroweth for my stead, or
my while, neither that telleth to me, for my son hath
raised my servant against me, setting treason to me, unto
this day. (Is that why all of you have conspired together
against me, and no one told me that my son hath made a
covenant with the son of Jesse; yea, none of you hath
concern for me, nor even telleth me that my own son
hath raised up my servant against me, setting treason for
me, unto this day.)
9 Soothly Doeg of Idumea answered, that stood nigh,
and was the first among the servants of Saul, and said, I
saw the son of Jesse in Nob, at Ahimelech, the priest, the
son of Ahitub; (And Doeg of Idumea, who stood near,
and was the first among Saul's officers, answered, and
said, I saw Jesse's son in Nob, with Ahimelech, the priest,
the son of Ahitub;)
10 and Ahimelech counselled with the Lord for David,
and gave him meats, (and gave him food, *or sustenance*),
but also he gave to David the sword of Goliath (the)
Philistine.
11 Therefore the king sent to call Ahimelech, the priest,
the son of Ahitub, and all the house of his father, of [the]
priests that were in Nob; which all came to the king.
(And so the king sent for Ahimelech, the priest, the son of
Ahitub, and all those in his family, who were also priests
in Nob; and they all came to the king.)
12 And Saul said to Ahimelech, Hear me, thou son of
Ahitub. Which answered, Lord, I am ready. (And Saul
said to Ahimelech, Listen to me, O son of Ahitub. Who
answered, My lord, I am listening.)
13 And Saul said to him, Why hast thou conspired
against me, thou, and the son of Jesse, and [thou] hast
given loaves and a sword to him, and hast counselled
with the Lord for him, that he should rise (up) against me,
and he dwelleth a traitor (now) unto this day?
14 And Ahimelech answered to the king, and said, Who
among all thy servants is so faithful as David, and he is thy
son-in-law, and going at thy behest, and glorious in all
thine house? (And Ahimelech answered the king, and
said, Who among all thy servants is as faithful as David,
and he is the king's son-in-law, and doeth thy bidding,
and who is more honourable in all thy household?)
15 Whether I began today to counsel (with) the Lord for
him? Far be this from me; suppose not the king such (a)
thing against his servant, (or) in all the house of my father
(or in all my family); for thy servant knew not anything,
either little, either great, of this cause.
16 And the king said, Ahimelech, thou shalt die by
death, thou, and all the house of thy father. (And the king
said, Ahimelech, thou shalt die, thou, and all thy family.)
17 And the king said to (the) men able to be sent out (to
do his bidding), that stood about him, Turn ye, and slay
the priests of the Lord, for the hand of them is with David;
and they knew that he fled, and they showed not to me.
Soothly the servants of the king would not hold forth their
hand into the priests of the Lord (But the king's guards
would not put their hands against the Lord's priests).
18 And the king said to Doeg, Turn thou, and hurtle
into the priests of the Lord. And Doeg of Idumea turned,
and hurtled into the priests, and strangled in that day
fourscore and five men, clothed with ephods of linen
cloth, *or linen priests' capes* (and killed eighty-five men
that day, each of whom could carry the ephod).
19 Forsooth he smote Nob (And then he struck Nob),
the city of the priests, by the sharpness of (the) sword, men
and women, little children and (those) sucking, and ox,
and ass, and sheep, (all) by the sharpness of (the) sword.
20 But one son of Ahimelech, the son of Ahitub,
escaped, of which son the name was Abiathar; and he
fled to David,
21 and (he) told him that Saul had slain the priests of
the Lord.
22 And David said to Abiathar, Soothly I knew in that
day, that when Doeg of Idumea was there, he would tell
without doubt to Saul; I am guilty of all the lives *that be
slain* of thy father('s) house. (And David said to Abiathar,
Truly I knew on that day, when Doeg the Idumean was
there, that without a doubt he would tell Saul; yea, I am
guilty for all the lives *that be lost* in thy father's family.)
23 Dwell thou with me, dread thou not; if any man
seeketh thy life, he shall seek also my life, and thou shalt

be kept with me. (Stay thou with me, and fear thou not; if
any man seeketh thy life, he shall also seek my life, but
thou shalt be kept safe with me.)

CHAPTER 23

1 And they told to David, and said, Lo! The Philistines
fight against Keilah, and ravish the cornfloors (and steal
the harvest/and rob the threshing floors).
2 Therefore David counselled (with) the Lord, and
said, Whether I shall go, and smite these Philistines? (And
so David counselled with the Lord, and asked, Shall I go,
and strike down these Philistines?) And the Lord said to
David, Go forth, and thou shalt smite the Philistines, and
thou shalt save Keilah.
3 And (the) men, that were with David, said to him,
Lo! we be here in Judah, and have dread (and be afraid);
how much more if we shall go into Keilah against the
companies of (the) Philistines.
4 Therefore again David counselled with the Lord; the
which answered (who answered), and said to David, Rise
thou up, and go into Keilah; for I shall betake [the]
Philistines into thine hand.
5 Therefore David went, and his men, into Keilah, and
fought against the Philistines; and he drove away their
work beasts, and smote them with [a] great wound; and
David saved the dwellers of Keilah. (And so David and
his men went to Keilah, and fought against the
Philistines; and he took away their work beasts, and
struck them down with a great slaughter; and so David
saved the inhabitants of Keilah.)
6 And in that time, wherein Abiathar, [the] son of
Ahimelech, fled to David into Keilah, he came down,
and had with him (the) ephod, *that is, the cloak of the
highest priest.* (And when Abiathar, the son of Ahimelech,
joined David at Keilah, he brought the ephod with him.)
7 And it was told to Saul, that David had come into
Keilah; and Saul said, The Lord hath taken him into mine
hands, and he is (en)closed, and entered into a city, in
which be gates and locks. (And Saul was told that David
had gone to Keilah; and Saul said, The Lord hath
delivered him into my hands, and now he is enclosed, for
he hath gone into a city, where there be gates and locks.)
8 And Saul commanded to all the people, that it should
go down to battle into Keilah (that they should go down
to do battle at Keilah), and besiege David and his men.
9 And when David perceived, that Saul made ready
evil privily to him, he said to Abiathar, the priest, Bring
hither [the] ephod. (And when David understood, that
Saul planned to attack him, he said to Abiathar, the
priest, Bring the ephod here.)
10 And David said, Lord God of Israel, thy servant hath
heard say, that Saul disposeth to come to Keilah, that he
destroy the city for me; (Then David said, Lord God of
Israel, thy servant hath heard say, that Saul disposeth to
come to Keilah, to destroy the city because of me;)
11 if the men of Keilah shall betake me into his hands,
and if Saul shall come down, as thy servant hath heard,
thou Lord God of Israel, show to thy servant? And the
Lord said, He shall come down. (will the men of Keilah
deliver me into his hands? and will Saul come down, as
thy servant hath heard? O Lord God of Israel, tell thy
servant. And the Lord said, He shall come down.)
12 And David said again, Whether the men of Keilah
shall betake me, and the men that be with me, into the
hands of Saul? And the Lord said, They shall betake *thee
to Saul, if thou abidest him there.* (And David asked,
Shall the men of Keilah deliver me, and my men, into the
hands of Saul? And the Lord said, They shall deliver *thee
to Saul, if thou waitest here for him.*)
13 Therefore David rose, and his men, as six hundred;
and they went out of Keilah, and wandered uncertain
hither and thither. And it was told to Saul, that David
had fled from Keilah, and was saved; wherefore Saul
dissembled to go out. (And so David and his men, about
six hundred in all, rose up; and they went out of Keilah,
and wandered about with uncertainty. And it was told to
Saul, that David had fled from Keilah, and so he was
saved; and for a short while Saul left off going after him.)
14 But David dwelled in the desert, in full strong
places, and he dwelled in the hill of (the) wilderness of
Ziph, in a dark hill; nevertheless Saul sought him in all
days, and the Lord betook not him into the hands of Saul.
(And David lived in the wilderness, in secure places, and
he stayed in the hill country of the wilderness of Ziph, on
a dark hill; and Saul continued to seek after him in all
days, but the Lord did not deliver him into Saul's hands.)
15 And David saw, that Saul went out, that he would
seek his life. And David was in the desert of Ziph, in a
wood. (And David saw, that Saul went out to seek his
life. And David was in the wilderness of Ziph, in a forest.)
16 And Jonathan, the son of Saul, rose up, and went to
David into the wood, and comforted his hands in God.
(And Saul's son Jonathan rose up, and went to David in
the forest, and strengthened his hand in God/and
encouraged him in the name of God.)
17 And he said to David, Dread thou not; for the hand
of Saul my father shall not find thee, and thou shalt reign
on Israel, and I shall be the second to thee; but also Saul
my father knoweth this. (And he said to David, Fear not;
for the hand of my father Saul shall not find thee, and
thou shalt reign upon Israel, and I shall be second to
thee; and my father Saul knoweth this.)
18 Therefore ever either smote (a) bond of peace before
the Lord. And David dwelled in the wood; and Jonathan
turned again into his house. (And so they both struck a
covenant before the Lord. And David stayed in the
forest; and Jonathan returned home.)
19 Certainly men of Ziph went up to Saul in Gibeah,

and said, Lo! whether not David is hid with us in the full
secure places in the thick wood(s), in the hill of Hachilah,
that is at the right side of desert? (Then men of Ziph went
up to Saul in Gibeah, and said, Lo! David is hid among
us in the most secure places, in the thick forest on Mount
Hachilah, which is to the south of Jeshimon.)
20 Now therefore come thou down, as thy soul desired,
that thou shouldest come down; forsooth it shall be our
doing, that we betake him into the hands of the king.
(And so now come thou down, as thy soul truly desireth
to come down; and it shall be our *doing* that we deliver
him into thy hands.)
21 And Saul said, Blessed be ye of the Lord, for ye
[have] sorrowed for my stead/for my while (for ye be
concerned about my situation).
22 Therefore, I pray *you*, go ye, and make ready more
diligently, and do ye more curiously, *either attentively*,
and behold ye swiftly, where his foot is, either who saw
him there, where ye said; for he thinketh on me, that
fellily I ambush him. (And so, I pray *you*, go ye, and
more diligently, *yea, most attentively*, seek ye him out,
and quickly see ye, where his foot is, and who saw him
there, where ye said; for he thinketh, that I am foolish to
even try to ambush him.)
23 Behold ye, and see all his hiding places, in which he
is hid, and then turn ye again to me at a certain thing,
that I go with you; that if he encloseth himself yea in [the]
earth, I shall seek him with(in) all the thousands of Judah.
(Seek ye out, and see all his hiding places, where he can
be hid, and return to me with this certain information,
and then I shall go back with you; yea, if he is hid there
in the land, I shall seek him out among all the thousands
of Judah.)
24 And they rose up, and went into Ziph before Saul.
And David and his men were in the desert of Maon, in
the field places, at the right half of Jeshimon (And David
and his men were in the wilderness of Maon, to the south
of Jeshimon).
25 Therefore Saul went and his fellows to seek David,
and it was told to David; and anon he went down to the
stone, and lived in the desert of Maon; and when Saul
had heard this, he pursued David in the desert of Maon.
(And so Saul and his fellows went to seek out David, and
this was told to David; and at once he went down to a
rocky hill, and lived there in the wilderness of Maon; and
when Saul had heard this, he pursued David in the
wilderness of Maon.)
26 And Saul went and his men at the side of the hill on
[the] one part; forsooth David and his men were in the
side of the hill on the tother part; soothly David
despaired, that he might (not) escape from the face of
Saul. And so Saul and his men compassed by the manner
of a crown *round about* David and his men, that they
should take them. (And Saul and his men went on one
side of the hill; and David and his men were on the other
side of the hill; and David truly despaired that he might
not escape from Saul. And Saul and his men
encompassed David and his men *round about* like a
crown, in order to capture them.)
27 And (then) a messenger came to Saul, and said,
Haste thou, and come, for the Philistines have spread
themselves on the land.
28 Therefore Saul turned again, and ceased to pursue
David; and went against the coming of (the) Philistines.
For this thing they called that place The Stone of Parting
(And because of this they called that place
Selahammahlekoth).
29 Therefore David went up from thence, and dwelled
in the most secure places of Engedi.

CHAPTER 24

1 And when Saul turned again, after that he pursued
[the] Philistines, they told to him, and said, Lo! David is
in the desert of Engedi (Lo! David is in the wilderness of
Engedi).
2 Therefore Saul took three thousand chosen men of
all Israel, and went to seek David and his men, yea upon
the most broken rocks, the which be thorough-ways to
wild goats alone (which be thoroughfares only for wild
goats).
3 And he came to the folds of sheep, that offered
themselves to the way-goer. And there was a cave, into
which Saul entered, that he would purge his womb;
forsooth David and his men were hid in the inner part of
the den. (And he came to the sheepfolds, *or the pens*,
that offered themselves to the way-goer. And there was a
cave, into which Saul entered, where he could empty his
bowels; and David and his men were hid in the inner
part of that cave.)
4 And the servants of David said to him, Lo! the day of
which the Lord spake to thee, (and said,) I shall betake to
thee thine enemy, that thou do to him as it pleaseth in
thine eyes. Therefore David rose up, and cutted the hem
off the mantle of Saul privily. (And David's servants said
to him, Lo! this is the day of which the Lord spoke to
thee, and said, I shall deliver thy enemy to thee, so that
thou can do to him as it pleaseth thee. And David rose
up, and secretly cut off the hem of Saul's mantle.)
5 After these things, David smote his heart, *that is, his
conscience reproved him*, for he had cut away the hem of
the mantle of Saul. (But after doing this, David's heart
struck him, *that is, his conscience reproved him*, for he
had cut away the hem of Saul's mantle.)
6 And David said to his men, The Lord be merciful to
me, lest I do this thing to my lord, the anointed of the Lord,
or that I send mine hand on him, for he is the christ of the
Lord. (And David said to his men, The Lord forbid that I
do this to my lord, who is the Lord's anointed, or that I

put my hand against him, for he is the Lord's anointed.)
7 The Lord liveth, for but the Lord smite him, either
his day come, that he die, either he go down into battle,
and perish, the Lord be merciful to me, that I send not
mine hand into the christ of the Lord; *and David brake
his men by such words, and suffered not them, that they
rised against Saul.* And Saul rose out of the den, and
went in the way begun. (As the Lord liveth, but the Lord
strike him down, or his day come that he die, or that he
go down to the battle, and perish, the Lord forbid that I
put my hand against the Lord's anointed; *and David
convicted his men with such words, and did not allow
them to rise up against Saul.* And so Saul left the cave
without any harm, and went on the way begun.)
8 And David rose up after him, and he went out of the
den, and cried after the back of Saul, and said, My lord,
the king! And Saul beheld behind himself; and David
bowed himself low to the earth, and worshipped him
(and David bowed low to the ground, and honoured him).
9 And David said to Saul, Why hearest thou the words
of men speaking, David seeketh evil against thee? (And
David said to Saul, Why hearest thou the words of men
who say that David seeketh to harm thee.)
10 Lo! today thine eyes saw, that the Lord betook thee
in mine hand in the den, and I thought that I would slay
thee, but mine eye spared thee; for I said, I shall not hold
forth mine hand into my lord, for he is the anointed of
the Lord. (Lo! today thine eyes can see that the Lord
delivered thee into my hands in the cave, and I thought
that I would kill thee, but instead, I spared thee; for I said,
I shall not put my hand against my lord, for he is the
Lord's anointed.)
11 But rather, my father, see thou, and know the hem
of thy mantle in mine hand; for when I cutted away the
hem off thy mantle, I would not hold forth mine hand
against thee (for when I cut off the hem of thy mantle, I
would not put forth my hand against thee); perceive thou,
and see, for neither evil neither wickedness is in mine
hand, neither I have sinned against thee; but thou
ambushest my life, that thou do it away.
12 The Lord deem betwixt me and thee, and the Lord
venge me of thee (and the Lord avenge me upon thee);
but mine (own) hand be not against thee,
13 as it is said in [the] eld proverb, Wickedness shall go
out of wicked men; therefore mine hand be not against
thee (and so my hand shall not be against thee).
14 Whom pursuest thou, king of Israel, whom pursuest
thou? Thou pursuest a dead hound, and a quick flea.
15 The Lord be judge, and the Lord deem betwixt me
and thee, and see, and deem my cause, and deliver me
from thine hand.
16 And when David had filled, *or ended*, speaking such
manner words to Saul, Saul said, Whether this is thy voice,
my son David? And Saul raised up his voice, and wept.
17 And he said to David, Thou art more just than I; for
thou gavest good things to me; but I have yielded evils to
thee. (And he said to David, Thou art more in the right
than I; for thou gavest good to me; but I yielded only evil
to thee.)
18 And thou hast showed to me today, what goods
thou hast done to me, how the Lord betook me in thine
hand, and thou killedest not me. (And thou hast shown
me today the good that thou hast done for me, yea, how
the Lord delivered me into thy hands, but thou didest not
kill me.)
19 For who, when he findeth his enemy, shall deliver
him into (a) good way? But the Lord yield to thee this
while, for that, (that) thou hast wrought today in me (for
what thou hast done for me today).
20 And now, for I know, that thou shalt reign most
certainly, and shalt have in thine hand the realm of Israel,
(And now, for I know, that most certainly thou shalt
reign, and shalt have in thy hands the kingdom of Israel,)
21 swear thou to me in the Lord, that thou do not away
my seed after me, neither take away my name from the
house of my father. (swear thou to me by the Lord, that
thou shalt not do away my descendants after me, nor take
away my name from my father's house.)
22 And David swore to Saul. Therefore Saul went into
his house (And then Saul went back to his house), and
David and his men went up to (the) secure places.

CHAPTER 25

1 Forsooth Samuel was dead; and all Israel was
gathered together, and they bewailed him greatly, and
buried him in his house in Ramah. And David rose up,
and went down into the desert of Paran. (And then
Samuel died; and all Israel was gathered together, and
they greatly bewailed him, and buried him at his house
in Ramah. And David rose up, and went down to the
wilderness of Paran.)
2 And in Maon there was a man, and his possession
was in Carmel; and that man was full great, and there
were to him three thousand sheep, and a thousand of
goats; and it befelled that his flock was shorn in Carmel.
(And in Maon there was a man, and his possession was in
Carmel; and that man was very rich, and there were to
him three thousand sheep, and a thousand goats; and it
befell that his flock was clipped in Carmel.)
3 And the name of that man was Nabal, and the name
of his wife was Abigail; and that woman was most
prudent and fair, (and that woman was very intelligent,
and beautiful); but her husband was hard and full wicked
and malicious; and he was of the kin of Caleb.
4 Therefore when David had heard in desert, that
Nabal clipped his flock, (And when David had heard in
the wilderness, that Nabal clipped his flock,)
5 he sent ten young men, and said to them, Go ye up

into Carmel, and ye shall come to Nabal, and ye shall
greet him of my name peaceably (and ye shall give him a
friendly greeting in my name);
6 and ye shall say thus (and so ye shall say), Peace be
to my brethren and to thee, and peace be to thine house,
and peace be to all things, whatever thou hast.
7 I have heard that thy shepherds, that were with us in
desert, have shorn thy flocks; we were never dis-easeful
to them, neither any time anything of the flock failed to
them, in all the time in which they were with us in
Carmel; (I have heard that thy shepherds, who were with
us in the wilderness, have clipped thy flocks; we never
threatened them, nor at any time did anything of theirs go
missing, in all the time when they were with us in Carmel;)
8 ask thy young men, and they shall show to thee.
Now therefore thy young men find grace in thine eyes;
for in a good day we come to thee; whatever thing thine
hand findeth, *or (it) pleaseth to thee*, give *it* to thy
servants, and to thy son David. (ask thy young men, and
they shall tell thee. And so now let *my* young men find
favour in thine eyes, for we come to thee on a good day;
and whatever thing that thy hand findeth, *or it pleaseth
thee*, give *it* to thy servants, and to thy son David.)
9 And when the young men of David had come, they
spake to Nabal all these words in the name of David, and
held [their] peace (and then they were silent).
10 Forsooth Nabal answered to the young men of
David, and said, Who is David? and who is the son of
Jesse? Today servants [have] increased that flee their lords
(Today too many servants have fled from their lords).
11 Therefore shall I take my loaves, and my waters, and
the flesh of (my) beasts, which I have slain to my shearers
(which I have killed for my shearers), and shall I give (it)
to men, that I know not of whence they be?
12 Therefore the young men of David went again by
their way; and they turned again, and came, and told to
him all (the) words which Nabal had said.
13 Then David said to his young men, (Let) Each man
be gird with his sword. And all (his) men were girded
with their swords, and David also was girded with his
sword; and as four hundred men followed David, for two
hundred (were) left at the fardels (and about four hundred
men followed David, for two hundred were left behind
with the bundles, *or the supplies*).
14 And one of the young men told to Abigail, the wife
of Nabal, and said, Lo! David sent messengers from
desert, that they should bless our lord, and he turned
them away (Lo! David sent messengers from the
wilderness to greet our lord, but he turned them away);
15 these men were good enough, and not dis-easeful to
us, and nothing of ours perished in all the time in which
we were with them in desert, (*or in the wilderness*);
16 they were to us for a wall, both in night and day, in
all the days in which we pastured flocks with them. (they
were like a wall for us, both night and day, all the days in
which we pastured the flocks with them.)
17 Wherefore behold thou, and think, what thou shalt
do; for malice is full-filled against thine husband, and
against thine house (for malice is now filled full against
thy husband, and against all thy family); and he is the son
of Belial, so that no man may speak (sense) to him.
18 Therefore Abigail hasted, and took two hundred
loaves, and two vessels of wine, and five wethers sodden,
and seven bushels and an half of flour (and five roasted
sheep, and seven and a half bushels of flour), and an
hundred bundles of dried grapes, *or raisins*, and two
hundred pieces of dried figs; and she put *all this* upon
asses,
19 and said to her servants, Go ye before me; lo! I shall
follow you behind your back. And she showed not *this*
to her husband Nabal (But she did not say anything about
this to her husband Nabal).
20 Therefore when she had gone upon an ass, and
came down to the foot of the hill, David and his men
came down into her coming; the which she met (and she
met them).
21 And (earlier) David (had) said, Verily in vain I have
kept all these things that were of this Nabal in the desert,
and nothing perished of all things that pertained to him,
and (yet) he hath yielded to me evil for good. (And earlier
David had said, Truly in vain have I kept watch over all
those things that were Nabal's in the wilderness, and
though nothing perished of all the things that pertained to
him, yet he hath yielded to me evil for good.)
22 The Lord do these things, and add he these things to
the enemies of David, if I shall leave (anything)
undestroyed of all things that pertain to him till tomorrow
(yea, even) a pisser to a wall. (May the Lord do these
things, and add he other things, to David's enemies, if I
leave anything *unwasted* until tomorrow out of all the
things that pertain to him, yea, even a pisser on the wall.)
23 And when Abigail saw David, she hasted, and went
down off the ass; and she fell down before David on her
face, and worshipped *him* on the earth (bowing low to
the ground before *him*).
24 And she felled down to his feet, and said, My lord
the king, this wickedness be in me; I beseech thee, speak
thine handmaid in thine ears, and hear thou the words of
thy servantess; (And she fell down at his feet, and said,
My lord the king, let this wickedness be upon me; I
beseech thee, let thy servantess speak to thee, and listen
thou to the words of thy servantess;)
25 I pray (thee), my lord the king, set not his heart on
this wicked man Nabal, for by his name he is a fool, and
folly is with him; but, my lord, I thine handmaid saw not
thy young men, which thou sentest (but my lord, I thy
servantess, did not see thy young men, whom thou
sentest).

26 Now therefore, my lord, the Lord liveth, and thy
soul liveth, the which Lord hath forbidden thee, that thou
shouldest come into blood, and the Lord saved thy life to
thee; and now thine enemies, and they that seek evil to
thee my lord, be they made as Nabal. (And so now, my
lord, as the Lord liveth, and as thy soul liveth, the which
Lord hath forbidden thee, that thou shouldest come to
shed blood, and so to avenge thyself with thy own hand;
yea, now let thy enemies, and they who seek evil for thee
my lord, be they made like Nabal.)
27 Wherefore receive thou this blessing, (*or this gift,*)
which thine handmaid [hath] brought to thee, my lord,
and give *it* to the young men that follow thee, my lord.
28 (And) Do thou away the wickedness of thy
servantess; for the Lord making shall make a faithful
house to thee, my lord (for the Lord shall make a faithful
family for thee, my lord), for thou, my lord, fightest the
battles of the Lord; therefore malice be not found in thee
in all the days of thy life.
29 For if a man riseth any time, and pursueth thee, and
seeketh thy life, the life of my lord shall be kept (safe) as
in a bundle of living *trees*, at thy Lord God (with the Lord
thy God); but the soul of thine enemies shall be hurled
round about as in [the] fierceness, and [the] circle of a
sling.
30 Therefore when the Lord hath done to thee, my lord,
all these good things, which he hath spoken of thee, and
hath ordained thee duke upon Israel (and hath ordained
thee ruler upon Israel),
31 this shall not be into sighing, *that is, into mourning
of soul, and into remorse of conscience*, and into doubt
of heart to thee, my lord, that thou hast shed out guiltless
blood, either that thou hast (a)venged thyself. And when
the Lord hath done well to thee, my lord, thou shalt have
mind on thine handmaid (thou shalt remember thy
servantess), and thou shalt do well to her.
32 And David said to Abigail, Blessed be the Lord God
of Israel, that sent thee today into my coming (who sent
thee today to meet me),
33 and blessed be thy speech; and blessed be thou, that
hast forbade me, lest I went *today* to (shed) blood, and
had venged me with mine hand (and had avenged myself
with my own hands);
34 else the Lord God of Israel liveth, which forbade
me, lest I did evil to thee, if thou haddest not soon come
into meeting to me, (yea, even) a pisser to the wall
should not have (been) left to Nabal till to the morrow
light. (else as the Lord God of Israel liveth, who forbade
me, lest I did evil to thee, if thou haddest not swiftly
come to meet me, yea, even a pisser on the wall would
not have been left to Nabal by the morning light.)
35 Therefore David received (out) of her hand all (the)
things which she had brought to him; and he said to her,
Go thou in peace into thine house; lo! I have heard thy
voice, and I honoured thy face (and I grant thy request).
36 Forsooth Abigail came to Nabal; and lo! a feast was
to him in his house, as the feast of a king; and the heart of
Nabal was merry, certainly he was full drunken; and she
showed not to him a word, little or great, till the morrow.
(And Abigail came back to Nabal; and lo! he was giving a
feast in his house, a feast fit for a king; and Nabal's heart
was merry, for he was very drunk; and so she did not tell
him anything, little or great, until the morning.)
37 But in the morrowtide, when Nabal had voided the
wine, his wife showed to him all these words; and his
heart was almost dead within, and he was made as a
stone. (But in the morning, when Nabal had voided the
wine, his wife told him everything; and his heart was
almost dead within, and he was made like a stone.)
38 And when ten days had passed, the Lord smote
Nabal, and he was dead (and he died).
39 The which thing when David had heard, Nabal *to
be* dead, he said, Blessed be the Lord God, that hath
venged the cause of my shame of the hand of Nabal, and
hath kept his servant from evil, and the Lord hath yielded
the malice of Nabal into the head of him. Therefore
David sent, and spake to Abigail, that he would take her
(as a) wife to him. (Which thing when David had heard,
that is, that Nabal *had* died, he said, Blessed be the Lord
God, who hath avenged the cause of my shame at the
hand of Nabal, and hath kept his servant from evil; yea,
the Lord hath yielded the malice of Nabal onto his own
head. Then David sent word to Abigail that he would
take her for his wife.)
40 And the servants of David came to Abigail into
Carmel, and spake to her, and said, David sent us to thee,
that he take thee into wife to him. (And so David's
servants came to Abigail at Carmel, and spoke to her, and
said, David sent us to tell thee, that he would take thee as
his wife.)
41 And she rose up, and worshipped low to the earth
(and bowed low to the ground), and said, Lo! (let) thy
servantess be into an handmaid, that she wash the feet of
the servants of my lord.
42 And Abigail hasted, and rose (up), and ascended on
an ass (and mounted her donkey); and five damsels, (the)
followers of her feet, went with her, and she followed the
messengers of David, and (so) was made [a] wife to him.
43 But also David took Ahinoam of Jezreel, and ever
either was wife to him (and they both became his wives);
44 and Saul gave Michal his daughter, [the] wife of
David, to Phalti, the son of Laish, that was of Gallim.

CHAPTER 26

1 And Ziphites came to Saul into Gibeah, and said,
Lo! David is hid in the hill of Hachilah, which is even
against the wilderness. (And the Ziphites came to Saul at
Gibeah, and said, Lo! David is hid on Mount Hachilah,

overlooking Jeshimon.)
2 And Saul rose up, and went down into the desert of
Ziph, and with him three thousand of men of the chosen
of Israel, that he should seek David in the desert of Ziph.
(And Saul rose up, and went down to the wilderness of
Ziph, and three thousand chosen men of Israel went with
him, to help him seek out David in the wilderness of Ziph.)
3 And Saul setted his tents in the hill of Hachilah, that
was even against the wilderness, in the way. And David
dwelled in the desert. Forsooth David saw that Saul had
come after him into desert; (And Saul pitched his tents on
Mount Hachilah, on the way overlooking Jeshimon. And
David stayed in the wilderness. And David knew that
Saul had come after him into the wilderness;)
4 and David sent spyers, and learned most certainly,
that Saul had come thither.
5 And David rose up privily, and came to the place
where Saul was. And when David had seen the place,
wherein Saul slept, and Abner, the son of Ner, the prince
of his chivalry; and Saul sleeping in the tent, and the
tother common people by his compass; (And David rose
up quickly, and came to the place where Saul was. And
when David had seen the place where Saul slept, and
Abner, the son of Ner, the leader of his cavalry, *or his
army*; and Saul was sleeping in his tent, and the other
common people were all around him;)
6 David said to Ahimelech, (the) Hittite, and to
Abishai, the son of Zeruiah, the brother of Joab, saying,
Who shall go down with me to Saul into his tents? And
Abishai said, I shall go down with thee.
7 Therefore David and Abishai came to the people in
the night, and they found Saul lying and sleeping in the
tent, and a spear set fast in the earth at his head; forsooth
they found Abner and the people sleeping in his compass
(and *they found* Abner and the other people sleeping all
around him).
8 And Abishai said to David, God hath closed today
thine enemy into thine hands; now therefore I shall
pierce him with the spear once (through, and) in(to) the
earth, and no need shall be (for) the second time. (And
Abishai said to David, God hath enclosed thy enemy in
thy hands today; and so now I shall pierce him once
through with the spear, and into the ground, and there
shall be no need for a second thrust.)
9 And David said to Abishai, Slay thou not him, for
who shall hold forth his hand into the christ of the Lord,
and shall be innocent? (And David said to Abishai, Kill
thou him not, for who shall put his hand against the
anointed of the Lord, and still be innocent?)
10 And David said, (As) The Lord liveth, for no but the
Lord smite him, either his day come that he die, either he
go down into battle, and perish;
11 the Lord be merciful to me, that I hold not forth
mine hand into the christ of the Lord; now therefore take
thou the spear, that is at his head, and the cup of water,
and go we away. (the Lord forbid/God forbid that I put
my hand against the Lord's anointed; and so now, let us
take the spear, that is at his head, and the cup of water,
and go we away.)
12 Then David took the spear, and the cup of water,
that was at the head of Saul, and they went forth, and no
man was that saw, and understood, and waked, but all
men slept (and there was no one who saw it, or knew it,
or even awoke, but all the men slept); for the sleep of the
Lord had fallen [up]on them.
13 And when David had passed [over] even against,
and had stood on the top of the hill afar (off), and a great
space was betwixt them,
14 David cried to the people, and to Abner, the son of
Ner, and said, Abner, whether thou wilt not answer?
(Abner, wilt thou not answer me?) And Abner answered,
and said, Who art thou, that criest, and dis-easest the king?
15 And David said to Abner, Whether thou art not a
man (Art thou not a man), and what other man is like
thee in Israel? why therefore hast thou not kept thy lord
the king (safe)? For one man of the company entered,
that he should slay thy lord the king;
16 this that thou hast done, is not good; the Lord liveth,
for ye be sons of death, that kept not your lord, the christ
of the Lord (this is not good, what thou hast done; as the
Lord liveth, for ye be the sons of death, who kept not
your lord safe, yea, the Lord's anointed). Now therefore
see thou, where is the spear of the king, and where is the
cup of water, that was at his head.
17 Forsooth Saul knew the voice of David, and said,
Whether this voice is thine, my son David? And David
said, My lord the king, it is my voice. (And Saul knew the
voice of David, and said, Is this thy voice, David my son?
And David said, My lord the king, it is my voice.)
18 And David said, For what cause pursueth my lord
his servant? What have I done, either what evil is in mine
hand?
19 Now therefore, my lord the king, I pray, hear the
words of thy servant; if the Lord stirreth thee against me,
the sacrifice be smelled; forsooth if [the] sons of men *stir
thee*, they be cursed in the sight of the Lord, which have
cast me out today, that I dwell not in the heritage of the
Lord, and say, Go thou, serve thou alien gods. (And so
now, my lord the king, I pray thee, listen to the words of
thy servant; if the Lord stirreth thee against me, let the
sacrifice be smelled; but if the sons of men *stir thee*, be
they cursed before the Lord, they who have thrown me
out today, so that I live not in the inheritance of the Lord,
and who say to me, Go thou, serve thou foreign, *or
other*, gods.)
20 And now my blood be not shed out in the earth
before the Lord; for the king of Israel hath gone out, that
he seek a quick flea, as a partridge is pursued in hills.

(And now let not my blood be shed out on the ground
before the Lord; for the king of Israel hath gone out, so
that he can seek after a quick, *or an insignificant*, flea,
like a partridge is pursued over the hills.)
21 And Saul said, I have sinned; turn thou again, my
son David, for I shall no more do evil to thee, for my life
was precious today in thine eyes; for it seemeth, that I
have done follily (that I have done foolishly), and I have
unknown full many things.
22 And David answered and said, Lo! the spear of the
king, one of the young men of the king pass (over *hither*),
and take it; (And David replied, Lo! the spear of the king;
one of the king's young men come over *here*, and take it
back;)
23 forsooth the Lord shall yield to each man after his
rightfulness and *his* faith; for the Lord betook thee today
into mine hand, and I would not hold forth mine hand
into the christ of the Lord; (and the Lord shall yield to
each man after his uprightness and *his* faithfulness, *or his
loyalty*; for the Lord delivered thee today into my hands,
but I would not put my hand against the Lord's anointed;)
24 and as thy life is magnified today in mine eyes, so
my life be magnified in the eyes of the Lord, and deliver
he me from all anguish. (and as thy life is magnified
today in my eyes, so let my life be magnified in the eyes
of the Lord, and let him deliver me from all anguish.)
25 Therefore Saul said to David, Blessed be thou, my
son David; and soothly thou doing shalt do, and thou
mighty shalt be mighty. Then David went forth into his
way, and Saul turned again into his place (Then David
went forth on his way, and Saul returned home).

CHAPTER 27

1 And David said in his heart, Sometime I shall fall in
one day in the hand of Saul (One day I shall fall by Saul's
hand); whether it is not better, that I flee, and be saved in
the land of (the) Philistines, (so) that Saul despair, and
cease to seek me in all the ends of Israel; therefore flee
we his hands.
2 And (so) David rose up, and went forth, he and six
hundred men with him, to Achish, the son of Maoch,
king of Gath.
3 And David dwelled with Achish in Gath, he, and his
men, and his house(hold) (And David lived with Achish
in Gath, he, and his men, and his family); *that is*, David,
and his two wives, Ahinoam of Jezreel, and Abigail, the
wife of Nabal of Carmel.
4 And it was told to Saul, that David (had) fled into
Gath; and he added no more that he should seek (after)
David [and he added no more for to seek him].
5 Forsooth David said to Achish, If I have found grace
in thine eyes, (let) a place be given to me in one of the
cities of this country, that I dwell there; for why dwelleth
thy servant in the city of the king with thee? (for why
should thy servant remain with thee in the king's city?)
6 Therefore Achish gave him Ziklag in that day (And
so Achish gave him Ziklag that day), for the which cause
Ziklag was made into *(a) possession* of the kings of Judah
unto this day.
7 And the number of days, in which David dwelled in
the country of (the) Philistines, was days, *that is a year*,
and four months.
8 And David went up, and his men, and they took
preys of Geshurites, and of Gezrites, and of men of
Amalek; for these towns were inhabited by (them in) eld
time(s) in the land, to men going to Shur, unto the land of
Egypt. (And David and his men went up, and they took
prey from the Geshurites, and the Gezrites, and the
Amalekites; for these people inhabited the land in old
times, unto Shur, and the land of Egypt.)
9 And David smote all the land of them, and he left
not man nor woman living (and he left no man or woman
alive); and he took sheep, and oxen, and asses, and
camels, and clothes, and turned again, and came to
Achish.
10 And Achish said to him, Into whom hurled ye
today?/Against whom have ye hurled today? And David
answered, Against the south of Judah, and against the
south of Jerahmeel, and against the south of Kenites. (And
Achish would say to him, Where did ye attack today?
And David would answer, In the south of Judah, or, In
the south of Jerahmeel, or, To the south of the Kenites.)
11 David left not quick man and woman (David left no
man or woman alive), neither brought (them back) into
Gath, and said, Lest peradventure they speak against us.
David did these things, and this was his doom, in all [the]
days in which he dwelled in the country of (the) Philistines.
12 Therefore Achish believed to David (And so Achish
trusted David), and said, Certainly he hath wrought many
evils against his people Israel, therefore he shall be a
servant to me for evermore.

CHAPTER 28

1 Forsooth it was done in those days, the Philistines
gathered together their companies, that they should be
made ready against Israel to battle. And Achish said to
David, Thou witting know now, for thou shalt go out
with me in tents, thou and thy men. (And it was done in
those days, the Philistines gathered together the
companies *of their troops*, to prepare for battle against
Israel. And Achish said to David, Thou must know, that
thou shalt go out with me to the battle, thou and thy men.)
2 And David said to Achish, (And) Now thou shalt
know what things thy servant shall do. And Achish said
to David, And I shall set thee (the) keeper of mine head
in all days.
3 Forsooth Samuel was dead, and all Israel bewailed
him, and they buried him in Ramah, his city. And Saul

did away from the land witches and false diviners.
4 And (the) Philistines were gathered, and came, and
setted tents in Shunem; soothly and Saul gathered all
Israel, and came into Gilboa.
5 And Saul saw the castles of Philistines [And Saul saw
the tents of (the) Philistines], and he dreaded, and his heart
dreaded greatly. (And Saul saw the army of the
Philistines, and he was afraid, and his heart greatly
dreaded/and his heart greatly feared.)
6 And he counselled (with) the Lord; and the Lord
answered not to him (but the Lord did not answer him),
neither by priests, nor by dreams, nor by prophets.
7 And Saul said to his servants, Seek ye to me a
woman having a fiend speaking in the womb; and I shall
go to her, and I shall inquire by her. And his servants
said to him, A woman having a fiend speaking in the
womb is in Endor. (And Saul said to his servants, Seek ye
out for me a woman who hath a familiar spirit; and I shall
go to her, and I shall inquire through her. And his
servants said to him, There is a woman who hath a
familiar spirit in Endor.)
8 Therefore Saul changed his clothing, and he was
clothed with other clothes; and he went, and two men
with him; and they came to the woman in the night. And
he said, Divine thou to me in a fiend speaking in the
womb, and raise thou up to me whom I shall say to thee
(And he said, Call thou for me thy familiar spirit, and
raise thou up for me whom I shall name to thee).
9 And the woman said to him, Lo! thou knowest how
great things Saul hath done, and how he hath done away
from the land witches, and false diviners (and how he
hath done away with witches, and false diviners, from the
land); why therefore settest thou treason to my life, that I
be slain?
10 And Saul swore to her in the Lord, and said, The Lord
liveth; for nothing of evil shall come to thee for this thing.
(And Saul swore to her by the Lord, and said, As the Lord
liveth; nothing of evil shall come to thee for this thing.)
11 And the woman said to him, Whom shall I raise up
to thee? And he said, Raise thou Samuel up to me. (And
the woman said to him, Whom shall I raise up for thee?
And he said, Raise thou up Samuel for me.)
12 Soothly when the woman had seen Samuel, she
cried with [a] great voice, and said to Saul, Why hast thou
deceived me? for thou art Saul.
13 And the king said to her, Do not thou dread (Fear
not); what hast thou seen? And the woman said to Saul, I
saw gods ascending from [the] earth.
14 And Saul said to her, What manner form is of him?
[What manner is the form of him?] And she said, An eld man
goeth up, and he is clothed with a mantle. And Saul
understood that it was Samuel; and Saul bowed himself
on his face to the earth, and worshipped. (And Saul said
to her, What is his form? And she said, An old man goeth
up, and he is clothed with a mantle. And Saul understood
that it was Samuel; and Saul bowed himself low to the
ground, and honoured him.)
15 And Samuel said to Saul, Why hast thou dis-eased
me, that I should be raised? And Saul said, I am
constrained greatly; for the Philistines fight against me,
and God hath gone away from me, and he would not
hear me, neither by the hand of prophets, nor by dreams;
therefore I called thee, that thou shouldest show to me
what I shall do. (And Samuel said to Saul, Why hast thou
disturbed me, so that I am raised up? And Saul said, I am
in great trouble; for the Philistines fight against me, and
God hath gone away from me, and he will not answer
me, not by prophets, nor by dreams; and so I called thee,
so that thou couldest tell me what I should do.)
16 And Samuel said, What askest thou me, when God
hath gone away from thee, and hath passed to thine
enemy? (And Samuel said, Why askest thou me, when
God hath gone away from thee, and hath become thy
enemy?)
17 For the Lord shall do to thee as he spake in mine
hand (For the Lord shall do to thee as he spoke through
me), and he shall cut away thy realm from thine hand,
and he shall give it to David, thy neighbour;
18 for thou obeyedest not the voice of the Lord, neither
thou didest the fierce wrath of the Lord in Amalek.
Therefore the Lord hath done to thee today that that thou
sufferest (And so the Lord hath done to thee what thou
sufferest today);
19 and the Lord shall give also Israel with thee in the
hand of Philistines. Forsooth tomorrow thou and thy
sons shall be with me; but also the Lord shall betake the
castles of Israel in the hand of the Philistines [but and the
Lord shall take the tents of Israel in the hand of the Philistines].
(and the Lord shall also give Israel along with thee into
the hands of the Philistines. Yea, tomorrow thou and thy
sons shall be with me; and the Lord shall deliver the
army of Israel into the hands of the Philistines.)
20 And anon Saul fell down and was stretched forth
upon the earth; for he dreaded the words of Samuel, and
strength was not in him, for he had not eaten bread in all
that day and all that night. (And at once Saul fell down
and was stretched out on the ground; for he feared
Samuel's words, and there was no strength in him, for he
had not eaten any food all that day and all that night.)
21 Therefore that woman entered to Saul, and said; for
he was troubled greatly (for he was greatly troubled); and
she said to him, Lo! thine handmaid hath obeyed to thy
voice, and I have put my life in mine hand, and I heard
thy words, which thou spakest to me.
22 And now therefore thou hear the voice of thine
handmaid, and I shall set a morsel of bread before thee,
and that thou eating wax strong, and mayest do thy
journey. (And so now listen thou to the voice of thy

servantess, for I shall set a morsel of food before thee,
and once that thou hast eaten it, thou shalt grow strong,
and then thou shalt go forth on thy journey.)
23 And he forsook it, and said, I shall not eat. But his
servants and the woman compelled him; and at the last,
when the voice of them was heard, he rose up from the
earth, and sat on the bed.
24 Soothly that woman had a fat calf in the house, and
she hasted, and killed it; and she took meal, and meddled
it together, and made therf bread (and she took meal, and
mixed it together, and made unleavened bread);
25 and she set (it) forth before Saul, and before his
servants, and when they had eaten, they rose up, and
walked in all the night (and walked through all that night).

CHAPTER 29

1 Therefore all the companies of the Philistines were
gathered in Aphek, but also Israel setted tents above the
well that was in Jezreel. (And so all the companies of the
Philistines were gathered together at Aphek, and Israel
pitched their tents by the well that was in Jezreel.)
2 And soothly the princes of the Philistines went in
companies of an hundred, and in thousands; but David
and his men were in the last company with Achish. (And
the princes of the Philistines led out their companies in
units of a hundred, and of a thousand; and David and his
men were in the last group with Achish.)
3 And the princes of Philistines said to Achish, What
will these Hebrews to themselves? And Achish said to
the princes of Philistines, Whether ye know not David,
that was the servant of Saul, king of Israel? and he was
with me many days, either years, and I found not in him
anything *of imagining to evil*, from the day in which he
fled to me unto this day. (And the princes of the
Philistines said to Achish, What be these Hebrews doing
here? And Achish said to the Philistine princes, Do ye
not know David, who was the servant of Saul, the king of
Israel? he hath been with me for many years, and I have
found nothing *of evil* in him, from the day in which he
fled to me until this day.)
4 Certainly the princes of (the) Philistines were wroth
against Achish, and they said to him, (Have) The man
turn again, and abide he in his place, in which thou hast
ordained him, and come he not down with us into battle,
lest he be made (an) adversary to us, when we have
begun to fight; for how may he please his lord in other
manner, but in our heads? (for how can he please his lord
in any other manner, but than with our heads?)
5 Whether this is not David, to whom they sang in
dances, and said, Saul smote in [his] thousands, and David
smote in his ten thousands? (Is this not David, whom they
sang about as they danced, and said, Saul struck down
thousands, but David struck down tens of thousands?)
6 Therefore Achish called David, and said to him, (As)
The Lord liveth; for thou art rightful (for thou art upright),
and good in my sight, and thy going out and thy coming
in is with me in [the] tents, and I have not found in thee
anything of evil, from the day in which thou camest to
me till to this day; but thou pleasest not the princes, *or
satraps*.
7 Therefore turn thou again, and go in peace (And so
return thou, and go home in peace), and offend thou not
the eyes of the princes, *or satraps*, of the Philistines.
8 And David said to Achish, And what have I done,
and what hast thou found in me thy servant, from the day
in which I was (first) in thy sight till into this day, that I
come not, and fight against the enemies of my lord the
king?
9 And Achish answered, and spake to David, (and
said,) I know that thou art good, and (be) as the angel of
God in my eyes; but the princes of Philistines said, He
shall not go up with us into battle.
10 Therefore rise thou up early, thou, and thy servants
that came with thee; and when ye have risen by night,
and it beginneth to be clear *day*, go ye forth. (And so rise
thou up early, thou, and thy servants who came with
thee; and when ye have risen in the night, and it
beginneth to be clear *daylight*, then go ye forth.)
11 Therefore David rose up by night, he and his men,
that they should go forth early, and turn again to the land
of Philistines; but the Philistines went up into Jezreel.
(And so David and his men rose up in the night, so that
they could go forth early, and return to the land of the
Philistines; and the Philistines went on to Jezreel.)

CHAPTER 30

1 And when David and his men had come into Ziklag
in the third day, (they learned that) men of Amalek had
made assault on the south part (of Judah,) (and) in Ziklag;
and (had) smitten Ziklag, and burnt it by fire. (And when
David and his men had come into Ziklag on the third
day, they learned that the Amalekites had made an
assault on the southern part of Judah, and in Ziklag; and
they had struck Ziklag, and had burned it down.)
2 And they led (away) the women (as) prisoners from
thence, from the least unto the most; and they had not
slain any, but they led them forth with them, and went in
their way. (And they took away the women as prisoners
from there, from the least unto the most; and they did not
kill any, but they took them away with them, and went
on their way.)
3 Therefore when David and his men had come to the
city, and had found it burnt with fire, and that their
wives, and their sons, and daughters were led away (as)
prisoners,
4 then David and the people that was with him raised
[up] their voices, and wailed, till the tears failed in them.
5 And also [the] two wives of David were led away

(as) prisoners, Ahinoam of Jezreel, and Abigail, the wife of Nabal of Carmel.
6 And David was full sorry; certainly all the people would have stoned David, for the soul of each man was bitter on their sons and daughters. Forsooth David was comforted in his Lord God. (And David was in great trouble; yea, all the men would have stoned David, for all of them were bitter over losing their sons and daughters. But David was strengthened by the Lord his God.)
7 And he said to Abiathar, the priest, the son of Ahimelech, Bring thou [the] ephod to me. And Abiathar brought the ephod to David;
8 and David counselled with the Lord, and said, Shall I pursue these thieves, either no? and shall I take them? And the Lord said to him, Pursue thou; for without doubt thou shalt take them, and thou shalt take away from them their prey. (and David counselled with the Lord, and said, Shall I pursue these thieves, or not? and shall I be able to overtake them? And the Lord said to him, Pursue thou them; for without a doubt thou shalt overtake them, and thou shalt take their prey away from them.)
9 Therefore David went forth, he and six hundred men that were with him, and they came unto the strand of Besor; and *there* the weary men *of the host of David* abode behind. (And so David went forth, he and the six hundred men who were with him, and they came to the Besor Stream; and the weary men *in David's army* stayed behind there.)
10 Forsooth David pursued, he and four hundred men; for two hundred abided (behind), that were weary, and might not pass [over] the strand of Besor.
11 And they found a (young) man of Egypt in the field, and they brought him to David; and they gave him bread, that he should eat, and water to drink (and they gave him some bread to eat, and some water to drink);
12 but also *they gave to him* a gobbet of a bundle of dried figs, and two clusters of dried grapes. And when he had eaten those, his spirit turned again *to him*, and he was comforted; for he had not eaten bread, neither had drunk water in three days and three nights. (and *they* also *gave him* a piece of a bundle of dried figs, and two clusters of dried grapes. And when he had eaten them, his spirit returned *to him*, and he was strengthened; for he had not eaten any bread, or drunk any water, for three days and three nights.)
13 Then David said to him, Whose *man* art thou, either from whence and whither goest thou? And he said, I am a young man of Egypt, the servant of a man of Amalek; but my lord forsook me, for I began to be sick the third day ago.
14 For we brake out at the south coast of (the) Cherethites, and against Judah (near Judah), and at the south of Caleb, and we burnt Ziklag with fire.
15 And David said to him, Mayest thou lead me to this
company? Which said (And the young man said), Swear thou to me by God, that thou shalt not slay me, and that thou shalt not betake me into the hands of my lord; and I shall lead thee to this company. And David swore to him.
16 And when the young man had led him *thither*, lo! they sat at the meat, upon the face of all the earth, eating and drinking, and as hallowing a feast day, for all the prey and spoils which they had taken of the land of Philistines, and of the land of Judah. (And when the young man had led him *there*, lo! they sat spread out over all the ground, eating and drinking, as if celebrating a feast day, because of all the prey and the spoils which they had taken from the land of the Philistines, and the land of Judah.)
17 And David smote them from the eventide unto the eventide of the tother day, and not any of them escaped, no but four hundred young men, that went upon camels, and fled (who went upon camels, and fled).
18 Forsooth David delivered all things which the men of Amalek took, and he delivered his two wives; (And so David recovered all that the Amalekites had taken, and he rescued his two wives;)
19 neither any of them failed, from little till to great, as well of sons as of daughters, and of spoils; and whatever things they had ravished, David led again all things; (no one was lost, from the least unto the greatest, sons as well as daughters; and all the spoils, yea, whatever they had taken, David brought home again.)
20 and he took all the flocks and great beasts, and drove them before his face. And they said, This is the prey of David (And the men said, This should all be David's prey).
21 Forsooth David came to the two hundred men, that were weary, and abided behind, and might not follow David; and he [had] commanded them to sit at the strand of Besor; which went out against David, and the people that was with him. Forsooth David nighed to the people, and he greeted it peaceably. (And David came back to the two hundred men who were weary, and had stayed behind, and did not follow David; and he had commanded them to remain there at the Besor Stream; and they went out to meet David, and the people who were with him. And David came to these men, and he greeted them warmly.)
22 And one man, the worst man and wicked of the men that were with David, answered, and said, For they came not with us, we shall not give to them anything of the prey, that we have ravished, but suffice it to each man his wife and his children; and when they have taken them, go they away. (But some men, the worst and the most wicked of those who went with David, said, For they did not come with us, we shall not give them any of the prey, that we have recovered, but let each man take only his wife and his children; and when they have taken them, go they away.)

23 And David said, My brethren, ye shall not do so, *as*
ye speak, of these things, which the Lord hath given to
us, and he hath kept us, and gave the thieves, that brake
out against us, into our hands; (But David said, My
brothers/My kinsmen, ye shall not do, *as ye speak*, with
these things, which the Lord hath given us, for he hath
kept us safe, and delivered the thieves, who broke out
against us, into our hands;)
24 neither any shall hear us *strive* on this word. For
even part shall be of him that goeth down to battle, and
of him that dwelleth at the fardels; and in like manner
they shall part *the prey*. (nor shall anyone hear us *arguing*
over this matter. For even portion shall be for him who
went down to the battle, as well as for him who stayed
with the bundles, *or the supplies*; yea, in like manner
they shall divide up *the prey*.)
25 And this was made a constitution and a doom from
that day and afterward, and as a law in Israel till into this
day. (And from that day forward, this was made a custom,
and a judgement, and a law in Israel, until this day.)
26 Then David came into Ziklag, and he sent gifts of
the prey to the elder men of Judah, his neighbours, and
said, Take ye blessing of the prey of [the] enemies of the
Lord (Have ye a gift out of the prey from the Lord's
enemies);
27 to them that were in Bethel, and that were in
Ramoth, at the south, and that were in Jattir,
28 and that were in Aroer, and that were in Siphmoth,
and that were in Eshtemoa,
29 and that were in Rachal, and that were in the cities
of Jerahmeel, and that were in the cities of Kenites,
30 and that were in Hormah, and that were in
Chorashan, and that were in Athach,
31 and that were in Hebron, and to other men, that were
in these places, in which David dwelled and his men.
(and those in Hebron, and to the other men who were in
those places, where David and his men had lived.)

CHAPTER 31

1 Forsooth the Philistines fought against Israel, and the
men of Israel fled before the face of Philistines, and they
fell down slain in the hill of Gilboa. (Then the Philistines
fought against Israel, and the men of Israel fled from the
Philistines, and they fell down dead on Mount Gilboa.)
2 And the Philistines hurled fiercely into Saul, and
into his sons, and they killed Jonathan, and Abinadab,
and Melchishua, [the] sons of Saul.
3 And (then) all the weight, or charge, of the battle
was turned against Saul; and (the) men archers pursued
him, and he was wounded greatly of the archers (and he
was seriously wounded by the archers).
4 And Saul said to his squire, Draw out thy sword, and
slay me, lest peradventure these uncircumcised men
come, and slay me, and scorn me. And his squire would
not, for he was afeared by full great dread; therefore Saul
took his sword, and felled thereon (But his squire would
not do it, for he was afraid with a very great fear; and so
Saul took his own sword, and fell on it).
5 And when his squire had seen this, that Saul was
dead, also he felled upon his sword (he also fell on his
sword), and was dead with him.
6 And so Saul was dead, and his three sons, and his
squire, and all his men in that day together. (And so Saul,
and his three sons, and his squire, and all his men, died
together on the same day.)
7 And the sons of Israel, that were beyond the valley,
and beyond Jordan, saw that the men of Israel had fled,
and that Saul was dead, and his sons, and they left their
cities, and fled; and the Philistines came, and dwelled
there. (And when the Israelites, who were beyond the
valley, and east of the Jordan River, saw that the other
Israelites had fled, and that Saul and his sons were dead,
they left their cities, and fled; and the Philistines came,
and lived there.)
8 Forsooth in the tother day made, Philistines came,
that they should despoil the slain men, and they found
Saul, and his three sons, lying in the hill of Gilboa; (And
the next day, the Philistines came to rob the dead men,
and they found Saul, and his three sons, lying there dead
on Mount Gilboa;)
9 and they cutted away the head of Saul, and
despoiled him of his armours; and sent into the land of
Philistines by compass, that it should be told in the
temple of idols, and in the peoples. (and they cut off
Saul's head, and stripped him of his armour/and robbed
him of his arms, *or of his weapons*; and then they sent
messengers into all the land of the Philistines, so that it
could be told to their idols, and to their people alike.)
10 And they putted his armours in the temple of
Ashtaroth; but they hanged his body in the wall of
Bethshan. (And they put his armour in the temple of
Ashtoreth/And they put his arms, *or his weapons*, in the
temple of Astarte, but they hung up his body on the wall
of Bethshan.)
11 And when the dwellers of Jabesh of Gilead had
heard this, and whatever things the Philistines had done
to Saul, (And when the inhabitants of Jabesh of Gilead
had heard this, and all the things that the Philistines had
done to Saul,)
12 and all the strongest men rose (up), and went forth
all that night, and they took (down) the dead body of
Saul, and the dead bodies of his sons, from the wall of
Bethshan; and the men of Jabesh of Gilead came, and
burnt those *dead bodies* with fire.
13 And they took the bones of them, and buried them
in the wood of Jabesh, and fasted by seven days. (And
they took their bones, and buried them under the
tamarisk tree in Jabesh, and then fasted for seven days.) ✡

2ND SAMUEL

CHAPTER 1

1 And it was done, after that Saul was dead, that
David turned again from the slaying of Amalek, and he
dwelled two days in Ziklag. (And it was done, after Saul
died, that David returned from the slaughter of the
Amalekites, and he stayed in Ziklag for two days.)
2 And in the third day a man appeared, coming from
the tents of Saul with a cloth rent, and his head sprinkled
with dust; and as he came to David, he felled upon his
face, and worshipped *him.* (And on the third day a man
appeared, coming from Saul's camp with a torn cloak,
and his head sprinkled with dirt, *or with earth*; and when
he came to David, he fell on his face, and honoured *him.*)
3 And David said to him, From whence comest thou?
And he said to David, I fled from the tents of Israel.
4 And David said to him, What is the word that is
done there; show thou to me (What happened there; tell
thou to me). And he said, The people of Israel hath fled
from the battle, and many of the people felled (by the
sword), and be dead; but also Saul, and Jonathan, his
son, have perished.
5 And David said to the young man, that told to him,
Whereof knowest thou, that Saul is dead, and Jonathan,
his son? (And David said to the young man, who told him
this, How knowest thou that Saul, and his son Jonathan,
be dead?)
6 And the young man said, that told to him, By hap I
came into the hill of Gilboa, and Saul leaned upon his
spear; and chariots and horsemen nighed to him; (And
the young man, who told him this, said, By happenstance
I was on Mount Gilboa, and Saul was leaning on his spear;
and the chariots and the horsemen came towards him;)
7 and he turned behind his back, and saw me, and
called. To whom when I had answered, I am present;
(and he looked behind his back, and saw me, and called
to me. To whom when I had answered, I am here;)
8 he said to me, Who art thou? And I said to him, I
am a man of Amalek.
9 And he spake to me, (and said,) Stand thou upon
me, and slay me (and kill me); for anguishes hold me,
and yet all my life is in me.
10 And (so) I stood upon him, and I slew him; for I
knew that he might not live after the falling (for I knew
that he could not live as soon as he fell); and I took the
diadem, that was on his head, and the band from his arm,
and I have brought them hither to thee, my lord.
11 Forsooth David took and rent his clothes, and
(likewise) [all] the men that were with him;
12 and they wailed, and wept, and fasted till to
eventide, on Saul, and Jonathan, his son, and on the
people of the Lord, and on the house of Israel, for they
had felled by sword. (and they wailed, and wept, and
fasted until evening, for Saul, and for Jonathan, his son,
and for the people of the Lord, and for the house of
Israel, because they had fallen by the sword.)
13 And David said to the young man, that told to him,
Of whence art thou? And he answered, I am the son of a
man comeling, of a man of Amalek. (And David said to
the young man, who told him the news, Where art thou
from? And he answered, I am the son of a newcomer, *or*
of a foreigner, I am an Amalekite.)
14 And David said to him, Why dreadest thou not to
send thine hand, that thou shouldest slay the christ of the
Lord? (And David said to him, Why fearest thou not, to
put forth thy hand to kill the Lord's anointed?)
15 And David called one of his young men, and said,
Go thou, and fall on him. And he smote that young man,
and he was dead (And he struck that young man, and he
died).
16 And David said to him, Thy blood be on thine head;
for thy mouth spake against thee, and said, I killed the
christ of the Lord/I killed the anointed of the Lord.
17 Forsooth David bewailed such a wailing on Saul,
and on Jonathan, his son; (And David bewailed this
wailing, *or this lament*, for Saul, and for his son Jonathan;)
18 and he commanded, that they should teach the sons
of Judah the bow, *that is, the craft of shooting*, as it is
written in the Book of Just Men. (and he commanded,
that they should teach the sons of Judah the use of the
bow, *that is, the craft of shooting arrows*, as it is written
in the Book of Jasher.)
19 And (so) David said, Israel, behold thou, for these
that be dead, be wounded on thine high places; the
noble men of Israel be slain upon thine hills. How have
fallen [the] strong men? (How the strong have fallen!)
20 do not ye tell *this* in Gath, neither tell ye (it) in the
way-lots of Askelon; lest peradventure the daughters of
Philistines be glad, lest the daughters of uncircumcised
men joy.
21 Hills of Gilboa, neither dew, neither rain come
upon you, neither be they the fields of first fruits (nor be
ye the fields of the first fruits); for the shield of (the) strong
men was cast away there, the shield of Saul, as if he had
not been anointed with oil.
22 Of the blood of slain men, of the fatness of strong
men, the arrow of Jonathan went never aback, and the
sword of Saul turned not again void.
23 Saul and Jonathan, amiable, and fair in their life,
were not parted also in their death; *they were* swifter
than eagles, stronger than lions. (Saul and Jonathan were
so loved, and delightful, in their lives, and were not
separated in their deaths; *they were* swifter than eagles,

stronger than lions.)
24 Daughters of Israel, weep ye on Saul, that clothed
you with fine red, and in (other) delights, that gave
golden ornaments to your attire. (Daughters of Israel,
weep ye for Saul, who clothed you in fine red, and in
other delights, who gave gold ornaments for your attire.)
25 How have strong men fallen down in battle?
Jonathan was slain in the high places. (How the strong
have fallen in battle! Jonathan was killed on the hills.)
26 I make sorrow upon thee, my brother Jonathan, full
fair and amiable more than the love of women; as a
mother loveth her only son, so I loved thee. (I have
sorrow for thee, my brother Jonathan, so delightful, and
whose love for me was more than even the love of
women; like a mother loveth her only son, so I loved
thee.)
27 How therefore felled down strong men, and armours
of battle perished? (How the strong have fallen, and the
arms, *or the weapons*, of battle have perished!)

CHAPTER 2

1 Therefore after these things David counselled with
the Lord, and said, Whether I shall go up into one of the
cities of Judah? (And after these things David counselled
with the Lord, and said, Shall I go up into one of the
cities of Judah?) And the Lord said to him, Go thou up.
And David said to the Lord, Whither shall I go up? And
the Lord answered to him, Into Hebron.
2 Therefore David went up, and his two wives,
Ahinoam of Jezreel, and Abigail, the wife of Nabal of
Carmel.
3 But also David led the men that were with him,
each man with his house(hold) (each man with his
family); and they dwelled in the towns of Hebron.
4 And the men of Judah came, and anointed there
David, that he should reign upon the house of Judah
(And the men of Judah came, and there they anointed
David to reign upon the house of Judah). And it was told
to David, that [the] men of Jabesh of Gilead had buried
Saul.
5 Therefore David sent messengers to the men of
Jabesh of Gilead, and said to them, Blessed be ye of the
Lord, that did this mercy with your lord Saul, and buried
him. (And so David sent messengers to the men of Jabesh
of Gilead, and said to them, May the Lord bless you, who
have shown this kindness to your lord Saul, and have
buried him.)
6 And now soothly the Lord shall yield to you mercy
and truth, but also I shall yield thanking, for ye did this
word. (And now surely the Lord shall show truth and
kindness to you, and I shall also give you thanks, for ye
did this thing.)
7 Your hands be comforted, and be ye the sons of
strength; for though your lord Saul is dead, nevertheless
the house of Judah hath anointed me king to him. (May
your hands be strengthened, and may ye be the sons of
strength; for though your lord Saul is dead, nevertheless
the house of Judah hath anointed me king upon them.)
8 Forsooth Abner, the son of Ner, prince of the host of
Saul, took Ishbosheth, the son of Saul, and led him about
by the castles, (Then Abner, the son of Ner, the leader of
Saul's army, took Ishbosheth, the son of Saul, and
brought him over to Mahanaim,)
9 and made him king on Gilead, and on Ashurites,
and on Jezreel, and on Ephraim, and on Benjamin, and
on all Israel.
10 Ishbosheth, the son of Saul, was of forty years, when
he began to reign upon Israel; and he reigned two years.
Soothly the house alone of Judah followed David.
(Ishbosheth, the son of Saul, was forty years old when he
began to reign upon Israel; and he reigned for two years.
Only the house of Judah followed David.)
11 And the number of days, by which David dwelled
reigning in Hebron on the house of Judah, was of seven
years and six months.
12 And Abner, the son of Ner, went out, and the
servants of Ishbosheth, the son of Saul, from the castles
in[to] Gibeon. (And Abner, the son of Ner, and the men
of Ishbosheth, the son of Saul, went out from Mahanaim
to Gibeon.)
13 And Joab, the son of Zeruiah, and the servants of
David, went out, and they came to them beside the
cistern of Gibeon. And when they had come together
into one place even against either *other*, these sat on one
part of the cistern, and they on the tother. (And Joab, the
son of Zeruiah, and David's men, went out, and they
came to them beside the pool of Gibeon. And when they
had come together at a place opposite each *other*, those
men sat on one side of the pool, and they sat on the other
side.)
14 And Abner said to Joab, The children rise, and play
before us[1] (And Abner said to Joab, Let the young men
rise up, and slay, *or kill*, each other). And Joab
answered, Rise they up.
15 Then they rose up, and passed forth twelve in
number of Benjamin, of the part of Ishbosheth, the son of
Saul; and twelve of the servants of David. (Then they rose
up, and came forth twelve in number for Benjamin, on
the part of Ishbosheth, Saul's son; and twelve of David's
men.)
16 And each man, when he had taken his fellow by the
head, fixed his sword into the side of his adversary; and
they felled down together. And (so) the name of that
place was called The Field of Men Slain Together, (which
is) in Gibeon.

---

[1] *That is, 'show their strength and nobility'; and here 'play' is set for 'slay' either 'fight'.*

17 And full hard battle rose in that day; and Abner and
the sons of Israel were driven (away) of the servants of
David. (And a hard fought battle arose that day; and Abner
and the men of Israel were driven back by David's men.)
18 Forsooth (the) three sons of Zeruiah were there,
Joab, and Abishai, and Asahel; and Asahel was a full swift
runner, as one of the caprets that dwell in woods (like
one of the gazelles that live in the forest).
19 And Asahel pursued Abner, and he bowed neither
to the right side, nor to the left side, ceasing to pursue
Abner.
20 Therefore Abner beheld behind his back, and said,
Whether thou art Asahel? Which answered, I am.
21 And Abner said to him, Go thou to the right side,
either to the left side; and take (down) one of the young
men, and take to thee his spoils. But Asahel would not
cease, that not he pursued him (But Asahel would not
cease from pursuing Abner).
22 And again Abner spake to Asahel, (and said,) Go
thou away; do not thou pursue me, lest I be compelled to
pierce thee into the earth, and I shall not be able to raise
then my face to Joab, thy brother. (And again Abner said
to Asahel, Go thou away; do not thou pursue me, lest I
be compelled to pierce thee through to the ground, and
then I shall not be able to face thy brother Joab.)
23 And Asahel despised to hear, and would not bow
away. Therefore Abner smote him with the spear turned
away, *that is, turned against him,* in the share-bone, *that
is, behind the maw, in the fifth rib, under which be the
members of life,* and pierced [him] through, and he was
dead in the same place; and all men that passed by the
place, in which *place* Asahel felled down, and was dead,
stood still. (And Asahel despised to hear him, and would
not turn away. And so Abner struck him with the spear
turned against him, in the *belly, at the fifth rib, under
which be the members of life,* and pierced him through,
and he died there; and all those who came to the place,
where Asahel fell down, and died, stopped and stood
there, *and gawked.*)
24 And while Joab and Abishai pursued Abner fleeing,
the sun went down; and they came to the little hill of a
water conduit, that is even against the valley, and the
way of desert in Gibeon. (And while Joab and Abishai
pursued after Abner, the sun went down; and they came
to the hill of Ammah, that is opposite Giah, on the way to
the wilderness of Gibeon.)
25 And the sons of Benjamin were gathered to Abner,
and they were gathered together into one company, and
they stood in the height of an heap of earth (and they
stood on the top of a hill).
26 And Abner cried to Joab, and said, Whether thy
sword shall be fierce unto slaying? Whether thou
knowest not, that despair is perilous? How long sayest
thou not to the people, that it cease to pursue his
brethren? (How long before thou sayest to thy people,
that they should cease pursuing their kinsmen?)
27 And Joab said, The Lord liveth, for if thou haddest
spoken *thus* early, the people pursuing his brother had
gone away. (And Joab said, As the Lord liveth, if thou
haddest not spoken, the people would have continued
pursuing their kinsmen until morning.)
28 And Joab sounded with a clarion, and all the host
stood still; and they pursued no further Israel, neither
began battle. (And then Joab sounded with a trumpet,
and all the army stood in place; and they no longer
pursued the men of Israel, and the fighting ceased.)
29 And Abner and his men went *(from) thence* by the
field places of Moab in all that night, and they passed
[over] Jordan; and when all Bithron was compassed, they
came to the castles. (And Abner and his men went *from
there* through the fields of Moab all that night, and then
they crossed over the Jordan River; and when all Bithron
had been traversed, they came to Mahanaim.)
30 And when Abner was left, Joab turned again, and
gathered together all his people; and ten men and nine,
besides Asahel, failed of the servants of David. (And
when Joab left off pursuing Abner, he returned, and
gathered together all his people; and *he found that*
nineteen of David's men, besides Asahel, were missing.)
31 Forsooth the servants of David smited of Benjamin,
and of the men that were with Abner, three hundred men
and sixty, which also were dead. (But David's men struck
and killed three hundred and sixty of the Benjaminites,
and of Abner's men.)
32 And they took Asahel, and buried him in the
sepulchre of his father in Bethlehem. And Joab, and the
men that were with him, went in all that night, and in
that morrowtide they came into Hebron (and in the
morning they came to Hebron).

CHAPTER 3

1 Therefore a long strife was made betwixt the house
of David and the house of Saul; and David profited and
ever[more] was stronger than himself, *in comparison of
time passed, for his power increased ever,* but the house
of Saul decreased each day. (And so for a long time there
was strife between the house of David and the house of
Saul; and David grew in strength, *that is, as more time
that passed, the more his power increased,* but the house
of Saul grew ever weaker.)
2 And sons were born to David in Hebron; and his
first begotten son was Amnon, of Ahinoam of Jezreel;
3 and after him was Chileab, of Abigail, the wife of
Nabal of Carmel; and the third was Absalom, the son of
Maacah, the daughter of Talmai, king of Geshur;
4 and the fourth was Adonijah, the son of Haggith;
and the fifth was Shephatiah, the son of Abital;
5 and the sixth was Ithream, of Eglah, the wife of

David. These (sons) were born to David in Hebron.
6 Therefore when battle was betwixt the house of Saul
and the house of David, Abner, the son of Ner, governed
the house of Saul.
7 And to Saul was a concubine, *that is, a secondary
wife*, Rizpah by name, the daughter of Aiah; and Abner
entered [in] to her. And Ishbosheth said to Abner, Why
hast thou entered [in] to the concubine of my father?
8 And Abner was wroth greatly for the words of
Ishbosheth, and said, Whether I am the head of a dog
against Judah today, and I have done mercy on the house
of Saul, thy father, and on his brethren, and neighbours,
and I betook not thee into the hands of David, and (yet)
thou hast sought in me that, that thou shouldest reprove
for a woman today? (And Abner was greatly angered by
Ishbosheth's words, and said, Am I the head of a dog,
that is, a traitor, and do I serve Judah today? have I not
shown mercy, *or loyalty*, to the house of Saul, thy father,
and to his brothers, and to his neighbours? I did not
deliver thee into the hands of David, and yet today thou
hast sought that for which thou wouldest reprove me for,
yea, for but a woman!)
9 God do these things to Abner, and add these things
to him, no but as the Lord swore to David, so I do with
him (so I shall do for him),
10 that the realm be translated from the house of Saul
(that the kingdom be transferred from the house of Saul),
and (that) the throne of David be raised on Israel and on
Judah, from Dan till to Beersheba.
11 And Ishbosheth might not answer anything to
Abner, for he dreaded Abner (for he feared Abner).
12 Therefore Abner sent messengers to David, and they
said for him, Whose is the land? and that the messengers
should (also) speak *thus*, Make thou friendships with me,
and mine hand shall be with thee, and I shall bring (over)
all Israel to thee.
13 And David said, Best, I shall make friendships with
thee; but I ask of thee one thing, and say, Thou shalt not
see my face, before that thou bring Michal, the daughter
of Saul, and so thou shalt come, and shalt see me. (And
David answered, Very well, I shall be friends with thee;
but I require one thing from thee, and that is, that thou
shalt not see my face, until thou bring Saul's daughter
Michal to me; only then shalt thou come, and see me.)
14 Therefore David sent messengers to Ishbosheth (And
David also sent messengers to Ishbosheth), the son of
Saul, and said, Yield thou my wife Michal, whom I
espoused to me for an hundred prepuces of Philistines.
15 Therefore Ishbosheth sent, and took her from her
husband, Phaltiel, the son of Laish; (And so Ishbosheth
sent some men, and took her away from her husband,
Phaltiel, the son of Laish;)
16 and her husband followed her, and wept till to
Bahurim. And Abner said to him, Go thou, and turn
again; and he turned again. (and her husband followed
her, and wept all the way to Bahurim. But Abner said to
him, Go thou back home! and so he went home.)
17 Also Abner brought in a word to the elder men of
Israel, and said, Both yesterday and the third day ago ye
sought David, that he should reign upon you.
18 Now therefore do ye; for the Lord spake to David,
and said, In the hand of my servant David I shall save my
people Israel from the hand of Philistines, and of all his
enemies. (And so now do ye it; for the Lord spoke to
David, and said, By my servant David I shall save my
people Israel from the hands of the Philistines, and from
all their enemies.)
19 And also Abner spake to Benjamin; and he went,
that he should speak to David, in Hebron, (of) all things
that pleased Israel and all Benjamin. (And Abner also
spoke to the Benjaminites; and then he went to speak to
David in Hebron, about all that the Israelites and the
Benjaminites had agreed to do.)
20 And he came to David, in Hebron, with twenty
men. And David made a feast to Abner, and to the men
that came with him (And David made a feast for Abner,
and the men who came with him).
21 And Abner said to David, I shall rise up, that I gather
all Israel to thee, my lord the king, and that I make (a)
bond of peace with thee, and that thou reign on all, as
thy soul desireth. Therefore when David had led forth
Abner, and he had gone in peace, (And Abner said to
David, I shall rise up, and gather all Israel to thee, my
lord the king, and they shall make a covenant with thee,
and thou shalt reign upon all of them, as thy soul
desireth. And after David had let Abner go away, with a
guarantee of surety, *or of safety*,)
22 anon the servants of David and Joab came with a
full great prey, when the thieves were slain; and Abner
was not then with David, in Hebron, for David had let
him go, and he went forth in peace. (shortly thereafter
David's men and Joab came back from a raid, with a
great deal of prey; and Abner was then not with David, in
Hebron, for David had let him go away, with a guarantee
of safety.)
23 And Joab, and the hosts that were with him, came
afterward; therefore it was told to Joab of tellers, (saying,)
Abner, the son of Ner, came to the king, and the king let
go him, and he went forth in peace. (And so Joab, and
the men who were with him, came shortly thereafter; and
people said to Joab, Abner, the son of Ner, came to the
king, and the king let him go away, with a guarantee of
safety.)
24 And Joab entered to the king, and said, What hast
thou done? Lo! Abner came to thee; why lettest go thou
him (why hast thou let him go), and he went, and
departed from thee?
25 Knowest thou not (that) Abner, the son of Ner, for

hereto he came to thee, that he should deceive thee, and
that he should know thy going out and thine entering,
and should know all things which thou doest? (Thou must
know that Abner, the son of Ner, came to thee so that he
could deceive thee, and learn thy going out and thy
coming in, and so know all the things that thou doest.)
26 Therefore Joab went out from David, and sent
messengers after Abner; and led him again from the
cistern of Sirah (and they brought him back from the Well
of Sirah), while David knew not.
27 And when Abner had come again into Hebron, Joab
led him asides half to the middle of the gate, (as if) that
he should speak to him in guile; and he smote Abner
there in the share-bone, and he was dead, into vengeance
of the blood of his brother Asahel (and Joab struck, *or
stabbed*, Abner in the belly, and he died there, in
revenge for killing Joab's brother Asahel).
28 That when David had heard this thing done, he said,
I am clean, and my realm, with God into without end
from the blood of Abner, the son of Ner; (And when
David had heard that this thing was done, he said, I and
my kingdom, be clean with God forevermore, of the
blood, *or of the murder*, of Abner, the son of Ner;)
29 and come it on the head of Joab, and upon all the
house of his father; and fail there not from the house of
Joab a man suffering flowing of seed, and a leprous man,
(and a man) holding a spindle, and a man falling by
sword, and (a man) having need to bread. (yea, let it
come upon Joab's head, and upon all his father's family;
and let there never fail to be in the house of Joab a man
suffering the flowing out of his seed, or a leprous man, or
a man holding a spindle, or a man falling by the sword,
or a man having need of bread.)
30 Therefore Joab, and Abishai, his brother, killed
Abner, for he had slain Asahel, their brother (for he had
killed their brother Asahel), in Gibeon, in battle.
31 And David said to Joab, and to all the people that
was with him, Rend ye your clothes, and be ye gird with
sackcloths, and bewail ye before the hearses, *either dirge*,
of Abner. Forsooth king David followed the bier. (And
David said to Joab, and to all the people who were with
him, Tear ye your clothes, and be ye gird with sackcloths,
and bewail ye the dirge for Abner. And King David
himself followed the bier.)
32 And when they had buried Abner in Hebron, king
David raised (up) his voice, and wept on the burial of
Abner; and certainly all the people wept.
33 And the king bewailed, and bemourned Abner, and
said, Abner, thou diedest not as dreadful men, *either
cowards*, be wont to die (Abner, thou hast not died like
fearful men, *or like cowards*, be wont to die).
34 Thine hands were not bound, and thy feet were not
grieved with stocks, but thou hast fallen down, as men be
wont to fall before the sons of wickedness. And all the
people doubled together, and wept on him. (Thy hands
were not bound, and thy feet were not put in the stocks,
but thou hast fallen, like men be wont to fall before the
sons of wickedness. And all the people wept again for
him.)
35 And when all the multitude came to take meat with
David, while the day was yet clear, David swore, and
said, God do to me these things, and add these things
too, if I shall taste bread, either any other thing, before
the going down of the sun.
36 And all the people heard *this*; and all things which
the king did in the sight of all the people pleased them;
37 and all the common people and all Israel knew in
that day, that it was not done of the king (that it was not
done by the king), that Abner, the son of Ner, was slain.
38 Also the king said to his servants, Whether ye know
not, that the prince and the greatest (man) hath fallen
down today in Israel?
39 And I am yet tender, and anointed king; and these
sons of Zeruiah be (too) hard to me; the Lord yield to him
that doeth evil after his (own) malice. (And I am yet
weak, though anointed the king; and these sons of
Zeruiah be too hard for me; may the Lord yield to him
who doeth evil after his own malice.)

CHAPTER 4

1 And Ishbosheth, the son of Saul, heard that Abner
had fallen down in Hebron; and his hands were
discomforted, and all Israel was troubled. (And
Ishbosheth, the son of Saul, heard that Abner had been
killed in Hebron; and his hands were enfeebled, *that is,
he was afraid*, and all Israel was troubled.)
2 And two men, princes of (raiding) companies, were
to the son of Saul; name to the one was Baanah, and
name to the tother was Rechab, the sons of Rimmon (the)
Beerothite, of the sons of Benjamin; for also Beeroth is
areckoned in Benjamin. (And two men, leaders of raiding
parties, were officers for Saul's son; one was named
Baanah, and the other was named Rechab; they were the
sons of Rimmon the Beerothite, of the sons of Benjamin,
for Beeroth is reckoned as part of Benjamin.)
3 And men of Beeroth fled into Gittaim; and they
were comelings there till to that time. (And the
Beerothites had fled to Gittaim; and they had lived there
until that time.)
4 And a son feeble in *his* feet was to Jonathan, the son
of Saul; and he was five years eld, when the messenger
came from Saul and Jonathan, from Jezreel, *telling that
they were dead* (and he was five years old, when a
message came from Jezreel about Saul and Jonathan,
saying that they were dead). Therefore his nurse took
him, and fled; and when she hasted to flee, she felled
down, and *the child* was made lame; and the name of the
child was Mephibosheth.

5 Therefore Rechab and Baanah, the sons of Rimmon
of Beeroth, came, and entered in the hot (of the) day into
the house of Ishbosheth, that slept upon his bed at
midday; and the woman that kept the doors of the house,
(who had been) purging wheat, (now also) slept fast. (And
so Rechab and Baanah, the sons of Rimmon of Beeroth,
came, and in the heat of the day entered into
Ishbosheth's house, while he slept on his bed at midday;
and the woman who kept the doors of the house, had
been purging wheat, but now she was also asleep.)
6 And they came till to the midst of the house, and
took wheat; and Rechab, and Baanah, his brother, smote
Ishbosheth in the share-bone, and fled. (And they came
into the midst of the house, carrying wheat; and Rechab,
and his brother Baanah, struck, *or stabbed,* Ishbosheth in
the belly, and then fled.)
7 Soothly when they had entered into the house, he
slept on his bed in a (bed-)closet; and they smited and
killed him; and when they had taken [off] his head, they
went by the way of desert in all that night. (Yea, when
they entered into the house, he slept on his bed in the
bed-chamber; and they struck, *or stabbed,* him and killed
him; and when they had cut off his head, they left, and
went by the way of the wilderness all that night.)
8 And they brought the head of Ishbosheth to David,
in Hebron, and they said to the king, Lo! the head of
Ishbosheth, the son of Saul, thine enemy, that sought thy
life; and the Lord hath given today to our lord the king
vengeance of Saul, and of his seed (yea, today the Lord
hath avenged our lord the king upon Saul, and upon his
descendants, *or his family*).
9 And David answered to Rechab, and Baanah, his
brother, the sons of Rimmon of Beeroth, and said to
them, The Lord liveth, that hath delivered my life from all
anguish (As the Lord liveth, who hath delivered my life
from all anguish);
10 for I held him that told to me, and said, Saul is dead,
which man guessed himself to tell prosperities, and I
killed him in Ziklag, to whom (he thought) it behooved
me (to) give meed for (his) message; (for I took hold of
him who told me, and said, Saul is dead, which man
thought that he told good news, and I killed him in
Ziklag, yea, he who thought it behooved me to give him
a reward for his message;)
11 how much more now, when wicked men have slain
a guiltless man in his house upon his bed, shall I not seek
his blood of your hand, and shall not I do away you from
the earth? (how much more now, when you wicked men
have killed an innocent man in his own house on his
own bed, will I not avenge his blood upon you, and shall
I not do you away from the face of the earth?)
12 Therefore David commanded to his servants, and
they killed them; and they cut off their hands and their
feet, and hanged them over the cistern in Hebron (and
hung them up near the pool in Hebron). Forsooth they
took the head of Ishbosheth, and they buried it in the
sepulchre of Abner, in Hebron.

CHAPTER 5

1 And all the lineages of Israel came to David, in
Hebron, and said, Lo! we be thy bone and thy flesh. (And
all the tribes of Israel came to David, in Hebron, and
said, Lo! we be thy flesh and blood.)
2 But also yesterday and the third day ago, when Saul
was king upon us, thou leddest out, and leddest again
Israel; forsooth the Lord said to thee, Thou shalt feed my
people Israel, and thou shalt be duke upon Israel. (And
yesterday and the third day ago, when Saul was king
upon us, thou leddest out *the people* Israel, and leddest
them in again; and the Lord said to thee, Thou shalt feed
my people Israel, and thou shalt be the leader of Israel.)
3 Also and the elder men of Israel came to the king,
into Hebron; and king David smote with them (a) bond of
peace in Hebron, before the Lord; and they anointed
David into king upon Israel. (And the elders of Israel
came to the king in Hebron; and King David struck a
covenant with them in Hebron, before the Lord; and they
anointed David king upon Israel.)
4 David was a son of thirty years, when he began to
reign, and he reigned forty years(.)
5 in Hebron; he reigned upon Judah seven years and
six months; and in Jerusalem he reigned thirty and three
years upon all Israel and Judah. (In Hebron, he reigned
seven years and six months upon Judah; and in Jerusalem,
he reigned thirty-three years upon all Israel and Judah.)
6 And the king went, and all [the] men that were with
him, into Jerusalem, to Jebusites, the dweller(s) of the
land. And it was said of them to David, Thou shalt not
enter hither, no but thou do away blind men and lame,
saying, David shall not enter hither. (And the king, and
all the men who were with him, went to Jerusalem, unto
the Jebusites, the inhabitants of the land. And they said
to David, Thou shalt not come in here until thou do away
all the blind and the crippled, that is to say, Thou, David,
shalt never come in here.)
7 Forsooth David took the tower of Zion; this is the
city of David. (But David captured the stronghold, *or the
fortress,* of Zion; this is known as the City of David.)
8 For David had purposed in that day to have given
meed to him, that had smitten Jebusites, and that had
touched the gutters of the house roofs, and that had taken
away lame men and blind, hating the life of David.
Therefore it is said in common speech, A blind man and
a lame shall not enter into the temple. (For David had put
forth a reward that day, to anyone who struck down the
Jebusites, yea, up to the gutters of the housetops, and
who did away even the crippled and the blind, yea, any
and all who hated the life of David. And so it is said in

common speech, No one blind or crippled shall enter
into the Temple.)
9 And David dwelled in the tower, and called it the
city of David; and he builded by compass from Millo,
and within. (And David lived in the stronghold, and
called it the City of David; and he built all around from
Millo, inwards.)
10 And he entered profiting, and increasing; and the
Lord God of hosts was with him.
11 Also Hiram, king of Tyre, sent messengers to David,
and cedar trees, and craftsmen of wood, and craftsmen of
stones to (make) walls; and they builded the house of
David.
12 And David knew, that the Lord had confirmed him
king upon Israel, and that he had enhanced his realm
upon his people Israel (and that he had raised up his
kingdom for the sake of his people Israel).
13 Therefore David took yet (more) concubines, and
wives of (the inhabitants of) Jerusalem, after that he came
from Hebron; and also other sons and daughters were
born to David.
14 And these be the names of them that were born to
him in Jerusalem; Shammuah, and Shobab, and Nathan,
and Solomon,
15 and Ibhar, and Elishua, and Nepheg, and Japhia,
16 and Elishama, and Eliada, and Eliphalet.
17 Then the Philistines heard, that they had anointed
David king upon Israel, and all the *Philistines* went up to
seek David. And when David had heard this, he went
down into a stronghold.
18 And the Philistines came, and they were spread
abroad in the valley of Rephaim. (And the Philistines
came, and they were spread all over the Rephaim Valley.)
19 And David counselled with the Lord, and said,
Whether I shall go up to Philistines, and whether thou
shalt give them in mine hand? And the Lord said to
David, Go thou up, for I shall betake the Philistines, and I
shall give them in thine hand. (And David counselled
with the Lord, and said, Shall I go up to the Philistines?
and shalt thou give them into my hands? And the Lord
said to David, Go thou up, for I shall deliver the
Philistines into thy hands.)
20 Therefore David came into Baalperazim, and smote
them there (and he struck them there), and said, The Lord
hath parted mine enemies before me, as waters be
parted. Therefore the name of that place was called
Baalperazim, *that is, The Field, either Plain, of Parting*.
21 And they left there their sculptures, (*or their images*,)
which David burnt, and his men. (And they left their
idols there, which David and his men burned *to ashes*.)
22 And [the] Philistines added yet, that they should
ascend, and they were spread abroad in the valley of
Rephaim. (And the Philistines attacked again, and they
were spread all over the Rephaim Valley.)
23 And David counselled with the Lord, and said,
Whether I shall go up against the Philistines, and whether
thou shalt betake them into mine hands? (And David
counselled with the Lord, and said, Shall I go up against
the Philistines, and shalt thou deliver them into my
hands?) And the Lord answered, Thou shalt not go up
against them, but compass thou them behind their back,
and (then) thou shalt come to them on the contrary side
of the pear trees.
24 And when thou shalt hear the sound of (a) cry going
in the top(s) of (the) pear trees, then thou shalt begin (the)
battle; for then the Lord shall go out before thy face, that
he smite the tents of Philistines (for then the Lord shall go
out before thee, and strike down the host, *or the army*, of
the Philistines).
25 Therefore David did as the Lord commanded to him;
and he smote the Philistines from Geba till they came to
Gazer.

CHAPTER 6

1 Forsooth David gathered again all the chosen men
of Israel, thirty thousand. (Then David gathered together
all the chosen, *or all the best*, out of Israel, yea, thirty
thousand men.)
2 And David rose, and went, and all the people that
was with him of the men of Judah, to bring the ark of
God, on which the name of the Lord of hosts, sitting in
cherubim on that ark, was called. (And David rose up,
and then he, and all the people who were with him, went
to Baalath in Judah, to bring back from there the Ark of
God, which beareth the name of the Lord of hosts, who is
enthroned upon, *or above*, the cherubim.)
3 And they putted the ark of God on a new wain, and
they took it from the house of Abinadab, that was in
Gibeah (And they put the Ark of God on a new wagon,
and they took it from Abinadab's house, which was on
the hill). And Uzzah and Ahio, the sons of Abinadab,
drove the new wain.
4 And when they had taken it from the house of
Abinadab, that was in Gibeah, and kept the ark of God,
Ahio went before the ark. (And so they took it from
Abinadab's house, which was on the hill, who had kept
the Ark of God safe; and Ahio went before the Ark.)
5 And David and all Israel played before the Lord, in
all treen instruments of melody, and in harps, and citoles,
and tympans, and trumps, and cymbals. (And David and
all Israel played music before the Lord, on all the wooden
instruments, and on harps, and lutes, and drums, *or
tambourines*, and trumpets, and cymbals.)
6 Forsooth after that they came to the cornfloor of
Nachon, Uzzah held forth his hand to the ark of God,
and held it, for the oxen kicked, and bowed it. (But when
they came to the threshing floor of Nachon, Uzzah put
forth his hand to the Ark of God, and held it, for the oxen

stumbled, and shook it.)
7 And the Lord was wroth by indignation against
Uzzah, and smote him on the folly (and struck him down
for his foolishness *in touching the Ark*); and he was dead
there beside the ark of God.
8 And David was sorry, for the Lord had slain Uzzah;
and the name of that place was called The Smiting of
Uzzah till into this day. (And David was grieved that the
Lord had killed Uzzah; and the name of that place is
called Perezuzzah, *or the Punishment of Uzzah*, unto
this day.)
9 And David dreaded the Lord in that day, and said,
How shall the ark of the Lord enter to me? (And David
feared the Lord that day, and said, How can I bring the
Ark of the Lord back with me?)
10 And (so) he would not turn [aside] the ark of the
Lord (un)to himself into the city of David, but he turned it
[aside] into the house of Obededom of Gath.
11 And the ark of the Lord dwelled in the house of
Obededom of Gath three months; and the Lord blessed
Obededom, and all his house(hold). (And the Ark of the
Lord stayed at the house of Obededom the Gittite for
three months; and the Lord blessed Obededom, and all
his family.)
12 And it was told to king David, that the Lord had
blessed Obededom, and all his things, for the ark of God.
And David said, I shall go, and bring the ark with
blessing into mine house. Therefore David went, and
brought the ark of God from the house of Obededom
into the city of David with joy. (And it was told to King
David, that the Lord had blessed Obededom, and all that
he had/and all that was his, for keeping the Ark of God
safe. And David said, Now I shall go, and bring the Ark
of God with blessing to my house. And so David went,
and brought the Ark of God from the house of
Obededom to the City of David with great joy.)
13 And when they, that bare the ark of the Lord, had
gone six paces, they offered an ox and a ram. (And when
they, who carried the Ark of the Lord, had gone six
paces, he offered an ox and a ram.)
14 And David smote in organs fastened to his arm (And
David played on an instrument fastened to his arm); and
he danced with all *his* strengths before the Lord; and
David was clothed with (only) a linen surplice.
15 And David, and all the house of Israel, led forth the
ark of [the] testament of the Lord/the ark of [the]
witnessing of the Lord in hearty song, and in sound of
trump. (And David, and all the house of Israel, brought
forth the Ark of the Lord with hearty song, and the sound
of trumpets.)
16 And when the ark of the Lord had entered into the
city of David, Michal, the daughter of Saul, beheld by a
window, and she saw the king skipping and
dancing/hopping and dancing before the Lord; and she
despised him in her heart.
17 And they brought in the ark of the Lord, and setted it
in his place, in the midst of the tabernacle, which
tabernacle David had made therefore/had made ready
thereto; and David offered burnt sacrifices and peaceable
(sacrifices) before the Lord. (And they brought in the Ark
of the Lord, and set it in its place, in the midst of the
Tent, which David had prepared for it; and David offered
burnt sacrifices and peace offerings before the Lord.)
18 And when David had ended those, and had offered
burnt sacrifices and peaceable (sacrifices), he blessed the
people in the name of the Lord of hosts. (And when
David had finished offering the burnt sacrifices and the
peace offerings, he blessed the people in the name of the
Lord of hosts.)
19 And he gave to all the multitude of Israel, as well to
man as to woman, to each a cake of bread, and one part
roasted of bugle flesh, and flour of wheat fried with oil;
and all the people went forth, each into his house. (And
he gave to all the multitude of Israel, yea, to each man
and woman, a cake of bread, and a piece of roasted ox
flesh, and wheat flour fried with oil; and then all the
people went home.)
20 And David turned again to bless his house, and
Michal, the daughter of Saul, went out into the coming of
David, and said, How glorious was the king of Israel
today, uncovering himself before the handmaids of his
servants, and he was made naked, as if one of the knaves
had been made naked? (And David returned to bless his
own house, and Michal, Saul's daughter, went out to
meet David, and said, How glorious was the king of
Israel today, uncovering himself before the slave-girls of
his servants, yea, he was made naked, just like one of the
knaves would be made naked!)
21 And David said to Michal, The Lord liveth, for I shall
play, (*or I shall dance*,) before the Lord, that chose me
rather than thy father, and rather than all the house of
him, and commanded to me, that I should be duke on
the people of the Lord of Israel; and I shall play, (And
David said to Michal, As the Lord liveth, I shall dance
before the Lord, who chose me rather than thy father, and
all of his family, and who commanded to me that I
should be the leader of the people of the Lord of Israel;
and so I shall dance,)
22 and I shall be made more vile than I am *yet* made,
and I shall be meek in mine eyes, and I shall appear more
glorious with those handmaidens, of which thou hast
spoken. (and I shall be made even more vile than I am
yet made, and I shall be abased in thine eyes, but I shall
appear more glorious to those slave-girls of whom thou
hast spoken.)
23 Therefore a son was not born to Michal, the
daughter of Saul, till into the day of her death. (And so no
child was ever born to Saul's daughter Michal, unto the

day of her death.)

CHAPTER 7

1 Forsooth it was done, when king David had sat in
his house, and the Lord had given rest to him on each
side from all his enemies,
2 he said to Nathan the prophet, Seest thou not, that I
dwell in an house of cedar (that I live in a cedar house),
and the ark of God is put in the midst of skins?
3 And Nathan said to the king, Go thou, and do all
thing that is in thine heart, for the Lord is with thee.
4 And it was done in that night, and lo! the word of
the Lord, was made to Nathan, [saying,]
5 Go thou, and speak to my servant David, (and say,)
The Lord saith these things, Whether thou shalt build to
me an house to dwell in? (Shalt thou build a house for
me to live in?)
6 Soothly I have not dwelled in an house from the day
in which I led the sons of Israel out of the land of Egypt
till into this day; but I have gone in a tabernacle and in a
tent,
7 by all places, to which I passed with all the sons of
Israel? Whether I speaking spake to (any)one of the
lineages of Israel, to whom I commanded, that he should
feed my people Israel, and said, Why buildedest thou not
an house of cedar to me? (to all the places, to which I
went with all the people of Israel. Did I speak to anyone
of the tribes of Israel, to whom I commanded, that they
should feed my people Israel, and did I ever ask them,
Why hast thou not built a cedar house for me?)
8 And now thou shalt say these things to my servant
David, The Lord of hosts saith these things, I took thee
from [the] pastures following flocks, that thou shouldest
be duke on my people Israel (so that thou couldest be the
leader of my people Israel),
9 and I was with thee in all things, wherever thou hast
gone, and I have killed all thine enemies from thy face,
and I have made to thee a great name, by the name of
great men that be in earth; (and I was with thee in all
things, wherever thou hast gone, and I have killed all thy
enemies before thee, and I have made a great name for
thee, like the names of the great men who be on the
earth;)
10 and I shall set a place to my people Israel, and I
shall plant him, and I shall dwell with him, and he shall
no more be troubled, and the sons of wickedness shall
not add to, that they torment him as before, (and I shall
set a place for my people Israel, and I shall plant them,
and I shall live with them, and they shall no more be
troubled, and the sons of wickedness shall not torment
them anymore, like they did in the past,)
11 (like they did) from the day in which I ordained
judges upon my people Israel; and I shall give rest to thee
from all thine enemies. And the Lord before-saith to
thee, that he shall make an house to thee (And the Lord
saith in advance to thee, that he shall make a house for
thee);
12 and when thy days be fulfilled, and thou hast slept
with thy fathers, (*that is, when thou hast died,*) I shall
raise up thy seed after thee, which shall go out of thy
womb, and I shall make steadfast his realm (and I shall
establish his kingdom).
13 (And) He shall build an house to my name, and I shall
make stable the throne of his realm till into without end;
14 I shall be to him into a father, and he shall be to me
into a son; and if he shall do anything wickedly, I shall
chastise him in the rod of men, and in the wounds of the
sons of men. (I shall be his father, and he shall be my son;
and if he doeth anything wicked, I shall chastise him with
the rod of men, and with wounds from the sons of men.)
15 Forsooth I shall not do away my mercy from him, as
I did it away from Saul, whom I removed from my face.
(But I shall not take away my love from him, like I took it
away from Saul, whom I removed from my presence.)
16 And thine house *shall be* faithful, and thy realm
shall be till into without end before my face, and thy
throne shall be steadfast continually (and thy throne shall
be established forever).
17 By all these words, and by all this revelation, so
Nathan spake to David.
18 Forsooth David the king entered *into the tabernacle,*
and he sat before the Lord, and said, Who am I, Lord
God, and what is mine house, that thou hast brought me
hitherto?
19 But also this is seen (as but a) little (thing) in thy
sight, my Lord God; no but (that) thou shouldest speak
also of the house of thy servant into long time. For this is
the law of Adam, Lord God (For this is the law of men, *or*
people's lot, O Lord God);
20 what therefore may David add yet, that he speak to
thee? (and so what can I say to thee?) For thou, Lord God,
knowest thy servant;
21 thou hast done all these great things, for thy word,
and by thine heart (for thy word's sake, and according to
thy heart), so that thou madest *those* known to thy servant.
22 Therefore, Lord God, thou art made great, for none
is like thee, nor there is no God except thee, in all things
which we have heard with our ears. (And so, Lord God,
thou art truly great, and from everything that we have
heard with our ears, no one is like thee, nor is there any
God except thee.)
23 Soothly what folk in (the) earth is as the people of
Israel, for which the Lord God went, that he should
again-buy it to him into a people, and should set to
himself a name, and should do to it great things, and
horrible, on [the] earth, *in casting out* thereof the folks,
and gods thereof, from the face of thy people, which thou
again-boughtest to thee from Egypt? (Yea, what nation on

earth is like the people of Israel, for whom the Lord God
went, and redeemed, *or rescued*, them in order to be a
people for himself, and to make a name for himself, and
to do for them great and wonderful things on the earth, *in
throwing out* from here the nations, and their gods, from
before thy people, whom thou hast redeemed, *or
rescued*, for thyself from Egypt?)
24 And thou hast confirmed to thee thy people Israel
into a people everlasting, and thou, Lord, art made into
God to them. (And thou hast confirmed thy people Israel
to be thy own people forevermore, and O Lord, thou hast
become their God.)
25 Now therefore, Lord God, raise up (into) without
end the word that thou hast spoken upon thy servant, and
upon his house, and do as thou hast spoken;
26 and thy name be magnified/and thy name be made
great till into without end, and be it said, The Lord of
hosts is God upon Israel; and the house of thy servant
David shall be stablished before the Lord;
27 for thou, Lord of hosts, God of Israel, hast made
revelation to the ear of thy servant, and saidest, I shall
build an house to thee; therefore thy servant hath found
by his heart, that he should pray thee by this prayer. (for
thou, O Lord of hosts, the God of Israel, hast made a
revelation in the ear of thy servant, and saidest, I shall
build a house for thee; and so thy servant hath found in
his heart, that he should pray to thee by this prayer.)
28 Now therefore, Lord God, thou art very God, and
thy words shall (always) be true; for thou hast spoken
these good things to thy servant;
29 therefore begin thou, and bless the house of thy
servant, that it be into without end before thee; for thou,
Lord God, hast spoken these things, and through thy
blessing the house of thy servant shall be blessed [into]
without end.

CHAPTER 8

1 And it was done after these things, David smote the
Philistines, and made low them; and David took away
the bridle of tribute from the hand of Philistines. (And it
was done after these things, that David struck the
Philistines, and made them low, *or conquered them*; and
David took away Methegammah from the Philistines.)
2 And David smote Moab, and meted them with a
cord, and he made them even to the earth; forsooth he
meted (them by) two cords, one to slay, and one to
quicken. And Moab served David under tribute. (And
David struck the Moabites, and he made his captives to
lie on the ground, and had them measured with a cord;
and for every two cord lengths of men that he killed, one
cord length was allowed to live. And then the Moabites
paid tribute, *or taxes*, to David.)
3 And David smote Hadadezer, the son of Rehob,
king of Zobah, when he went forth to be lord over the
flood Euphrates. (And then David struck Hadadezer, the
son of Rehob, the king of Zobah, as he went to recover
his land by the Euphrates River.)
4 And when a thousand and seven hundred horsemen
of his part were taken, and twenty thousand of footmen,
David hocked all [the] drawing beasts in chariots; but
David left of those an hundred chariots, *that is, the
horses of an hundred chariots*. (And David took from
him, *or captured*, a thousand and seven hundred
horsemen, and twenty thousand footmen, and he hocked
all the drawing beasts for the chariots; but he left
unharmed the horses for a hundred chariots.)
5 Also Syrians of Damascus came, that it should bear
help to Hadadezer, king of Zobah; and David smote of
(the) Syrians two and twenty thousand of men. (And the
Syrians of Damascus came to help Hadadezer; and David
struck down twenty-two thousand of the men of Syria.)
6 And David setted a stronghold in Syria of Damascus,
and Syria was made serving David under tribute. And
the Lord kept David in all things, to whatever things he
went forth. (And David set up strongholds in Syria of
Damascus, and the Syrians were made to serve David,
and to pay tribute, *or taxes*, to him. And the Lord gave
victory to David in all his battles, wherever he went.)
7 And David took golden armours and bands (And
David took the gold arms, *or the weapons*), which the
servants of Hadadezer had, and he brought those into
Jerusalem.
8 And of Betah, and of Berothai (And from Betah, and
Berothai), the cities of Hadadezer, David [the] king took
full much brass.
9 Forsooth Toi, king of Hamath, heard that David had
smitten all the host of Hadadezer.
10 And Toi sent Joram, his son, to king David, that he
should greet him, and thank (him), and do thankings, for
he had overcome Hadadezer, and had smitten him; for
Toi was enemy of Hadadezer; and vessels of silver, and
vessels of gold, and vessels of brass were in his hand.
(And King Toi sent his son Joram to King David, to greet
him, and to congratulate him on his victory, for he had
overcome Hadadezer, and had beaten him; for Toi was
Hadadezer's enemy; and his son brought with him
vessels of silver, and gold, and brass, for David.)
11 And the same vessels king David hallowed to the
Lord, with the silver and gold, which he had hallowed of
all heathen men, which he had made subject. (And King
David dedicated these vessels to the Lord, along with the
silver and the gold which he had dedicated from all the
heathen whom he had made subject,)
12 of Syria, and of Moab, and of the sons of Ammon,
and of Philistines, and of Amalek, and of the spoils of
Hadadezer, the son of Rehob, king of Zobah.
13 Also David made to him a name, when he turned
again when Syria was taken, for eighteen thousand men

were slain in the valley, where salt was made, and in
Helam, to three and twenty thousand.[2] (And so David
had made a name for himself, by the time he returned
after the Syrians were killed, for eighteen thousand men
were slain in the Salt Valley, and twenty-two thousand in
Helam.)
14 And he setted keepers in Idumea, and ordained [a]
stronghold, and all Idumea was made serving to David;
and the Lord kept David in all things, to whatever things
he went forth. (And he set up strongholds in Edom, *or
Idumea*, and all the Edomites served David; and so the
Lord gave victory to David everywhere he went.)
15 And David reigned upon all Israel, and David did
doom, and rightwiseness to all his people. (And David
reigned over all Israel, and David brought justice, *or
judgement*, and righteousness unto all his people.)
16 And Joab, the son of Zeruiah, was over the host *of
David*; and Jehoshaphat, the son of Ahilud, was recorder;
(And Joab, the son of Zeruiah, was the leader of *David's*
army; and Jehoshaphat, the son of Ahilud, was the officer
in charge of the records;)
17 and Zadok, the son of Ahitub, and Ahimelech, the
son of Abiathar, were priests; and Seraiah was a scribe
(and Seraiah was the writer).
18 But Benaiah, the son of Jehoiada, was over
Cherethites and Pelethites, *that is, over archers and
arrow-blasters*; and the sons of David were priests. (And
Benaiah, the son of Jehoiada, was the leader of the
Cherethites and Pelethites, *that is, the archers and the
arrow-blasters*; and David's sons were priests.)

CHAPTER 9

1 And David said, Whether any man is, that (is) left of
the house of Saul, that I do mercy with him for Jonathan?
(And David asked, Is there any man who is left of Saul's
family, to whom I can show kindness for Jonathan's sake?)
2 And there was a servant, Ziba by name, of the house
of Saul; whom when the king had called to himself, the
king said to him, Whether thou art not Ziba? (Art thou
Ziba?) And he answered, I am thy servant.
3 And the king said, Whether any man liveth of the
house of Saul, that I do with him the mercy of God? And
Ziba said to the king, A son of Jonathan liveth, feeble in
the feet. (And the king said, Is there any man left of Saul's
family, to whom I can show the kindness that God
commandeth? And Ziba said to the king, A son of
Jonathan liveth, who is lame, *or crippled*.)
4 And the king said, Where is he? And Ziba said to
the king, Lo! he is in the house of Machir, the son of
Ammiel, in Lodebar.
5 Therefore king David sent, and took Jonathan's son
from the house of Machir, the son of Ammiel, from
Lodebar. (And so King David sent for Jonathan's son, and
brought him to Jerusalem from the house of Machir, the
son of Ammiel, in Lodebar.)
6 And when Mephibosheth, the son of Jonathan, [the]
son of Saul, had come to David, he felled into his face,
and worshipped. And David said, Mephibosheth! And
he answered, I am present, thy servant. (And when
Mephibosheth, the son of Jonathan, the son of Saul, had
come to David, he fell on his face, and honoured him.
And David said, Mephibosheth! And he answered, I am
thy servant.)
7 And David said to him, Dread thou not, for I doing
shall do mercy to thee for Jonathan, thy father; and I shall
restore to thee all the fields of Saul, thy father, and thou
shalt eat bread in my table ever[more]. (And David said
to him, Fear not, for I shall do kindness to thee because
of thy father Jonathan; and I shall restore to thee all the
fields of Saul, thy grandfather, and thou shalt have a
place at my table forevermore.)
8 Which worshipped him (Who bowed low before
him again), and said, Who am I, thy servant, for thou hast
beheld on a dead dog like me?
9 Therefore the king called Ziba, the servant of Saul;
and said to him, I have given to the son of thy lord all
things, whichever were of Saul, and all the house of him;
(And so the king called Ziba, Saul's servant, and said to
him, I have given to thy lord's grandson everything that
belonged to Saul, and his family;)
10 therefore work thou the land to him, thou, and thy
sons, and thy servants, and thou shalt bring in meats to the
son of thy lord, that he be fed; but Mephibosheth, the son
of thy lord, shall eat ever bread on my board. And fifteen
sons and twenty servants were to Ziba. (and so work thou
the land for him, thou, and thy sons, and thy servants, and
thou shalt bring in the harvest for the family of thy lord,
so that they can be fed; but Mephibosheth, the grandson
of thy lord, shall have a place at my table forevermore.
And Ziba had fifteen sons and twenty servants.)
11 And Ziba said to the king, As thou, my lord (the)
king, hast commanded to thy servant, so thy servant shall
do; and Mephibosheth, as one of the sons of the king,
shall eat on thy board (and Mephibosheth, like one of the
king's sons, ate at the king's table).
12 And Mephibosheth had a little son, Micha by name;
and all the family of the house of Ziba served
Mephibosheth.
13 And Mephibosheth dwelled in Jerusalem; for he ate
continually of the king's board, and was crooked, or halt,
on either foot. (And so Mephibosheth lived in Jerusalem;
and he always ate at the king's table, and he was lame, or
crippled, in both feet.)

CHAPTER 10

1 Forsooth it was done after these things, that Nahash,

[2] See 2ND Samuel 10:16-19.

[the] king of the sons of Ammon, died; and Hanun, his
son, reigned for him (and his son Hanun reigned in his
place).
2 And David said, I shall do mercy with Hanun, the
son of Nahash, as his father did mercy with me.
Therefore David sent comforting (to) him by his servants
on the death of the father (And David said, I shall show
friendship to Nahash's son Hanun, like his father showed
to me. And so, by his servants, David sent words of
comfort to Hanun on the death of his father). And when
the servants of David had come into the land of the sons
of Ammon,
3 the princes of the sons of Ammon said to Hanun,
their lord, Guessest thou, that for the honour of thy father
David hath sent comforters to thee; and not *rather*
therefore David sent his servants to thee, that he should
espy, and ensearch the city, and destroy it? (and not *rather,*
that David sent his servants to thee to spy out, and to
search through the city, so that later he could destroy it?)
4 Therefore Hanun took the servants of David, and
shaved half the part of the beard of them, and he cutted
away the middle clothes of them, till to the buttocks; and
let go them. (And so Hanun took David's servants, and
shaved off half of their beards, and cut away half of their
clothes, unto the buttocks, and then let them go.)
5 And when this was told to David, he sent into the
coming of them, for the men were shamed full vilely
(And when this was told to David, he sent men to meet
them, for these men had been vilely shamed). And David
commanded to them, (and said,) Dwell ye in Jericho, till
your beard (hath) waxed, and then turn ye again.
6 And the sons of Ammon saw, that they had done
wrong to David, and they sent, and hired with meed of
Bethrehob of Syria, and of Zoba of Syria, twenty
thousand of footmen, and of king Maacah, a thousand
men, and of Ishtob, twelve thousand of men. (And the
Ammonites saw that they had wronged David, and so
they sent for, and hired for pay, Syrians from Bethrehob
and from Zoba, yea, twenty thousand footmen, and a
thousand men from King Maacah, and twelve thousand
men from Tob.)
7 And when David had heard this, he sent (out) Joab,
and all the host of fighters (and all his army of fighting
men).
8 Therefore the sons of Ammon went out, and dressed
battle array before them in the entering of the gate. And
Zoba, and Rehob of Syria, and Ishtob, and Maacah, were
asides half in the field. (And so the Ammonites went out,
and dressed the battle array before them at the entrance
to the city gate. And the Syrians from Zoba and from
Rehob, and the men from Tob, and from Maacah, were
asides half in the field.)
9 Therefore Joab saw, that the battle was made ready
against him, both even against him and behind his back;
and he chose to himself of all the chosen men of Israel
(and he chose for himself the best men out of all Israel),
and ordained (the) battle array against (the) Syrians.
10 Forsooth he betook to Abishai, his brother, the
tother part of the people, which dressed (the) battle array
against the sons of Ammon.
11 And Joab said, If (the) men of Syria have the mastery
against me, thou shalt be to me into help; and if the sons
of Ammon have the mastery against thee, I shall help thee;
12 be thou a strong man (be thou of good courage), and
fight we for our people, and for the city of our God; for
the Lord shall do that, that is good in his sight.
13 Therefore Joab and the people that was with him,
began battle against men of Syria, which fled anon from
his face. (And so Joab, and the men who were with him,
began to fight against the Syrians, who fled at once from
before them.)
14 And the sons of Ammon saw, that [the] men of Syria
had fled; and they fled also from the face of Abishai, and
entered into the city; and Joab turned again from the sons
of Ammon, and came into Jerusalem (and then Joab left
off fighting the Ammonites, and went back to Jerusalem).
15 And [the] men of Syria saw that they had fallen
before Israel, and they were gathered together. (And
when the Syrians saw that they had fallen before Israel,
they gathered themselves together.)
16 And Hadadezer[3] sent, and led out [the] men of Syria
that were beyond the flood, and he brought forth the host
of them; and Shobach, [the] master of the chivalry of
Hadadezer, was the prince of them. (And Hadadezer sent
for the Syrians who were on the other side of the
Euphrates River, and they came forth to Helam; and
Shobach, the master of Hadadezer's cavalry, *or of his
army,* was their leader.)
17 And when this was told to David, he drew together
all Israel, and he passed over Jordan (and he crossed over
the Jordan River), and came into Helam. And [the] men of
Syria dressed (the) battle array against David, and fought
against him.
18 And Syrians fled from the face of Israel; and David
killed of the Syrians (the men in) seven hundred chariots,
and forty thousand of horsemen; and he smote Shobach,
the prince of the chivalry, the which was dead anon.
(And the Syrians fled from the Israelites; and David killed
of those Syrians the men in seven hundred chariots, and
forty thousand horsemen; and he struck down Shobach,
the leader of the cavalry, *or of the army,* who died on the
battlefield.)
19 And all the kings, that were in help of Hadadezer,
saw that they were overcome of Israel, and they made
peace with Israel, and served them; and the Syrians
dreaded to give (more) help to the sons of Ammon. (And

[3] Also known as Hadarezer.

when all the kings, who were subject to Hadadezer, saw
that they were overcome by Israel, they made peace with
Israel, and served them; and from then on the Syrians
were afraid to give any more help to the Ammonites.)

CHAPTER 11

1 And it was done, when the year turned again, in that
time in which kings be wont to go forth to battles, David
sent forth Joab, and with him his servants, and all Israel;
and they destroyed the sons of Ammon, and besieged
Rabbah; and David dwelled in Jerusalem. (And it was
done, when the year turned again, at the time when kings
be wont to go forth to battle, David sent out Joab, and
with him his officers, and all of Israel's army; and they
destroyed the Ammonites, and besieged Rabbah; but
David stayed in Jerusalem.)
2 While these things were done, it befelled, that
David rose in a day from his bed after midday, and
walked in the solar of the king's house; and he saw a
woman washing herself even against *him* upon her solar;
and the woman was full fair. (While these things were
done, it befell one day, that David rose from his bed after
midday, and walked on the roof of his palace; and he
saw a woman opposite *him* washing herself on her roof;
and the woman was truly beautiful.)
3 Therefore the king sent, and inquired, what woman
it was; and it was told to him that she was Bathsheba, the
daughter of Eliam, *and (that) she was* the wife of Uriah
(the) Hittite.
4 Then by messengers sent, David took her; and when
she entered to him, he slept with her, and anon she was
hallowed from her uncleanness[4]. And she turned again
into her house, (Then David sent messengers, who
brought her to him; and after she came to him, he slept
with her, and at once she was hallowed from her
uncleanness. And she returned to her house,)
5 with a child conceived; and she sent, and told to
David, and said, I have conceived.
6 And David sent to Joab, and said, Send thou Uriah
(the) Hittite to me; and Joab sent Uriah to David.
7 And Uriah came to David; and David asked, how
rightfully Joab did and the people, and how the battle
was (ad)ministered, *or served.* (And Uriah came to David;
and David asked him how well Joab and the men were
doing, and how the battle was going.)
8 And David said to Uriah, Go into thine house, and
wash thy feet. [And] Uriah went out from the house of
the king, and the king's meat followed him (and the
king's gift followed him home).
9 Soothly Uriah slept before the gate of the king's
house with other servants of his lord, and went not down
to his house. (But Uriah slept by the palace gate with
other servants of his lord, and did not go down to his
house.)
10 And it was told to David of men, saying, Uriah went
not to his house (And it was told to David by men,
saying, Uriah did not go down to his house). And David
said to Uriah, Whether thou camest not from the way?
why wentest thou not down into thine house?
11 And Uriah said to David, The ark of God, [and]
Israel, and Judah (all) dwell in tents, and my lord Joab,
and the servants of my lord dwell upon the face of the
earth, and shall I (then) go into mine house, to eat and
drink, and sleep with my wife? By thine health, and by
the health of thy soul, I shall not do this thing.
12 Therefore David said to Uriah, Dwell thou here also
today, and tomorrow I shall deliver thee. Uriah dwelled
in Jerusalem in that day, and the tother (And so Uriah
stayed in Jerusalem that day, and the next day as well).
13 And David called him, that he should eat and drink
before him, and David made drunken Uriah (and David
made Uriah drunk); and he went out in the eventide, and
slept in his bed with the servants of his lord; and went
not down into his house.
14 Therefore when the morrowtide was made, David
wrote [an] epistle to Joab, and sent (it) by the hand of
Uriah,
15 and wrote in the epistle, Put ye Uriah even against
the battle, where the battle is strongest, *that is, where the
adversaries be (the) strong(est),* and forsake ye him, that
he be smitten and perish (and leave ye him there, so that
he can be struck down and die).
16 Therefore when Joab besieged the city, he setted
Uriah in the place where he knew that (the) strongest
men were.
17 And [the] men went out of the city, and fought
against Joab, and they killed of the people of the servants
of David, and also Uriah (the) Hittite was dead there.
(And the men came out of the city, and fought against
Joab, and they killed some of David's officers, and Uriah
the Hittite was also killed.)
18 Therefore Joab sent, and told all the words of the
battle; (And so Joab sent a message to David, telling him
all about the battle;)
19 and he commanded to the messenger, and said,
When thou hast fulfilled all the words of the battle to the
king (When thou hast finished telling the king everything
about the battle),
20 if thou seest, that he is wroth, and saith, Why nighed
ye to the wall to fight? whether ye knew not, that many
darts, (*or arrows,*) (would) be sent out from the wall above?
21 who smote Abimelech, the son of Jerubbesheth?
whether not a woman sent on him a gobbet of a
millstone from the wall, and killed him in Thebez? why
nighed ye beside the wall? thou shalt say, Also thy

[4] *That is, from (the) flux of unclean blood that should come till to the child bearing, for she conceived in that lying-by.*

servant, Uriah (the) Hittite, died. (do ye not recall who
struck down Abimelech, the son of Jerubbesheth? did not
a woman send down a piece of a millstone upon him
from the wall above, and killed him there in Thebez?
why did ye go beside the wall? thou shalt say, And thy
officer, Uriah the Hittite, also died.)
22 Therefore the messenger went, [and came] (to the
king), and told to David all things which Joab had
commanded to him.
23 And the messenger said to David, [The] Men had the
mastery against us, and they went out to us into the field;
and with great fierceness we pursued them unto the gate
of the city.
24 And [the] archers sent (out) darts to thy servants from
the wall above, and some of the king's servants be dead;
and also thy servant, Uriah (the) Hittite, is dead. (And
their archers sent out arrows at thy servants, *or thy
officers*, from the wall above, and some of the king's
servants were killed; and thy servant, Uriah the Hittite,
also died.)
25 And David said to the messenger, Thou shalt say
these things to Joab, This thing break not thee; for the hap
of battle is diverse, and sword wasteth now this man,
[and] now that man; comfort thy fighters against the city,
that thou destroy it, and excite thou them. (And David
said to the messenger, Thou shalt say these things to
Joab, Do not let this thing break thee; for the
happenstance of battle is diverse, and the sword wasteth
now this man, and now that one; make thy fighting men
strong against the city, so that thou destroy it, yea,
encourage thou them.)
26 And the wife of Uriah heard, that Uriah her husband
was dead, and she bewailed him.
27 And when the mourning was passed, David sent,
and brought her into his house; and she was made (a)
wife to him, and she childed a son to him. And this word
that David had done displeased before the Lord (But this
thing that David had done greatly displeased the Lord).

CHAPTER 12

1 Therefore the Lord sent Nathan to David; and when
he had come to David, he said to him, Answer thou a
doom to me (Give thou to me your judgement on this);
two men were in one city; one man *was* rich, and the
tother was poor.
2 The rich man had full many sheep, and oxen;
3 and the poor man had utterly nothing, except one
little sheep, which he had bought, and nourished, and
which had waxed at him, (and) with his sons, and ate
together (with them) of his bread, and drank of his cup,
and slept in his bosom; and it was as a daughter to him.
(and the poor man had utterly nothing, except one little
lamb, which he had bought, and nourished, and which
had grown up with him, and with his sons, and together
with them ate his food, and drank from his cup, and slept
in his bosom; yea, it was like a daughter to him.)
4 But when a pilgrim came to this rich man, he spared
to take of his own sheep and oxen, that he should make a
feast to that pilgrim, that came to him; and he took the
sheep of the poor man, and prepared meats to the man
that came to him. (But when a visitor came to the rich
man, he would not take his own sheep and oxen to make
a feast for that visitor, who came to him; but instead he
took the poor man's lamb, and prepared food for the man
who came to him.)
5 Certainly David was full wroth with indignation
against that man, and he said to Nathan, (As) The Lord
liveth, for the man that did this thing is the son of death,
*that is, is worthy of death, for the hideousness of the
deed*;
6 he shall yield the sheep into fourfold, for he did this
word, and spared not. (he shall give him four sheep, for
he did this thing, and yet could care less.)
7 And Nathan said to David, Thou art that man, that
hast done this thing. The Lord God of Israel saith these
things, I anointed thee into king on Israel (I anointed thee
king upon Israel), and I delivered thee from the hand of
Saul,
8 and I gave to thee the house of thy lord, and the
wives of thy lord in(to) thy bosom, and I gave to thee the
house of Israel, and of Judah; and if these things be little,
I shall add to thee much greater things (and if these things
were too little, I would have added much greater things
for thee).
9 Why therefore hast thou despised the word of the
Lord, that thou didest evils in my sight? Thou hast killed
by sword Uriah (the) Hittite, and thou hast taken his wife
into wife to thee, and thou hast slain him with the sword
of the sons of Ammon. (And so why hast thou despised
the word of the Lord, so that thou didest evils in my
sight? Thou hast killed Uriah the Hittite with the sword,
and thou hast taken his wife for thy wife, and thou hast
killed him by the sword of the Ammonites.)
10 Wherefore a sword shall not go away from thine
house till into without end; for thou hast despised me,
and hast taken the wife of Uriah (the) Hittite, that she
should be thy wife.
11 Therefore the Lord saith these things, Lo! I shall raise
on thee evil (out) of thine house, and I shall take thy
wives in thine eyes, and I shall give to thy neighbour, and
he shall sleep with thy wives in the eyes of this sun. (And
so the Lord saith these things, Lo! I shall raise up evil
against thee from thy own house, and I shall take thy
wives from before thee, and I shall give them to thy
neighbour, *or to another man*, and he shall sleep with thy
wives in broad daylight.)
12 For thou hast done (*thy sin*) privily; forsooth I shall
do this word in the sight of all Israel, and in the sight of

this sun. (Yea, thou hast done *thy sin* in secret; but I shall
do this thing before all Israel, and in broad daylight.)
13 And David said to Nathan, I have sinned to the
Lord. And Nathan said to David, Also the Lord hath
turned away thy sin; thou shalt not die. (And David said
to Nathan, I have sinned against the Lord. And Nathan
said to David, The Lord hath turned away thy sin; thou
shalt not die.)
14 Nevertheless for thou hast made [the] enemies to
blaspheme the name of the Lord, for this word the child
that is born to thee shall die by death (because of this, the
child who is born to thee shall die).
15 And Nathan turned again into his house. And the
Lord smote the little child, whom the wife of Uriah
childed to David, and he despaired. (And Nathan
returned to his house. And the Lord struck the young
child, whom Uriah's wife had borne to David, and he
became very ill.)
16 And David prayed to the Lord for the little child; and
David fasted by fasting, and entered asides half, and lay
on the earth (and lay on the floor *all night*).
17 And the elder men of his house came, and
constrained him, that he should rise up from the earth;
and he would not, neither he ate meat with them. (And
the older men of his household came, and compelled
him to get up off the floor; but he would not, nor would
he eat any food with them.)
18 And it befelled in the seventh day, that the young
child died; and the servants of David dreaded to tell to
him, that the little child was dead; for they said, Lo! while
the little child lived yet, we spake to him, and he heard
not our voice; how much more (now), if we say the child
is dead, he shall torment himself? (And it befell that on
the seventh day, the young child died; and David's
servants feared to tell him that the young child was dead;
for they said, Lo! while the young child yet lived, we
spoke to him, and he would not listen to us; how much
more now shall he torment himself, if we tell him that the
child is dead?)
19 Therefore when David had heard his servants
speaking privily, *either muttering*, he understood that the
young child was dead; and he said to his servants,
Whether the child is dead? (Is the child dead?) Which
answered to him, He is dead.
20 Therefore David rose up from the earth, and was
washed, and anointed; and when he had changed his
clothes, he entered into the house of the Lord, and
worshipped, and came into his house; and he asked, that
they should set bread to him, and he ate. (And so David
got up off the floor, and washed, and anointed himself;
and when he had changed his clothes, he went to the
House of the Lord, and worshipped, and then came back
to the palace; and he asked them to set food before him,
and he ate it.)
21 And his servants said to him, What is the word that
thou hast done? Thou hast fasted, and wept for the young
child, while he lived yet; but when the child was dead,
thou risedest/thou hast risen up, and atest bread? (And his
servants said to him, What is this? Thou hast fasted, and
wept for the young child, while yet he lived; but when
the child was dead, thou hast risen up, and eaten food?)
22 And David said, I fasted and wept for the young
child, when he lived yet; for I said, Who knoweth, if
peradventure the Lord give him to me, and the young
child live? (And David said, Yes, I fasted and wept for the
young child, while yet he lived; for I said, Who knoweth,
perhaps the Lord shall give him back to me, and the
young child shall live.)
23 But now for he is dead, why fast I? whether I shall
be able to again-call him more? I shall go more to him,
but he shall not turn again to me. (But now that he is
dead, why should I fast? can I call him back again? One
day, I shall go to him, but he shall never return to me.)
24 And David comforted Bathsheba, his wife; and he
entered [in] to her, and slept with her. And she
engendered a son, and *David* called his name Solomon;
and the Lord loved him.
25 And he sent him in the hand of Nathan, the prophet;
and he called his name Amiable to the Lord, for the Lord
loved him. (And he sent word through Nathan, the
prophet; and he called his name Jedidiah, *that is,
Beloved of the Lord*, for the Lord loved him.)
26 Then Joab fought against Rabbah, of the sons of
Ammon, and he fought against the king's city.
27 And Joab sent messengers to David, and said, I have
fought against Rabbah, and the city of waters shall be
taken (and I have taken the city's water supply).
28 Now therefore gather thou the tother part of the
people, and besiege thou the city, and take thou it, lest
when the city is wasted of me (lest when I have destroyed
the city), the victory be areckoned to my name.
29 Therefore David gathered together all the people,
and he went forth against Rabbah; and when he had
fought *against that city*, he took it.
30 And he took the diadem of the king of them[5] from
his head, by weight [of] a talent of gold, (and) having
precious pearls; and it was put on the head of David; but
also David bare away full much prey of the city. (And he
took the crown off the head of their king/And he took the
crown off the head of their idol, which weighed a talent
of gold, and was adorned with precious pearls; and it was
put on David's head; and David also took away a great
deal of prey, *or of spoils*, from the city.)
31 And he led forth the people thereof, and sawed
(them), and did about them iron instruments of torment,

[5] *That is, '(the crown) of the idol of them', which is called Malcham, (or Milcom,) that is interpreted 'the king of them'.*

and parted (them) with knives, and led (them) over by the
likeness of tilestones; so he did to all the cities of the sons
of Ammon. And David turned again, and all his host,
into Jerusalem (And then David, and all his army,
returned to Jerusalem).

CHAPTER 13

1 And it was done after these things, that Amnon, the
son of David, loved the fairest sister, Tamar by name, of
Absalom, the son of David. (And it was done after these
things, that Amnon, one of David's sons, loved Tamar,
the fairest sister *of Amnon, and* of Absalom, another of
David's sons.)
2 And Amnon perished greatly for her, so that he was
sick for her love. For since she was a virgin, it seemed
hard to him, that he should do anything unhonestly with
her. (And Amnon greatly burned for her, so that he was
sick for her love. But since she was a virgin, it was hard
for him to do anything dishonourable to her.)
3 But there was a friend to Amnon, Jonadab by name,
the son of Shimeah, the brother of David; and *Jonadab
was* a full prudent man, [(*that is*), a full sly man].
4 Which said to Amnon, Son of the king, why art thou
made feeble so by leanness, by all days? why showest
thou not to me? (And he said to Amnon, Son of the king,
why art thou made so weak and thin, day after day? why
not tellest thou to me?) And Amnon said to him, I love
Tamar, the sister of my brother Absalom.
5 And Jonadab answered to him, Lie thou on thy bed,
and feign thou sickness; and when thy father cometh, that
he visit thee, say thou to him, I pray, come Tamar, my
sister, that she give meat to me, and make a stew, that I
eat it of her hand. (And Jonadab answered to him, *Do
thou this*. Lie thou on thy bed, and pretend to be sick;
and when thy father cometh to visit thee, say thou to
him, I pray thee, let my sister Tamar come, and give food
to me, yea, to make me a stew, and I shall eat it by her
hand/and she shall serve it to me.)
6 Therefore Amnon lay down, and feigned to be sick.
And when the king had come to visit him, Amnon said to
the king, I beseech, come Tamar, my sister, that she make
two suppings before my eyes, and that I take of her hand
the meat made ready. (And so Amnon lay down, and
pretended to be sick. And when the king had come to
visit him, Amnon said to the king, I beseech thee, that my
sister Tamar come, and make supper for me, and when
the food is ready, I shall eat it by her hand/she shall serve
it to me.)
7 Therefore David sent to the house of Tamar, and
said, Come thou into the house of Amnon, thy brother,
and make thou a stew to him. (And so David sent word
to Tamar's house, and said, Go thou to thy brother
Amnon's house, and make thou a stew for him.)
8 And Tamar came into the house of Amnon, her
brother. And he lay down; and she took meal, and
mixed (it) together, and made (it) moist before his eyes,
and seethed [the] suppings (and boiled the supper);
9 and she took that, that she had sodden, and poured
it out, and set it before him, and he would not eat (and
she took what she had boiled, and poured *it* out, and set
it before him, but he would not eat it). And Amnon said,
Put ye out all men from me. And when they had put out
all (the) men,
10 Amnon said to Tamar, Bear the meat into the (bed-)
closet, that I eat of thine hand. Therefore Tamar took the
suppings which she had made, and brought in to Amnon,
her brother, in the (bed-)closet. (Amnon said to Tamar,
Bring the food into the bed-chamber, so that I can eat it
by thy hand/so that thou can serve it to me. And so
Tamar took the supper which she had made, and brought
it to her brother Amnon, in the bed-chamber.)
11 And when she had proffered the meat to him, he
took her, and said, Come thou, my sister, lie thou with
me. (And when she offered him the food, he took hold of
her, and said, Come thou, my sister, lie thou with
me/sleep with me.)
12 And she answered to him, My brother, do not thou,
do not thou oppress me, for this is not leaveful in Israel
(for this is not lawful in Israel); do not thou do this folly.
13 For I shall not be able to bear my shame, and thou
shalt be as one of the unwise men, (*or the fools*,) in Israel;
but rather speak thou to the king, and he shall not deny
me to thee.
14 Soothly he would not assent to her prayers; but he
was stronger in mights, and oppressed her, and lay with
her.
15 And then (afterward,) with full great hatred Amnon
hated her, so that the hatred was greater, by which he
hated her, than the love by which he (had) loved her
before. And Amnon said to her, Rise thou (up), and go.
16 And she answered to him, This evil is more which
thou doest now against me, and puttest me out, than that,
that thou didest before. And he would not hear her; (And
she answered to him, This evil which thou now doest
against me, by putting me out, is worse, than what thou
didest before. But he would not listen to her;)
17 but when the servant was called, that ministered to
him (who served him), he said, Put thou out this woman
from me, and close thou the door after her.
18 And she was clothed with a coat down to the heel;
for the king's daughters (who were) virgins used such
clothes. Then the servant of Amnon put her out, and
closed the door after her.
19 And she sprinkled ashes (on)to her head, and when
her long coat was rent, and her hands put on her head,
she went entering [in] and crying.
20 And Absalom, her brother, said to her, Whether
Amnon, thy brother, hath lain with thee? But now, sister,

be still; he is thy brother, and torment thou not thine
heart for this thing. Therefore Tamar dwelled mourning
in the house of Absalom, her brother (And so Tamar
stayed in the house of her brother Absalom, and
mourned *her state*).
21 Forsooth when king David had heard these words,
he was full sorry, and he would not make sore the spirit
of Amnon, his son (And when King David heard about
this, he was very upset, but he would not punish his son
Amnon); for he loved Amnon, for he was his first
begotten son.
22 And Absalom spake not to Amnon, neither evil nor
good; for Absalom hated Amnon, for he had defouled
Tamar, his sister (for he had defiled his sister Tamar).
23 And it was done after the time of two years, that the
sheep of Absalom were shorn in Baalhazor, which is
beside Ephraim. And Absalom called all the sons of the
king (And Absalom invited all the king's sons to be there).
24 And he came to the king, and said to him, Lo! the
sheep of thy servant be shorn; I pray (thee), come the
king with his servants to his servant.
25 And the king said to Absalom, Do not thou, my son,
do not thou pray, that all we come, and charge thee.
And when he constrained David, and he would not go,
he blessed Absalom. (And the king said to Absalom, Do
not thou, my son, do not thou pray, that we all come,
and be a burden to thee. And when Absalom pressed
David, he still would not go, but he blessed Absalom.)
26 And Absalom said to David, If thou wilt not come, I
beseech thee, come namely Amnon, my brother, with us
(And Absalom said to David, If thou wilt not come, I
beseech thee, then let my brother Amnon come with us).
And the king said to him, It is no need, that he go with
thee.
27 Therefore Absalom constrained him; and he
delivered with him Amnon, and all the sons of the king.
(But Absalom pressed him; and so he let Amnon, and all
his other sons, go with him.)
28 And Absalom had made a feast as the feast of a king.
And Absalom [had] commanded to his servants, and said,
Espy ye, when Amnon is drunken of wine, and *when* I
say to you, Smite ye, and slayeth him. Do not ye dread,
for I am that command to you; be ye strengthened, and
be ye strong men. (And Absalom made a feast like the
feast of a king. And Absalom commanded to his
servants, and said, Watch ye, so that when Amnon is
drunk with wine, and I say to you, Strike ye him! that you
kill him. Do not ye fear, for I am the one who command
you to do this; be ye of good courage, and be ye strong
men.)
29 Therefore the servants of Absalom did against
Amnon, as Absalom had commanded to them; and (then)
all the sons of the king (swiftly) rose up, and ascended
each upon his mule, and fled.
30 And when they went yet in the way, (the) fame
came *thereof* to the king, and it was said, Absalom hath
slain all the sons of the king, and namely not one (is) left
of them. (And when they were yet on the way, the report
came to the king, and it was said, Absalom hath killed all
of the king's sons, and not one of them is left alive.)
31 Therefore the king rose up, and rent his clothes, and
felled down on the earth (and fell down on the ground);
and all his servants that stood nigh to him, rent their
clothes.
32 But Jonadab, the son of Shimeah, brother of David,
answered and said, My lord the king, guess thou not, that
all the young men, and sons of the king, be slain; Amnon
alone is dead, for he was set in hatred to Absalom, from
the day in which he oppressed Tamar, his sister. (But
Jonadab, the son of Shimeah, David's brother, said, My
lord the king, think thou not, that all of the king's sons be
killed; no, only Amnon is dead, for Absalom hath hated
him, from the day that he oppressed his sister Tamar.)
33 Now therefore, my lord the king, set not this word
on his heart, and say, All the sons of the king be slain; for
Amnon alone is dead. (And so now, my lord the king, put
not this thing upon thy heart, and say, All the king's sons
be killed; for only Amnon is dead.)
34 Forsooth Absalom fled. And a young man, (an)
espyer, raised [up] his eyes, and beheld, and lo! much
people came by a way out of the common way, by the
side of the hill. (And so Absalom fled away. And a young
man, a watchman, raised up his eyes, and looked, and lo!
a crowd of people came by the road, on the side of the
hill behind him.)
35 And Jonadab said to the king, Lo! the sons of the
king come; after the word of thy servant, so it is done
(yea, so it is done, just as thy servant hath said).
36 And when he had ceased to speak, also the sons of
the king appeared; and they entered, and raised up their
voice, and wept; but also the king and all his servants
wept with full great weeping.
37 Forsooth Absalom fled, and went to Talmai, the son
of Ammihud, the king of Geshur. Therefore David
bewailed his son Amnon in many days (And so David
bewailed his son Amnon for many days).
38 Forsooth Absalom, when he had fled, and had come
into Geshur, was there (for) three years.
39 And [king] David ceased to pursue Absalom, for he
was comforted upon the death of Amnon. (And after King
David resigned himself to Amnon's death, he longed for
his son Absalom.)

CHAPTER 14

1 Forsooth Joab, the son of Zeruiah, understood, that
the heart of the king was turned to(ward) Absalom;
2 and he sent to Tekoah, and took from thence a wise
woman, and he said to her, Feign thee to mourn, and be

thou clothed with a cloak of dole, and be thou not
anointed with oil, that thou be as a woman by mourning
now in full much time a dead man (so that thou be like a
woman now after a great deal of time mourning for her
husband).
3 And thou shalt enter to the king, and thou shalt
speak to him such *manner* words. And Joab put the
words in her mouth.
4 Therefore when the woman of Tekoah had entered
to the king, she felled before him on the earth, and
worshipped, and said, O! king, keep thou me. (And so
when the woman from Tekoah had entered before the
king, she fell on the ground before him, and honoured
him, and said, O! king, help thou me.)
5 And the king said to her, What hast thou of cause?
And she answered, Alas! I am a woman widow, for mine
husband is dead; (And the king said to her, What is thy
problem? And she answered, Alas! I am a widow
woman, for my husband is dead;)
6 and twain sons were of thine handmaid, which
debated against themselves in the field, and none was
that might forbid them, and the one smote the tother, and
killed him. (and thy servantess had two sons, who raged
against each other out in the field, and no one could
separate them, and one of them struck the other, and
killed him.)
7 And lo! all the kindred riseth against thine
handmaid, and saith, Give thou him *to us* that killed his
brother, that we slay him, for the life of his brother whom
he killed, and that we do away the heir; and they seek to
quench my spark that is left, that the name dwell not to
mine husband, and that remnants *be not to him* on earth.
(And lo! all the kinsmen riseth against thy servantess, and
saith, Give thou *to us* he who killed his brother, so that
we can kill him for taking his brother's life, and so that
we can do away the heir; yea, they seek to quench what
is left of my spark, so that my husband's name not
remain, and that there be no remnant *of him* left here on
the earth.)
8 And the king said to the woman, Go into thine
house, and I shall (give a) command for thee.
9 And the woman of Tekoah said to the king, My lord
the king, this wickedness be on me, and on the house of
my father; forsooth (let) the king and his throne be
innocent/be guiltless.
10 And the king said, Bring thou him to me, that
against-saith thee, and he shall no more add to (it,) that
he touch thee.
11 And she said, The king have mind on his Lord God,
and the next (kins)men of blood to take vengeance be not
multiplied, and they shall not slay my son. And the king
said, The Lord liveth, for none of the hairs of thy son shall
fall upon the earth. (And she said, May the king pray to
the Lord his God, that the kinsmen who be next of blood,
and who desire vengeance, be not able to take it, and so
they shall not kill my son. And the king said, As the Lord
liveth, none of the hairs of thy son shall fall on the ground!)
12 Therefore the woman said, Thine handmaid speak a
word to my lord the king (And the woman said, May thy
servantess speak a word to my lord the king?). And the
king said, Speak thou.
13 And the woman said, Why hast thou thought such a
thing against the people of God? and the king spake this
word, that he do sin, and bring not again his *son* (who is)
cast out? (And the woman said, Why then hast thou done
this same thing against the people of God? and so by
speaking this word, the king hath sinned, for he hath not
brought back his own *son* who is cast out.)
14 All we die, and as waters that shall not turn again,
we slide into the earth; and God will not that a soul
perish, but he withdraweth, and thinketh, lest he perish
utterly, which is cast away. (We shall all die, and we
shall slide into the earth, like water that shall not return;
but God desireth that no soul perish, but he withdraweth,
and thinketh, lest he, who is cast away, utterly perish.)
15 Now therefore come thou, that I speak to my lord
the king this word, while the people is present; and thine
handmaid said, I shall speak to the king, if in any manner
the king do the word of his handmaid. (And so now, I
have come that I may speak of this thing to my lord the
king, because the people have threatened me; and so thy
servantess said to herself, I shall speak to the king, if by
any chance the king will do what I request.)
16 And the king heard the words, that he should deliver
his handmaid from the hands of all men, that would do
away me, and my son together, from the heritage of the
Lord. (And for the king to hear these words, so that he
might deliver his servantess from the hands of all those
who would do away me, and my son, from the Lord's
inheritance.)
17 Therefore thine handmaid say, that the word of my
lord the king be made as sacrifice, *that is, that the
sentence given of him be pleasant to God, as sacrifice
pleaseth God* (And so thy servantess said to herself, that
the words of my lord the king would be like a sacrifice,
*that is, that his judgement would be pleasing to God, like
a sacrifice pleaseth God*); for as an angel of the Lord, so is
my lord the king, that he be not moved by blessing neither
by cursing. Wherefore and thy Lord God is with thee.
18 And the king answered, and said to the woman,
Hide thou not from me the word which I ask thee (Hide
thou not from me what I ask thee). And the woman said
to him, Speak thou, my lord the king.
19 And the king said, Whether the hand of Joab is with
thee in all these things? The woman answered, and said,
By the health of thy soul, my lord the king, neither to the
left side neither to the right side is *anything* of all these
things, which my lord the king hath spoken. For thy

servant Joab himself commanded to me, and he putted all
these words into the mouth of thine handmaid,
20 that I should turn the figure of this word (so that I
might help straighten out this matter); for thy servant Joab
commanded this thing. Forsooth thou, my lord the king,
art wise, as an angel of God that hath wisdom, that thou
understand all things on (the) earth.
21 And (later,) the king said to Joab, Lo! I am pleased,
and I have done thy word; therefore go thou, and again-
call thou the child Absalom. (And later, the king said to
Joab, Lo! I grant thy request; go thou, and bring back the
young man Absalom.)
22 And Joab felled upon his face to the earth, and he
worshipped, and blessed the king; and Joab said, Thy
servant hath understood today, that I have found grace in
thine eyes, my lord (the) king, for thou hast done the
word of thy servant. (And Joab fell down on the ground,
or the floor, and he honoured the king, and blessed him;
and Joab said, Thy servant knoweth today, that I have
found favour in thine eyes, my lord the king, for thou hast
granted my request.)
23 Therefore Joab rose up, and went into Geshur, and
brought Absalom into Jerusalem. (And so Joab rose up,
and went to Geshur, and brought Absalom back to
Jerusalem.)
24 And the king said, Turn he again into his house, and
see not he my face. Therefore Absalom turned again into
his house, and saw not the face of the king. (And the king
said, Go he back to his own house, for he shall not come
before me, *or into my presence*. And so Absalom
returned to his own house, and did not come before the
king.)
25 Soothly no man in all Israel was so fair as Absalom,
and full comely; from the step of the foot unto the top,
there was no wem in him (there was no flaw, *or blemish*,
on him);
26 and inasmuch as he clipped more his hairs, by so
much the more they waxed; but he was clipped once in
the year, for his hair grieved him. And when he clipped
the hairs, he weighed the hairs of his head by two
hundred shekels by common weight (And when he cut
his hair, the hairs of his head weighed two hundred
shekels by common weight).
27 And three sons, and a daughter, Tamar by name,
(and she was) of seemly shape, *or excellent form*, were
born to Absalom.
28 And Absalom dwelled in Jerusalem two years, and
he saw not the face of the king. (And Absalom lived in
Jerusalem for two years, but he never came before the
king.)
29 Therefore he sent to Joab, that he should send him
to the king; and Joab would not come to him. And when
he had sent the second time, and Joab would not come,
(And so he sent for Joab, so that he could take a message
to the king; but Joab would not come to him. And when
he had sent for him a second time, and Joab would still
not come,)
30 Absalom said to his servants, Ye know the field of
Joab beside my field, (the field of his) having ripe barley;
therefore go ye, and burn ye it [up] with fire. Therefore
the servants of Absalom burnt the (barley) corn with fire.
(Absalom said to his servants, Ye know Joab's field beside
my field, the one with the ripe barley; go ye, and burn it
down. And so Absalom's servants burned down the crop.)
31 And Joab rose up, and came to Absalom into his
house, and said, Why have thy servants burnt [up] my
(barley) corn with fire? (And Joab rose up, and came to
Absalom at his house, and said, Why have thy servants
burned down my crop?)
32 And Absalom answered to Joab, I sent to thee, and
besought that thou shouldest come to me, and that I
should send thee to the king, that thou shouldest say to
him, Why came I from Geshur? It was better to me to
have been there; therefore I beseech, that I see the face of
the king, that if he is mindful of my wickedness, slay he
me. (And Absalom answered to Joab, I sent for thee, and
desired that thou wouldest come to me, so that I could
send thee to the king, and thou couldest say to him for
me, Why did I come back from Geshur? It was better for
me to have stayed there; and so I beseech thee, let me go
before the king, and if he thinketh on my wickedness,
then let him kill me.)
33 (So) Joab entered to the king, and told to him. And
Absalom was called, and he entered to the king, and he
worshipped on the face of [the] earth before him (and
honouring him, he bowed low to the ground before him),
and the king kissed Absalom.

CHAPTER 15

1 Therefore after these things, Absalom made a chariot
to him, and (had) knights and fifty men, that should go
before him. (And so after these things, Absalom got a
chariot and horses for himself, and had fifty men who
went before him.)
2 And Absalom rose early, and stood beside the
entering of the gate in the way; and Absalom called to
him each man, that had a cause, [(*or*) a need,] that he
should come to the doom of the king, and Absalom said,
Of what city art thou? Which answered, and said, Of one
lineage of Israel I am, thy servant. (And Absalom would
rise up early, and stand beside the entrance to the city
gate on the road; and then he would call over each man
who had a case, *or a dispute*, that should have gone
before the king for judgement, and Absalom would say,
Of what city art thou? And each one would answer, and
say, I, thy servant, am from such and such tribe of Israel.)
3 And Absalom answered to him, Thy words seem to
me good and just, but none is ordained of the king to

hear thee. (And then Absalom would say to him, Thy
words seem good and just to me, but no one is ordained
by the king to hear thee.)
4 And Absalom said, Who shall ordain me judge on
the land, that all men that have (a) cause come to me,
and I deem justly? (And Absalom would add, Who shall
ordain me judge over the land, so that all who have a
case, *or a dispute*, can come before me, and I shall give
them justice?)
5 But when a man came to Absalom to greet him, he
held forth his hand, and took, and kissed that man; (And
whenever a man came to Absalom to greet him, he
would stretch out his hand, and take hold of him, and
kiss him;)
6 and Absalom did this to all Israel, that came to
doom to be heard of the king (and Absalom did this for
all of Israel who came to the king for a judgement); and
(so) Absalom stole the hearts of [the] men of Israel.
7 But after four years, Absalom said to king David, I
shall go, and shall yield my vows, which I vowed to the
Lord in Hebron; (And after four years, Absalom said to
King David, I shall now go to Hebron, and yield my
vows, which I vowed to the Lord;)
8 for thy servant vowing vowed, when he was in
Geshur of Syria, and said, If the Lord bringeth again me
into Jerusalem, I shall make sacrifice to the Lord. (for thy
servant made a vow, when he was in Geshur of Syria,
and said, If the Lord bringeth me back again to Jerusalem,
I shall go and make sacrifice to the Lord in Hebron.)
9 And the king said to him, Go thou in peace. And
Absalom rose up, and went into Hebron (And so
Absalom rose up, and went to Hebron).
10 Forsooth Absalom sent spyers into all the lineage[s]
of Israel, and said, Anon as ye hear the sound of [the]
clarion, say ye, Absalom shall reign in Hebron. (But
Absalom also sent messengers to all the tribes of Israel,
who said, As soon as ye hear the sound of the trumpet,
say ye, Absalom is king in Hebron.)
11 And two hundred men called (out) of Jerusalem
went forth with Absalom, and went with simple heart,
and utterly they knew not the cause. (And Absalom
invited two hundred men to go out of Jerusalem with
him, and they went innocently, *that is, in good faith*, and
utterly knew nothing about his true intentions.)
12 Also Absalom called (for) Ahithophel of Giloh, the
counsellor of David, from his city Giloh. And when he
offered sacrifices, a strong swearing together was made,
and the people running together was increased with
Absalom. (And Absalom summoned Ahithophel the
Gilonite, David's counsellor, from his city of Giloh. And
so while he offered his sacrifices, the conspiracy
strengthened, and the number of people joining Absalom
increased.)
13 Therefore a messenger came to David, and said,
With all [the] heart all Israel followeth Absalom,
14 And David said to his servants that were with him in
Jerusalem, Rise ye up, and flee we; for none escaping
shall be to us from the face of Absalom; therefore haste
ye to go out, lest he come, and occupy us, and fulfill
upon us his falling, and smite the city with sharpness of
[the] sword. (And David said to his servants who were
with him in Jerusalem, Rise ye up, and flee we; for there
shall be no escape for us from Absalom; and so haste ye
to go out, lest he come, and occupy us, and fulfill his
falling on us, *that is, that he destroy us*, and strike down
the people of the city with the sharpness of his sword.)
15 And the servants of the king said to him, We thy
servants shall perform gladly all things (We thy servants
shall gladly do all things), whatever our lord the king
shall command.
16 Then the king went out, and all his house, upon
their feet; and the king left ten women concubines, *that
is, secondary wives*, to keep the house. (Then the king
departed, and all his household followed him; but the
king left ten of his concubines, *or his secondary wives*, to
look after the palace.)
17 And (so) the king went out, and all Israel, upon their
feet, and the king stood far from the house (and they
stopped far away from the palace).
18 And all his servants went beside him, and the
legions of Cherethites and of Pelethites, and all the strong
fighting men of Gath, six hundred men, that followed
him from Gath, went on foot before the king.
19 And the king said to Ittai of Gath, Why comest thou
with us? Turn thou again, and dwell with the (new) king,
for thou art a pilgrim, and wentest out from thy place.
20 Thou camest yesterday, and today thou art
compelled to go out with us. Soothly I shall go, whither I
shall go; (but thou) turn again, and lead again thy
brethren with thee, and the Lord do mercy and truth with
thee, for thou hast showed *to me* grace and faith. (Thou
camest but yesterday, and so today, art thou compelled
to go out with us? Nay! Truly I shall go, wherever I shall
go; but thou return, and take thy kinsmen with thee, and
may the Lord show kindness and truth to thee, for thou
hast shown favour and faith *to me*.)
21 And Ittai answered to the king, and said, (As) The
Lord liveth, and (as) my lord the king liveth, for in
whatever place thou shalt be, my lord the king, either in
death either in life, there thy servant shall be.
22 And David said to Ittai, Come thou, and pass forth.
And Ittai of Gath passed forth, and the king, and all men
that were with him, and the tother multitude. (And David
said to Ittai, Then come thou, and let us go. And so Ittai
the Gittite, and the king, and the men who were with
him, and all the other people, went forth.)
23 And all men wept with great voice, and all the
people passed forth; and the king went over the strand of

Kidron, and all the people went against the way of the
olive tree(s), that beholdeth to the desert. (And all the
people wept loudly, as they all went forth; and the king
led the people over the Kidron Stream/over the Kidron
Gorge, and they went toward the way of the olive trees
which looketh toward the wilderness.)
24 Forsooth and Zadok the priest came, and all the
deacons with him, and they bare the ark of [the] bond of
peace of God, and they setted down the ark of God; and
Abiathar went up, till all the people was passed forth that
went out of the city. (And Zadok the priest came, and all
the Levites with him, carrying the Ark of the Covenant of
God; and they set down the Ark of God beside Abiathar,
until all the people who went out of the city had passed
by.)
25 And the king said to Zadok, Bear again the ark of
God into the city; if I shall find grace in the eyes of the
Lord, he shall lead me again, and he shall show to me
that ark, and his tabernacle. (And the king said to Zadok,
Take the Ark of God back to the city; if I shall find favour
before the Lord, he shall bring me back here, and he shall
let me see that Ark, and its resting place again.)
26 Soothly if the Lord saith, Thou pleasest not me; I am
ready, do he that, that is good before himself. (But if the
Lord saith, Thou pleasest me not; I am ready; do he what
he desireth with me.)
27 And the king said to Zadok, the priest, O! thou seer,
that is, (a) prophet, turn again into the city, with peace;
and Ahimaaz, thy son, and Jonathan, the son of Abiathar,
your two sons, be with you. (And the king said to Zadok,
the priest, O! thou prophet, return to the city in peace;
and thy son Ahimaaz, and Jonathan, the son of Abiathar,
these two young men, go they with you.)
28 Lo! I shall be hid in [the] field places of the desert,
till word come from you, and show to me. (Lo! I shall
hide at the Fords, *or the river crossings*, of the
Wilderness, until word come from thee to me.)
29 Therefore Zadok and Abiathar bare again the ark of
God into Jerusalem, and they dwelled there (and they
stayed there).
30 Forsooth David went up upon the hill of olive trees,
going up and weeping, with his head covered, and with
bare feet passing forth; but also all the people that was
with him, went up with their head(s) covered, and (they
also) wept. (And David went up on the Mount of Olives,
walking and weeping, with his head covered, and going
forth with bare feet; and all the people who were with
him also went up weeping, and with their heads covered.)
31 And it was told to David, that Ahithophel was in the
swearing together with Absalom; and David said, Lord, I
beseech, make thou fond the counsel of Ahithophel.
(And it was told to David that Ahithophel was in the
conspiracy with Absalom; and David said, Lord, I
beseech thee, turn thou Ahithophel's advice into
foolishness.)
32 And when David went up into [the] highness of the
hill, in which he should worship the Lord, lo! Hushai of
Archi, with *his* cloth rent, and with *his* head full of earth,
came to him. (And when David reached the top of the
hill, where he would worship the Lord, lo! Hushai the
Archite came to him, with *his* cloak torn, and with earth,
or with dirt, on *his* head.)
33 And David said to him, If thou comest with me, thou
shalt be to me (a) charge (thou shalt be a burden to me);
34 soothly if thou turnest again to the city, and sayest to
Absalom, I am thy servant, O king, suffer thou me to live;
as I was the servant of thy father, so I shall be thy servant;
thou shalt destroy the counsel of Ahithophel (then thou
shalt be able to destroy Ahithophel's advice).
35 And thou hast with thee Zadok and Abiathar, the
priests; and whatever word thou shalt hear in the house
of the king, thou shalt show it to the priests, Zadok and
Abiathar. (And thou shalt have with thee Zadok and
Abiathar, the priests; and whatever thing that thou shalt
hear in the king's house, thou shalt tell it to those priests,
Zadok and Abiathar.)
36 And their two sons be with them, Ahimaaz, the son
of Zadok, and Jonathan, the son of Abiathar; and ye shall
send by them to me each word that ye shall hear (and ye
shall send them to me with all that ye hear).
37 Therefore when Hushai, friend of David, came into
the city, also Absalom entered into Jerusalem. (And so
David's friend Hushai came into the city, just as Absalom
was entering Jerusalem.)

CHAPTER 16

1 And when David had passed a little (by) the top of
the hill, Ziba, the servant of Mephibosheth, appeared into
his coming, with twain asses, that were charged with two
hundred loaves, and with an hundred bundles of dried
grapes, and with an hundred gobbets/an hundred pieces
of pressed figs, and with two vessels of wine. (And after
David had just left the hilltop, Mephibosheth's servant
Ziba appeared before him, with two donkeys that were
loaded with two hundred loaves, a hundred bundles of
dried grapes, a hundred pieces of pressed figs, and two
vessels of wine.)
2 And the king said to Ziba, What will these things to
themselves? And Ziba answered, My lord the king, the
asses be to the menials of the king, that they sit *on them*;
and the loaves and the pressed figs be to thy children to
eat; forsooth the wine is, that if any man fail in desert, he
(may) drink. (And the king said to Ziba, What doest thou
with these things? And Ziba answered, My lord the king,
the donkeys be for the king's menials to sit *on*; and the
loaves and the pressed figs be for thy young men to eat;
and the wine, so that if any man feel faint in the
wilderness, he hath something to drink.)

3 And the king said, Where is the son of thy lord?
And Ziba answered to the king, He dwelled [still] in
Jerusalem, and said, Today the Lord of the house of Israel
shall restore to me the realm of my father. (And the king
said, Where is the grandson of thy lord? And Ziba
answered to the king, He remaineth in Jerusalem, and
said, Today the house of Israel shall restore my
grandfather's kingdom to me.)
4 And the king said to Ziba, All things that were of
Mephibosheth be thine. And Ziba said, I pray, find I
grace before thee, my lord the king. (And the king said to
Ziba, All the things that were Mephibosheth's now be
thine. And Ziba said, I pray thee, that I may find favour
before thee, my lord the king.)
5 Therefore king David came to Bahurim, and lo! a
man of the family of the house of Saul, Shimei by name,
[the] son of Gera, went out from thence; he went forth
going out, and cursed (and he cursed *David* as he went
forth).
6 And he sent stones against David, and against all the
servants of king David; and all the people, and all the
fighting men went at the right side and at the left side of
the king.
7 And Shimei spake thus, when he cursed the king,
Go out, go out, thou man of bloods, *that is, the shedder
out of much guiltless blood*, and man of Belial!
8 The Lord hath yielded to thee all the blood of the
house of Saul, for thou hast ravished the realm from him
(for thou hast stolen the kingdom from him); and the Lord
hath given the realm into the hand of Absalom, thy son;
and lo! thine evils oppress thee, for thou art a man of
bloods.
9 And Abishai, the son of Zeruiah, said to the king,
Why curseth this dog, that shall die, my lord the king? I
shall go, and I shall gird off his head. (And Abishai, the
son of Zeruiah, said to the king, Why let this dead dog
curse my lord the king? I shall go, and I shall cut off his
head!)
10 And the king said, Ye sons of Zeruiah, what is (it) to
me and to you? Suffer ye him, that he curse (But the king
said, Ye sons of Zeruiah, what is it to me, or to you?
Allow ye him to curse me); forsooth the Lord hath
commanded to him, that he should curse David; and
who is he that dare say, Why did he so?
11 And the king said to Abishai, and to all his servants,
Lo! my son, that went out of my womb, seeketh my life;
how much more now this son of Benjamin? Suffer ye
him, that he curse (me) by [the] commandment of the
Lord;
12 if in hap the Lord behold my tormenting, and yield
good to me for this day's cursing. (perhaps the Lord shall
behold my torments, and shall yield good to me for this
day's curses.)
13 Therefore David went forth, and his fellows, by the
way with him; but Shimei went aside by the slade of the
hill (over) against David; and cursed *David*, and threw
stones against him, and sprinkled earth. (And so David,
and his fellows, went forth by the way; but Shimei went
alongside by the ridge of the hill opposite David; and
cursed *David*, and threw stones at him, and threw dirt.)
14 And so king David came, and all the people weary
with him, and they were refreshed there. (And so the
king, and all the people who were with him, came weary
to the Jordan River, and they were refreshed there.)
15 And Absalom, and all the people of Israel entered
into Jerusalem, but also Ahithophel with him (and
Ahithophel was with him).
16 And when Hushai of Archi, the friend of David, had
come to Absalom, he said to him, Hail, king! hail, king!
17 To whom Absalom said, This is thy grace to thy
friend (This is how thou showest thy loyalty to thy
friend?); why wentest thou not with thy friend?
18 And Hushai answered to Absalom, Nay, for I shall
be the *servant* of him, whom the Lord hath chosen, and
all this people, and all Israel; and I shall dwell with him
(and I shall stay with him).
19 But that I say also this, to whom shall I serve?
whether not to the son of the king? as I obeyed to thy
father, so I shall obey to thee.
20 And Absalom said to Ahithophel, Take ye counsel
(Give ye advice to me), what we ought to do.
21 And Ahithophel said to Absalom, Enter thou [in] to
the concubines of thy father, which he left to keep the
house; that when all Israel heareth, that thou hast
defouled thy father's *bed*, the hands of them be
strengthened with thee. (And Ahithophel said to
Absalom, Enter thou in to thy father's concubines, whom
he left in charge of the palace; and when all Israel
heareth, that thou hast defiled thy father's bed, the hands
of them who be with thee shall be strengthened.)
22 Therefore they stretched out (for) Absalom a
tabernacle in the solar, and he entered [in] to the
concubines of his father before all Israel. (And so they
stretched out a tent on the roof for Absalom, and he lay
with his father's concubines in the sight of all Israel.)
23 And the counsel of Ahithophel, which he gave in
those days, was as if a man had counselled with God; so
was all the counsel of Ahithophel, both when he was
with David, and when he was with Absalom.

CHAPTER 17

1 Then Ahithophel said to Absalom, I shall choose to
me twelve thousand of men, and I shall rise up, and
pursue David in this night. (Then Ahithophel said to
Absalom, Let me choose twelve thousand men, and then
I shall rise up, and pursue David this very night.)
2 And I shall fall on him, for he is weary, and with
unbound hands I shall smite him. And when all the

people fleeth that is with him, I shall smite the king left
alone. (And I shall fall on him, for he is weary, and with
enfeebled hands, and I shall strike him down. Yea, when
all the people who be with him fleeth away, then I shall
strike down only the king/then I shall strike down the
king alone.)
3 And I shall lead again all the people, as one man is
wont to be turned again; for thou seekest (only) one man,
and (then) all the people shall be in peace. (And I shall
bring back all the people, and they shall return as if but
one man; for thou seekest only one man, and all the
other people shall be unharmed.)
4 And the word(s) of Ahithophel pleased Absalom,
and all the greater men in birth of Israel. (And
Ahithophel's plan pleased Absalom, and all the men of
great age, *that is, the elders*, of Israel.)
5 And Absalom said, Call ye also Hushai of Archi, and
hear we what also he saith. (And Absalom said, Now call
ye Hushai the Archite, and let us hear what he saith.)
6 And when Hushai had come to Absalom, Absalom
said to him, Ahithophel hath spoken such a word; ought
we (to) do thereafter, either nay? what counsel givest
thou?
7 And Hushai said to Absalom, This is not good
counsel, that Ahithophel hath given in this time. (And
Hushai said to Absalom, This is not good advice which
Ahithophel hath given thee at this time.)
8 And again Hushai said, Thou knowest, that thy
father, and the men that be with him, be most strong, and
in bitter soul, as if a she bear is fierce in the forest, when
her whelps be ravished *from her*; but also thy father is a
man warrior, and he shall not dwell with the people.
(And Hushai said, Thou knowest, that thy father, and the
men who be with him, be most strong, and with bitter
souls, like when a she bear is fierce in the forest, after her
cubs be stolen *from her*; but also thy father is a fighting
man, and he shall not stay with the army.)
9 In hap now he is hid, *either lurketh*, in ditches,
either in one place, in which he will *hide him*; and when
any man falleth in the beginning, whoever shall hear (of)
it, he shall hear, and shall say, Vengeance is done in the
people that followed Absalom. (Perhaps even now he is
hid, *or lurketh*, in a ditch, or some other place, where he
hideth himself; and when any of your men falleth at the
beginning, whoever shall hear of *it*, he shall say, Revenge
is now taken on the people who followed Absalom.)
10 And each full strong man, whose heart is as *the
heart* of a lion, shall be discomforted for dread; for all the
people of Israel knoweth, that thy father is strong, and
that all the men be strong, that be with him. (And then
even the strongest man, whose heart is like *the heart* of a
lion, shall be enfeebled by fear; for all the people of
Israel know that thy father is strong, and that all the men
who be with him also be strong.)
11 But this seemeth to me to be rightful counsel; (let)
all Israel be gathered to thee, from Dan till to Beersheba,
(and they shall be as) unnumberable as the sand of the
sea; and thou shalt be in the midst of them.
12 And we shall fall upon him, in whatever place he is
found, and we shall cover him, as dew is wont to fall on
the earth; and we shall not leave (any) of the men that be
with him, soothly not one. (And then we shall fall on
David wherever he is found, and we shall cover him like
dew is wont to fall on the ground; and we shall not leave
alive any of the men who be with him, no not one.)
13 That if he entereth into any city, all Israel shall
compass that city with ropes, and we shall draw it into
the strand, yea that nothing be found, soothly not a little
stone thereof. (And if he entereth into any city, all Israel
shall surround that city with ropes, and we shall draw it
into the stream, yea so that nothing be found of it, truly
not even a little stone of it.)
14 And Absalom said, and all the men of Israel, The
counsel of Hushai of Archi is better than the counsel of
Ahithophel; and the profitable counsel of Ahithophel was
destroyed by God's will, that the Lord should bring in
evil on Absalom. (And Absalom, and all the men of
Israel, said, Hushai the Archite's advice is better than
Ahithophel's; and so Ahithophel's good advice was
destroyed by God's will, so that the Lord could bring in
evil upon Absalom.)
15 And Hushai said to Zadok and to Abiathar, the
priests, Ahithophel gave counsel to Absalom, and to the
elder men of Israel in this and this manner, and I gave
such and such counsel.
16 Now therefore send ye soon, and tell ye to David,
and say ye, Dwell thou not this night in [the] field places
of the desert, but pass thou [over] without delay; lest
peradventure the king be swallowed up, and all the
people that is with him. (And so now send ye to him
soon, and tell ye to David, Stay thou not this night at the
Fords, *or the crossings*, of the Wilderness, but cross thou
over the river without delay; lest perhaps the king be
swallowed up, and all the people who be with him.)
17 And Jonathan and Ahimaaz stood beside the well of
Rogel (And Jonathan and Ahimaaz were waiting at
Enrogel); (and) an handmaid went, and told to them, and
(then) they went forth to tell the message to king David;
for they might not be seen, neither (could) enter into the
city.
18 And a child saw them, and he showed *it* to
Absalom; and they entered with swift going into the
house of a man in Bahurim, that had a pit in his place,
and they went down into that pit. (But a boy saw them,
and he went and told Absalom; and going swiftly,
Jonathan and Ahimaaz entered into the house of a man in
Bahurim, who had a well at his place, and they went
down into that well.)

19 And a woman took, and spread abroad a covering
over the mouth of the pit, as (if) drying barley with the
peel taken away, and so the thing was hid. (And a
woman took, and spread out a covering over the mouth
of the well, and then put some peeled barley on top of it,
as if to dry it, and so they were hid.)
20 And when the servants of Absalom had come into
the house, they said to the woman, Where is Ahimaaz
and Jonathan? And the woman answered to them, They
passed (over) the river of waters, *that is, (over the) Jordan*.
And when they that sought them had not found them,
they turned again into Jerusalem (And so when the men
who sought them could not find them, they returned to
Jerusalem).
21 And when they had gone forth, they went up from
the pit; and they went, and told to king David, and said,
Rise ye up, and passeth soon (over) the flood, for
Ahithophel hath given such counsel against you. (And
when the men had gone, Ahimaaz and Jonathan went up
from the well; and they went, and said to King David,
Quickly rise ye up, and cross ye over the river, and *know
ye also* that Ahithophel hath spoken such and such a plan
against you.)
22 Therefore David rose up, and all the people that was
with him, and they passed (over) Jordan, till it was clear
day, before that the word was published; and soothly not
one was left, that passed not (over) the flood. (And so
David, and all the people who were with him, rose up,
and they crossed the Jordan River before anyone knew it;
and by daylight, everyone had crossed over the river.)
23 And Ahithophel saw, that his counsel was not done,
and he saddled his ass, and rose up, and went into his
house, and into his city; and when his house was
disposed, he perished by hanging himself, and he was
buried in the sepulchre of his father. (And Ahithophel
saw that his advice was not followed, and so he saddled
up his donkey, and went back to his house in his city;
and after his affairs were in order, he hanged himself, and
he was buried in his father's tomb, *or his grave*.)
24 And David came into the castles, and Absalom
passed [over] Jordan, he and all the men of Israel with
him. (And as David came to Mahanaim, Absalom, and all
the men of Israel who were with him, crossed over the
Jordan River.)
25 And Absalom ordained Amasa for Joab upon *his*
host; and Amasa was the son of a man that was called
Ithra of Jezreel, the which entered to Abigail, the
daughter of Nahash, (and) the sister of Zeruiah, that was
the mother of Joab. (And Absalom ordained Amasa upon
his army, in Joab's place; and Amasa was the son of a
man called Ithra, an Ishmaelite, who entered in to
Abigail, who was Nahash's daughter, and Zeruiah's sister,
Joab's mother.)
26 And Israel setted tents with Absalom in the land of
Gilead.
27 And when David had come into the castles (And
when David had come to Mahanaim), Shobi, the son of
Nahash of Rabbah, of the sons of Ammon, and Machir,
the son of Ammiel, of Lodebar, and Barzillai, of Gilead,
of Rogelim,
28 brought to him beddings, and tapets (brought him
bedding, and blankets), and earthen vessels, and wheat,
and barley, and meal, and flour, and beans, and
lentils/vetches, and fried chick(pea)s,
29 and honey, and butter, and sheep, and fat calves.
And they gave *those* to David, and to the people that
were with him, to eat; for they supposed the people to be
made faint for hunger and thirst in desert (for they knew
that the people would be made hungry and thirsty in the
wilderness).

CHAPTER 18

1 Therefore David, when he had beheld his people,
ordained chieftains of thousands, and (chieftains) of
hundreds upon them.
2 And he gave the third part of the people under the
hand of Joab; and the third part under the hand of
Abishai, the son of Zeruiah, the brother of Joab; and the
third part under the hand of Ittai, that was of Gath. And
the king said to the people, Also I shall go out with you.
(And he sent out a third part of the people under Joab's
command; and a third part under Abishai, the son of
Zeruiah, Joab's brother; and a third part under Ittai the
Gittite. And the king said to the people, And I shall go
out with all of you.)
3 And the people answered, Thou shalt not go out; for
whether we flee, it shall not pertain to them by great
work of us; whether half the part fall down of us, they
shall not reckon (it) enough, for thou art reckoned for ten
thousand; therefore it is better, that thou be to us in the
city in strong succour. (And the people answered, Thou
shalt not go out with us; for if we flee, it shall not pertain
to them to make any great effort against us; and even if
half of us shall fall down, *or shall die*, they shall not
reckon it enough/they shall not reckon it much, for thou
art reckoned for ten thousand; and so it is better for us, if
thou be in the city, and support us from here.)
4 And the king said to them, I shall do that, that
seemeth rightful to you. Therefore the king stood beside
the gate, and the people went out by their companies, by
hundreds, and by thousands.
5 And the king commanded to Joab, and to Abishai,
and to Ittai, and said, Keep ye to me the child Absalom.
And all the people heard the king commanding to all the
princes for Absalom. (And the king commanded to Joab,
and Abishai, and Ittai, and said, For my sake, do not ye
harm the young man Absalom. And all the people heard
the king commanding to all his officers about Absalom.)

6 Therefore the people went out into the field against
Israel; and the battle was made in the forest of Ephraim.
7 And the people of Israel was slain there of the host
of David, and a great slaughter of twenty thousand was
made in that day. (And many Israelites were killed there
by David's army, yea, there was a great slaughter of
twenty thousand that day.)
8 And the battle was scattered there upon the face of
all the land, and many more were of the people which
the forest wasted, than they which the sword devoured in
that day. (And the battle there was scattered over all the
countryside, and the forest killed many more people that
day, than they whom the sword devoured.)
9 Soothly it befelled, that Absalom, sitting on a mule,
came against the servants of David; and when the mule
had entered under a thick oak, and great, the head of
Absalom cleaved to the oak; and when he was hanged
betwixt heaven and earth, the mule, on which he sat,
passed (forth). (And it befell, that Absalom, sitting on a
mule, came toward David's men; and when the mule had
entered under a great thick oak, Absalom's head got
caught in the branches; and while he hung in the air
above the ground, the mule, on which he sat, went forth.)
10 And some man saw this, and told it to Joab, and
said, I saw Absalom hanged on an oak (and said, I saw
Absalom hung up in an oak).
11 And Joab said to the man that told to him, If thou
saw *him*, why piercedest thou not him through to the
earth, and I should have given to thee ten shekels of
silver, and a girdle? (And Joab said to the man who told
him this, If thou saw *him thus*, why didest thou not
pierce him through to the ground, and then I would have
gladly given thee ten silver shekels, and a girdle.)
12 And he said to Joab, Though thou paidest in mine
hands a thousand pieces of silver, I would not send mine
hand into the son of the king; for while we heard, the
king commanded to thee, and to Abishai, and to Ittai, and
said, Keep ye to me the child Absalom. (And he said to
Joab, Though thou paidest me a thousand pieces of silver,
I would not raise my hand against the king's son; for
while we heard, the king commanded to thee, and to
Abishai, and to Ittai, and said, For my sake, do not ye
harm the young man Absalom.)
13 But and though I had done fool hardily against my
life (But if I had acted so foolishly against my own life),
this might not be hid from the king, and thou wouldest
stand on the contrary side.
14 And Joab said, Not as thou wilt, but I shall assail
him before thee. Therefore Joab took three spears in his
hand, and fixed those in(to) the heart of Absalom. And
when he sprawled, yet cleaving in the oak (And yet while
he sprawled, still caught up in the oak),
15 ten young squires of Joab ran, and smote, and killed
him. (ten young squires of Joab ran over to him, and
struck, *or stabbed*, and killed him.)
16 And Joab trumped with a clarion, and held with him
the people, lest it pursued Israel fleeing, and he would
spare the multitude. (And then Joab sounded with a
trumpet, to hold back the army with him, lest they
pursued the men of Israel fleeing away, for he would
spare the multitude.)
17 And they took Absalom, and casted forth him into a
great ditch in the forest, and bare together a full great
heap of stones on him; and all Israel fled into their
tabernacles. (And they took Absalom's body, and threw it
forth into a great ditch in the forest, and put a great heap
of stones on it; and all Israel fled back to their homes.)
18 Forsooth Absalom, while he lived yet, had raised to
him a memorial, which is in the valley of the king; for he
said, I have no son, and this shall be the mind of my
name; and he called the memorial by his name, and it is
called The Hand, *that is, (the) Work*, of Absalom, till to
this day. (And Absalom, while yet he lived, had raised up
a memorial to himself, in the King's Valley; for he said, I
have no son, and this shall be in remembrance of my
name; and he called the memorial after his own name,
and unto this day it is still called The Work of Absalom.)
19 And Ahimaaz, the son of Zadok, said, I shall run,
and I shall tell to the king, that the Lord hath made doom
to him of the hand of his enemies. (And Ahimaaz, the son
of Zadok, said, I shall run, and I shall tell the king, that
the Lord hath made judgement for him, *that is, hath
avenged him*, upon his enemies.)
20 To whom Joab said, Thou shalt not be a messenger
in this day, but thou shalt tell in another day; I will not
that thou tell this today, for the son of the king is dead (I
do not desire that thou tell this news today, for the king's
son is dead).
21 And Joab said to Cushi, Go thou, and tell to the king
those things that thou hast seen. Cushi worshipped Joab,
and ran forth (Cushi bowed to Joab, and ran off).
22 And again Ahimaaz, the son of Zadok, said to Joab,
What hindereth, if also I run after Cushi? And Joab said
to him, What wilt thou run, my son? Come thou hither,
thou shalt not be a bearer of good message (And Joab
said to him, Why would thou run, my son? It is better to
stay here, for thou shalt not be a bearer of good news).
23 The which answered, But what if I shall run? And
Joab said to him, Run thou. Therefore Ahimaaz ran by
the way of shortness, and speed, and passed Cushi.
24 And David sat betwixt (the) two gates; soothly the
espyer, that was in the highness of the gate on the wall,
raised up his eyes, and he saw a man alone running;
(And David sat between the two gates of the city; and the
watchman, who was on the roof of the gate by the wall,
raised up his eyes, and he saw a man running alone;)
25 and the espyer cried, and showed to the king. And
the king said to him, If he is alone, good message is in his

mouth. But while he hasted, and nighed near, (and the
watchman cried aloud, and told the king. And the king
said to himself, If he is alone, then he hath good news.
But while he hastened, and drew near,)
26 the espyer saw another man running; and the espyer
cried on high, and said, Another man running alone
appeareth to me. And the king said to him, And this man
is a good messenger. (the watchman saw another man
running; and the watchman cried out on high, and said,
Another man also running alone appeareth to me. And
the king said to himself, This man must also have good
news.)
27 Soothly the espyer said (And the watchman said), I
behold the running of the former, as the running of
Ahimaaz, the son of Zadok. And the king said, He is a
good man, and he cometh bringing a good message.
28 And Ahimaaz cried, and said to the king, Hail king!
And he worshipped the king lowly before him to the
earth, and said, Blessed be thy Lord God, that hath closed
together the men, that raised their hands against my lord
the king. (And Ahimaaz cried out, and said to the king,
Hail king! And honouring the king, he bowed low to the
ground before him, and said, Blessed be the Lord thy
God, who hath given thee victory over the men who
raised up their hands, *that is, who rebelled*, against my
lord the king.)
29 And the king said, Whether peace is to the child
Absalom? And Ahimaaz said, I saw, *that is, I heard*, a
great noise, when Joab, thy servant, thou king, sent me,
thy servant; I know none other thing. (And the king said,
Is all well with the young man Absalom? And Ahimaaz
said, I saw a great tumult/I heard a great noise, when thy
servant Joab, O king, sent me, thy servant; I know
nothing else.)
30 To whom the king said, Pass thou, and stand here.
And when he had passed, and stood, (To whom the king
said, Stand thou over there. And when he had stepped
aside, and stood in silence,)
31 Cushi appeared; and he came and said, My lord the
king, I bring good message; for the Lord hath deemed
today for thee of the hand of all men that rised against
thee. (Cushi appeared; and he came and said, My lord
the king, I bring good news; for the Lord hath given thee
victory today over all the men who rebelled against thee.)
32 And the king said to Cushi, Whether peace is to the
child Absalom? To whom Cushi answered, and said, The
enemies of my lord the king, and all men that rise against
him into evil, be made as the child. (And the king said to
Cushi, Is all well with the young man Absalom? To
whom Cushi answered, May all the enemies of my lord
the king, and all the men who rebel against him, be made
like that young man!)
33 Therefore the king was sorry, and went up into the
solar of the gate, and he wept, and spake thus going (And
so the king was deeply grieved, and went up to the roof
of the gate, and as he went, he wept, and spoke thus), My
son, Absalom! Absalom, my son! who giveth to me, that I
die for thee? Absalom, my son! my son, Absalom!

CHAPTER 19

1 Forsooth it was told to Joab, that the king wept, and
bewailed his son;
2 and the victory in that day was turned into mourning
to all the people; for the people heard, that it was said in
that day, The king maketh sorrow on his son. (and so the
victory that day was turned into mourning for all the
people; for the people heard, that it was said that day,
The king sorroweth for his son.)
3 And the people eschewed to enter into the city in
that day, as the people turned and fleeing from [the]
battle is wont to bow away. (And the people entered into
the city on that day in shameful quiet, like the people
who turned, and fled away from a battle, be wont to go.)
4 And the king covered his head, and cried with great
voice (and cried with a loud voice), My son, Absalom!
Absalom, my son!
5 Therefore Joab entered to the king into the house,
and said, Thou hast shamed today the cheers of all thy
servants, that have made safe thy life, and the life of thy
sons and of thy daughters, and the life of thy wives, and
the life of thy secondary wives. (And so Joab entered into
the palace, and said to the king, Today thou hast brought
shame upon all of thy servants who have made thy life
safe, and also upon the lives of thy sons and thy
daughters, and thy wives, and thy secondary wives, *or
thy concubines*.)
6 Thou lovest them that hate thee, and thou hatest
them that love thee; and thou hast showed today that
thou reckest not of thy dukes and of thy servants; and
verily I have known now, that if Absalom lived, and all
we had been dead, then it should please thee. (Thou
lovest them who hate thee, and thou hatest them who
love thee; and thou hast shown today that thou carest not
for thy leaders or for thy men; and now I truly know, that
if Absalom had lived, and all of us had died, it would
have pleased thee.)
7 Now therefore rise up, and go thou forth, and speak
thou, and make satisfaction to thy servants; for I swear to
thee by the Lord, that if thou shalt not go forth, soothly
not one man shall dwell with thee in this night; and this
shall be worse to thee, than all the evils that came [up]on
thee from thy young waxing age till into *this* present
time. (And so now rise up, and go thou out, and speak
thou, and give satisfaction to thy men; for I swear by the
Lord to thee, that if thou shalt not go out to them, truly
not one man shall stay with thee through this night; and
this shall be worse for thee, than all the evil that hath come
upon thee from thy youngest age unto *this* present time.)

8 Therefore the king rose up, and sat in the gate; and it
was told to all the people, that the king sat in the gate,
and all the multitude came before the king. Forsooth
Israel fled into their tabernacles (Meanwhile all the
Israelites had fled to their homes).
9 And all the people strived in all the lineages of
Israel, and said, The king delivered us from the hand of
all our enemies, and he saved us from the hand of
Philistines; and now he hath fled from the land for
Absalom (and now he hath fled from the land because of
Absalom).
10 Certainly Absalom, whom we anointed upon us, is
dead in battle; how long be ye still, and bring not again
the king? (how long shall ye be silent, and not bring back
the king?) And the counsel of all Israel came to the king.
11 And king David sent to Zadok and to Abiathar, the
priests, and said, Speak ye to the greater men in birth of
Judah, and say ye, Why came ye the last to bring again
the king into his house? Soothly the word of all Israel
came to the king, that they would bring him again into
his house. For the king said, Ye shall say these things to
the people, (And King David sent word to Zadok and
Abiathar, the priests, and said, Speak ye to the men of
great age, *that is, to the elders,* of Judah, and say ye, Why
be ye the last to help bring back the king to his palace?
Truly the word of all Israel had come to the king, that
they would bring him back to his palace. And so the
king said, Ye shall say these things to the elders,)
12 Ye be my brethren, ye be my bone and my flesh;
why the last bring ye again the king? (Ye be my kinsmen,
ye be my flesh and blood; so why be ye the last to bring
back the king?)
13 And say ye to Amasa, Whether thou art not my bone
and my flesh? God do these things to me, and add these
things too, if thou shalt not be master of chivalry (if thou
shalt not be the leader of the cavalry, *or of the army*),
before me in all time after Joab.
14 And David bowed *to him* the heart of all [the] men
of Judah as of one man; and they sent to the king, and
said, Turn thou again, and all thy servants. (And so David
turned *to himself* the hearts of all the men of Judah as if
one man; and they sent word to the king, and said, Come
thou back again with all thy men.)
15 And the king turned again, and came till to Jordan
(And so the king returned, and came to the Jordan River);
and all Judah came till into Gilgal to meet the king, and
to lead him over (the) Jordan.
16 But Shimei, the son of Gera, the son of Benjamin, of
Bahurim, hasted, and came down with the men of Judah
into the meeting of king David, (And Shimei, the son of
Gera, the son of Benjamin, hastened from Bahurim, and
came down with the men of Judah to meet King David,)
17 with a thousand men of Benjamin; and Ziba, the
servant of the house of Saul, and (the) fifteen sons of him,
and (his) twenty servants were with him; and they brake
into (the) Jordan, before the king (and they went over the
Jordan River before the king),
18 and they passed the fords, that they should lead over
the house of the king, and do by the behest of the king.
Soothly Shimei, the son of Gera, kneeled before the king,
when he had passed now Jordan, (and they passed over
the crossing, in order to bring over the king's household,
and to do whatever the king commanded. And Shimei,
the son of Gera, kneeled before the king, when he had
crossed over the Jordan River,)
19 and said to the king, My lord the king, areckon thou
not wickedness to me, neither have thou mind of the
wrongs of thy servant in the day (nor remember the
wrongs of thy servant on the day), in which thou, my lord
the king, wentest out of Jerusalem, neither set thou, king,
those wrongs in thine heart;
20 for I thy servant acknowledge my sin; and therefore
today I came the first of all the house of Joseph, and I
came down into the meeting of my lord the king (and I
came down to meet my lord the king).
21 And Abishai, the son of Zeruiah, answered and said,
Whether Shimei, that cursed the christ of the Lord, shall
not be slain for these words? (And Abishai, the son of
Zeruiah, answered to him and said, Should not Shimei,
who cursed the Lord's anointed, be killed for those
words?)
22 And David said, What is (it) to me and to you, ye
sons of Zeruiah? Why be ye made to me today into
Satan, *that is, (an) adversary*? Therefore whether a man
shall be slain today in Israel? Whether I know not (that)
me (am) made king today on Israel? (And David said,
What is it to me or to you, ye sons of Zeruiah? Why be ye
made into my adversaries today? Should any man be put
to death on this day in Israel? The day that I am made
king upon Israel? Nay!)
23 And the king said to Shimei, Thou shalt not die; and
the king swore to him.
24 Also Mephibosheth, the son of Saul, came down
with unwashed feet, and with his beard unclipped, into
the coming of the king. And Mephibosheth had not
washed his clothes, from the day in which the king went
out of Jerusalem till to the day of his coming again in
peace. (And Mephibosheth, Saul's son, came down with
unwashed feet, and with his beard unclipped, to meet the
king. And Mephibosheth had not washed his clothes
from the day in which the king went out of Jerusalem
until the day that he returned in victory/until the day that
he safely returned home.)
25 And when at Jerusalem he had come to the king
(And when he had come from Jerusalem to meet the
king), the king said to him, Mephibosheth, why camest
thou not with me?
26 And he answered and said, My lord the king, my

servant despised me; and I thy servant said to him, that
he should saddle the ass to me, and I should ascend, and
I should go with the king; for I thy servant am crooked.
(And he answered, My lord the king, my servant
deceived me; for I thy servant had said to him, that he
should saddle up the donkey for me, and then I would
get on it, and I would go with the king; for I thy servant
am crippled.)
27 Moreover and he accused me, thy servant, to thee,
my lord the king; but thou, my lord the king, art as the
angel of God; do thou that, that is pleasant to thee. (And
moreover he hath accused me, thy servant, to thee, my
lord the king; but thou, my lord the king, art like the
angel of God to me; so do thou what is pleasing to thee.)
28 For the house of my father was not no but guilty of
death to my lord the king; soothly thou hast set me thy
servant among the guests of thy board; what therefore
have I of just complaint, either (of) what may I more cry
to the king? (For my father's family was guilty of death
before my lord the king; but thou hast put me thy servant
among the guests at thy table; so what right have I of any
complaint, or what more may I ask for from the king?)
29 And the king said to him, What speakest thou more?
that that I have spoken is steadfast; thou and Ziba part the
possessions. (And the king said to him, Why sayest thou
anything more? my decision is final; thou and Ziba will
share the possessions.)
30 And Mephibosheth answered to the king, Yea, take
he all things, after that my lord the king turned again
peaceably into his house (now that my lord the king hath
returned home in victory/now that my lord the king hath
safely returned home).
31 Also Barzillai of Gilead, a full eld man, came down
from Rogelim, and led the king over Jordan, ready also to
follow him over the flood. (And Barzillai of Gilead, a very
old man, came down from Rogelim, and joined in
escorting the king over the Jordan River.)
32 And Barzillai of Gilead was full eld, that is, of
fourscore years; and he gave meats to the king, when the
king dwelled in castles; for Barzillai was a full rich man.
(And Barzillai of Gilead was very old, that is, eighty years
old; and he gave food to the king, when the king lived at
Mahanaim; for Barzillai was a very rich man.)
33 And so the king said to Barzillai, Come thou with
me, that thou rest securely with me in Jerusalem. (And so
the king said to Barzillai, Come thou with me, so that
thou can have a peaceful life there in Jerusalem with me.)
34 And Barzillai said to the king, How many (more) be
the days of [the] years of my life, that I (should) go up
with the king into Jerusalem?
35 I am of fourscore years today; whether my wits be
quick to deem sweet thing either bitter, either meat and
drink may delight thy servant, either may I hear more the
voice of singers either of singsters? Why is thy servant to
(be a) charge to my lord the king? (I am eighty years old
now; can my wits still judge a thing bitter or sweet? or
can food and drink still delight thy servant? or can I still
hear the voice of singers and singsters? No! So why
should thy servant be a burden to my lord the king?)
36 I thy servant shall go forth a little from (the) Jordan
with thee, I have no need to this yielding; (I thy servant
shall go forth a little from the Jordan River with thee, but I
have no need for this reward;)
37 but I beseech *thee*, that I thy servant turn again, and
die in my city, and be buried beside the sepulchre of my
father and of my mother; forsooth (my son) Chimham is
thy servant, my lord the king, (so) go he with thee, and
do thou to him that that seemeth good to thee.
38 Therefore the king said to Barzillai, Chimham (shall)
go forth with me; and I shall do to him whatever thing
pleaseth thee (and I shall do for him whatever pleaseth
thee), and thou shalt get all thing, that thou askest of me.
39 And when all the people and the king had passed
[over] Jordan, the king abode; and the king kissed
Barzillai, and blessed him; and he turned again into his
place. (And when the king and all the people had crossed
over the Jordan River, the king stopped there; and he
kissed Barzillai, and blessed him; and then Barzillai
returned to his home.)
40 Then the king passed forth into Gilgal, and
Chimham (was) with him. And all the people of Judah
had led the king over, and the half part only of the people
of Israel was present (and also half the people of Israel).
41 Therefore all the men of Israel came together to the
king, and said to him, Why have our brethren, the men of
Judah, stolen thee, and have led the king and his house
over Jordan, and all the men of David with him? (And so
all the men of Israel who were there came together to the
king, and said to him, Why have our brothers, the men of
Judah, stolen thee away, and have led the king, and his
household, and all the men of David with him, over the
Jordan River?)
42 And each man of Judah answered to the men of
Israel, (and said,) For the king is near (of kin) to me (For
the king is our next of kin); why art thou wroth upon this
thing? Whether we have eaten anything of the king('s),
either gifts be given to us?
43 And a man of Israel answered to the men of Judah,
and said, I am greater by ten parts to the king, and David
pertaineth more to me than to thee; why hast thou done
wrong to me, and it was not told to me the former, that I
should bring again my king? Forsooth the men of Judah
answered harder to the men of Israel. (And the men of
Israel answered to the men of Judah, and said, We have a
greater stake in the king by ten parts, and David
pertaineth more to us than to thee; why hast thou done
us this wrong? were we not the first to say that we should
bring back our king? But the men of Judah answered

back even harder to the men of Israel.)

CHAPTER 20

1 Also it befelled, that a man of Belial was there,
Sheba by name, the son of Bichri, a man of the
generation of Benjamin; and he sounded with a trump,
and said, No part is to us in David, neither heritage in the
son of Jesse; thou Israel, turn again into thy tabernacles.
(And it befell, that a man of Belial was there, named
Sheba, the son of Bichri, a man of the tribe of Benjamin;
and he sounded with a trumpet, and said, There is no
part for us with David, nor inheritance with the son of
Jesse; O Israel, return to thy homes!)
2 And all Israel was parted from David, and followed
Sheba, the son of Bichri; and the men of Judah cleaved to
their king, from Jordan till to Jerusalem. (And so all Israel
deserted David, and followed Sheba, the son of Bichri;
but the men of Judah cleaved to their king, from the
Jordan River unto Jerusalem.)
3 And when the king had come into his house in
Jerusalem, he took [the] ten women, his secondary wives,
which he had left to keep the house, and he betook them
into keeping, and gave meat to them; and he entered not
[in] to them; but they were closed (up) till to the day of
their death, and lived in widowhood. (And when the king
had come to his palace in Jerusalem, he took his
secondary wives, the ten women whom he had left in
charge of the palace, and he put them under guard, and
gave them food; but he did not sleep with them any
more; and they were enclosed until the day of their
death, and lived in widowhood.)
4 And David said to Amasa, Call thou together to me
all the men of Judah into the third day, and be thou
present. (And David said to Amasa, Call thou together for
me all the men of Judah in three days' time, and be thou
present with them.)
5 Therefore Amasa went forth, that he call together the
people of Judah; and he dwelled over the covenanted
time, which the king had set to him. (And so Amasa went
out to call together the people of Judah; but he took more
time to arrange matters than what the king had set for him.)
6 And (so) David said to Abishai, Now Sheba, the son
of Bichri, shall torment us (even) more than Absalom *did*;
therefore take the servants of thy lord (and so take my
bodyguards), and pursue him, lest in hap he find
strengthened, (or fortified,) cities, and escape us.
7 Therefore the men of Joab went out with Abishai,
and (the) Cherethites and Pelethites, and all the strong
men, (and they) went out of Jerusalem to pursue Sheba,
the son of Bichri.
8 And when they were beside the great stone, which
is in Gibeon, Amasa came, and ran to them; and Joab
was clothed with a strait coat at the measure of his shape,
and he was girded above with a sword hanging down unto
his entrails in a sheath; and it went out, and felled down.
(And when they were beside the great stone, which is in
Gibeon, Amasa came over to them; and Joab was clothed
with a narrow coat tight to his body, and he was girded
with a sword in a sheath hanging down to his entrails; and
as Amasa came over, it fell out/he secretly took it out.)
9 And so Joab said to Amasa, Hail, my brother! And
Joab held with his right hand the chin of Amasa, as
kissing him (And Joab held Amasa's chin with his right
hand, as if to kiss him).
10 Forsooth Amasa took not keep of the sword, which
sword Joab had, and Joab smote Amasa in the side, and
shedded out his entrails into the earth, and Amasa was
dead; and Joab added not the second wound. And (then)
Joab, and Abishai, his brother, pursued Sheba, the son of
Bichri. (But Amasa was not on guard for the sword which
Joab had, and *suddenly* Joab struck, *or stabbed*, Amasa in
the side with it, and poured out his entrails onto the
ground, and so Amasa died; and Joab did not need to add
a second wound. And then Joab, and his brother
Abishai, pursued Sheba, the son of Bichri.)
11 In the meantime, when some of the children of
David, of the fellows of Joab, had stood beside the dead
body of Amasa, they said, Lo! he that would be the
fellow of David, (be) for Joab. (In the meantime, one of
Joab's young men stood beside Amasa's dead body, and
he said, Lo! he who would be the fellow of Joab and of
David, follow he Joab!)
12 And Amasa was besprinkled with blood, and lay in
the middle of the way. Some man saw this/A man saw
this, that all the people abode to see Amasa, and he
removed Amasa from the way into the field, and he
covered Amasa with a cloth, lest men passing should
abide [still] for him. (And Amasa was covered with blood,
and lay in the middle of the road. And some man saw
that all the people stood about looking at Amasa, and so
he moved Amasa's body from the road to a nearby field,
and he covered it with a cloak, lest men passing by
should stand there, and gawk at him.)
13 Therefore when he was removed from the way, each
man passed forth, following Joab to pursue Sheba, the
son of Bichri.
14 Forsooth Sheba had passed by all the lineages of
Israel till into Abel, and into Bethmaachah; and all the
chosen men were gathered to him. (And Sheba passed
through *the territories of* all the tribes of Israel unto Abel
of Bethmaachah; and all the men of Bichri/and all the
Berites were gathered to him, and followed him.)
15 Therefore they came, and fought against him in
Abel, and in Bethmaachah, and (en)compassed the city
with strongholds; and the city was besieged. And all the
company, that was with Joab, enforced to destroy the
walls. (And then Joab and his men came, and fought
against him in Abel of Bethmaachah, and surrounded the

city with strongholds; and the city was besieged. And all
the men who were with Joab endeavoured to destroy the
walls.)
16 And a wise woman of the city cried (out from) on
high, Hear ye! hear ye! say ye to Joab, Nigh thou hither
(Come thou here), and I shall speak with thee.
17 And when he had nighed to her, she said to him, Art
thou Joab? And he answered, I am. To whom she spake
thus, Hear thou the words of thine handmaid. Joab
answered, I hear (And Joab answered, I am listening).
18 And again she said, A word was said in (an) eld
proverb, They that ask, ask in Abel; and so they profited.
19 Whether I am not, that answer truth to Israel? and
seekest thou to destroy a city, and to do away a mother
city in Israel?[6] why castedest thou down/why throwest
thou down the heritage of the Lord? (My city is one of the
most peaceful, and faithful, in all of Israel; so why seekest
thou to destroy such a city, and to do away such a mother
in Israel? why throwest thou down the Lord's inheritance?)
20 And Joab answered, and said, Far be (this), far be
this from me; I cast not down, neither I destroy (I do not
want to destroy *this city*).
21 The thing hath not so itself; but a man of the hill of
Ephraim, Sheba, the son of Bichri, by surname, raised his
hand against king David; betake ye him alone *to us*, and
we shall go away from the city (That is not my goal; but a
man named Sheba, the son of Bichri, of the hill country
of Ephraim, raised a rebellion against King David; deliver
ye him *to us*, and him alone, and we shall go away from
your city). And the woman said to Joab, Lo! his head
shall be sent to thee by the wall.
22 Then the woman went in to all the people, and she
spake to them wisely; and they threw (out) to Joab the
head of Sheba, the son of Bichri, girded off. And Joab
sounded with a trump, and they departed from the city,
each man into his tabernacles; and Joab turned again to
Jerusalem to the king. (Then the woman went to all the
people, and she spoke wisely to them; and so they cut off
the head of Sheba, the son of Bichri, and threw it out to
Joab. And then Joab sounded with a trumpet, and they
left the city, and each man went back to his home; and
Joab returned to the king in Jerusalem.)
23 Therefore Joab was on all the host of Israel; forsooth
Benaiah, [the] son of Jehoiada, was on Cherethites and
Pelethites; (And so Joab was over all of Israel's army; and
Benaiah, the son of Jehoiada, was over the Cherethites
and Pelethites;)
24 and Adoram was upon the tributes (and Adoram was
over the forced labour/was over the taxation); and
Jehoshaphat, the son of Ahilud, was (the) chancellor;
25 and Sheva was scribe; but Zadok and Abiathar were
priests; (and Sheva was the writer; and Zadok and
Abiathar were the priests;)
26 and Ira of Jairites was the priest of David.

CHAPTER 21

1 And hunger was made *in the land of Israel* in the
days of David, by three years continually. And David
counselled the answer of the Lord, *that is, asked counsel
of the Lord in the answering place*; and the Lord said, *It is*
for Saul, and for his house, and for [the] blood, for he
killed the men of Gibeon. (And in the days of David, there
was hunger *in the land of Israel*, for three years without
ceasing. And David counselled with the Lord; and the
Lord said, *It is* because Saul, and his family, were guilty
of the blood, *or of murder*, for he killed the Gibeonites.)
2 Therefore when [the] Gibeonites were called, the
king said to them; soothly Gibeonites be not of the sons
of Israel, *but they be* the relics of Amorites; and the sons
of Israel had sworn to them, *that they should not slay
them*, and Saul would smite them for (his) fervent love, as
for the sons of Israel and of Judah; (And so when the
Gibeonites were called, the king said to them; now the
Gibeonites be not Israelites, *but they be* the remnants of
the Amorites; and the Israelites had sworn to them, *that
they would not kill them*, but Saul did strike many of
them down in his fervent love for the people of Israel and
of Judah;)
3 therefore David said to Gibeonites, What shall I do
to you, and what shall be your amends, that ye bless the
heritage of the Lord? (and so David said to the
Gibeonites, What can I do for you? and what shall be
your amends, so that ye bless the Lord's inheritance, *that
is, his people*?)
4 And Gibeonites said to him, No question is to us
upon gold and silver, but against Saul, and against his
house; neither we will, that a man of Israel be slain. To
whom the king said, What therefore will ye, that I do to
you? (And the Gibeonites said to him, No answer shall be
for us in gold or silver, but rather with Saul and his
family; and we do not desire that just any man of Israel
be killed. To whom the king said, And so what do ye
desire, that I do for you?)
5 And they said to the king, We ought so to do away
the man, that defouled and oppressed us wickedly, that
not one soothly be left of his generation in all the coasts
of Israel. (And they said to the king, We want to
completely do away the man, who defiled and wickedly
oppressed us, so that truly not one of his generation be
left in all the coasts of Israel.)
6 Seven men of his sons be given to us, that we
crucify them to the Lord in Gibeah of Saul, sometime the
chosen man of the Lord. And the king said, I shall give

[6] The woman speaketh in the person of the city, as if she said, 'This city held ever truth and faith to the king'; and therefore in Hebrew it is thus, 'I am one of peaceable and true', that is, one of the number of cities (that be) peaceable and true to the king.

them to you. (Let seven of his kinsmen be given to us, so
that we can hang them before the Lord in Gibeah of Saul,
who was, at one time, the Lord's chosen man. And the
king said, I shall give them to you.)
7 And the king spared Mephibosheth (But the king
spared Mephibosheth), the son of Jonathan, the son of
Saul, for the oath of the Lord, that was betwixt David and
Jonathan, the son of Saul.
8 And so the king took (the) two sons of Rizpah, the
daughter of Aiah, which she childed to Saul, Armoni, and
(another) Mephibosheth; and *he took* [the] five sons of
Michal, the daughter of Saul (and *he took* the five sons of
Saul's daughter Merab), which she engendered to Adriel,
the son of Barzillai, that was of (the) Meholathites.
9 And he gave them (up) into the hands of (the)
Gibeonites, and they did those seven sons upon (a) cross
in an hill before the Lord (and they hanged those seven
kinsmen on a hill before the Lord); and (so) these seven
fell down slain together in the days of the first reap(ing),
when the reaping of barley began.
10 Forsooth Rizpah, (the) daughter of Aiah, took an
hair-shirt, and arrayed to herself *a place* above the
stone/and laid it under her(self) upon a stone (and arrayed
for herself *a place* on the rock where their bodies lay),
from the beginning of harvest till water dropped on them
from (the) heaven(s); and she suffered not (the) birds to
tear them by day, neither (the) beasts by night.
11 And those things which Rizpah, the secondary wife of
Saul, the daughter of Aiah, had done, were told to David.
12 And David went, and took the bones of Saul, and
the bones of Jonathan, his son, from the men of Jabesh of
Gilead; which had stolen those bones from the street of
Bethshan, in which Philistines had hanged them, when
they had slain Saul in Gilboa (for they had stolen those
bones from the street in Bethshan, where the Philistines
had hung them, after they had killed Saul at Gilboa).
13 And David bare out from thence the bones of Saul,
and the bones of Jonathan, his son; and they gathered the
bones of them that were crucified (and they also gathered
up the bones of the seven men who were hanged),
14 and they buried those with the bones of Saul and of
Jonathan, his son, in the land of Benjamin, in the side of
the sepulchre of Kish, the father of Saul (in the tomb, *or
the grave*, of Saul's father Kish). And they did all things,
whatever the king commanded *them*; and the Lord did
mercy to the land after these things.
15 Forsooth battle of the Philistines was made again
against Israel; and David went down, and his servants
with him, and fought against the Philistines. Soothly
when David failed, (And again the Philistines made battle
against Israel; and David and his men went down, and
fought against the Philistines. And when David grew
weary,)
16 Ishbibenob, that was of the kin of Harapha, *that is,
(the father) of the giants*, and the iron of his spear
weighed three hundred ounces, and he was girded with a
new sword, enforced to smite David. (Ishbibenob, who
was a descendant of Harapha, *that is, the father of the
giants*, whose iron of his spear weighed three hundred
ounces, and who was girded with a new sword,
endeavoured to strike down David.)
17 And Abishai, the son of Zeruiah, was in help to
David; and he smote and killed the Philistine. Then the
men of David swore, and said, Now thou shalt not go out
with us into battle, lest thou quench the lantern of Israel.
(But Abishai, the son of Zeruiah, helped David; and he
struck and killed the Philistine. And then the men of
David swore, and said, From now on, thou shalt not go
out with us into battle, lest thou quench Israel's lantern.)
18 Also the second battle was in Gob against [the]
Philistines; then Sibbechai of Hushathites smote Saph, of
the generation of Harapha, of the kin of giants. (And there
was a second battle against the Philistines at Gob; there
Sibbechai of the Hushathites struck down Saph, a
descendant of Harapha, that is, the father of the giants.)
19 Also the third battle was in Gob against [the]
Philistines; in which battle a man given of God, the son
of a forest, and a(n) (em)broiderer, a man of Bethlehem,
smote (the brother of) Goliath of Gath, whose spear shaft
was as a beam of webs. (And the third battle against the
Philistines was also at Gob; in which battle Elhanan, the
son of Jair/the son of Jaareoregim, a man of Bethlehem,
struck down *the brother of* Goliath of Gath, whose spear
shaft was like a weaver's beam.)
20 The fourth battle was in Gath; wherein was an high
man, that had six fingers in his hands and (six toes) in his
feet, that is, four and twenty (digits); and he was of the
kin of Harapha, (the father of the giants); (And the fourth
battle was at Gath; and there was a very tall man there,
who had six fingers on each hand, and six toes on each
foot, that is, twenty-four digits altogether; and he was a
descendant of Harapha, *that is, the father of the giants*;)
21 and he blasphemed Israel; and Jonathan, the son of
Shimeah, the brother of David, killed him.
22 These four were born of Harapha in Gath, and they
felled down in the hand of David, and of his servants.
(These four were descendants of Harapha of Gath, *that is,
the father of the giants*, and they all fell down at the
hands of David and his men.)

CHAPTER 22

1 Soothly David spake to the Lord the words of this
song, in the day in which the Lord delivered him from
the hand of all his enemies, and from the hand of Saul.
2 And David said, The Lord is my stone, and my
strength/and my stronghold, and my saviour;
3 my God, my strength, I shall hope into him; my
shield, and the horn of mine health, my raiser (up), and

my refuge; my saviour, thou shalt deliver me from
wickedness, *that is, (thou) hast delivered (me from
violence).* (my God, my strength/my stronghold, yea, I
have hope in him; my shield, and the horn of my
salvation, *or of my victory*, my raiser-up, and my refuge;
my saviour, thou hast delivered me from all violence.)
4 I shall inwardly call (upon) the Lord, worthy to be
praised; and I shall be safe from mine enemies. (I shall
call to the Lord, who is worthy to be praised; and I shall
be saved from my enemies.)
5 For the sorrows of death compassed me; the strands
of Belial made me afeared.
6 The cords of hell (en)compassed me; the snares of
death have gone before me. (The cords of hell
surrounded me; the snares of death were set to catch me.)
7 In tribulation I shall call thee, Lord, *that is, I have
called thee, Lord,* and I shall cry to my God; and he
heard from his holy temple my voice, and my cry shall
come to his ears. (In tribulation I called on thee, Lord,
yea, I cried to my God; and he heard my voice in his
holy Temple, and my cry came to his ears.)
8 The earth was moved, and trembled; the
foundaments of hills were smitten and shaken together,
for the Lord was wroth to them. (The earth was moved,
and trembled; the foundations of heaven were altogether
shaken, for the Lord was angry.)
9 Smoke went up from his nostrils, and fire of his
mouth shall devour; coals were kindled of it. (Smoke
went up from his nostrils, and devouring fire came out of
his mouth; coals were kindled by it.)
10 And he bowed (the) heavens, and came down; and
mist (was) under his feet.
11 And he went upon cherubim, and flew; and he slid
on the pens/on the feathers of the wind (and he went
upon the wings of the wind).
12 He put darkness (a) hiding place in his compass, and
riddled, or winnowed, waters from the clouds of
heavens; (He hid himself in darkness, and the clouds of
the heavens, which were filled with water, encompassed,
or surrounded, him;)
13 for brightness in his sight coals of fire were kindled.
(coals of fire were kindled from the brightness going out
before him.)
14 The Lord shall thunder from (the) heaven(s); and
[the] high *God* shall give his voice.
15 He sent his arrows, and scattered them; *and sent*
lightnings, and wasted them.
16 And the sheddings out of the sea appeared, and the
foundaments of the world were showed; from the
blaming of the Lord, from the breathing of the spirit of his
strong vengeance. (And the seabed appeared, and the
foundations of the world were uncovered; at the Lord's
rebuke, and at the blast of the breath of his nostrils.)
17 He sent from heaven, and took (hold of) me; and
drew me out of many waters.
18 He delivered me from my mightiest enemy, and
from them that hated me; for they were stronger than I.
19 They came before me in the day of my tormenting;
and the Lord was made my steadfastness.
20 And he led me out into largeness, and he delivered
me; for I pleased him. (And he led me out into a large
place, and he saved me; because he delighted in me.)
21 The Lord shall yield to me after my rightwiseness;
and he shall yield to me after the cleanness of mine hands.
22 For I [have] kept the ways of the Lord; and I did not
(turn) wickedly from my God. (For I have followed the
Lord's ways; and I have not wickedly turned from my
God.)
23 For all his dooms *were* in my sight; and I did not
away from me his behests. (For all his laws were before
me; and I did not turn away from his commands.)
24 And I shall be perfect with him (And I shall be
upright before him); and I shall keep me from my
wickedness.
25 And the Lord shall restore to me after my
rightwiseness; and after the cleanness of mine hands in
the sight of his eyes.
26 With the holy thou shalt be holy, and with the
strong, *that is, to suffer adversities patiently*, thou shalt be
perfect; (With the holy thou shalt be holy, and with the
upright, thou shalt be upright;)
27 and with a chosen man thou shalt be chosen, and
with a wayward man thou shalt be made wayward[7]. (and
with the pure, thou shalt be pure, but to the wicked, thou
shalt be hostile *to them*.)
28 And thou shalt make safe a poor people; and with
thine eyes thou shalt make low them that be high. (And
thou shalt save the poor; and thou shalt humble those
who be high in their own eyes/and thou shalt look with
contempt upon the proud.)
29 For thou, Lord, art my lantern, and thou, Lord, shalt
lighten my darkness.
30 For I girded, *that is, made ready to battle*, shall run
in thee, *that is, in thy strength*; and in my God I shall skip
over the wall. (For when I am girded, *that is, made ready
for battle*, I shall run by thy strength; and so, with God's
help, I shall leap over the wall.)
31 God, his way is without wem; the speech of the
Lord is examined with fire, *that is, is (as) pure and clean
as metal proved in the furnace*; he is a shield of all men
hoping in him. (As for God, his way is without fault; the
word of the Lord is examined with fire, *that is, is as pure
and clean as metal proved in the furnace*; he is a shield

[7] *For when wayward men be justly punished of God, they say that God doeth waywardly with them.* (*For when wicked men be justly punished by God, they say that God doeth wickedly to them.*)

for all men hoping in him.)
32 For who is God, except the Lord; and who is strong,
except our God?
33 God, that hath girded me with strength, and hath
made plane my perfect way; (Yea, God, who hath girded
me with strength, and hath made my way perfect, *or
without blame*;)
34 and he hath made even my feet with harts' (feet),
and hath set me upon mine high things; (and he hath
made my feet like the feet of a hart, *or of a deer*, and hath
set me on high places, *that is, on the mountains*;)
35 and he taught mine hands to battle, and a brassen
bow was granted to mine arm(s). (and he taught my hands
in battle, and now my arms can break a bronze bow.)
36 Thou hast given to me the shield of thine health;
and thy mildness hath multiplied me. (Thou hast given
me the shield of thy salvation; and thy gentleness hath
made me great.)
37 Thou shalt alarge my steps under me; and mine
heels shall not fail. (Thou hast broadened my steps under
me; and my feet have not slipped.)
38 I shall pursue mine enemies, and I shall all-brake
them; and I shall not turn again, till I waste them (and I
shall not return, until I destroy them).
39 I shall waste them, and I shall break *them*, that they
rise not; they shall fall under my feet. (I shall break them,
and I shall destroy *them*, so that they shall not rise again;
they shall all fall under my feet.)
40 Thou hast girded me with strength to battle; thou
hast bowed under me them that stood against me. (Thou
hast girded me with strength for the battle; thou hast put
those who stood against me under me.)
41 Thou hast given mine enemies' aback to me, men
hating me; and I shall destroy them. (Thou hast given me
the backs of my enemies; and I destroy those who hate
me.)
42 They shall cry, *that is, to idols either to men's help*,
and none shall be that shall save *them*; *they shall* cry to
the Lord, and he shall not hear them. (They cry *to their
idols, or to men, for help*, but no one can save them; they
cry to the Lord, but he will not answer them.)
43 I shall do away them as the dust of [the] earth; I shall
pound them, and I shall do [them] away as the clay, or
the fen, of streets. (I shall do them away like the dust of
the earth; I shall pound them, and I shall do them away
like the fen, or the clay, of the streets.)
44 Thou shalt save me from [the] against-sayings of my
people; thou shalt keep me into the head of folks (thou
shalt make me the head of the nations/thou shalt keep me
the head of the nations); the people, whom I know not,
shall serve me.
45 Alien sons shall (not) against-stand me; by hearing of
[the] ear, they shall obey to me. (The sons of foreigners
shall bow low to me; and after hearing me, they shall
obey me.)
46 Alien sons floated away; and they shall be drawn
together in their enclosings. (*The courage of* the sons of
foreigners shall fade away; and they shall slink out of
their strongholds together.)
47 The Lord liveth, and my God is blessed; and the
strong God of mine health shall be enhanced. (The Lord
liveth, and blessed is my God; yea, the strong God of my
salvation shall be exalted.)
48 God, that givest vengeances to me, and hast cast
down peoples under me. (The God, who grantest me
vengeance, and hast thrown down peoples, *or nations*,
under me.)
49 Which leadest me out from mine enemies, and
raisest me from men against-standing me; thou shalt
deliver me from the wicked man. (Who leadest me out
from my enemies, and raisest me up from those who
stand against me; yea, thou shalt deliver me from violent
people.)
50 Therefore, Lord, I shall acknowledge to thee in
heathen men; and I shall sing to thy name. (And so, Lord,
I shall praise thee before the heathen; and I shall sing
praises to thy name.)
51 That he maketh great the healths of his king; and
doeth mercy to his christ, David, and to his seed till into
without end. (Yea, he who maketh the great victories of
his king; and who doeth mercy to his anointed, yea, to
David, and to his descendants forevermore.)

CHAPTER 23

1 Forsooth these be the last words, which David, the
son of Jesse, said. (The words that) The man said, to
whom it is ordained of Christ, of the God of Jacob, the
noble psalm-maker of Israel; (These be the last words
which David, the son of Jesse, said. The words that the
man to whom it was ordained to be the anointed of the
God of Jacob, the noble psalm-maker of Israel, yea, the
last words that he said;)
2 The spirit of the Lord spake by me, and his word by
my tongue.
3 *David* said, God of Israel spake to me, the strong
help of Israel, the just Lord of men, *is* Lord in the dread of
God. (The God of Israel spoke, the Strong One of Israel
said to me, The lord, *or the leader*, of men should be just,
ruling in the fear of God.)
4 As the light of the morrowtide, when the sun riseth
early, (and) is bright without clouds; and as an herb
cometh forth of the earth by rains. (He is like the morning
light, when the sun riseth early, and it is bright without
clouds; and like a herb that cometh forth out of the
ground after the rain.)
5 And mine house is not so great with God, that he
should make with me everlasting covenant, steadfast and
made strong in all things; for all mine health *is of him*,

and all my will, *that is, all my desire, goeth into him*, and
nothing is thereof, that maketh not fruit[8]. (And though my
house is not so great before God, yet he hath made with
me an everlasting covenant, steadfast and strong in all
things; for all my salvation *is from him*, and all my desire
is for him, and there is nothing of it, that maketh not fruit.)
6 Forsooth all trespassers shall be drawn out as thorns,
that be not taken with hands. (And all trespassers shall be
drawn out like thorns, which cannot be picked, *or
touched*, by hand.)
7 And if any man will touch those, he shall be armed
with iron, and with a (piece of) wood formed into a
spear; and (then) the thorns shall be kindled, and shall be
burnt till to nought.
8 These be the names of the strong men of David.
David sitteth in the chair, the wisest prince among (the)
three; he is as a most tender worm of a tree, that killed
eight hundred with one fierceness. (These be the names
of David's strong men. The Hachmonite sitteth in the
chair, *he is* the wise leader of The Three/The first,
Jashobeam, the son of Hachmoni, *was* the leader of The
Three; he raised up his spear against eight hundred men,
and killed all of them at one time.)
9 After him was Eleazar, the son of his father's brother,
(the) Ahohite; (he was) among [the] three strong men, that
were with David, when they said shame to the
Philistines, and were gathered thither into battle. And
when the men of Israel had gone up, (After him was
Eleazar, the son of Dodo, the Ahohite; he was one of The
Three, who were with David, when they said shame to,
or taunted, the Philistines, and were gathered there in
battle. And when the men of Israel had gone away,)
10 he/Eleazar stood *in battle, when his fellows went
aback*, and smote the Philistines, till that his hand failed,
and was stark with the sword. And the Lord made great
health in that day; and the people that fled turned again,
to draw away the spoils of [the] slain men. (Eleazar stood
his ground *in the battle, while his fellows fled*, and he
struck down the Philistines, until his hand failed, and was
fixed, *or frozen*, to the sword. And the Lord gave great
victory that day; and the people who had fled returned to
take away the spoils from the dead.)
11 And after him was Shammah, the son of Agee, of
Hararites. And Philistines were gathered in the station; and
there was a field full of lentils, *or vetches*; and when the
people *of Israel* [had] fled from the face of Philistines, (And
the third member of The Three was Shammah, the son of
Agee, of the Hararites. And when the Philistines were
gathered at Lehi; and there was a field full of lentils; and
the people *of Israel* had fled from before the Philistines,)
12 he stood in the midst of the field, and beheld it, *for
he defended the field*; and he smote the Philistines, and
the Lord made there [a] great health. (he stood there in
the midst of the field, and held it, *and he defended that
field*; and he struck down the Philistines, and the Lord
gave a great victory there.)
13 Also and three men went down before, that were
princes among (the) thirty, and came to David in the time
of reap(ing) into the den of Adullam. And the tents of
Philistines were set in the valley of giants. (And three of
The Thirty came down at the beginning of the harvest to
join David at the cave of Adullam. And the Philistines'
tents were pitched in the Rephaim Valley.)
14 And David was in a stronghold; and the station of
Philistines was then in Bethlehem. (And David was in a
stronghold; and a Philistine garrison was at Bethlehem.)
15 Then David desired water of the well (Then David
desired water out of the cistern), and said, (O!) If any man
would give to me (a) drink of the water (out) of the
cistern, which is in Bethlehem, beside the gate.
16 Therefore (the) three strong men brake into the tents
of Philistines, and drew water of the cistern of
Bethlehem, that was beside the gate, and they brought it
to David; and he would not drink, but offered it to the
Lord, (And so The Three broke into the camp of the
Philistines, and drew water out of the cistern of Bethlehem,
that was beside the gate, and they brought it to David;
but he would not drink it, but offered it to the Lord,)
17 and said, The Lord be merciful to me, that I do not
this; whether I shall drink the blood of these men, that
went forth, and the peril of their lives? Therefore he
would not drink. (The) Three full strong men did these
things. (and said, May the Lord be merciful to me, so that
I do not do this; for should I drink the blood of these
men, who went down there, risking their own lives? And
so he would not drink it. The Three did these things.)
18 Also Abishai, the brother of Joab, the son of Zeruiah,
was prince of [the] three; he it is that raised his spear
against three hundred men, which he killed; *he was*
named among [the] three, (And Abishai, Joab's brother, the
son of Zeruiah, was the leader of The Thirty; it was he who
raised up his spear against three hundred men, whom he
killed; *he had* the famous name among The Thirty,)
19 and was the nobler among (the) three, and he was
the prince of them; but he came not to the three first
men. (yea, he was the most famous of The Thirty, and he
was their leader; but he did not come up to, *or rival*, The
Three.)
20 And Benaiah, the son of Jehoiada, the strongest man
of great works, of Kabzeel, he smote [the] two lions of
Moab, *that is, two knights hardy as lions/two strong
hardy knights*; and he went down, and smote a lion in
the middle (of a) cistern in the days of snow.
21 Also he killed a man of Egypt, a man worthy of
beholding, having a spear in his hand; and so when he

[8] *And this is done, when all thing that cometh forth of the will, either of advisement, is done into the glory of God.*

had gone down with a rod to that man, by might he
wrung out the spear from the hand of the man of Egypt,
and killed him with his own spear. (And he killed an
Egyptian man, a man worthy of beholding, who had a
spear in his hand; for he had gone down to that man with
a staff, and by might he wrung the spear out of the hand
of the Egyptian, and then killed him with his own spear.)
22 Benaiah, the son of Jehoiada, did these things; and
he was named among [the] three strong men (and he had
a famous name among The Thirty),
23 that were among the thirty nobler men; nevertheless
he came not (up) to the *first* three. And David made him
a counsellor of private to himself. (indeed *some said* he
was the most famous of The Thirty; nevertheless he came
not up to, *or rivaled*, The Three. And David made him
his personal counsellor/the head of his bodyguard.)
24 Asahel, the brother of Joah, was among the thirty
men; Elhanan, the son of his father's brother, of
Bethlehem; (And other members of The Thirty; Asahel,
Joah's brother; and Elhanan, the son of Dodo, of
Bethlehem;)
25 Shammah, of Harodites; Elika, of Harodites;
26 Helez, of Paltites; Ira, the son of Ikkesh, of Tekoa;
(Helez, of Pelet; Ira, the son of Ikkesh the Tekoite;)
27 Abiezer, of Anathoth (Abiezer the Anethothite);
Mebunnai, of Hushathites;
28 Zalmon, of Ahohites; Maharai, of Netophah;
29 Heleb, the son of Baanah, and he was of Netophah;
Ittai, the son of Ribai, of Gibeah, of the sons of Benjamin;
30 Benaiah, of Pirathon; Hiddai, of the strand of Gaash;
31 Abialbon, of Arabah; Azmaveth, of Barhumites;
32 Eliahba, of Shaalbonites; the sons of Jashen, Jonathan,
and Jashen; (Eliahba, of Shaalbon; the sons of Jashen;
Jonathan;/Eliahba, of Shaalbon; Hashem the Gizonite;)
33 Shammah, of Hararites; Ahiam, the son of Sharar, of
Hararites; (Jonathan, the son of Shammah the Hararite;
Ahiam, the son of Sharar the Hararite;)
34 Eliphelet, the son of Ahasbai, the son of (the)
Maachathite; Eliam, the son of Ahithophel, of Giloh;
35 Hezrai, of Carmel; Paarai, of Arbites;
36 Igal, the son of Nathan, of Zobah; Bani, of Gadites;
37 Zelek, of Ammonites; Nahari, of Beeroth, the squire
of Joab, the son of Zeruiah;
38 Ira, of Ithrites; Gareb, and he was of Ithrites;
39 Uriah of Hittites; all these were seven and thirty
men (in all, there were thirty-seven famous fighting men).

CHAPTER 24

1 And the strong vengeance of the Lord added to be
wroth against Israel, and he stirred against them David,
saying to Joab, Go thou, and number thou Israel and
Judah. (And again the Lord was angry with Israel, and in
his strong vengeance he stirred David against them, so
that he said to Joab, Go thou, and count the people of
Israel and Judah.)
2 And the king said to Joab, the prince of his host, Go
thou by all the lineages of Israel, from Dan till to
Beersheba, and number thou the people, that I know the
number thereof. (And the king said to Joab, the leader of
his army, Go thou through all the tribes of Israel, from
Dan unto Beersheba, and count the people, so that I can
know their number.)
3 And Joab said to the king, Thy Lord God increase to
this people, how great it is now, and again multiply he it
an hundredfold in the sight of my lord the king; but what
will my lord the king to himself in such a thing? (And
Joab said to the king, May the Lord thy God increase this
people to be more numerous than they be now, and may
he multiply them a hundredfold before my lord the king;
but why would my lord the king desire to do such a thing
as to count the people?)
4 But the word of the king overcame the words of
Joab, and of the princes of the host; and Joab went out,
and the princes of the knights, from the face of the king,
that they should number the people of Israel. (But the
king's word overruled what Joab and the other leaders of
the army said; and so Joab, and the leaders of the
horsemen, went out from before the king, to count the
people of Israel.)
5 And when they had passed [over] Jordan (And when
they had crossed over the Jordan River), they came into
Aroer, to the right side of the city that is in the valley of
Gad; and they passed forth by Jazer
6 into Gilead, and into the lower land of Hodshi, and
they came into the woody places of Dan; and they went
about beside Sidon, (to Gilead, and to the land of
Tahtimhodshi, and they came to Danjaan; and they went
about beside Sidon,)
7 and passed nigh the walls of Tyre, and nigh all the
land of Hivites, and of Canaanites; and they came to the
south of Judah, in[to] Beersheba.
8 And when all the land was compassed, they came
after nine months and twenty days into Jerusalem. (And
when they had gone throughout all the land, they came
back to Jerusalem after nine months and twenty days.)
9 And so Joab gave the number of [the] describing of
the people to the king. And of Israel were found nine
hundred thousand of strong men, that drew out sword;
and of Judah five hundred thousand of fighters. (And so
Joab gave the census count to the king. And there were
found in Israel eight hundred thousand strong men who
drew out the sword; and in Judah five hundred thousand
fighting men.)
10 And the heart of David smote him, *that is, his
conscience reproved him*, after that the people was
numbered; and David said to the Lord, I have sinned
greatly in this deed; but, Lord, I pray, that thou turn away
the wickedness of thy servant, for I have done full follily.

(And then David's heart struck him, *that is, his*
conscience rebuked him, after that the people were
counted; and David said to the Lord, I have greatly
sinned by doing this deed; but, Lord, I pray thee, that
thou turn away thy servant's wickedness, yea, what I
have done so foolishly.)
11 Therefore David rose (up) early; and the word of the
Lord was made to Gad, the prophet and seer, and said,
12 Go thou, and speak to David (Go thou, and say to
David), The Lord saith these things, The choice of three
things is given to thee; choose thou one, which thou wilt
of these, that I do to thee.
13 And when Gad had come to David, he told to him,
and said, Either hunger shall come to thee in thy land
seven years; either three months thou shalt flee thine
adversaries, and they shall pursue thee; either certainly
three days pestilence shall be in thy land; now therefore
deliver thou, *either advise thou/examine thou*, and see,
what word I shall answer to him that sent me. (And so
when Gad had come to David, he told him, and said,
Either seven years of hunger, *or of famine*, shall come
upon thee in thy land; or for three months thou shalt flee
thy adversaries, and yet they shall pursue thee; or for
three days a pestilence shall be in thy land; and so now
thou deliberate, *and examine thou it*, and see, what I
shall answer to him who sent me.)
14 And David said to Gad, I am constrained on each
side greatly (I am greatly constrained on every side); but it
is better that I fall into the hands of the Lord, for his
mercies be many, than into the hands of men.
15 And (so) the Lord sent (a) pestilence into Israel from
the morrowtide till to the time ordained; and seventy
thousand of men were dead of the people from Dan till
to Beersheba.
16 And when the angel of the Lord had held forth his
hand over Jerusalem, that he should destroy it, the Lord
had mercy on the tormenting; and said to the angel
smiting the people, It sufficeth now; withhold thine hand.
And the angel of the Lord was beside the cornfloor of
Araunah (the) Jebusite. (And when the angel of the Lord
had put forth his hand over Jerusalem, to destroy it, the
Lord had mercy on the tormenting; and he said to the
angel striking the people, That is enough; withdraw thy
hand. And the angel of the Lord was beside the threshing
floor of Araunah the Jebusite.)
17 And David said to the Lord, when he had seen the
angel slaying the people, I am *he* that have sinned, and I
have done wickedly; what have these done, that be
sheep? I beseech, thine hand be turned against me, and
against the house of my father. (And David said to the
Lord, when he had seen the angel killing the people, I am
the one who hath sinned, and I have done wickedly;
what have these people done, yea, they who be but
sheep? I beseech thee, let thy hand be turned against me,
and against the house of my father.)
18 Forsooth Gad, the prophet, came to David in that
day, and said to him, Go thou up, and ordain an altar to
the Lord in the cornfloor of Araunah (the) Jebusite. (And
that same day, the prophet Gad came to David, and said
to him, Go thou up, and build an altar to the Lord on the
threshing floor of Araunah the Jebusite.)
19 And David went up, after the word of Gad, which
the Lord had commanded to him.
20 And Araunah beheld, and perceived, that the king
and his servants passed over to him; and he went out,
and worshipped the king with low cheer to the earth;
(And Araunah looked up, and saw the king and his
servants coming over to him; and he went over, and
bowed before the king, with his face low to the ground;)
21 and said, What is the cause, that my lord the king
cometh to his servant? To whom David said, That I buy of
thee the cornfloor, and build an altar to the Lord, and the
slaying cease, that is cruel in the people. (and he said,
What is the reason that my lord the king cometh to his
servant? To whom David said, To buy the threshing floor
from thee, and to build on it an altar to the Lord, so that
the slaughter that is so cruel upon the people will cease.)
22 And Araunah said to David, My lord the king take,
and offer, as it pleaseth to him; thou hast oxen into burnt
sacrifice, and a wain and yokes of oxen into uses of
wood. (And Araunah said to David, My lord the king take
it, and offer, as it pleaseth thee; lo! thou hast here oxen
for a burnt sacrifice, and a wagon, and the yokes of the
oxen for wood.)
23 Araunah gave, *that is, would give*, all (these) things
to the king. And Araunah said to the king, Thy Lord God
receive thy vow. (And so Araunah would gladly have
given all these things to the king. And Araunah said to
the king, May the Lord thy God receive thy vow.)
24 To whom the king answered, and said, Not as thou
wilt, but I shall buy *it* of thee for (a) price, and I shall not
offer to the Lord my God burnt sacrifices given freely.
Therefore David bought the cornfloor *for six hundred*
shekels of gold[9], and the oxen for fifty shekels of silver.
(To whom the king answered, No, not as thou wilt, but I
shall buy *it* from thee for a price; for I shall not offer to
the Lord my God burnt sacrifices that cost nothing. And
then David bought the threshing floor *for six hundred*
shekels of gold, and the oxen for fifty shekels of silver.)
25 And David builded there an altar to the Lord, and
offered burnt sacrifices and peaceable sacrifices; and the
Lord did mercy to the land, and the vengeance was
refrained from Israel. (And David built an altar there to
the Lord, and offered burnt sacrifices and peace offerings;
and then the Lord gave mercy to the land, and the plague
in Israel was stopped.) ✡

---

[9] *(As written) in the first book of Chronicles, 21st Chapter.*

1ST KINGS

CHAPTER 1

1 And king David waxed eld (And King David grew
old), and had full many days of age; and when he was
covered with clothes, he was (still) not made hot.
2 Therefore his servants said to him, Seek we to our
lord the king a young waxing virgin; and stand she before
the king, and nurse she him, and sleep in his bosom, and
make hot our lord the king. (And so his servants said to
him, Let us seek for our lord the king a youthful virgin;
and stand she before the king, and nurse she him, and
sleep in his bosom, and make our lord the king warm.)
3 Therefore they sought a young waxing virgin, fair in
all the coasts of Israel; and they found Abishag of
Shunem, and they brought her to the king. (And so they
searched for a young, beautiful virgin in all the coasts of
Israel; and they found Abishag of Shunem, and they
brought her to the king.)
4 And the damsel was full fair, and she slept with the
king, and ministered to him; forsooth the king knew not
her fleshly. (And the young woman was very beautiful,
and she slept with the king, and ministered to him; but
the king did not know her fleshly.)
5 And Adonijah, the son of Haggith, was raised up,
and said, I shall reign. And he made to him a chariot,
and knights, and fifty men, that ran before him (And he
got himself a chariot, and horsemen/and horses, and fifty
men who ran before him).
6 Neither *David*, his father, reproved him any time,
nor said, Why hast thou done this? But also he was full
fair, the second child after Absalom; (And *David*, his
father, did not rebuke him at any time, nor said to him,
Why hast thou done this? And he was very handsome,
and the second child after Absalom;)
7 and his word was with Joab, the son of Zeruiah, and
with Abiathar, priest, that helped the parts of Adonijah.
(and he talked with Joab, the son of Zeruiah, and with
Abiathar, the priest, and they supported Adonijah.)
8 But Zadok, the priest, and Benaiah, the son of
Jehoiada, and Nathan, the prophet, and Shimei, and (the)
Cherethites and Pelethites, and all the strength of the host
of David, were not with Adonijah. (But Zadok, the priest,
and Benaiah, the son of Jehoiada, and Nathan, the
prophet, and Shimei, and Rei, and all the strong men
who were David's bodyguards, were not with Adonijah.)
9 Therefore when rams were offered, and calves, and
all fat things, beside the stone [of] Zoheleth, that was nigh
the well of Rogel (And when rams, and calves, and all the
fat things, were offered beside the stone of Zoheleth, that
was near Enrogel), Adonijah called all his brethren, the
sons of the king, and all the men of Judah, (the) servants
of the king.
10 Soothly he called not Nathan, the prophet, and
Benaiah, and all the strong men, and Solomon, his
brother.
11 And so Nathan said to Bathsheba, the mother of
Solomon, Whether thou hast heard, that Adonijah, the
son of Haggith, hath reigned, and our lord David
knoweth not this? (And so Nathan said to Bathsheba,
Solomon's mother, Hast thou heard, that Adonijah, the
son of Haggith, hath made himself king, and our lord
David knoweth it not?)
12 Now therefore come thou, take thou counsel of me,
and save thy life, and (the life) of Solomon, thy son.
13 Go thou, and enter to king David, and say thou to
him, Whether not thou, my lord the king, hast sworn to
me, thine handmaid, and saidest, that Solomon thy son
shall reign after me, and he shall sit in my throne? (and
he shall sit on my throne?) Why therefore reigneth
Adonijah?
14 And yet while thou shalt speak there with the king, I
shall come after thee, and fulfill thy words (and confirm
thy words).
15 Therefore Bathsheba entered to the king in the
closet/in the bed place; and the king was full eld, and
Abishag of Shunem ministered to him.
16 And Bathsheba bowed herself, and worshipped the
king; to whom the king said, What wilt thou to thee?
(And Bathsheba bowed herself down, and honoured the
king; to whom the king said, What wilt thou that I do for
thee?)
17 And she answered, and said, My lord the king, thou
hast sworn to thine handmaid by thy Lord God, (and
said,) Solomon thy son shall reign after me, and he shall
sit in my throne (and he shall sit on my throne);
18 and lo! Adonijah hath reigned now (and lo!
Adonijah hath made himself king now), while thou, my
lord the king, knowest (it) not;
19 (and) he hath slain oxen, and all fat things, and full
many rams; and he hath called all the sons of the king,
also Abiathar [the] priest, and Joab, the prince of the
chivalry (the leader of the cavalry, *or of the army*); but he
called not Solomon, thy servant.
20 Nevertheless, my lord the king, the eyes of all Israel
behold into thee, that thou show to them, who oughteth
to sit in thy throne, my lord the king, after thee; (Now,
my lord the king, the eyes of all Israel look to thee, for
thou to tell them, who ought to sit on thy throne, my lord
the king, after thee;)
21 and it shall be, (that) when my lord the king hath
slept with his fathers, I and my son Solomon shall be
(reckoned as) sinners, *that is, Adonijah shall put on us
crimes, to deprive us from life.* (or else it shall be, that

when my lord the king sleepeth with his forefathers, *that*
is, when he dieth, I and my son Solomon shall be
reckoned as sinners, *that is, Adonijah shall put crimes*
upon us to deprive us of life.)
22 While she spake yet with the king, Nathan, the
prophet, came. (Yet while she spoke with the king,
Nathan the prophet came in.)
23 And they told to the king, and said, Nathan, the
prophet, is present. And when he had entered in the
sight of the king, and had worshipped him lowly to the
earth (and had bowed low to the ground before him),
24 Nathan said, My lord the king, saidest thou,
Adonijah reign after me, and sit he on my throne?
(Nathan said, My lord the king, hast thou said, Adonijah
shall reign after me, and he shall sit on my throne?)
25 For he came down today, and offered oxen, and fat
things, and full many wethers; and he called all the sons
of the king, [and the prince(s) of the host,] and also
Abiathar, [the] priest; and when they ate, and drank
before him, and said, King Adonijah live (and when they
ate, and drank before him, they said, Long live King
Adonijah!);
26 (but) he called not me, thy servant, and Zadok, the
priest, and Benaiah, the son of Jehoiada, and Solomon,
thy son.
27 Whether this word went out from my lord the king,
and thou showedest not to me, thy servant, who should
sit on the throne of my lord the king after him? (Did this
word go out from my lord the king, but thou hast not told
me, thy servant, who should sit on the throne of my lord
the king after him?)
28 And king David answered, and said, Call ye
Bathsheba to me. And when she had entered before the
king, and had stood before him,
29 the king swore, and said, The Lord liveth, that hath
delivered my life from all anguish; (the king swore, and
said, As the Lord liveth, who hath delivered my life from
all anguish;)
30 for as I swore to thee by the Lord God of Israel, and
said, Solomon, thy son, shall reign after me, and he shall
sit on my throne for me, so I shall do today (so I shall
make this happen today).
31 And Bathsheba, with her cheer bowed down into
the earth, worshipped the king, and said, My lord king
David live without end. (And Bathsheba, with her face
bowed down to the ground, honoured the king, and said,
My lord King David, may thou live forever!)
32 And king David said, Call ye Zadok, the priest, to
me, and Nathan, the prophet, and Benaiah, the son of
Jehoiada. And when they had entered before the king,
33 the king said to them, Take with you the servants of
your lord, and put ye my son Solomon upon my mule,
and lead ye him into Gihon.
34 And [there] Zadok, the priest, and Nathan, the
prophet, anoint him into king upon Israel and Judah; and
ye shall sing with a trump, and ye shall say, Live king
Solomon! (And there Zadok, the priest, and Nathan, the
prophet, anoint him king upon Israel; and ye shall sing
with a trumpet, and ye shall say, Long live King
Solomon!)
35 (Then) Ye shall go up after him, and ye shall come
to Jerusalem; and he shall sit upon my throne, and he
shall reign for me; and I shall command to him, that he
be duke on Israel and on Judah (and I shall command to
him, to be the ruler of Israel and of Judah).
36 And Benaiah, the son of Jehoiada, answered to the
king, and said, Amen; so speak the Lord God of my lord
the king (and may the Lord God of my lord the king also
say thus.)
37 As the Lord was with my lord the king, so be he
with Solomon, and make he the throne of Solomon
higher than the throne of my lord king David.
38 Then Zadok, the priest, went down, and Nathan, the
prophet, and Benaiah, the son of Jehoiada, and (the)
Cherethites, and Pelethites; and they putted Solomon
upon the mule of David, the king, and they brought him
into Gihon. (Then Zadok, the priest, and Nathan, the
prophet, and Benaiah, the son of Jehoiada, and the
Cherethites, and Pelethites, went down; and they put
Solomon on King David's mule, and they brought him to
Gihon.)
39 And Zadok, the priest, took an horn of oil (out) of
the tabernacle, and anointed Solomon; and they sang
with a clarion (and they sang with a trumpet); and all the
people said, (Long) Live king Solomon!
40 And all the multitude went up after him, and the
people of men singing with pipes, and being glad with
great joy; and the earth sounded of the cry of them (and
the earth sounded with their cry).
41 And Adonijah heard, and all that were called of him
to the feast; and then the feast was ended. But also Joab
said, when the voice of the trump was heard, What will it
to itself the cry of the city making (such a) noise? (And
Adonijah, and all who were called by him to the feast,
heard the noise, as the feast was ending. And when Joab
heard the sound of the trumpet, he said, What is the
meaning of all this noise in the city?)
42 Yet while he spake, Jonathan, the son of Abiathar,
the priest, came; to whom Adonijah said, Enter thou, for
thou art a strong man, and telling good things.
43 And Jonathan answered to Adonijah, Nay; for our
lord king David hath ordained Solomon (as) king;
44 and David hath sent with Solomon Zadok, the
priest, and Nathan, the prophet, and Benaiah, the son of
Jehoiada, and (the) Cherethites, and Pelethites; and they
have put Solomon upon the mule of the king.
45 And Zadok, the priest, and Nathan, the prophet,
have anointed him (as) king in Gihon; and they came

down from thence being glad, and the city (re)sounded;
this is the voice that ye heard (that is the noise that ye
heard).
46 But also Solomon sitteth on the throne of (the)
realm; (And so now Solomon sitteth on the throne of the
kingdom;)
47 and the servants of the king have entered, and have
blessed our lord king David, and said, God make large
the name of Solomon above thy name, and make great
his throne above thy throne. And king David worshipped
in his bed; (and the king's servants have entered, and
have blessed our lord King David, and said, God make
the name of Solomon greater than thy name, and make
his throne greater than thy throne. And King David hath
bowed himself in worship on his bed;)
48 and furthermore he spake these things, Blessed be
the Lord God of Israel, that hath given today a sitter in my
throne, while mine eyes see. (and furthermore he spoke
these things, and said, Blessed be the Lord God of Israel,
who today hath given such a man to sit on my throne,
while I have lived to see *it*.)
49 Therefore all that were called of Adonijah to the
feast, were afeared, and rose up, and each man went into
his way. (And so all who were called by Adonijah to the
feast were afraid, and they rose up, and each man went
on his way.)
50 And Adonijah dreaded Solomon, and rose up, and
went into the tabernacle of the Lord, and he held the
horn, *or corner*, of the altar. (And Adonijah feared
Solomon, and he rose up, and went into the Tabernacle,
or the Tent, of the Lord, and he held onto the horns, *or
the corners*, of the altar.)
51 And they told to Solomon, and said, Lo! Adonijah
dreadeth the king Solomon, and he holdeth the horn, *or
corner*, of the altar (and he holdeth onto the horns, *or the
corners*, of the altar), and said, (Let) King Solomon swear
to me today, that he shall not slay his servant with (the)
sword.
52 And Solomon said, If he is a good man, soothly not
an hair of him shall fall into the earth (If he is a good
man, truly not one hair of his head shall fall to the
ground); but if evil be found in him, he shall die.
53 Therefore king Solomon sent, and led out Adonijah
from the altar; and he entered, and worshipped king
Solomon (and he entered, and bowed low before King
Solomon); and Solomon said to him, Go into thine
house.

CHAPTER 2

1 Forsooth the days of David nighed, that he should
die; and he commanded to Solomon, his son, and said,
2 Lo! I enter into the way of all (the) earth; be thou
strengthened (take thou courage), and be thou a strong
man.
3 And keep thou the keepings and the behests of thy
Lord God, that thou go in his ways, and keep his
ceremonies, and his behests, and his dooms, and (his)
witnessings, as it is written in the law of Moses; that thou
understand all things which thou doest, and whither ever
thou shalt turn thee. (And obey thou the orders and the
commands of the Lord thy God, so that thou go in his
ways, and keep his statutes, and his commands, and his
laws, *or his judgements*, and his testimonies, as it is
written in the Law of Moses; so that thou understand all
the things that thou doest, and wherever thou shalt turn
thyself.)
4 That the Lord confirm his words, which the Lord
spake of me, and said, If thy sons keep my ways, and go
before me in truth, in all their heart, and in all their soul,
a man shall not be taken away of thee from the throne of
Israel. (So that the Lord shall establish his words, which
the Lord spoke about me, saying, If thy sons follow my
ways, and go before me in truth, with all their heart, and
with all their soul, a man of thee shall not be taken away
from the throne of Israel.)
5 Also thou knowest what things Joab, the son of
Zeruiah, did to me; (and) what things he did to [the] two
princes of the host of Israel, to Abner, the son of Ner, and
to Amasa, the son of Jether, which he killed, and shedded
the blood of battle in peace; and putted the blood of
battle in his girdle, that was about his loins, and in his
shoe(s), that was in his feet (and put the blood of battle
upon his girdle, that was about his loins, and in his
shoes, that were upon his feet).
6 Therefore thou shalt do by thy wisdom, and thou
shalt not lead forth his hoariness peaceably to hells,
either (the) sepulchre. (And so do thou by thy wisdom,
and do not let his hoar hairs go down peacefully to
Sheol, *or into the grave, or into the tomb*.)
7 But also thou shalt yield grace to the sons of
Barzillai of Gilead, and they shall be eating in thy board
(and they shall eat at thy table); for they met me, when I
fled from the face of Absalom, thy brother.
8 Also thou hast with thee Shimei, the son of Gera,
the son of Benjamin, of Bahurim, the which Shimei
cursed me by the worst cursing, when I went to the
defensible places; but for-thy he came down to me into
my meeting, when I passed (the) Jordan, and I swore to
him by the Lord, and said, I shall not slay thee with
sword, (Also thou hast with thee Shimei, the son of Gera,
the son of Benjamin, of Bahurim, the which Shimei
cursed me by the worst cursing, when I went to
Mahanaim; but he came down to meet me when I
crossed over the Jordan River, and I swore to him by the
Lord, and said, I shall not kill thee with the sword,)
9 do not thou suffer him to be unpunished; forsooth
thou art a wise man, and thou shalt know what thou shalt
do to him, and thou shalt lead forth his hoar hairs with

blood to hells. (but now do not thou allow him to go
unpunished; thou art a wise man, and thou knowest what
thou shalt do to him, *and that is,* thou shalt lead forth his
hoar hairs in blood down to Sheol, *or into the grave*!)
10 And (then) David slept with his fathers, and was
buried in the city of David.
11 And the days, in which David reigned upon Israel,
be forty years; in Hebron he reigned seven years, and in
Jerusalem three and thirty years.
12 Forsooth Solomon sat upon the throne of David, his
father, and his realm was made steadfast greatly (and his
reign was firmly established).
13 And Adonijah, the son of Haggith, entered to
Bathsheba, the mother of Solomon; and she said to him,
Whether thine entering is peaceable? And he answered,
It is peaceable (and she said to him, Cometh thou here in
peace? And he answered, I have come in peace).
14 And he added, A word of me is to thee (And he
added, I have a word to say to thee). And she said, Speak
thou.
15 And he said, Thou knowest that the realm was mine,
and all Israel purposed to make me into king to them; but
the realm is translated, and is made my brother's; for of
the Lord it is ordained to him. (And he said, Thou
knowest that the kingdom was mine, and all Israel
purposed to make me king over them; but the kingdom
was taken away *from me*, and made my brother's; for the
Lord ordained it to him.)
16 Now therefore I pray of thee one asking; shame thou
not my face. And she said to him, Speak thou.
17 And he said, I pray, that thou say to Solomon the
king; for he may not deny anything to thee; that he give
me Abishag of Shunem to wife (that he give me Abishag
of Shunem for a wife).
18 And Bathsheba said, Well, I shall speak for thee to
the king.
19 Therefore Bathsheba came to king Solomon, to
speak to him for Adonijah; and the king rose against the
coming of her, and worshipped her, and sat on his
throne; and a throne was set to the mother of the king,
and she sat at his right side. (And so Bathsheba went to
King Solomon, to speak to him for Adonijah; and the king
rose up to greet her, and honoured her, and then sat
down on his throne; and a throne was put in place for the
king's mother, and she sat at his right side.)
20 And she said to him, I pray of thee one little asking;
shame thou not my face. And the king said to her, My
mother, ask thou; for it is not leaveful that I turn away thy
face (for it would not be right for me to refuse thee).
21 And she said, (Let) Abishag of Shunem be given (for
a) wife to Adonijah, thy brother.
22 And king Solomon answered, and said to his
mother, Why askest thou (only for) Abishag of Shunem to
Adonijah? Ask thou to him also the realm (Why askest
thou only for Abishag of Shunem for Adonijah? Why not
ask thou also for the kingdom for him?); certainly he is
mine elder brother, and he hath Abiathar, (the) priest, and
Joab, the son of Zeruiah.
23 Therefore king Solomon swore by the Lord, and
said, God do to me these things, and add these things
too, for Adonijah hath spoken this word against his (own)
life.
24 And now the Lord liveth, that hath confirmed me,
and hath set me on the throne of [David,] my father, and
that hath made to me an house, as he spake, for Adonijah
shall be slain today. (And now as the Lord liveth, who
hath firmly established me, and hath put me on the
throne of my father David, and who hath made a house
for me, as he promised, let Adonijah be killed today!)
25 And king Solomon sent by the hand of Benaiah, the
son of Jehoiada; and Benaiah slew Adonijah, and he was
dead (and so he died).
26 Also the king said to Abiathar, the priest, Go thou
into Anathoth, to thy field; and soothly thou art a man of
death, *that is, worthy of death, for conspiring against me,
and David, my father*; but today I shall not slay thee, for
thou barest the ark of the Lord God before David, my
father, and thou sufferedest travail in all things, in which
my father travailed.
27 Therefore Solomon putted out Abiathar, that he
should not be priest of the Lord (And so Solomon put out
Abiathar, so that he would no longer be the Lord's priest),
(so) that the word of the Lord were [ful]filled, which he
spake on the house of Eli in Shiloh.
28 And a messenger came to Solomon, and said that
Joab had bowed after Adonijah, and that he had not
bowed after Solomon. Therefore Joab fled into the
tabernacle of the Lord, and took the horn of the altar.
(And a message concerning all of this came to Joab; for
he had sided with Adonijah, but not with Absalom. And
so Joab fled into the Tabernacle, *or the Tent*, of the Lord,
and took hold of the horns of the altar.)
29 And it was told to king Solomon, that Joab had fled
into the tabernacle of the Lord, and was beside the altar;
and Solomon sent Benaiah, the son of Jehoiada, and said,
Go thou, and slay him.
30 And Benaiah came to the tabernacle of the Lord,
and said to Joab, The king saith these things, Go thou
out. And he said, I shall not go out, but I shall die here.
Benaiah told the word to the king (Benaiah told this to
the king), and said, Joab spake these things, and
answered these things to me.
31 And the king said to Benaiah, Do thou as he hath
spoken, and slay thou him, and (then) bury *him*; and thou
shalt remove the innocent blood, that was shed out of
Joab, from me, and from the house of my father (and so
thou shalt remove the innocent blood that was shed by
Joab, from me, and from my father's house).

32 And the Lord yield on(to) his (own) head his (own)
blood, for he killed two just men, and better than himself,
and he killed them by (the) sword, while David, my
father, knew not, Abner the son of Ner, the prince of the
chivalry of Israel, and Amasa, the son of Jether, the prince
of the host of Judah (that is, Abner the son of Ner, the
leader of Israel's cavalry, *or army*, and Amasa, the son of
Jether, the leader of Judah's army).
33 And the blood of them shall turn again into the head
of Joab, and into the head of his seed without end; but
peace be of the Lord till into without end to David, and
to his seed, and to the house, and [the] throne of him.
(And their blood shall return onto Joab's head, and onto
the head of his descendants forevermore; but let peace,
or prosperity, be from the Lord forevermore for David,
and for his descendants, and for his house, and his
throne.)
34 Therefore Benaiah, the son of Jehoiada, went up,
and assailed Joab, and killed him; and Joab was buried in
his house in (the) desert.
35 And the king ordained Benaiah, the son of Jehoiada,
upon the host for Joab; and the king put Zadok the priest
(in place) for Abiathar. (And the king ordained Benaiah,
the son of Jehoiada, over the army in place of Joab; and
he made Zadok the priest in place of Abiathar.)
36 Also the king sent, and called (for) Shimei, and said
to him, Build to thee an house in Jerusalem, and dwell
thou there (Build a house for thyself in Jerusalem, and
live thou in it), and thou shalt not go out from thence
hither and thither;
37 for in whatever day thou goest out, and passest
[over] the strand of Kidron, know thou thee worthy to be
slain; thy blood shall be on thine head. (for in whatever
day thou goest out, and passest over the Kidron Stream/
and passest over the Kidron Gorge, know thou that thou
shalt be killed; thy blood shall be upon thy own head.)
38 And Shimei said to the king, The word of the king is
good; as my lord the king spake, so thy servant shall do.
And so Shimei dwelled in Jerusalem many days.
39 But it was done after three years, that the servants of
Shimei fled to Achish, the son of Maachah, king of Gath;
and it was told to Shimei, that his servants had gone into
Gath.
40 And Shimei rose up, and saddled his ass (and
saddled up his donkey), and went to Achish, into Gath,
to seek his servants; and he brought them (back) again
from Gath.
41 And it was told to king Solomon, that Shimei had
gone to Gath from Jerusalem, and had come (back) again.
42 And Solomon sent, and called him, and said to him,
Whether I witnessed not to thee by the Lord, and before-
said to thee, In whatever day thou shalt go out hither and
thither, know thou that thou shalt die; and thou
answeredest to me, The word is good, which I heard?
(And Solomon sent, and called for him, and said to him,
Did I not make thee swear by the Lord? and did I not say
to thee, On whatever day that thou shalt go out here and
there, know thou that thou shalt die? and didest thou not
answer to me, The word, which I heard, is good?)
43 Why therefore keptest thou not the oath of the Lord,
and the commandment which I commanded to thee?
44 And the king said to Shimei, Thou knowest all the
evil, of which thine heart is guilty to thee, which evil
thou didest to [David] my father; the Lord hath yielded
thy malice into thine head. (And the king said to Shimei,
Thou knowest all the evil which thy heart is guilty of,
which evil thou didest to my father David; and now the
Lord shall yield thy malice onto thy own head.)
45 And king Solomon *shall be* blessed; and the throne
of David shall be stable before the Lord till into without
end.
46 Therefore the king commanded to Benaiah, the son
of Jehoiada; and he assailed Shimei, and smote him, and
he was dead. Therefore the realm was confirmed into the
hands of Solomon; (And so the king commanded to
Benaiah, the son of Jehoiada; and he assailed Shimei, and
struck him down there, and he died. And so the kingdom
was firmly established in Solomon's hands;)

CHAPTER 3

1 and (then) by affinity, *either alliance*, he was joined
to Pharaoh, king of Egypt; for he took the daughter of
Pharaoh, and brought (her) into the city of David, till he
[ful]filled building his house, and the house of the Lord,
and the wall of Jerusalem by compass.
2 Nevertheless the people offered in high places; for
the temple was not builded to the name of the Lord till
into that day. (But the people still offered at the hill
shrines; for the Temple was not yet built in honour of the
name of the Lord unto that day.)
3 Soothly Solomon loved the Lord, and went in the
behests of David, his father, except that Solomon offered
in high places and burnt incense. (And Solomon loved
the Lord, and followed his father David's commands,
except that Solomon offered sacrifices and burned
incense at the hill shrines.)
4 And so Solomon went into Gibeon, to offer there;
for that was the most high place (for that was the most
important, *or the most famous*, hill shrine). Solomon
offered upon that altar in Gibeon a thousand offerings
into burnt sacrifice.
5 Soothly the Lord appeared to Solomon by sleep in
the night, and said, Ask thou that, that thou wilt, that I
give *it* to thee.
6 And Solomon said, Thou hast done great mercy with
thy servant David, my father, as he went in thy sight, in
truth, and [in] rightwiseness, and in rightful heart with
thee; thou hast kept to him thy great mercy (thou hast

shown him thy great love), and hast given to him a son,
sitting on his throne, as it is today.
7 And now, Lord God, thou hast made thy servant to
reign for David, my father; forsooth I am a little child (but
I am like a little child), and not knowing mine out-going
and mine in-coming.
8 And thy servant is in the midst of the people, which
thou hast chosen, of [a] people without number, that may
not be numbered and reckoned, for multitude. (And thy
servant is in the midst of the people, whom thou hast
chosen, of a people without number, who cannot be
counted, or reckoned, for their multitude.)
9 Therefore thou shalt give to thy servant an heart able
to be taught, *that is, enlightened of thee,* that he may
deem thy people, and judge betwixt good and evil; for
who may deem this people, thy people, this much
people? (And so give thou to thy servant a heart able to
be taught, *that is, able to be enlightened by thee,* so that
he can judge, *or rule,* thy people, and judge between
good and evil; for who can judge, *or rule,* this people,
this great people of thine?)
10 Therefore the word pleased before the Lord, that
Solomon had asked (for) such a thing.
11 And the Lord said to Solomon, For thou askedest
this word, and askedest not to thee many days, neither
riches, neither the lives of thine enemies, but thou
askedest to thee wisdom to deem doom, (And the Lord
said to Solomon, For thou askedest for this thing, and
askedest not for many days for thyself, nor riches, nor the
lives of thy enemies, but thou askedest for wisdom to
judge justly, *or wisely,*)
12 lo! I have done to thee after thy words, and I have
given to thee a wise heart and an understanding (one), in
so much that no man before thee was like thee, neither
shall rise (up) after thee.
13 But also I have given to thee these things, which
thou askedest not, that is, riches, and glory, that no man
be like thee in kings in all times afterward (so that there
shall not be any man like thee among the kings in all thy
days).
14 Forsooth if thou goest in my ways, and keepest my
biddings and [my] commandments, as thy father went *in
them,* (then) I shall make thy days long.
15 Therefore Solomon waked, and understood what the
sweven was. And when he had come to Jerusalem, he
stood before the ark of [the] bond of peace of the Lord,
and he offered burnt sacrifices, and made peaceable
sacrifices, and (made) a great feast to all his household/to
all his menials. (And so Solomon awoke, and understood
the dream. And when he had come to Jerusalem, he
stood before the Ark of the Covenant of the Lord, and he
offered burnt sacrifices, and made peace offerings, and
made a great feast for all his household/for all his
menials.)
16 Then two women whores came to the king, and
stood before him;
17 of which one said, My lord, I beseech, I and this
woman dwelled in one house, and I childed at her in a
couch (and I brought forth my child in a bed when she
was there).
18 And in the third day after that I had childed, also this
woman childed (And on the third day after that I had
given birth, this woman also gave birth); and we were
together in the house, and none other was (there) with us
in the house, except us twain.
19 And the son of this woman was dead in the night,
for she slept, and over-lay him; (And this woman's son
died in the night, for while she was sleeping, she rolled
over, and laid upon him;)
20 and she rose up in the fourth part of the night in
silence, and took my son from the side of me, (while)
thine handmaid (was) sleeping, and she laid it in her
bosom; and she putted in my bosom her son, that was
dead.
21 And when I had risen early, to give milk to my son,
he appeared dead; whom I beheld more diligently by
clear light, and I perceived, that he was not mine, whom
I had engendered (whom I had begat).
22 The tother woman answered, It is not as thou sayest,
but thy son is dead; forsooth my son liveth. The contrary,
she said, Thou liest (But the other woman said, Thou
liest); for my son liveth, and thy son is dead. And by this
manner they strove before the king.
23 Then the king said, This woman saith, My son
liveth, and thy son is dead; and this woman answereth,
Nay, but thy son is dead, and my son liveth.
24 Therefore the king said, Bring ye to me a sword.
And when they had brought a sword before the king,
25 he said, Part ye the quick young child in two parts
(Divide ye, *or cut ye,* the young living child in two), and
give ye the half part to the one, and the half part to the
tother.
26 And the woman, whose son was quick, said to the
king; for her entrails were moved on her son; Lord, I
beseech, give ye to her the quick child, and do not ye
slay him. The contrary, she said, Be he neither to me,
neither to thee, but be he parted. (And the woman,
whose son was living, said to the king; for she was
moved with love for her son; Lord, I beseech thee, give
ye to her the child alive, and do not ye kill him. But the
other woman said, Be he neither to me, nor to thee, but
be he divided, *or cut in two.*)
27 The king answered, and said, Give ye to this (first)
woman the young child quick, and be he not slain (Give
ye this first woman the young child alive, and do not kill
him); forsooth this is his mother.
28 Therefore all Israel heard the doom, which the king
had deemed; and they dreaded the king, and saw, that

the wisdom of God was in him, to make doom. (And so
all Israel heard the judgement, which the king had
decreed; and they revered the king, and saw, that God's
wisdom was in him, to make judgements, *or justice*.)

CHAPTER 4

1 Forsooth king Solomon was reigning on all Israel.
2 And these were the princes which he had; Azariah,
the son of Zadok, the priest; (And these were the leaders
that he had; Azariah, the son of Zadok, was the priest
who was over-the-year, that is, the calendar of events;)
3 Elihoreph, and Ahiah, (the) sons of Shisha, *were*
scribes; Jehoshaphat, the son of Ahilud, *was* chancellor;
4 Benaiah, the son of Jehoiada, *was prince* upon the
host (was *the leader* of the army); and Zadok and
Abiathar *were* priests;
5 Azariah, the son of Nathan, *was* upon them that
stood nigh [to] the king (*was* over those who stood close
to the king/*was* over the regional governors); Zabud, the
son of Nathan, *was* [a] priest, a friend of the king;
6 and Ahishar *was* steward of the house; and
Adoniram, the son of Abda, *was* upon the tributes (*was* in
charge of the taxes, *or the levies*/*was* in charge of the
forced labour).
7 Forsooth Solomon had twelve prefects, *either chief
ministers*, on all Israel, that gave lifelode to the king, and
to his house; soothly by each month by itself in the year,
each prefect by himself ministered necessaries. (And
Solomon had twelve prefects, *or chief ministers*, over all
Israel, who gave sustenance, *or food*, to the king, and to
his household; and each month of the year, one prefect
by himself administered the necessities.)
8 And these be the names of them; Ben-hur, in the hill
(country) of Ephraim;
9 Ben-dekar, in Makaz, and in Shaalbim, and in
Bethshemesh, and in Elon, and in Bethhanan (and in
Elonbethhanan);
10 Ben-hesed, in Aruboth; and Sochoh, and all the land
of Hepher, was (also) his;
11 Ben-abinadab, whose was all Naphath, had Dor
Taphath, the daughter of Solomon, to wife. (Ben-
abinadab, whose had all of Naphath-dor, *that is, the
region of Dor*, and he had Taphath, Solomon's daughter,
for a wife.)
12 Baana, the son of Ahilud, governed Taanach, and
Megiddo, and all Bethshean, which is beside Zartanah,
under Jezreel, from Bethshean unto Abelmeholah, even
against Jokneam (as far as Jokneam).
13 Ben-geber, in Ramoth of Gilead, had Havoth-jair, of
the son of Manasseh, in Gilead; he was sovereign in all
the country of Argob, which is in Bashan, to sixty great
cities and walled, that had brazen locks. (Ben-geber, in
Ramoth of Gilead, had Havoth-jair, *that is, the tent
villages of* Jair, who was the son of Manasseh, in Gilead;
he was the sovereign, *or the ruler*, in all the country of
Argob, which is in Bashan, yea, to sixty great walled
cities that had bronze locks.)
14 Ahinadab, the son of Iddo, was sovereign in
Mahanaim;
15 Ahimaaz *was* in Naphtali, but also he had Basmath,
the daughter of Solomon, in wedlock;
16 Baanah, the son of Hushai, *was* in Asher, and in
Aloth;
17 Jehoshaphat, the son of Paruah, *was* in Issachar;
18 Shimei, the son of Elah, *was* in Benjamin:
19 Geber, the son of Uri, *was* in the land of Gilead,
and in the land of Sihon, king of Amorites, and (in the
land) of Og, king of Bashan, and upon all things that
were in that land.
20 (The people of) Judah and Israel were
unnumberable, as the sand of the sea in multitude,
eating, and drinking, and being glad.
21 Forsooth Solomon was in his lordship, and had all
the realms, as from the flood of the land of Philistines,
unto the last part of Egypt, of men offering gifts, *that is,
tributes*, to him, and serving to him, in all the days of his
life. (For Solomon was in his lordship, and had all the
kingdoms, from the Euphrates River unto the land of the
Philistines, and unto the last part of Egypt; and the men of
these places offered tribute, *or taxes*, to him, and served
him, all the days of his life.)
22 Forsooth the meat of Solomon was by each day,
thirty cors of clean flour of wheat, and sixty cors of meal,
(And each day the food for Solomon *and his household*,
was thirty cors of fine wheat flour, and sixty cors of
meal,)
23 ten fat oxen, and twenty oxen of the pasture(s), and
an hundred wethers, besides (the) hunting of harts, of
goats, and of bugles (and of buffalo, *or wild oxen*), and of
birds made fat.
24 For he held all the country that was beyond the
flood, as from Tiphsah unto Azzah (from Tiphsah to
Azzah), and all the kings of those countries; and he had
peace by each part in compass.
25 And Judah and Israel dwelled without any dread
(And the people of Judah and Israel lived without any
fear), each man under his vine, and under his fig tree,
from Dan unto Beersheba, in all the days of Solomon.
26 And Solomon had forty thousand cratches of horses
for chariots, and twelve thousand of road horses; (And
Solomon had forty thousand stalls for the horses for his
chariots, and twelve thousand road horses;)
27 and the foresaid prefects/the chief masters of the
king nourished those horses. But also with great busyness
they gave [the] necessaries to the board of king Solomon,
in their time (But also with great diligence they gave the
necessities for King Solomon's table, each in his turn);
28 also they brought barley, and forage of horses and of

work beasts, into the place where the king was, after it
was ordained to them. (they also brought barley, and
forage, for the horses and the work beasts, to the place
where the king was, as it was ordained to them.)
29 Also God gave to Solomon wisdom, and prudence
full much (and a great deal of prudence), and largeness of
heart, as the sand that is in the brink of the sea.
30 And the wisdom of Solomon passed the wisdom of
all [the] east men, and Egyptians; (And Solomon's
wisdom surpassed the wisdom of all the men of the East,
and of all the Egyptians;)
31 and he was wiser than all men; he was wiser than
Ethan (the) Ezrahite, and than Heman, and than Chalcol,
and than Darda, the sons of Mahol; and he was named
among all folks by compass.
32 And Solomon spake three thousand parables, and
his songs were a thousand and five;
33 and he disputed of trees, from a cedar which is in
Lebanon, till to the hyssop that goeth out of the wall; he
disputed of work beasts, and (of) birds, and of creeping
beasts, and of fishes.
34 And they came from all peoples to hear the wisdom
of Solomon, and from all the kings of [the] earth, that
heard his wisdom (who heard of his wisdom).

CHAPTER 5

1 Also Hiram, king of Tyre, sent his servants to
Solomon; for he heard that they had anointed him king
for his father (for he had heard that they had anointed
him king in place of his father); for Hiram was (a) friend
of David in all time.
2 And also Solomon sent to Hiram, and said,
3 Thou knowest the will of David, my father, and for
he might not build an house to the name of his God
(Thou knowest the desire of my father David, and that he
could not build a house in honour of the name of the
Lord his God), for [the] battles nighing by compass, till
the Lord gave them under the step of his feet.
4 But now my Lord God hath given rest to me by
compass, and none adversary is, neither evil assailing;
(But now the Lord my God hath given peace to me all
around, and there is no adversary, nor evil, assailing me;)
5 wherefore I think to build a temple to the name of
my Lord God, as God spake to David, my father, and
said, Thy son, whom I shall give to thee for thee upon thy
throne, he shall build an house to my name. (and so I
shall build a Temple in honour of the name of the Lord
my God, as God spoke to my father David, and said, Thy
son, whom I shall put on thy throne in thy place, he shall
build a House in honour of my name.)
6 Therefore command thou, that *thy servants* hew
down to me cedars of the Lebanon (And so command
thou, that *thy servants* cut down cedars in Lebanon for
me); and my servants (shall) be with thy servants; and I
shall give to thee the meed of thy servants, whatever thou
shalt ask; for thou knowest, that in my people (there) is
not a man that can hew trees, as (well as the) Sidonians
can (do it)/as (well as) the men of Sidon.
7 Therefore when Hiram had heard the words of
Solomon, he was full glad, and said, Blessed be the Lord
God today, that hath given to David the son most wise
upon this people full much. (And so when Hiram had
heard Solomon's words, he was very glad, and said,
Blessed be the Lord God today, who hath given David a
most wise son to rule over this great people.)
8 And Hiram sent to Solomon, and said, I have heard
whatever things thou sentest to me (for); I shall do all thy
will, in trees of cedars, and in trees of box (and I shall
provide all the cedar, and fir, *or pine*, trees, that thou
needeth, *or wanteth*).
9 My servants shall put down those trees from the
Lebanon to the sea, and I shall array those trees in ships
in the sea, unto the place that thou shalt signify *to* me;
and I shall direct those there, that thou take those; and
thou shalt give necessaries to me, that meat be given to
mine house. (My servants shall bring down that wood
from Lebanon to the sea, and I shall convey it in sea-
worthy ships, to the place that thou shalt signify to me;
and I shall send them there, so that thou can have them;
and thou shalt give necessities to me, so that food shall
be given to all my household.)
10 And so Hiram gave to Solomon cedar trees, and box
trees, by all his will; (And so Hiram gave Solomon all the
cedar, and fir, *or pine*, trees, that he needed, *or wanted*;)
11 and Solomon gave to Hiram twenty thousand cors of
wheat, into meat to his house, and twenty cors of purest
oil; Solomon gave these things to Hiram by all years. (and
Solomon gave to Hiram twenty thousand cors of wheat,
for food for his household, and twenty cors of purest oil;
Solomon gave these things to Hiram annually.)
12 Also the Lord gave wisdom to Solomon, as he spake
to him; and peace was betwixt Hiram and Solomon, and
both they smote together (a) bond of peace. (And the
Lord gave wisdom to Solomon, as he said he would; and
there was peace between Hiram and Solomon, and they
struck a covenant together.)
13 And king Solomon chose workmen (out) of all Israel;
and the sum was thirty thousand of men.
14 And Solomon sent them into the Lebanon, ten
thousand by each month by whiles, so that in two
months by whiles they were in their houses; and
Adoniram was on such a sum. (And Solomon sent them
to Lebanon, ten thousand each month by turn, and then
for two months by turn, they went back to their own
houses; and Adoniram was in charge of them all.)
15 And so seventy thousand of them, that bare burdens,
were to Solomon, and fourscore thousand of masons in
the hill(s), (And so working for Solomon were seventy

thousand men who carried loads, and fourscore thousand stonemasons in the hills,)
16 without the sovereigns, that were masters of all the works, by the number of three thousand and three hundred, commanding to the people, and to them that made work. (besides the sovereigns, *or the foremen*, who were masters over all the work, three thousand and three hundred in number, commanding the people who did the work.)
17 And the king commanded, that they should take great stones, and precious stones/heavy stones, into the foundament of the temple, (And the king commanded, that they should cut great fine stones/great heavy stones, for the foundation of the Temple,)
18 and that they should make those square; which stones the masons of Solomon and the masons of Hiram hewed. And [the] men of Byblos made ready [the] trees and stones, to the house to be builded (And the men of Byblos prepared the wood and the stones, needed to build the Temple).

CHAPTER 6

1 Forsooth it was done in the four hundred and fourscore year of the going out of the sons of Israel from the land of Egypt, in the fourth year of the realm of Solomon (in the fourth year of Solomon's reign), in the month Zif; that is, the second month of the fourth year of the realm of Solomon on Israel; he began to build an house to the Lord.
2 Forsooth the house which king Solomon builded to the Lord, had sixty cubits in length, and twenty cubits in breadth, and thirty cubits in height.
3 And a porch was before the temple of twenty cubits of length, by the measure of the breadth of the temple; and the porch had ten cubits of breadth, before the face of the temple. (And there was a vestibule in front of the Temple, twenty cubits in length, equal to the measure of the breadth of the Temple; and the vestibule was ten cubits deep, projecting out in front of the Temple.)
4 And Solomon made in the temple narrow windows withoutforth and large within.
5 And he builded on the wall of the temple, buildings of boards by compass, in the walls of the house, by compass of the temple, and of God's answering place; and he made [the] sides in the compass. (And he made chambers, *or rooms*, out of boards, against the walls of the Temple, all around the Temple, and the Inner Temple, *that is, the Most Holy Place, or the Holy of Holies*, on the sides, and at the back.)
6 The building of boards, that was under, had five cubits of breadth; and the middle building of boards was of six cubits of breadth; and the third building of boards was having seven cubits of breadth (The bottom story, made out of boards, was five cubits in breadth; and the middle story, also made out of boards, was six cubits in breadth; and the third story, also made out of boards, was seven cubits in breadth). And he put beams in the house by compass withoutforth, (so) that those cleaved not to the walls of the temple.
7 And when the house was builded, it was built of perfect(ly) hewn stones; and hammer, and ax, and all thing made of iron, were not heard in the house, while it was in building (while it was being built).
8 The door of the middle side was in the wall of the right half of the house; and by a vice men went up into the middle solar, and from the middle solar into the third solar. (The door for the bottom story was in the wall for the right side of the House of the Lord; and by a stairway, men went up to the middle story, and from the middle story to the third story.)
9 And Solomon builded the house, and ended it. And Solomon covered the house with couples of cedar, (And Solomon built the House, and finished it. And he braced the House with cedar couplings,)
10 and he builded a building of boards over all the house, by five cubits of height, and covered the house with cedar wood. (and he built a building out of boards all around the sides of the House, *or the Temple*, five cubits in height, and joined it to the Temple with cedar beams.)
11 And the word of the Lord was made to Solomon, and said,
12 This is the house, which thou buildest; if thou goest in my behests, and doest my dooms, and keepest all my commandments, and goest by those, I shall make steadfast my word to thee, which word I spake to David, thy father; (This is the House, which thou should built; and then if thou followest my commands, and doest my judgements, and obeyest all my commandments, and goest by them, I shall make steadfast my word to thee, which word I spoke to thy father David;)
13 and I shall dwell in the midst of the sons of Israel, and I shall not forsake my people Israel. (and I shall live in the midst of the Israelites, and I shall never desert my people Israel.)
14 Therefore Solomon builded the house, and ended it; (And so Solomon built the House, and finished it;)
15 and he builded the walls of the house within with boards of cedar, from the pavement of the house unto the highness of the wall, and unto the couples; and he covered *them* with wood of cedar within; and he covered the pavement of the house with boards of box. (and he built the walls of the House within out of cedar boards, from the floor of the House unto the top of the wall, and unto the couplings; and he covered *them* with cedar wood within; and he covered the floor of the House with fir, *or pine*, boards.)
16 And he builded a wall of boards of cedar of twenty

cubits at the hinder part of the temple, from the
pavement unto the higher parts; and he made the inner
house of God's answering place into the holy of holy
things, (and he made the Inner Temple, *that is, the Most
Holy Place, or the Holy of Holies*).
17 And that temple before the doors of God's answering
place was of forty cubits. (And the chamber in front of the
doors of the Inner Temple was forty cubits in length.)
18 And all the house within was clothed with cedar,
and had his smoothnesses, and his joinings made subtly,
and gravings appearing above; all things were clothed
with boards of cedar, and utterly a stone might not
appear in the wall. (And all the House within was
covered with cedar, and had carvings of knops, *or of
gourds*, and open flowers; everything was covered with
cedar boards, and no stone appeared, *or was visible*,
utterly anywhere on the wall.)
19 And Solomon made God's answering place in the
midst of the house, in the inner part, that he should set
there the ark of (the) bond of peace of the Lord (where he
would put the Ark of the Covenant of the Lord).
20 And God's answering place had twenty cubits of
length, and twenty cubits of breadth, and twenty cubits of
height (And the Inner Temple was twenty cubits in
length, and twenty cubits in breadth, and twenty cubits in
height); and he covered (it), and clothed it with purest
gold; but also he clothed the altar with cedar.
21 Also he covered with purest gold the house before
God's answering place, *or the oracle*, and he fastened the
plates with golden nails. (And he covered the inside of
the Temple all around the Inner Temple, *or the oracle*,
with the purest gold; and he fastened plates to the walls
with gold nails.)
22 Nothing was in the temple that was not covered
with gold; but also he covered with gold all the altar of
God's answering place. (There was nothing in the
Temple that was not covered with gold; and he also
covered all of the altar for the Inner Temple with gold.)
23 And he made in God's answering place two
cherubims of the trees of olives, of ten cubits of height
(each ten cubits in height);
24 one wing of (the) cherub *was* of five cubits, and the
tother wing of (the) cherub *was* (also) of five cubits, that
is, having ten cubits, from the highness of the one wing
till to the highness of the tother wing.
25 And the second cherub was of ten cubits in even
measure; and one work was in the two cherubims, (And
the second cherub was also ten cubits in equal measure;
and the two cherubim were of the same work, or design,)
26 that is, one cherub had the height of ten cubits, and
in like manner the tother cherub.
27 And he set [the] cherubims in the midst of the inner
temple; and the cherubims held forth their wings, and
one wing touched the one wall, and the wing of the
second cherub touched the tother wall; and the other
wings in the middle part of the temple touched
themselves together (and the other wings touched each
other in the middle of the Inner Temple).
28 And he covered the cherubims with gold, and (also)
all the walls of the (whole) temple by compass/about;
29 and he graved them with diverse gravings and
smoothness; and he made in those *walls* cherubims, and
palms, and diverse paintures, as standing forth and going
out of the wall. (and he carved into them diverse
carvings; he made cherubim, and palms, and open
flowers on those *walls*, standing forth from the walls, and
going out of them.)
30 But also he covered with gold the pavement of the
house, within and withoutforth. (And he also covered the
floor of the Temple, within and without, with gold.)
31 And in the entering of God's answering place he
made two little doors of the trees of olives; and *he made*
posts of five corners, (And at the entrance to the Inner
Temple, he made two doors of olive wood; and *he made*
posts with five corners,)
32 and [the] two doors (were) of the trees of olives; and
he graved in those the painture of cherubims, and the
likenesses of palms, and gravings above standing forth
greatly; and he covered those with gold; and he covered
as well the cherubims, as [the] palms, and (the) other
things, with gold. (and the two doors were made out of
olive wood; and he carved on them the likenesses of
cherubim, and palms, and open flowers; and he covered
them with gold; and he *also* covered the cherubim, and
the palms, and the other things, with gold.)
33 And in the entering of the temple he made posts
four-cornered of (the) trees of olives; (And for the
entrance to the Temple he made four-cornered posts out
of olive wood;)
34 and he made [the] two doors of the trees of box,
each against (the) other (and he made the two doors out
of fir, *or pine*, wood, each against the other); and ever
either door was double, and it was opened holding itself
together.
35 And he graved cherubims, and palms, and gravings
appearing greatly (And he carved cherubim, and palms,
and open flowers); and he covered all things with golden
plates, by square work at rule.
36 And he builded a large street, *or an alley*, within, by
three orders of stones made fair, and by one order of
wood of cedar. (And he built a large courtyard within,
with three rows of hewn stones, and one row of cedar
beams.)
37 The house of the Lord was founded in the fourth
year of the realm of Solomon, in the month (of) Zif; (The
House of the Lord was begun in the fourth year of
Solomon's reign, in the month of Zif;)
38 and the house was made perfect, *or ended*, in all his

work, and in all his vessels, *either purtenances,* in the
eleventh year, in the month [of] Bul; that is the eighth
month; and he builded that house in seven years. (and
the House was finished with all of its work, and all of its
vessels, *or its purtenances,* in the eleventh year, in the
month of Bul; that is, the eighth month; and so he built
that House in seven years.)

CHAPTER 7

1 Forsooth Solomon builded his own house in thirteen
years, and brought *it* till to perfection, *or (a) perfect end
(or unto completion).*
2 He builded an house (made) of the forest, (*or out of
the wood,*) of Lebanon, of an hundred cubits of length,
and of fifty cubits of breadth, and of thirty cubits of
height; and *he builded* four alleys betwixt the pillars of
cedars (and *he built* four rows of cedar pillars); for he had
hewn down [the] trees of cedars into pillars.
3 And he clothed all the chamber(s) with walls of
cedar; the which chamber was sustained, or borne up,
with five and forty pillars. And one order had fifteen
pillars, set against themselves together, (And he covered
all the walls of the chambers, *or of the rooms,* with cedar;
and the roof was sustained, or borne up, by forty-five
pillars. And each row had fifteen pillars, set in line with
each other,)
4 and beholding themselves each even against (the)
other by even space betwixt the pillars; (and there were
three rows of windows, one row on each floor, each
window in line with the one above, or below;)
5 and on the pillars *were* foursquare posts, even in all
things. (and the pillars *were* square posts, even in all
things.)
6 And he made a porch of pillars of fifty cubits of
length, and of thirty cubits of breadth; and *he made*
another porch in the face of the greater porch; and he
made (the) pillars, and [the] pommels on the pillars. (And
he made a colonnade of pillars which was fifty cubits in
length, and thirty cubits in breadth; and *he made* another
colonnade in front of the greater colonnade; and so he
made the pillars, and the capitals on the pillars.)
7 Also he made a porch of the king's seat, in which
the seat of doom was; and he covered it with wood of
cedar, from the pavement unto the highness. (And he
made a hall for the king's throne, in which was the
throne of judgement; and he covered all the hall with
cedar wood, from the floor to the ceiling.)
8 And a little house, in which he sat to deem, was in
the middle porch, by like work. Also Solomon made an
house to the daughter of Pharaoh, whom he had wedded,
by such work, by what manner work he made and this
porch. (And his own house, where he would live, had
another hall within a colonnade, by like work. And
Solomon made a house for Pharaoh's daughter, whom he
had wedded, in the same manner of work with which he
had made this hall.)
9 He made all things of precious stones, that were
sawed at a rule and measure, both within and
withoutforth, from the foundament unto the highness of
[the] walls (from the foundation to the top of the walls),
and within and till to the great street, *either court(yard).*
10 And the foundaments *were* of precious stones, great
stones of ten, either of eight cubits; (And the foundations
were made out of precious stones, great stones of eight or
ten cubits;)
11 and precious stones hewn of even measure were
above; in like manner and of cedar. (and above were
precious stones, hewn, *or cut,* of equal measure; and
cedar, in like manner.)
12 And the greater court, *either void space,* was round,
of three orders of hewn stones, and of one order of hewn
cedar beams; also and in the inner large street of the
house of the Lord, and in the porch of the house of the
Lord. (And the great courtyard all around had three rows
of hewn stones, and one row of hewn cedar beams; as
did the inner courtyard of the House of the Lord, and the
vestibule of the House of the Lord.)
13 Also king Solomon sent, and brought from Tyre,
Hiram[1], (And King Solomon sent for, and brought there
Hiram from Tyre,)
14 the son of a woman widow (the son of a widow
woman), of the lineage of Naphtali, of the father of a man
of Tyre, a craftsman of brass, and full of wisdom, and
understanding, and doctrine, *or teaching,* to make all
work of brass. And when he had come to king Solomon,
he made all his work.
15 And he made two pillars of brass, one pillar of
eighteen cubits of height; and a line of twelve cubits
compassed ever either pillar. (And he made two bronze
pillars, each pillar eighteen cubits in height; and *it took* a
cord twelve cubits long to go all around either pillar.)
16 Also he made two pommels, molten of brass, which
were set on the heads of the pillars; one pommel of five
cubits of height, and the tother pommel of five cubits of
height; (And he cast two bronze capitals, which were set
on the tops of the pillars; each capital was five cubits in
height;)
17 and by the manner of a net, and of chains knit
together to themselves, by wonderful work. Ever either
pommel of the pillars was molten; seven works like nets
of orders were in one pommel, and seven works like nets
in the tother pommel. (and they were decorated with
networks of chains knit together. Each capital for the
pillars was cast; and seven rows of networks were on
each capital.)
18 And he made perfectly the pillars, and two orders

[1] Also known as 'Huram'.

about all the works like nets, that those should cover the
pommels, which were upon the highness of [the]
pomegranates; in the same manner he did also to the
second pommel. (And he finished the pillars, with two
rows of pomegranates, all around the tops of the pillars,
above the networks; he did this in the same manner for
each of the capitals.)
19 And the pommels, that were upon the heads of the
pillars in the porch, were made as by work of lily, of four
cubits; (And the capitals, that were on the tops of the
pillars in the vestibule, were shaped like lilies, four cubits
in height;)
20 and again other pommels in the highness of [the]
pillars above, by the measure of the pillar, *set* against the
works like nets; and two hundred orders of pomegranates
were in the compass of the second pommel. (and on the
capitals, on the tops of the two *bronze* pillars, above the
networks, were two hundred pomegranates in two rows,
around each capital.)
21 And he set the two pillars in the porch of the
temple; and when he had set the right half pillar, he
called it by name Jachin, *that is, steadfast*; in like manner
he raised up the second pillar, and he called the name
thereof Boaz, *that is, strength*. (And he placed the two
pillars in the vestibule of the Temple; and when he had
raised up the right-hand pillar, he named it Jachin, *that is,
Steadfast*; and in like manner he raised up the left-hand
pillar, and he named it Boaz, *that is, Strength*.)
22 And he set upon the heads of the pillars a work by
the manner of a lily; and (so) the work of the pillars was
made perfect. (And on the very top of the pillars was lily
work; and so the work of the pillars was finished, *or
completed*.)
23 Also he made a molten sea, *that is, a washing vessel
for priests*, round in compass, of ten cubits from brink to
brink; the highness thereof was of five cubits; and a cord
of thirty cubits went about it by compass. (And he cast
the *bronze* Sea, *that is, a washing vessel for the priests*,
and it was ten cubits across from brim to brim; its
highness was five cubits; and *it took* a cord thirty cubits
long to go all around it.)
24 And the engraving under the brink compassed it,
and compassed the sea by ten cubits/and it came about
the sea by ten cubits; twain orders of gravings containing
some stories were molten (two rows of knops, *or of
gourds*, were cast together, and joined with the Sea),
25 and (it) stood upon twelve oxen; of which oxen
three beheld to the north, and three to the west, and
three to the south, and three to the east; and the sea was
above upon those oxen, of which all the hinder things
were hid within.
26 And the thickness of the sea was of four *fingers, or a
palm*, and the brink thereof was as the brink of a cup
(and its brim was like the brim of a cup), and as the leaf
of a lily crooked again; the sea contained two thousand
baths, *that is, three thousand metretes*.
27 And he made ten brazen foundaments, each
foundament of four cubits of length, and of four cubits of
breadth, and of three cubits of highness.
28 And that work of the foundaments was raised
betwixt; and gravings were between the jointures.
29 And between the little crowns and the circles were
lions, oxen, and cherubims; and in the jointures in like
manner above; and under the lions and the oxen were as
reins of bridles of brass hanging down (and under the
lions and the oxen were like reins of bridles made of
bronze hanging down, *or spiral work*).
30 And by each foundament were four wheels, and
brazen axletrees; and by (the) four parts were as little
shoulderings under the washing vessel, *the shoulderings,
that is, short pillars to sustain the washing vessel*, molten,
and beholding against themselves together (the short
pillars were cast, and they were placed opposite each
other).
31 And the mouth of the washing vessel within was in
the highness of the head, and that, that appeared
withoutforth, was of one cubit, and it was all-round, and
had altogether one cubit and an half; and diverse
gravings were in the corners of [the] pillars (and diverse
engravings were on the corners of the pillars), and the
middle pillar between was square, not round.
32 And the four wheels, which were by [the] four
corners of the foundament, cleaved together to
themselves under the foundament; one wheel had one
cubit and an half of height.
33 And the wheels were such, which manner wheels
be wont to be made in a chariot; and the axletrees, and
the nave-stocks, and the spokes, and [the] felloes/and the
dowels of those wheels, all things were molten. (And the
wheels were such, as be wont to be made for a chariot;
and the axle-rods, and the nave-stocks, and the spokes,
and the felloes/and the dowels for those wheels, all of
these things were cast.)
34 For also the four little shoulderings, by all the
corners of one foundament, were joined together, and
[were] molten of that foundament, *that is, were molten
together with that foundament (that is, were cast together
with that foundation), and made one body*.
35 And in the highness of the foundament was a
roundness, of one cubit and an half, so made craftily, that
the washing vessel might be set above, having his
portrayings, and diverse gravings of itself. (And at the top
of the foundation was a circular band, one and a half
cubits in height, skillfully made, so that the washing
vessel could be put above, having portrayings, and
diverse engravings, upon it.)
36 Also he graved in those walls, that were of brass,
and in the corners, cherubims, and lions, and palms, as

by the likeness of a man standing, that those seemed not
graven, but put to by compass. (And he engraved on their
bronze walls, and on their corners, cherubim, and lions,
and palms, like the likeness of a man standing there,
wherever there was an empty space, with spiral work all
around it.)
37 By this manner he made ten foundaments, by one
melting out, and one measure, and like engraving.
38 Also he made ten washing vessels of brass; one
washing vessel took, (*or held,*) forty baths, and it was of
four cubits; and he put each washing vessel by itself by
each foundament by itself, that is, ten (and he put one
washing vessel by itself on one foundation by itself, that
is, ten altogether).
39 And he made ten foundaments, five at the right half
of the temple, and five at the left half; and he set the sea
at the right half of the temple, against the east, at the
south. (And he put ten foundations, five on the right side
of the Temple, and five on the left side; and he put the
Sea on the right side of the Temple, at the southeast
corner.)
40 Also Hiram made cauldrons, and pans, and wine
vessels; and he made perfectly all the work of king
Solomon in the temple of the Lord. (And Hiram made
cauldrons, and pans, and basins; and so he finished all
the work for King Solomon for the Temple of the Lord.)
41 *He made* (the) two pillars, and (the) two cords of the
pommels, *that is, (the) circles compassing the pommels,
at the manner of cords,* upon the pommels of the pillars,
and (the) two works like nets, that those should cover the
two cords, that were upon the heads of the pillars. (*He
made* the two pillars, and the two bowl-shaped capitals,
that were on the tops of the pillars, and the two networks,
to cover the two bowl-shaped capitals, that were on the
tops of the pillars.)
42 And *he made* pomegranates four hundred in two
works like nets; and two orders of pomegranates in each
work like a net, to cover the cords of the pommels, that
were on the heads of [the] pillars. (And *he made* four
hundred pomegranates for the two networks; and there
were two rows of pomegranates for each network, to
cover the bowl-shaped capitals, that were on the tops of
the pillars.)
43 And *he made* [the] ten foundaments, and [the] ten
washing vessels on the foundaments;
44 and one sea, and twelve oxen under the sea;
45 and cauldrons, and pans, and wine vessels. All the
vessels, which Hiram made to king Solomon in the house
of the Lord, were of latten. (and the cauldrons, and pans,
and basins. All the vessels, which Hiram made for King
Solomon for the House of the Lord, were cast in bronze.)
46 And the king melted out those vessels in the field
country of Jordan (And the king had those vessels cast in
the field country of Jordan), in [the] clay land, betwixt
Succoth and Zarthan.
47 And Solomon setted all the vessels (in their places);
but for the great multitude, no weight was of the brass.
(And Solomon put all the vessels in their places; and
because of their great multitude, the weight of the bronze
could not be reckoned.)
48 And Solomon made all the vessels in the house of
the Lord; soothly he made the golden altar, *that is, the
altar of incense, that was within the temple,* and the
golden board, upon which the loaves of setting forth
were set; (And Solomon made all the vessels for the
House of the Lord; yea, he made the gold altar, *that is,
the altar of incense, that was within the Temple,* and the
gold table, on which the loaves of setting forth, *or the
loaves of proposition,* were placed;)
49 and *he made* of most pure gold (the) golden
candlesticks, five at the right half, and five at the left half,
against God's answering place; and *he made* as the
flowers of a lily, and (the) golden lanterns above, and
(the) golden tongs; (and *he made* the candlesticks out of
pure gold, five on the right side, and five on the left side,
that stood in front of the Inner Temple, *that is, the Most
Holy Place, or the Holy of Holies*; and *he made* the lily
flowers, and the lanterns, and the tongs *out of pure gold*;)
50 and pots, and hooks, and vials, and mortars, and
censers of purest gold; and the hinges of the doors of the
inner house of the holy of holy things, and of the doors of
the house of the temple, were of gold. (and the pots, and
hooks, and basins, and spoons, and censers out of pure
gold; and the hinges for the doors of the Inner Temple,
that is, the Most Holy Place, or the Holy of Holies, and
for the doors of the Temple itself, were *also made* out of
gold.)
51 And Solomon performed all the work, that he made
in the house of the Lord; and he brought in the things,
which David, his father, had hallowed; silver, and gold,
and vessels; and he kept those in the treasures of the
house of the Lord. (And so Solomon finished all the work
that he had ordained for the House of the Lord; and he
brought in the things, which his father David had
dedicated; the silver, and the gold, and the vessels; and
he kept them all in the treasuries of the House of the
Lord.)

CHAPTER 8

1 Then all the greater men in birth in Israel, with [the]
princes of the lineages, and the dukes of [the] families of
the sons of Israel, were gathered to king Solomon, into
Jerusalem, that they should bear the ark of [the] bond of
peace of the Lord from the city of David, that is, from
Zion. (Then all the men of great age, *that is, the elders,* of
Israel, with the leaders of the tribes and the families of
the Israelites, were gathered unto King Solomon, in
Jerusalem, so that they could bring the Ark of the Covenant

of the Lord from the City of David, that is, from Zion.)
2 And all Israel came together [to king Solomon] in the
month [of] Ethanim, *that is September,* in the solemn day;
which is the seventh month. (And all Israel came together
to King Solomon on the feast day in the month of
Ethanim, *that is September,* which is the seventh month.)
3 And all the eld men of Israel came; and the priests
took the ark,
4 and they bare the ark of the Lord, and the tabernacle
of [the] bond of peace, and all the vessels of the
saintuary, that were in the tabernacle; and the priests and
deacons bare those. (and they carried the Ark of the Lord,
and the Tabernacle of the Covenant, and all the vessels of
the sanctuary, that were in the Tabernacle; yea, the
priests and the Levites carried all of it.)
5 And king Solomon, and all the multitude of Israel,
that came together to him, went with him before the ark;
and they offered sheep and oxen, without guessing and
number[2]. (And King Solomon, and all the multitude of
Israel, who came together to him, went with him before
the Ark; and they offered sheep and oxen, beyond
estimating, or counting.)
6 And [the] priests brought the ark of [the] bond of
peace of the Lord into his place, into God's answering
place of the temple, into the holy of holy things, under
the wings of the cherubims. (And the priests brought the
Ark of the Covenant of the Lord into its place, into God's
answering place at the Temple, yea, into the Inner
Temple, *that is, the Most Holy Place, or the Holy of
Holies,* under the wings of the cherubim.)
7 And the cherubims spreaded forth their wings over
the place of the ark; and they covered the ark, and the
bars thereof above.
8 And when the bars stood forth, and the highness of
those appeared without the saintuary, before God's
answering place, those *bars* appeared no further
withoutforth; the which bars also were there unto this
present day. (And when the bars were drawn out, the
ends of them could be seen outside the sanctuary, in
front of the Inner Temple, but those *bars* could not be
seen otherwise; and these bars be there to this present
day.)
9 And in the ark was none other thing, no but [the]
two tables of stone, which Moses in Horeb had put in the
ark, when the Lord made (a) bond of peace with the sons
of Israel, when they went out of the land of Egypt. (And
there was nothing else in the Ark, but the two stone
tablets, which Moses had put in the Ark at Horeb, *that is,
at Mount Sinai,* when the Lord made a covenant with the
Israelites, when they went out of the land of Egypt.)
10 And it was done when the priests had gone out of
the saintuary, a cloud filled the house of the Lord;
11 and the priests might not stand and minister, for the
cloud; for why the glory of the Lord had filled the house
of the Lord.
12 Then Solomon said, The Lord said, that he would
dwell in a cloud/in a mist.
13 I building have builded an house into thy dwelling
place, into thy most steadfast throne without end. (I have
built a house for thy dwelling place, *to be* thy most
steadfast throne forevermore.)
14 And the king turned his face, and blessed all the
church in Israel; for all the church of Israel stood. (And
the king turned himself, and blessed all the congregation
of Israel; for all the congregation of Israel stood there.)
15 And Solomon said, Blessed be the Lord God of
Israel, that spake with his mouth to David, my father, and
performed (it) in his hands, and said, (And Solomon said,
Blessed be the Lord God of Israel, who spoke with his
mouth to my father David, and fulfilled his word with his
hands, and said,)
16 From the day in which I led my people Israel out of
Egypt, I chose not a city of all the lineages of Israel, that
an house should be builded, and my name should be
there; but I chose David, that he should be over my
people Israel. (From the day in which I led my people
Israel out of Egypt, I chose not a city out of all the tribes
of Israel, where a House should be built, for my name to
be honoured there; but I chose David, that he should rule
over my people Israel.)
17 And David, my father, would build/would have
builded an house to the name of the Lord God of Israel.
(And my father David desired to build a House in honour
of the name of the Lord God of Israel.)
18 And the Lord said to David, my father, That thou
thoughtest in thine heart to build an house to my name,
thou didest well, treating (also) this same thing in thy
soul; (And the Lord said to my father David, That thou
desiredest in thy heart to build a House in honour of my
name, thou didest well, treating this in thy soul, *that is,
taking it to heart*;)
19 nevertheless thou shalt not build an house to me,
but thy son, that shall go out of thy reins, he shall build
an house to my name. (but thou shalt not build a House
for me, but thy son, who shall go out of thy loins, he shall
build a House in honour of my name.)
20 The Lord hath *now* confirmed his word, that he
spake; and I stood for David, my father, and I sat upon
the throne of Israel, as the Lord spake; and I have builded
an house to the name of the Lord God of Israel. (The Lord
hath *now* fulfilled his word, that he spoke; and I have
stood in place of my father David, and now I sit on the
throne of Israel, as the Lord spoke; and I have built a
House in honour of the name of the Lord God of Israel.)
21 And I have ordained there a place of the ark, in

[2] This is said by figurative speech, called hyperbole, to signify the multitude of sacrifices.

which ark the bond of peace of the Lord is, which he
smote with our fathers, when they went out of the land of
Egypt. (And I have ordained a place there for the Ark, in
which Ark is the Covenant of the Lord, which he struck
with our forefathers, when they went out of the land of
Egypt.)
22 And Solomon stood before the altar of the Lord, in
the sight of the church of Israel; and he held forth his
hands against heaven, (And Solomon stood before the
altar of the Lord, before the congregation of Israel; and he
held forth his hands toward heaven,)
23 and said, Lord God of Israel, no God in heaven
above, neither on earth beneath, is like thee, which
keepest covenant and mercy to thy servants, that go before
thee in all their heart; (and said, Lord God of Israel, there
is no god like thee, in heaven above, or on the earth
beneath, which keepest covenant and mercy with thy
servants, who go before thee with all their heart;)
24 and thou keepest to David, my father, thy servant,
those things which thou hast spoken to him (and thou
hast kept thy promise to thy servant David, my father); by
mouth thou hast spoken (it), and by hands thou hast
fulfilled (it), as this day proveth.
25 Now therefore, Lord God of Israel, keep thou to thy
servant David, my father, those things which thou spakest
to him, and saidest, A man of thee shall not be taken
away (from) before me, which man shall sit on the throne
of Israel, so nevertheless if thy sons keep thy way (as long
as thy sons obey thy ways), (so) that they go before me,
as thou wentest in my sight.
26 And now, Lord God of Israel, thy words be made
steadfast, which thou spakest to thy servant David, my
father.
27 Therefore whether it is to guess, that God dwelleth
verily on earth; for if heaven, and (the) heaven of heavens
be not able to take thee, how much more this house, that
I have builded to thee. (And so, is it only a guess, that
truly God liveth not on the earth? for if heaven, and the
heaven of heavens be not able to hold thee, then how
much less this House, that I have built for thee?)
28 But, my Lord God, behold thou to the prayer of thy
servant, and to the beseechings of him; hear thou the
hymn, *either praising*, and [the] prayer, which thy servant
prayeth before thee today;
29 that thine eyes be opened on this house by night
and day, on the house of which thou saidest, My name
shall be there; that thou hear the prayer, which thy
servant prayeth to thee in this place;
30 that thou hear the beseeching of thy servant, and of
thy people Israel, whatever thing he prayeth in this place,
and hear thou in the place of thy dwelling in heaven; and
when thou hast heard, thou shalt be merciful. (that thou
hear the beseeching of thy servant, and of thy people
Israel, whatever thing they prayeth in this place, and hear
thou in heaven, in thy dwelling place; and that when
thou hast heard, thou shalt be merciful.)
31 If a man sinneth against a man, and hath any oath,
by which he is holden bound, and cometh for the oath
into thine house, before thine altar (and cometh for the
oath before thy altar in thy House),
32 (then) thou shalt hear in heaven, and thou shalt do,
and thou shalt deem thy servants; and thou shalt
condemn the wicked man, and shalt yield his way on(to)
his head, and thou shalt justify the just man, and shalt
yield to him after his rightfulness.
33 If thy people Israel fleeth his enemies, for he shall
do sin to thee (When thy people Israel fleeth their
enemies, for they have sinned against thee), and they do
penance, *or repent their sin*, and acknowledge to thy
great name, and come, and worship, and beseech thee in
this house,
34 (then) hear thou in heaven, and forgive thou the sin
of thy people [Israel]; and thou shalt lead them again into
the land, which thou hast given to the fathers of them.
35 If heaven is closed (When the heavens be closed
up), and (it) raineth not for the sins of them, and they
pray in this place, and do penance to thy name, and be
converted, or altogether turned, from their sins for their
torment,
36 (then) hear thou them in heaven, and forgive thou
the sins of thy servants, and of thy people Israel, and
show thou to them a good way, by which they shall go,
and give thou rain to them upon the land, which thou
hast given to them into possession (which thou hast given
to them for a possession).
37 If hunger riseth in the land, either pestilence is,
either corrupt air is (If famine riseth in the land, or
pestilence, or corrupt air), either rust, either locust, either
mildew, and if his enemy tormenteth him, and besiegeth
the gates of him, and (bringeth in) all wound, all sickness,
38 all cursing, and all wishing *of evil*, that befalleth to
each man of thy people Israel, if any man knoweth the
wound of his heart, and holdeth forth his hands in this
house,
39 thou shalt hear in heaven, in the place of thy
dwelling (then thou shalt hear in heaven, in thy dwelling
place), and thou shalt do mercy, and thou shalt do that
thou give to each man after all his ways, as thou seest his
heart; for thou alone knowest the heart of all the sons of
men,
40 that they dread thee in all days in which they live on
the face of the land, which thou hast given to our fathers.
(that they fear thee/that they revere thee all the days in
which they live on this land, which thou hast given to
our forefathers.)
41 Furthermore and when an alien, that is not of thy
people Israel, cometh from a far land for thy name; (And
furthermore when a foreigner, who is not of thy people

Israel, cometh from a far land because of thy fame;)
42 for thy great name, and thy strong hand, and thine
arm stretched out (and thy outstretched arm), shall be
heard (of) everywhere; therefore when he cometh, and
prayeth in this place,
43 thou shalt hear in heaven, in the firmament of thy
dwelling place, and thou shalt do all things, for which the
alien calleth thee; that all peoples of lands learn to dread
thy name, as thy people Israel *doeth*, and prove [they],
that thy name is called on this house, which I [have]
builded. (thou shalt hear in heaven, in the firmament of
thy dwelling place, and thou shalt do all the things, for
which the foreigner calleth thee; so that all the peoples of
the lands learn to fear thy name/learn to revere thy name,
as thy people Israel *doeth*, and they learn that this House,
which I have built, is called by thy name.)
44 If thy people goeth out to battle against his enemies,
by the way whither ever thou sendest them, they shall
pray (to) thee against the way of the city which thou hast
chosen, and over against the house that I have builded to
thy name, (If thy people goeth out to battle against their
enemies, by the way wherever thou sendest them, they
shall pray to thee toward the way of the city which thou
hast chosen, and toward the House that I have built in
honour of thy name,)
45 and (then) thou shalt hear in heaven the prayers of
them, and the beseechings of them, and thou shalt make
the doom of them (and thou shalt grant them justice).
46 That if they sin to thee (But when they sin against
thee), for no man is that sinneth not, and thou art wroth,
and betakest them to their enemies, and they be led
prisoners into the land of (their) enemies, far either nigh,
47 and (if) they do penance in their heart in the place of
their imprisoning, and be converted, or altogether turned,
and beseech (thee) in their imprisoning, and say, We
have sinned, we have done wickedly, we have done
unfaithfully;
48 and they turn again to thee in all their heart, and in
all their soul, in the land of their enemies, to which they
be led prisoners, and they pray (to) thee over against the
way of their land, which thou hast given to their fathers,
and of the city which thou hast chosen, and of the temple
which I [have] builded to thy name, (and they return to
thee with all their heart, and with all their soul, in the
land of their enemies, to which they be led prisoners, and
they pray to thee toward the way of their land, which
thou hast given to their forefathers, and the city which
thou hast chosen, and the Temple which I have built in
honour of thy name,)
49 thou shalt hear in heaven, in the firmament of thy
seat, the prayers of them, and the beseechings of them,
and thou shalt make the doom of them; (then thou shalt
hear in heaven, in the firmament of thy dwelling place,
their prayers, and their beseechings, and thou shalt grant
them justice;)
50 and thou shalt be merciful to thy people, that have
sinned to thee, and to all the wickednesses, by which
they have trespassed against thee; and thou shalt do
mercy before those men, that had them prisoners, that
those men do mercy to them. (and thou shalt be merciful
to thy people, who have sinned against thee, and all the
wickednesses, by which they have trespassed against
thee; and thou shalt give them mercy before those who
took them prisoners, so that those men also do mercy to
them.)
51 For it is thy people, and thine heritage, which thou
leddest out of the land of Egypt (whom thou leddest out
of the land of Egypt), from the midst of the iron furnace;
52 that thine eyes (may) be open to the beseeching of
thy servant, and of thy people Israel; and thou shalt hear
them in all things, for which they call thee.
53 For thou hast separated them to thee into (thine)
heritage from all the peoples of [the] earth, as thou
spakest by Moses, thy servant, when thou, Lord God,
leddest our fathers out of Egypt.
54 Forsooth it was done, when Solomon, praying the
Lord, had filled all this prayer and beseeching, he rose up
from [the] sight of the altar of the Lord; for he had set fast
ever either knee to the earth, and he had held forth his
hands to heaven. (And it was done, when Solomon,
praying to the Lord, had finished all this prayer and
beseeching, he rose up from before the altar of the Lord;
for he had set both of his knees upon the ground, and he
had held forth his hands toward heaven.)
55 Therefore he stood, and blessed all the church of
Israel, and said with [a] great voice, (And he stood, and
blessed all the congregation of Israel, and said with a
loud voice,)
56 Blessed be the Lord God of Israel, that hath given
rest to his people Israel (who hath given peace to his
people Israel), (as) by all things which he spake; a word
felled not down, soothly neither one, of all [the] goods/of
all the good things which he spake by Moses, his servant.
57 Our Lord God be with us, as he was with our
fathers, and forsake not us (and desert us not), neither
cast us away;
58 but bow he our hearts to himself, that we go in all
his ways, and keep his commandments, and ceremonies,
and dooms, whichever he commanded to our fathers.
(but bow he our hearts to himself, so that we go in all his
ways, and obey his commandments, and statutes, and
judgements, whatever he commanded to our forefathers.)
59 And these words of me, by which I have prayed
before the Lord, be they nighing to our Lord God by day
and night, that he make doom to *me* his servant, and to
his people Israel by all days; (And these words of mine,
with which I have prayed before the Lord, be they close
to the Lord our God day and night, so that he may grant

justice to *me* his servant, and to his people Israel by all
days;)
60 and (so that) all the peoples of [the] earth know, that
the Lord himself is God, and [there is] none other without
him (and there is no one else but him).
61 Also our heart be perfect with our Lord God, that we
go in his dooms, and keep his commandments, as also
today. (And let our hearts be perfect with the Lord our
God, so that we walk in his judgements, and obey his
commandments, as we do this day.)
62 Therefore the king, and all Israel with him, offered
sacrifices before the Lord.
63 And Solomon slew peaceable sacrifices, which he
offered to the Lord; of oxes two and twenty thousand,
and of sheep sixscore thousand; and the king and the
sons of Israel hallowed the temple of the Lord. (And
Solomon killed the peace offerings, which he offered to
the Lord; *yea, they killed* twenty-two thousand oxen, and
sixscore thousand sheep; and so the king and the
Israelites dedicated the Temple of the Lord.)
64 In that day the king hallowed the middle of the great
street, that was before the house of the Lord; for he made
there burnt sacrifice[s], and offering(s), and the inner
fatness of peaceable things; for the brazen altar that was
before the Lord was too little, and it might not take the
burnt sacrifice(s), and the offering(s), and the inner fatness
of peaceable things. (On that day the king dedicated the
center of the great courtyard that was before the House of
the Lord; for he offered there the burnt sacrifices, and the
offerings, and the inner fatness of the peace offerings; for
the bronze altar that was before the Lord was too small,
and it could not take, *or handle*, all the burnt sacrifices,
and the offerings, and the inner fatness of the peace
offerings.)
65 Therefore Solomon made in that time a solemn
feast, and all Israel with him, a great multitude, from the
entering of Hamath unto the strand of Egypt, before our
Lord God, in seven days and seven days, that is, fourteen
days (altogether). (And so Solomon, and all Israel with
him, a great multitude from the entering of Hamath unto
the River of Egypt, celebrated the Feast of Shelters before
the Lord our God, for seven days altogether.)
66 And in the eighth day he delivered the peoples,
which blessed the king, and went forth into their
tabernacles, and they were glad and of joyful heart on all
the goods that God had done to David, his servant, and
to Israel, his people. (And on the eighth day he let the
people go, who blessed the king, and went back to their
homes, and they were glad and had joyful hearts for all
the good things that God had done for his servant David,
and for his people Israel.)

CHAPTER 9

1 And it was done, when Solomon had performed the
building of the house of the Lord, and the building of the
king, and all thing that he coveted, and would make,
(And it was done, when Solomon had finished building
the House of the Lord, and the king's house, and all the
things that he desired, and would make,)
2 the Lord appeared to Solomon the second time, as
he (had) appeared to him (before) in Gibeon.
3 And the Lord said to him, I have heard thy prayer,
and thy beseeching, that thou hast besought before me; I
have hallowed this house, that thou hast builded, that I
should set there my name without end (I have dedicated,
or consecrated, this House which thou hast built, and I
have set my name there forevermore); and mine eyes and
mine heart shall be there in all days.
4 Also if thou goest before me, as thy father went, in
simpleness of heart, and in equity, and doest all things
which I have commanded to thee, and keepest my
dooms, and my lawful things, (And if thou goest before
me, as thy father went, with integrity, and uprightness,
and doest all the things which I have commanded to
thee, and obeyest my judgements, and my laws,)
5 I shall set the throne of thy realm upon Israel
without end, as I spake to David, thy father, and said, A
man of thy kin shall not be taken away from the throne of
Israel.
6 Forsooth if by turning away, ye and your sons turn
away, and follow not me, and keep not my behests and
ceremonies, which I have set forth to you, but ye go, and
worship alien gods, and honour them, (But if by turning
away, ye or your sons turn away, and do not follow me,
and do not obey my commands and statutes, which I
have set forth to you, but ye go, and worship other gods,
and honour them,)
7 I shall do away Israel from the face of the land
which I gave to them; and I shall cast away from my sight
the temple, which I [have] hallowed to my name (and I
shall throw away from my sight the Temple which I have
dedicated, *or consecrated*, in honour of my name); and
Israel shall be into a proverb and into a fable, to all
peoples.
8 And this house shall be into (an) ensample *of God's
offence*; each man that shall pass by it, shall wonder, and
shall hiss, and shall say, Why hath the Lord done thus to
this land, and to this house?
9 And they shall answer, For they forsook their Lord
God, that led the fathers of them out of Egypt; and they
followed alien gods (and they followed other gods), and
worshipped them, and honoured them; therefore the
Lord hath brought in upon them all this evil.
10 Soothly when twenty years were [ful]filled, after that
Solomon had builded (the) twain houses (after that
Solomon had begun to build the two houses), that is, the
house of the Lord, and the house of the king,
11 while Hiram, king of Tyre, gave to Solomon trees of

cedar, and of fir, and gold, by all thing that he had
needful; then Solomon gave to Hiram twenty cities in the
land of Galilee. (and Hiram, the king of Tyre, had given
to Solomon cedar, and fir, *or pine*, trees, and gold, yea,
all the things that he had need of; then Solomon gave
Hiram twenty cities in the land of Galilee.)
12 And Hiram went out of Tyre that he should see the
cities, which Solomon had given to him, and those
pleased not him; (And Hiram went out from Tyre to see
the cities which Solomon had given to him, and they did
not please him;)
13 and he said, Whether these be the cities, which
thou, brother, hast given to me? And he called those
cities the land of Cabul, *that is, displeasing (that is, The
Displeasing Land*), unto this day.
14 Also Hiram (had) sent to king Solomon sixscore
talents of gold.
15 This is the rent, which Solomon raised, to build the
house of the Lord, and his own house, (and the) Millo,
and the wall of Jerusalem, and Hazor, and Megiddo, and
Gezer.
16 (For) Pharaoh, king of Egypt, (had) ascended, and
took Gezer, and burnt it by fire; and he killed (the)
Canaanites, that dwelled in the city, and gave it into (a)
dower to his daughter, the wife of Solomon. (For
Pharaoh, the king of Egypt, had gone up, and took Gezer,
and burned it down; and he killed the Canaanites, who
lived in that city, and gave it as a dowry to his daughter,
Solomon's wife.)
17 Therefore Solomon builded Gezer (And so Solomon
rebuilt Gezer), and the lower Bethhoron,
18 and Baalath, and Tadmor in the land of (the)
wilderness;
19 and he made strong all the towns, that pertained to
him, and were without (a) wall, and the cities of chariots,
and the cities of knights, and whatever thing (it) pleased
him to build in Jerusalem, and in Lebanon, and in all the
land of his power.
20 (And) Solomon made tributaries unto this day (of) all
the people, that (were) left of the Amorites, Hittites, and
Perizzites, and Hivites, and Jebusites, which be not of the
sons of Israel,
21 the sons of these *heathen men*, that dwelled in the
land, that is, which the sons of Israel might not destroy.
(the sons of these *heathen*, who continued to live in the
land, that is, they whom the Israelites did not destroy.)
22 Soothly king Solomon ordained not any man of the
sons of Israel to serve, *that is, in vile works, and of the
fields*, but they were men of war, and servants of him,
and princes, and dukes, and masters of his chariots and
horses. (And King Solomon did not let any man of the
Israelites serve *in slavery, or in the fields*, but they all
were warriors, and his servants, and the leaders, and the
masters, of his chariots and of his horsemen.)
23 And five hundred and fifty princes were sovereigns
over all the works of Solomon, the which princes had the
people subject *to them*, and commanded to [the] works
ordained (and were in charge of the ordained works).
24 And the daughter of Pharaoh went up from the city
of David into her house, which house Solomon had
builded to her (which house Solomon had built for her);
then he builded (the) Millo.
25 Also Solomon offered in three times by all years
burnt sacrifices and peaceable sacrifices, on the altar
which he had builded to the Lord; and he burnt incense
before the Lord, and the temple was performed. (And
three times each year Solomon offered burnt sacrifices
and peace offerings, on the altar which he had built to
the Lord, and he burned incense before the Lord. And so
the Temple was completed.)
26 Also king Solomon made a navy in Eziongeber,
which is beside Elath, in the brink of the Red Sea, in the
land of Idumea. (And King Solomon also made a navy in
Eziongeber, which is beside Elath, on the Gulf of Akabah,
or Aqaba, in the land of Edom.)
27 And Hiram sent in that navy his servants, (those who
were) shipmen, and knowing of the sea, with the servants
of Solomon; (And Hiram sent some of his servants, those
who were shipmen, and knowledgeable about the sea, to
be in that navy with Solomon's servants;)
28 and when they had come into Ophir, they brought
from thence gold of four hundred and twenty talents to
king Solomon. (and when they had gone to Ophir, they
brought back gold from there worth four hundred and
twenty talents for King Solomon.)

CHAPTER 10

1 But also the queen of Sheba, when the fame of
Solomon was heard, came in the name of the Lord to
assay him in dark and doubtful questions. (And the queen
of Sheba, when she heard of Solomon's fame, *regarding
his knowledge* concerning the name of the Lord, came to
test him with dark and doubtful questions.)
2 And she entered with much fellowship and riches
into Jerusalem, and with camels bearing sweet smelling
things, and gold greatly without number, and precious
stones; and she came to king Solomon, and spake to him
all things which she had in her heart.
3 And Solomon taught her all [the] words which she
had put forth; no word was, that might be hid from the
king, and *which* he answered not to her. (And Solomon
taught her all the things that she asked him about; there
was nothing that was hid from the king, and *which* he did
not answer to her, *or share with her*.)
4 And the queen of Sheba saw all the wisdom of
Solomon, and the house that he had builded,
5 and the meats of his table (and the food on his
table), and the dwelling places of his servants, and the

orders of the men serving him, and the clothes of them,
and the butlers, and the burnt sacrifices which he offered
in the house of the Lord; and she had no more spirit.
6 And she said to the king, The word is true, that I
heard in my land, of thy words, and of thy wisdom;
7 and I believed not to men telling to me, till I myself
came, and saw with mine eyes, and proved that the half
part was not told to me; thy wisdom is more and thy
works, than the fame that I heard. (and I did not believe
what they told me, until I came myself, and saw with my
eyes, and proved that the half part was not told to me; thy
wisdom and thy works be more than the reports that I
have heard.)
8 Thy men be blessed, and thy servants be blessed,
these that stand before thee ever[more] (those who stand
before thee forevermore), and hear thy wisdom.
9 Blessed be thy Lord God, whom thou pleasedest,
and hath set thee on the throne of Israel; for the Lord
loved Israel without end, and hath ordained thee king,
that thou shouldest do doom and rightfulness (so that
thou can give judgement and show uprightness).
10 Therefore she gave to the king sixscore talents of
gold, and full many sweet smelling things, and precious
stones; so many sweet smelling things were no more
brought (there were never brought there again so many
sweet smelling things), as those which the queen of
Sheba gave to king Solomon.
11 But also the ship(s) of Hiram, that brought gold from
Ophir, brought from Ophir full many trees of thyine, and
precious stones. (And the ships of Hiram, that brought
gold from Ophir, also brought from Ophir a great deal of
thyine wood, and precious stones.)
12 And king Solomon made of the trees of thyine
undersettings of the house of the Lord, and of the king's
house, and harps, and citoles to singers; such (fine) trees
of thyine were not brought (there), neither seen (again),
till into this present day. (And King Solomon made from
the thyine wood undersettings for the House of the Lord,
and for the king's house, and harps and lutes for the
singers; there was never such fine thyine wood brought
there, nor seen again, unto this present day.)
13 Soothly king Solomon gave to the queen of Sheba
all things which she would have, and asked of him,
besides these things which he had given to her by the
king's gift willfully; and she turned again, and went into
her land with her servants. (And King Solomon gave the
queen of Sheba everything that she desired, and asked for
from him, besides those things which he had willingly, *or
freely*, given to her by the king's gift; and then she
returned, and went back to her land with her servants.)
14 Forsooth the weight of gold, that was offered to
Solomon by each year, was of six hundred and six and
sixty talents of gold,
15 besides that which the men that were on the
tollages, *that is, rents of things borne about in the land
(that is, the rents for things borne about in the land)*, and
that (the) merchants, and all men selling shields, and that
all the kings of Arabia, and the dukes of the land, gave.
16 And king Solomon made two hundred shields of
purest gold; he gave six hundred shekels of gold into the
plates of one shield (he gave six hundred shekels of gold
to make the plates for one shield);
17 and *he made* three hundred bucklers of proved
gold; three hundred talents of gold covered one buckler
(three pounds of gold covered one buckler). And the
king put those bucklers in the house of the forest of
Lebanon.
18 Also king Solomon made a great throne of ivory,
and covered it with full fine gold;
19 and the throne had six degrees; and the highness of
the throne was round in the hinder part (and the throne
had six steps; and the top of the throne was round on the
back part); and twain hands *were* on this side and on that
side, holding the seat, and two lions stood beside each
hand;
20 and twelve little lions standing on [the] six degrees,
(and twelve little lions standing on the six steps), on this
side and on that side; such a work was not made in all
realms.
21 But also all the vessels, of which king Solomon
drank, were of gold, and all the purtenance of the house
of the forest of Lebanon was of purest gold; silver was not
(used at all), neither it was areckoned of any price in the
days of Solomon.
22 For the ship(s) of the king went once by three years
with the ship(s) of Hiram into Tharshish, and brought
(back) from thence gold, and silver, and teeth of
elephants, and apes, and peacocks.
23 Therefore king Solomon was magnified above all
[the] kings of [the] earth in riches and wisdom.
24 And all earth desired to see the cheer of Solomon, to
hear the wisdom of him, which *wisdom* God had given
in his heart. (And the whole earth desired to come see
Solomon's face, to hear his wisdom, which *wisdom* God
had placed in his heart.)
25 And all men brought gifts to him, vessels of gold,
and of silver, clothes, and armours of battle (and arms, *or
weapons*, of battle), and sweet smelling things, and
horses, and mules, by each year.
26 And Solomon gathered together chariots, and
horsemen; and a thousand and four hundred chariots
were made to him, and twelve thousand horsemen; and
he disposed them by [the] strengthened cities, and with
the king in Jerusalem. (And Solomon gathered together
chariots, and horsemen; and a thousand and four
hundred chariots were made for him, and he had twelve
thousand horsemen; and he stationed them in the
fortified cities, and with the king himself in Jerusalem.)

27 And he made, that so great abundance of silver was
in Jerusalem, (as) how great was also (that) of (the) stones;
and he gave the multitude of cedars as (the) sycamores,
that grow in field places (and he made cedars to be like
the multitude of sycamores, which grow in the fields).
28 And the horses of Solomon were led out of Egypt,
and (out) of Coa; for (the) merchants of the king bought
them of Coa, and brought them to him, for [the] price
ordained. (And Solomon's horses were brought out of
Egypt, and out of Coa; for the king's merchants bought
them in Coa, and then brought them to him, for the
ordained price.)
29 For a chariot went out of Egypt for six hundred
shekels of silver, and an horse for an hundred and fifty
shekels; and by this manner all the kings of Hittites, and
of Syria, sold horses.

CHAPTER 11

1 Forsooth king Solomon loved burningly many alien
women, and the daughter of Pharaoh, and women of
Moab, and Ammonites, and Idumeans, and Sidonians,
and Hittites; (And King Solomon burningly loved many
foreign women, including the daughter of Pharaoh, and
women of Moab, and of the Ammonites, and Edomites,
and Sidonians, and Hittites;)
2 of the folks of which the Lord said to the sons of
Israel, Ye shall not enter to those folks, neither any of
them shall enter to you; for most certainly they shall turn
away your hearts, that ye follow the gods of them. And
so king Solomon was coupled to these women, by most
burning love (But King Solomon was coupled to these
women with a most burning love).
3 And wives as queens were seven hundred to him,
and three hundred secondary wives; and the women
turned away his heart.
4 And when he was then eld, his heart was depraved
by women, that he followed alien gods (And then when
he was old, his heart was so depraved by these women,
that he followed other gods); and his heart was not
perfect with his Lord God, as the heart of David, his
father, *was perfect*.
5 But Solomon worshipped Astarte, the goddess of
Sidonians, and Chemosh, the god of Moabites, and
Moloch, the idol of Ammonites; (For Solomon
worshipped Ashtoreth, the goddess of the Sidonians, and
Chemosh, the god of the Moabites, and Milcom, the god
of the Ammonites;)
6 and Solomon did that, that pleased not before the
Lord, and he full-filled not that he followed the Lord, as
David, his father. (and Solomon did what did not please
the Lord, and he did not follow fully after the Lord, as his
father David did.)
7 Then Solomon builded a temple to Chemosh, the
idol of Moab, in the hill which is (over) against Jerusalem,
and to Moloch, the idol of the sons of Ammon. (Then on
the hill that is east of Jerusalem, Solomon built a temple
for Chemosh, the false god of Moab, and for Moloch, the
false god of the Ammonites.)
8 And by this manner he did to all his alien wives, the
which burnt incenses, and offered to their gods. (And so
in this manner he did for all his foreign wives, who
burned incense, and offered to their gods.)
9 Therefore the Lord was wroth to Solomon, for his
soul was turned away from the Lord God of Israel; that
appeared to him the second time, (And so the Lord was
angry with Solomon; for his soul was turned away from
the Lord God of Israel, who had appeared to him twice,)
10 and [had] commanded of this word, that he should
not follow alien gods; and he kept not those things,
which the Lord commanded to him. (and had
commanded this thing, that he should not follow other
gods; but he did not obey those things, which the Lord
had commanded to him.)
11 Therefore the Lord said to Solomon, For thou
haddest this thing with thee, and keptest not my
covenant, and my behests, which I commanded to thee, I
shall break, and I shall part thy realm, and I shall give it
to thy servant. (And so the Lord said to Solomon, For
thou hast done this thing, and did not keep my covenant,
and obey my commands, which I commanded to thee, I
shall break up, and I shall divide thy kingdom, and I shall
give it to thy servant.)
12 Nevertheless I shall not do (it) in thy days, for David,
thy father (for the sake of thy father David); I shall cut it
(off) from the hand of thy son;
13 neither I shall do away all the realm, but I shall give
one lineage to thy son, for David, my servant, and for
Jerusalem, which I chose. (nor shall I take away all the
kingdom, but I shall give one tribe to thy son, for the sake
of my servant David, and for Jerusalem, which I have
chosen.)
14 Forsooth the Lord raised to Solomon an adversary,
Hadad (the) Idumean, of the king's seed, that was in
Edom. (And the Lord raised up an adversary to Solomon,
Hadad the Edomite, of the king's descendants, who was
in Edom, *or Idumea*.)
15 For when David was in Idumea, and Joab, the
prince of *his* chivalry, had gone up to bury them that
were slain, and he had slain each male kind in Idumea;
(For when David was in Edom, Joab, the leader of *his*
cavalry, *or of his army*, had gone to bury those who were
killed, after that he had killed each male in Edom;)
16 for Joab, and all Israel, dwelled there by six months,
till they had killed each male kind in Idumea; (for Joab,
and all Israel, stayed there for six months, until they had
killed each male in Edom;)
17 Hadad himself fled, and (some) men of Idumea, of
the servants of his father, with him, that he should enter

into Egypt; soothly Hadad was a little child. (and Hadad
himself had fled, with some Edomites, some of his
father's servants, so that he could escape to Egypt; for
Hadad was still a young boy.)
18 And when they had risen from Midian, they came
into Paran; and they took with them men of Paran, and
entered into Egypt, to Pharaoh, king of Egypt; and
Pharaoh gave an house to him, and ordained to him
meats, and assigned to him land. (And after they had left
Midian, they came to Paran; and they took with them
men from Paran, and then went to Egypt, unto Pharaoh,
the king of Egypt; and Pharaoh gave him a house, and
ordained him sustenance, and assigned him some land.)
19 And Hadad found grace before Pharaoh greatly, in
so much that Pharaoh gave to him a wife, the sister of his
wife, (that is,) the sister of the queen, (the sister) of
Tahpenes. (And Hadad found much favour before
Pharaoh, so much so that Pharaoh eventually gave him a
wife, his own wife's sister, that is, the sister of Queen
Tahpenes.)
20 And the sister of Tahpenes engendered to him a son,
Genubath; and Tahpenes nursed him in the house of
Pharaoh; and Genubath dwelled before Pharaoh (and
Genubath lived with Pharaoh), with the sons of Pharaoh.
21 And when Hadad had heard in Egypt, that David
slept with his fathers, and that Joab, the prince of (the)
chivalry, was dead, he said to Pharaoh, Suffer thou me,
that I go into my land. (And when Hadad had heard in
Egypt, that David slept with his forefathers, *that is, that he
had died*, and that Joab, the leader of the cavalry, *or of
the army*, had also died, he said to Pharaoh, Allow me to
go back to my own land.)
22 And Pharaoh said to him, And of what thing hast
thou need with me, that thou seekest to go to thy land?
And he answered, Of nothing; but I beseech thee, that
thou deliver me/that thou let me go. (And Pharaoh said to
him, And what thing hast thou still need of from me, that
thou now seekest to go back to thy own land *to get*? And
he answered, Nothing; but I beseech thee, that thou let
me go.)
23 And God raised (up) an*other* adversary to Solomon,
Rezon, the son of Eliadah, that fled Hadadezer, king of
Zobah, his lord (who fled from Hadadezer, the king of
Zobah, his lord);
24 and [he] gathered men against him, and was made
the prince of thieves, when David killed them (of Zobah);
and they went to Damascus, and dwelled there (and
stayed there); and they made him king in Damascus.
25 And he was [an] adversary of Israel in all the days of
Solomon; and this is (besides) the evil of Hadad, and his
hatred against Israel; and he reigned in Syria. (And he
was an adversary of Israel in all the days of Solomon,
besides the evil that Hadad did; and he hated Israel, and
he reigned upon Syria.)
26 (And) Also Jeroboam, the son of Nebat, of Ephraim
of Zereda, the servant of Solomon, of which Jeroboam, a
woman widow (a widow woman), Zeruah by name, was
(his) mother, he (also) raised (up) his hand against the
king.
27 And this was [the] cause of (his) rebelty against the
king; for Solomon builded Millo, and made even the
swallow of the city of David, his father. (And this was the
story of his rebellion against the king; it happened when
Solomon had built the Millo, and closed the breach in
the wall of the City of David, his father.)
28 Forsooth Jeroboam was a mighty man and strong;
and Solomon saw the young waxing man (to be) of good
kindred, and witting in things to be done, and Solomon
made him prefect, *either sovereign*, upon the tributes of
all the house of Joseph. (And Jeroboam was a strong and
mighty man; and Solomon saw that the young man was
from a good family, and knowing how to do things, and
so Solomon made him prefect, *or the ruler*, over all the
taxes, *or all the levies*, in the house, *or the territory*, of
the tribe of Joseph.)
29 Therefore it was done in that time, that Jeroboam
went out of Jerusalem; and Ahijah of Shiloh, a prophet,
covered with a new mantle, found him in the way (met
him on the way); and they twain were alone in the field.
30 And Ahijah took his new mantle, with which he was
covered, and he cut *it* into twelve parts;
31 and said to Jeroboam, Take to thee ten cuttings *of
the mantle*; for the Lord God of Israel saith these things,
Lo! I shall cut (off) the realm from the hand of Solomon,
and I shall give to thee ten lineages (and I shall give ten
tribes to thee);
32 but one lineage shall dwell to him, for David, my
servant, and for Jerusalem, the city which I chose of all
the lineages of Israel; (but one tribe shall stay with him,
for the sake of my servant David, and for the sake of
Jerusalem, the city which I have chosen out of all the
tribes of Israel;)
33 *this cutting of the realm shall be*; for Solomon
forsook me, and worshipped Astarte, the goddess of
Sidonians, and Chemosh, the god of Moab, and Moloch,
the god of the sons of Ammon; and [he] went not in my
ways, that he did rightwiseness before me, and my
behests, and my dooms, as David, his father, *did*. (*this
breaking of his kingdom shall be* because Solomon
deserted me, and worshipped Ashtoreth, the goddess of
the Sidonians, and Chemosh, the god of the Moabites,
and Milcom, the god of the Ammonites; and he went not
in my ways, so that he did what was right before me, and
followed my laws, and my judgements, like his father
David *did*.)
34 And I shall not take away all the realm from his
hand, but I shall put him duke in all the days of his life,
for David, my servant, whom I chose, which kept my

behests, and my commandments. (And I shall not take
away the whole kingdom from him, but I shall keep him
as the leader in all the days of his life, for the sake of my
servant David, whom I chose, who obeyed my laws, and
my commandments.)
35 Soothly I shall take away the realm from the hand of
his son, and I shall give [the] ten lineages to thee;
36 forsooth I shall give one lineage to his son, that a
lantern dwell to David, my servant (so that a light, *or a
flame*, shall remain for my servant David), in all days
before me in Jerusalem, the city which I chose, that my
name should be there.
37 Forsooth I shall take thee, and thou shalt reign on all
things which thy soul desireth, and thou shalt be king
upon Israel.
38 Therefore if thou shalt hear all things which I shall
command to thee, and if thou shalt go in my ways, and if
thou shalt do that, that is rightful before me, and if thou
shalt keep my commandments, and my behests, as
David, my servant, did, I shall be with thee, and I shall
build a faithful house to thee, as I builded an house to
David, and I shall give Israel to thee; (And so if thou shalt
obey all the things which I shall command to thee, and if
thou shalt go in my ways, and if thou shalt do what is
right before me, and if thou shalt obey my
commandments, and my laws, as my servant David did, I
shall be with thee, and I shall build thee a steadfast
house, like I built a house for David, and I shall give
Israel to thee;)
39 and I shall torment the seed of David on this thing,
nevertheless not in all days. (and I shall torment David's
descendants because of this, but not forever.)
40 Therefore Solomon would slay Jeroboam, which
rose (who rose up), and fled into Egypt, to Shishak, king
of Egypt; and he was in Egypt unto the death of Solomon.
41 Forsooth the residue of the words of Solomon, and
all things which he did, and his wisdom, lo! all *those*
things be written in the book of [the] words of [the] days
of Solomon.
42 And the days in which Solomon reigned in
Jerusalem upon all Israel, be forty years.
43 And Solomon slept with his fathers, and was buried
in the city of David, his father; and Rehoboam, his son,
reigned for him.

CHAPTER 12

1 Forsooth Rehoboam came into Shechem; for all
Israel was gathered thither to make him king.
2 And soothly Jeroboam, the son of Nebat, when he
was yet in Egypt, and fled from the face of king Solomon,
turned again from Egypt, for the death of Solomon was
heard; (And Jeroboam, the son of Nebat, when he was
still in Egypt, where he had fled from King Solomon,
heard of Solomon's death, and returned from Egypt;)
3 and they sent, and called him. Therefore Jeroboam
came, and all the multitude of Israel, and they spake to
Rehoboam, and said,
4 Thy father putted the most hard yoke upon us,
therefore abate thou a little now of the hardest
commandment of thy father, and of the full grievous yoke
that he hath put upon us, and we shall serve to thee. (Thy
father put the hardest yoke upon us, but now, if thou
abate a little thy father's hardest commands, and the most
grievous yoke that he hath put upon us, then we shall
serve thee.)
5 And Rehoboam said to them, Go ye till to the third
day, and turn ye again to me (Go ye away until the third
day, and then return ye here). And when the people had
gone,
6 king Rehoboam took counsel with the elder men,
that stood before Solomon, his father, while he lived yet
(while yet he lived); and Rehoboam said, What counsel
give ye to me, that I answer to the people?
7 Which said to him, If thou obeyest today to this
people, and servest this people, and givest stead to their
asking, and speakest to them light, or easy, words, they
shall be servants to thee in all days (they shall be thy
servants forevermore).
8 And Rehoboam forsook the counsel of [the] eld
men, which they gave to him, and took (counsel with
the) young men, that were nourished with him, and stood
nigh [to] him; (But Rehoboam forsook the elders' counsel,
which they gave him, and sought counsel with the young
men, who grew up with him, and stood close to him;)
9 and he said to them, What counsel give ye to me,
that I answer to this people, that said to me, Make thou
easier the yoke that thy father hath put upon us?
10 And the young men, that were nourished with him
(who grew up with him), said to him, Thus speak thou to
this people, that spake to thee, and said, Thy father made
grievous our yoke, relieve thou us; thus thou shalt speak
to them, My least finger is greater than the back of my
father;
11 and now (though) my father putted on you a
grievous yoke, forsooth I shall add on(to) your yoke (but I
shall add to your yoke); my father beat you with
scourges, but I shall beat you with scorpions[3].
12 Therefore Jeroboam, and all the people, came to
Rehoboam, in the third day, as the king spake, saying,
Turn ye again to me in the third day (Come ye back to
me in three days).
13 And the king answered hard things to the people,
while the counsel of [the] elder men was forsaken, that
they had given to him;
14 and he spake to them by the counsel of [the] young

[3] That is, a kind of (the) hardest scourge, that hath knots of lead, either of iron, in the end of cords (on the end of the cords).

men, and said, My father made grievous your yoke,
forsooth I shall add to your yoke; my father beat you with
scourges, but I shall beat you with scorpions.
15 And the king assented not to the people, for the Lord
had turned *him* away, that the Lord should raise up his
word, that he had spoken in the hand of *the prophet*
Ahijah of Shiloh to Jeroboam, the son of Nebat. (And the
king assented not to the people, for the Lord had turned
him away *from them*, so that the Lord could raise up his
word, which he had spoken by *the prophet* Ahijah of
Shiloh to Jeroboam, the son of Nebat.)
16 Then the people saw, that the king would not hear
them, and the people answered to the king, and said,
What part is to us in David, either what heritage in the
son of Jesse? Israel, turn thou again into thy tabernacles;
now, David, see thou (to) thine house. And Israel went
into his tabernacles. (Then the people saw that the king
would not listen to them, and the people answered to the
king, and said, What part is for us with David, or what
inheritance with the son of Jesse? Israel, return thou to
thy homes; and David, see thou to thy own house. And
the people of Israel went back to their homes.)
17 Forsooth Rehoboam reigned on the sons of Israel,
which dwelled in the cities of Judah. (And so Rehoboam
reigned only upon those Israelites, who lived in the cities
of Judah.)
18 Therefore king Rehoboam sent Adoram, that was on
the tributes; and all the people of Israel stoned him, and
he was dead (And so King Rehoboam sent out Adoram,
who was over the taxes, *or the levies*; and all the people
of Israel stoned him, and he died). Forsooth king
Rehoboam went up hastily upon his chariot, and fled into
Jerusalem;
19 and Israel departed from the house of David, till into
this present day. (and so Israel, *that is, the Northern
Kingdom*, hast been in rebellion against the house of
David, unto this present day.)
20 Forsooth it was done, when all Israel had heard that
Jeroboam [was] turned again, they sent, and called him,
when the company was gathered together, and they
made him king upon all Israel; and no man followed the
house of David, except the lineage alone of Judah. (And
so it was done, when all Israel had heard that Jeroboam
had returned, they sent for him, and when the people
were gathered together, they made him king upon all
Israel; and no man followed the house of David, except
the tribe of Judah.)
21 And Rehoboam came to Jerusalem, and gathered
together all the house of Judah, and the lineage of
Benjamin, an hundred and fourscore thousand of chosen
men and warriors, that they should fight against the
house of Israel, and should bring again the realm to
Rehoboam, the son of Solomon (to fight against the
house of Israel, and bring back the kingdom to
Rehoboam, the son of Solomon).
22 Forsooth the word of God was made to Shemaiah,
the man of God, and said,
23 Speak thou to Rehoboam, the son of Solomon, king
of Judah, and to all the house of Judah and of Benjamin,
and to the residue of the people, and say thou,
24 The Lord saith these things, Ye shall not go up,
neither ye shall fight against your brethren, the sons of
Israel; turn *each* man again into his house, for this word
is done of me (*every* man return to his house, for this
word is from me). (And) They heard the word of the
Lord, and they turned again from the journey, as the Lord
commanded to them.
25 And Jeroboam builded Shechem, in the hill of
Ephraim, and dwelled there (Then Jeroboam built
Shechem, in the hill country of Ephraim, and lived there);
and he went out from thence, and builded Penuel.
26 And Jeroboam said in his heart, Now the realm shall
turn again to the house of David, (And Jeroboam said in
his heart, Even now the kingdom shall return to the house
of David,)
27 if this people ascendeth to Jerusalem, that it make
sacrifice in the house of the Lord in Jerusalem; and *then*
the heart of this people shall turn again to their lord,
Rehoboam, king of Judah; and they shall slay me, and
shall turn again to him. (if these people goeth up to
Jerusalem, to make sacrifice in the House of the Lord in
Jerusalem; *for then* the heart of these people shall return
to their lord, Rehoboam, the king of Judah; and they shall
kill me, and they shall return to him.)
28 And by counsel thought out, Jeroboam made twain
golden calves, and he said to the people, Do not ye
ascend more into Jerusalem; Israel, lo! thy gods, that led
thee out of the land of Egypt. (And so, by counsel
carefully thought out, Jeroboam made two gold calves,
and he said to the people, Do not ye go up to Jerusalem
any more; Israel, lo! thy gods, that led thee out of the
land of Egypt.)
29 And he set one *calf* in Bethel, and the tother in Dan.
30 And this word was made to Israel into sin; for the
people went into Dan, to worship the calf. (And this thing
became a sin in Israel; and some people went all the way
up to Dan to worship the calf there.)
31 And Jeroboam made temples in high places (And
Jeroboam made temples at the hill shrines), and *he made*
priests (out) of the last men of the people, the which were
not of the sons of Levi.
32 And the king ordained a solemn day in the eighth
month, in the fifteen day of the month, by [the] likeness
of the solemnity that was hallowed in Judah. And the
king went up, and made in like manner an altar in Bethel,
that he should offer to the calves, which he had made;
and he ordained in Bethel priests of the high places,
which he had made. (And the king ordained a feast in the

eighth month, on the fifteen day of the month, like the feast that was kept in Judah. And the king went up to Bethel, and offered on the altar that he had made to the calves, which he had made; and he ordered the priests of the hill shrines, to serve at the altar in Bethel, which he had made.)

33 And he went up upon the altar, which he had builded in Bethel, in the fifteenth day of the eighth month, which he had feigned of his heart; and he made a solemnity to the sons of Israel, and he went upon the altar, that he should burn incense. (And so he went up to the altar, which he had built in Bethel, on the fifteenth day of the eighth month, which *month* he had chosen out of his own heart; and he made a feast for the sons of Israel, and he went up to the altar, so that he could burn incense on it.)

CHAPTER 13

1 And lo! a man of God came from Judah, by the word of the Lord, into Bethel, while Jeroboam stood upon the altar, casting incense (while Jeroboam stood by the altar, throwing incense).

2 And he cried out against the altar, by the word of the Lord, and said, Altar! altar! the Lord saith these things, Lo! a son, Josiah by name, shall be born to the house of David; and he shall offer upon thee the priests of (the) high things, the which burn now incense in thee, and he shall burn the bones of men upon thee (and he shall offer upon thee the priests of the hill shrines, who now burn incense upon thee, and he shall burn men's bones upon thee).

3 And he gave a sign in that day, and said, This shall be the sign that the Lord spake, Lo! the altar shall be cut, and the ash which is therein, shall be shed out. (And he gave a sign on that day, and said, This shall be the sign that the Lord spoke, Lo! the altar shall be split open, and the ashes that are upon it, shall be poured out.)

4 And when the king had heard the word of the man of God, which he had cried against the altar in Bethel, the king held forth his hand from the altar, and said, Take ye him. And his hand dried (up), which he had held forth, and he might not draw it again to himself.

5 Also the altar was cut, and the ash was shed out of the altar, by the sign which the man of God before-said, in the word of the Lord. (And the altar was split open, and the ashes were poured out of the altar, by the sign which the man of God had foretold, by the word of the Lord.)

6 And the king said to the man of God, Beseech thou (before) the face of the Lord thy God, and pray thou for me, that mine hand be restored to me. And the man of God prayed (before) the face of the Lord; and the hand of the king turned again to him (and the king's hand was restored to him), and it was made as it was before.

7 And the king spake to the man of God, (and said,) Come thou home with me, that thou eat, and I shall give gifts to thee.

8 And the man of God said to the king, Though thou shalt give to me the half part of thine house, I shall not come with thee, neither I shall eat bread, neither I shall drink water in this place.

9 for so it was commanded to me by the word of the Lord, commanding, Thou shalt not eat bread, neither thou shalt drink water, neither thou shalt turn again by the way by which thou camest.

10 Therefore he went by another way, and turned not again by the way, by which he came into Bethel.

11 Forsooth an eld prophet dwelled *then* in Bethel, to whom his sons came, and told to him all the works which the man of God had done in that day in Bethel; and they [also] told to their father the words which he spake to the king.

12 And the father of them said to them, By what way went he? His sons showed to him the way, by which the man of God went, that came from Judah (who came from Judah).

13 And he said to his sons, Saddle ye an ass to me. And when they had saddled *the ass*, he went up, (And he said to his sons, Saddle ye up a donkey for me. And when they had saddled up *the donkey*, he rode on it,)

14 and went after the man of God, and found him sitting under a terebinth. And he said to the man of God, Whether thou art the man of God, that camest from Judah? He answered, I am.

15 And he said to him, Come thou with me home, that thou eat bread. (And he said to him, Come thou home with me, so that thou can eat some bread.)

16 And he said, I may not turn again (I cannot return), neither come with thee, neither I shall eat bread, neither I shall drink water in this place;

17 for the Lord spake to me in the word of the Lord (for the Lord spoke to me by the word of the Lord), and said, Thou shalt not eat bread, and thou shalt not drink water there, neither thou shalt turn again by the way by which thou wentest *thither*.

18 And he said to him, And I am a prophet like thee; and an angel spake to me by the word of the Lord, and said, Lead again him into thine house, that he eat bread, and drink water (Bring him back to thy house, so that he can eat some food, and drink some water). (But) He deceived the man of God,

19 and brought *him* (back) again with him. Therefore he ate bread in his house, and drank water.

20 And when he sat at the table, the word of the Lord was made to the prophet[4] that brought him (back) again;

---

[4] *(The) revelation of prophesy is given sometime to evil men, as to Balaam, in (the) 22ND Chapter of Numbers.*

21 and he cried [out] to the man of God that came from
Judah, and said, The Lord saith these things, For thou
obeyedest not to the mouth of the Lord, and keptest not
the commandment which thy Lord God commanded to
thee,
22 and thou turnedest (back) again, and atest bread,
and drankest water in the place in which I commanded to
thee, that thou shouldest not eat bread, neither shouldest
drink water, thy dead body shall not be borne into the
sepulchre of thy fathers.
23 And when he had eaten and drunk, the prophet,
whom he had brought again, saddled his ass (the
prophet, whom he had brought back, saddled up his
donkey).
24 And when he had gone forth, a lion found him in
the way, and killed *him*. And his dead body was cast
forth in the way; soothly the ass stood beside him, and
the lion also stood beside the dead body. (And when he
had gone forth, a lion found him on the way, and killed
him. And his dead body was thrown down on the way;
and the donkey stood beside him, and the lion also stood
beside his dead body.)
25 And lo! men passing saw the dead body cast forth in
the way (And lo! men passing by saw the dead body
thrown down on the way), and the lion standing beside
the dead body; and they came, and published *it* in the
city, in which the eld prophet dwelled.
26 And when that prophet, that brought him (back)
again from the way, had heard this, he said, It is the man
of God, that was unobedient to the mouth of God; and
the Lord betook him to the lion, that hath broken him,
and killed him, by the word of the Lord which he spake
to him.
27 And he said to his sons, Saddle ye an ass to me
(Saddle ye up a donkey for me). And when they had
saddled (it up),
28 and he had gone, he found his dead body cast forth
in the way, and the ass and the lion standing beside the
dead body; and the lion ate not the dead body, neither
hurted the ass. (and he had gone there, he found his dead
body thrown down on the way, and the donkey and the
lion standing beside the dead body; and the lion had not
eaten the dead body, nor had hurt the donkey.)
29 Therefore the prophet took the dead body of the
man of God, and put it on the ass; and he turned again,
and brought it into the city of the eld prophet, that he
should bewail him. (And so the prophet took the dead
body of the man of God, and put it on his donkey; and
then the old prophet returned, and brought the body
back to the city, so that he could bewail, *or mourn*, him.)
30 And he put his dead body in his (own) sepulchre,
and they bewailed him, *and said*, Alas! alas! my brother!
31 And when they had bewailed him, he said to his
sons, When I shall be dead (When I shall die), bury me in
the sepulchre, in which the man of God is buried; put ye
my bones beside his bones.
32 For soothly the word shall come, which he before-
said in the word of the Lord, against the altar that is in
Bethel, and against all the temples of [the] high places,
which be in the cities of Samaria. (For truly the word
shall come to pass, which he foretold by the word of the
Lord, against the altar that is in Bethel, and against all the
temples of the hill shrines, which be in the cities of
Samaria.)
33 After these words Jeroboam turned not again from
his worst way, but on the contrary, of the last of the
people he made priests of (the) high places; whoever
would, [he] fulfilled his hand, and he was made [a] priest
of (the) high places. (And after this thing Jeroboam turned
not away from his worst ways, but on the contrary, he
made priests for the hill shrines from the lowest people;
yea, whoever desired it, he consecrated him, and he was
made a priest of the hill shrines.)
34 And for this cause the house of Jeroboam sinned,
and it was destroyed, and done away from the face of the
earth.

CHAPTER 14

1 In that time Abijah, (the) son of Jeroboam, was sick.
2 And Jeroboam said to his wife, Rise thou up, and
change clothing, that thou be not known, that thou art
the wife of Jeroboam; and go thou into Shiloh, where
Ahijah, the prophet, is, which spake to me, that I should
reign upon this people. (And Jeroboam said to his wife,
Rise thou up, and change your clothes, so that thou shalt
not be known, that thou art Jeroboam's wife; and go thou
to Shiloh, where the prophet Ahijah is, who spoke to me,
and said that I would reign upon this people.)
3 Also take thou in thine hand ten loaves, and a cake,
and a vessel of honey, and go thou to him; for he shall
show to thee, what shall befall to this child.
4 The wife of Jeroboam did as he said, and she rose
up, and went into Shiloh, and came into the house of
Ahijah; and Ahijah might not see, for his eyes dimmed
for eld (age). (And Jeroboam's wife did as he said, and
she rose up, and went to Shiloh, and came to Ahijah's
house; and Ahijah could not see, for his eyes had
dimmed because of old age.)
5 Forsooth the Lord said to Ahijah, Lo! the wife of
Jeroboam entereth, that she counsel (with) thee on her
son, which is sick (who is sick); thou shalt speak these
and these things to her. Therefore when she had entered,
and had feigned herself to be *that* (which) she was not,
6 Ahijah heard the sound of the feet of her entering by
the door, and he said, Enter thou, the wife of Jeroboam;
why feignest thou thee to be another? Forsooth I am sent
(to be) an hard messenger, *that is, (one) telling hard
things*, to thee (For I am sent with a hard message for

thee).
7 Go thou, and say to Jeroboam, The Lord God of
Israel saith these things, For I enhanced thee from the
midst of the people, and I gave thee (to be) duke on my
people Israel (and I made thee the leader of my people
Israel),
8 and I cutted the realm of the house of David, and I
gave it to thee, and (yet) thou were not as my servant
David, that kept my behests, and followed me in all his
heart, and did that that was pleasant in my sight; (and I
cut away the kingdom from the house of David, and I
gave it to thee, and yet thou were not like my servant
David, who obeyed my commands, and followed me
with all his heart, and did what was pleasing in my sight;)
9 but thou hast wrought evil, over all men that were
before thee, and madest to thee alien gods, and welled
those together, that thou shouldest excite me/thou
shouldest stir me to wrathfulness, soothly thou hast cast
forth me behind thy back. (but thou hast brought forth
evil, more than all the men who were before thee, and
madest other gods for thyself, and welded those together,
so that thou shouldest stir me to anger, truly thou hast
thrown me behind thy back.)
10 Therefore lo! I shall bring in evils upon the house of
Jeroboam, and I shall smite the house of Jeroboam unto a
pisser *to the wall*, and unto him that is imprisoned, and
the last in Israel (and I shall strike down the house of
Jeroboam unto a pisser *on the wall*, and unto him who is
imprisoned, and the last in Israel); and I shall cleanse the
relics, *or remnants*, of the house of Jeroboam, as dung is
wont to be cleansed unto purity, *either cleanness*[5];
11 soothly dogs shall eat them, that shall die of the
house of Jeroboam in the city; and birds of the air shall
devour them, that shall die in the field; for the Lord
spake. (truly the dogs shall eat those of the house of
Jeroboam who shall die in the city; and the birds of the
air shall devour those who shall die in the field; for the
Lord hath spoken.)
12 Therefore rise thou, and go into thine house; and in
that entering of thy feet into the city, the child shall die.
(And so rise thou up, and go to thy house; and with the
entry of thy feet into the city, the child shall die.)
13 And all Israel shall bewail him, and shall bury *him*;
for this *child* alone of Jeroboam shall be borne into the
sepulchre, for a good word is found on him of the Lord
God of Israel, in (all) the house of Jeroboam. (And all
Israel shall bewail, *or mourn*, him, and shall bury *him*; for
only this *child* of Jeroboam shall have a proper burial,
because only in him is there found any good toward the
Lord God of Israel, in all the house of Jeroboam.)
14 Forsooth the Lord shall ordain to him(self) a king
upon Israel, that shall smite the house of Jeroboam, in
this day, and in this time, *that is, of nigh*; (And the Lord
shall ordain for himself a king upon Israel, who shall
strike the house of Jeroboam, on this day, and at this
time, *that is, very soon*;)
15 and the Lord God of Israel shall smite, as a reed in
the water is wont to be moved; and he shall draw out
Israel from this good land, which he gave to their fathers,
and he shall winnow them over the flood, for they made
to them *maumet* woods, that they should stir the Lord to
ire. (and the Lord God shall strike Israel, like a reed in the
water is wont to be shaken; and he shall pull Israel out of
this good land, which he gave to their forefathers, and he
shall scatter them beyond the Euphrates River, for they
made for themselves *sacred* groves, *and poles*, and stirred
the Lord to anger.)
16 And the Lord God shall betake Israel *to his enemies*,
for the sins of Jeroboam, that sinned, and made Israel to
do sin. (And the Lord God shall abandon Israel, for the
sins of Jeroboam, who sinned, and made Israel to do sin.)
17 Therefore the wife of Jeroboam rose (up), and went
(away), and came into Tirzah; and when she entered into
the threshold of the house, the child was dead (the child
died).
18 And they buried him; and all Israel bewailed him,
by the word of the Lord, which he spake in the hand of
his servant, Ahijah the prophet (which he spoke by his
servant, the prophet Ahijah).
19 Forsooth, lo! the residue of the words of Jeroboam,
how he fought, and how he reigned, be written in the
book of [the] words of the days of [the] kings of Israel.
20 Forsooth the days, in which Jeroboam reigned, be
two and twenty years; and Jeroboam slept with his
fathers, and Nadab, his son, reigned for him.
21 Forsooth Rehoboam, the son of Solomon, reigned in
Judah; Rehoboam was of one and forty years, when he
began to reign, and he reigned seventeen years in
Jerusalem, the city which the Lord chose of all the
lineages of Israel (the city which the Lord chose out of all
the tribes of Israel), that he should set his name there.
And the name of his mother was Naamah (the)
Ammonite.
22 And Judah did evil before the Lord, and they stirred
him to ire on all things, which their fathers did in their
sins, by which they sinned. (And *the people of* Judah did
evil before the Lord, and they stirred him to anger with
their sins which they sinned, more than all the things that
their forefathers had done.)
23 For also they builded to themselves altars, and
images, and woods (For they also built altars for
themselves, and poles, and sacred groves), on each high
hill, and under each tree full of boughs.
24 But also men of women's conditions/womanish men
were in the land, and they did all the abominations of

[5] (That is,) dung is not cleansed in itself, but the place in which the dung is, is cleansed, when the dung is cast out.

heathen men, which the Lord all-brake before the face of
the sons of Israel. (And also male and female whores
were in the land, *serving* at the hill shrines, and they did
all the abominations of the heathen, whom the Lord had
cast out before the Israelites.)
25 Forsooth in the fifth year of the realm of Rehoboam
(Now in the fifth year of Rehoboam's reign), Shishak, the
king of Egypt, went up into Jerusalem;
26 and he took the treasures of the house of the Lord,
and the king's treasures, and he ravished all things; also
he ravished the golden shields which Solomon made.
(and he took away the treasures of the House of the Lord,
and the king's treasures, and he took everything *that he
could get his hands on*; and *he also took away* the gold
shields which Solomon had made.)
27 For which king Rehoboam made brazen shields, and
gave those in(to) the hands of [the] dukes of (the) shield-
makers, and of them that watched before the door of the
house of the king. (And King Rehoboam replaced them
with bronze shields, and gave them to the officers who
guarded the door of the house of the king.)
28 And when the king entered into the house of the
Lord, they that had office to go before (they who had the
duty to go before him), bare those, and (then) they bare
those again to the place of armour of [the] shield-makers.
29 Forsooth, lo! the residue of the words of Rehoboam,
and all things which he did, be written in the book of
[the] words of [the] days of [the] kings of Judah.
30 And battle was betwixt Rehoboam and Jeroboam, in
all (their) days.
31 And Rehoboam slept with his fathers, and was
buried with them in the city of David. And the name of
his mother *was* Naamah (the) Ammonite; and Abijam, his
son, reigned for him.

CHAPTER 15

1 Therefore in the eighteenth year of the realm of
Jeroboam, the son of Nebat, Abijam reigned upon Judah.
(And so in the eighteenth year of the reign of Jeroboam,
the son of Nebat, Abijam began to reign upon Judah.)
2 Three years he reigned in Jerusalem (He reigned for
three years in Jerusalem); the name of his mother was
Maachah, the daughter of Abishalom.
3 And he went in all the sins of his father, which he
did before him; and his heart was not perfect with his
Lord God, as the heart of David, his father, *was perfect*.
4 But for David, his Lord God gave to him a lantern in
Jerusalem, that he should raise (up) his son after him, and
that he should stand in Jerusalem; (But for David's sake,
the Lord his God gave him a light, *or a flame*, in
Jerusalem, so that he would raise up his son after him,
and keep Jerusalem secure;)
5 for David had done rightfulness in the eyes of the
Lord, and had not bowed [away] from all things that the
Lord had commanded to him, in all the days of his life,
except the word of Uriah (the) Hittite[6]. (for David had
done what was right in the eyes of the Lord, and had not
turned away from all the things that the Lord had
commanded to him, in all the days of his life, except in
the matter of Uriah the Hittite.)
6 Nevertheless battle was betwixt Abijam and
Jeroboam, in all the time of his life. (And there was
always battle between Rehoboam and Jeroboam, in all
the time of Abijam's life.)
7 Soothly the residue of the words of Abijam, and all
things that he did, whether these be not written in the
book of [the] words of [the] days of the kings of Judah?
And battle was betwixt Abijam and Jeroboam (And there
was always battle between Abijam and Jeroboam).
8 And Abijam slept with his fathers; and they buried
him in the city of David; and Asa, his son, reigned for him.
9 And Asa, king of Judah, reigned in the twentieth
year of Jeroboam, king of Israel; (And Asa, the king of
Judah, began to reign in the twentieth year of Jeroboam,
the king of Israel;)
10 and Asa reigned one and forty years in Jerusalem.
The name of his (grand)mother *was* Maachah, the
daughter of Abishalom.
11 And Asa did rightfulness in the sight of the Lord, as
David, his father, *did*;
12 and he took away from the land men of women's
conditions, and he purged all the filths of idols, which his
fathers (had) made.
13 Furthermore and he removed Maachah, his
(grand)mother, that she should not be princess in the
solemn things of *the idol* Priapus, and in his maumet
wood that she had hallowed; and he destroyed the den of
him, and he brake the foulest simulacrum, and burnt it in
the strand of Kidron; (And furthermore he removed
Maachah, his grandmother, so that she would no longer
be the queen mother, for she had erected *an idol of*
Priapus in a grove, and worshipped it/for she had made
an obscene idol for the worship of Asherah; and he broke
up, and destroyed, that most foul idol, and burned it by
the Kidron Stream/and burned it in the Kidron Gorge;)
14 soothly he did not (do) away the high things[7] (but he

[6] David sinned in the numbering of the people, and in sentence given against Mephibosheth, as it is told in (the) 2ND book (of Samuel), but these sins were full little (sic*), in comparison of the sin in the deed of Uriah, and therefore these be not areckoned; for a little thing is areckoned as nothing, as the Philosopher saith in (the) 2ND book of Physics. (*David's decision to number, or to count, the people led to the death of 70,000 innocent Israelites. TPN.)

[7] That is, (the) high places, in which the sons of Israel made sacrifice to God, before that the temple was builded; and for that time it was leaveful, (or lawful,) (but) not afterward.

did not do away the hill shrines); nevertheless the heart
of Asa was perfect with his Lord God, in all his days.
15 And he brought into the house of the Lord those
things, which his father had hallowed, and avowed, (the)
silver, and gold, and vessels.
16 Forsooth battle was betwixt Asa and Baasha, king of
Israel, in all the days of them.
17 And Baasha, king of Israel, went up into Judah, and
builded Ramah, that no man of the part of Asa, king of
Judah, might go out, either go in. (And Baasha, the king
of Israel, went up to Judah, and fortified Ramah, so that
no man of Asa, the king of Judah, could come in, or
could go out.)
18 Therefore Asa took all the silver and gold, that
(were) left in the treasuries of the house of the Lord, and
in the treasuries of the king's house, and gave it into the
hands of his servants; and he sent it to Benhadad, the son
of Tabrimon, son of Hezion, the king of Syria, that
dwelled in Damascus (who lived in Damascus), and said,
19 A bond of peace is betwixt me and thee, and
betwixt my father and thy father, and therefore I sent to
thee gifts, gold, and silver; and I ask, that thou come, and
make void the bond of peace, that thou hast with Baasha,
king of Israel, and that he go away from me. (There is a
covenant between me and thee, and between my father
and thy father, and so I sent gifts of gold and silver to
thee; and I ask that thou come, and dissolve the
covenant, that thou hast with Baasha, the king of Israel,
so that then he shall go away from me.)
20 Benhadad assented to king Asa, and sent the princes
of his host into the cities of Israel; and they smote Ijon,
and Dan, and Abel, the house of Maachah (and
Abelbethmaachah), and all Cinneroth, that is, all the land
of Naphtali.
21 And when Baasha had heard this thing, he left (off)
to build Ramah, and turned again into Tirzah. (And when
Baasha had heard of this thing, he stopped fortifying
Ramah, and returned to Tirzah.)
22 Forsooth king Asa sent [a] message into all Judah,
and said, No man be excused. And (so) they (all came,
and) took (away) the stones of Ramah, and the trees
thereof, by which Baasha had builded (it); and king Asa
builded of the same *stones and trees* Geba of Benjamin,
and Mizpah. (And King Asa sent a message to all Judah,
and said, No man shall be excused. And so they all
came, and took away the stones, and the timber, from
Ramah, with which Baasha had fortified it; and King Asa
used these same *stones and timber* to fortify Geba of
Benjamin, and Mizpah.)
23 Soothly the residue of all the words of Asa, and of
all his strength, and all things that he did, and the cities
which he builded, whether these be not written in the
book of [the] words of [the] days of [the] kings of Judah?
Nevertheless Asa had (an) ache in *his* feet, in the time of
his eld (age).
24 And Asa slept with his fathers, and he was buried
with them in the city of David, his father; and
Jehoshaphat, his son, reigned for him.
25 Forsooth Nadab, the son of Jeroboam, reigned on
Israel, in the second year of Asa, king of Judah; and he
reigned on Israel two years. (And Nadab, the son of
Jeroboam, began to reign upon Israel in the second year
of Asa, the king of Judah; and he reigned upon Israel for
two years.)
26 And he did that, that was evil in the sight of the
Lord, and he went in the ways of his father, and in the
sins of him, in which he made Israel to do sin.
27 And Baasha, the son of Ahijah, of the house of
Issachar, setted treason to him, and he smote him in
Gibbethon[8], which is a city of Philistines; and Nadab and
all Israel besieged Gibbethon. (And Baasha, the son of
Ahijah, of the house of Issachar, set treason for him, and
he struck him down in Gibbethon, which is a city of the
Philistines; for Nadab and all Israel besieged Gibbethon.)
28 Therefore Baasha killed him, in the third year of Asa,
king of Judah, and reigned for him.
29 And when he had reigned, he smote all the house of
Jeroboam; he left not one man of his seed, till he did
away him, by the word of the Lord, which he spake in
the hand of his servant, Ahijah of Shiloh, a prophet, (And
once he began to reign, he struck down all the house of
Jeroboam; he left not one of his descendants, until he had
done away all of them, by the word of the Lord, which
he spoke by his servant, the prophet Ahijah of Shiloh,)
30 for the sins of Jeroboam which he sinned, and in
which he made Israel to do sin, and for the trespass, by
which he wrathed the Lord God of Israel. (for the sins of
Jeroboam which he sinned, and in which he made Israel
to do sin, and for the trespass by which he stirred the
Lord God of Israel to anger.)
31 Soothly the residue of the words of Nadab, and all
things which he wrought, whether these be not written in
the book of [the] words of [the] days of the kings of Israel?
32 And battle was betwixt Asa and Baasha, king of
Israel, in all the days of them. (And there was battle
between Asa and Baasha, the king of Israel, in all their
days.)
33 In the third year of Asa, king of Judah, Baasha, the
son of Ahijah, reigned upon all Israel, in Tirzah, four and
twenty years. (In the third year of Asa, the king of Judah,
Baasha, the son of Ahijah, began to reign upon all Israel
in Tirzah, and he reigned twenty-four years.)
34 And he did evil before the Lord, and he went in the
ways of Jeroboam, and in his sins, by which he made

[8] Gibbethon was a city in the lineage of Dan, but (the) Philistines occupied it, against which city Nadab went to recover it (and so Nadab went to recover it).

Israel to do sin.

CHAPTER 16

1 Forsooth the word of the Lord was made to Jehu, the
son of Hanani, against Baasha, and said,
2 For that that I raised thee from dust, and setted thee
duke on Israel, my people; soothly thou wentest in the
way of Jeroboam, and thou hast made my people Israel to
do sin, that thou shouldest stir me to ire, in the sins of
them; (For though I raised thee up out of the dust, and
made thee the leader of my people Israel; yet thou
wentest in the way of Jeroboam, and thou hast made my
people Israel to do sin, so that thou stirrest me to anger
with their sins;)
3 lo! I shall cut away the hinder things of Baasha, and
the hinder things of his house, and I shall make thine
house as the house of Jeroboam, the son of Nebat. (lo! I
shall cut away the posterity, *or the descendants*, of
Baasha, and of his household, *or of his family*, and I shall
make thy house like the house of Jeroboam, the son of
Nebat.)
4 Dogs shall eat that man of Baasha, that shall be dead
in the city, and [the] birds of the air shall eat that man of
Baasha, that shall die in the field. (The dogs shall eat
those of Baasha's family, who shall die in the city, and
the birds of the air shall eat those of Baasha's family, who
shall die in the field.)
5 Soothly the residue of the words of Baasha, and
whatever things he did, and his battles, whether these be
not written in the book of [the] words of [the] days of the
kings of Israel?
6 And so Baasha slept with his fathers, and he was
buried in Tirzah; and Elah, his son, reigned for him.
7 Forsooth when the word of the Lord was made in
the hand of Jehu, the son of Hanani, against Baasha, and
against his house, and against all the evil which he did
before the Lord, to stir him to ire in the works of his
hands, that he should be as the house of Jeroboam, for
this cause he killed him[9]. (And the word of the Lord was
made to Jehu, the son of Hanani, against Baasha, and
against his house, and against all the evil which he did
before the Lord, to stir him to anger with the works of his
hands, because he sinned like the house of Jeroboam,
and also because he killed them.)
8 In the six and twentieth year of Asa, king of Judah,
Elah, the son of Baasha, reigned upon Israel, in Tirzah,
two years. (In the twenty-sixth year of Asa, the king of
Judah, Elah, the son of Baasha, began to reign upon Israel
in Tirzah, and he reigned for two years.)
9 And Zimri, his servant, duke of the half part of *his*
knights, rebelled against him; soothly Elah was in Tirzah,
and drank and was drunken in the house of Arza, prefect
of Tirzah. (And Zimri, his officer, the leader of half of *his*
horsemen, rebelled against him; and Elah was in Tirzah,
and drank until he was drunk in the house of Arza, the
prefect of Tirzah.)
10 Therefore Zimri felled in, and smote Elah, and killed
him, in the seven and twentieth year of Asa, king of
Judah; and [he] reigned for him.
11 And when he had reigned, and sat upon his throne,
he smote all the house of Baasha, and he left not thereof
a pisser to the wall, and his kinsmen, and friends. (And
once he began to reign, and sat on his throne, he struck
down all the house of Baasha, and he left not of it a
pisser on the wall, nor any of his kinsmen, nor any of his
friends.)
12 And Zimri did away all the house of Baasha, by the
word of the Lord, which he spake to Baasha, in the hand
of Jehu, the prophet (which he spoke to Baasha, by the
prophet Jehu),
13 for all the sins of Baasha, and for the sins of Elah, his
son, which sinned, and made Israel to do sin, and
wrathed the Lord God of Israel in their vanities. (because
of all the sins of Baasha, and because of the sins of his
son Elah, both of whom sinned, and made Israel to do
sin, and stirred the Lord God of Israel to anger with their
worthless idols.)
14 Soothly the residue of the words of Elah, and all
things which he did, whether these be not written in the
book of [the] words of [the] days of the kings of Israel?
15 In the seven and twentieth year of Asa, king of
Judah, Zimri reigned (for) seven days in Tirzah (In the
twenty-seventh year of Asa, the king of Judah, Zimri
reigned in Tirzah for seven days); forsooth the host of
Israel besieged Gibbethon, the city of (the) Philistines.
16 And when it had heard, that Zimri had rebelled, and
had slain the king, all Israel made Omri king to them, that
was prince of the chivalry, on Israel, in that day, in their
tents. (And when they had heard that Zimri had rebelled,
and had killed the king, all Israel made Omri, who was
the leader of the cavalry, *or of the army*, king upon Israel,
that very day, in the camp.)
17 Therefore Omri went up, and all Israel with him,
from Gibbethon, and besieged Tirzah. (And then Omri,
and all Israel with him, went up from Gibbethon, and
besieged Tirzah.)
18 And Zimri saw, that the city should be overcome,
and he entered into the palace, and burnt himself with
the king's house; and he was dead (And Zimri saw that
the city would be overcome, and so he entered into the
palace, and burned himself up, along with the palace;
and so he died)
19 in his sins which he sinned, doing evil before the
Lord, and going in the way of Jeroboam, and in his sins,
by which he made Israel to do sin.

[9] The words that follow, 'that is, Jehu, the prophet, the son of Hanani, (the prophet,)' are not in Hebrew; it is a gloss.

20 Soothly the residue of the words of Zimri, and of his
treasons, and tyranny, whether these be not written in the
book of [the] words of [the] days of the kings of Israel?
21 Then the people of Israel was parted into two parts;
the half part of the people followed Tibni, the son of
Ginath, to make him king, and the *other* half part
followed Omri.
22 And the people that was with Omri, had the mastery
over the people that followed Tibni, the son of Ginath;
and Tibni was dead, and Omri reigned. (And the people
who were with Omri, had the mastery over the people
who followed Tibni, the son of Ginath; and so Tibni was
killed, and Omri reigned.)
23 In the one and thirtieth year of Asa, king of Judah,
Omri reigned upon Israel, twelve years; in Tirzah, he
reigned six years. (In the one and thirtieth year of Asa, the
king of Judah, Omri began to reign upon Israel, and he
reigned for twelve years; the first six years he reigned in
Tirzah.)
24 And he bought of Shemer, for two talents of silver,
the hill of Samaria, and builded (on) that *hill*; and he
called the name of the city, which he had builded, by the
name of Shemer, [the] lord of the hill of Samaria. (And he
bought the hill of Samaria from Shemer, for two talents of
silver, and built *a city* on that *hill*; and he called the
name of the city, which he built, Samaria, after the name
of Shemer, the former lord of that hill.)
25 Forsooth Omri did evil in the sight of the Lord, and
wrought waywardly, *or wickedly*, over all men that were
before him. (But Omri did evil before the Lord, and acted
more wickedly than all the kings who were before him.)
26 And he went in all the way of Jeroboam, the son of
Nebat, and in his sins, by which he made Israel to do sin,
that he should stir to ire, in his vanities, the Lord God of
Israel. (And he went in all the ways of Jeroboam, the son
of Nebat, and in his sins, by which he made Israel to do
sin, so that they stirred the Lord God of Israel to anger
with their worthless idols.)
27 Forsooth the residue of the words of Omri, and his
battles, which he did, whether these be not written in the
book of [the] words of [the] days of the kings of Israel?
28 And Omri slept with his fathers, and was buried in
Samaria; and Ahab, his son, reigned for him.
29 Forsooth Ahab, the son of Omri, reigned upon
Israel, in the eight and thirtieth year of Asa, king of Judah;
and Ahab, the son of Omri, reigned upon Israel, in
Samaria, two and twenty years. (Then Ahab, the son of
Omri, began to reign upon Israel in the thirty-eighth year
of Asa, the king of Judah; and Ahab, the son of Omri,
reigned upon Israel, in Samaria, for twenty-two years.)
30 And Ahab, the son of Omri, did evil in the sight of
the Lord, over all men that were before him; (And Ahab,
the son of Omri, did evil before the Lord, more than all
the kings who were before him;)
31 and it sufficed not to him that he went in the sins of
Jeroboam, the son of Nebat, furthermore and he wedded
a wife, Jezebel, the daughter of Ethbaal, king of
Sidonians; and he went and served Baal, and worshipped
him. (and it was not sufficient for him that he merely
went in the sins of Jeroboam, the son of Nebat, but
moreover he wedded Jezebel for a wife, Ethbaal's
daughter, the king of the Sidonians; and he went and
served Baal, and worshipped him.)
32 And he set up an altar to Baal in the temple of Baal,
which he had builded in Samaria,
33 and he planted a maumet wood; and Ahab added to
(that) in his work, and stirred to ire the Lord God of Israel,
more than all [the] kings of Israel that were before him.
(and he planted an idol grove/and he put up a sacred
pole; and Ahab did more with his deeds, to stir the Lord
God of Israel to anger, than all the kings of Israel who
were before him.)
34 Forsooth in his days Hiel of Bethel builded Jericho;
in Abiram, his first *son*, he founded it[10], and in Segub, his
last *son*, he setted the gates thereof, by the word of the
Lord, which he had spoken in the hand of Joshua, the son
of Nun. (And in his days Hiel of Bethel rebuilt Jericho; *he
lost* Abiram, his first *son*, at the time that he founded it,
and *he lost* Segub, his last *son*, when he put up its gates,
by the word of the Lord, which he had spoken by Joshua,
the son of Nun.)

CHAPTER 17

1 And Elijah (the) Tishbite, of the dwellers of Gilead,
said to Ahab, (As) The Lord God of Israel liveth, in whose
sight I stand, dew and rain shall not be in these years, no
but by the words of my mouth.
2 And the word of the Lord was made to him, and
said,
3 Go thou away from hence, and go against the east,
and be thou hid in the strand of Cherith, that is against
Jordan, (Go thou away from here, and go toward the east,
and be thou hid by the Cherith Stream/by the Cherith
Gorge, that is east of the Jordan River,)
4 and there thou shalt drink of the strand (and there
thou shalt drink out of the stream); and I have
commanded to [the] crows, that they feed thee there.
5 Therefore he went, and did by the word of the Lord;
and when he had gone, he sat in the strand of Cherith,
that is against Jordan. (And so he went, and did by the
word of the Lord; and when he had gone forth, he sat by
the Cherith Stream/he sat by the Cherith Gorge, that is

[10] That is, when he setted the foundaments, Abiram, his first engendered son, died, and when he went forth in building, his sons died each after (the) other, till to the last son, that was dead in the filling of the work (who died when the rebuilding was completed).

east of the Jordan River.)
6 And [the] crows bare to him bread and flesh early;
and in like manner in the eventide; and he drank of the
strand. (And each morning the crows brought him bread
and meat; and likewise in the evening; and he drank from
the stream.)
7 And after some days the strand was dried (And after
some days the stream dried up); for it had not rained on
the earth.
8 Therefore the word of the Lord was made to him,
and said,
9 Rise thou (up), and go into Zarephath of (the)
Sidonians, and thou shalt dwell there; for I have
commanded to a woman widow there, that she feed thee
(for I have commanded to a widow woman there, that
she should feed thee).
10 He rose, and went into Zarephath of Sidonians; and
when he had come to the gate of the city, a woman
widow gathering sticks appeared to him; and he called
her, and said to her, Give thou to me a little of water in a
vessel, that I drink. (He rose up, and went to Zarephath of
the Sidonians; and when he had come to the city gate, a
widow woman gathering sticks appeared before him; and
he called to her, and said to her, Give thou to me a little
water in a vessel, so that I can have a drink.)
11 And when she went to bring it, he cried behind her
back, and said, I beseech, bring thou to me also a morsel
of bread in thine hand.
12 And she answered, (As) Thy Lord God liveth, for I
have no bread, no but as much of meal in a pot, as a
fist[ful] may take, and a little of oil in a vessel; lo! I gather
two sticks, that I enter, and make it to me, and to my son,
that we eat, and die (lo! I am gathering only two sticks, so
that I can go in, and make it up for me, and my son, so
that we can eat, and then die).
13 And Elijah said to her, Do not thou dread, but go,
and make as thou saidest; nevertheless make thou first to
me of that little meal a little loaf, baken under ashes, and
bring thou *it* to me; soothly thou shalt make afterward to
thee and to thy son. (And Elijah said to her, Do not thou
fear, but go, and make as thou saidest; but first make thou
for me a small loaf from that little amount of meal, baked
under ashes, and bring thou *it* to me; then afterward thou
shalt make some for thee and thy son.)
14 Forsooth the Lord God of Israel saith these things (to
you), The pot of meal shall not fail, and the vessel of oil
shall not be abated, till to the day in which the Lord shall
give rain on the face of the earth.
15 And she went, and did by the word of Elijah; and he
ate, and she, and her house (and he, and she, and all of
her household, *or her family*, ate for many days).
16 And from that day the pot of meal failed not, and the
vessel of oil was not abated, by the word of the Lord,
which he had spoken in the hand of Elijah (which he had
spoken by Elijah).
17 Forsooth it was done after these words, (that) the son
of a woman housewife, was sick, and the sickness was
full strong, so that breath dwelled not in him. (And it was
done after these things, that the son of that woman
housewife, was sick, and the sickness grew very strong,
so that finally no breath remained in him.)
18 Therefore she said to Elijah, What to me and to thee,
thou man of God? Enteredest thou to me, that my
wickedness should be remembered, and that thou
shouldest slay my son?
19 And Elijah said to her, Give thy son to me. And he
took that *son* from her bosom, and bare into the solar,
where he dwelled; and he put him on his bed. (And he
took her *son* from her bosom, and carried him up to the
solarium, where he stayed; and he put him on his bed.)
20 And he cried to the Lord, and said, My Lord God,
whether thou hast tormented also the widow (hast thou
tormented this widow), with whom I am sustained in all
manner, (so) that thou killedest her son?
21 He spread abroad himself, and was meted upon the
child by three times; and he cried to the Lord, and said,
My Lord God, I beseech, the soul of this child turn again
into the entrails of him. (Then he stretched himself over,
or above, the child three times; and he cried to the Lord,
and said, O Lord my God, I beseech thee, let the soul of
this child return to his entrails.)
22 The Lord heard the voice of Elijah, and the soul of
the child turned again within him, and he lived again.
23 And Elijah took the child, and put him down of the
solar into the lower house (and took him down from the
solarium to the lower part of the house), and betook *him*
to his mother; and he said to her, Lo! thy son liveth.
24 And the woman said to Elijah, Now in this I have
known, that thou art a man of God, and the word of the
Lord is sooth in thy mouth. (And the woman said to
Elijah, Now by this I know, that thou art a man of God,
and that the word of the Lord from thy mouth is truth.)

CHAPTER 18

1 After many days the word of the Lord was made to
Elijah, in the third year, and said, Go, and show thee to
Ahab, that I give rain upon the face of the earth (Go, and
show thyself to Ahab, and I shall send rain upon the face
of the earth).
2 Therefore Elijah went to show himself to Ahab;
forsooth a great hunger was made in Samaria (and there
was then a great famine in Samaria).
3 And Ahab called Obadiah, the dispenser, *either
steward*, of his house; forsooth Obadiah dreaded greatly
the Lord God of Israel (and Obadiah greatly feared/greatly
revered the Lord God of Israel).
4 For when Jezebel killed the prophets of the Lord, he
took an hundred prophets, and hid them, by fifties and

fifties, in dens (and hid them in caves, fifty by fifty), and
fed them with bread and water.
5 Then Ahab said to Obadiah, Go thou into the land,
to all the wells of waters, and into all (the) valleys, if in
hap we may find grass, and save (the) horses and mules;
and [the] work beasts perish not utterly (and so the work
beasts shall not utterly perish).
6 And they parted the countries to themselves, that
they should compass those; Ahab went by one way, and
Obadiah went by another way, by himself.
7 And when Obadiah was in the way, Elijah met him
(And when Obadiah was on the way, Elijah met him);
and when he had known Elijah, he felled on his face, and
said, Whether thou art my lord Elijah?
8 To whom he answered, I *am*. And Elijah said, Go
thou, and say to thy lord, Elijah is present (Elijah is here).
9 And Obadiah said, What have I sinned, for thou
betakest me in(to) the hand of Ahab, that he slay me?
10 Thy Lord God liveth, for no folk either realm is,
whither my lord, seeking thee, sent not; and when all
men answered, He is not here, he charged greatly all
realms and folks, for thou were not found; (As the Lord
thy God liveth, for there is no nation, or kingdom, where
my lord hath not sent, seeking thee; and when all people
answered, He is not here, he greatly charged each
kingdom, and nation, to swear, that thou were not found
there;)
11 and now thou sayest to me, Go, and say to thy lord,
Elijah is present (Elijah is here).
12 And when I shall depart from thee, the Spirit of the
Lord shall bear thee away into a place which I know not;
and I shall enter, and tell to Ahab, and he shall not find
thee, and he shall slay thee; forsooth thy servant dreadeth
the Lord from his young childhood. (And when I shall
leave thee, the Spirit of the Lord shall carry thee away to
a place which I know not; and I shall go, and tell Ahab,
but he shall not find thee, and then he shall kill me; and
know ye that thy servant feareth the Lord/revereth the
Lord, from his young childhood.)
13 Whether it is not showed to thee, my lord, what I
did, when Jezebel killed the prophets of the Lord, that I
hid of the prophets of the Lord an hundred men, by fifty
and fifty, in dens, and I fed them with bread and water?
(Was it not told to thee, my lord, what I did, when
Jezebel killed the prophets of the Lord, that I hid a
hundred of the prophets of the Lord in caves, fifty by fifty,
and that I fed them with bread and water?)
14 And now thou sayest, Go, and say to thy lord, Elijah
is present/Elijah is nigh, that he slay me. (And now thou
sayest, Go, and say to thy lord, Elijah is here. No! he shall
kill me!)
15 And Elijah said, The Lord of hosts liveth, before
whose sight I stand, for today I shall appear to him. (And
Elijah said, As the Lord of hosts liveth, whom I stand
before, I shall appear before him today.)
16 Therefore Obadiah went into the meeting of Ahab,
and showed it to him; and Ahab came into the meeting of
Elijah. (And so Obadiah went to find Ahab, and told him
everything; and Ahab came to meet with Elijah.)
17 And when he had seen Elijah, he said, Whether
thou art he, that troublest Israel? (And when he had seen
Elijah, he said, Art thou he who troublest Israel?)
18 And he said, Not I trouble Israel, but thou, and the
house of thy father, which have forsaken the
commandments of the Lord, and followed Baalim. (And
Elijah said, It is not I who trouble Israel, but thou, and the
house of thy father, who have deserted the
commandments of the Lord, and followed Baalim.)
19 Nevertheless now send thou, and gather to me all
Israel, into the hill of Carmel, and the four hundred and
fifty prophets of Baal, and [the] four hundred prophets of
(the) maumet woods, that eat of the table of Jezebel. (But
now send thou, and gather together for me all Israel on
Mount Carmel, and the four hundred and fifty prophets of
Baal, and the four hundred prophets of Asherah, who eat
at Jezebel's table.)
20 Ahab sent to all the sons of Israel, and gathered
together the prophets in the hill of Carmel. (And so Ahab
sent for all the Israelites, and gathered together the
prophets on Mount Carmel.)
21 Forsooth Elijah nighed to all the people of Israel,
and said, How long halt ye into two parts? (How long
shall ye waver between two paths?) If the Lord is God,
follow ye him; and if Baal *is God*, follow ye him. And
the people answered not one word to him.
22 And Elijah said again to the people, I dwelled alone
a prophet of the Lord; soothly the prophets of Baal be
four hundred and fifty, and the prophets of the maumet
woods be four hundred men. (And Elijah said to the
people, I am the only prophet of the Lord still left; but
there be four hundred and fifty prophets of Baal, and four
hundred prophets of Asherah.)
23 (Let) Twain oxes be given to us; and choose they
one ox, and they shall cut (it) into gobbets, and put it on
wood, but put they not fire under (it); and I shall make
(ready) the tother ox *into sacrifice* (and I shall prepare the
other ox *for sacrifice*), and I shall put (it) on the wood,
and I shall not put fire under (it either).
24 Call ye the name of your gods, and I shall call the
name of my God; and the God that heareth by fire *falling
down, given from heaven to waste the sacrifice*, be he
God. And all the people answered, and said, The reason
is best, that Elijah hath spoken. (Then call ye on the name
of your god, and I shall call on the name of my God; and
the God who answereth with fire *falling down*, that is,
with fire given from heaven to consume the sacrifice, he
is God. And all the people answered, and said, What
Elijah hath spoken is reasonable.)

25 Therefore Elijah said to the prophets of Baal, Choose
ye one ox to you, and make ye (ready) first *your sacrifice*,
for ye be the more; and call ye the names of your gods,
and put ye not fire under. (And so Elijah said to the
prophets of Baal, Choose ye one ox for yourselves, and
prepare ye first *your sacrifice*, for ye be the more; and
then call ye on the name of your god, but put ye no fire
under it.)
26 And when they had taken the ox, whom Elijah gave
to them, they made (ready the) *sacrifice*, and called the
name of Baal, from the morrowtide till to midday, and
said, Baal, hear us! And no voice was, neither any that
answered; and they skipped over the altar, which they
had made. (And when they had taken the ox, which was
given to them, they prepared the *sacrifice*, and called on
the name of Baal, from the morning until midday, and
said, Baal, hear us! But there was no voice, nor anyone
who answered; even as they leapt all around the altar,
which they had made.)
27 And when it was then midday, Elijah scorned them,
and said, Cry ye with [a] greater voice, for *Baal* is your
god, and in hap he speaketh with another, either he is in
a harbourgerie, either in the way, either certainly he
sleepeth, that he be raised up. (And when it was midday,
Elijah scorned them, and said, Cry ye with a greater
voice, for *Baal* is your god, and perhaps he speaketh with
another, or else he is at an inn, or he is on the way, or
certainly he sleepeth, so that he must be raised up.)
28 Therefore they cried with [a] great(er) voice, and
they cut themselves with knives and lancets, after their
custom, till they were beshed with blood.
29 But after that midday passed, and while they
prophesied, *or prayed*, the time came, in which the
sacrifice is wont to be offered, neither voice was heard *of
their gods*, neither any answered, neither perceived *them*
praying. (But after that midday had passed, and yet while
they prophesied, *and prayed*, the time came, in which
the evening sacrifice was wont to be offered, and still
neither the voice was heard *of their god*, nor did anyone
answer them, nor did anyone perceive *their* prayers.)
30 [And] Elijah said to all the people, Come ye to me.
And when the people came to him, he arrayed the altar
of the Lord, that was destroyed. (And Elijah said to all the
people, Come ye close to me. And when the people
came close to him, he repaired the altar of the Lord that
was destroyed.)
31 And he took twelve stones, by the number of the
lineages of the sons of Jacob (which was the number of
the tribes of Jacob), to which *Jacob* the word of the Lord
was made, and said, Israel shall be thy name.
32 And he builded an altar of stones, in the name of the
Lord, and he made a leading-to of water, *either a ditch*
(and he made a leading-to, *or a ditch*, for the water), as
by two little ditches, *or furrows*, in the compass of the
altar[11].
33 And he dressed [the] wood, and he parted the ox by
(its) members, and put *it* upon the wood, and said, Fill ye
four pots with water, and pour ye *it* upon the burnt
sacrifice (to be), and upon the wood.
34 And again he said, Also the second time do ye this.
And they did (it) the second time. And he said, Do ye the
same thing the third time; and they did (it) the third time.
35 And the waters ran about the altar, and the ditch, *or
rut*, of [the] leading-to of water was filled. (And the water
ran about the altar, and the ditch, *or the rut*, of the
leading-to for the water, was completely filled.)
36 And when the time was then, that the burnt sacrifice
should be offered, Elijah the prophet nighed, and said,
Lord God of Abraham, of Isaac, and of Israel, show thou
today that thou art God of Israel, and *that I am* thy
servant, and have done all these words by thy
commandment. (And when it was the time, that the burnt
sacrifice should be offered, Elijah the prophet came near,
and said, Lord God of Abraham, and Isaac, and Israel, *or
Jacob*, show thou today that thou art the God of Israel,
and *that I am* thy servant, and that I have done all these
things by thy commandment.)
37 Lord, hear thou me; Lord, hear thou me; that this
people learn, that thou art the Lord God, and that thou
hast converted again the heart of them. (Lord, hear thou
me; Lord, hear thou me; so that this people shall learn
that thou art the Lord God, and thou shalt turn their
hearts back to thee again.)
38 Soothly [the] fire of the Lord felled down *then*, and
devoured the burnt sacrifice, the wood, and the stones,
and it licked up also the powder, and the water that was
in the leading-(to), (*or the rut*,) of (the) water. (Then the
fire of the Lord fell down, and devoured the burnt
sacrifice, and the wood, and the stones, and the dust, and
it also licked up the water that was in the ditch, *or in the
rut*, for the water.)
39 And when all the people had seen this, *the people*
felled into his face (*the people* fell down on their faces),
and said, The Lord, he is God; the Lord, he is God.
40 And Elijah said to them, Take ye the prophets of
Baal; not one soothly escape of them. And when they
had taken them, Elijah led them to the strand of Kishon,
and killed them there. (And Elijah said to them, Take ye
hold of the prophets of Baal; do not let one of them
escape. And when they had taken hold of them, Elijah
led them to the Kishon Stream/to the Kishon Gorge, and

[11] In Hebrew it is thus, 'And he made a furrow of three bushels of seed, that is, so much seed (as) might be sown within the compass of the furrow (And he made a furrow, or ditch, around the altar, deep enough to hold three bushels of seed that might be sown within the compass of the furrow)', as Rabbi Solomon saith.

they killed them there.)
41 And Elijah said to Ahab, Go thou up, and eat, and
drink, for the sound of much rain is *nigh.* (And Elijah said
to Ahab, Go thou to eat, and drink, for there is the sound
of much rain coming.)
42 Ahab went up to eat and drink; but Elijah went up
into (the top of) the hill of Carmel, and he set lowly his
face to the earth, betwixt his knees; (So Ahab went to eat
and drink; but Elijah went up to the top of Mount Carmel,
and he put his face low to the ground, between his
knees;)
43 and said to his servant, Go thou up, and behold
thou against the sea. And when he had gone up, and
beheld, he said, Nothing is (there). And again *Elijah* said
to him, Turn thou again seven times. (and said to his
servant, Go thou up now, and behold the sea. And when
he had gone, and beheld it, he said, There is nothing
there. And *Elijah* said to him, Do it again; and in all, he
commanded him to do it seven times.)
44 And in the seventh time, lo! a little cloud, as the step
of a man, went up from the sea. And *Elijah* said, Go thou
up, and say to Ahab, Join thy chariot, and go down, lest
the rain before-occupy thee. (And on the seventh time,
lo! a little cloud, like the hand of a man, went up from
the sea. And *Elijah* said, Go thou up now, and say to
Ahab, Join up thy chariot, and get going, or the rain shall
stop thee!)
45 And when they turned them hither and thither, lo!
heavens were made dark, and cloud, and wind, and great
rain was made. Therefore Ahab went up (into his chariot),
and went into Jezreel; (And when they turned themselves
here and there, lo! the skies were made dark with clouds
and wind, and a great rain came. And so Ahab went up
into his chariot, and went back to Jezreel;)
46 and the hand of the Lord was made upon Elijah, and
when his loins were girded, he ran before Ahab, till he
came into Jezreel. (and the hand of the Lord was made
upon Elijah, and when his loins were girded up, he ran
ahead of Ahab, all the way back to Jezreel.)

CHAPTER 19

1 Forsooth Ahab told to Jezebel all things that Elijah
had done, and how he had slain with (the) sword all the
prophets of Baal.
2 And Jezebel sent a messenger to Elijah, and said,
Gods do these things to me (The gods do these things to
me), and add these things too, no but tomorrow in this
hour I shall put thy life as the life of one of them.
3 Therefore Elijah dreaded, and rose (up), and went
whither ever *his* will bare him; and he came into
Beersheba of Judah, and he left there his servant (and he
left his servant there);
4 and went into (the) desert, the way of one day. And
when he came, and sat under one juniper tree, he asked
to his soul, that he should die (he prayed that he should
die); and he said, Lord, it sufficeth to me, take my soul
(now); for I am not (any) better than my fathers.
5 And he casted forth himself (And he threw himself
down), and slept in the shadow of the juniper tree. And
lo! the angel of the Lord touched him, and said to him,
Rise thou (up), and eat.
6 (And) He beheld, and, lo! at his head *was* a loaf
baken under ashes, and a vessel of water. Therefore he
ate, and drank, and slept again.
7 And the angel of the Lord turned again the second
time, and touched him; and he said to him, Rise thou,
and eat; for a great way is to thee (Rise thou up, and eat,
or the way shall be too much for thee),
8 And when he had risen, he ate, and drank; and he
went in the strength of that meat forty days and forty
nights, unto Horeb, the hill of God. (And when he had
risen, he ate, and drank; and he went in the strength of
that food for forty days and forty nights, unto Mount
Sinai, the mountain of God.)
9 And when he had come thither, he dwelled in a den
(And when he had come there, he lived in a cave); and
lo! the word of the Lord *was made* to him, and said to
him, Elijah, what doest thou here?
10 And he answered, By fervent love, *that is, of all the
heart,* I have loved fervently, for the Lord God of hosts;
for the sons of Israel have forsaken the covenant of the
Lord; they have destroyed thine altars, and killed with
(the) sword thy prophets; and I am left alone, and they
seek my life, that they do it away. (And he answered,
With fervent love, *that is, with all of my heart,* I have
fervently loved for the Lord God of hosts; but the
Israelites have deserted the covenant of the Lord; they
have destroyed thy altars, and killed thy prophets with
the sword; and I alone am left, and now they seek my
life, so that they can do me away.)
11 And he said to Elijah, Go thou out, and stand in the
hill, before the Lord. And lo! the Lord passeth, and a
great wind, and strong, turning upside-down hills, and
all-breaking stones before the Lord; not in the wind is the
Lord. And after the wind is a stirring; not in the stirring is
the Lord. (And he said to Elijah, Go thou out, and stand
on the mount before the Lord. And lo! the Lord then
passed by, and there was a great strong wind, that turned
the mountains upside-down, and broke up the stones
before the Lord; but the Lord was not in the wind. And
after the wind there was a great shaking; but the Lord was
not in that shaking.)
12 And after the stirring is a fire; not in the fire is the
Lord. And after the fire is an hissing of thin wind, *or
breathing softly*; there is the Lord. (And after the stirring,
or the shaking, there was a fire; but the Lord was not in
the fire. And after the fire there was a hissing of the
wind, *as if softly breathing*; and there was the Lord/and

the Lord was there.)
13 And when Elijah had heard this, he covered his face
with a mantle, and he went out, and stood in the door of
the den (and stood at the entrance to the cave). And a
voice spake to him, and said, Elijah, what doest thou
here?
14 And he answered, With fervent love I have loved
fervently, for the Lord God of hosts; for the sons of Israel
have forsaken thy covenant; they have destroyed thine
altars, and they have killed with (the) sword thy prophets;
and I am left alone, and they seek my life, that they do it
away. (And he answered, and said, With fervent love I
have fervently loved for the Lord God of hosts; but the
Israelites have deserted thy covenant; they have
destroyed thy altars, and they have killed thy prophets
with the sword; and I alone am left, and now they seek
my life, so that they can do me away.)
15 And the Lord said to him, Go, and turn again into
thy way, by the desert, into Damascus (And the Lord said
to him, Go, and return on the way, by the wilderness, to
Damascus); and when thou shalt come thither, thou shalt
anoint Hazael king upon Syria;
16 and thou shalt anoint (unto) king upon Israel, Jehu,
the son of Nimshi; and thou shalt anoint a prophet for
thee, Elisha, the son of Shaphat, that is of Abelmeholah.
(and thou shalt anoint Jehu, the son of Nimshi, to be king
upon Israel; and thou shalt anoint Elisha, the son of
Shaphat, of Abelmeholah, to be the prophet in thy place.)
17 And it shall be, whoever shall flee the sword of
Hazael, Jehu shall slay him; and whoever shall flee the
sword of Jehu, Elisha shall slay him.
18 And I shall leave to me in Israel seven thousand of
men, of which the knees be not bowed before Baal, and
each mouth that worshipped not him, and kissed not his
hand. (But I shall leave for me seven thousand men in
Israel, who have not bowed their knees before Baal, and
whose mouths have not worshipped him, nor kissed his
hand.)
19 Therefore Elijah went forth from thence, and found
Elisha, the son of Shaphat, earing in twelve yokes of
oxen; and he was one in the twelve yokes of oxen,
earing. And when Elijah had come to him, Elijah casted
his mantle upon him. (And so Elijah went forth from
there, and found Elisha, the son of Shaphat, plowing with
twelve yokes of oxen; and he was plowing alongside the
twelfth yoke of them. And when Elijah had come to him,
he threw his mantle upon him.)
20 And he ran anon after Elijah, when the oxen were
left, and said, I pray thee, kiss I my father and my mother,
and so I shall follow thee. And Elijah said to him, Go
thou, and turn again, for I have done to thee that that was
mine (to do). (And leaving the oxen behind, Elisha ran at
once after Elijah, and said, I pray thee, let me kiss my
father and my mother good-bye, and then I shall follow
thee. And Elijah said to him, Go thou, and return, for I
have done to thee what was mine to do.)
21 Soothly he turned again from Elijah, and took twain
oxen, and killed them; and with the plow of the oxen he
seethed the flesh, and gave (the meat) to the people, and
they ate; and he rose (and then he rose up), and went,
and followed Elijah, and ministered to him.

CHAPTER 20

1 Forsooth Benhadad, king of Syria, gathered together
all his host, and two and thirty kings with him, and
horses, and chariots; and he went up against Samaria,
and fought, and besieged it.
2 And he sent messengers to Ahab, king of Israel, into
the city, and (they) said (to him), Benhadad saith these
things,
3 Thy silver and thy gold is mine, and thy wives, and
thy best sons be mine.
4 And the king of Israel answered, By thy word, my
lord the king, I am thine, and all my things *be thine.*
5 And the messengers turned again, and said,
Benhadad, that sent us to thee, saith these things (again),
Thou shalt give to me thy silver, and thy gold, and thy
wives, and thy sons.
6 Therefore tomorrow, in this same hour, I shall send
my servants to thee, and they shall seek (throughout)
thine house, and the house of thy servants; and they shall
put in their hands, and take away all thing that shall
please them.
7 Forsooth the king of Israel called all the elder men of
the land, and said, Perceive ye, and see, that he setteth
treason to us; for he sent to me for my wives, and sons,
and for (my) silver, and gold, and I forsook not. (And the
king of Israel called all the elders of the land, and said,
Perceive ye, and see, that this man hath set treason for us;
for he sent to me for my wives, and my sons, and my
silver, and my gold, and I agreed to it all.)
8 And all the greater men in birth (And all the men of
great age, *that is, the elders*), and all the people said to
him, Hear thou not, neither assent thou to him.
9 And he answered to the messengers of Benhadad,
Say ye to my lord the king, I shall do all things, for which
thou sentest in the beginning to me, thy servant; but I
may not do this thing. And the messengers turned again,
and told all things to him. (And so he answered to the
messengers of Benhadad, and said, Say ye to my lord the
king, I, thy servant, shall do all the things for which thou
sentest to me at the beginning; but I cannot do this thing.
And the messengers returned, and told all these things to
Benhadad.)
10 Which sent again, and said, Gods do these things to
me, and add these things too (And Benhadad sent them
back again to Ahab, to say *to him*, The gods do these
things to me, and add these things too), if the dust of

Samaria shall suffice to the fist[ful]s of all the people that
followeth me.
11 And the king of Israel answered, and said, Say ye to
him, A girded man, *that is, he that goeth to battle*, have
not glory evenly as a man ungirded, *that is, as he that
hath the victory, and hath put off his armours.* (And
Ahab, the king of Israel, answered, and said, Say ye to
him, A girded man, *that is, he who goeth to battle*, hath
not equal glory to an ungirded man, *that is, he who
already hath the victory, and hath put off his armour.*)
12 And it was done, when Benhadad had heard this
word, he drank, and also the kings, in shadowing places
(in a shady place in their tents); and he said to his
servants, Compass ye the city. And they compassed it.
13 And lo! one prophet nighed to Ahab, king of Israel,
and said to him, The Lord God saith these things,
Certainly thou hast seen all this multitude full great
(Certainly thou hast seen all this very great multitude); lo!
I shall betake it into thine hand today, that thou know
that I am the Lord.
14 And Ahab said, By whom? And he said to Ahab,
The Lord saith these things, By the squires, *or the
footmen*, of the princes of (the) provinces. And Ahab
said, Who shall begin to fight? And the prophet said,
Thou.
15 Therefore he numbered the young men of the
princes of [the] provinces, and he found the number of
two hundred and two and thirty; and after them he
numbered the people, all the sons of Israel, seven
thousand. (And so he called for the young men who
served the leaders of the provinces, and he found them to
number two hundred and thirty-two; and after them he
called for the people, yea, all the Israelites/the whole
Israelite army, seven thousand of them.)
16 And they went out in midday. Forsooth Benhadad
drank, and was drunken in his shadowing place, and
(the) two and thirty kings with him, that came to the help
of him. (And they went out at midday. And in a shady
place in their tents, Benhadad drank, and became drunk,
as did the thirty-two kings who were with him, who came
to help him.)
17 And the young men of the princes of (the) provinces
went out in the first front. Therefore Benhadad sent *men*,
which told to him, and said, Men went out of Samaria
(And Benhadad sent out *men*, who reported back to him,
and said, Some men have come out of Samaria).
18 And he said, Whether they come for peace, take ye
them quick; whether to fight, take ye them quick. [And he
saith, Whether for peace they come, taketh them alive; whether
that they fight, taketh them alive.]
19 Therefore the young men of the princes of (the)
provinces went out, and the residue host followed (them);
20 and each smote the man that came against him.
And (the) men of Syria fled, and Israel pursued them; also
Benhadad, the king of Syria, fled on an horse with his
knights.
21 Also the king of Israel went out, and smote (the)
horses and chariots, and he smote Syria with a full great
vengeance. (And the king of Israel went out, and struck
down the horses and the chariots, and he struck down
the Syrians with a very great slaughter.)
22 Forsooth a prophet nighed to the king of Israel, and
said, Go thou, and be strengthened, and know, and see,
what thou shalt do; for the king of Syria shall ascend
against thee in the year following (for the king of Syria
shall also come against thee next year).
23 Soothly the servants of the king of Syria said to him,
The Gods of hills be the Gods of the sons of Israel (The
gods of the hills be the gods of the Israelites), therefore
they overcame us; but it is better that we fight against
them in [the] field places, and we shall get them *there*.
24 Therefore do thou this word, *or counsel*; remove
thou all [the] kings from thine host, and set thou princes
for them; (And so do thou this thing, *or follow thou this
counsel*; remove thou all the kings from thy army, and
put thou other leaders in their place;)
25 and restore thou the number of knights, that felled of
thine, and [the] horses after the former horses, and *restore
thou* [the] chariots, by the chariots which thou haddest
before; and we shall fight against them in [the] field
places, and thou shalt see, that we shall get them. He
believed to the counsel of them, and did so (He believed
in their counsel, and did so).
26 Therefore after that the year had passed, Benhadad
numbered men of Syria (Benhadad called for the Syrians),
and he went up into Aphek, to fight against Israel.
27 Forsooth the sons of Israel were numbered; and
when meats were taken, they went forth even against
(them); and they, as two little flocks of goats, setted tents
against men of Syria. Forsooth men of Syria filled the
land. (And the Israelites were also called for; and when
provisions were taken, they went forth opposite them;
and they, as but two little flocks of goats, pitched their
tents opposite the Syrians. And the Syrians filled the
land.)
28 And one prophet of God nighed, and said to the
king of Israel, The Lord God saith these things, For (the)
men of Syria said, God of hills is the Lord of them, and
he is not God of valleys (The god of the hills is their Lord,
and he is not the god of the valleys), (and so) I shall give
all this great multitude in(to) thine hand, and ye shall
know that I am the Lord.
29 And seven days these and they dressed battle arrays
even against *each other*; and in the seventh day the battle
was joined altogether, and the sons of Israel smote of the
men of Syria an hundred thousand of footmen in one
day. (And for seven days these and they directed battle
arrays opposite *each other*; and then on the seventh day

the battle was joined, and the Israelites struck down a
hundred thousand Syrian footmen in one day.)
30 And they that (were) left fled into the city of Aphek,
and the wall felled down upon seven and twenty
thousand of (the) men that (were) left. Forsooth
Benhadad fled, and entered into the city, into a closet
that was within a closet;
31 and his servants said to him, [Lo!] We have heard
that the kings of the house of Israel be merciful, therefore
put we sackcloths in our loins, and cords in our heads
(and so let us put sackcloths on our loins, and cords on
our heads), and go we out to the king of Israel; in hap he
shall save our lives.
32 They girded their loins with sackcloths, and put
cords in their heads, and they came to the king of Israel,
and said to him, Thy servant Benhadad saith, I pray thee,
let my soul live. And he said, If Benhadad liveth yet, he
is my brother. (And so they girded up their loins with
sackcloths, and put cords on their heads, and they came
to the king of Israel, and said to him, Thy servant
Benhadad saith, I pray thee, *let* me live. And Ahab said, If
Benhadad yet liveth, he is my brother, *that is, I will make
peace with him.*)
33 Which thing the men *of Syria* took for a gracious
word, and they ravished hastily the word of his mouth
(and they hastily took hold of the word of his mouth), and
said, Thy brother Benhadad liveth. And Ahab said to
them, Go ye, and bring ye him to me. Therefore
Benhadad went out to him, and he raised up Benhadad
into his chariot.
34 [The] Which Benhadad said to him, I shall yield the
cities which my father took from thy father, and make
thou streets to thee in Damascus, as my father made in
Samaria; and I shall be bound to peace, and I shall depart
from thee. Therefore Ahab made [a] bond of peace *with
him*, and delivered him. (And Benhadad said to Ahab, I
shall give back the cities which my father took from thy
father, and then thou can make streets *of commerce, or
for trading*, for thyself in Damascus, like my father made
in Samaria. And Ahab said, On those terms I shall be
bound in peace with thee, and then thou can depart from
me. And so he made a covenant *with him*, and let him
go.)
35 Then a man of the sons of the prophets said to his
fellow, in the word of the Lord (by the word of the Lord),
Smite thou me. And he would not smite (him).
36 To whom the prophet said, For thou wouldest not
hear the voice of the Lord, lo! thou shalt go [away] from
me, and a lion shall smite thee. And when he had gone a
little from him, a lion found him, and slew *him*.
37 But also the prophet found another man, and he said
to that man, Smite thou me. And he smote him, and
wounded *him*.
38 Therefore the prophet went, and met the king in the
way; and he changed with a cloth, *that is, by (the)
wrapping of a cloth*, his mouth and eyes. (And so the
prophet went, and met the king on the way; and he
covered his mouth and his eyes with a cloth, *that is, he
disguised his face by wrapping it in a cloth.*)
39 And when the king had passed (And as the king
passed by), he cried to the king, and said, Thy servant
went out to fight anon, and when one man had fled, a
man brought him to me, and said, Keep thou this man;
and if he escapeth, thy life shall be for his life, either thou
shalt pay a talent of silver.
40 Soothly while I was troubled, and turned me hither
and thither, suddenly he appeared not. And the king of
Israel said to him, This is thy doom that thou [thyself] hast
deemed. (And while I was troubled, and turned myself
here and there, suddenly he was gone. And the king of
Israel said to him, This is thy judgement, or *thy sentence*,
that thou thyself hast pronounced, *or declared.*)
41 And anon he removed the cloth, *either binding*,
from his face (And at once he removed the cloth, *or the
wrapping*, from his face), and the king of Israel knew him,
that he was (one) of the prophets.
42 The which said to the king, The Lord saith these
things, For thou deliveredest from thine hand a man
worthy (of) death, thy life shall be for his life, and thy
people for his people.
43 Therefore the king of Israel turned again into his
house, and despised to hear *God's word*, and came
wroth into Samaria.[12] (And so the king of Israel returned
to his house, despising *the word of God* that he had
heard, and came back angry to Samaria.)

CHAPTER 21

1 Forsooth after these words, in that time, the vinery
of Naboth of Jezreel, that was in Jezreel, was beside the
palace of Ahab, king of Samaria. (Now after these things,
at that time, Naboth the Jezreelite had a vineyard which
was in Jezreel, beside the palace of Ahab, the king of
Samaria, *that is, the king of Israel.*)
2 Therefore Ahab spake to Naboth, and said, Give
thou to me thy vineyard, that I make to me *thereof* a
garden of worts, for it is nigh *to me*, and nigh mine
house; and I shall give to thee a better vinery for it; either
if thou guessest it more profitable to thee, I shall give thee
the price of silver, as much as it is worth. (And so Ahab
spoke to Naboth, and said, Give thou thy vineyard to me,
so that I can make a herb garden *out of it* for myself, for it
is close to *me*, and close to my house; and I shall give
thee a better vineyard for it; or if thou guessest that it be
more profitable to thee, I shall give thee the price of it in
silver, for as much as it is worth.)
3 To whom Naboth answered, The Lord be merciful

[12] Josephus saith that he killed the prophet.

to me, that I give not to thee the heritage of my fathers.
4 Therefore Ahab came into his house, having
indignation, and gnashing on the word which Naboth of
Jezreel had spoken to him, and said, I shall not give to
thee the heritage of my fathers. And Ahab casted down
himself into his bed, and turned away his face to the
wall, and ate not bread (And Ahab threw himself down
onto his bed, and turned his face to the wall, and ate no
food).
5 And Jezebel, his wife, entered to him, and said to
him, What is this thing, whereof thy soul is made sorry?
and why eatest thou not bread? (and why eatest thou no
food?)
6 Which answered to her, I spake to Naboth of
Jezreel, and I said to him, Give thy vineyard to me for
money taken, either if it pleaseth thee, I shall give to thee
a better vinery for it. And he said, I shall not give to thee
my vineyard.
7 Therefore Jezebel, his wife, said to him, Thou art of
great authority, and thou governest well [the realm of]
Israel; rise thou (up), and eat bread, and be thou patient,
either comforted; I shall give to thee the vinery of Naboth
of Jezreel (I shall get the vineyard of Naboth of Jezreel for
thee).
8 Therefore she wrote letters in the name of Ahab, and
sealed those with the ring of him; and she sent to the
greater men in birth, and to the best men, that were in
the city of Naboth, and dwelled with him (and she sent
them to the men of great age, *that is, to the elders,* and to
the best men, who lived in the city of Naboth with him).
9 And this was the sentence of the letter(s); Preach ye
fasting, and make ye Naboth to sit among the first men of
the people;
10 and send ye (in) privily two men, the sons of Belial,
against him, and say they (this) false witnessing, Naboth
hath blessed God, and the king[13], *that is, hath cursed*;
and lead ye out him, and stone ye *him*, and die he so.
(and privately, *or stealthily*, send ye in two men, the sons
of Belial, opposite him, and then say they this false
witness against him, Naboth hath cursed God, and the
king; and then lead ye him out, and stone ye *him*, and so
he shall die.)
11 Therefore his citizens, the greater men in birth, and
the best men that dwelled with him in the city (And so
his fellow citizens, the men of great age, *that is, the
elders*, and the best men who lived with him in the city),
did as Jezebel had commanded [to them], and as it was
written in the letters, which she had sent to them.
12 They preached fasting, and made Naboth to sit
among the first men of the people;
13 and when two men, (the) sons of the devil, were
brought (in), they made them to sit against him (they had
them sit opposite him), and they, that is, as men of the
devil, said (false) witnessing against him before all the
multitude, (saying,) Naboth blessed God, and the king,
that is, Naboth hath cursed God, and the king; for which
thing they led him without the city, and killed *him* with
stones.
14 And they sent to Jezebel, and said, Naboth is stoned
(Naboth was stoned), and is dead.
15 Forsooth it was done, when Jezebel had heard
Naboth stoned and dead, she spake to Ahab, Rise thou,
take in possession the vinery of Naboth of Jezreel, which
would not assent to thee, and give it for [the] money
taken; for Naboth liveth not, but is dead. (And it was
done, when Jezebel had heard that Naboth had been
stoned and was dead, she spoke to Ahab, and said, Rise
thou up, and take in possession the vineyard of Naboth
of Jezreel, who would not assent to thee, and give it to
thee for the money received; for Naboth no longer liveth,
but now is dead.)
16 And when Ahab had heard this, that is, Naboth *to
be* dead, he rose, and went down into the vinery of
Naboth of Jezreel, to have it into possession. (And when
Ahab had heard this, that is, that Naboth was dead, he
rose up, and went down to the vineyard of Naboth of
Jezreel, to take possession of it.)
17 Therefore the word of the Lord was made to Elijah
of Tishbe, and said,
18 Rise thou, go down into the coming of Ahab, king of
Israel, which is in Samaria; lo! he goeth down to the
vinery of Naboth, that he have it in possession. (Rise thou
up, and go down to meet with Ahab, the king of Israel,
who is in Samaria; lo! he goeth down to the vineyard of
Naboth, to take possession of it.)
19 And thou shalt speak to him, and say, The Lord saith
these things, Thou hast slain *Naboth*, furthermore and
thou hast taken *his vineyard* in possession; and after
these things thou shalt add, [These things saith the Lord,]
In this place, wherein dogs licked the blood of Naboth,
they shall lick also thy blood. (And thou shalt speak to
him, and say, The Lord saith these things, Hast thou
killed *Naboth*, and furthermore, hast thou taken
possession of *his vineyard*? and after these things thou
shalt add, The Lord saith these things, In this place,
where the dogs licked up the blood of Naboth, they shall
also lick up thy blood.)
20 And Ahab said to Elijah, Whether thou hast found
me thine enemy? And Elijah said, I have found *thee so*,
for thou art sold *to the devil* that thou shouldest do evil in
the sight of the Lord. (And when Ahab saw Elijah, he
said, Hast thou found me, O my enemy? And Elijah said,
Yes, I have found *thee*, for thou hath sold thyself *to the
devil*, and thou doest evil before the Lord.)

---

[13] *That is, 'cursed', as in the 2ND Chapter of Job, 'Bless thou God, and die thou'; for the horror of cursing, (the) Jews signified it by the contrary name.*

21 Therefore the Lord saith these things, Lo! I shall
bring in upon thee evil, and I shall cut away thine hinder
things, and I shall slay of Ahab a pisser to the wall, and
the imprisoned, and the last in Israel; (And so the Lord
saith these things, Lo! I shall bring in evil upon thee, and
I shall cut away thy posterity, *or thy descendants*, and I
shall kill all who be of Ahab, unto a pisser on the wall,
and the imprisoned, and the last in Israel;)
22 and I shall give thine house *to be* as the house of
Jeroboam, the son of Nebat, and as the house of Baasha,
the son of Ahijah; for thou didest evil to excite me to
wrathfulness, and madest Israel to do sin. (and I shall
make thy house *to be* like the house of Jeroboam, the son
of Nebat, and like the house of Baasha, the son of Ahijah;
for thou didest evil to stir me to anger, and madest Israel
to do sin.)
23 But also the Lord spake of Jezebel, and said, (The)
Dogs shall eat (up) Jezebel in the field of Jezreel;
24 if Ahab shall die in the city, dogs shall eat him;
soothly if he shall die in the field, birds of the air shall eat
him. (and if Ahab shall die in the city, the dogs shall eat
him; and if he shall die in the field, the birds of the air
shall eat him.)
25 Therefore none other was such as Ahab, that was
sold to do evil in the sight of the Lord; for Jezebel his
wife excited him thereto; (And there was no one else like
Ahab, who sold himself to do evil before the Lord; for
Jezebel his wife stirred him to do it;)
26 and he was made abominable, in so much that he
followed the idols that (the) Amorites made, which men
the Lord wasted from (before) the face of the sons of
Israel.
27 Therefore when Ahab had heard these words, he
rent his cloth (he tore his cloak), and covered his flesh
with an hair-shirt, and he fasted, and slept in a sackcloth,
and went with the head cast down.
28 And the word of the Lord was made to Elijah of
Tishbe, and said,
29 Whether thou hast not seen Ahab made low before
me? Therefore for he is made low for the cause of me, I
shall not bring in evil in his days, but in the days of his
son I shall bring in evil to his house. (Hast thou seen that
Ahab hath made himself low, *or hath humbled himself*,
before me? And so because he hath made himself low, I
shall not bring in evil in his days, but later I shall bring in
evil upon his household, *or his family*, yea, in the days of
his son.)

CHAPTER 22

1 Therefore three years passed without battle betwixt
Syria and Israel.
2 And in the third year Jehoshaphat, king of Judah,
went down to the king of Israel.
3 And the king of Israel said to his servants, Know ye
not, that Ramoth of Gilead is ours, and (that) we be
negligent to (not) take it (back) from the hand of the king
of Syria?
4 And he said to Jehoshaphat, Whether thou shalt
come with me to fight in Ramoth of Gilead? And
Jehoshaphat said to the king of Israel, As I am, so and
thou (I am ready when thou art/What is mine is yours);
my people and thy people be one; and my knights and
thy knights *be one*.
5 And Jehoshaphat said to the king of Israel, I pray
thee, ask thou today the word of the Lord.
6 Therefore the king of Israel gathered together [the]
prophets, about four hundred men, and he said to them,
Ought I to go into Ramoth of Gilead to fight, either *ought
I* to rest? Which answered, Go thou up, and the Lord
shall give it in(to) the hand of the king.
7 Forsooth Jehoshaphat said, Is there not here any
(other) prophet of the Lord, that we (may) ask by him?
8 And the king of Israel said to Jehoshaphat, One man,
Micaiah, the son of Imlah, is left, by whom we may ask
the Lord; but I hate him, for he prophesieth not good to
me, but evil. To whom Jehoshaphat said, King, speak
thou not so. (And the king of Israel said to Jehoshaphat,
There is one man left, Micaiah, the son of Imlah, by
whom we can ask the Lord; but I hate him, for he never
prophesieth good things for me, but only evil. To whom
Jehoshaphat said, O king, do not thou say such things!)
9 Therefore the king of Israel called some
chamberlain, and said to him, Haste thou to bring
Micaiah, [the] son of Imlah.
10 Forsooth the king of Israel, and Jehoshaphat, king of
Judah, sat, each in his throne, clothed with king's
ornament, in the large house beside the door, or wicket,
of the gate of Samaria; and all the prophets prophesied in
the sight of them. (And so the king of Israel, and
Jehoshaphat, the king of Judah, each sat on their throne,
clothed with king's adornment, at the entrance to the gate
of Samaria; and all the prophets prophesied before them.)
11 Also Zedekiah, the son of Chenaanah, made to
himself horns of iron, and said, The Lord God saith these
things, With these thou shalt scatter Syria, till thou do
away it. (And Zedekiah, the son of Chenaanah, made
iron horns for himself, and said, The Lord God saith these
things, With these *horns* thou shalt scatter Syria, until
thou do it away.)
12 And all [the] prophets prophesied in like manner,
and said, Ascend thou into Ramoth of Gilead, and go
thou with prosperity; and the Lord shall betake thine
enemies in(to) the hand of the king.
13 Soothly the messenger, that went to call Micaiah,
spake to him, and said, Lo! the words of the prophets
with one mouth preach goods to the king; therefore thy
word be like them, and speak thou goods. (And the
messenger who went to call Micaiah, spoke to him, and

said, Lo! the words of the prophets preach with one
mouth good things for the king; and so let thy word/s be
like them, and say thou what is good.)
14 To whom Micaiah said, (As) The Lord liveth, for
whatever thing the Lord shall say to me, I shall speak this.
15 Therefore he came to the king. And the king said to
him, Micaiah, ought we (to) go into Ramoth of Gilead to
fight, either cease (we)? To which king he answered,
Ascend thou, and go in prosperity; and the Lord shall
betake it into the hand of the king.
16 Forsooth the king said to him, Again and again I
conjure thee (Again and again I adjure thee), that thou
speak not to me, no but that that is sooth in the name of
the Lord.
17 And he said, I saw all Israel scattered in the hills, as
sheep not having a shepherd; and the Lord said, These
have no lord, each man turn again into his house in
peace (and the Lord said, They have no lord, so let each
one now return to his house in peace).
18 Therefore the king of Israel said to Jehoshaphat,
Whether I said not to thee, that he prophesieth not good
to me, but ever[more] evil? (And the king of Israel said to
Jehoshaphat, Did I not say to thee, that he never
prophesieth good for me, but always evil?)
19 Soothly that Micaiah added, and said, Therefore
hear thou the word of the Lord; I saw the Lord sitting on
his throne, and *I saw* all the host of heaven standing nigh
[to] him, on the right side and on the left side.
20 And the Lord said, Who shall deceive Ahab, king of
Israel, that he ascend, and fall in Ramoth of Gilead? And
one said such words, and another in another manner.
21 Soothly a spirit went out, and went before the Lord,
and said, I shall deceive him.
22 To whom the Lord spake, In what thing? And he
said, I shall go out, and I shall be a spirit of leasing in the
mouth of all his prophets (and I shall be a lying spirit in
the mouth of all his prophets). And the Lord said, Thou
shalt deceive (him), and shalt have the mastery; go thou
out, and do so.
23 Now therefore, lo! the Lord gave a spirit of leasing
in the mouth of all (these) prophets that be here; and the
Lord spake evil against thee. (And so now, lo! the Lord
hath put a lying spirit in the mouths of all these prophets
of thine that be here; and the Lord hath spoken evil
against thee.)
24 Forsooth Zedekiah, [the] son of Chenaanah, nighed,
and smote Micaiah on the cheek, and said, Whether the
Spirit of the Lord forsook me, and spake to thee?
25 And Micaiah said, Thou shalt see in that day (Thou
shalt see on that day), when thou shalt go into a closet
within (a) closet, (so) that thou be hid.
26 And the king of Israel said, Take Micaiah, and dwell
he at Amon, [the] prince of the city, and at Joash, the son
of Amalek; (And the king of Israel said, Take hold of
Micaiah, and deliver him to Amon, the ruler of the city,
and Joash, the son of Ahab;)
27 and say ye to them, The king saith these things,
Send ye this man into prison, and sustain ye him with
bread of tribulation, and with water of anguish, till I turn
again in peace (until I safely return).
28 And Micaiah said, If thou shalt turn again in peace,
the Lord spake not in me (If thou shalt safely return, then
the Lord hath not spoken by me). And he said, Hear ye,
all peoples.
29 Therefore the king of Israel ascended, and
Jehoshaphat, king of Judah, into Ramoth of Gilead. (And
so the king of Israel, and Jehoshaphat, the king of Judah,
went up to Ramoth of Gilead.)
30 Therefore the king of Israel said to Jehoshaphat,
Take thou armours, and enter thou into battle, and be
thou clothed in thy clothes, *that is, in (the) noble signs of
the king.* Certainly the king of Israel changed his
clothing, and entered into battle. (And so the king of
Israel said to Jehoshaphat, Take thou up thy arms, *or thy
weapons,* and enter thou into the battle, and be thou
clothed in thy clothes, *that is, in the noble signs of the
king.* But the king of Israel changed his own clothes, and
only then entered into the battle.)
31 Soothly the king of Syria had commanded to [the]
two and thirty princes of chariots, and said, Ye shall not
fight against any man [the] less, either [the] more, but
against the king of Israel only. (And the king of Syria had
commanded to the thirty-two leaders of his chariots, and
said, Ye shall not fight against any lesser man, or against
any greater man, but only against the king of Israel.)
32 Therefore when the princes of (the) chariots had
seen Jehoshaphat, they supposed that he was (the) king of
Israel, and by fierceness made, they fought against him.
And Jehoshaphat cried [out], *calling (for) God's help, and
declaring his banner;*
33 and the princes of [the] chariots understood, that it
was not the king of Israel, and they ceased from
(pursuing) him.
34 Soothly some man bent a bow, and directed an
arrow into uncertain, and by hap he smote the king of
Israel betwixt the lung and the stomach. And the king
said to his charioteer, Turn thine hand, and cast me out
of the host, for I am wounded grievously (And the king
said to his charioteer, Turn thy hand, and take me out of
the battle, for I am grievously wounded).
35 Therefore [the] battle was joined in that day, and the
king of Israel stood in his chariot against (the) men of
Syria, and he was dead at eventide. Forsooth the blood
of the wound floated down into the bottom of the
chariot. (And so the battle was joined on that day, and
the king of Israel stood in his chariot facing the Syrians,
and then he died that evening. And the blood from his
wound flowed down into the bottom of his chariot.)

36 And a crier sounded in all the host, before that the
sun went down, and said, Each man turn again into his
city, and into his land (Each man return to his own city,
and to his own land).
37 Forsooth the king was dead, and was borne into
Samaria; and they buried the king in Samaria.
38 And they washed his chariot in the cistern of
Samaria, and dogs licked his blood, and they washed the
armours, by the word of the Lord which he had spoken.
(And they washed his chariot at the pool of Samaria, and
the dogs licked up his blood, and they washed his arms,
or his weapons/and the whores washed themselves in it,
according to the word which the Lord had spoken.)
39 Soothly the residue of [the] words of Ahab, and all
things which he did, and the house of ivory which he
builded, and of all [the] cities which he builded (and the
ivory house and all the cities which he built), whether
these be not written in the book of [the] words of [the]
days of the kings of Israel?
40 Therefore Ahab slept with his fathers, and Ahaziah,
his son, reigned for him. (And so Ahab died, and his son
Ahaziah reigned for him.)
41 Forsooth Jehoshaphat, [the] son of Asa, began to
reign on Judah in the fourth year of Ahab, king of Israel.
42 Jehoshaphat was of five and thirty years, when he
began to reign, and he reigned five and twenty years in
Jerusalem; the name of his mother *was* Azubah, [the]
daughter of Shilhi.
43 And he went in all the way of Asa, his father, and
[he] bowed not [aside] from it; and he did that, that was
rightful in the sight of the Lord. Nevertheless he did not
away [the] high things, for yet the people made sacrifice,
and burnt incense, in high places. (And he went in all the
ways of his father Asa, and he turned not aside from
them; and he did what was right before the Lord. But he
did not do away the hill shrines, for yet the people
offered sacrifices, and burned incense, at the hill shrines.)
44 And Jehoshaphat had peace with the king of Israel.
45 Soothly the residue of [the] words of Jehoshaphat,
and the works and (the) battles, which he did, whether
these be not written in the book of [the] words of [the]
days of the kings of Judah?
46 But also he took away from the land the relics of
[the] men turned into women's conditions, that (were) left
in the days of Asa, his father. (And he also did away from
the land the male and female whores, who served at the
hill shrines, who were still there from the days of his
father Asa.)
47 Neither a king was ordained then in Edom (And
there was not a king then in Edom, *that is, Idumea*); (but
a deputy, appointed by the king of Judah, ruled over it).
48 Forsooth king Jehoshaphat made ships in the sea,
that should sail into Ophir for gold, and those might not
go, for they were broken in Eziongeber. (And King
Jehoshaphat made ships of the sea, to sail to Ophir for
gold, but they never arrived there, for they were wrecked
at Eziongeber.)
49 Then Ahaziah, [the] son of Ahab, said to
Jehoshaphat, My servants (shall) go with thine in (our)
ships. And Jehoshaphat would not (But Jehoshaphat
would not consent to that).
50 And Jehoshaphat slept with his fathers, and was
buried with them in the city of David, his (fore)father;
and Jehoram[14], his son, reigned for him.
51 Forsooth Ahaziah, [the] son of Ahab, began to reign
on Israel, in Samaria, in the seventeenth year of
Jehoshaphat, king of Judah; and Ahaziah reigned on
Israel two years.
52 And he did evil in the sight of the Lord, and went in
the way of his father, and of his mother, and in the way
of Jeroboam, [the] son of Nebat, that made Israel to do
sin.
53 And he served Baal, and worshipped him, and
wrathed the Lord God of Israel, by all things which his
father had done. (And he served Baal, and worshipped
him, and stirred the Lord God of Israel to anger, by doing
all the evil things which his father had done.) ✡

[14] Also known as Joram.

2ND KINGS

CHAPTER 1

1 Forsooth Moab trespassed against Israel, after that
Ahab was dead. (After Ahab died, Moab rebelled against
Israel.)
2 And Ahaziah felled through the alures of his solar,
which he had in Samaria, and was (made) sick; and he
sent messengers, and said to them, Go ye, and counsel
(with) Baalzebub, [the] god of Ekron, whether I may live
after this sickness of me. (And Ahaziah fell through the
lattice of his solarium, which he had in Samaria, and was
injured; and he sent out messengers, and said to them,
Go ye, and counsel with Baalzebub, the god of Ekron, to
see whether I shall recover from this injury of mine.)
3 Forsooth the angel of the Lord spake to Elijah of
Tishbe, and said, Rise thou, and go down into the
meeting of the messengers of the king of Samaria; and
thou shalt say to them, Whether God is not in Israel, that
ye go to counsel Baalzebub, [the] god of Ekron? (Is God
not in Israel, so that ye must go to counsel with
Baalzebub, the god of Ekron?)
4 For which thing the Lord saith these things, Thou
shalt not go down off the bed, on which thou
ascendedest, (but thou shalt die). And Elijah went (forth).
5 And the messengers turned again to Ahaziah. And
he said to them, Why turned ye again? (And the
messengers returned to Ahaziah. And he said to them,
Why have ye returned?)
6 And they answered to him, A man met us, and said
to us, Go ye, turn ye again to the king, that sent you; and
ye shall say to him, The Lord saith these things, Whether
for God was not in Israel, thou sendest, that Baalzebub,
[the] god of Ekron, be counselled? Therefore thou shalt
not go down off the bed, on which thou ascendedest, but
thou shalt die by death. (And they answered to him, A
man met us, and said to us, Go ye, return ye to the king,
who sent you; and ye shall say to him, The Lord saith
these things, Thinkest thou that God was not in Israel,
and thou sentest out messengers, so that Baalzebub, the
god of Ekron, could be counselled with? And so thou
shalt not go down off the bed, on which thou liest, but
thou shalt die.)
7 Which Ahaziah said to them, Of what figure and
habit is that man, that met you, and spake to you these
words?
8 And they said, An hairy man, and gird with a girdle
of leather in the reins. Which said to them, It is Elijah of
Tishbe. (And they said, A hairy man, and girded with a
girdle of leather about his loins. And he said to them, It
is Elijah of Tishbe.)
9 And he sent to Elijah a prince of fifty, and [the] fifty
men that were under him. Which prince ascended to
him, and said to him, sitting in the top of the hill, Man of
God, the king commandeth, that thou come down. (And
he sent to Elijah a leader of fifty men, and the fifty men
who were under him. Which leader went up to him, and
said to him, as he was sitting on the hill-top, Man of God,
the king commandeth, that thou come down.)
10 And Elijah answered, and said to the prince of fifty
men (and said to the leader of fifty men), If I am the man
of God, (let) fire come down from heaven, and devour
thee and thy fifty men. Therefore fire came down from
heaven, and devoured him, and the fifty men that were
with him.
11 Again he sent to Elijah another prince of fifty, and
fifty men with him, which spake to Elijah, Man of God,
the king saith these things, Haste thou, come thou down.
(And he sent to Elijah another leader of fifty men, and the
fifty men who were with him, who spoke to Elijah, and
said, Man of God, the king saith these things, Hasten
thou, come thou down.)
12 Elijah answered, and said, If I am the man of God,
(let) fire come down from heaven, and devour thee and
thy fifty men. Therefore the fire of God came down from
heaven, and devoured him and his fifty men.
13 Again he sent the third prince of fifty men, and [the]
fifty men that were with him. And when the prince had
come, he bowed the knees against Elijah (And when the
leader had come near, he bowed his knees before Elijah),
and prayed him, and said, Man of God, do not thou
despise my life, and the lives of (these fifty men,) thy
servants, that be with me.
14 Lo! fire came down from heaven, and devoured
twain, the first (two) princes of fifty men, and the fifty
men that were with them; but now, I beseech, that thou
have mercy on my life. (Lo! fire came down from heaven,
and devoured the first two leaders of fifty men, and the
fifty men who were with each of them; but now, I
beseech thee, that thou have mercy on my life.)
15 Forsooth the angel of the Lord spake to Elijah of
Tishbe, and said, Go thou down with him; dread thou
not (do not thou fear). Therefore Elijah rose (up), and
came down with him to the king;
16 and he spake to the king, (and said,) The Lord saith
these things, For thou sentest messengers to counsel
Baalzebub, god of Ekron, as if no God were in Israel, of
whom thou mightest ask a word; therefore thou shalt not
go down off the bed, on which thou ascendedest, but
thou shalt die by death. (and he spoke to the king, and
said, The Lord saith these things, Because thou sentest out
messengers to counsel with Baalzebub, the god of Ekron,
as if God were not in Israel, of whom thou mightest ask a
word; and so thou shalt not go down off the bed, on

which thou liest, but thou shalt die.)
17 Therefore he was dead by the word of the Lord,
which word Elijah spake; and Joram[1], his brother, reigned
for him, in the second year of Jehoram[2], the son of
Jehoshaphat, king of Judah; for Ahaziah had no son.
18 Soothly the residue of [the] words of Ahaziah, which
he wrought, whether these be not written in the book of
[the] words of [the] days of the kings of Israel?

CHAPTER 2

1 Forsooth it was done, when the Lord would raise
(up) Elijah by a whirlwind into heaven, Elijah and Elisha
went from Gilgal.
2 And Elijah said to Elisha, Sit thou here, for the Lord
[hath] sent me till into Bethel. To whom Elisha said, The
Lord liveth, and thy soul liveth, for I shall not forsake thee
(To whom Elisha said, As the Lord liveth, and as thy soul
liveth, I shall not desert thee). And when they had come
down to Bethel,
3 the sons of (the) prophets, that were in Bethel, went
out to Elisha, and said to him, Whether thou knowest,
that the Lord shall take away thy lord today from thee?
(Knowest thou, that the Lord shall take away thy lord from
thee today?) Which answered, And I know; be ye still.
4 Forsooth Elijah said to Elisha, Sit thou here, for the
Lord [hath] sent me into Jericho. And he said, (As) The
Lord liveth, and (as) thy soul liveth, for I shall not forsake
thee. And when they had come to Jericho,
5 the sons of (the) prophets, that were in Jericho,
nighed to Elisha, and said to him, Whether thou knowest,
that the Lord shall take away thy lord today from thee?
(Knowest thou, that the Lord shall take away thy lord
from thee today?) And he said, I know; be ye still.
6 Forsooth Elijah said to Elisha, Sit thou here, for the
Lord [hath] sent me to (the) Jordan (River). Which said,
(As) The Lord liveth, and (as) thy soul liveth, for I shall
not forsake thee. Therefore (they) both went together;
7 and fifty men of the sons of (the) prophets followed,
which also stood far even against; soothly they both
stood over (the) Jordan. (and fifty men of the sons of the
prophets followed, and stood looking from afar; and they
both stood by the Jordan River.)
8 And Elijah took his mantle, and wrapped it, and
smote the waters; which were parted into ever either part,
and both went by the dry. (And Elijah took his mantle, *or
his cloak*, and rolled it up, and struck the water; which
was divided into two parts, and they went across on dry
ground.)
9 And when they had passed [over], Elijah said to
Elisha, Ask thou that, that thou wilt that I do to thee,
before that I be taken away from thee. And Elisha said, I
beseech, that thy double spirit be made in me/I beseech,
that thy double spirit be with me[3]. (And when they had
crossed over, Elijah said to Elisha, Ask thou what thou
wilt that I can do for thee, before that I be taken away
from thee. And Elisha said, I beseech thee, that a double
portion of thy spirit be given to me/be upon me.)
10 Which Elijah answered, Thou askest an hard thing;
nevertheless if thou shalt see me, when I shall be taken
away from thee, that that thou askest shall be (so); soothly
if thou shalt not see (me), (then) it shall not be (so).
11 And when they went, and spake going (And as they
went forth, speaking as they went), lo! a chariot of fire,
and horses of fire, parted ever either; and Elijah ascended
by a whirlwind into heaven[4].
12 Forsooth Elisha saw, and cried, My father! my father!
the chariot of Israel, and the charioteer thereof. And he
saw no more Elijah. And he took his clothes, and rent
those into two parts. (And Elisha saw it, and cried, My
father! my father! the chariot of Israel, and its charioteer.
And then he saw Elijah no more. And he took his own
mantle, *or his own cloak*, and tore it in two.)
13 And he raised the mantle of Elijah, that felled down
to him; and he turned again, and stood over the river of
Jordan (And he picked up Elijah's mantle, that fell down
to him; and he returned, and stood by the Jordan River.)
14 And with the mantle of Elijah, that felled down to
him, he smote the waters, which were not parted. And
he said, Where is [the] God of Elijah also now? And (so)
he smote the waters, and those were parted hither and
thither; and Elisha passed [over]. (And using Elijah's
mantle, that fell down to him, he struck the water, for it
was not parted. And he said, Where is the God of Elijah?
And after that he struck the water, it was again parted
here and there; and Elisha crossed over *again*.)
15 Soothly the sons of [the] prophets, that were in
Jericho even against, saw, and said, The spirit of Elijah
rested on Elisha. And they came into the meeting of him,
and worshipped him lowly to [the] earth. (And the sons of
the prophets from Jericho, were watching, and when they
saw this, they said, The spirit of Elijah now resteth upon
Elisha. And they came to meet him, and honoured
him/and bowed low before him, down to the ground.)
16 And they said to him, Lo! with thy servants be fifty
strong men, that may go, and seek thy lord, lest
peradventure the Spirit of the Lord hath taken him, and
hath cast forth him in one of the hills, either in one of the
valleys. And Elisha said, Do not ye send. (And they said

[1] Also known as Jehoram.

[2] Also known as Joram(!).

[3] As Elijah's successor, Elisha asked for the share that the first-born son inherited by law from his father. (Good News Bible)

[4] Not into (the) heaven of stars, neither of brightness in bliss, but into (the) heaven of the air; and by the air Elijah was born into (the) earthly paradise, whither Enoch was translated before... (from a "Later Version" gloss).

to him, Lo! among thy servants be fifty strong men, who
can go, and search for thy lord, for perhaps the Spirit of
the Lord hath taken him up, and hath thrown him forth
onto one of the hills, or into one of the valleys. And
Elisha said, Do not ye go.)
17 And they constrained him, till he assented to them,
and said, Send ye (them out). And they sent (out the) fifty
men; and when they had sought *him* by three days, they
found him not (and after they had looked for him for
three days, they still could not find him).
18 And they turned again to Elisha; and he dwelled in
Jericho. And he said to them, Whether I said not to you,
Do not ye send (them out)? (And they returned to Elisha,
who had stayed in Jericho. And he said to them, Did I
not say to you, Do not ye go?/Do not ye send them out?)
19 Therefore the men of the city said to Elisha, Lo! the
dwelling of this city is full good, as thou thyself, lord,
seest; but the waters be most evil, and the land is barren.
20 And he said, Bring ye to me a new vessel, and put
ye salt into it. And when they had brought it to him,
21 he went out to the well of waters, and sent salt into
it, and said, The Lord saith these things, I have healed
these waters, and neither death, nor barrenness, shall be
more in them. (he went to the well of water, *or to the
spring*, and put the salt into it, and said, The Lord saith
these things, I have healed this water, and no more shall
there be death, or barrenness, in it.)
22 Therefore the waters were healed till into this day,
by the word of Elisha, which he spake. (And so the
waters were healed unto this day, by the word of Elisha,
that he spoke.)
23 Forsooth Elisha went up from thence into Bethel;
and when he went up by the way, little children went out
of the city, and scorned him, and said, Go up, thou bald
one! go up, thou bald one! (Go away, O bald one! go
away, Baldy!)
24 And when he had beheld, he saw them, and cursed
them in the name of the Lord. And two bears went out of
the forest, and rent (two and) forty children of them. (And
when he had looked back, and beheld them, he cursed
them in the name of the Lord. And two bears went out of
the forest, and tore forty-two of those children to death.)
25 Soothly Elisha went from thence into the hill of
Carmel, and from thence he turned again to Samaria.
(And Elisha went from there to Mount Carmel, and then
returned to Samaria.)

CHAPTER 3

1 Forsooth Joram[5], [the] son of Ahab, reigned on
Israel, in Samaria, in the eighteenth year of Jehoshaphat,
king of Judah. And he reigned twelve years, (Now Joram,
Ahab's son, began to reign upon Israel, in Samaria, in the
eighteenth year of Jehoshaphat, the king of Judah. And
he reigned for twelve years,)
2 and he did evil before the Lord, but not as his father
and his mother (had done); for he took away the images
of Baal, which his father had made,
3 nevertheless he cleaved to the sins of Jeroboam, the
son of Nebat, that made Israel to do sin (who made Israel
to do sin); and he went not away from them.
4 Forsooth Mesha, king of Moab, nourished many
beasts, and paid to the king of Israel an hundred
thousand of lambs, and an hundred thousand wethers,
with their fleeces.
5 And when Ahab was dead, he brake the bond of
peace, which he had with the king of Israel. (But when
Ahab died, he broke the covenant which he had with the
king of Israel.)
6 Therefore king Joram went out of Samaria in that
day, and numbered all Israel. (And King Joram went out
of Samaria that day, and gathered together Israel's army.)
7 And he sent to Jehoshaphat, king of Judah, and said,
The king of Moab hath gone away from me; come thou
with me against him to battle. And Jehoshaphat
answered, I shall go up with thee; he that is mine, is thine
(all that is mine, is thine); my people is thy people; and
mine horses be thine horses.
8 And he said, By what way shall we ascend? And
Joram answered, By the desert of Idumea (And Joram
answered, Through the wilderness of Edom).
9 Therefore the king of Israel, and the king of Judah,
and the king of Edom, went forth, and compassed by the
way of seven days; and (then) there was not water to the
host, and to the beasts, that followed them. (And so the
king of Israel, and the king of Judah, and the king of
Edom, went forth, and travelled on the way for seven
days; and then there was no more water for the army,
and for the beasts, that followed them.)
10 And the king of Israel said, Alas! alas! alas! the Lord
hath gathered together us three kings to betake *us* in(to)
the hand of Moab. (And the king of Israel said, Alas! alas!
alas! the Lord hath gathered us three kings together to
deliver *us* into the hands of the Moabites.)
11 And Jehoshaphat said, Whether any prophet of the
Lord is here, (so) that we (can) beseech the Lord by him?
And one of the servants of the king of Israel answered,
Elisha, the son of Shaphat, is here, that poured water
upon the hands of Elijah (Elisha, the son of Shaphat, is
here, who poured water upon Elijah's hands).
12 And Jehoshaphat said, Is the word of the Lord at
him? Which said, Yea/It is (And Jehoshaphat said, And
the word of the Lord is with him). And (so) the king of
Israel, and Jehoshaphat, king of Judah, and the king of
Edom, went down to him.
13 And Elisha said to the king of Israel, What is to me
and to thee, *an idolater*? Go thou to the prophets of thy

[5] Also known as Jehoram.

father and of thy mother. And the king of Israel said to
him, Why hath the Lord gathered together these three
kings, to betake them into the hands of Moab? (But the
king of Israel said to him, Nay! for the Lord hath gathered
these three kings together, to deliver them into the hands
of the Moabites.)
14 And Elisha said to him, The Lord of hosts liveth, in
whose sight I stand, if I were not ashamed[6] of the cheer
of Jehoshaphat, king of Judah, truly I had not perceived,
neither I had beheld thee. (And Elisha said to him, As the
Lord of hosts liveth, before whom I stand, if I did not
have such great respect for Jehoshaphat, the king of
Judah, truly I would not have bothered to look upon thee,
nor receive thee *into my presence*.)
15 Now forsooth bring ye to me a psalterer (But now
bring ye to me a singer of psalms, *or of songs*). And
when the psalterer sang, the hand of the Lord was made
upon Elisha,
16 and he said, The Lord saith these things, Make ye
the womb, *either the depth*, of this strand, ditches and
ditches. (and he said, The Lord saith these things, Make
ye the trough of this dry stream, *or this dry river-bed*, into
ditches and ditches.)
17 For the Lord saith these things, Ye shall not see
wind, neither rain, and this depth shall be filled with
waters, and ye shall drink, and your families, and your
beasts. (For the Lord saith these things, Though ye shall
not see wind, or rain, yet this depth shall be filled with
water, so that ye, and your families, and your beasts, shall
have water to drink.)
18 And this is (but a) little thing in the sight of the Lord.
Furthermore also he shall betake Moab into your hands
(And furthermore he shall deliver the Moabites into your
hands);
19 and ye shall smite each strengthened city, and each
chosen city, and ye shall cut down each tree bearing
fruit, and ye shall stop all the wells of waters, and ye shall
cover with stones each noble field. (and ye shall strike
down each fortified city, and each chosen city, and ye
shall cut down each fruit-bearing tree, and ye shall stop,
or close up, all the water wells, *or all the springs*, and ye
shall cover each fertile field with stones.)
20 Therefore it was done early, when (the) sacrifice is
wont to be offered, and, lo! waters came by the way of
Edom, and the land was filled with waters.
21 Soothly all the men of Moab heard, that *these* kings
had gone up to fight against them; *and they* called
together all men, that were gird with a knight's girdle
above, and they stood in the terms. (And all the Moabites
heard, that *these* kings had gone up to fight against them;
and they called together all the men who were girded
with a horseman's girdle, and who were stationed at the
border.)
22 And men of Moab rose full early, and when the sun
was risen then even against the waters, they saw the
waters (as) red as blood even against them. (And the men
of Moab rose up very early, and when the sun rose up
over the water, they saw that the water before them was
as red as blood/was red like blood.)
23 And they said, It is the blood of (the) sword, *that is,
shed out by (the) sword*; [the] kings have fought against
themselves, and they be slain together (and they have
killed one another); now go thou, Moab, to the prey.
24 And they went into the castles of Israel; forsooth
Israel rose, and smote Moab, and they fled before the
men of Israel. Then they that had over-come, came, and
smote Moab, (And they went to the tents, *or to the camp*,
of the Israelites; but Israel rose up, and struck down the
Moabites, and they fled before the men of Israel. Then
the Israelites came forth, and entered, and struck down
the Moabites in their own land,)
25 and destroyed their cities; and all men sending
stones filled each best field, and stopped all the wells of
waters, and cut down all the trees bearing fruit, so that
only [the] earthen walls were left; and the city was
compassed of men setting engines, and it was smitten by
great part *thereof*. (and destroyed their cities; and all the
men threw stones, and filled up each best field, and they
stopped, *or closed up*, all the water wells, *or all the
springs*, and cut down all the fruit-bearing trees, so that
only the walls in Kirhareseth were left; and the city was
encompassed, *or surrounded*, with men setting up engines,
or bulwarks, and a great part *of it* was struck down.)
26 And when the king of Moab had seen this, that is,
that the enemies had the mastery, he took with him seven
hundred men drawing out swords, that they should break
(through) into the king of Edom; and they might not. (And
when the king of Moab had seen this, that is, that the
enemies had the mastery, he took with him seven
hundred men drawing out swords, to try to break through
to the king of Edom; but they could not do so.)
27 And he took his first engendered son, that should
reign for him, and offered *him* (as) a burnt sacrifice on the
wall; and great indignation was made in Israel; and anon
they went away from him, and turned again into their land.
(And so he took his first-born son, who would reign for
him, and offered *him* as a burnt sacrifice on the wall; and
great indignation was felt by all the Israelites; and at once
they went away from him, and returned to their own land.)

CHAPTER 4

1 Forsooth a woman of the wives of prophets cried to
Elisha, and said, Thy servant, mine husband, is dead, and
thou knowest that thy servant dreaded God; and lo! the
creancer, *that is, he to whom debt is owed*, cometh to take

---

[6] *Ashamed; in denying his asking to him (in denying his request), since he is faithful and devout.*

my two sons to serve him. (And a woman of the wives of
the sons of the prophets cried to Elisha, and said, Thy
servant, my husband, is dead, and thou knowest that thy
servant feared God/revered God; and lo! the creditor
cometh to take away my two sons to serve him.)
2 To whom Elisha said, What wilt thou that I do to
thee? (What wilt thou that I do for thee?) say thou to me,
what hast thou in thine house? And she answered, I
thine handmaid have not anything in mine house, no but
a little of oil, with which I shall be anointed.
3 To whom he said, Go thou, and ask by borrowing of
all thy neighbours void vessels, not a few. (To whom he
said, Go thou, and ask to borrow empty vessels from all
of thy neighbours, and borrow not just a few.)
4 And enter, and close thy door, when thou art within,
thou and thy sons (And go inside, and when thou and thy
sons be within, close the door); and put ye thereof into
all these vessels; and when those shall be full, thou shalt
take (them, and put them) away.
5 Therefore the woman went, and closed the door on
herself and on her sons, (and) they brought the vessels,
and she poured in(to them).
6 And when the vessels were full, she said to her son,
Bring yet a vessel to me. And he answered, I have not.
And *then* the oil stood, *increasing no more*. (And when
all the vessels were full, she said to her son, Bring me
another vessel. And he answered, I have no more. And
then the oil stood still, *or stopped, and increased no
more*.)
7 Forsooth she came, and showed it to the man of
God; and he said, Go thou, sell the oil, and yield to thy
creancer; and thou and thy children live ye off the
remnant, *or the residue*. (And she came, and showed it to
the man of God; and he said, Go thou, sell the oil, and
yield *what thou owest* to thy creditor; and then thou and
thy children live ye on the rest.)
8 Forsooth a day was made, and Elisha passed by a
city, Shunem; and a great woman was there, which held
him, that he should eat bread, *that is, busily prayed (him
to come) to meat*. And when he passed oft thereby, he
turned to her, that he would eat bread *with her* (And
often when he passed by, he would turn in at her home,
so he could share a meal *with her*).
9 And she said to her husband, I perceive that this is
an holy man of God, that passeth oft by us (who often
passeth by us);
10 therefore make we a little solar to him, and put we
therein a little bed to him, and a board, and a chair, and a
candlestick; that when he cometh to us, he dwell there.
(and so let us make a solarium for him, and put we a bed
in it, and a table, and a chair, and a candlestick for him;
so that when he cometh to us, he can rest there.)
11 Therefore a day was made, and Elisha came, and
turned in to the solar (and went up to the solarium), and
rested there.
12 And he said to Gehazi, his servant, Call thou this
Shunammite. And when he had called her, and she had
stood before him,
13 he said to his servant, Speak thou to her, Lo! thou
hast ministered to us busily in all things; what wilt thou
that I do to thee? Whether thou hast a cause, and wilt that
I speak to the king, either to the prince of the chivalry?
And she answered, I dwell in the midst of my people.
(And then she went away.) (he said to his servant, Speak
thou to her, and say, Lo! thou hast busily served us in all
things; what wilt thou that I do for thee? Hast thou a case,
that I speak about to the king, or to the leader of the
cavalry, *or of the army*? And she answered, All is well; I
live here in the midst of my people. And then she went
away.)
14 And he said, What then will she that I do to her?
(And he said, What then desireth her that I should do for
her?) [And] Gehazi said to him, Ask thou not (me), for she
hath no son, and her husband is eld.
15 Therefore Elisha commanded, that he should call
her (back). And when she was called, and stood before
the door,
16 he said to her, In this time, as in (the) time of life (At
this time, next year), thou shalt embrace a son.[7] And she
answered, Do not thou, my lord, the man of God, I
beseech (thee), do not thou lie to thine handmaid.
17 And the woman conceived, and childed a son in the
time, and in the same hour, in which Elisha had said.
(And the woman conceived, and bare a son at the time,
and at the hour, in which Elisha had said.)
18 Soothly the child increased; and when some day
was, and the child was gone out, and went to his father,
and to the reapers, (And the child grew; and then one
day, when the child went out to his father, and to the
reapers,)
19 he said to his father, Mine head acheth, mine head
acheth. And his father said to a servant, Take (him), and
lead him to his mother.
20 And when he had taken (him), and had brought him
to his mother, she setted him on her knees unto midday,
and he was dead (and then he died).
21 Certainly she went up, and laid him on the little bed
of the man of God, and closed the door. And she went
out,
22 and called her husband, and said, I beseech, send
thou with me one of the servants, and an ass, and I shall
run out unto the man of God, and I shall turn again (and
then I shall return).
23 And he said to her, For what cause goest thou to

---

[7] *That is, 'In the year turned about (When the year is turned about), thou shalt live (as) whole as now, and thou shalt embrace a son born then,' as Rabbi Solomon saith.*

him? today be not calends, neither sabbath. And she
answered, I shall go.
24 And she saddled the ass, and commanded to the
servant, Drive thou, and haste thee; make thou no
tarrying to me in going (do not thou go slow for me), and
do thou this thing which I command to thee.
25 Then she went forth, and came to the man of God,
into the hill of Carmel. And when the man of God had
seen her even against him, he said to Gehazi, his servant,
Lo! that Shunammite; (Then she went forth, and came to
the man of God, on Mount Carmel. And when the man
of God had seen her some way off, he said to Gehazi, his
servant, Lo! that Shunammite;)
26 go thou therefore into the meeting of her, and say
thou to her, Whether it is done rightfully about thee, and
about thine husband, and about thy son? And (when the
servant came to her, and asked her,) she answered (to
him), *It is done* rightfully. (and so go thou to meet her,
and say thou to her, Is all well with thee, and thy
husband, and thy son? And when the servant came to
her, and asked her, she answered to him, *All is* well.)
27 And when she had come to the man of God, into
the hill, she took (hold of) his feet; and Gehazi nighed,
that he should remove her. And the man of God said,
Suffer thou her; for her soul is in bitterness, and the Lord
hath held it privy from me, and showed it not to me. (But
when she had come to the man of God, on the hill, she
took hold of his feet; and Gehazi came over, so that he
could move her away. And the man of God said, Allow
thou her; for her soul is bitter for some reason, and the
Lord hath kept it secret from me, and hath not showed it
to me.)
28 And she said to him, Whether I asked a son of *thee*,
my lord? Whether I said not to thee, Scorn thou not me?
(And she said to him, Did I ask for a son from *thee*, my
lord? Did I not say to thee, Do not thou scorn me?)
29 And he said to Gehazi, Gird thy loins, and take my
staff in thine hand, and go; and if a man meet thee, greet
thou not him; and if any man greeteth thee, answer thou
not him; and put thou my staff upon the face of the child.
(And he said to Gehazi, Gird up thy loins, and take my
staff in thy hand, and go; and if thou meet any man, greet
thou him not; and if any man greeteth thee, answer thou
him not; and put thou my staff on the child's face.)
30 Forsooth the mother of the child said, (As) The Lord
liveth, and (as) thy soul liveth, I shall not leave thee.
Therefore he rose (up), and followed her.
31 And Gehazi went before them, and putted the staff
upon the face of the child; and there was not voice in
him, neither wit. And Gehazi turned again into the
meeting of him; and told to him, and said, The child rose
not (And Gehazi returned to meet him; and said to him,
The child did not get up).
32 Therefore Elisha entered into the house, and, lo! the
dead child lay in his bed. (And so Elisha went into the
house, and, lo! the child lay dead on his bed.)
33 And he entered, and closed the door on himself,
and on the child; and prayed to the Lord.
34 And (then) Elisha went up, and lay upon the child;
and he putted his mouth upon the mouth of the child,
and his eyes upon the eyes of the child, and his hands
upon the hands of the child. And he bowed himself
(down) upon the child; and the flesh of the child was
made hot.
35 And he turned again, and walked in the house once
hither and thither; and (then) again Elisha went up, and
lay upon the child, and the child coughed seven times,
and opened the eyes (and opened his eyes).
36 And he called Gehazi, and said to him, Call thou
this Shunammite. And she was called, and entered to
him. And he said, Take thy son.
37 She came, and felled down to his feet, and
worshipped on the earth; and she took her son, and went
out. (She came, and fell down at his feet, and bowed low
to the ground; and she took her son, and went out.)
38 And Elisha turned again into Gilgal. Forsooth
hunger was in the land, and the sons of (the) prophets
dwelled before him. And Elisha said to one of his
servants, Set thou a great pot (on the fire), and seethe
thou pottage to the sons of (the) prophets[8]. (And Elisha
returned to Gilgal. And there was a famine in the land.
And when the sons of the prophets sat before him, Elisha
said to one of his servants, Put thou a great pot on the
fire, and boil thou some broth, *or some stew*, for these
sons of the prophets.)
39 And one went out into the field to gather herbs of
the field; and he found as *it were* a wild vine, and he
gathered thereof gourds of the field. And he [full-]filled
his mantle, and he turned again, and shredded *those* into
the pot of pottage; for he knew not what it was (And he
filled his mantle, *or his cloak*, full, and he returned, and
shredded *them* into the pot of broth, *or of stew*; but he
did not know what it was).
40 Therefore they poured in to fellows to eat; and when
they had tasted of the seething, they cried out, and said,
Death is in the pot! death is in the pot! thou man of God.
And they might not eat *it*. (And so they poured it out for
the fellows to eat; but when they had tasted the broth, *or
the stew*, they cried out, and said, Death is in the pot!
death is in the pot, O man of God! And they could not
eat *it*.)
41 And he said, Bring ye meal. And when they had
brought, he put *it* into the pot, and said, Pour ye out to
the company, that they eat; and anything of bitterness
was no more in the pot. (And he said, Bring ye some
meal. And when they had brought it, he put *it* into the

[8] *That is, disciples of him, for they lived religiously.*

pot, and said, Pour ye it out for the group, so that
everyone can eat some; and there was no longer anything
of bitterness in the pot.)
42 Forsooth some man came from Baalshalisha, and
bare to the man of God loaves of the first fruits, twenty
loaves of barley, and thing made of corns, in his scrip.
And the man of God said, Give thou to the people, that it
eat. (And some man came from Baalshalisha, and brought
in his bag, to the man of God, loaves of the first fruits,
yea, twenty barley loaves, and some full ears of corn.
And the man of God said, Give thou to the people, so
that they can eat.)
43 And his servant answered to him, What is this, that I
set before an hundred men? Again Elisha said, Give thou
to the people, that it eat; for the Lord saith these things,
They shall eat, and there shall leave [over]. (And his
servant answered to him, This is not enough to put before
a hundred men! But again Elisha said, Give thou to the
people, so that they can eat; for the Lord saith these
things, They shall eat, and there shall be some left over.)
44 Then he put before them, the which ate; and there
(was) left (some) meat, after the word of the Lord. (Then
he put it before them, and they ate; and indeed, there
was some food left over, according to the word of the
Lord.)

CHAPTER 5

1 Naaman, prince of the chivalry of the king of Syria,
was a great man, and worshipped with his lord; for by
him the Lord gave health to Syria; soothly he was a strong
man and rich, but he was leprous. (Naaman, the leader of
the cavalry, *or of the army*, of the king of Syria, was a
great man, and honoured by his lord; and by him the
Lord gave victory to Syria; truly he was a strong man, and
a rich one, but he was also a leper.)
2 Forsooth thieves went out of Syria, and led (away as)
prisoner from the land of Israel a little damsel, that was in
the service of the wife of Naaman (who was now in the
service of Naaman's wife).
3 And she said to her lady, Would God, that my lord
had been at the prophet that is in Samaria (If only my lord
had been to the prophet who is in Samaria); soothly the
prophet would have cured him of [the] leprosy that he
hath.
4 Therefore Naaman entered to his lord, and told to
him, and said, A damsel of the land of Israel spake so and
so.
5 Therefore the king of Syria said to him, Go thou,
and I shall send letters to the king of Israel. And when
Naaman had gone forth, and had taken with him ten
talents of silver, and six thousand golden pieces, *either
florins*, and ten changings of clothes (and ten changes of
clothing),
6 he brought (the) letters to the king of Israel by these
words (he brought the letter to the king of Israel, which
read thus); When thou hast taken this epistle, know thou,
that I have sent to thee Naaman, my servant, (so) that
thou (can) cure him of his leprosy.
7 And when the king of Israel had read the letters, he
rent his clothes, and said, Whether I am God, that may
slay and quicken, for this king sent to me, that I cure a
man of his leprosy? Perceive ye, and see, that he seeketh
occasions against me. (And when the king of Israel had
read the letter, he tore his clothes, and said, Am I God,
who may kill and make alive, for this king sent to me,
that I should cure a man of his leprosy? See ye, and
understand, that he seeketh a reason, *or an excuse*, to
attack me.)
8 And when Elisha, the man of God, had heard this,
that is, that the king of Israel had rent his clothes, he sent
to the king, and said, Why rentest thou thy clothes? come
he to me, and know he, that there is a prophet in Israel.
(And when Elisha, the man of God, had heard this, that
is, that the king of Israel had torn his clothes, he sent to
the king, and said, Why tearest thou thy clothes? Let him
come to me, and then know he, that there is a prophet in
Israel.)
9 Then Naaman came with horses and chariots, and
stood at the door of the house of Elisha.
10 And Elisha sent to him a messenger (And Elisha sent
a messenger to him), and said, Go, and be thou washed
seven times in Jordan; and thy flesh shall receive health,
and thou shalt be cleansed.
11 Naaman was wroth, and went away, and said, I
guessed, that he would have gone out to me, and that he
would have stood, and inwardly have called (on) the
name of the Lord his God, and that he should have
touched with his hand the place of the leprosy, and
should have cured me *so*. (And Naaman was angry, and
went away, and said, I guessed, that he would have come
out to me, and that he would have stood there, and
inwardly called on the name of the Lord his God, and
then he would have touched the place of the leprosy
with his hand, and *thus* he would have cured me.)
12 Whether Abana and Pharpar, the floods of
Damascus, be not better than all the waters of Israel, that
I be washed in them, and be cleansed? Therefore when
he had turned himself, and went away, having
indignation, (Be not Abana and Pharpar, the rivers of
Damascus, better than all the waters of Israel, and that I
be washed in them, and be cleansed? And so when he
had turned, and went away, having indignation,)
13 his servants nighed to him, and spake to him, Father,
though the prophet had said to thee a great thing,
certainly thou oughtest to do it; how much more for now
he said to thee, Be thou washed, and thou shalt be
cleansed. (his servants came to him, and spoke to him,
and said, Father, if the prophet had said to thee to do a

great thing, certainly thou wouldest have done it; how
much more now for that he hath *simply* said to thee, Be
thou washed, and thou shalt be cleansed, *or healed.*)
14 Then Naaman went down, and washed *him(self)*
seven times in Jordan, by the word of the man of God;
and his flesh was restored as the flesh of a little child, and
he was cleansed (and his flesh was restored like the flesh
of a young child, and he was healed).
15 And he turned again with all his fellowship to the
man of God, and came, and stood before him; and said,
Verily I know (now), that none other God is in all [the]
earth, no but only [the] God of Israel; therefore, I
beseech, that thou take [a] blessing, *that is, a gift,* of thy
servant (and so I beseech thee, that thou receive a gift
from thy servant).
16 And Elisha answered, The Lord liveth before whom I
stand, for I shall not take it *of thee.* And when he made
great force *thereto,* (*that is, had pressed him greatly,*)
Elisha assented not utterly. (And Elisha answered, As the
Lord liveth, whom I stand before, I shall not take it *from
thee.* And when Naaman *greatly* pressed him, and
insisted, Elisha would still not agree.)
17 Then Naaman said, As thou wilt; but, I beseech,
grant thou to me, thy servant, that I take of this earth the
charge of two burdens; for thy servant shall no more
make burnt sacrifice, either slain sacrifice, to alien gods
(to foreign, *or other,* gods), no but (only) to the Lord.
18 Forsooth this thing is only (And this thing only), of
which thou shalt pray (to) the Lord for thy servant, (that)
when my lord shall enter into the temple of Rimmon, that
he worship (there), and while he shall lean on mine
hand, if I worship in the temple of Rimmon, while he
worshippeth in the same place, that the Lord forgive to
thy servant, for this thing.
19 And Elisha said to him, Go thou in peace. And so
Naaman went from Elisha in a chosen time of the land.
20 And Gehazi, the servant of the man of God, said *in
his heart,* My lord hath spared this man of Syria, that he
took not of him that, that he brought; (as) the Lord liveth,
for I shall run after him, and I shall take of him
something. (And Gehazi, the servant of the man of God,
said *in his heart,* My lord hath spared this Naaman of
Syria, and he took not from him, what he brought for
him; as the Lord liveth, I shall run after him, and I shall
get something from him.)
21 And Gehazi followed after the back of Naaman; and
when Naaman had seen Gehazi running to him, he
skipped down off the chariot into the meeting of Gehazi;
and said, Whether all things be rightful? (Is everything all
right?)
22 And he said, Rightfully; my lord sent me to thee,
and said, Two young men of the hill of Ephraim, of the
sons of (the) prophets, came now to me; give thou to
them a talent of silver, and double changing (of) clothes.
(And he said, All is well; but my lord hath sent me to
thee, and said, Two young men, of the sons of the
prophets, have now come to me, from the hill country of
Ephraim; give thou to them a talent of silver, and two
changes of clothing.)
23 And Naaman said, It is better that thou take two
talents. And Naaman constrained him; and Naaman
bound the two talents of silver in two bags, and the
double clothes (with the two changes of clothing), and he
put *those* upon his two servants, the which also bare *it*
before Gehazi.
24 And when Gehazi had come (back) then in the
eventide, he took *it* from the hand of them, and laid it up
in the house; and he delivered the men, and they went
forth. (And when Gehazi had come back in the evening,
he took *the bundles* out of their hands, and laid them up
in the house; and he let the men go, and they went
away.)
25 And *then* Gehazi entered, and stood before his lord.
And Elisha said, Gehazi, from whence comest thou?
Which answered, Thy servant went not to any place.
26 And Elisha said, Whether mine heart was not
present *there,* when the man turned again from his
chariot into the meeting of thee? Now therefore thou
hast taken silver, and thou hast taken clothes, (so) that
thou (can) buy places of olives, and vineries, and sheep,
and oxen, and servants, and handmaids;
27 but also the leprosy of Naaman shall cleave to thee,
and to thy seed without end. And Gehazi went out from
him leprous as snow. (but now Naaman's leprosy shall
cleave to thee, and to thy descendants, forevermore. And
so Gehazi went away from him leprous, as white as
snow.)

CHAPTER 6

1 Forsooth the sons of prophets said to Elisha, Lo! the
place in which we dwell before thee, is strait to us; (And
the sons of the prophets said to Elisha, Lo! the place in
which we live before thee, is too narrow, *or too small,*
for us;)
2 go we *therefore* to Jordan, and each man take a
portion of wood for himself, that we build to us there a
place to dwell *therein* (so that we can build a place there
for all of us to live *in*). And Elisha said, Go ye.
3 And one of them said, Therefore and thou come
with thy servants. (And) He answered, I shall come.
4 And he went with them. And when they came to
Jordan, they hewed trees (they cut down some wood).
5 And it befelled, that when a man *of them* had cut
down [a] matter, *or (a piece of) wood,* the iron of the ax
felled into the water; and he cried [out], and said, Alas!
alas! alas! my lord, and I had taken this same thing by
borrowing (for I have borrowed this thing from
someone!).

6 Soothly the man of God said, Where felled it? And
he showed to him the place. Therefore he cutted down a
tree, and sent *it* thither *where the iron was*; and the iron
floated (And so he cut off a stick, and sent *it* down *to
where the piece of iron was*; and the iron floated up).
7 And Elisha said, Take thou (*it*). Which held forth the
hand, and took it (And he put forth his hand, and took it).
8 Forsooth the king of Syria fought against Israel; and
he took counsel with his servants, and said, Set we
ambushments in this place, and in that.
9 And therefore the man of God sent to the king of
Israel, and said, Beware, lest thou pass to that place, for
(the) men of Syria be there in ambushments.
10 Therefore the king of Israel sent to the place, which
the man of God had said to him, and before-occupied it,
and kept himself there, not once, neither twice. (And so
the king of Israel sent word to the place about which the
man of God had warned him, and took precautions
whenever he was there, and not just once, or twice.)
11 And the heart of the king of Syria was troubled for
this thing; and when his servants were called together, he
said, Why show ye not to me, who is my traitor with the
king of Israel?
12 And one of his servants said, Nay, my lord the king,
but Elisha, the prophet, that is in Israel (who is in Israel),
showeth to the king of Israel all things, whatever things
thou speakest in thy closet.
13 And the king said to them, Go ye, and see, where he
is, that I send, and take him. And they told to him, and
said, Lo! he dwelleth in Dothan.
14 And the king sent thither horses, and chariots, and
the strength of his host; which, when they had come by
night, compassed the city. (And the king sent there
horses, and chariots, and the strong force of his army;
which, when they had come by night, encompassed, *or
surrounded*, the city.)
15 Soothly the minister of the man of God rose early,
and went out, and he saw an host in the compass of the
city, and horses, and chariots (And the servant of the man
of God rose up early, and went out, and he saw an army
all around the city, with horses, and chariots). And he
told to the man of God, and said, Alas! alas! alas! my
lord, what shall we do?
16 And he answered, Do not thou dread (Do not thou
fear); for more be with us than with them.
17 And when Elisha had prayed, he said, Lord, open
thou the eyes of this young man, that he (may) see. And
the Lord opened the eyes of the young man, and he saw.
And, lo! the hill (was) full of horses, and of chariots of
fire, in the compass of Elisha (all around Elisha).
18 And the enemies came down to him; but Elisha
prayed to the Lord, and said, I beseech *thee*, smite this
folk with blindness (I beseech *thee*, strike these people
with blindness). And the Lord smote them, (so) that they
saw not, by the word of Elisha.
19 Forsooth Elisha said to them, This is not the way,
neither this is the city; follow ye me, and I shall show you
the man, whom ye seek. And he led them into Samaria.
20 And when they had entered into Samaria, Elisha
said, Lord, open the eyes of these men, (so) that they
(can) see *now*. And the Lord opened their eyes, and they
saw, that they were in the midst of Samaria.
21 And the king of Israel, when he had seen them, said
to Elisha, My father, whether I shall smite them? (My
father, shall I strike them down?)
22 And he said, Thou shalt not smite them, for thou
hast not taken them by thy sword and bow, that thou
smite them; but set thou bread and water before them,
that they eat and drink, and go to their lord *again*. (And
he said, Thou shalt not strike them down, for thou hast
not taken them with thy sword and bow, so that thou
may strike them down; but put thou bread and water
before them, so that they can eat and drink, and then let
them go back to their lord *again*.)
23 And much preparing of meats was set forth to them;
and they ate, and drank. And the king let go them, and
they went to their lord; and [the] thieves of Syria came no
more into the land of Israel (And then the king let them
go, and they went back to their lord; and after that, the
thieves of Syria no longer came into the land of Israel).
24 Forsooth it was done after these things, Benhadad,
king of Syria, gathered all his host (called up all his army),
and went up, and besieged Samaria.
25 And great hunger was made in Samaria; and so long
it was besieged (and it was besieged for so long), till [that]
the head of an ass were sold for fourscore pieces of silver,
and the fourth part of a measure called [a] cab, (out) of
the craw of culvers[9], *was sold* for five pieces of silver.
26 And when the king of Israel passed by the wall *of
the city*, a woman cried to him, and said, My lord the
king, save thou me.
27 Which said (Who said), Nay, the Lord save thee;
whereof may I save thee? (out) of [the] cornfloor, either
(out) of [the] presser?
28 And the king said to her, What wilt thou that I do to
thee? (What wilt thou that I do for thee?) And she
answered, This woman said to me, Give thy son, that we
eat him today, and we shall eat my son tomorrow.
29 Therefore we seethed my son, and ate *him*. And I
said to her in the tother day, Give thy son, that we eat
him; and she hid her son. (And so we boiled my son, and
ate *him*. And I said to her the next day, Give thy son to
us now, so that we can eat him; but she hid her son.)

---

[9] *In Latin it is said, 'of the drit of culvers'; but 'drit' is not taken here properly, but unproperly, for 'the throat', where corns, eaten of culvers, be gathered, and cooks of rich men sold these corns to the people, for (the) hunger (because of the famine).*

30 And when the king had heard this, he rent his
clothes, and passed by the wall; and all the people saw
the hair-shirt, with which the king was clothed at the
flesh within; (And when the king had heard this, he tore
his clothes, and passed forth by the wall; and all the
people saw the hair-shirt, *or the sackcloth*, with which
the king was clothed upon his flesh;)
31 And the king said, God do to me these things, and
add these things too, if the head of Elisha, the son of
Shaphat, shall stand on him today (shall remain on him
this day).
32 Soothly Elisha sat in his house, and (the) eld men sat
with him; then the king before-sent a man to Elisha, and
before that that messenger came, Elisha said to the eld
men, Whether ye know, that the son of (a) man-queller
[hath] sent hither, that mine head be girded off? Therefore
see ye, when the messenger cometh, shut ye the door,
and suffer ye not him to enter; for lo! the sound of the
feet of his lord is behind him. (And Elisha sat in his
house, and the old men, *or the elders*, sat with him; then
the king sent out a man from before himself to Elisha, but
before that the messenger came, Elisha said to the old
men, *or the elders*, Do ye not know, that this son of a
man-killer hath sent a man here, to gird off my head? And
so see ye, when the messenger cometh, that ye shut the
door, and do not allow him to enter; for lo! the sound of
the feet of his lord is behind him.)
33 And yet while he spake to them, the messenger that
came to him appeared; and (then also) *the king* (who)
said, Lo! so great evil is of the Lord; soothly what more
shall I abide of the Lord? (And yet while he spoke to
them, the messenger who came to him appeared; and
then also *the king*, who said, Lo! this great evil is from the
Lord; how more longer shall I have to wait for the Lord?)

CHAPTER 7

1 Forsooth Elisha said, Hear ye the word of the Lord;
the Lord saith these things, In this time tomorrow (At this
time tomorrow), a bushel of [tried] flour shall be *sold* for
a stater, and two bushels of barley for a stater, in the gate
of Samaria.
2 And one of the dukes, on whose hand the king
leaned, answered to the man of God, and said, (Yea,)
Though the Lord make also the gutters of heaven to be
opened, whether that, that thou speakest, may be? And
Elisha said, Thou shalt see *it* with thine eyes, and thou
shalt not eat thereof. (And one of the leaders, on whose
hand the king leaned, answered to the man of God, and
said, Even if the Lord shall make the gutters of the
heavens to open up, what thou sayest could not be true!
And Elisha said, Thou shalt see *it* with thine eyes, but
thou shalt not eat any of it.)
3 Therefore four leprous men were beside the entering
of the *city's* gate, which said together, What will we be
here, till we die? (And so four lepers were beside the
entrance to the *city* gate, and they said together, Why
should we stay here, and just wait until we all die?)
4 Whether we will enter into the city, we shall die for
hunger; whether we dwell here (or if we stay here), we
shall (also) die. Therefore come ye, and flee we over to
the tents of Syria; if they shall spare us, we shall live;
soothly if they will slay *us*, nevertheless we shall (still
just) die.
5 Then they rose up in the eventide, to come to the
tents of Syria; and when they had come to the beginning
of the tents of Syria, they found not any man there.
6 Forsooth the Lord had made a sound of chariots,
and of horses, and of a full much host to be heard in the
tents of Syria; and they said together, Lo! the king of
Israel hath hired by meed against us the kings of Hittites,
and of Egyptians; and they came *suddenly* upon us. (For
the Lord had made the sound of chariots, and of horses,
and of a very large army to be heard among the tents, *or
in the camp*, of the Syrians; and they had said together,
Lo! the king of Israel hath hired for money the kings of
the Hittites, and of the Egyptians, to come against us; and
they have *suddenly* come upon us!)
7 Therefore they rose up, and fled in darkness, and left
their tents, and their horses, and mules, and asses, in the
castles (with the tents); and they fled, coveting to save
their lives only. (And so they rose up, and fled away in
the darkness, and left their tents, and their horses, and
mules, and donkeys, with the tents, *or in the camp*; and
they fled, desiring only to save their own lives.)
8 Therefore when those leprous men had come to the
beginning of the castles, *or tents*, they entered into one
tabernacle, and ate, and drank; and they took from
thence silver, and gold, and clothes; and went, and hid *it*;
and again they turned again to another tabernacle, and in
like manner they took away from thence, and hid. (And
so when those lepers had come to the beginning of the
tents, *or of the camp*, they went into one tent, and ate,
and drank; and they took from there silver, and gold, and
clothes; and went, and hid *it*; and then they turned to
another tent, and in like manner they took away from
there, and hid it all.)
9 And they said together, We do not rightfully, for this
is a day of good message; if we hold *it* still, and do not
tell till the morrowtide, we shall be reproved of
trespassing (if we keep it quiet, and do not tell anyone
until the morning, we shall be blamed for not reporting
it); come ye, go we, and tell *it* in the king's hall.
10 And when they had come to the gate of the city,
they told to them, and said, We went to the castles of
Syria (We went to the tents, *or the camp*, of the Syrians),
and we found not any man there, but (all the) horses and
asses tied (up), and [the] tents fastened (in place).
11 And so the porters went (And so the guards went),

and told these things in the palace of the king within.
12 And the king rose up by night, and said to his
servants, I say to you, what the men of Syria have done to
us; they know, that we travail with hunger, therefore they
have gone out of the castles, and be hid in the fields, and
say, When they shall go out of the city, we shall take
them quick, and then we shall be able to enter into the
city. (And the king rose up in the night, and said to his
servants, I shall tell you, what the men of Syria have done
to us; they know, that we be hungry, and so they have
gone out of their tents, and be hid in the fields, and they
say, When they shall go out of the city, we shall take
them alive, and then we shall be able to enter into their
city.)
13 And one of his servants answered, Take we (some
of) [the] five horses, that [be] left in the city; for those be
left only in all the multitude of Israel, for [the] other
horses be wasted (for those be the only ones *left* in all the
multitude of Israel, for all the others have died, or have
been eaten); and we sending may espy.
14 Therefore they brought forth two horses; and the
king sent (men upon them) into the tents of the men of
Syria, and said, Go ye, and see. (And so they brought
forth two horses; and the king sent out men upon them to
follow after the Syrian army, saying, Go ye, and see what
you can see.)
15 The which went after them unto (the) Jordan; lo!
forsooth all the way was full of clothes, and of vessels,
which the men of Syria (had) casted forth, when they
were troubled. And the messengers turned again, and
showed *it* to the king (And the messengers returned, and
reported to the king about all these things).
16 And the people went out, and ravished the castles of
Syria (And the people went out, and spoiled the tents, *or
the camp*, of the Syrians); and a bushel of tried flour was
made *sold* for a stater, and two bushels of barley for a
stater, by the word of the Lord.
17 Forsooth the king ordained at the gate that duke, in
whose hand the king leaned; whom the company trode
with *their* feet, and he was dead, by the word, which the
man of God spake, when the king came down to him.
(And the king ordered that leader, on whose hand he had
leaned, to go to the city gate; and the people then trode
upon him with *their* feet, and he died, according to the
word, which the man of God spoke, when the king had
come down to him.)
18 And (so) it was done by the word of the man of
God, that he [had] said to the king, when he said, Two
bushels of barley shall be *sold* for a stater, and a bushel
of tried wheat flour for a stater, in this same time
tomorrow in the gate of Samaria;
19 when that duke answered to the man of God, and
said, Yea, though the Lord shall make the gutters in
heaven to be opened, whether this that thou speakest
may be? and *the man of God* said, Thou shalt see it with
thine eyes, and thou shalt not eat thereof. (when that
leader had answered the man of God, and said, Even if
the Lord shall make the gutters of the heavens to open
up, what thou sayest could not be true! and *the man of
God* said, Thou shalt see it with thine eyes, but thou shalt
not eat any of it.)
20 Therefore it befelled to him, as it was before-said;
and the people trode him with *their* feet in the gate, and
he was dead. (And so it befell to him, as it had been
foretold; and the people trode upon him with *their* feet at
the city gate, and he died.)

CHAPTER 8

1 Forsooth Elisha spake to the woman, whose son he
made to live, and said, Rise thou, and go, both thou and
thine house, and go in pilgrimage/and make pilgrimage,
wherever thou shalt find *it best*; for the Lord shall call
hunger, and it shall come upon the land seven years. (For
Elisha spoke to the woman, whose son he had made to
live again, and said, Rise thou up, and go away, both
thou and thy household, *or thy family*, and go in
pilgrimage, wherever thou shalt find *it best*; for the Lord
shall call for a famine, and it shall come upon the land
for seven years.)
2 And she rose (up), and did after the word of the man
of God; and she went with her house, and was in
pilgrimage in the land of Philistines many days (and she
went away with her family, and was in pilgrimage in the
land of the Philistines for seven years).
3 And when (the) seven years were ended, the woman
turned again from the land of Philistines (the woman
returned from the land of the Philistines); and she went
out, to ask the king for her house, and [for] her fields.
4 And (it happened that) the king spake (then) with
Gehazi, the servant of the man of God, and said, Tell
thou to me all the great deeds that Elisha did.
5 And when he told to the king (And as he told the
king), how *Elisha* had raised (up) a dead man, the woman
appeared, whose son he had made to live (again), and
she cried to the king for her house, and for her fields.
And Gehazi said, My lord the king, this is the (very)
woman, and this is her son, whom Elisha raised (back to
life).
6 And the king asked the woman, and she told to him,
that the things were sooth. And the king gave, *or
assigned*, to her a chamberlain, and said, Restore thou to
her all things that be hers, and all [the] fruits of the fields,
from the day in which she left the land unto this present
time.
7 Also Elisha came to Damascus (And Elisha came to
Damascus), and Benhadad, king of Syria, was sick; and
they told to him, and said, The man of God came hither.
8 And the king said to Hazael, Take with thee gifts,

and go thou into the meeting of the man of God, and ask
thou counsel by him of the Lord, and say thou, Whether I
may escape from this my sickness? (And the king said to
Hazael, Take gifts with thee, and go to meet the man of
God, and ask thou for counsel with the Lord by him, and
ask thou, Shall I recover from this sickness of mine?)
9 Therefore Hazael went in to the meeting of him, and
had with him gifts, and all the goods of Damascus, the
burdens of forty camels. And when he had stood before
Elisha, he said, Thy son, Benhadad, king of Syria, sent me
to thee, and said, Whether I may be healed of this my
sickness? (And so Hazael went to meet him, and had gifts
with him, and all the good things of Damascus, yea, the
loads of forty camels. And when he had stood before
Elisha, he said, Thy son, Benhadad, the king of Syria, sent
me to thee, and said, Shall I be healed of my sickness?)
10 And Elisha said, Go thou, and say to him, Thou shalt
be healed; forsooth the Lord [hath] showed to me that he
shall die by death (but the Lord hath shown me that he
shall die).
11 And he stood with him, and he was troubled, unto
the casting down of his cheer (and he cast down his face);
and the man of God wept.
12 And Hazael said, Why weepeth my lord? And he
answered, For I know what evils thou shalt do to the sons
of Israel; thou shalt burn [up] by fire the strengthened
cities of them, and thou shalt slay by (the) sword the
young men of them, and thou shalt hurtle down the little
children of them, and thou shalt part the women with
child. (And Hazael said, Why weepeth my lord? And he
answered, For I know what evils thou shalt do to the
Israelites; thou shalt burn down their fortified cities, and
thou shalt kill with the sword their young men, and thou
shalt hurtle down their little children, and thou shalt
carve up their women with child.)
13 And Hazael said, What soothly am I, thy servant, a
dog, that I do this great thing? (And Hazael said, Truly
what am I, thy servant, nothing but a dog? for how can I
do such a great thing?) And Elisha said, The Lord hath
showed to me that thou shalt be king of Syria.
14 And when he had departed from Elisha, he came to
his lord; which said to Hazael, What said Elisha to thee?
And he answered, Elisha said to me, Thou shalt receive
health (Thou shalt recover).
15 And when the tother day had come, Hazael took the
cloth that lay on the bed *of Benhadad*, and he beshedded
it with water, and he spreaded it abroad upon the face of
Benhadad; and when he was dead, Hazael reigned for
him.
16 In the fifth year of Joram[10], son of Ahab, king of
Israel, and of Jehoshaphat, king of Judah, Jehoram[11], the
son of Jehoshaphat, king of Judah, reigned. (In the fifth
year of Joram, the son of Ahab, the king of Israel,
Jehoram, the son of Jehoshaphat, the king of Judah, began
to reign.)
17 He was of two and thirty years when he began to
reign, and he reigned eight years in Jerusalem.
18 And he went in the ways of the kings of Israel, as the
house of Ahab had gone; for the daughter of Ahab was
his wife; and he did that, that was evil in the sight of the
Lord.
19 Forsooth the Lord would not destroy Judah, for
David, his servant, as he promised to David, that he
should give to him a lantern, and to his sons in all days.
(But the Lord did not destroy Judah, for the sake of his
servant David, as he had promised David, that he would
give him, and his sons, a light, *or a flame*, to burn
forever.)
20 In those days Edom, *that is, Idumea*, went away, that
it should not be under Judah; and made a king to itself
(and got themselves a king).
21 And Jehoram came to Zair, and all the chariots with
him; and he rose by night, and smote Idumeans, that
compassed him, and the princes of chariots; soothly the
people fled into their tabernacles. (And Jehoram came to
Zair, and all the chariots with him; and he rose up by
night, and struck the Edomites, who surrounded him, and
the leaders of their chariots; and the people fled into their
tents.)
22 Therefore Edom went away, that it was not under
(the hand of) Judah till to this day; then also Libnah went
away in that time. (And so Edom went away, and they
were not under the hand of Judah unto this day; and also
Libnah went away at that time.)
23 Certainly the residue of the words of Jehoram, and
all things which he did, whether these be not written in
the book of [the] words of [the] days of the kings of
Judah?
24 And Jehoram slept with his fathers, and was buried
with them in the city of David; and Ahaziah, his son,
reigned for him.
25 In the twelfth year of Joram, the son of Ahab, king of
Israel, Ahaziah, the son of Jehoram, king of Judah,
reigned (began to reign).
26 Ahaziah, the son of Jehoram, was of two and twenty
years, when he began to reign, and he reigned one year
in Jerusalem; the name of his mother *was* Athaliah, the
daughter of Omri, king of Israel.
27 And he went in the ways of the house of Ahab, and
did that, that is evil (and he did what was evil), in (the)
sight of the Lord, as the house of Ahab *did*; for he was
[the] husband of a daughter of the house of Ahab.
28 Also he went with Joram, the son of Ahab, to fight
against Hazael, king of Syria, in Ramoth of Gilead; and
men of Syria wounded Joram.

[10] Also known as Jehoram.

[11] Also known as Joram.

29 Which turned again, to be healed in Jezreel; for men
of Syria wounded him in Ramoth, fighting against
Hazael, king of Syria. And Ahaziah, the son of Jehoram,
the king of Judah, came down to see Joram, the son of
Ahab, into Jezreel, that was sick there. (Who returned
home, to recover in Jezreel; for the Syrians had wounded
him at Ramah, fighting against Hazael, the king of Syria.
And Ahaziah, the son of Jehoram, the king of Judah,
came down to Jezreel to see Joram, the son of Ahab,
because he was sick.)

CHAPTER 9

1 Forsooth Elisha, the prophet, called one of the sons
of (the) prophets, and said to him, Gird (up) thy loins, and
take this vessel of oil in thine hand, and go into Ramoth
of Gilead.
2 And when thou shalt come thither, thou shalt see
Jehu, the son of Jehoshaphat, the son of Nimshi; and thou
shalt enter, and shalt raise him (up) from the midst of his
brethren, and thou shalt lead him into an inner closet.
3 And thou shalt hold the vessel of oil, and thou shalt
pour *it* on his head, and thou shalt say, The Lord saith
these things, I have anointed thee into king upon Israel (I
have anointed thee king upon Israel); and *then* thou shalt
open the door, and shalt flee *(from) thence*, and thou
shalt not abide there.
4 Therefore the young waxing man, the child of the
prophet, went into Ramoth of Gilead, (And so the young
man, the young prophet, went to Ramoth of Gilead.)
5 and entered thither. Lo! soothly the princes of the
host sat *there*; and he said, O! prince, I have a word to
thee (O! prince, I have a word for thee). And Jehu said,
To whom of all (of) us? And he said, To thee, thou prince.
6 And he rose, and entered into the closet. And that
young man poured (the) oil upon the head of him, and
said, The Lord God of Israel saith these things, I have
anointed thee into king on the people of the Lord, of
Israel; (And he rose up, and they went inside. And that
young man poured the oil upon his head, and said, The
Lord God of Israel saith these things, I have anointed thee
king upon Israel, yea, upon the people of the Lord;)
7 and thou shalt smite the house of Ahab, thy lord,
that I venge the blood of my servants (the) prophets, and
the blood of all the servants of the Lord, of the hand of
Jezebel. (and thou shalt strike down the house of Ahab,
thy lord, so that I avenge the blood of my servants the
prophets, and the blood of all the servants of the Lord, at
the hands of Jezebel.)
8 And I shall lose all the house of Ahab, and I shall
slay of the house of Ahab a pisser to the wall, and the
enclosed, and the last in Israel. (And I shall destroy all the
house of Ahab, and I shall kill all the house of Ahab unto
a pisser on the wall, and the captive, and the last in
Israel.)
9 And I shall give the house of Ahab as the house of
Jeroboam, the son of Nebat, and as the house of Baasha,
the son of Ahijah. (And I shall make the house of Ahab
like the house of Jeroboam, the son of Nebat, and like the
house of Baasha, the son of Ahijah.)
10 Also dogs shall eat Jezebel in the field of Jezreel
(And the dogs shall eat up Jezebel in the field of Jezreel);
and there shall be none that shall bury her. And (then)
the young man opened the door, and fled.
11 And Jehu went out to the servants of his lord, which
said to him, Whether all things be rightful? (Is everything
all right?) (For) What came this mad man to thee? Which
said to them, Ye know the man, and what he spake.
12 And they answered, It is false; but more *rather* tell
thou us *what he said* (but *rather* now tell thou us *what he
said*). The which said to them, He spake these things and
these to me, and said, The Lord saith these things, I have
anointed thee king of Israel.
13 Therefore they hasted, and each man took his
mantle, and putted under his feet by the likeness of a
throne. And they sang with a trump, and said, Jehu shall
reign.
14 Therefore Jehu, the son of Jehoshaphat, the son of
Nimshi, swore *with others* together against Joram[12].
Forsooth Joram had besieged Ramoth of Gilead, he and
all Israel, against Hazael, king of Syria.
15 And Joram turned again to be healed in Jezreel for
wounds *that he had*; for men of Syria had smitten him
fighting against Hazael, king of Syria (Now Joram had
returned to Jezreel to recover from the wounds *that he
had*; for the men of Syria had struck him when he fought
against Hazael, the king of Syria). And Jehu said (to
them), If it please you, (then let) no man go out fleeing
from the city, lest he go, and tell (it) in Jezreel.
16 And (then) Jehu went up, and went forth into
Jezreel; for Joram was sick there; and Ahaziah, king of
Judah, came down to visit Joram.
17 Therefore a watchman, that stood above (in) a tower
of Jezreel, saw the multitude of Jehu coming, and he said,
I see a multitude. And Joram said, Take thou a chariot,
and send *it* into the meeting of him; and say the goer,
Whether all things be rightful? (and let the goer, *or the
driver*, say to him, Is everything all right?)
18 Then he, that went upon the chariot, went into the
meeting of Jehu, and said, The king saith these things,
Whether all things be peaced? (Is everything at peace
with you?) And Jehu said to him, What to thee and to
peace? Pass thou *from Joram*, and follow me. And the
watchman told to Joram, and said, The messenger came
to them, and he turneth not again.
19 Also *the king* sent the second chariot of horses, and
he came to them, and said, The king saith these things,

---

[12] Also known as Jehoram.

Whether peace is *with you*? (And *the king* sent a second
chariot of horses, and the man came to them, and said,
The king saith these things, Is everything at peace *with
you*?) And Jehu said, What to thee and to peace? Pass
thou forth, and follow me.
20 And the espyer told *to Joram*, and said, He came
unto them, and he turneth not again; forsooth the going
of the duke is as the going of Jehu, son of Nimshi (and
the driving *of the leader* is like the driving of Jehu, the
son of Nimshi); certainly he goeth fast.
21 And Joram said, Join ye (up) a chariot. And they
joined (up) his chariot. And Joram, king of Israel, went
out, and Ahaziah, king of Judah, went out, each in his
chariot; and they went out into the meeting of Jehu, and
they found him in the field of Naboth of Jezreel.
22 And when Joram had seen Jehu, he said, Jehu, is (it)
peace? (And when Joram had seen Jehu, he said, Jehu, is
everything at peace *with you*?) And he answered, What
peace? Yet the fornications, *that is, (the) idolatries*, of
Jezebel, thy mother, and (the) many poisonings of her be
in strength.
23 And Joram turned his hand, and fled, and said to
Ahaziah, Treasons! treasons! (O!) Ahaziah.
24 Certainly Jehu bent a bow with *his* hand, and smote
Joram betwixt the shoulders, and the arrow went out
through his heart; and at once he felled down in his
chariot.
25 And Jehu said to Bidkar the duke, Take thou (him)
away, and cast forth him in the field of Naboth of Jezreel;
for I have mind, when I and thou sat in the chariot, and
followed Ahab, his father, that the Lord raised on him this
burden, and said, (And Jehu said to Bidkar, his officer,
Take thou him away, and throw him forth into the field of
Naboth of Jezreel; for I remember, when I and thou sat in
the chariot, and followed his father Ahab, that the Lord
raised on him this burden, and said,)
26 If not for the blood of Naboth, and for the blood of
his sons, which I saw yesterday, saith the Lord, I shall
yield to thee in this field, saith the Lord. Now therefore
do thou away him, and cast forth him in the field, by the
word of the Lord. (For the blood of Naboth, and for the
blood of his sons, which I saw yesterday, saith the Lord, I
shall yield to thee in this field, saith the Lord. And so now
do thou him away, and throw him forth into the field, by
the word of the Lord.)
27 Forsooth Ahaziah, king of Judah, saw this, and fled
by the way of the house of the garden; and Jehu pursued
him, and said, Also smite ye this man in his chariot. And
men smote Ahaziah in the going up of Gur, that is beside
Ibleam; and Ahaziah fled into Megiddo, and was dead
there (and Ahaziah fled to Megiddo, and died there).
28 And his servants putted him on his chariot, and
brought *him* into Jerusalem; and they buried him in a
sepulchre with his fathers, in the city of David.
29 In the eleventh year of Joram, the son of Ahab, king
of Israel, Ahaziah reigned upon Judah (Ahaziah began to
reign upon Judah).
30 And Jehu came into Jezreel. Forsooth when his
entering was heard (And when she heard him coming),
Jezebel painted her eyes with (the) ointment of *lecherous*
women, and adorned her head; and she beheld by a
window
31 Jehu entering by the gate, and she said, Whether
peace may be to Zimri, that killed his lord?/that slew his
lord? (Jehu entering by the gate, and she said, Can there
be peace for Zimri, who killed his lord?)
32 And Jehu raised up his face to the window, and said,
What *woman* is this? And twain either three
chamberlains bowed themselves to him, and said to him,
This is that Jezebel.
33 And he said to them, Cast ye her down. And they
casted down her (And they went, and threw her down);
and the wall was besprinkled with (her) blood, and (also)
the hooves of (the) horses, that treaded (upon) her.
34 And when he had entered to eat and drink, he said,
Go ye, and see that cursed woman, and bury ye her, for
she is a king's daughter.
35 And when they had gone to bury her, they found
not *of her*, no but the skull, and the feet, and the ends of
her hands;
36 and they turned again, and told to him (and they
returned, and told him). And Jehu said, This is the word
of the Lord, which he spake by his servant, Elijah of
Tishbe/Elijah (the) Tishbite, and said, (The) Dogs shall eat
(up) the flesh of Jezebel in the field of Jezreel;
37 and the fleshes of Jezebel shall be as dung upon the
face of the earth in the field of Jezreel, so that men
passing forth thereby say, Lo! this is that Jezebel.

CHAPTER 10

1 Forsooth seventy sons in Samaria were to Ahab.
Therefore Jehu wrote letters, and sent into Samaria to the
best men of the city, and to the greater men in birth, and
to all the nurses *of the sons* of Ahab, and said, (Now
Ahab had seventy sons in Samaria. And so Jehu wrote
letters, and sent them to Samaria, to the best men of the
city, and to the men of great age, *that is, to the elders*,
and to all the nurses, *or the guardians, of the sons* of
Ahab, and said,)
2 Anon as ye have taken these letters, ye that have the
sons of your lord, and the chariots, and horses, and
strong cities, and armours, (As soon as ye have received
these letters, ye who have the sons of your lord, and the
chariots, and horses, and fortified cities, and arms, *or
weapons*,)
3 choose the best, and him that pleaseth to you of the
sons of your lord, and set him on the throne of his father,
and fight ye for the house of your lord.

4 And they dreaded greatly, and said, Lo! two kings
might not stand before him, and how shall we be able to
against-stand him? (And they greatly feared, and said, Lo!
two kings could not stand against him, so how shall we
be able to stand against him?)
5 Therefore the sovereigns of the house, and the
prefect of the city, and the greater men of birth, and the
nurses (of the sons) sent to Jehu, and said, We be thy
servants; whatever things thou commandest, we shall do,
and we shall not make a king to us; do thou whatever
thing pleaseth thee. (And so the sovereign, *or the ruler*, of
the household, and the prefect of the city, and the men of
great age, *that is, the elders*, and the nurses, *or the
guardians*, of Ahab's sons sent to Jehu, and said, We be
thy servants; whatever thou commandest, we shall do,
and we shall not make a king for us; do thou whatever
thing pleaseth thee.)
6 Forsooth he wrote again to them letters the second
time, and said, If ye be mine, and obey to me, take ye
(off) the heads of the sons of your lord, and come ye to
me in this same hour tomorrow into Jezreel. And the
sons of the king, seventy men, were nursed at the best
men of the city. (And he wrote letters to them a second
time, and said, If ye be mine, and obey me, then bring ye
to me the heads of the sons of your lord, and come ye to
me in Jezreel at this same hour tomorrow. And the sons
of the king, seventy men, were nourished, *or were cared
for*, by the best men of the city.)
7 And when the letters had come to them, they took
the sons of the king, and killed *those* seventy men, and
they putted the heads of them in coffins; and sent *those*
to Jehu into Jezreel (and sent them to Jehu in Jezreel).
8 And a messenger came to him, and showed to him
(and told him), and said, They have brought the heads of
the sons of the king. Which answered, Put ye those
heads (in)to twain heaps, beside the entering of the gate,
till the morrowtide.
9 And when it was clear day, he went out, and stood,
and said to all the people, Ye be just men; if I conspired
against my lord, and killed him, who killed all these?
10 Therefore see ye now, that none of the words of the
Lord hath fallen down into the earth, which the Lord
spake on the house of Ahab; and the Lord hath done that,
that he spake in the hand of his servant, Elijah. (And so
see ye now, that none of the words of the Lord hath
fallen to the ground, words which the Lord spoke about
the house of Ahab; yea, the Lord hath done what he
spoke by his servant Elijah.)
11 Therefore Jehu smote all that were left of the house
of Ahab in Jezreel, and all the best men of him, and his
known men, and his priests, till no relics of him (were)
left. (And so Jehu struck down all who were left of the
house of Ahab in Jezreel, and all his best men, and his
friends, and his priests, until none was left.)
12 And he rose, and came into Samaria; and when he
had come to the chamber of the shepherds in the way,
(And he rose up, and went to Samaria; and when he had
come to the shepherds' shelter on the way,)
13 he found *there* the brethren of Ahaziah, king of
Judah (he found *there* the kinsmen of Ahaziah, the king
of Judah); and he said to them, Who be ye? And they
answered, We be the brethren of Ahaziah, and we came
down to greet the sons of the king, and the sons of the
queen.
14 And *Jehu* said, Take ye them quick. And when they
had taken them quick, they strangled them in the cistern,
beside the chamber, two and forty men; and he left not
any of them (alive). (And *Jehu* said, Take ye them alive.
And when they had taken them alive, then they strangled
them there at the well, beside the shelter, forty-two men;
and he left none of them alive.)
15 And when he had gone from thence, he found
Jehonadab, the son of Rechab, (coming) into (the)
meeting of him; and he blessed him. And Jehu said to
him, Whether thine heart is rightful with mine heart, as
mine heart is with thine heart? (Is thy heart right with my
heart, as my heart is with thy heart?) And Jehonadab said,
It is. And Jehu said, If it is, give me thine hand. Which
gave his hand to him; and Jehu raised him up to him(self)
into his chariot.
16 And he said to him, Come thou with me, and see
my fervent love for the Lord. And he led him, put in his
chariot, into Samaria (And they rode together, in his
chariot, to Samaria).
17 And (once they arrived,) he killed all (the) men that
were residue, or left, of Ahab in Samaria, till to one, by
the word of the Lord, which he spake by Elijah.
18 Therefore Jehu gathered together all the people (And
then Jehu gathered together all the people), and said to
them, Ahab worshipped Baal a little, but I shall worship
him more.
19 Now therefore call ye to me all the prophets of Baal,
and all his servants, and all his priests; (let) none be that
come not, for (a) great sacrifice is of me to Baal; whoever
shall fail (*to come*), he shall not live. Forsooth Jehu did
this by treason, that he should destroy all the worshippers
of Baal. (And so now call unto me all the prophets of
Baal, and all his servants, and all his priests; let there be
no one who shall not come, for I shall make a great
sacrifice to Baal; whoever shall fail *to come*, he shall not
live. But Jehu did this to deceive them, so that he could
destroy all the worshippers of Baal.)
20 And he said, Hallow ye a solemn day to Baal. And
Jehu called, (And he said, Proclaim ye a sacred day for
Baal. And they proclaimed it,)
21 and sent into all the terms of Israel; and all the
servants of Baal came, none was left, and soothly not one
was that came not. And they entered into the temple of

Baal; and the house of Baal was [full-]filled, from one end
till to the tother. (and Jehu sent into all the land of Israel;
and all the servants of Baal came, and truly there was not
one who did not come. And they entered into the temple
of Baal; and the house of Baal was filled full, from one
end unto the other.)
22 And Jehu said to them that were sovereigns over the
priests' clothes, Bring ye forth [the] vestments to all the
servants of Baal; and they brought forth [the] vestments to
them. (And Jehu said to them who looked after the
priests' clothing, Bring ye forth the vestments for all of
Baal's servants; and they brought forth the vestments for
them.)
23 And Jehu entered, and Jehonadab, the son of
Rechab, into the temple of Baal. And *Jehu* said to the
worshippers of Baal, Inquire ye, and see, lest
peradventure any of the servants of the Lord be with you;
but that the servants be alone of Baal. (And Jehu, and
Jehonadab, the son of Rechab, entered into the temple of
Baal. And *Jehu* said to the worshippers of Baal, Inquire
ye, and see, lest perhaps any of the servants of the Lord
be with you; make certain that only Baal's servants be
here.)
24 Then they entered, to make slain sacrifices, and
burnt sacrifices. Soothly Jehu had made ready to him
withoutforth fourscore men, and had said to them,
Whoever shall flee away of all these, which I shall bring
into your hands, the life of him *that suffereth any (to)
escape* shall be for the life of him *that escapeth.* (Then
they entered, to offer slain sacrifices, and burnt sacrifices.
Now Jehu had prepared eighty men outside, and had said
to them, Of all these whom I shall bring into your hands,
whoever shall let anyone of them flee away, his life shall
be for the life of him *who escapeth.*)
25 Forsooth it was done, when the burnt sacrifice was
[full]filled, Jehu commanded to his knights and [his]
dukes, (and said,) Enter ye, and slay them, that none
escape. And the knights and dukes smote [them] with the
sharpness of [the] sword, and cast forth. And they went
into the city of the temple of Baal, (And it was done,
when the burnt sacrifice was finished, Jehu commanded
to his horsemen and his leaders, and said, Go ye in, and
kill them all, so that none escape. And the horsemen and
the leaders struck them down with the sharpness of their
swords, and cast them forth. And then they went into the
inner chamber of the temple of Baal,)
26 and they brought forth the image from the temple of
Baal, and burnt *it*, (and they brought forth the sacred
pillar from the temple of Baal, and burned *it*,/and they
brought forth the images, *or the idols*, from the temple of
Baal, and burned *them*,)
27 and all-brake it. Also they destroyed the house of
Baal, and made privies for it unto this day. (and broke it
all up/and broke them all up. And they utterly destroyed
the house of Baal, and made it into latrines, as it still is
unto this day.)
28 Therefore Jehu did away Baal from Israel; (And so
Jehu did away Baal from Israel;)
29 nevertheless he went not away from the sins of
Jeroboam, the son of Nebat, that made Israel to do sin,
neither he forsook the golden calves, that were in Bethel
and in Dan.
30 Forsooth the Lord said to Jehu, For thou didest
busily that that was rightful (For thou didest what was
right), and that pleased in mine eyes, and hast done
against the house of Ahab all things that were in mine
heart, thy sons till to the fourth generation shall sit on the
throne of Israel.
31 Forsooth Jehu kept not, that he went in the law of
the Lord God of Israel in all his heart; for he went not
away from the sins of Jeroboam, that made Israel to do
sin. (But Jehu did not follow the Law of the Lord God of
Israel with all his heart; for he went not away from the
sins of Jeroboam, who made Israel to do sin.)
32 In those days the Lord began to be annoyed upon
Israel[13] (In those days the Lord began to do harm to
Israel); and Hazael smote them in all the coasts of Israel,
33 from Jordan against the east coast, all the land of
Gilead, and of Gad, and of Reuben, and of Manasseh,
from Aroer, which is on the strand of Arnon (which is by
the Arnon Stream), and (even unto) Gilead, and Bashan.
34 Forsooth the residue of [the] words of Jehu, and all
things that he did, and his strength, whether these be not
written in the book of [the] words of [the] days of the
kings of Israel?
35 And Jehu slept with his fathers; and they buried him
in Samaria; and Jehoahaz, his son, reigned for him.
36 Forsooth the days, in which Jehu reigned upon Israel
in Samaria, be eight and twenty years.

CHAPTER 11

1 Forsooth Athaliah, the mother of Ahaziah, saw (that)
her son (was) dead, and she rose up, and killed all the
seed of the king (and killed all of the king's descendants).
2 And Jehosheba, the daughter of king Jehoram[14],
(and) the sister of Ahaziah, took Joash[15], the son of
Ahaziah, and stole him from the midst of the sons of the
king, that were slain (who were killed); and *she (also)
took* the nurse of him from the house of three stages; and
she hid him from the face of Athaliah, so that he were not

[13] *That is, to have abomination of her deeds, for the worshipping of idols had endured long then (for worshipping idols had long endured then), and many other evils came forth with those, and therefore that realm was suffered, (or allowed,) to be tormented by Hazael in many manners.*

[14] Also known as Joram.

[15] Also known as Jehoash.

slain.
3 And he was with her in the house of the Lord privily
six years (And he was hid with her in the House of the
Lord for six years). Forsooth Athaliah reigned upon the
land six years.
4 But in the seventh year Jehoiada, *the priest*, sent,
and took (the) chieftains upon hundreds, and (the)
knights, and he brought *them* to him into the temple of
the Lord; and covenanted with them a bond of peace
(and made a covenant with them), and he made them to
swear in the temple of the Lord, and showed to them the
son of the king.
5 And he commanded to them, and said, This is the
word, that ye ought to do; the third part of you enter in
(on) the sabbath day, and keep ye the watches of the
king's house; (And he commanded to them, and said,
This is the thing, that ye ought to do; a third part of you
be on duty on the sabbath day, and keep ye watch over,
or guard, the palace;)
6 and another third part be at the gate of Sur; and the
third part be at the gate that is behind the dwelling place
of the makers of shields; and ye shall keep the watches of
the house of Masah. (and a third part be at the Sur Gate;
and a third part be at the gate that is behind the dwelling
place of the shield-makers; and so ye shall keep watch
over the House *of the Lord* behind the other guards.)
7 Forsooth two parts of you all going out in the
sabbath, keep they the watches of the house of the Lord
about the king. (And so the two parts of you that be off-
duty on the sabbath, keep they watch over the king in the
House of the Lord.)
8 And ye shall compass the king, and ye shall have
arms in your hands; and if any man enter into the closing
of the temple, be he slain; and ye shall be with the king
going in and going out. (And ye shall encompass, *or
surround*, the king, and ye shall have weapons in your
hands; and if anyone enter into the enclosing, *or the
interior*, of the Temple, they shall be killed; and ye shall
be with the king coming in and going out.)
9 And the chieftains upon hundreds did by all things
that Jehoiada, the priest, had commanded to them; and
they all taking their men that entered to the sabbath day,
with them that went out from the sabbath day, came to
Jehoiada, the priest (and they all took their men who
went on duty on the sabbath day, with those who went
off-duty on the sabbath day, and came to Jehoiada, the
priest).
10 Which gave to them [the] spears, and [the] armours
of king David, that were in the house of the Lord. (And
he gave them King David's spears and shields, that were
in the House of the Lord.)
11 And all stood having arms in their hand (And they
all stood with weapons in their hands), from the right side
of the temple unto the left side of the altar and of the
house, (all) about the king.
12 And he brought forth the son of the king, and put
upon his head a diadem, and the witnessing; and they
made him king, and anointed *him*; and they clapped with
the hand[s], and said, The king live! (And he brought
forth the king's son, and put the crown on his head, and
gave him the warrant; and then they anointed him king;
and they clapped their hands, and said, Long live the
king!)
13 Forsooth Athaliah heard the voice(s) of the people
running, and she entered to the companies into the
temple of the Lord, (And Athaliah heard all the noise that
the people made, and she came into the Temple of the
Lord,)
14 and she saw the king standing on the throne (and
she saw the king standing by the throne), (as) by custom,
and singers, and companies nigh him, and all the people
of the land being glad, and singing with trumps. And she
rent her clothes, and cried, Swearing together! swearing
together!/Conjuration! conjuration! *either treason*.
15 Certainly Jehoiada commanded to the chieftains
(upon hundreds), that were upon the host, and said to
them, Lead ye her out of the closings of the temple; and
whoever followeth her, be he smitten with [a] sword.
And the priest said, Be she not slain in the temple of the
Lord. (And Jehoiada commanded to the chieftains upon
hundreds, who were over the army, and said to them,
Take ye her out of the enclosings of the Temple; and
whoever followeth her, let him be struck down with a
sword. And the priest said, She shall not be killed in the
Temple of the Lord.)
16 And they putted hands on her, and hurled her by the
way of the entering of [the] horses beside the palace; and
she was slain there.
17 Therefore Jehoiada made (a) bond of peace betwixt
the Lord and the king, and betwixt the people, that it
should be the people of the Lord; and (also) betwixt the
king and the people. (And so Jehoiada made a covenant
between the Lord and the king and the people, that they
would be the people of the Lord; and also between the
king and the people.)
18 [And] All the people of the land entered into the
temple of Baal; and they destroyed the altars of him, and
all-brake strongly the images; and they killed before the
altar Mattan, the priest of Baal. And Jehoiada the priest
set keepings in the house of the Lord; (And all the people
of the land entered into the temple of Baal; and they
destroyed his altars, and broke up all the images, *or all
the idols*; and they killed Mattan, Baal's priest, in front of
the altar. And Jehoiada the priest put guards in the House
of the Lord;)
19 and he took [the] chieftains upon hundreds, and
[the] legions of Cherethites, and Pelethites, and all the
people of the land. And they led forth the king from the

house of the Lord; and they came by the way of the gate
of the makers of shields into the palace; and Joash sat
upon the throne of kings.
20 And all the people of the land was glad, and the city
rested. Forsooth Athaliah was slain by (the) sword in the
house of the king.
21 And Joash was of seven years, when he began to
reign. (And Joash was seven years old, when he began to
reign.)

CHAPTER 12

1 Joash[16] reigned in the seventh year of Jehu (Joash
began to reign in the seventh year of Jehu); he reigned
forty years in Jerusalem; the name of his mother *was*
Zibiah of Beersheba.
2 And Joash did rightfulness before the Lord in all the
days, in which Jehoiada, the priest, taught him. (And
Joash did what was right before the Lord in all the days,
in which Jehoiada, the priest, taught him.)
3 Nevertheless he did not away the high things; for yet
the people made sacrifice, and burnt incense in (the) high
things. (But he did not do away the hill shrines; for yet
the people made sacrifice, and burned incense at the hill
shrines.)
4 And Joash said to the priests, All the money of [the]
holy things, that is brought of men passing forth into the
temple of the Lord, and that is offered for the price of
[the] soul, and that men bring willfully, and by freedom
of their heart, into the temple of the Lord, [the] priests by
their order take it. (And Joash said to the priests, All the
money of the dedicated things, that is brought into the
Temple of the Lord by men passing forth, and that is
offered for the price of the soul, and that men willingly
bring, in the freedom of their hearts, into the Temple of
the Lord, the priests take it by their order.)
5 And *the priests* repair the coverings of the house, if
they see anything needful in repairing.
6 Soothly the priests repaired not the coverings of the
temple, unto the three and twentieth year of king Joash.
(But the priests did not make any repairs to the Temple,
unto twenty-third year of King Joash.)
7 And Joash, the king, called Jehoiada, the bishop,
and the priests, and said to them, Why have ye not
repaired the coverings of the temple? Therefore do not
ye more take money by your order, but yield it to the
reparation of the temple. (And King Joash called the High
Priest Jehoiada, and the other priests, and said to them,
Why have ye not made any repairs to the Temple?
Henceforth do not ye take any more money for
yourselves, but all of it must be used to repair the
Temple.)
8 And the priests were forbidden to take [any] more
money of the people, and to repair the coverings of the
house. (And so the priests were forbidden to take any
more money from the people, or to make any repairs to
the House *of the Lord*.)
9 And Jehoiada, the bishop, took a coffer of the
treasury, and opened an hole [there]above, and setted it
beside the altar, at the right side of men entering into the
house of the Lord; and [the] priests, that kept the doors,
sent, *or put*, into it all the money that was brought to the
temple of the Lord. (And the High Priest Jehoiada took a
treasury box, and made a hole in the lid, and put it
beside the altar, to the right of the entrance to the House
of the Lord; and the priests on duty, at the entrance, put
into it all the money that was brought to the Temple of
the Lord.)
10 And when they saw that full much money was in the
treasury, the scribe of the king and the bishop went up,
and poured *it* out, and they numbered the money that
was found in the house of the Lord. (And whenever they
saw that a great deal of money was in the treasury box,
the king's writer, *or his secretary*, and the High Priest
went, and poured *it* out, and they counted the money
that was brought to the House of the Lord.)
11 And they gave it by number and measure in(to) the
hand of them, that were sovereigns to the masons of the
house of the Lord, the which gave it in carpenters, and in
these masons, that wrought in the house of the Lord, and
made the coverings, (And then they gave it in number
and measure into the hands of those, who were the
foremen of the masons for the House of the Lord, who
then gave it to the carpenters, and the masons, who
worked at the House of the Lord, and made the repairs,)
12 and in these men that hewed stones; and that they
should buy trees and stones, that were hewn down; so
that the reparation of the house of the Lord was [ful]filled
in all things, that needed cost to make strong the house.
(and to the men who cut stones, so that they could buy
timber, and hewn stone; and so the repairs of the House
of the Lord were made, and also all the other expenses
paid for.)
13 Nevertheless waterpots of the temple of the Lord
were not made of the same money, and fleshhooks, and
censers, and trumps; (and) each vessel of gold and of
silver *were not made* of the money, that was brought into
the temple of the Lord. (But the waterpots for the Temple
of the Lord, and the fleshhooks, and the censers, and the
trumpets, were not paid for with this money; and also all
the gold and silver vessels *were not bought* with the
money, that was brought into the Temple of the Lord.)
14 For it was given to them that made the work, (so)
that the temple of the Lord should be repaired.
15 And reckoning was not made to these men that took
the money, that they should deal it (out) to [the]
craftsmen; but they treated, *or spended*, it in faith. (And

[16] Also known as Jehoash.

no reckoning, *or accounting*, was done with the men
who took the money, how they dealt it out to the
craftsmen, for they did so by faith, *or in trust*.)
16 Soothly they brought not into the temple of the Lord
the money *offered* for trespass, and the money for sins,
for it was the priests'.
17 Then Hazael, king of Syria, went up, and fought
against Gath; and he took it, and (ad)dressed his face (and
directed his face), (so) that he should ascend into
Jerusalem.
18 Wherefore Joash, king of Judah, took all the
hallowed things, that Jehoshaphat had hallowed, and
Jehoram[17], and Ahaziah, the fathers of him, kings of
Judah, and which things he had offered, and all the silver,
that might be found in the treasures of the temple of the
Lord, and in the palace of the king. And he sent (*these*)
to Hazael, king of Syria; and he went away from
Jerusalem. (And so Joash, the king of Judah, took all the
dedicated things, that Jehoshaphat, and Jehoram, and
Ahaziah, his forefathers, the kings of Judah, had
dedicated, and which things he had offered, and all the
silver that was found in the treasuries of the Temple of
the Lord, and in the king's palace. And he sent *these* to
Hazael, the king of Syria; and then Hazael went away
from Jerusalem.)
19 Soothly the residue of the words of Joash, and all
things that he did, whether these be not written in the
book of [the] words of [the] days of the kings of Judah?
20 And the servants of Joash rose (up), and swore
together betwixt themselves, and smote Joash in the
house of Millo, and in the going down of Silla (at the
going down to Silla).
21 For Jozachar, the son of Shimeath, and Jehozabad,
the son of Shomer, his servants, smote him, and he was
dead (and he died); and they buried him with his fathers
in the city of David; and Amaziah, his son, reigned for
him.

CHAPTER 13

1 In the three and twentieth year of Joash[18], the son of
Ahaziah, king of Judah, Jehoahaz, the son of Jehu,
reigned upon Israel, in Samaria seventeen years. (In the
twenty-third year of Joash, the son of Ahaziah, the king of
Judah, Jehoahaz, the son of Jehu, began to reign upon
Israel, in Samaria, and he reigned for seventeen years.)
2 And he did evil before the Lord, and he followed the
sins of Jeroboam, the son of Nebat, that made Israel to do
sin; and he bowed not away from those *sins*.
3 And the strong vengeance of the Lord was wroth
against Israel, and he betook them into the hand of
Hazael, king of Syria, and in(to) the hand of Benhadad,
son of Hazael, in all (their) days.
4 Forsooth Jehoahaz besought the face of the Lord,
and the Lord heard him; for he saw the anguish of Israel,
for the king of Syria had all-broken them.
5 And the Lord gave a saviour to Israel, and he was
delivered from the hand of the king of Syria; and the sons
of Israel dwelled in their tabernacles, as yesterday and the
third day ago. (And the Lord gave a saviour to Israel, and
they were rescued from the hands of the king of Syria;
and then the Israelites lived in their homes, like yesterday
and the third day ago.)
6 Nevertheless they departed not from the sins of the
house of Jeroboam, that made Israel to do sin; but they
went in those sins; soothly also the [maumet] wood
dwelled in Samaria (and also the idol grove/the sacred
pole remained in Samaria).
7 And to Jehoahaz were not left of the people, but five
hundred knights, and ten chariots, and ten thousand of
footmen (And there were left of the people to Jehoahaz,
but five hundred horsemen, and ten chariots, and ten
thousand footmen); for the king of Syria had slain them,
and had driven them [down] as into powder in the
threshing of a cornfloor.
8 Forsooth the residue of [the] words of Jehoahaz, and
all things that he did, and the strength of him, whether
these be not written in the book of [the] words of [the]
days of the kings of Israel?
9 And Jehoahaz slept with his fathers, and they buried
him in Samaria; and Jehoash[19], his son, reigned for him.
10 In the seven and thirtieth year of Joash, king of
Judah, Jehoash, the son of Jehoahaz, reigned upon Israel
in Samaria sixteen years.[20] (In the thirty-seventh year of
Joash, the king of Judah, Jehoash, the son of Jehoahaz,
began to reign upon Israel in Samaria, and he reigned for
sixteen years.)
11 And he did that, that is evil in the sight of the Lord
(And he did what was evil in the sight of the Lord); for he
bowed not away from all the sins of Jeroboam, the son of
Nebat, that made Israel to do sin; but he went in those
sins.
12[21] Forsooth the residue of [the] words of Jehoash, and
all things that he did, but also his strength, how he fought
against Amaziah, king of Judah, whether these be not
written in the book of [the] words of [the] days of the
kings of Israel?
13 And Jehoash slept with his fathers; forsooth
Jeroboam (II) sat upon his throne (and his son, Jeroboam
II, sat on his throne). And Jehoash was buried in Samaria

[17] Also known as Joram.

[18] Also known as Jehoash.

[19] Also known as Joash.

[20] Joash, king of Judah, was also known as Jehoash; Jehoash, king of Israel, was also known as Joash! For a time they reigned concurrently.

[21] Compare verses 13:12-13 with 14:15-16.

with the kings of Israel.
14 Forsooth Elisha was sick in a sickness, by which and
he was dead (Now Elisha was sick with the sickness from
which he would die); and Jehoash, king of Israel, went
down to him, and wept before him, and said, My father!
my father! the chariot of Israel, and the charioteer thereof!
15 And Elisha said to him, Bring thou a bow and
arrows. And when he had brought to Elisha a bow and
arrows,
16 he said to the king of Israel, Set thine hand on the
bow. And when he had set his hand (on it), Elisha setted
his hands on the hands of the king,
17 and (he) said, Open thou the east window. And
when he had opened (it), Elisha said, Shoot thou an
arrow; and he shot (it). And Elisha said, *This is* an arrow
of [the] health of the Lord, and an arrow of health against
Syria; and thou shalt smite Syria in Aphek, till thou waste
it (And Elisha said, *This is* an arrow of the Lord's victory,
yea, an arrow of victory over Syria; and thou shalt strike
Syria in Aphek, until thou destroy it).
18 And *Elisha* said, Take away the arrows. And when
he had taken (them) away, Elisha said to him, Smite thou
the earth with a dart (Strike thou the earth with this
arrow). And when he had smitten three times, and had
stood,
19 the man of God was wroth against him, and said, If
thou haddest smitten five times, either six times, either
seven times, thou shouldest have smitten Syria unto the
ending (of it); now forsooth thou shalt smite it three times
(but now thou shalt strike it only three times).
20 Then Elisha was dead (Then Elisha died), and they
buried him. And the thieves of Moab came into the land
in that year.
21 Forsooth some men buried a man (And some men
were burying a man), and they saw the thieves, and they
cast forth the dead body into the sepulchre of Elisha; and
when it had touched the bones of Elisha, the man lived
again, and stood up on his feet.
22 Then Hazael (But Hazael), king of Syria, tormented
Israel in all the days of Jehoahaz.
23 And the Lord had mercy on them, and turned again
to them for his covenant, that he had *made* with
Abraham, Isaac, and Jacob; and he would not destroy
them, neither cast *them* away utterly, into this present
time. (But the Lord had mercy on the Israelites, and
returned to them, because of the covenant that he had
made with Abraham, Isaac, and Jacob; and he would not
destroy them, nor throw *them* utterly away, even into this
present time.)
24 And Hazael, king of Syria, died; and Benhadad, his
son, reigned for him.
25 Forsooth Jehoash, the son of Jehoahaz, took away
[the] cities from the hand of Benhadad, the son of Hazael,
which he had taken by the right of battle from the hand
of Jehoahaz, his father (which he had taken from the
hand, *or the power*, of his father Jehoahaz, by right of
battle); Jehoash smote him three times, and he yielded
those cities to Israel.

CHAPTER 14

1 In the second year of Jehoash[22], the son of Jehoahaz,
king of Israel, Amaziah, the son of Joash[23], king of Judah,
reigned (began to reign).
2 *Amaziah* was of five and twenty years, when he
began to reign; and he reigned in Jerusalem nine and
twenty years; the name of his mother was Jehoaddan of
Jerusalem.
3 And he did rightfulness before the Lord,
nevertheless not as David, his father, did; he did by all
things that Joash, his father, did, (And he did what was
right before the Lord, but not as his forefather David did;
he did all things, that his father Joash did,)
4 no but this only, that he did not away (the) high
things; for yet the people made sacrifice, and burnt
incense in (the) high things. (in all but this only, that he
did not do away the hill shrines; for yet the people made
sacrifice, and burned incense at the hill shrines.)
5 And when he had gotten the realm, he smote his
servants, that had killed the king, his father;
6 but he killed not the sons of them that had slain *the
king*/that had slain *his father*, by that that is written in the
book of the law of Moses, as the Lord commanded to
Moses, and said, [The] Fathers shall not die for the sons,
neither the sons for the fathers, but each man shall die in
his own sin (but each man shall die for his own sin).
7 He smote Edom in the valley of (the) makings of salt,
he smote ten thousand (men), and took the Stone in
battle (and took Selah in battle); and he called the name
thereof Joktheel[24], (which it is still called) unto this
present day.
8 Then Amaziah sent messengers to Jehoash, the son
of Jehoahaz, the son of Jehu, king of Israel, and said,
Come thou, and see we us *in battle*/Come thou, and see
we us (Come thou, let us have a meeting).
9 And Jehoash, king of Israel, sent again to Amaziah,
king of Judah, and said *mystically*, The carduus, *or
thistle, that is, a low herb, and full of thorns*, of the
Lebanon sent to the cedar, that is in the Lebanon, and
said, Give thy daughter (as) wife to my son; and the
beasts of the forest, that be in the Lebanon, passed forth,
and trode down the carduus.
10 Thou hast smitten Edom, and haddest the mastery
upon *it*, and thine heart hath raised thee (up); be thou

[22] Also known as Joash.
[23] Also known as Jehoash(!).
[24] *That is, '(the) soreness of teeth', for they that were slain there gnashed with (their) teeth, for the horror and sorrow of death.*

satisfied with *this* glory, and sit in thine house; why
excitest thou evil, *or stirrest thou (up) evil*, so that thou
fall, and Judah with thee?
11 And Amaziah assented not *to be in peace*; and
Jehoash, king of Israel, went up, and he and Amaziah,
king of Judah, saw themselves (*when they met in battle*)
in Bethshemesh, a city of Judah. (But Amaziah assented
not *to be at peace*; and so Jehoash, the king of Israel,
went up, and he and Amaziah, the king of Judah, faced
each other *when they met in battle*, in Bethshemesh, a
city of Judah.)
12 And Judah was smitten before Israel; and they fled
each man into his tabernacles.
13 Soothly Jehoash, king of Israel, took in Bethshemesh
Amaziah, king of Judah, the son of Joash, the son of
Ahaziah, and brought him into Jerusalem (And Jehoash,
the king of Israel, captured Amaziah, the king of Judah,
the son of Joash, the son of Ahaziah, at Bethshemesh, and
brought him to Jerusalem); and he brake the wall of
Jerusalem, from the gate of Ephraim unto the gate of the
corner, by four hundred cubits.
14 And he took all the gold and silver, and all the
vessels, that were found in the house of the Lord, and in
the treasures of the king('s) (house); and *he took* hostages,
and turned again into Samaria. (And he took all the gold
and silver, and all the vessels, that were found in the
House of the Lord, and in the treasuries of the palace;
and *he also took some* hostages, and then returned to
Samaria.)
15[25] Soothly the residue of [the] words of Jehoash, which
he did, and his strength, by which he fought against
Amaziah, king of Judah, whether these be not written in
the book of [the] words of [the] days of the kings of Israel?
16 And Jehoash slept with his fathers, and was buried
in Samaria with the kings of Israel; and Jeroboam (II), his
son, reigned for him.
17 Forsooth Amaziah, the son of Joash, king of Judah,
lived five and twenty years, after that Jehoash, the son of
Jehoahaz, king of Israel, was dead. (And Amaziah, the
son of Joash, the king of Judah, lived for fifteen years after
that Jehoash, the son of Jehoahaz, the king of Israel, died.)
18 Forsooth the residue of the words of Amaziah,
whether these be not written in the book of [the] words of
[the] days of the kings of Judah?
19 And swearing together, *that is, conspiracy*, in
Jerusalem was made against him, and he fled into
Lachish; and they sent after him into Lachish, and killed
him there. (And a conspiracy was made against him in
Jerusalem, and he fled to Lachish; but they went after him
to Lachish, and killed him there.)
20 And they bare out him in horses (And they brought
back his body on a horse), and he was buried in
Jerusalem with his fathers, in the city of David.
21 Forsooth all the people of Judah took Azariah,
having sixteen years; and made him king for his father
Amaziah. (And all the people of Judah took Azariah, *also
known as Uzziah*, who was sixteen years old; and made
him king for his father Amaziah.)
22 He builded Elath, and restored it to Judah, after that
the king slept with his fathers. (And he built Elath, and
restored it to Judah, after that King Amaziah slept with his
forefathers, *or died*.)
23 In the fifteenth year of Amaziah, the son of Joash,
king of Judah, Jeroboam (II), the son of Jehoash, king of
Israel, reigned in Samaria one and forty years; (In the
fifteenth year of Amaziah, the son of Joash, the king of
Judah, Jeroboam II, the son of Jehoash, the king of Israel,
began to reign in Samaria, and he reigned for forty-one
years;)
24 and did that, that is evil before the Lord (and he did
what was evil before the Lord); he went not away from all
the sins of Jeroboam, [the] son of Nebat, that made Israel
to do sin.
25 He restored the terms of Israel, from the entering of
Hamath unto the sea of (the) wilderness, by the word of
the Lord God of Israel, which he spake by his servant
Jonah, the son of Amittai, (*that is,*) *by Jonah*, the prophet,
that was of Gath, that is in Hepher. (He restored the
borders of Israel, from the entering of Hamath unto the
Sea of the Wilderness, *that is, the Dead Sea*, according to
the word of the Lord God of Israel, which he spoke by his
servant Jonah, the son of Amittai, *that is, by* the prophet
Jonah, who was of Gath-hepher.)
26 For the Lord saw the full bitter torment of Israel, and
that they were wasted unto the closed men of prison (and
that they were wasted unto the enclosed men in prison),
and to the last men, and there was none that helped Israel.
27 And the Lord spake not, that he should do away [the
name of] Israel from under heaven, but he saved them in
the hand of Jeroboam (II), the son of Jehoash. (And the
Lord spoke not, that he would do away the name of Israel
from under heaven, but he saved them by the hand, *or by
the power*, of Jeroboam II, the son of Jehoash.)
28 Forsooth the residue of the words of Jeroboam (II),
and all things that he did, and the strength of him, by
which he fought, and how he restored Damascus, and
Hamath of Judah, in Israel (to Israel), whether these be
not written in the book of [the] words of [the] days of the
kings of Israel?
29 And Jeroboam (II) slept with his fathers, the kings of
Israel; and Zachariah[26], his son, reigned for him.

CHAPTER 15

1 In the seven and twentieth year of Jeroboam (II),

[25] Compare verses 14:15-16 with 13:12-13.

[26] Also spelled Zechariah.

king of Israel, Azariah[27], the son of Amaziah, king of
Judah, reigned; (In the twenty-seventh year of Jeroboam
II, the king of Israel, Azariah, *also known as Uzziah*, the
son of Amaziah, the king of Judah, began to reign;)
2 he was of sixteen years, when he began to reign,
and he reigned two and fifty years in Jerusalem; the name
of his mother *was* Jecholiah of Jerusalem.
3 And he did that, that was pleasant before the Lord
(And he did what was pleasing before the Lord), by all
things that Amaziah, his father, had done;
4 nevertheless he destroyed not [the] high things; (for)
yet the people made sacrifice, and burnt incense in (the)
high things. (but he did not destroy the hill shrines; for
yet the people made sacrifice, and burned incense at the
hill shrines.)
5 Forsooth the Lord smote the king, and he was
leprous till into the day of his death; and he dwelled in
an house freely by himself (and he lived alone in a
house, free of all duties). Soothly Jotham, [the] son of the
king, governed the palace, and deemed the people of the
land.
6 Forsooth the residue of the words of Azariah, and all
things that he did, whether these be not written in the
book of [the] words of [the] days of the kings of Judah?
7 And Azariah slept with his fathers; and they buried
him with his elder men in the city of David; and Jotham,
his son, reigned for him.
8 In the eight and thirtieth year of Azariah, king of
Judah, Zachariah[28], the son of Jeroboam, reigned upon
Israel in Samaria six months. (In the thirty-eighth year of
Azariah, *or Uzziah*, the king of Judah, Zachariah, the son
of Jeroboam, began to reign upon Israel in Samaria, and
he reigned for six months.)
9 And he did that, that was evil before the Lord, as his
fathers did; he departed not from the sins of Jeroboam,
the son of Nebat, that made Israel to do sin.
10 Forsooth Shallum, the son of Jabesh, conspired
against him in Samaria; and *Shallum* smote him before
the people, and killed *him*, and reigned for him.
11 And the residue of the words of Zachariah, whether
these be not written in the book of [the] words of [the]
days of the kings of Israel?
12 This is the word of the Lord, which he spake to Jehu,
and said, Thy sons till to the fourth generation shall sit on
the throne of thee of Israel; and it was done so. (This was
the word of the Lord, which he spoke to Jehu, and said,
Thy sons unto the fourth generation shall sit on the
throne of Israel; and so it was done.)
13 Shallum, the son of Jabesh, reigned in the ninth and
thirty year of Azariah, king of Judah; soothly he reigned
one month in Samaria. (Shallum, the son of Jabesh, began
to reign in the thirty-ninth year of Azariah, *or Uzziah*, the
king of Judah; and he reigned for one month in Samaria.)
14 And Menahem, the son of Gadi, went up from
Tirzah, and came into Samaria; and he smote Shallum,
the son of Jabesh, in Samaria, and killed him, and reigned
for him (and reigned in his place).
15 Soothly the residue of the words of Shallum, and his
conspiracy, by which he setted treasons, whether these
be not written in the book of [the] words of [the] days of
the kings of Israel(?).
16 Then Menahem smote *the city* Tiphsah, and all the
men that were therein, and the terms thereof from Tirzah,
for they would not open *their gates* to him[29]; and he
killed all the women thereof with child, and carved them
(up).
17 In the nine and thirtieth year of Azariah, king of
Judah, Menahem, the son of Gadi, reigned upon Israel
ten years in Samaria. (In the thirty-ninth year of Azariah,
or Uzziah, the king of Judah, Menahem, the son of Gadi,
began to reign upon Israel, and he reigned ten years in
Samaria.)
18 And he did that, that was evil before the Lord; he
departed not from the sins of Jeroboam, the son of Nebat,
that made Israel to do sin.
19 In all the days of him, Pul, the king of Assyria, came
into Tirzah. And Menahem gave to Pul a thousand
talents of silver, that he should be to him into help, and
should make steadfast his realm; (In all his days, Pul, the
king of Assyria, came against the land. And Menahem
gave Pul a thousand talents of silver, so that he would
help him, and strengthen Menahem's hold on his
kingdom;)
20 and Menahem setted tollage of silver on Israel, to all
[the] mighty men and rich, that he would give to the king
of Assyria; *he setted* fifty shekels of silver to one man,
that is, to each man; and the king of Assyria turned again,
and dwelled not in Tirzah. (and Menahem put a toll, *or a
tax*, of silver on Israel, on all the rich and mighty men, to
give to the king of Assyria; *he set* the toll at fifty shekels
of silver from each man; and after receiving this payment,
then the king of Assyria left, and did not stay in the land.)
21 Forsooth the residue of the words of Menahem, and
all things that he did, whether these be not written in the
book of [the] words of [the] days of the kings of Israel?
22 And Menahem slept with his fathers; and Pekahiah,
his son, reigned for him.
23 In the fiftieth year of Azariah, king of Judah,
Pekahiah, the son of Menahem, reigned on Israel in
Samaria two years. (In the fiftieth year of Azariah, *or
Uzziah*, the king of Judah, Pekahiah, the son of
Menahem, began to reign upon Israel in Samaria, and he

[27] He is called Uzziah throughout Chapter 15 in numerous translations.

[28] Also spelled Zechariah.

[29] *That is, receive him as king in the city.*

reigned for two years.)
24 And he did that, that was evil before the Lord; he
departed not from the sins of Jeroboam, the son of Nebat,
that made Israel to do sin.
25 Forsooth Pekah, the son of Remaliah, (a) duke of his
host, conspired against him, and smote him in Samaria,
in the tower of the king's house, *that is, (in) the palace,*
besides Argob, and besides Arieh; and he *smote* him with
fifty men of the sons of Gileadites; and Pekah killed him,
and reigned for him. (And Pekah, the son of Remaliah, a
leader of Pekahiah's army, conspired against him, and
struck him down in Samaria, in the tower of the palace,
with Argob and Arieh; and he *struck down* with him fifty
men of the Gileadites; and Pekah killed him, and reigned
for him.)
26 Soothly the residue of the words of Pekahiah, and all
things that he did, whether these be not written in the
book of [the] words of [the] days of the kings of Israel?
27 In the two and fiftieth year of Azariah, king of Judah,
Pekah, the son of Remaliah, reigned [upon Israel] in
Samaria twenty years. (In the fifty-second year of Azariah,
or Uzziah, the king of Judah, Pekah, the son of Remaliah,
began to reign upon Israel in Samaria, and he reigned for
twenty years.)
28 And he did that, that was evil before the Lord; he
departed not from the sins of Jeroboam, the son of Nebat,
that made Israel to do sin.
29 In the days of Pekah, king of Israel, Tiglathpileser,
king of Assur, came, and took Ijon, and Abel, the house
of Maachah, and Janoah, and Kedesh, and Hazor, and
Gilead, and Galilee, and all the land of Naphtali; and
translated them into (the) Assyrians. (In the days of Pekah,
the king of Israel, Tiglathpileser, the king of Assyria,
came, and captured Ijon, and Abelbethmaachah, and
Janoah, and Kedesh, and Hazor, and Gilead, and Galilee,
and all the land of Naphtali; and carried away all the
people to Assyria.)
30 Forsooth Hoshea, the son of Elah, conspired, and set
treasons against Pekah, the son of Remaliah, and smote
him, and killed *him*; and he reigned for him, in the
twentieth year of Jotham, the son of Uzziah, (*that is, the
son of Azariah*).
31 Forsooth the residue of the words of Pekah, and all
things that he did, whether these be not written in the
book of [the] words of [the] days of the kings of Israel?
32 In the second year of Pekah, the son of Remaliah,
king of Israel, Jotham, the son of Uzziah, king of Judah,
reigned; (In the second year of Pekah, the son of
Remaliah, the king of Israel, Jotham, the son of Uzziah,
that is, the son of Azariah, the king of Judah, began to
reign;)
33 he was of five and twenty years, when he began to
reign, and he reigned sixteen years in Jerusalem; the
name of his mother was Jerusha, the daughter of Zadok.
34 And he did that, that was pleasant before the Lord;
he wrought by all things, that his father Uzziah had done;
(And he did what was pleasing before the Lord; he did all
the things, that his father Uzziah, *that is, Azariah,* had
done;)
35 nevertheless he did not away [the] high things; (for)
yet the people made sacrifice, and burnt incense in (the)
high things; he builded the highest gate of the house of
the Lord. (but he did not do away the hill shrines; for yet
the people made sacrifice, and burned incense at the hill
shrines; he built the highest gate of the House of the
Lord.)
36 Forsooth the residue of [the] words of Jotham, and
all things that he did, whether these be not written in the
book of [the] words of [the] days of the kings of Judah?
37 In those days the Lord began to send into Judah
Rezin, the king of Syria, and Pekah, the son of Remaliah.
(In those days the Lord began to send against Judah
Rezin, the king of Syria, and Pekah, the son of Remaliah.)
38 And Jotham slept with his fathers, and was buried
with them in the city of David, his father; and Ahaz, his
son, reigned for him.

CHAPTER 16

1 In the seventeenth year of Pekah, the son of
Remaliah, Ahaz, the son of Jotham, king of Judah,
reigned (began to reign).
2 Ahaz was of twenty years, when he began to reign,
and he reigned sixteen years in Jerusalem; he did not
that, that was pleasant in the sight of his Lord God, as
David, his father, *did* (he did not do what was pleasing
before the Lord his God, as his forefather David *did*),
3 but he went in the way of the kings of Israel.
Furthermore and he hallowed his son, and bare, *or drew
him,* through the fire, after the idols of heathen men,
which the Lord destroyed before the sons of Israel. (but
he went in the way of the kings of Israel. And
furthermore, he offered his own son in the fire, as a
sacrifice to the idols of the heathen, whom the Lord had
destroyed before the Israelites.)
4 And he offered sacrifices, and burnt incense in (the)
high places, and in (the) hills, and under each tree full of
boughs. (And he offered sacrifices, and burned incense at
the hill shrines, and on the hills, and under each tree full
of boughs.)
5 Then Rezin, king of Syria, and Pekah, son of
Remaliah, king of Israel, went up into Jerusalem to fight
with Ahaz; and when they besieged Ahaz, they might not
overcome him (but when they besieged Ahaz, they could
not overcome him).
6 In that time Rezin, king of Syria, restored Elath to
Syria, and casted out the Jews from Elath; and Idumeans
and men of Syria came into Elath, and dwelled there till
into this day. (At that time Rezin, the king of Syria,

restored Elath to Syria, and cast out the Jews from Elath;
and the Edomites and the Syrians came into Elath, and
live there unto this day.)
7 Forsooth Ahaz sent messengers to Tiglathpileser,
king of Assyrians, and said, I am thy servant and thy son;
go thou up (come thou up), and make me safe from the
hand of the king of Syria, and from the hand of the king
of Israel, that have risen (up) together against me.
8 And when Ahaz had gathered together silver and
gold, that might be found in the house of the Lord, and in
the treasures of the king, he sent (it as) gifts to the king of
Assyrians; (And when Ahaz had gathered together the
silver and gold, that could be found in the House of the
Lord, and in the treasuries of the palace, he sent it as gifts
to the king of Assyria;)
9 and he assented to his will. Soothly the king of
Assyrians went up into Damascus, and wasted it, and
translated the dwellers thereof to Kir (and carried away all
of its inhabitants to Kir); soothly he killed Rezin.
10 And king Ahaz went into meeting to Tiglathpileser,
king of Assyrians; and when king Ahaz had seen the altar
of Damascus, he sent *into Jerusalem* to Urijah, the priest,
the exemplar and [the] likeness thereof, by all the work
thereof. (And King Ahaz went to meet Tiglathpileser, the
king of Assyria; and when King Ahaz had seen the altar of
Damascus, he sent *back to Jerusalem* an exact description
and a model of it, to Urijah the priest.)
11 And (then) Urijah, the priest, builded an altar by all
things that king Ahaz had commanded from Damascus;
so did the priest Urijah, till king Ahaz came from
Damascus (so did Urijah the priest, until King Ahaz came
back from Damascus).
12 And when the king came from Damascus, he saw
the altar, and worshipped (on) it;
13 and he went up, and offered burnt sacrifices, and his
sacrifice; and he offered moist sacrifices, and he poured
the blood of peaceable things, which he had offered, on
the altar. (and he went up, and offered his burnt
sacrifices, and his grain sacrifices; and he offered a wine
offering, and he poured the blood of his peace offering
on the altar.)
14 Forsooth he did away the brazen altar, that was
before the Lord, from the face of the temple, and from
(between) the place of the (new) altar, and the place of
the temple of the Lord; and setted it on the side of the
(new) altar at the north/and he set *God's* altar at the north
side of his altar. (And he did away the bronze altar, that
was before the Lord, from the front of the Temple, and
from between the place of the new altar, and the Temple
of the Lord; and put it to the side of the new altar at the
north/and he put *God's* altar at the north side of his altar.)
15 Also king Ahaz commanded to Urijah, the priest,
and said, Offer thou upon the more altar, *that is, (up)on
the new altar*, the burnt sacrifice of the morrowtide, and
the sacrifice of the eventide, and the burnt sacrifice of the
king, and the (grain) sacrifice of him, and the burnt
sacrifice of all the people of the land, and the (grain)
sacrifices of them, and the moist sacrifices of them (and
their wine offerings); and thou shalt pour out upon that
new altar all the blood of [the] burnt sacrifice, and all the
blood of [the] slain sacrifice; soothly the brazen altar shall
be [made] ready at my will.
16 Therefore Urijah, the priest, did by all things that
king Ahaz had commanded to him.
17 Forsooth king Ahaz took (away) the painted
foundaments *of (the) pillars*, and the washing vessel, that
was set above (them), and he put down the sea, *that is,
the washing vessel for priests*, from [off] the brazen oxen
(from off the bronze oxen), that sustained *it*, and he setted
(it) on the pavement arrayed with stone.
18 Also he turned (around) the chamber of [the]
sabbath, which he had builded in the temple, and *he
turned (around)* the entering of the king (from)
withoutforth into the temple of the Lord, for (to please)
the king of Assyrians. (And he turned around the
chamber used on the sabbath, which he had built in the
Temple, and *he turned around* the entrance for the king
from withoutforth into the Temple of the Lord, all to
please the king of Assyria.)
19 Forsooth the residue of [the] words of Ahaz, and all
things which he did, whether these be not written in the
book of [the] words of [the] days of the kings of Judah?
20 And Ahaz slept with his fathers, and was buried with
them in the city of David; and Hezekiah, his son, reigned
for him.

CHAPTER 17

1 In the twelfth year of Ahaz, king of Judah, Hoshea,
the son of Elah, reigned in Samaria upon Israel nine
years. (In the twelfth year of Ahaz, the king of Judah,
Hoshea, the son of Elah, began to reign in Samaria upon
Israel, and he reigned for nine years.)
2 And he did evil before the Lord, but not as the kings
of Israel, that were before him.
3 Shalmaneser, king of Assyrians, went up against
Hoshea, and Hoshea was made (a) servant to him, and
yielded tributes to him (and paid him taxes).
4 And when the king of Assyrians had perceived, that
Hoshea enforced to rebel, and (that he) had sent
messengers to So, king of Egypt, that he should not give
tributes to the king of Assyrians, as he was wont (to do)
by all years, *the king of Assyrians* besieged him, and sent
him bound into prison. (And when the king of Assyria
had perceived that Hoshea endeavoured to rebel, for he
had sent messengers to So, the king of Egypt, *asking for
help*, and thereafter paid no taxes to the king of Assyria,
as he had done before by all years, *the king of Assyria*
besieged him, and bound him, and put *him* in prison.)

5 And *Shalmaneser* went through[out] all the land,
and he went up to Samaria, and besieged it three years.
6 Forsooth in the ninth year of Hoshea, the king of
Assyrians took Samaria, and translated Israel into (the)
Assyrians (and carried away all the Israelites to Assyria);
and he put them in Halah, and in Habor, beside the flood
[of] Gozan, (and) in the cities of (the) Medes.
7 Forsooth it was done, when the sons of Israel had
sinned before their Lord God, that led them out of the
land of Egypt, from (under) the hand of Pharaoh, king of
Egypt, they worshipped alien gods; (For it was, that the
Israelites had sinned before the Lord their God, who had
led them out of the land of Egypt, from under the hand of
Pharaoh, the king of Egypt, for they worshipped foreign,
or other, gods,)
8 and went by the custom of heathen men, which the
Lord had wasted in the sight of the sons of Israel (whom
the Lord had destroyed before the Israelites), and (the
custom) of the kings of Israel, for they had done in like
manner.
9 And the sons of Israel offended their Lord God by
words not rightful, and they builded to themselves high
things in all their cities, from the tower of (the) keepers
unto a strengthened city. (And the Israelites offended the
Lord their God with things that were not right, and they
built for themselves hill shrines in all their cities, from a
watchman's tower unto a fortified city.)
10 And they made to them(selves) images, and maumet
woods, in each high hill, and under each tree full of
boughs; (And they set up images, *or idols*, for themselves,
and idol groves, *or sacred poles*, on each high hill, and
under each tree full of boughs;)
11 and they burnt there incense on the altars, by the
custom of heathen men, which the Lord had translated
from the face of them. And they did [the] worst words,
that is, (the) worst works, and they wrathed the Lord;
(and they burned incense on the altars there, by the
custom of the heathen, whom the Lord had carried away
from before them. And they did the worst works, and
they stirred the Lord to great anger;)
12 and [they] worshipped [the] uncleannesses, of which
the Lord commanded to them, that they should not do
this word. (and they worshipped idols, which the Lord
had commanded to them, that they should not do this
thing.)
13 And the Lord witnessed in Israel and in Judah, by
the hand of all (the) prophets, and [the] seers, and said,
Turn ye again from your worst ways/your full evil ways,
and keep my commandments, and [my] ceremonies, by
all the law which I commanded to your fathers, and as I
sent to you in the hand of my servants (the) prophets.
(And the Lord witnessed against Israel and Judah, by all
of his prophets, and seers, and said, Turn ye away from
your worst ways/from your full evil ways, and keep my
commandments, and my statutes, by all the Law which I
commanded to your forefathers, and as I sent word to
you by my servants the prophets.)
14 Which heard not, but made hard their noll by the
noll of their fathers, that would not obey to their Lord
God. (But they would not listen, but hardened, *or
stiffened*, their necks, *or were stubborn*, like their
forefathers, who also would not obey the Lord their God.)
15 And they casted away the lawful things of him, and
the covenant that he covenanted with their fathers, and
the witnessings by which he witnessed to them; and they
followed vanities, *that is, idols*, and did vainly; and
followed heathen men, that were about them; of which
things the Lord commanded to them, that they should not
do as also those *heathen men* did. (And they threw away
his laws, and the covenant that he had covenanted with
their forefathers, and the witnessings, or the testimonies,
by which he had witnessed to them; and they followed
vain, or worthless, idols; and followed the heathen, who
were about them; of which *things* the Lord commanded
to them, that they should not do as those *heathen* did.)
16 And they forsook all the commandments of their
Lord God, and they made to them two molten calves,
and maumet woods, and worshipped all the knighthood
of (the) heaven(s) (and they made for themselves two cast
metal calves, and idol groves, *or poles*, and worshipped
all the host of heaven), *that is, (the) sun, and moon, and
other planets*; and they served Baal,
17 and [they] hallowed to him their sons, and their
daughters, through fire, and they served to false divining,
and to divining by chittering of birds; and they gave
themselves to do evil before the Lord, and they wrathed
him. (and they sacrificed their sons and their daughters to
him, by burning them in the fire, and they served false
divining, and divining by the twittering of birds; and they
gave themselves to do evil before the Lord, and they
stirred him to great anger.)
18 And the Lord was wroth greatly to Israel; and he
took away them from his sight, and none (was) left, no
but the lineage of Judah only. (And the Lord was greatly
angered with Israel; and he put them away from before
him, and no one was left, but only the tribe of Judah.)
19 But neither Judah himself kept the behests of the
Lord his God, *but* nevertheless he erred, and went in the
error of Israel, which it wrought. (Yet even the people of
Judah themselves did not obey the commandments of the
Lord their God, but they also erred, and went in the error
of Israel, which they also did.)
20 And the Lord casted away all the seed of Israel, and
tormented them, and betook them in the hand of
raveners; till he had cast away them from his face, (And
so the Lord threw away all the descendants of Israel, and
tormented them, and delivered them into the hands of
robbers, *or of plunderers*; until he had thrown them all

away from before his face,)
21 from that time in which Israel was parted from the
house of David, and [they] made to them a king (and they
made a king for themselves), Jeroboam, the son of Nebat.
For Jeroboam separated Israel from the Lord, and made
them to do great sin.
22 And the sons of Israel went in all the sins of
Jeroboam, which he had done (And the Israelites went in
all the sins of Jeroboam, which he had done); and they
departed not from those *sins,*
23 till the Lord did away Israel from his face, as he
spake in the hand of all his servants (the) prophets; and
Israel was translated/was brought over from his land into
Assyrians till into this day (and the Israelites were carried
away/were brought over from their own land into Assyria,
and they be there unto this day).
24 Forsooth the king of Assyrians brought people from
Babylon, and from Cuthah, and from Ava, and from
Hamath, and from Sepharvaim, and set them in the cities
of Samaria for the sons of Israel (and put them in the
cities of Samaria in place of the Israelites); and these had
in possession Samaria, and they dwelled in the cities
thereof.
25 And when they began to dwell there, they dreaded
not the Lord; and the Lord sent to them lions, the which
killed them. (And when they began to live there, they did
not fear the Lord/they did not revere the Lord; and the
Lord sent lions among them, which killed some of them.)
26 And it was told to the king of Assyrians, and was
said, The folks which thou hast translated, and madest to
dwell in the cities of Samaria, know not the lawful things
of [the] God of the land; and the Lord hath sent lions into
them, and lo! those slay them; for they know not the
custom of [the] God of the land. (And it was told to the
king of Assyria, and it was said, The peoples whom thou
hast transferred, and madest to live in the cities of
Samaria, know not the laws of the God of the land; and
so the Lord hath sent lions among them, and lo! they
have killed some of the people; for they know not the
customs of the God of the land.)
27 Soothly the king of Assyrians commanded, and said,
Led ye thither one of the priests, which ye brought (as)
prisoners from thence, that he go, and dwell with them,
and teach them the lawful things of (the) God of the land
(and teach them the laws of the God of the land).
28 Therefore when one of these priests had come, that
were led (away as) prisoners from Samaria, he dwelled in
Bethel, and taught them, how they should worship the
Lord. (And so when one of those priests, who were led
away as prisoners from Samaria, had come, he lived in
Bethel, and taught them how they should worship the
Lord.)
29 And each folk made his god, and they setted those
gods in the high temples, which the men of Samaria had
made, folk and folk in their cities, in which they dwelled.
(But each people made their own god, and they put those
gods in the high temples, which the men of Samaria had
made, yea, each people in their city, in which they lived.)
30 For men of Babylon made Succothbenoth; and men
of Cuth made Nergal; and men of Hamath made Ashima;
31 and (the) Avites made Nibhaz and Tartak; soothly
they that were of Sepharvaim burnt their sons in fire to
Adrammelech and Anammelech, the gods of Sepharvaim.
32 And nevertheless they (still) worshipped the Lord;
forsooth of the last men, *that is, of vile persons, that were
not of (the) priests' kin, by the law of Moses,* they made
priests of the high things, and setted them in (the) high
temples. (And though they still worshipped the Lord, they
made the lowest men, *that is, the most vile persons, who
were not of the priests' kin, after the law of Moses,* to be
the priests of the hill shrines, and put them in the temples
there.)
33 And when they worshipped God, they served also
their gods, by the custom of heathen men, from which
they were translated to Samaria; (And while they
worshipped God, they also served their own gods, after
the custom of the heathen, from where they had been
brought back to Samaria;)
34 till to this present day they follow the eld custom;
they dreaded not the Lord, neither they keep his
ceremonies, and dooms (and judgements), and law, and
commandment, which the Lord commanded to the sons
of Jacob, whom he named Israel;
35 and the Lord [had] smote a covenant with them, and
[had] commanded to them, and said, Do not ye dread
alien gods, and honour ye not outwardly them, neither
worship ye inwardly them, and make ye not sacrifice to
them; (and the Lord had made a covenant with them, and
had commanded to them, and said, Do not ye fear
foreign, *or other,* gods/Do not ye revere foreign, *or other,*
gods, nor outwardly honour ye them, nor inwardly
worship ye them, and make ye not sacrifice to them;)
36 but your Lord God, that led you out of the land of
Egypt in great strength, and in an arm stretched out,
dread ye him, and worship ye him, and make ye sacrifice
to him. (but the Lord your God, who led you out of the
land of Egypt with great strength, and with an outstretched arm, fear ye him/revere ye him, and worship ye
him, and make ye sacrifice to him.)
37 Also keep ye the ceremonies, and [the] dooms, and
the law, and the commandment, which he wrote to you,
that ye do *it* in all days; and dread ye not alien gods.
(And obey ye the statutes, and the judgements, and the
laws, and the commandments, which he wrote for you,
and that ye do *them* in all days; and fear ye not foreign,
or other, gods/and revere ye not foreign, *or other,* gods.)
38 And do not ye forget the covenant, which he/the
Lord smote with you, neither worship ye alien gods (nor

worship ye foreign, *or other*, gods);
39 but dread ye your Lord God, and he shall deliver
you from the hand of all your enemies. (but fear ye/but
revere ye the Lord your God, and he shall rescue you
from all of your enemies.)
40 Forsooth they heard not, but did by their former
custom.
41 Therefore soothly these heathen men dreaded God;
but nevertheless they served also their idols, for both
their sons and the sons of their sons do so, till into this
present day, as their fathers did. (And so these heathen
feared God/revered God; but nevertheless they also
served their idols, for both their sons and the sons of their
sons do so, as their forefathers did, unto this present day.)

CHAPTER 18

1 In the third year of Hoshea, the son of Elah, king of
Israel, reigned Hezekiah, son of Ahaz, king of Judah. (In
the third year of Hoshea, the son of Elah, the king of
Israel, Hezekiah, the son of Ahaz, the king of Judah,
began to reign.)
2 He was of five and twenty years, when he began to
reign, and he reigned in Jerusalem nine and twenty years;
the name of his mother *was* Abi, the daughter of
Zachariah[30].
3 And he did that, that was good before the Lord, by
all things that David, his father, had done.
4 And he destroyed [the] high places, and all-brake
[the] images, and cut down [the maumet] woods, and he
brake the brazen serpent, whom Moses had made; for
unto that time the sons of Israel burnt incense to it; and
he called the name of it Nehushtan. (And he destroyed
the hill shrines, and broke up all the images, *or all the
idols*, and cut down the idol groves, *or the sacred poles*,
and broke apart the bronze serpent that Moses had made;
for unto that time the sons of Israel had burned incense to
it; and they called it Nehushtan.)
5 And he hoped in the Lord God of Israel; therefore
after him none was like him of all the kings of Judah, but
neither also in the *kings* that were before him. (And he
hoped in the Lord God of Israel; and after him there was
no one like him out of all the kings of Judah, but also not
any of the *kings* who were before him *were like him*.)
6 And he cleaved to the Lord, and went not away
from his steps, and he did the commandments of the
Lord, which the Lord commanded to Moses;
7 wherefore and the Lord was with him, and he
governed wisely himself in all things, to which he went
forth. Also he rebelled against the king of Assyrians, and
therefore he served not to him; (wherefore the Lord was
with him, and he wisely governed himself in all the
things, to which he went forth. And he rebelled against
the king of Assyria, and he served him not;)
8 and he smote [the] Philistines till to Gaza, and all
the terms of them, from the tower of the keepers unto a
city made strong.
9 In the fourth year of king Hezekiah, that was the
seventh year of Hoshea, the son of Elah, king of Israel,
Shalmaneser, king of Assyrians, went up to Samaria, and
fought against it,
10 and took *it*. For after three years, in the sixth year of
Hezekiah, that is, in the ninth year of Hoshea, king of
Israel, Samaria was taken;
11 and the king of Assyrians translated Israel into (the)
Assyrians, and he set them in Halah, and in Habor, (by
the) rivers of Gozan, (and) in the cities of (the) Medes;
(and the king of Assyria carried away the Israelites to
Assyria, and he put them in Halah, and on the banks of
the Habor River, *that is*, the river in Gozan, and in the
cities of the Medes;)
12 for they heard not the voice of their Lord God, but
they brake his covenant (because they did not listen to, *or
obey*, the voice of the Lord their God, but they broke his
covenant); they heard not, neither did all things, which
Moses, the servant of the Lord, [had] commanded.
13 In the fourteenth year of king Hezekiah,
Sennacherib, king of Assyrians, went up to all the
strengthened cities of Judah, and took them.
14 Then Hezekiah, king of Judah, sent messengers to
the king of Assyrians into Lachish, and said, I have sinned
(I have done wrong); go away from me, and I shall bear
all things, that thou shalt put to me. Therefore the king of
Assyrians putted on Hezekiah, king of Judah, (a fine of)
three hundred talents of silver, and thirty talents of gold.
15 And Hezekiah gave all the silver, that was found in
the house of the Lord, and in the king's treasures, *to the
king of Assyrians*. (And Hezekiah gave all the silver, that
was found in the House of the Lord, and in the treasuries
of the palace, *to the king of Assyria*.)
16 In that time Hezekiah (also) brake (up) the gates of
the temple of the Lord, and the plates of gold, which he
had fastened (to them), and he gave those to the king of
Assyrians. (And at that time Hezekiah also broke apart the
gates of the Temple of the Lord; and he gave the gold
plates, which he had fastened to the gates, to the king of
Assyria.)
17 Forsooth the king of Assyrians sent Tartan (and
Rabsaris) and Rabshakeh from Lachish to king Hezekiah,
with strong hand to Jerusalem; and when they had gone
up, they came to Jerusalem, and stood beside the water
conduit of the higher cistern, which is in the way of the
fuller, *or of (the) tucker*. (And the king of Assyria sent
Tartan, and Rabsaris, and Rabshakeh, from Lachish to
King Hezekiah, with a strong army against Jerusalem; and
when they had gone up, they came to Jerusalem, and
stood beside the water conduit of the higher cistern,

[30] Also spelled Zechariah.

which is on the way to the fullers, *or to the tuckers*.)
18 And they called (for) the king; soothly Eliakim, the
son of Hilkiah, the sovereign of the house, and Shebna,
the scribe, and Joah, (the) chancellor, the son of Asaph,
went out to them.
19 And Rabshakeh said to them, Speak ye to Hezekiah,
(and say,) The great king, the king of Assyrians, saith
these things, What is this trust, in which thou
endeavourest *thee*?
20 In hap thou hast taken counsel, that thou wouldest
make thee ready to battle. In whom trustest thou, that
thou be (so) (fool-)hardy to rebel *against Sennacherib*?
21 Whether thou hopest in a staff of (a) reed and
broken, (that is, upon) Egypt (Hopest thou in the staff of a
broken reed, that is, upon Egypt), on which, if a man
leaneth, it shall be broken, and shall enter into his hand,
and shall pierce it. So is Pharaoh, king of Egypt, to all
men that trust in him.
22 That if thou sayest to me, We have trust in the Lord
our God; whether this is not he, whose high things and
altars Hezekiah took away, and commanded to Judah and
to Jerusalem, *saying*, Ye shall worship before this altar in
Jerusalem? (But if thou sayest to me, We have trust in the
Lord our God; is this not he, whose hill shrines and altars
Hezekiah took away, and commanded to Judah and
Jerusalem, *saying*, Ye shall worship only before this altar
in Jerusalem?)
23 Now therefore, give ye pledges to my lord, the king
of Assyrians, and I shall give to you two thousand of
horses, and see ye, whether ye be able to have riders of
them? (And so now, give ye pledges to my lord, the king
of Assyria, and I shall give you two thousand horses, and
see ye, if ye be able to have enough riders for them.)
24 And how may ye withstand before one prince of the
least servants of my lord? Whether thou hast trust in
Egypt, for chariots and knights *thereof*?
25 Whether I ascended without God's will to this place,
that I should destroy it? The Lord said to me, Ascend
thou to this land, and destroy thou it. (Did I come up to
destroy this place outside of God's will? No! The Lord
said to me, Go thou up to this land, and destroy it!)
26 Forsooth Eliakim, the son of Hilkiah, and Shebna,
and Joah, said to Rabshakeh, We pray thee, that thou
speak by the language of Syria to us, thy servants; for we
understand this language; and that thou speak not to us
by the language of Jews, while the people heareth, which
is on the wall. (And Eliakim, the son of Hilkiah, and
Shebna, and Joah, said to Rabshakeh, We pray thee, that
thou speak to us, thy servants, in the Syrian language; for
we understand that language; and that thou do not speak
to us by the language of the Jews, while the people, who
be on the wall, might hear.)
27 And Rabshakeh answered, and said, Whether my
lord sent me to thy lord and to thee, that I should speak
these words, and not rather to the men that sit on the
wall, that they eat their turds, and drink their piss with
you? (And Rabshakeh answered, and said, Did my lord
send me to thy lord and to thee, to speak these words,
and not rather to those who sit on the wall, and who shall
eat their own turds, and drink their own piss, as you
shall?)
28 Therefore Rabshakeh stood, and cried with [a] great
voice by (the) language of (the) Jews, and said, Hear ye
the words of the great king, the king of Assyrians. (And so
Rabshakeh stood, and cried with a great voice in the
language of the Jews, and said, Hear ye the words of the
great king, the king of Assyria.)
29 The king saith these things, Hezekiah deceive not
you (Do not let Hezekiah deceive you), for he may not
deliver you from mine hand;
30 neither give he trust to you on the Lord (nor let him
make you to trust in the Lord), and say, The Lord
delivering shall deliver us, and this city shall not be
betaken in(to) the hand of the king of Assyrians;
31 do not ye hear Hezekiah. For the king of Assyrians
saith these things, Do ye with me that, that is profitable to
you, and go ye out to me; and each man shall eat of his
vinery, and of his fig tree, and ye shall drink waters of
your cisterns, (do not ye listen to Hezekiah. For the king
of Assyria saith these things, Do ye what is profitable for
yourselves with me, and come ye out to me; and then
each person shall eat from his own vineyard, and from
his own fig tree, and ye shall drink water out of your own
wells,)
32 till I come, and translate you, or bear you over, into
a land which is like your land, into a fruitful land, and
plenteous of wine, a land of bread, and of vineries, a land
of olive trees, and of oil, and of honey; and ye shall live,
and ye shall not die. Do not ye hear Hezekiah, that
deceiveth you, and saith, The Lord shall deliver you.
(until I come, and take you away, to a land which is like
your land, to a fruitful land, with plenteous wine, a land
of bread, and vineyards, a land of olive trees, and of oil,
and of honey; and ye shall live, and ye shall not die. Do
not ye listen to Hezekiah, who deceiveth you, and saith,
The Lord shall rescue you.)
33 Whether the gods of heathen men delivered their
land from the hand of the king of Assyrians? (Have the
gods of the heathen delivered their land from the power
of the king of Assyria?)
34 Where is [the] god of Hamath, and of Arpad?
Where is [the] god of Sepharvaim, of Hena, and of Ivah?
Whether they delivered Samaria from mine hand?
35 For who be they in all [the] gods of (the) lands, that
(have) delivered their country from mine hand, that the
Lord may deliver Jerusalem from mine hand? (so how can
even the Lord rescue Jerusalem out of my hands?)
36 Therefore the people was still (But the people were

silent), and answered not anything to him; for they had
taken commandment of the king, that they should not
answer to him.
37 And Eliakim, the son of Hilkiah, the sovereign of the
house, and Shebna, the scribe, and Joah, the chancellor,
the son of Asaph, came with rent clothes to Hezekiah
(came with torn clothes to Hezekiah); and told to him the
words of Rabshakeh.

CHAPTER 19

1 And when king Hezekiah had heard these things, he
rent his clothes, and was covered with a sackcloth; and
he entered into the house of the Lord. (And when King
Hezekiah had heard these things, he tore his clothes, and
was covered with a sackcloth; and he went to the House
of the Lord.)
2 And he sent Eliakim, [the] sovereign of the house,
and Shebna, the scribe, and [the] eld men of the priests,
covered with sackcloths, to Isaiah, the prophet, the son of
Amoz.
3 The which said to him, Hezekiah saith these things,
This day is a day of tribulation, and of blaming, and of
blasphemy; (for the) sons came unto the birth, and the
mother travailing hath not strength *thereto* (for we be like
a woman come to the childbirth, but who hath no
strength to bring forth *her child*).
4 If peradventure thy Lord God hear all the words of
Rabshakeh, whom the king of Assyrians, his lord hath
sent, that he should despise the Lord living, and reprove
by words, which thy Lord God (hath) heard; and (so)
make thou prayer for these remnants *of the people*, that
be found. (Perhaps the Lord thy God hath heard all the
words of Rabshakeh, whom the king of Assyria, his lord,
hath sent, his insulting words towards the living Lord;
and he shall rebuke him for those words, that he, the
Lord thy God, hath heard; so pray thou for these
remnants *of the people*, who be found here.)
5 Therefore the servants of king Hezekiah came to
Isaiah; (And so the servants of King Hezekiah came to
Isaiah;)
6 and Isaiah said to them, Say ye these things to your
lord, The Lord saith these things, Do not thou dread of
the face, *or (the) showing*, of the words, that thou
heardest (Do not thou fear the words which thou hast
heard), by which the servants of the king of Assyrians
blasphemed me.
7 Lo! I shall send to him a spirit, and he shall hear a
messenger, and he shall turn again into his land; and I
shall cast him down by sword in his own land. (Lo! I shall
send a spirit to him, and he shall hear a message, and he
shall return to his own land; and then I shall throw him
down by the sword in his own land.)
8 Therefore Rabshakeh turned again (And so
Rabshakeh returned), and found the king of Assyrians
fighting against Libnah; for he had heard, that *the king*
had gone away from Lachish.
9 And when he had heard of Tirhakah, king of
Ethiopia, men saying, Lo! he went out, that he fight
against thee; that he should go against that *king*, he sent
messengers to Hezekiah, and said, (And when he had
heard men saying of Tirhakah, the king of Ethiopia, Lo!
he went out, so that he could fight against thee; then
before he went out against Tirhakah, he sent messengers
to Hezekiah, and said,)
10 Say ye these things to Hezekiah, king of Judah, Thy
Lord God, in whom thou hast trust, deceive not thee
(deceive thee not), neither say thou, Jerusalem shall not
be betaken into the hands of the king of Assyrians;
11 for thou thyself hast heard what things the kings of
Assyrians have done in all lands, how they have wasted
them; whether therefore thou alone mayest be delivered?
(and so can thou alone escape?)
12 Whether the gods of heathen men delivered all (the)
men which my fathers destroyed, that is, Gozan, and
Haran, and Rezeph, and the sons of Eden, that were in
Thelasar? (who were in Thelasar?)
13 Where is the king of Hamath, and the king of Arpad?
and the king of the city of Sepharvaim, of Hena, and of
Ivah?
14 Therefore when Hezekiah had taken the letters from
the hand of the messengers, and had read them, he went
up into the house of the Lord, and spreaded abroad those
letters before the Lord;
15 and prayed in his sight, and said, Lord God of Israel,
that sittest upon cherubim, thou art (the) God alone of all
kings of [the] earth; thou madest heaven and earth. (and
prayed before him, and said, Lord God of Israel, who
sittest above the cherubim, thou alone art the God of all
the kingdoms of the earth; thou madest heaven and earth.)
16 Bow [down] thine ear, (Lord,) and hear; open thine
eyes, Lord, and see; and hear all the words of
Sennacherib, the which (he) hath sent to us, that he
would despise the living God (yea, his insulting words
toward the living God).
17 Truly, Lord, the kings of Assyrians have destroyed
heathen men, and the lands of all men,
18 and they have sent the gods of them into (the) fire;
for they were not gods, but [the] works of men's hands, of
wood and of stone; and they destroyed them.
19 Now therefore, our Lord God, make us safe from the
hand of them, that all the realms of [the] earth (may)
know that thou art the Lord God alone. (And so now,
Lord our God, make us safe from them, so that all the
kingdoms of the earth can know that thou alone art the
Lord God.)
20 Forsooth Isaiah, the son of Amoz, sent to Hezekiah,
and said, The Lord God of Israel saith these things, I have
heard those things, which thou prayedest (to) me on

Sennacherib, king of Assyrians.
21 This is the word, that the Lord hath spoken of him,
Thou virgin the daughter of Zion, the king *of Assyria* hath
despised thee, and scorned thee; thou daughter of
Jerusalem, he moved his head after thy back. (This is the
word that the Lord hath spoken about him, saying, The
virgin daughter of Zion hath despised thee, and scorned
thee; the daughter of Jerusalem hath moved her head
behind thy back.)
22 *O! Sennacherib,* whom hast thou despised, and
whom hast thou blasphemed? Against whom hast thou
raised thy voice, and hast raised (up) thine eyes on high?
Against the Holy (One) of Israel.
23 By the hand of thy servants thou hast despised the
Lord, and saidest, In the multitude of my chariots I went
up into the high things of (the) hills, in the highness of
Lebanon, and [I] cutted down the high cedars thereof,
and the chosen box trees thereof; and I entered unto the
terms, *or uttermost coasts,* thereof, and I cutted down the
forest of Carmel thereof; (By the words of thy servants
thou hast despised the Lord, and saidest, With the
multitude of my chariots I went up into the high places of
the hills, into the heights of Lebanon, and I cut down its
tall cedars, and its chosen pine trees; and I entered unto
its uttermost coasts, and I cut down the fartherest forest
there;)
24 and I drank alien waters, and I made dry with the
steps of my feet all [the] waters enclosed. (and I drank
foreign waters, and with the steps of my feet I made dry
all the rivers and streams.)
25 Whether thou heardest not, what I made at the
beginning? From eld days I made it, and now I have
brought *it* forth; and strengthened cities of fighters shall
be into (the) falling of hills (and thou shalt bring down
fortified cities into heaps of rubble).
26 And they that sit meek in hand in those *cities,*
trembled together, and be shamed; they be made as the
hay of the field, and as green herb of roofs, which dried,
or withered, before that it came to ripeness. (And they
who sit in those *cities,* be made meek, *or weak,* and
shake and tremble, and be ashamed; they be made like
the hay of the field, and like the green herb of the roofs,
which dried, *or withered,* before that it became ripe.)
27 And I knew thy dwelling [place], and thy going out,
and thine entering/and thy going in, and thy way, and thy
strong vengeance against me. (And I know thy dwelling
place, and thy going out, and thy coming in, and thy
way, and thy strong vengeance against me.)
28 Thou were wroth against me, and thy pride went up
into mine ears; therefore I shall put a ring in thy nostrils,
and a barnacle in thy lips (and a bit between thy lips),
and I shall lead thee again into the way by which thou
camest.
29 Forsooth Hezekiah, this shall be a sign to thee; eat
thou in this year that, that thou findest; forsooth in the
second year, those things that grow by their own will;
soothly in the third year, sow ye, and reap ye, and plant
ye vineries, and eat the fruits of those.
30 And whatever thing shall be residue, *or left over,* of
the house of Judah, it shall send (a) root downward, and
shall make fruit upward.
31 For the relics, *or folk left,* shall go out of Jerusalem,
and those who shall be saved, *shall go out* of the hill of
Zion (For those who be left shall go out from Jerusalem,
and those who shall be saved, *shall go forth* from Mount
Zion); the fervent love of the Lord of hosts shall do this.
32 Wherefore the Lord saith these things of the king of
Assyrians, He shall not enter into this city *(of) Jerusalem,*
neither he shall send an arrow into it, neither shield *of
him* shall occupy it, neither strong hold, *either besieging,*
shall compass it.
33 He shall turn again by the way by which he came,
and he shall not enter into this city, saith the Lord;
34 and I shall defend this city, and I shall save it for
myself, and for David, my servant. (and I shall defend this
city, and I shall save it for my sake, and for the sake of my
servant David.)
35 Therefore it was done, in that night the angel of the
Lord came, and smote in the castles of the Assyrians an
hundred fourscore and five thousand (And so it was done
that night, that the angel of the Lord came, and killed a
hundred and eighty-five thousand men in the tents, *or the
camp,* of the Assyrians). And when *Sennacherib* had
risen early, he saw all the bodies of [the] dead men;
36 and he departed, and went away. And Sennacherib,
king of Assyrians, turned again, and dwelled in Nineveh
(And Sennacherib, the king of Assyria, returned home,
and lived in Nineveh).
37 And when he worshipped in the temple (of) Nisroch
his god, Adrammelech and Sharezer, his sons, killed him
with (the) sword; and (then) they fled into the land of
Armenia; and Esarhaddon, his son, reigned for him.

CHAPTER 20

1 In those days Hezekiah was sick unto the death; and
Isaiah, the prophet, the son of Amoz, came to him, and
said to him, The Lord God saith these things, Command
to thine house, *that is, make thy (last will and)
testament*/Dispose to thine house (Put thy house in
order), for thou shalt die, and thou shalt not live.
2 And Hezekiah turned his face to the wall, and
worshipped the Lord, and said,
3 I beseech, Lord, have mind, how I have gone before
thee in truth, and in a perfect heart, and I did that, that
was pleasant before thee. Then Hezekiah wept with a
great weeping. (I beseech thee, Lord, remember, how I
have gone before thee in truth, and with a perfect heart,
and I did what was pleasing before thee. Then Hezekiah

wept with a great weeping.)
4 And before that Isaiah went out half the part of the
court(yard), the word of the Lord was made to Isaiah, and
said,
5 Turn thou again, and say to Hezekiah, the duke of
my people (Return thou, and say to Hezekiah, the leader,
or the ruler, of my people), The Lord, (the) God of David,
thy father, saith these things, I have heard thy prayer, and
I saw thy tears, and lo! I have healed thee. In the third
day thou shalt go up into the temple of the Lord,
6 and I shall add fifteen years to thy days; but also I
shall deliver thee and this city from the hand of the king
of Assyrians, and I shall defend this city for me, and for
David, my servant (and I shall defend this city for my
sake, and for the sake of my servant David).
7 And Isaiah said, Bring ye to me a gobbet of figs.
And when they had brought it, and had put (it) on his
botch/and had put it on the botch of Hezekiah, he was
healed.
8 And Hezekiah said to Isaiah, What shall be the sign,
that the Lord shall heal me, and *also* that in the third day
I shall go up into the temple of the Lord?
9 To whom Isaiah said, This shall be a sign of the
Lord, that the Lord shall do the word which he spake;
wilt thou, that the shadow (*of the sun*) go further by ten
lines, either turn again by so many degrees? (To whom
Isaiah said, This shall be the sign from the Lord, that the
Lord shall do the thing which he spoke; wilt thou, that
the *sun's* shadow go forward by ten degrees, or turn back
by as many degrees?)
10 And Hezekiah said, It is light, *or easy*, that the
shadow increase by ten lines, neither I will that this be
done, but that it turn again backward by ten degrees.
(And Hezekiah said, It is easy for the shadow to increase
by ten degrees, so I do not desire that this be done, but
rather, that it go backward by ten degrees.)
11 Then Isaiah, the prophet, called inwardly (upon) the
Lord, and brought again backward by ten degrees the
shadow by *the same* lines, by which it had gone down
then in the horologe of Ahaz. (Then the prophet Isaiah
inwardly called to the Lord, and brought the shadow
backward by ten degrees, by the same lines by which it
had gone forward on Ahaz's sundial.)
12 In that time, Berodach-baladan, the son of Baladan,
the king of Babylon, sent letters and gifts to Hezekiah; for
he had heard that Hezekiah had been sick, and had
recovered. (Now at that time, Berodach-baladan, the son
of Baladan, the king of Babylon, sent letters and gifts to
Hezekiah; for he had heard that Hezekiah had been sick.)
13 And Hezekiah was glad in the coming of them (And
Hezekiah welcomed the messengers), and he showed to
them the house of spiceries, and (the) gold, and silver,
and diverse pigments, (and) also (the) ointments, and the
house of his vessels, and all (the) things that he might
have in his treasures; there was not any word, *or thing*, in
his house, and in all his power, that Hezekiah showed
not to them.
14 Soothly Isaiah, the prophet, came to king Hezekiah,
and said to him, What said these men, either from
whence came they to thee? To whom Hezekiah said,
They came to me from a far land, from Babylon. (And the
prophet Isaiah came to King Hezekiah, and said to him,
What did these men say to thee, and from where did they
come? To whom Hezekiah said, They came to me from a
far land, from Babylon.)
15 And he answered, What have they seen in thine
house? Hezekiah said, They have seen all things,
whatever things be in mine house; nothing is in my
treasures, which I showed not to them. (And Isaiah asked,
What have they seen in thy house? And Hezekiah said,
They have seen everything that is in my house; there is
nothing among my treasures, which I have not shown
them.)
16 Therefore Isaiah said to Hezekiah, Hear thou the
word of the Lord.
17 Lo! days (shall) come, and all things that be in thine
house, and which things thy fathers made till into this
day, shall be taken away into Babylon; not anything shall
(still) dwell, saith the Lord (nothing shall be left, saith the
Lord).
18 But also of thy sons, that shall go out of thee, which
thou shalt beget, shall be taken [away], and they shall be
geldings in the palace of the king of Babylon (and they
shall be eunuchs in the palace of the king of Babylon).
19 And Hezekiah said to Isaiah, The word of the Lord,
which he spake, is good; only peace and truth be in my
days. (And Hezekiah said to Isaiah, The word of the Lord,
which thou spoke, is good; let there be only peace and
truth in my days.)
20 Forsooth the residue of [the] words of Hezekiah, and
all his strength, and how he made a cistern, and a water
conduit, and brought water into the city, whether these
be not written in the book of [the] words of [the] days of
the kings of Judah?
21 And Hezekiah slept with his fathers, and Manasseh,
his son, reigned for him.

CHAPTER 21

1 Manasseh was of twelve years, when he began to
reign, and he reigned five and fifty years in Jerusalem; the
name of his mother was Hephzibah.
2 And he did evil in the sight of the Lord, after the
evils of heathen men, the which men the Lord did away
from the face of the sons of Israel.
3 And he was turned, and builded [up] (again the)
high things, which Hezekiah, his father (had) destroyed;
and he raised up altars of Baal, and he made maumet
woods, as Ahab, king of Israel, had done; and he

worshipped withoutforth all the knighthood of (the)
heaven(s), and worshipped it *in heart*. (And he rebuilt the
hill shrines, which his father Hezekiah had destroyed;
and he raised up altars for Baal, and he made idol groves,
or a sacred pole, like Ahab, the king of Israel, had done;
and he worshipped withoutforth all the host of heaven,
and also worshipped them *with his heart*.)
4 And he builded altars in the house of the Lord, of
which the Lord said, I shall set my name in Jerusalem.
(And he built altars in the House of the Lord, of which
the Lord had said, I shall set my name in Jerusalem *there*.)
5 And he builded altars to all the knighthood of (the)
heaven(s) in the two large places of the temple of the
Lord; (And he built altars for all the host of heaven in the
two large courtyards of the Temple of the Lord;)
6 and he led over his son through the fire; and he
used false divinings in altars, on which sacrifice was
made to fiends, and he kept false divinings by chittering
of birds; and he made men to have evil spirits speaking in
the womb, and he multiplied false diviners in entrails of
beasts sacrificed to fiends, that he should do evil before
the Lord, and stir him to ire. (and he burned, *or
sacrificed*, his own son in the fire; and he practiced false
divinings at altars on which sacrifice was made to fiends,
and he did false divinings by the twittering of birds; and
he made men to have evil spirits speaking in their
wombs, and he increased *the number of* false diviners of
the entrails of beasts sacrificed to fiends, and he did evil
before the Lord, and stirred him to anger.)
7 And he set an idol of wood, that he had made, in
the temple of the Lord, of which *temple* the Lord spake to
David, and to Solomon, his son, *saying*, I shall set my
name without end in this temple, and in Jerusalem,
which I chose (out) of all the lineages of Israel. (And he
set up a wooden idol, that he had made, in the Temple of
the Lord, of which *Temple* the Lord spoke to David, and
to his son Solomon, *saying*, I shall set my name without
end in this Temple, and in Jerusalem, which I chose out
of all the tribes of Israel.)
8 And I shall no more make the foot of Israel to be
moved from the land which I gave to the fathers of them;
so nevertheless if they keep in work all things that I have
commanded to them, and all the law that Moses, my
servant, commanded to them.
9 Soothly they heard not, but were deceived of
Manasseh, that they did evil over heathen men, which
the Lord all-brake from the face of the sons of Israel. (But
they would not listen, and were deceived by Manasseh,
and they did more evil than the heathen, whom the Lord
had destroyed before the Israelites.)
10 And the Lord spake in the hand of his servants (the)
prophets, and said, (And the Lord spoke by his servants
the prophets, and said,)
11 For Manasseh, king of Judah, did these worst
abominations over all things which (the) Amorites did
before him, and made also the people of Judah to do sin
in his uncleannesses (and also made the people of Judah
to do sin with his idols);
12 therefore the Lord God of Israel saith these things,
Lo! I shall bring in evils upon Jerusalem and Judah, that
whoever heareth (of it), both his ears [shall] tingle, *or
ring*;
13 and I shall hold forth upon Jerusalem the cord of
Samaria, and the burden of the house of Ahab, and I shall
do away Jerusalem, as tables be wont to be done away;
and I shall do (it) away and overturn *it*, and I shall lead
full oft a pointel upon the face thereof. (and I shall hold
forth upon Jerusalem the cord of Samaria, and the
plummet, *or the plumb-line*, of the house of Ahab; and I
shall wipe Jerusalem clean like dishes be wont to be
wiped clean, and turned upside-down; and I shall do it
away and overturn *it*, and I shall scratch a stylus over its
face.)
14 Forsooth I shall leave [the] remnants of mine
heritage, and I shall betake them into the hand of
enemies thereof; and they shall be in destroying, and in
raven to all their adversaries; (And I shall abandon the
remnants of my inheritance, and I shall deliver them into
the hands of their enemies; and they shall be destroyed,
and become spoils for all their adversaries;)
15 for they did evil before me, and they continued in
stirring me to ire, from the day in which their fathers
went out of the land of Egypt, unto this day.
16 Furthermore also Manasseh shedded full much
innocent blood, till he filled Jerusalem unto the mouth,
without his sins by which he made Judah to do sin, to do
evil before the Lord. (And furthermore Manasseh shed a
great deal of innocent blood, until he had filled Jerusalem
up to the mouth, and this is besides his sins by which he
made Judah to do sin, yea, to do evil before the Lord.)
17 Forsooth the residue of the words of Manasseh, and
all things that he did, and his sin that he sinned, whether
these be not written in the book of [the] words of [the]
days of the kings of Judah?
18 And Manasseh slept with his fathers, and was buried
in the garden of his house, in the garden of Uzza; and
Amon, his son, reigned for him.
19 Amon was of two and twenty years, when he began
to reign; and he reigned two years in Jerusalem; the name
of his mother was Meshullemeth, the daughter of Haruz
of Jotbah.
20 And he did evil in the sight of the Lord, as Manasseh,
his father, had done.
21 And he went in all the way, by which his father had
gone, and he served to [the] uncleannesses, *that is, (the)
idols*, to which his father had served, and he worshipped
those;
22 and he forsook the Lord God of his fathers, and he

went not in the way of the Lord.
23 And his servants setted treasons to him, and killed
the king in his house. (And his servants set treason
against him, and killed the king in his own house.)
24 Soothly the people of the Lord smote all the men,
that had conspired against king Amon, and they ordained
to them a king, Josiah, his son, for him. (And the people
of the Lord struck down all those who had conspired
against King Amon, and they ordained for themselves
Josiah, Amon's son, to be king in his place.)
25 Forsooth the residue of [the] words of Amon, (and all
the things) which he did, whether these be not written in
the book of [the] words of [the] days of the kings of Judah?
26 And he slept with his fathers, and they buried him in
the sepulchre in the garden of Uzza; and Josiah, his son,
reigned for him.

CHAPTER 22

1 Josiah was of eight years, when he began to reign,
and he reigned one and thirty years in Jerusalem; the
name of his mother *was* Jedidah, the daughter of Adaiah
of Boscath.
2 And he did that, that was pleasant before the Lord,
and he went by all the ways of David, his father; he
bowed not, neither to the right side, nor of the left side.
(And he did what was pleasing before the Lord, and he
went in all the ways of his forefather David; he turned
not, neither to the right, nor to the left.)
3 Forsooth in the eighteenth year of king Josiah, the
king sent Shaphan, the son of Azaliah, the son of
Meshullam, [the] scribe, *either doctor*, of the temple of
the Lord (to the Temple of the Lord), and said to him,
4 Go thou to Hilkiah, the great priest, (and command)
that the money, which is borne into the temple of the
Lord, be molten together, which *money* the porters of the
temple have gathered of the people; (Go thou to the High
Priest Hilkiah, and command that the money, which is
brought into the Temple of the Lord, be melted down,
which *money* the guards, *or the door-keepers*, of the
Temple have gathered from the people;)
5 and that it be given to craftsmen by the sovereigns of
the house of the Lord; which also parted that money to
them that work in the temple of the Lord, to repair the
roofs of the temple of the Lord, (and that it be given to
the craftsmen by the foremen of the House of the Lord;
and they deal out that money to those who work in the
Temple of the Lord, to make the needed repairs to the
Temple of the Lord,)
6 that is, to carpenters, and to masons, and to them
that make [together] broken things (and to those who put
together broken things), and (also) that timber and stones
of quarriers be bought, to repair the temple of the Lord;
7 nevertheless the silver, which they take/that the
workmen take, be not reckoned to them, but have they it
in (their own) power, and in faith (but trust them to have
it under their own power, *or control*).
8 And Hilkiah, the bishop, said to Shaphan, the scribe,
I have found the book of the law in the house of the Lord.
And Hilkiah gave the book to Shaphan, the scribe, which
also read it. (And the High Priest Hilkiah said to Shaphan,
the writer, I have found The Book of the Law in the
House of the Lord. And Hilkiah gave the book to
Shaphan, the writer, and he read it.)
9 Also Shaphan, the scribe, came to the king, and told
to him those things, which Hilkiah had commanded, and
he said, Thy servants have spended the money, that was
found in the house of the Lord, and they have given, that
it should be parted to [the] craftsmen of the sovereigns of
[the] works of the temple of the Lord. (And Shaphan, the
writer, came to the king, and reported to the king about
those things which he had commanded, and he said, Thy
servants have spent the money that was found in the
House of the Lord, and they have ordained that it be
dealt out to the craftsmen by the foremen of the repairs to
the Temple of the Lord.)
10 Also Shaphan, the scribe, told to the king, and said,
Hilkiah, the priest of God, hath given to me a book; and
when Shaphan had read that book before the king,
11 and the king had heard the words of the book of the
law of the Lord, he rent his clothes. (and the king had
heard the words of The Book of the Law of the Lord, he
tore his clothes.)
12 And he commanded to Hilkiah, the priest, and to
Ahikam, the son of Shaphan, and to Achbor, the son of
Michaiah, and to Shaphan the scribe, and to Asahiah, (a)
servant of the king, and said,
13 Go ye, and ask, *or counsel ye*, the Lord on me, and
on the people, and on all Judah, of the words of this
book, that is found; for (the) great ire of the Lord is
kindled against us, for our fathers heard not the words of
this book, to do all thing which is written to us. (Go ye,
and ask ye the Lord's counsel for me, and for the people,
and for all Judah, about the words of this book, that is
found; for great is the Lord's anger that is kindled against
us, for our forefathers did not listen to the words of this
book, to do all the things which be written to us.)
14 Therefore Hilkiah, the priest, and Ahikam, and
Achbor, and Shaphan, and Asahiah, went to Huldah, the
prophetess, the wife of Shallum, the son of Tikvah, the
son of Harhas, keeper of the clothes, the which *Huldah*
dwelled in Jerusalem, in the second *dwelling*/in the
second environing of the wall (in the second quarter);
and they spake to her.
15 And she answered to them, The Lord God of Israel
saith these things, Say ye to the man, that sent you to me,
16 The Lord God of Israel saith these things, Lo! I shall
bring evils upon this place, and upon the dwellers thereof
(and upon its inhabitants), *and I shall fulfill* all the words

[of the law], which the king of Judah read;
17 for they forsook me, and made sacrifice to alien
gods, and stirred me to ire in all the works of their hands;
and mine indignation shall be kindled in this place, and
shall not be quenched. (for they deserted me, and made
sacrifice to foreign, *or other*, gods, and stirred me to
anger with all the works of their hands; and my
indignation shall be kindled against this place, and it
shall not be quenched.)
18 Soothly to the king of Judah, that sent you, that ye
shall counsel (with) the Lord/that ye shall ask the Lord('s)
counsel, ye shall say thus, The Lord God of Israel saith
these things, For thou heardest the words of the book,
19 and thine heart was afeared, and thou were made
meek before the Lord, when *his* words were heard
against this place, and against the dwellers thereof, that
is, that they should be made into wondering, and into
cursing, and thou rentest thy clothes, and weptest before
me, and I heard, saith the Lord; (and that thy heart was
afraid, and thou were humbled before the Lord, when *his*
words were heard against this place, and against its
inhabitants, that is, that they should be made into
wondering, and into cursing, and that thou torest thy
clothes, and weptest before me, and for thou hath done
all these things, I have heard thee, saith the Lord;)
20 therefore I shall gather thee to thy fathers, and thou
shalt be gathered to thy sepulchre in peace; (so) that thine
eyes see not all the evils, which I shall bring in upon this
place. And they told to the king that, that she said (And
they told the king what she said);

CHAPTER 23

1 which king sent, and all the eld men of Judah, and
of Jerusalem, were gathered to him. (and the king sent for
all the elders of Judah, and of Jerusalem, and they were
gathered unto him.)
2 And the king went up into the temple of the Lord,
and all the men of Judah, and all the men that dwelled in
Jerusalem with him, the priests and the prophets, and all
the people from little unto great; and the king read, while
all men heard, all the words of the book of [the] bond of
peace of the Lord, the which was found in the house of
the Lord. (And the king went up into the Temple of the
Lord, and all the men of Judah, and all the men who
lived in Jerusalem with him, the priests and the prophets,
and all the people from the little unto the great; and the
king read, while all the men listened, all the words of The
Book of the Covenant of the Lord, which had been found
in the House of the Lord.)
3 And the king stood on the degrees; and smote a
bond of peace before the Lord, that they would go after
the Lord, and keep his commandments and witnessings
and ceremonies in all their heart and in all their soul, and
that they should raise up the words of this bond of peace,
that were written in that book; and the people assented to
the covenant. (And the king stood on the steps; and
struck a covenant before the Lord, that they would follow
the Lord, and keep his commandments and testimonies
and statutes, with all their heart and with all their soul,
and that they would raise up the words of this covenant
that were written in that book; and the people agreed to
the covenant.)
4 And the king commanded to Hilkiah, the bishop,
and to the priests of the second order, and to the porters,
that they should cast out of the temple [of the Lord] all
the vessels, that were made to Baal, and in the maumet
wood, and to all the knighthood of (the) heaven(s); and
he burnt those *vessels* without Jerusalem, in the even
valley of Kidron, and he bare the powder of those *vessels*
into Bethel. (And the king commanded to the High Priest
Hilkiah, and to the priests of the second order, and to the
guards, that they should throw out of the Temple of the
Lord all the vessels that were made for Baal, and for
Asherah, and for all the host of heaven; and he burned
those *vessels* outside Jerusalem, in the Kidron Valley, and
he brought the powder of those *vessels* to Bethel.)
5 And he did away [the] false diviners, which the
kings of Judah had set to make sacrifice in (the) high
things by the cities of Judah, and in the compass of
Jerusalem; and *he did away* them that burnt incense to
Baal, and to the sun, and to the moon, and to (the) twelve
signs, and to all the knighthood of (the) heaven(s). (And
he did away the false diviners, whom the kings of Judah
had ordained to make sacrifice in the hill shrines in the
cities of Judah, and all around Jerusalem; and *he did
away* those who burned incense to Baal, and to the sun,
and to the moon, and to the twelve signs, yea, to all the
host of heaven.)
6 And the king made the wood *of maumetry* to be
borne out of the house of the Lord, without Jerusalem,
in(to) the even valley of Kidron, and he burnt it there; and
he drove *it* into powder, and casted *it* forth upon the
sepulchres of the common people. (And the king ordered
the sacred pole of *that idol, or that false god,* Asherah to
be taken out of the House of the Lord, and out of
Jerusalem, to the Kidron Valley, and he burned it there;
and he drove *it* down into powder, and threw *it* forth
onto the tombs, *or the graves,* of the common people.)
7 Also he destroyed the little houses of [the]
womanish men, the which houses were in the house of
the Lord; for the which *houses* women weaved, *or
wattled,* as little houses of the wood. (And he destroyed
the little houses of the male whores *of the Temple,* which
houses were attached to the House of the Lord; and
where women weaved, *or wattled,* vestments used in
honouring and worshipping Asherah.)
8 And he gathered all the priests from the cities of
Judah, and he defouled the high things, where the priests

made sacrifice, from Geba unto Beersheba; and he
destroyed the altars of the gates (that were) in the entering
of the door of Joshua, (who was the) prince of a city,
which door was at the left half of the gate of the city.
(And he gathered all the priests from the cities of Judah,
and he defiled the hill shrines, where the priests made
sacrifice, from Geba unto Beersheba; and he destroyed
the altars of the demons that were at the entrance of the
gate of Joshua, who was the ruler of the city, which gate
was on the left side of the city gate.)
9 Nevertheless the priests of [the] high things went not
up to the altar of the Lord in Jerusalem, but only they ate
therf loaves in the midst of their brethren. (Now the
priests of the hill shrines did not go up to the altar of the
Lord in Jerusalem, but they did eat the unleavened bread
in the midst of their kinsmen.)
10 Also he defouled Topheth, which is in the even
valley of the son of Hinnom, (so) that no man should
hallow his son either his daughter by fire to Moloch.
(And he defiled Topheth, which is in the Valley of Ben-hinnom, so that no man would sacrifice his son or his
daughter in the fire to Moloch.)
11 Also he did away [the] horses, that the kings of
Judah had given to the sun, in the entering of the temple
of the Lord, beside the chamber of Nathanmelech, the
gelding, that was in (the) Parvarim, (*that is, the suburbs,
or the living quarters*); forsooth he burnt by fire the
chariots of the sun. (And he did away the horses, that the
kings of Judah had erected to the sun, at the entrance to
the Temple of the Lord, beside the chamber of
Nathanmelech, the eunuch, that was in the Parvarim, *that
is, in the suburbs, or the living quarters*; and he burned
up the chariots of the sun.)
12 Also the king destroyed the altars, that were on the
roofs of the solar of Ahaz, which the kings of Judah had
made; and *the king destroyed* the altars, which Manasseh
had made in the two great places of the temple of the
Lord; and he ran from thence, and scattered the ashes of
those *altars* into the strand of Kidron. (And the king
destroyed the altars that were on the roof of the solarium
of Ahaz, which the kings of Judah had made; and *the
king destroyed* the altars which Manasseh had made in
the two great courtyards of the Temple of the Lord; and
he went from there, and scattered the ashes of those
altars in the Kidron Valley.)
13 Also the king defouled the high things, that were in
Jerusalem at the right half of the hill of offence, *that is,
the hill of Olivet*, which Solomon, king of Israel, had
builded to Ashtoreth, the idol of Sidonians, and to
Chemosh, the offence of Moab, and to Malcham, the
abomination of the sons of Ammon; (And the king defiled
the hill shrines that were east of Jerusalem, on the right
side of the hill of offence, *that is, south of the Mount of
Olives*, which Solomon, the king of Israel, had built for
Ashtoreth, the false god of the Sidonians, and for
Chemosh, the offensive god of Moab, and for Milcom,
the abominable god of the Ammonites;)
14 and he all-brake [the] images, and cutted down (the)
[maumet] woods (and cut down the sacred poles of
Asherah), and filled the places of those with the bones of
dead men.
15 Furthermore also *he destroyed* the altar that was in
Bethel, and the high *solemn* thing, which Jeroboam, the
son of Nebat, had made, that made Israel to do sin; and
he destroyed that high altar, and burnt *it*, and all-brake *it*
into powder, and cutted down also the [maumet] wood.
(And furthermore *he destroyed* the altar that was in
Bethel, and the hill shrine, which Jeroboam, the son of
Nebat, had made, who had made Israel to do sin; and he
destroyed that high altar, and burned *it*, and broke *it* all
into powder, and also cut down the sacred pole of
Asherah.)
16 And Josiah turned, and saw there sepulchres that
were in the hill; and he sent, and took the bones from the
sepulchres, and burnt those on the altar, and defouled it,
after the word of the Lord, that the man of God spake,
that before-said these words. (And Josiah turned, and saw
the tombs, *or the graves*, that were there on the hill; and
he sent for, and took all the bones from those tombs, *or
those graves*, and burned them on the altar, and defiled
it, after the word of the Lord, that the man of God spoke,
who foretold these things.)
17 And *the king* said, What is this burial, that I see?
[Whose is this tomb that I see?] And the citizens of that city
answered to him, It is the sepulchre of the man of God,
that came from Judah, and before-said these words (and
foretold these things), which thou hast done upon the
altar of Bethel.
18 And *the king* said, Suffer ye him (Do not ye touch
him); no man move his bones. And (*so*) his bones
dwelled untouched with the bones of the prophet, that
came from Samaria.
19 Furthermore also Josiah did away all the temples of
[the] high things, that were in the cities of Samaria, which
the kings of Israel had made to stir the Lord to ire; and he
did to those *temples* by all things which he had done in
Bethel. (And furthermore Josiah did away all the temples
of the hill shrines that were in the cities of Samaria,
which the kings of Israel had built, and had so stirred the
Lord to anger; and he did to those *temples* all the things
which he had done to the temples in Bethel.)
20 And he killed all the priests of [the] high things, that
were there upon the altars, and he burnt men's bones on
those *altars*; and he turned again to Jerusalem; (And he
killed all the priests of the hill shrines, who were there at
the altars, and he burned the bones of people upon those
altars; and then he returned to Jerusalem;)
21 and he commanded to all the people, and said,

Make ye pask to the Lord your God, after that, that is
written in the book of this bond of peace. (and he
commanded to all the people, and said, Keep ye the
Passover to the Lord your God, after what is written in
this Book of the Covenant.)
22 Certainly such a pask was not made, from the days
of judges that deemed Israel, and of all the days of the
kings of Israel, and of Judah, (Certainly such a Passover
was not kept, from the days of the judges who judged
Israel, nor in all the days of the kings of Israel, or of
Judah,)
23 as this pask (that) was made to the Lord in Jerusalem
in the eighteenth year of king Josiah.
24 But also Josiah did away men having fiends
speaking in their wombs, and false diviners in altars, and
he did away the figures of idols, and *all* [the]
uncleannesses, and [the] abominations, that were in the
land of Judah and in Jerusalem, that he should do the
words of the law, that were written in the book, that
Hilkiah, the priest, found in the temple of the Lord. (And
Josiah also did away men having fiends speaking in their
wombs, and false diviners at altars, and the figures of
idols, and *all* the uncleannesses, and the abominations,
that were in the land of Judah and in Jerusalem, so that
he would do all the words of the Law, that were written
in the book that the High Priest Hilkiah had found in the
Temple of the Lord.)
25 No king before him was like him, that turned again
to the Lord in all his heart, and in all his soul, and in all
his strength, after all the law of Moses; neither after him
rose (up) any like him. (There was no king like him
before him, who had turned again to the Lord with all his
heart, and with all his soul, and with all his strength, after
all the Law of Moses; nor did there rise up any king like
him after him.)
26 Nevertheless the Lord was not turned away from the
ire of his great vengeance, by which his strong vengeance
was wroth against Judah, for the stirrings to ire by which
Manasseh had stirred him to ire.
27 Therefore the Lord said, I shall do away also Judah
from my face, as I did away Israel; and I shall cast away
this city Jerusalem, which I chose, and the house of
which I said, My name shall be there. (And so the Lord
said, I shall also do away Judah from before me, as I did
away Israel; and I shall throw away this city of Jerusalem,
which I chose, and the House of which I said, My name
shall *always* be there.)
28 Forsooth the residue of the words of Josiah, and all
things that he did, whether these be not written in the
book of [the] words of [the] days of the kings of Judah?
29 In the days of Josiah, Pharaoh Necho, the king of
Egypt, went up against the king of Assyrians, to the flood
Euphrates; and Josiah, king of Judah, went into the
meeting of Pharaoh, *to forbid him to pass through Judah*;
and *Josiah* was slain in Megiddo, when he had seen
Pharaoh. (In the days of Josiah, Pharaoh Necho, the king
of Egypt, went up to the Euphrates River to help the king
of Assyria; and Josiah, the king of Judah, went out against
Pharaoh, *to forbid him to pass through Judah*; and *Josiah*
was killed at Megiddo, when he met Pharaoh in battle.)
30 And his servants bare him dead from Megiddo, and
brought him into Jerusalem, and buried him in his
sepulchre; and the people of the land took Jehoahaz[31],
the son of Josiah, and anointed him, and made him king
for his father (and made him king in place of his father).
31 Jehoahaz was of three and twenty years, when he
began to reign, and he reigned three months in
Jerusalem; the name of his mother *was* Hamutal, the
daughter of Jeremy of Libnah.
32 And he did evil before the Lord, by all things which
his fathers had done.
33 And Pharaoh Necho bound him *in prison* in Riblah,
that is in the land of Hamath, that he should not reign in
Jerusalem; and Pharaoh set a pain, *either a fine*, to the
land *of Judah*, in an hundred talents of silver, and in one
talent of gold (and Pharaoh put a fine on the land *of
Judah*, of a hundred talents of silver, and a talent of gold).
34 And Pharaoh Necho made king Eliakim, the son of
Josiah, for Josiah, his father; and he turned the name of
him to Jehoiakim; forsooth *Pharaoh* took Jehoahaz, and
led *him* into Egypt, (and he died there). (And Pharaoh
Necho made Eliakim, Josiah's son, to be king in place of
his father; and he changed his name to Jehoiakim; but
Pharaoh took away Jehoahaz, and led *him* into Egypt,
and he died there.)
35 Soothly Jehoiakim gave silver and gold to Pharaoh,
when he had commanded to the land by all years, that it
should be brought, by the commandment of Pharaoh;
and Jehoiakim raised of each man by his mights, or after
his power, both silver and gold, of the people of the land,
that he should give to Pharaoh Necho. (And Jehoiakim
paid the silver and gold to Pharaoh, in all the years that
he commanded over the land, that it should be brought
in, by Pharaoh's commandment; and Jehoiakim raised
both the silver, and the gold, from the people of the land,
yea, out of each man's own wealth, so that he could pay
it to Pharaoh Necho.)
36 Jehoiakim was of five and twenty years, when he
began to reign, and he reigned eleven years in Jerusalem;
the name of his mother *was* Zebudah, the daughter of
Pedaiah of Rumah.
37 And he did evil before the Lord, by all things which
his fathers had done.

CHAPTER 24

1 In the days of Jehoiakim, Nebuchadnezzar, king of

[31] Also known as Joahaz.

Babylon, went up *into Judah*, and Jehoiakim was made
(a) servant to him by three years; and again Jehoiakim
rebelled against him. (Now in the days of Jehoiakim,
Nebuchadnezzar, the king of Babylon, went up *into
Judah*, and Jehoiakim was made his servant for three
years; and then Jehoiakim rebelled against him.)
2 And the Lord sent to him thieves of Chaldees, and
thieves of Syria, and thieves of Moab, and thieves of the
sons of Ammon; and he sent them into Judah, that he
should destroy it, by the word of the Lord, which he
spake by his servants (the) prophets. (And the Lord sent
against him thieves of the Chaldeans, and thieves from
Syria, and from Moab, and of the Ammonites; and he
sent them into Judah to destroy it, by the word of the
Lord, which he spoke by his servants the prophets.)
3 Forsooth this was done by the word of the Lord
against Judah, that he should do away it (from) before
himself, for the sins of Manasseh, and all things which he
did, (This was done by the word of the Lord against the
people of Judah, so that he would do them away from his
sight, for the sins of Manasseh, and all the things which
he did,)
4 and for the guiltless blood that he shed out; and he
filled Jerusalem with the blood of innocents; and for this
thing the Lord would not do mercy.
5 Forsooth the residue of [the] words of Jehoiakim,
and all things which he did, whether these be not written
in the book of [the] words of (the) days of the kings of
Judah?
6 And Jehoiakim slept with his fathers, and Jehoiachin,
his son, reigned for him.
7 And the king of Egypt added no more to go out of
his land; for the king of Babylon had taken all things that
were the king's of Egypt, from the strand of Egypt unto
the flood Euphrates (from the River of Egypt unto the
Euphrates River).
8 Jehoiachin was of eighteen years, when he began to
reign, and he reigned three months in Jerusalem; the
name of his mother *was* Nehushta, the daughter of
Elnathan of Jerusalem.
9 And he did evil before the Lord, by all things that his
father had done.
10 In that time the servants of Nebuchadnezzar, king of
Babylon, went up against Jerusalem, and the city was
compassed with besiegings.
11 And Nebuchadnezzar, king of Babylon, came to the
city with his servants, that he should fight against it (so
that he could fight against it).
12 And Jehoiachin, king of Judah, went out to the king
of Babylon, he, and his mother, and his servants, and his
princes, and his chamberlains; and the king of Babylon
received him, in the eighth year of his realm (and the
king of Babylon took him prisoner in the eighth year of
his reign).
13 And he brought forth from thence all the treasures of
the house of the Lord, and the treasures of the king's
house; and he beat together all the golden vessels, which
Solomon, king of Israel, had made in the temple of the
Lord, by the word of the Lord. (And he brought back from
there all the treasures from the House of the Lord, and
the treasures from the king's palace; and he broke up all
the gold vessels, which Solomon, the king of Israel, had
made for the Temple of the Lord, by the word of the
Lord.)
14 And he translated all Jerusalem, and all the princes,
and all the strong men of the host, ten thousand, into
captivity, and each craftsman, and goldsmith; and
nothing was left, except the poor people/s of the land.
(And he carried away all the people of Jerusalem, and all
the leaders, and all the strong men of the army, ten
thousand altogether, into captivity, and also each
craftsman, and each goldsmith; and no one was left,
except the poor people of the land.)
15 Also he translated Jehoiachin into Babylon, and the
mother of the king, the wives of the king, and the
chamberlains of the king; and he led the judges of the
land into captivity from Jerusalem into Babylon; (And he
carried away Jehoiachin to Babylon, and the king's
mother, and the king's wives, and the king's
chamberlains; and he led away the judges of the land
from Jerusalem into captivity in Babylon;)
16 and all the strong men, seven thousand; and
craftsmen and goldsmiths, a thousand; yea, all (of the)
strong men and warriors; and the king of Babylon led
them (away as) prisoners into Babylon.
17 And he ordained Mattaniah, the brother of his
father, (that is, Jehoiachin's uncle,) (to reign) for him; and
putted to him the name Zedekiah. (And he ordained
Mattaniah, the brother of Jehoiachin's father, to be king
in place of him; and he changed his name to Zedekiah.)
18 Zedekiah had one and twenty years of age, when he
began to reign, and he reigned eleven years in Jerusalem;
the name of his mother was Hamutal, the daughter of
Jeremy of Libnah. (Zedekiah was twenty-one years old,
when he began to reign, and he reigned for eleven years
in Jerusalem; the name of his mother was Hamutal, the
daughter of Jeremiah of Libnah.)
19 And he did evil before the Lord, by all things that
Jehoiakim had done.
20 For the Lord was wroth against Jerusalem, and
against Judah, till he casted them away from his face; and
Zedekiah went away from the king of Babylon. (And
because of that, the Lord was so angry against Jerusalem,
and Judah, that he threw them away from his face; and
then Zedekiah rebelled against the king of Babylon.)

CHAPTER 25

1 Forsooth it was done in the ninth year of his realm,

in the tenth month, in the tenth day of the month,
Nebuchadnezzar, king of Babylon, came, he, and all his
host, into Jerusalem; and they compassed it, and builded
strongholds in the compass thereof. (And it was done in
the ninth year of his reign, in the tenth month, on the
tenth day of the month, Nebuchadnezzar, the king of
Babylon, came, he, and all his army, into Jerusalem; and
they encompassed, *or surrounded*, it, and built
strongholds all around it.)
2 And the city was closed, and compassed, till to the
eleventh year of king Zedekiah, (And the city was
enclosed, and encompassed, *or surrounded*, until the
eleventh year of King Zedekiah.)
3 in the ninth day of the month; and hunger had
mastery in the city, and there was not bread to the people
of the land. (And on the ninth day of the month, famine
had the mastery in the city, and there was no food for the
people of the land.)
4 And the city was broken (into), and all (the) men
warriors fled in the night by the way of the gate, that is
betwixt the double wall, toward the garden of the king;
soothly the Chaldees besieged the city in compass/about.
Therefore Zedekiah fled by the way that leadeth to the
field places of the wilderness;
5 and the host of Chaldees pursued the king, and took
him in the plain of Jericho; and all the warriors, that were
with him, were scattered abroad, and left him. (and the
Chaldean army pursued the king, and overtook him/and
took hold of him on the plains of Jericho; and all the
warriors, who were with him, scattered everywhere, and
left him all alone.)
6 Therefore they led the king taken to the king of
Babylon, into Riblah, which spake doom with him, *that
is, with Zedekiah.* (And so they captured the king, and
led him to the king of Babylon, at Riblah, who spoke
judgement upon him, *that is, upon Zedekiah.*)
7 Soothly he killed the sons of Zedekiah before him,
and putted out his eyes, and bound him with chains, and
led *him* into Babylon.
8 In the fifth month, in the seventh day of the month,
that is the nineteenth year of (Nebuchadnezzar,) the king
of Babylon, Nebuzaradan, prince of the host, [the]
servant of the king of Babylon, came into Jerusalem; (In
the fifth month, on the seventh day of the month, that is
the nineteenth year of Nebuchadnezzar, the king of
Babylon, Nebuzaradan, the leader of the army/the
captain of the guard, the servant of the king of Babylon,
came into Jerusalem;)
9 and he burnt the house of the Lord, and the house of
the king, and the houses of Jerusalem, and he burnt by
fire each house *thereof*; (and he burned down the House
of the Lord, and the house of the king, and the houses of
Jerusalem, yea, he burned down every house *there*;)
10 and all the host of Chaldees, that was with the
prince of knights, destroyed the walls of Jerusalem in
compass. (and all the army of the Chaldeans, that was
with the leader of the horsemen, *or of the army*,
destroyed the walls of Jerusalem all around.)
11 Forsooth Nebuzaradan, prince of the chivalry,
translated the tother part of the people, that dwelled in
the city, and the fleers, that had fled over to the king of
Babylon, and the remnant common people; (And
Nebuzaradan, the leader of the cavalry, *or of the
army*/the captain of the guard, carried away the other part
of the people, who lived in the city, and the fleers, who
had fled over to the king of Babylon, and the remnant of
the common people;)
12 and he left of the poor men of the land vine-tillers,
and earth-tillers. (but he left of the poor people of the
land the vine-tillers, and the earth-tillers.)
13 Soothly Chaldees brake the brazen pillars, that were
in the temple, and the foundaments, and the sea of brass,
that was in the house of the Lord; and they translated, or
bare over, all the metal into Babylon. (And the Chaldeans
broke up the bronze pillars, that were in the Temple, and
their bases, and the Sea of bronze, that was in the House
of the Lord; and they carried away all the bronze to
Babylon.)
14 And they took the pots of brass, and trowels, and
fleshhooks, and cups, and mortars, and all [the] brazen
vessels, in which they ministered; (And they took away
the bronze pots, and the trowels, and fleshhooks, and
cups, and spoons, and all the other bronze vessels, with
which they ministered;)
15 and censers also, and vials. The prince of the
chivalry took those things that were of gold, and those
that were of silver, (and also the censers, and basins. The
leader of the cavalry, *or of the army*/The captain of the
guard took away those things that were made out of gold,
and made out of silver,)
16 that is, two pillars, one sea, and the foundaments, *or
bases*, which king Solomon had made to the temple of
the Lord (that is, the two pillars, the one Sea, and the
foundations, *or the bases*, which King Solomon had
made for the Temple of the Lord); and there was no
certain weight of [the] metal of all the vessels.
17 One pillar had eighteen cubits of height, and a
brazen pommel upon it of the height of three cubits, and
a work like a net, and pomegranates upon the pommel of
the pillar, all things of brass; and the second pillar had
like adorning. (One pillar was eighteen cubits in height,
and had a bronze capital upon it the height of three
cubits, and a network, and pomegranates upon the
capital of the pillar, all things made out of bronze; and
the second pillar had like adorning.)
18 Also the prince of the chivalry took Seraiah, the first
priest, and Zephaniah, the second priest, and [the] three
porters, (And the leader of the cavalry, *or of the army*/the

captain of the guard took Seraiah, the first priest, and
Zephaniah, the second priest, and the three guards,)
19 and an honest (and chaste) servant of the city, that
was sovereign over [the] men warriors, and five men of
them that stood before the king, which he found in the
city; and *he took* (the) Sopher, (that is,) the prince of the
host, that proved [the] young knights, *either (the) men
able to battle*, of the people of the land, and six(ty) men
of the commons, that were found in the city; (and a
eunuch of the city, who was the ruler over the warriors,
and five men of those who stood before the king, whom
he found in the city; and *he took* the Sopher, that is, the
leader in the army, who proved the young soldiers *to be
able for battle*, of the people of the land, and sixty
common men, who were also found in the city;)
20 (all of) which Nebuzaradan, prince of the chivalry,
took, and led to the king of Babylon, into Riblah. (all of
whom Nebuzaradan, the leader of the cavalry, *or of the
army*/the captain of the guard, took hold of, and led
captive to the king of Babylon, in Riblah.)
21 And the king of Babylon smote them, and killed
them in Riblah, in the land of Hamath; and Judah was
translated from his land. (And the king of Babylon struck
them down, and killed them in Riblah, in the land of
Hamath; and so *the people of* Judah were taken away
from their land.)
22 Soothly Nebuchadnezzar made Gedaliah, the son of
Ahikam, the son of Shaphan, sovereign to the people,
that was left in the land of Judah; which people
Nebuchadnezzar, king of Babylon, had left *in Judah.*
(And Nebuchadnezzar made Gedaliah, the son of
Ahikam, the son of Shaphan, to be the ruler of the
people, who were left in the land of Judah; which people
Nebuchadnezzar, the king of Babylon, had left there *in
Judah*.)
23 And when all the dukes of knights had heard these
things, they, and all the men that were with them, that is,
that the king of Babylon had ordained Gedaliah *to be
their sovereign in Judah*, they came to Gedaliah, in
Mizpah, (that is,) Ishmael, son of Nethaniah, and
Johanan, son of Careah, and Seraiah, son of Tanhumeth
of Netophah, and Jaazaniah, son of (a) Maachathite, they,
and the fellows of them. (And when all the leaders of the
horsemen, they and all the men who were with them,
had heard these things, that is, that the king of Babylon
had ordained Gedaliah *to be their ruler in Judah*, they
came to Gedaliah in Mizpah; that is, Ishmael, the son of
Nethaniah, and Johanan, the son of Careah, and Seraiah,
the son of Tanhumeth of Netophah, and Jaazaniah, the
son of a Maachathite, they, and all their fellows *came*.)
24 And Gedaliah swore to them, and to the fellows of
them, and said, Do not ye dread to serve the Chaldees;
dwell ye in the land, and serve ye the king of Babylon,
and it shall be well to you. (And Gedaliah swore to them,
and to their fellows, and said, Do not ye fear to serve the
Chaldeans; live ye in the land, and serve ye the king of
Babylon, and it shall be well with you.)
25 Forsooth it was done in the seventh month, *that is,
since Gedaliah was made sovereign*, (that) Ishmael, the
son of Nethaniah, the son of Elishama, of the king's seed,
came, and ten men with him, and they smote Gedaliah,
which died; but also *they smited* [the] Jews and [the]
Chaldees, that were with him in Mizpah. (And it was
done in the seventh month, *that is, since Gedaliah was
made the ruler*, that Ishmael, the son of Nethaniah, the
son of Elishama, of the king's descendants, came, and ten
men with him, and they struck down Gedaliah, and he
died; and *they* also *struck down* the Jews and the
Chaldeans, who were with him in Mizpah.)
26 And all the people rose, from the little unto the
great, and the princes of knights, and they came, *or fled*,
into Egypt, and dreaded the Chaldees. (And all the
people, from the little unto the great, and the leaders of
the horsemen, rose up, and they fled to Egypt, for they
feared the Chaldeans.)
27 Therefore it was done in the seven and thirtieth year
of the transmigration, *either passing over*, of Jehoiachin,
king of Judah, in the twelfth month, in the seven and
twentieth day of the month, Evilmerodach, king of
Babylon, in the year in which he began to reign, raised
[up] the head of Jehoiachin, king of Judah, from
prison,(And so it was done in the thirty-seventh year of
the captivity of Jehoiachin, the king of Judah, in the
twelfth month, on the twenty-seventh day of the month,
that Evilmerodach, the king of Babylon, in the year in
which he began to reign, raised up the head of
Jehoiachin, the king of Judah, *and released him* from
prison,)
28 and spake to him benignly; and he set the throne of
Jehoiachin above the throne of (the) kings, that were with
him in Babylon. (and spoke kindly to him; and he put
Jehoiachin's seat above the seats of the other kings, who
were with him *for meals* in Babylon.)
29 And Evilmerodach changed the clothes *of
Jehoiachin* that he had (worn) in prison; and he ate bread
ever[more] in the sight of Evilmerodach, in all the days of
his life.
30 Also Evilmerodach ordained sustenance for
Jehoiachin without ceasing; which sustenance also was
given of the king to him by all days, in all the days of his
life. (And Evilmerodach ordered a regular allowance for
Jehoiachin; yea, each day this allowance was given to
him by the king, for all the *remaining* days of his life.) ✡

1ST CHRONICLES

CHAPTER 1

1 Adam *begat* Seth; and Seth, Enos, [Adam, Seth, Enos,]
2 Kenan, Mahalaleel, Jered,
3 Henoch, Methuselah, Lamech,
4 Noe, Shem, Ham, and Japheth.
5 The sons of Japheth *were* Gomer, Magog, Madai,
and Javan, Tubal, Meshech, and Tiras.
6 Forsooth the sons of Gomer *were* Ashchenaz, and
Riphath, and Togarmah.
7 And the sons of Javan *were* Elishah, and Tarshish,
Kittim, and Dodanim.
8 The sons of Ham *were* Cush, and Mizraim, Put, and
Canaan.
9 And the sons of Cush *were* Seba, and Havilah,
Sabta, and Raamah, and Sabtecha. And the sons of
Raamah *were* Sheba, and Dedan.
10 And Cush begat Nimrod; this *Nimrod* began to be
mighty in [the] earth.
11 And Mizraim begat Ludim, and Anamim, and
Lehabim, and Naphtuhim,
12 and Pathrusim, and Casluhim, of which the
Philistines and Caphthorim went out, *or came.* (and
Pathrusim, and Casluhim, and Caphthorim, from whom
the Philistines came.)
13 And Canaan begat Sidon, his first begotten son (his
first-born son), and Heth,
14 and (the) Jebusite, and Amorite, and Girgashite,
15 and Hivite, and Arkite, and Sinite,
16 and Arvadite, and Zemarite, and Hamathite.
17 The sons of Shem *were* Elam, and Asshur, and
Arphaxad, and Lud, and Aram. And the sons of Aram
were Uz, and Hul, and Gether, and Meshech.
18 And Arphaxad begat Shelah; which himself
engendered Eber. (And Arphaxad begat Shelah; and
Shelah begat Eber.)
19 And to Eber were born two sons; the name of [the]
one *was* Peleg, for the land was parted in his days (for the
land was divided in his days); and the name of his
brother *was* Joktan.
20 And Joktan begat Almodad, and Sheleph, and
Hazarmaveth, and Jerah,
21 and Hadoram, and Uzal, and Diklah,
22 Ebal, and Abimael, and Sheba,
23 and Ophir, and Havilah, and Jobab; all these *were*
the sons of Joktan.
24 Shem, Arphaxad, Shelah,
25 Eber, Peleg, Reu,
26 Serug, Nahor, Terah,
27 Abram; this is Abraham.
28 The sons of Abraham were Isaac, and Ishmael.
29 And these be the generations of them; the first
begotten of Ishmael *was* Nebaioth, and then Kedar, and
Adbeel, and Mibsam, (And these be their descendants;
the first-born son of Ishmael *was* Nebaioth, and then
Kedar, and Adbeel, and Mibsam,)
30 and Mishma, and Dumah, and Massa, Hadad, and
Tema,
31 Jetur, Naphish, and Kedemah; these be the sons of
Ishmael.
32 And the sons of Keturah, the secondary wife of
Abraham, the which she engendered, *or conceived, were*
Zimran, Jokshan, Medan, Midian, Ishbak, and Shuah.
And the sons of Jokshan *were* Sheba, and Dedan. And
the sons of Dedan *were* Asshurim, and Letushim, and
Leummim.
33 And the sons of Midian *were* Ephah, and Epher, and
Henoch, and Abida, and Eldaah. All these *were* the sons
of Keturah.
34 Forsooth Abraham begat Isaac; whose sons were
Esau, and Israel (whose sons were Esau, and Jacob).
35 The sons of Esau *were* Eliphaz, Reuel, Jeush, and
Jaalam, and Korah.
36 The sons of Eliphaz *were* Teman, Omar, Zephi,
Gatam, Kenaz, and Timna, and Amalek.
37 The sons of Reuel *were* Nahath, Zerah, Shammah,
and Mizzah.
38 The sons of Seir *were* Lotan, Shobal, Zibeon, Anah,
Dishon, Ezar, and Dishan.
39 The sons of Lotan *were* Hori, and Homam; soothly
the sister of Lotan was Timna.
40 The sons of Shobal *were* Alian, and Manahath, and
Ebal, and Shephi, and Onam. The sons of Zibeon *were*
Aiah, and Anah.
41 The son of Anah *was* Dishon. The sons of Dishon
were Amram, and Eshban, and Ithran, and Cheran.
42 The sons of Ezer *were* Bilhan, and Zavan, and Jakan.
The sons of Dishan *were* Uz and Aran.
43 These be the kings that reigned in the land of Edom,
before that a king was on the sons of Israel (before that
the Israelites had a king). Bela, the son of Beor; and the
name of his city *was* Dinhabah.
44 And when Bela was dead, and Jobab (then Jobab),
the son of Zerah of Bozrah, reigned for him.
45 And when Jobab was dead, Husham of the land of
Temanites reigned for him.
46 And Husham died; and Hadad, the son of Bedad,
that smote Midian in the land of Moab, reigned for him;
and the name of the city of *Hadad was* Avith.
47 And when Hadad was dead, Samlah of Masrekah
reigned for him.
48 But also Samlah was dead, and Saul of Rehoboth,
which is set beside the river, reigned for him. (And when

Samlah died, Saul of *the city of* Rehoboth, that is set on
the banks of the river, reigned for him.)
49 Also when Saul was dead (And when Saul died),
Baalhanan, the son of Achbor, reigned for him.
50 But also he was dead, and Hadad, the name of
whose city was Pai, reigned for him (And when
Baalhanan died, Hadad reigned for him; and his city was
named Pai); and his wife was called Mehetabel, the
daughter of Matred, the daughter of Mezahab.
51 And when Hadad was dead, dukes began to be in
Edom for kings (And after Hadad died, the leaders of
Edom, *or of Idumea,* were these); duke Timnah, duke
Aliah, duke Jetheth,
52 duke Oholibamah, duke Elah, duke Pinon,
53 duke Kenaz, duke Teman, duke Mibzar,
54 duke Magdiel, duke Iram. These *were* the dukes of
Edom (These were the chiefs, *or the leaders,* of Idumea).

CHAPTER 2

1 Forsooth the sons of Israel *were* Reuben, Simeon,
Levi, Judah, Issachar, and Zebulun,
2 Dan, Joseph, and Benjamin, Naphtali, Gad, and Asher.
3 The sons of Judah *were* Er, Onan, and Shelah; these
three were born to him of Shua, a daughter of Canaan.
And Er, the first begotten (son) of Judah, was evil before
the Lord, and the Lord killed him. (The sons of Judah
were Er, Onan, and Shelah; these three were born to him
of the daughter of Shua, of Canaan/these three were born
to him of Bathshua, a Canaanite. And Er, the first-born
son of Judah, was evil before the Lord, and the Lord
killed him.)
4 And Tamar, the wife of the son of Judah, childed to
him Pharez, and Zerah (bare him Perez, and Zerah); and
all the sons of Judah *were* five.
5 And the sons of Pharez *were* Hezron, and Hamul.
(And the sons of Perez *were* Hezron, and Hamul.)
6 And the sons of Zerah *were* Zimri, and Ethan, and
Heman, and Calcol, and Dara; five (al)together.
7 The son of Carmi was Achar, that troubled Israel,
and sinned in the theft of (the) thing hallowed to the
Lord.
8 The son of Ethan was Azariah.
9 And the sons of Hezron, that were born to him,
were Jerahmeel, and Ram, and Chelubai.
10 And Ram begat Amminadab. And Amminadab
begat Nahshon, prince of the sons of Judah.
11 And Nahshon begat Salma; of whom Boaz was
born. (And Nahshon begat Salma; and Salma begat
Boaz.)
12 And Boaz begat Obed; which himself begat Jesse.
(And Boaz begat Obed; and Obed begat Jesse.)
13 And Jesse begat his first son, Eliab; the second,
Abinadab; the third, Shimma;
14 the fourth, Nethaneel; the fifth, Raddai;
15 the sixth, Ozem; the seventh, David;
16 whose sisters were Zeruiah, and Abigail. The sons
of Zeruiah *were* three, Abishai, Joab, and Asahel.
17 And Abigail childed Amasa (And Abigail bare
Amasa), whose father was Jether (the) Ishmaelite.
18 And Caleb, the son of Hezron, took a wife, Azubah,
by name, of whom he begat Jerioth; and his sons were
Jesher, and Shobab, and Ardon (and her sons were
Jesher, and Shobab, and Ardon).
19 And when Azubah was dead, Caleb took a wife,
Ephrath, which childed Hur to him (who bare him Hur).
20 And Hur begat Uri; (and) Uri begat Bezaleel.
21 After these things Hezron entered to the daughter of
Machir, the father of Gilead, and he took her *to wife,*
when he was of sixty years; and she childed Segub to
him. (After these things Hezron went to the daughter of
Machir, the father of Gilead, and he took her *for his wife,*
when he was sixty years old; and she bare him Segub.)
22 But also Segub begat Jair; and he had in possession
three and twenty cities in the land of Gilead;
23 and he took Geshur, and Aram, the cities of Jair, and
Kenath, and the towns thereof, of seventy cities (but
Geshur and Aram captured the cities of Jair, and Kenath,
and their towns, sixty towns in all). All these *were* (of) the
sons of Machir, the father of Gilead.
24 And when Hezron was dead, Caleb entered into
Ephratah. And Hezron had a wife Abiah, the which
childed to him Ashhur, the father of Tekoa. (And when
Hezron died, Caleb went to Ephratah, the wife of his
father Hezron, *and married her.* And she bare him
Ashhur, the founder of Tekoa.)
25 And sons were born of Jerahmeel, the first begotten
(son) of Hezron; (and) Ram *was* the first begotten son of
him, and *then* Bunah, and Oren, and Ozem, and Ahijah.
(And sons were born to Jerahmeel, the first-born son of
Hezron; and Ram *was* his first-born son, and *then* Bunah,
and Oren, and Ozem, and Ahijah.)
26 Also Jerahmeel wedded another wife, Atarah by
name, that was the mother of Onam. (And Jerahmeel wed
another wife, who was named Atarah; she was the
mother of Onam.)
27 But and the sons of Ram, the first begotten (son) of
Jerahmeel, were Maaz, and Jamin, and Eker.
28 And Onam begat sons, Shammai, and Jada. And the
sons of Shammai were Nadab, and Abishur;
29 and the name of the wife of Abishur was Abihail,
that childed to him Ahban, and Molid (who bare him
Ahban, and Molid).
30 And the sons of Nadab were Seled and Appaim;
forsooth Seled died without children.
31 And the son of Appaim *was* Ishi, the which Ishi
begat Sheshan; certainly Sheshan begat Ahlai.
32 And the sons of Jada, the brother of Shammai, *were*
Jether, and Jonathan; but Jether died without sons;

33 and Jonathan begat Peleth, and Zaza. These were
the sons of Jerahmeel.
34 And Sheshan had not sons, but daughters, and a
servant of Egypt (and an Egyptian servant), Jarha by name;
35 and he gave his daughter to wife to Jarha, which
childed Attai to him. (and Sheshan gave his daughter to
Jarha for a wife, and she bare him Attai.)
36 And Attai begat Nathan, and Nathan begat Zabad.
37 Also Zabad begat Ephlal, and Ephlal begat Obed.
38 Obed begat Jehu, Jehu begat Azariah,
39 Azariah begat Helez, Helez begat Eleasah,
40 Eleasah begat Sisamai, Sisamai begat Shallum,
41 Shallum begat Jekamiah, (and) Jekamiah begat
Elishama.
42 And the sons of Caleb, the brother of Jerahmeel,
were Mesha, the first begotten son of him, that is the
father of Ziph; and the sons of Mareshah, the father of
Hebron. (And the sons of Caleb, the brother of Jerahmeel,
were Mesha, his first-born son, who is the founder of
Ziph; and Mareshah, the founder of Hebron.)
43 Certainly the sons of Hebron *were* Korah, and
Tappuah, Rekem, and Shema.
44 And Shema begat Raham, the father of Jorkoam; and
Rekem begat Shammai.
45 The son of Shammai *was* Maon; and Maon *was* the
father of Bethzur.
46 And Ephah, the secondary wife of Caleb, childed
Haran, and Moza, and Gazez; and Haran begat Gazez.
47 The sons of Jahdai *were* Regem, and Jotham, and
Gesham, and Pelet, and Ephah, and Shaaph.
48 Maachah, the secondary wife of Caleb (the
concubine of Caleb), childed Sheber, and Tirhanah.
49 And (Maachah also bare) Shaaph, the father of
Madmannah, (and she also) engendered Sheva, the father
of Machbenah, and the father of Gibea; and the daughter
of Caleb was Achsa. (And Maachah also bare Shaaph, the
founder of Madmannah, and Sheva, the founder of
Machbenah, and the founder of Gibea; and Caleb's
daughter was Achsa.)
50 These were (also) the sons of Caleb. The sons of
Hur, the first begotten son of Ephratah, *were* Shobal, the
father of Kiriathjearim (the founder of Kiriathjearim);
51 Salma, the father of Bethlehem; Hareph, the father
of Bethgader. (Salma, the founder of Bethlehem; and
Hareph, the founder of Bethgader.)
52 And the sons of Shobal, the father of Kiriathjearim,
that saw the half of [the] restings, (And the sons of
Shobal, the founder of Kiriathjearim; and Haroeh/and
Reaiah, and half of the Manahethites.)
53 and was of the kindred of Kiriathjearim, were
Ithrites, and Puhites, and Shumathites, and Mishraites.
Of these were born Zareathites, and Eshtaulites. (And
those of the kindred of Kiriathjearim, were the Ithrites,
and Puhites, and Shumathites, and Mishraites. From these
were born the Zareathites, and the Eshtaulites.)
54 The sons of Salma, the father of Bethlehem, and of
Netophathites, *were* the crowns of the house of Joab, and
half of the resting of Zorites. (The sons of Salma *were*
Bethlehem, and the Netophathites, Ataroth, the house of
Joab, half of the Manahethites, and the Zorites./The sons
of Salma, the founder of Bethlehem, *were* the
Netophathites, Ataroth, the house of Joab, half of the
Manahethites, and the Zorites.)
55 And the kindreds of scribes, dwelling in Jabez,
singing, and sounding, and dwelling in tabernacles.
These be Kenites, that came of the heat of the father of
the house of Rechab. (And the kindreds, *or the families*,
of the writers, *or the copyists*, living in Jabez; the
Tirathites, and Shimeathites, and Suchathites. These be
the Kenites, who joined with the house of Rechab.)

CHAPTER 3

1 Forsooth David had these sons, that were born to
him in Hebron; the first begotten son *of him was* Amnon,
of Ahinoam of Jezreel; the second son, Daniel, of Abigail
of Carmel;
2 the third, Absalom, the son of Maachah, the
daughter of Talmai, king of Geshur; the fourth, Adonijah,
the son of Haggith;
3 the fifth, Shephatiah, of Abital; the sixth, Ithream, of
Eglah his wife.
4 Therefore six sons were born to him in Hebron;
where he reigned seven years and six months; and he
reigned three and thirty years in Jerusalem.
5 Forsooth four sons, *that is*, Shimea, and Shobab, and
Nathan, and Solomon, were born of Bathsheba, the
daughter of Ammiel, to him in Jerusalem; (And four sons,
that is, Shimea, and Shobab, and Nathan, and Solomon,
were born to him of Bathsheba, the daughter of Ammiel,
in Jerusalem;)
6 (and) also Ibhar, and Elishama, and Eliphelet,
7 and Nogah, and Nepheg, and Japhia,
8 also Elishama, and Eliada, and Eliphelet, nine
(others).
9 All these *were* the sons of David, without the sons of
his secondary wives; and they had a sister, Tamar.
10 Soothly the son of Solomon *was* Rehoboam, whose
son Abia begat Asa; and Jehoshaphat, the father of
Jehoram[1], was born of this Asa (and Asa begat
Jehoshaphat, and Jehoshaphat begat Jehoram);
11 the which Jehoram begat Ahaziah, of whom Joash
was born, *or begotten*.
12 And Amaziah, the son of this Joash, begat Azariah;
*and Azariah (begat) Jotham,
13 *(and Jotham) begat Ahaz, the father of Hezekiah, of

---

[1] Also known as Joram.

* Original text confused in these two phrases.

whom Manasseh was born.
14 But also Manasseh begat Amon, the father of Josiah.
15 And the sons of Josiah were *these*, the first begotten
son *was* Johanan; the second, Jehoiakim; the third,
Zedekiah; and the fourth, Shallum.
16 Of Jehoiakim was born Jeconiah[2], and Zedekiah. (Of
Jehoiakim were born Jehoiachin, and Zedekiah.)
17 The sons of Jeconiah were Assir, Salathiel, (The sons
of Jehoiachin, a prisoner, were Shealtiel,)
18 Malchiram, Pedaiah, Shenazar, and Jecamiah,
Hoshama, and Nedabiah.
19 Of Pedaiah were born Zerubbabel, and Shimei.
Zerubbabel begat Meshullam, Hananiah, and Shelomith,
the sister of them;
20 and Hashubah, and Ohel, and Berechiah, and
Hasadiah, and Jushabhesed, five (others).
21 And the son of Hananiah *was* Pelatiah, the father of
Jesaiah, whose son *was* Rephaiah. And the son of him
was Arnan, of whom was born Obadiah, whose son was
Shechaniah. (And the sons of Hananiah *were* Pelatiah,
and Jesaiah, whose son *was* Rephaiah. And the son of
Rephaiah *was* Arnan, of whom Obadiah was born,
whose son was Shechaniah.)
22 The son of Shechaniah *was* Shemaiah, whose sons
were Hattush, and Igeal, and Bariah, and Neariah, and
Shaphat; six in number.
23 The sons of Neariah *were* three, Elioenai, and
Hezekiah, and Azrikam.
24 The sons of Elioenai *were* seven, Hodaiah, and
Eliashib, and Pelaiah, and Akkub, and Johanan, and
Dalaiah, and Anani.

CHAPTER 4

1 The sons of Judah *were* Pharez (The sons of Judah
were Perez), and Hezron, and Carmi, and Hur, and
Shobal.
2 And Reaiah, the son of Shobal, begat Jahath; of
whom were born Ahumai, and Lahad. These were the
kindreds of Zorathites.
3 And this is the generation of Etam (And these be the
descendants of Etam); Jezreel, Ishma, and Idbash; and the
name of the sister of them *was* Hazelelponi.
4 And Penuel *was* the father of Gedor, and Ezer *was*
the father of Hushah; these be the sons of Hur, the first
begotten son of Ephratah, the father of Bethlehem.
5 And Ashhur, the father of Tekoa, had two wives,
Helah, and Naarah;
6 and Naarah childed to him Ahuzam, and Hepher,
and Temeni, and Haahashtari; these be the sons of
Naarah.
7 And the sons of Helah *were* Zereth, Jezoar, and
Ethnan.
8 And Coz begat Anub, and Zobebah, and the
kindreds of Aharhel, the son of Harum.
9 And Jabez was noble before all his brethren; and his
mother called his name Jabez, and said, For I childed him
in sorrow. (And Jabez was more respected than all his
brothers; and his mother called him Jabez, *or He who
maketh sorrow*, saying, For I gave birth to him in pain.)
10 And Jabez called inwardly (to the) God of Israel, and
said, If thou blessing shalt bless me, and shalt enlarge my
terms, and if thine hand shall be with me, and thou shalt
make me to be not oppressed of malice. And God gave
to him that thing, that he prayed. (And Jabez inwardly
called on the God of Israel, and said, If thou blessing
shalt bless me, and shalt enlarge my borders, and thy
hand shall be with me, and thou shalt keep me from
being oppressed by malice, *I shall be blessed indeed*.
And God gave him what he prayed for.)
11 And Chelub, the brother of Shuah, begat Mehir, that
was the father of Eshton;
12 and Eshton begat Bethrapha, and Paseah, and
Tehinnah, the father of the city [of] Nahash (the founder
of Irnahash). These be the sons of Rechah.
13 And the sons of Kenaz *were* Othniel, and Seraiah.
And the sons of Othniel *were* Hathath,
14 and Meonothai, that begat Ophrah. And Seraiah
begat Joab, the father of the valley of craftsmen; for they
were craftsmen. (and Meonothai, who begat Ophrah.
And Seraiah begat Joab, the founder of the Valley of
Charashim, *or the Ge-harashim Valley*; for the people
there were craftsmen.)
15 And the sons of Caleb, the son of Jephunneh, *were*
Iru, and Elah, and Naam. And the sons of Elah *were*
Kenaz (And the son of Elah *was* Kenaz).
16 Also the sons of Jehaleleel *were* Ziph, and Ziphah,
Tiria, and Asareel.
17[3] And the sons of Ezra *were* Jether, and Mered, and
Epher, and Jalon; and he begat Marie, and Shammai, and
Ishbah, the father of Eshtemoa.
18 Also Jehudijah, his wife, childed Jered, the father of
Gedor; and Heber, the father of Socho; and Jekuthiel, the
father of Zanoah. And these *were* the sons of Bithiah, the
daughter of Pharaoh, whom Mered took *to wife*.
19 And the sons of the wife of Hodiah, the sister of

[2] Also known as Jehoiachin and Coniah.

[3] Verses 17 & 18, as found in the original text, and presented above unchanged, are a confused rendering (as they also are in the KJV). A better ordering of these phrases would be:
17 And the sons of Ezra *were* Jether, and Mered, and Epher, and Jalon. And the children of Mered and Bithiah, the daughter of Pharaoh, whom Mered took *for a wife*; were Miriam, and Shammai, and Ishbah, the founder of Eshtemoa.
18 And Mered's Jewish wife/And his wife from the tribe of Judah bare Jered the founder of Gedor, and Heber the founder of Soco, and Jekuthiel the founder of Zanoah.

Naham, father of Keilah, *were* (the) Garmite, and Eshtemoa,
that was of Maachathites. (And the sons of Hodiah and
his wife, Naham's sister, were Daliah the father of Keilah
the Garmite, and Eshtemoa the Maachathite.)
20 Also the sons of Shimon *were* Amnon, and Rinnah;
the son of Hanan *was* Tilon (And the sons of Shimon
were Amnon, and Rinnah, and Benhanan, and Tilon);
and the sons of Ishi *were* Zoheth, and Benzoheth.
21 The sons of Shelah, the son of Judah, *were* Er, the
father of Lecah, and Laadah, the father of Mareshah; and
these *were* the kindreds of the house of men working bis,
in the house of an oath (and these *were* the families of
the house of those who made fine linen, of the house of
Ashbea/at Beth-ashbea),
22 and which made the sun to stand, and the men of
lying, secure, and going, that were princes in Moab, and
that turned again into Bethlehem; and these be [the] old
words. (and Jokim, and the men of Chozeba, and Joash,
and Saraph, who were the leaders in Moab, and
Jashubilehem; and these be the old words.)
23 These be (the) potters dwelling in plantings, and in
hedges, with kings in their works; and they dwelled there.
(These be the potters, and those living among plants and
hedges; and they lived there with the king, to be in his
service./These be the potters, living in Netaim and
Gederah; and they lived there, and worked for the king.)
24 The sons of Simeon *were* Nemuel, and Jamin, Jarib,
Zerah, (and) Saul;
25 Shallum *was* his son; Mibsam *was* his son; Mishma
was his son.
26 The sons of Mishma; Hamuel, his son; and Zacchur,
his son; [and] Shimei, his son.
27 The sons of Shimei *were* sixteen, and six daughters;
soothly his brethren had not many sons, and all the
kindred might not be even to the sum of the sons of
Judah. (And Shimei had sixteen sons, and six daughters;
but his brothers did not have many children, and so all
the kindred of Simeon was not equal to the number of
people in the tribe of Judah.)
28 And they dwelled in Beersheba (And they lived in
Beersheba), and in Moladah, and in Hazarshual,
29 and in Bilhah, and in Ezem, and in Tolad,
30 and in Bethuel, and in Hormah, and in Ziklag,
31 and in Bethmarcaboth, and in Hazarsusim, and in
Bethbirei, and in Shaaraim; these *were* the cities of them,
unto *the time of* king David.
32 Also the towns of them *were* Etam, and Ain, and
Rimmon, and Tochen, and Ashan; five cities.
33 And all the villages of them by the compass of these
cities, till to Baal; this is the dwelling of them, and the
parting of their cities. (And all their villages around these
cities, unto Baal; these be their dwelling places, and the
division of their cities.)
34 Also Meshobab, and Jamlech, and Joshah, the son of
Amaziah,
35 and Joel, and Jehu, the son of Josibiah, and the sons
of Seraiah, the sons of Asiel, (and Joel, and Jehu, the son
of Josibiah, the son of Seraiah, the son of Asiel,)
36 and Elioenai, and Jaakobah, and Jeshohaiah, and
Asaiah, and Adiel, and Jesimiel, and Benaiah;
37 and Ziza, the son of Shiphi, the son of Allon, the son
of Jedaiah, the son of Shimri, the son of Shemaiah.
38 These be [the] princes named in their kindreds, and
be multiplied greatly in the house of their allies. (These
were the princes, *or the leaders*, named in their kindreds;
and the house of their forefathers had greatly multiplied.)
39 And they went forth to enter into Gedor, unto the
east of the valley, and to seek pastures to their sheep.
(And they went forth unto the entrance of Gedor, east of
the valley, to seek pastures for their sheep.)
40 And they found pastures full plenteous, and full
good, and a full large land, and restful, and plenteous,
wherein men of the generation of Ham had dwelled
before. (And they found plentiful, and good pastures, and
a very large, and restful, and plentiful land, where Ham's
descendants had lived before.)
41 Therefore these men, which we have described
before by name, came in the days of Hezekiah, king of
Judah; and smote the tabernacles of them, and the
dwellers that were found there; and they destroyed them
unto this present day; and they dwelled for them, for they
found there full plenteous pastures. (And so these men,
whom we have described above by name, came in the
days of Hezekiah, the king of Judah; and struck the tents,
or the camps, of those who they found there, and also the
Meunites, and no trace remaineth of them, unto this
present day; and they lived in their place, for they found
plentiful pastures there.)
42 Also five hundred men of the sons of Simeon went
in to the hill of Seir, and they had (for) princes Pelatiah,
and Neariah, and Rephaiah, and Uzziel, the sons of Ishi;
(And five hundred men of the sons of Simeon went to the
hill country of Seir, and they had for leaders Pelatiah, and
Neariah, and Rephaiah, and Uzziel, the sons of Ishi;)
43 and they smote the remnants of Amalekites, that
might escape; and they dwelled there for them unto this
day. (and they struck down the remnants of the
Amalekites, who had escaped; and they have lived there
in their place unto this day.)

CHAPTER 5

1 Also the sons of Reuben, the first begotten son of
Israel; for he was the first begotten son of Israel, but when
he had defouled the bed of his father, the dignity of his first
begetting was given to the sons of Joseph, the son of Israel;
and Reuben was not areckoned into the first begotten son
(and so Reuben was not reckoned as the first-born son).
2 Forsooth (of) Judah, that was the strongest among his

brethren, princes were gathered of his generation (But
from Judah, who was the strongest among his brothers,
came the leader for all the tribes); forsooth the right of
first begetting was areckoned to Joseph.
3 Therefore the sons of Reuben, the first begotten son
of Israel, *were* Hanoch, and Pallu, Hezron, and Carmi.
4 The sons of Joel *were* Shemaiah; his son, Gog; his
son, Shimei;
5 his son, Micah; his son, Reaia; his son, Baal;
6 his son, Beerah; whom Tilgathpilneser, king of
Assyrians, led (away) prisoner; and he was prince in the
lineage of Reuben (and he was a leader of the tribe of
Reuben).
7 Soothly his brethren, and all the kindred, when they
were numbered by their families, had princes Jeiel, and
Zechariah. (And his kinsmen, and all their kindred, when
they were listed by their families, had Jeiel as their leader,
and then Zechariah,)
8 Forsooth Bela, the son of Azaz, son of Shema, son of
Joel, he dwelled in Aroer till to Nebo and Baalmeon;
(and Bela, the son of Azaz, the son of Shema, the son of
Joel, and they lived in Aroer unto Nebo and Baalmeon;)
9 and he dwelled against the east coast, till to the
entering of (the) desert, and to the flood Euphrates. And
he had in possession much number of beasts in the land
of Gilead. (and they lived toward the east coast, unto the
edge of the wilderness/unto the entrance to the desert,
and the Euphrates River. And they had in possession a
great number of beasts in the land of Gilead.)
10 Forsooth in the days of Saul *the sons of Reuben*
fought against (the) Hagarites, and killed them; and
dwelled for them in the tabernacles of them (and they
lived in their tents, *or their camps*), in all the coast that
beholdeth to the east of Gilead.
11 Soothly the sons of Gad even against them dwelled
in the land of Bashan till to Salcah; (And the sons of Gad
lived beside them in the land of Bashan unto Salcah;)
12 Joel *was* in the beginning, and Shapham *was* the
second; also Jaanai and Shaphat *were* in Bashan. (Joel
was the leader, and Shapham *was* the second; and Jaanai
and Shaphat *were* in Bashan.)
13 Also their brethren by the houses of their kindreds,
Michael, and Meshullam, and Sheba, and Jorai, and
Jachan, and Zia, and Heber, seven. (And their kinsmen in
the houses of their kindreds, that is, *the families* of
Michael, and Meshullam, and Sheba, and Jorai, and
Jachan, and Zia, and Heber, seven in all.)
14 These *were* the sons of Abihail, the son of Huri, son
of Jaroah, son of Gilead, son of Michael, son of Jeshishai,
son of Jahdo, son of Buz.
15 Also the brethren of the son of Abdiel, son of Guni,
was prince of the house in his families. (And Ahi, the son
of Abdiel, the son of Guni, *was* the leader of the house of
their family.)
16 And they dwelled in Gilead (And they lived in
Gilead), and in Bashan, and in the towns thereof, (and) in
all the suburbs of Sharon, till to the ends.
17 All these were numbered in the days of Jotham, king
of Judah, and in the days of Jeroboam (II), king of Israel.
18 The sons of Reuben, and of Gad, and of half the
lineage of Manasseh, were men warriors, bearing shields
and swords, and bending bow, and taught in battles, four
and forty thousand seven hundred and sixty, and they
went forth to battle, (The sons of Reuben, and of Gad,
and of the eastern half of the tribe of Manasseh, were
men of war, bearing shields and swords, and bending
bow, and taught in battles, forty-four thousand seven
hundred and sixty, and they went forth to battle,)
19 and fought against Hagarites. Forsooth Jetur, and
Nephish, and Nodab,
20 gave help to them; and Hagarites, and all men that
were with them, were betaken into the hands of Reuben,
and Gad, and Manasseh; for they called inwardly the
Lord, while they fought, and the Lord heard them, for
they believed in to him. (gave them help; and the
Hagarites, and all the men who were with them, were
delivered into the hands of Reuben, and Gad, and eastern
Manasseh; for they inwardly called on the Lord, while
they fought, and the Lord heard them, for they believed
in him.)
21 And they took (away) all things which (the)
Hagarites had in possession, fifty thousand of camels, and
two hundred and fifty thousand of sheep, two thousand
of asses (two thousand donkeys), and an hundred
thousand persons of men;
22 for many men were wounded and felled down; for it
was the battle of the Lord. And they dwelled (there) for (the)
Hagarites till to the conquest. (for many men were killed
and fell down; for the battle was the Lord's making. And
they lived there in place of the Hagarites until the captivity.)
23 Also the sons of the half lineage of Manasseh had in
possession the land, from the ends of Bashan till to
Baalhermon, and Senir, and the hill of Hermon; for it was
a great number. (And the sons of the eastern half of the
tribe of Manasseh, had in possession the land from
Bashan to Baalhermon, and Senir, and Mount Hermon;
for they were great in number.)
24 And these were the princes of the house of their
kindred; Epher, and Ishi, and Eliel, and Azriel, and
Jeremy, and Hodaviah, and Jahdiel, full strong men and
mighty, and named dukes in their families. (And these
were the leaders of the house of their kindred; Epher, and
Ishi, and Eliel, and Azriel, and Jeremy, and Hodaviah,
and Jahdiel, very strong and mighty men, with famous
names, yea, the leaders of their families.)
25 Forsooth they forsook the God of their fathers, and
did fornication after the gods of [the] peoples of the land,
which the Lord took away before them. (But they left the

God of their fathers, and did idolatry, worshipping the
gods of the peoples of the land, whom the Lord had
destroyed before them.)
26 And the Lord God of Israel raised (up) the spirit[4] of
Pul, king of Assyrians, and the spirit of Tilgathpilneser,
king of Assur; and he translated Reuben, and Gad, and
the half lineage of Manasseh, and brought them into
Halah, and Habor, and Hara, and into the river of Gozan,
till to this day. (And the Lord God of Israel stirred up the
will, *or the desire*, of Pul, the king of Assyria, who is also
known as Tilgathpilneser, the king of Assyria, to fight
against Israel; and he carried away Reuben, and Gad, and
the eastern half of the tribe of Manasseh, and brought
them to Halah, and Habor, and Hara, and the Gozan
River, where they live unto this day.)

CHAPTER 6

1 The sons of Levi *were* Gershon[5], Kohath, and Merari.
2 The sons of Kohath *were* Amram, Izhar, Hebron,
and Uzziel.
3 The sons of Amram *were* Aaron, Moses, and Marie
(The children of Amram *were* Aaron, Moses, and
Miriam). The sons of Aaron *were* Nadab, and Abihu,
Eleazar, and Ithamar.
4 Eleazar begat Phinehas, and Phinehas begat
Abishua,
5 Abishua begat Bukki, and Bukki begat Uzzi,
6 Uzzi begat Zerahiah, and Zerahiah begat Meraioth.
7 Forsooth Meraioth begat Amariah, Amariah begat
Ahitub,
8 Ahitub begat Zadok, Zadok begat Ahimaaz,
9 Ahimaaz begat Azariah, Azariah begat Johanan,
10 Johanan begat Azariah; he it is that was set in
priesthood, in the house that Solomon builded in
Jerusalem. (Johanan begat Azariah; it was he who served
as High Priest, in the House that Solomon built in
Jerusalem.)
11 Forsooth Azariah begat Amariah, and Amariah begat
Ahitub,
12 Ahitub begat Zadok, Zadok begat Shallum,
13 Shallum begat Hilkiah, Hilkiah begat Azariah,
14 Azariah begat Seraiah, Seraiah begat Jehozadak.
15 Forsooth Jehozadak went out, when the Lord
translated Judah and Jerusalem, by the hands of
Nebuchadnezzar the king. (And Jehozadak went into
captivity, when the Lord carried away Judah and
Jerusalem, by the hand, *or the power*, of King
Nebuchadnezzar.)
16 Therefore the sons of Levi *were* Gershon, Kohath,
and Merari.
17 And these *were* the names of the sons of Gershon;
Libni, and Shimei.
18 The sons of Kohath *were* Amram, and Izhar, and
Hebron, and Uzziel.
19 The sons of Merari *were* Mahli, and Mushi. Soothly
these *were* the kindreds of Levi by the families of them;
20 (of) Gershon; Libni, his son; Jahath, his son;
Zimmah, his son;
21 Joah, his son; Iddo, his son; Zerah, his son; Jeaterai,
his son.
22 The sons of Kohath; Amminadab, his son; Korah, his
son; Assir, his son;
23 Elkanah, his son; Ebiasaph, his son; Assir, his son;
24 Tahath, his son; Uriel, his son; Uzziah, his son; Saul,
his son.
25 The sons of Elkanah *were* Amasai, and Ahimoth;
26 and (the son of Ahimoth *was*) Elkanah. The sons of
(this) Elkanah; Zophai, his son; Nahath, his son;
27 Eliab, his son; Jeroham, his son; Elkanah, his son.
28 The sons of Samuel; the first begotten Vashni, and
Abiah. (The sons of Samuel; Joel, the first-born son, and
Abijah.)
29 Soothly the sons of Merari; Mahli, his son; Libni, his
son; Shimei, his son; Uzza, his son;
30 Shimea, his son; Haggiah, his son; Asaiah, his son.
31 These it be that David ordained on the singers of the
house of the Lord, since the ark of the Lord was set
(there); (These it be whom David ordained over the
music in the House of the Lord, after the Ark of the Lord
was moved there;)
32 and they ministered before the tabernacle of
witnessing, and sang, till Solomon builded the house of
the Lord in Jerusalem; forsooth they stood by their order
in [their] service. (and they served before, *or in front of*,
the Tabernacle, *or the Tent*, of the Witnessing, and sang,
until Solomon built the House of the Lord in Jerusalem;
and they did their duty in their proper turn.)
33 And these it be that stood nigh with their sons. Of
the sons of Kohath; Heman the chanter, the son of Joel,
son of Shemuel, (And these were they who did their duty
with their kinsmen. Of the sons of Kohath; Heman the
cantor, *or the singer*, the son of Joel, the son of Shemuel,)
34 son of Elkanah, son of Jeroham, son of Eliel, son of
Toah,
35 son of Zuph, son of Elkanah, son of Mahath, son of
Amasai,
36 son of Elkanah, son of Joel, son of Azariah, son of
Zephaniah,
37 son of Tahath, son of Assir, son of Ebiasaph, son of
Korah,
38 son of Izhar, son of Kohath, son of Levi, the son of
Israel.
39 And his brethren; Asaph, that stood at the right half

[4] *Yea, 'the spirit', that is, (the) will to fight against the children of Israel.*

[5] Spelled 'Gershom' in some translations in Chapter 6, verses 16, 17, 20, 43, 62, and 71.

of him, (that is) Asaph, the son of Berachiah, son of
Shimea, (And his kinsman, Asaph, who stood at his right
hand, that is Asaph, the son of Berachiah, the son of
Shimea,)
40 son of Michael, son of Baaseiah, son of Malchiah,
41 son of Ethni, son of Zerah, son of Adaiah,
42 son of Ethan, son of Zimmah, son of Shimei,
43 son of Jahath, son of Gershon, the son of Levi.
44 Forsooth the sons of Merari, the brethren of them,
were at the left side; Ethan, the son of Kishi, son of Abdi,
son of Malluch, (And their kinsman, Ethan, the son of
Merari, who stood at their left side, that is, Ethan, the son
of Kishi, the son of Abdi, the son of Malluch,)
45 son of Hashabiah, son of Amaziah, son of Hilkiah,
46 son of Amzi, son of Bani, son of Shamer,
47 son of Mahli, son of Mushi, son of Merari, son of Levi.
48 And deacons, the brethren of them, that were ordained
into all the service of the tabernacle of the house of the
Lord. (And the Levites, their kinsmen, who were ordained to
do all the service of the Tabernacle, the House of the Lord.)
49 Forsooth Aaron and his sons burnt incense upon the
altar of brunt sacrifices, and upon the altar of incense,
into all the work of the holy of holy things; and that they
should pray for Israel, by all things which Moses, the
servant of God, commanded (and they prayed for Israel,
following the commands which Moses, the servant of
God, had given).
50 And these be the sons of Aaron; Eleazar, his son;
Phinehas, his son; Abishua, his son;
51 Bukki, his son; Uzzi, his son; Zerahiah, his son;
52 Meraioth, his son; Amariah, his son; Ahitub, his son;
53 Zadok, his son; Ahimaaz, his son.
54 And these *were* the dwelling places, by the towns
and coasts of them, that is, of the sons of Aaron, by the
kindreds of Kohathites; for those befelled to them by lot.
55 Therefore *the children of Israel* gave to them
Hebron in the land of Judah, and the suburbs thereof by
compass; (And so *the children of Israel* gave them
Hebron in the land of Judah, and its suburbs all around;)
56 and *they gave* the fields and towns of the cities to
Caleb, the son of Jephunneh.
57 And they gave cities to the sons of Aaron, Hebron to
refuge, and *they gave* Libnah, with his suburbs, and Jattir,
and Eshtemoa, with their suburbs, (And they gave to the
sons of Aaron, the city of Hebron for refuge, and also
Libnah, with its suburbs, and Jattir, and Eshtemoa, with
their suburbs,)
58 but also Hilen, and Debir, with their suburbs; (and
Hilen, and Debir, with their suburbs;)
59 also *they gave* Ashan, and Bethshemesh, and the
suburbs of those. (and Ashan, and Bethshemesh, and
their suburbs.)
60 And of the lineage of Benjamin *they gave* Geba, and
the suburbs thereof, and Alemeth with his suburbs,
Anathoth also with his suburbs; all the cities *were*
thirteen with their suburbs, by the kindreds of them. (And
from the tribe of Benjamin *they gave* Geba, and its
suburbs, and Alemeth with its suburbs, and Anathoth
with its suburbs; so all the cities with their suburbs, *were*
thirteen, for their kindreds, *or families*.)
61 And [to] the sons of Kohath, (to) the residues of their
kindred, they gave of the half lineage of Manasseh, ten
cities into possession. (And to the sons of Kohath, for the
rest of their kindred, they gave from the *western* half of
the tribe of Manasseh, ten cities for a possession.)
62 And to the sons of Gershon by their kindreds, *they
gave* fourteen cities in Bashan, of the lineage of Issachar,
and of the lineage of Asher, and of the lineage of
Naphtali, and of the lineage of Manasseh. (And to the
sons of Gershon by their kindreds, *they gave* thirteen
cities from the tribes of Issachar, and Asher, and Naphtali,
and *the eastern half* of the tribe of Manasseh in Bashan.)
63 And to the sons of Merari by their kindreds, they gave
by lots twelve cities, of the lineage of Reuben, of the lineage
of Gad, and of the lineage of Zebulun. (And to the sons
of Merari by their kindreds, they gave by lot twelve cities,
from the tribes of Reuben, and Gad, and Zebulun.)
64 And the sons of Israel gave to [the] deacons (the)
cities and suburbs of those; (And the Israelites gave these
cities, and their suburbs, to the Levites;)
65 and they gave by lot, of the sons of the lineage of
Judah, and of the lineage of the sons of Simeon, and of
the lineage of the sons of Benjamin, these cities, which
the deacons called by their names; (and they gave by lot,
from the tribes of Judah, and of Simeon, and of Benjamin,
these cities, which be named above.)
66 and of them that were of the kindred of the sons of
Kohath, and in the terms of them, were the cities of the
lineage of Ephraim. (And for those who were of the
kindred of the sons of Kohath, there were cities in the
land of the tribe of Ephraim.)
67 And *the sons of Israel* gave to them (the) cities of
refuge, Shechem with his suburbs, in the hill of Ephraim;
and Gezer with his suburbs, (Yea, *the Israelites* gave
them the city of refuge, Shechem with its suburbs, in the
hill country of Ephraim; and Gezer with its suburbs,)
68 also Jokmeam with his suburbs, and Bethhoron also.
(and Jokmeam, and Bethhoron, with their suburbs.)
69 Also of the lineage of Dan *they gave* Aijalon, with
her suburbs, and Gathrimmon by the same manner. (And
from the tribe of Dan *they gave* Aijalon with its suburbs,
and Gathrimmon with its suburbs.)
70 And of the half lineage of Manasseh *they gave* Aner,
and the suburbs thereof, (and) Bileam, and the suburbs
thereof; that is, to them that were residue/that were left of
the kindred of the sons of Kohath. (And from the *western*
half of the tribe of Manasseh *they gave* Aner, and its
suburbs, and Bileam, and its suburbs; that is, to those

who were left of the kindred of the sons of Kohath.)
71 And to the sons of Gershon *they gave* of the kindred
of half the lineage of Manasseh, Golan in Bashan, and the
suburbs thereof, and Ashtaroth with his suburbs. (And to
the sons of Gershon *they gave* from the kindred of the
eastern half of the tribe of Manasseh, Golan in Bashan,
and its suburbs, and Ashtaroth with its suburbs.)
72 Of the lineage of Issachar *they gave* Kedesh, and the
suburbs thereof, and Daberath with his suburbs; (And
from the tribe of Issachar *they gave* Kedesh, and its
suburbs, and Daberath with its suburbs;)
73 also Ramoth, and his suburbs, and Anem with his
suburbs. (and Ramoth, and its suburbs, and Anem with its
suburbs.)
74 Also of the lineage of Asher *they gave* Mashal with his
suburbs, and Abdon also, (And from the tribe of Asher, *they
gave* Mashal with its suburbs, and Abdon with its suburbs,)
75 and Hukok, and the suburbs thereof, and Rehob
with his suburbs. (and Hukok, and its suburbs, and
Rehob with its suburbs.)
76 And of the lineage of Naphtali *they gave* Kedesh in
Galilee, and the suburbs thereof, Hammon with his suburbs,
and Kiriathaim, and the suburbs thereof. (And from the tribe
of Naphtali *they gave* Kedesh in Galilee, and its suburbs,
Hammon with its suburbs, and Kiriathaim, and its suburbs.)
77 Soothly to the residue sons of Merari *they gave* of
the lineage of Zebulun, Rimmon, and the suburbs
thereof, and Tabor with his suburbs. (And to the rest of
the sons of Merari *they gave* from the tribe of Zebulun,
Rimmon, and its suburbs, and Tabor with its suburbs.)
78 Also beyond (the) Jordan, even against Jericho,
against the east of (the) Jordan, *they gave* of the lineage of
Reuben, Bezer in the wilderness with his suburbs, and
Jahzah with his suburbs, (And beyond the Jordan River,
opposite Jericho, on the east side of the Jordan River,
they gave from the tribe of Reuben, Bezer in the
wilderness with its suburbs, and Jahzah with its suburbs,)
79 also Kedemoth, and his suburbs, and Mephaath with
his suburbs. (and Kedemoth, and its suburbs, and
Mephaath with its suburbs.)
80 Also of the lineage of Gad, *they gave* Ramoth in
Gilead, and the suburbs thereof, Mahanaim with his
suburbs, (And from the tribe of Gad, *they gave* Ramoth in
Gilead, and its suburbs, Mahanaim with its suburbs,)
81 but also Heshbon with his suburbs, and Jazer with
his suburbs. (and Heshbon with its suburbs, and Jazer
with its suburbs.)

CHAPTER 7

1 Forsooth the sons of Issachar were four; Tola, and
Puah, Jashub, and Shimrom.
2 The sons of Tola *were* Uzzi, and Rephaiah, and
Jeriel, and Jahmai, and Jibsam, and Shemuel, princes by
the houses of their kindreds. Of the generation of Tola
were numbered (the) strongest men in the days of David,
two and twenty thousand and six hundred. (The sons of
Tola *were* Uzzi, and Rephaiah, and Jeriel, and Jahmai,
and Jibsam, and Shemuel, the leaders of the houses of
their kindreds. They were the strongest men of the
descendants of Tola, who, in the days of David,
numbered twenty-two thousand and six hundred.)
3 The sons of Uzzi *were* Izrahiah (The son of Uzzi
was Izrahiah); of whom were born Michael, and
Obadiah, and Joel, and Ishiah, five, all princes.
4 And with them *were* by their families and peoples,
six and thirty thousand most strong men girded to battle; for
they had many wives and sons. (And with them, by their
families and peoples, *were* thirty-six thousand most strong
men girded for battle; for they had many wives and sons.)
5 And their brethren, by all the kindreds of Issachar,
most strong to fight, were numbered fourscore and seven
thousand (numbered eighty-seven thousand).
6 The sons of Benjamin *were* Bela, and Becher, and
Jediael, three.
7 The sons of Bela *were* Ezbon, and Uzzi, and Uzziel,
and Jerimoth, and Iri, five; princes of families (the leaders
of their families), most strong to fight; for the number of
them was two and twenty thousand and four and thirty.
8 And the sons of Becher *were* Zemira, and Joash, and
Eliezer, and Elioenai, and Omri, and Jerimoth, and Abiah,
and Anathoth, and Alameth; all these *were* the sons of
Becher.
9 And the princes of (their) kindreds were numbered
by their families twenty thousand and two hundred most
strong men to battles. (And the leaders of their kindreds
were listed, *or registered*, by their families, and there
were found *to be* twenty thousand and two hundred most
strong men for battle.)
10 And the sons of Jediael *were* Bilhan (And the son of
Jediael *was* Bilhan); soothly the sons of Bilhan *were*
Jeush, and Benjamin, and Ehud, and Chenaanah, and
Zethan, and Tharshish, and Ahishahar.
11 All these the sons of Jediael *were* princes of their
families, seventeen thousand and two hundred, strongest
men going forth to battle. (All these sons of Jediael, the
leaders of their families, and their most strong men, were
seventeen thousand and two hundred going forth to battle.)
12 Also Shuppim (And Shuppim), and Huppim, *were*
the sons of Ir; and Hushim *was* the son of Aher.
13 And the sons of Naphtali *were* Jahziel, and Guni,
and Jezer, and Shallum, the sons of Bilhah.
14 And the son of Manasseh *was* Asriel; and Sira[6], his
secondary wife, childed Machir, the father of Gilead.

---

[6] Here the Hebrew text speaks of 'an Aramean', that is, 'a citizen of Aram'. In Wycliffe's time, 'Aram' was also called 'Syria'. From this word, the translators mistakenly made the 1ST person name, 'Sira'.

(And the sons of Manasseh *were* Ashriel, and Machir, the
father of Gilead, whom his secondary wife, the Syrian, *or
the Aramean*, bare for him.)
15 And Machir took wives to his sons Huppim and
Shuppim; and he had a sister, Maachah by name (And
Machir took for a wife the sister of Huppim and
Shuppim, whose name was Maachah/And Machir took
for a wife a woman whose name was Maachah); and the
name of the second son was Zelophehad, and daughters
were born to Zelophehad.
16 And Maachah, the wife of Machir, childed a son
(bare a son), and called his name Peresh; and the name of
his brother *was* Sheresh; and his sons *were* Ulam and
Rakem.
17 And the son of Ulam *was* Bedan. These were the
sons of Gilead, son of Machir, son of Manasseh;
18 and Hammoleketh his sister childed a fair man,
Abiezer, and Mahalah. (and his sister Hammoleketh gave
birth to Ishod, and Abiezer, and Mahalah.)
19 And the sons of Shemidah were Ahian, and
Shechem, and Likhi, and Aniam.
20 And the sons of Ephraim *were* Shuthelah; Bered, his
son; Tahath, his son; Eladah, his son; and Tahath, his son;
21 and Zabad, his son; and Shuthelah, his son; and
Ezer, and Elead, his sons. And [the] men of Gath born in
the land killed them, for they went down to assail their
possessions.
22 Therefore Ephraim, the father of them, wailed by
many days; and his brethren came to comfort him. (And
their father Ephraim bewailed them for many days; and
his kinsmen came to comfort him.)
23 And he entered [in] to his wife, which conceived,
and childed a son (and bare a son); and he called his
name Beriah, for he was born in the evils of his house.
24 And his daughter was Sherah; that builded
Bethhoron, the lower, and the higher, and Uzzen, and
Sherah. (And his daughter was Sherah, who built Lower
Bethhoron, and Upper Bethhoron, and Uzzensherah.)
25 And his son *was called* Rephah, and (his son was)
Resheph, and (his son was) Telah, of whom was born
Tahan; (And Ephraim's son *was called* Rephah, and his
son was Resheph, and his son was Telah, and his son was
Tahan;)
26 that engendered Laadan; and Ammihud, the son of
him, begat Elishama; (and Tahan begat Laadan; and
Laadan's son Ammihud, begat Elishama;)
27 of whom was born Nun; that had a son Joshua.
28 And the possession and the dwelling places of them
was Bethel with his villages, and against the east, Naaran;
at the west coast, Gezer, and his villages, also Shechem
with his villages, and Gaza with his villages. (And their
possession and their dwelling places *were* Bethel with its
villages, and to the east, Naaran; and to the west, Gezer,
and its villages, and Shechem with its villages, and Gaza
with its villages.)
29 Also beside the sons of Manasseh, Bethshean and
his towns, Taanach and his towns, Megiddo and his
towns, Dor and his towns; and the sons of Joseph, son of
Israel, dwelled in these *towns*. (And the sons of Manasseh
had Bethshean and its towns, Taanach and its towns,
Megiddo and its towns, and Dor and its towns; and the
sons of Joseph, the son of Israel, lived in these *towns*.)
30 The sons of Asher *were* Imnah, and Isuah, and
Ishuai, and Beriah; and Serah *was* the sister of them.
31 And the sons of Beriah *were* Heber, and Malchiel;
he is the father of Birzavith.
32 And Heber engendered Japhlet, and Shomer, and
Hotham, and Shua, the sister of them.
33 And the sons of Japhlet *were* Pasach, and Bimhal,
and Ashvath; these *were* the sons of Japhlet.
34 And the sons of Shamer *were* Ahi, and Rohgah, and
Jehubbah, and Aram.
35 And the sons of Helem, his brother, *were* Zophah,
and Imna, and Shelesh, and Amal. (And the sons of his
brother Hotham *were* Zophah, and Imna, and Shelesh,
and Amal.)
36 The sons of Zophah *were* Suah, and Harnepher, and
Shual, and Beri, and Imrah,
37 and Bezer, and Hod, and Shamma, and Shilshah,
and Ithran, and Beera.
38 The sons of Jether *were* Jephunneh, and Pispah, and
Ara.
39 And the sons of Ulla *were* Arah, and Haniel, and
Rezia.
40 All these *were* the sons of Asher, princes of
kindreds, chosen men and full strong dukes of dukes; and
the number, of the age of them that were able to battle,
was six and twenty thousand. (All these *were* the sons of
Asher, the leaders of their kindreds, chosen and very
strong men, leaders of leaders; and the number of them
of the age who were able to do battle, was twenty-six
thousand.)

CHAPTER 8

1 Forsooth Benjamin begat Bela his first begotten son,
Ashbel the second, Aharah the third,
2 Nohah the fourth, and Rapha the fifth.
3 And the sons of Bela were Addar, and Gera, and
Abihud,
4 and Abishua, and Naaman, and Ahoah,
5 but also Gera (and Gera), and Shephuphan, and
Huram.
6 These be the sons of Ehud, princes of [the] kindreds
dwelling in Geba, that were translated into Manahath
(who were sent away to Manahath).
7 And Naaman, and Ahiah, and Gera, he translated
them (whom he removed), and he begat Uzza and Ahihud;
8 and Shaharaim, he begat (children) in the country of

Moab, after that he let go of Hushim and Baara, his
wives; (and Shaharaim begat children in the country of
Moab, after he divorced his wives, Hushim and Baara;)
9 and he begat of Hodesh, his (new) wife, Jobab, and
Zibia, and Mesha, and Malcham,
10 also Jeuz, and Shachia, and Mirma; those be the sons
of him, princes in their families. (and Jeuz, and Shachia, and
Mirma; these be his sons, the leaders in their families.)
11 And Hushim begat Abitub, and Elpaal.
12 And the sons of Elpaal *were* Eber, and Misham, and
Shamed; he builded Ono, and Lod, and his villages; (And
the sons of Elpaal *were* Eber, and Misham, and Shamed; it
was Shamed who built Ono, and Lod, and their villages;)
13 and Beriah and Shema *were* princes of [the] kindreds
dwelling in Aijalon; these drove away the dwellers of
Gath; (and Beriah and Shema *were* the leaders of the
kindreds, *or of the families*, living in Aijalon; they drove
away the inhabitants of Gath;)
14 and Ahio, and Shashak, and Jeremoth,
15 and Zebadiah, and Arad, and Ader,
16[E][7] Michael forsooth (and Michael), and Ispah, and
Joha, the sons of Beriah;
17[E] Zebadiah, and Meshullam, and Hezeki, and Heber,
18[E] and Ishmerai, and Jezliah, and Jobab, (the) sons of
Elpaal;
19[E] Jakim, and Zichri, and Zabdi,
20[E] and Elienai, and Zilthai, and Eliel,
21[E] and Adaiah, and Beraiah, and Shimrath, the sons of
Shimhi;
22[E] Ishpan, and Heber, Eliel,
23[E] and Abdon, and Zichri, and Hanan,
24[E] and Hananiah, and Elam, and Antothijah,
25[E] and Iphedeiah, and Penuel, the sons of Shashak;
26[E] Shamsherai, and Shehariah, and Athaliah,
27 and Jaresiah, and Eliah, and Zichri, the sons of
Jeroham.
28 These *were* [the] patriarchs and princes of (the)
kindreds, that dwelled in Jerusalem (who lived in
Jerusalem).
29 And in Gibeon dwelled Abigibeon, (*that is, Jehiel,
the founder of Gibeon,*) and Maachah (was) the name of
his wife;
30 and his first begotten son Abdon, and Zur, and Kish,
and Baal, and Nadab,
31 and Gedor, and Ahio, and Zacher,
32 and Mikloth. And Mikloth begat Shimeah; and they
dwelled even against their brethren in Jerusalem, with
their brethren. (and Mikloth. And Mikloth begat Shimeah;
and they lived alongside their kinsmen in Jerusalem.)
33 And Ner begat Kish, and Kish begat Saul; and Saul
begat Jonathan, and Malchishua, and Abinadab, and
Eshbaal.
34 And the son of Jonathan was Meribbaal; and
Meribbaal begat Micah.
35 The sons of Micah *were* Pithon, and Melech, and
Tarea, and Ahaz.
36 And Ahaz begat Jehoadah; and Jehoadah begat
Alemeth, and Azmaveth, and Zimri. And Zimri begat Moza,
37 and Moza begat Binea, whose son was Rapha, of
whom was begotten Eleasah, that begat Azel.
38 Soothly Azel had six sons by these names, Azrikam,
Bocheru, Ishmael, Sheariah, Obadiah, and Hanan; all
these were the sons of Azel.
39 And the sons of Eshek, his brother, *were* Ulam, the
first begotten son, and Jehush, the second, and Eliphelet,
the third.
40 And the sons of Ulam were full strong men, and
bending bow with great strength, and having many sons,
and sons of sons, till to an hundred and fifty. All these
were the sons of Benjamin.

CHAPTER 9

1 Therefore all Israel was numbered, and the sum of
them was written in the book of [the] kings of Israel and
of Judah; and they were translated into Babylon for their
sin. (And so all Israel was listed, *or registered*, and their
sum was written down in The Book of the Kings of Israel
and of Judah; but they were carried away to Babylon
because of their sins.)
2 And they that dwelled first in their cities, and in the
possessions of Israel, and the priests, and the deacons,
and Nethinims, (And the first to return, and to live on
their own possessions, *or on their own property*, in their
cities, were the Israelites, and the priests, and the Levites,
and the Nethinims.)
3 dwelled in Jerusalem. Of the sons of Judah, and of
the sons of Benjamin, also of the sons of Ephraim, and of
Manasseh; (And they who lived in Jerusalem *were* of the
sons of Judah, and of Benjamin, and of Ephraim, and of
Manasseh;)
4 (of the sons of Judah;) Uthai, the son of Ammihud,
the son of Omri, the son of Imri, the son of Bani, of the
sons of Pharez (of the sons of Perez), the son of Judah;
5 and of Shelah (and of the Shilonites/and of the
Shelanites); Asaiah, the first begotten (son), and his sons;
6 and (of) the sons of Zerah; Jeuel, and his brethren
(and his kinsmen); six hundred, fourscore and ten.
7 And of the sons of Benjamin; Sallu, the son of
Meshullam, the sons of Hodaviah, the sons of Hasenuah,
(And of the sons of Benjamin; Sallu, the son of
Meshullam, the son of Hodaviah, the son of Hasenuah,)
8 and Ibneiah the son of Jeroham, and Elah the son of
Uzzi, the sons of Michri (the son of Michri), and

[7] Because of more accurate punctuation, verses 16-26 are taken from the "Early Version" of the "Wycliffe Bible"; there are no major wording differences with the same verses of the "Later Version".

Meshullam the son of Shephathiah, the son of Reuel,
(the) son of Ibnijah,
9 and the brethren of them, by their families; nine
hundred [and] six and fifty. All these *were* princes of their
kindreds by the houses of their fathers. (and their kinsmen,
by their families; nine hundred and fifty-six. All these *were*
leaders of their kindreds by the houses of their forefathers.)
10 And of the priests, Jedaiah, (and) Jehoiarib, and Jachin;
11 and Azariah, the son of Hilkiah, (the) son of
Meshullam, the son of Zadok, the son of Meraioth, (the)
son of Ahitub, *was* [the] bishop of the house of the Lord
(was the High Priest, *or the ruler*, of the House of the Lord).
12 (And) Adaiah, son of Jeroham, son of Pashur, son of
Malchijah, and Maasiai, son of Adiel, son of Jahzerah,
son of Meshullam, son of Meshillemith, son of Immer,
13 also their brethren, princes by their families, *were* a
thousand seven hundred and fourscore (and their
kinsmen, leaders of their families, *were* a thousand seven
hundred and sixty), men full strong in bodily might, to
make the work of [the] service in the house of the Lord.
14 And of the deacons (And of the Levites); Shemaiah,
the son of Hasshub, the son of Azrikam, the son of
Hashabiah, of the sons of Merari;
15 also Bakbakkar, the carpenter, and Galal, and
Mattaniah, the son of Micah, son of Zichri, son of Asaph,
(and Bakbakkar, and Heresh, and Galal, and Mattaniah,
the son of Micah, the son of Zichri, the son of Asaph,)
16 and Obadiah, the son of Shemaiah, (the) son of Galal,
the son of Jeduthun, and Berechiah, the son of Asa, the son
of Elkanah, that dwelled in the porches of Netophathites
(who lived in the villages of the Netophathites).
17 And the porters *were* Shallum, and Akkub, and
Talmon, and Ahiman, and the brethren of them; Shallum
was the prince; (And the guards, *or the doorkeepers*,
were Shallum, and Akkub, and Talmon, and Ahiman, and
their kinsmen; and Shallum *was* the leader;)
18 till to that time they kept by their whiles in the gate
of the king at the east, of the sons of Levi. (until that time,
they had all been guards, *or doorkeepers*, in the
companies of the Levites, at the King's Gate, on the east.)
19 Shallum forsooth, the son of Kore, the son of
Ebiasaph, the son of Korah, with his brethren, and with
the house of his father; these be the sons of Korah upon
the works of the service, keepers of the porches of the
tabernacle, and the families of them kept by whiles, *or
times*, the entering of the castles of the Lord. (And
Shallum, the son of Kore, the son of Ebiasaph, the son of
Korah, with his kinsmen, of the house of his father; these
Korahites were in charge of the guards at the entrance to
the Tabernacle; for their families had long guarded the
entrances to the tents, *or to the camp*, of the Lord.)
20 And Phinehas, the son of Eleazar, *was* the duke of
them before the Lord. (And Phinehas, the son of Eleazar,
had been their leader before, the Lord be with him!)
21 And Zechariah, the son of Meshelemiah, *was* porter
of the gate of the tabernacle of witnessing. (And
Zechariah, the son of Meshelemiah, *was* the guard at the
gate to the Tabernacle of the Witnessing.)
22 All these chosen into porters by (the) gates *were* two
hundred and twelve, and they were described, *or
presented*, in their own towns, which *deacons, or
ministers*, David and Samuel, the prophet, ordained in
their faith, (All these chosen to be guards at the gates
were two hundred and twelve, and they were listed in
their own towns, and David, and the prophet Samuel,
had ordained these *Levites, or these ministers*, for their
faithfulness,)
23 both them and the sons of them in the doors of the
house of the Lord, and in the tabernacle of witnessing, by
their whiles. (both them and their sons *to be* at the doors
of the House of the Lord, that is, at the entrance to the
Tabernacle of the Witnessing, by their watches.)
24 Porters were by four coasts (Guards were on four
sides), that is, at the east, at the west, at the north, and at
the south.
25 And their brethren dwelled in towns, and came in
their sabbaths from time till to time. (And their kinsmen
lived in their towns, and came for seven days at a time,
each in their turn.)
26 All the number of porters was betaken to these four
deacons, and they kept (charge of) the chambers, and the
treasures of the house of the Lord. (These four chief
guards, *or doorkeepers*, were Levites; and they were
greatly trusted, and kept charge of the rooms, and the
supplies of the House of the Lord.)
27 Also they dwelled in their keepings by the compass
of the temple of the Lord, that when time were, they
should open the gates early. (And they lived in their
residences about the Temple of the Lord, so that at the
proper time, they could open the gates every morning.)
28 *Men* of their kin were also on the vessels of [the]
service; for the vessels were borne in at the number, and
were borne out of them. (*Men* of their kin were also in
charge of the vessels used in the service; for the vessels
were borne in and borne out by them, by number.)
29 And they that had the vessels of the saintuary
betaken to their keeping, were sovereigns of [the tried]
flour, and [the] wine, and oil, and incense, and sweet
smelling spiceries. (And they who had the vessels of the
sanctuary under their charge, *or their care*, were also
responsible for the fine flour, and the wine, and the oil,
and the incense, and the sweet smelling spices.)
30 And (some of) the sons of [the] priests made
ointments of (the) sweet smelling spiceries.
31 And Mattithiah, deacon (the Levite), the first
begotten son of Shallum of the kindred of Korah, was the
sovereign of all things that were fried in the frying pan.
32 And *men* of the sons of Kohath, the brethren of

them, were on the loaves of setting forth, that they should
make ready ever new loaves by each sabbath. (And *some*
of the sons of Kohath, their kinsmen, were responsible for
the loaves of setting forth, *or the loaves of proposition*,
and they prepared new loaves every sabbath.)
33 These be the princes of chanters, by the families of
Levites, that dwelled in chambers, so that they should
serve continually day and night in their service. (These be
the leaders of the cantors, *or of the singers*, by the families
of the Levites, who lived in rooms set apart for them, so that
they could continually serve day and night in their service.)
34 The heads of (the) Levites, by their families, the
princes, dwelled in Jerusalem. (The heads of the Levites,
their leaders, lived in Jerusalem, by their families.)
35 And there dwelled in Gibeon, Jeiel, the father of
Gibeon, and the name of his wife (was) Maachah; (And
Jeiel, the founder of Gibeon, lived in Gibeon, and his
wife's name was Maachah;)
36 (and) Abdon, his first begotten son, and Zur, and
Kish, and Baal, and Ner, and Nadab,
37 and Gedor, and Ahio, and Zechariah, and Mikloth;
38 and Mikloth begat Shimeam; these dwelled even
against their brethren in Jerusalem, with their brethren.
(and Mikloth begat Shimeam; they lived with their
kinsmen in Jerusalem.)
39 And Ner begat Kish; and Kish begat Saul; and Saul
begat Jonathan, and Malchishua, and Abinadab, and
Eshbaal.
40 And the son of Jonathan *was* Meribbaal; and
Meribbaal begat Micah.
41 And the sons of Micah *were* Pithon, and Melech,
and Tahrea, (and Ahaz);
42 and Ahaz begat Jarah; and Jarah begat Alemeth, and
Azmaveth, and Zimri; and Zimri begat Moza;
43 and Moza begat Binea, whose son Rephaiah begat
Eleasah, of whom Azel was begotten.
44 And Azel had six sons by these names, Azrikam,
Bocheru, Ishmael, Sheariah, Obadiah, (and) Hanan; these
were the sons of Azel.

CHAPTER 10

1 Forsooth the Philistines fought against Israel, and the
sons of Israel fled (from) the Philistines, and felled down
wounded in the hill of Gilboa. (And the Philistines fought
against *the men of* Israel, and the Israelites fled from the
Philistines, and fell down dead on Mount Gilboa.)
2 And when the Philistines had nighed pursuing Saul
and his sons, they killed Jonathan, and Abinadab, and
Malchishua, the sons of Saul.
3 And the battle was aggrieved against Saul; and men
archers found him, and wounded *him* with darts. (And
the battle was grievous against Saul; and the archers
found him, and *mortally* wounded *him* with arrows.)
4 And Saul said to his squire, Draw out thy sword, and
slay me, lest these uncircumcised men come, and scorn
me. But his squire was afeared by dread, and would not
do this; therefore Saul took a sword, and felled upon it.
5 And when his squire had seen this, that is, that Saul
was dead, he felled also on his sword, and was dead.
6 Therefore Saul perished (And so Saul died), and his
three sons, and all his house felled down together.
7 And when the men of Israel, that dwelled in field
places, had seen this, they fled; and when Saul and his
sons were dead, they forsook their cities, and were
scattered hither and thither; and Philistines came, and
dwelled in those. (And when the men of Israel, who lived
in the valley, had seen this, they fled; yea, when they
heard that Saul and his sons were dead, they deserted
their cities, and were scattered here and there; and the
Philistines came, and lived in them/and lived there.)
8 Therefore in the tother day, the Philistines drew
away the spoils of [the] slain men, and found Saul and his
sons lying in the hill of Gilboa. (And so the next day, as
the Philistines took away the spoils of the slain men, they
found Saul and his sons lying dead on Mount Gilboa.)
9 And when they had spoiled him, and had girded off
the head, and had made *him* naked of the armours, they
sent *his head* into their land, that it should be borne
about, and should be showed in the temples of idols, and
to (the) peoples;
10 and they hallowed his armours in the temple of their
god(s), and they setted the head in the temple of Dagon.
11 When men of Jabesh of Gilead had heard this, that
is, all things which the Philistines did on Saul, (And when
some men of Jabesh of Gilead had heard about this, that
is, all the things that the Philistines had done to Saul,)
12 all [the] strong men rose (up) together, and took the
dead bodies of Saul and of his sons, and brought those
into Jabesh; and they buried the bones of them under an
oak, that was in Jabesh; and fasted seven days.
13 Therefore Saul was dead for his wickednesses, for he
brake the behest of the Lord, which he [had]
commanded, and kept not it, but furthermore also he
took counsel at a woman having a fiend speaking in the
womb, (And so Saul died for his wickedness, for he broke
the word of the Lord/for he broke the command of the
Lord, which the Lord had commanded, and he did not
obey, but he also took counsel with a woman having a
spirit speaking in her womb,)
14 and he hoped not in the Lord; for which thing both
the Lord killed him, and translated his realm to David,
the son of Jesse. (and he asked not of the Lord; for which
thing the Lord killed him, and turned his kingdom over to
Jesse's son David.)

CHAPTER 11

1 Therefore all Israel was gathered to David in
Hebron, and said, We be thy bone and thy flesh; (And so

all Israel was gathered unto David in Hebron, and said,
We be thy flesh and blood;)
2 also yesterday and the third day ago, when Saul
reigned yet upon Israel, thou it was that leddest out and
leddest in Israel; for the Lord thy God said to thee, Thou
shalt feed my people Israel, and thou shalt be prince
upon it. (and yesterday and the third day ago, when Saul
yet ruled Israel, it was thou who leddest out Israel and
leddest them in again; for the Lord thy God said to thee,
Thou shalt feed my people Israel, and thou shalt be
prince upon them/and thou shalt be their leader.)
3 Therefore all the greater men in birth of Israel came
to the king in Hebron; and David made with them a
bond of peace before the Lord, and they anointed him
king upon Israel, by the word of the Lord, which he
spake in the hand of Samuel. (And so all the men of Israel
of great age, *that is, the elders,* came to the king in
Hebron; and David made a covenant with them before
the Lord, and they anointed him king upon Israel, by the
word of the Lord, which he spoke through Samuel.)
4 Therefore David went, and all Israel, into Jerusalem;
this *Jerusalem* is Jebus, where Jebusites, inhabiters of the
land, were. (And so David, and all Israel, went to
Jerusalem; this *Jerusalem* is Jebus, where the Jebusites,
who inhabited the land, were.)
5 And they that dwelled at Jebus said to David, Thou
shalt not enter hither. Forsooth David took the high
tower of Zion, which is the city of David; (And those who
lived at Jebus said to David, Thou shalt not come in here.
But David took the high tower, *or the stronghold,* of
Zion, which is now called the City of David;)
6 and he said, Each man that slayeth first (a) Jebusite,
shall be prince and duke. Therefore Joab, the son of
Zeruiah, went up first, and was made prince. (and he
said, The first man who killeth a Jebusite shall be the
leader of the army. And so Joab, the son of Zeruiah, went
up first, and he was made the leader.)
7 And David dwelled in the high tower, and therefore
it was called the city of David; (And David lived in the
high tower, *or the stronghold,* and so it was called the
City of David.)
8 and he builded the city in compass, from Millo till to
the compass (about); and Joab builded the tother part of
the city. (and he built the city all around, from the Millo
all around; and Joab built the other part of the city.)
9 And David profited going and waxing (And David
grew stronger and stronger), and the Lord of hosts was
with him.
10 These *be* the princes of the strong men of David,
that helped him, that he should be king upon all Israel,
by the word of the Lord which he spake to Israel. (These
be the leaders of the strong men of David, who helped
him, so that he could be king upon all Israel, by the word
of the Lord which he spoke to Israel.)
11 And this *is* the number of the strong men of David;
Jashobeam, the son of Hachmoni, *was* prince among
(the) thirty; this raised up his shaft, *either spear,* upon
three hundred, (and) wounded (these) men in one time.
(And this *is* the list of the strong men of David;
Jashobeam, the son of Hachmoni, *was* the leader of The
Three; he raised up his spear against three hundred, and
killed all these men at one time.)
12 And after him *was* Eleazar, the son of his father's
brother, *that* was of (the) Ahohites, the which *Eleazar* was
among [the] three mighty men. (And after him *was*
Eleazar, the son of Dodo, *who* was of the Ahohites, and
Eleazar was also one of The Three mighty men.)
13 This was with David in Pasdammim, when
Philistines were gathered to one place into battle (He was
with David in Pasdammim, when the Philistines had
gathered together for battle); and a field of that country
was full of barley, and the people fled from the face of
(the) Philistines.
14 This *Eleazar* stood in the midst of the field, and
defended it; and when he had slain the Philistines, the
Lord gave great health to his people (the Lord gave them
a great victory).[8]
15 Soothly three of [the] thirty princes went down to
the stone, wherein David was, to the den of Adullam,
when the Philistines setted tents in the valley of Rephaim.
(And three of the thirty leaders went down to the stone,
where David was, to Adullam's cave, when the
Philistines pitched their tents in the Rephaim Valley.)
16 And David was in a stronghold, and the station, *that
is, the host gathered,* of Philistines *was* in Bethlehem.
(And David was then in a stronghold, and the garrison,
that is, the gathered army, of the Philistines *was* in
Bethlehem.)
17 Therefore David desired water, and said, I would,
that some man gave to me water (out) of the cistern of
Bethlehem, which is in the gate. (And so David desired
water, and said, I wish that someone would give me some
water from the well, which is by the gate of Bethlehem.)
18 Therefore these three went through the middle of
the castles, *or of the hosts,* of [the] Philistines, and drew
water (out) of the cistern of Bethlehem, that was in the
gate, and they brought to David, that he should drink;
and David would not *drink it,* but rather he offered it to
the Lord, (And so The Three went through the middle of
the Philistines' camp, *or tents,* and drew water from the
well, that was by the gate of Bethlehem, and they brought
it back to David, so that he could drink it; but David
would not *drink it,* but rather he offered it to the Lord,)
19 and said, Far be it, that I do this thing in the sight of
my God, and that I drink the blood of these men, for in

[8] The third member of The Three mighty men was Shammah, the son of Agee, from Harar (2ND Samuel 23:11).

the peril of their lives they brought water to me; and for
this cause he would not drink (for at the peril of their
lives they brought this water to me; and for this reason he
would not drink it). [The] Three strongest men did these
things.
20 Also Abishai, the brother of Joab, he was the prince
of (the second) three men, and he raised up his spear
against three hundred, (and) wounded (those) men; and
he was most named among (these) three, (And Abishai,
Joab's brother, he was the leader of The Thirty *mighty
men*, and he raised up his spear against three hundred,
and he killed those men; and he was famous among The
Thirty,)
21 [and] among the second three, he was noble, and
the prince of them; nevertheless he came not to the first
three. (yea, among The Thirty, he was famous, and was
their leader; but he did not achieve the fame, *or the
stature*, of The Three *mighty men*.)
22 Benaiah, the son of Jehoiada, (was) the strongest man
of Kabzeel, that did many works (who did many works); he
killed two strong men of Moab; and he went down, and
killed a lion in the midst of a cistern, in the time of snow;
23 and he killed a man of Egypt, whose stature was of
five cubits, and he had a spear as the beam of webs;
therefore Benaiah went down to him with a rod, and
ravished the spear, which he held in his hand, and killed
him with his own spear. (and he killed a man of Egypt,
who was five cubits tall, and his spear was like a
weaver's beam; and so Benaiah went down to him with a
rod, *or a club*, and seized his spear, which he held in his
hand, and killed him with his own spear.)
24 Benaiah, the son of Jehoiada, did these things, (he)
that was most named among (the second) three strong
men, (Benaiah, the son of Jehoiada, did these things, and
he was the most famous among The Thirty *mighty men*,)
25 and he was the first among [the] thirty; nevertheless
he came not to the (first) three; and David set him at his
ear *for a good counsellor*. (yea, he was the most famous
among The Thirty; but he did not achieve the fame of The
Three; and David put him in charge of his bodyguard.)
26 Forsooth the strongest men in the host *were* Asahel,
the brother of Joab, and Elhanan, the son of his father's
brother of Bethlehem, (And so the strongest men in the
army *were* Asahel, Joab's brother, and Elhanan, the son
of Dodo of Bethlehem,)
27 Shammoth (the) Harorite, Helez (the) Pelonite,
28 Ira, the son of Ikkesh of Tekoa, Abiezer of Anathoth,
29 Sibbecai (the) Hushathite, Ilai (the) Ahohite,
30 Maharai (the) Netophathite, Heled, the son of
Baanah (the) Netophathite,
31 Ithai, the son of Ribai of Gibeah, of the sons of
Benjamin; Benaiah (the) Pirathonite,
32 men of the strand [of] Gaash, Abiel (the) Arbathite,
(Hurai, of the Gorge of Gaash, Abiel the Arbathite,)
33 Azmaveth (the) Baharumite, Eliahba (the) Shaalbonite,
34 the sons of Hashem (the) Gizonite, Jonathan, the son
of Shage (the) Hararite, (Hashem the Gizonite, Jonathan,
the son of Shage the Hararite,)
35 Ahiam, the son of Sacar (the) Hararite, Eliphal, the
son of [Ur],
36 Hepher (the) Mecherathite, Ahijah (the) Pelonite,
37 Hezro (the) Carmelite, Naarai, the son of Ezbai,
38 Joel, the brother of Nathan, Mibhar, the son of
Haggeri,
39 Zelek (the) Ammonite, Naharai (the) Berothite, the
squire of Joab, son of Zeruiah,
40 Ira (the) Ithrite, Gareb (the) Ithrite,
41 Uriah (the) Hittite, Zabad, the son of Ahlai,
42 Adina, the son of Shiza (the) Reubenite, prince of
Reubenites (a leader of the Reubenites), and thirty men
with him;
43 Hanan, the son of Maachah, and Joshaphat (the)
Mithnite,
44 Uzzia (the) Ashterathite, Shama and Jehiel, the sons
of Hothan (the) Aroerite,
45 Jediael, the son of Shimri, and Joha, his brother,
(the) Tizite,
46 Eliel (the) Mahavite, Jeribai, and Joshaviah, the sons
of Elnaam, Ithmah (the) Moabite,
47 Eliel, and Obed, and Jasiel of (the) Mesobaites. (and
Eliel, and Obed, and Jasiel, from Zobah.)

CHAPTER 12

1 Also these came to David in Ziklag, when he fled yet
from Saul, the son of Kish; the which were full strong men
and noble fighters, (And these men also came to David in
Ziklag, when he had fled from Saul, the son of Kish; and
they were very strong men, and able and valiant fighters,)
2 bending bow, and casting stones with slings with
ever either hand, and directing arrows; of the brethren of
Saul of Benjamin (of the kinsmen of Saul of Benjamin),
3 the prince Ahiezer (the leader was Ahiezer), and
Joash, the sons of Shemaah of Gibeah; and Jeziel, and
Pelet, the sons of Azmaveth; and Berachah, and Jehu of
Anathoth;
4 also Ismaiah of Gibeon *was* (one of) the strongest
among (the) thirty, and above (the) thirty; Jeremy, and
Jahaziel, and Johanan, and Josabad (the) Gederathite,
(and Ismaiah of Gibeon *was* one of the strongest among
The Thirty, and a leader of The Thirty; Jeremiah, and
Jahaziel, and Johanan, and Josabad the Gederathite,)
5 Eluzai, and Jerimoth, and Bealiah, and Shemariah,
and Shephatiah (the) Haruphite,
6 Elkanah, and Jesiah, and Azareel, and Joezer, and
Jashobeam, of Korhites,
7 and Joelah, and Zebadiah, the sons of Jeroham of
Gedor.
8 But also (some) of (the) Gadites' strongest men, and

best fighters, holding shield and spear, fled over to
David, when he was hid in desert; the faces of them as
the face of a lion, and they were swift as caprets in hills.
(And some of the Gadites strongest men, and best
fighters, holding shield and spear, fled over to David,
when he was hid in the wilderness; their faces were like
the faces of lions, and they were as swift as the gazelles
on the hills.)
9 Ezer was the prince (Ezer was their leader), Obadiah
the second, Eliab the third,
10 Mishmannah the fourth, Jeremy the fifth,
11 Attai the sixth, Eliel the seventh,
12 Johanan the eighth, Elzabad the ninth,
13 Jeremy the tenth (Jeremiah the tenth), Machbanai the
eleventh;
14 these of the sons of Gad *were* princes of the host;
and the least, *that is, he that had the least power*, was
sovereign over an hundred knights, and the most *was*
over a thousand. (these of the Gadites *were* leaders of the
army; and the least, *that is, he who had the least power*,
was the ruler of a hundred horsemen, and *he who had*
the most *power, ruled* over a thousand.)
15 These it be that passed over (the) Jordan in the first
month, when it was wont to flow over his brinks; and
they drove away all men, *that is, heathen men*, that
dwelled in the valleys at the east coast, and [at the] west
coast. (These it were who passed over the Jordan River in
the first month, when it was wont to overflow its banks;
and they drove away all the people, *that is, all the heathen*,
who lived in the valleys to the east, and to the west.)
16 And also (some) men of Benjamin and of Judah
came to the stronghold, wherein David dwelled (where
David lived).
17 And David went out against them, and said, If ye
come peaceable to me, for to help me, mine heart be
joined to you; forsooth if ye set ambush to me for mine
adversaries, since I have not wickedness in the hands,
God of our fathers see and deem. (And David went out to
meet them, and said, If ye have come in peace to me,
yea, to help me, my heart shall be joined to you; but if ye
set ambush against me for my adversaries, since I have no
wickedness in my hands, let the God of our fathers see
and judge.)
18 And the spirit clothed Amasai, the prince among
(the) thirty, and he said, O! David, we be thine, and thou,
son of Jesse, we shall be with thee; peace, peace to thee,
and peace to thine helpers, for thy Lord God helpeth
thee. Therefore David received them, and made [them]
princes of the company. (And the spirit clothed Amasai,
later the leader of The Thirty, and he said, O! David, we
be thine, and thou, son of Jesse, we shall be with thee;
peace, peace to thee, and peace to thine helpers, for the
Lord thy God helpeth thee. And so David received them,
and made them leaders in his army.)
19 And (some) men of Manasseh fled over to David,
when he came with Philistines to fight against Saul, and
he fought not with them; for after that the princes of
Philistines had taken counsel, they sent him again, and
said, With peril of our head, he shall turn again to Saul
his lord. (And some men of Manasseh fled over to David,
when he came with the Philistines to fight against Saul,
though he did not fight with them; for after that the
princes, *or the leaders*, of the Philistines had taken
counsel, they sent him away, for they said, He shall
return to his lord Saul, at the peril of our own heads.)
20 Therefore when David turned again into Ziklag, men
of Manasseh fled over to him, Adnah, and Jozabad,
Jediael, and Michael, and Jozabad, and Elihu, and Zilthai,
princes of knights in Manasseh. (And so when David
returned to Ziklag, these men of Manasseh fled over to
him; Adnah, and Jozabad, Jediael, and Michael, and
Jozabad, and Elihu, and Zilthai; each of them was a
leader of a thousand horsemen in Manasseh.)
21 These men gave help to David against [the] thieves;
for all were full strong [men], and were made princes in
the host. (These men gave help to David against the
thieves; for they were all very strong men, and were
made leaders in his army.)
22 But also by each day men came to David, for to help
him, till that the number was made (as) great as the host
of God.
23 Also this is the number of [the] princes of the host that
came to David, when he was in Hebron, that they should
translate the realm of Saul to him, by the word of the Lord;
(And these are the numbers of the armed companies who
came to David, when he was in Hebron, so that they could
help get Saul's kingdom for him, by the word of the Lord;)
24 (of) the sons of Judah, bearing shield and spear, six
thousand and eight hundred, ready to battle (ready for
battle);
25 of the sons of Simeon, seven thousand and an
hundred, of (the) strongest men (for) to fight;
26 of the sons of Levi, four thousand and six hundred;
27 also Jehoiada, prince of the generation of Aaron, and
three thousand and seven hundred with him; (and
Jehoiada, the leader of Aaron's descendants, and three
thousand and seven hundred men with him;)
28 also Zadok (and Zadok), a young man of noble wit,
and the house of his father, two and twenty princes;
29 and of the sons of Benjamin, the brethren of Saul,
three thousand; for a great part of them followed yet the
house of Saul; (and of the sons of Benjamin, Saul's
kinsmen, three thousand men; for a great part of them
still followed the house of Saul;)
30 and of the sons of Ephraim, twenty thousand and
eight hundred, full strong men in bodily might, men
named in their families (famous men in their families);
31 and of the half part of the lineage of Manasseh,

eighteen thousand; all came by their names, to make
David king; (and of the western half of the tribe of
Manasseh, eighteen thousand; each chosen by their
name, to come and help make David king;)
32 also of the sons of Issachar, two hundred princes,
learned men, that knew (at) each time to command what
the people of Israel ought to do; and all the remnant *of
the* lineage followed the counsels of them; (and of the
sons of Issachar, two hundred leaders, learned men, who
knew every time what to command the people of Israel to
do; and all the remnant *of their* tribe followed their counsel;)
33 and of Zebulun came fifty thousand into his help, not
in double heart, which went out to battle, and stood in the
battle array, and were made ready with armours of battle;
(and of Zebulun came fifty thousand to help him, not of
double heart, but who went out to battle, and stood in the
battle array, ready with the arms, *or the weapons,* of battle;)
34 and of Naphtali a thousand princes, and with them
came seven and thirty thousand men, arrayed with shield
and spear; (and of Naphtali a thousand leaders, and with
them *came* thirty-seven thousand men, arrayed with
shield and spear;)
35 also of Dan, eight and twenty thousand and six
hundred men, made ready to battle; (and of Dan, twenty-
eight thousand and six hundred men, ready for battle;)
36 and of Asher forty thousand men, going out to
battle, and stirred to battle in the battle array.
37 And beyond (the) Jordan, of the sons of Reuben, and
of Gad, and of the half part of the lineage of Manasseh,
sixscore thousand men, arrayed with armours of battle.
(And from the east side of the Jordan River, of the sons of
Reuben, and of Gad, and of the eastern half of the tribe of
Manasseh, one hundred and twenty thousand men, ready
with the arms, *or the weapons,* of battle.)
38 All these men warriors and ready to battle, came
with perfect heart into Hebron, to make David king upon
all Israel (All these men of war and ready for battle, came
with perfect heart to Hebron, to make David king upon
all Israel); but also all the residue of Israel were of one
heart, that David should be made king upon all Israel.
39 And they were there at David three days, and ate
and drank; for their brethren had made ready to them;
(And they were there with David for three days, and ate
and drank; for their kinsmen had made provisions for them;)
40 but also they that were nigh them, till to Issachar
and Zebulun and Naphtali, brought loaves on asses, and
camels, and mules, and oxen, for to eat; (and also) meal,
bundles of pressed figs, and dried grapes, wine, and oil,
oxen and wethers, to all plenty (in all plenty); for joy was
in Israel.

CHAPTER 13

1 Forsooth David took counsel with [the] tribunes, and
centurions, and all [the] princes (and all the leaders);
2 and he said to all the company of the sons of Israel, If it
pleaseth you, and if the word that I speak goeth out from the
Lord our God, send we to the remnant of our brethren to
all the countries of Israel, and to [the] priests and deacons
that dwell in the suburbs of cities, that they be gathered
to us, (and he said to all the company of the Israelites, If it
pleaseth you, and if the word that I speak goeth out from the
Lord our God, then send we for the rest of our kinsmen in
all the land of Israel, and for the priests and the Levites who
live in the suburbs of the cities, that they be gathered to us,)
3 and that we bring again to us the ark of our God; for
we sought not (at) it in the days of Saul. (and then we
shall bring back the Ark of our God to us; for in the days
of Saul we did not resort to it/we did not make use of it;)
4 And all the multitude answered, that it should be
done so; for the word pleased all the people.
5 Therefore David gathered together all Israel, from
Shihor of Egypt till that thou enter into Hamath, that he
should bring the ark of God from Kiriathjearim. (And so
David gathered together all Israel, from Shihor of Egypt unto
Hamath, to bring back the Ark of God from Kiriathjearim.)
6 And David went up, and all the men of Israel, to the
hill of Kiriathjearim, which is in Judah, that he should
bring from thence the ark of the Lord God sitting on
cherubim, where his name was inwardly called (on).
(And David went up, and all the men of Israel, to Baalah,
that is, Kiriathjearim, which is in Judah, to bring back
from there the Ark of the Lord God, which sat on
cherubim, yea, the Ark which bare his name.)
7 And they putted the ark of the Lord God on a new
wain from the house of Abinadab; and Uzza and his
brethren drove the wain. (And they put the Ark of the
Lord God on a new wagon at the house of Abinadab; and
Uzza and Ahio drove the wagon.)
8 And David and all Israel played before the Lord,
with all might, in songs, and in harps, and psalteries, and
in tympans, and in cymbals, and trumps. (And David and
all Israel played before the Lord with all their might, with
songs, and harps, and lutes, and tympans, and cymbals,
and trumpets.)
9 And when they had come to the cornfloor of Chidon
(And when they had come to the threshing floor of Chidon),
Uzza stretched forth his hand to sustain, *or (to) stable,* the
ark; for the oxes waxing wild had bowed it [down] a little.
10 Therefore the Lord was wroth against Uzza, and
smote him (and struck him down), for he had touched the
ark; and he was dead there before the Lord.
11 And David was sorry, for the Lord had parted, *or
(had) slain,* Uzza; and he called that place The Parting of
Uzza, (as it is still called) unto this present day.
12 And David dreaded the Lord in that time, and said,
How may I bring into me the ark of the Lord? (And David
feared the Lord at that time, and said, How can I bring
the Ark of the Lord back home with me?)

13 And for this cause he brought not it to him, that is,
into the city of David, but he turned it into the house of
Obededom of Gath. (And for this reason he did not bring
it back with him, that is, to the City of David, but he left
it at the house of Obededom the Gittite.)
14 Therefore the ark of God dwelled in the house of
Obededom of Gath three months; and the Lord blessed
his house, and all things that he had. (And so the Ark of
God stayed at the house of Obededom the Gittite for
three months; and the Lord blessed his house, and all that
he had.)

CHAPTER 14

1 And Hiram, the king of Tyre, sent messengers to
David, and trees of cedar, and workmen of walls and of
trees, that they should build to him an house. (And
Hiram, the king of Tyre, sent messengers to David, and
cedar timber, and workmen of walls and of wood, so that
they could build a house for him.)
2 And David knew that the Lord had confirmed him
into king upon Israel; and that his realm was raised upon
his people Israel. (And David knew that the Lord had
established him as king upon Israel; and that his kingdom
was raised up on high for the sake of his people Israel.)
3 And David took other wives in Jerusalem, and he
begat sons and daughters.
4 And these be the names of them that were born to
him in Jerusalem; Shammua, and Shobab, Nathan, and
Solomon,
5 Ibhar, and Elishua, and Elpalet,
6 and Nogah, and Nepheg, and Japhia,
7 and Elishama, and Beeliada, and Eliphalet.
8 Forsooth the Philistines heard that David was
anointed king on all Israel, and [they] all ascended to
seek (out) David, (*to destroy him*). And when David had
heard this thing, he went out against them.
9 And [the] Philistines came, and were spread abroad
in the valley of Rephaim;
10 and David counselled (with) the Lord, and said,
Whether I shall go up to the Philistines? and whether
thou shalt betake them into mine hands? And the Lord
said to him, Go thou up, and I shall betake them into
thine hand. (and David counselled with the Lord, and
said, Should I go up against the Philistines? and shalt thou
deliver them into my hands? And the Lord said to him,
Go thou up, and I shall deliver them into thy hands.)
11 And when the Philistines had gone up into
Baalperazim, David smote them there (David struck them
down there), and said, God hath parted mine enemies by
mine hand, as waters be parted. And therefore the name
of that place was called Baalperazim, (*that is, the Lord of
the Breakthrough*);
12 and they left there their gods, which David
commanded to be burnt. (and they left their gods there,
which David commanded to be burned.)
13 And another time the Philistines felled in, and were
spread abroad in the valley; (And the Philistines came
another time, and were spread across the valley;)
14 and again David counselled (with) the Lord, and the
Lord said to him, Thou shalt not go up after them; go
[thou] away from them, and thou shalt come against them
even against the pear trees (and thou shalt meet them
opposite the pear trees).
15 And when thou shalt hear the sound of a goer in the
top, *or height*, of the pear trees, then thou shalt go out to
battle; for the Lord is gone out before thee, to smite the
powers of [the] Philistines (to strike down the army of the
Philistines).
16 Therefore David did as God commanded to him,
and he smote the castles/the powers of the Philistines,
from Gibeon till to Gazer. (And so David did as God
commanded him, and he struck down the army of the
Philistines, from Gibeon unto Gazer.)
17 And the name of David was published in all
countries, and the Lord gave his dread on all folks. (And
so David's name was published in every land, and the
Lord brought the fear of him upon all nations.)

CHAPTER 15

1 And David made to him(self) houses in the city of
David, and he builded a place to the ark of the Lord, and
arrayed a tabernacle to it. (And David prepared quarters
for himself in the City of David, and he built a place for
the Ark of the Lord, and prepared a Tent for it.)
2 Then David said, It is unleaveful, that the ark of God
be borne about of any others, no but of the deacons,
which the Lord chose to bear it, and for to minister to
him into without end. (Then David said, It is unlawful, for
the Ark of God to be carried about by any others, except
the Levites, whom the Lord hath chosen to carry it, and to
serve him forevermore.)
3 And David gathered together all Israel into
Jerusalem, that the ark of God should be brought into his
place, which he had made ready to it; (And David
gathered together all Israel into Jerusalem, so that the Ark
of God could be brought to the place, which he had
prepared for it;)
4 also and *he gathered together* the sons of Aaron,
and the deacons; (and *he* also *gathered together* the sons
of Aaron, and the Levites;)
5 of the sons of Kohath, Uriel was prince, and his
brethren two hundred and twenty; (of the sons of Kohath,
Uriel was the leader, with one hundred and twenty of his
kinsmen;)
6 of the sons of Merari, Asaiah *was* prince, and his
brethren two hundred and thirty; (of the sons of Merari,
Asaiah *was* the leader, with two hundred and twenty of
his kinsmen;)

7 of the sons of Gershon[9], the prince *was* Joel, and his
brethren an hundred and thirty; (of the sons of Gershon, Joel
was the leader, with one hundred and thirty of his kinsmen;)
8 of the sons of Elizaphan, Shemaiah *was* prince, and his
brethren two hundred; (of the sons of Elizaphan, Shemaiah
was the leader, with two hundred of his kinsmen;)
9 of the sons of Hebron, Eliel *was* prince, and his
brethren fourscore; (of the sons of Hebron, Eliel *was* the
leader, with eighty of his kinsmen;)
10 of the sons of Uzziel, Amminadab *was* prince, and
his brethren an hundred and twelve. (of the sons of
Uzziel, Amminadab *was* the leader, with one hundred
and twelve of his kinsmen.)
11 And David called (for) Zadok and Abiathar (the)
priests, and the deacons (and the Levites), Uriel, Asaiah,
and Joel, Shemaiah, Eliel, and Amminadab;
12 and said to them, Ye that be princes of the families
of Levi, be ye hallowed with your brethren, and bring ye
the ark of the Lord God of Israel to the place, that is made
ready to it; (and said to them, Ye who be the leaders of
the families of the Levites, be ye consecrated, *or purified*,
along with your kinsmen, and bring ye the Ark of the
Lord God of Israel to the place, that was prepared for it;)
13 lest, as at the beginning, for ye were not present, the
Lord smote us, so and now it be done, if we do any
unleaveful thing. (because the first time, for ye were not
present, the Lord struck us down, and so now it could be
done to us *again*, if we do any unlawful thing.)
14 Therefore the priests and deacons were hallowed,
that they should bear the ark of the Lord God of Israel.
(And so the priests and the Levites purified themselves, so
that they could carry the Ark of the Lord God of Israel.)
15 And the sons of Levi took the ark of God with bars
upon their shoulders, as Moses commanded by the word
of the Lord. (And the Levites took the Ark of God on bars
upon their shoulders, as Moses commanded by the word
of the Lord.)
16 And David said to the princes of (the) deacons, that
they should ordain of their brethren singers in organs of
musics, that is, in gitterns, and harps, and cymbals; that
the sound of gladness should sound on high. (And David
said to the leaders of the Levites, that they should ordain
among their kinsmen singers, and players of musical
instruments, that is, of lutes, and harps, and cymbals; so
that the sound of gladness could be heard on high.)
17 And they ordained deacons, Heman, the son of Joel,
and of his brethren, Asaph, the son of Berechiah; soothly
of the sons of Merari, [the] brethren of them, *they
ordained* Ethan, the son of Kushaiah, (And the Levites
ordained Heman, the son of Joel, and of his kinsmen,
Asaph, the son of Berechiah; and of the sons of Merari,
their kinsmen, *they ordained* Ethan, the son of Kushaiah;)

[9] Also known as Gershom.

18 and the brethren of them with them; in the second
order Zechariah, and Ben, and Jaaziel, and Shemiramoth,
and Jehiel, and Unni, Eliab, and Benaiah, and Maaseiah,
and Mattithiah, and Elipheleh, and Mikneiah, and
Obededom, and Jeiel, porters; (and with them, their
kinsmen of the second order, *or degree*, Zechariah, and
Ben, Jaaziel, Shemiramoth, Jehiel, Unni, Eliab, Benaiah,
Maaseiah, Mattithiah, Elipheleh, and Mikneiah, and the
guards, *or the doorkeepers*, Obededom, and Jeiel;)
19 and the singers, Heman, Asaph, and Ethan,
sounding in brazen cymbals; (and the musicians, Heman,
Asaph, and Ethan, sounding with brass cymbals;)
20 and Zechariah, and Aziel, and Shemiramoth, and
Jehiel, and Unni, and Eliab, and Maaseiah, and Benaiah,
these sang privates in gitterns (these played lutes in
Alamoth);
21 and Mattithiah, and Elipheleh, and Mikneiah, and
Obededom, and Jeiel, and Azaziah, sang in harps for the
eighth (played harps for the eighth), and (also the)
epinicion, *that is, thankings that ought to be done to
God, (the) overcomer and (the) victor*;
22 and Chenaniah, the prince of deacons, and of
prophecy, was sovereign to before-sing [the] melody, for
he was full wise; (and Chenaniah, a leader of the Levites,
led the singing by the singers, for he was very wise;)
23 and Berechiah, and Elkanah, *were* porters of the ark;
(and Berechiah, and Elkanah, *were* the guards, *or the
doorkeepers*, for the Ark;)
24 and Shebaniah, and Jehoshaphat, and Nethaneel,
and Amasai, and Zechariah, and Benaiah, and Eliezer,
(the) priests, sounded with trumps before the ark of the
Lord; and Obededom, and Jehiah, were porters of the ark
(and Obededom, and Jehiah, were also guards, *or
doorkeepers*, for the Ark).
25 Therefore David, and the greater men in birth of
Israel, and the tribunes, went to bring the ark of [the]
bond of peace of the Lord from the house of Obededom
with gladness. (And so David, and the men of great age,
that is, the elders, of Israel, and the tribunes, went with
great gladness to bring back the Ark of the Covenant of
the Lord from the house of Obededom.)
26 And when God had helped the deacons that bare
the ark of [the] bond of peace of the Lord, seven bulls
and seven rams were offered. (And because God had
helped the Levites who carried the Ark of the Covenant
of the Lord, they offered seven bulls and seven rams.)
27 And David was clothed with a white stole, and all
the deacons that bare the ark, and the singers, and
Chenaniah, the prince of the prophecy among [the]
singers, *were clothed in white stoles (too)*; and also
David was clothed with a linen surplice. (And David was
clothed with a white robe, and all the Levites who carried
the Ark, and the singers, and Chenaniah, the leader of the
singing by the singers, *were also clothed in white robes*;

and David was also clothed with a linen ephod.)
28 And all Israel led forth the ark of [the] bond of peace
of the Lord, and sounded in joyful song, and in sound of
clarions, and in trumps, and in cymbals, and in gitterns,
and harps. (And all Israel brought forth the Ark of the
Covenant of the Lord, and sounded with joyful song, and
with the sound of horns, and trumpets, and cymbals, and
lutes, and harps.)
29 And when the ark of [the] bond of peace of the Lord
had come into the city of David, Michal, the daughter of
Saul, beheld forth by a window, and saw king David
dancing and playing; and she despised him in her heart.
(And when the Ark of the Covenant of the Lord had come
into the City of David, Michal, Saul's daughter, watched
from a window, and saw King David dancing and
playing; and she despised him in her heart.)

CHAPTER 16

1 Therefore they brought the ark of God, and setted it
in the midst of the tabernacle, that David had arrayed
thereto; and they offered burnt sacrifices and peaceable
sacrifices before the Lord. (And so they brought the Ark
of God, and put it in the midst of the Tent that David had
prepared for it; and they offered burnt sacrifices and
peace offerings before the Lord.)
2 And when David offering burnt sacrifices and
peaceable sacrifices had fulfilled, he blessed the people
in the name of the Lord; (And when David had finished
offering the burnt sacrifices and the peace offerings, he
blessed the people in the name of the Lord;)
3 and he parted to all, to each by himself, from man to
woman, one cake of bread/a cake of bread, and a part of
roasted flesh of a bugle, and flour fried in oil. (and he
gave to all of them, yea, to each one, every man and
woman, a loaf of bread, and a piece of the roasted flesh
of a wild ox, *or of a buffalo*, and flour fried in oil.)
4 And he ordained before the ark of the Lord, of the
Levites, *that is, deacons*, that should minister, *that is,
serve*, and have mind of the works of the Lord, and
glorify and praise the Lord God of Israel; (And he
ordained before the Ark of the Lord some of the Levites
to serve, and to remember *aloud* the works of the Lord,
and to glorify and to praise the Lord God of Israel;)
5 Asaph the prince, and Zechariah his second;
forsooth Jeiel, and Shemiramoth, and Jehiel, and
Mattithiah, and Eliab, and Benaiah, and Obededom, and
Jeiel, on the organs of the psaltery, and on the harps; but
he ordained Asaph to sound with cymbals; (Asaph *to be*
the leader, and Zechariah *to be* his second; and Jaaziel,
and Shemiramoth, and Jehiel, and Mattithiah, and Eliab,
and Benaiah, and Obededom, and Jeiel, to play the lutes
and the harps; and Asaph to sound with the cymbals;)
6 and *he ordained* Benaiah and Jahaziel, priests,
before the ark of the bond of peace of the Lord, for to
trump continually. (and Benaiah and Jahaziel, the priests,
to blow the trumpets continuously before the Ark of the
Covenant of the Lord.)
7 In that day, David made Asaph prince, and his
brethren, for to acknowledge to the Lord. (On that day,
David first ordained Asaph, and his kinsmen, to give
praise and thanks to the Lord, *and to proclaim to the
people, saying,*)
8 Acknowledge ye to the Lord, and inwardly call ye
(on) his name; make ye his findings known among
peoples. (Give ye thanks to the Lord, and call ye on his
name; make ye his deeds known among the peoples.)
9 Sing ye to him, and say ye psalm to him, and tell ye
all his marvels (and tell ye of all his marvellous deeds).
10 Praise ye his holy name; the heart of men seeking
the Lord be glad (let the hearts of those seeking the Lord
be glad).
11 Seek ye the Lord and his strength; seek ye
ever[more] his face (seek ye his face forevermore).
12 Have ye mind of his marvels that he hath done; of
his signs, and of the dooms of his mouth. (Remember the
marvels that he hath done; his signs, and the judgements
from his mouth.)
13 The seed of Israel, his servant, *praise thou God*; the
sons of Jacob, his chosen, *praise ye God*. (Let the
descendants of his servant Israel, *praise ye God*; let the
children of Jacob, his chosen, *praise ye God*.)
14 He *is* the Lord our God; his dooms *be* in each land
(let his judgements *be* in every land).
15 Have ye mind without end of his covenant; of the
word which he covenanted into a thousand generations.
(Remember his covenant forevermore; yea, the word
which he covenanted to a thousand generations.)
16 Which word he covenanted with Abraham; and of
his oath to Isaac.
17 And he ordained that *word* to Jacob into a
commandment; and to Israel into (an) everlasting covenant.
(And he ordained that *word* to Jacob for a commandment;
and to Israel for an everlasting covenant.)
18 And he said, To thee I shall give the land of Canaan;
the part of your heritage (the portion of your inheritance).
19 When they were few in number; little, and pilgrims
thereof (yea, only a few, and strangers there).
20 And they passed from folk into folk; and from a
realm to another people. (And they went from nation to
nation; and from one kingdom to another.)
21 He suffered not any man (to) falsely challenge them;
but he blamed kings for them. (He did not allow anyone
to oppress them; and he admonished kings for them.)
22 (*And he said*,) Do not ye touch my christs, *that is,
(the) patriarchs anointed with the anointing of grace*; and
do not ye do wickedly against my prophets.
23 All [the] earth, sing ye to the Lord; tell ye from day
into day his health (tell ye of his victory day after day/tell

ye of his salvation, *or his deliverance*, day after day).
24 Tell ye among heathen men his glory (Tell ye of his
glory among the heathen); his marvels among all peoples.
25 For the Lord *is* great, and worthy to be praised full
much; and he *is* horrible, *that is, fearful*, over all gods.
(For the Lord *is* great, and worthy to be greatly praised;
and he it *is* who *should be* feared/and it *is* he who *should
be* revered, more than all the gods.)
26 For all the gods of (the) peoples *be* (but) idols; but
the Lord made (the) heavens.
27 Acknowledging and great doing *be* before him;
strength and joy *be* in the place of him. (Acknowledgement
and great accomplishment, *that is, honour and glory, be*
before him; strength and joy *be* in his dwelling.)
28 Ye families of peoples, bring ye to the Lord; bring ye
to the Lord glory and empire.
29 Give ye the glory to his name, raise ye up sacrifice,
and come ye in his sight; and worship ye the Lord in holy
fairness. (Give ye the glory due to his name, raise ye up a
sacrifice, and come ye before him; and worship ye the
Lord in the beauty of holiness.)
30 All earth be moved from his face; for he hath
founded the world unmoveable. (All the earth tremble
before him; for he hath made the world immovable.)
31 (The) Heavens be glad, and the earth make full out
joy; and say they among (the) nations, The Lord reign.
32 The sea thunder, and his fullness (Let the sea
thunder, and all of its fullness); the fields fully joy they,
and all things that be in those.
33 Then the trees of the forest shall praise before the
Lord; for he cometh to deem the earth (for he cometh to
judge the earth).
34 Acknowledge to the Lord, for he is good; for his
mercy *is* without end. (Give thanks to the Lord, for he is
good; for his mercy *is* forevermore.)
35 And say ye, Thou God, our saviour, save us, and
gather us together, and deliver *us* from heathen men; that
we acknowledge to thine holy name, and be fully glad in
thy songs. (And say ye, Thou God, our saviour, save us,
and gather us together, and deliver *us* from the heathen;
so that we may give thanks to thy holy name, and rejoice
in thy songs, *or in thy praise*.)
36 Blessed be the Lord God of Israel from without
beginning and into without end; and all the people say,
Amen, and *say* praising to God.
37 Therefore David left there, before the ark of [the] bond
of peace of the Lord, Asaph and his brethren, for to minister
in the sight of the ark, *or before the ark*, continually, by
all days and their whiles. (And so David left Asaph and
his kinsmen there, before the Ark of the Covenant of the
Lord, to serve continually before the Ark, in all the days
of their service, *that is, first one, and then another*.)
38 And David ordained (as) porters, Obededom and his
brethren, eight and sixty; and Obededom, the son of
Jeduthun, and Hosah. (And David ordained Obededom,
the son of Jeduthun, and Hosah, to be the guards, *or the
doorkeepers*; and Obededom and his kinsmen were sixty-
eight in number.)
39 And *he ordained* Zadok (the) priest, and his
brethren, (the) priests, before the tabernacle of the Lord,
in the high place that was in Gibeon, (And *he ordained*
Zadok the priest, and his kinsmen, the priests, *to be*
before the Tabernacle of the Lord, that was at the hill
shrine in Gibeon,)
40 for to offer burnt sacrifices to the Lord upon the altar
of burnt sacrifice continually, in the morrowtide and
eventide, by all things that be written in the law of the
Lord (by all the things that be written in the Law of the
Lord), which he commanded to Israel.
41 And after him *David ordained* Heman and Jeduthun,
and [the] other(s) chosen, each man by his name, for to
acknowledge to the Lord; for his mercy is without end.
(And with them *David ordained* Heman and Jeduthun,
and the others who were chosen, each man by his name,
to give thanks to the Lord; for his mercy is forevermore.)
42 And *he ordained* Heman and Jeduthun, (with)
trumping, and shaking (of) cymbals, and all organs of
musics, for to sing to God; forsooth he made the sons of
Jeduthun to be porters. (And *he ordained* Heman and
Jeduthun, and the others, to sing to God with trumpets,
and cymbals, and all the other musical instruments; and
he made the sons of Jeduthun to be the guards, *or the
doorkeepers*.)
43 And all the people turned again into their house,
and David *turned again*, to bless also his house. (And all
the people returned to their houses, and David also
returned home to bless his house.)

CHAPTER 17

1 Forsooth when David dwelled in his house, he said
to Nathan, the prophet, Lo! I dwell in an house of cedars;
and the ark of [the] bond of peace of the Lord is under
skins. (And when David was in his house, he said to the
prophet Nathan, Lo! I live in a cedar house; but the Ark of
the Covenant of the Lord is under curtains, *or in a tent*.)
2 And Nathan said to David, Do thou all things that
be in thine heart, for God is with thee.
3 Therefore in that night (But in that night), the word
of the Lord was made to Nathan, and (he) said,
4 Go thou, and speak to David, my servant, (and say,)
The Lord saith these things, Thou shalt not build to me an
house to dwell in (Thou shalt not built a House for me to
live in);
5 certainly I have not dwelled in an house, from that
time in which I led Israel out of the land of Egypt till to
this day, but ever[more] I have changed places of the
tabernacle, and have dwelled in a tent with all Israel.
(truly I have not lived in a House, from that time in which

I led Israel out of the land of Egypt unto this day, but
always I have gone from place to place, and have lived in
a tabernacle, yea, a tent, like all Israel.)
6 Whether I have spoken namely to one of the judges
of Israel, to which I commanded that they should feed my
people, and said, Why hast thou not builded to me an
house of cedar? (Have I spoken to any of the judges of
Israel, to whom I commanded that they should feed my
people, and said, Why hast thou not built a cedar House
for me?)
7 Now therefore thou shalt speak thus to my servant
David, The Lord of hosts saith these things, I took thee,
when thou followedest the flock in the pastures, that thou
shouldest be duke upon my people Israel; (And so now
thou shalt say thus to my servant David, The Lord of
hosts saith these things, I took thee from the pastures,
where thou followedest the flocks, so that thou wouldest
be the leader of my people Israel;)
8 and I was with thee whither ever thou wentest, and I
killed all thine enemies before thee, and I made to thee a
name, as of one of the great men that be made
worshipful, *either famous*, in [the] earth. (and I was with
thee wherever thou wentest, and I killed all thy enemies
before thee, and I made a name for thee, as of one of the
great men to be honoured, *or famous*, on the earth.)
9 And I gave a place to my people Israel; it shall be
planted, and shall dwell therein, and it shall no more be
moved, and the sons of wickedness shall not defoul
them, as from the beginning, (And I gave a place to my
people Israel; they shall be planted there, and shall live
there; and they shall no longer be oppressed, and the
sons of wickedness shall not defile them, as they did at
the beginning,)
10 from the days in which I gave judges to my people
Israel; and I made low all thine enemies. Therefore I tell
to thee, that the Lord shall build an house to thee. (in the
days when I gave judges to my people Israel; yea, I shall
humble all thy enemies. And so I tell thee, that the Lord
shall build a house for thee.)
11 And when thou hast fulfilled thy days, that thou go
to thy fathers, I shall raise up thy seed after thee, that
shall be of thy sons, and I shall stablish his realm; (And
when thou hast finished thy days, and thou shalt go to
thy fathers, *that is, when thou shalt die*, I shall raise up
thy descendant after thee, who shall be one of thy sons,
and I shall stablish his kingdom;)
12 he shall build to me an house, and I shall make
steadfast his seat into without end. (he shall build a House
for me, and I shall make his throne steadfast forevermore.)
13 I shall be to him into a father, and he shall be to me
into a son; and I shall not do away my mercy from him,
as I took it away from him that was before thee; (I shall
be a father to him, and he shall be a son to me; and I
shall not take away my love from him, as I took it away
from him who was before thee;)
14 and I shall ordain him in mine house and in my
realm into without end; and his throne shall be most
steadfast without end. (and I shall ordain him in my
House and in my kingdom forevermore; and his throne
shall be most steadfast forevermore.)
15 By all these words, and by all this revelation, so
Nathan spake to David.
16 And when king David had come, and had set before
the Lord, he said, Lord God, who am I, and what is mine
house, that thou shouldest give such things to me?
17 But also this is seen (as) little in thy sight, and therefore
thou hast spoken of the house of thy servant, yea, into
time to coming (in the time to come); and thou hast made
me worthy to be beholden over all men. My Lord God,
18 what may David add more, since thou hast so
glorified thy servant, and hast known him? (what more
can David add, *or say*, since thou hast so glorified thy
servant, even though thou knowest him *so well*?)
19 Lord, for thy servant, thou hast done by thine heart
all this great doing, and thou wouldest that all (these)
great things be known. (Lord, for thy servant's sake, and
after thy own heart, thou hast done all this great doing,
and thou desirest that all these great things be known.)
20 Lord, none is like thee, and none other God is without
thee, of all which we have heard with our ears. (Lord, no
one is like thee, and there is no other God besides thee,
out of all which we have heard with our ears.)
21 For who is another (such) as thy people Israel, (this)
one folk in [the] earth, to whom God went, to deliver and
make a people to himself, and to cast out by his greatness
and dreads nations from the face thereof, the which
people he delivered from Egypt? (For who is another such
as thy people Israel, this one nation in all the earth, to
whom God went, and delivered from servitude, *or from
slavery*, to make them his people, and to make a great and
fearful name for himself, by throwing out nations from
before them, yea, the *people* whom he rescued from Egypt?)
22 And thou hast set thy people Israel into a people to
thee into without end, and thou, Lord, art made the God
thereof (and thou, Lord, art made their God).
23 Now therefore (And so now), Lord, the word which
thou hast spoken to thy servant, and on his house, be it
confirmed without end, and do, as thou hast spoken;
24 and thy name dwell, and be (it) magnified without
end; and be it said, The Lord of hosts *is* God of Israel,
and the house of David, his servant, dwelling before him
(and the house of his servant David shall live before him).
25 For thou, my Lord God, hast made revelation in the ear
of thy servant, that thou wouldest build to him an house
(that thou wouldest build a house for him); and therefore
thy servant hath found trust, that he pray before thee.
26 Now therefore, Lord, thou art God, and hast spoken
to thy servant so great benificences; (And so now, Lord,

thou art God, and hast promised to thy servant such good
and great things;)
27 and thou hast begun to bless the house of thy
servant, that it be ever[more] before thee; for, Lord, for
thou blessest, it shall be blessed without end. (and thou
hast begun to bless the house of thy servant, that it be
before thee forevermore; for, Lord, because thou blessest,
it shall be blessed forevermore.)

CHAPTER 18

1 Soothly it was done after these things, that David
smote the Philistines (that David struck the Philistines),
and made them low, and he took away Gath and the
villages thereof from the hand of (the) Philistines;
2 and he smote Moab (and he struck Moab); and
Moabites were made the servants of David, and brought
gifts to him.
3 In that time David smote also Hadadezer[10], king of
Zobah, of the country of Hamath, when he went to alarge
his empire till to the flood Euphrates. (At that time David
also struck down Hadadezer, the king of Zobah, of the
country of Hamath, when he went to enlarge his empire
unto the Euphrates River.)
4 Therefore David took a thousand four-horsed carts
of his, and seven thousand of horsemen, and twenty
thousand of footmen; and he hocked all the horses of the
chariots, except an hundred four-horsed carts, which he
kept to himself. (And so David took from him a thousand
four-horsed chariots, and seven thousand horsemen, and
twenty thousand footmen; and he hocked all the horses
for the chariots, except *the horses for* a hundred four-
horsed chariots, which he kept for himself.)
5 Forsooth also (the) Syrians of Damascus came
above, to give help to Hadadezer, king of Zobah, but
David smote also of his two and twenty thousand of men;
(And when the Syrians of Damascus came over, to give
help to Hadadezer, the king of Zobah, David struck
down twenty-two thousand of them;)
6 and David set knights in Damascus, that (the)
Syrians also should serve him, and bring *to him* gifts.
And the Lord helped David in all things to which he
went. (and David put horsemen, *or garrisons*, in
Damascus, so that the Syrians would also serve him, and
bring *him* gifts/and pay *him* taxes, *or tribute*. And so the
Lord helped David in everything that he did.)
7 And David took [the] golden arrow cases, which the
servants of Hadadezer had, and he brought those into
Jerusalem;
8 also and of Tibhath, and of Chun, the cities of
Hadadezer, *he took* full much of brass, whereof Solomon
made the brazen sea, *that is, (the) washing vessel*, and
(the) pillars, and (the) brazen vessels. (and also from
Tibhath, and from Chun, the cities of Hadadezer, *he took*
a great deal of bronze, from which Solomon made the
bronze Sea, *that is, the washing vessel*, and the pillars,
and the bronze vessels.)
9 And when Tou, king of Hamath, had heard this
thing, that is, that David had smitten all the host of
Hadadezer, king of Zobah, (And when Tou, the king of
Hamath, had heard that David had struck down all the
army of Hadadezer, the king of Zobah,)
10 he sent Hadoram, his son, to David the king, for to
ask of him peace, and for to thank him, for he had
overcome and smitten Hadadezer; for why king
Hadadezer was adversary of Tou. (And Hadoram brought
vessels of gold and silver and bronze, as gifts.) (he sent
his son Hadoram to King David, to greet him, and to
congratulate him, for he had overcome and struck down
Hadadezer; for King Hadadezer was an adversary of Tou.
And Hadoram brought vessels of gold and silver and
bronze, as gifts.)
11 But also king David hallowed to the Lord all the
vessels of gold, and of silver, and of brass; and the silver,
and the gold, which the king had taken of all folks, as
well of Idumea, and of Moab, and of the sons of Ammon,
as of [the] Philistines, and of Amalek. (And King David
dedicated these gifts to the Lord; and also the silver and
gold which he had taken from all the nations, yea, from
Edom, and from Moab, and from the Ammonites, and
from the Philistines, and from Amalek.)
12 And Abishai, the son of Zeruiah, smote Edom in the
valley of salt pits, (killing) eighteen thousand (men).
13 And he set stronghold(s) in Edom, that Idumeans
should serve David (And David put strongholds, *or
garrisons*, in Edom, so that the Edomites would serve
him). And the Lord saved David in all things, to which
he went.
14 Therefore David reigned on all Israel, and did doom
and rightwiseness to all his people. (And so David
reigned upon all Israel, and decreed righteous
judgements for all of his people.)
15 Forsooth Joab, the son of Zeruiah, was on the host;
and Jehoshaphat, the son of Ahilud, *was* chancellor; (And
Joab, the son of Zeruiah, was in command of the army;
and Jehoshaphat, the son of Ahilud, *was* the chancellor;)
16 and Zadok, the son of Ahitub, and Abimelech, the
son of Abiathar, *were* priests; and Shavsha *was* scribe;
(and Zadok, the son of Ahitub, and Abimelech, the son of
Abiathar, *were* the High Priests; and Shavsha *was* the
writer, *or the royal secretary*;)
17 and Benaiah, the son of Jehoiada, *was* on the
legions (of the) Cherethites and Pelethites, *keepers of
David's head*; soothly the sons of David *were* the first at
the hand of the king. (and Benaiah, the son of Jehoiada,
was over the legions of the Cherethites and Pelethites,
who were David's bodyguards; and David's sons *were*

[10] Also known as Hadarezer.

the first in line at the hand of the king.)

CHAPTER 19

1 Forsooth it befelled, that Nahash, [the] king of the
sons of Ammon, died, and his son reigned for him. (And
it befell, that Nahash, the king of the Ammonites, died,
and his son reigned for him.)
2 And David said, I shall do mercy with Hanun, the
son of Nahash; for his father gave mercy to me. And
David sent messengers, to comfort him on the death of
his father. And when they were come into the land of
the sons of Ammon, for to comfort Hanun (And when
they were come into the land of the Ammonites, to
comfort Hanun),
3 the princes of the sons of Ammon said to Hanun, In
hap thou guessest, that David, for cause of honour into
thy father, sent *men*, that should comfort thee; and thou
perceivest not, that his servants be come to thee to espy,
and inquire, and to seek (through) thy land. (the princes
of the Ammonites/the leaders of the Ammonites said to
Hanun, Perhaps thou guessest that David, in honour of
thy father, sent these *men* to comfort thee; and thou
perceivest not, that his servants came to thee to spy, and
to inquire, and to search out thy land.)
4 Therefore Hanun made bald and shaved the servants
of David, and cutted the coats off them from the buttocks
of them till to the feet; and let go them (and then he let
them go).
5 And when they had gone forth, and had sent this to
David, he sent into the meeting of them; for they had
suffered great despite; and he commanded, that they should
dwell in Jericho, till their beard(s) waxed, and then they
should turn again. (And when they had gone forth, and
had sent word about this to David, he sent a message to
them; for they had suffered great despising, *or great shame*;
and he commanded, that they should live in Jericho, until
their beards grew again, and then they could return home.)
6 And the sons of Ammon saw, that they had done
wrong to David, both Hanun and the other people, and
they sent a thousand talents of silver, for to hire to them
chariots and horsemen of Mesopotamia, and of Syria, of
Maachah, and of Zobah; (And when the Ammonites saw
that they had wronged David, Hanun and the other
people sent a thousand talents of silver, to hire for
themselves chariots and horsemen from Mesopotamia,
and Syriamaachah, and Zobah;)
7 and they hired to them two and thirty thousand of
chariots, and the king of Maachah with his people. And
when they were come, they set their tents even against
Medeba; and the sons of Ammon were gathered together
from their cities, and came to battle. (and they hired for
themselves thirty-two thousand chariots, and the king of
Maachah with his people. And when they were come,
they pitched their tents opposite, *or near*, Medeba; and
the Ammonites were gathered together from their cities,
and came to do battle.)
8 And when David heard this, he sent Joab, and all
the host of strong men. (And when David heard of this,
he sent Joab, and all his army of strong men.)
9 And the sons of Ammon went out, and dressed
battle array beside the gate of the city; but the kings, that
were come to help them, stood asides-half in the field.
(And the Ammonites went out, and directed the battle
array beside the gate of the city; and the kings, who had
come to help them, stood half-aside in the field.)
10 Therefore Joab understood, that [the] battle was
made against him even against and behind *his* back, and
he chose the strongest men of all Israel, and went against
(the) Syrians; (And so Joab understood, that the battle was
made against him both in front, and behind *his* back, and
he chose the strongest men out of all Israel, and went out
against the Syrians;)
11 soothly he gave the residue part of the people under
the hand of Abishai, his brother; and they went forth against
the sons of Ammon. (and he left the rest of the people
under the hand, *or the power*, of his brother Abishai; and
then they went forth against the Ammonites.)
12 And Joab said, If Syrians shall overcome me, thou
shalt help me; and if the sons of Ammon shall overcome
thee, I shall help thee; (And Joab said, If the Syrians
overcome me, thou shalt help me; and if the Ammonites
overcome thee, I shall help thee;)
13 be thou comforted, and do we manly for our
people, and for the cities of our God; and the Lord do
that, that is good in his sight. (be thou strengthened, and
be thou confident, for our people, and for the cities of
our God; and may the Lord do what is good in his sight.)
14 Therefore Joab went forth, and the people that was
with him, against (the) Syrians to (the) battle, and he
drove them away. (And so Joab, and the people who
were with him, went forth to do battle against the
Syrians, and they drove them away.)
15 And the sons of Ammon saw, that (the) Syrians had
fled, and they [also] fled from Abishai, his brother, and
entered into the city; and Joab turned again into Jerusalem.
(And when the Ammonites saw that the Syrians had fled,
then they also fled from his brother Abishai, and entered
into the city; and then Joab returned to Jerusalem.)
16 And (the) Syrians saw, that he had fallen down
before Israel, and he sent messengers, and brought [forth]
to them (the) Syrians, that was beyond the flood; and
Shophach, the prince of [the] chivalry of Hadadezer[11],
was the duke of them. (And when the Syrians saw that
they had fallen down before Israel, they sent messengers,
and brought over *to themselves* the Syrians who were on
the east side of the Euphrates River; and Shophach, the

[11] Also known as Hadarezer.

prince of Hadadezer's cavalry, *or of his army*, was their leader.)

17 And when this was told to David, he gathered all Israel, and passed (over the) Jordan; and he felled in on them, and dressed (the) battle array even against them, fighting on the contrary. (And when this was told to David, he gathered all Israel, and crossed the Jordan River; and he fell in on them, and directed the battle array opposite them, and began to fight.)

18 And (the) Syrians fled from Israel, and David killed of the men of Syria seven thousand of chariots, *that is, seven thousand men fighting in chariots*[12], and forty thousand of footmen, and Shophach, the prince of the host (and also Shophach, the leader of the army).

19 And the servants of Hadadezer saw, that they were overcome of Israel, and they fled over to David, and served him; and Syria would no more give help to the sons of Ammon. (And the servants of Hadadezer saw that they were overcome by Israel, and they fled over to David, and served him; and from that time on, Syria no longer gave any help to the Ammonites.)

CHAPTER 20

1 Forsooth it was done after the end of a year, in that time wherein kings be wont to go forth to battles, Joab gathered the host, and the strength of (the) chivalry, and he wasted the land of the sons of Ammon, and went, and besieged Rabbah; forsooth David dwelled in Jerusalem, when Joab smote Rabbah, and destroyed it. (And it was done after the end of the year, at that time when kings be wont to go forth to battle, Joab gathered the army, and the power of the cavalry, *or the horsemen*, and he wasted the land of the Ammonites, and went, and besieged Rabbah; but David stayed in Jerusalem, while Joab struck Rabbah, and destroyed it.)

2 And David took the crown of Malcham from his head, and found therein the weight of gold (of) a talent, and most precious gems, and he made thereof a diadem to himself; also he took full many spoils of the city. (And David took the crown from the head of *their idol* Milcom, and found that it weighed a talent of gold, and had a most precious gemstone, and he made it his own crown; and he took full many spoils from the city.)

3 And he led out the people that was therein, and made brads, *either instruments by which corns be broken*, and sleds, and iron chariots, to pass (over) on them, so that all men were cut into diverse parts, and were all-broken; David did thus to all the cities of the sons of Ammon, and he turned again with all his people into Jerusalem. (And he led out the people who were there, and made brads, *that is, instruments by which corn is broken*, and sleds, and iron chariots, to pass over the top of them, so that all the people were cut into many parts, and were killed; and David did this to all the cities of the Ammonites, and then he returned with all of his people to Jerusalem.)

4 After these things, a battle was made in Gezer against (the) Philistines, wherein Sibbechai (the) Hushathite slew Sippai of the kin of Rephaim, *that is, of the kind of giants*, and he meeked them (and he made them low, *or he humbled them*).

5 Also another battle was done against the Philistines, in which a man given of God, the son of the forest, a man of Bethlehem, killed Goliath of Gath, the brother *of giants*, of whose shaft, *or spear*, the wood was as the beam of webs. (And another battle was made against the Philistines, in which Elhanan, the son of Jair, a man of Bethlehem, killed Lahmi, the brother of Goliath of Gath, and the wood of his shaft, *or his spear*, was like a weaver's beam.)

6 But also another battle befelled in Gath, in which a full long man was, having six fingers (on each hand, and six toes on each foot), that is, altogether four and twenty, and he was (also) begotten of the generation of Rephaim; (And another battle befell in Gath, in which there was a very tall man, who had six fingers on each hand, and six toes on each foot, that is, twenty-four digits altogether, and he was also born of the descendants of the Rephaim, *that is, of the giants*;)

7 and he blasphemed Israel, and Jonathan, the son of Shimea, (the) brother of David, killed him.

8 These be the sons of Rephaim in Gath, that felled down in the hand of David, and of his servants. (These be the sons of the Rephaim in Gath, who fell at the hands of David, and his men.)

CHAPTER 21

1 Soothly Satan rose against Israel, and stirred David for to number Israel. (And Satan rose up against Israel, and stirred David to count the Israelites.)

2 And David said to Joab, and to the princes of the people, Go ye, and number *all* Israel from Beersheba till to Dan, and bring ye the number to me, that I know *what it is*. (And David said to Joab, and to the leaders of the people, Go ye, and count up *all* Israel from Beersheba unto Dan, and bring ye the number to me, so that I know *what it is*.)

3 And Joab answered, The Lord increase his people an hundredfold more than they be; (but) my lord the king, whether (they) all be not thy servants? Why seeketh my lord this thing, that shall be areckoned into sin to Israel? (that shall be reckoned as a sin by Israel?)

4 But the word of the king had more the mastery; and Joab went out, and compassed all Israel, and turned again into Jerusalem. (But the word of the king had more the

[12] For there were seven hundred of chariots, (as it says) in the second book of Kings, 10TH chapter (that is, as it says in the 10TH Chapter of 2ND Samuel), and in each chariot were 10 men, and these make seven thousand men fighting in chariots.

mastery; and Joab went out, and went all around Israel,
and then returned to Jerusalem.)
5 And he gave to David the number of them, which
he had compassed; and all the number of Israel was
found a thousand thousand, and an hundred thousand of
men, drawing out sword; forsooth of Judah were three
hundred thousand, and seventy thousand warriors. (And
he gave David the number of them, which he had
counted; and all the number of Israel was found to be a
thousand thousand, and a hundred thousand men
drawing out the sword; and in Judah there were four
hundred and seventy thousand warriors.)
6 But Joab numbered not Levi and Benjamin, for
against his will he did the commandment of the king.
(But Joab did not count the Levites and the Benjaminites,
for he did the king's commandment against his own will.)
7 Forsooth that thing that was commanded displeased
the Lord, therefore he smote Israel. (But what was
commanded displeased the Lord, and so he struck Israel.)
8 And David said to God, I have sinned greatly, that I
would do this thing; I beseech thee, Lord, do thou away
the wickedness of thy servant, for I did follily. (And David
said to God, I have greatly sinned, that I would do this
thing; I beseech thee, Lord, do thou away the wickedness
of thy servant, for I did foolishly.)
9 And the Lord spake to Gad, the prophet of David,
and said to him,
10 Go thou, and speak to David, and say to him, The
Lord saith these things, I give to thee the choosing of
three things; choose thou one which thou wilt, that I do
to thee.
11 And when Gad was come to David, he said to
David, The Lord saith these things, Choose thou that that
thou wilt *of these* (Choose thou what thou wilt *from these
three punishments*),
12 either pestilence three years, either that three months
thou flee thine enemies, and be not able to escape their
sword, either that the sword of the Lord and death reign
three days in the land, and that the angel of the Lord slay in
all the coasts of Israel. Now therefore see thou, what I shall
answer to him that sent me. (either three years of famine,
or for three months thou shalt flee thy enemies, and not
be able to escape their swords, or for three days the
sword of the Lord, *that is, pestilence*, shall reign in the
land, and the angel of the Lord shall kill in all of Israel's
coasts. And so now say thou, what shall I answer to him
who sent me.)
13 And David said to Gad, Anguishes oppress me on
each part, but it is better to me (but it is better for me),
that I fall into the hands of the Lord, for his merciful
doings be many, then into the hands of men.
14 Therefore the Lord sent pestilence into Israel, and
seventy thousand of men felled down of Israel. (And so
the Lord sent pestilence into Israel, and seventy thousand
Israelites died.)
15 Also the Lord sent an angel into Jerusalem, that he
should smite it; and when it was smitten, the Lord saw,
and had mercy upon the greatness of (the) evil; and he
commanded to the angel that smote, and said, It
sufficeth, now thine hand cease. And the angel of the
Lord stood beside the cornfloor of Ornan (the) Jebusite.
(And the Lord sent an angel into Jerusalem, to strike it;
and when it was struck, the Lord saw, and had mercy on
the greatness of the evil; and he commanded to the angel
who struck it, and said, It sufficeth, now stay thy hand.
And the angel of the Lord stood still beside the threshing
floor of Ornan the Jebusite.)
16 And David raised up his eyes, and saw the angel of
the Lord standing betwixt heaven and (the) earth, and a
drawn sword in his hand, turned against Jerusalem. And
both he and the greater men in birth were clothed with hair-
shirts, and they fell down upon the earth (And both he
and the men of great age, *that is, the elders*, were clothed
with hair-shirts, and they fell down on the ground).
17 And David said to the Lord, Whether I am not he
that commanded that the people should be numbered? I
it am that sinned, I it am that did evil; what hath this flock
deserved? My Lord God, I beseech thee, (let) thine hand
be turned against me, and against the house of my father;
but thy people be not smitten. (And David said to the
Lord, Was it not I who commanded that the people
should be counted? It is I who sinned, it is I who did the
evil; what hath this flock done to deserve this? My Lord
God, I beseech thee, let thy hand be turned against me,
and against the house of my father; but do not let thy
people be struck down.)
18 And the angel of the Lord commanded [to] Gad, that
he should say to David, that he should go up, and build
an altar to the Lord God in the cornfloor of Ornan (the)
Jebusite. (And the angel of the Lord commanded to Gad,
that he should say to David, that he should go up, and
build an altar to the Lord God at the threshing floor of
Ornan the Jebusite.)
19 Therefore David went up by the word of Gad,
which he spake to him by the word of the Lord. (And so
David went up by the word of Gad, which he spoke to
him in the name of the Lord.)
20 And when Ornan had beheld, and saw the angel,
and his four sons with him *had seen* (him also), they hid
them[selves], for in that time Ornan threshed wheat in the
cornfloor. (And when Ornan, and his four sons who were
with him, beheld, and saw the angel, his sons ran and hid
themselves; for at that time Ornan threshed wheat at the
threshing floor.)
21 Therefore when David came to Ornan, Ornan
beheld David, and went forth from the cornfloor against
him, and worshipped him lowly upon the ground. (And
so when David came to Ornan, Ornan saw David, and

went out from the threshing floor to greet him, and he
bowed low before him, with his face to the ground.)
22 And David said to him, Give the place of the
cornfloor to me, that I build therein an altar to the Lord;
so (long as) that thou take as much silver as it is worth,
and that the vengeance cease from the people. (And
David said to him, Give me the place of the threshing
floor, so that I can build on it an altar to the Lord; yea,
take thou as much silver as it is worth; so only that this
vengeance cease from destroying the people.)
23 And Ornan said to David, Take thou *it*, and my lord
the king do *he* whatever thing pleaseth him; but also I
give oxen into burnt sacrifice, and instruments of wood,
whereby corns be threshed, into sticks to be burnt, and
wheat into sacrifice; I give gladly all *these* things. (And
Ornan said to David, Take thou *it*, and my lord the king do
he whatever thing pleaseth him; and also I give oxen for the
burnt sacrifices, and the wooden instruments, with which
the corns be threshed, for sticks to be burned, and wheat for
the offering; I willingly, *or I gladly*, give you all *these* things.)
24 And king David said to him, It shall not be done so,
but I shall give *to thee* silver (for) as much as it is worth;
for I ought not to take away from thee, and offer so to the
Lord burnt sacrifices freely given. (And King David said to
him, It shall not be done so, but I shall give *thee* as much
silver as it is worth; for I ought not to take what is thine to
give to the Lord, nor to offer burnt sacrifices given for free.)
25 Therefore David gave to Ornan for the place six
hundred shekels of gold of full just weight. (And so David
gave Ornan six hundred shekels of gold of full just weight
for the place.)
26 And David builded there an altar to the Lord, and
offered thereon burnt sacrifices and peaceable sacrifices,
and he inwardly called (on) God; and God heard him in
fire from heaven upon the altar of burnt sacrifice. (And
David built there an altar to the Lord, and offered on it
burnt sacrifices and peace offerings, and he inwardly
called on God; and God answered him from heaven with
fire on the altar of burnt sacrifice.)
27 And the Lord commanded to the angel, and he
turned his sword again into the sheath.
28 Then anon David saw, that the Lord had heard him
in the cornfloor of Ornan (the) Jebusite, and he offered
there slain sacrifices. (And David saw at once, that the
Lord had answered him at the threshing floor of Ornan
the Jebusite, and he offered slain sacrifices there.)
29 Forsooth the tabernacle of the Lord, that Moses had
made in the desert, and the altar of burnt sacrifices, was
in that tempest in the high place of Gibeon; (For the
Tabernacle of the Lord, that Moses had made in the
wilderness, and the altar of burnt sacrifices, were at that
time at the hill shrine in Gibeon;)
30 and David might not go to the altar, to beseech God
there, for he was afeared with full great dread (for he was
afraid with a very great fear), seeing the sword of the
angel of the Lord.

CHAPTER 22

1 And David said, This is the house of God, and this
altar is into burnt sacrifice of Israel. (And David said, This
is the House of God, and this is the altar of burnt sacrifice
for Israel.)
2 And David commanded that all converts, *that is*, all
men turned from heathenness to the law of Israel, should
be gathered together of the land of Israel (And David
commanded that all *male* converts, *that is*, all men turned
from heathenness to the Law of Israel, in the land of
Israel, should be gathered together); and he ordained
(some) of them (to be) masons for to cut, *or (to) hew*,
stones and to polish *them*, and that the house of the Lord
should be builded;
3 also David made ready full much iron to the nails of
the gates, and to the mixings and jointures, and
unnumberable weight of brass; (and David made ready a
great deal of iron for the nails of the gates, and for the
joints, and innumerable weight of bronze;)
4 also the (number of) trees of cedar might not be
guessed (and the amount of cedar timber could not be
guessed), which the men of Sidon and the men of Tyre
brought to David.
5 And David said, Solomon, my son, is a little child
and delicate, *that is, for tenderness of age*; soothly the
house, which I will (to) be builded to the Lord, oughteth
to be such, that it be named in all countries; therefore I
shall make ready necessaries to him. And for this cause
David before his death made ready all [the] costs. (And
David said, My son Solomon is a young and delicate
man, *that is, of tender age*; and the House, which I desire
to build to the Lord, ought to be such that it be famous in
every country; and so I shall prepare its necessities. And
for this reason David prepared all the expenses and the
materials before his death.)
6 And he called Solomon, his son, and commanded to
him, that he should build an house to the Lord God of
Israel. (And he called for his son Solomon, and commanded
him to build a House for the Lord God of Israel.)
7 And David said to Solomon, My son, it was my will
to build an house to the name of the Lord my God; (And
David said to Solomon, My son, it was my desire to build
a House to honour the name of the Lord my God;)
8 but the word of the Lord was made to me, and said,
Thou hast shed out (too) much blood, and thou hast fought
full many battles; thou mayest not build an house to my
name (so thou mayest not build a House to honour my
name), for thou hast shed out so much blood before me;
9 the son that shall be born to thee, shall be a man
most peaceable; for I shall make him to have rest of all
his enemies by compass, and for this cause he shall be

called Peaceable; and I shall give peace and rest in Israel
in all his days. (the son who shall be born to thee shall be
a man of peace; for I shall give him rest from all his enemies
about, and for this reason he shall be called Solomon;
and I shall give peace and rest to Israel in all his days.)
10 He shall build an house to my name; he shall be to
me into a son, and I shall be to him into a father; and I
shall make steadfast the seat of his realm on Israel
without end. (He shall build a House to honour my
name; he shall be a son to me, and I shall be a father to
him; and I shall make steadfast the throne of his kingdom
upon Israel forevermore.)
11 Now therefore, my son, the Lord be with thee; and
have thou prosperity, and build thou an house to the
Lord thy God, as he hath spoken of thee. (And so now,
my son, the Lord be with thee; and be thou prosperous,
and build thou the House of the Lord thy God, as he hath
said of thee.)
12 And the Lord give to thee prudence and wit, that
thou may govern Israel, and keep the law of the Lord thy
God (and obey the Law of the Lord thy God).
13 For then thou mayest profit, if thou keepest the behests
and dooms, which the Lord commanded to Moses, that
he should teach Israel; be thou strengthened, and do thou
manly, dread thou not withoutforth, neither dread thou
within. (For then thou shalt prosper, if thou obeyest the
commands and the judgements, *or the laws,* which the
Lord commanded to Moses, that he should teach Israel;
be thou strengthened, and be thou confident, fear thou
not anything withoutforth, nor fear thou anything within.)
14 Lo! in my poverty I have made ready the costs of the
house of the Lord; an hundred thousand talents of gold,
and a thousand thousand talents of silver; soothly of brass
and iron is no weight, for the number is overcome by
greatness; I have (also) made ready wood and stones at all
costs. (Lo! in spite of my tribulations I have prepared the
expenses and the materials for the House of the Lord; a
hundred thousand talents of gold, and a thousand thousand
talents of silver; and of bronze and iron there is no weight,
for the number hath overpassed greatness; I have also
prepared some timber and stones, but you will need more.)
15 Also thou hast full many craftsmen, masons, and
layers of stones, and craftsmen of timber, and of all crafts,
most prudent to make work (most able to do the work),
16 in gold, and silver, and brass (and bronze), and in
iron, of which (there) is no number; therefore rise thou
up, and make *it,* and the Lord shall be with thee.
17 Also David commanded to all the princes of Israel,
that they should help Solomon, his son, and said,
18 Ye see, that the Lord your God is with you, and he
hath given to you rest by compass/about, and he hath
betaken all [the] enemies in your hand, and the earth is
subject before the Lord, and before his people. (Ye see,
that the Lord your God is with you, and he hath given
you rest all around, and he hath delivered all the enemies
into your hands, *or your power,* and the land is subject
before the Lord, and before his people.)
19 Therefore give ye your hearts and your souls, that ye
seek the Lord your God; and rise ye up together, and
build ye a saintuary to the Lord our God, that the ark of
[the] bond of peace of the Lord be brought in thither, and
that vessels hallowed to the Lord *be brought* into the
house, that is builded to the name of the Lord. (And so
give ye your hearts and your souls, that ye seek the Lord
your God; and rise ye up together, and build ye a
sanctuary for the Lord our God, so that the Ark of the
Covenant of the Lord can be brought in there, and that
vessels dedicated, *or consecrated,* to the Lord *can be*
brought into the House, that is built to honour the name
of the Lord.)

CHAPTER 23

1 Then David was eld and full of days, and he
ordained Solomon, his son, king upon Israel.
2 And he gathered together all the princes of Israel,
and the priests, and deacons; (And he gathered together
all the leaders of Israel, and the priests, and the Levites;)
3 and the deacons were numbered from twenty years
and above, and eight and thirty thousand of men were
found of them. (and the Levites twenty years of age and
older were counted, and thirty-eight thousand men were
found of them.)
4 And four and twenty thousand men were chosen of
them, and were parted into the service of the house of
the Lord; and of sovereigns, and judges, six thousand;
(And twenty-four thousand men were chosen from them,
and were put in service in the House of the Lord; and six
thousand were overseers, *or officers,* and judges, *or*
magistrates;)
5 and four thousand that were porters of gates and doors,
and so many singers, singing to the Lord in organs, which
David had made for to sing with. (and four thousand
were made the guards, *or the doorkeepers,* of the gates
and the doors, and as many singers sang to the Lord with
the instruments which David had made to sing with.)
6 And David parted them by the whiles of the sons of
Levi, that is, of Gershon, and Kohath, and Merari. (And
David divided them into *three* groups, *or divisions,* by
the families of the Levites, that is, of Gershon, and
Kohath, and Merari.)
7 And the sons of Gershon *were* Laadan and Shimei.
8 The sons of Laadan *were* three; the prince Jehiel (the
leader *was* Jehiel), and Zetham, and Joel.
9 The sons of Shimei *were* three, Shelomith, and Haziel,
and Haran; these *were* the princes of the families of
Laadan (these *were* the leaders of the families of Laadan).
10 And the sons of Shimei *were* Jahath, and Zina, and
Jeush, and Beriah; these four *were* the sons of Shimei.

11 And Jahath was the former, and Zizah, the second; and Jeush and Beriah had not full many sons, and therefore they were reckoned in one family, and in one house. (And Jahath was the first-born son, and Zizah, the second; and Jeush and Beriah did not have many sons, and so they were reckoned as one family, and one house.)

12 The sons of Kohath *were* four, Amram, and Izhar, and Hebron, and Uzziel.

13 The sons of Amram *were* Aaron and Moses; and Aaron was separated, that he should minister in the holy of holy things, he and his sons without end, and to burn incense to the Lord by his custom, and to bless his name without end. (The sons of Amram *were* Aaron and Moses; and Aaron was set apart, so that he could be in charge of the holy things, he and his sons forevermore, and to burn incense to the Lord as by its custom, and to bless his name forevermore.)

14 Also the sons of Moses, the man of God, were numbered in the lineage of Levi. (But the sons of Moses, the man of God, were counted in the tribe of Levi.)

15 The sons of Moses *were* Gershom and Eliezer.

16 The sons of Gershom; Shebuel the first (son).

17 And the sons of Eliezer were Rehabiah the first (son), and other sons were not to Eliezer; forsooth the sons of Rehabiah were multiplied full much.

18 The sons of Izhar; Shelomith the first (son).

19 The sons of Hebron; Jeriah the first (son), Amariah the second, Jahaziel the third, Jekameam the fourth.

20 The sons of Uzziel; Micah the first (son), Jesiah the second.

21 The sons of Merari *were* Mahli and Mushi. The sons of Mahli *were* Eleazar, and Kish.

22 And Eleazar was dead, and had not sons, but daughters; and the sons of Kish, the brethren of them, *that is, (the) cousins-german*, wedded them. (And Eleazar died, and had no sons, but only daughters; and the sons of Kish, their kinsmen, *that is, their first cousins*, wedded them.)

23 The sons of Mushi *were* three, Mahli, and Eder, and Jeremoth.

24 These *were* the sons of Levi in their kindreds and families, *and they were* princes by whiles, and the number of all the heads, that did the travail of the service of the house of the Lord, from twenty years and above. (These *were* the Levites in their kindreds and families, and the list of all their leaders, yea, those who did the work in the service of the House of the Lord, from twenty years of age and older.)

25 For David said, The Lord God of Israel hath given rest to his people, and a dwelling in Jerusalem into without end; (For David said, The Lord God of Israel hath given rest to his people, and shall make his dwelling place in Jerusalem forevermore;)

26 and it shall not be the office of (the) deacons for to bear [any] more the tabernacle, and all the vessels thereof for to minister *therein*. (and it shall not be the duty of the Levites to carry about the Tabernacle any more, or any of the vessels for its service.)

27 Also by the last behests of David the number of the sons of Levi shall be reckoned from twenty years and above; (And by the last commands of David the number of the Levites shall be reckoned from twenty years of age and above;)

28 and they shall be under the hand of the sons of Aaron, into the worship of the house of the Lord, in porches, and in chambers, and in the place of cleansing, and in the saintuary, and in all works of the service of the temple of the Lord. (and they shall be under the power of the sons of Aaron in the service of the House of the Lord, yea, in the courtyards, and in the rooms, and in the cleansing of all the holy things, and in all the works in the service of the Temple of the Lord.)

29 And [the] priests *shall* be over the loaves of proposition, *that is, (the loaves of) setting forth*, and to the sacrifice of [tried] flour, and to the pastes sodden in water, and to the therf loaves, and to the frying pan, and to [the] hot flour, and to singe, and over all weight and measure. (And the priests *shall* be in charge of the loaves of proposition, *that is, the loaves of setting forth*, and the sacrifice of fine flour, and the pastries boiled in water, and the unleavened bread, and the frying pan, and the hot flour, and the singeing, and over all the weights and measures.)

30 And the deacons *shall be*, that they stand early, for to acknowledge and sing to the Lord, and in like manner at eventide, (And every morning, the Levites shall be on duty to give thanks and to sing to the Lord, and in like manner every evening,)

31 as well in the offering of burnt sacrifices of the Lord, as in sabbaths, and calends, and other solemnities, by the number and ceremonies of each thing, continually before the Lord; (as well as at the offering of burnt sacrifices to the Lord, on sabbaths, and calends, and the other Feast Days, by their prescribed number, continually before the Lord;)

32 and that they keep the observances of the tabernacle of the bond of peace of the Lord, and the custom of the saintuary, and the observance of the sons of Aaron, their brethren, that they minister in the house of the Lord. (and that they keep the observances of the Tabernacle of the Covenant of the Lord, *that is, the Tabernacle of the Witnessing*, and the customs of the sanctuary, and the observances of the sons of Aaron, their kinsmen, and so serve in the House of the Lord.)

CHAPTER 24

1 Forsooth to the sons of Aaron these portions shall be; the sons of Aaron *were* Nadab, and Abihu, Eleazar, and Ithamar; (And these shall be the divisions of the sons of Aaron; Aaron's sons *were* Nadab, and Abihu, Eleazar, and Ithamar;)

2 but Nadab and Abihu were dead without free
children before their father, and Eleazar and Ithamar were
set in priesthood. (and Nadab and Abihu died before
their father did, and had no children, and so Eleazar and
Ithamar became priests, *that is, the High Priests*.)
3 And David parted them, that is, (with the help of)
Zadok, of the sons of Eleazar, and Ahimelech, of the sons
of Ithamar, by their whiles, and their service; (And David,
with the help of Zadok, of the sons of Eleazar, and
Ahimelech, of the sons of Ithamar, divided them for their
duties, and their service;)
4 and the sons of Eleazar were found many more in
the men princes, than the sons of Ithamar. And David
parted to them, that is, to the sons of Eleazar, sixteen
princes by their families (and houses); and to the sons of
Ithamar eight *princes* by their families and houses. (and
there were found many more leaders of the sons of
Eleazar, than of the sons of Ithamar. And David ordained
to them, that is, to the sons of Eleazar, sixteen leaders by
their families and houses; and to the sons of Ithamar eight
leaders by their families and houses.)
5 And he parted ever either families among themselves
by lots; for there were princes of the saintuary, and
princes of the house of God, as well of the sons of
Eleazar, and of the sons of Ithamar. (And he divided both
families among themselves by lots; for there were officers
of the sanctuary, and officers of the House of God, from
the sons of Eleazar, and from the sons of Ithamar.)
6 And Shemaiah, the son of Nethaneel, a scribe of the
lineage of Levi, described them before the king and [the]
princes, and before Zadok, the priest, and Ahimelech, the
son of Abiathar, and to the princes of the families of the
priests and of the deacons; *he described* one house of
Eleazar, that was sovereign to [the] others, and the tother
house of Ithamar, that had [the] other *priests and deacons*
under him. (And Shemaiah, the son of Nethaneel, a
writer, *or a secretary*, of the Levite tribe, listed them
before the king, and the officers, and Zadok, the priest,
and Ahimelech, the son of Abiathar, and the leaders of
the families of the priests and the Levites; *he listed* one
household, *or family*, of Eleazar, that was the leader of
the others, and another household, *or family*, of Ithamar,
that had the other *priests and Levites* under him.)
7 Forsooth the first lot went out to Jehoiarib, the
second to Jedaiah,
8 the third to Harim, the fourth to Seorim,
9 the fifth to Malchijah, the sixth to Mijamin,
10 the seventh to Hakkoz, the eighth to Abiah (the
eighth to Abijah),
11 the ninth to Jeshuah, the tenth to Shecaniah,
12 the eleventh to Eliashib, the twelfth to Jakim,
13 the thirteenth to Huppah, the fourteenth to Jeshebeab,
14 the fifteenth to Bilgah, the sixteenth to Immer,
15 the seventeenth to Hezir, the eighteenth to Aphses,
16 the nineteenth to Pethahiah, the twentieth to
Jehezekel,
17 the one and twentieth to Jachin, the two and
twentieth to Gamul,
18 the three and twentieth to Delaiah, and the four and
twentieth to Maaziah.
19 These were the whiles, *or times*, of them by their
services, that they enter into the house of God, and by
their custom under the hand of Aaron, their father, as the
Lord God of Israel commanded.
20 Forsooth Shubael was prince of the sons of Levi that
were residue/that were left, of the sons of Amram; and
the son of Shubael *was* Jehdeiah; (And of the Levites who
were left; of the sons of Amram, Shubael was the leader;
and the son of Shubael *was* Jehdeiah;)
21 also Isshiah *was* prince of the sons of Rehabiah. (and
Isshiah *was* the leader of the sons of Rehabiah.)
22 And Shelomoth *was prince* of Izharites; and the son
of Shelomoth *was* Jahath; (And Shelomoth *was the leader*
of the Izharites; and Shelomoth's son *was* Jahath;)
23 and (the sons of Hebron); his first son was Jeriah,
Amariah the second, Jahaziel the third, Jekameam the
fourth.
24 The son of Uzziel *was* Michah; the son of Michah
was Shamir;
25 the brother of Michah *was* Isshiah; and the son of
Isshiah *was* Zechariah.
26 The sons of Merari *were* Mahli and Mushi; the son
of Jaaziah *was* Beno; (The sons of Merari *were* Mahli, and
Mushi, and Jaaziah his son;)
27 and the son of Merari *was* Jaaziah, and Shoham, and
Zaccur, and Ibri. (and the sons of Merari, of Jaaziah, *were*
Beno, and Shoham, and Zaccur, and Ibri.)
28 And the son of Mahli *was* Eleazar, which had not free
sons; (And the son of Mahli *was* Eleazar, who had no sons;)
29 and the son of Kish *was* Jerahmeel;
30 the sons of Mushi *were* Mahli, Eder, and Jerimoth.
These *were* the sons of Levi, by the houses of their
families.
31 Also and they sent lots (over) against their brethren,
the sons of Aaron, before David the king, and before
Zadok, and Ahimelech, and *before* the princes of the
families of [the] priests, and of deacons; [the] lot parted
evenly all *things*, both the greater and the less. (And they
cast lots side by side with their kinsmen, the sons of
Aaron, before King David, and Zadok, and Ahimelech,
and the leaders of the families of the priests, and of the
Levites; and the lot evenly divided all, both the greater
and the lesser alike.)

CHAPTER 25

1 Therefore David, and the magistrates of the host,
separated to the service of the sons of Asaph, and of
Heman, and of Jeduthun, the which should prophesy in

harps, and in psalteries, and in cymbals, by their number,
and serve the office hallowed, *or enjoined*, to them. (And
so David, and his officers/and his leaders, set apart for
service the sons of Asaph, and of Heman, and of
Jeduthun, who would prophesy to the accompaniment of
harps, and lutes, and cymbals, by their number, and so
do the work assigned to them.)
2 Of the sons of Asaph; Zaccur, and Joseph, and
Nethaniah, and Asarelah; and the sons of Asaph, under
the hand of Asaph, prophesied beside the king
(prophesied by order of the king).
3 And the sons of Jeduthun *were these*; Gedaliah,
Zeri, Jeshaiah, (Shimei,) and Hashabiah, and Mattithiah,
six; under the hand of their father Jeduthun, that
prophesied in an harp, upon men acknowledging and
praising the Lord (who prophesied to the accompaniment
of a harp, giving thanks, and praising the Lord).
4 Also the sons of Heman *were* (*these* of) Heman;
Bukkiah, Mattaniah, Uzziel, Shebuel, and Jerimoth,
Hananiah, Hanani, Eliathah, Giddalti, and Romamtiezer,
and Joshbekashah, Mallothi, Hothir, and Mahazioth;
5 all these the sons of Heman *were* prophets of the
king in the words of God, that he should enhance the
horn, *or strength*. And God gave to Heman fourteen sons
and three daughters. (all these *were* the sons of Heman,
the prophet of the king, by the promises of God, to lift up
his horn, *or his strength*. And God gave Heman fourteen
sons and three daughters.)
6 All these under the hand of their father were dealed,
either assigned, to sing in the temple of the Lord, in
cymbals, and psalteries, and harps, into the service of the
house of the Lord, nigh the king, that is say, Asaph, and
Jeduthun, and Heman. (All these were under the hand, *or
the power*, of their father, and were assigned to play, in
the Temple of the Lord, cymbals, and lutes, and harps, for
service in the House of the Lord, while Asaph, and
Jeduthun, and Heman, were under the direction of the
king.)
7 And the number of them, with their brethren that
taught the song[s] of the Lord, all the teachers, was two
hundred fourscore and eight. (And their number, with
their kinsmen who taught the songs of the Lord, yea, all
of the teachers, was two hundred and eighty-eight.)
8 And they sent lots by their whiles evenly, as well the
greater as the less, also a wise man and an unwise. (And
they all cast lots for their duties, both the greater and the
lesser alike, and a wise man as well as an unwise one.)
9 And the first lot went out to Joseph, that was of
Asaph, (and to his sons and to his brothers, twelve); the
second to Gedaliah, to him, and to his sons and to his
brethren, twelve;
10 the third to Zaccur, to his sons and to his brethren,
twelve;
11 the fourth to Izri, to his sons and to his brethren,
twelve;
12 the fifth to Nethaniah, to his sons and to his
brethren, twelve;
13 the sixth to Bukkiah, to his sons and to his brethren,
twelve;
14 the seventh to Jesharelah, to his sons and to his
brethren, twelve;
15 the eighth to Jeshaiah, to his sons and to his
brethren, twelve;
16 the ninth to Mattaniah, to his sons and to his
brethren, twelve;
17 the tenth to Shimei, to his sons and to his brethren,
twelve;
18 the eleventh to Azareel, to his sons and to his
brethren, twelve;
19 the twelfth to Hashabiah, to his sons and to his
brethren, twelve;
20 the thirteenth to Shubael, to his sons and to his
brethren, twelve;
21 the fourteenth to Mattithiah, to his sons and to his
brethren, twelve;
22 the fifteenth to Jeremoth, to his sons and to his
brethren, twelve;
23 the sixteenth to Hananiah, to his sons and to his
brethren, twelve;
24 the seventeenth to Joshbekashah, to his sons and to
his brethren, twelve;
25 the eighteenth to Hanani, to his sons and to his
brethren, twelve;
26 the nineteenth to Mallothi, to his sons and to his
brethren, twelve;
27 the twentieth to Eliathah, to his sons and to his
brethren, twelve;
28 the one and twentieth to Hothir, to his sons and to
his brethren, twelve;
29 the two and twentieth to Giddalti, to his sons and to
his brethren, twelve;
30 the three and twentieth to Mahazioth, to his sons
and to his brethren, twelve;
31 the four and twentieth to Romamtiezer, to his sons
and to his brethren, twelve.

CHAPTER 26

1 Forsooth these *were* the partings of [the] porters; of
the sons of Korah, Meshelemiah *was* the son of Kore, of
the sons of Asaph. (Now these *were* the divisions of the
guards, *or the doorkeepers*; of the Korahites, there *was*
Meshelemiah, the son of Kore, of the sons of Asaph.)
2 The sons of Meshelemiah *were* Zechariah the first
begotten, Jediael the second, Zebadiah the third, Jathniel
the fourth,
3 Elam the fifth, Jehohanan the sixth, Elioenai the
seventh.
4 And the sons of Obededom *were these*; Shemaiah

the first begotten, Jehozabad the second, Joah the third,
and Sacar the fourth, Nethaneel the fifth,
5 Ammiel the sixth, Issachar the seventh, Peulthai the
eighth, for the Lord blessed him.
6 And to Shemaiah, his son, were born sons,
sovereigns of their families (leaders of their families); for
they were full strong men.
7 Therefore the sons of Shemaiah *were* Othni, and
Rephael, and Obed, and Elzabad; and his brethren, full
strong men, also Elihu, and Semachiah. (And so the sons
of Shemaiah *were* Othni, and Rephael, and Obed, and
Elzabad, and their other brothers, Elihu, and Semachiah,
who were all very strong men.)
8 All these *were* of the sons of Obededom; they and
their sons and their brethren, full strong men for to serve,
two and sixty of Obededom. (All these *were* of the sons
of Obededom; they and their sons and their brothers, all
very strong men fit for service *in the Temple*, were sixty-
two of Obededom.)
9 And of Meshelemiah *were* eighteen sons and
brethren, full strong men (all very strong men).
10 And of Hosah, that is, of the sons of Merari, Simri
was (the) prince; and for he had no first begotten son,
therefore his father ordained him into [a] prince; (And of
Hosah, that is, of the sons of Merari, Simri was the leader;
and though he was not the first-born son, his father had
ordained him to be the leader;)
11 and Hilkiah the second, Tebaliah the third,
Zechariah the fourth; all these thirteen *were* the sons and
brethren of Hosah.
12 These were parted into porters, that ever[more] the
princes of [the] keepings, as also their brethren, should
minister in the house of the Lord. (These were the
divisions of the guards, *or the doorkeepers*, and
forevermore the leaders of the divisions, and their
kinsmen, would serve in the House of the Lord.)
13 Therefore lots were sent, *or cast*, evenly, both to the
little and to the great, by their families, into each of the
gates. (And so they all cast lots, both the lesser and the
greater alike, by their families, for each of the gates.)
14 Therefore the lot of the east *coast* befelled to
Shelemiah; and the north coast befelled by lot to
Zechariah, his son, a full prudent man and well learned;
(And so the east *gate* fell by lot to Shelemiah; and the
north gate to his son Zechariah, a well-learned and very
prudent man;)
15 and to Obededom and to his sons *(the) lot fell* at the
south *coast*, in which part of the house was the council of
the elder men; (and the south *gate fell by lot* to
Obededom, and the gatehouse to his sons;)
16 Shuppim and Hosah were at the west *coast*, besides
the (Shallecheth) gate that leadeth to the way of going up,
keeping against keeping [ward against ward]. (Shuppim and
Hosah were at the west *gate*, as well as the Shallecheth
Gate that leadeth to the way of ascending; they guarded
one, then the other.)
17 And at the east *part were* six deacons, and at the
north were four by day; and at the south also were four at
midday; and, where the council was, *were* twain and
twain. (And on the east *side there were* six Levites every
day, and on the north there were four every day; and on
the south there were also four every day; and two *were* at
each gatehouse.)
18 And in the cells, *either little houses*, of [the] porters
at the west *side*, *were* four in the way, and twain by the
cells. (And by the cells, *or the little houses*, of the guards
on the west *side*, *there were* four by the road, and two by
the cells.)
19 These were [the] partings of the porters, of the sons
of Kore and of Merari. (These were the divisions of the
guards, *or the doorkeepers*, of the sons of Kore, and the
sons of Merari.)
20 And (of the Levites,) Ahijah was over the treasures of
the house of the Lord, and over [the] vessels of the holy
things. (And fellow Levites were in charge of the
treasuries of the House of the Lord, and the vessels of the
holy things.)
21 The sons of Laadan, the son of Gershon; of Laadan
were the princes of the families of Laadan, and of
Gershon, and of Jehiel. (Of the sons of Laadan, the son of
Gershon; of Laadan, the leader of the families of Laadan
the Gershonite *was* Jehiel.)
22 The sons of Jehiel *were* Zetham, and Joel, his
brother, (who were) over the treasures of the house of the
Lord, (The other sons of Laadan *were* Zetham, and his
brother Joel, who were in charge of the treasuries of the
House of the Lord.)
23 (of) Amramites, and Izharites, and Hebronites, and
Uzzielites. (Of the Amramites, and Izharites, and
Hebronites, and Uzzielites,)
24 And Shebuel, the son of Gershom, son of Moses,
was sovereign of the treasures; (Shebuel, the son of
Gershom, the son of Moses, *was* in charge of the
treasures/*was* in charge of the treasuries;)
25 and his brother, Eliezer (and his brother *was*
Eliezer); whose son *was* Rehabiah; and his son *was*
Jeshaiah; and his son *was* Joram; and his son *was* Zichri;
but and his son *was* Shelomith.
26 That Shelomith, and his brethren, *were* over the
treasures of the holy things, which David the king
hallowed, and the princes of families, and the tribunes,
and the centurions, and the dukes of the host, (This
Shelomith, and his kinsmen, *were* over all the treasures
of the holy things, which King David, and the leaders of
the families, and the tribunes, and the centurions, and the
leaders of the army, had dedicated, *or had given*,)
27 of the battles, and of the spoils of battles, which they
hallowed to the reparation and purtenance of the temple

of the Lord. (from the battles, and the spoils of battles,
which they had dedicated for use in the Temple of the
Lord /which they had dedicated for the upkeep of the
Temple of the Lord.)
28 And Samuel, the prophet, hallowed all these things,
and Saul, the son of Kish, and Abner, the son of Ner, and
Joab, the son of Zeruiah; and all these hallowed those
things by the hand of Shelomith, and of his brethren.
(And all those things which the prophet Samuel, and
Saul, the son of Kish, and Abner, the son of Ner, and
Joab, the son of Zeruiah, had dedicated; indeed, all the
dedicated things were under the hand of Shelomith, and
his kinsmen.)
29 And Chenaniah was sovereign, and his sons, to
Izharites, to the works withoutforth on Israel, to teach and
to deem them. (And of the Izharites, Chenaniah and his
sons were in charge of the works withoutforth in Israel,
that is, in keeping the records, and resolving disputes.)
30 And of (the) Hebronites, Hashabiah, and his
brethren, full strong men, a thousand and seven hundred,
were sovereigns upon Israel beyond (the) Jordan against
the west, in all the works of the Lord, and into the service
of the king. (And of the Hebronites, Hashabiah, and his
kinsmen, very strong men, a thousand and seven hundred,
were in charge of Israel west of the Jordan River, in all
the works of the Lord, and in the service of the king.)
31 And Jerijah was prince of Hebronites, by their
families and kindreds. In the fortieth year of the realm of
David there were numbered, and were found full strong
men in Jazer of Gilead; (And Jerijah was the leader of the
Hebronites, by their families and kindreds. In the fortieth
year of David's reign they were sought out, and many
strong men of them were found at Jazer of Gilead;)
32 and his brethren, of stronger age, two thousand and
seven hundred, princes of families. And king David
made them sovereigns of Reubenites, and Gadites, and of
the half lineage of Manasseh, into all the service of God,
and of the king. (yea, of his kinsmen, men of ability, two
thousand and seven hundred, all leaders of their families.
And King David made them rulers over the Reubenites,
and Gadites, and the eastern half of the tribe of Manasseh,
concerning all service to God, and to the king.)

CHAPTER 27

1 Forsooth the sons of Israel by their number, the
princes of families, the tribunes, and centurions, and
prefects, that ministered to the king by their companies *of
knights,* entering in and going out by each month in the
year, were sovereigns, each by himself, upon four and
twenty thousand. (Now the number of Israelites, that is,
the leaders of the families, and the tribunes, and the
centurions, and the prefects, who served the king with
their companies *of horsemen,* coming in and going out
each month of the year, was twenty-four thousand in
each company, *or division.*)
2 Jashobeam, the son of Zabdiel, was sovereign of the
first company in the first month, and under him *were* four
and twenty thousand; (Jashobeam, the son of Zabdiel,
was the leader of the first company in the first month, and
under him *were* twenty-four thousand;)
3 of the sons of Pharez, *was* the prince of all [the] princes
in the host, in the first month. (of the sons of Perez, *he was*
the leader of all the leaders in the army, in the first month.)
4 Dodai (the) Ahohite had the company of the second
month, and after himself *he had* another man, Mikloth by
name, that governed a part of the host of four and twenty
thousand. (Dodai the Ahohite led the second company in
the second month, and *he had* another man, named
Mikloth, who helped him govern his division of twenty-
four thousand./And Eleazar, the son of Dodai the
Ahohite, led the second company in the second month,
and he governed his division of twenty-four thousand.)
5 And Benaiah, the son of Jehoiada, the priest, was
duke of the third company in the third month, and four
and twenty thousand *were* in his parting; (And Benaiah,
the son of Jehoiada, the priest, was the leader of the third
company in the third month, and twenty-four thousand
were in his division;)
6 that is Benaiah, the strongest man among (the) thirty,
and above (the) thirty; and Ammizabad, his son, was
sovereign of his company (after him). (this is Benaiah, the
strongest man among The Thirty, and he *was* a leader of
The Thirty; and his son Ammizabad was the leader of his
company after him.)
7 In the fourth month, the fourth *prince was* Asahel,
the brother of Joab, and Zebadiah, his son, (was the
leader) after him, and four and twenty thousand *were* in
his company.
8 In the fifth month, the fifth *prince was* Shamhuth
(the) Izrahite, and four and twenty thousand *were* in his
company.
9 In the sixth month, the sixth *prince was* Ira, the son
of Ikkesh, (the) Tekoite, and four and twenty thousand
were in his company.
10 In the seventh month, the seventh *prince was* Helez
(the) Pelonite, of the sons of Ephraim, [and] four and
twenty thousand *were* in his company.
11 In the eighth month, the eighth *prince was* Sibbecai
(the) Hushathite, of the generation of Zarhites (of the sons of
Zareh), and four and twenty thousand *were* in his company.
12 In the ninth month, the ninth *prince was* Abiezer
(the) Anetothite, of the generation of Benjamin (of the
sons of Benjamin), and four and twenty thousand *were* in
his company.
13 In the tenth month, the tenth *prince was* Maharai,
and he *was* (a) Netophathite, of the generation of Zarhites
(of the sons of Zareh), and four and twenty thousand
were in his company.

14 In the eleventh month, the eleventh *prince was*
Benaiah (the) Pirathonite, of the sons of Ephraim, and
four and twenty thousand *were* in his company.
15 In the twelfth month, the twelfth *prince was* Heldai
(the) Netophathite, of the generation of Othniel (of the
sons of Othniel), and four and twenty thousand *were* in
his company.
16 Forsooth *these* were the sovereigns of the lineages
of Israel (And *these* were the rulers of the tribes of Israel);
duke Eliezer, the son of Zichri, *was sovereign* to
Reubenites; duke Shephatiah, the son of Maachah, *was
sovereign* to Simeonites;
17 Hashabiah, the son of Kemuel, *was sovereign* to the
Levites; Zadok *was sovereign* to Aaronites;
18 Elihu, the brother of David, *was sovereign* to the
lineage of Judah (Elihu, David's brother, *was the ruler* of
the tribe of Judah); Omri, the son of Michael, *was
sovereign* to Issacharites.
19 Ishmaiah, the son of Obadiah, *was sovereign* to
Zebulunites; Jerimoth, the son of Azriel, *was sovereign* to
Naphtalites;
20 Hoshea, the son of Azaziah, *was sovereign* to the
sons of Ephraim; Joel, the son of Pedaiah, *was sovereign*
to the half lineage of Manasseh (Joel, the son of Pedaiah,
was the ruler of the western half of the tribe of Manasseh);
21 and Iddo, the son of Zechariah, *was sovereign* to the
(other) half lineage of Manasseh in Gilead; and Jaasiel,
the son of Abner, *was sovereign* to Benjamin; (and Iddo,
the son of Zechariah, *was the ruler* of the eastern half of
the tribe of Manasseh in Gilead; and Jaasiel, the son of
Abner, *was the ruler* of Benjamin;)
22 and Azareel, the son of Jeroham, *was sovereign* to
Dan; these *were* the princes of the sons of Israel. (and
Azareel, the son of Jeroham, *was the ruler* of Dan; these
were the leaders of the Israelites.)
23 And David would not number them *that were* within
twenty years, for the Lord [had] said, that he would multiply
Israel as the stars of heaven. (But David did not list those
who were under twenty years of age, for the Lord had said
that he would multiply Israel like the stars in the heavens.)
24 Joab, the son of Zeruiah, began for to number *Israel*,
but he fulfilled not; for ire *of God* fell upon Israel for this
thing, and therefore the number of them that were
numbered, was not told in the books of (the) chronicles
of king David. (Joab, the son of Zeruiah, began to count
the Israelites, but he did not finish the census; for *God's*
anger fell upon the Israelites for this thing, and so the
number of them who were counted, was not told in the
books of The Chronicles of King David.)
25 Forsooth Azmaveth, the son of Adiel, was
(sovereign) on the treasuries of the king; but Jehonathan,
the son of Uzziah, was sovereign over these treasures,
that were in cities, and in towns, and in towers. (And
Azmaveth, the son of Adiel, was in charge of the king's
treasuries; and Jehonathan, the son of Uzziah, was in
charge of his treasures, *or of his treasuries*, that were in
the cities, and in the towns, and in the towers.)
26 And Ezri, the son of Chelub, was sovereign upon the
work of husbandry, and upon [the] earth-tillers, that tilled
the land (who worked the land);
27 and Shimei (the) Ramathite *was sovereign* upon [the]
tillers of (the) vineries; and Zabdi (the) Shiphmite *was
sovereign* upon the wine cellars;
28 for Baalhanan (the) Gederite *was (sovereign)* [up]on
the olive places, and the fig places, that were in the field
places; and Joash *was sovereign* upon the shops, *either
cellars*, of oil;
29 and Shitrai (the) Sharonite *was sovereign* upon the
droves that were pastured in Sharon; and Shaphat, the
son of Adlai, *was* over the oxen in valleys; (and Shitrai
the Sharonite *was in charge* of the herds that were
pastured in Sharon; and Shaphat, the son of Adlai, *was in
charge* of the oxen in the valleys;)
30 and Obil of Ishmael *was* over the camels; and
Jehdeiah (the) Meronothite *was* over the asses; (and Obil
of Ishmael *was in charge* of the camels; and Jehdeiah the
Meronothite *was in charge* of the donkeys;)
31 and Jaziz (the) Hagerite *was* over the sheep; all these
were princes of the chattel of king David. (and Jaziz the
Hagerite *was in charge* of the sheep; all these *were* the
overseers of King David's possessions.)
32 And Jonathan, the brother of David's father, *was* a
counsellor, a mighty man, and prudent, and lettered; he
and Jehiel, the son of Hachmoni, were with the sons of
the king.
33 Also Ahithophel *was* a counsellor of the king; and
Hushai (the) Archite *was* a friend of the king.
34 After Ahithophel was Jehoiada, the son of Benaiah,
and Abiathar; but Joab was prince of the host of the king
(and Joab was the leader of the king's army).

CHAPTER 28

1 Therefore David called together all the princes of
Israel, the dukes of lineages, and the sovereigns of
companies, that ministered to the king/that served the
king, also the tribunes, and centurions, and them that
were sovereigns over the cattle, *or over the chattel*, and
the possessions of the king, and (of) his sons, with [the]
eunuchs, and all the mighty and strong men in the host of
Jerusalem. (And so David called together all the leaders
of Israel, the leaders of the tribes, and the leaders of the
companies, who served the king, and the tribunes, and
the centurions, and those who were in charge of the
king's cattle and his possessions, and those of his sons,
along with the eunuchs, and all the strong and mighty
men in his kingdom, to come to Jerusalem.)
2 And when the king had risen, and stood up, he said,
My brethren and my people, hear ye me. I thought for to

build an house, wherein the ark of [the] bond of peace of
the Lord (where the Ark of the Covenant of the Lord), and
the stool of the feet of our God, should rest; and I have
made ready all things to build it.
3 But God said to me, Thou shalt not build an house
to my name, for thou art a man warrior, and hast shed
blood. (But God said to me, Thou shalt not build a House
to honour my name, for thou art a man of war, and hast
shed blood.)
4 But the Lord God of Israel chose me of all the house
of my father, that I should be king on Israel without end;
for of Judah he hath chosen princes, soothly of the house
of Judah, he hath chosen the house of my father, and of
the sons of my father, it pleased him to choose me king
on all Israel (it pleased him to make me king upon all
Israel).
5 But also of (all) my sons, for the Lord hath given to
me many sons, he hath chosen Solomon, my son, that he
should sit in the throne of the realm of the Lord on Israel.
(And of all my sons, for the Lord hath given me many
sons, he hath chosen my son Solomon, to sit on the
throne of the Lord's kingdom upon Israel.)
6 And he said to me, Solomon, thy son, shall build
mine house, and mine altars; for I have chosen him to me
into a son, and I shall be to him into a father; (And he
said to me, Thy son Solomon shall build my House, and
my altars; for I have chosen him to be a son to me, and I
shall be a father to him;)
7 and I shall make steadfast his realm into without
end, if he shall continue to do my behests and [my]
dooms, as and today. (and I shall establish his kingdom
forevermore, if he shall continue to do my commands
and my judgements/if he shall continue to obey my
commands and my laws, as in this day.)
8 Now therefore before all the company of Israel, (and)
in the hearing of God, (I say,) keep ye and seek ye all the
commandments of your Lord God (obey ye and seek ye
to understand all the commands of the Lord your God),
(so) that ye (can) have in possession a good land, and that
ye leave it to your sons after you into without end.
9 But thou, Solomon, my son, know [thou] the God of
thy father, and serve thou him with (a) perfect heart, and
with a willful soul, *or mind* (and *with* a willing mind); for
the Lord searcheth all hearts, and he understandeth all
the thoughts of souls; if thou seekest him, thou shalt find
him; forsooth if thou forsakest him, he shall cast thee
away without end.
10 Now therefore, for the Lord hath chosen thee, for to
build the house of [the] saintuary, be thou comforted, and
perform *it.* (And so now, for the Lord hath chosen thee,
to build the House of the sanctuary, be thou
strengthened, and do *it.*)
11 And David gave to Solomon, his son, the describing,
either the ensample, of the porch of the temple, and of
[the] cellars, and of the solar, and of [the] closets in (the)
privy places, and of the house of propitiation, *or of mercy
doing, that is, of the holy of holy things, where the
propitiatory was;*
12 also and *he gave him (the) ensample* of all (the)
things which he thought, of the large places, and of [the]
chambers by compass, into the treasures of the house of
the Lord, and into the treasures of [the] holy things, (and
he also gave him the example for all the things which he
had in mind, for the courtyards, and the rooms around
them, and the treasuries of the House of the Lord, and the
treasuries of the holy things,)
13 and of the partings of [the] priests and deacons, into
all the works of the house of the Lord, and all [the]
vessels of service of the temple of the Lord. (and for the
divisions of the priests and the Levites, for all the works
of the House of the Lord, and for all the vessels for
service in the Temple of the Lord.)
14 Of gold in weight by each vessel of service, and of
silver, for [the] diversity of vessels, and of works; (And he
told him the weight of the gold for each gold vessel used
in its service, and the weight of the silver for the other
vessels used for diverse services;)
15 but also to [the] golden candlesticks, and to their
lanterns, *he gave* gold, for the measure of each
candlestick, and of (its) lanterns; also and in [the] silveren
candlesticks, and in their lanterns, he betook to them the
weight of silver, for the diversity of (the) measure *of
those.* (and the weight of the gold for the gold
candlesticks, and their lanterns; and the weight of the
silver for the silver candlesticks, and their lanterns, by the
diversity of *their* service.)
16 And he gave gold into the board[s] of setting forth,
for the diversity of measure, also and *he gave* silver into
other silveren boards; (And he told him the weight of the
gold for the tables for the loaves of proposition, *or the
loaves of setting forth,* and the weight of the silver for the
other silver tables;)
17 also to [the] fleshhooks, and vials, and to censers of
purest gold; and to golden basins, for the manner of
measure, he separated a weight into a basin and a basin;
also and into silveren basins he separated diverse weight of
silver. (and the weight of the pure gold for the fleshhooks,
and the bowls, and the censers; and also the weight of the
gold for the gold basins, in the manner of the measure;
and the diverse weight of the silver for the silver basins.)
18 And he gave most fine gold to the altar, wherein
incense was burnt, (and) that a likeness of the cart of
cherubims, holding forth (their) wings, and covering the
ark of [the] bond of peace of the Lord, should be made
thereof. (And he told him the weight of the most fine gold
for the altar, on which the incense was burned, and also
for the likeness, *or the model,* of the chariot of the
cherubim, with them holding forth their wings, and

covering the Ark of the Covenant of the Lord.)
19 *And* David said, All (these) things came written by
the hand of the Lord to me, that I should understand all
the works of the exemplar/of the ensampler (so that I
could understand all the works in the example).
20 And David said to Solomon, his son, Do thou
manly, and be thou comforted, and make; dread thou not
withoutforth, neither dread thou within; for my Lord God
shall be with thee, and he shall not leave thee, neither
shall forsake thee, till thou perform all the work of the
service of the house of the Lord. (And David said to his
son Solomon, Be thou confident, and be thou
strengthened, and make *it*; fear thou not anything from
withoutforth, nor fear thou anything from within; for the
Lord my God shall be with thee, and he shall not leave
thee, nor shall desert thee, until thou finish all the work
needed in the service of the House of the Lord.)
21 Lo! the partings of priests and of deacons, into all
the work of the service of the house of the Lord, shall
stand nigh [to] thee; and they be ready *to do their service*,
and both the princes and the people know to do all thy
commandments. (Lo! the divisions of the priests, and the
Levites, shall do their duties, ready to do all the work in
the service of the House of the Lord; and all the craftsmen
be ready *to do their service*; and also the leaders, and all
the people, shall be wholly at thy command.)

CHAPTER 29

1 And king David spake to all the church, (and said,)
God hath chosen Solomon, my son, yet a child and tender;
forsooth the work is great, and a dwelling is not made
ready to man, but to God. (And King David spoke to all
the congregation, and said, God hath chosen my son
Solomon, yet a tender young man; and the work is great,
but this dwelling place is not made for man, but for God.)
2 Soothly I in all my mights have made ready the costs
of the house of my God; gold to golden vessels, silver to
silveren vessels, brass to brazen vessels, iron to iron
vessels, and tree to treen vessels, onyx stones, and stones
as of the colour of women's ointment, and each precious
stone of diverse colours, and marble of diverse colours,
most plenteously. (And with all my power I have
prepared the expenses and the materials for the House of
my God; gold for the gold vessels, silver for the silver
vessels, bronze for the bronze vessels, iron for the iron
vessels, and wood for the wooden vessels, and onyx
stones, and stones the colour of women's ointment, and
each precious stone of diverse colour, and most plentiful
marble of diverse colours.)
3 And over these things, I give gold and silver into the
temple of my God, which I have offered of my proper
chattel into the house of my God, besides these things
which I have made ready into the holy house, (And in
addition to these things, I have given gold and silver for
the Temple of my God, which I have offered out of my
own substance, *or possessions*, for the House of my God,
besides these things which I have prepared for the Holy
House,)
4 (namely) three thousand talents of gold, of the gold
of Ophir, and seven thousand of talents of silver most
proved (and seven thousand talents of most proved
silver), to overgild the walls of the temple;
5 and (for the) works (which) be made by the hands of
craftsmen, wherever gold is needful, of gold, and wherever
silver is needful, of silver; and if any man offereth by his
free will, [full-]fill he his hand today, and offer he that that
he will to the Lord. (and for the works which be made by
the hands of craftsmen, yea, the gold, wherever gold is
needed, and the silver, wherever silver is needed; and if
anyone else will offer by his free will, open he his hand
today, and offer he what he will to the Lord.)
6 Therefore the princes of [the] families, and the dukes
of the lineages of Israel, and the tribunes, and the
centurions, and the princes of the possessions of the king,
promised *to give thereto*/promised *to give gifts to the
temple*; (And so the leaders of the families, and the
leaders of the tribes of Israel, and the tribunes, and the
centurions, and the overseers of the king's possessions,
promised *to give gifts for the Temple*;)
7 and they gave into the works of the house of the Lord,
five thousand talents of gold, and ten thousand shillings;
and ten thousand talents of silver, and eighteen thousand
talents of brass, and an hundred thousand talents of iron.
(and they gave for the work of the House of the Lord, five
thousand talents of gold, and ten thousand shillings; and
ten thousand talents of silver, and eighteen thousand
talents of bronze, and a hundred thousand talents of iron.)
8 And at whomever precious stones were found, they
gave (them) into the treasure/into the treasury of the
house of the Lord, by the hand of Jehiel (the) Gershonite.
(And whoever had precious stones, gave them to the
treasury of the House of Lord, where Jehiel the
Gershonite was in charge.)
9 And the people was glad, when they promised (their)
avows by their free will, for with all the heart they offered
those to the Lord (for with all their hearts they offered them
to the Lord). But also king David was glad with great joy,
10 and he blessed the Lord before all the multitude,
and said, Lord God of Israel, our father, thou art blessed
from without beginning [and] into without end; (and he
blessed the Lord before all the multitude, and said,
Blessed art thou, Lord God of our father Israel, from
without beginning, and forevermore;)
11 Lord, worthy doing is thine, *that is, thy doing is
worthy and great*, and power, and glory, and victory, and
praising is to thee; for all things that be in heaven and in
earth be thine; Lord, the realm is thine, and thou art over
all princes; (Lord, thy doing is worthy and great, and

power, and glory, and victory, and praising be to thee; for
everything that is in heaven and on earth be thine; Lord,
the kingdom is thine, and thou art over all the leaders;)
12 riches be thine, and glory is thine; thou art Lord of
all; in thine hand is strength, and power, and in thine
hand is greatness, and lordship of all.
13 Now therefore, our God (And so now, our God), we
acknowledge to thee, and we praise thy noble name.
14 Who am I, and who is my people, that we may
promise all these things to thee? All things be thine, and
we have (but) given (back) to thee those things, which we
have taken of thine hand. (But who am I, and who be my
people, that we can give anything to thee? For all things
be thine, and we have only given back to thee those
things, which we have received from thy own hands.)
15 For we be pilgrims and comelings before thee, as all
our fathers *were* (For we be foreigners and newcomers
before thee, as all our forefathers *were*); our days be as (a)
shadow on the earth, and there is no tarrying.
16 Our Lord God, all this plenty *of diverse goods* which
we have made ready, that an house should be builded to
thine holy name, is of thine hand; and all things be thine.
(Lord our God, all this plenty *of diverse goods* which we
have prepared, so that a House could be built to honour thy
holy name, is from thy own hands; and all things be thine.)
17 My God, I know, that thou provest hearts, and that
thou lovest simpleness, *that is, lowness, or meekness,* of
heart; wherefore in the simpleness of mine heart, I have
offered gladly all these things; and I have seen with great
joy thy people, which is found here, to offer gifts to thee
(and so with an honest heart, I have gladly offered all
these things; and I have seen with great joy thy people,
who be found here, to willingly offer their gifts to thee).
18 Lord God of Abraham, and of Isaac, and of Israel, our
fathers, keep thou without end this will of their hearts; and
this mind dwell ever[more] into the worshipping of thee.
(Lord God of our fathers Abraham, and of Isaac, and of
Jacob, keep thou this desire forevermore in their hearts;
and may their hearts forevermore worship thee.)
19 Also give thou to Solomon, my son, a perfect heart,
that he keep thy behests, and thy witnessings, and thy
ceremonies; and do all *these* things, and that he build the
house, whose costs I have made ready. (And give thou to
my son Solomon a perfect heart, that he obey thy
commands, and thy testimonies, and thy statutes; and do
all *these* things, and that he build the House, whose
materials and expenses I have prepared.)
20 Soothly David commanded to all the church, *that is,
(to) all the people gathered together,* Bless ye the Lord
our God. And all the church, *that is, the people,* blessed
the Lord God of their fathers, and they bowed
themselves, and worshipped God, and [then] afterward
the king. (And David commanded to all the congregation,
Bless ye the Lord your God. And all the congregation
blessed the Lord God of their fathers, and they bowed
themselves, and worshipped God, and then the king.)
21 And they offered slain sacrifices to the Lord, and
they offered burnt sacrifices in the day following; a
thousand bulls, and a thousand rams, and a thousand
lambs, with their flowing sacrifices, and with all the
custom, most plenteously, into all Israel. (And they
offered slain sacrifices to the Lord, and then they offered
burnt sacrifices on the following day; a thousand bulls, a
thousand rams, and a thousand lambs, with their wine
offerings, by all the custom, most plentifully, for all
Israel.)
22 And they ate and drank before the Lord in that day,
with great gladness. And they anointed the second time
Solomon, the son of David; and they anointed him into
prince to the Lord, and Zadok into bishop. (And they ate
and drank before the Lord on that day, with great
gladness. And a second time, they anointed David's son
Solomon, as king; yea, they anointed him as the Lord's
prince, and Zadok as the High Priest.)
23 And Solomon sat on the throne of the Lord into
king, for David, his father; and it pleased all men, and all
Israel obeyed to him. (And Solomon sat on the throne of
the Lord as king, in place of his father David; and it
pleased everyone, and all Israel obeyed him.)
24 But also all [the] princes, and mighty men, and all
the sons of king David, gave (the) hand, *that is, (in)
swearing or steadfast(ly) promising to be faithful,* and
were (made) subject to Solomon the king. (And all the
princes/all the leaders, and the mighty men, and also all
the sons of King David, raised up their hands *to swear, or
to steadfastly promise, to be faithful,* and were made
subject to King Solomon.)
25 Therefore the Lord magnified, *or made great,*
Solomon upon all Israel, and gave to him (such) glory of
the realm, what manner (of) glory no king of Israel (had
ever) had before him.
26 And (so) David, the son of Jesse, reigned upon all
Israel;
27 and the days in which he reigned upon Israel were
forty years; in Hebron he reigned seven years, and in
Jerusalem he reigned three and thirty years.
28 And he died in [a] good eld (age), and was full of
days, and riches, and glory; and Solomon, his son,
reigned for him.
29 Forsooth the former and the last deeds of king David
(And the first and the last deeds of King David), be written
in the book of Samuel, the prophet, and in the book of
Nathan, the prophet, and in the book of Gad, the prophet;
30 and of all his realm, and strength, and times, that
passed under him, either in Israel, either in all realms of
lands. (yea, all about his kingdom, and power, and the
times through which he, and Israel, and all the kingdoms
of the lands, had passed.) ✡

2ND CHRONICLES

CHAPTER 1

1 Therefore Solomon, the son of David, was
comforted in his realm (And so Solomon, the son of
David, was strengthened, *or confirmed,* in his kingdom),
and the Lord was with him, and magnified him on high.
2 And Solomon commanded to all Israel, to tribunes,
and centurions, and to dukes, and to doomsmen of all
Israel, and to the princes of families; (And Solomon
commanded to all Israel, to the tribunes, and the
centurions, and the leaders, and the judges of all Israel,
and the leaders of the families;)
3 and Solomon went with all the multitude into the
high place of Gibeon, where the tabernacle of [the] bond
of peace of the Lord was, which tabernacle Moses, the
servant of the Lord, made in wilderness. (and Solomon
went with all the multitude to the hill shrine of Gibeon,
where the Tabernacle of the Covenant of the Lord was,
that is, the Tabernacle of the Witnessing, which
Tabernacle Moses, the Lord's servant, had made in the
wilderness.)
4 Forsooth David had brought the ark of God from
Kiriathjearim into the place which he had made ready to
it, and where he had set a tabernacle to it, that is, in
Jerusalem. (But David had brought the Ark of God from
Kiriathjearim to the place which he had prepared for it,
and where he had set up a Tent for it, that is, in
Jerusalem.)
5 And the brazen altar, which Bezaleel, the son of Uri,
the son of Hur, had made, was there before the
tabernacle of the Lord; which also Solomon and all the
church sought. (And the bronze altar, which Bezaleel, the
son of Uri, the son of Hur, had made, was there in front
of the Tabernacle of the Lord; and Solomon and all the
congregation sought *the Lord* at that altar.)
6 And Solomon went up to the brazen altar, before
the tabernacle of the bond of peace of the Lord, and
offered in it a thousand sacrifices. (And Solomon went up
to the bronze altar, before the Tabernacle of the Covenant
of the Lord, and offered on it a thousand sacrifices.)
7 Lo! forsooth in that night God appeared to him, and
said, Ask that that thou wilt, that I give to thee (Ask what
thou wilt, that I give it to thee).
8 And Solomon said to God, Thou hast done great
mercy with David, my father, and hast ordained me king
for him. (And Solomon said to God, Thou hast shown
great love for my father David, and hast made me king in
his place.)
9 Now therefore, Lord God, thy word be fulfilled,
which thou promisedest to David, my father; for thou
hast made me king upon thy great people, which is so
unnumberable as the dust of [the] earth. (And so now,
Lord God, let thy word be fulfilled, which thou hast
promised to my father David; for thou hast made me king
upon thy great people, who be as innumerable as the
dust of the earth.)
10 Give thou to me wisdom and understanding, that I
go in and go out before thy people; for who may deem
worthily this thy people, which is so great? (Give thou to
me wisdom and understanding, so that I can come in and
go out before thy people; for who can worthily judge this
thy people, who be so great *in number*?)
11 And God said to Solomon, For that this thing
pleased more thine heart, and thou askedest not riches,
and chattel, and glory, neither the lives of them that hate
thee, but neither full many days of *thy* life; but thou hast
asked (for) wisdom and knowing, that thou mayest deem
my people, upon which I have ordained thee king, (And
God said to Solomon, For that this thing more pleased
thy heart, and thou hast asked not for riches, or
possessions, or glory, or for the lives of those who hate
thee, or for a great many days for *thy* own life; but thou
hast asked for wisdom and knowledge, so that thou can
judge my people, on whom I have ordained thee to be
king,)
12 wisdom and knowing (shall) be given to thee; and
over this, I shall give to thee riches, and chattel, and glory
(and in addition to this, I shall give to thee riches, and
possessions, and glory), so that none among kings,
neither before thee, nor after thee, (shall) be like thee.
13 Then Solomon came from the high place of Gibeon
into Jerusalem, (from) before the tabernacle of the bond
of peace, and he reigned upon Israel. (Then Solomon
came from the hill shrine at Gibeon to Jerusalem, from
before the Tabernacle of the Covenant, and he reigned
upon Israel.)
14 And Solomon gathered together to him chariots and
knights, and a thousand and four hundred chariots were
made to him, and twelve thousand knights; and he made
them to be in the cities of carts, and with the king in
Jerusalem. (And Solomon gathered to himself chariots
and horsemen, and he had a thousand and four hundred
chariots, and twelve thousand horsemen; and he
ordained some of them to be in the cities for the chariots,
and some of them to be with the king in Jerusalem.)
15 And the king gave in Jerusalem gold and silver as
stones *in plenty,* and *he gave* cedar *trees* as sycamores,
that come forth in field places in great multitude. (And
the king made gold and silver to be as plentiful as stones
in Jerusalem, and cedar *trees* to be like the sycamores
that come forth in the fields in great multitude.)
16 And horses were brought to him from Egypt, and
from Coa, by the merchants of the king, which went, and

bought by price (who went there, and bought them for money),

17 a chariot of horses for six hundred pieces of silver, and an horse for an hundred and fifty. In like manner buying was made of all the realms of cities, and of the kings of Syria (In like manner, purchases were made from all the kings of the Hittites, and from the kings of Syria).

CHAPTER 2

1 Forsooth Solomon deemed, *or purposed,* to build an house to the name of the Lord, and a palace to himself. (And Solomon decided to build a House in honour of the name of the Lord, and a palace for himself.)

2 And he numbered seventy thousand of men bearing (burdens) in shoulders, and fourscore thousand that should cut, *or hew,* stones in hills; and the sovereigns of them *were* three thousand and six hundred. (And he called up seventy thousand men who would carry burdens on *their* shoulders, and eighty thousand who would cut stones in the hills; and they had three thousand and six hundred rulers, *or overseers.*)

3 And Solomon sent to Hiram[1], the king of Tyre, and said, As thou didest with my father David, and sentest him trees of cedar, that he should build to him an house, in which also he dwelled; so do thou with me, (And Solomon sent word to Hiram, the king of Tyre, and said, As thou didest with my father David, and sentest cedar wood to him, so that he could build a house for himself, in which he would live, so do thou also with me;)

4 that I build an house to the name of the Lord my God, and that I hallow it, to burn incense before him, and to make odour of sweet smelling spiceries, and to [the] everlasting setting forth of loaves, and to [the] burnt sacrifices in the morrowtide and eventide, and in [the] sabbaths, and (on) new moons, *that is, (at) feasts in the beginnings of months,* and in solemnities of the Lord our God into without end, which *observances and hallowings* be commanded to Israel. (so that I can build a House in honour of the name of the Lord my God, and I shall consecrate it, so that I can burn incense before him, to make the odour of sweet smelling spices, and for the everlasting setting forth of loaves, and for burnt sacrifices in the morning and in the evening, and on sabbaths, and on new moons, *that is, at feasts at the beginning of the month,* and at the solemn, *or annual,* Feasts of the Lord our God forevermore, which *observances and consecrations* be commanded to Israel.)

5 For the house which I covet to build is great; forsooth the Lord our God is great over all gods.

6 Who therefore may have might to build a worthy house to him? For if heaven and heavens of heavens may not take, *or hold,* him, how great am I, that I may build an house to him, but to this thing only, that incense be burnt *there* before him? (And so who is able to build a House worthy of him? For if heaven and the heavens of heavens cannot hold him, who am I, that I build him a House, but only for this, so that incense can be burned *there* before him?)

7 Therefore send thou to me a learned man, that can work in gold, and in silver, in brass, and iron, in purple, and in red silk, and in jacinth; and that can grave graving with these craftsmen, which I have with me in Judah and in Jerusalem, the which men David, my father, before made ready. (And so send thou to me a learned man, who knoweth how to work with gold, and silver, and bronze, and iron, and purple, and red silk, and jacinth; one who knoweth how to engrave engravings with these craftsmen who I have with me in Judah and in Jerusalem, which men my father David provided.)

8 But also send thou to me cedar trees, and pine trees, and thyine trees of the Lebanon; for I know, that thy servants can cut trees of the Lebanon; and my servants shall be with thy servants, (And also send thou to me cedar, and pine, and algum timber from Lebanon; for I know, that thy servants know how to cut down the trees of Lebanon; and my servants shall be with thy servants,)

9 that full many trees be made ready to me (so that a great deal of timber can be prepared for me); for the house which I covet to build is full great and noble.

10 Furthermore to thy servants, workmen that shall cut trees, I shall give into meats twenty thousand cors of wheat, and so many cors of barley, and twenty thousand measures of oil, that be called baths. (And for thy servants, the workmen who shall cut down the trees, I shall give for food twenty thousand cors of wheat, and as many cors of barley, and twenty thousand measures of oil, that be called baths.)

11 And Hiram, king of Tyre, said by letters which he sent to Solomon, For the Lord [hath] loved his people, therefore he hath made thee to reign upon it (and so he hath made thee to reign upon them).

12 And *Hiram* added to (that), saying, Blessed be the Lord God of Israel, that made heaven and earth, which hath given to king David a wise son, and learned, and witting, and prudent, that he should build an house to the Lord, and a palace to himself. (And *Hiram* added to that, saying, Blessed be the Lord God of Israel, who made heaven and earth, and who hath given to King David a wise and learned son, knowledgeable and prudent, who shall build a House for the Lord, and a palace for himself.)

13 Therefore I have sent to thee a prudent man and most knowing, Hiram[2], my father, (And so I am sending to thee a prudent and most knowledgeable man, Hiram, my master craftsman,)

[1] Also known as Huram.

[2] Also known as Huram(!).

14 the son of a woman of the lineage of Dan, whose
father was a man of Tyre; the which Hiram can work in
gold, and silver, in brass, and in iron, and in marble, and
in trees, also in purple, and jacinth, and bis, and in red
silk; and the which Hiram can grave in all graving, and
can find prudently, whatever thing is needful in work
with thy craftsmen, and with the craftsmen of my lord
David, thy father. (the son of a woman of the tribe of
Dan, whose father was a man of Tyre; this Hiram
knoweth how to work with gold, and silver, and bronze,
and iron, and marble, and wood, and purple, and jacinth,
and fine linen, and red silk; and this Hiram knoweth how
to engrave in all manner of engraving, and knoweth how
to prudently do whatever is needed to work with thy
craftsmen, and with the craftsmen of thy father, my lord
David.)
15 Therefore, my lord, send thou to (us) thy servants the
wheat, and barley, and oil, and wine, which thou hast
promised.
16 And we shall cut (down) trees of the Lebanon, how
many ever thou hast need of; and we shall bring those
trees in ships by the sea into Joppa; and it shall be thine
doing to lead those over into Jerusalem.
17 Then Solomon numbered all men converted from
heathenness, that were in the land of Israel, after the
numbering that David, his father, had numbered; and an
hundred thousand and three and fifty thousand and six
hundred were found *of them.* (Then Solomon counted all
the men converted from heathenness who were in the
land of Israel, like in the census that his father David had
taken; and a hundred and fifty-three thousand and six
hundred were found *of them.*)
18 And he made of them seventy thousand, that should
bear burdens on their shoulders, and fourscore thousand,
that should cut, *or hew,* stones in hills; and *he made*
three thousand and six hundred sovereigns of [the] works
of the people. (And he ordained seventy thousand of
them, who would carry burdens on their shoulders, and
eighty thousand, who would cut stones in the hills; and
he made three thousand and six hundred to be the rulers,
or the overseers, who would make these people work.)

CHAPTER 3

1 And Solomon began to build the house of the Lord
in Jerusalem, in the hill of Moriah, that was showed to
David, his father, in the place that David had made ready
in the cornfloor of Ornan (the) Jebusite. (And so Solomon
began to build the House of the Lord in Jerusalem, on
Mount Moriah, where the Lord had appeared to his father
David, on the place that David had prepared at the
threshing floor of Ornan the Jebusite.)
2 Forsooth he began to build in the second day of the
(second) month, in the fourth year of his realm. (And he
began to build on the second day of the second month,
in the fourth year of his reign, *or of his kingdom.*)
3 And these were the foundaments, which Solomon
setted, that he should build the house of God; sixty cubits
of length in the first measure, and twenty cubits of
breadth. (And these were the foundations, which
Solomon laid, that he would build for the House of God;
sixty cubits in length, at the old measure, and twenty
cubits in breadth.)
4 And he builded a porch before the front, that was
stretched forth along beside, *or at* the measure of, the
breadth of the house, of twenty cubits, and the highness
was of an hundred and twenty cubits; and he overgilded
it within with cleanest gold. (And he built a vestibule, *or
an entrance room,* at the front, that was stretched forth
along beside, *or at* the measure of, the breadth of the
House, of twenty cubits, and its highness was a hundred
and twenty cubits; and he overgilded it within with the
purest gold.)
5 Also he covered the greater house with boards of
box, and he fastened plates of gold of the best colour all
about; and he graved therein palm trees, and as small
chains embracing themselves together. (And he covered
the large inner chamber with box boards, and he fastened
gold plates of the best colour, *that is, most pure,* all
about; and he carved on them palm trees, and small
chains linked together.)
6 And he arrayed the pavement of the temple with
most precious marble, in much fairness. And the gold
was most proved, (And he arrayed the Temple with most
precious marble, in much fairness, *or for great beauty.*
And the gold was from Parvaim,)
7 of whose plates he covered the house, and the
beams thereof, and the posts, and the walls, and the
doors; and he graved cherubims, *that is, angels,* in the
walls. (of whose plates he covered the House, and its
beams, and the posts, and the walls, and the doors; and
he carved cherubim, *that is, angels,* on the walls.)
8 Also he made an house to the holy of holy things, in
length by the breadth of the house, of twenty cubits, and
the breadth also of twenty cubits; and he covered it with
golden plates, as with six hundred talents *in value.* (And
he made the Holy of Holies, *that is, the Most Holy Place,*
twenty cubits in length, which was equal to the breadth
of the Temple, and also twenty cubits in breadth; and he
covered it with gold plates worth six hundred talents *in
value.*)
9 And also he made golden nails, so that each nail
weighed fifty shekels; and he covered the solars with
gold. (And he made gold nails, and each nail weighed
fifty shekels; and he covered the solariums, *or the upper
rooms,* with gold.)
10 Also he made in the house of the holy of holy things
(And he made in the Holy of Holies, *that is, in the Most
Holy Place*), two cherubims by the work of an image

maker, and covered them with gold.
11 The wings of cherubims were holden forth by
twenty cubits (The cherubim's wings were stretched out
twenty cubits), so that one wing had five cubits, and it
touched the wall of the house; and the tother wing had
five cubits, and it touched the wing of the other cherub.
12 In like manner the one wing of the other cherub had
five cubits, and it touched the wall, and the other wing
thereof *that was (also)* of five cubits, touched the wing of
the other cherub.
13 Therefore the wings of ever either cherub were
spread abroad, and they were holden forth by twenty
cubits; and those cherubims stood upon [the] feet raised
up, and their faces were turned to the outermore house.
(And so the wings of both cherubim were spread out, and
they stretched out twenty cubits; and the cherubim stood,
raised up on their feet, and their faces were turned to the
outer chamber.)
14 Also he made a veil of jacinth, and purple, of red
silk, and bis; and weaved cherubims therein. (And he
made the Veil, *or the Curtain,* out of jacinth, and purple,
and red silk, and fine linen; and he weaved figures of
cherubim into it.)
15 Also before the gates of the temple *he made* two
pillars, which had five and thirty cubits of height; and the
heads of those *pillars were* of five cubits *in height.* (And
in front of the gates of the Temple *he made* two pillars,
which were thirty-five cubits tall; and the pommels, *or
the capitals,* of those pillars were five cubits tall.)
16 Also *he made* as it were little chains in God's
answering place, and he putted them on the heads of the
pillars (And *he made* little chains, as there were in the
Most Holy Place, *that is, the Holy of Holies,* and he put
them on the capitals of the pillars); also *he made* an
hundred pomegranates, which he setted betwixt the little
chains.
17 And he setted those pillars in the porch of the
temple (And he set up those pillars at the front of the
Temple), one at the right side, and the other at the left
side; he called that *pillar* that was at the right side Jachin,
and that that was at the left side he called Boaz.

CHAPTER 4

1 Also he made a brazen altar of twenty cubits of length,
and of twenty cubits of breadth, and of ten cubits of height;
(And he made a bronze altar twenty cubits in length, and
twenty cubits in breadth, and ten cubits in height;)
2 *he made* also a molten sea, *that is, a great washing
vessel for priests,* of ten cubits from brink to brink, round
by compass; it had five cubits of height; and a cord of
thirty cubits (en)compassed the compass thereof. (and *he*
made a round Sea, *that is, a great washing vessel for the
priests,* cast in bronze, ten cubits in diameter from brim
to brim; it had five cubits of height; and it took a cord
thirty cubits long to go all around its circumference.)
3 And the likeness of oxen was under it, and by ten
cubits some gravings withoutforth (en)compassed the
brink of the sea, as with twain orders; and the oxen were
molten. (And under it were the likeness of oxen, and for
thirty cubits some engravings on the outside went all
around the brim of the Sea, in two rows; and they were
cast together with it.)
4 And that sea was set upon twelve oxen, of which
oxen three beheld to the north, and (an)other three to the
west, and three others *beheld* to the south, and [the] three
that were residue *beheld* (to) the east, and *these* had the
sea set above *them* (and the Sea was set upon *them*); but
the hinder parts of the oxen were within under the sea.
5 And the thickness of the sea had the measure of the
palm of an hand, and the brink thereof was as the brink
of a cup (and its brim was like the brim of a cup), either
as of a lily crooked again, and the sea held three
thousand metretes of measure.
6 Also he made ten hollow vessels, and setted five at
the right side, and five at the left side, that they should
wash in those all things, which they should offer into
burnt sacrifice; soothly the priests were washed in the
sea. (And he made ten hollow vessels, and put five at the
right side, and five at the left side, so that they could
wash all the things in them that they would offer for the
burnt sacrifice; but the priests washed in the Sea.)
7 Soothly he made ten golden candlesticks by the
likeness which he had commanded to be made, and he
setted those in the temple, five at the right side, and five
at the left side.
8 And *he made* also ten tables, and he setted those in
the temple, five at the right side, and five at the left side.
Also *he made* an hundred golden vials, *or basins* (And *he
made* a hundred gold basins).
9 Also he made a large place of (the) priests, and a
great house, and [the] doors in the great house, which he
covered with brass. (And he made a courtyard for the
priests, and the great courtyard, and he covered the doors
of both courtyards with bronze.)
10 And he setted the sea in the right side *of the porch*
against the east at the south. (And he put the Sea on the
right side *of the courtyard* toward the east at the south.)
11 Also Hiram made cauldrons, and fleshhooks, and
vials, *or basins,* and he fulfilled all the work of the king in
the house of God, (And Hiram made cauldrons, and
fleshhooks, and basins, and so he finished all the work
for the king for the House of God,)
12 that is, *he made* (the) two pillars, and their
pommels, and (the) heads, and as some nets, that covered
the heads above the pommels; (that is, *he made* the two
pillars, and two bowl-shaped capitals on the tops of the
pillars, and the networks that covered the bowl-shaped
capitals on the tops of the pillars;)

13 also *he made* forty pomegranates, and two works
like nets, so that the two orders of pomegranates were
joined to each work like nets, which covered the
pommels, and the heads of the pillars. (and *he made* four
hundred pomegranates on the two networks, with two
rows of pomegranates on each network, that covered the
bowl-shaped capitals, that were on the tops of the pillars.)
14 He made also (the) foundaments, and (the) hollow
vessels, which he set upon the foundaments;
15 *he made* one sea, and twelve oxen under the sea,
(*he made* the one Sea, and the twelve oxen under the
Sea,)
16 and cauldrons, and fleshhooks, and vials, *or basins*.
Hiram, the father of Solomon, *that is, (called so) for
reason of age, either of excellence of craft,* made to him
all the vessels in the house of the Lord of cleanest brass.
(and the cauldrons, and fleshhooks, and basins. Hiram,
the father of Solomon, *so called because of his age, or
because of the excellence of his craftsmanship,* made all
the vessels for Solomon for the House of the Lord out of
burnished bronze.)
17 The king melted out those *vessels* in the country(side)
of Jordan, in [the] clay land between Succoth and
Zeredathah.
18 Forsooth the multitude of vessels was
unnumberable, so that the weight of brass was not
known (so that the weight of the bronze was unknown).
19 And Solomon made all the vessels of God's house,
the golden altar, and (the) boards/the meat tables, and the
loaves of setting forth upon those; (And Solomon also
made all the vessels for God's House, the gold altar, and
the tables, on which the loaves of proposition, *or the
loaves of setting forth,* were put;)
20 and candlesticks of purest gold, with their lanterns,
that those should shine before God's answering place, by
the custom; (and the candlesticks, with their lanterns, out
of the purest gold, which would shine before the Most
Holy Place, *that is, the Holy of Holies,* after the custom;)
21 and *he made* some works like flowers, and lanterns,
and golden tongs; all these things were made of cleanest
gold (all these things were made out of the purest gold);
22 also *he made* pans for coals to burn incense, and
censers, and vials, *or basins,* and mortars, of purest gold.
And he engraved the doors of the inner temple, that is, in
the holy of holy things, and the golden doors of the
temple withoutforth; (and *he made* the pans for the coals
to burn the incense, and the censers, and basins, and
spoons, out of the purest gold. And the doors of the
Inner Temple, that is, the doors for the Holy of Holies, *or
the Most Holy Place,* and the outer doors of the Temple,
were also made out of gold;)

CHAPTER 5

1 and so all the work was [ful]filled that Solomon
made in the house of the Lord. Therefore Solomon
brought in all things, that is, silver, and gold, which
David, his father had avowed; and he putted all the
vessels in the treasuries of the house of the Lord. (and so
all the work that Solomon did for the House of the Lord
was finished. And so Solomon brought in all the things
which his father David had vowed; and he put all the
silver, and the gold, and the vessels in the treasuries of
the House of the Lord.)
2 After which things he gathered together all the
greater men in birth of Israel, and all the princes of
lineages, and the heads of families, of the sons of Israel,
into Jerusalem, that they should bring the ark of [the]
bond of peace of the Lord from the city of David, which
is Zion. (After which he gathered together all the men of
great age, *that is, the elders,* of Israel, and all the leaders
of the tribes, and the heads of the families of the
Israelites, to Jerusalem, so that they could bring the Ark of
the Covenant of the Lord from the City of David, which is
called Zion.)
3 Therefore all [the] men of Israel came to the king, in
the solemn day of the seventh month. (And so all the
men of Israel came to the king, on the Feast day of the
seventh month, *that is, the Feast of Tabernacles.*)
4 And when all the elder men of Israel came, the
deacons bare the ark, (And when all the elders of Israel
came, the Levites carried the Ark,)
5 and they brought it, and all the array of the
tabernacle, *into the temple*. And the priests with the
deacons bare the vessels of the saintuary, that were in the
tabernacle. (and they brought it, and all the array of the
Tabernacle, *into the Temple*. And the priests, and the
Levites, carried the vessels of the sanctuary, that had been
in the Tabernacle, *into the Temple*.)
6 And king Solomon, and all the companies of Israel,
and all that were gathered together, offered before the ark
wethers and oxen without number; for the multitude of
slain sacrifices was so great that it might not be
numbered. (And King Solomon, and all the congregation
of Israel, and all who were gathered together in front of
the Ark, offered rams and oxen without number; for the
multitude of slain sacrifices was so great that it could not
be counted.)
7 And [the] priests brought the ark of [the] bond of
peace of the Lord into the place thereof, that is, to God's
answering place of the temple, into the holy of holy things,
under the wings of cherubims; (And the priests brought
the Ark of the Covenant of the Lord into its place, the
Inner Temple, that is, into the Holy of Holies, *or the Most
Holy Place,* under the wings of the cherubim;)
8 so that (the) cherubims spreaded forth their wings
over the place, in which the ark was put, and covered
that ark with his bearing bars. (and the cherubim spread
out their wings over the place, where the Ark was put,

and covered the Ark and its bearing bars.)
9 Soothly the heads, *or pommels*, (of the bars,) with
which the ark was borne, were open, *or uncovered*,
before God's answering place, for those heads were a
little longer *than the stretching (out) of (the) cherubs'
wings*; but if a man had been a little withoutforth, he
might not see those bearing bars. Therefore the ark was
there till into the present day; (And the heads, *or the
ends*, of the bars, with which the Ark was carried, could
be seen when standing in front of the Most Holy Place, *or
the Holy of Holies*, for the heads were a little longer *than
the stretching out of the cherubim's wings*; but if anyone
was a little withoutforth, he would not see those bars.
And they still be there unto this present day;)
10 and there was none other thing in the ark, but [the]
two tables, which Moses had put therein in Horeb, when
the Lord gave the law to the sons of Israel going out of
Egypt. (and there was nothing else in the Ark, but the two
tablets, which Moses had put in it at Mount Sinai, when
the Lord gave the Law to the Israelites going out of Egypt.)
11 And *after this* the priests went out of the saintuary,
for all the priests, that might be found there, were
hallowed, and the whiles, *or certain times*, and the order
of services among (the) priests, was not parted yet in that
time; (And *after this* the priests went out of the sanctuary,
for all the priests, who might be found there, had
consecrated, *or purified*, themselves, but their appointed
times, and the order of their service, was not yet divided
among the priests at that time;)
12 *and* both deacons and singers, that is, both they that
were under Asaph, and they that were under Heman, and
they that were under Jeduthun, their sons and brethren,
clothed with white linen clothes, sounded with cymbals
and psalteries and harps, and stood at the west coast, *or
corner*, of the altar, and with them *were* sixscore priests
trumping. (*and* the levitical singers and musicians, that is,
they who were under Asaph, and they who were under
Heman, and they who were under Jeduthun, with their
sons and kinsmen, were clothed in white linen clothes,
and played cymbals and lutes and harps, and stood at the
east side of the altar, and with them *were* one hundred
and twenty priests who blew the trumpets.)
13 Therefore when they all sang together, both with
trumps, and voice, and cymbals, and organs, and of
diverse kinds of musics, and they raised [up] their voice
on high, the sound was heard [a]far, so that when they
had begun to praise the Lord, and to say, Acknowledge
ye to the Lord, for he is good, for his mercy is into the
world, *either without end*; the house of God was filled
with a cloud, (And so when they all sang together, with
trumpets, and voices, and cymbals, and diverse kinds of
instruments, and they raised up their voices on high, the
sound was heard afar, so that when they began to praise
the Lord, and to sing, Praise ye the Lord, for he is good,
his love is forevermore; suddenly the House of God was
filled with a cloud,)
14 and the priests might not stand to serve for the
darkness; for the glory of the Lord had filled the house of
the Lord. (and the priests could not continue to minister
because of the darkness; for the glory of the Lord had
filled the House of the Lord.)

CHAPTER 6

1 Then Solomon said, The Lord promised, that he
would dwell in [the] darkness;
2 and I have built an house to his name, that he
should dwell therein without end. (and I have built a
House in honour of his name, so that he can live in it
forevermore.)
3 And Solomon turned his face, and blessed all the
multitude of Israel; for all the company stood attentive
(for all the congregation stood attentive);
4 and he said, Blessed *be* the Lord God of Israel, for
he hath fulfilled in work that thing, that he spake to
David, my father, and said,
5 From the day in which I led my people out of the
land of Egypt, I chose not a city of all the lineages of
Israel, that an house should be builded therein to my
name, neither I chose any other man, that he should be
duke upon my people Israel; (From the day in which I led
my people out of the land of Egypt, I chose no city out of
all the tribes of Israel, where a House would be built in
honour of my name, nor did I choose any man, who
would be the leader of my people Israel;)
6 but (then) I chose Jerusalem, that my name (would)
be therein, and I chose David, to ordain him upon my
people Israel.
7 And when it was of the will of David, my father, to
build an house to the name of the Lord God of Israel,
(And when it was the desire of my father David, to build
a House in honour of the name of the Lord God of Israel,)
8 the Lord said to him, For this was thy will, to build
an house to my name, soothly thou didest well, having
such a will, (the Lord said to him, For this was thy desire,
to build a House in honour of my name, truly thou didest
well, having such a desire,)
9 but *yet* thou shalt not build an house to me;
nevertheless the son, that shall go out of thy loins, he
shall build an house to my name. (but *yet* thou shalt not
build a House for me; but the son, who shall go out of
thy loins, he shall build a House in honour of my name.)
10 Therefore the Lord hath fulfilled his word, that he
spake; and I rose up for David, my father, and I sat on the
throne of Israel, as the Lord spake, and I have builded an
house to the name of the Lord God of Israel (and I have
built a House in honour of the name of the Lord God of
Israel);
11 and I have put therein the ark, in which is the covenant

of the Lord, which he covenanted with the sons of Israel.
(and I have put the Ark in it, in which is the covenant of
the Lord, which he covenanted with the Israelites.)
12 Therefore Solomon stood before the altar of the Lord
even against all the multitude of Israel, and stretched
forth his hands. (And so Solomon stood before the altar of
the Lord in front of all the multitude of Israel, and
stretched out his hands.)
13 For Solomon had made a brazen foundament, and
had set it in the midst of the great house, and it had five
cubits of length, and five (cubits) of breadth, and three
cubits of height, and he stood there upon [it]; and from
that time he kneeled against all the multitude of Israel,
and he raised up his hands into heaven, (For Solomon
had made a bronze foundation, *or platform*, and had set
it in the midst of the great courtyard, and it had five
cubits of length, and five cubits of breadth, and three
cubits of height, and he stood upon it; and then he knelt
before all the multitude of Israel, and he raised up his
hands toward heaven,)
14 and said, Lord God of Israel, none is like thee; *thou
art* God in heaven, and in earth, which keepest covenant
and mercy with thy servants, that go before thee in all
their heart; (and said, Lord God of Israel, there is no god
like thee, in heaven, or on earth, who keepest covenant
with thy servants, and showest them love, yea, to those
who go before thee with all their heart;)
15 thou hast given to David thy servant, my father,
whatever thing thou hast spoken, *or promised*, to him;
and thou hast fulfilled in work those things, which thou
promisedest by mouth, as also this present time proveth.
(thou hast given to thy servant David, my father,
whatever thou hast promised to him; and thou hast
fulfilled in work those things, which thou promisedest
with thy mouth, as this present time proveth.)
16 Now therefore, Lord God of Israel, fulfill thou to thy
servant, my father David, whatever things thou hast
spoken, saying, A man of thee shall not fail before me,
that shall sit upon the throne of Israel; so nevertheless if
thy sons keep my ways (so shall it be if thy sons keep my
ways), and go in my law, as and thou hast gone before me.
17 And now, Lord God of Israel, thy word be made
steadfast, which thou spakest to thy servant David.
18 Therefore whether it is believeful, that the Lord
dwell with men on earth? If heaven and the heavens of
heavens (may not) take, either may not hold thee, *Lord*,
how much more this house, which I have builded? (And
so is it believable, that the Lord can live with people here
on earth? If heaven and the heavens of heavens cannot
hold thee, *Lord*, how much less this House, *Lord*, which I
have built *for thee*?)
19 But hereto only it is made, that thou, my Lord God,
behold there the prayer of thy servant, and the
beseeching of him, and that thou hear the prayers, which
thy servant poureth [out] before thee;
20 that thou open thine eyes upon this house by days
and nights, upon the place in which thou promisedest,
that thy name should be in-called, and that thou wouldest
hear the prayer, which thy servant prayeth therein. (and
that thou open thine eyes upon this House day and night,
yea, upon the place in which thou promisedest, that thy
name would be there, and that thou wouldest hear the
prayer, which thy servant prayeth in it.)
21 Hear thou the prayers of thy servant, and of thy
people Israel; whoever prayeth in this place, hear thou
from thy dwelling place, that is, from heaven, and do
thou mercy *to him*.
22 If any man sinneth against his neighbour, and
cometh ready to swear against him, and bindeth himself
with cursing before the altar in this house, (If any man
sinneth against his neighbour, and must swear an oath,
and bindeth himself with that oath before the altar in this
House,)
23 thou shalt hear from heaven, and shalt do the doom
of thy servants; so that thou yield to the wicked man his
way into his own head, and that thou venge the just man,
and yield to him after his rightwiseness. (thou shalt hear
from heaven, and shalt do justice for thy servants/and
shalt make judgement for thy servants; so that thou yield
to the wicked person his way upon his own head, and
that thou avenge the just person, and reward him
because of his righteousness.)
24 If thy people Israel is overcome of enemies, for they
shall do sin against thee, and if they converted do
penance, and beseech thy name, and pray in this place,
(And if thy people Israel be overcome by enemies, for they
have sinned against thee, and if they be turned and do
penance, and beseech thy name, and pray in this place,)
25 thou shalt hear from heaven, and do thou mercy to
the sin of thy people Israel (and forgive the sin of thy
people Israel), and bring them again into the land, which
thou hast given to them, and to their fathers.
26 If when heaven is closed, rain come not down for
the sin of thy people, and they beseech thee in this place,
and acknowledge to thy name, and be turned from their
sins, when thou hast tormented them, (And when the
heavens be closed up, and rain come not down for the
sin of thy people, and they beseech thee in this place,
and acknowledge, *or confess*, thy name, and be turned
from their sins, when thou hast tormented them,)
27 hear thou, Lord, from heaven, and forgive thou the
sins to thy servants, and to thy people Israel (and forgive
thou the sins of thy servants, and of thy people Israel),
and teach thou them a good way, by which they shall
enter, and give thou rain to the land, which thou hast
given to thy people to have in possession.
28 (And) If that hunger riseth in the land, and
pestilence, and rust, and wind destroying corns, (*or*

crops,) and if that a locust, and (a) bruchus *cometh*; and if
enemies besiege the gates of the city, after that the
countries be destroyed (after that the countryside is
destroyed); and if (in) any manner vengeance and
sickness oppresseth *thy people*;
29 if any of thy people Israel beseecheth, and knoweth
his vengeance, *that is, his sin wherefore he hath deserved*
(this) vengeance, and sickness, and if he spreadeth
abroad his hands in this house,
30 thou shalt hear from heaven, that is, from thine high
dwelling place, and do thou mercy, and yield thou to
each man after his ways, which thou knowest, that he
hath in his heart; for thou alone knowest the hearts of the
sons of men; (thou shalt hear from heaven, that is, from
thy high dwelling place, and then do thou mercy, and
yield thou to each person after their ways, which thou
knowest, that they have in heir heart; for thou alone
knowest the hearts of people;)
31 that they dread thee (so that they shall fear thee/so
that they shall revere thee), and go in thy ways in all
days, in which they live on the face of [the] earth, which
thou hast given to our fathers.
32 Also thou shalt hear from heaven, thy most steadfast
dwelling place, a stranger, which is not of thy people
Israel, if he cometh from a far land for thy great name,
and for thy strong hand, and thine arm stretched forth,
and prayeth in this place; (And thou shalt hear from
heaven, thy most steadfast dwelling place, a stranger,
who is not of thy people Israel, if he cometh from a far
land for thy great name's sake, and for thy strong hand,
and thy out-stretched arm, and prayeth in this place;)
33 and thou shalt do all things, for which that pilgrim
inwardly calleth thee, that all the people of (the) earth
know thy name, and dread thee, as thy people Israel
doeth; and that they know, that thy name is called on (in)
this house, which I have builded to thy name. (and thou
shalt do all the things, for which that pilgrim inwardly
calleth thee, so that all the people of the earth can know
thy name, and fear thee/and revere thee, as thy people
Israel *doeth*; and so that they can know, that thy name is
called on in this House, which I have built in honour of
thy name.)
34 If thy people goeth out to battle against his
adversaries, by the way in which thou sendest them, they
shall worship thee against the way in which this city is
set, which thou hast chosen, and the house which I
[have] builded to thy name, (If thy people goeth out to
battle against their adversaries, by the way in which thou
sendest them, they shall worship thee toward the way in
which this city is *set*, which thou hast chosen, and the
House which I have built in honour of thy name,)
35 that thou hear from heaven their prayers and their
beseeching, and do thou vengeance *to their adversaries*.
36 And if they sin against thee, for no man is *alive* that
sinneth not, and if thou art wroth with them, and betakest
them to their enemies (and deliverest them to their
enemies); and (the) enemies lead them (away as) prisoners
into a far land, either certainly which land is nigh;
37 and if they be converted in their heart in the land, to
which they be led prisoners, and they do penance, and
beseech thee in the land of their captivity, and say, We
have sinned, we have done wickedly, we did unjustly;
38 and if they turn again to thee in all their heart, and
in all their soul, in the land of their captivity, to which
they be led, *and if* they shall worship thee against the
way of their land, which thou hast given to the fathers of
them, and *against the way* of the city which thou hast
chosen, and of the house which I [have] builded to thy
name; (and if they turn again to thee with all their heart,
and with all their soul, in the land of their captivity to
which they be led away, *and if* they shall worship thee
toward the way of their land, which thou hast given to
their fathers, and *toward the way* of the city which thou
hast chosen, and *toward the way* of the House which I
have built in honour of thy name;)
39 that thou hear from heaven, that is, from thy
steadfast dwelling place, the prayers of them, and that
thou make doom, and forgive to thy people, though they
be sinful; (that thou hear from heaven, that is, from thy
steadfast dwelling place, their prayers, and that thou give
them justice/and that thou make judgement, and forgive
thy people, even though they have been sinful;)
40 for thou art my God; I beseech thee, be thine eyes
opened (let thine eyes be opened), and thine ears be
attentive to the prayer that is made in this place.
41 Now therefore, Lord God, rise up into thy rest, thou
and the ark of thy strength; Lord God, thy priests be
clothed with health (Lord God, let thy priests be clothed
with salvation), and thy holy men be glad in good things.
42 Lord God, turn thou not away the face of thy christ;
have thou mind on the mercies of David thy servant.
(Lord God, turn thou not away the face of thy anointed;
remember thy abiding love for thy servant David.)

CHAPTER 7

1 And when Solomon shedding out his prayers had
full ended *them*, fire came down from heaven, and it
devoured the burnt sacrifices, and the slain sacrifices; and
the majesty, *or shining*, of the Lord full-filled the house
(and the majesty, *or the shining*, of the Lord filled the
House full).
2 And the priests might not enter into the temple of
the Lord; for the mighty shining of the Lord had full-filled
the temple of the Lord. (And the priests could not enter
into the Temple of the Lord; for the mighty shining of the
Lord had fully filled the Temple of the Lord.)
3 But also all the sons of Israel saw fire coming down,
and the glory of the Lord upon the house, and they felled

down low to the earth, upon the pavement arrayed, *or*
paved, with stone, and they worshipped, and praised the
Lord, (and said,) For he is good, for his mercy is into the
world. (And all the Israelites saw the fire coming down,
and the glory of the Lord on the House, and they fell
down low to the ground, on the pavement paved with
stone, and they worshipped, and praised the Lord, and
said, For he is good, for his love is forevermore.)
4 And the king and all the people offered slain
sacrifices before the Lord.
5 Therefore king Solomon killed sacrifices of oxen two
and twenty thousand, of wethers sixscore thousand; and
the king and all the people hallowed the house of God.
(And so King Solomon and the people killed for a
sacrifice twenty-two thousand oxen, and one hundred
and twenty thousand rams; and the king and all the
people dedicated the House of God.)
6 And the priests stood in their offices, and [the]
deacons in organs of songs of the Lord, which king David
made to praise the Lord (with), For his mercy is into the
world; and they sang the hymns of David by their hands
in organs and other instruments; and the priests sang with
trumps before them, and all the people of Israel stood.
(And the priests stood in their places, and the Levites with
the musical instruments for the Lord, which King David
had made to praise the Lord with, For his love is
forevermore; and they sang the hymns of David *with the*
instruments; and the priests blew their trumpets opposite
them, and all the people of Israel stood.)
7 Therefore Solomon hallowed the middle of the large
place before the temple of the Lord; for he had offered
there burnt sacrifices, and the inner fatnesses of peaceable
sacrifices, for the brazen altar which he had made might
not sustain, *or hold*, the burnt sacrifices, and slain
sacrifices, and inner fatnesses of peaceable sacrifices. (And
so Solomon consecrated the centre of the *courtyard*, in
front of the Temple of the Lord; for he offered the burnt
sacrifices, and the inner fatnesses of the peace offerings
there, because the bronze altar which he had made could
not hold all the burnt sacrifices, and the slain sacrifices,
and the inner fatnesses of the peace offerings.)
8 Therefore Solomon made a solemnity in that time in
seven days, and all Israel with him, a full great church, *or*
congregation, from the entering of Hamath unto the
strand of Egypt. (And so Solomon made a feast at that
time for seven days, and all Israel with him, the full great
congregation, from the entrance to Hamath unto the
River of Egypt, *that is, unto the Nile*.)
9 And in the eighth day he made a gathering of
money, *that is, for necessaries of the temple*, for he had
hallowed the altar in seven days, and had made [the]
solemnity in seven (more) days. (And on the eighth day
they gathered money *for the necessities of the Temple*, for
they had celebrated the dedication of the altar for seven
days, and then had kept the feast for another seven days.)
10 Therefore in the three and twentieth day of the
seventh month, he let the peoples go to their tabernacles
(he let the people go back to their tents, *or their homes*),
joying and gladding upon the goodness that God had
done to David, and to Solomon, and to his people Israel.
11 And Solomon performed the house of the Lord, and
the house of the king, and all things which he had
disposed in his heart for to do in the house of the Lord,
and in his own house; and he had prosperity. (And
Solomon finished the House of the Lord, and the king's
house, and all the things that he had disposed in his heart
to do for the House of the Lord, and for his own house;
and he prospered.)
12 Forsooth the Lord appeared to him in the night, and
said, I have heard thy prayer, and I have chosen this
place to me into an house of sacrifice. (And the Lord
appeared to him in the night, and said, I have heard thy
prayer, and I have chosen this place to be a House of
sacrifice to me.)
13 If I close heaven, and rain cometh not down, and if I
send, and command to the locust, that he devour the
land, and if I send pestilence into my people; (And if I
close up the heavens, and rain cometh not down, or if I
command to the locusts, that they devour the land, or if I
send pestilence into my people;)
14 forsooth if my people is converted, on which my
name is called, and if it beseecheth me, and seeketh my
face, and doeth penance of his full evil ways, then I shall
hear from heaven, and I shall be merciful to the sins of
them, and I shall heal the land of them. (and if my
people, who be called by my name, be turned, and if
they beseech me, and seek my face, and do penance for
their full evil ways, then I shall hear from heaven, and I
shall be merciful to their sins, and I shall heal their land.)
15 And mine eyes shall be opened, and mine ears shall
be raised up to the prayer of him, that prayeth in this
place (who prayeth in this place);
16 for I have chosen, and hallowed this place, that my
name be there without end, and that mine eyes and mine
heart dwell there in all days.
17 Also if thou goest before me, as David thy father
went, and doest by all those things which I commanded
to thee, and keepest my rightfulnesses and my dooms,
(And if thou goest before me, as thy father David went,
and doest by all those things which I commanded to
thee, and obeyest my statutes and my judgements,)
18 I shall raise up the throne of thy realm, as I promised
to David thy father, and said, A man of thy generation
shall not be taken away, that shall be prince in Israel. (I
shall raise up the throne of thy kingdom, as I promised to
thy father David, and said, There shall always be a man
of thy descendants, who shall be the leader of Israel.)
19 But if ye turn away, and forsake my rightfulnesses

and my commandments, which I have set forth to you,
and ye go, and serve alien gods, and worship them, (But
if ye turn away, and abandon my statutes and my
commandments, which I have set forth to you, and ye go,
and serve other gods, and worship them,)
20 I shall draw you away from my land, which I gave to
you, and I shall cast away from my face this house which
I have builded to my name, and I shall give it into a
parable, and into ensample to all peoples. (I shall draw
you away from my land, which I gave you, and this
House, which I have consecrated in honour of my name,
I shall throw it away from my face, and I shall make it
into a parable, and into an example, for all the peoples.)
21 And this house shall be into a proverb to all men
passing forth; and they shall say, wondering *in
themselves*, Why did the Lord so to this land, and to this
house? (And this House shall be like a proverb for all
people passing forth; and they shall say, wondering *to
themselves*, Why hath the Lord done so to this land, and
to this House?)
22 And they shall answer, For they forsook the Lord
God of their fathers, that led them out of the land of
Egypt, and they took (hold of) alien gods, and
worshipped [them], and praised them; therefore all these
evils came upon them. (And they shall answer to them,
For they deserted the Lord God of their fathers, who led
them out of the land of Egypt, and they clung to foreign,
or other, gods, and worshipped them, and praised them;
and so all these evils came upon them.)

CHAPTER 8

1 Forsooth when twenty years were [ful]filled, after
that Solomon had builded the house of the Lord, and his
own house,
2 he builded the cities, which Hiram[3] had given to
Solomon; and he made the sons of Israel to dwell there.
(he rebuilt the cities, which Hiram had given to Solomon;
and he ordered the Israelites to live there.)
3 Also he went into Hamath of Zobah, and got it.
4 And he builded Palmyra in (the) desert, and he
builded other full strong cities in Hamath.
5 And he builded the higher Bethhoron and the lower
Bethhoron, walled cities, having gates, and locks, and bars;
6 also *he builded* Baalath, and all the strong cities that
were of Solomon; and all the cities of carts, and the cities
of knights (and all the cities for the chariots, and the cities
for the horsemen), (and) king Solomon builded, and
disposed all things, whichever he would, in Jerusalem,
and in Lebanon, and in all the land of his power.
7 And Solomon made subject into tributaries till into
this day all the people that was left of (the) Hittites, and
Amorites, and Perizzites, and Hivites, and Jebusites, that
were not of the generations of Israel,
8 and of the sons of them, and of the after-comers of
them, which the sons of Israel had not slain, (and their
descendants, and their after-comers, whom the Israelites
had not killed.)
9 For of the sons of Israel Solomon set not, that they
should serve the works of the king; for they were men
warriors, and the first, *or chief*, dukes, and princes of his
chariots, and of his knights; (For Solomon ordained, that
the Israelites should not serve in the forced labour for the
public works of the king; for they were men of war, and
the first, *or the chief*, officers, and the leaders of his
chariots, and of his horsemen;)
10 and all the princes of the host of king Solomon were
two hundred and fifty, that taught, *or ruled*, the people.
11 And Solomon translated the daughter of Pharaoh
from the city of David into an house, that he had builded
to her; for the king said, My wife shall not dwell in the
house of David, king of Israel, for it is hallowed, for the
ark of the Lord entered into that house. (And Solomon
brought Pharaoh's daughter up from the City of David to
the house, that he had built for her; for the king said, My
wife shall not live in the house of David, the king of
Israel, for it is holy, for the Ark of the Lord hath entered
into that house.)
12 Then Solomon offered burnt sacrifices to the Lord
on the altar of the Lord, which he had builded before the
porch (which he had built in front of the vestibule),
13 that by all days offering should be offered in it, by
the commandment of Moses, in sabbaths, and in calends,
and in feast days, thrice by the year, that is, in the
solemnity of therf loaves, and in the solemnity of weeks,
and in the solemnity of tabernacles. (so that by all days
the offerings would be offered on it, by the command of
Moses, yea, on sabbaths, and calends, and Feast days,
three times in the year, that is, on the Feast of
Unleavened Bread, and the Feast of Weeks, and the Feast
of Tabernacles.)
14 And he ordained by the ordinance of David, his
father, the offices of priests in their services, and the
deacons in their order, that they should praise and
minister before [the] priests by the custom of each day;
and *he ordained* [the] porters in their partings by gate and
gate. For David, the man of God, had commanded so;
(And he ordained by the ordinance of his father David,
the offices of the priests in their services, and the Levites
in their order, to praise and to minister before the priests
by the custom of each day; and *he ordained* the guards,
or the doorkeepers, in their divisions by each gate. For
David, the man of God, had so commanded;)
15 and both priests and deacons passed not from the
commandments of the king of all things which he had
commanded. (and the priests and the Levites followed all
the king's commands concerning everything which he

[3] Also known as Huram.

commanded, including his orders about the treasuries.)
16 And Solomon had all [the] costs, *or dispenses (or
expenses)*, made ready in the keepings of [the] treasuries,
from that day in which he founded the house of the Lord,
till into the day in which he performed it. (And so
Solomon founded the House of the Lord, and he finished
it; and he successfully completed all of his work.)
17 Then Solomon went into Eziongeber, and into Elath,
at the brink of the Red Sea (and into Elath, on the Gulf of
Akabah), which is in the land of Edom.
18 Therefore Hiram sent to him, by the hands of his
servants, ships, and shipmen knowing of the sea (And so
Hiram sent to him, under the command of his servants,
ships, and shipmen who were knowledgeable about the
sea), and they went with the servants of Solomon into
Ophir, and they took from thence four hundred and fifty
talents of gold, and they brought it (back) to king Solomon.

CHAPTER 9

1 And the queen of Sheba, when she had heard (of)
the fame of Solomon, came into Jerusalem for to assay
him in dark figures[4], *or likenesses* (came to Jerusalem to
test him with hard questions), (along) with great riches,
and camels, that bare sweet smelling spices, and full
much of gold, and precious gems, *either pearls.* And
when she was come to Solomon, she spake to him
whatever things were in her heart.
2 And Solomon expounded to her (on) all things
which she had put forth *to him,* and nothing was, that he
made not open, *or known,* to her.
3 And after that she saw these things, that is, the
wisdom of Solomon, and the house that he had builded,
4 also and the meats of his board (and also the food
on his table), and the dwelling places of his servants, and
the offices of his ministers, and the clothes of them, and
the butlers, and their clothes, and the sacrifices which he
offered in the house of the Lord, there was no more spirit
(left) in her for wondering, *for these things passed her
understanding.*
5 And she said to the king, The word is true, which I
heard in my land, of thy virtues (of thy works, *or thy
deeds*), and [of thy] wisdom;
6 I believed not to [the] tellers, till I myself had come,
and mine eyes had seen, and I had proved that scarcely
the half of thy wisdom was told to me; thou hast
overcome, *or (sur)passed,* the fame by thy virtues (thou
hast even surpassed the reports that I heard).
7 Blessed be thy men, and blessed be thy servants,
these that stand before thee in all time (these who always
stand in thy presence), and hear thy wisdom.
8 Blessed be the Lord God, that would ordain thee on
his throne king of the people of the Lord thy God; truly
for God loveth Israel, and will save him without end,
therefore he hath set thee king upon him, that thou do
dooms and rightfulness. (Blessed be the Lord thy God,
who hath ordained thee upon his throne to be the king of
the people of the Lord thy God; for God truly loveth
Israel, and will save them forevermore, and so he hath set
thee *to be* king upon them, so that thou can give them
judgements and laws.)
9 And she gave to the king sixscore talents of gold,
and full many sweet smelling spices, and most precious
gems; there were not such sweet smelling spices, as these
which the queen of Sheba gave to king Solomon (there
were never such sweet smelling spices in Israel, as those
which the queen of Sheba gave to King Solomon).
10 But also the servants of Hiram[5], with the servants of
Solomon, brought gold from Ophir, and trees of thyine
(and algum wood), and most precious gems;
11 of which, that is, of the thyine trees, the king made
degrees in the house of the Lord, and in the house of the
king, and also *he made* harps, and psalteries to singers;
such trees were never seen in the land of Judah. (of
which, from the algum wood, the king made stairs in the
House of the Lord, and in the house of the king, and also
he made harps, and lutes for the singers; such wood was
never seen before in the land of Judah.)
12 And [king] Solomon gave to the queen of Sheba all
things which she would, and which she asked, many
more than she had brought to him. And she turned
again, and went into her land with her servants. (And
King Solomon gave to the queen of Sheba all the things
which she desired, and which she asked for, indeed
many more things than she had brought to him. And
then she returned to her land with her servants.)
13 And the weight of gold, that was brought to
Solomon by each year, was six hundred and six and sixty
talents of gold,
14 besides that sum which the legates of diverse folks,
and merchants were wont to bring, and all the kings of
Arabia, and the princes of (other) lands, which brought
together gold and silver to Solomon (who all brought
gold and silver to Solomon).
15 Therefore king Solomon made two hundred golden
spears of the sum of six hundred florins, *either pieces of
gold,* that were spended in each spear; (And so King
Solomon made two hundred gold spears, where six
hundred florins, *or pieces of gold,* were used to make
each spear;)
16 and he made three hundred golden shields of three
hundred florins/three hundred pieces of gold, with which
each shield was covered; and the king putted those in the
armoury place, that was set in the wood (and the king put

[4] Figurative speech is to speak one thing, and to understand another. (Gloss from Original Text)

[5] Also known as Huram.

them all in the House of the Forest of Lebanon).
17 Also the king made a great seat, *or throne*, of ivory,
and he covered it with most clean gold; (And the king
made a great ivory throne, and he covered it with the
purest gold;)
18 and *he made* six degrees by which men went up to
the seat, and a golden stool, and twain arms, one against
the tother, and two lions standing beside the arms; (and *he*
made six steps by which people went up to the throne,
and a gold stool, and it had two arms, one opposite the
other, and two lions standing beside the arms;)
19 but also *he made* twelve little lions standing upon
[the] six degrees on ever either side of the throne (and *he*
also *made* twelve little lions standing on the six steps on
either side of the throne). Such a throne was not in all
realms, *that is, in none of all the realms of the world.*
20 And all the vessels of the feast of the king were
(made) of gold, and the vessels of the house of the forest
of Lebanon *were* (made) of most pure gold; for silver in
those days was areckoned for nought.
21 For also the ships of the king went into Tarshish with
the servants of Hiram once in three years, and they
brought (back) from thence gold, and silver, and ivory,
and apes, and peacocks.
22 And king Solomon was magnified over all [the]
kings of the earth for *his* riches and glory.
23 And all the kings of (the) lands desired to see the
face of Solomon, for to hear the wisdom that God had
given in his heart;
24 and they brought to him gifts, vessels of silver and of
gold, clothes, and armours (and arms, *or weapons*), and
sweet smelling spices, horses and mules, by each year.
25 And Solomon had forty thousand of horses in
stables, and twelve thousand of chariots and of knights;
and he ordained them in the cities of chariots, and where
the king was in Jerusalem. (And Solomon had four
thousand chariots and their horses in *his* stables, and
twelve thousand cavalry horses; and he ordained them to
be in the cities for the chariots, and where the king was
in Jerusalem.)
26 Forsooth he used power on all the kings, from the
flood of Euphrates unto the land of Philistines, and unto
the terms of Egypt. (And he exercised power over all the
kings from the Euphrates River unto the land of the
Philistines, and the border with Egypt.)
27 And he gave so great plenty of silver in Jerusalem, as
of stones, and so great multitude of cedar trees, as of
sycamores that grow in field places. (And he made silver
in Jerusalem *to be* as plentiful as stones, and cedar trees
to be as plentiful as the sycamores that grow in the fields.)
28 And horses were brought to Solomon from Egypt,
and from all countries.
29 Soothly the residue of the former works and the last
of Solomon (And the rest of the first and the last deeds of
Solomon), be written in the words of Nathan, the
prophet, and in the words of Ahijah of Shiloh, and in the
vision, *either prophecy*, of Iddo, the prophet, against
Jeroboam, the son of Nebat.
30 Soothly Solomon reigned in Jerusalem on all Israel
(for) forty years,
31 and he slept with his fathers; and they buried him in
the city of David, and Rehoboam, his son, reigned for him.

CHAPTER 10

1 Forsooth Rehoboam went forth into Shechem; for all
Israel came together thither to make him king.
2 And when Jeroboam, the son of Nebat, that was in
Egypt, for he fled thither (from) before Solomon, had
heard this, he turned again anon. (And when Jeroboam,
the son of Nebat, who was in Egypt, for he had fled there
from Solomon, had heard this, he returned at once.)
3 And they called him, and he came with all Israel,
and they spake to Rehoboam, and said,
4 Thy father oppressed us with a full hard yoke;
command thou lighter things *on us* than thy father, the
which set upon us a grievous servage; and release thou a
little of *our* burden, that we serve thee. (Thy father
oppressed us with a very hard yoke; command thou
lighter things *upon us* than thy father, who set upon us a
grievous slavery; and if thou release a little of *our* burden,
then we shall *gladly* serve thee.)
5 And he said, After three days turn ye again to me
(And he said, Return to me after three days). And when
the people was gone [away],
6 he took counsel with [the] eld men, that stood
before his father Solomon, while he lived yet (he took
counsel with the old men, *or the elders*, who stood
before his father Solomon, while yet he lived), and said,
What counsel give ye, that I answer to the people?
7 And they said to him, If thou pleasest this people,
and makest them soft, *or quietest them*, by meek words,
they shall serve thee in all time. (And they said to him, If
thou pleasest this people, and quietest them, with
humble words, they shall *loyally* serve thee always.)
8 And he forsook the counsel of the eld men, and
began to treat (this in thought) with (the) young men, that
were nourished with him, and were in his company. (But
he forsook the counsel of the old men, *that is, the elders*,
and began to discuss this with the young men, who grew
up with him, and were his friends.)
9 And he said to them, What seemeth to you? either
what thing ought I (to) answer to this people, that said to
me, Release thou the yoke, that thy father hath put upon
us?
10 And they answered, as young men, and nourished
with him in delights, and said, Thus thou shalt speak to
the people that said to thee, Thy father made grievous
our yoke, release thou *it*; and thus thou shalt answer to

them, My least finger is greater than the loins of my
father; (And these young men, who had grown up with
him in ease, said, Thus shalt thou say to the people who
said to thee, Thy father made our yoke grievous, release
thou *it*; thou shalt answer this to them, My least finger is
greater than my father's loins;)
11 my father put upon you a grievous yoke, and I shall
lay to (you) a greater burden (but I shall put upon you a
far greater burden); my father beat you with scourges, but
I shall beat you with scorpions, *that is, hard-knotted
ropes.*
12 And Jeroboam and all the people came to
Rehoboam in the third day, as he had commanded to
them.
13 And the king answered (to them) hard things, after
that he had forsaken the counsel of the elder men,
14 and he spake by the will of the young men, (*and
said,*) My father putted on you a grievous yoke, which I
shall make grievouser; my father beat you with scourges,
soothly I shall beat you with scorpions.
15 And Rehoboam assented not to the prayers of the
people; for it was the will of God, that his word should
be [ful]filled, which he had spoken by the hand of Ahijah
of Shiloh to Jeroboam, the son of Nebat.
16 And when the king had said *these* harder things, all
the people spake thus to him, No part be to us in David,
neither heritage in the son of Jesse; Israel, turn thou again
into thy tabernacles; and thou, David, feed thine own
house. And Israel went into his tabernacles. (And when
the king had said *these* hard things, all the people spoke
thus to him, We shall have no part with David, nor
inheritance with the son of Jesse; Israel, return thou to thy
tents, *or to thy homes*; and thou, David, feed thy own
house. And the people of Israel went back to their
tents/went back home.)
17 And Rehoboam reigned upon the sons of Israel, that
dwelled in the cities of Judah. (And so Rehoboam reigned
only upon the Israelites who lived in the cities of Judah.)
18 And king Rehoboam sent Hadoram, that was
sovereign over the tributes; and the sons of Israel stoned
him, and he was dead. And king Rehoboam hasted
him(self) to go up into his chariot, and fled into
Jerusalem. (And King Rehoboam sent out Hadoram, who
was the ruler over the tributes, *or the taxes*; and the
Israelites stoned him, and he died. And King Rehoboam
hastened to go up into his chariot, and fled into
Jerusalem.)
19 And Israel went away from the house of David unto
this day.

CHAPTER 11

1 Forsooth Rehoboam came into Jerusalem, and he
called together all the house of Judah and of Benjamin,
unto ninescore thousand of chosen men and warriors, for
to fight against Israel, and for to turn again his realm to
him (and to bring back his kingdom to him).
2 And the word of the Lord was made to Shemaiah,
the man of God, and said,
3 Speak thou to Rehoboam, the son of Solomon, king
of Judah, and to all Israel, which is in Judah and
Benjamin; (and say,) (Speak thou to Solomon's son
Rehoboam, the king of Judah, and to all Israel, who be in
Judah and Benjamin; and say,)
4 The Lord saith these things, Ye shall not go up,
neither ye shall fight against your brethren; each man
turn again to his house, for this thing is done by my will.
And when they had heard the word of the Lord, they
turned again, and went not against king Jeroboam. (The
Lord saith these things, Ye shall not go up, nor shall ye
fight against your kinsmen; each man return to his house,
for this thing is done by my will. And when they had
heard the word of the Lord, they returned to their homes,
and did not go up against King Jeroboam.)
5 And Rehoboam dwelled in Jerusalem, and he
builded walled cities in Judah; (And Rehoboam lived in
Jerusalem, and he built walls for many cities in Judah;)
6 and he builded Bethlehem, and Etam, and Tekoa,
(yea, he fortified Bethlehem, and Etam, and Tekoa,)
7 and Bethzur; and Shoco, and Adullam;
8 also and Gath, and Mareshah, and Ziph;
9 but also Adoraim, and Lachish, and Azekah;
10 and Zorah, and Aijalon, and Hebron, which were in
Judah and Benjamin, full strong cities (all well-fortified
cities).
11 And when he had closed those with walls, he set
princes in them, and barns of meats, that is, of oil, and of
wine. (And when he had enclosed them with walls, he
put leaders in them, and storehouses of food, and oil, and
wine.)
12 But also in each city he made places of armours of
shields, and spears, and he made those strong with most
diligence; and he reigned on Judah and Benjamin. (And
also in each city he made places for arms, *or for
weapons*, that is, for shields and spears, and he fortified
the cities with most diligence; and so he reigned upon
Judah and Benjamin.)
13 And the priests and the deacons, that were in all
Israel, came to Rehoboam from all their cities, (And the
priests and the Levites, who were in all Israel, came to
Rehoboam from all their cities,)
14 and they forsook their suburbs and their possessions,
and they passed into Judah and to Jerusalem (and they
abandoned their suburbs and their possessions, and they
went to Judah and Jerusalem); for Jeroboam and his after-
comers had cast them away, that they should not be set
in the priesthood of the Lord;
15 the which *Jeroboam* made to him[self] priests of
high places, and of fiends, and of calves, which he had

made. (and *Jeroboam* made for himself priests for the hill
shrines, and for the fiends, and for the calves, *or the
idols*, which he had made.)
16 But also of all the lineages of Israel, whichever gave
their heart to seek the Lord God of Israel, they came to
Jerusalem for to offer their sacrifices before the Lord God
of their fathers. (And from all the tribes of Israel, whoever
gave their heart to seek after the Lord God of Israel, they
came to Jerusalem, to offer their sacrifices to the Lord
God of their fathers.)
17 And they strengthened the realm of Judah, and
strengthened Rehoboam, the son of Solomon, by three
years; for they went in the ways of David, and of
Solomon, only by three years. (And so they strengthened
the kingdom of Judah, and Solomon's son Rehoboam, for
three years; for they went in the ways of David, and
Solomon, but only for three years.)
18 Forsooth Rehoboam wedded a wife, Mahalath, the
daughter of Jerimoth, the son of David, and (of) Abihail,
the daughter of Eliab, the son of Jesse;
19 and she childed to him sons (and she bare for him
three sons), Jeush, and Shamariah, and Zaham.
20 Also after this *wife* he took Maachah, the daughter
of Absalom, and she childed to him Abijah (and she bare
for him Abijah), and Attai, and Ziza, and Shelomith.
21 And Rehoboam loved Maachah, the daughter of
Absalom, above all his wives and his secondary wives.
And he had wedded eighteen wives, and he had sixty
secondary wives; and he begat eight and twenty sons,
and sixty daughters (And he wedded eighteen wives, and
he had sixty concubines; and he begat twenty-eight sons,
and sixty daughters).
22 And he ordained Abijah, the son of Maachah, the
head, (and) duke over all his brethren; for he thought to
make Abijah king, (And he ordained Abijah, Maachah's
son, to be the head, and the ruler, over all his brothers;
for he thought to make Abijah king.)
23 for *he was* wiser and mightier over all his sons; and
in all the coasts of Judah and of Benjamin, and in all the
walled cities, *he set his sons*; and he gave to them full
many meats, and he had many wives/and he took to
them many wives. (And *he* treated all his sons wisely,
and *he placed them in authority*, in all the land of Judah
and of Benjamin, in all the fortified cities; and he gave
them a great deal of food, *or provisions*, and many wives.)

CHAPTER 12

1 And when the realm of Rehoboam was made strong
and strengthened, he forsook the law of the Lord, and all
Israel with him. (But when Rehoboam's kingdom was
made strong and established, he abandoned the Law of
the Lord, and all Israel with him.)
2 And in the fifth year of the realm of Rehoboam,
Shishak, king of Egypt, went up into Jerusalem, for they,
that is, the men of Jerusalem, [had] sinned against the
Lord; (And in the fifth year of the reign of Rehoboam,
Shishak, the king of Egypt, went up against Jerusalem, for
they, *that is, the people of Jerusalem*, had sinned against
the Lord;)
3 and *he ascended* with a thousand and two hundred
chariots, and with sixty thousand horsemen, and no
number was of the common people, that came with him
from Egypt, that is, Libyans, and Troglodytes, and
Ethiopians. (and *he went up* with a thousand and two
hundred chariots, and sixty thousand horsemen, and
there was no number of the common people, who came
with him from Egypt, that is, Libyans, and Sukkiims, and
Ethiopians.)
4 And he took [the] full strong cities in Judah, and he
came to Jerusalem. (And he took the fortified cities in
Judah, and then he came to Jerusalem.)
5 And Shemaiah, the prophet, entered to Rehoboam,
and to the princes of Judah, which, fleeing from Shishak,
were gathered together in Jerusalem. And he said to
them, The Lord saith these things, Ye have forsaken me,
and I have forsaken you in the hand of Shishak. (And the
prophet Shemaiah went in to Rehoboam, and to the
leaders of Judah, who, fleeing from Shishak, were
gathered together in Jerusalem. And he said to them, The
Lord saith these things, Ye have deserted me, and so now
I have deserted you unto the power of Shishak.)
6 And the princes of Israel and the king were
astonished, and said, The Lord is just. (And Israel's
leaders and the king were astonished, but they said, The
Lord is just.)
7 And when the Lord had seen that they were
meeked, the word of the Lord was made to Shemaiah,
and said, For they be meeked, I shall not destroy them,
and I shall give to them a little help, and my strong
vengeance shall not drop upon Jerusalem by the hand of
Shishak. (And when the Lord had seen that they were
humbled, the word of the Lord was made to Shemaiah,
and said, For they be humbled, I shall not destroy them,
and I shall give them a little help, and my strong
vengeance shall not drop upon Jerusalem by the hand of
Shishak.)
8 Nevertheless they shall serve him, that they know
the diversity of my service, and of the service of the realm
of lands. (But they shall still serve him, so that they know
the difference between serving me, and serving the rulers
of other lands.)
9 Therefore Shishak, the king of Egypt, went away
from Jerusalem, after that he had taken away the treasures
of the house of the Lord, and of the king's house; and he
took all things with him, and (even) the gold shields
which Solomon had made,
10 for which *golden shields* king *Rehoboam* made
brazen shields, and he betook those to the princes of

[the] shield-makers, that kept the porch of the palace. (for
which *gold shields* King *Rehoboam* then made bronze
shields, and he gave them to the leaders of the guards,
who guarded the entrance to the palace.)
11 And when the king entered into the house of the
Lord, the shield-makers came, and took those *shields,*
and (then) they brought them again to his armoury place.
(And when the king entered into the House of the Lord,
the guards came, and brought those *shields,* and
afterward they took them back to his armoury.)
12 Nevertheless for they were meeked, the ire of the
Lord was turned away from them, and they were not
done away utterly; for good works were found also in
Judah. (But because they were humbled, the Lord's anger
was turned away from them, and they were not utterly
done away with; for good works were also found in
Judah.)
13 Therefore king Rehoboam was comforted in
Jerusalem, and reigned (And so King Rehoboam
strengthened himself in Jerusalem, and reigned). And he
was of one and forty years, when he began to reign, and
he reigned seventeen years in Jerusalem, the city which
the Lord chose (out) of all the lineages of Israel, that he
should confirm his name there. And the name of his
mother was Naamah (an) Ammonitess.
14 And he did evil, and he made not ready his heart to
seek God. (But he did evil, and he did not ordain his
heart to seek God's will.)
15 And the first and the last works of Rehoboam be
written, and diligently declared, in the books of
Shemaiah the prophet, and of Iddo the prophet. And
Rehoboam and Jeroboam fought in all days against
themselves (And Rehoboam and Jeroboam fought against
each other in all their days).
16 And Rehoboam slept with his fathers, and was
buried in the city of David; and Abijah, his son, reigned
for him.

CHAPTER 13

1 In the eighteenth year of king Jeroboam Abijah
reigned upon Judah; (In the eighteenth year of King
Jeroboam, Abijah began to reign upon Judah;)
2 he reigned three years in Jerusalem; and the name of
his mother *was* Michaiah, the daughter of Uriel of
Gibeah. And battle was betwixt Abijah and Jeroboam.
3 And when Abijah had begun battle, and had *with
him* most chivalrous men, and four hundred thousand of
chosen men, Jeroboam arrayed on the contrary the battle
array with eight hundred thousand of men, and they were
chosen men, and most strong men to battle. (And when
Abijah began the battle, he had *with him* four hundred
thousand most able, chosen men, and Jeroboam arrayed
his battle array opposite him, with eight hundred
thousand men, who were also very strong, and chosen
for battle.)
4 And Abijah stood upon the hill Zemaraim (And
Abijah stood on Mount Zemaraim), that was in Ephraim,
and he said, Hear thou, Jeroboam, and all Israel;
5 whether ye know not, that the Lord God of Israel
gave to David the realm on Israel without end, to him
and to his sons into the covenant of salt, *that is, steadfast
and stable*? (do ye not know that the Lord God of Israel
gave David the kingdom of Israel forevermore, yea, to
him and to his sons by a covenant of salt?)
6 And now Jeroboam, the son of Nebat, the servant of
Solomon, the son of David, hath risen up, and hath
rebelled against his lord.
7 And most vain men, the sons of Belial, were
gathered together to him, and they had might against
Rehoboam, the son of Solomon. Certainly Rehoboam
was boistous, *either fond/or untaught,* and of fearedful
heart, and might not against-stand them (and could not
stand against them).
8 Now therefore ye say, that ye be able to against-
stand the realm of the Lord, that he holdeth in possession
by the sons of David; and ye have a great multitude of
people, and ye have golden calves, which Jeroboam
made into gods to you. (And so now ye say, that ye be
able to stand against the kingdom of the Lord, that he
gave to the sons of David to have in possession; and ye
have a great multitude of people, and ye have gold
calves, which Jeroboam made to be your gods.)
9 And ye have cast away the priests of the Lord, the
sons of Aaron, and the deacons, and ye have made
priests to you, as all the peoples of (other) lands *have
priests;* whoever cometh and halloweth his hand in a
bull, in oxes, and in seven wethers, anon he is made
priest of them that be not gods. (And ye have thrown
away the priests of the Lord, the sons of Aaron, and the
Levites, and ye have made priests for yourselves, like all
the peoples of other lands *have;* so that whoever cometh
to consecrate himself with a young bull, and with seven
rams, he at once is made a priest of them that be not
gods.)
10 But our Lord is God, whom we forsake not; and
[the] priests of the sons of Aaron minister to the Lord, and
(the) deacons be in their order; (But our Lord is God,
whom we will not abandon; and the priests of the sons of
Aaron serve the Lord, and the Levites assist them;)
11 and they offer burnt sacrifices to the Lord by each
day in the morrowtide and eventide, and *also* incense
made by commandments of the law; and loaves be set
forth in a most clean board; and at us is the golden
candlestick, and the lantern thereof, that it be tended ever
at eventide; and we keep the behests of our God, whom
ye have forsaken. (and they offer burnt sacrifices to the
Lord each day in the morning and in the evening, and
also burn the incense as commanded by the Law; and the

loaves be set forth on a most clean table; and with us is
the gold candlestick, and its lanterns, that they light every
evening; for we follow the orders, *or the commands*, of
our God, whom ye have deserted.)
12 Therefore God is duke in our host, and his priests,
that trump and sound against you; do not ye, sons of
Israel, fight against the Lord God of your fathers, for it
speedeth not to you. (And so God is the leader of our
army, and of his priests, who be ready to sound against
you with trumpets; do not, ye Israelites, fight against the
Lord God of your fathers, for it shall not profit you/for ye
shall not prosper.)
13 While Abijah spake these things, Jeroboam made
ready treasons behind (them); and when Jeroboam stood
even against his enemies, he (en)compassed (them) with
his host, Judah unwitting. (And while Abijah spoke all
these things, Jeroboam prepared an attack behind them;
and so while Jeroboam stood in front of his enemies, he
was also behind them with his army, but Judah was
unwitting, *or unknowing*.)
14 And Judah beheld, and he saw battle nigh even
against *before* them, and behind *their* back; and he cried
to the Lord, and [the] priests began to trump. (But then
the men of Judah looked about, and they saw that the
battle was to come from in front of them, and also from
behind *their* backs; and they cried to the Lord, and the
priests began to sound their trumpets.)
15 And all the men of Judah cried out, and, lo! while
they cried on high, God made afeared Jeroboam and all
Israel, that stood even against Judah and Abijah/which
stood [over] against Judah and Abijah. (And all the men
of Judah cried out, and, lo! while they cried on high, God
made Jeroboam and all Israel afraid, who stood opposite,
or in front of, Judah and Abijah.)
16 And the men of Israel fled from Judah, and God
betook them into the hands of the men of Judah.
17 Therefore Abijah and his people smote them with a
great wound, and there felled down of them five hundred
thousand of strong men wounded. (And so Abijah and his
people struck them down there with a great slaughter,
and five hundred thousand strong men of them fell down
slain.)
18 And the sons of Israel were made low in that time,
and the sons of Judah were comforted full greatly, for
they had hoped in the Lord God of their fathers. (And the
Israelites were brought low at that time, and the sons of
Judah prevailed, for they had hoped in the Lord God of
their fathers.)
19 And Abijah pursued Jeroboam fleeing, and took his
cities, *that is*, Bethel and his villages, and Jeshanah with
his villages, and Ephron and his villages; (And Abijah
pursued after Jeroboam, and took his cities, *that is*,
Bethel, and its villages, and Jeshanah with its villages,
and Ephron, and all its villages;)
20 and Jeroboam might no more against-stand (*Judah*)
in the days of Abijah, whom the Lord smote, and he was
dead. (and Jeroboam never regained his power in the
days of Abijah, and finally the Lord struck him down, and
he died.)
21 Therefore Abijah, when his empire was comforted,
took fourteen wives, and he begat two and twenty sons,
and sixteen daughters. (And so Abijah, when his empire
was strengthened, *or confirmed*, took fourteen wives, and
he begat twenty-two sons, and sixteen daughters.)
22 The residue of [the] words of Abijah, and of his ways
and his works, be written full diligently in the book of
Iddo, the prophet. (And the rest of the deeds of Abijah,
his ways and his works, be very diligently written down
in The Book of Iddo, the prophet.)

CHAPTER 14

1 And Abijah slept with his fathers, and they buried
him in the city of David; and Asa, his son, reigned for
him. In whose days the land rested in peace ten years (In
whose days the land was at peace for ten years).
2 And Asa did that, that was good and pleasant in the
sight of his God, (And Asa did what was good and
pleasing before his God,)
3 and he destroyed the altars of strange worshipping,
that is, of idolatry, and the high places, and brake
altogether the images, and cutted down [the] maumet
woods; (and he destroyed the altars of idolatry, and the
hill shrines, and broke in pieces the sacred pillars, and
cut down the idol groves, *or the sacred poles*;)
4 and he commanded Judah to seek the Lord God of
their fathers, and to do the law and all [the]
commandments. (and he commanded the people of
Judah to seek the Lord God of their fathers, and to obey
the Law and all the commandments.)
5 And he took away from all the cities of Judah (the)
altars and (the) temples of idols, and he reigned in peace.
6 And he builded strong cities in Judah; for he was in
rest (for the land was at rest), and no battles rose (up) in
his times, for the Lord gave him peace.
7 And Asa said to Judah, Build we [up] these cities,
and (en)compass we *them* with walls (and surround we
them with walls), and strengthen we *them* with towers,
and gates, and locks, as long as all things be restful from
battle; for we have sought the Lord God of our fathers,
and he hath given to us rest by compass. Therefore they
builded, and there was no hindering in the building.
8 And Asa had in his host three hundred thousand of
(the) men of Judah bearing shields and spears; and of
Benjamin, he had two hundred thousand and fourscore
thousand of shield-bearers and of archers; all these *were*
full strong men.
9 Forsooth Zerah of Ethiopia went out against them
with his host (of) ten hundred thousand (men), and with

three hundred chariots, and came unto Mareshah.
10 Certainly Asa went (out) against *them*, and (they)
arrayed (the) battle array in the valley of Zephathah,
which is beside Mareshah.
11 And Asa inwardly called (upon) the Lord God, and
said, Lord, no diversity is with thee, whether thou help in
few, either in many; our Lord God, help thou us, for we
have trust in thee, and in thy name, and we came against
this multitude; Lord, thou art our God, a man have not
the mastery against thee. (And Asa inwardly called on the
Lord God, and said, Lord, there is no difference for thee,
whether thou help a few, or many; Lord our God, help
thou us, for we have trust in thee, and we have gone out
against this multitude in thy name; Lord, thou art our
God, let no man have the mastery against thee.)
12 Therefore the Lord made afeared (the) Ethiopians
before Asa and Judah, and (the) Ethiopians fled; (And so
the Lord made the Ethiopians afraid of Asa and the
people of Judah, and the Ethiopians fled;)
13 and Asa and his people, that was with him (who
were with him), pursued them unto Gerar. And (the)
Ethiopians felled down to (the) death, for they were all-
broken by the Lord slaying (them), and by his host
fighting (them). Then they took many spoils,
14 and they smote all the cities about Gerar; for great
dread had assailed all men. And they spoiled the
cities/And they rifled the cities, and bare away much
prey; (and they struck all the cities about Gerar; for great
fear had assailed all people. And they spoiled the cities/
And they rifled the cities, and carried away much prey;)
15 and also they destroyed the folds of sheep, and they
took multitude without number of sheep and of camels,
and they turned again into Jerusalem. (and they also
destroyed the sheepfolds, and they took away a multitude
without number of sheep and camels, and then they
returned to Jerusalem.)

CHAPTER 15

1 Forsooth Azariah, the son of Oded, when the spirit
of the Lord was come into him, (And Azariah, the son of
Oded, after the spirit of the Lord came upon him,)
2 he went out into the meeting of Asa (he went out to
meet Asa); and said to him, Asa, and all Judah and
Benjamin, hear ye me; the Lord *is* with you, for ye were
with him; if ye seek him, ye shall find *him*; soothly if ye
forsake him, he shall forsake you.
3 Forsooth many days shall pass in Israel without (the)
very God, and without priest, and without teacher, and
without law. (But many days have passed in Israel
without the true God, and without a priest, and without a
teacher, and without the Law.)
4 And when they turn again in their anguish, and cry
to the Lord God of Israel, and seek him, they shall find
him. (But when, in their anguish, they turned to the Lord
God of Israel, and cried to him, and sought him, they
found him.)
5 In that time [there] shall not be peace to go out and
to go in, but dreads on all side(s) on all the dwellers of
the land. (At that time there was no safety, *or security*, to
come in or to go out, but fear was on all sides for all the
inhabitants of the land.)
6 For folk shall fight against folk, and a city against a
city, for the Lord shall disturb them in all anguish; (And
nation fought against nation, and a city against a city, for
the Lord troubled them with all kinds of anguish;)
7 but be ye comforted, and your hands be not slacked;
for meed shall be to your work. (but be ye strengthened,
and do not let your hands be limp; for your work shall be
rewarded.)
8 And when Asa had heard this thing, that is, the
words and [the] prophecy of Azariah, the son of Oded,
the prophet, he was comforted, and he did away all the
idols from all the land of Judah and of Benjamin, and
from the cities which he had taken of the hill of Ephraim.
And he hallowed the altar of the Lord, that was before the
porch of the house of the Lord. (And when Asa had heard
this, that is, the words and the prophecy of the prophet
Azariah, the son of Oded, he was strengthened, *or
encouraged*, and he did away all the idols from all the
land of Judah and of Benjamin, and from the cities which
he had taken in the hill country of Ephraim. And he
repaired the altar of the Lord, that was in front of the
vestibule of the House of the Lord.)
9 And he gathered together all Judah and Benjamin,
and with them the comelings of Ephraim, and of
Manasseh, and of Simeon (and with them the newcomers
from Ephraim, and Manasseh, and Simeon); for many of
Israel, seeing that his Lord God was with him, fled over
to him.
10 And when they had come into Jerusalem, in the
third month, in the fifteen year of the realm of Asa,
11 they offered to the Lord in that day, both of the
spoils and of the prey, which they had brought, seven
hundred oxen, and seven thousand wethers. (they offered
to the Lord on that day, out of the spoils and the prey,
which they had brought back, seven hundred oxen, and
seven thousand rams.)
12 And Asa entered by custom to make strong the bond
of peace, that they should seek the Lord God of their
fathers in all their heart, and in all their soul. (And they
entered into a covenant, that they would seek the Lord
God of their fathers with all their heart, and with all their
soul.)
13 And *the king* said, If any man seeketh not the Lord
God of Israel, die he, from the least unto the most, from
man unto woman. (And that whoever would not seek the
Lord God of Israel should be put to death, from the least
unto the most, man or woman.)

14 And all that were in Judah swore with cursing to the
Lord, *that is, obliging themselves to cursing and pain of death, if they did against the oath,* with [a] great voice, in hearty song, and in sound of trump, and in sound of clarions; (And they swore *an oath, or a pledge,* to the Lord with a loud voice, and a hearty shout, and the sounding of trumpets and horns.)
15 for they swore in all their heart, and in all their will
they sought him, and found him; and the Lord gave to them rest by compass. (And all who were in Judah had great joy over the pledge; for they swore with all their heart, and they sought him with all their will, and they found him; and the Lord gave them rest, *or peace,* all about.)
16 But also he put down Maachah, the (grand)mother
of Asa the king, *that is, his own (grand)mother,* from the strait empire, for she had made in a wood a simulacrum, *or a likeness,* of a man's rod; and he all-brake that simulacrum, and pounded *it* into gobbets, and burnt it in the strand of Kidron. (And Asa also removed his grandmother Maachah, from her place of honour, for she had made an image, *or a likeness,* of a man's rod in the forest/for she had made an obscene idol for the worship of Asherah; and he broke up that image, and pounded *it* into pieces, and burned it by the Kidron Stream/and burned it in the Kidron Gorge.)
17 But yet [the] high places were left in Israel;
nevertheless the heart of Asa was rightful in all his days. (But yet there were still hill shrines in Israel; but Asa's heart was upright in all his days.)
18 And he brought into the house of the Lord those
things that his father [had] avowed, silver and gold, and diverse purtenance of vessels;
19 and battle was not unto the five and thirtieth year of
the realm of Asa. (and there was no battle *with any nation* until the thirty-fifth year of Asa's reign.)

CHAPTER 16

1 Forsooth in the six and thirtieth year of his realm,
Baasha, king of Israel, went up into Judah, and (en)compassed Ramah with a wall, that no man of the realm of Asa might go out, either enter in securely. (But in the thirty-sixth year of Asa's reign, Baasha, the king of Israel, went up into Judah, and surrounded Ramah with a wall, so that no man in Asa's kingdom could safely come in, or go out.)
2 And Asa brought forth gold and silver from the
treasur[i]es of the house of the Lord, and from the king's treasuries; and sent (it) to Benhadad, king of Syria, that dwelled in Damascus (who lived in Damascus), and said,
3 (A) Bond of peace is betwixt me and thee, and my
father and thy father had accord together; wherefore I have sent to thee silver and gold, that when thou hast broken the bond of peace, which thou hast with Baasha, king of Israel, thou make him to go away from me. (There is a covenant between me and thee, and my father and thy father had an accord together; and so I have sent to thee my silver and gold, so that when thou hast broken the covenant which thou hast with Baasha, the king of Israel, then thou shalt make him go away from me.)
4 And when this was found (acceptable), Benhadad
sent the princes of his hosts to the cities of Israel, which smote Ijon, and Dan, and Abelmaim, and all the walled cities of Naphtali. (And when this was found acceptable, Benhadad sent the leaders of his armies against the cities of Israel, who struck Ijon, and Dan, and Abelmaim, and all the walled cities of Naphtali.)
5 And when Baasha had heard this, he ceased to build
(up) Ramah, and left [off] his work.
6 And king Asa took all Judah, and they took from
Ramah the stones, and [the] wood, which Baasha had made ready to building; and he builded of those Geba, and Mizpah. (And King Asa commanded to all Judah, and they took away the stones, and the timber from Ramah, with which Baasha had fortified it; and Asa used them to fortify Geba and Mizpah.)
7 In that time Hanani, the prophet (At that time the
prophet Hanani), came to Asa, king of Judah, and said to him, For-thy that thou haddest trust in the king of Syria, and not in the Lord thy God, therefore the host of the king of Syria escaped from thine hand.
8 Whether (the) Ethiopians and Libyans were not
many more in chariots, and knights, and in full great multitude; which, when thou haddest believed to the Lord, he betook them into thine hands? (Did not the Ethiopians and the Libyans, with such a great multitude, have many more chariots, and horsemen *than thee*? yet, when thou had believed in the Lord, he delivered them into thy hands.)
9 For the eyes of the Lord behold all the earth, and
give strength to them, that with perfect heart believe into him (and give strength to those, who with a perfect heart believe in him). Therefore thou hast done follily, and for this *trust in men,* yea, in *this* present time battles shall rise against thee.
10 And Asa was wroth against the prophet, and
commanded him to be sent into the stocks. Forsooth the Lord had indignation greatly upon this thing, and he killed full many of the people in that time (And the king had great indignation because of this word, and he killed a great many people at that time).
11 Soothly the first and [the] last works of Asa be
written in the book of [the] kings of Judah and of Israel.
12 And Asa was sick full greatly in the aching of *his*
feet, in the nine and thirtieth year of his realm; and neither in his sickness he sought the Lord, but he trusted more in the craft of leeches. (And Asa was greatly sick, *or pained,* with aching feet, in the thirty-ninth year of his

kingdom; yet even in his sickness he did not seek the
Lord, but he trusted more in the craft of physicians.)
13 And Asa slept with his fathers, and was dead in the
one and fortieth year of his realm. (And Asa went to be
with his ancestors, and died in the forty-first year of his
reign.)
14 And they buried him in his sepulchre, which he had
made to himself in the city of David; and they put him, *or laid him*, on his bed full of sweet smelling spices and
ointments of whores, that where made (al)together by the
craft of ointment makers, and they burnt *these* upon him
with full great cost. (And they buried him in his tomb,
which he had made for himself in the City of David; and
they laid him on his bed full of sweet smelling spices and
ointments, which were made by the craft of ointment
makers; and they burned a great bonfire to mourn his
death.)

CHAPTER 17

1 Forsooth Jehoshaphat, his son, reigned for him; and
he had the mastery against Israel.
2 And he set numbers of knights in all the cities of
Judah, that were (en)compassed with walls (And he put
numbers of horsemen in all the cities of Judah, that were
surrounded with walls), and he disposed strongholds in
the land of Judah, and in the cities of Ephraim, which
Asa, his father, had taken.
3 And the Lord was with Jehoshaphat, which went in
the first ways of David, his father; he hoped not in
Baalim, (And the Lord was with Jehoshaphat, who went
in the early ways of his father *Asa;* he did not trust in, *or follow*, the Baalim,)
4 but *he hoped* in the Lord God of David, his father
(but *he hoped* in the Lord God of his father *Asa*), and he
went in the commandments of God, and not after the sins
of Israel.
5 And the Lord confirmed the realm in his hand; and
all Judah gave gifts to Jehoshaphat, and riches without
number, and much glory was made to him.
6 And when his heart had taken hardiness for the
ways of the Lord, he took away also (the) high places and
[maumet] woods from Judah. (And he took pride in
following the ways of the Lord, and he also did away the
hill shrines and the idol groves, *or the sacred poles*, in
Judah.)
7 And in the third year of his realm, he sent of his
princes (he sent his officials), Benhail, and Obadiah, and
Zechariah, and Nethaneel, and Michaiah, that they
should teach in the cities of Judah;
8 and with them *he sent nine* deacons, (*or Levites,) that is*, Shemaiah, and Nethaniah, and Zebadiah, and
Asahel, and Shemiramoth, and Jehonathan, and
Adonijah, and Tobijah, and Tobadonijah, deacons (all
Levites); and with them Elishama and Jehoram, priests;
9 and they taught the people in Judah, and had the
book of the law of the Lord; and they compassed all the
cities of Judah, and taught all the people. (and they taught
the people in Judah, and had The Book of the Law of the
Lord; and they went all around the cities of Judah, and
taught all the people.)
10 Therefore the dread of the Lord was made upon all
the realms of (the) lands, that were (round) about Judah;
and those durst not fight against Jehoshaphat.
11 But also [the] Philistines brought gifts to
Jehoshaphat, and toll, *or tribute*, of silver; and men of
Arabia brought *to him* sheep, seven thousand and seven
hundred wethers, and so many bucks of goats (and as
many goat bucks).
12 Then Jehoshaphat increased, and was magnified till
to on high; and he builded in Judah houses at the
likeness of towers, and full strong cities;
13 and he made ready many works in the cities of
Judah. Also men warriors and strong men were in
Jerusalem; (and he had much work done in the cities of
Judah. And there were men of war and strong men in
Jerusalem;)
14 of which this is the number, by the houses and
families of all *(the) men* (*who were*) in Judah. Duke
Adnah *was* prince of the host (Adnah *was* the leader of
the army), and with him were three hundred thousand
full strong men.
15 And after him was Jehohanan (the) prince (And
second in command was Jehohanan), and with him *were*
two hundred thousand and fourscore thousand *men*.
16 After this also Amasiah, the son of Zichri, *was*
hallowed to the Lord (And after him *was* Amasiah, the
son of Zichri, *who was* dedicated to the Lord), and with
him *were* two hundred thousand of strong men.
17 (And of Benjamin;) Eliada, a mighty *man* to battles,
followed this *Amasiah*, and with him *were* two hundred
thousand of men holding bow and shield. (And of
Benjamin; Eliada, a mighty *man* of battles, and with him
were two hundred thousand men holding bow and
shield.)
18 After this *was* also Jehozabad, and with him *were* an
hundred thousand and fourscore thousand of ready
knights. (And after him *was* Jehozabad, and with him
were a hundred and eighty thousand fully-armed
horsemen.)
19 All these were at the hand of the king, besides
others, which he had put in walled cities in all Judah. (All
of these were at the hand of the king, besides others,
whom he had put in the fortified cities in all of Judah.)

CHAPTER 18

1 Forsooth Jehoshaphat was full rich, and noble, and
by affinity he was joined to Ahab. (Now Jehoshaphat was
very rich, and noble, and by marriage he was joined to

Ahab.)
2 And after *certain* years *Jehoshaphat* came down to
Ahab into Samaria; at whose coming Ahab killed full
many wethers and oxen, and to the people that came
with him; and *Ahab* counselled *Jehoshaphat* to go up
with him into Ramoth of Gilead. (And after *some* years
Jehoshaphat came down to *Ahab* in Samaria; and Ahab
killed a great many rams and oxen for him, and for the
people who came with him; and *Ahab* counselled
Jehoshaphat to go up *with him* into Ramoth of Gilead.)
3 And Ahab, king of Israel, said to Jehoshaphat, king
of Judah, Come thou with me into Ramoth of Gilead. To
whom he answered, As and I am, so and thou art; and as
thy people, so and my people; and we shall be with thee
in battle. (And Ahab, the king of Israel, said to
Jehoshaphat, the king of Judah, Come thou with me to
Ramoth of Gilead. And Jehoshaphat answered, I am
ready when thou art/What is mine is yours; and my
people be as thy people; and we shall be with thee in
battle.)
4 And Jehoshaphat said to the king of Israel, I beseech
thee, counsel thou in *this* present time the word of the
Lord.
5 Therefore the king of Israel gathered together four
hundred men of (the) prophets, and said to them, Ought
we to go into Ramoth of Gilead for to fight, either take
rest? (or should we not?) And *the prophets* said, Go ye
up, and God shall betake *it* into the hand of the king.
6 And Jehoshaphat said, Whether no (other) prophet
of the Lord is here, that we may also ask of him?
7 And the king of Israel said to Jehoshaphat, One man
is, of whom we may ask the will of the Lord, but I hate
him, for he prophesieth not good, but evil to me, in all
time; soothly it is Micaiah, the son of Imla. And
Jehoshaphat said to him, King, speak thou not in this
manner. (And the king of Israel said to Jehoshaphat,
There is one man, of whom we can ask the will of the
Lord, but I hate him, for every time he prophesieth not
good, but only evil for me; this is Micaiah, the son of
Imla. And Jehoshaphat said to him, O king, do not thou
say such things.)
8 Then the king of Israel called one of his geldings, *or*
(his honest and) chaste servants, and said to him, Call
thou anon Micaiah, the son of Imla. (Then the king of
Israel called one of his eunuchs, and said to him, Call
thou at once Micaiah, the son of Imla.)
9 And the king of Israel and Jehoshaphat, king of
Judah, sat ever either in his seat, and they were clothed in
king's array; and they sat in the cornfloor, beside the gate
of Samaria; and all the prophets prophesied before them.
(And the king of Israel, and Jehoshaphat, the king of
Judah, both sat on their thrones, and they were clothed in
king's clothing; and they sat at the entrance to the gate of
Samaria; and all the prophets prophesied before them.)
10 And Zedekiah, the son of Chenaanah, made to him
iron horns (made iron horns for himself), and said, The
Lord saith these things, With these, thou shalt winnow
the men of Syria, till thou all-brake *them*.
11 And all the prophets prophesied in like manner, and
said, Go thou up into Ramoth of Gilead, and thou shalt
have prosperity; and the Lord shall betake them into the
hands of the king (yea, the Lord shall deliver them into
the hands of the king).
12 And the messenger, that went to call Micaiah (who
went to call Micaiah), said to him, Lo! the words of all the
prophets tell with one mouth good things to the king;
therefore, I pray thee, that thy word dissent not from
them, and that thou speak prosperities *to him*.
13 To whom Micaiah answered, (As) The Lord liveth,
for whatever things my Lord *God* speaketh to me, I shall
say those things.
14 Therefore he came to the king (And so he came to
the king). To whom the king said, Micaiah, ought we (to)
go into Ramoth of Gilead to fight, either (should we) take
rest, *and not to go thither*? To whom Micaiah answered,
Go ye up *thither*, for all prosperities shall come *to you*,
and [the] enemies shall be taken into your hands.
15 And the king said *to him*, Again and again I charge
thee, that thou speak not to me no but that that is sooth
in the name of the Lord.
16 And he said, I saw all Israel scattered abroad in the
hills, as sheep without a shepherd. And the Lord said,
These men have not lords; each man *therefore* turn again
into his house in peace. (And then Micaiah said, I saw all
Israel scattered over the hills, like sheep without a
shepherd. And the Lord said, These men have no leader;
so let each man return to his house in peace.)
17 The king of Israel said to Jehoshaphat, Whether I
said not to thee, that he prophesied not any good to me,
but those things that be evil? (And the king of Israel said
to Jehoshaphat, Did I not say to thee, that he would not
prophesy any good for me, but only those things that be
evil?)
18 And then *Micaiah* said, Hear ye the word of the
Lord. I saw the Lord sitting in his throne (I saw the Lord
sitting on his throne), and all the host of heaven standing
nigh [to] him at the right side and *at the* left.
19 And the Lord said, Who shall deceive Ahab, king of
Israel, (so) that he go up, and fall down in Ramoth of
Gilead? And when one said in this manner, and another
said in another manner,
20 a spirit came forth, and stood before the Lord, and
said, I shall deceive him. To whom the Lord said, And
wherein shalt thou deceive *him*? (And how shalt thou
deceive *him*?)
21 And he answered, I shall go out, and I shall be a
lying spirit in the mouth of all his prophets. And the Lord
said, Thou shalt deceive *him*, and thou shalt have the

mastery; go thou out, and do so.
22 Now therefore, lo! the Lord hath given a spirit of
leasing in the mouth of all thy prophets, and the Lord
hath spoken evil things of thee, *that is, he hath said (of
the) evil things to come to thee*. (And so now, lo! the
Lord hath put a lying spirit in the mouth of all thy
prophets, and the Lord hath spoken evil things for thee,
that is, he hath said that evil things shall come to thee.)
23 And Zedekiah, the son of Chenaanah, nighed, and
he smote Micaiah upon the cheek (and he struck Micaiah
upon his cheek), and said, By what way hath the Spirit of
the Lord passed from me to speak with thee?
24 And Micaiah said, Thou thyself shalt see in that day,
when thou shalt enter from closet into closet, that thou
be hid. (And Micaiah said, Thou thyself shalt see, *or shalt
discover*, on that day, when thou shalt go from closet to
closet, so that thou can be hid.)
25 And the king of Israel commanded, saying, Take ye
Micaiah, and lead ye him to Amon, [the] prince of the
city, and to Joash, the son of Amalek (the son of Ahab);
26 and ye shall say *to them*, The king saith these things,
Send ye this man into prison, and give ye to him a little
of bread, and a little of water, till I turn again in peace
(until I return home safely).
27 And Micaiah said, If thou turnest again in peace, the
Lord spake not to me. And he said, All peoples hear ye.
(And Micaiah said, If thou returnest home safely, the Lord
did not speak through me. And he said, Hear ye, all the
people.)
28 Then the king of Israel, and Jehoshaphat, the king of
Judah, went up into Ramoth of Gilead.
29 And the king of Israel said to Jehoshaphat, I shall
change *my* clothing, and so I shall go to fight; but be thou
clothed in thy (*king's*) clothes. Therefore when the king of
Israel had changed (*his*) clothing, he came to (the) battle.
30 And the king of Syria commanded to the dukes of
the multitude of his knights, and said, Fight ye not against
the least, nor against the most; but against the king alone
of Israel. (And the king of Syria had commanded to the
leaders of his multitude of horsemen, and said, Do not ye
fight against the least, or against the most, but only
against the king of Israel.)
31 Therefore when the princes of the multitude of
knights had seen Jehoshaphat, they said, This is the king
of Israel; and they (en)compassed him, and fought *against
him* (And so when the leaders of the multitude of
horsemen had seen Jehoshaphat, they said, This is the
king of Israel; and they surrounded him, and fought
against him). And Jehoshaphat cried to the Lord; and the
Lord helped him, and turned them away from him.
32 And when the dukes of the multitude of knights had
heard, *or understood*, that it was not the king of Israel,
they left him/they let him go. (And when the leaders of
the multitude of horsemen had understood that he was
not the king of Israel, they let him go.)
33 And it befelled, that one man of the people shot an
arrow into uncertain(ty), and he smote the king of Israel
betwixt the neck and the shoulders. And he said to his
charioteer, Turn thine hand, and lead me out of the battle
array; for I am wounded.
34 And the battle was ended in that day. Certainly the
king of Israel stood in his chariot against (the) men of
Syria till to eventide, and he died, when the sun went
down. (And the battle ended that day. And the king of
Israel stood in his chariot facing the men of Syria until the
evening, and then he died, when the sun went down.)

CHAPTER 19

1 Forsooth Jehoshaphat, king of Judah, turned again
peaceably into his house into Jerusalem. (And
Jehoshaphat, the king of Judah, returned safely to his
house, *that is, his palace*, in Jerusalem.)
2 Whom the prophet Jehu, the son of Hanani met, and
said to him, Thou givest help to a wicked man, and thou
art joined by friendship to them that hate the Lord; and
therefore soothly thou deservedest the wrath of the Lord;
3 but good works be found in thee, for thou hast done
away [the] maumet woods from the land of Judah, and
thou hast made ready thine heart, for to seek the Lord
God of thy fathers. (but good works be found done by
thee, for thou hast done away the idol groves, *or the
sacred poles*, from the land of Judah, and thou hast
directed thy heart to seek the Lord God of thy fathers.)
4 Therefore Jehoshaphat dwelled in Jerusalem; and
again he went out to the people from Beersheba to the
hill of Ephraim, and he called them again to the Lord
God of their fathers. (And so Jehoshaphat lived in
Jerusalem; but he went out among the people, from
Beersheba to the hill country of Ephraim, and he brought
them back to the Lord God of their fathers.)
5 And he ordained judges of the land in all the
strengthened cities of Judah, by each place. (And he
ordained judges of the land in all the fortified cities of
Judah, at each place.)
6 And he commanded to the judges, and said *to them*,
See ye, *that is, be ye ware*, what ye do; for ye use not the
doom of man, but *doom* of the Lord; and whatever thing
ye deem *unjustly*, it shall turn against you; (And he
commanded to the judges, and said *to them*, Be ye ware
what ye do; for ye judge not for man, but for the Lord;
and whatever thing ye judge *unjustly*, it shall return to
you;)
7 the dread of the Lord be with you (let the fear of the
Lord/let reverence for the Lord be with you), and do ye
all things with diligence, *that is, with discretion*; forsooth
with the Lord your God (there) is no wickedness, neither
taking, *or accepting*, of persons, neither covetousness of
gifts.

8 And also in Jerusalem Jehoshaphat ordained
deacons, and priests, and the princes of the families of
Israel, that they should deem the doom and the cause of
the Lord, to the dwellers of Jerusalem. (And in Jerusalem
Jehoshaphat ordained the Levites, and the priests, and the
leaders of the families of Israel, to declare the judgement
of the Lord, and to administer the civil laws, for the
inhabitants of Jerusalem.)
9 And he commanded to them, and said, Thus ye shall
do in the dread of the Lord, faithfully, and in perfect
heart. (And he commanded to them, and said, Thus ye
shall do in the fear of the Lord/in reverence for the Lord,
faithfully, and with a perfect heart.)
10 Each cause that cometh to you of your brethren, that
dwell in their cities, betwixt kindred and kindred,
wherever is question of the law, (*or*) of the
commandment, *or* of ceremonies, *either sacrifices, or* of
justifyings, show ye to them, that they do not sin against
the Lord, and that wrath *of the Lord* come not upon you,
and upon your brethren. Therefore ye doing thus shall
not do sin. (Each cause, *or case*, that cometh to you of
your kinsmen, who live in their cities, between kindred
and kindred, wherever there is a question of the law, *or*
of the commandment, *or* of ceremonies, *or sacrifices, or*
of statutes, show ye to them, so that they do not sin
against the Lord, and that the Lord's anger come not
upon you, and upon your kinsmen. And by doing so, ye
shall do no sin.)
11 And Amariah, your priest and bishop, shall be
sovereign in these things, that pertain to God. And
Zebadiah, the son of Ishmael, that is duke in the house of
Judah, shall be *sovereign* upon the works that pertain to
the office of the king, and ye (shall also) have master
deacons before you; be ye comforted, and do ye
diligently, *that is, studiously, or busily*, and the Lord shall
be with you in goods. (And your High Priest Amariah,
shall be the ruler in these things that pertain to God. And
Zebadiah, the son of Ishmael, who is the leader in the
house of Judah, shall be *the ruler, or the overseer*, of the
works that pertain to the office of the king, and ye shall
also have the Levites before you; so be ye strengthened,
and do ye diligently, *that is, studiously, or busily*, and the
Lord shall be on the side of the good.)

CHAPTER 20

1 After these things the sons of Moab, and the sons of
Ammon, and with them Idumeans, were gathered
together, *and they came* to Jehoshaphat, for to fight
against him. (And after these things the Moabites, and the
Ammonites, and with them the Meunites, were gathered
together, *and they came* to Jehoshaphat, to fight against
him.)
2 And messengers came, and showed *this* to
Jehoshaphat, saying, A great multitude of those places
that be beyond the sea, and of Syria, is come against
thee; and lo! they stand *together* in Hazazontamar, which
is Engedi. (And messengers came, and told *this* to
Jehoshaphat, saying, A great multitude from that place on
the other side of the Dead Sea, yea, from Edom, hath
come against thee; and lo! they stand *together* in
Hazazontamar, which is Engedi.)
3 Forsooth Jehoshaphat was afeared by dread, and
gave himself all for to pray the Lord, and preached fasting
to all Judah. (And Jehoshaphat was filled with fear, and
gave his all to pray to the Lord, and preached a fast for all
of Judah.)
4 And Judah was gathered together for to pray (to) the
Lord, and also all men came from their cities for to
beseech him.
5 And when Jehoshaphat had stood in the midst of the
company of Judah and of Jerusalem, in the house of the
Lord, before the new large place *of the temple*, (And
when Jehoshaphat had stood in the middle of the
congregation of Judah and of Jerusalem, in the House of
the Lord, in front of the new courtyard *of the Temple*,)
6 he said, Lord God of our fathers, thou art God in
heaven, and thou art Lord of all (the) realms of folks;
strength and power be in thine hand, and none may
against-stand thee. (he said, Lord God of our fathers, thou
art God in heaven, and thou art Lord of all the kingdoms
of the nations; strength and power be in thine hand, and
no one can stand against thee.)
7 Whether not thou, our God, hast slain all the
dwellers of this land before thy people Israel, and hast
given it to the seed of Abraham, thy friend, [into] without
end? (Hast not thou, our God, killed all the inhabitants of
this land before thy people Israel, and hast thou not given
it to the descendants of Abraham, thy friend,
forevermore?)
8 And they dwelled therein, and builded therein a
saintuary to thy name, and said, (And they lived here,
and built a sanctuary in honour of thy name, and said,)
9 If evils come [up]on us, the sword of doom,
pestilence, or hunger (yea, the sword, or judgement, or
pestilence, or hunger), we shall stand before this house
(into) without end in thy sight, in which house thy name
is called (upon), and we shall cry to thee in our
tribulations; and thou shalt hear us, and shalt make us
safe.
10 Now therefore lo! the sons of Ammon, and of Moab,
and the hill (country) of Seir, by whom thou grantedest
not to the sons of Israel for to pass (through their lands),
when they went out of Egypt, but they bowed away from
them, and killed not them, (And so now lo! the
Ammonites, and the Moabites, and those of the hill
country of Seir, whom thou grantedest not to the
Israelites to pass through their lands, when they went out
of Egypt, but they turned away from them, and did not

kill them,)
11 *but* (*now*) they do on the contrary, and endeavour to
cast us out of the possession, which thou, our God, hast
given to us;
12 therefore whether thou, *Lord*, shalt not deem them?
Truly in us is not so great strength, that we may against-
stand this multitude, that falleth in upon us; but since we
know not what we ought to do, we, the residue, have *this*
only, that we (ad)dress our eyes to thee. (and so shalt
thou not judge them? Truly there is not in us so great a
strength, that we can stand against this multitude, who
falleth in against us; but since we know not what we
ought to do, we, who remain, have only *this*, that we
direct our eyes to thee.)
13 And all Judah stood before the Lord, with their little
children, and their wives, and with their free children.
14 And Jahaziel, the son of Zechariah, the son of
Benaiah, the son of Jeiel, the son of Mattaniah, was a
deacon, and of the sons of Asaph, upon whom the Spirit
of the Lord was made in the midst of the company, (And
Jahaziel, the son of Zechariah, the son of Benaiah, the
son of Jeiel, the son of Mattaniah, was a Levite of the sons
of Asaph, upon whom the Spirit of the Lord came in the
middle of the congregation,)
15 and he said, All Judah, and ye that dwell in
Jerusalem, and thou, king Jehoshaphat, perceive ye, *or
taketh heed*, The Lord saith these things to you, Do not
ye dread, neither be ye afeared of this multitude, for it is
not your battle, but God's battle. (and he said, All Judah,
and ye who live in Jerusalem, and thou, king
Jehoshaphat, take heed, The Lord saith these things to
you, Do not ye fear, nor be ye afraid of this multitude, for
it is not your battle, but God's battle.)
16 Tomorrow ye shall go up against them; for they shall
go up by the side of the hill, called Ziz by name, and ye
shall find them in the height of the strand, that is against
the wilderness of Jeruel. (Tomorrow ye shall go out
against them; for they shall go up by the Ziz Pass, and ye
shall find them at the end of the valley, east of the
wilderness of Jeruel.)
17 For it shall not be ye, that shall fight; but only stand
ye trustily (For it shall not be ye, who shall fight; but only
stand ye there with trust/in faith), and ye shall see the
help of the Lord upon you. O! Judah and Jerusalem, do
not ye dread, neither be ye afeared; tomorrow ye shall go
out against them, and the Lord shall be with you.
18 Therefore Jehoshaphat, and Judah, and all the
dwellers of Jerusalem, fell lowly upon the earth before
the Lord, and worshipped him. (And so Jehoshaphat, and
Judah, and all the inhabitants of Jerusalem, fell low on
the ground before the Lord, and worshipped him.)
19 And the deacons of the sons of Kohath, and of the
sons of Korah (And the Levites of the Kohathites, and of
the Korahites), praised the Lord God of Israel with [a]
great voice on high.
20 And when *upon the morrow* they had risen early,
they went out by the desert of Tekoa; and when they had
gone forth, Jehoshaphat stood in the midst of them, and
said, Judah, and all the dwellers of Jerusalem, hear ye
me; believe ye in the Lord your God, and ye shall be
secure; believe ye to his prophets, and all prosperities
shall come *to you*. (And when they had risen early *the
next morning*, they went out by the wilderness of Tekoa;
and when they had gone forth, Jehoshaphat stood in their
midst, and said, Judah, and all the inhabitants of
Jerusalem, listen ye to me; believe ye in the Lord your
God, and ye shall be secure; believe ye his prophets, and
ye shall prosper.)
21 And he gave counsel to the people, and he ordained
the singers of the Lord, that they should praise him in
their companies, and that they should go before the host,
and say with according voice, Acknowledge ye to the
Lord, for he is good; for his mercy is without end. (And
he consulted with the people, and he ordained the
singers of the Lord, to praise him in their companies, and
to go before the army, and to sing together with a loud
voice, Praise ye the Lord, for he is good; for his love
endureth forevermore.)
22 And when they began to sing praisings, the Lord
turned the ambushments of them against themselves, that
is, of the sons of Ammon, and of Moab, and of the hill of
Seir, which went out to fight against Judah; and they were
slain. (And when they began to sing their praises, the
Lord turned their enemies' ambushes back against
themselves, that is, against the Ammonites, and the
Moabites, and those of the hill country of Seir, yea, all
who went to fight against Judah; and they were killed.)
23 For why the sons of Ammon and of Moab rose
together against the dwellers of the hill of Seir, to slay,
and to do away them; and when they had done this thing
in work, they were *then* also turned against themselves,
and they fell down together by wounds, each *slaying*
(the) other. (For the Ammonites and the Moabites rose up
together against the inhabitants of the hill country of Seir,
to kill them, and to do them away; and when they had
done this thing, *then* they turned against each other, and
they fell down wounded together, each *killing* the other.)
24 Certainly when Judah was come to the den, (*or the
cave*,) that beholdeth, *or is over against*, the wilderness,
he saw afar all the large country full of dead bodies, and
that none was left, that might escape death. (And when
the men of Judah came to the watch-tower, that
overlooketh the wilderness, they saw all the countryside
far and wide full of dead bodies, and that no one was left,
who had escaped death.)
25 Therefore Jehoshaphat came, and all the people
with him, to draw away the spoils of [the] dead men, and
they found among the dead bodies diverse purtenance of

household, and clothes, and full precious vessels; and
they ravished, *or took those things away*, in diverse
manners, so that they might not bear all things, neither
they might take away the spoils by three days, for the
greatness of [the] prey. (And so Jehoshaphat, and all the
people with him, came to take away the dead men's
spoils, and they found among the dead bodies diverse
purtenance of household, and clothes, and very precious
vessels; and they took those things away, by many
means, but even over *the course* of three days, they
could not carry away all those things, and take away all
the spoils, for the greatness of the prey.)
26 Soothly in the fourth day they were gathered
together in the valley of Blessing; for-thy that they blessed
the Lord there, they called that place the valley of
Blessing, unto this present day. (And on the fourth day
they gathered together in the Berachah Valley, *that is, in
the Valley of Blessing*; for because they blessed the Lord
there, that place is called the Valley of Blessing, unto this
present day.)
27 And each man of Judah turned again, and the
dwellers of Jerusalem, and Jehoshaphat (went) before
them, into Jerusalem with great gladness; for the Lord
God had given to them (the) joy of their enemies. (And
each man of Judah, and the inhabitants of Jerusalem, with
Jehoshaphat going before them, returned to Jerusalem
with great gladness; for the Lord God had given them
victory over their enemies/for the Lord God had given
them joy over their enemies' defeat.)
28 And they entered into Jerusalem with psalteries, and
harps, and trumps, into the house of the Lord. (And they
entered into Jerusalem with lutes, and harps, and
trumpets, and went to the House of the Lord.)
29 Forsooth the dread of the Lord felled on all the
realms of (the) lands, when they had heard, that the Lord
had fought against the enemies of Israel.
30 And the realm of Jehoshaphat rested *from war*; and
the Lord gave peace to him all about.
31 And Jehoshaphat reigned upon Judah; and he was of
five and thirty years, when he began to reign; and he
reigned five and twenty years in Jerusalem; and the name
of his mother *was* Azubah, the daughter of Shilhi.
32 And he went in the way of Asa his father, and
bowed not from it, and he did whatever things were
pleasant before the Lord. (And he went in the way of his
father Asa, and turned not from it, and he did whatever
things were pleasing in the sight of the Lord.)
33 Nevertheless he did not away the high places; *and*
yet the people had not (ad)dressed their heart to the Lord
God of their fathers. (But still he did not do away the hill
shrines; *and* the people had not yet directed their hearts
toward the Lord God of their fathers.)
34 Forsooth the residue of the former and the last deeds
of Jehoshaphat be written in the book of Jehu, the son of
Hanani, which he ordained in the book of [the] kings of
Israel. (And the rest of the first and the last deeds of
Jehoshaphat be written in The Book of Jehu, the son of
Hanani, which is part of The Book of the Kings of Israel.)
35 After these things Jehoshaphat, king of Judah, made
friendships with Ahaziah, king of Israel, whose works
were full evil/were most evil;
36 and he was partner *to him*, and they made ships,
which should go into Tarshish; and they made one ship
(*to go*) into Eziongaber. (and he was *his* partner, and they
made ships in order to go to Tarshish; and they built the
ships at Eziongaber.)
37 And Eliezer, the son of Dodavah, of Mareshah,
prophesied to Jehoshaphat, and said, For thou hast had
bond of peace with Ahaziah, the Lord hath destroyed thy
works; and the ships be broken, and [they] might not go
into Tarshish (But Eliezer, the son of Dodavah, of
Mareshah, prophesied to Jehoshaphat, and said, For thou
hast had a covenant with Ahaziah, the Lord shall destroy
thy works; and so the ships were destroyed, and they
never did go to Tarshish.)

CHAPTER 21

1 And Jehoshaphat slept with his fathers, and was
buried with them in the city of David; and Jehoram[6], his
son, reigned for him.
2 And he had brethren, the sons of Jehoshaphat,
Azariah, Jehiel, and Zechariah, and (another) Azariah,
and Michael, and Shephatiah; all these *were* the sons of
Jehoshaphat, king of Judah.
3 And their father gave to them many gifts of gold and
of silver, and *he gave them* pensions, *or rents*, with full
strong cities in Judah; but he gave the realm to Jehoram,
for he was his first begotten *son*. (And their father gave
them many gifts of gold and of silver, and *he gave them*
pensions, *or rents*, along with fortified cities in Judah; but
he gave the kingdom to Jehoram, for he was his first-born
son.)
4 And Jehoram rose up on the realm of his father; and
when he had confirmed himself *in the realm*, he slew all
his brethren by sword, and *also* some of the princes of
Judah. (And when Jehoram had taken his father's
kingdom, and established himself *on the throne*, he killed
all of his brothers by the sword, and *also* some of the
leaders of Israel.)
5 Jehoram was of two and thirty years, when he began
to reign; and he reigned eight years in Jerusalem.
6 And he went in the ways of the kings of Israel, as the
house of Ahab had done, for the daughter of Ahab was
his wife; and he did evil in the sight of the Lord.
7 But the Lord would not destroy the house of David,
for the covenant which he had made with David, and for

[6] Also known as Joram.

he had promised to give to him a lantern, and to his sons,
in all time. (But the Lord would not destroy the house of
David, because of the covenant which he had made with
David, and because he had promised to give a light, *or a
flame*, to him, and to his sons, for all time.)
8 In those days Edom rebelled, so that it was not
subject to Judah, and it ordained a king to itself. (In those
days the Edomites rebelled, so that they were not subject
to Judah, and they ordained a king for themselves.)
9 And when Jehoram had passed forth with his
princes, and all the multitude of knights, that was with
him, he rose up by night, and smote Edom, that
(en)compassed him, and all the dukes of his multitude of
knights. (And when Jehoram had come forth with his
leaders, and all the multitude of his horsemen who were
with him, he rose up by night, and struck the army of
Edom, who had surrounded him, and his leaders, and all
his multitude of horsemen.)
10 Nevertheless Edom rebelled, (so) that it was not
under the lordship of Judah unto this day. In that time
also Libnah went away, that it was not under the hand of
him (At that time Libnah also went away *from Jehoram*,
so that they were not under his power); for he had
forsaken the Lord God of his fathers.
11 Furthermore he made high places in the cities of
Judah, and made the dwellers of Jerusalem to do
fornication, *that is, idolatry*, and Judah to break the law.
(And furthermore he made hill shrines in the cities of
Judah, and made the inhabitants of Jerusalem to do
idolatry, and the people of Judah to break *God's* Law.)
12 And letters were brought to him from Elijah, the
prophet, in which it was written, The Lord God of David,
thy father, saith these things, For that thou hast not gone
in the ways of Jehoshaphat, thy father, and in the way(s)
of Asa, king of Judah,
13 but thou hast gone by the way of the kings of Israel,
and thou hast made Judah and the dwellers of Jerusalem
to do fornication, and thou hast followed the fornication
of the house of Ahab; furthermore and thou hast slain thy
brethren in the house of thy father, *that is, (the) princes of
the house of thy father, which were* better than thou; (but
thou hast gone in the ways of the kings of Israel, and thou
hast made Judah and the inhabitants of Jerusalem to do
idolatry, and thou hast followed the idolatry of the house
of Ahab; and furthermore thou hast killed thy brothers in
the house of thy father, *that is, the princes of the house of
thy father, who were* better than thou;)
14 lo! the Lord shall smite thee with a great vengeance,
and thy people, and thy sons, and thy wives, and all thy
chattel; (lo! the Lord shall strike thee with a great
vengeance, and also thy people, and thy sons, and thy
wives, and all thy substance, *or thy possessions*;)
15 and thou shalt be sick with the worst sorrow of thy
womb, (*or thy belly*,) till that thine entrails go out little
and little by each day.
16 Therefore the Lord raised up against Jehoram the
spirit of Philistines, and of Arabians, that march with
Ethiopians; (And so the Lord raised up against Jehoram
the spirit of the Philistines, and of the Arabs, who march
with the Ethiopians;)
17 and these went up into the land of Judah, and they
wasted it, and they took away all the substance, that was
found in the house of the king, furthermore and his sons,
and his wives *they took away* (and furthermore *they took
away* his sons, and his wives); and no son was left to
him, but Jehoahaz, that was his least *son, or youngest
son*, in birth.
18 And over all these things the Lord smote him with
uncurable sorrow of the womb. (And after all these things
the Lord struck him with an incurable disease in his
bowels.)
19 And when day came after day, and the spaces of
time were turned about, the course of two years was
fulfilled; and so he was wasted by long rot, so that he
casted out also his own entrails, and so he wanted sorrow
and life together, and he was dead in the worst sickness.
And the people did not to him [the] service of dead men
by the custom of burning, as it had done to his greaters,
either ancestors. (And when day came after day, and the
space of time was turned about, the course of two years
was fulfilled; and he was wasted by long rot, so that he
cast out his own bowels, and he wanted to live and to die
at the same time, and finally he died of the worst
sickness. And the people did not do for him the service
of the dead by the custom of honouring him with a
bonfire, as they had done with his greaters, *or his
ancestors*.)
20 He was of two and thirty years when he began to
reign, and he reigned eight years in Jerusalem, and he
went not rightfully; and they buried him in the city of
David, nevertheless not in the sepulchre(s) of kings. (He
was thirty-two years old when he began to reign, and he
reigned eight years in Jerusalem, and at his death he was
not mourned; and they buried him in the City of David,
but not in the tombs of the kings.)

CHAPTER 22

1 Forsooth the dwellers of Jerusalem ordained
Ahaziah, the youngest son of Jehoram[7], *to be* king for
him; for the thieves of Arabia, that felled into the castles
of Judah, had slain all his greater, *or elder brethren*,
which were *begotten* before him. And Ahaziah, the son
of Jehoram, king of Judah, reigned. (And the inhabitants
of Jerusalem ordained Ahaziah, the youngest son of
Jehoram, *to be* king for him; for the Arab thieves, who
fell upon the tents, *or the camps, of Judah*, had killed all

[7] Also known as Joram.

his *elder* brothers, who were *born* before him. And so
Ahaziah, the son of Jehoram, the king of Judah, reigned.)
2 Ahaziah was of two and forty years (Ahaziah was
twenty-two years old), when he began to reign, and he
reigned one year in Jerusalem; the name of his mother
was Athaliah, the daughter of Omri.
3 But he entered by the way of the house of Ahab (But
he went in the ways of the house of Ahab); for his mother
compelled him to do evil.
4 Therefore he did evil in the sight of the Lord, as the
house of Ahab; for they were counsellors to him into his
perishing, after the death of his father; (And so he did evil
before the Lord, like the house of Ahab; for they were his
counsellors after his father's death, yea, unto his
perishing;)
5 and he went in the counsel of them. And he went
with Joram[8], the son of Ahab, king of Israel, into battle
against Hazael, king of Syria, into Ramoth of Gilead (at
Ramoth of Gilead). And men of Syria wounded Joram;
6 which turned again for to be healed in Jezreel; for
he had taken many wounds in the foresaid battle.
Therefore Ahaziah[9], king of Judah, the son of Jehoram,
went down to visit Joram, the son of Ahab, *that was* sick
in Jezreel; (who returned home to Jezreel to recover; for
he had received many wounds in the foresaid battle.
And so Ahaziah, the son of Jehoram, the king of Judah,
went down to visit Joram, the son of Ahab, the king of
Israel, *who was* sick in Jezreel;)
7 for it was God's will against Ahaziah, that he came
to Joram. And when he was come, he went out with him
against Jehu, the son of Nimshi, whom God (had)
anointed, that he should do away the house of Ahab.
8 Therefore when Jehu destroyed the house of Ahab,
he found the princes of Judah, and the sons of the
brethren of Ahaziah, that ministered to him; and he killed
them. (And so when Jehu destroyed the house of Ahab,
he found the leaders of Judah, and the sons of the
kinsmen of Ahaziah, who served him; and he killed
them.)
9 And he sought that Ahaziah, and caught him hid in
Samaria, and after that he was brought to Jehu, Jehu
killed him; and they buried him, for he was the son of
Jehoshaphat, that had sought God in all his heart. And
none hope was more, that any of the generation of
Ahaziah should reign. (And he sought out Ahaziah, and
they caught him hiding in Samaria, and after that he was
brought to Jehu, Jehu killed him; and they buried him, for
he was the son of Jehoshaphat, who had sought God with
all his heart. And then there was no more hope, that any
of Ahaziah's family would ever reign again.)
10 And Athaliah, the mother of Ahaziah, saw that her
son was dead, and she rose up, and killed all the king's
generation of the house of Jehoram. (And Athaliah,
Ahaziah's mother, saw that her son was dead, and she
rose up, and killed all the king's family of the house of
Judah.)
11 Forsooth Jehoshabeath, the daughter of the king,
took Joash, the son of Ahaziah, and stole him from the
midst of the sons of the king, when they were slain; and
she hid him with his nurse in a closet of beds. For
Jehoshabeath, that hid him, was the daughter of king
Jehoram, and (the) wife of Jehoiada, the bishop, and the
sister of Ahaziah; and therefore Athaliah killed not her.
(But Jehoshabeath, the king's daughter, took Joash,
Ahaziah's son, and stole him away from the midst of the
king's sons, when they were being killed; and she hid
him with his nurse in a bed-closet. For Jehoshabeath,
who hid him, was King Jehoram's daughter, and the wife
of the High Priest Jehoiada, and Ahaziah's sister; and so
Athaliah did not kill Joash.)
12 Therefore he was hid with them in the house of God
(for) six years, in which Athaliah reigned on the land.

CHAPTER 23

1 Forsooth in the seventh year Jehoiada was
comforted, and took [the] centurions, that is, Azariah, the
son of Jeroham, and Ishmael, the son of Jehohanan, and
Azariah, the son of Obed, and Maaseiah, the son of
Adaiah, and Elishaphat, the son of Zichri; and he made
with them a counsel and a bond of peace. (But in the
seventh year Jehoiada was strengthened, and called for
the centurions, that is, Azariah, the son of Jeroham, and
Ishmael, the son of Jehohanan, and Azariah, the son of
Obed, and Maaseiah, the son of Adaiah, and Elishaphat,
the son of Zichri; and he made a covenant with all of
them.)
2 The which compassed Judah, and gathered together
deacons (out) of all the cities of Judah, and the princes of
the families of Israel, and they came into Jerusalem. (And
then they went around Judah, and gathered together the
Levites from all the cities of Judah, and the leaders of the
families of Israel, and they came into Jerusalem.)
3 And all the multitude made (a) covenant in the
house of the Lord with the king. And Jehoiada said to
them, Lo! *Joash* the son of the king shall reign, as the
Lord spake on the sons of David. (And all the multitude
made a covenant with the king in the House of the Lord.
And Jehoiada said to them, Lo! *Joash*, the king's son, shall
reign, as the Lord hath said of the sons of David.)
4 Therefore this is the word, that ye shall do. The third
part of you that be come to the sabbath, of priests, and of
deacons, and of porters, shall be in the gates; (And so this
is the thing that ye shall do. A third of the priests and the
Levites, who come to the sabbath, shall guard the gates;)
5 and a third part shall be at the house of the king;

[8] Also known as Jehoram(!).

[9] Here the KJV erroneously has "Azariah".

and the *other* third part shall be at the gate, *which is*
called of the foundament. And all the other common
people be in the large places of the house of the Lord;
(and a third shall be at the house of the king; and the
other third shall be at the Foundation Gate. And all the
other common people shall be in the courtyards of the
House of the Lord;)
6 and none other man enter into the house of the
Lord, no but [the] priests, and they that minister of the
deacons; only enter they, that be hallowed, and all the
other common people keep *they* the keepings of the
Lord. (and no other person shall enter into the House of
the Lord, but the priests, and those of the Levites who
serve there; only they shall enter, for they be consecrated,
or purified, but all the other common people shall keep
the Lord's watch.)
7 Forsooth the deacons (en)compass the king, and
each man have his armours; and if any other man
entereth into the temple, be he slain; and be they with
the king entering and going out. (And the Levites shall
stand about the king, and each man shall be armed/and
each man shall have his weapon; and if any other man
cometh into the Temple, let him he killed; and be they
with the king coming in and going out.)
8 Therefore the deacons and all Judah did by all things
which Jehoiada, the bishop, had commanded; and (they)
all took the men, that were with them, and came by the
order of [the] sabbath with them, that had [ful]filled now
the sabbath, and should go out. For Jehoiada, the bishop,
suffered not the companies to go away, that were wont to
come one after the tother by each week. (And so the
Levites, and all the men of Judah, did all that the High
Priest Jehoiada had commanded; and they took the men
who were with them, and had come in by the order of
the sabbath, with them who had fulfilled the sabbath, and
should now go out. For the High Priest Jehoiada, did not
allow any of the companies, who were wont to come one
after the other by each week, to go away.)
9 And Jehoiada, the priest, gave to the centurions
spears, and shields, and bucklers, of king David, which
he had hallowed in the house of the Lord. (And the High
Priest Jehoiada gave the centurions the spears, and
shields, and bucklers, of King David, which he had kept
in the House of the Lord.)
10 And he ordained all the people, of them that held
swords, at the right side of the temple unto the left side of
the temple, before the altar and the temple, by compass
of the king (all around the king).
11 And they led out *Joash* the son of the king, and they
set a diadem upon his head; and they gave to him in his
hand the law to be holden, and they made him king.
And Jehoiada, the bishop, and his sons, anointed him;
and they prayed heartily, and said, The king live! (And
the High Priest Jehoiada, and his sons, anointed him; and
they prayed, and heartily said, Long live the king!)
12 And when Athaliah had heard this thing, that is, the
voice of men running and praising the king (that is, the
sound of men running and praising the king), she entered
in to the people, into the temple of the Lord.
13 And when she had seen the king, standing on the
degrees in the entering (*of the temple*), and the princes
and the companies of knights about him, and all the
people of the land joying, and sounding with trumps, and
singing together with organs of diverse kind, and the
voice of men praising, she rent her clothes, and said,
Treasons! treasons! (And when she had seen the king
standing on the steps at the entrance *to the Temple*, and
the leaders and the companies of horsemen all about
him, and all the people of the land rejoicing, and
sounding with trumpets, and singers, and musicians with
diverse kinds of instruments, and people praising him,
she tore her clothes, and said, Treasons! treasons!)
14 And Jehoiada, the bishop, went out to the
centurions, and to the princes of the host, and said to
them, Lead ye her without the precincts, *either*
enclosings, of the temple, and be she slain withoutforth
by sword; and the priest commanded, that she should not
be slain in the house of the Lord. (And the High Priest
Jehoiada went out to the centurions, and to the leaders of
the army, and said to them, Lead ye her without the
precincts of the Temple, and let her be killed outside
with the sword; and the High Priest commanded, that she
should not be killed in the House of the Lord.)
15 And they setted hands on her noll (And so they put
their hands on her); and when she had entered into the
gate of the horses, of the king's house, they killed her
there.
16 Forsooth Jehoiada covenanted a bond of peace
betwixt himself and all the people and the king, that it
should be the people of the Lord. (And then Jehoiada
made a covenant between himself and all the people and
the king, that they should be the people of the Lord.)
17 Therefore all the people entered into the house of
Baal, and they destroyed it, and they brake the altars and
the simulacra thereof; but they killed before the altars
Mattan, the priest of Baal (and they killed Mattan, the
priest of Baal, before the altars).
18 And Jehoiada ordained sovereigns in the house of
the Lord, that under the hands of priests, and of deacons,
which David parted in the house of the Lord, they should
offer burnt sacrifices to the Lord, as it is written in the
book of Moses, in joy and in songs, by the ordinance of
David. (And then Jehoiada ordained as the rulers of the
House of the Lord, the priests, and the Levites, whom
David had assigned to the House of the Lord, to offer the
burnt sacrifices to the Lord, as it is written in The Book of
Moses, with joy and with songs, by David's ordinance.)
19 Also he ordained porters in the gates of the house of

the Lord, that an unclean man in anything should not
enter into it. (And he ordained the guards, *or the doorkeepers*, at the gates of the House of the Lord, so that no unclean person could enter into it.)
20 And he took the centurions, and the strongest men,
and princes of the people, and all the common people of the land. And they made the king to go down from the house of the Lord, and to enter by the midst of the higher gate into the house of the king; and they set him in the king's throne. (And he took the centurions, and the strongest men, and the people's leaders, and all the common people of the land. And together they brought the king down from the House of the Lord, and they entered through the Upper Gate into the house of the king, and they put him on the king's throne.)
21 And all the people of the land was glad, and the city
rested; forsooth Athaliah was slain by (the) sword.

CHAPTER 24

1 Joash was of seven years (Joash was seven years
old), when he began to reign, and he reigned forty years in Jerusalem; the name of his mother *was* Zibiah of Beersheba.
2 And he did that, that was good before the Lord, in
all the days of Jehoiada, the priest.
3 And Joash took two wives, of which he begat sons
and daughters. (And Jehoiada chose two wives for him, of whom Joash begat sons and daughters.)
4 And after which things it pleased Joash to repair the
house of the Lord.
5 And he gathered together [the] priests and deacons,
and said to them, Go ye out to the cities of Judah, and gather ye of all Israel money, to the repairing of the temple of your Lord God, by each year; and do ye this *thing* hastily. Certainly the deacons did *this thing* negligently. (And he gathered together the priests and the Levites, and said to them, Go ye out to the cities of Judah, and gather ye the yearly money, *or the annual tax*, from all Israel, for repairs to the Temple of the Lord your God; and do ye this *thing* promptly, *or quickly*. But the Levites did *it* negligently, *or slovenly*.)
6 And the king called Jehoiada, the prince *of priests*,
and said to him, Why was it not (a) charge to thee, to constrain the deacons to bring in (the) money of Judah and of Jerusalem, which money was ordained of Moses, the servant of the Lord, that all the multitude of Israel should bring it into the tabernacle of witnessing? (And so the king called the High Priest Jehoiada, and said to him, Why was it not a concern for thee, to require the Levites to bring in the money, *that is, the tax*, from Judah and Jerusalem, which was ordained by Moses, the Lord's servant, that all the multitude of Israel should bring to the Tabernacle of the Witnessing?)
7 For the wicked *woman* Athaliah, and her sons,
destroyed the house of God; and of all the things, that were hallowed to the temple of the Lord, they adorned the temple of Baalim. (For that wicked *woman* Athaliah, and her sons, destroyed the House of God; and they adorned the temple of the Baalim, with all the things that were dedicated to the Temple of the Lord.)
8 Therefore the king commanded, and they made an
ark, and setted it beside the gate (of the House) of the Lord withoutforth. (And so the king commanded, and they made a box, and put it outside the gate of the House of the Lord.)
9 And it was preached in Judah and Jerusalem, that
each man should bring to the Lord the price, that Moses, the servant of God, ordained upon all Israel, in desert. (And it was preached in Judah and Jerusalem, that everyone should bring to the Lord the tax, that Moses, the servant of God, had ordained upon all Israel, in the wilderness.)
10 And all the princes and all the people were glad,
and they entered, and brought, and sent *freely their gifts* into the ark of the Lord (and *freely* put *their gifts* into the box for the Lord), so that it was filled *with treasure*.
11 And when it was time, that they should bear the ark
before the king('s) (officials) by the hands of deacons, for they saw much money, the clerk of the king entered, and he whom the first, *or chief*, priest had ordained, and they poured out the money, that was in the ark; and they bare again the ark to his place (And when it was time, that they should carry the box to the king's officials by the hands of the Levites, for they saw much money *in it*, the king's clerk entered, and he whom the High Priest had ordained, and they poured out the money, that was in the box; and then they put the box back in its place). And so they did by all days, and money without number was gathered together;
12 which the king and Jehoiada gave to them that were
(the) sovereigns of the works of the house of the Lord. And they hired thereof cutters of stones, and craftsmen of all works, that they should repair the house of the Lord; also *they hired* smiths of iron, and of brass, that that thing should be underset, that began to fall (and *they hired* ironsmiths, and bronze-workers, so that what had begun to fall, *or to fail*, could be strengthened).
13 They that wrought did craftily, and the crazing of the
walls was stopped by the hands of them; and they raised the house of the Lord into the former state, and made it to stand steadfastly. (They who did the work did so with craftsmanship, and they repaired the breaches in the walls; and so they raised the House of the Lord back to its former state, and made it stand strong and steadfast.)
14 And when they had fulfilled all the works, they
brought before the king and Jehoiada the tother part of the money, of which money vessels were made into the service of the temple, and to burnt sacrifices (and from

that money vessels were made for service in the Temple,
and for the burnt sacrifices); also vials, *or basins*, and
other vessels of gold and of silver *were made thereof.*
And burnt sacrifices were offered in the house of the Lord
continually, in all the days of Jehoiada.
15 And Jehoiada full of days waxed eld, and he was
dead, when he was of an hundred years and thirty; (And
Jehoiada grew old, and full of days, and he died when he
was a hundred and thirty years old;)
16 and they buried him in the city of David with (the)
kings; for he had done good with Israel, (for God,) and
with his house. (and they buried him in the City of David
with the kings; for he had done good in Israel, for God,
and for his House.)
17 But after that Jehoiada died, the princes of Judah
entered, and worshipped the king, which was flattered
with their services, and assented to them. (But after that
Jehoiada died, the leaders of Judah entered, and
worshipped, *or honoured*, the king, who was flattered by
them, and he assented to them.)
18 And they forsook the temple of the Lord God of
their fathers, and served idols in woods, and graven
images (and worshipped sacred poles, and carved idols);
and the ire of the Lord was made against Judah and
Jerusalem for this sin.
19 And he sent to them prophets, that they should turn
again to the Lord (so that they would return to the Lord);
the which prophets' witnessing, they would not hear.
20 Then the Spirit of the Lord clothed, *or environed*,
Zechariah, the priest, the son of Jehoiada; and he stood in
the sight of the people, and said to them, The Lord saith
these things, Why break ye the commandment of the
Lord, which thing shall not profit to you, and ye have
forsaken the Lord, that he should forsake you? (Then the
Spirit of the Lord came upon Zechariah, the son of the
High Priest Jehoiada; and he stood before the people,
and said to them, The Lord saith these things, Why have
ye broken the Lord's commands? truly that shall not profit
you; but because ye have abandoned the Lord, now he
hath abandoned you.)
21 Which were gathered together against him, and
casted stones (*at him*), by commandment of the king, in
the large place of the house of the Lord. (And they
gathered together against him, and threw stones *at him*,
by the command of the king, in the courtyard of the
House of the Lord.)
22 And king Joash had not mind on the mercy, (*or
goodness*,) which Jehoiada, the father of Zechariah, had
done with him; but he killed the son of Jehoiada. And
when Zechariah died, he said, The Lord see *this thing*,
and again-seek *it.* (And King Joash forgot about the
loyalty which Jehoiada, Zechariah's father, had shown to
him; and so he had Jehoiada's son killed. And as
Zechariah died, he said, May the Lord see *what thou hast
done*, and avenge *it.*)
23 And when a year was turned about, *either ended*,
the host of Syria went up against Joash, and it came into
Judah and into Jerusalem, and it killed all the princes of
the people (and they came into Judah and Jerusalem, and
they killed all the leaders of the people); and they sent all
the prey to the king of Damascus.
24 And certain(ly), when a full little number of men of
Syria was come *into Judah*, the Lord betook in(to) their
hands a multitude *of Jews* without number, for they had
forsaken the Lord God of their fathers. Also they used
shameful dooms against Joash (And so they executed
judgement against Joash);
25 and they went away *from him*, and they left him in
great sorrows. And his servants rose up against him, into
vengeance of the blood of the son of Jehoiada, priest; and
killed him in his bed, and he was dead. And they buried
him in the city of David, but not in the sepulchres of
kings. (and then they went away *from him*, and they left
him in great sorrows. And then his servants rose up
against him, in vengeance for the blood of the son of the
High Priest Jehoiada; and they killed him in his bed, and
he was dead. And they buried him in the City of David,
but not in the tombs of the kings.)
26 And Zabad, the son of Shimeath of Ammon, and
Jehozabad, the son of Shimrith of Moab, setted treasons
to him. (And it was Zabad, the son of Shimeath of
Ammon, and Jehozabad, the son of Shimrith of Moab,
who set treason against him.)
27 Soothly his sons, and the sum of money that was
gathered under him, and the repairing of the house of
God, be written diligently in the book of Kings (all be
diligently written about in The Book of the Kings). And
Amaziah, his son, reigned for him;

CHAPTER 25

1 Amaziah was of five and twenty years, when he
began to reign, and he reigned nine and twenty years in
Jerusalem; the name of his mother *was* Jehoaddan, of
Jerusalem.
2 And he did good in the sight of the Lord,
nevertheless not in perfect heart. (And he did good before
the Lord, but not with a perfect heart.)
3 And when he saw the empire strengthened to
himself, he strangled the servants that killed the king, his
father; (And once he saw himself confirmed, *or
established*, in power, he strangled the servants who had
killed his father the king;)
4 but he killed not the sons of them; as it is written in
the book of the law of Moses, where the Lord
commanded, saying, [The] Fathers shall not be slain for
the sons, neither the sons for their fathers; but each man
shall die in, *or for*, his own sin.
5 Therefore Amaziah gathered together Judah, and

ordained them by families, and tribunes, and centurions,
in all Judah and Benjamin; and he numbered *them* from
twenty years and above, and he found thirty thousand of
able young men, that went out to battle, and held spear
and shield. (And so Amaziah gathered the men of Judah
together, and ordained them by families, under tribunes,
and centurions, in all Judah and Benjamin; and he
counted *them* from twenty years of age and older, and he
found thirty thousand *able* young men, who went out to
battle, and held a spear and shield.)
6 Also for meed, he hired of Israel an hundred
thousand of strong men, for an hundred talents of silver,
that they should fight against the sons of Edom. (And for
reward, *or for money*, he hired out of Israel a hundred
thousand strong men, for a hundred talents of silver, to
fight against the Edomites.)
7 Forsooth a man of God came to him, and said, A!
king, the host of Israel go not out with thee, for the Lord
is not with Israel, and with all the sons of Ephraim; (But a
man of God came to him, and said, O! king, do not let
Israel's army go out with thee, for the Lord is not with
Israel, and with all these Ephraimites;)
8 for if thou guessest that battles stand in the might of
an host, the Lord shall make thee to be overcome of thine
enemies, forsooth it is of God for to help, and to turn
men into flight. (for if thou thinkest that battles stand, *or
fall*, by the strength of an army, then the Lord shall make
thee to be overcome by thy enemies; for it is of God to
help thee, or to turn *men* to flight.)
9 And Amaziah said to the man of God, What then
shall be done of the hundred talents, which I gave to the
knights of Israel? And the man of God answered to him,
The Lord hath, whereof he may yield to thee much more
things than these.
10 Therefore Amaziah separated the host that came to
him from Ephraim, that it should turn again into his
place; and they were wroth greatly against Judah, and
they turned again into their country. (And so Amaziah
separated out the army that came to him from Ephraim,
and told them to return home; and they were greatly
angered against the people of Judah, but they returned to
their own country.)
11 And Amaziah led out trustily his people, and went
into the valley of (the) makings of salt, and he killed of
the sons of Seir ten thousand. (And then Amaziah trustily
led out his people, and went into the Salt Valley, and he
killed ten thousand of the sons of Seir there.)
12 And the sons of Judah took (an)other ten thousand of
men, and brought (*them*) to the high scarp of a stone; and
they cast them down from the highest *part* into a pit;
which all brake (and they were all killed there).
13 And that host that Amaziah had sent again, that it
should not go with him to battle, was spread abroad in
the cities of Judah from Samaria unto Bethhoron; and
after (that) *the host of Israel* had slain three thousand *of
Judah*, it took away a great prey (they took away a great
deal of prey).
14 And Amaziah, after the slaying of Idumeans, and
after that he had brought *thence with him* the gods of the
sons of Seir, *he* ordained them *to be* into gods to himself,
and he worshipped them, and burnt incense to them.
(And Amaziah, after the slaughter of the Edomites,
brought back *from there* the gods of the sons of Seir *with
him*, and *he* ordained them *to be* his gods, and he
worshipped them, and burned incense to them.)
15 Wherefore the Lord was wroth against Amaziah, and
he sent to him a prophet, that said to him, Why
worshippest thou gods which have not delivered their
(own) people from thine hand?
16 *And* when the prophet spake these things, Amaziah
answered to him, Whether thou art a counsellor of the
king? cease thou, lest peradventure I slay thee. And the
prophet went away *from him*, and said, I know, that the
Lord hath thought to slay thee (And as the prophet went
away *from him*, he said, I know that the Lord hath
decided to kill thee); for thou hast done this evil, and
furthermore thou assentedest not to my counsel.
17 Therefore Amaziah, the king of Judah, when he had
taken a full evil counsel, sent to the king of Israel,
Jehoash[10], the son of Jehoahaz, the son of Jehu, and said,
Come thou, and see we us together. (And so Amaziah,
the king of Judah, when he had taken very evil counsel,
sent to Jehoash, the son of Jehoahaz, the son of Jehu, the
king of Israel, and said, Come thou, and see we each
other *in battle*.)
18 And *Jehoash, the king of Israel*, sent messengers
(back) *to him*, and said (*mystically*), A thistle, that is in
the Lebanon, sent to a cedar tree of the Lebanon, and
said, Give thy daughter (as a) wife to my son; and lo! [the]
beasts that were in the wood of the Lebanon went and
defouled the thistle.
19 Thou saidest, I have smitten Edom, and therefore
thine heart is raised into pride (Thou saidest, I myself
have struck down Edom, and so thy heart is raised up in
pride); sit thou *still* in thine house; why stirrest thou (up)
evil against thyself, (so) that thou fall, and Judah with
thee?
20 (But) Amaziah would not hear *this*, for it was the
will of the Lord, that he should be betaken into the hands
of his enemies, for the gods of Edom *which he
worshipped* (because *he and the people of Judah
worshipped* the gods of Edom).
21 Therefore Jehoash, king of Israel, ascended, and they
saw themselves together. Soothly Amaziah, the king of
Judah, was in Bethshemesh of Judah; (And so Jehoash,
the king of Israel, went forth, and they saw each other *in*

[10] Also known as Joash.

battle. And he and Amaziah, the king of Judah, were in
Bethshemesh of Judah;)
22 and Judah felled down before Israel, and fled into
his tabernacles. (and the men of Judah fell down before
the men of Israel, and they fled back to their tents.)
23 And [Jehoash,] the king of Israel, took in
Bethshemesh Amaziah, the king of Judah, the son of
Joash, the son of Jehoahaz[11], and brought *him* into
Jerusalem; and he destroyed the walls thereof from the
gate of Ephraim to the gate of the corner, by four hundred
cubits (*in length*). (And Jehoash, the king of Israel, the son
of Jehoahaz, captured Amaziah, the king of Judah, the
son of Joash, the son of Ahaziah, at Bethshemesh, and
brought *him* to Jerusalem; and he destroyed its walls from
the Ephraim Gate unto the Corner Gate, a distance of
four hundred cubits.)
24 And he led again into Samaria all the gold and
silver, and all the vessels that he found in the house of
the Lord, and at Obededom, in the treasuries also of the
king's house, also and the sons of (the) hostages. (And he
took back to Samaria all the gold and silver, and all the
vessels that he found in the House of the Lord, under the
care, *or the protection*, of Obededom, and also the
treasures from the king's house, and the hostages as well.)
25 And Amaziah, king of Judah, the son of Joash, lived
fifteen years after that Jehoash, king of Israel, the son of
Jehoahaz, was dead (died).
26 Soothly the residue of the former and the last words
of Amaziah, be written in the book of [the] kings of Judah
and of Israel. (And the rest of the first and the last deeds
of Amaziah, be written in The Book of the Kings of Judah
and of Israel.)
27 And after that he had gone away from the Lord, they
set to him treasons in Jerusalem; and when he had fled to
Lachish, they sent *thither*, and killed him there; (And after
that Amaziah had gone away from the Lord, they set
treasons against him in Jerusalem; and when he fled to
Lachish, they followed him *there*, and killed him there;)
28 and they brought *him* again upon horses (and they
brought back *his body* on a horse), and buried him with
his fathers in the city of David.

CHAPTER 26

1 Forsooth all the people of Judah made Uzziah[12], his
son, of sixteen years *age*, king for his father Amaziah.
(Then all the people of Judah took Uzziah, *or Azariah*,
Amaziah's son, *who was* sixteen years old, and made
him king in place of his father.)
2 He builded Eloth (And he rebuilt Eloth), and restored
it to the lordship of Judah, after that the king slept with
his fathers.
3 Uzziah was of sixteen years (Uzziah was sixteen
years old), when he began to reign; and he reigned two
and fifty years in Jerusalem; and the name of his mother
was Jecoliah, of Jerusalem.
4 And he did that, that was rightful in the sight of the
Lord, by all things which Amaziah, his father, had done.
5 And he sought the Lord in the days of Zechariah,
understanding and seeing God (who had understanding
in the visions of God); and when he sought God, God
ruled him in all things.
6 And he went out, and fought against (the)
Philistines, and destroyed the wall of Gath, and the wall
of Jabneh, and the wall of Ashdod; and he builded strong
places in Ashdod, and in Philistines (and he built fortified
cities in Ashdod, and among the Philistines).
7 And the Lord helped him both against Philistines,
and against Arabians that dwelled in Gurbaal, and against
Ammonites. (And the Lord helped him against the
Philistines, and against the Arabs who lived in Gurbaal,
and against the Meunites/and the Mehunims.)
8 [And] Ammonites paid gifts to Uzziah (And the
Ammonites paid tribute, *or taxes*, to Uzziah), and his
name was published unto the entering of Egypt for *his* oft
victories.
9 And Uzziah builded towers in Jerusalem over the
gate of the corner, and over the gate of the valley, and
other towers in the same side of the wall (and other
towers on the same side of the wall); and he made those
steadfast, *or strong*.
10 Also he builded towers in the wilderness, and
digged full many cisterns; for he had many beasts, as well
in the field places, as in the vastness of desert (for he had
many beasts, in the fields, and in the vast wilderness).
Also he had vineries, and tillers of vines in the hills/in the
great mountain(s), and in Carmel; for he was a man given
to earth-tilling.
11 And (he had) the host of his warriors, that went forth
to battles, under the hand of Jeiel, (the) scribe, and of
Maaseiah, the teacher, and under the hand of Hananiah,
that was of the dukes of the king. (And he had the army
of his warriors, who went forth to battle, all listed, *or
registered*, by Jeiel, the writer, *or the royal secretary*, and
Maaseiah, the teacher, and Hananiah, who was one of
the king's leaders;)
12 and all the number of (the) princes, by their families,
was of strong men two thousand and six hundred. (and
the number of all the leaders of his fighting men, by their
families, was two thousand and six hundred.)
13 And under them was all the host, three hundred
thousand and seven thousand and five hundred, that
were able to battle (who were well able for battle), and
fought for the king against (*his*) adversaries.
14 And Uzziah made ready to them, that is, to all the
host, shields, and spears, and basinets, and habergeons,

[11] A variant form of 'Ahaziah' (the son of Jehoram, king of Judah).
[12] Also known as Azariah.

and bows, and slings to cast stones. (And Uzziah had
made for all his army, many shields, and spears, helmets,
and breastplates, and bows, and slings to throw stones.)
15 And he made in Jerusalem engines of diverse kind,
which he set in towers, and in the corners of walls, that
those should cast out arrows and great stones (from
which they would send out arrows and great stones); and
his name went out far, for the Lord helped him, and had
made him strong.
16 But when he was made strong, his heart was raised
up into his perishing; and he despised the Lord his God
(for he defied the Lord his God); and he entered into the
temple of the Lord, and would burn incense upon the
altar of incense.
17 And anon Azariah, the priest, entered after him, and
with him sixty priests of the Lord, men full noble; (And at
once, the High Priest Azariah went in after him, and with
him were eighty priests of the Lord, and all of them were
very noble men;)
18 which against-stood the king, and said *to him*,
Uzziah, it is not of thine office, that thou burn incense to
the Lord, but of the priests of the Lord, that is, the sons of
Aaron, that be hallowed to such service; go thou out of
the saintuary; *and* despise thou not *God*; for this thing
shall not be areckoned of the Lord God to thee into glory.
(who stood against the king, and said *to him*, Uzziah, it is
not thy duty to burn incense to the Lord, but only the
duty of the priests of the Lord, that is, the sons of Aaron,
who be consecrated for such service; go thou out of the
sanctuary; offend thou not; for this thing shall not be
counted as glory for thee by the Lord God.)
19 And Uzziah was wroth, and he held in his hand the
censer for to offer incense, and he menaced the priests;
and anon leprosy was sprung forth in his forehead, before
the priests in the house of the Lord, upon the altar of
incense. (And Uzziah was angry, and he held in his hand
the censer to offer incense, and he threatened the priests;
and at once leprosy sprung out on his forehead, in front
of the priests in the House of the Lord, as they stood by
the altar of incense.)
20 And when Azariah, the bishop, had beheld him, and
also all the other priests, they saw leprosy in his
forehead, and anon they putted the king out *of the
temple*; but also he was afeared, and hasted to go out; for
he feeled anon the vengeance of the Lord. (And when the
High Priest Azariah, and all the other priests, beheld him,
and they saw that leprosy had sprung out on his
forehead, they put the king out *of the Temple* at once;
and he was afraid, and hastened to go out; for he felt at
once the vengeance of the Lord.)
21 Therefore king Uzziah was leprous unto the day of
his death, and dwelled in an house by itself (and lived in
a house set apart), *and he was* full of leprosy; for which
he was cast out of the house of the Lord. And Jotham, his
son, governed the house of the king, and deemed the
people of the land.
22 And Isaiah, the prophet, the son of Amoz, wrote the
residue of the former and of the last words of Uzziah.
(And the prophet Isaiah, the son of Amoz, wrote down
the rest of the first and the last deeds of Uzziah.)
23 And Uzziah slept with his fathers, and they buried
not him in the field of the kings' sepulchres, for he was
leprous; and Jotham, his son, reigned for him. (And
Uzziah slept with his fathers, and they buried him in a
field, and not in the tombs of the kings, for he was
leprous; and his son Jotham reigned for him.)

CHAPTER 27

1 Jotham was of five and twenty years (Jotham was
twenty-five years old), when he began to reign, and he
reigned sixteen years in Jerusalem; the name of his
mother *was* Jerushah, the daughter of Zadok.
2 He did that, that was rightful before the Lord, by all
things which Uzziah, his father, had done; except that he
entered not into the temple of the Lord, and the people
trespassed yet. (And he did what was right before the
Lord, as by all the things which his father Uzziah had
done; but he did not enter into the Temple of the Lord
like his father did, and the people still continued to
trespass.)
3 He builded the high gate of the house of the Lord,
and he builded many things in the wall of Ophel; (He
built the Upper Gate of the House of the Lord, and he
built many things on the wall of Ophel;)
4 also he builded cities in the hills of Judah, and *he
builded* castles and towers in forests. (and he built cities
in the hill country of Judah, and forts and towers in the
forests.)
5 He fought against the king of the sons of Ammon,
and overcame him; and the sons of Ammon gave to him
in that time an hundred talents of silver, and ten thousand
cors of barley, and so many of wheat; the sons of Ammon
gave these things to him in the second, and the third
years. (He fought against the king of the Ammonites, and
overcame him; and the Ammonites gave him at that time
a hundred talents of silver, and ten thousand cors of
barley, and as many cors of wheat; the Ammonites gave
these things to him in the second, and the third years.)
6 And Jotham was made strong, for he had (ad)dressed
his ways before the Lord his God. (And Jotham was made
strong, for he had directed his ways before the Lord his
God, *that is, he obeyed him*.)
7 Forsooth the residue of [the] words of Jotham, and
all his battles, and works, be written in the book of the
kings of Israel and of Judah. (And the rest of the deeds of
Jotham, and all his battles, and works, be written in The
Book of the Kings of Judah and of Israel.)
8 He was of five and twenty years (He was twenty-five

years old), when he began to reign, and he reigned
sixteen years in Jerusalem.
9 And Jotham slept with his fathers, and they buried
him in the city of David; and Ahaz, his son, reigned for
him.

CHAPTER 28

1 Ahaz was of twenty years, when he began to reign,
and he reigned sixteen years in Jerusalem; he did not
rightfulness in the sight of the Lord, as David, his father,
did (he did not go rightfully before the Lord, like his
forefather David *did*);
2 but he went in the ways of the kings of Israel.
Furthermore and he melted out images to Baalim (And
furthermore he cast metal images of the Baalim).
3 He it is that burnt incense in the valley of Ben-
hinnon, and purged his sons by fire (It was he who
burned incense in the Valley of Ben-hinnon, and who
burned his sons in the fire), (as) by the custom of heathen
men, whom the Lord (had) killed in the coming of the
sons of Israel *from Egypt/*in the coming of the sons of
Israel *to the land of promise.*
4 Also he made sacrifice, and burnt incense in high
places, and in hills, and under each tree full of boughs.
(And he made sacrifices, and burned incense at the hill
shrines, and on the hills, and under each tree full of
boughs.)
5 And the Lord his God betook him in(to) the hand of
the king of Syria, which smote Ahaz, and took a great
prey of his empire, and brought into Damascus. Also
Ahaz was betaken to the hands of the king of Israel, and
he was smitten with a great wound. (And the Lord his
God delivered him into the hands of the king of Syria,
who struck Ahaz, and took away many captives from his
empire, and brought them to Damascus. And then Ahaz
was delivered into the hands of the king of Israel, who
struck down his army with a great slaughter.)
6 And Pekah, the son of Remaliah, killed of Judah
sixscore thousand in one day, all the men warriors; for
they had forsaken the Lord God of their fathers. (And
Pekah, the son of Remaliah, killed one hundred and
twenty thousand of the men of Judah on one day, all very
strong men of war; because they had abandoned the Lord
God of their fathers.)
7 In the same time Zichri, a mighty man of Ephraim,
killed Maaseiah, the son of Jotham, the king; and *he
killed* Azrikam, the duke of his house, and Elkanah, the
second *person* from the king. (At the same time Zichri, a
mighty man of Ephraim, killed Maaseiah, the son of
Jotham, the king; and *he also killed* Azrikam, the leader
of his household, and Elkanah, the second *person* from
the king.)
8 And the sons of Israel took of their brethren two
hundred thousand of women and of children and of
damsels, and prey without number, and bare it into
Samaria. (And the Israelites captured two hundred
thousand of their kinsmen's women and children and
young women, and also took prey without number, and
brought them and the spoils back to Samaria.)
9 In that tempest, *or (time of) vengeance*, a prophet of
the Lord, Oded by name, was there, which went out
against the host *of Israel* coming into Samaria, and he
said to them, Lo! the Lord God of your fathers was wroth
against Judah, and he hath betaken them in your hands;
and ye have slain them cruelly, so that your cruelty
stretcheth forth into heaven. (And in that tempest, *or at
that time of vengeance*, a prophet of the Lord named
Oded was there, and he went out to meet the army *of
Israel* coming back to Samaria, and he said to them, Lo!
the Lord God of your fathers was angry against Judah,
and so he delivered them into your hands; but ye have
cruelly killed them, so that your cruelty stretcheth forth
unto heaven.)
10 Furthermore and ye will (to) make subject to you the
sons of Judah and of Jerusalem into servants and
handmaids; which thing is not needful to be done;
certainly ye have sinned in this thing to the Lord your
God. (And furthermore ye desire to make the sons of
Judah and of Jerusalem subject to you, to make them be
your servants and your sevantesses; but this should not
be done, for ye have also sinned against the Lord your
God.)
11 But hear ye my counsel, and lead again the
prisoners, which ye have brought *thence* of your brethren
(whom ye have brought *here* from your kinsmen); for
(the) great vengeance of the Lord nigheth to you.
12 Therefore men of the princes of the sons of Ephraim,
Azariah, the son of Johanan, Berechiah, the son of
Meshillemoth, Jehizkiah, the son of Shallum, and Amasa,
the son of Hadlai, stood against them that came from the
battle; (And so some leaders of the Ephraimites, Azariah,
the son of Johanan, Berechiah, the son of Meshillemoth,
Jehizkiah, the son of Shallum, and Amasa, the son of
Hadlai, stood against them who came from the battle;)
13 and said to them, Ye shall not bring in hither the
prisoners, lest we do (more) sin against the Lord; why will
ye lay to on your sins, and heap (more on) *your* old
trespasses? Certainly this is great sin; the wrath of the
strong vengeance of the Lord nigheth on Israel. (and said
to them, Ye shall not bring in the prisoners here, lest we
do more sin against the Lord; why add ye more onto our
sins, and heap up more onto *our* old trespasses? For our
sin is great; and the anger of the strong vengeance of the
Lord cometh upon Israel.)
14 And the men warriors left the prey, and all things
which they had taken, before the princes and all the
multitude. (And so the men of war left the prisoners, and
all the things which they had taken, in front of the leaders

and all the multitude.)
15 And the men stood *there*, which we remembered
before, and they took the prisoners, and they clothed of
the spoils all that were naked; and when they had
clothed them, and shod *them*, and refreshed *them* with
meat, and with drink, and anointed *them* for (their)
travail, and gave cure, *either medicine*, to them; which
ever of *them were feeble*, and might not go, they putted
on horses, and they brought *them* to Jericho, the city of
palms, to their brethren; and they turned again into
Samaria. (And the men stood *there*, whom we named
before, and they took the prisoners, and they clothed all
who were naked with the spoils; and when they had
clothed them, and shod *them*, and refreshed *them* with
food, and with drink, and anointed *them* for their travail,
and gave a cure, *or medicine*, to them; whomever of
them were feeble, or were weak, and could not walk,
they put on horses, and they brought *them* to Jericho, the
City of Palms, back to their kinsmen; and then they
returned to Samaria.)
16 In that time (At that time), king Ahaz sent to the king
of Assyrians, and asked help *of him*.
17 And Idumeans came (For the Edomites had
returned), and killed many men of Judah, and took great
prey.
18 Also [the] Philistines were spread abroad by (the)
cities of the fields, and at the south of Judah; and they
took Bethshemesh, and Ajalon, and Gederoth, and
Shocho, and Timnah, and Gimzo, with their villages; and
they dwelled in those (and they lived there).
19 For the Lord made low Judah for Ahaz, the king of
Judah[13]; for he had made him naked of help, and (he had)
despised the Lord. (For the Lord had humbled Judah
because of Ahaz, the king of Judah; for he had made
Judah naked, *or void*, of any help, and he had defied the
Lord.)
20 And the Lord brought against him Tilgathpilneser,
king of Assyrians, that tormented him (who tormented
him), and wasted *him*, while no man against-stood (him).
21 Therefore Ahaz, after that he had spoiled the house
of the Lord, and the house of the king, and (those) of the
princes, gave gifts to the king of Assyrians, and
nevertheless it profited nothing to him. (And so Ahaz,
after that he had spoiled the House of the Lord, and the
house of the king, and those of the leaders, gave gifts to
the king of Assyria, but nevertheless it profited nothing to
him.)
22 Furthermore also in the time of his anguish he
increased despite against God; that king Ahaz, himself,
(And furthermore in the time of his anguish he increased
his defiance against God; for King Ahaz, himself,)
23 offered sacrifices to the gods of Damascus, his
smiters, *or destroyers*, and he said, The gods of the kings
of Syria help them, which gods I shall please by
sacrifices, and they shall help me; when, on the contrary,
they were (the cause of) falling to him, and to all Israel.
(offered sacrifices to the gods of Damascus, his
destroyers, and he said, Because the gods of the kings of
Syria help them, I shall please these gods, and then they
shall also help me; when, on the contrary, they were the
cause of his downfall, and that of all Israel.)
24 Therefore after that Ahaz had taken away, and
broken all the vessels of the house of God, he closed the
gates of God's temple, and he made altars to himself in
all the corners of Jerusalem (and he made altars for
himself in all the corners of Jerusalem).
25 And in all the cities of Judah he builded altars to
burn incense (to other gods), and he stirred the Lord God
of his fathers to wrathfulness.
26 Soothly the residue of his words and of all his
works, the former and the last, be written in the book of
[the] kings of Judah and of Israel. (And the rest of the first
and the last deeds of Ahaz, be written in The Book of the
Kings of Judah and of Israel.)
27 And Ahaz slept with his fathers, and they buried him
in the city of Jerusalem; for they received not him into the
sepulchres of the kings of Israel (for they would not lay
him in the tombs of the kings of Israel); and Hezekiah, his
son, reigned for him.

CHAPTER 29

1 And Hezekiah began to reign, when he was of five
and twenty years, and he reigned in Jerusalem nine and
twenty years (And Hezekiah began to reign, when he was
twenty-five years old, and he reigned in Jerusalem for
twenty-nine years); the name of his mother *was* Abijah,
the daughter of Zechariah.
2 And Hezekiah did that, that was pleasing in the sight
of the Lord, by all things that David, his father, had done.
(And Hezekiah did what was pleasing before the Lord, by
all the things that his forefather David had done.)
3 In that year, and in the first month of his realm, he
opened the gates of the house of the Lord, and restored,
or repaired, those *gates*;
4 and he brought (in) the priests, and deacons (and the
Levites), and he gathered them *together* into the east
street,
5 and said to them, Sons of Levi, hear ye me, and be
ye hallowed; cleanse ye the house of the Lord God of
your fathers; and do ye away all uncleanness from the
saintuary. (and said to them, Sons of Levi/Levites, listen
ye to me, and be ye consecrated, *or purified*, now; and
cleanse ye the House of the Lord God of your fathers;
and do ye away all uncleanness from the sanctuary.)
6 Our fathers have sinned, and done evil in the sight
of the Lord our God, and forsook him; they turned away

13 Here the KJV mistakenly says, "king of Israel".

their faces from the tabernacle of the Lord our God, and
gave their back (and they turned their backs on him).
7 They closed the doors that were in the porch (They
closed the doors of the vestibule), and quenched the
lanterns; and they burnt not incense, and they offered not
burnt sacrifices in the saintuary of (the) God of Israel.
8 Therefore the strong vengeance of the Lord was
raised upon Judah and Jerusalem; and he gave them into
stirring/into moving, *or unstableness*, and into perishing,
and into hissing, *either scorning*, as ye see with your
eyes.
9 Lo! our fathers have fallen down by swords; our
sons, and our daughters, and our wives be led (away as)
prisoners for this great trespass.
10 Now therefore it pleaseth me, that we make a bond
of peace with the Lord God of Israel, and that he turn
from us the strong vengeance of his wrath. (And so now it
pleaseth me, that we make a covenant with the Lord God
of Israel, so that he turn away the strong vengeance of his
anger from us.)
11 My sons, do not ye *herein* be reckless; the Lord hath
chosen you, that ye stand before him, and serve him, that
ye praise him, and burn incense to him.
12 Therefore the deacons rose up (And so the Levites
rose up), Mahath, the son of Amasai, and Joel, the son of
Azariah, of the sons of Kohath; and of the sons of Merari,
Kish, the son of Abdi, and Azariah, the son of Jehalelel;
and of the sons of Gershon, Joah, the son of Zimmah,
and Eden, the son of Joah;
13 and of the sons of Elizaphan, Shimri, and Jeiel; and
of the sons of Asaph, Zechariah, and Mattaniah;
14 also of the sons of Heman, Jehiel, and Shimei; but
also of the sons of Jeduthun, Shemaiah, and Uzziel. (and
of the sons of Heman, Jehiel, and Shimei; and of the sons
of Jeduthun, Shemaiah, and Uzziel.)
15 And they gathered together their brethren, and they
were hallowed (And they gathered their kinsmen
together, and they were consecrated, *or were purified*);
and (then) they entered by the commandment of the king,
and by [the] commandment of the Lord, for to cleanse the
house of the Lord.
16 Also [the] priests entered into the temple of the Lord,
for to hallow it, and they bare out all the uncleanness,
that they found therein in(to) the porch, *either large
place*, of the house of the Lord; which uncleanness the
deacons took, and they bare *it* out to the strand of Kidron
withoutforth. (And the priests entered into the Temple of
the Lord to cleanse it, and they brought out all the
unclean things, that they found there, into the courtyard
of the House of the Lord; and then the Levites took away
these unclean things, and they carried *them* to the Kidron
Stream/to the Kidron Gorge.)
17 Soothly they began to cleanse in the first day of the
first month, and in the eighth day of the same month they
entered into the porch of the house of the Lord, and they
cleansed the temple eight days; and in the sixteenth day
of the same month they [ful]filled that, that they had
begun. (And they began to cleanse it on the first day of
the first month, and on the eighth day of the same month
they reached the vestibule of the House of the Lord, and
then they cleansed the Temple for eight days; and on the
sixteenth day of the same month, they finished what they
had begun.)
18 And they entered to Hezekiah, the king, and said to
him, We have hallowed, *or cleansed*, all the house of the
Lord, and the altar of burnt sacrifice thereof, and the
vessels thereof, also and the board of setting forth with all
his vessels, (And they came to King Hezekiah, and said to
him, We have cleansed all the House of the Lord, and
also the table for the loaves of proposition, *or the loaves
of setting forth*, with all its vessels,)
19 and all the purtenance of the temple, that king Ahaz
had defouled in his realm (that King Ahaz had defiled
during his reign), after that he brake the law; and lo! all
things be set forth before the altar of the Lord.
20 And Hezekiah, the king, rose up in the morrowtide,
and he gathered together all the princes of the city, and
he went up into the house of the Lord; (And King
Hezekiah rose up in the morning, and he gathered
together all the leaders of the city, and he went to the
House of the Lord;)
21 and they offered together seven bulls, and seven
rams, seven lambs, and seven bucks of goats, for [the] sin,
for the realm, for the saintuary, and for Judah (and they
offered seven bulls, and seven rams, and seven lambs,
and seven goat bucks as a sin offering for the kingdom,
and for the sanctuary, and for Judah). And he said to
[the] priests, the sons of Aaron, that they should offer
sacrifices on the altar of the Lord.
22 Therefore they killed (the) bulls, and the priests took
the blood, and poured it upon the altar; also they killed
(the) rams, and they poured the blood of those upon the
altar; and they (also) offered (the) lambs, and they poured
the blood upon the altar.
23 And they brought [the] bucks of goats for (the) sin
(offering) before the king and all the multitude, and they
setted their hands on those (and they put their hands on
them);
24 and the priests offered them, and they sprinkled the
blood of them before the altar, for the cleansing of all
Israel. For the king commanded, that burnt sacrifice
should be made for all Israel, and for (the) sin *thereof.*
(and the priests offered them, and they sprinkled their
blood on the altar, for the cleansing of all Israel. For the
king commanded, that the burnt sacrifice, and the sin
offering, should be made for all Israel.)
25 Also he ordained deacons in the house of the Lord,
with cymbals, and psalteries, and harps (And he ordained

Levites in the House of the Lord, with cymbals, and lutes,
and harps), by the ordinance of David the king, and of
Gad, the prophet, and of Nathan, the prophet; for it was
the commandment of the Lord by the hand of his
prophets.
26 And the deacons stood, and held the organs of
David; and priests *held* [the] trumps. (And the Levites
stood ready with the instruments of David, and the priests
with the trumpets.)
27 And Hezekiah commanded, that they should offer
burnt sacrifices upon the altar; and when burnt sacrifices
were offered, they began to sing praisings to the Lord,
and to sound with trumps, and with diverse organs,
which David, king of Israel, had made ready to sound
with. (And Hezekiah commanded, that they should offer
burnt sacrifices upon the altar; and when the burnt
sacrifices were offered, they began to sing praises to the
Lord, and to sound with the trumpets, and the other
instruments, which David, the king of Israel, had made to
sound *with.*)
28 Forsooth when all the company worshipped/And
when all the company worshipped *the Lord,* [the] singers
and they that held trumps were in their office, till the
burnt sacrifice was filled (the singers sang, and those who
had the trumpets blew them, until the burnt sacrifice was
finished).
29 And when the offering was ended, the king was
bowed *down,* and all that were with him (the king bowed
down, and all who were with him), and they worshipped
God.
30 And Hezekiah and the princes commanded to the
deacons, that they should praise the Lord with the words
of David, and of Asaph, the prophet; which praised *him*
with great gladness, and kneeled, and worshipped. (And
Hezekiah and his leaders commanded to the Levites, that
they should praise the Lord with the words of David, and
with those of the prophet Asaph; and so they praised *him*
with great gladness, and kneeled, and worshipped.)
31 Soothly Hezekiah added also these things, (and
said,) Ye have filled your hands *with blessings* to the
Lord; nigh ye, and offer sacrifices and praisings in the
house of the Lord. Therefore all the multitude offered
with devout soul sacrifices, and praisings, and burnt
sacrifices. (And Hezekiah added these things, and said,
Ye have consecrated yourselves to the Lord; now come
ye, and offer sacrifices and praises in the House of the
Lord. And so with devout soul, all the multitude offered
sacrifices, and praises, and burnt sacrifices.)
32 And this was the number of burnt sacrifices, which
the multitude offered; seventy bulls, and an hundred
rams, and two hundred lambs.
33 Also they hallowed to the Lord six hundred oxen,
and three thousand sheep.
34 And the priests were few, and they might not suffice
for to draw, *or flay off,* the skins of [the] burnt sacrifices;
wherefore and the deacons their brethren helped them,
till the work was [ful]filled, and the priests were
hallowed; for the deacons be hallowed by lighter custom
than the priests. (And the priests were too few, to be able
to draw away, *or to flay off,* all the skins of the burnt
sacrifices; and so their kinsmen the Levites helped them,
until the work was finished, and the other priests had
consecrated themselves; for more of the Levites had kept
themselves purified than had the priests.)
35 Therefore there were full many burnt sacrifices, and
inner fatness of peaceable sacrifices, and the moist
sacrifices of burnt sacrifices, and *thereby* the worship of
the house of the Lord was (ful)filled. (And so there were a
great many burnt sacrifices, as well as the inner fatness of
the peace offerings, and the wine sacrifices for all the
burnt sacrifices, and *by this* the service of the House of
the Lord was restored.)
36 And Hezekiah was glad, and all the people, for the
service of the Lord was fulfilled; for it pleased (them all),
that this was done suddenly. (And Hezekiah and all the
people were glad, that the service of the House of the
Lord had begun again, *or was restored*; and it pleased
them all, that it had all been done so quickly.)

CHAPTER 30

1 And Hezekiah sent to all Israel and to Judah, and he
wrote epistles to Ephraim and to Manasseh, that they
should come into the house of the Lord in Jerusalem, and
make pask to the Lord God of Israel. (And Hezekiah sent
word to all Israel and to Judah, and also wrote letters to
Ephraim and to Manasseh, that they should come to the
House of the Lord in Jerusalem, and keep the Passover of
the Lord God of Israel.)
2 Therefore when counsel was taken of the king, and
of [the] princes, and of all the company of Jerusalem, they
deemed, *or purposed,* to make pask in the second month.
(And so when the king, and the leaders, and all the
company of Jerusalem, had taken counsel together, they
decided to keep the Passover in the second month.)
3 For they deemed not to *be able to* do *this* in his
time, *that is, the first month* (For they deemed that they
could not do *it* at that time, *that is, in the first month*); for
the priests which might suffice *thereto* were not *yet*
hallowed, and the people was not yet gathered into
Jerusalem.
4 And the word pleased the king, and all the
multitude. (And this decision pleased the king, and all the
multitude.)
5 And they deemed to send messengers into all Israel,
from Beersheba unto Dan, that they should come, and
make (the) pask to the Lord God of Israel in Jerusalem; for
(so) many men had not done *it,* as it is before-written in
the law (for so many had not kept *it* before, as it was

described in the Law).
6 And couriers went forth with epistles, by [the]
commandment of the king and of his princes, into all
Israel and Judah, and preached by that, that the king had
commanded, (and said,) Sons of Israel, turn ye again to
the Lord God of Abraham, and of Isaac, and of Israel; and
he shall turn again to the remnant of men, that escaped
the hands of the king(s) of Assyrians. (And couriers went
forth with the letters, by the command of the king and of
his leaders, into all Israel and Judah, and preached what
the king had commanded, and said, Israelites, return ye
to the Lord God of Abraham, and of Isaac, and of Jacob;
and he shall return to the remnant of people, who
escaped from the hands, *or from the power*, of the kings
of Assyria.)
7 Do not ye be made as your fathers and *your*
brethren, which went away from the Lord God of their
fathers; and he gave them into perishing, as ye see. (Do
not ye be made like your fathers and *your* kinsmen, who
went away from the Lord God of their fathers; and he
gave them into perishing, as ye see.)
8 Do not ye make hard your nolls, as your fathers *did*
(Do not ye be stiff-necked, *or stubborn*, like your fathers);
give ye *your* hands to the Lord *in promising that ye shall
serve him faithfully*, and come ye to his saintuary, which
he hath hallowed (into) without end; serve ye the Lord
God of your fathers, and the wrath of his strong
vengeance shall turn away from you.
9 For if ye turn again to the Lord, your brethren and
your sons shall have mercy before their lords that led
them prisoners; and they shall turn again into this land
(For if ye return to the Lord, your kinsmen and your
children shall have mercy before their lords who led
them away as prisoners; and they shall return to this
land). For the Lord our God is pious, *either benign*, and
merciful; and he will not turn away his face from you, if
ye turn again to him.
10 Therefore the couriers went swiftly from city into
city through the land of Ephraim and Manasseh unto
Zebulun, while they scorned and bemocked them (but
the people *of those territories* scorned and mocked
them).
11 Nevertheless some men of Asher, and of Manasseh,
and of Zebulun, assented to the counsel, and came into
Jerusalem.
12 Forsooth the hand of the Lord was made in Judah,
that he gave to them one heart, and that they did the
word of the Lord, by the commandment of the king and
of the princes. (But the hand of the Lord was made in
Judah, so that he gave them one heart, and that they did
the word of the Lord, by the command of the king and
his leaders.)
13 And many peoples were gathered into Jerusalem, for
to make the solemnity of therf loaves in the second
month. (And many people gathered in Jerusalem to keep
the Feast of Unleavened Bread in the second month.)
14 And they rose, and destroyed the altars, that were in
Jerusalem; and they destroying all things in which
incense was burnt to idols, casted forth into the strand of
Kidron. (And they rose up, and destroyed the altars, that
were in Jerusalem; and to destroy all the things in which
incense was burned to idols, they threw *them* forth into
the Kidron Stream/into the Kidron Gorge.)
15 And they offered pask in the fourteenth day of the
second month; also the priests and the deacons were
hallowed at the last, and (then they) offered burnt
sacrifices in the house of the Lord. (And they offered the
Passover on the fourteenth day of the second month; and
the priests and the Levites were ashamed, *for they were
not ritually clean*, and so at last they consecrated
themselves, and then they offered the burnt sacrifices in
the House of the Lord.)
16 And they stood in their order, by the ordinance and
law of Moses, the man of God. Soothly the priests took
of the hands of deacons the blood to be shed out (And
the priests took the blood to be shed out from the hands
of the Levites),
17 for much (of the) company was not hallowed; and
therefore the deacons offered pask for them, that might
not be hallowed to the Lord. (for many of the people
were not yet purified, and so the Levites sacrificed, *or
killed*, the Passover lambs for those who had not yet been
consecrated to the Lord.)
18 Also a great part of the people of Ephraim, and of
Manasseh, and of Issachar, and of Zebulun, that was not
hallowed, ate (the) pask not by that that is written. And
Hezekiah prayed for them, and said, The good Lord shall
do mercy to all men, (And a great part of the people of
Ephraim, and of Manasseh, and of Issachar, and of
Zebulun, who were not purified, ate the Passover not by
what was written. But Hezekiah prayed for them, and
said, The good Lord shall do mercy to all,)
19 which seek in all their heart the Lord God of their
fathers (who seek in all their hearts the Lord God of their
fathers); and it shall not be areckoned to them *into sin*,
that they be not hallowed *by (the) offering of gifts.*
20 And the Lord heard him, and was pleased to the
people. (And the Lord heard him, and healed the
people/and forgave the people.)
21 And the sons of Israel, that were found in Jerusalem,
made the solemnity of therf loaves seven days in great
gladness, and they praised the Lord by each day; and the
deacons and [the] priests *praised the Lord* by organs,
which accorded to their office. (And the Israelites, who
were found in Jerusalem, kept the Feast of Unleavened
Bread for seven days with great gladness, and they
praised the Lord each day; and the Levites and the priests
praised the Lord with mighty instruments.)

22 And Hezekiah spake to the heart of all the deacons,
that had good understanding of the Lord; and they ate by
(the) seven days of the solemnity, offering sacrifices of
peaceable things, and praising the Lord God of their
fathers. (And Hezekiah spoke to the hearts of all the
Levites, who had a good understanding of the Lord; and
they ate throughout the seven days of the Feast, offering
the peace offerings, and praising the Lord God of their
fathers.)
23 And it pleased all the multitude to hallow also other
seven days; which thing also they did with great joy.
(And it pleased all the multitude to also dedicate another
seven days; and so they did that with great joy.)
24 Forsooth Hezekiah, king of Judah, gave to the
multitude a thousand bulls, and seven thousand of sheep;
and the princes gave to the people a thousand bulls, and
ten thousand sheep (and the leaders gave the people a
thousand bulls, and ten thousand sheep). Therefore a full
great multitude of priests was hallowed[14];
25 and all the company of Judah was filled with
gladness, as well of priests and deacons, as of all the
multitude that came from Israel, and of [the] converts of
the land of Israel, and of [the] dwellers in Judah. (and all
the congregation of Judah was filled with gladness, *that
is,* the priests and the Levites, and all the multitude who
came from Israel, and the converts in the land of Israel,
and the inhabitants of Judah.)
26 And great solemnity was made in Jerusalem, what
manner was not in that city from the days of Solomon,
the son of David, king of Israel. (And there was great joy
in Jerusalem, such as was not in that city since the days of
Solomon, the son of David, king of Israel.)
27 And [the] priests and deacons rose up, and blessed
the people; and the voice of them was heard, and their
prayer came into the holy dwelling place of heaven. (And
the priests and the Levites rose up, and blessed the
people; and their voices were heard, and their prayers
came unto the holy dwelling place of heaven.)

CHAPTER 31

1 And when these things were done rightfully, all
Israel went out, that was found in the cities of Judah; and
they brake [the] simulacra, and cutted down (the)
[maumet] woods, and wasted [the] high places, and
destroyed [the] altars, not only of all Judah and Benjamin,
but also of Ephraim and Manasseh, till that they had
destroyed *those altars/their idols* utterly. And *then* all the
sons of Israel turned again into their possessions and
cities. (And when all these things were finished, all Israel
went out, who were found in the cities of Judah; and they
broke up the idols, and cut down the idol groves, *or the
sacred poles,* and wasted the hill shrines, and destroyed
the altars, not only of all Judah and Benjamin, but also of
Ephraim and Manasseh, until they had utterly destroyed
those altars/their idols. And *then* all the Israelites
returned to their possessions, *or their own property,* in
their cities.)
2 And Hezekiah ordained companies of priests and
deacons by their partings, each man in his own office,
that is, as well of priests as of deacons, to burnt sacrifices
and peaceable sacrifices, that they should minister, and
acknowledge, and sing in the gates of the castles of the
Lord. (And Hezekiah ordained companies of the priests
and the Levites, by their divisions, and each man
according to his duty, that is, the priests as well as the
Levites, for the offering of the burnt sacrifices and the
peace offerings, to serve, or to give thanks, or to sing in
the Temple of the Lord.)
3 And the part of the king's *sacrifice* was, that of his
own substance, or chattel, burnt sacrifice should be
offered evermore in the morrowtide and in the eventide,
also in sabbaths, and calends, and in other solemnities, as
it is written in the law of Moses. (And the king's portion
of the *sacrifice,* out of his own substance, or chattel,
provided the burnt sacrifice that was offered every
morning and every evening, and also on the sabbaths,
and the calends, and the other Feasts, as it is written in
the Law of Moses.)
4 Also he commanded to the people of them that
dwelled in Jerusalem, to give parts to the priests and
deacons, that they might give attention to the law of the
Lord. (And he commanded to the people who lived in
Jerusalem, to give portions to the priests and the Levites,
so that they would be able to devote their full attention to
the Law of the Lord.)
5 And when this was known in the ears of the
multitude, the sons of Israel offered full many first fruits of
wheat, of wine, of oil, and of honey; and of all things
which the earth bringeth forth, they offered tithes. (And
when this was heard by the multitude, the Israelites
offered a great many first fruits of wheat, of wine, of oil,
and of honey; and they offered tithes of all the things
which the earth brought forth.)
6 But also the sons of Israel and of Judah, that dwelled
in the cities of Judah, offered tithes of oxen, and of sheep,
and the tithes of holy things, which they avowed to their
Lord God, and they brought all things, and made full
many heaps. (And the Israelites and the people of Judah,
who lived in the cities of Judah, offered their tithes of
oxen, and of sheep, and of the holy things which they
vowed to the Lord their God, and they brought all these
things to the Temple, and made a large number of heaps.)
7 In the third month they began to lay the
foundaments of the heaps, and in the seventh month they
filled, *or ended (or completed),* those heaps.
8 And when Hezekiah and his princes had entered

[14] *That is, ordained to kill and offer to the Lord these beasts.*

(And when Hezekiah and his officials came), they saw
the heaps, and they blessed the Lord, and the people of
Israel.
9 And Hezekiah asked the priests and deacons why
the heaps lay so.
10 And Azariah, the first, *or chief*, priest of the
generation of Zadok (And the High Priest Azariah, a
descendant of Zadok), answered to him and said, Since
the first fruits began to be offered in the house of the
Lord, we have eaten *of those fruits*, and been fulfilled,
and full many things be left; for the Lord hath blessed his
people; and this plenty, which thou seest, is of the
remnants.
11 Therefore Hezekiah commanded, that they should
make ready barns in the house of the Lord; and when
they had done this thing, (And so Hezekiah commanded,
that they should prepare storerooms in the House of the
Lord; and when they had done this thing,)
12 they brought in faithfully both the first fruits, and
(the) tithes, and whatever things they had avowed. And
Conaniah, the deacon, was [the] sovereign of those things
(And Conaniah, the Levite, was the ruler, *or the overseer*,
of those things); and Shimei, his brother was the second,
next (to) him;
13 after whom Jehiel, and Azaziah, and Nahath, and
Asahel, and Jerimoth, and Jozabad, and Eliel, and
Ismachiah, and Mahath, and Benaiah, were sovereigns
under the hands, *or powers*, of Conaniah and Shimei, his
brother, by the commandment of Hezekiah the king, and
of Azariah, the bishop of the house of the Lord (by the
command of King Hezekiah, and of Azariah, the High
Priest of the House of the Lord), to whom all things
pertained.
14 But Kore, the son of Imnah, deacon, and porter of
the east gate, was sovereign of those things that were
offered by free will to the Lord, and of the first fruits, and
of [the] things hallowed into the holy things *of the
number* of holy things; (And Kore, the son of Imnah, the
Levite, and the guard, *or the doorkeeper*, at the East Gate,
was in charge of the things that were offered by free will
to the Lord, and of the first fruits, and of the things
dedicated for the holiest of holy things;)
15 and under his care, (*or his charge*,) *were* Eden, and
Miniamin, Jeshua, and Shemaiah, and Amariah, and
Shecaniah, in the cities of (the) priests, that they should
part faithfully to their brethren the parts, to the less and to
the greater (who should faithfully distribute the portions
to their kinsmen, to the greater and the lesser alike),
16 besides males from three years and above, these
things to all that entered into the temple of the Lord, and
whatever thing by each day was hired in the service and
observances, by their partings. (yea, to males three years
of age and older, these things were distributed to all who
entered into the Temple of the Lord each day, for their
part in the service and observances, by their divisions.)
17 To (the) priests by *their* families, and to deacons
from twenty years and above (and to the Levites from
twenty years of age and older), by their orders and
companies,
18 and to all the multitude, *that is*, both to the wives,
and the free children of them of ever either kind, meats,
(*or foods*,) were given faithfully of these things that were
hallowed. (and to all their multitude, *that is*, to their
wives, and their sons and their daughters, for they were
required to perform their sacred duties at any time.)
19 But also men of the sons of Aaron were ordained, by
the fields and by suburbs of all the cities, which men
should deal parts to all the male kind of priests, and
deacons. (And men of the sons of Aaron were ordained,
who were in the fields of the suburbs of all their cities, to
distribute portions to all the priests, and the Levites.)
20 Therefore Hezekiah did all *these* things, which we
have said, in all Judah, and he wrought that, that was
rightful and good and true before the Lord his God,
21 in all the religion of the service of the house of the
Lord, by the law and by the ceremonies; and he would
seek his Lord God in all his heart, and he did *so*, and had
prosperity. (in all the work of the service of the House of
the Lord, and by the Law and the commandments/and by
the Law and the statutes; for he sought the Lord his God
with all his heart, yea, he did *so*, and he prospered.)

CHAPTER 32

1 After which things and such truth (After these things
and such loyalty, *or such faithfulness*), Sennacherib, the
king of Assyrians, came and entered into Judah; and he
besieged (the) strong cities, and would take those.
2 And when Hezekiah had heard this thing, that is,
that Sennacherib had come, and that all the fierceness of
his battle was turned against Jerusalem,
3 he took counsel with [the] princes and with (the)
most strong men, that they should stop the heads of
wells, which were without the city; and when the
sentence of all men deemed this *profitable*, (he took
counsel with the leaders and the most strong men, who
said that they should stop up, *or close up*, the heads of
the wells, which were outside the city; and when the
judgement of all the men judged this *profitable*,)
4 he gathered together a full great multitude *of men*,
and they stopped (up) all the wells, and the river, that
flowed in the midst of the land; and said, Lest the kings of
Assyrians come, and find (an) abundance of waters (here).
5 Also Hezekiah did wittingly, and he builded all the
wall that was destroyed, and he builded towers on *the
wall*, and another wall withoutforth. And he repaired
Millo in the city of David; and made armour of all kind,
and shields. (And Hezekiah did knowingly, *or with
intent*, and he rebuilt all the wall that was destroyed, and

he built towers on *the wall*, and another wall outside it.
And he repaired the Millo in the City of David; and he
made all kinds of arms, *or weapons*, and shields.)
6 And he ordained princes of warriors in the host; and
he called together all (the) men in(to) the street of the gate
of the city, and spake to the heart(s) of them, and said,
7 Do ye manly, and be ye comforted (Be ye brave,
and be ye strong); do not ye dread, neither be ye afeared
of the king of Assyrians, nor of all the multitude that is
with him; for many more be with us than with him.
8 A fleshly arm is with him; and the Lord our God is
with us, which is our helper, and shall fight for us. And
the people was comforted with such words of Hezekiah,
king of Judah. (An arm of flesh is with him; but the Lord
our God is with us, he is our helper, and shall fight for us.
And the people were encouraged by such words from
Hezekiah, the king of Judah.)
9 And after that these things were done, Sennacherib,
[the king of Assyria,] sent his servants to Jerusalem; for he
himself (but he himself), with all the host, besieged
Lachish. *He sent* (them) to Hezekiah, king of Judah, and
to all the people that was in the city *of Jerusalem*, and
(they) said,
10 Sennacherib, king of Assyrians, saith these things, In
whom have ye trust, and sit besieged in Jerusalem?
(Sennacherib, the king of Assyria, saith these things, In
whom do ye trust, when ye now sit besieged in
Jerusalem?)
11 Whether not Hezekiah deceiveth you, that ye betake
you to death in hunger and thirst, and he affirmeth, that
the Lord your God shall deliver you from the hand of the
king of Assyrians? (Did not Hezekiah deceive you, so that
now ye deliver *yourselves* unto death by hunger and
thirst, while he yet affirmeth, that the Lord your God shall
rescue you from the hands of the king of Assyria?)
12 Whether this is not Hezekiah, that destroyed (the)
high places, and altars of him, and commanded to Judah
and Jerusalem, and said, Ye shall worship before one
altar, and therein ye shall burn incense? (Is this not the
same Hezekiah, who destroyed the *Lord's* hill shrines,
and his altars, and commanded to Judah and Jerusalem,
and said, Ye shall worship before one altar, and ye shall
burn incense on it?)
13 Whether ye know not what things I have done, and
my fathers, to all the peoples of (other) lands? Whether
the gods of (those) folks and of all (those) lands might
deliver their country from mine hand? (Do ye not know
what I and my forefathers have done, to all the peoples of
other lands? Did the gods of those nations deliver their
lands out of my hands?)
14 Who is, of all the gods of (those) folks, which my
fathers destroyed, that might deliver his people from
mine hand, that also your God may deliver you from
mine hand? (Who was there, of all the gods of the nations
whom my forefathers destroyed, that could rescue his
people out of my hands? *no one!* yet ye think that your
God shall rescue you out of my hands?)
15 Therefore Hezekiah deceive not you, neither scorn
he *you* by vain counselling, neither believe ye to him; for
if no god of all (those) folks and countries might deliver
his people from mine hand, and from the hand of my
fathers, followingly neither your God shall be able to
deliver you from this mine hand. (And so do not let
Hezekiah deceive you, nor scorn he *you* with vain
counselling, nor believe ye him; for if no god of any of
those other nations or lands could rescue his people out
of my hands, or out of the hands of my forefathers, then it
followeth, that your God shall not be able to rescue you
out of my hands either.)
16 But also his servants spake many other things against
the Lord God, and against Hezekiah, his servant.
17 Also he wrote epistles full of blasphemy against the
Lord God of Israel, and he spake against God, *and said*,
As the gods of other folks might not deliver their people
from mine hand, so and the God of Hezekiah may not
deliver his people from mine hand.
18 Furthermore, and with [a] great cry in the language
of Jews, he sounded against the people, that sat on the
walls of Jerusalem, to make them afeared, and to take the
city. (And furthermore, with a great cry in the language of
the Jews, they shouted at the people who sat on the walls
of Jerusalem, to make them afraid, so it would be easier
to take the city.)
19 And he spake against [the] God of Israel, as against
the gods of the peoples of [the] earth, the works of men's
hands. (And they spoke against the God of Jerusalem, like
they spoke against the gods of the other peoples of the
earth, which were the work of men's hands.)
20 Therefore Hezekiah, the king, and Isaiah, the
prophet, the son of Amoz, prayed against this blasphemy,
and cried [out] till into heaven (and cried out to heaven).
21 And the Lord sent his angel, the which killed each
strong man and warrior, and the prince of the host of the
king of Assyrians; and he/*Sennacherib* turned again with
shame to his land. And when he had entered into the
house of his god, the sons, which went out of his womb,
killed him *there* with sword. (And the Lord sent his angel,
who killed each strong man and warrior, and the leader
of the army of the king of Assyria; and he/*Sennacherib*
returned with shame to his own land. And when he had
gone into the house of his god, the sons, who went out of
his womb, killed him *there* with the sword.)
22 And the Lord saved Hezekiah, and the dwellers of
Jerusalem, from the hand of Sennacherib, king of
Assyrians, and from the hand of all men; and he gave to
them rest by compass. (And the Lord saved Hezekiah,
and the inhabitants of Jerusalem, from the hands, *or the
power*, of Sennacherib, the king of Assyria, and from the

hands of all men; and he gave them peace all around.)
23 Also many men brought offerings and sacrifices to
the Lord into Jerusalem, and gifts to Hezekiah, king of
Judah; which was enhanced after these things before all
folks. (And many people brought offerings and sacrifices
for the Lord to Jerusalem, and gifts for Hezekiah, the king
of Judah; and after these things he was exalted, *or held in
high honour,* before all the nations.)
24 In those days Hezekiah was sick unto the death, and
he prayed the Lord; and he heard him, and gave to him a
sign;
25 but he yielded not *thankings to the Lord* after the
benefits which he had taken, for his heart was raised *into
pride* (but Hezekiah did not give *thanks to the Lord* for the
benefits which he had received, for his heart was raised
up *in pride*); and (then the) wrath *of the Lord* was made
against him, and against Judah, and against Jerusalem.
26 And he was meeked afterward, for-thy that his heart
was raised; both he *was meeked,* and the dwellers of
Jerusalem (And he was humbled afterward, because his
heart had been raised up; both he, and the inhabitants of
Jerusalem, *were humbled*); and therefore the wrath of the
Lord came not upon them in the days of Hezekiah.
27 And Hezekiah was rich, and full noble, and he
gathered to himself full many treasures of silver, and of
gold, and of precious stones, and of sweet smelling
spices, and of armours of all kind, and of vessels of great
price. (And Hezekiah was rich, and very glorious, and he
made for himself many treasuries for his silver, and gold,
and precious stones, and sweet smelling spices, and for
all kinds of arms, *or weapons,* and for his vessels of great
value.)
28 Also he builded large (store)houses of wheat, [and]
of wine, and of oil, and cratches of all beasts, and folds to
sheep, (And he built large storehouses for his wheat, and
wine, and oil, and stalls for all kinds of beasts, and
sheepfolds,)
29 and *he builded* six cities. And he had unnumberable
flocks of sheep and of great beasts; for the Lord had given
to him full much chattel.
30 That is Hezekiah, that stopped the higher well of the
waters of Gihon, and he turned those away under *the
earth* at the west side of the city of David; in all his works
he did by prosperity, whatever thing he would (and he
prospered in all his works, whatever he did).
31 Nevertheless in the message of the princes of
Babylon, that were sent to him for to ask of the great
wonder, that befelled on the land, God forsook him, that
he were assayed, and that all things were known that
were in his heart. (Even when the messengers of the
leaders of Babylon came, who were sent to ask him
about the great wonder, that befell the land, and God
abandoned him, so that he was tested, *or tried,* and so
that all things could be known that were in his heart.)
32 Soothly the residue of [the] words of Hezekiah, and
of his mercies, be written in the prophecy of Isaiah, the
prophet, the son of Amoz, and in the book of kings of
Judah and of Israel. (And the rest of the deeds, and the
mercies, *or the righteous works,* of Hezekiah, be written
in the prophecy of the prophet Isaiah, the son of Amoz,
and in The Book of the Kings of Judah and of Israel.)
33 And Hezekiah slept with his fathers, and they buried
him above the sepulchres of the sons of David. And all
Judah and all the dwellers of Jerusalem made solemn the
services of his burying; and Manasseh, his son, reigned
for him. (And Hezekiah joined his ancestors, and they
buried him in the uppermost of the tombs of the sons of
David. And all Judah and all the inhabitants of Jerusalem
paid him honour at the services for his burial; and his son
Manasseh reigned for him.)

CHAPTER 33

1 Manasseh was of twelve years, when he began to
reign, and he reigned in Jerusalem five and fifty years.
(Manasseh was twelve years old, when he began to reign,
and he reigned in Jerusalem for fifty-five years.)
2 And he did evil before the Lord after the
abominations of heathen men, whom the Lord destroyed
before the sons of Israel. (And he did evil before the Lord
after the abominations of the heathen, whom the Lord
had destroyed before the Israelites.)
3 And he turned, and restored the high places, which
Hezekiah, his father, had destroyed. And he builded
altars to Baalim, and made woods, and worshipped all
the knighthood of heaven, and praised it. (And he turned,
and restored the hill shrines, which his father Hezekiah
had destroyed. And he built altars to the Baalim, and
made idol groves, *or sacred poles,* and worshipped all
the host of heaven, *that is, the moon, and the stars, and
the planets,* and praised them.)
4 And he builded altars in the house of the Lord, of
which the Lord had said, My name shall be in Jerusalem
(into) without end.
5 Soothly he builded those altars to all the knighthood
of heaven in the two large places of the house of the
Lord. (Yea, he built those altars to all the host of heaven
in the two courtyards of the House of the Lord.)
6 And he made his sons to pass through the fire in the
valley of Ben-hinnom; he kept (watch over) dreams; he
followed false divining by (the) chittering of birds; and he
served witchcrafts; and he had with him astrologers and
enchanters, *either tregetours, that deceived men's wits
(who deceived men's minds),* and he wrought many evils
before the Lord to stir him to wrath.
7 And he set a graven and a molten sign in the house
of the Lord (And he put a carved image, an idol, in the
House of the Lord), of which house God spake to David,
and to Solomon, his son, and said, I shall set my name

[into] without end in this house, and in Jerusalem, which
I chose of all the lineages of Israel;
8 and I shall not make the foot of Israel to move from
the land which I gave to their fathers, so only that they
take heed to do those things that I have commanded to
them, and all the law, and ceremonies, and dooms, by
the hand of Moses. (and I shall not make the foot of Israel
to move from the land which I gave to their fathers, if
only they take heed to do those things which I have
commanded to them, and all the Law, and the statutes,
and the judgements, *or the laws*, through Moses.)
9 But Manasseh deceived the men of Judah, and the
dwellers of Jerusalem, so that they did evil, more than all
heathen men, which the Lord had destroyed from the
face of the sons of Israel. (But Manasseh deceived the
people of Judah, and the inhabitants of Jerusalem, so that
they did evil, more than all the heathen, whom the Lord
had destroyed before the Israelites.)
10 And the Lord spake to him, and to his people; and
they would not take heed (but they would not take heed,
or listen to him).
11 Therefore the Lord brought upon them the princes of
the host of the king of Assyrians (And so the Lord brought
upon them the leaders of the army of the king of Assyria);
and they took Manasseh, and bound him with chains,
and stocks, and led him into Babylon.
12 And after that he was anguished, he prayed (to) the
Lord his God, and did penance greatly before the God of
his fathers (and did great penance before the God of his
fathers).
13 And he prayed (to) God, and beseeched him
intently; and God heard his prayer, and brought him
again into Jerusalem into his realm (and he brought him
back to Jerusalem, and to his throne); and *then* Manasseh
knew, that the Lord himself is God *alone*.
14 After these things he builded the wall without the
city of David, at the west *side* of Gihon, in the valley,
from the entering of the gate of fishes, by compass unto
Ophel; and he raised it up greatly; and he ordained
princes of the host in all the strong cities of Judah. (After
these things he built the outside wall of the City of David,
at the west *side* of Gihon, in the valley, unto the entrance
at the Fish Gate, and all around Ophel; and he raised it
up to a great height; and he stationed leaders of his army
in all the fortified cities of Judah.)
15 And he did away alien gods and simulacra from the
house of the Lord; and *he did away* the altars, which he
had made in the hill of the house of the Lord, and in
Jerusalem, and he casted them away all without the city.
(And he took away the foreign, *or other*, gods and the
idols from the House of the Lord; and *he did away* the
altars which he had built on the Temple Mount, and in
Jerusalem, and he threw all of them out of the city.)
16 Certainly he restored the altar of the Lord, and
offered thereon slain sacrifices, and peaceable sacrifices,
and praising (And he restored the altar of the Lord, and
offered slain sacrifices, and peace offerings, *or thank
offerings*, upon it); and he commanded Judah to serve the
Lord God of Israel.
17 Nevertheless the people offered yet in high places to
the Lord their God. (But still the people offered at the hill
shrines, but only to the Lord their God.)
18 Forsooth the residue of [the] deeds of Manasseh, and
his beseeching to his Lord God, and the words of [the]
prophets, that spake to him in the name of the Lord God
of Israel, be contained in the words of the kings of Israel.
(And the rest of the deeds of Manasseh, and his
beseeching to the Lord his God, and the words of the
prophets, who spoke to him in the name of the Lord God
of Israel, be contained in The Book of the Kings of Israel.)
19 And his prayer, and the hearing *that the Lord heard
him*, and all *his* sins, and *all his* despising, and also the
places in which he builded high things, and made
maumet woods and images, before that he did penance,
these be written in the book of Hozai. (And his prayer,
and the answer that he received *from the Lord*, and all *his*
sins, and offences, and also where he built the hill
shrines, and made idol groves/and set up sacred poles,
and carved images, before that he did penance, these be
written in The Book of the Seers.)
20 And Manasseh slept with his fathers, and they
buried him in his house; and Amon, his son, reigned for
him.
21 Amon was of two and twenty years, when he began
to reign; and he reigned two years in Jerusalem.
22 And he did evil in the sight of the Lord, as
Manasseh, his father, had done; and he offered, and
served to all the idols, which Manasseh had made.
23 And he reverenced not the face of the Lord, as
Manasseh, his father, reverenced (And he did not humble
himself before the Lord, like his father Manasseh had
humbled himself); and he did much greater trespasses
than his father did.
24 And when his servants had sworn together against
him, they killed him in his house.
25 Soothly the residue multitude of the people, after
that they had slain them that had slain Amon, ordained
Josiah, his son, king for him.

CHAPTER 34

1 Josiah was of eight years, when he began to reign,
and he reigned in Jerusalem one and thirty years.
2 And he did that, that was rightful in the sight of the
Lord; and went in the ways of David, his father, and
bowed not to the right side, neither to the left side.
3 And in the eighth year of the realm of his empire,
when he was yet a boy, (*that is, sixteen years of age*,) he
began to seek the God of his father David; and in the

twelfth year after that he began, he cleansed Judah and
Jerusalem from high places, and woods, and simulacra,
and graven images (and in the twelfth year after that he
began to reign, he cleansed Judah and Jerusalem from the
hill shrines, and the idol groves/and the sacred poles, and
the idols, and the carved images).
4 And they destroyed before him the altars of Baalim,
and they destroyed the simulacra, that were put above
(them). Also he hewed down the maumet woods, and
the graven images, and brake to small gobbets; and
scattered abroad the small gobbets on the burials of
them, that were wont to offer *to those.* (And they
destroyed before him the altars of the Baalim, and they
destroyed the idols, that were put upon them. And he cut
down the idol groves, *or the sacred poles*, and the carved
idols, and broke them into small pieces; and he scattered
those small pieces all over the burials of those, who were
wont to offer *to those idols.*)
5 Furthermore *the king* burnt the bones of (the) priests
upon the altars of (the) idols, and (so) he cleansed Judah
and Jerusalem *of idolatry.*
6 But also he destroyed all the idols in the cities of
Manasseh, and of Ephraim, and of Simeon, unto
Naphtali.
7 And when he had scattered the altars, and had all-
broken into gobbets the maumet woods, and the graven
images, and had destroyed all [the] temples of idols from
all the land of Israel, he turned again into Jerusalem. (And
when he had destroyed the altars, and the idol
groves/and the sacred poles, and had broken the carved
idols into pieces, and destroyed all the temples of idols in
all the land of Israel, he returned to Jerusalem.)
8 Therefore in the eighteenth year of his realm, when
the land and the temple was cleansed now, he sent
Shaphan, the son of Hilkiah, and Maaseiah, the prince of
the city, and Joah, the son of Joahaz, his chancellor, that
they should repair the house of the Lord his God. (And so
in the eighteenth year of his reign, when the land and the
Temple had been cleansed, he sent Shaphan, the son of
Azaliah, and Maaseiah, the leader of the city, and Joah,
the son of Joahaz, his chancellor, to repair the House of
the Lord his God.)
9 Which came to Hilkiah, the great priest; and when
they had taken of him the money, that was brought into
the house of the Lord, which *money* the deacons and
porters had gathered of *men of* Manasseh, and of
Ephraim, and of all the remnant men of Israel, and of
Judah and of Benjamin, and of the dwellers of Jerusalem,
(And they came to the High Priest Hilkiah; and when
they had delivered the money to him, that was brought to
the House of the Lord, which *money* the Levites, who
were the guards, *or the doorkeepers*, had gathered from
the people of Manasseh, and of Ephraim, and from all the
remnant of Israel, and of Judah and of Benjamin, and
from the inhabitants of Jerusalem,)
10 they gave it in(to) the hands of them that were
sovereigns of the workmen in the house of the Lord, that
they should restore the temple, and repair all the feeble
things *thereof.* (they gave it to those who were the rulers,
or the overseers, of the workmen in the House of the
Lord, so that they could restore the Temple, and repair all
its weakened, *or its broken*, parts.)
11 And they gave that money to the craftsmen and
masons, for to buy stones hewed out of the quarries, and
wood to the joinings of the building(s), and to the
coupling(s) of [the] houses, which the kings of Judah had
destroyed. (And they gave that money to the craftsmen
and the masons, to buy stones cut out of the quarries, and
timber for the joints of the buildings, and for the
couplings of the houses, which the kings of Judah had
destroyed.)
12 The which workmen did faithfully all things. And
the sovereigns of workers were Jahath, and Obadiah, of
the sons of Merari; and Zechariah, and Meshullam, of the
sons of Kohath, which hasted the work; all *were* deacons,
knowing how to sing with organs. (And the workmen
faithfully did their work. And the rulers, *or the overseers*,
of the workers were Jahath, and Obadiah, *Levites* of the
sons of Merari; and Zechariah, and Meshullam, of the
Kohathites, who hastened the work; all of them were
Levites, who knew how to play instruments.)
13 And over them that bare burdens to diverse uses
were scribes, and masters of deacons, and porters. (And
they were over those who carried burdens, and did
diverse types of work; and other Levites were writers, *or
secretaries*, and clerks, and guards, *or doorkeepers.*)
14 And when they bare out the money, that was
brought into the temple of the Lord, Hilkiah, the priest,
found a book of the law of the Lord by the hand of
Moses. (And when they took out the money, that was
brought into the Temple of the Lord, the High Priest
Hilkiah found The Book of the Law of the Lord, written
by Moses.)
15 And *Hilkiah* said to Shaphan, the writer, I have
found the book of the law in the house of the Lord. And
Hilkiah took *it* to Shaphan, (And *Hilkiah* said to Shaphan,
the writer, I have found The Book of the Law in the
House of the Lord. And Hilkiah gave *it* to Shaphan,)
16 and he bare in the book to the king (and he took the
book to the king); and he told to him, and said, Lo! all
things be fulfilled, *or ended*, which thou hast given into
the hands of thy servants.
17 And they have welled together the silver, which is
found in the house of the Lord; and it is given to the
sovereigns of the craftsmen, and (to those) making
diverse works; (And they have melted together the silver,
which was kept in the House of the Lord; and it was
given to the rulers, *or the overseers*, of the craftsmen, and

to those doing diverse types of work;)
18 furthermore Hilkiah, the priest, took to me this
book. And when he had rehearsed this book in the
presence of the king, (and furthermore, the High Priest
Hilkiah gave me this book. And when he had read the
book before the king,)
19 and *when the king* had heard the words of the law,
he rent his clothes; (and *the king* had heard the words of
the Law, he tore his clothes;)
20 and he commanded to Hilkiah, and to Ahikam, the
son of Shaphan, and to Abdon, the son of Micah, and to
Shaphan, the scribe, and to Asaiah, the servant of the
king, and said,
21 Go ye, and pray the Lord for me, and for the
remnant of men of Israel and of Judah, on all the words of
this book, that is found (Go ye, and pray to the Lord for
me, and for the rest of the people who remain in Israel
and Judah, concerning all the words of this book, that is
found). For great (is the) vengeance of the Lord (that)
hath dropped upon us, for our fathers kept not the words
of the Lord, to do all things that be written in this book.
22 Therefore Hilkiah, and they that were sent together
(with him) from the king, *went* to Huldah, the prophetess,
the wife of Shallum, the son of Tikvath, the son of
Hasrah, (the) keeper of the *king's* clothes, the which
Huldah dwelled in Jerusalem in the second *ward* (who
lived in Jerusalem's second *ward*); and they spake to her
the words, which we told before.
23 And she answered to them, The Lord God of Israel
saith these things, Say ye to the man, that sent you to me,
24 The Lord saith these things, Lo! I shall bring evils
upon this place, and upon the dwellers thereof (and upon
its inhabitants), and all the cursings that be written in this
book, that they have read before the king of Judah.
25 For they have forsaken me, and have sacrificed to
alien gods, for to stir me to wrathfulness in all the works
of their hands (For they have abandoned me, and have
sacrificed to foreign, *or other*, gods, and have stirred me
to anger with all the works of their hands); therefore my
strong vengeance shall drop upon this place, and it shall
not be quenched.
26 But speak ye thus to the king of Judah, that sent you
to pray (to) the Lord, The Lord God of Israel saith these
things, For thou heardest the words of the book,
27 and thine heart *thereby* is made nesh, and thou art
meeked in the sight of the Lord of these things which be
said against this place, and *against* the dwellers of
Jerusalem, and thou hast reverenced my face, and hast
rent thy clothes, and hast wept before me; also I have
heard thee, saith the Lord. (and thy heart is softened *by it*,
and thou art humbled before the Lord by these things
which be said against this place, and *against* the
inhabitants of Jerusalem, and thou hast reverenced my
face, and hast torn thy clothes, and hast wept before me;
yea, I have heard thee, saith the Lord.)
28 For now I shall gather thee to thy fathers, and thou
shalt be borne into thy sepulchre in peace; and thine eyes
shall not see all the evil, *that is, none of all the evils*, that
I shall bring in upon this place, and upon the dwellers
thereof (and upon its inhabitants). Then they told to the
king all things, that Huldah had said.
29 And after that *the king* had called together all the
elder men of Judah and of Jerusalem,
30 he went up into the house of the Lord, and *there
went up* together *with him* all the men of Judah, and the
dwellers of Jerusalem, priests, and deacons, and all the
people, from the least unto the most; to whose hearing in
the house of the Lord, the king read all the words of the
foresaid book. (he went up to the House of the Lord, and
there went up together *with him* all the men of Judah,
and the inhabitants of Jerusalem, and the priests, and the
Levites, and all the people, from the least unto the most;
to whom the king then read aloud all the words of the
foresaid book that was found in the House of the Lord.)
31 And he stood in his throne, and smote, *or made*, a
bond of peace before the Lord, for to follow him, and to
keep the commandments, and the witnessings, and the
justifyings of him, in all his heart, and in all his soul; and
to do those things which were written in that book, that
he had read. (And he stood by his throne, and struck a
covenant before the Lord, to follow him, and to keep his
commandments, and his testimonies, and his statutes,
with all his heart, and with all his soul; and to do those
things that were written in that book, that he had read.)
32 And he charged greatly upon this thing all men, that
were found in Jerusalem and Benjamin; and the dwellers
of Jerusalem did after the covenant of the Lord God of
their fathers. (And he greatly charged all who were found
in Jerusalem and Benjamin to keep this oath, *or this
pledge*; and the inhabitants of Jerusalem did after the
covenant of the Lord God of their fathers.)
33 Therefore Josiah did away all the abominations from
all the countries of the sons of Israel; and made all men,
that were left in Israel, to serve the Lord God (And so
Josiah did away all the abominations from all the
territories of the Israelites; and made all, who were left in
Israel, to serve the Lord God); and in all the days of his
life they went not away from the Lord God of their
fathers.

CHAPTER 35

1 Forsooth Josiah made pask to the Lord in Jerusalem,
the which *pask* was offered in the fourteenth day of the
first month; (And Josiah kept a Passover to the Lord in
Jerusalem, and *the Passover beasts* were killed on the
fourteenth day of the first month;)
2 and he ordained priests in their offices; and
commanded them for to serve in the house of the Lord.

(and he ordained the priests in their offices; and
encouraged them to do their service well in the House of
the Lord.)
3 And he spake to the deacons, at whose teaching all
Israel was hallowed to the Lord, Set ye, *he said*, the ark *of*
the Lord in the saintuary of the temple, that Solomon,
king of Israel, the son of David builded; for ye shall no
more bear it *about* (And he said to the Levites, who
taught all Israel, and were dedicated to the Lord, Put ye
the Ark *of the Lord* in the sanctuary of the Temple, that
Solomon, the king of Israel, the son of David, built; for no
more shall ye carry it *about*). But now serve ye the Lord
your God, and his people Israel,
4 and make you(rselves) ready by your houses and
families, in the partings of each by himself (in each of
your divisions), as David, king of Israel, commanded, and
as Solomon, his son, ordained;
5 and serve ye in the saintuary by the families and
(the) companies of (the) deacons,
6 and be ye hallowed, and offer ye (the) pask; also
make ready your brethren, that they may do after the
words, which the Lord spake by the hand of Moses. (and
be ye consecrated, *or purified*, and kill ye the Passover
lambs; and prepare for your kinsmen, to do after the
words, which the Lord spoke through Moses.)
7 Furthermore Josiah gave to all the people, that was
found there in the solemnity of pask, *that is, to make the*
solemnity, lambs and kids of the flocks, and of residue
sheep *he gave* thirty thousand, and of oxes three
thousand; these things *were given* of the substance of the
king. (And Josiah gave to all the people who were there
for the Passover Feast, *that is, to all who were there to*
keep the Feast, lambs and goat kids of the flocks, and *he*
gave thirty thousand sheep, and three thousand oxen;
these things *were given* out of the king's substance, *or*
from his own possessions.)
8 And his dukes offered those things which they
avowed by their free will, as well to the people, as to
priests and deacons (And his leaders offered those things
which they vowed by their own free will, to the people, as
well as to the priests, and the Levites). And Hilkiah, and
Zechariah, and Jehiel, princes of the house of the Lord,
gave to [the] priests, to make (the) pask in common, two
thousand and six hundred sheep, and three hundred oxen.
9 And Conaniah, and Shemaiah, and Nethaneel, and
his brethren, and also Hashabiah, and Jeiel, and Jozabad,
the princes of deacons, gave to other deacons, to make
[the] pask, five thousand of sheep, and five hundred
oxen. (And Conaniah, and Shemaiah, and Nethaneel, and
his kinsmen, and also Hashabiah, and Jeiel, and Jozabad,
the leaders of the Levites, gave to the other Levites, to
make the Passover, five thousand sheep, and five
hundred oxen.)
10 And the service was made ready; and [the] priests
stood in their office, and deacons in their companies (and
the Levites in their divisions), by the commandment of
the king;
11 and pask was offered. And [the] priests sprinkled
their hands with blood, and deacons drew off the skins of
sacrificed beasts, (and so the Passover beasts were killed.
And the priests sprinkled the blood with their hands, and
the Levites drew off the skins of the sacrificed beasts,)
12 and they parted those sacrifices, for to give *them* by
the houses and families of all men *that were come thither*
to make (the) pask; and that those *sacrifices* should be
offered to the Lord, as it is written in the book of Moses;
and of oxen they did in like manner. (and they separated
those sacrifices, in order to distribute *them* by the houses
and the families of all those *who were come there to*
keep the Passover; and so that those *sacrifices* should be
offered to the Lord, as it is written in The Book of Moses;
and they did in like manner with the oxen.)
13 And they roasted the pask *lamb* upon the fire, after
that that is written in the law. And they seethed
peaceable sacrifices in pans, and in cauldrons, and in
pots, and in haste they dealed *it* to all the people; (And
they roasted the Passover *lamb* upon the fire, after what
is written in the Law. And they boiled the peace
offerings in pans, and cauldrons, and pots, and then they
gave *it* out hastily, *or quickly*, to all the people;)
14 but they made ready afterward to themselves, and to
priests; for the priests were occupied unto [the] night in
the offering of burnt sacrifices and of the inner fatnesses.
Wherefore the deacons made ready *their part* at the last
to themselves, and to the priests, the sons of Aaron. (and
afterward *the Levites* prepared for themselves, and for the
priests; for the priests were occupied into the night in
offering the burnt sacrifices and the inner fatnesses. And
so the Levites prepared *their portion* lastly for themselves,
and for the priests, the sons of Aaron.)
15 And [the] singers, the sons of Asaph, stood in their
order, by the commandment of David, and of Asaph, and
of Heman, and of Jeduthun, the prophets of the king; but
the porters kept *their office* by each gate, so that they
went not away from their service, soothly (not) in a point,
that is, they were in no time absent from their office;
wherefore and the deacons, their brethren, made ready
meats to them (and the guards, *or the doorkeepers*, kept
watch at each gate, so that they went not away from their
service, truly at no point, *that is, they were never absent*
from their station; and so the Levites, their kinsmen,
prepared their meats).
16 Therefore all the religion of the Lord was fulfilled
rightfully in that day, that they made pask (And so all the
service of the Lord was rightfully done on that day, so that
they kept the Passover), and offered burnt sacrifices upon
the altar of the Lord, by the commandment of king Josiah.
17 And the sons of Israel, that were found there, made

pask in that time, and the solemnity of therf loaves seven
days. (And the Israelites, who were found there, kept the
Passover at that time, and then the Feast of Unleavened
Bread for seven days.)
18 No pask was like this in Israel, from the days of
Samuel, the prophet; but neither any of the kings of Israel
made pask as Josiah *did*, to [the] priests and deacons, and
to all Judah and Israel, that was found *there*, and to the
dwellers of Jerusalem. (There was no Passover like this in
Israel, since the days of the prophet Samuel; nor did any
of the kings of Israel keep such a Passover as Josiah *did*,
with the priests and the Levites, and all Judah and Israel,
who were found *there*, and the inhabitants of Jerusalem.)
19 This pask was hallowed in the eighteenth year of the
realm of Josiah. (This Passover was kept in the eighteenth
year of Josiah's reign.)
20 After that Josiah had repaired the temple, Necho, the
king of Egypt, went up to fight in Charchemish beside
Euphrates; and Josiah went forth into his meeting. (After
that Josiah had repaired the Temple, Necho, the king of
Egypt, went up to fight in Charchemish, which was on
the banks of the Euphrates River; and Josiah went out
against him.)
21 And *Necho* said by messengers sent to Josiah, King
of Judah, what *cause of strife* is to me and to thee? I come
not against thee today, but I fight against another
household, to which God bade me go in haste; cease
thou to do *thus* against God, that is with me, lest he slay
thee. (And *Necho* sent messengers who said to Josiah,
King of Judah, what *cause of strife* is there between me
and thee? I did not come against thee today, but I fight
against another household, to whom God hath ordered
me to go in haste; cease thou to do *thus* against God,
who is with me, lest he kill thee.)
22 But Josiah would not turn again, but he made ready
battle against him; and he assented not to the words of
Necho, by God's mouth, but he went for to fight in the
field of Megiddo. (But Josiah would not turn back, but he
prepared battle array against him; and he assented not to
the words of Necho, which were from God's mouth, but
he went out to fight in the field of Megiddo.)
23 And there he was wounded of archers, and *Josiah*
said to his servants, Lead ye me out of the battle, for I am
wounded greatly. (And there he was wounded by
archers, and *Josiah* said to his servants, Lead ye me out of
the battle, for I am greatly wounded.)
24 And they bare him over from that chariot into
another chariot, that followed him, by custom of the king,
and they brought him *forth* into Jerusalem; and he died
there, and was buried in the sepulchre of his fathers.
And all Judah and Jerusalem bewailed him,
25 Jeremy most (of all), of whom all [the] singers and
singeresses till into [the] present day rehearse (*his*)
lamentations, *either wailings*, on Josiah (and Jeremiah
bewailed him most of all, and all the singers and
singeresses recite *his* lamentations, *or his wailings*, upon
Josiah unto this present day); and it came forth as a law in
Israel, Lo! it is said written in [the] Lamentations.
26 Forsooth the residue of [the] words of Josiah, and of
his mercies, that be commanded in the law of the Lord,
(And the rest of the words concerning Josiah, and the
mercies that he did, *that is, his righteous works*, which be
commanded in the Law of the Lord,)
27 and his works, the first and the last, be written in the
book of [the] kings of Israel and of Judah. (and his first
and last works, be written in The Book of the Kings of
Judah and of Israel.)

CHAPTER 36

1 Therefore the people of the land took Jehoahaz, the
son of Josiah, and ordained him king for his father in
Jerusalem. (And so the people of the land took Jehoahaz,
Josiah's son, and made him king in place of his father in
Jerusalem.)
2 Jehoahaz was of three and twenty years, when he
began to reign, and he reigned three months in Jerusalem.
3 And *when* the king of Egypt had come to Jerusalem,
he removed him, and he condemned the land in an
hundred talents of silver and in a talent of gold. (And
when the king of Egypt came to Jerusalem, he removed
Jehoahaz, and made *the people of* the land pay him, *the
king of Egypt*, tribute, *or taxes*, of a hundred talents of
silver, and a talent of gold.)
4 And he ordained for him Eliakim, his brother, (to be)
king upon Judah and Jerusalem; and he turned his name
(and he changed his name), *and called him* Jehoiakim.
And he took that Jehoahaz (back) with himself, and he
brought *him* into Egypt.
5 Jehoiakim was of five and twenty years, when he
began to reign, and he reigned eleven years in Jerusalem,
and he did evil before the Lord his God.
6 And Nebuchadnezzar, king of Chaldees (the king of
the Chaldeans, *that is, the king of Babylon*), went up
against this Jehoiakim, and he led him bound with chains
into Babylon.
7 To which Babylon he translated also the vessels of
the house of the Lord, and he set those in his temple.
(And he also carried away the vessels of *the House of* the
Lord, and he put them in his temple in Babylon.)
8 Soothly the residue of [the] words of Jehoiakim (And
the rest of the deeds of Jehoiakim), and of his
abominations which he wrought, and which were found
in him, be contained in the book of [the] kings of Israel
and of Judah. And Jehoiachin, his son, reigned for him.
9 Jehoiachin was of eight years (Jehoiachin was
eighteen years old), when he began to reign, and he
reigned three months and ten days in Jerusalem, and he
did evil in the sight of the Lord.

10 And when the circle of the year was turned about,
Nebuchadnezzar the king sent men, which also brought
him into Babylon, when the most precious vessels of the
house of the Lord were borne out together (And at the
turn of the year, King Nebuchadnezzar sent men *to*
Jerusalem, who brought Jehoiachin back to Babylon, and
the most precious vessels, from the House of the Lord,
were brought back with him). And Nebuchadnezzar
ordained Zedekiah, his father's brother, king upon Judah
and Jerusalem.
11 Zedekiah was of one and twenty years, when he
began to reign, and he reigned eleven years in Jerusalem.
12 And he did evil in the sight of the Lord his God, and
he was not ashamed of the face of Jeremy, the prophet,
that spake to him by the mouth of the Lord. (And he did
evil before the Lord his God, and he was not ashamed
before the face of the prophet Jeremiah, who spoke to
him the words of the Lord.)
13 Also he went [away] from king Nebuchadnezzar,
which made him to swear by God, *that is, to promise*
steadfastly to be true to him; and *Zedekiah* made hard his
noll and his heart, that he would not turn again to the
Lord *God* of Israel. (And he also rebelled against King
Nebuchadnezzar, who had made him to swear by God,
that is, to promise steadfastly to be true to him; and
Zedekiah stiffened his neck, *that is, he became stubborn*,
and he hardened his heart, and he would not return to
the Lord *God* of Israel.)
14 But also all the princes of priests, and the people,
trespassed wickedly, by all the abominations of heathen
men; and they defouled the house of the Lord, which he
had hallowed to himself in Jerusalem. (But also all the
leaders of the priests, and the people, wickedly
trespassed, by all the abominations of the heathen; and
they defiled the House of the Lord, which he had
consecrated in Jerusalem.)
15 And the Lord God of their fathers sent to them by
the hand of his messengers, and the Lord rose up by
night, and *he* admonished *them* each day; for-thy that he
would spare his people, and his dwelling place.
16 And they mocked the messengers of God, and they
despised his words, and they scorned his prophets; till
the great vengeance of the Lord ascended upon his
people, and no cure, *or healing*, were *to them*. (But they
mocked God's messengers, and they despised his
words/and they defied his words, and they scorned his
prophets; until the great vengeance of the Lord
descended upon his people, and then there was no cure,
or healing, for them.)
17 And he brought on them the king of Chaldees; and
[he] killed the young men of them by sword in the house
of [the] saintuary; he had not mercy of a young man, and
of a virgin, and of an eld man, and soothly neither of a
man nigh the death for eldness, but he betook all in the
hand of that *king of Chaldees*. (And he brought in upon
them the king of the Chaldeans; and he killed their young
men with the sword in the House of the sanctuary; and
he had no mercy for a young man, or a virgin, or an old
man, or a man near death because of old age, but he
delivered them all into the hands of that *king of the*
Chaldeans.)
18 And he translated into Babylon all the vessels of the
house of the Lord (And he carried away to Babylon all
the vessels of the House of the Lord), both the greater and
the less(er) vessels, and the treasures of the temple, and
of the king *of Judah*, and of the princes *thereof*.
19 *And* (the) enemies burnt the house of the Lord; *and*
they destroyed the wall of Jerusalem; they burnt all the
towers; and they destroyed whatever thing was precious
therein. (And the enemies burned down the House of the
Lord; *and* they destroyed the wall of Jerusalem; they
burned down all the towers; and they destroyed whatever
precious things were *there*.)
20 If any man escaped the sword, he was led (away)
into Babylon, and served the king and his sons; *this*
subjection (this subjugation)/this thralldom continued
upon the men of Judah, till the king of Persia reigned,
21 and till the word of the Lord by the mouth of Jeremy
was fulfilled, and till the land hallowed his sabbaths (and
until the word of the Lord given by Jeremiah was fulfilled,
and until the land consecrated its sabbaths). Soothly
Judah in all the days of (its) desolation, *or of the*
destroying or forsaking thereof, it made sabbath, till that
seventy years were fulfilled.
22 Forsooth in the first year of Cyrus, king of Persia, to
fulfill the word of the Lord, which he had spoken by the
mouth of Jeremy, the Lord raised (up) the spirit of Cyrus,
king of Persia, that commanded to be preached in all his
realm, yea, by writing, and said, (But in the first year of
Cyrus, the king of Persia, to fulfill the word of the Lord,
which he had spoken by the mouth of Jeremiah, the Lord
raised up the spirit of Cyrus, the king of Persia, who
commanded to be preached in all his kingdom, by word
of mouth, and in writing, *the following edict*,)
23 (I) Cyrus, king of Persia, saith these things, The Lord
God of heaven hath given to me all the realms of [the]
earth, and he commanded to me, that I should build to
him an house in Jerusalem, which is in Judah. Who of
you is in all his people? the Lord his God be with him,
and go he up *thither* (To every man among you who is of
his people, the Lord his God be with him, and go he up
there now *to Jerusalem*). ✡

Printed in Great Britain
by Amazon